ORGANIZATION
THEORY AND DESIGN

Richard L. Daft

Vanderbilt University

Sixth Edition

With cases contributed by Richard Ivey School of Business, The University of Western Ontario
Workbook and Workshop exercises written and prepared by Dorothy Marcic

SOUTH-WESTERN College Publishing

An International Thomson Publishing Company

Publishing Team Director: John Szilagyi
Developmental Editor: Esther Craig
Production Editor: Kelly Keeler
Production House: Pre-Press Company, Inc.
Internal Designer: Ellen Pettengell
Photo Researcher: Mary Goljenboom

Library of Congress Cataloging-in-Publication Data

Daft, Richard L.
   Organization theory and design/Richard L. Daft.—6th ed.
      p. cm.
   Includes bibliographical references and index.
   ISBN 0-538-87902-5 (hc)
    1. Organization. 2. Organizational sociology—Case studies.
  I. Title.
   HD31.D135 1997
   658.4—dc21   97-20922
                                          CIP

Printed in the United States of America

   4 5 WST 0 9 8

I(T)P®

International Thomson Publishing
South-Western College Publishing is an ITP company. The ITP trademark is used under license.

Contents

chapter three
The External Environment   80

part three
Organization Structure and Design   117

chapter four
Manufacturing, Service, and Advanced Information Technologies   118

Preface

The sixth edition of *Organization Theory and Design* has undergone a complete revitalization. To attain my vision of presenting the most recent thinking about organizations in a way that is interesting and enjoyable for students, I have changed many parts of the book. These changes include a new chapter, new case examples, new book reviews, new examples of paradigm-breaking companies, new end-of-chapter cases, new exercises for student application, and new end-of-book integrative cases. The research and theories in the field of organization studies are insightful, rich, and help students and managers understand their organizational world and solve real-life problems. My mission is to integrate the concepts and models from organizational theory with changing events in the real world to provide the most up-to-date view of organizations available.

FEATURES NEW TO THE SIXTH EDITION

Many students in a typical organization theory course do not have extensive work experience, especially at the middle and upper levels, where organization theory is most applicable. To engage students in today's world of organizations, the sixth edition adds or expands significant features: a new chapter on interorganizational relationships, a feature called The New Paradigm, student experiential activities called Workbooks (which appear in every chapter) and Workshops (which appear in selected chapters), new concepts, new Book Marks, new case examples, and new integrative cases for student analysis. The total set of features substantially improves and expands the book's content and accessibility. The glossary has also been expanded in the sixth edition.

The New Paradigm

The New Paradigm boxes describe companies that have undergone a major shift in strategic direction, values, or culture to cope with today's turbulent and competitive international environment. The New Paradigm examples illustrate company transformations toward empowerment, new structures, new cultures, new technologies, the breaking down of barriers between departments or divisions, and the joining together of employees in a common mission. Examples of New Paradigm organizations include Springfield Remanufacturing, Arizona Public Service Company, Progressive Corporation, the Agricultural Department, the Intranet, Starbucks Coffee, GE Plastics/Borg Warner, and Volkswagen.

New Chapter

The new chapter, Chapter 14, describes the recent evolution in interorganizational relationships. Today more organizations act as part of an ecosystem. Collaboration is often as important as competition. The collaborative networks that emerge represent a new challenge for management. Other perspectives in this chapter include population ecology, resource dependence, and institutionalism. The term *institutionalism* is new to this edition. It describes an organization's need for legitimacy with external stakeholders and explains why organizations tend to resemble one another. The three core mechanisms are mimetic isomorphism, normative isomorphism, and coercive isomorphism. Chapter 14 helps students learn about interorganizational relationships and how to consciously manage them.

New Concepts

Many concepts have been added or expanded in this edition. New material has been added on the postmodern organization, strategies for organizational excellence, reengineering, global teams, the transnational model of organization, leadership for change, forces driving the need for major change, stages in commitment to change, the balance of empowerment and control, intranets, strategy-structure-technology link, the learning organization, organizational transformations, and the new concepts of institutionalism and interorganizational relationships described in Chapter 14.

New Book Marks

Book Marks, a unique feature of this text, are book reviews that reflect current issues of concern to researchers and managers. These reviews describe how organizations are dealing with today's changing environment. New Book Marks in this edition include *Sacred Cows Make the Best Burgers, What America Does Right, Hypercompetition, Lean Thinking, The Self-Defeating Organization, Jumping the Curve, Real Change Leaders, Levers of Control, Built to Last, The We-Force in Management, The Boundaryless Organization,* and *Open-Book Management.*

New Case Examples

This edition contains many new examples to illustrate theoretical concepts. Many examples are international, and all are about real organizations. New chapter opening cases include Zeneca Agricultural Products, Ryder Systems, Chrysler Corporation, Marmot Mountain, French Rags, Matsushita Electric, 3M, KPMG Peat Marwick, Southwest Airlines, Intel, and the USIA. In addition, many In Practice cases are used within chapters to illustrate specific concepts. These new cases include Delta Airlines, Sun Microsystems, Greyhound Lines, General Electric, Taco Bell, MADD, Karolinska Hospital, TopsyTail, Nu-Skin International, Rolls-Royce, Imperial Oil, Rhone-Poulenc, Herman Miller, Texas Instruments, Lantech, and Corsair Communications.

New Integrative Cases

In addition, several new integrative cases have been added to encourage student discussion and involvement. The new integrative cases include both national and international situations, such as Littleton Manufacturing (A) and (B), Victoria Heavy Equipment Limited, The Food Terminal (A) and (B), and Bhiwar Enterprises.

Student Applications

This edition includes new student application exercises at the end of every chapter. Each chapter contains a Workbook—an exercise through which students gain more experience with chapter concepts. Selected chapters also have a Workshop exercise that engages a student group in a larger learning experience. In addition, challenging new cases have been added to the end of each chapter, and include S-S Technologies, The Acetate Department, Mason & Lynch, C&C Groceries, The University Art Museum, London Free Press, The Bay Kitchener, Cherie Cosmetics, and W.L. Gore and Associates.

Other Features

Many of the features from previous editions have been so well received that the general approach has been retained.

1. Multiple pedagogical devices are used to enhance student involvement in text material. A Look Inside introduces each chapter with a relevant and interesting organizational example. In Practice cases illustrate theoretical concepts in organizational settings. Frequent exhibits are used to help students visualize organizational relationships, and the artwork has been redone to communicate concepts more clearly. The Summary and Interpretation section tells students which points are important in the broader context of organization theory. The Briefcase feature tells students how to use concepts to analyze cases and manage organizations. Cases for Analysis are tailored to chapter concepts and provide a vehicle for student analysis and discussion.

2. Each chapter is highly focused and is organized into a logical framework. Many organization textbooks treat material in sequential fashion, such as Here's View A, Here's View B, Here's View C, and so on. *Organization Theory and Design* shows how they apply to organizations. Moreover, each chapter sticks to the essential point. Students are not introduced to extraneous material or confusing methodological squabbles that occur among organizational researchers. The body of research in most areas points to a major trend, which is reported here. Several chapters develop a framework that organizes major ideas into an overall scheme.

3. This book has been extensively tested on students. Feedback from students and faculty members has been used in the revision. The combination of organization theory concepts, book reviews, examples of paradigm-breaking organizations, case illustrations, experiential exercises, and other new teaching devices is designed to meet student learning needs, and students have responded very favorably.

Acknowledgments

Textbook writing is a team enterprise. The sixth edition has integrated ideas and hard work from many people to whom I am very grateful. The reviewers of the fifth edition made an especially important contribution. They praised many features, were critical about things that didn't work well, and offered several suggestions. I thank the following individuals for their significant contributions to this text.

Henry J. Bazan
Western New England College

Richard Paulson
Mankato State University

Christine Borycki
University of South Carolina—Sumter

Preston Probasco
San Jose State Unversity

Tina Dacin
Texas A&M University

Sudhir K. Saha
Memorial University of Newfoundland

Gordon E. Dehler
University of Dayton

Udo Staber
University of New Brunswick

Lynne E. Miller
LaSalle University

Dana Stover
University of Idaho

I especially thank and acknowledge Karen Dill Bowerman, California State University—Fresno, for her terrific contribution to the *Instructor's Manual* that accompanies *Organization Theory and Design*. Karen did a superb job developing new questions for the test bank, creating new teaching ideas and auxiliary lectures, and writing teaching notes for the cases. Karen's work provides many additional resources for instructors to use in class.

Among my professional colleagues, I owe a special debt to Arie Lewin, who over the last few years has made excellent suggestions for new material about international structures, advanced information technology, and top-management direction. I also thank Tina Dacin for her excellent ideas about institutional theory for the new chapter on interorganizational relationships, and Ken Friedman for his excellent suggestions for the text and Book Marks. I appreciate, too, the intellectual stimulation from friends and colleagues at the Owen School: Alice Andrews, Bruce Barry, Ray Friedman, Barry Gerhart, Tom Mahoney, Rich Oliver, and Greg Stewart. Marty Geisel, the dean at the Owen School, maintained a positive scholarly atmosphere and supported me with the time and resources needed to complete this book.

I want to extend special thanks to my editorial assistant, Pat Lane. Pat provided outstanding help throughout the revision of this text. She skillfully drafted materials on a variety of cases and topics, found resources, and did an outstanding job with the copyedited manuscript, page proofs, and ancillary materials. Pat's personal enthusiasm and care added to the high level of excellence in the sixth edition. I am also grateful to Chad Payne and Linda Roberts. Chad Payne, an MBA student at Vanderbilt, did a wonderful job of researching and drafting materials for the Book Marks. Linda Roberts took responsibility for the completion of several projects, including permissions, that provided me time to focus on revising this book.

The editors at South-Western also deserve special mention. Esther Craig, the developmental editor, did her usual great job of moving the project forward while providing significant ideas for improvements. In addition, Kelly Keeler, the production editor, combined her creativity with a smooth management style to facilitate the book's on-time completion.

Finally, I want to acknowledge the love and contributions of my wife, Dorothy Marcic. Dorothy was very supportive and helped me grow emotionally during the revision, and she took the book a giant step forward with her creation of the Workbook and Workshop student exercises, which are a significant addition to the text. I also want to acknowledge the love and support of all my daughters, who make my life special during our precious time together.

part one

Introduction to Organizations

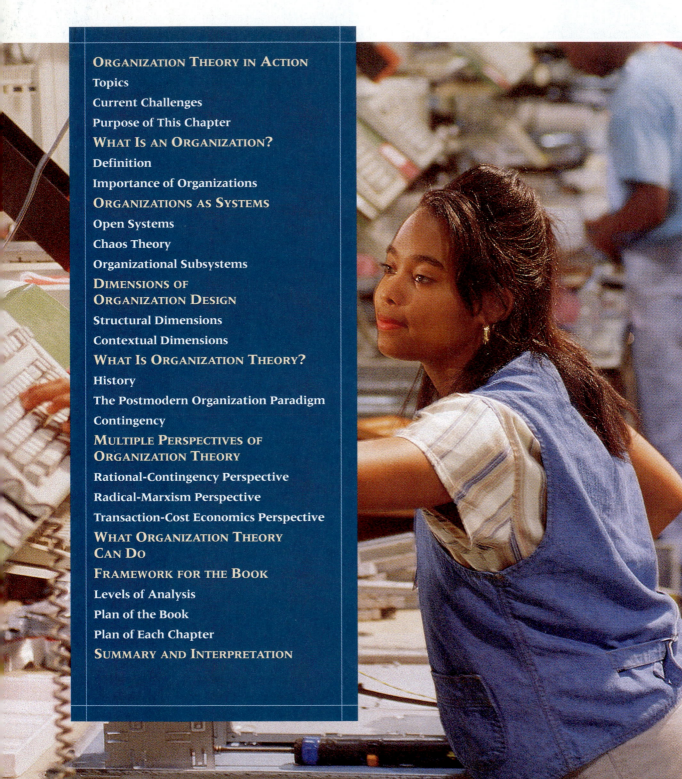

chapter one

Organizations and Organization Theory

International Business Machines Corporation

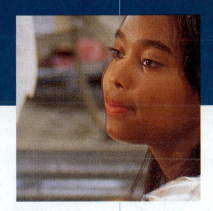

Owning stock in IBM was like owning a gold mine. The overwhelming success of the IBM PC sent the company's already high profits soaring, and IBM was ranked as the world's largest company in terms of stock market value. Big Blue, as the company was known, was creating jobs around the world, its work force ultimately swelling to 407,000.

A decade later, those who had invested their lives—or their money—in a company they thought could never fail watched long-cherished dreams go down the drain. The company went from earning a $6 billion profit to reporting a whopping $5 billion loss two years later. IBM stock lost more than $75 billion in value, an amount equal to the gross domestic product of Sweden. Everyone associated with the once-great company suffered.

- More than 140,000 IBM workers lost their jobs. Entire towns that sprang up because of IBM watched their economies disappear. New York's middle Hudson Valley was devastated, and when IBM announced layoffs in 1993, local officials requested that gun shops close for the day.
- As IBM stock fell from $176 to the low $40s, so did the retirement hopes of hundreds of thousands of investors, from IBM executives to the small-town grandmother who thought she'd made the safest investment in the world.
- By the time IBM gave up its no-layoffs policy, damaged employee morale was reinforced by former employees who sold T-shirts with the IBM logo spelling out "I've Been Misled."
- After a long career of rising to the top of one of the world's greatest companies, the chairman of IBM, John Akers, resigned under heavy pressure, taking other top executives with him. But more than careers were tarnished that day. On the same day, the company shook the financial world by announcing that for the first time in history, it was slashing its quarterly dividend from $1.21 to $.54 a share.

The fall of IBM, the giant of the computer industry for eighty years, is a classic story of organizational failure. The company went from literally being at the top of the world to fighting for its life. How did it happen? Just as importantly, what changes have current IBM executives implemented to bring new life to the company and regain status as a leader in the computer industry?

Background

IBM grew out of a conglomerate formed in 1911 that primarily made scales, coffee grinders, cheese slicers, and time clocks. The so-called "Computer-Tabulating-Recording" component of the conglomerate grew quickly, and the name change to International Business Machines Corporation in 1924 signaled a significant shift in focus.

For fifty-seven years, until 1971, IBM was led by the Thomas Watsons (senior and junior). The leaders who followed them were not as forceful or visionary as the Watsons, but they inherited a strong company that clearly dominated the computer market. In the mid-1960s, IBM introduced the System/360 family of mainframe computers—six models launched simultaneously, requiring five new factories and creating thousands of new jobs. An outstanding success, the 360 sealed IBM's leadership in the computer industry. Some think it may have marked another turning point as well.

"Bureaucracy Run Amok"

Retired IBM executive Malcolm Robinson, who rose to a senior post in IBM Europe, said, "The scale of the [System/360 project] created a complexity in the business that almost couldn't be handled. It was chaos for a while. So an organization had to be created to bring things under control and make sure that kind of breakdown never happened again. And that really may have been what made the bureaucracy take off."[1] Statistics indicate that Robinson was right. IBM's personnel count went up almost 130 percent between 1963 and 1966, while sales rose about 97 percent.

Many mistakes made by IBM executives were caused by too many people and too many meetings. Decisions that should have been made quickly in response to changes in the computer market were delayed or ignored because of the cumbersome management system that demanded everything be done "the IBM way." For one thing, the IBM way demanded consensus through meetings, so any time a participating staff member "nonconcurred," in the jargon of the company, decisions were referred to another meeting. IBM choked on the bureaucratic culture. When IBM's new chairman took over after the resignation of John Akers, he said of the troubled company, "It was bureaucracy run amok."

The IBM culture led to such things as the ridiculous—but relatively harmless—file of IBM-approved jokes for executives to tell at luncheons or other speaking engagements. But it also led to disaster.

"The Times They Are A-Changin'"

Around the time IBM introduced its 360 line of computers in the mid-1960s, folk singer Bob Dylan's song "The Times They Are A-Changin'" was released. Unfortunately, IBM didn't change with the times. The company staked its claim in the world of multimillion-dollar mainframes. It was late getting into the personal computer market, choosing to steer what company leaders in the 1970s thought was a safe course—preserving the company's mainframe profits.

By the time IBM decided to enter the personal computer game in earnest, the death knell was already starting to toll on the profits from mainframes. The values that guided IBM and its mainframe leadership—the caution, the obsessive training of employees, a focus on following rather than anticipating customer needs, and a guarantee of lifetime employment to its workers—didn't work when IBM moved into the fast-paced, ever-changing, competitive world of personal computers.

It's Not What They Did; It's What They Didn't Do

The IBM PC was an instant success for IBM, but the PC war was already lost. It's what the company *didn't* do, both before and after the introduction of the PC, that ultimately caused its downfall.

The first big mistake IBM made was in not taking advantage of a new technology the company itself invented in the mid-1970s. The reduced instruction-set computing (RISC) microprocessor offered simplified, faster computing, well-suited to the minicomputers that were gaining popularity. But the new technology threatened the huge profits from the company's mainframe business. The decision to develop smaller, less expensive machines with new technology kept getting delayed until the competition stepped way ahead of IBM at its own game.

At least as damaging to IBM's future was its subsequent failure to grab a larger share of PC profits when it had the opportunity. The company signed on with Microsoft for the PC's software and Intel for the microprocessor. IBM might, at the time, have purchased all or part of both of these companies, allowing Big Blue to cash in on the huge profits that are now accruing to the two smaller firms. Several years later, Bill Gates again encouraged IBM to purchase around 10 percent of Microsoft, believing it would be beneficial to his own company as well as to IBM. Again, IBM declined—a very expensive mistake. If IBM had bought 10 percent of Microsoft then, the company would today have turned a $100 million investment into more than $3 billion.

Another thing IBM didn't do quickly was accept that its no-layoffs policy was simply no longer working in the fast-paced world in which the company was operating. As one former manager put it, the policy was defended "like virginity." Rather than admitting the organization needed to be streamlined and the workforce cut, IBM began several years of "reorganizing"—eliminating positions here, firing employees there for the slightest infractions of the rules. The company gradually increased the pressure for workers to accept severance offers. All the time, IBM's then-Chairman John Akers kept insisting that no one was being laid off. Though some championed Akers's efforts to maintain this distinctive piece of IBM's culture, employee morale and company image were severely damaged by these word games by the time IBM finally gave up its sacred no-layoffs policy.

IBM Today

In January 1993, John Akers finally announced that he was stepping down as chairman of IBM, a move that many thought was long overdue. Though Akers wasn't responsible for the problems at IBM, he failed to solve them. The media attention surrounding the announcement of his resignation tarnished IBM's image even further.

IBM's current chairman and CEO, Louis V. Gerstner, Jr., stepped into this mess with the determination to shine up that image and create a culture in which IBM people waste fewer opportunities, minimize bureaucracy, and put the good of the company ahead of their separate divisions. In his first year on the job, he revamped IBM's finances, brought in outsiders to head up several critical divisions, and dramatically altered financial incentives for top executives, basing about 75 percent of their variable pay on the overall performance of the company. Today, sweaters, chinos, and loafers have replaced starched white shirts and suits in many IBM offices, an outward symbol that the company's stiff, bureaucratic culture has given way to a more relaxed, adaptable one. Gerstner, known for his sometimes lightning-quick decisions, dismantled a top-management committee that often stifled action and began talking to employees and customers directly through e-mail. Results so far are impressive. IBM has shifted into growth mode once again, profits have doubled, and share prices are on the rebound.

IBM suffered by missing opportunities and delaying action; Gerstner wants to make sure the same thing doesn't happen in the new networking era. He's pulling together resources from all over the giant company and focusing them on the goal of bringing customers all sorts of network computing services. In addition, Big Blue is ironing out the details of a strategic partnership with Intel to penetrate the growing business of managing networks of PCs all over corporate America. The company is turning out a string of hot new products, including PCs as well as new types of mainframes and midsize computers by the tens of thousands to supply the Internet and the networked corporate world.

Gerstner envisions a future in which major corporations will buy computing power and applications software the way they buy electric service, never even knowing or caring where the computer that does the work is located. Can his wide-ranging vision once again put IBM at the top of the computer world? Or has that world been altered so dramatically that IBM can never catch up? One thing is certain—Lou Gerstner isn't afraid of change: "If the organization doesn't work right one way, we'll change it."[2] On the eve of the twenty-first century, as Gerstner continues his efforts to lead the biggest corporate transformation of all time, the world will be watching.[3]

Welcome to the real world of organization theory. The shifting fortunes of IBM illustrate organization theory in action. IBM managers were deeply involved in organization theory each day of their working lives—but they never realized it. Company managers didn't fully understand how the organization related to the environment or how it should function internally. Familiarity with organization theory can help current IBM managers analyze and diagnose what is happening to the company and the changes needed to turn the company around. Organization theory gives us the tools to explain what happened to IBM. Organization theory also helps us understand what may happen in the future, so we can manage our organizations more effectively.

ORGANIZATION THEORY IN ACTION

Topics

Each of the topics to be covered in this book is illustrated in the IBM case. Consider, for example, IBM's failure to respond to or control such elements as customers, suppliers, and competitors in the fast-paced external environment; its inability to coordinate departments and design control systems that promoted efficiency; slow decision making, such as delaying action on exploiting the potential of new technology; handling the problem of large size; the absence of a forceful top management team that allowed IBM to drift further and further into chaos; and an outmoded corporate culture that stifled innovation and change. These are the subjects with which organization theory is concerned. Organization theory can also help Lou Gerstner find the right organizational structure and strategy to revitalize the giant company.

Of course, organization theory is not limited to IBM. Every organization, every manager in every organization, is involved in organization theory. Johnsonville Foods, a Sheboygan, Wisconsin, sausage maker, turned a floundering family business into a dynamic fast-growing company by reorganizing into self-managed teams. Hewlett-Packard Company—which was suffering from some of the same problems as IBM in the 1980s—went through a major, highly successful reorganization, using concepts based in organization theory. By the mid-1990s, HP was one of the fastest growing PC companies in the computer industry. Eastman Kodak Company is undergoing a similar structural transformation, as leaders struggle to turn an organization characterized by rigid bureaucracy, indecisive management, and demoralized workers into one marked by teamwork, focus on the customer, and willingness to take risks.[4]

Organization theory draws lessons from these organizations and makes those lessons available to students and managers. The story of IBM's decline is important because it demonstrates that even large, successful organizations are vulnerable, that lessons are not learned automatically, and that organizations are only as strong as their decision makers. The stories of Johnsonville Foods, Hewlett-Packard, Eastman Kodak, and IBM also illustrate that organizations are not static; they continuously adapt to shifts in the external environment. Today, many companies are facing the need to transform themselves into dramatically different organizations because of new challenges in the environment.

Current Challenges

Research into hundreds of organizations provides the knowledge base to make IBM and other organizations more effective. For example, challenges facing or-

Book Mark 1.0

Have You Read About This?

Sacred Cows Make the Best Burgers: Paradigm-Busting Strategies for Developing Change-Ready People and Organizations

by Robert Kriegal and David Brandt

The huge spotlight on and the necessity for rapid corporate change have revealed a set of obstacles that inhibit companies from realizing new opportunities. Through a witty and humorous approach, *Sacred Cows Make the Best Burgers* exposes a change-inhibiting set of sacred cows—outmoded beliefs, assumptions, practices, policies, systems and strategies. These old-paradigm cows, such as the paper cow, the downsizing cow, and the work-till-you-drop cow, can be "put out to pasture" to ensure the development of a change-ready organization that "can respond quickly to the challenges and opportunities of the twenty-first century." Such an organization makes people open and receptive to ideas, excited about change, challenged versus threatened by transition, and committed to change as an ongoing process.

Five Steps to Change-Readiness

Kriegal and Brandt offer a five-step approach to creating a change-ready organization:

1. *Round up sacred cows.* Challenge your well-worn beliefs, assumptions, and practices and identify those that have outlived their usefulness. Deal with people who are resistant to change.
2. *Develop a change-ready environment.* Create an environment in which people are more open to innovation and new ideas.
3. *Turn resistance into readiness.* Coach yourself and others to recognize and overcome resistance to change.
4. *Motivate people to change.* Get people excited about change and motivate them to act.
5. *Develop personal change-ready traits.* Cultivate the personal characteristics needed to thrive in a changing environment.

Conclusion

With a starting place of fourteen sacred cows, each with a change-ready thinking tip, the authors uncover and eliminate old-paradigm blind habits—the things we do because we've always done them that way. Using real-world, practical examples of prominent companies, *Sacred Cows* illustrates the ill effect of detrimental ruts and ineffective beliefs and provides workable strategies and anecdotes to overcome a ruinous paradigm.

By removing barriers to becoming change-ready, an organization will create a new paradigm that encourages risk, challenges convention, and chases dreams. It makes "life richer, more rewarding, and much more fun."

Sacred Cows Make the Best Burgers: Paradigm-Busting Strategies for Developing Change-Ready People and Organizations, by Robert Kriegal and David Brandt, is published by Warner Books.

ganizations on the eve of the twenty-first century are quite different from those of the 1970s and 1980s, and thus the concept of organizations and organization theory is evolving. For one thing, the world is changing more rapidly than ever before. In a recent survey, coping with rapid change emerged as the most common problem facing managers and organizations today.[5] As discussed in Book Mark 1.0, today's managers can challenge outmoded assumptions and practices to create change-ready organizations. Some specific challenges facing IBM and other organizations are global competition, the need for organizational renewal, finding strategic advantage, managing new employee relationships, supporting diversity, and maintaining high standards of ethics and social responsibility.

Global Competition. Every company, large and small, faces international competition on its home turf at the same time as it confronts the need to be competitive in international markets. After Japan's economic bubble burst in the early

1990s, many American managers thought Japanese companies were no longer a threat. Japanese leaders, however, are quietly rebuilding their recession-battered companies, once again gaining a competitive edge in speed, quality, and efficiency.[6] Today's managers also deal with increasing global interdependence, with products, services, capital, and human resources crossing borders at a dizzying pace. It's difficult to tell these days which country a product actually comes from—your Mercury Tracer may have come from Mexico, and a neighbor's Nissan may have been built in Tennessee. A Gap polo shirt may be made from cloth cut in the United States but sewn in Honduras. Eat an all-American Whopper and you've just purchased from a British company.[7] At the McDonald's in Cracow, the burgers come from a Polish plant, partly owned by Chicago-based OSI Industries, the onions come from Fresno, California, the buns from a production and distribution center near Moscow, and the potatoes from a plant in Aldrup, Germany.[8] In the face of this growing interdependence, companies such as IBM and Ford are working to globalize their management structures.

Organizational Renewal.   Companies throughout the United States and Canada face the formidable task of reinventing themselves because of dramatic economic and social changes that have forever altered the playing field and the rules for business success. Never before have so many companies across an array of industries simultaneously faced such a challenge. The patterns of behavior and attitude that were once successful no longer work, yet new patterns are just emerging. As one management scholar put it, "Most managers today have the feeling that they are flying the airplane at the same time they are building it."[9]

One of the hottest trends in recent years is called *reengineering,* a radical redesign of business processes that can lead to big results—and usually big layoffs. Organization structures are flatter, with middle management being eliminated and teams of employees empowered to make decisions. The concept of teamwork is a fundamental change in the way work is organized, as companies recognize that the best way to meet the challenges of higher quality, faster service, and total customer satisfaction is through an aligned and coordinated effort by motivated workers. At the Frito-Lay plant in Lubbock, Texas, team members handle everything from potato processing to equipment maintenance. In addition, the team has the authority to select new hires, determine crew scheduling, and discipline team members that aren't pulling their load.[10]

Teamwork and empowerment of employees are key elements in companies that are shifting to what has been called the *learning organization,* an organization in which everyone is engaged in identifying and solving problems, enabling the organization to continuously experiment, improve, and increase its capability. Changing employee behaviors and attitudes is key to the continuous organizational renewal needed in today's rapidly changing world.[11]

Strategic Advantage.   What still matters most for an organization to remain successful is producing results for customers—having a product or service that people want and getting it to them quickly at a competitive price.[12] U.S. and Canadian companies have made dramatic improvements in product and service quality over the past two decades. Although quality and cost are still important, the distinguishing competitive issue today is how fast products and services can be delivered to customers. As part of his efforts to revitalize IBM, one of Lou Gerstner's top priorities is getting products to market faster than competitors. 3M's giant electronics operation in Austin, Texas, cut its product development time from two years to about two months. Through aggressive use of new information technology, GTE Telephone Operations managers reduced the time it takes to complete a customer order from four days to less than two hours.

Information technology facilitates communication and group formation in whatever way is needed to accomplish tasks or projects. Technology dramatically flattens organization structures, so that there may be hundreds of far-flung sites, such as stores or offices, all transmitting information to a single headquarters.[13] New information technology also empowers employees, giving them access to complete information, which enables them to get the job done in less time than if they had to solicit information from superiors or colleagues.

Employee Relationships. The demand for speed and advances in information technology also play a role in another challenge facing today's workers and organizations. As companies become more flexible, employees become more flexible as well. At IBM's Cranford, New Jersey, sales office, six hundred sales representatives do most of their work on the road or from home via modem. Gone are the fancy offices and chats around the water cooler. "This isn't about importance, about epaulets," says manager Duke Mitchell, "It's about what you get done."[14] At the start of 1996, 9.2 million Americans were defined as telecommuters, and the number is predicted to triple within the next fifteen to twenty years.[15]

Working one's way up the career ladder has become a thing of the past as work is being repackaged to meet new economic realities. Managers spend more time moving along a horizontal ladder than a vertical one, as strong project managers become increasingly important in flatter organizations. There is no longer a single career path, but various paths: the entrepreneurial path, the small business path, temporary and contract work, and a multitude of freelancing opportunities.[16] Careers may be defined less by companies than by professions as more people become permanent freelancers or contract workers. Yet, in the new work world, everyone—not just the part-time and contract worker—becomes a "contingent" worker, with employment contingent on the results the organization can achieve.

At IBM today, as at other organizations, the name of the game is no longer "lifetime employment," but "lifelong employability." Both employees and organizations are called on to rethink traditional roles and relationships. Whereas employees have to take charge of their own careers, employers have an obligation to provide opportunities for growth and self-improvement. For example, Raychem Corporation is creatively confronting workplace changes with an in-house career center that gives workers the tools and training they need to continually reinvent themselves and move into new positions, either within or outside the company.[17]

Diversity. Diversity is a fact of life that no organization can afford to ignore. The workforce—as well as the customer base—is changing in terms of age, gender, race, national origin, sexual orientation, and physical ability. Estimates are that by the year 2000 only 15 percent of new entrants to the workforce will be white males.[18] Recent studies also project that in the twenty-first century Asian Americans, African Americans, and Hispanics will make up 85 percent of U.S. population growth and constitute about 30 percent of the total workforce.[19] The growing diversity of the workforce brings a variety of challenges, such as maintaining a strong corporate culture while supporting diversity, balancing work and family concerns, and coping with the conflict brought about by varying cultural styles. For example, Service Merchandise, in Nashville, Tennessee, wisely hired about a dozen Hispanic workers to answer calls from Spanish-speaking customers. The company, however, became embroiled in a serious employee-rights controversy by dictating that the workers could use their native language only while on the phone with customers or in the break room for lunch.[20]

People from diverse ethnic and cultural backgrounds offer varying styles, and organizations must learn to welcome and incorporate this diversity into the upper ranks. For example, recent research has indicated that women's style of doing business may hold important lessons for success in the emerging world of the twenty-first century. Yet the glass ceiling persists, keeping women from reaching positions of top leadership.[21]

Ethics and Social Responsibility.   Ethics and social responsibility have become hot topics in corporate America. Companies of all sizes are rushing to adopt codes of ethics, and most are also developing other policies and structures that encourage ethical conduct. Organizations get into trouble when they fail to pay attention to ethical issues in the blind pursuit of making money. For example, under pressure from CEO Dan Gill to maintain Bausch & Lomb's double-digit sales and earnings growth, managers resorted to inflating revenues by faking sales, shipping products that customers never ordered, and accepting cash and third-party checks that may have indirectly helped launder drug money. After the juggling act at B&L's Hong Kong division began to unravel, a full-scale investigation was launched and the widespread corruption ultimately led to the company's financial downfall.[22]

More companies are recognizing the benefits of contributing to the community. St. Paul Companies, a major insurance company that tops the list of *Business Ethics*'s one hundred most socially responsible companies, gave $2.5 million for a new Science Museum of Minnesota and provides numerous employee programs, such as an on-site day-care facility, which leaders believe attracts better workers. Campbell's Soup Company has for more than two decades sponsored the Camden Summer Program, which provides educational, recreational, and employment opportunities to young people.[23] The public is tired of unethical and socially irresponsible business practices, and organizations will increasingly face the challenge of maintaining high standards in this area.

Purpose of This Chapter

The purpose of this chapter is to explore the nature of organizations and organization theory today. Organization theory has developed from the systematic study of organizations by scholars. Concepts are obtained from living, ongoing organizations. Organization theory can be practical, as illustrated in the IBM case. It helps people understand, diagnose, and respond to emerging organizational needs and problems.

The next section begins with a formal definition of organization and then explores introductory concepts for describing and analyzing organizations. Next, the scope and nature of organization theory are discussed more fully. Succeeding sections consider what organization theory can and cannot do, its usefulness, and how organization theory can help people manage complex organizations. The chapter closes with a brief overview of the important themes to be covered in this book.

WHAT IS AN ORGANIZATION?

Organizations are hard to see. We see outcroppings, such as a tall building or a computer workstation or a friendly employee; but the whole organization is vague and abstract and may be scattered among several locations. We know organizations are there because they touch us every day. Indeed, they are so common we take them for granted. We hardly notice that we are born in a hospital, have our birth records registered in a government agency, are educated in schools and universities, are raised on food produced on corporate farms, are treated by doctors engaged in a joint practice, buy a house built by a construction company and sold by a real estate agency, borrow money from a bank, turn to police and fire departments when trouble erupts, use moving companies to change residences, receive an array of benefits from government agencies, spend forty hours a week working in an organization, and are even laid to rest by an undertaker.[24]

Definition

Organizations as diverse as a church, a hospital, and the International Business Machines Corporation have characteristics in common. The definition used in this book to describe organizations is as follows: **organizations** are (1) social entities that (2) are goal directed, (3) are designed as deliberately structured and coordinated activity systems, and (4) are linked to the external environment.

The key element of an organization is not a building or a set of policies and procedures; organizations are made up of people and their relationships with one another. An organization exists when people interact with one another to perform essential functions that help attain goals. Recent trends in management recognize the importance of human resources, with most new approaches designed to empower employees with greater opportunities to learn and contribute as they work together toward common goals. Managers deliberately structure and coordinate organizational resources to achieve the organization's purpose. However, even though work may be structured into separate departments or sets of activities, most organizations today are striving for greater horizontal coordination of work activities, often using teams of employees from different functional areas to work together on projects. Boundaries between departments as well as those between organizations are becoming more flexible and diffuse as companies face the need to respond to changes in the external environment more rapidly. An organization cannot exist without interacting with customers, suppliers, competitors, and other elements of the external environment. Today, some companies are even cooperating with their competitors, sharing information and technology to their mutual advantage.

Importance of Organizations

Organizations are all around us and shape our lives in many ways. But what contributions do organizations make? Why are they important? Exhibit 1.1 lists seven reasons organizations are important to you and to society. First, organizations bring together resources to accomplish specific goals. Consider the 1996 Summer Olympics. After Atlanta won the bid to host the games, the Atlanta

Exhibit 1.1

Importance of Organizations

1. Bring together resources to achieve desired goals and outcomes
2. Produce goods and services efficiently
3. Facilitate innovation
4. Use modern manufacturing and computer-based technology
5. Adapt to and influence a changing environment
6. Create value for owners, customers, and employees
7. Accommodate ongoing challenges of diversity, ethics, career patterns, and the motivation and coordination of employees

Committee for the Olympic Games (ACOG) had to pull together $1.7 billion, thousands of staff members and volunteers, security and sanitation services, venues for the various activities, computer technology and broadcasting services, and many other types of resources, all directed toward the goal of presenting the Olympics without any city or state support.[25]

Organizations also produce goods and services that customers want at competitive prices. Companies look for innovative ways to produce and distribute goods and services more efficiently. One way is through the use of modern manufacturing technology and new information technology. Redesigning organizational structures and management practices can also contribute to increased efficiency. Organizations create a drive for innovation rather than a reliance on standard products and outmoded ways of doing things. The trend toward the learning organization reflects the desire to improve in all areas. Computer-aided design and manufacturing and new information technology also help promote innovation.

Organizations adapt to and influence a rapidly changing environment. Some large companies have entire departments charged with monitoring the external environment and finding ways to adapt to or influence that environment. One of the most significant changes in the external environment today is globalization. In an effort to influence the environment, for example, Coca-Cola entered into a joint venture with Romania's largest bottler of soft drinks, Ci-Co S.A., to be more competitive with Pepsi in newly opened Eastern European markets.[26]

Through all of these activities, organizations create value for their owners, customers, and employees. Managers need to understand which parts of the operation create value and which parts do not; a company can be profitable only when the value it creates is greater than the cost of resources. McDonald's made a thorough study of how to use its core competencies to create better value for customers. The study resulted in the introduction of Extra Value Meals and the decision to open restaurants in different locations, such as inside Wal-Mart and Sears stores. [27] Finally, organizations have to cope with and accommodate today's challenges of workforce diversity, growing concerns over ethics and social responsibility, and changing career patterns, as well as find effective ways to motivate employees to work together to accomplish organizational goals.

Organizations shape our lives, and well-informed managers can shape organizations. An understanding of organization theory enables managers to design organizations to function more effectively.

ORGANIZATIONS AS SYSTEMS

Open Systems

One significant development in the study of organizations was the distinction between closed and open systems.[28] A **closed system** would not depend on its environment; it would be autonomous, enclosed, and sealed off from the outside world. Although a true closed system cannot exist, early organization studies focused on internal systems. Early management concepts, including scientific management, leadership style, and industrial engineering, were closed-system approaches because they took the environment for granted and assumed the organization could be made more effective through internal design. The management of a closed system would be quite easy. The environment would be stable and predictable and would not intervene to cause problems. The primary management issue would be to run things efficiently.

An **open system** must interact with the environment to survive; it both consumes resources and exports resources to the environment. It cannot seal itself off. It must continuously change and adapt to the environment. Open systems can be enormously complex. Internal efficiency is just one issue—and sometimes a minor one. The organization has to find and obtain needed resources, interpret and act on environmental changes, dispose of outputs, and control and coordinate internal activities in the face of environmental disturbances and uncertainty. Every system that must interact with the environment to survive is an open system. The human being is an open system. So is the planet earth, the city of New York, and IBM. Indeed, one problem at IBM was that top managers seemed to forget they were part of an open system. They isolated themselves within the IBM culture and failed to pay close attention to what was going on with their customers, suppliers, and competitors.

To understand the whole organization, it should be viewed as a system. A **system** is a set of interacting elements that acquires inputs from the environment, transforms them, and discharges outputs to the external environment. The need for inputs and outputs reflects dependency on the environment. Interacting elements mean that people and departments depend on one another and must work together.

Exhibit 1.2 illustrates an open system. Inputs to an organization system include employees, raw materials and other physical resources, information, and financial

Exhibit 1.2

An Open System and Its Subsystems

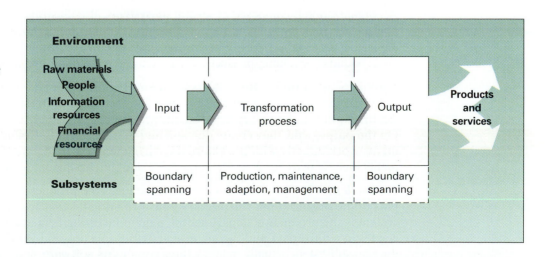

resources. The transformation process changes these inputs into something of value that can be exported back to the environment. Outputs include specific products and services for customers and clients. Outputs may also include employee satisfaction, pollution, and other by-products of the transformation process.

Chaos Theory

The new science of **chaos theory** tells us that we live in a complex world full of randomness and uncertainty. Our world is characterized by surprise, rapid change, and confusion, and often seems totally out of our control. Managers can't measure, predict, or control in traditional ways the unfolding drama inside or outside the organization. However, chaos theory recognizes that this randomness and disorder occurs within certain constraints or larger patterns of order.

One characteristic of chaotic systems, called the *butterfly effect,* is relevant for today's managers. The butterfly effect means small events can have giant effects. A butterfly flapping its wings over Peking can cause air disturbances that will eventually affect the weather in the United States. Today's companies are like the weather—small events may have consequences far beyond their initial strength. For example, an insignificant lawsuit against AT&T had far-reaching effects, resulting in the emergence of MCI and other long-distance carriers and ultimately creating a whole new world of telecommunications.

Today's businesses must be able to respond to the completely unpredictable, within certain bounds of the organization's mission and guiding principles. The rapid change in our world requires organizations to be fluid, perhaps replacing jobs, roles, structures, and even products or services weekly or monthly. In a chaotic world, the big picture is more important than the parts. Managers must imprint the organization's larger mission and values in the minds of employees, thus enabling empowered employees to respond on their own to a random, unpredictable environment. Managers can also flood the organization with information, keeping everyone fully informed. Trends associated with managing chaotic organizations are a shift to worker teams, staying connected to the customer, the empowerment of employees, and a structure based on horizontal work processes rather than vertical functions. Organizations develop subsystems to help cope with rapid change and uncertainty in the external environment.

Organizational Subsystems

An organization is composed of several **subsystems,** also illustrated in Exhibit 1.2. The specific functions required for organization survival are performed by departments that act as subsystems. Organizational subsystems perform five essential functions: boundary spanning, production, maintenance, adaptation, and management.[29]

Boundary Spanning.   Boundary subsystems handle input and output transactions; in other words, they are responsible for exchanges with the environment. On the input side, boundary departments acquire needed supplies and materials. On the output side, they create demand and market outputs. Boundary departments work directly with the external environment. At IBM, boundary departments include marketing on the output side and purchasing on the input side.

Production.   The production subsystem produces the product and service outputs of the organization. The primary transformation takes place here. This subsystem is the production department in a manufacturing firm, the teachers and classes in a university, and the medical activities in a hospital. At IBM, the production subsystem actually manufactures computers, software, and workstations.

Maintenance.   The maintenance subsystem is responsible for the smooth operation and upkeep of the organization. Maintenance includes the cleaning and painting of buildings and the repair and servicing of machines. Maintenance activities also try to meet human needs, such as morale, compensation, and physical comfort. Maintenance functions in a corporation like IBM are performed by such subsystems as the human resources department, the employee cafeteria, and the janitorial staff.

Adaptation.   The adaptive subsystem is responsible for organizational change. The adaptive subsystem scans the environment for problems, opportunities, and technological developments. It is responsible for creating innovations and for helping the organization change and adapt. At IBM, the technology, research, and marketing research departments are responsible for the adaptive function.

Management.   Management is a distinct subsystem, responsible for directing and coordinating the other subsystems of the organization. Management provides direction, strategy, goals, and policies for the entire organization. In addition, the managerial subsystem is responsible for developing organization structure and directing tasks within each subsystem. At IBM the management subsystem consists of the chairman, the vice president, and the managers of its several divisions.

In ongoing organizations, the five subsystems are interconnected and often overlap. Departments often have multiple roles. Marketing is primarily a boundary spanner but may also sense problems or opportunities for innovation. Managers coordinate and direct the entire system, but they are also involved in maintenance, boundary spanning, and adaptation. People and resources in one subsystem may perform other functions in organizations.

DIMENSIONS OF ORGANIZATION DESIGN

The systems view pertains to dynamic, ongoing activities within organizations. The next step for understanding organizations is to look at dimensions that describe specific organizational design traits. These dimensions describe organizations much the same way that personality and physical traits describe people.

Organizational dimensions fall into two types: structural and contextual, illustrated in Exhibit 1.3. **Structural dimensions** provide labels to describe the internal characteristics of an organization. They create a basis for measuring and comparing organizations. **Contextual dimensions** characterize the whole organization, including its size, technology, environment, and goals. They describe the organizational setting that influences and shapes the structural dimensions. Contextual dimensions can be confusing because they represent both the organization and the environment. Contextual dimensions can be envisioned as a set of overlapping elements that underlie an organization's structure and work processes. To understand and evaluate organizations, one must examine both structural and contextual dimensions.[30] These dimensions of organization design interact with one another and can be adjusted to accomplish the purposes listed earlier in Exhibit 1.1.

Structural Dimensions

1. *Formalization* pertains to the amount of written documentation in the organization. Documentation includes procedures, job descriptions, regulations, and policy manuals. These written documents describe behavior and activities. Formalization is often measured by simply counting the number of pages of documentation within the organization. Large state universities,

for example, tend to be high on formalization because they have several volumes of written rules for such things as registration, dropping and adding classes, student associations, dormitory governance, and financial assistance. A small, family-owned business, in contrast, may have almost no written rules and would be considered informal.

2. *Specialization* is the degree to which organizational tasks are subdivided into separate jobs. If specialization is extensive, each employee performs only a narrow range of tasks. If specialization is low, employees perform a wide range of tasks in their jobs. Specialization is sometimes referred to as the *division of labor.*

3. *Standardization* is the extent to which similar work activities are performed in a uniform manner. In a highly standardized organization like McDonald's, work content is described in detail, and similar work is performed the same way at all locations.

4. *Hierarchy of authority* describes who reports to whom and the span of control for each manager. The hierarchy is depicted by the vertical lines on an organization chart, as illustrated in Exhibit 1.4. The hierarchy is related to *span of control* (the number of employees reporting to a supervisor). When spans of control are narrow, the hierarchy tends to be tall. When spans of control are wide, the hierarchy of authority will be shorter.

5. *Complexity* refers to the number of activities or subsystems within the organization. Complexity can be measured along three dimensions: vertical,

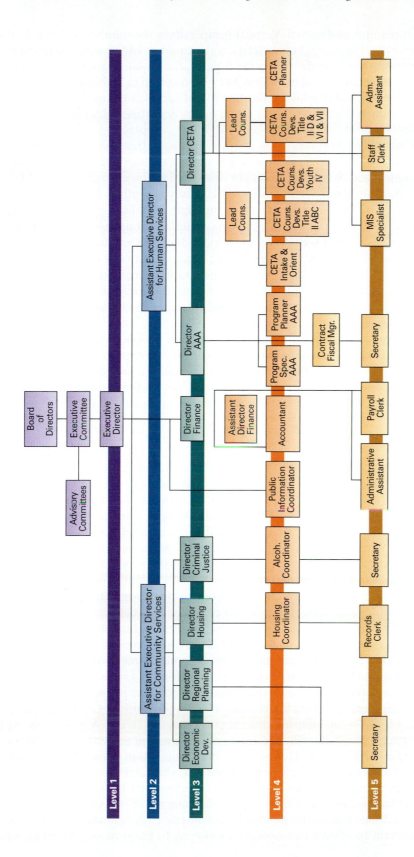

Exhibit 1.4
Organization Chart Illustrating the Hierarchy of Authority and the Structural Complexity for a Community Job Training Program

horizontal, and spatial. Vertical complexity is the number of levels in the hierarchy. Horizontal complexity is the number of job titles or departments existing horizontally across the organization. Spatial complexity is the number of geographical locations. The organization in Exhibit 1.4 has a vertical complexity of five levels. The horizontal complexity can be calculated as either thirty-four job titles or seven major departments. Spatial complexity is low because the organization is located in one place.

6. *Centralization* refers to the hierarchical level that has authority to make a decision. When decision making is kept at the top level, the organization is centralized. When decisions are delegated to lower organizational levels, it is decentralized. Organizational decisions that might be centralized or decentralized include purchasing equipment, establishing goals, choosing suppliers, setting prices, hiring employees, and deciding marketing territories.

7. *Professionalism* is the level of formal education and training of employees. Professionalism is considered high when employees require long periods of training to hold jobs in the organization. Professionalism is generally measured as the average number of years of education of employees, which could be as high as twenty in a medical practice and less than ten in a construction company.

8. *Personnel ratios* refer to the deployment of people to various functions and departments. Personnel ratios include the administrative ratio, the clerical ratio, the professional staff ratio, and the ratio of indirect to direct labor employees. A personnel ratio is measured by dividing the number of employees in a classification by the total number of organizational employees.

Contextual Dimensions

1. *Size* is the organization's magnitude as reflected in the number of people in the organization. It can be measured for the organization as a whole or for specific components, such as a plant or division. Because organizations are social systems, size is typically measured by the number of employees. Other measures such as total sales or total assets also reflect magnitude, but they do not indicate the size of the human part of the social system.

2. *Organizational technology* is the nature of the production subsystem, and it includes the actions and techniques used to change organizational inputs into outputs. An assembly line, a college classroom, and an oil refinery are technologies, although they differ from one another.

3. The *environment* includes all elements outside the boundary of the organization. Key elements include the industry, government, customers, suppliers, and the financial community. Environmental elements that affect an organization the most are often other organizations.

4. The organization's *goals and strategy* define the purpose and competitive techniques that set it apart from other organizations. Goals are often written down as an enduring statement of company intent. A strategy is the plan of action that describes resource allocation and activities for dealing with the environment and for reaching the organization's goals. Goals and strategies define the scope of operations and the relationship with employees, clients, and competitors.

5. An organization's *culture* is the underlying set of key values, beliefs, understandings, and norms shared by employees. These underlying values may pertain to ethical behavior, commitment to employees, efficiency, or cus-

tomer service, and they provide the glue to hold organization members together. An organization's culture is unwritten but can be observed in its stories, slogans, ceremonies, dress, and office layout.

The thirteen contextual and structural dimensions discussed here are interdependent. For example, large organization size, a routine technology, and a stable environment all tend to create an organization that has greater formalization, specialization, and centralization. More detailed relationships among the thirteen dimensions are explored in later chapters of this book.

These dimensions provide a basis for the measurement and analysis of characteristics that cannot be seen by the casual observer, and they reveal significant information about an organization. Consider, for example, the dimensions of W. L. Gore & Associates compared with those of Wal-Mart and a welfare agency.

W. L. Gore & Associates

In Practice 1.1

When Jack Dougherty began work at W. L. Gore & Associates, Inc., he reported to Bill Gore, the company's founder, to receive his first assignment. Gore told him, "Why don't you find something you'd like to do." Dougherty was shocked at the informality but quickly recovered and began interrogating various managers about their activities. He was attracted to a new product called Gore-Tex, a membrane that was waterproof but breathable when bonded to fabric. The next morning, he came to work dressed in jeans and began helping feed fabric into the maw of a large laminator. Five years later, Dougherty was responsible for marketing and advertising in the fabrics group.

Bill Gore died in 1986, but the organization he designed still runs without official titles, orders, or bosses. People are expected to find a place where they can contribute and manage themselves. The company has some 4,200 associates (not employees) in twenty-nine plants. The plants are kept small—up to two hundred people—to maintain a family atmosphere. "It's much better to use friendship and love than slavery and whips," Bill Gore said. Several professional employees are assigned to develop new products, but the administrative structure is lean. Good human relations is a more important value than is internal efficiency, and it works. New plants are being built almost as fast as the company can obtain financing.

Contrast that approach to Wal-Mart's, where efficiency is the goal. Wal-Mart achieves its competitive edge through employee commitment and internal cost efficiency. A standard formula is used to build each store, with uniform displays and merchandise. Wal-Mart has more than 1,300 stores, and its administrative expenses are the lowest of any chain. The distribution system is a marvel of efficiency. Goods can be delivered to any store in less than two days after an order is placed. Stores are controlled from the top, but store managers are also given some freedom to adapt to local conditions. Performance is high, and employees are satisfied because the pay is good and more than half of them share in corporate profits.

An even greater contrast is seen in the welfare office at Newark, New Jersey. The office is small, but workers are overwhelmed with rules. One employee pointed to a four-inch stack of memos about recent rule changes resulting from Congress's rewriting the laws concerning food stamp distribution. Employees don't have time to read the memos, much less learn the new rules. Applicants have to fill out four-page forms without a single mistake or food stamps will be delayed for weeks. Along with the rules, the number of applicants has also been increasing. Most office employees have been thrown into the role of serving clients, and there is little staff to do typing and filing. Employees are frustrated, and so are welfare applicants. Fights break out occasionally. One employee commented, "We're lucky we don't have a riot."[31]

Exhibit 1.5
Characteristics of Three Organizations

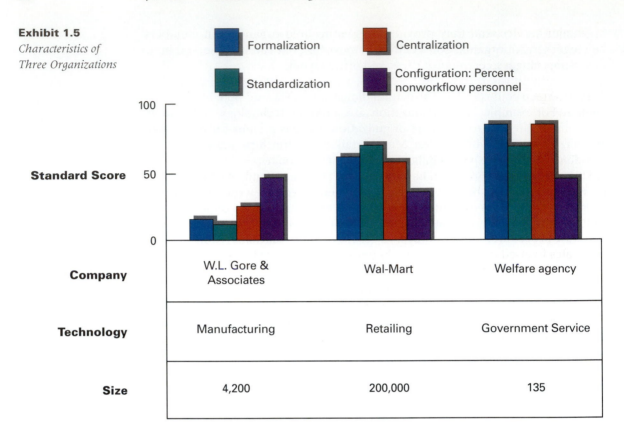

Several structural and contextual dimensions of Gore & Associates, Wal-Mart, and the welfare agency are illustrated in Exhibit 1.5. Gore & Associates is a medium-sized manufacturing organization that ranks very low with respect to formalization, standardization, and centralization. A number of professional staff are assigned to nonworkflow activities to do the research and development needed to stay abreast of changes in the fiber industry. Wal-Mart is much more formalized, standardized, and centralized. Efficiency is more important than new products, so most activities are guided by standard regulations. The percentage of nonworkflow personnel is kept to a minimum. The welfare agency, in contrast to the other organizations, reflects its status as a small part of a large government bureaucracy. The agency is overwhelmed with rules and standard ways of doing things. Rules are dictated from the top. Most employees are assigned to work-flow activities, although in normal times a substantial number of people are devoted to administration and clerical support.

Structural and contextual dimensions can thus tell a lot about an organization and about differences among organizations. Organization design dimensions are examined in more detail in later chapters to determine the appropriate level of each dimension needed to perform effectively in each organizational setting.

WHAT IS ORGANIZATION THEORY?

Organization theory is not a collection of facts; it is a way of thinking about organizations. Organization theory is a way to see and analyze organizations more accurately and deeply than one otherwise could. The way to see and think about organizations is based on patterns and regularities in organizational design and behavior. Organization scholars search for these regularities, define them, measure them, and make them available to the rest of us. The facts from the research are not as important as the general patterns and insights into organizational functioning.

History

You may recall from an earlier management course that the modern era of management theory began early in this century with the classical management perspective, which included both scientific management and administrative principles approaches. **Scientific management,** pioneered by Frederick Taylor, claimed decisions about organization and job design should be based on precise, scientific procedures after careful study of individual situations. **Administrative principles** focused more on the total organization and grew from the insights of practitioners. For example, Henry Fayol proposed fourteen principles of management, such as "each subordinate receives orders from only one superior" (unity of command) and "similar activities in an organization should be grouped together under one manager" (unity of direction).[32] Scientific management and administrative principles were closed systems approaches that did not anticipate the uncertain environment and rapid changes facing today's companies.

Following classical management theory, other academic approaches emerged. The Hawthorne studies showed that positive treatment of employees increased motivation and productivity and laid the groundwork for subsequent work on leadership, motivation, and human resource management. The work of sociologists on bureaucracy, beginning with Weber, appeared in the 1950s and 1960s and helped establish the notions of bureaucracy that will be discussed in Chapter 5. Later organizations came to be characterized as rational, problem-solving, decision-making systems.[33]

Scientific management, administrative principles, and bureaucratic approaches to organizing seemed to work well into the 1950s and 1960s. Now we see that success during this period occurred because the economies of Europe and Japan had been shattered by World War II, so North American companies had the playing field to themselves. Organizations became horrendously overmanaged, with bloated administrative ratios and professional staff ratios that would sink many organizations in the 1970s and 1980s. International competition from Europe and Japan provided the rude awakening. For example, Xerox discovered it was using 1.3 overhead workers for every direct worker, while its Japanese affiliate needed only 0.6 overhead workers. By the 1980s North American companies had to find a better way. AT&T cut thirty thousand managers during the 1980s. The merger of Chevron and Gulf led to the dismissal of eighteen thousand employees, many of whom were managers. GE laid off fifty thousand salaried employees.[34]

The 1980s produced new corporate cultures that valued lean staff, flexibility, rapid response to the customer, motivated employees, caring for customers, and quality products. The world was changing fast because corporate boundaries were altered by waves of merger activity, much of it international, and increased international competition.

Today, the world—and thus the world of business—is undergoing a change more profound and far-reaching than any experienced since the dawn of the modern age and the scientific revolution about five hundred years ago. Just as civilization was altered irrevocably in the transition from the agrarian to the industrial age, emerging events will change the ways in which we interact with one another in our personal and professional lives. Old organization forms and management methods are inadequate to cope with new problems in the emerging postmodern world.[35] The net effect of the evolving business environment and the evolving study of organization theory is a new, more flexible approach to management and the use of contingency theory to describe and convey organizational concepts.

The Postmodern Organization Paradigm

The challenges produced by today's rapidly changing environment—global competitiveness, diversity, ethical issues, rapid advances in technology and communications, a shift away from an exploitative to an ecologically sensitive approach to the natural environment, and the growing expectation of workers for meaningful work and opportunities for personal and professional growth—require dramatically different responses from people and organizations. A recent book argued that most business schools are not preparing students for the postmodern world but rather are stuck in the old way of doing things, essentially offering degrees in "bureaucratic" administration rather than business administration.[36] Yet it is the managers of tomorrow who will have to design and orchestrate new responses to a dramatically new world.

Significant changes are already occurring in organizations in response to changes in the society at large. These changes are reflected in Exhibit 1.6 as a shift from the modern to the postmodern organization paradigm.[37] A **paradigm** is a shared mind-set that represents a fundamental way of thinking, perceiving, and understanding the world. Our beliefs and understandings direct our behavior. In today's fast-paced society, a number of shifts in ways of thinking and understanding are occurring, and these in turn are associated with shifts in understanding and behavior taking place in organizations.

Before the Industrial Revolution, most organizations were related to agriculture or craft work. Communication was primarily face-to-face. Organizations were small, with simple structures and fuzzy boundaries, and were generally not

Exhibit 1.6

Modern Versus Postmodern Organization Paradigms

Modern	Contextual Variables	Postmodern
Stable	Environment	Turbulent
Money, buildings, machines	Form of capital	Information
Routine	Technology	Nonroutine
Large	Size	Small to moderate
Growth, efficiency	Goals	Learning, effectiveness
Employees taken for granted	Culture	Employees empowered
Organizational Outcomes		
Rigid & centralized, distinct boundaries	Structure	Flexible & decentralized, diffuse boundaries
Autocratic	Leadership	Servant leadership
Formal, written	Communication	Informal, oral
Bureaucratic	Control	Decentralized, self-control
Managers	Planning & decision making	Everyone
Patriarchal	Guiding principles	Egalitarian

interested in growing larger. In the modern, industrial age, however, a new organization paradigm emerged. Growth became a primary criterion for success. Organizations became large and complex, and boundaries between functional departments and between organizations were distinct. Environments were relatively stable, and technologies tended to be mass-production manufacturing processes. The primary forms of capital in the modern age were money, buildings, and machines. Internal structures became more complex, vertical, and bureaucratic. Leadership was based on solid management principles and tended to be autocratic; communication was primarily through formal, written documents, such as memos, letters, and reports. Managers did all the planning and "thought work," while employees did the manual labor in exchange for wages and other compensation.

In the postmodern world of today, the environment is anything *but* stable, and the postmodern organization recognizes the chaotic, unpredictable nature of the world. In a world characterized by rapid change, complexity, and surprise, managers can't measure, predict, or control in traditional ways the unfolding drama inside or outside the organization. To cope with this chaos, organizations need a newer paradigm, in which they tend toward moderate size, with flexible, decentralized structures that emphasize horizontal cooperation. In addition, boundaries between organizations again become more diffuse, as even competitors learn to cooperate to meet turbulent environmental conditions. The primary form of capital in the postmodern organization is not money or machines but *information,* and methods of motivation provide workers more intrinsic satisfaction from their jobs. Workers are often empowered to make decisions once reserved for managers, and emphasis on a clear and powerful vision or mission helps to ensure that decisions are made to achieve the organization's overriding purpose. Sound management is still important in postmodern organizations; however, leadership qualities are often quite different. "Servant" leadership takes center stage, as managers serve employees who in turn serve customers. In addition, informal leaders frequently emerge for limited periods of time in response to specific problems and then fade back into organizational teams as new conditions require other leaders with different skills and capabilities.

Qualities traditionally considered egalitarian—equality, empowerment, horizontal relationships, and consensus building—are particularly important in the postmodern organization. Chrysler's oldest plant, a machine-and-forge facility in New Castle, Indiana, experienced a remarkable turnaround by shifting to the postmodern form of organization, as described in The New Paradigm box.

Contingency

Despite the changes in the environment, organizations are not all alike. A great many problems occur when all organizations are treated as similar, which was the case with both the administrative principles and bureaucratic approaches that tried to design all organizations alike. The organization charts and financial systems that work in the retail division of a conglomerate will not be appropriate in the manufacturing division.

Contingency means that one thing depends on other things, and for organizations to be effective, there must be a "goodness of fit" between their structure and the conditions in their external environment.[38] What works in one setting may not work in another setting. There is not one best way. Contingency theory means "it depends." For example, the terms in Exhibit 1.6 illustrate contingency

The New Paradigm

Chrysler's New Castle Plant

In the mid-1980s, Chrysler's dank, dirty machine-and-forge facility in New Castle, Indiana, was on the verge of being written off by headquarters as a rust-belt dinosaur not worth keeping. Today, it is a competitive showcase of lean production and a model for the twenty-first century organization. Thirty million dollars' worth of new equipment turns out parts for everything from the Neon to minivans, and for the first time in almost twenty years, the plant is hiring new workers for around-the-clock production. Worker absenteeism is down to 2.8 percent, one of the lowest among Chrysler's plants, and grievances, which reached as high as eight hundred in 1985, now total only thirty to forty per year.

The United Auto Workers and Chrysler management worked together to save the aging plant by creating self-directed teams and a new work ethic. The spark for the transformation was provided by what everyone at New Castle calls the MOA, short for Modern Operating Agreement—a radical new blueprint that calls for management and labor working cooperatively to manage the plant. The MOA manifests itself in both small changes and radical shifts. For example, no neckties or time clocks are allowed in the plant. Responsibility for plant production rests in the hands of seventy-one small teams of factory workers who make decisions, handle discipline, and coach one another to peak performance. The number of supervisors has been cut from fifty-six to twenty-six, and these act as advisers to the teams.

There are frequent town-hall style meetings between labor and management to air concerns, and a new $250,000 video communications network facilitates the exchange of information between the two groups. Workers are encouraged to stop by the plant manager's office anytime to offer suggestions or criticism without fear of reprisals. The open atmosphere helps keep motivation and morale high. Other motivational techniques are also used. For example, there are informal awards sessions where workers can win service pins or baseball caps. A Capability Pay Progression Plan gives workers a chance to earn more by voluntarily learning more jobs. Continuous training is available, from basic literacy classes, to computer training, to role-playing exercises designed to promote diversity awareness.

By working cooperatively, Chrysler and the UAW have created a new environment in which workers want to better themselves and have the opportunity to do so. Plant manager Dennis Mason explains that "fear drove the change," but he and everyone else at New Castle expects the plant to continue to evolve in response to turbulent conditions of the emerging postmodern world.

Source: Anita Lienert, "Forging a New Partnership," *Management Review,* October 1994, 39–43.

---

theory. Some organizations may experience a certain environment, use a routine technology, and desire efficiency. In this situation, a management approach that uses bureaucratic control procedures, a functional structure, and formal communication would be appropriate. Likewise, free-flowing management processes work best in an uncertain environment with a nonroutine technology. The correct management approach is contingent on the organization's situation.

MULTIPLE PERSPECTIVES OF ORGANIZATION THEORY

Organization theorists—and some managers—tend to align themselves with distinct perspectives or frames of reference toward organizations. The perspective adopted throughout most of this book is sometimes called the rational-contingency perspective. Two alternative perspectives are radical-Marxism and transaction-cost economics.

Rational-Contingency Perspective

The **rational-contingency perspective** carries an implicit manager orientation toward efficiency and maintenance of the organizational status quo.[39] Researchers adopting this perspective accept the organization status quo as given and simply search for regularities to test to predict and control the organization toward greater efficiency and performance. This perspective assumes that managers are intentionally rational. Managers may not always have the correct answer, but they try to do what is logically best for the organization. Rationality means that goals are selected, effectiveness criteria are established, and managers adopt strategies to achieve designated outcomes in the manner best for the organization. Moreover, managers try to logically design structure and processes to fit the contingencies of environment, technology, and other factors in the organization's situation. The rational-contingency view is widely held, and adherents believe that organizations are instruments for accomplishing tasks that benefit everyone in the organization.[40] Again, most of the concepts in this book are based on the rational-contingency perspective.

Radical-Marxism Perspective

Organization theorists who adopt a **radical-Marxism** perspective agree that managers are intentionally rational, but with a twist. Managers are believed to make decisions to maintain themselves in the capitalist class, keeping power and resources for themselves. Managers make decisions not for organizational efficiency and productivity but to maintain or enhance their positions. Thus, workers are given small jobs not to increase output but because it "de-skills" workers and prevents them from having a larger claim on the organization. The radical-Marxism perspective is driven by egalitarian values, and CEO salaries that can be two hundred times larger than employee salaries add legitimacy to this argument.

A second aspect of this perspective is the belief in changing the status quo. The goal of organizational theory should be to free organization employees from alienation, exploitation, and repression. Radical-Marxists believe organization theory should have a political agenda that examines the legitimacy of what organizations do and uncovers power and resource distortions. Indeed, the most extreme proponents of this view would like to see a societal transformation that would stop members high in the social hierarchy from dominating lower members.[41]

Transaction-Cost Economics Perspective

This approach developed out of the field of economics and has received attention from a number of organizational theorists and organization sociologists.[42] The **transaction-cost economics** perspective assumes that individuals act in their self-interest and that exchanges of goods and services could theoretically occur in the free marketplace. However, as environments become complex and uncertain, the transaction costs become prohibitive. Contracts become lengthy, number in the hundreds, and cannot all be supervised; hence, transactions are brought within the hierarchy of an organization. Behavior can be monitored through supervision, control systems, and audits less expensively than through contracts. A particular organization structure occurs because it is most cost efficient. The goal of individuals in organizations is to reduce transaction costs.

Thus, the focus of this perspective is on the exchange of goods and services rather than on production, and it takes a rather narrow, economic view of organization events. Proponents of the transaction-cost perspective agree it cannot explain all behavior in organizations. Most people and organizations want to behave in ways that minimize costs. However, many activities within organizations are based on trust and social relationships rather than on supervision, contracts, and economic relationships.

WHAT ORGANIZATION THEORY CAN DO

Why study organizations? Most people who study organization theory belong to one of two groups: those who are organization managers or potential managers, and those who will not be managers. For the second group, the reason is to appreciate and understand more about the world around them. Organization theory can provide an appreciation and understanding of what is happening in organizations. North America is a society of organizations, and organizations are the key social entities of our time. By studying organizations, you can learn more about a significant aspect of your environment, just as you would by studying geography, astronomy, or music.

For people who are or will be managers, organization theory provides significant insight and understanding to help them become better managers. As in the case of IBM, many managers learn organization theory by trial and error. At IBM, the managers did not understand the situation they were in or the contingencies to which they should respond. The same thing happened at People Express Airlines. In 1984 it was considered one of the best-managed companies; twenty-four months later, it flopped. People Express's informal organization structure and control systems were not suited to a large airline. Organization theory identifies variables and provides models so managers know how to diagnose and explain what is happening around them and thus can organize for greater effectiveness.

In a very real sense, organization theory can make a manager more competent and more influential. Understanding how and why organizations act lets managers know how to react. The study of organizations enables people to see and understand things other people cannot see and understand. The topic of organizational culture has been increasingly important in recent years as organizations shift to structures emphasizing teamwork and consensus building. Companies such as Xerox are finding that by using social scientists to help them understand their culture, they can improve productivity and cut costs.

| In Practice 1.2 | *Xerox* |

When Xerox set out in the 1980s to devise less expensive and more productive training programs for its service technicians, it asked for the help of anthropologist Julian Orr. By going on service calls himself, Orr found that repairing copy machines wasn't the technicians' most difficult job—it was handling the people who were trying to use the machines. He found that a large number of service calls were from customers who simply didn't know how to use the complex copiers, not from users whose machines broke down. The technicians often found themselves acting as teachers. While Xerox was focusing on adding more in-depth and complex technological training, the problems service technicians encountered most often were problems of relationships. With this new knowledge, Xerox could develop methods for helping technicians deal with both the machine and the human aspects of their jobs.[43]

The experience at Xerox shows the positive side of what organization theory can do in the area of corporate culture. Organization theory also covers many additional topics that are discussed in this book. The next section provides an overview of these topic areas.

FRAMEWORK FOR THE BOOK

What topic areas are relevant to organization theory and design? How does a course in management or organizational behavior differ from a course in organization theory? The answer is related to the concept called level of analysis.

Levels of Analysis

In systems theory, each system is composed of subsystems. Systems are nested within systems, and one **level of analysis** has to be chosen as the primary focus. Four levels of analysis normally characterize organizations, as illustrated in Exhibit 1.7. The individual human being is the basic building block of organizations. The human being is to the organization what a cell is to a biological system. The next higher system level is the group or department. These are collections of individuals who work together to perform group tasks. The next level of analysis is the organization itself. An organization is a collection of groups or departments that combine into the total organization. Organizations themselves can be grouped together into the next higher level of analysis, which is the interorganizational set and community. The interorganizational set is the group of organizations with which a single organization interacts. Other organizations in the community also make up an important part of an organization's environment.

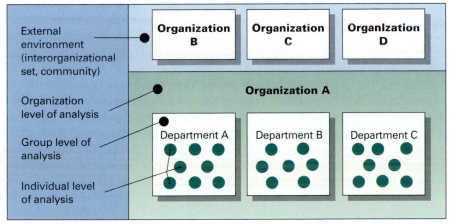

Exhibit 1.7

Levels of Analysis in Organizations

Source: Based on Andrew H. Van de Ven and Diane L. Ferry, *Measuring and Assessing Performance* (New York: Wiley, 1980), p. 8; and Richard L. Daft and Richard M. Steers, *Organizations: A Micro/Macro Approach* (Glenview, Ill.:Scott, Foresman, 1986), p. 8.

Organization theory focuses on the organizational level of analysis but with concern for groups and the environment. To explain the organization, one should look not only at its characteristics but also at the characteristics of the environment and of the departments and groups that make up the organization. The focus of this book is to help you understand organizations by examining their specific characteristics, the nature and relationships among groups and departments that make up the organization, and the collection of organizations that make up the environment.

Are individuals included in organization theory? Organization theory does consider the behavior of individuals, but in the aggregate. People are important, but they are not the primary focus of analysis. Organization theory is distinct from organizational behavior. **Organizational behavior** is the micro approach to organizations because it focuses on the individuals within organizations as the relevant units of analysis. Organizational behavior examines concepts such as motivation, leadership style, and personality and is concerned with cognitive and emotional differences among people within organizations. **Organization theory** is a macro examination of organizations because it analyzes the whole organization as a unit. Organization theory is concerned with people aggregated into departments and organizations and with the differences in structure and behavior of the organization level of analysis. Organization theory is the sociology of organizations, while organizational behavior is the psychology of organizations.

A new approach to organization studies is called meso theory. Most organizational research and many management courses specialize in either organizational behavior or organization theory. **Meso theory** (*meso* means "in between") concerns the integration of both micro and macro levels of analysis. Individuals and groups affect the organization and the organization in return influences individuals and groups. To thrive in organizations, managers and employees need to understand multiple levels simultaneously. For example, research may show that employee diversity enhances innovation. To facilitate innovation, managers need to understand how structure and context (organization theory) are related to interactions among diverse employees (organizational behavior) to foster innovation, because both macro and micro variables account for innovations.[44]

For its part, organization theory is directly relevant to top- and middle-management concerns and partly relevant to lower management. Top managers are responsible for the entire organization and must set goals, develop strategy, interpret the external environment, and decide organization structure and design. Middle management is concerned with major departments, such as marketing or research, and must decide how the department relates to the rest of the organization. Middle managers must design their departments to fit work-unit technology and deal with issues of power and politics, intergroup conflict, and information and control systems, each of which is part of organization theory. Organization theory is only partly concerned with lower management because this level of supervision is concerned with employees who operate machines, type letters, teach classes, and sell goods. Organization theory is concerned with the big picture of the organization and its major departments.

Plan of the Book

The topics within the field of organization theory are interrelated. Chapters are presented so that major ideas unfold in logical sequence. The framework that guides the organization of the book is shown in Exhibit 1.8. Part 1 introduces the

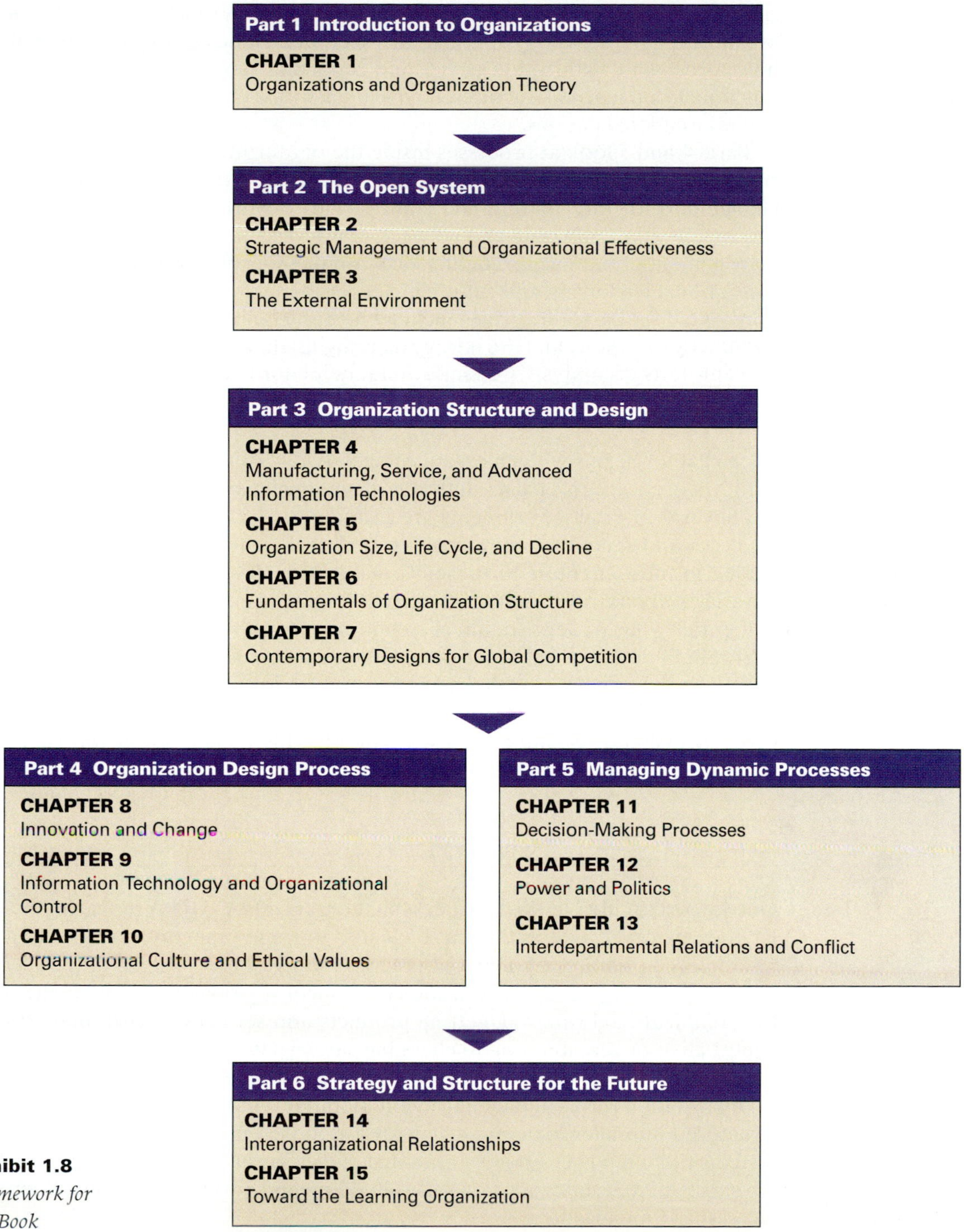

Part 1 Introduction to Organizations

CHAPTER 1
Organizations and Organization Theory

Part 2 The Open System

CHAPTER 2
Strategic Management and Organizational Effectiveness

CHAPTER 3
The External Environment

Part 3 Organization Structure and Design

CHAPTER 4
Manufacturing, Service, and Advanced
Information Technologies

CHAPTER 5
Organization Size, Life Cycle, and Decline

CHAPTER 6
Fundamentals of Organization Structure

CHAPTER 7
Contemporary Designs for Global Competition

Part 4 Organization Design Process

CHAPTER 8
Innovation and Change

CHAPTER 9
Information Technology and Organizational
Control

CHAPTER 10
Organizational Culture and Ethical Values

Part 5 Managing Dynamic Processes

CHAPTER 11
Decision-Making Processes

CHAPTER 12
Power and Politics

CHAPTER 13
Interdepartmental Relations and Conflict

Part 6 Strategy and Structure for the Future

CHAPTER 14
Interorganizational Relationships

CHAPTER 15
Toward the Learning Organization

Exhibit 1.8
*Framework for
the Book*

basic idea of organizations as social systems and the nature of organization theory. This discussion provides the groundwork for Part 2, which is about top management, goals and effectiveness, and the external environment. Organizations
are open systems that exist for a purpose. The nature of the environment and the
achievement of that purpose are the topics of Part 2. Part 3 describes how to de-

sign the organization's structure. Organization design is related to such factors as organizational technology and size. This section includes a chapter that explains how to design organization charts and reporting relationships for divisional, functional, and matrix structures. It concludes with a chapter on new team-based and international designs.

Parts 4 and 5 look at processes inside the organization. Part 4 describes how structure can be designed to influence internal systems for innovation and change and for information and control. Part 5 shifts to dynamic behavioral processes that exist within and between major organizational departments. The management of intergroup conflict, decision making, power and politics, and organizational leadership and culture are covered there. Part 6 considers organizational issues of the future, which include the burgeoning network of relationships among organizations and the newly emerging learning organization.

Plan of Each Chapter

Each chapter begins with an organizational case to illustrate the topic to be covered. Theoretical concepts are introduced and explained in the body of the chapter. Several In Practice segments are included in each chapter to illustrate the concepts and show how they apply to real organizations. Book Marks are included in most chapters to present organizational issues managers face right now. These book reviews discuss current concepts and applications to deepen and enrich your understanding of organizations. The New Paradigm examples illustrate the dramatic changes taking place in management thinking and practice. Each chapter closes with a Summary and Interpretation section and a Brief-case section. Summary and Interpretation reviews and interprets important theoretical concepts. The Briefcase section highlights key points for use in designing and managing organizations.

SUMMARY AND INTERPRETATION

One important idea in this chapter is that organizations are systems. In particular, they are open systems that must adapt to the environment to survive. Change has replaced stability as a key trait in today's organizations. Some of the specific challenges managers and organizations face include global competition, the need for organizational renewal, getting products and services to customers fast at competitive prices, adapting to changing career patterns, coping with diversity, and maintaining high ethical standards. These challenges are leading to changes in organization forms and management methods. The trend is away from highly structured bureaucratic approaches toward looser, more flexible management systems that empower employees to make decisions and provide more intrinsic job satisfaction. Teamwork, consensus building and horizontal collaboration are increasingly important.

The focus of analysis for organization theory is not individual people but the organization itself. Relevant concepts include the dimensions of organization structure and context. The dimensions of formalization, specialization, standardization, hierarchy of authority, complexity, centralization, professionalism, personnel ratios, size, organizational technology, environment, goals and strategy, and culture provide labels for measuring and analyzing organizations. These dimensions vary widely from organization to organization. Subsequent chapters provide frameworks for analyzing organizations with these concepts.

Another important idea is that organization theory consists of multiple perspectives. This book tends to adopt the managerial, rational-contingency approach to organization theory. Other equally valid approaches include the radical-Marxist and the transaction-cost economics perspectives.

Finally, most concepts pertain to the top- and middle-management levels of the organization. This book is concerned more with the topics of those levels than with the operational level topics of supervision and motivation of employees, which are discussed in courses on organizational behavior.

Key Concepts

administrative principles	organization theory
chaos theory	paradigm
closed system	radical-Marxism
contextual dimensions	rational-contingency perspective
contingency	scientific management
level of analysis	structural dimensions
meso theory	subsystems
open system	system
organizational behavior	transaction-cost economics
organizations	

Discussion Questions

1. What is the definition of *organization*? Briefly explain each part of the definition.
2. What is the difference between an open system and a closed system? Can you give an example of a closed system?
3. What are the five subsystems in organizations? If an organization had to give up one system, which one could it survive the longest without? Explain.
4. Why might human organizations be considered more complex than machine-type systems? What is the implication of this complexity for managers?
5. What is the difference between formalization, specialization, and standardization? Do you think an organization high on one of these three dimensions would also be high on the others? Discuss.
6. Discuss ways in which your own life has been affected by the shift from the modern to the postmodern age. What advantages and disadvantages can you see in working for a team-based organization such as Chrysler's New Castle plant?
7. What does *contingency* mean? What are the implications of contingency theories for managers?
8. What levels of analysis are typically studied in organization theory? How would these contrast with the level of analysis studied in a course in psychology? Sociology? Political science?
9. What is the value of organization theory for nonmanagers? For managers?
10. Early management theorists believed that organizations should strive to be logical and rational, with a place for everything and everything in its place. Discuss the pros and cons of this approach for today's organizations.

Briefcase

As an organization manager, keep the following guides in mind:

1. Do not ignore the external environment or protect the organization from it. Because the environment is unpredictable, do not expect to achieve complete order and rationality within the organization. Strive for a balance between order and flexibility.
2. Assign people and departments to perform the subsystem functions of production, boundary spanning, maintenance, adaptation, and management. Do not endanger the organization's survival and effectiveness by overlooking these functions.
3. Think of the organization as an entity distinct from the individuals who work in it. Describe the organization according to its size, formalization, decentralization, complexity, specialization, professionalism, personnel ratios, and the like. Use these characteristics to analyze the organization and to compare it with other organizations.
4. Be cautious when applying something that works in one situation to another situation. All organizational systems are not the same. Use organization theory to identify the correct structure, goals, strategy, and management systems for each organization.
5. Make yourself a competent, influential manager by using the frameworks that organization theory provides to interpret and understand the organization around you. Be aware of which perspective you adopt and believe in. Use organization theory to handle such things as intergroup conflict, power and politics, organization structure, environmental change, and organizational goals.

Chapter One Workbook *Measuring Dimensions of Organizations**

Analyze two organizations along the dimensions shown below. Indicate where you think each organization would fall on all of the scales. Use an "X" to indicate the first organization and an "*" to show the second.

You may choose any two organizations you are familiar with, such as your place of work, the university, a student organization, your church or synagogue, or your family.

Formalization

| Many written rules | 1 2 3 4 5 6 7 8 9 10 | Few rules |

Specialization

| Separate tasks and roles | 1 2 3 4 5 6 7 8 9 10 | Overlapping tasks |

Hierarchy

| Tall hierarchy of authority | 1 2 3 4 5 6 7 8 9 10 | Flat hierarchy of authority |

Technology

| Product | 1 2 3 4 5 6 7 8 9 10 | Service |

External Environment

| Stable | 1 2 3 4 5 6 7 8 9 10 | Unstable |

Culture

| Clear norms and values | 1 2 3 4 5 6 7 8 9 10 | Ambiguous norms and values |

Professionalism

| High professional training | 1 2 3 4 5 6 7 8 9 10 | Low professional training |

Goals

| Well-defined goals | 1 2 3 4 5 6 7 8 9 10 | Goals not defined |

Size

| Small | 1 2 3 4 5 6 7 8 9 10 | Large |

Organizational Paradigm

| Modern | 1 2 3 4 5 6 7 8 9 10 | Postmodern |

Questions

1. What are the main differences between the two organizations you evaluated?

2. Would you recommend that one or both of the organizations have different ratings on any of the scales? Why?

Case for Analysis *S-S Technologies Inc. (A)—Introduction**

In January 1994, Rick Brock and Keith Pritchard, owners of S-S Technologies Inc. (SST) were concerned with the rapid rate of growth facing their company. SST had revenues of $6.3 million in 1993 and employed 30 highly skilled workers. These numbers could double or triple in the next couple of years. To determine how well SST was structured to achieve its future goals, Brock hired a consultant he had worked with successfully in the past. The consultant's major role was to make recommendations as to the appropriate organizational design (culture, people, layers of management and administrative systems) in the event that SST grew from 30 to 60 or even 120 employees. As a by-product of his activities at SST, the consultant also questioned whether some marketing opportunities were being missed with the current operations. In addition, questions regarding employee compensation had begun to surface, and the owners wanted to address this issue as soon as possible. Finally, the consultant wondered if a more formalized measurement system, directly tied to the company's strategic objectives, was necessary for SST's growth and prosperity.

Company Information

S-S Technologies Inc., incorporated in 1992, was a 100 percent Canadian-owned company which had focused on industrial software and hardware development. Previously, the same business had operated for 12 years

Exhibit 1.9

*SS-Technologies
Organization Chart*

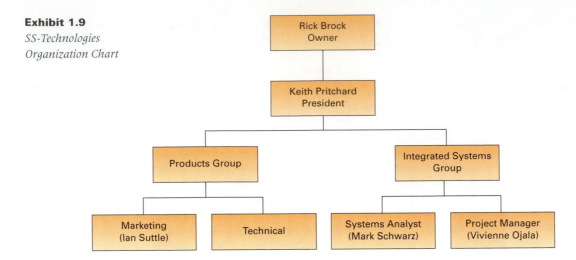

as a division of Sutherland-Schultz Limited, a large integrated engineering and construction company. When Sutherland-Schultz changed ownership, the new owner sold the SST portion of the company to Brock. Ultimately, SST was owned by its CEO Rick Brock, former president of Sutherland-Schultz, and by Keith Pritchard, president of SST. A brief organization chart is provided as Exhibit 1.9

SST had unique expertise in the factory automation market. The company brought together engineers and technicians with different but synergistic expertise to focus on projects that other systems integrators were unable or unwilling to handle. Out of these efforts, several unique communication and simulation products evolved. The company recognized the opportunities these products represented, and expanded its capabilities to successfully bring these products to the global automation market. Over the last three years, SST had grown an average of 33 percent per year (the Products Group had grown an average of 64 percent and the Integrated Systems Group an average of 30 percent), as shown in Exhibit 1.10.

Operating Groups

As Exhibit 1.9 indicates, SST was divided into two distinct groups: the Products Group (PG), and the Integrated Systems Group (ISG), each with its own characteristics.

Products Group

PG was involved in the development and marketing of the company's unique hardware and software products. The products were sold around the world through licensed representatives, distributors and direct sales. There were two key types of products:

Direct-Link Interface Cards were totally programmable interfaces designed to make it easier and quicker to exchange data between personal computers and industrial computers/programmable controllers. In layman's terms, the product allowed office computers to communicate with factory floor computers (commonly termed PLC's, or Programmable Logic Controllers). SST designed and manufactured the interfaces for both the factory floor computers and desktop computers, as well as com-

Exhibit 1.10

*SS-Technologies
Revenues*

Year	Products	Integrated Systems	Total*
1990	$931,000	$1,100,000	$2,685,202
1991	$1,638,000	$1,200,000	$3,570,797
1992	$2,763,000	$1,300,000	$4,521,987
1993	$4,036,000	$2,270,000	$6,306,000
1994**	$5,200,000	$3,500,000	$8,700,000

*Includes other sources of income and expenses
**Projection

plementary diagnostic software to ensure that computer networks were performing optimally. The Direct-Link cards received the *Canada Award for Business Excellence in Innovation* from Industry, Science and Technology Canada in 1991.

PICS (Programmable Industrial Control Simulator) was a hardware and software package that allowed a personal computer (PC) to simulate, in real-time, an automated factory floor environment. To use PICS, a PC (running the PICS software) is connected directly to a PLC via a Direct-Link card. An experienced software developer then programs, under the PICS environment, a set of routines which send input to and receive output from the PLC, allowing the PC to act as if it were one or more automated factory machines. The PLC is, in essence, "tricked" into thinking it is actually running the automated factory floor, allowing the user to ensure that the PLC software is performing properly. The system can be used for debugging new industrial software, re-tooling, and employee training, all of which result in substantial time and cost savings for the user.

These products, developed by SST, were often the result of a solution to a technical problem no other company could solve. PG also had a number of other products and ideas under consideration for possible launch in 1994 or 1995.

PG's key success factors fell into two categories: products and marketing. Quality product performance was imperative. In case of faulty products, a replacement had to be provided quickly. In addition, new products were needed to maintain pace with a rapidly changing plant electronic environment. PG's growth also depended highly on marketing. Product awareness by systems integration engineers complemented by an efficient and effective distribution network was vital for PG's successful growth.

Integrated Systems Group

ISG was involved in three distinct, yet often interrelated areas of services: consulting, system engineering, and customer support. ISG employed computer professionals and engineers who were dedicated to the development of software and hardware solutions for complex factory floor systems. Clients were provided with tested, reliable and sophisticated solutions for data collection, custom control software, batching systems, diagnostic systems and programmable controller simulation. ISG also implemented and commissioned packaged control software, and provided project management for large and technically complex projects. ISG customers included industrial manufacturers and institutional organizations.

ISG's key success factors were to complete projects on time, on budget and of high quality. To date, ISG had received excellent feedback from clients. ISG's performance depended highly on the quality of its employees. Its goals were for manageable growth, focusing on projects within the company's scope and skills.

Environment

In early 1990, the North American economy was in a recession. Although recovery was widely predicted, some results of the recession were permanent. Companies sought to maintain margins during this recession through downsizing and reducing production costs. SST's Products Group benefited from this trend because PICS and Direct-Link cards offered ways of reducing the cost of automating a plant, a move which often reduced production costs. The market for PG grew despite the recession. The recession also meant that many companies eliminated or drastically reduced their in-house engineering capabilities and sought to subcontract this work, a trend that benefited ISG.

Case for Analysis *S-S Technologies Inc. (D)—Organizational Design**

The task of designing an organization to support S-S Technologies Inc.'s (SST) growth was taken on by the company's CEO (Richard Brock), president (Keith Pritchard) and a consultant hired by Brock. They were to develop a structure and set of administrative systems (policies, performance appraisal, compensation and partnering program) that would achieve the company's key success factors (see S-S Technologies Inc. (A)—Introduction), maintain the existing culture and attract the kind of people they wanted working for them.

SST's Top Management and Human Resources

SST was directed by its two owners:

> Richard R. Brock, P. Eng., was the CEO of SST. During his eight years as President of Sutherland-Schultz Limited, Brock recognized and nurtured the potential of the Products Group (PG) and Information Systems Group (ISG) which eventually formed S-S Technologies Inc. He continued to be involved in all aspects of the new company, and brought to it his extensive knowledge of business management and development.

> Keith Pritchard was the president of SST. Pritchard had risen through the company ranks, starting as a systems analyst, becoming project manager, then group manager, and finally, president in 1992. Pritchard also developed the PICS product which accounted for $500K of company sales. His unique set of skills in both management and technical areas made him an excellent leader for the company.

SST had a flat organizational structure that allowed it to respond quickly to technical and market changes. Anyone who had a door, left it open; employees felt free to take their concerns to whomever they believed could help. Decisions were often made using a consultative approach which empowered those involved and which led to "ownership" of problems and their solutions

Projects were assigned to individuals or teams, depending on the size. The individuals and teams were self-managed. Responsibility for project scheduling, budgeting and execution was left largely in team members' hands. Such responsibility created commitment to the project for those who worked on it and led to the high motivation evident within the company.

Overhead resources, such as marketing and administration, were kept to a minimum. For example, there were only four people on the marketing team which managed over $4 million in revenues. Administrative support was provided by two, or at times, three people. Even the controller (Doug Winger) shared his time with two other related organizations (SAF and Wilson Gas). SST was truly a lean organization.

Resources—PG

PG had highly competent, highly motivated technical teams. The technical people were leaders in their respective fields, with extensive and varied educations and backgrounds. They worked well together to meet R&D challenges, and to respond quickly and effectively to customers' inquiries. Many team members were involved in the original product development and expressed a personal commitment to PG's continued market success.

> Linda Oliver, B. Math., the lead programmer for the PICS product, had worked on the project as a designer and programmer since its inception.

> Bruce Andrews, Ph.D., was involved in the ongoing development of the PICS product, especially the communications tasks and testing; he also wrote the manuals.

> Lorne Diebel, C.E.T., developed a reputation as a communications "guru." Lorne often travelled to far-off sites, on a moment's notice, to debug a customer's application problem.

> Jonathan Malton, B. Sc., a talented hardware designer, had been instrumental in advancing the Direct-Link cards from the old "through hole" format to the new "surface mount" technology.

Newer members were added to PG as the pace of R&D increased and customer support became more demanding. Newcomers brought their own areas of expertise, and worked alongside the more senior team members, whose enthusiasm for their work was infectious.

As a result of its progressive and applied R&D program, the technical team members were advanced on the learning curve. This allowed SST to keep ahead of the competition. As a result, large PLC vendors often came to SST to solve their communication and simulation problems, rather than investing in the learning curve themselves.

The marketing team had grown over the past few years as PG revenues grew. People from both a marketing and a technical background combined to create a well rounded, effective marketing department:

Ian Suttie, P.Eng., the marketing manager, was involved in design review, marketing, distribution and sales of all products. His main function was to set up a network of distributors and representatives to reach all major markets in the U.S., Europe, and beyond.

Colleen Richmond had experience in marketing with other high-tech firms. She handled all the trade shows, promotional material and advertising activities.

Steve Blakely was the inside sales person, and came to SST with a technical background. He responded to enquiries for information, and was the first contact within SST for customers having technical difficulties.

Colleen Dietrich was recently hired by SST to determine the extent to which leads generated through the various advertising media used by PG eventually resulted in sales.

The marketing team worked well together, buoyed by PG's success. However, they were stretched to the limit and team members admitted they were unable to do everything they wished to do because of personnel constraints. All known product complaints were acted upon; however, there was no formal audit of customer satisfaction.

Resources—ISG

ISG's most important resource was its people. The engineers and technicians were not only technically competent, but were highly motivated and loyal. The following is a brief summary of ISG people and the unique skills they brought to the company:

Mark Schwarz, P.Eng., an accomplished systems analyst, wrote sales proposals, estimated projects, and did most of the marketing for ISG. He was very good at business development, seeking out large, extremely complicated projects, and often helping the customer define the scope and approach to the project. Convincing a customer that you could handle their large, technically complex job was tricky business, but Schwarz exhibited a talent for it. Schwarz also had a talent for scheduling personnel and was interested in ensuring that everyone had something interesting to do.

Vivienne Ojala, P.Eng., an experienced and talented project manager, designer and programmer, was more than capable of handling all aspects of design and project management for the $2 million-plus projects ISG hoped to attract. She was excellent with customers who preferred her "straight" talk to the "techno-babble" others gave them. Ojala made the customer confident that the project was in good hands, which is very important when you have asked a manufacturer to give you a production system which could determine business success or failure. Ojala was also good at training those who worked on her projects, as well as developing people in general.

Peter Roeser, P.Eng., was a systems analyst with special skills in the area of communications and various operating systems.

Brian Thomson, P.Eng., was an expert in the area of real-time software development. He also managed projects.

Ted Hannah, P.Eng., was a project manager and systems analyst with extensive skills and experience.

Bruce Travers, who marketed ISG capabilities in Ontario and provided technical direction for projects, had over 20 years experience with industrial applications of information systems.

Due to the diverse skills of its people, ISG was able to tackle large, complex systems integration projects that most of the competitors could not. ISG had in-house expertise covering nearly every technology that would be applied to a project. Also, because ISG was not tied to a single supplier of PLC's or PC's (as many competitors were), it was able to be more flexible and innovative in the solutions that were presented to customers.

Another important ISG resource was its excellent reputation and relationship with a large Canadian manufacturer which had given ISG substantial repeat business. As well, ISG had completed many projects for several large North American companies and had never failed to deliver on its promises.

ISG was advanced on the learning curve. New customers benefited from the fact that ISG had faced many challenges before, and solved them successfully. ISG's experience was more rounded, and hence more innovative and current than an in-house engineering department which had only worked in one type of factory.

Consultant's Interviews

The consultant interviewed all SST employees. Some of the observations which resulted from his interviews are grouped below by issues:

(i) Goals and Strategies

Other than Brock, Pritchard, Suttie and Schwarz, few employees were aware of SST's goals and strategies or even those of their own Group. In addition, even within top management (Pritchard, Suttie and Schwarz), significant differences existed regarding SST's goals and strategy.

(ii) Hierarchical Structure

Pritchard viewed Suttie and Schwarz as PG and ISG managers respectively. However, PG members generally saw themselves as reporting to Pritchard and saw Suttie as performing the marketing function. When apprised of this situation by the consultant, Pritchard said it would take time for Suttie to establish his position.

The ISG situation also proved somewhat confusing. A number of ISG members saw Schwarz as the manager. However, there was some confusion as to his position vis-à-vis Ojala, who had recently returned to SST after leaving to work for a much larger technology company in Montreal. Ojala tells the story of Pritchard begging her to return to SST, a story which Pritchard confirms. Ojala saw herself as reporting to Pritchard (and so did Pritchard). Her "formal" relationship to Schwarz had to be worked out.

Before Ojala left SST (she was away for five months), both she and Schwarz reported to Pritchard directly. When Ojala left, many of her responsibilities, such as some of the proposal writing and personnel scheduling, were given to Schwarz. Now that Ojala was back, to everyone's relief, there was the question of how to structure her role, particularly in relation to Pritchard and Schwarz. Ojala would not report to Schwarz, and Schwarz would not report to Ojala.

(iii) Physical Space

SST had outgrown the location which it shared with two other companies, Wilson Gas and SAF. Brock owned SAF, which was part of SST holdings, and rented space out to Wilson Gas. Each company had about one-third of the building they shared. SST added a trailer to house additional personnel. Any expansion in the same building required evicting SAF, Wilson or both. Pritchard was adamant that all SST personnel be housed in one location and have easy access to one another.

(iv) Compensation

One of the most contentious issues that arose from the interviews dealt with bonuses and compensation. Historically, bonuses had been promised if the company succeeded. The amount and date of the bonus were at the discretion of Brock and Pritchard. To date, no bonuses had been paid. Given the company's growth and success, many employees were expecting a Christmas bonus. There was no policy regarding bonus or merit pay. Both Brock and Pritchard wondered what the policy should be and how that policy should be developed. Existing compensation tended to be at the low end of the spectrum for engineers. This was particularly true for the longer-term employees in ISG.

It became apparent during the interviews that it was important to formalize the bonus plan to end the speculation, uncertainty and disappointment caused by the present, seemingly random (to the employees at least) system. Historically, when SST was part of Sutherland-Schultz, the company had a few good years and generous bonuses were paid. However, when the recession hit, the construction side of Sutherland-Schultz slumped considerably and, although PG and ISG held their profitability, the company as a whole could not afford to pay bonuses. In fact, SST people were laid off and some of those who remained felt cheated. Now that SST was on its own, there was an opportunity to tie bonuses directly to the company's performance. Management wanted the bonus system to achieve the following goals:

- To develop a co-operative, team spirit.
- To foster cooperation between ISG and PG, and limit interpersonal competition.
- To provide extra reward for unique contributions.
- To not reward weak performance.

(v) Partnering

Given the experience of losing Ojala to another firm (albeit temporarily), Brock was anxious to develop a "partnering" system in which those crucial to the company's success could participate. He wanted to make people like Suttie, Schwarz and Ojala feel like owners or partners committed to the company, so they would not be lured away by the promise of greener pastures; after all, the job market for people of this calibre was extremely promising. This was true not only of those in management positions, but also of the best systems analysts and programmers: people like Linda Oliver and Lorne Diebel.

Brock wanted part of the partners' bonus to consist of stock in the company. The problem was that these people were all young, with growing families, and could not afford to have their money tied up in stock when they had mortgage payments and daycare costs to worry about. Generally, their immediate concern was cash flow, as they knew their long-term earning potential was excellent. Brock's concern was how to structure the partners' bonuses and compensation to keep key people on-side, while allowing room for more partners to be brought in as the company grew. The company had recently hired a half-dozen talented engineering and computer science students, all of whom had the potential to become the next Schwarz, Suttie or Ojala. On top of all this, Brock still had his own return on equity to consider.

(vi) Commitment and Motivation

The consultant was overwhelmed by the high commitment to SST and the task motivation expressed by employees. The people loved the work environment, the lack of politics, the quick response to their technical needs (equipment and/or information), and the lack of talk-for-talk's-sake meetings. They were confident in their future and happy to come to work. For the consultant, this was a refreshing contrast to the downsizing gloom and doom that permeated many other companies he worked with in the 1990s.

The employees set their own working hours. They had to put in 40 hours per week, but could do this at any time. The flexible working hours allowed them to engage in other activities that occurred between 9 and 5, such as their children's school events. Employees kept track of their overtime and were paid either straight time or took the equivalent in extra holidays. Each employee recorded his/her overtime weekly and passed on the information to Pritchard. Previously, employees had noted the overtime information mentally. Pritchard had them write it out and report it weekly because he observed that their mental calculations erred on the side of the company (they remembered fewer hours than they worked overtime).

(vii) Personnel Function and Communications

New employees were generally assigned to a project manager who informally took on the induction and training role. In that way, new employees immediately tied into a task, and it was left to them to learn the culture and expectations of SST by osmosis. Should the employees not perform well, or fit into the culture, their employment was terminated.

Periodically, Pritchard would have a meeting of all employees to inform them of SST's progress, success and direction. Given these meetings, Pritchard was surprised to learn that only a few employees were aware of SST's goals and strategy.

One issue mentioned by a couple of employees dealt with performance appraisal and company benefits. Performance appraisal was conducted by Pritchard; however, he did not keep a record of the meeting and it was not done at regular intervals. Also, anyone interested in learning about benefits or salary ranges for various jobs did not know whom to contact. In contrast, all employees knew whom to contact for technical information. In fact, performance appraisal, compensation and benefits were managed in an ad hoc manner.

Where Do We Go from Here?

Brock, Pritchard and the consultant wanted to design an organization that would contemplate an expansion to double or triple SST's existing size. They knew the existing SST culture attracted and nurtured highly motivated and committed employees who expanded the company successfully and rapidly (Exhibit 1.11). They

Culture	People
• Open communications at all levels	• Highly motivated
• Flexible working hours	• Highly skilled (tech)
• Few policies	• Entrepreneurial
• Profit sharing at all levels	• Team players
• Quick decision making	• High performers
• Encourage initiative, not bureaucracy	• Committed to SST

Exhibit 1.11

SS-Technologies' Desired Culture and People

also knew that they could not manage $50 million in revenue and 120 to 150 people as they managed $6 million in revenue and 30 people.

The trio's task was to design an organization that would allow SST to grow successfully. Given SST's culture and the kind of people it wanted to attract as shown in Exhibit 1.11, what were the best structure, performance appraisal, compensation/bonus plan, company policies, and partnering program that should be implemented?

Notes

1. Carol J. Loomis, "Dinosaurs?" *Fortune,* 3 May 1993, 36–42.

2. Stratford Sherman, "Is He Too Cautious to Save IBM?" *Fortune,* 3 October 1994, 78–90.

3. The analysis of IBM was based on Paul Carroll, *Big Blues: The Unmaking of IBM* (New York: Crown, 1993); Brent Schlender, "Big Blue Is Betting on Big Iron Again," *Fortune,* 29 April 1996, 102–112; Sherman, "Is He Too Cautious to Save IBM?"; Ira Sager, "The View from IBM," *Business Week,* 30 October 1995, 142–152; John Greenwald, "A Blue Chip Case of Blues," *Time,* 16 May 1994, 71–72; David Kirkpatrick, "First: With New PCs and a New Attitude, IBM Is Back," *Fortune,* 11 November 1996, 28–29; Judith H. Dobrzynski, "Rethinking IBM," *Business Week,* 4 October 1993, 86–97; Michael W. Miller and Laurence Hooper, "Akers Quits at IBM Under Heavy Pressure; Dividend Is Slashed," *Wall Street Journal,* 27 January 1993, A1, A6; John W. Verity, "IBM: A Bull's-Eye and a Long Shot," *Business Week,* 13 December 1993, 88–89; and G. Pascal Zachary and Stephen Kreider Yoder, "Computer Industry Divides into Camps of Winners and Losers," *Wall Street Journal,* 27 January 1993, A1, A4.

4. John A. Byrne, "Management Meccas," *Business Week,* 18 September 1995, 122–134; Catherine Arnst, "Now HP Stands for Hot Products," *Business Week,* 14 June 1993, 36; Ronald E. Yates, "Fisher Exposes Kodak to Motorola Experience," *Chicago Tribune,* 14 April 1996, Section 5, p. 1, 2.

5. Eileen Davis, "What's on American Managers' Minds?" *Management Review* (April 1995): 14–20.

6. Ronald Henkoff, "New Management Secrets from Japan—Really," *Fortune,* 27 November 1995, 135–146.

7. Richard L. Daft, *Management,* 3rd ed. (Fort Worth: Dryden, 1994), 80; James L. Gibson, John M. Ivancevich, and James H. Donnelly, Jr., *Organizations,* 8th ed. (Burr Ridge, Ill.: Irwin, 1994), 54–55.

8. Karen Lowry Miller, with Bill Javetski, Peggy Simpson, and Tim Smart, "Europe: The Push East," *Business Week,* 7 November 1994, 48–49; Andrew E. Serwer, "McDonald's Conquers the World," *Fortune,* 17 October 1994, 103–116.

9. Nicholas Imparato and Oren Harari, "When New Worlds Stir," *Management Review* (October 1994): 22–28.

10. Patricia Booth, "Embracing the Team Concept," *Canadian Business Review* (Autumn 1994): 10–13; Jeffrey Pfeffer, "Producing Sustainable Competitive Advantage Through the Effective Management of People," *Academy of Management Executive* 9, no. 1 (1995): 55–72; Wendy Zellner, "Team Player: No More Same Ol'-Same Ol'," *Business Week,* 17 October 1994, 95–96.

11. Christopher A. Bartlett and Sumantra Ghoshal, "Rebuilding Behavioral Context: Turn Process Reengineering into People Rejuvenation," *Sloan Management Review* (Fall 1995): 11–23.

12. Byrne, "Management Meccas."

13. Walter Kiechell III, "How We Will Work in the Year 2000," *Fortune,* 17 May 1993, 38–52.

14. Keith H. Hammonds, Kevin Kelly, and Karen Thurston, "The New World of Work," *Business Week,* 17 October 1994, 76–87.

15. Patricia Galagan, "Signs of the Times," *Training and Development* (February 1996): 32–36.

16. William Bridges, "A Nation of Owners," *The State of Small Business 1995* (Special Issue), *Inc.,* 16 May 1995, 89–91; Arno Penzias, "New Paths to Success," *Fortune,* 12 June 1995, 90–94; John P. Kotter, *The New Rules: How to Succeed in Today's Post-Corporate World* (New York: The Free Press, 1994); Judith H. Dobrzynski, "New Secret of Success: Getting Off the Ladder," an interview with John P. Kotter, *New York Times,* 19 March 1995, F14.

17. Keith H. Hammonds, Kevin Kelly, and Karen Thurston, "The New World of Work," 76–87.

18. Genevieve Capowski, "Managing Diversity," *Management Review* (June 1996): 13–19.

19. Octave V. Baker, "Meeting the Challenge of Managing Cultural Diversity," in Roger A. Ritvo, Anne H. Litwin, and Lee Butler, eds., *Managing in the Age of Change: Essential Skills to Manage Today's Diverse Workforce* (Burr Ridge, Ill.: Irwin, 1995).

20. Bonna M. de la Cruz, "Language Battle Flares in the Office," *The Tennessean,* 5 June 1996, A1, A2.

21. Joline Godfrey, "Been There, Doing That," *Inc.,* March 1996, 21–22; Paula Dwyer, Marsha Johnston, and Karen Lowry Miller, "Out of the Typing Pool, into Career Limbo," *Business Week,* 15 April 1996, 92–94.

22. Mark Maremont, "Blind Ambition," *Business Week,* 23 October 1995, 78–92.

23. Dale Kurschner, "The 100 Best Corporate Citizens," *Business Ethics,* May/June 1995, 24–35.

24. Howard Aldrich, *Organizations and Environments* (Englewood Cliffs, N.J.: Prentice-Hall, 1979), 3.

25. David Greising, "The Virtual Olympics," *Business Week,* 29 April 1996, 64–66.

26. Nathaniel C. Nash, "Coke's Great Romanian Adventure," *New York Times,* 26 February 1995, F1.

27. Michael A. Hitt, R. Duane Ireland, and Robert E. Hoskisson, *Strategic Management: Competitiveness and Globalization* (St. Paul, Minn.: West, 1995), 238.

28. James D. Thompson, *Organizations in Action* (New York: McGraw-Hill, 1967), 4–13.

29. Daniel Katz and Robert L. Kahn, *The Social Psychology of Organizations* (New York: Wiley, 1978).

30. The following discussion was heavily influenced by Richard H. Hall, *Organizations: Structures, Processes, and Outcomes* (Englewood Cliffs, N.J.: Prentice-Hall, 1991); D. S. Pugh, "The Measurement of Organization Structures: Does Context Determine Form?" *Organizational Dynamics* 1 (Spring 1973): 19–34; and D. S. Pugh, D. J. Hickson, C. R. Hinings, and C. Turner, "Dimensions of Organization Structure," *Administrative Science Quarterly* 13 (1968): 65–91.

31. Adapted from John Huey, "The New Post-Heroic Leadership," *Fortune,* 21 February 1994, 42–50; John Huey, "Wal-Mart: Will It Take Over the World?" *Fortune,* 30 January 1989, 52–61. Howard Rudnitsky, "How Sam Walton Does It," *Forbes,* 16 August 1982, 42–44; and Janet Guyan, "Food-

Stamp Red Tape Raises Tension Levels in Understaffed Offices," *Wall Street Journal,* 27 June 1984, 1, 16.

32. Richard L. Daft, *Management,* 3rd ed. (Chicago: Dryden, 1994).

33. Richard L. Daft and Arie Y. Lewin, "Can Organization Studies Begin to Break out of the Normal Science Strait-jacket? An Editorial Essay," *Organization Science* 1 (1990): 1–9.

34. Amanda Bennett, *The Death of the Organization Man* (New York: William Morrow, 1990).

35. Ian I. Mitroff, Richard O. Mason, and Christine M. Pearson, "Radical Surgery: What Will Tomorrow's Organizations Look Like?" *Academy of Management Executive* 8, no. 2 (1994): 11–21; Nicholas Imparato and Oren Harari, "When New Worlds Stir," *Management Review* (October 1994): 22–28; William Bergquist, *The Postmodern Organization: Mastering the Art of Irreversible Change* (San Francisco: Jossey-Bass, 1993).

36. David M. Boje and Robert F. Dennehy, *Managing in the Postmodern World: America's Revolution Against Exploitation,* 2nd ed. (Dubuque, Iowa: Kendall/Hunt, 1994).

37. This discussion is based on Bergquist, *The Postmodern Organization,* 1993, and Richard L. Daft, *Organization Theory and Design,* 5th ed. (Minneapolis/St. Paul: West, 1995), 13–14, 22–23.

38. Johannes M. Pennings, "Structural Contingency Theory: A Reappraisal," *Research in Organizational Behavior* 14 (1992): 267–309.

39. Dennis A. Gioia and Evelyn Pitre, "Multiparadigm Perspectives on Theory Building," *Academy of Management Review* 15 (1990): 584–602.

40. Richard H. Hall, *Organizations: Structures, Processes, and Outcomes* (Englewood Cliffs, N.J.: Prentice-Hall, 1991).

41. Gioia and Pitre, "Multiparadigm Perspectives on Theory Building."

42. Peter Moran and Sumantra Ghoshal, "Theories of Economic Organization: The Case for Realism and Balance," *Academy of Management Review* 21, no. 1 (1996): 58–72; Todd H. Chiles and John F. McMackin, "Integrating Variable Risk Preferences, Trust, and Transaction Cost Economics," *Academy of Management Review* 21, no. 1 (1996): 73–99; Oliver E. Williamson, "Economics and Organization: A Primer," *California Management Review* 38, no. 2 (Winter 1996): 131–46; William S. Hesterly, Julia Liebeskind, and Todd R. Zenger,

"Organizational Economics: An Impending Revolution in Organization Theory?" *Academy of Management Review* 15 (1990): 402–20; Oliver E. Williamson and William G. Ouchi, "The Markets and Hierarchy Program of Research: Origins, Implications, Prospects," in Andrew H. Van de Ven and William E. Joyce, eds., *Perspectives on Organizational Design and Behavior* (New York: Wiley-Interscience, 1981).

43. Christina Elnora Garza, "Studying the Natives on the Shopfloor," *Business Week,* 30 September 1991, 74–78.

44. Robert House, Denise M. Rousseau, and Melissa Thomas-Hunt, "The Meso Paradigm: A Framework for the Integration of Micro and Macro Organizational Behavior," *Research in Organizational Behavior* 17 (1995): 71–114.

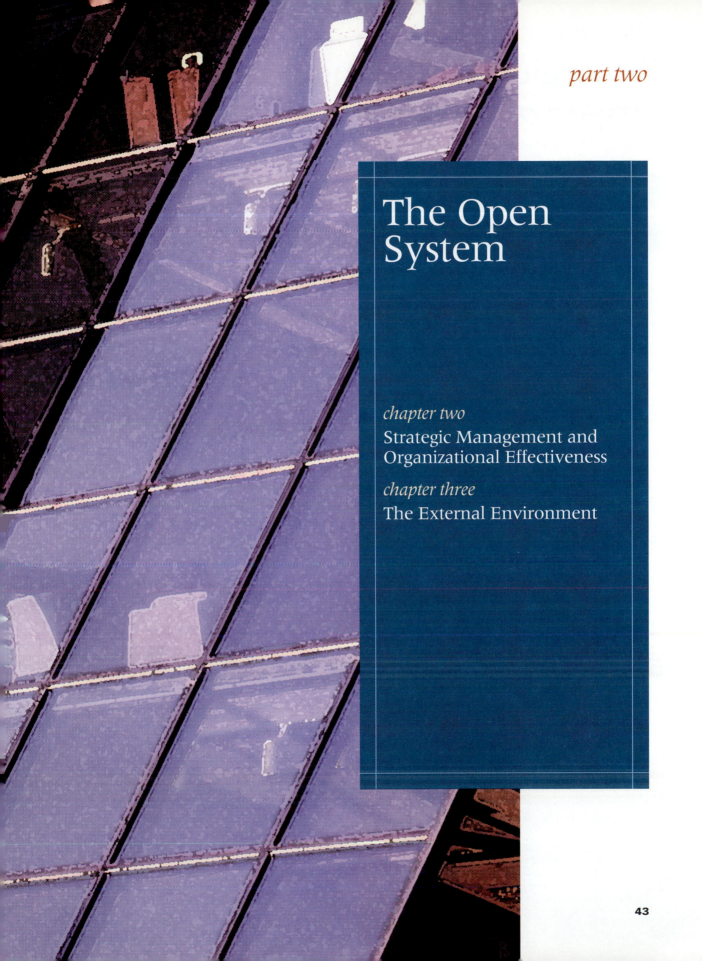

part two

The Open System

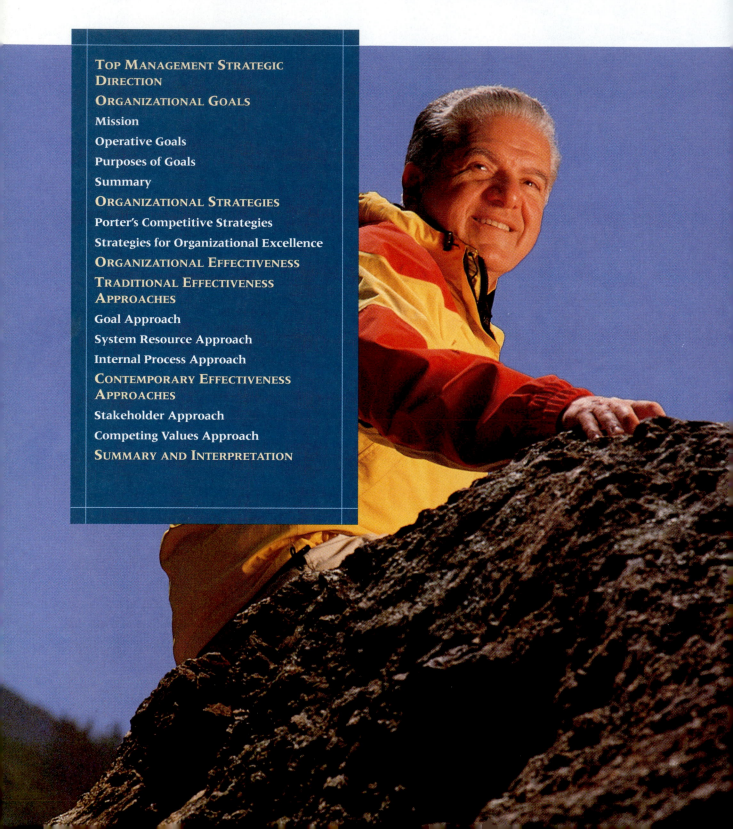

chapter two

Strategic Management and Organizational Effectiveness

A look inside

Marmot Mountain

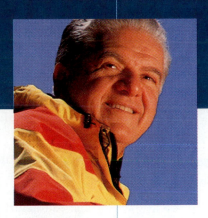

When it comes to making high-performance outdoor clothing and equipment, no one does it better than Marmot Mountain. But when Steve Crisafulli took over as president, he "had never before seen a company this screwed up operationally." Early in Crisafulli's tenure, Marmot faced a disaster: the parent company, Odyssey International, filed for Chapter 11 bankruptcy protection, and many observers believed the small, shaky Marmot would simply perish. Yet employees were so convinced they could overcome their problems that the entire management team pitched in and bought the company. What has happened since has stunned the outdoor-apparel industry.

Crisafulli believes the best way for a small company to succeed is to concentrate on one or two major goals at a time. Managers first tackled the company's biggest problem, agreeing that on-time delivery would be Marmot's first priority for the next year. To reach its goal, Marmot had to temporarily limit growth—sales reps were forbidden to open any new accounts for eighteen months, until Marmot could service its loyal buyers. Anything that might have a negative impact on delivery had to wait—meetings were postponed, new product features were abandoned, and other projects were delayed. By working late nights and weekends, Marmot met its goal, shipping products two weeks ahead of schedule. Crisafulli and the Marmot staff continued to hammer away at the company's problems one at a time, setting a primary goal for each year:

- Believing its product line was going stale, Marmot next directed resources to new product development, eventually releasing a line of more than a dozen new sleeping bags, plus a waterproof breathable fabric to rival Gore-Tex.
- Managers then focused on broadening market visibility and brand recognition, tripling the marketing and advertising budget. From running one ad in two publications, Marmot's marketing department reached out with a half dozen creative new ads that ran for nine months in six publications. A new vice president was hired to expand sales.
- Marmot is now focusing on improving customer service by installing an 800 number and upgrading the company's computer systems.

Crisafulli's strategy is working. The year after employees bought the company was the first profitable year in Marmot's twenty-year history. Sales have been nothing short of spectacular ever since, growing from around $5 million in the early 1990s to $11 million in 1994, and Crisafulli predicts Marmot will grow around 40 percent annually for the next several years. The company has outpaced competitors to become the third-largest-selling brand of outdoor clothing, after Patagonia and the North Face. Focusing employee energy on clear, limited goals has not only brought Marmot back from the brink of disaster, but has the company once again ascending the peaks in the outdoor clothing and equipment industry.[1]

An **organizational goal** is a desired state of affairs that the organization attempts to reach.[2] A goal represents a result or end point toward which organizational efforts are directed. The goals for Marmot Mountain include on-time delivery, new product development, expanded market visibility and sales, and better customer service.

Purpose of This Chapter

Top managers give direction to organizations. They set goals and develop the strategies for their organization to attain those goals. The purpose of this chapter is to help you understand the types of goals organizations pursue and some of the competitive strategies managers develop to reach those goals. We will examine characteristics common to successful organizations and discuss how managers help their organizations achieve excellence. The chapter also describes the most popular approaches to measuring the effectiveness of organizational efforts. To manage organizations well, managers need a clear sense of how to measure effectiveness.

TOP MANAGEMENT STRATEGIC DIRECTION

An organization is created and designed to achieve some end, which is decided by the chief executive officer and/or the top management team. Organization structure and design is an outcome of this purpose. Indeed, *the primary -sibility of top management is to determine an organization's goals, strategy, and design, therein adapting the organization to a changing environment.*[3] Middle managers do much the same thing for major departments within the guidelines provided by top management. The relationships through which top managers provide direction and then design are illustrated in Exhibit 2.1.

The direction setting process typically begins with an assessment of the opportunities and threats in the external environment, including the amount of change, uncertainty, and resource availability, which we discuss in more detail in Chapter 3. Top management also assesses internal strengths and weaknesses to define the company's distinctive competence compared with other firms in the industry.[4] The assessment of internal environment often includes an evaluation of each department and is shaped by past performance and the leadership style of the CEO and top management team. The next step is to define overall mission and official goals based on the correct fit between external opportunities and internal strengths. Specific operational goals or strategies can then be formulated to define how the organization is to accomplish its overall mission.

In Exhibit 2.1, organization design reflects the way goals and strategies are implemented. Organization design is the administration and execution of the strategic plan. *This is the role of organization theory*. Organization direction is achieved through decisions about structural form, information technology and control systems, the type of production technology, human resource policies, culture, and linkages to other organizations. Changes in structure, technology, human resource policies, culture, and interorganization linkages will be discussed in subsequent chapters. Also note the arrow in Exhibit 2.1 running from organization design back to strategic management. This means that strategies are often made within the current structure of the organization, so that current design constrains or puts limits on goals and strategy. More often than not, however, the

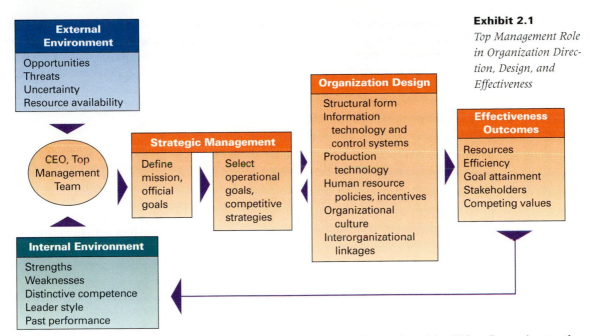

Exhibit 2.1

Top Management Role in Organization Direction, Design, and Effectiveness

Source: Adapted from Arie Y. Lewin and Carroll U. Stephens, "Individual Properties of the CEO as Determinants of Organization Design," unpublished manuscript, Duke University, 1990; and Arie Y. Lewin and Carroll U. Stephens, "CEO Attributes as Determinants of Organization Design: An Integrated Model," *Organization Studies* 15, no. 2 (1994): 183–212.

new goals and strategy are selected based on environmental needs, and then the top management attempts to redesign the organization to achieve those ends.

Finally, Exhibit 2.1 illustrates how managers evaluate the effectiveness of organizational efforts—that is, the extent to which the organization realizes its goals. This chart reflects the most popular ways of measuring performance, each of which is discussed later in this chapter. It is important to note here that performance measurements feed back into the internal environment, so that past performance of the organization is assessed by top management in setting new goals and strategies for the future.

The role of top management is important because managers can interpret the environment differently and develop different goals. An interesting example occurred in New York City, where the crime rate plunged farther and faster than anywhere else in the nation after former Police Commissioner William Bratton issued a clear, simple goal: "Cut crime." Top managers before Bratton had started with the premise that lawbreaking was caused by factors in the external environment that were beyond the control of the police department. Thus, cops reacted to crime rather than actually trying to reduce crime. Bratton, however, believed his department could have an impact on the environment and dramatically cut the crime rate by managing resources more effectively. He devised strategies to target specific criminal behaviors and invested in new information technology so crime trends and problems could be spotted immediately. Precinct commanders were given unprecedented autonomy to run their station houses and deploy resources as they saw fit. Bratton's strategies led to a 39 percent decline in the murder rate and a reduction in overall crime of more than 15 percent.[5] Top management choices about goals, strategies, and organization design can have a tremendous impact on organizational effectiveness.

Remember that goals and strategy are not fixed or taken for granted. Top managers and middle managers must select goals for their respective units, and the ability to make these choices largely determines firm success. Organization design is used to implement goals and strategy and also determines organizational success. We will now discuss further the concept of organizational goals and strategy, and in the latter part of this chapter, we will discuss various ways to evaluate organizational effectiveness.

ORGANIZATIONAL GOALS

Many types of goals exist in an organization, and each type performs a different function. One major distinction is between the officially stated goals, or mission, of the organization and the operative goals the organization actually pursues.

Mission

The overall goal for an organization is often called the **mission**—the organization's reason for existence. The mission describes the organization's vision, its shared values and beliefs, and its reason for being. It can have a powerful impact on an organization.[6] The mission is sometimes called the **official goals**, which are the formally stated definition of business scope and outcomes the organization is trying to achieve. Official goal statements typically define business operations and may focus on values, markets, and customers that distinguish the organization. Whether called a mission statement or official goals, the organization's general statement of its purpose and philosophy is often written down in a policy manual or the annual report. The mission statement for Hallmark is shown in Exhibit 2.2. Note how the overall mission, values, and goals are all defined.

Operative Goals

Operative goals designate the ends sought through the actual operating procedures of the organization and explain what the organization is actually trying to do.[7] Operative goals describe specific measurable outcomes and are often concerned with the short run. Operative versus official goals represent actual versus stated goals. Operative goals typically pertain to the primary tasks an organization must perform, similar to the subsystem activities identified in Chapter 1.[8] These goals concern overall performance, boundary spanning, maintenance, adaptation, and production activities. Specific goals for each primary task provide direction for the day-to-day decisions and activities within departments.

Overall Performance.   Profitability reflects the overall performance of for-profit organizations. Profitability may be expressed in terms of net income, earnings per share, or return on investment. Other overall goals are growth and output volume. Growth pertains to increases in sales or profits over time. Volume pertains to total sales or the amount of products or services delivered. At Pier 1 Imports, beating last year's Christmas sales numbers by 5 percent is a chainwide goal set by CEO Clark Johnson. Some stores then set even higher performance goals, as did Paula Hankins and Eva Goldyn, managers of Pier 1's smallest Nashville, Tennessee, store. Meeting the goal of a 36 percent increase in Christ-

Exhibit 2.2
*Hallmark's Mission
Statement*

THIS IS HALLMARK

We believe:

That our *products and services* must enrich people's lives
and enhance their relationships.
That *creativity and quality*—in our concepts, products
and services—are essential to our success.
That the *people* of Hallmark are our company's
most valuable resource.
That distinguished *financial performance* is a must,
not as an end in itself, but as a means
to accomplish our broader mission.
That our *private ownership* must be preserved.

The values that guide us are:

Excellence in all we do.
Ethical and moral conduct at all times
and in all our relationships.
Innovation in all areas of our business as a means
of attaining and sustaining leadership.
Corporate social responsibility to Kansas City
and to each community in which we operate.

*These beliefs and values guide our business strategies,
our corporate behavior, and our relationships
with suppliers, customers, communities and each other.*

Source: Patricia Jones and Larry Kahaner, *Say It and Live It: 50 Corporate Mission Statements That Hit the Mark* (New York: Currency Doubleday, 1995).

mas season sales became a storewide obsession, with clerks constantly checking
the backroom computer for an up-to-the-minute tally.[9]

Not-for-profit organizations such as labor unions do not have goals of profitability, but they do have goals that attempt to specify the delivery of services to
members within specified budget expense levels. Growth and volume goals also
may be indicators of overall performance in not-for-profit organizations.

Resources.   Resource goals pertain to the acquisition of needed material and financial resources from the environment. They may involve obtaining financing
for the construction of new plants, finding less expensive sources for raw materials, or hiring top-quality college graduates.

Market.   Market goals relate to the market share or market standing desired by the organization. Market goals are the responsibility of marketing, sales, and advertising departments. An example of a market goal is Bausch & Lomb's desire to capture at least 50 percent of every segment of the contact lens market. PepsiCo's Frito-Lay division controls more than half of the market share for salty snacks. Both companies have the operative goal of having the largest market share in a specific industry.[10]

Employee Development.   Employee development pertains to the training, promotion, safety, and growth of employees. It includes both managers and workers. At Franciscan Health System in Tacoma, Washington, a top goal is to "create an organizational environment that values, empowers, enriches, and supports those with whom we work." The goal includes supporting educational activities for employees, providing change-management seminars and retraining, developing reward and recognition systems, and encouraging diversity. These activities improve employee morale and help workers continue to learn and grow.[11]

Innovation.   Innovation goals pertain to internal flexibility and readiness to adapt to unexpected changes in the environment. Innovation goals are often defined with respect to the development of specific new services, products, or production processes. For example, 3M has a goal of generating enough new products so that 30 percent of sales come from products introduced within the past four years.[12]

Productivity.   Productivity goals concern the amount of output achieved from available resources. They typically describe the amount of resource inputs required to reach desired outputs and are thus stated in terms of "cost for a unit of production," "units produced per employee," or "resource cost per employee." For example, Rubbermaid has a productivity goal of increasing the number of units produced per worker per day. Total output increased from three hundred units per worker per day in 1952 to five hundred units in 1980 and 750 in 1988. Another productivity goal was to reduce the number of sales representatives and to increase the workforce by only 50 percent while doubling sales. The resulting increases in productivity have produced fresh profits for Rubbermaid.[13]

Successful organizations use a carefully balanced set of operative goals. For example, although achieving profitability is important, some of today's best companies recognize that a single-minded focus on bottom-line profits may not be the best way to achieve high performance, as discussed in Book Mark 2.0.

Purposes of Goals

Both official goals and operative goals are important for the organization, but they serve very different purposes. Official goals provide legitimacy; operative goals provide employee direction, decision guidelines, and criteria of performance. These purposes are summarized in Exhibit 2.3.

Legitimacy.   A mission statement (or official goals) communicates legitimacy to external and internal stakeholders. The mission describes the purpose of the organization so people know what it stands for and accept its existence. Moreover, employees join and become committed to an organization when they identify with the organization's stated goals.

What America Does Right: Learning from Companies That Put People First

By Robert H. Waterman, Jr.

Robert Waterman's book *What America Does Right* might aptly be subtitled "Treat People Well; The Money will Follow." Waterman believes that for companies to be successful, bottom-line profits should not be the top priority. Through in-depth case histories of some of America's most admired and successful companies, Waterman concludes that "Today's top enterprise does the best job for its shareholders by treating them as only one of the three main constituent groups essential to their success. The other two are quite clearly their people and their customers." Profits accrue to companies that inspire and motivate employees and listen to and satisfy customers.

Company Examples

The book offers fascinating studies of companies that consistently perform well because they build relationships with employees, customers, and suppliers that are hard for competitors to duplicate. For example,

- Rubbermaid's highly motivated teams, obsessed with meeting customer needs, consistently outinnovate competitors—they introduce a new product every day, and 90 percent of these products succeed.
- Motorola added $3.2 billion to its bottom line in five years by making total quality manufacturing and total customer satisfaction one and the same.

- Levi Strauss went from mediocre performance to profits and growth, managing to pay off massive debt early, by implementing programs that make work exciting and meaningful for its front-line workers.
- Procter & Gamble's Lima, Ohio, plant improved worker productivity 30 to 40 percent by giving factory workers the power to make important decisions, including how to arrange production and voting on promotions.

Sustaining Success

What do these companies have in common? First and foremost, they think long term and have the commitment, patience, and tenacity to make big things happen. Most provide opportunities for employees to better themselves through formal education and job-related training. Companies that remain successful also tend to break themselves into small, autonomous units that stay in close touch with customers and provide motivation and autonomy for workers. The interplay between pay for performance and the maintenance of high standards is another common feature of these companies. Waterman's case studies clearly indicate that worker involvement, high expectations, and fair treatment are all necessary ingredients to success.

What America Does Right, by Robert H. Waterman, Jr., is published by W. W. Norton & Company.

Most top managers want their company to look good to other companies in their environment. Managers want customers, competitors, suppliers, and the local community to look on them in a favorable light. The dynamics of a company's interaction with the organizational environment often depend as much on cultural norms, symbols, and beliefs as on technological or material factors; and the concept of organizational legitimacy plays a critical role.[14] The mision statement is a powerful first step in communicating legitimacy to external and internal stakeholders and creating a positive impression.

Fortune magazine reflects the corporate concern for legitimacy with ratings of the reputations of corporations in each of thirty-seven industries. Mirage Resorts, which runs gambling casinos, popped into the number 2 spot based largely on its strong commitment to high-quality service—employees are empowered to do whatever it takes to keep guests smiling. The company's treatment of its workers keeps them smiling too; with turnover in the hotel-casino game at about 43 percent

Exhibit 2.3
Goal Type and Purpose

Type of Goals	Purpose of Goals
Official goals, mission:	Legitimacy
Operative goals:	Employee direction and motivation Decision guidelines Standard of performance

per year, Mirage's 12 percent turnover rate is the envy of the industry. Mirage's mission and goal statements help communicate the company's commitment to its workers and emphasis on total customer satisfaction. As another example, telephone companies in the United States have been criticized for offering sexually explicit dial-up message services. Public sentiment has caused many companies to shut them down and develop mission and goal statements that communicate legitimacy and social responsibility. A similar situation in Norway led to the cancellation of quite lucrative dial-up services offered by a national tabloid newspaper. Managers determined that these services were detrimental to their image of corporate responsibility and their goal of serving as a major national news medium.[15]

Employee Direction and Motivation. Goals give a sense of direction to organization participants. The stated end toward which an organization is striving and strategies for how to get there tell employees what they are working for. Goals help motivate participants, especially if participants help select the goals. At 3M, for example, the overall goal that "30 percent of sales should come from products developed in the past four years" is widely accepted and pursued by employees. All employees work toward innovation.

Decision Guidelines. The goals of an organization also act as guidelines for employee decision making. Organizational goals are a set of constraints on individual behavior and decisions.[16] They help define the correct decisions concerning organization structure, innovation, employee welfare, or growth. When Owens-Illinois, a glass container manufacturer, established the goal of reducing volume to improve profits, internal decisions were redirected. Owens-Illinois had been running marginal plants just to maintain volume. The new goal of increased profits provided decision guidelines that led to the closing of these marginal plants.

Criteria of Performance. Goals provide a standard for assessment. The level of organization performance, whether in terms of profits, units produced, or number of complaints, needs a basis for evaluation. Is a profit of 10 percent on sales good enough? The answer lies in goals. Goals reflect past experience and describe the desired state for the future. If the profit goal is 8 percent, then a 10 percent return is excellent. When Owens-Illinois shifted from volume to profit goals, profits increased by 30 percent. This increase occurred during the period when two competitors reported profit declines of 61 percent and 76 percent. Profit thus replaced production volume as the criterion of performance.[17]

Summary

Official goals and mission statements describe a value system for the organization; operative goals represent the primary tasks of the organization. Official goals legitimize the organization; operative goals are more explicit and well defined. For example, when Datapoint Corporation was trying to achieve greater efficiency in customer service, managers adopted the operative goals of schedule, cost, and quality. Manufacturing was expected to "deliver a product to the customer on time, deliver it at minimal cost, and deliver a good quality product."[18] These operative goals provided direction to employees and helped attain the overall company goal of continuing to have consecutive quarterly increases in net revenues, net earnings, and shipments.

ORGANIZATIONAL STRATEGIES

A **strategy** is a plan for interacting with the competitive environment to achieve organizational goals. Some managers think of goals and strategies as interchangeable, but for our purposes, goals define where the organization wants to go and strategies define how it will get there. For example, a goal may be to achieve 15 percent annual sales growth; strategies to reach that goal might include aggressive advertising to attract new customers, motivating salespeople to increase the average size of customer purchases, and acquiring other businesses that produce similar products. Strategies can include any number of techniques to achieve the goal. The Porter model of competitive strategies provides one framework for competitive action. Managers try to develop strategies that will be congruent with the external environment.

Porter's Competitive Strategies

Michael E. Porter studied a number of businesses and introduced a framework describing three competitive strategies.[19] These strategies and the organizational characteristics associated with each are summarized in Exhibit 2.4.

Strategy	Organizational Characteristics
Low-cost Leadership	Strong central authority; tight cost control
	Standard operating procedures
	Easy-to-use manufacturing technologies
	Highly efficient procurement and distribution systems
	Close supervision; limited employee empowerment
	Frequent, detailed control reports
Differentiation	Acts in an organic, loosely-knit way, with strong coordination among departments
	Creative flair, thinks "out-of-the-box"
	Strong capability in basic research
	Strong marketing abilities
	Rewards employee innovation
	Corporate reputation for quality or technological leadership
Focus	Combination of above policies directed at specific strategic target
	Values and rewards flexibility and customer intimacy
	Measures cost of providing service and maintaining customer loyalty
	Pushes empowerment to employees with customer contact

Exhibit 2.4
Organizational Characteristics for Porter's Competitive Strategies

Source: Based on Michael E. Porter, *Competitive Strategy: Techniques for Analyzing Industries and Competitors* (New York: The Free Press, 1980); Michael Treacy and Fred Wiersema, "How Market Leaders Keep Their Edge," *Fortune,* 6 February 1995, 88–98; and Michael A. Hitt, R. Duane Ireland, and Robert E. Hoskisson, *Strategic Management* (St. Paul, Minn.: West, 1995). 100–113.

1. Low-Cost Leadership.   The **low-cost leadership** strategy tries to increase market share by emphasizing low cost compared to competitors. With a low-cost leadership strategy, the organization aggressively seeks efficient facilities, pursues cost reductions, and uses tight controls to produce products more efficiently than its competitors.

This strategy is concerned primarily with stability rather than taking risks or seeking new opportunities for innovation and growth. A low-cost position means the company can undercut competitor's prices and still offer comparable quality and earn a reasonable profit. Compaq Computer used a low-cost leadership strategy to reach its goal of being the world's No. 1 PC supplier. Compaq has been cutting costs better than anyone in the industry and is therefore able to supply price-busting products that are creating huge demand from consumers.[20] Being the low-cost producer can help a company defend against current competitors because customers cannot find lower prices elsewhere. In addition, if substitute products or potential new competitors enter the picture, the low-cost producer is in a better position to prevent loss of market share. Low cost is an effective strategy, but getting there can be difficult for a high-cost company, as Delta Airlines is discovering.

In Practice 2.1

Delta Airlines

The kind of aggressive cost cutting going on at Delta Airlines is likely to happen only when a company has no choice. According to CEO Ronald W. Allen, a combination of terrible industry economics and Delta's own blunders meant, "We were talking about survival." Delta hadn't turned a profit since 1990, and only troubled USAir operated less efficiently than Delta's 9.76 cents per mile.

In April of 1994, Allen announced a radical program to cut $2 billion in costs and reduce operating expenses to only 7.5 cents per mile, making Delta the second-lowest-cost major carrier next to Southwest Airlines. He set up eleven restructuring teams charged with reaching broad cost-cutting goals: $400 million from marketing, $300 million from layoffs, and $310 million from onboard services. The numbers are making for significant operational changes—for example, a shift to cross-functional work teams and to outsourcing some work, leading to a 23 percent cut in jobs. But Allen has been doing more than slashing jobs and services in his quest for efficiency. He's redrawn Delta's route map, formed innovative partnerships, and revamped everything from baggage handling to maintenance.[21]

Delta still has a long way to go in its quest to be a low-cost provider, but the company is ahead of schedule and recently earned its first profit in five years. Allen is convinced Delta's fierce cost cutting will help the company attain a low-cost leadership position in the airline industry.

2. Differentiation.   In a **differentiation** strategy, organizations attempt to distinguish their products or services from others in the industry. An organization may use advertising, distinctive product features, exceptional service, or new technology to achieve a product perceived as unique. This strategy usually targets customers who are not particularly concerned with price, so it can be quite profitable. Mercedes-Benz automobiles, Maytag appliances, and Tylenol are the products of companies that have benefited from a differentiation strategy.

A differentiation strategy can reduce rivalry with competitors and fight off the threat of substitute products because customers are loyal to the company's brand. However, companies must remember that successful differentiation strategies require a number of costly activities, such as product research and design and extensive advertising. Companies that pursue a differentiation strategy need strong marketing abilities and creative employees who are given the time and resources to seek innovations.

3. Focus.   With Porter's third strategy, the **focus strategy**, the organization concentrates on a specific regional market or buyer group. The company will try to achieve either a low-cost advantage or a differentiation advantage within a narrowly defined market. One example of focus strategy is Enterprise Rent-a-Car, which has made its mark by focusing on a market in which the major companies like Hertz and Avis don't even compete—the low-budget insurance replacement market. Customers whose cars have been wrecked or stolen have one less thing to worry about when Enterprise delivers a rental car right to their driveway. Enterprise has been able to grow rapidly by using a focus strategy.[22]

Strategies for Organizational Excellence

Managers not only develop strategies for interacting with the external environment, they also want to build internal organizational characteristics that contribute to long-lasting company success. As we saw in Chapter 1, today's competitive organizations exhibit a number of shifts in thinking in response to changes in society. Successful organizations remain flexible to adapt quickly to a chaotic international environment. Another shift is a concern for empowering employees and a stronger interest in corporate values and culture. One recent book, *Built to Last: Successful Habits of Visionary Companies,* examines companies that have remained successful over long time periods and argues that there are certain "timeless fundamentals" that help companies achieve and sustain long-term organizational excellence.[23] Other publications, such as *Reengineering the Corporation* about corporate redesign and *Control Your Destiny or Someone Else Will* about Jack Welch's revolution at General Electric, have also added new understanding about organizational excellence.[24] Some of the major ideas from these publications are summarized in Exhibit 2.5. They are organized into four categories: strategic orientation, top management, organization design, and corporate culture.

Exhibit 2.5
Factors Associated with Organization Excellence

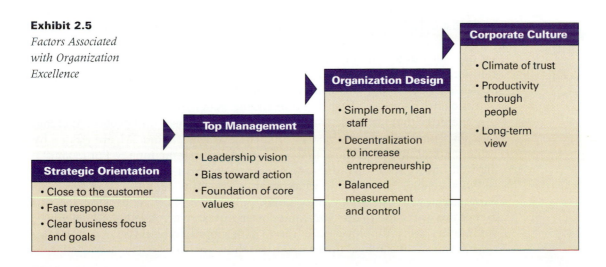

Strategic Orientation	Top Management	Organization Design	Corporate Culture
• Close to the customer • Fast response • Clear business focus and goals	• Leadership vision • Bias toward action • Foundation of core values	• Simple form, lean staff • Decentralization to increase entrepreneurship • Balanced measurement and control	• Climate of trust • Productivity through people • Long-term view

Strategic Orientation. Three characteristics identified in corporate research pertain to an organization's strategic orientation: being *close to the customer,* providing *fast response,* and having *a clear business focus and goals.*

Excellent organizations are customer driven. Organizations are increasingly looking at customers as their most important stakeholders, and a dominant value in successful organizations is satisfying customer needs.[25] For example, the president of Pepsi Cola North America makes a point of calling at least four customers directly per day.[26]

A fast response means successful companies respond quickly to problems and opportunities. They lead rather than follow. They take chances. They make continuous improvement a way of life and often achieve their greatest accomplishments through constant experimentation and improvement. 3M is a classic example. The company encourages employees to try just about anything and gives them 15 percent of their time to do it.[27]

Moreover, to sustain excellence, companies need to have a clear focus and goals. They know that to be successful, they should do what they do best. At Gerber, for example, the motto is "Babies are our business . . . our only business." Eastman Kodak, which thrived for decades on its camera and film business, suffered disastrous results when managers lost sight of the core business and moved into pharmaceutical and consumer health products.[28] As part of his ongoing transformation of the company, CEO George Fisher is selling off these product lines to refocus Kodak on its core imaging business.

Top Management. Management techniques and processes are another dimension of excellent organizations. Three factors unique to managers are part of a highly successful company: *leadership vision, a bias toward action,* and *promoting a foundation of core values.*

To achieve and maintain excellence, an organization needs a special kind of leadership vision that provides leadership of the organization, not just leadership within the organization. Leaders must provide a vision of what the organization can be and what it stands for; they give employees a sense of direction, shared purpose, and meaning that persists despite changes in product line or manager turnover. When asked to name the most important decisions contributing to Hewlett-Packard's immense growth, David Packard speaks entirely in terms of organizational characteristics, such as creating an environment that encourages creativity, rather than in terms of technological breakthroughs.[29]

Managers and employees in excellent organizations are also oriented toward action—they don't talk problems to death before making decisions or creating solutions. Successful companies "do it, try it, fix it." The decision philosophy at Pepsi Co., for example, is "Ready, Fire, Aim."[30]

Yet decisions are not based on thin air; top managers support and promote a core ideology that permeates organizational life and guides all decision making. The best companies, like Johnson & Johnson, Wal-Mart, and 3M, are guided by values and a sense of purpose that go beyond just making money. For example, the well-known Johnson & Johnson Credo, the code of ethics that tells employees what to care about and in what order, puts profits dead last—yet the company has never lost money since going public in 1944.[31] At McDonald's, no exceptions are made to the core values of quality, service, cleanliness, and value; yet in other areas, employees are free to experiment, to be flexible, and to take risks in ways that can help the company reach its goals.

Organization Design. Excellent organizations are characterized by three design attributes: *simple form and lean staff, decentralization to increase entrepreneurship*, and *a balance between financial and nonfinancial measures of performance.*

Simple form and lean staff means that the underlying form and systems of excellent organizations are elegantly simple and few personnel are in staff positions. There is little bureaucracy. Large companies are divided into small divisions for simplicity and adaptability.

Organization structure is decentralized to encourage innovation and change. Creativity and innovation by employees at all levels are encouraged and rewarded. Technical people are located near marketing people so they can lunch together. Organizational units are kept small to create a sense of belonging and shared problem solving.

In addition, successful organizations measure more than the bottom line, recognizing that excellence depends on a diverse set of competencies and values.[32] Balancing financial and nonfinancial measures provides a better picture of the company's performance and also helps managers align all employees toward key strategic goals.[33] Organizations such as Mobil Corporation's Americas Marketing and Refining division gauge progress by a constellation of measures, including key strategic performance areas like customer satisfaction, employee performance, innovation/change, and community/environmental issues. One study found that companies that carefully track these "soft" competencies along with "hard" data like financial performance and operating efficiency, were more successful over the long term.[34]

4. *Corporate Culture.* Companies throughout the United States and Canada are discovering that employee commitment is a vital component of organization success. Excellent companies manage to harness employee energy and enthusiasm. They do so by creating a *climate of trust*, encouraging *productivity through people*, and taking a *long-term view.*

A climate of trust is necessary so that employees can deal openly and honestly with one another. Collaboration across departments requires trust. Managers and workers must trust one another to work together in joint problem solving. At Ford Motor Company, where workers were historically suspicious of management, a new climate of trust has led to increased productivity and reduced costs.[35]

Productivity through people simply means that everyone must participate. Rank-and-file workers are considered the root of quality and productivity. People are empowered to participate in production, marketing, and new product improvements. Conflicting ideas are encouraged rather than suppressed. The ability to move ahead through consensus preserves the sense of trust, increases motivation, and facilitates both innovation and efficiency. As described in The New Paradigm box, leaders at Springfield Remanufacturing Corporation believe giving workers a voice in how the company operates is the only sensible way to run a business.

Another lesson from successful companies is the importance of taking a long-term view. Organizational success is not built in a day. Successful companies realize they must invest in training employees and commit to employees for the long term. Career paths are designed to give employees broad backgrounds rather than rapid upward mobility.

The ideas summarized in Exhibit 2.5 are important, but they may not always translate into short-term success. Some research suggests that organizations that

The New Paradigm

Springfield Remanufacturing Corporation

Jack Stack, chairman and CEO of Springfield Remanufacturing Corporation (SRC), has built a highly successful company based on the philosophy that "the best, most efficient, most profitable way to operate a business is to give everybody a voice in how the company is run and a stake in the financial outcome, good or bad."

Stack involves every employee in the planning and goal-setting process and established a bonus system, based on hitting the plan's targets, as well as a stock ownership plan. SRC's planning officially kicks off when Stack and other top executives meet with the sales and marketing managers of SRC's fifteen divisions in a formal two-day event. But before that meeting, the sales and marketing managers have done their homework by meeting with managers, supervisors, and front-line workers throughout their divisions. If a manager's plan is beyond the plant's capacity, the workers suggest workable alternatives. "We take everyone's ideas," says Bob Bigos, national sales manager for the Heavy Duty Division. "Then we blend them down to what we think is realistic." By the time managers present their plan to the top brass, everyone in the various divisions has had a say and thus developed a sense of ownership and commitment to the goals.

SRC also gives all employees access to the company's financial data so they can compare performance to the plan. SRC has invested heavily in financial education for all workers—everyone learns what's at risk and what's to be gained, and everyone knows how to make a difference. According to Kevin Dotson, an ex-marine who works in the Heavy Duty warehouse, he learns something new about the financial statements every time he goes to a meeting. "It's not like you have just one meeting and learn everything. . . . But you do understand the lines on the statement that you actually affect. That's how you see how you can be more efficient or how we as a small team within a large team can improve so the next group can take the handoff more smoothly. We all have different jobs, but we're all pulling for the same goals."

Source: Jay Finegan, "Everything According to Plan," *Inc.,* March 1995, 78–85.

have these characteristics often go through periods of lower performance.[36] A preponderance of these characteristics, however, can help organizations adapt and evolve as the environment changes and thus sustain a long-term commitment to excellence.

ORGANIZATIONAL EFFECTIVENESS

Understanding organizational goals and strategies is the first step toward understanding organizational effectiveness. Organizational goals represent the reason for an organization's existence and the outcomes it seeks to achieve. The next few sections of the chapter explore the topic of effectiveness and how effectiveness is measured in organizations.

Goals were defined earlier as the desired future state of the organization. Organizational **effectiveness** is the degree to which an organization realizes its goals.[37] Effectiveness is a broad concept. It implicitly takes into consideration a range of variables at both the organizational and departmental levels. Effectiveness evaluates the extent to which multiple goals—whether official or operative—are attained.

Efficiency is a more limited concept that pertains to the internal workings of the organization. Organizational efficiency is the amount of resources used to produce a unit of output.[38] It can be measured as the ratio of inputs to outputs. If one organization can achieve a given production level with fewer resources than another organization it would be described as more efficient.[39]

Sometimes efficiency leads to effectiveness. In other organizations, efficiency and effectiveness are not related. An organization may be highly efficient but fail to achieve its goals because it makes a product for which there is no demand. Likewise, an organization may achieve its profit goals but be inefficient.

Overall effectiveness is difficult to measure in organizations. Organizations are large, diverse, and fragmented. They perform many activities simultaneously. They pursue multiple goals. And they generate many outcomes, some intended and some unintended.[40] As we have just discussed, many organizations are recognizing that the bottom line is not the only measure of effectiveness. In a review of management literature, two Canadian scholars identified twenty-seven characteristics of successful firms that go beyond hard data; yet their studies also revealed that many managers have difficulty with the concept of evaluating performance on goals that are imprecise and not subject to quantitative measurement.[41] However, when managers tie performance measurement to strategy execution, it can be a valuable tool for helping organizations reach their goals.[42] For example, Federal Express developed a list of "service quality indicators"—service problems ranked according to their seriousness based on customer satisfaction surveys. By giving workers specific goals to shoot for, Federal Express ties performance measurement to the everyday operation and success of the company.[43]

TRADITIONAL EFFECTIVENESS APPROACHES

The measurement of effectiveness has focused on different parts of the organization. Organizations bring resources in from the environment, and those resources are transformed into outputs delivered back into the environment, as shown in Exhibit 2.6. The **goal approach** to organizational effectiveness is concerned with the output side and whether the organization achieves its goals in terms of desired levels of output.[44] The **system resource approach** assesses

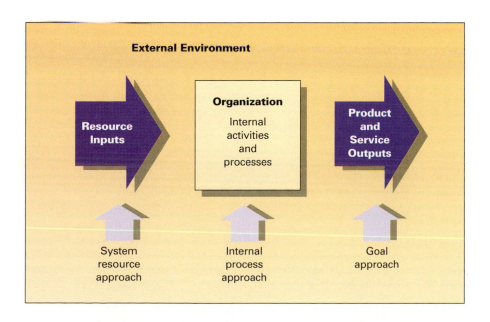

Exhibit 2.6

Traditional Approaches to the Measurement of Organizational Effectiveness

effectiveness by observing the beginning of the process and evaluating whether the organization effectively obtains resources necessary for high performance. The **internal process approach** looks at internal activities and assesses effectiveness by indicators of internal health and efficiency.

This section first examines effectiveness as evaluated by the goal approach. Then it turns to the system resource and internal process approaches to effectiveness. The following section of this chapter examines contemporary approaches that integrate these perspectives.

Goal Approach

The goal approach to effectiveness consists of identifying an organization's output goals and assessing how well the organization has attained those goals.[45] This is a logical approach because organizations do try to attain certain levels of output, profit, or client satisfaction. The goal approach measures progress toward attainment of those goals.

Indicators.   The important goals to consider are operative goals. Efforts to measure effectiveness have been more productive using operative goals than using official goals.[46] Official goals tend to be abstract and difficult to measure. Operative goals reflect activities the organization is actually performing.

One example of multiple goals is from a survey of U.S. business corporations.[47] Their reported goals are shown in Exhibit 2.7. Twelve goals were listed as being important to these companies. These twelve goals represent outcomes that cannot be achieved simultaneously. They illustrate the array of outcomes organizations attempt to achieve.

Usefulness.   The goal approach is used in business organizations because output goals can be readily measured. Business firms typically evaluate performance in terms of profitability, growth, market share, and return on investment. However, identifying operative goals and measuring performance of an organization are not always easy. Two problems that must be resolved are the issues of multiple goals and subjective indicators of goal attainment.

Exhibit 2.7

Reported Goals of U.S. Corporations

Goal	% Corporations
Profitability	89
Growth	82
Market share	66
Social responsibility	65
Employee welfare	62
Product quality and service	60
Research and development	54
Diversification	51
Efficiency	50
Financial stability	49
Resource conservation	39
Management development	35

Source: Adapted from Y. K. Shetty, "New Look at Corporate Goals," *California Management Review* 22, no. 2 (1979), pp. 71–79.

Since organizations have multiple and conflicting goals, effectiveness often cannot be assessed by a single indicator. High achievement on one goal may mean low achievement on another. Moreover, there are department goals as well as overall performance goals. The full assessment of effectiveness should take into consideration several goals simultaneously.

The other issue to resolve with the goal approach is how to identify operative goals for an organization and how to measure goal attainment. For business organizations, there are often objective indicators for certain goals. The stated objectives of top management and such measures as profit or growth are available in published reports. Subjective assessment is needed in business organizations for such outcomes as employee welfare or social responsibility. The following example shows how Granite Rock Company measures goal performance related to customer satisfaction and ties this information back into its daily operations.

Granite Rock Company

In Practice 2.2

Granite Rock believes if something is worth doing, it's worth measuring. The century-old, family-owned company tracks its various operations in about forty different ways. Graphs and charts are plotted and posted on bulletin boards at company headquarters and at each plant.

One of these charts shows employees how they measure up in the eyes of their customers. Granite Rock charges premium rates for high-quality construction materials and has to work hard to convince customers that its products and services are worth the extra cost.

The company regularly surveys customers to find out not only how they rate Granite Rock but how they rate the company's major competitors as well. Granite Rock's operations then aim to outperform the group average by at least 33 percent.

- On-time delivery is at the top of the list of factors customers are concerned about, and therefore it's at the top of the list of Granite Rock's customer-satisfaction goals. Recent performance measurement charts told workers they ranked 59 percent above the average for on-time delivery.
- Maintaining high product quality is a goal Granite Rock reached easily: 69 percent above the norm.
- But the company ranked highest of all on scheduling, or the ability to deliver needed products on short notice. Customers rated the company 76 percent better than the average.

Granite Rock has to be rated effective based on achieving its customer satisfaction goals. Ratings are not always so high in a company that tracks its performance forty different ways. When they're not, a top manager says, it "sounds an alarm. We believe you don't stress a negative—you chart it. Our people . . . will look at that negative and want to do something about it."[48]

Many goals cannot be measured objectively. Someone has to go into the organization and learn what are the actual goals. Since goals reflect the values of top management, the best informants are members of the top-management coalition.[49] These managers can report on the actual goals of the organization. Once goals are identified, subjective perceptions of goal achievement can be obtained if quantitative indicators are not available. Top managers rely on information from customers, competitors, suppliers, and employees, as well as on their own intuition, when considering these goals.[50]

The goal approach seems to be the most logical way to assess organizational effectiveness. Effectiveness is defined as the ability of an organization to attain its goals. However, the actual measurement of effectiveness is a complex problem. Organizations have many goals, so there is no single indicator of effectiveness. Some goals are subjective and must be identified by managers within the organization. The assessment of organizational effectiveness using the goal approach requires that the evaluator be aware of these issues and allow for them in the evaluation of effectiveness.

System Resource Approach

The system resource approach looks at the input side of the transformation process shown in Exhibit 2.6. It assumes organizations must be successful in obtaining resource inputs and in maintaining the organizational system to be effective. Organizations must obtain scarce and valued resources from other organizations. From a systems view, organizational effectiveness is defined as the ability of the organization, in either absolute or relative terms, to exploit its environment in the acquisition of scarce and valued resources.

Indicators.   Obtaining resources to maintain the organization system is the criterion by which organizational effectiveness is assessed. In a broad sense, indicators of system resource effectiveness encompass the following dimensions:

1. Bargaining position—the ability of the organization to exploit its environment in the acquisition of scarce and valued resources
2. Ability of the system's decision maker to perceive and correctly interpret the real properties of the external environment
3. Maintenance of internal day-to-day organizational activities
4. Ability of the organization to respond to changes in the environment.[51]

Usefulness.   The system resource approach is valuable when other indicators of performance are difficult to obtain. In many not-for-profit and social welfare organizations, for example, it is hard to measure output goals or internal efficiency. George Mason University recently received a lot of attention for increasing its academic reputation. The indicators used to evaluate George Mason's effectiveness were its ability to obtain scarce and valued resources. At one time, its faculty was considered second-rate, but George Mason has since been able to hire top professors to fill endowed chairs in several departments. Another indicator is the ability to obtain gifts of money. In four years, George Mason went from an endowment of less than $1 million and no professorships to an endowment of $20 million and twenty-nine professorships. Another scarce and valued resource is students. George Mason was able to increase the diversity of its student body and attract students with higher scholastic aptitude test scores. The ability to attract better students and faculty, plus winning large gifts from businesses and foundations, are used by George Mason administrators to indicate effective performance.[52]

Although the system resource approach is valuable when other measures of effectiveness are not available, it does have shortcomings. Often the ability to acquire resources seems less important than the utilization of those resources. For example, a college football program that recruits many star players would not be considered effective if the program did not develop the players to produce a winning team. This approach is most valuable when measures of goal attainment cannot be obtained.

Internal Process Approach

In the internal process approach, effectiveness is measured as internal organizational health and efficiency. An effective organization has a smooth, well-oiled internal process. Employees are happy and satisfied. Departmental activities mesh with one another to ensure high productivity. This approach does not consider the external environment. The important element in effectiveness is what the organization does with the resources it has, as reflected in internal health and efficiency.

Indicators.   The best-known proponents of a process model are from the human relations approach to organizations. Such writers as Chris Argyris, Warren G. Bennis, Rensis Likert, and Richard Beckhard have all worked extensively with human resources in organizations and emphasize the connection between human resources and effectiveness.[53] Writers on corporate culture and organizational excellence have stressed the importance of internal processes. Results from a recent study of nearly two hundred secondary schools showed that both human resources and employee-oriented processes were important in explaining and promoting effectiveness in those organizations.[54]

Indicators of an effective organization as seen from an internal process approach are:

1.   Strong corporate culture and positive work climate
2.   Team spirit, group loyalty, and teamwork
3.   Confidence, trust, and communication between workers and management
4.   Decision making near sources of information, regardless of where those sources are on the organizational chart
5.   Undistorted horizontal and vertical communication; sharing of relevant facts and feelings
6.   Rewards to managers for performance, growth, and development of subordinates and for creating an effective working group
7.   Interaction between the organization and its parts, with conflict that occurs over projects resolved in the interest of the organization.[55]

A second indicator of internal process effectiveness is the measurement of economic efficiency. William Evan developed a method that uses quantitative measures of efficiency.[56] The first step is to identify the financial cost of inputs (I), transformation (T), and outputs (O). Next, the three variables can be combined in ratios to evaluate various aspects of organizational performance. The most popular assessment of efficiency is O/I. For an automaker, this would be the number of cars produced per employee. For a hospital, the O/I ratio is the number of patients per annual budget. For a university, it is the number of students graduated divided by the resource inputs. The O/I ratio indicates overall financial efficiency for an organization.

Usefulness.   The internal process approach is important because the efficient use of resources and harmonious internal functioning are ways to measure effectiveness. As discussed in Chapter 1, a significant recent trend in management is the empowerment of human resources as a source of competitive advantage. Most managers believe participative management approaches and positive corporate culture are important components of effectiveness.

The financial approach to efficiency is useful for measuring the performance of departments concerned with efficiency, such as manufacturing. For example, the manufacturing efficiency of Chrysler enabled it to become the low-cost producer in the automobile industry. The assembly line was reorganized, and the number of robots was increased from 300 to 1,242. The payoff in productivity was an increase from 4,500 to 8,000 cars and trucks a day, while the number of worker-hours to build a vehicle shrank from 175 to 102.[57]

The internal process approach does have shortcomings. Total output and the organization's relationship with the external environment are not evaluated. Also, evaluations of internal health and functioning are often subjective, because many aspects of inputs and internal processes are not quantifiable. Managers should be aware that efficiency alone represents a limited view of organizational effectiveness.

CONTEMPORARY EFFECTIVENESS APPROACHES

The three approaches—goal, system resource, internal process—to organizational effectiveness described earlier all have something to offer, but each one tells only part of the story. Recently, integrative approaches to organizational effectiveness have been introduced. These new approaches acknowledge that organizations do many things and have many outcomes. These approaches combine several indicators of effectiveness into a single framework. They include the stakeholder and competing values approaches.

Stakeholder Approach

One proposed approach integrates diverse organizational activities by focusing on organizational stakeholders. A **stakeholder** is any group within or outside an organization that has a stake in the organization's performance. Creditors, suppliers, employees, and owners are all stakeholders. In the **stakeholder approach** (also called the constituency approach), the satisfaction of such groups can be assessed as an indicator of the organization's performance.[58] Each stakeholder will have a different criterion of effectiveness because it has a different interest in the organization. Each stakeholder group has to be surveyed to learn whether the organization performs well from its viewpoint.

Indicators. The initial work on evaluating effectiveness on the basis of stakeholders included ninety-seven small businesses in Texas. Seven stakeholder groups relevant to those businesses were surveyed to determine the perception of effectiveness from each viewpoint.[59] The following table shows each stakeholder and its criterion of effectiveness:

Stakeholder	Effectiveness Criteria
1. Owners	Financial return
2. Employees	Worker satisfaction, pay, supervision
3. Customers	Quality of goods and services
4. Creditors	Creditworthiness
5. Community	Contribution to community affairs
6. Suppliers	Satisfactory transactions
7. Government	Obedience to laws, regulations

The survey of stakeholders showed that a small business found it difficult to simultaneously fulfill the demands of all groups. One business may have high employee satisfaction, but the satisfaction of other groups may be lower. Nevertheless, measuring all seven stakeholders provides a more accurate view of effectiveness than any single measure. Evaluating how organizations perform across each group offers an overall assessment of effectiveness.

Usefulness. The strength of the stakeholder approach is that it takes a broad view of effectiveness and examines factors in the environment as well as within the organization. The stakeholder approach includes the community's notion of social responsibility, which was not formally measured in traditional approaches. The stakeholder approach also handles several criteria simultaneously—inputs, internal processing, outputs—and acknowledges that there is no single measure of effectiveness. The well-being of employees is just as important as attaining the owner's goals.

The stakeholder approach is gaining in popularity, based on the view that effectiveness is a complex, multidimensional concept that has no single measure.[60] Recent research has shown that the assessment of multiple stakeholder groups is an accurate reflection of effectiveness, especially with respect to organizational adaptability.[61] Moreover, research shows that firms really do care about their reputational status and do attempt to shape stakeholders' assessments of their performance.[62] If an organization performs poorly according to several interest groups, it is probably not meeting its effectiveness goals. However, satisfying some stakeholders may alienate others, as illustrated by the following example of the Safeway grocery chain.

Safeway, Inc.

In Practice 2.3

Safeway, Incorporated's chief executive is just the kind of man shareholders like to see leading the Oakland-based supermarket chain. By slashing costs, reducing prices, and steadily improving service, Steve Burd has turned Safeway into a tough competitor in the struggling supermarket business. The company reported a 110 percent increase in profits and a 3 percent rise in sales in the third quarter of 1993, and analysts predicted a tripling of income for the entire year. As a result, the price of Safeway's stock increased more than 70 percent.

The drastic cost cutting has benefited customers as well, and employees have been cautiously satisfied with their role in the restructuring. But suppliers are complaining, as cutting costs for Safeway sometimes means transferring more expenses to vendors. Competition for shelf space is fierce, and although Safeway denies charging vendors for space, it admits it might ask them to help pay for advertising. Suppliers gasped at a recent convention when Safeway's director of marketing suggested the chain take goods from vendors on consignment, to be returned if they don't sell promptly.

Burd has obviously improved the company's operating success. There may, however, be a limit to how far suppliers will go in the effort to cut costs within the organization.[63]

Competing Values Approach

Recall that organizational goals and performance criteria are defined by top and middle managers. The **competing values approach** to organizational effectiveness was developed by Robert Quinn and John Rohrbaugh to combine the diverse indicators of performance used by managers and researchers.[64] Using a comprehensive list of performance indicators, a panel of experts in organizational effectiveness rated the indicators for similarity. The analysis produced underlying dimensions of effectiveness criteria that represented competing management values in organizations.

Indicators. The first value dimension pertains to organizational **focus**, which is whether dominant values concern issues that are *internal* or *external* to the firm. Internal focus reflects a management concern for the well-being and efficiency of employees, and external focus represents an emphasis on the well-being of the organization itself with respect to the environment. The second value dimension pertains to organization **structure**, and whether *stability* versus *flexibility* is the dominant structural consideration. Stability reflects a management value for top-down control, whereas flexibility represents a value for adaptation and change.

The value dimensions of structure and focus are illustrated in Exhibit 2.8. The combination of dimensions provides four models of organizational effectiveness, which, though seemingly different, are closely related. In real organizations, these competing values can and often do exist together. Each model reflects a different management emphasis with respect to structure and focus.[65]

The **open systems model** reflects a combination of external focus and flexible structure. Management's primary goals are growth and resource acquisition. The organization accomplishes these goals through the subgoals of flexibility, readiness, and a positive external evaluation. The dominant value in this model is establishing a good relationship with the environment to acquire resources and grow. This model is similar in some ways to the system resource model described earlier.

The **rational goal model** represents management values of structural control and external focus. The primary goals are productivity, efficiency, and profit. The organization wants to achieve output goals in a controlled way. Subgoals that fa-

Exhibit 2.8
Four Models of Effectiveness Values

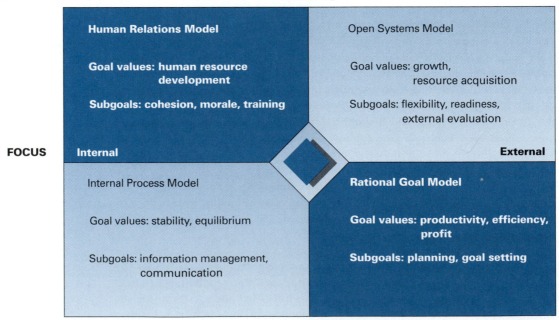

Source: Adapted from Robert E. Quinn and John Rohrbaugh, "A Spatial Model of Effectiveness Criteria: Toward a Competing Values Approach to Organizational Analysis," *Management Science* 29 (1983): 363–77; and Robert E. Quinn and Kim Cameron, "Organizational Life Cycles and Shifting Criteria of Effectiveness: Some Preliminary Evidence," *Management Science* 29 (1983): 33–51.

cilitate these outcomes are internal planning and goal setting, which are rational management tools. The rational goal model is similar to the goal approach described earlier.

The **internal process model** is in the lower left section of Exhibit 2.8; it reflects the values of internal focus and structural control. The primary outcome is a stable organizational setting that maintains itself in an orderly way. Organizations that are well established in the environment and simply want to maintain their current position would fit this model. Subgoals for this model include mechanisms for efficient communication, information management, and decision making.

The **human relations model** incorporates the values of an internal focus and a flexible structure. Here, management concern is on the development of human resources. Employees are given opportunities for autonomy and development. Management works toward the subgoals of cohesion, morale, and training opportunities. Organizations adopting this model are more concerned with employees than with the environment.

The four models in Exhibit 2.8 represent opposing organizational values. Managers must decide which goal values will take priority in their organizations. The way two organizations are mapped onto the four models is shown in Exhibit 2.9.[66] Organization A is a young organization concerned with finding a niche and becoming established in the external environment. Primary emphasis is given to flexibility, innovation, the acquisition of resources from the

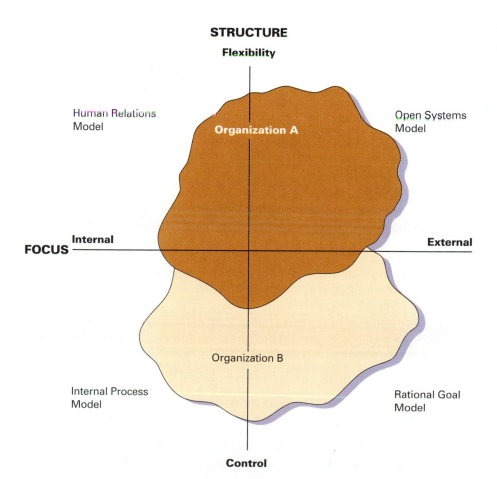

STRUCTURE

Flexibility

Human Relations
Model

Organization A

Open Systems
Model

FOCUS   Internal   External

Internal Process
Model

Organization B

Rational Goal
Model

Control

Exhibit 2.9

*Effectiveness Values for
Two Organizations*

environment, and the satisfaction of external constituencies. This organization gives moderate emphasis to human relations and even less emphasis to current productivity and profits. Satisfying and adapting to the environment are more important. The emphasis given to open systems values means that the internal process model is practically nonexistent. Stability and equilibrium receive little emphasis.

Organization B, in contrast, is an established business in which the dominant value is productivity and profits. This organization is characterized by planning and goal setting. Organization B is a large company that is well established in the environment and is primarily concerned with successful production and profits. Flexibility and human resources are not major concerns. This organization prefers stability and equilibrium to readiness and innovation because it wants to take advantage of its established customers.

Usefulness.   The competing values approach makes two contributions. First, it integrates diverse concepts of effectiveness into a single perspective. It incorporates the ideas of output goals, resource acquisition, and human resource development as goals the organization tries to accomplish. Second, the model calls attention to effectiveness criteria as management values and shows how opposing values exist at the same ¬time. Managers must decide which values they wish to pursue and which values will receive less emphasis. The four competing values exist simultaneously, but not all will receive equal priority. For example, a new, small organization that concentrates on establishing itself within a competitive environment will give less emphasis to developing employees than to the external environment.

The dominant values in an organization often change over time as organizations experience new environmental demands or new top leadership. Ford Motor Company, for example, has been shifting its values to a growth-oriented strategy since the hiring of a new chairman.

| In Practice 2.4 | *Ford Motor Company* |

For most of the six decades since GM's Alfred Sloan overtook and then passed Henry Ford as the world's biggest carmaker in 1932, Ford Motor Company has been content to be No. 2. Ford focused on maintaining internal efficiency and maximizing profits, reflecting the values of the rational goal model of Exhibit 2.8. Since taking the top job in January of 1994, Chairman Alex Trotman, however, has been orchestrating a new world order at Ford. In a recent speech to Ford executives, Trotman issued the challenge: "We make five out of the top ten vehicles in America. . . . There are five slots left."

Trotman has led the company through a massive reorganization, cutting out three layers of management and combining the North American and European divisions into a single $92 billion-a-year business. He wants the company to be fast, flexible, and ready to face the global auto wars of the next century. Ford's U.S. sales of cars and trucks have neared the 4 million mark, and market share is up a remarkable 7 percentage points. The company is also mounting an aggressive push in Europe, Latin America, and Asia. Trotman is investing heavily to boost capacity at Ford's plants, as well as to develop a "global" line of cars that will use the same chassis and basic parts while tailoring styling to suit tastes around the world. By aggressively combining rebates, special lease deals, and fleet discounts, Ford continues to push up sales and market share.[67]

Ford's recent moves reflect a shift in values from the rational goal model to the open-systems model. Managers are primarily concerned with growth and are investing time and resources to gain the internal flexibility and the positive relationship with the external environment needed to reach No. 1.

SUMMARY AND INTERPRETATION

This chapter discussed organizational goals and the strategies top managers use to help organizations achieve those goals. Goals specify the mission or purpose of an organization and its desired future state; strategies define how the organization will reach its goals. The chapter also discussed the most popular approaches to measuring effectiveness, that is, how well the organization realizes its purpose and attains its desired future state.

Organizations exist for a purpose; top managers define a specific mission or task to be accomplished. The mission statement, or official goals, makes explicit the purpose and direction of an organization. Official and operative goals are a key element in organizations because they meet these needs—establishing legitimacy with external groups and setting standards of performance for participants.

Managers must develop strategies that describe the actions required to achieve goals. They attempt to develop strategies that are compatible with the external environment. Porter's model of competitive strategies provides one framework for competitive action. In addition, managers can develop a number of internal organization characteristics that contribute to organizational excellence. Today's most successful companies remain flexible to adapt quickly to a chaotic international environment. This chapter examined characteristics of strategic orientation, top management, organization design, and corporate culture that are usually found in excellent companies.

Assessing organizational effectiveness is complex and reflects the complexity of organizations as a topic of study. No easy, simple, guaranteed measure will provide an unequivocal assessment of performance. Organizations must perform diverse activities well—from obtaining resource inputs to delivering outputs—to be successful. Traditional approaches used output goals, resource acquisition, or internal health and efficiency as the criteria of effectiveness. Contemporary approaches consider multiple criteria simultaneously. Organizations can be assessed by surveying constituencies that have a stake in organizational performance or by evaluating competing values for effectiveness. No approach is suitable for every organization, but each offers some advantage that the others may lack.

From the point of view of managers, the goal approach to effectiveness and measures of internal efficiency are useful when measures are available. The attainment of output and profit goals reflects the purpose of the organization, and efficiency reflects the cost of attaining those goals. Other factors such as top-management preferences, the extent to which goals are measurable, and the scarcity of environmental resources may influence the use of effectiveness criteria. In not-for-profit organizations, where internal processes and output criteria are often not quantifiable, stakeholder satisfaction or resource acquisition may be the only available indicators of effectiveness.

From the point of view of people outside the organization, such as academic investigators or government researchers, the stakeholder and competing values approaches to organizational effectiveness may be preferable. The stakeholder approach evaluates the organization's contribution to various stakeholders, including owners, employees, customers, and the community. The competing values approach acknowledges different areas of focus (internal, external) and structure (flexibility, stability) and allows for managers to choose one value to emphasize.

Key Concepts

competing values approach	mission
differentiation	official goals
effectiveness	open systems model
efficiency	operative goals
focus	organizational goal
focus strategy	rational goal model
goal approach	stakeholder
human relations model	stakeholder approach
internal process approach	strategy
internal process model	structure
low-cost leadership	system resource approach

Briefcase

As an organization manager, keep these guides in mind:

1. Establish and communicate organizational mission and goals. Communicate official goals to provide a statement of the organization's mission to external constituents. Communicate operational goals to provide internal direction, guidelines, and standards of performance for employees.
2. After goals have been defined, select a strategy for achieving those goals that is compatible with the external environment, based on Porter's framework of three competitive strategies: low-cost leadership, differentiation, and focus.
3. Implement strategies for achieving internal company characteristics that contribute to long-term organizational excellence. Factors such as the company's strategic orientation, top-management characteristics, organization design, and corporate culture strongly influence company success.
4. Assess the effectiveness of the organization. Use the goal approach, internal process approach, and system resource approach to obtain specific pictures of effectiveness. Assess stakeholder satisfaction or competing values to obtain a broader picture of effectiveness.

Discussion Questions

1. Discuss the role of top management in setting organizational direction.
2. How do operative market goals differ from resource and productivity goals?
3. Compare the twelve qualities associated with organizational excellence with the internal process, goal, and competing values approaches to *measuring effectiveness*. Which approach would seem to best measure excellence in a company?
4. What is the difference between a goal and a strategy?
5. Discuss the difference between a low-cost leadership and a differentiation strategy described in Porter's model of competitive strategies. Identify a company you are familiar with that illustrates each strategy and explain why.

6. Do you believe mission statements and official goal statements provide an organization with genuine legitimacy in the external environment? Discuss.
7. Suppose you have been asked to evaluate the effectiveness of the police department in a medium-sized community. Where would you begin, and how would you proceed? What effectiveness approach would you prefer?
8. What are the advantages and disadvantages of the system resource approach versus the goal approach for measuring organizational effectiveness?
9. What are the similarities and differences between assessing effectiveness on the basis of competing values versus stakeholders? Explain.
10. A noted organization theorist once said, "Organizational effectiveness can be whatever top management defines it to be." Discuss.

Chapter Two Workbook *Identifying Company Goals and Strategies**

Choose three companies, either in the same industry or in three different industries. Search the Internet for information on the companies, including annual reports.

In each company look particularly at the goals expressed. Refer back to the goals in Exhibit 2.7 and also to Porter's competitive strategies in Exhibit 2.4.

	Goals from Exhibit 2.7 articulated	Strategies from Porter used
Company #1		
Company #2		
Company #3		

Questions

1. Which goals seem most important?
2. Look for differences in the goals and strategies of the three companies and develop an explanation for those differences.
3. Which of the goals or strategies should be changed? Why?
4. *Optional:* Compare your table with those of other students and look for common themes. Which companies seem to articulate and communicate their goals and strategies the best?

* Copyright 1996 by Dorothy Marcic. All rights reserved.

Case for Analysis *The University Art Museum**

Visitors to the campus were always shown the University Art Museum, of which the large and distinguished university was very proud. A photograph of the handsome neoclassical building that housed the museum had long been used by the university for the cover of its brochures and catalogues.

The building, together with a substantial endowment, was given to the university around 1912 by an alumnus, the son of the university's first president, who had become very wealthy as an investment banker. He also gave the university his own small, but high quality, collections—one of Etruscan figurines, and one, unique in America, of English pre-Raphaelite paintings. He then served as the museum's unpaid director until his death. During his tenure he brought a few additional collections to the museum, largely from other alumni of the university. Only rarely did the museum purchase anything. As a result, the museum housed several small collections of uneven quality. As long as the founder ran the museum, none of the collections was ever shown to anybody except a few members of the university's art history faculty, who were admitted as the founder's private guests.

After the founder's death, in the late 1920s, the university intended to bring in a professional museum director. Indeed, this had been part of the agreement under which the founder had given the museum. A search committee was to be appointed; but in the meantime a graduate student in art history, who had shown interest in the museum and who had spent a good many hours in it, took over temporarily. At first, she did not even have a title, let alone a salary. But she stayed on acting as the museum's director and over the next thirty years was promoted in stages to that title. But from the first day, whatever her title, she was in charge. She immediately set about changing the museum altogether. She catalogued the collections. She pursued new gifts, again primarily small collections from alumni and other friends of the university. She organized fund raising for the museum. But, above all, she began to integrate the museum into the work of the university. When a space problem arose in the years immediately following World War II, Miss Kirkoff offered the third floor of the museum to the art history faculty, which moved its offices there. She remodeled the building to include classrooms and a modern and well-appointed auditorium. She raised funds to build one of the best research and reference libraries in art history in the country. She also began to organize a series of special exhibitions built around one of the museum's own collections, complemented by loans from outside collections. For each of these exhibitions, she had a distinguished member of the university's art faculty write a catalogue. These catalogues speedily became the leading scholarly texts in the fields.

Miss Kirkoff ran the University Art Museum for almost half a century. But old age ultimately defeated her. At the age of 68, after suffering a severe stroke, she had to retire. In her letter of resignation she proudly pointed to the museum's growth and accomplishment under her stewardship. "Our endowment," she wrote, "now compares favorably with museums several times our size. We never have had to ask the university for any money other than our share of the university's insurance policies. Our collections in the areas of our strength, while small, are of first-rate quality and importance. Above all, we are being used by more people than any museum of our size. Our lecture series, in which members of the university's art history faculty present a major subject to a university audience of students and faculty, attracts regularly three hundred to five hundred people; and if we had the seating capacity, we could easily have a larger audience. Our exhibitions are seen and studied by more visitors, most of them members of the university community, than all but the most highly publicized exhibitions in the very big museums ever draw. Above all, the courses and seminars offered in the museum have become one of the most popular and most rapidly growing educational features of the university. No other museum in this country or anywhere else," concluded Miss Kirkoff, "has so successfully integrated art into the life of a major university and a major university into the work of a museum."

Miss Kirkoff strongly recommended that the university bring in a professional museum director as her successor. "The museum is much too big and much too important to be entrusted to another amateur such as I was 45 years ago," she wrote. "And it needs careful thinking regarding its direction, its basis of support, and its future relationship with the university."

*Case #3, "The University Art Museum: Defining Purpose and Mission" (pp. 28–35), from *Management Cases* by Peter F. Drucker. Copyright © 1977 by Peter F. Drucker. Reprinted by permission of Harper & Row, Publishers, Inc.

The university took Miss Kirkoff's advice. A search committee was duly appointed and, after one year's work, it produced a candidate whom everybody approved. The candidate was himself a graduate of the university who had then obtained his Ph.D. in art history and in museum work from the university. Both his teaching and his administrative record were sound, leading to his present museum directorship in a medium-sized city. There he converted an old, well-known, but rather sleepy museum to a lively, community-oriented museum whose exhibitions were well publicized and attracted large crowds.

The new museum director took over with great fanfare in September 1981. Less than three years later he left—with less fanfare, but still with considerable noise. Whether he resigned or was fired was not quite clear. But that there was bitterness on both sides was only too obvious.

The new director, upon his arrival, had announced that he looked upon the museum as a "major community resource" and intended to "make the tremendous artistic and scholarly resources of the museum fully available to the academic community as well as to the public." When he said these things in an interview with the college newspaper, everybody nodded in approval. It soon became clear that what he meant by "community resource" and what the faculty and students understood by these words were not the same. The museum had always been "open to the public" but, in practice, it was members of the college community who used the museum and attended its lectures, its exhibitions, and its frequent seminars.

The first thing the new director did, however, was to promote visits from the public schools in the area. He soon began to change the exhibition policy. Instead of organizing small shows, focused on a major collection of the museum and built around a scholarly catalogue, he began to organize "popular exhibitions" around "topics of general interest" such as "Women Artists through the Ages." He promoted these exhibitions vigorously in the newspapers, in radio and television interviews, and, above all, in the local schools. As a result, what had been a busy but quiet place was soon knee-deep with school children, taken to the museum in special buses that cluttered the access roads around the museum and throughout the campus. The faculty, which was not particularly happy with the resulting noise and confusion, became thoroughly upset when the scholarly old chairman of the art history department was mobbed by fourth-graders who sprayed him with their water pistols as he tried to push his way through the main hall to his office.

Increasingly, the new director did not design his own shows, but brought in traveling exhibitions from major museums, importing their catalogue as well rather than have his own faculty produce one.

The students too were apparently unenthusiastic after the first six or eight months, during which the new director had been somewhat of a campus hero. Attendance at the classes and seminars held at the art museum fell off sharply, as did attendance at the evening lectures. When the editor of the campus newspaper interviewed students for a story on the museum, he was told again and again that the museum had become too noisy and too "sensational" for students to enjoy the classes and to have a chance to learn.

What brought all this to a head was an Islamic art exhibit in late 1983. Since the museum had little Islamic art, nobody criticized the showing of a traveling exhibit, offered on very advantageous terms with generous financial assistance from some of the Arab governments. But then, instead of inviting one of the university's own faculty members to deliver the customary talk at the opening of the exhibit, the director brought in a cultural attaché of one of the Arab embassies in Washington. The speaker, it was reported, used the occasion to deliver a violent attack on Israel and on the American policy of supporting Israel against the Arabs. A week later, the university senate decided to appoint an advisory committee, drawn mostly from members of the art history faculty, which, in the future, would have to approve all plans for exhibits and lectures. The director thereupon, in an interview with the campus newspaper, sharply attacked the faculty as "elitist" and "snobbish" and as believing that "art belongs to the rich." Six months later, in June 1984, his resignation was announced.

Under the bylaws of the university, the academic senate appoints a search committee. Normally, this is pure formality. The chairperson of the appropriate department submits the department's nominees for the committee who are approved and appointed, usually without debate. But when the academic senate early the following semester was asked to appoint the search committee, things were far from "normal." The dean who presided, sensing the tempers in the room, tried to smooth over things by saying, "Clearly, we picked the wrong person the last time. We will have to try very hard to find the right one this time."

He was immediately interrupted by an economist, known for his populism, who broke in and said, "I admit that the late director was probably not the right personality. But I strongly believe that his personality was not at the root of the problem. He tried to do what needs doing, and this got him in trouble with the faculty. He tried to make our museum a community resource, to bring in the community and to make art accessible to broad masses of people, to the blacks and the Puerto Ricans, to the kids from the ghetto schools and to a lay public. And this is what we really resented. Maybe his methods were not the most tactful ones—I admit I could have done without those interviews he gave. But what he tried to do was right. We had better commit ourselves to the policy he wanted to put into effect, or else we will have deserved his attacks on us as 'elitist' and 'snobbish.'"

"This is nonsense," cut in the usually silent and polite senate member from the art history faculty. "It makes absolutely no sense for our museum to become the kind of community resource our late director and my distinguished colleague want it to be. First, there is no need. The city has one of the world's finest and biggest museums, and it does exactly that and does it very well. Secondly, we have neither the artistic resources nor the financial resources to serve the community at large. We can do something different but equally important and indeed unique. Ours is the only museum in the country, and perhaps in the world, that is fully integrated with an academic community and truly a teaching institution. We are using it, or at least we used to until the last few unfortunate years, as a major educational resource for all our students. No other museum in the country, and as far as I know in the world, is bringing undergraduates into art the way we do. All of us, in addition to our scholarly and graduate work, teach undergraduate courses for people who are not going to be art majors or art historians. We work with the engineering students and show them what we do in our conservation and restoration work. We work with architecture students and show them the development of architecture through the ages. Above all, we work with liberal arts students, who often have had no exposure to art before they came here and who enjoy our courses all the more because they are scholarly and not just 'art apprecia-

tion.' This is unique and this is what our museum can do and should do."

"I doubt that this is really what we should be doing," commented the chairman of the mathematics department. "The museum, as far as I know, is part of the graduate faculty. It should concentrate on training art historians in its Ph.D. program, on its scholarly work, and on its research. I would strongly urge that the museum be considered an adjunct to graduate and especially to Ph.D. education, confine itself to this work, and stay out of all attempts to be 'popular,' both on campus and outside of it. The glory of the museum is the scholarly catalogues produced by our faculty, and our Ph.D. graduates who are sought after by art history faculties throughout the country. This is the museum's mission, which can only be impaired by the attempts to be 'popular,' whether with students or with the public."

"These are very interesting and important comments," said the dean, still trying to pacify. "But I think this can wait until we know who the new director is going to be. Then we should raise these questions with him."

"I beg to differ, Mr. Dean," said one of the elder statesmen of the faculty. "During the summer months, I discussed this question with an old friend and neighbor of mine in the country, the director of one of the nation's great museums. He said to me: 'You do not have a personality problem, you have a management problem. You have not, as a university, taken responsibility for the mission, the direction, and the objectives of your museum. Until you do this, no director can succeed. And this is your decision. In fact, you cannot hope to get a good man until you can tell him what your basic objectives are. If your late director is to blame—I know him and I know that he is abrasive—it is for being willing to take on a job when you, the university, had not faced up to the basic management decisions. There is no point talking about who should manage until it is clear what it is that has to be managed and for what.'"

At this point the dean realized that he had to adjourn the discussion unless he wanted the meeting to degenerate into a brawl. But he also realized that he had to identify the issues and possible decisions before the next faculty meeting a month later.

Case for Analysis *Quality Circle Consequence**

John Stevens, plant manager of the Fairlee Plant of Lockstead Corporation, which manufactures structural components for aircraft wings and bodies, became interested in using quality circles to improve performance in his plant. "Quality circles" was the name used to describe joint labor-supervision participation teams operating at the shop-floor level at Lockstead. Other companies called quality circles names such as "productivity groups," "people involvement programs," and "departmental teams." By whatever name, the purpose of quality circles was to improve the quality of manufacturing performance.

The subject of quality-circles was a hot topic in the press. Stevens had seen books on Japanese management and productivity successes, which featured the use of quality circles. In these books, the slogan "None of us is as smart as all of us" was prominent.

Other books related quality circles to productivity gains. Articles on quality circles appeared often in trade journals and in business magazines, including *Business Week*.

Stevens also had a pamphlet from a management consulting firm announcing a "new and improved" training course for quality-circle leaders, scheduled consecutively in Birmingham, Alabama; Williamsburg, Virginia; and Orlando, Florida. Another consultant offered "A program that will teach your managers and supervisors how to increase productivity and efficiency without making costly investments . . . by focusing on techniques germane to the quality-circle process." Stevens was impressed enough to attend an advanced management seminar at a large midwestern university. A large part of the program concentrated on quality circles.

Professor Albert Mennon particularly impressed Stevens with his lectures on group discussion, team problem solving, and group decision making. Mennon convinced Stevens that employees meeting in quality-circle teams with adequate leaders could effectively consider problems and formulate quality decisions that would be acceptable to employees. The staff conducting this state-of-the-art seminar covered five areas, including: (1) training quality-circle members in the six-step problem sequence, (2) describing what leaders and facilitators should do during the quality-circle sessions, (3) planning and writing a policy guide, (4) developing an implementation plan, and (5) measuring quality-circle progress and success.

The potential benefits of a successfully implemented quality-circle program were expected to affect workers and the company. The list of such payoffs included improved job satisfaction, productivity improvements, efficiency gains, and better quality of performance and labor relations. It was expected, moreover, that a reduction would occur in such areas as grievance loads, absenteeism, and costs.

Returning to his plant after the seminar, Stevens decided to practice some of the principles he had learned. He called together the 25 employees of Department B and told them that production standards established several years ago were too low in view of the recent installation of automated equipment. He gave the workers the opportunity to discuss the mitigating circumstances and to decide among themselves, as a group, what their standards should be. On leaving the room, he believed that the workers would establish much higher standards than he would have dared propose.

After an hour of discussion, the group summoned Stevens and notified him that, contrary to his opinion, their decision was that the standards were already too high, and since they had been given the authority to establish their own standards, they were making a reduction of 10 percent. Stevens knew these standards were way too low to provide a fair profit on the owner's investment. Yet he believed his refusal to accept the group decision would be disastrous. Stevens thought of telephoning Professor Mennon for consultation about the quality-circle dilemma, but he chose to act on his own.

Options filled Stevens' mind: (1) He could accept the blame for the quality-circle experiment having gone awry and tell them to begin anew; (2) he could establish incentive pay adjustment linkage between the quality circle's decisions and productivity improvements; (3) he might even operate for a short while at a loss to prove that the original quality-circle decision had been unacceptable; and (4) he might abandon the participative team program. Stevens knows that he needs a decision, an operational policy for the quality-circle program, and an implementation plan.

*John M. Champion and John H. James, *Critical Incidents in Management: Decision and Policy Issues*, 6th ed. (Homewood, Ill.: Irwin, 1989), 214–215.

Chapter Two Workshop *Competing Values and Organizational Effectiveness**

1. Divide into groups of four to six members.
2. Select an organization to "study" for this exercise. It should be an organization one of you has worked at, or it could be the university.
3. Using the exhibit "Four Models of Effectiveness Values" (Exhibit 2.8), your group should list eight

potential measures that show a balanced view of performance. These should relate not only to work activities, but also to goal values for the company. Use the table below.

Goal or subgoal		Performance gauge	How to measure	Source of data	What do you consider effective?
(Example) Equilibrium		Turnover rates	Compare percentages of workers who left	HRM files	25% reduction in first year
Open system	1.				
	2.				
Human relations	3.				
	4.				
Internal process	5.				
	6.				
Rational goal	7.				
	8.				

4. How will achieving these goal values help the organization to become more effective? Which values could be given more weight than others? Why?
5. Present your competing values chart to the rest of the class. Each group should explain why it chose those particular values and which are more impor-

tant. Be prepared to defend your position to the other groups, which are encouraged to question your choices.

* Adapted by Dorothy Marcic from general ideas in Jennifer Howard and Larry Miller, *Team Management,* The Miller Consulting Group, 1994, p. 92.

Notes

1. David Goodman, "One Step at a Time," *Inc.,* August 1995, 64–70.

2. Amitai Etzioni, *Modern Organizations* (Englewood Cliffs, N.J.: Prentice-Hall, 1964), 6.

3. John P. Kotter, "What Effective General Managers Really Do," *Harvard Business Review* (November-December 1982): 156–67; Henry Mintzberg, *The Nature of Managerial Work* (New York: Harper & Row, 1973).

4. Charles C. Snow and Lawrence G. Hrebiniak, "Strategy, Distinctive Competence, and Organizational Performance," *Administrative Science Quarterly* 25 (1980): 317–35.

5. Elizabeth Lesly, "A Safer New York," *Business Week*, 11 December 1995, 81–84; and Eric Pooley, "One Good Apple," *Time*, 15 January 1996, 54–56.

6. David L. Calfee, "Get Your Mission Statement Working!" *Management Review,* January 1993, 54–57; John A. Pearce II and Fred David, "Corporate Mission Statements: The Bottom Line," *Academy of Management Executive* 1 (1987): 109–16; Fred R. David, "How Companies Define Their Mission," *Long-Range Planning* 22 (1989): 90–97.

7. Charles Perrow, "The Analysis of Goals in Complex Organizations," *American Sociological Review* 26 (1961): 854–66.

8. Johannes U. Stoelwinder and Martin P. Charns, "The Task Field Model of Organization Analysis and Design," *Human Relations* 34 (1981): 743–62; Anthony Raia, *Managing by Objectives* (Glenview, Ill.: Scott, Foresman, 1974).

9. Kevin Helliker, "Pressure at Pier 1: Beating Sales Numbers of Year Earlier Is a Storewide Obsession," *Wall Street Journal*, 7 December 1995, B1, B2.

10. Myron Magnet, "Let's Go For Growth," *Fortune*, 7 March 1994, 60–72; Patricia Sellars, "Pepsi Keeps on Going after No. 1," *Fortune,* 11 March 1991, 64; and "Bausch & Lomb: Hardball Pricing Helps It to Regain Its Grip in Contact Lenses," *Business Week*, 16 July 1984, 78–80.

11. William W. Arnold, "Lessons of Value-Driven Leadership," *Healthcare Executive*, July/August 1995, 12–15.

12. Rahul Jacob, "Corporate Reputations," *Fortune*, 6 March 1995, 54–67.

13. Alex Taylor III, "Why the Bounce at Rubbermaid," *Fortune*, 13 April 1987, 77–78.

14. Mark C. Suchman, "Managing Legitimacy: Strategic and Institutional Approaches," *Academy of Management Review* 20, no. 3 (1995): 571–610.

15. Edward A. Robinson, "America's Most Admired Companies," *Fortune*, 3 March 1997, 68–75; Anne B. Fisher, "Corporate Reputations, "*Fortune*, 4 March 1996, 90–98; Ken Friedman, Norwegian School of Management, Oslo, Norway, personal communication.

16. James D. Thompson, *Organizations in Action* (New York: McGraw-Hill, 1967), 83–98.

17. "Owens-Illinois: Giving up Market Share to Improve Profits," *Business Week*, 11 May 1981, 81–82.

18. Richard Crone, Bruce Snow, and Ricky Waclawcayk, "Datapoint Corporation," unpublished manuscript, Texas A&M University, 1981.

19. Michael E. Porter, *Competitive Strategy: Techniques for Analyzing Industries and Competitors* (New York: Free Press, 1980).

20. Peter Burrows, "Compaq Stretches for the Crown," *Business Week*, 11 July 1994, 140–42.

21. David Greising, "It Hurts So Good at Delta," *Business Week*, 11 December 1995, 106–107.

22. Greg Burns, "It Only Hertz When Enterprise Laughs," *Business Week*, 12 December 1994, 44.

23. James C. Collins and Jerry I. Porras, *Built to Last: Successful Habits of Visionary Companies* (New York: HarperBusiness, 1994).

24. Michael Hammer and James Champy, *Reengineering the Corporation* (New York, Harper-Collins, 1993); Noel M. Tichy and Stratford Sherman, *Control Your Destiny or Someone Else Will* (New York: Currency Doubleday, 1993).

25. Oren Harari, "You're Not in Business to Make a Profit," *Management Review*, July 1992, 53–55.

26. Sellers, "Pepsi Keeps on Going after No. 1."

27. James C. Collins, "Building Companies to Last," *The State of Small Business 1995* (Special Issue), *Inc.,* 16 May 1995, 83–85.

28. Kenneth Labich, "Why Companies Fail," *Fortune*, 14 November 1994, 52–68.

29. James C. Collins and Jerry I. Porras, "Building a Visionary Company," *California Management Review* 37, no. 2 (Winter 1995): 80–100.

30. Amy Dunkin, "Pepsi's Marketing Magic: Why Nobody Does It Better," *Business Week*, 10 February 1986, 52–57.

31. James C. Collins, "Building Companies to Last"; Brian O'Reilly, "J&J Is on a Roll," *Fortune*, 26 December 1994, 178–91.

32. James V. Koch and Richard J. Cebula, "In Search of Excellent Management," *Journal of Management Studies* 31, no. 5 (September 1994): 681–99.

33. Robert S. Kaplan and David P. Norton, "Using the Balanced Scorecard as a Strategic Management System," *Harvard Business Review* (January-February 1996): 75–85.

34. Brian McWilliams, "The Measure of Success," *Across the Board* (February 1996): 16–20; John H. Lingle and William A. Schiemann, "From Balanced Scorecard to Strategic Gauges: Is Measurement Worth It?" *Management Review* (March 1996): 56–61.

35. Neil Templin, "A Decisive Response to Crisis Brought Ford Enhanced Productivity," *Wall Street Journal*, 15 December 1992, A1, A8.

36. Michael A. Hitt and R. Duane Ireland, "Peters and Waterman Revisited: The Unended Quest for Excellence," *Academy of Management Executive* 1 (1987): 91–98.

37. Etzioni, *Modern Organizations,* 8.

38. Etzioni, *Modern Organizations,* 8; Gary D. Sandefur, "Efficiency in Social Service Organizations," *Administration and Society* 14 (1983): 449–68.

39. Richard M. Steers, *Organizational Effectiveness: A Behavioral View* (Santa Monica, Calif.: Goodyear, 1977), 51.

40. Karl E. Weick and Richard L. Daft, "The Effectiveness of Interpretation Systems," in Kim S. Cameron and David A. Whetten, eds., *Organizational Effectiveness: A Comparison of Multiple Models* (New York: Academic Press, 1982).

41. David L. Blenkhorn and Brian Gaber, "The Use of 'Warm Fuzzies' to Assess Organizational Effectiveness," *Journal of General Management*, 21, no. 2 (Winter 1995): 40–51.

42. Robert S. Kaplan and David P. Norton, "Using the Balanced Scorecard as a Strategic Management System," *Harvard Business Review* (January-February 1996): 75–85; Craig Eric Schneider, Douglas G. Shaw, and Richard W. Beatty, "Performance Measurement and Management: A Tool for Strategy Execution," *Human Resource Management* 30 (Fall 1991): 279–301.

43. Frank Rose, "Now Quality Means Service Too," *Fortune*, 22 April 1991, 99–108.

44. Steven Strasser, J. D. Eveland, Gaylord Cummins, O. Lynn Deniston, and John H. Romani, "Conceptualizing the Goal and Systems Models of Organizational Effectiveness—Implications for Comparative Evaluation Research," *Journal of Management Studies* 18 (1981): 321–40.

45. James L. Price, "The Study of Organizational Effectiveness," *Sociological Quarterly* 13 (1972): 3–15.

46. Richard H. Hall and John P. Clark, "An Ineffective Effectiveness Study and Some Suggestions for Future Research," *Sociological Quarterly* 21 (1980): 119–34; Price, "Study of Organizational Effectiveness;" Perrow, "Analysis of Goals."

47. George W. England, "Organizational Goals and Expected Behaviors in American Managers," *Academy of Management Journal* 10 (1967): 107–17.

48. Edward O. Welles, "How're We Doing?" *Inc.*, May 1991, 80–83.

49. Johannes M. Pennings and Paul S. Goodman, "Toward a Workable Framework," in Paul S. Goodman, Johannes M. Pennings, et al., *New Perspectives on Organizational Effectiveness* (San Francisco: Jossey-Bass, 1979), 152.

50. David L. Blenkhorn and Brian Gaber, "The Use of 'Warm Fuzzies' to Assess Organizational Effectiveness."

51. J. Barton Cunningham, "A Systems-Resource Approach for Evaluating Organizational Effectiveness," *Human Relations* 31 (1978): 631–56; Ephraim Yuchtman and Stanley E. Seashore, "A System Resource Approach to Organizational Effectiveness," *Administrative Science Quarterly* 12 (1967): 377–95.

52. David Shribeman, "University in Virginia Creates a Niche, Aims to Reach Top Ranks," *Wall Street Journal,* 30 September 1985, 1, 9.

53. Chris Argyris, *Integrating the Individual and the Organization* (New York: Wiley, 1964); Warren G. Bennis, *Changing Organizations* (New York: McGraw-Hill, 1966); Rensis Likert, *The Human Organization* (New York: McGraw-Hill, 1967); Richard Beckhard, *Organization Development Strategies and Models* (Reading, Mass.: Addison-Wesley, 1969).

54. Cheri Ostroff and Neal Schmitt, "Configurations of Organizational Effectiveness and Efficiency," *Academy of Management Journal* 36 (1993): 1345–

61; Peter J. Frost, Larry F. Moore, Meryl Reise Louis, Craig C. Lundburg, and Joanne Martin, *Organizational Culture* (Beverly Hills, Calif.: Sage, 1985).

55. J. Barton Cunningham, "Approaches to the Evaluation of Organizational Effectiveness," *Academy of Management Review* 2 (1977): 463–74; Beckhard, *Organization Development*.

56. William M. Evan, "Organization Theory and Organizational Effectiveness: An Exploratory Analysis," *Organization and Administrative Sciences* 7 (1976): 15–28.

57. Alex Taylor III, "Lee Iacocca's Production Whiz," *Fortune*, 22 June 1987, 36–44.

58. Anne S. Tusi, "A Multiple-Constituency Model of Effectiveness: An Empirical Examination at the Human Resource Subunit Level," *Administrative Science Quarterly* 35 (1990): 458, 483; Charles Fombrun and Mark Shanley, "What's in a Name? Reputation Building and Corporate Strategy," *Academy of Management Journal* 33 (1990): 233–58; Terry Connolly, Edward J. Conlon, and Stuart Jay Deutsch, "Organizational Effectiveness: A Multiple-Constituency Approach," *Academy of Management Review* 5 (1980): 211–17.

59. Frank Friedlander and Hal Pickle, "Components of Effectiveness in Small Organizations," *Administrative Science Quarterly* 13 (1968): 289–304.

60. Kim S. Cameron, "The Effectiveness of Ineffectiveness," in Barry M. Staw and L. L. Cummings, eds., *Research in Organizational Behavior* (Greenwich, Conn.: JAI Press, 1984), 235–86; Rosabeth Moss Kanter and Derick Brinkerhoff, "Organizational Performance: Recent Developments in Measurement," *Annual Review of Sociology* 7 (1981): 321–49.

61. Tusi, "A Multiple-Constituency Model of Effectiveness."

62. Fombrun and Shanley, "What's in a Name?"

63. Russell Mitchell, "Safeway's Low-Fat Diet," *Business Week*, 18 October 1993, 60–61.

64. Robert E. Quinn and John Rohrbaugh, "A Spatial Model of Effectiveness Criteria: Toward a Competing Values Approach to Organizational Analysis," *Management Science* 29 (1983): 363–77.

65. Regina M. O'Neill and Robert E. Quinn, "Editor's Note: Applications of the Competing Values Framework," *Human Resource Management* 32 (Spring 1993): 1–7.

66. Robert E. Quinn and Kim Cameron, "Organizational Life Cycles and Shifting Criteria of Effectiveness: Some Preliminary Evidence," *Management Science* 29 (1983): 33–51.

67. Robert L. Simison and Oscar Suris, "Alex Trotman's Goal: To Make Ford No. 1 in World Sales," *Wall Street Journal*, 18 July 1995, A1, A8; Keith Naughton, "Ford's Global Gladiator," *Business Week*, 11 December 1995, 116, 118.

chapter three

The External Environment

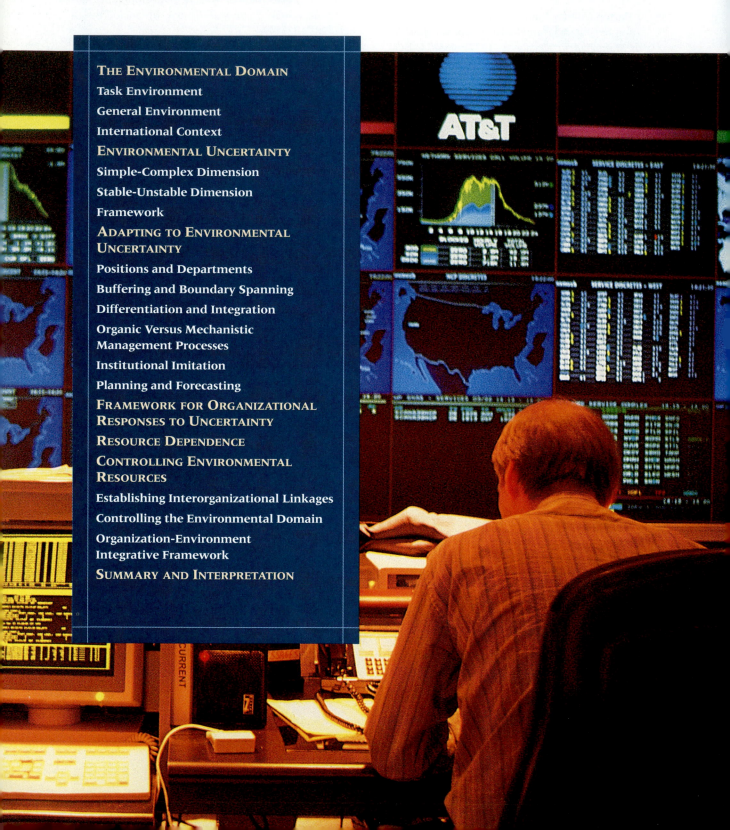

A look inside

AT&T

Just as you sit down to dinner, the phone rings, and another long distance company is promising you lower rates if you'll switch carriers. Here's the bad news—it's going to get worse. The most competitive business war in memory is looming on the horizon, and AT&T is gearing up for the fight by cutting jobs and operating costs, spinning off its equipment and computer units, and spending billions on advertising, new technology, and acquisitions.

After a lawsuit in the mid-1980s paved the way for MCI, Sprint, and other long-distance carriers to threaten AT&T's turf, the company lost 30 percent of the long-distance market share. By the mid-1990s, as part of its efforts to win back business, AT&T was airing hundreds of television spots, many of them accusing major rival MCI of misleading and annoying customers. The company also beefed up its systems for scanning the external environment by computerizing its network of intelligence professionals so that everyone in the company can be aware of competitive threats.

Now, government deregulation is sparking more upheaval, clearing the way for regional Bell operating companies and GTE, the nation's largest local phone company, to compete with AT&T in the long-distance market, while AT&T, MCI, and Sprint will be able to offer local as well as long-distance services. If government regulators approve the merger of British Telecommunications and MCI, AT&T will face its toughest battle yet. The company is investing millions in developing local networks and is acquiring other companies and developing strategic alliances, such as a partnership with Unisource, a group of European firms, to expand its capabilities to serve new markets. To further strengthen its competitive position, AT&T is poised for the possibility of eventually reacquiring one of the regional Bell units or a Bell asset such as a cable television company. In these unpredictable times, where new competitors dart out of nowhere because of deregulation, privatization, and rapid technological change, AT&T managers know they can't afford to be complacent.[1]

AT&T was surprised by the external environment in the mid-1980s, and managers are working overtime to ensure that the same thing doesn't happen again. AT&T managers know they are operating in a highly competitive and rapidly changing industry, and they search for ways to interpret, influence, and adapt to the environment. Similar turbulence and uncertainty face major European telecommunications companies, such as British Telecommunications, France Telecom, and Deutsche Telekom AG, as countries in the European Union prepare to open their phone markets to full competition by 1998. British firm Cable & Wireless, founded in the 1850s and a long-time global player, failed to heed warning signs in the external environment and lost customers rapidly to price cutting rivals ushered in by deregulation in Britain. In addition, as smaller rivals rushed into international alliances, Cable & Wireless spurned potential partners, seriously damaging the company's ability to remain competitive.[2]

The problem of a changing environment is not unique to telecommunications firms. Companies in all industries confront difficulties because of changes in the environment. Apple Computer is struggling to survive in an industry that has become dominated by PC clones based on Intel and Microsoft technology.[3] Small retailers have long suffered threats from huge discount stores, such as Wal-Mart. But even the mighty Wal-Mart is vulnerable to changes in the environment. Small retailers are challenging some of the giant chain's competitive tactics in court, claiming it is violating antitrust laws, and stubborn New Englanders have slowed the expansion of Wal-Mart into that region largely with zoning requirements and legal arguments that it will have a detrimental impact on the local environment.[4]

Firms that attempt to grow through mergers and acquisitions have run into brick walls in the form of tough regulations in many states. For other firms, new technology such as digital communications, microrobots from Japan, or Nucor's highly efficient thin-slab steel casting poses major threats. Also, firms in all industries agree that international competition worries everyone. The list could go on and on. The external environment is the source of important threats facing major corporations today.[5]

Purpose of This Chapter

The purpose of this chapter is to develop a framework for assessing environments and how organizations can respond to them. First, we will identify the organizational domain and the sectors that influence the organization. Then, we will explore two major environmental forces on the organization—the need for information and the need for resources. Organizations respond to these forces through structural design, planning systems, imitation, and attempts to change and control elements in the environment.

THE ENVIRONMENTAL DOMAIN

In a broad sense the environment is infinite and includes everything outside the organization. However, the analysis presented here considers only the aspects of the environment to which the organization is sensitive and must respond to survive. Thus, **organizational environment** is defined as all elements that exist outside the boundary of the organization and have the potential to affect all or part of the organization.

The environment of an organization can be understood by analyzing its domain within external sectors. An organization's **domain** is the chosen environmental field of action. It is the territory an organization stakes out for itself with respect to products, services, and markets served. Domain defines the organization's niche and defines those external sectors with which the organization will interact to accomplish its goals. For example, the domain of AT&T brings it into contact with customers, competitors, suppliers, and government rules and regulations.

The environment comprises several **sectors** or subdivisions of the external environment that contain similar elements. Ten sectors can be analyzed for each organization: industry, raw materials, human resources, financial resources, market, technology, economic conditions, government, sociocultural, and international.

Exhibit 3.1

An Organization's Environment

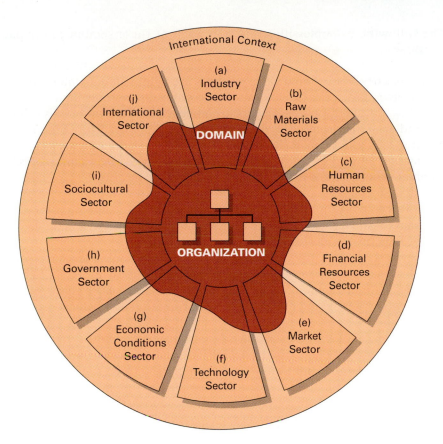

(a) Competitors, industry size and competitiveness, related industries
(b) Suppliers, manufacturers, real estate, services
(c) Labor market, employment agencies, universities, training schools, employees in other companies, unionization
(d) Stock markets, banks, savings and loans, private investors
(e) Customers, clients, potential users of products and services
(f) Techniques of production, science, research centers, automation, new materials

(g) Recession, unemployment rate, inflation rate, rate of investment, economics, growth
(h) City, state, federal laws and regulations, taxes, services, court system, political processes
(i) Age, values, beliefs, education, religion, work ethic, consumer and green movements
(j) Competition from and acquisition by foreign firms, entry into overseas markets, foreign customs, regulations, exchange rate

The sectors and a hypothetical organizational domain are illustrated in Exhibit 3.1. For most companies, the sectors in Exhibit 3.1 can be further subdivided into the task environment and general environment.

Task Environment

The **task environment** includes sectors with which the organization interacts directly and that have a direct impact on the organization's ability to achieve its goals. The task environment typically includes the industry, raw materials, and market sectors, and perhaps the human resources and international sectors.

The following examples illustrate how each of these sectors can impact organizations:

- In the *industry sector,* brand name products are fighting it out with lower-cost store brands. Procter & Gamble cut prices on Joy dishwashing liquid, Era detergent, and Luvs disposable diapers to compete with discount brands of similar products. Other companies decided if they couldn't beat store brands, they might as well join them. RJR Nabisco, for example, has announced plans to test-market lower-priced private label cookies and crackers in some stores.[6]
- An interesting example in the *raw materials sector* concerns the beverage can industry. Steelmakers owned the beverage can market until the mid-1960s, when Reynolds Aluminum Company launched a huge aluminum recycling program to gain a cheaper source of raw materials and make aluminum cans price-competitive with steel.[7]
- In the *market sector,* toy companies such as Mattel and Tyco have introduced African-American dolls in response to the growing buying power of African-Americans; and major cosmetics companies, such as Maybelline, are investing heavily in development and promotion of products geared to darker skins.[8]
- Labor unions have always been a significant force in the *human resources sector*. More than 32,000 unionized machinists went on strike at Boeing plants in Washington, Oregon, and Kansas, demanding higher wages and job security provisions. With a number of orders for new planes from major airlines, Boeing saw a need to settle, agreeing to most of the union's demands.[9]
- For U.S. automobile manufacturers, the *international sector* is part of the task environment because these companies face tough foreign competition, including an increasing number of foreign-owned manufacturing plants built on U.S. soil. The international sector as part of the general environment is discussed in more detail later in this chapter.

General Environment

The **general environment** includes those sectors that may not have a direct impact on the daily operations of a firm but will indirectly influence it. The general environment often includes the government, sociocultural, economic conditions, technology, and financial resources sectors. These sectors affect all organizations eventually. Consider the following examples:

- In response to well-publicized problems with medical devices such as heart valves and breast implants, the FDA introduced more stringent regulations that significantly slowed the rate of reviewing and approving new products. ISS, a small company that manufactures surgical assistant systems that use 3-D computer imaging and robotic tools, could once bring a new product to market in two or three years; it is now lucky to make it in six because of these changes in the *government sector*.[10]
- In the *sociocultural sector,* a growing concern for environmental protection and animal welfare is impacting numerous companies. Companies such as Aveda and John Paul Mitchell include in their marketing campaigns a commitment to environmental protection and "cruelty free" products, whereas Procter & Gamble and Gillette have both been targeted for a boycott because of their continued use of animals for testing.[11]

- General economic conditions often affect the way a company does business. To remain competitive in an era of low inflation, furniture maker Ethan Allen needed to keep prices low. To make a profit without raising prices, the company turned to making simpler furniture designs and increasing its technological efficiency.[12]
- The most striking changes in the *technology sector*, which are affecting every business today, have been in the computer industry. A greeting card that plays "Happy Birthday" holds more computing power than existed in the entire world before 1950.[13] Ford Motor Company is taking advantage of a vast array of modern technologies in assembly, safety testing, quality assurance, manufacturing, and design. For example, by linking computers on a network, designers around the world can collaborate on new car designs. These global design teams may also use teleconferencing to meet and discuss modifications "face-to-face."
- All businesses have to be concerned with *financial resources*, but this sector is often first and foremost in the minds of entrepreneurs starting a new business. When Bill Dayton and Phil Cooper had no cash to finance Encore Productions, which produces audiovisual shows for conventions and stockholder meetings, they amassed a hundred credit cards and $500,000 in credit lines to avoid a cash flow problem. Personal credit cards are sometimes the only way to obtain the financial resources needed for a new business, whereas more-established businesses rely on private investors or bank loans.[14]

International Context

The international sector can directly affect many organizations, and it has become extremely important in the last few years. In addition, all domestic sectors can be affected by international events. Despite the significance of international events for today's organizations, many students fail to appreciate the importance of international events and still think domestically. Think again. Even if you stay in your hometown, your company may be purchased tomorrow by the English, Canadians, Japanese, or Germans. The Japanese alone own more than one thousand U.S. companies, including steel mills, rubber and tire factories, automobile assembly plants, and auto parts suppliers. Nationwide, more than 350,000 Americans work for Japanese companies. People employed by Pillsbury, Shell Oil, Firestone, and CBS Records are working for foreign bosses.[15]

The impact of the international sector has grown rapidly with advances in technology and communications. Ideas, capital investments, business strategies, products, and services flow freely and rapidly around the world. One small company, Montague Corporation, designs unique folding mountain bikes in Cambridge, Massachusetts, makes them in Taiwan, and sells most of them in Europe. Design changes are sent back and forth across three continents, sometimes on a daily basis. U.S.-based Coca-Cola, Canada's Northern Telecom, Switzerland's Nestlé, and France's Carrefour, the retailer that invented the *hypermarket* concept, all get a large percentage of their sales from outside their home countries.[16] In this global environment, it is no surprise that foreign-born people with international experience have been appointed to run such U.S. companies as Coca-Cola, Ford, Gerber, NCR, and Heinz. Consider the following predictions:[17]

- One analyst believes that in the twenty-first century, most of the economic activity in the world will take place in Asia and the Pacific Basin.[18] Nine of ten of the world's largest banks are Japanese, sharply affecting the financial resources sector.

- The North American Free Trade Agreement is spurring many companies, including small businesses, to move into Canada and Mexico, affecting the market and human resources sectors.
- Japan, United Germany, and the European Union of 1992 may spawn large, powerful companies that compete easily with U.S. firms. These companies could reshape the industry and market sectors as we now know them.
- Newly industrialized countries such as Korea, Taiwan, Singapore, and Spain produce huge volumes of low-cost, high-quality commodities that will have an impact on the competitiveness of many industries, markets, and raw materials in North America.
- Eastern Europe, Russia, and China are all shifting toward market economies that also will affect markets, raw materials, industry competition, and worldwide economic conditions.
- Hundreds of partnerships are taking place between North American firms and firms in all parts of the world, facilitating the exchange of technology and production capability, thereby redefining the technology, raw materials, and industry sectors.
- Many companies in the United States build twin plants—one in Texas and one in Mexico. The Mexican plants provide component assembly, and that helps combat Mexico's high unemployment. Called maquiladoras, these plants reshape the human resources and raw materials sectors.
- All of these international connections are spawning new state and federal regulations, thereby affecting the government sector; and beliefs and values are becoming shared worldwide, shaping the sociocultural sector.

What kind of chaos does global competition create for organizations? Consider this. By making and designing more of their autos in the United States, Japanese auto firms are intensifying their challenge to Detroit. Honda, Nissan, Toyota, Mazda, Mitsubishi, Subaru, and Isuzu have all shifted manufacturing to the United States, and they already own a 30 percent share of the U.S. car market.

In addition, the United States is sinking like a rock in the consumer electronics industry. In the 1990s, production in Japan grew three times and production in Europe grew nearly two times faster than in the United States. Zenith is the only remaining U.S. maker of television sets, and it will soon be producing all of its televisions in Mexico, while foreign-owned companies such as Sony and Thomson (once General Electric) produce TVs in the United States.

AT&T, once the world's largest telecommunications company, loses that status with the purchase of MCI by British Telecommunications. The No. 3 U.S. long-distance company, Sprint, is already 20 percent owned by French and German phone companies.[19]

Yet there is also a positive side. When companies think globally, the whole world is their marketplace, and there is evidence that U.S. companies are becoming more competitive on a worldwide scale. The Global 1000, a ranking of the world's one thousand most valuable corporations compiled by Geneva-based Morgan Stanley Capital International, found that U.S. corporations have gained a lead over Japanese and European rivals.[20] For the first time in the nine-year history of the Global 1000, a U.S. company, General Electric, topped the list.

General Electric

When Jack Welch took over as Chairman and CEO of General Electric in the early 1980s, GE was a lumbering giant heavily dependent on industrial businesses and tied to unionized manufacturing and big-ticket orders that rode the waves of the U.S. economy. Welch soon began talking of turning the industrial giant into the "most globally competitive" company in the world. According to one ranking, he has reached his goal.

One way he's done it is by putting together a portfolio of products and services, such as power-generating equipment, jet engines, and financial services, that fit the needs of emerging-market nations investing heavily in infrastructure. Today, GE's international sales equal 40 percent of the company's total revenues and are expected to reach the half-way mark soon. Welch's ongoing productivity campaign has helped GE slash debt to 11 percent of capital and generate $6 billion a year in cash flow, most of which the company is pumping back into fast-growing markets such as India and China.

These moves position GE to outmaneuver less flexible global competitors, but Welch realizes the global game of business is never won. He keeps a close eye on such multinational competitors as Siemens, Asea Brown Boveri, Toshiba, and Mitsubishi. "We've just got to be faster," Welch says. "We come to work every day on the razor's edge of a competitive battle."[21]

Jack Welch realizes that the international environment is ever-changing and companies must be poised for rapid response. Every organization faces environmental uncertainty domestically as well as globally. In the following section, we will discuss in greater detail how companies cope with and respond to this uncertainty.

ENVIRONMENTAL UNCERTAINTY

How does the environment influence an organization? The patterns and events occurring across environmental sectors can be described along several dimensions, such as whether the environment is stable or unstable, homogeneous or heterogeneous, concentrated or dispersed, simple or complex; the extent of turbulence; and the amount of resources available to support the organization.[22] These dimensions boil down to two essential ways the environment influences organizations: (1) the need for information about the environment and (2) the need for resources from the environment. The environmental conditions of complexity and change create a greater need to gather information and to respond based on that information. The organization also is concerned with scarce material and financial resources and with the need to ensure availability of resources. Each sector can be analyzed relative to these three analytical categories. The remainder of this section will discuss the information perspective, which is concerned with the uncertainty that environmental complexity and change create for the organization. Later in the chapter, we will discuss how organizations control the environment to acquire needed resources.

Organizations must cope with and manage uncertainty to be effective. **Uncertainty** means that decision makers do not have sufficient information about environmental factors, and they have a difficult time predicting external changes. Uncertainty increases the risk of failure for organizational responses and makes it difficult to compute costs and probabilities associated with decision alternatives.[23] Characteristics of the environmental domain that influence uncertainty are the extent to which the external domain is simple or complex and the extent to which events are stable or unstable.[24]

Simple-Complex Dimension

The **simple-complex dimension** concerns environmental complexity, which refers to heterogeneity, or the number and dissimilarity of external elements relevant to an organization's operations. In a complex environment, many diverse external elements interact with and influence the organization. In a simple environment, as few as three or four similar external elements influence the organization.

Telecommunications firms such as AT&T have a complex environment, as do universities. Universities span a large number of technologies and are a focal point for cultural and value changes. Government regulatory and granting agencies interact with a university, and so do a variety of professional and scientific associations, alumni, parents, foundations, legislators, community residents, international agencies, donors, corporations, and athletic teams. A large number of external elements thus make up the organization's domain, creating a complex environment. On the other hand, a family-owned hardware store in a suburban community is in a simple environment. The only external elements of any real importance are a few competitors, suppliers, and customers. Government regulation is minimal, and cultural change has little impact. Human resources are not a problem because the store is run by family members or part-time help.

Stable-Unstable Dimension

The **stable-unstable dimension** refers to whether elements in the environment are dynamic. An environmental domain is stable if it remains the same over a period of months or years. Under unstable conditions, environmental elements shift abruptly. Instability may occur when competitors react with aggressive moves and countermoves regarding advertising and new products. For example, aggressive advertising and introduction of new services create instability for long-distance companies like AT&T. In one year alone, the three major U.S. long-distance carriers pumped over $1 billion into advertising.[25] Sometimes specific, unpredictable events—such as reports of syringes in cans of Pepsi or glass shards in Gerber's baby foods, the poisoning of Tylenol, or Union Carbide's gas leak in Bhopal, India—create unstable conditions. The Church of Scientology's attack on the antidepression drug Prozac, which it claimed drove people to murder and suicide, caused sales of the drug to weaken considerably before rebounding.[26]

Although environments are becoming more unstable for most organizations today, an example of a traditionally stable environment is a public utility.[27] In the rural Midwest, demand and supply factors for a public utility are stable. A gradual increase in demand may occur, which is easily predicted over time. Toy companies, by contrast, have an unstable environment. Hot new toys are difficult to predict, a problem compounded by the fact that toys are subject to fad buying. Coleco Industries, makers of the once-famous Cabbage Patch Kids, and Worlds of Wonder, creators of Teddy Ruxpin, went bankrupt because of the unstable nature of the toy environment, their once-winning creations replaced by Bandai's Mighty Morphin Power Rangers or Playmate Toys' Teenage Mutant Ninja Turtles.[28]

Framework

The simple-complex and stable-unstable dimensions are combined into a framework for assessing environmental uncertainty in Exhibit 3.2. In the *simple, stable* environment, uncertainty is low. There are only a few external elements to contend with, and they tend to remain stable. The *complex, stable* environment represents somewhat greater uncertainty. A large number of elements have to be scanned, analyzed, and acted upon for the organization to perform well. External elements do not change rapidly or unexpectedly in this environment.

Even greater uncertainty is felt in the *simple, unstable* environment.[29] Rapid change creates uncertainty for managers. Even though the organization has few external elements, those elements are hard to predict, and they react unexpectedly

Exhibit 3.2 *Framework for Assessing Environmental Uncertainty*

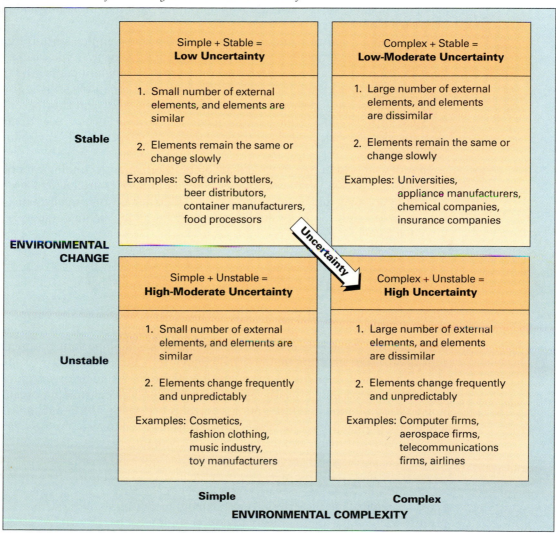

Source: Adapted and reprinted from "Characteristics of Perceived Environments and Perceived Environmental Uncertainty" by Robert B. Duncan, published in *Administrative Science Quarterly* 17 (1972): 313-27, by permission of *The Administrative Science Quarterly.* Copyright © 1972 by Cornell University.

to organizational initiatives. The greatest uncertainty for an organization occurs in the *complex, unstable* environment. A large number of elements impinge upon the organization, and they shift frequently or react strongly to organizational initiatives. When several sectors change simultaneously, the environment becomes turbulent.[30]

A beer distributor functions in a simple, stable environment. Demand for beer changes only gradually. The distributor has an established delivery route, and supplies of beer arrive on schedule. State universities, appliance manufacturers, and insurance companies are in somewhat stable, complex environments. A large number of external elements are present, but although they change, changes are gradual and predictable.

Toy manufacturers are in simple, unstable environments. Organizations that design, make, and sell toys, as well as those that are involved in the clothing or music industry, face shifting supply and demand. Mattel is currently trying to regain ground in the toy business with an ambitious push into designing and marketing toys for boys.[31]

The computer industry and the airline industry face complex, unstable environments. Many external sectors are changing simultaneously. In the case of airlines, in just a few years they were confronted with deregulation, the growth of regional airlines, surges in fuel costs, price cuts from competitors such as Southwest Airlines, shifting customer demand, an air-traffic controller shortage, overcrowded airports, and a reduction of scheduled flights.[32] A recent series of major air traffic disasters has further contributed to the complex, unstable environment for the industry.

In today's world of increased global competition, rapid technological breakthroughs, and shifting markets, companies in all industries are facing a greater level of uncertainty and change. Book Mark 3.0 discusses how organizations and managers can shift their ways of thinking and acting to remain competitive in this environment.

ADAPTING TO ENVIRONMENTAL UNCERTAINTY

Once you see how environments differ with respect to change and complexity, the next question is, "How do organizations adapt to each level of environmental uncertainty?" Environmental uncertainty represents an important contingency for organization structure and internal behaviors. An organization in a certain environment will be managed and controlled differently from an organization in an uncertain environment with respect to positions and departments, organizational differentiation and integration, control processes, institutional imitation, and future planning and forecasting. Organizations need to have the right fit between internal structure and the external environment.

Positions and Departments

As the complexity in the external environment increases, so does the number of positions and departments within the organization, which in turn increases internal complexity. This relationship is part of being an open system. Each sector in the external environment requires an employee or department to deal with it. The human resources department deals with unemployed people who want

Have You Read About This?

Hypercompetition: Managing the Dynamics of Strategic Maneuvering

by Richard A. D'Aveni

In a world where each day brings new global competitors, technological breakthroughs, and shifting markets, many companies have seen their competitive advantage ripped apart. The new level of environmental uncertainty, called *hypercompetition,* has created a condition of constant disequilibrium and change, not only in fast-moving, high-tech industries, but across the board. Richard A. D'Aveni suggests that managers need a fundamental shift in thinking to cope with this environmental change and competitiveness.

The 7S Framework

In today's constantly changing world, D'Aveni argues, it is impossible for a company to build a sustainable competitive advantage. Rather than merely adapting to the environment, successful organizations adapt the world to themselves. Based on studies of both successful and unsuccessful companies, D'Aveni proposes seven key elements of a dynamic approach to strategy. The "7S" framework is based on a strategy of finding and building a series of *temporary* advantages rather than trying to sustain advantage and maintain equilibrium:

1. Superior stakeholder satisfaction—Put customers' needs first and find a way to temporarily serve those needs better than competitors can.
2. Strategic soothsaying—Learn to see and create *future* customer needs by predicting future trends, understanding the evolution of markets, and controlling the development of key technologies.
3. Positioning for speed—Create and move to a new competitive advantage before your competitors do.

4. Positioning for surprise—Use the element of surprise to extend the time period before competitors respond with defensive actions or by duplicating your advantage.
5. Shifting the rules of the game—Reshape the competitive playing field and confuse competitors by actions such as moving into new areas of business.
6. Signaling strategic intent—Signaling can delay or dampen your competitor's actions to create advantage or throw the competitor off balance.
7. Simultaneous and sequential strategic thrusts—Use competitive thrusts as either a sequence of moves or a set of simultaneous actions to upset the equilibrium of the industry, disrupt the status quo, and open opportunities for new competitive advantage.

Conclusion

The new realities of the business world mean it is not enough for organizations to create a static set of competencies; dynamic skills are crucial. Companies in slower and less aggressive markets could concentrate on making great swords; in today's hypercompetitive environment, they must concentrate much more on the art of fencing. The 7S framework is proposed to guide organizations toward simultaneously making the right swords, learning how to fence, and pointing them in the right direction.

Hypercompetition: Managing the Dynamics of Strategic Maneuvering, by Richard A. D'Aveni, is published by The Free Press.

to work for the company. The marketing department finds customers. Procurement employees obtain raw materials from hundreds of suppliers. The finance group deals with bankers. The legal department works with the courts and government agencies.

Buffering and Boundary Spanning

The traditional approach to coping with environmental uncertainty was to establish buffer departments. The **buffering role** is to absorb uncertainty from the environment.[33] The technical core performs the primary production activity of an organization. Buffer departments surround the technical core and exchange materials, resources, and money between the environment and the organization. They help the technical core function efficiently. The purchasing department buffers the technical core by stockpiling supplies and raw materials. The human resources department buffers the technical core by handling the uncertainty associated with finding, hiring, and training production employees.

A newer approach some organizations are trying is to drop the buffers and expose the technical core to the uncertain environment. These organizations no longer create buffers because they believe being well connected to customers and suppliers is more important than internal efficiency. For example, John Deere has assembly-line workers visiting local farms to determine and respond to customer concerns. Whirlpool pays hundreds of customers to test computer-simulated products and features.[34] Opening up the organization to the environment makes it more fluid and adaptable.

Boundary-spanning roles link and coordinate an organization with key elements in the external environment. Boundary spanning is primarily concerned with the exchange of information to (1) detect and bring into the organization information about changes in the environment and (2) send information into the environment that presents the organization in a favorable light.[35]

To detect important information, boundary personnel scan the environment. For example, a market research department scans and monitors trends in consumer tastes. Boundary spanners in engineering and research and development (R&D) departments scan new technological developments, innovations, and raw materials. Boundary spanners prevent the organization from stagnating by keeping top managers informed about environmental changes. Often, the greater the uncertainty in the environment, the greater the importance of boundary spanners.[36]

Today, with global trade barriers falling and competition becoming more fierce, one of the fastest growing areas of boundary spanning is competitive intelligence. Companies large and small are setting up competitive intelligence departments or hiring outside specialists to gather information on competitors. Competitive intelligence gives top executives a systematic way to collect and analyze public information about rivals and use it to make better decisions.[37] Using techniques that range from Internet surfing to digging through trash cans, intelligence professionals dig up information on competitors' new products, manufacturing costs, or training methods and share it with top leaders. For example, Nutrasweet's competitive intelligence department helped the company delay a costly advertising campaign when it learned that a rival sweetener from Johnson & Johnson was at least five years away from FDA approval.[38] In today's uncertain environment, competitive intelligence is a trend that is likely to increase.

The boundary task of sending information into the environment to represent the organization is used to influence other people's perception of the organization. In the marketing department, advertising and sales people represent the organization to customers. Purchasers may call on suppliers and describe purchasing needs. The legal department informs lobbyists and elected officials about the organization's needs or views on political matters.

All organizations have to stay in touch with the environment. Here's how one small company spans the boundary in a shifting environment to stay close to the customer.

Characters, Inc.

In the mid-1980s, Houston-based Characters, Inc. was a business firmly rooted in typesetting, and Compaq, then a fledgling computer company, was one of its biggest customers. The day Compaq called and said they planned to start using desktop publishing sounded like disaster for the small company. Yet CEO David Steitz soon learned that there were areas such as client support and training, color separation, and other prepress work that could keep the company's revenues from Compaq steady and growing even after it stopped using their typesetting services. The discovery put Characters, Inc. on the cutting edge of a new field and taught Steitz the value of finding out what customers want and need *before* they come to you.

Today, Characters gets customer input in a number of ways. Executives hold monthly focus groups, meeting with current and potential customers to learn about their current technology or plans for new systems, giving Characters the foresight to develop the services and expertise its customers need. In addition, customers are surveyed twice a year about the type and level of technical support they expect from the company. Characters, Inc. also recently polled customers in a blind survey to help determine if the company should enter the digital short-run color printing industry, which is expected to grow rapidly over the next five years. Investing in the new venture would cost more than $2 million, but responses to the survey convinced company leaders it was an investment well worth making.

For Characters, Inc., customers are more than a sales outlet. They are a resource that can help determine and build the company's future.[39]

Differentiation and Integration

Another response to environmental uncertainty is the amount of differentiation and integration among departments. Organization **differentiation** is "the differences in cognitive and emotional orientations among managers in different functional departments, and the difference in formal structure among these departments."[40] When the external environment is complex and rapidly changing, organizational departments become highly specialized to handle the uncertainty in their external sector. Success in each sector requires special expertise and behavior. Employees in a research and development department thus have unique attitudes, values, goals, and education that distinguish them from employees in manufacturing or sales departments.

A study by Paul Lawrence and Jay Lorsch examined three organizational departments—manufacturing, research, and sales—in ten corporations.[41] This study found that each department evolved toward a different orientation and structure to deal with specialized parts of the external environment. The market, scientific, and manufacturing subenvironments identified by Lawrence and Lorsch are illustrated in Exhibit 3.3. Each department interacted with different external groups. The differences that evolved among departments within the organizations are shown in Exhibit 3.4. To work effectively with the scientific subenvironment, R&D had a goal of quality work, a long-time horizon (up to five years), an informal structure, and task-oriented employees. Sales was at the opposite extreme. It had a goal of customer satisfaction, was oriented toward the short term (two weeks or so), had a very formal structure, and was socially oriented.

Exhibit 3.3

Organizational Departments Differentiate to Meet Needs of Subenvironments

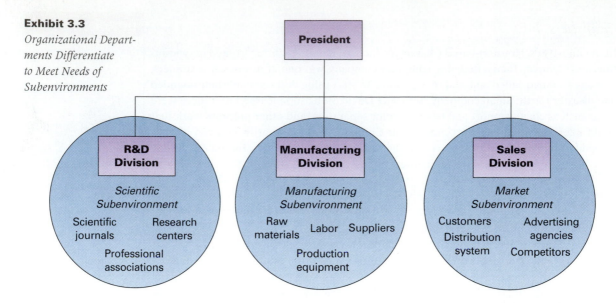

One outcome of high differentiation is that coordination among departments becomes difficult. More time and resources must be devoted to achieving coordination when attitudes, goals, and work orientation differ so widely. **Integration** is the quality of collaboration among departments.[42] Formal integrators are often required to coordinate departments. When the environment is highly uncertain, frequent changes require more information processing to achieve coordination, so integrators become a necessary addition to the organization structure. Sometimes integrators are called liaison personnel, brand managers, or coordinators. As illustrated in Exhibit 3.5, organizations with highly uncertain environments and a highly differentiated structure assign about 22 percent of management personnel to integration activities, such as serving on committees, on task forces, or in liaison roles.[43] In organizations characterized by very simple, stable environments, almost no managers are assigned to integration roles. Exhibit 3.5 shows that, as environmental uncertainty increases, so does differentiation among departments; hence, the organization must assign a larger percentage of managers to coordinating roles.

Lawrence and Lorsch's research concluded that organizations perform better when the levels of differentiation and integration match the level of uncertainty

Exhibit 3.4   *Differences in Goals and Orientations Among Organizational Departments*

Characteristic	R & D Department	Manufacturing Department	Sales Department
Goals	New developments, quality	Efficient production	Customer satisfaction
Time horizon	Long	Short	Short
Interpersonal orientation	Mostly task	Task	Social
Formality of structure	Low	High	High

Source: Based on Paul R. Lawrence and Jay W. Lorsch, *Organization and Environment* (Homewood, Ill.: Irwin, 1969), pp. 23–29.

Exhibit 3.5 *Environmental Uncertainty and Organizational Integrators*

	Plastics	Industry Foods	Container
Environmental uncertainty	High	Moderate	Low
Departmental differentiation	High	Moderate	Low
Percent management in integrating roles	22%	17%	0%

Source: Based on Jay W. Lorsch and Paul R. Lawrence, "Environmental Factors and Organizational Integration," *Organization Planning: Cases and Concepts* (Homewood, Ill.: Irwin and Dorsey, 1972), 45.

in the environment. Organizations that performed well in uncertain environments had high levels of both differentiation and integration, while those performing well in less uncertain environments had lower levels of differentiation and integration.

Organic Versus Mechanistic Management Processes

Another response to environmental uncertainty is the amount of formal structure and control imposed on employees. Tom Burns and G. M. Stalker observed twenty industrial firms in England and discovered that external environment was related to internal management structure.[44] When the external environment was stable, the internal organization was characterized by rules, procedures, and a clear hierarchy of authority. Organizations were formalized. They were also centralized, with most decisions made at the top. Burns and Stalker called this a **mechanistic** organization system.

In rapidly changing environments, the internal organization was much looser, free-flowing, and adaptive. Rules and regulations often were not written down or, if written down, were ignored. People had to find their own way through the system to figure out what to do. The hierarchy of authority was not clear. Decision-making authority was decentralized. Burns and Stalker used the term **organic** to characterize this type of management structure.

Exhibit 3.6 summarizes the differences in organic and mechanistic systems. As environmental uncertainty increases, organizations tend to become more organic, which means decentralizing authority and responsibility to lower levels, encouraging employees to take care of problems by working directly with one

Exhibit 3.6 *Mechanistic and Organic Organization Forms*

Mechanistic	Organic
1. Tasks are broken down into specialized, separate parts.	1. Employees contribute to the common task of the department.
2. Tasks are rigidly defined.	2. Tasks are adjusted and redefined through employee teamwork.
3. There is a strict hierarchy of authority and control, and there are many rules.	3. There is less hierarchy of authority and control, and there are few rules.
4. Knowledge and control of tasks are centralized at the top of organization.	4. Knowledge and control of tasks are located anywhere in the organization.
5. Communication is vertical.	5. Communication is horizontal.

Source: Adapted from Gerald Zaltman, Robert Duncan, and Jonny Holbek, *Innovations and Organizations* (New York: Wiley, 1973), 131.

The New Paradigm

Arizona Public Service Company

Electric utility companies have traditionally functioned in a stable, noncompetitive environment. However, increasing deregulation, the growth of small, independent power producers, strict government mandates, and growing environmental concerns have created a highly uncertain environment for many of today's public utility companies.

During most of its forty-year history, the predominant management style at Arizona Public Service Company (APS) was control oriented, with decisions made at the top and passed down to lower levels. Following a massive downsizing to reduce costs quickly, APS was left with a group of demoralized workers still following the command and control rules of the past. New CEO Mark De Michele realized major organizational changes were needed to cope with the uncertain environment—and that workers needed to be in control of the process. He began by meeting with large groups of employees to stress that the company's very survival depended on radical changes. About the same time, Pacificorp, a Northwestern utility, attempted to take over APS, an event that sounded a clear wake up call and galvanized employees into a sense of community.

To create a culture of employee involvement at APS, a program referred to as "Focus" involved cross-functional teams of workers in week-long marathon simulations designed to increase their awareness of how to operate strategically in an increasingly competitive environment. Sessions culminated with each team proposing a new project designed to significantly improve operations. The Focus program gave workers a sense of empowerment and proved to be a strong motivator. In addition to higher morale, APS began to realize other significant successes, including lowered costs, improved customer service, and reduced red tape. In 1992, APS was honored with the prestigious Edison Award for its "transformation from a traditional rate-driven utility to a customer-focused company."

But APS didn't stop there. Managers knew that for the company to remain competitive, workers had to be prepared for ongoing change and uncertainty. As a follow-up to Focus, the Breakthrough Leadership program involves employees from all levels of the company in discussing the organizational characteristics and systems needed to cope in a rapidly changing environment. Executives are also planning an organization-wide reengineering, again involving workers from throughout the company, to totally redesign work flow and complete the transformation.

Source: Samuel M. DeMarie and Barbara W. Keats, "Deregulation, Reengineering, and Cultural Transformation at Arizona Public Service Company," *Organizational Dynamics* (Winter 1995): 70–76.

another, encouraging teamwork, and taking an informal approach to assigning tasks and responsibility. Thus, the organization is more fluid and is able to adapt continually to changes in the external environment.[45]

As described in The New Paradigm box, Arizona Public Service Company, the largest investor-owned utility in Arizona, shifted to a more organic management system to meet the challenges of a rapidly changing environment.

Institutional Imitation

An emerging view, called the **institutional perspective**, argues that under high uncertainty, organizations mimic or imitate other organizations in the same institutional environment. The institutional environment includes other similar organizations in the industry that deal with similar customers, suppliers, and regulatory agencies.[46]

One example is the current trend toward mergers in some industries, such as banking. The trend began when a few banks merged to combine their capabilities and become more competitive. Others followed suit and eventually small, locally owned banks became a thing of the past. Today, the entertainment industry too is merging, with Disney and ABC Television, Westinghouse and CBS Television, and Time Warner and Turner Broadcasting System all joining the merger trend to compete in this rapidly changing industry.

Managers in an organization experiencing great uncertainty assume that other organizations face similar uncertainty. These managers will copy the structure, management techniques, and strategies of other firms that appear successful. Such mimicking serves to reduce uncertainty for managers, but it also means that organizations within an industry will tend to look alike over time. For example, all retail department stores will tend to operate in a similar way, as will airlines, banks, and drug companies.

In general, corporations do not want to be criticized by shareholders for being too different. As a result, if a successful company in an industry establishes a formal intelligence department, other firms are likely to do the same.

Organizations experience fads and fashions just as people do. In addition to the establishment of intelligence departments and the trend toward mergers, other recent fads include downsizing to eliminate excess personnel, MBWA (management by wandering around), and "intrapraneuring" (promoting change from within).[47] The institutional perspective will be discussed in greater detail in Chapter 14.

Planning and Forecasting

The final organizational response to uncertainty is to increase planning and environmental forecasting. When the environment is stable, the organization can concentrate on current operational problems and day-to-day efficiency. Long-range planning and forecasting are not needed because environmental demands in the future will be the same as they are today.

With increasing environmental uncertainty, planning and forecasting become necessary.[48] Planning can soften the adverse impact of external shifting. Organizations that have unstable environments often establish a separate planning department. In an unpredictable environment, planners scan environmental elements and analyze potential moves and countermoves by other organizations. Planning can be extensive and may forecast various scenarios for environmental contingencies. As time passes, plans are updated through replanning. However, planning does not substitute for other actions, such as boundary spanning. Indeed, under conditions of extraordinarily high uncertainty, planning may not be helpful because the future is so difficult to predict.

FRAMEWORK FOR ORGANIZATIONAL RESPONSES TO UNCERTAINTY

The ways environmental uncertainty influences organizational characteristics are summarized in Exhibit 3.7. The change and complexity dimensions are combined and illustrate four levels of uncertainty. The low uncertainty environment is simple and stable. Organizations in this environment have few departments and a mechanistic structure. In a low-moderate uncertainty environment, more departments are needed along with more integrating roles to coordinate the departments. Some planning and imitation may occur. Environments that are

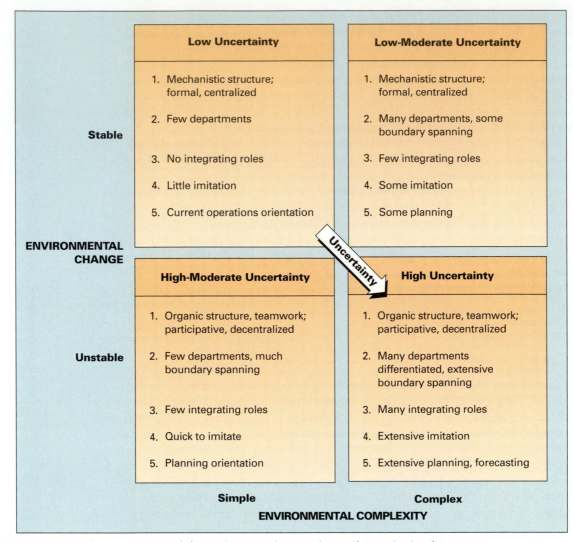

Exhibit 3.7   *Contingency Framework for Environmental Uncertainty and Organizational Responses*

high-moderate uncertainty are unstable but simple. Organization structure is organic and decentralized. Planning is emphasized and managers are quick to imitate successful attributes of competitors. The high uncertainty environment is both complex and unstable and is the most difficult environment from a management perspective. Organizations are large and have many departments, but they are also organic. A large number of management personnel are assigned to coordination and integration, and the organization uses boundary spanning, imitation, planning, and forecasting.

RESOURCE DEPENDENCE

Thus far, this chapter has described several ways in which organizations adapt to the lack of information and to the uncertainty caused by environmental change and complexity. We turn now to the third characteristic of the organization-environment relationship that affects organizations, which is the need for material and financial resources. The environment is the source of scarce and valued resources essential to organizational survival. Research in this area is called the resource dependence perspective. **Resource dependence** means that organizations depend on the environment but strive to acquire control over resources to minimize their dependence.[49] Organizations are vulnerable if vital resources are controlled by other organizations, so they try to be as independent as possible. When costs and risks are high, however, companies also team up to reduce resource dependence and the possibility of bankruptcy. In today's volatile environment, companies are collaborating as never before to share scarce resources and be more competitive. For example, as a new wave of technology based on digital communications builds, companies all over the world are racing into alliances to share the risks in this uncharted territory. [50]

Formal relationships with other organizations, however, present a dilemma to managers. North American organizations seek to reduce vulnerability with respect to resources by developing links with other organizations, but they also like to maximize their own autonomy and independence. Organizational linkages require coordination,[51] and they reduce the freedom of each organization to make decisions without concern for the needs and goals of other organizations. Interorganizational relationships thus represent a tradeoff between resources and autonomy. To maintain autonomy, organizations that already have abundant resources will tend not to establish new linkages. Organizations that need resources will give up independence to acquire those resources.

Dependence on shared resources gives power to other organizations. Once an organization relies on others for valued resources, those other organizations can influence managerial decision making. When a large company like DuPont, Motorola, or Xerox forges a partnership with a supplier for parts, both sides benefit, but each loses a small amount of autonomy. For example, some of these large companies are now putting strong pressure on vendors to lower costs, and the vendors have few alternatives but to go along.[52] In much the same way, dependence on shared resources gives advertisers power over print and electronic media companies. For example, as newspapers face increasingly tough financial times, they are less likely to run stories that are critical of advertisers. Though newspapers insist advertisers don't get special treatment, some editors admit there is growing talk around the country of the need for "advertiser-friendly" newspapers.[53]

In another industry, Microsoft is so large and powerful that it has a virtual monopoly in personal computer operating systems, so its every technical change adversely affects producers of application software. Microsoft has been accused of abusing this power and of squashing small competitors that would like to link up with it. Gradually, Microsoft is learning to use these dependencies in a positive way.[54]

CONTROLLING ENVIRONMENTAL RESOURCES

In response to the need for resources, organizations try to maintain a balance between linkages with other organizations and their own independence. Organizations maintain this balance through attempts to modify, manipulate, or control other organizations.[55] To survive, the focal organization often tries to reach

Establishing Interorganizational Linkages	Controlling the Environmental Domain
1. Ownership 2. Contracts, joint ventures 3. Cooptation, interlocking directorates 4. Executive recruitment 5. Advertising, public relations	1. Change of domain 2. Political activity, regulation 3. Trade associations 4. Illegitimate activities

out and change or control elements in the environment. Two strategies can be adopted to manage resources in the external environment: (1) establish favorable linkages with key elements in the environment and (2) shape the environmental domain.[56] Techniques to accomplish each of these strategies are summarized in Exhibit 3.8. As a general rule, when organizations sense that valued resources are scarce, they will use the strategies in Exhibit 3.8 rather than go it alone. Notice how dissimilar these strategies are from the responses to environmental change and complexity described in Exhibit 3.7. The dissimilarity reflects the difference between responding to the need for information rather than to the need for resources.

Establishing Interorganizational Linkages

Ownership.   Companies use ownership to establish linkages when they buy a part of or a controlling interest in another company. This gives the company access to technology, products, or other resources it doesn't currently have. The communications industry has become particularly complex, and many companies have been teaming up worldwide.

A greater degree of ownership and control is obtained through acquisition or merger. An *acquisition* involves the purchase of one organization by another so that the buyer assumes control. A *merger* is the unification of two or more organizations into a single unit.[57] In the world of computer software, Novell and Digital Research merged in an $80 million deal. The creation of Bristol Myers Squibb from the Bristol Myers and Squibb companies was a merger. Acquisition occurred when Philip Morris Company purchased Kraft Foods and when Maytag bought Magic Chef.[58] These forms of ownership reduce uncertainty in an area important to the acquiring company.

Formal Strategic Alliances.   When there is a high level of complementarity between the business lines, geographical positions, or skills of two companies, the firms often go the route of a strategic alliance rather than ownership through merger or acquisition.[59] Such alliances are formed through contracts and joint ventures.

Contracts and joint ventures reduce uncertainty through a legal and binding relationship with another firm. Contracts come in the form of *license agreements* that involve the purchase of the right to use an asset (such as a new technology) for a specific time and *supplier arrangements* that contract for the sale of one firm's output to another. Contracts can provide long-term security by tying customers and suppliers to specific amounts and prices. For example, McDonald's contracts for an entire crop of russet potatoes to be certain of its supply of french fries. McDonald's also gains influence over suppliers through these contracts and has changed the way farmers grow potatoes and the profit margins they earn, which is consistent with the resource dependence perspective.[60] Large retailers such as Wal-Mart, Kmart, Toys 'R' Us, and Home Depot are gaining so much clout that they can almost dictate contracts telling manufacturers what to make, how to make it, and how much to charge for it. As one manufacturing representative put it, "Most suppliers would do absolutely anything to sell Wal-Mart."[61] *Joint ventures* result in the creation of a new organization that is formally independent of the parents, although the parents will have some control.[62] In a joint venture, organizations share the risk and cost associated with large projects or innovations, such as when Pratt & Whitney joined a consortium to develop a new engine or Tenneco created a joint venture with other oil companies to drill for oil in Africa.

Cooptation, Interlocking Directorates. **Cooptation** occurs when leaders from important sectors in the environment are made part of an organization. It takes place, for example, when influential customers or suppliers are appointed to the board of directors, such as when the senior executive of a bank sits on the board of a manufacturing company. As a board member, the banker may become psychologically coopted into the interests of the manufacturing firm. Community leaders also can be appointed to a company's board of directors or to other organizational committees or task forces. These influential people are thus introduced to the needs of the company and are more likely to include the company's interests in their decision-making.

An **interlocking directorate** is a formal linkage that occurs when a member of the board of directors of one company sits on the board of directors of another company. The individual is a communications link between companies and can influence policies and decisions. When one individual is the link between two companies, this is typically referred to as a **direct interlock**. An **indirect interlock** occurs when a director of company A and a director of company B are both directors of company C. They have access to one another but do not have direct influence over their respective companies.[63] Recent research shows that, as a firm's financial fortunes decline, direct interlocks with financial institutions increase. Financial uncertainty facing an industry also has been associated with greater indirect interlocks between competing companies.[64]

Executive Recruitment. Transferring or exchanging executives also offers a method of establishing favorable linkages with external organizations. For example, each year the aerospace industry hires retired generals and executives from the Department of Defense. These generals have personal friends in the department, so the aerospace companies obtain better information about technical specifications, prices, and dates for new weapon systems. They can learn the needs of the defense department and are able to present their case for defense contracts in a more effective way. Companies without personal contacts find it nearly impossible to get a defense contract. Having channels of influence and communication between organizations serves to reduce financial uncertainty and dependence for an organization.

Advertising and Public Relations. A traditional way of establishing favorable relationships is through advertising. Organizations spend large amounts of money to influence the taste of consumers. Advertising is especially important in highly competitive consumer industries and in industries that experience variable demand. Because of the declining demand for health care, hospitals have begun to advertise through billboards, newspapers, and broadcast commercials to promote special services and bonuses, such as steak dinners and champagne. Dow Chemical used skillful advertising to create a new image on college campuses. It invested $50 million over five years in its "Dow lets you do great things" advertising campaign, the success of which has enabled Dow to hire excellent college graduates, an important resource.[65]

Public relations is similar to advertising, except that stories often are free and aimed at public opinion. Public relations people cast an organization in a favorable light in speeches, in press reports, and on television. Public relations attempts to shape the company's image in the minds of customers, suppliers, and government officials. For example, in an effort to survive in this anti-smoking era, tobacco companies have launched an aggressive public relations campaign touting smokers' rights and freedom of choice. Levi Strauss is taking full advantage of the trend toward casual business attire by introducing a campaign to help companies teach workers how to be casual without being sloppy. Levi provides brochures, videos, and personal presentations, and while there is no overt sales pitch, the campaign clearly benefits the company.[66]

Summary. Organizations can use a variety of techniques to establish favorable linkages that ensure the availability of scarce resources. Linkages provide control over vulnerable environmental elements. Strategic alliances, interlocking directorates, and outright ownership provide mechanisms to reduce resource dependency on the environment. American companies like IBM, Apple, AT&T, and Motorola have been quick in recent years to turn rivalry into partnership. Perhaps surprisingly, Japan's electronic companies have been slower to become involved in joint ventures and other strategic alliances. Toshiba, however, has been living in the age of high-tech alliances for years and has the competitive edge to show for it.

| In Practice 3.3 | *Toshiba* |

Strategic alliances have been a key element in Toshiba's corporate strategy since the early 1900s, when the company contracted to make light bulb filaments for General Electric. Since then, Toshiba has taken advantage of partnerships, licensing agreements, and joint ventures to become one of the world's leading manufacturers of electronic products. A joint venture with Motorola has made Toshiba the top maker of large-scale memory chips. Other partnerships aid the company in producing computers, fax machines, copiers, medical equipment, advanced semiconductors, home appliances, and nuclear and steam power-generating equipment, just for starters. Exhibit 3.9 shows some of the many linkages Toshiba shares with other companies.

Toshiba is involved in more than two dozen major partnerships or joint ventures for two reasons. One is money: the company estimates that the next-generation dynamic random-access memory chip will cost more than $1 billion to develop (it is working with IBM and Siemens on the project). The other is speed: Toshiba's management thinks that carefully chosen partners offer the best means of harnessing the resources needed to move quickly in today's volatile high-tech marketplace.[67]

Toshiba illustrates how linkages can be used to control resources and reduce dependency. The other major strategy companies can use to manage resource dependency is to control or redefine the external environmental domain.

Exhibit 3.9

Interorganizational Linkages of Toshiba Corporation

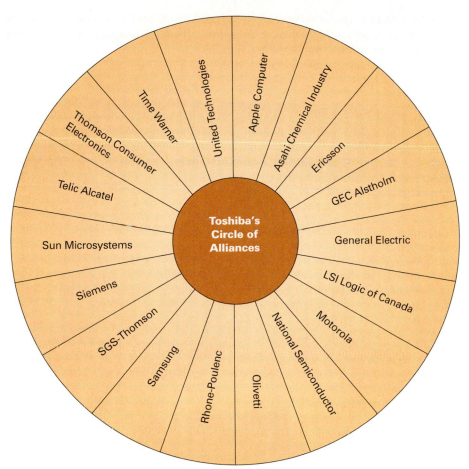

Source: Brenton R. Schlender, "How Toshiba Makes Alliances Work," *Fortune,* 4 October 1993, 116–120.

Controlling the Environmental Domain

In addition to establishing favorable linkages to obtain resources, organizations often try to change the environment. There are four techniques for influencing or changing a firm's environmental domain.

Change of Domain.   The ten sectors described earlier in this chapter are not fixed. The organization decides which business it is in, the market to enter, and the suppliers, banks, employees, and location to use, and this domain can be changed.[68] An organization can seek new environmental relationships and drop old ones. An organization may try to find a domain where there is little competition, no government regulation, abundant suppliers, affluent customers, and barriers to keep competitors out.

Acquisition and divestment are two techniques for altering the domain. Rockwell International felt vulnerable with 63 percent of its revenues coming from the federal government; thus, it acquired Allen Bradley to move into factory automation—a new domain that was not dependent on the government. Robert Mercer, CEO of Goodyear Tire & Rubber Company, changed Goodyear's domain to get the company away from the cutthroat competition in tires. He did this by reallocating resources into nontire lines of businesses, such as auto parts, aerospace products, and plastics. Goodyear also acquired an oil and gas company. Entering these new domains has taken the pressure off the tire business and enabled Goodyear to prosper. When British conglomerate Grand Metropolitan acquired Pillsbury, it also sold Bennigans, Steak & Ale, and Bumble Bee fish-canning operations, thereby redefining its domain in the food processing industry.

Political Activity, Regulation.   Political activity includes techniques to influence government legislation and regulation. For example, General Motors used political activity to successfully settle a battle with the U.S. Transportation Department over the safety of some of its pickup trucks. The settlement requires that GM spend $51 million on safety programs over a five-year period but saved the company the cost of a $1 billion recall.[69]

In one technique, organizations pay lobbyists to express their views to members of federal and state legislatures. In the telecommunications industry, the Baby Bells hired powerful lobbyists to influence a sweeping new telecommunications bill giving local phone companies access to new markets.[70] Many CEOs, however, believe they should do their own lobbying. CEOs have easier access than lobbyists and can be especially effective when they do the politicking. The CEOs of companies such as Raychem Corp., Citicorp, and MCI talked with powerful legislators to challenge a plan proposed by the Financial Accounting Standards Board that would require companies to calculate employee stock options and discharge that amount against earnings.[71] Political activity is so important that "informal lobbyist" is an unwritten part of almost any CEO's job description.[72]

Political strategy can be used to erect regulatory barriers against new competitors or to squash unfavorable legislation. Corporations also try to influence the appointment to agencies of people who are sympathetic to their needs. The value of political activity is illustrated by Bethlehem Steel's effort to roll back foreign steel imports by 15 percent. Assuming domestic consumption remained the same, the average price for steel would have increased about $50 a ton, and the increase in tons for Bethlehem would have meant a quarter of a billion dollars of new business.

Trade Associations.   Much of the work to influence the external environment is accomplished jointly with other organizations that have similar interests. Most manufacturing companies are part of the National Association of Manufacturers and also belong to associations in their specific industry. By pooling resources, these organizations can pay people to carry out activities such as lobbying legislators, influencing new regulations, developing public relations campaigns, and making campaign contributions. For example, the National Tooling and Machining Association (NTMA) devotes a quarter of a million dollars each year to lobbying, mainly on issues that affect small business, such as taxes, health insurance, or government mandates. NTMA also gives its members statistics and information that help them become more competitive in the global marketplace.[73]

Illegitimate Activities.   Illegitimate activities represent the final technique companies sometimes use to control their environmental domain. Certain conditions, such as low profits, pressure from senior managers, or scarce environmental resources, may lead managers to adopt behaviors not considered legitimate.[74] Many well-known companies have been found guilty of behavior considered unlawful. Example behaviors include payoffs to foreign governments, illegal political contributions, promotional gifts, and wire tapping. Intense competition among cement producers and in the oil business during a period of decline led to thefts and illegal kickbacks.[75] In the defense industry,

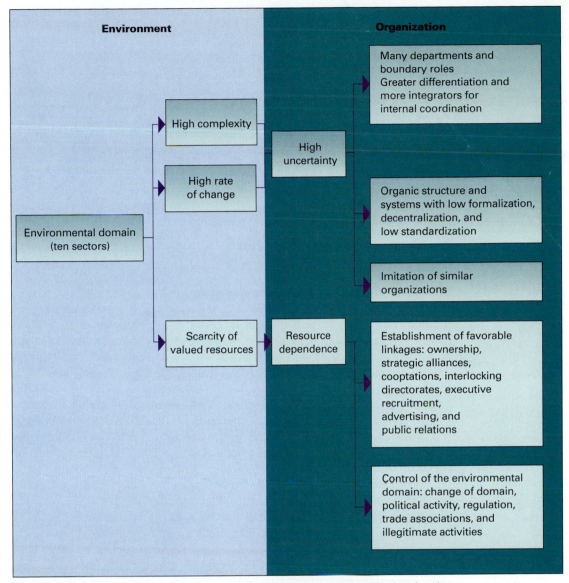

Exhibit 3.10 *Relationship Between Environmental Characteristics and Organizational Actions*

the intense competition for declining contracts for major weapon systems led some companies to do almost anything to get an edge, including schemes to peddle inside information and to pay off officials.[76] One study found that companies in industries with low demand, shortages, and strikes were more likely to be convicted for illegal activities, implying that illegal acts are an attempt to cope with resource scarcity.[77] In another study, social movement organizations such as Earth First! and the AIDS Coalition to Unleash Power (ActUp) were found to have acted in ways considered illegitimate or even illegal to bolster their visibility and reputation.[78]

Organization-Environment Integrative Framework

The relationships illustrated in Exhibit 3.10 summarize the two major themes about organization-environment relationships discussed in this chapter. One theme is that the amount of complexity and change in an organization's domain influences the need for information and hence the uncertainty felt within an organization. Greater information uncertainty is resolved through greater structural flexibility, the assignment of additional departments and boundary roles, and imitation. When uncertainty is low, management structures can be more mechanistic, and the number of departments and boundary roles can be fewer. The second theme pertains to the scarcity of material and financial resources. The more dependent an organization is on other organizations for those resources, the more important it is to either establish favorable linkages with those organizations or control entry into the domain. If dependence on external resources is low, the organization can maintain autonomy and does not need to establish linkages or control the external domain.

SUMMARY AND INTERPRETATION

The external environment has an overwhelming impact on management uncertainty and organization functioning. Organizations are open social systems. Most are involved with hundreds of external elements. The change and complexity in environmental domains have major implications for organizational design and action. Most organizational decisions, activities, and outcomes can be traced to stimuli in the external environment.

Organizational environments differ in terms of uncertainty and resource dependence. Organizational uncertainty is the result of the stable-unstable and simple-complex dimensions of the environment. Resource dependence is the result of scarcity of the material and financial resources needed by the organization.

Organization design takes on a logical perspective when the environment is considered. Organizations try to survive and achieve efficiencies in a world characterized by uncertainty and scarcity. Specific departments and functions are created to deal with uncertainties. The organization can be conceptualized as a technical core and departments that buffer environmental uncertainty. Boundary-spanning roles provide information about the environment.

The concepts in this chapter provide specific frameworks for understanding how the environment influences the structure and functioning of an organization. Environmental complexity and change, for example, have specific impact on internal complexity and adaptability. Under great uncertainty, more resources are allocated to departments that will plan, deal with specific environmental elements, and integrate diverse internal activities. Moreover, when risk is great or resources are scarce, the organization can establish linkages through the acquisition of ownership and through strategic alliances, interlocking directorates, executive recruitment, or advertising and public relations that will minimize risk and maintain a supply of scarce resources. Other techniques for controlling the environment include a change of the domain in which the organization operates, political activity, participation in trade associations, and perhaps illegitimate activities.

Two important themes in this chapter are that organizations can learn and adapt to the environment and that organizations can change and control the environment. These strategies are especially true for large organizations that command many resources. Such organizations can adapt when necessary but can also neutralize or change problematic areas in the environment.

Key Concepts

boundary-spanning roles
buffering roles
cooptation
differentiation
direct interlock
domain
general environment
indirect interlock
institutional perspective
integration

interlocking directorate
mechanistic
organic
organizational environment
resource dependence
sectors
simple-complex dimension
stable-unstable dimension
task environment
uncertainty

Briefcase

As an organization manager, keep these guides in mind:

1. Organize elements in the external environment into ten sectors for analysis: industry, raw materials, human resources, financial resources, market, technology, economic, government, sociocultural, and international. Focus on sectors that may experience significant change at any time.

2. Scan the external environment for threats, changes, and opportunities. Use boundary-spanning roles, such as market research and competitive intelligence departments, to bring into the organization information about changes in the environment. Enhance boundary-spanning capabilities when the environment is uncertain.

3. Match internal organization structure to the external environment. If the external environment is complex, make the organization structure complex. Associate a stable environment with a mechanistic structure and an unstable environment with an organic structure. If the external environment is both complex and changing, make the organization highly differentiated and organic, use mechanisms to achieve coordination across departments, and be prepared to imitate other organizations.

4. Reach out and control external sectors that threaten needed resources. Influence the domain by engaging in political activity, joining trade associations, and establishing favorable linkages. Establish linkages through ownership, strategic alliances, cooptation, interlocking directorates, executive recruitment, advertising, and public relations. Reduce the amount of change or threat from the external environment so the organization will not have to change internally.

Discussion Questions

1. Define *organizational environment*. Is it appropriate to include only the elements that actually interact with the organization?
2. What is environmental uncertainty? Which has the greatest impact on uncertainty—environmental complexity or environmental change? Why?
3. Why does environmental complexity lead to organizational complexity? Explain.

4. Is changing the organization's domain a feasible strategy for coping with a threatening environment? Explain.
5. Describe differentiation and integration. In what type of environmental uncertainty will differentiation and integration be greatest? Least?
6. Under what environmental conditions is organizational planning emphasized? Is planning an appropriate response to a turbulent environment?
7. What is an organic organization? A mechanistic organization? How does the environment influence organic and mechanistic structures?
8. Why do organizations become involved in interorganizational relationships? Do these relationships affect an organization's dependency? Performance?
9. Assume you have been asked to calculate the ratio of staff employees to production employees in two organizations—one in a simple, stable environment and one in a complex, shifting environment. How would you expect these ratios to differ? Why?

Chapter 3 Workbook *Organizations You Rely On**

Below, list eight organizations you somehow rely on in your daily life. Examples might be a restaurant, a clothing or CD store, university, family, post office, telephone company, airline, pizza delivery, your place of work, and so on. In the first column, list those eight organizations. Then, in column 2, choose another organization you could use in case the ones in column 1 were not available. In column 3, evaluate your level of dependence on the organizations listed in column 1 as: Strong, Medium, or Weak. Finally, in column 4, rate the certainty of that organization being able to meet your needs as: High (certainty), Medium, or Low.

Column 1 Organization	Column 2 Backup	Column 3 Level of dependence	Column 4 Level of certainty
1.			
2.			
3.			
4.			
5.			
6.			
7.			
8.			

*Adapted by Dorothy Marcic from "Organizational Dependencies," in Ricky W. Griffin and Thomas C. Head, *Practicing Management*, 2nd ed. (Dallas: Houghton Mifflin), 2–3.

Questions

1. Do you have adequate backup organizations for those of high dependence? How might you create even more backups?
2. What would you do if an organization you rated high dependence and high certainty suddenly became high dependence and low certainty? How would your behavior relate to the concept of resource dependence?
3. Have you ever used any behaviors similar to those in Exhibit 3.8 to manage your relationships with the organizations listed in column 1?

Case for Analysis *The Paradoxical Twins: Acme and Omega Electronics**

Part I

In 1965, Technological Products of Erie, Pennsylvania, was bought out by a Cleveland manufacturer. The Cleveland firm had no interest in the electronics division of Technological Products and subsequently sold to different investors two plants that manufactured printed circuit boards. One of the plants, located in nearby Waterford, was renamed Acme Electronics; the other plant, within the city limits of Erie, was renamed Omega Electronics, Inc.

Acme retained its original management and upgraded its general manager to president. Omega hired a new president who had been a director of a large electronic research laboratory and upgraded several of the existing personnel within the plant. Acme and Omega often competed for the same contracts. As subcontractors, both firms benefited from the electronics boom of the early 1970s, and both looked forward to future growth and expansion. Acme had annual sales of $10 million and employed 550 people. Omega had annual sales of $8 million and employed 480 people. Acme regularly achieved greater net profits, much to the chagrin of Omega's management.

Inside Acme

The president of Acme, John Tyler, was confident that, had the demand not been so great, Acme's competitor would not have survived. "In fact," he said, "we have been able to beat Omega regularly for the most profitable contracts, thereby increasing our profit." Tyler credited his firm's greater effectiveness to his managers' abilities to run a "tight ship." He explained that he had retained the basic structure developed by Technological Products because it was most efficient for the high-volume manufacture of printed circuits and their subsequent assembly. Acme had detailed organization charts and job descriptions. Tyler believed everyone should have clear responsibilities and narrowly defined jobs, which would lead to efficient performance and high company profits. People were generally satisfied with their work at Acme; however, some of the managers voiced the desire to have a little more latitude in their jobs.

Inside Omega

Omega's president, Jim Rawls, did not believe in organization charts. He felt his organization had departments similar to Acme's, but he thought Omega's plant was small enough that things such as organization charts just put artificial barriers between specialists who should be working together. Written memos were not allowed since, as Rawls expressed it, "the plant is small enough that if people want to communicate, they can just drop by and talk things over."

The head of the mechanical engineering department said, "Jim spends too much of his time and mine making sure everyone understands what we're doing and listening to suggestions." Rawls was concerned with employee satisfaction and wanted everyone to feel part of the organization. The top management team reflected Rawls's attitudes. They also believed that employees should be familiar with activities throughout the organization so that cooperation between departments would be increased. A newer member of the industrial engineering department said, "When I first got here, I wasn't sure what I was supposed to do. One day I worked with some mechanical engineers and the next day I helped the shipping department design some packing cartons. The first months on the job were hectic, but at least I got a real feel for what makes Omega tick."

Part II

In 1976, integrated circuits began to cut deeply into the demand for printed circuit boards. The integrated circuits (ICs) or "chips" were the first step into micro-

---

*Adapted from John F. Veiga, "The Paradoxical Twins: Acme and Omega Electronics," in John F. Veiga and John N. Yanouzas, *The Dynamics of Organization Theory* (St. Paul: West, 1984), 132–38.

miniaturization in the electronics industry. Because the manufacturing process for ICs was a closely guarded secret, both Acme and Omega realized the potential threat to their futures, and both began to seek new customers aggressively.

In July 1976, a major photocopier manufacturer was looking for a subcontractor to assemble the memory unit of its new experimental copier. The projected contract for the job was estimated to be $5 to $7 million in annual sales.

Both Acme and Omega were geographically close to this manufacturer, and both submitted highly competitive bids for the production of one hundred prototypes. Acme's bid was slightly lower than Omega's; however, both firms were asked to produce one hundred units. The photocopier manufacturer told both firms speed was critical because its president had boasted to other manufacturers that the firm would have a finished copier available by Christmas. This boast, much to the designer's dismay, required pressure on all subcontractors to begin prototype production before the final design of the copier was complete. This meant Acme and Omega would have at most two weeks to produce the prototypes or delay the final copier production.

Part III

Inside Acme

As soon as John Tyler was given the blueprints (Monday, July 11, 1976), he sent a memo to the purchasing department asking to move forward on the purchase of all necessary materials. At the same time, he sent the blueprints to the drafting department and asked that it prepare manufacturing prints. The industrial engineering department was told to begin methods design work for use by the production department supervisors. Tyler also sent a memo to all department heads and executives indicating the critical time constraints of this job and how he expected that all employees would perform as efficiently as they had in the past.

The departments had little contact with one another for several days, and each seemed to work at its own speed. Each department also encountered problems. Purchasing could not acquire all the parts on time. Industrial engineering had difficulty arranging an efficient assembly sequence. Mechanical engineering did not take the deadline seriously and parceled its work to vendors so the engineers could work on other jobs scheduled previously. Tyler made it a point to stay in touch with the photocopier manufacturer to let it know things were progressing and to learn of any new devel-

opments. He traditionally worked to keep important clients happy. Tyler telephoned someone at the photocopier company at least twice a week and got to know the head designer quite well.

On July 15, Tyler learned that mechanical engineering was way behind in its development work, and he "hit the roof." To make matters worse, purchasing did not obtain all the parts, so the industrial engineers decided to assemble the product without one part, which would be inserted at the last minute. On Thursday, July 21, the final units were being assembled, although the process was delayed several times. On Friday, July 22, the last units were finished while Tyler paced around the plant. Late that afternoon, Tyler received a phone call from the head designer of the photocopier manufacturer, who told Tyler that he had received a call on Wednesday from Jim Rawls of Omega. He explained that Rawls's workers had found an error in the design of the connector cable and taken corrective action on their prototypes. He told Tyler that he had checked out the design error and that Omega was right. Tyler, a bit overwhelmed by this information, told the designer that he had all the memory units ready for shipment and that, as soon as they received the missing component on Monday or Tuesday, they would be able to deliver the final units. The designer explained that the design error would be rectified in a new blueprint he was sending over by messenger and that he would hold Acme to the Tuesday delivery date.

When the blueprint arrived, Tyler called in the production supervisor to assess the damage. The alterations in the design would call for total disassembly and the unsoldering of several connections. Tyler told the supervisor to put extra people on the alterations first thing Monday morning and to try to finish the job by Tuesday. Late Tuesday afternoon, the alterations were finished and the missing components were delivered. Wednesday morning, the production supervisor discovered that the units would have to be torn apart again to install the missing component. When John Tyler was told this, he again "hit the roof." He called industrial engineering and asked if it could help out. The production supervisor and the methods engineer couldn't agree on how to install the component. John Tyler settled the argument by ordering that all units be taken apart again and the missing component installed. He told shipping to prepare cartons for delivery on Friday afternoon.

On Friday, July 29, fifty prototypes were shipped from Acme without final inspection. John Tyler was concerned about his firm's reputation, so he waived the final inspection after he personally tested one unit and found it operational. On Tuesday, August 2, Acme shipped the last fifty units.

Inside Omega

On Friday, July 8, Jim Rawls called a meeting that included department heads to tell them about the potential contract they were to receive. He told them that as soon as he received the blueprints, work could begin. On Monday, July 11, the prints arrived and again the department heads met to discuss the project. At the end of the meeting, drafting had agreed to prepare manufacturing prints, while industrial engineering and production would begin methods design.

Two problems arose within Omega that were similar to those at Acme. Certain ordered parts could not be delivered on time, and the assembly sequence was difficult to engineer. The departments proposed ideas to help one another, however, and department heads and key employees had daily meetings to discuss progress. The head of electrical engineering knew of a Japanese source for the components that could not be purchased from normal suppliers. Most problems were solved by Saturday, July 16.

On Monday, July 18, a methods engineer and the production supervisor formulated the assembly plans, and production was set to begin on Tuesday morning. On Monday afternoon, people from mechanical engineering, electrical engineering, production, and industrial engineering got together to produce a prototype just to ensure that there would be no snags in production. While they were building the unit, they discovered an error in the connector cable design. All the engineers agreed, after checking and rechecking the blueprints, that the cable was erroneously designed. People from mechanical engineering and electrical engineering spent Monday night redesigning the cable, and on Tuesday morning, the drafting department finalized the changes in the manufacturing prints. On Tuesday morning, Rawls was a bit apprehensive about the design changes and decided to get formal approval. Rawls received word on Wednesday from the head designer at the photocopier firm that they could proceed with the design changes as discussed on the phone. On Friday, July 22, the final units were inspected by quality control and were then shipped.

Part IV

Ten of Acme's final memory units were defective, while all of Omega's units passed the photocopier firm's tests. The photocopier firm was disappointed with Acme's delivery delay and incurred further delays in repairing the defective Acme units. However, rather than give the entire contract to one firm, the final contract was split between Acme and Omega with two directives added: (1) maintain zero defects and (2) reduce final cost. In 1977, through extensive cost-cutting efforts, Acme reduced its unit cost by 20 percent and was ultimately awarded the total contract.

Chapter Three Workshop *The External Environment**

1. Divide into groups of four to seven members. This exercise may be done in class or as an assignment to do with your group outside of class.
2. Consider the external environment for two organizations. Choose the place of work of one member of the group, the university, or some other organizations familiar to group members.
3. As a group, complete the table below. Consider changes that have occurred in the past few years and changes you expect in the next few years in economic conditions, government regulations, technology, socially, and in the global marketplace that would impact on the two organizations you have chosen. Expand on the ideas given as possibilities below, or write down other relevant issues.

Economy: Boom versus recession/depression, unemployment versus full-employment economy, high investment versus overspending and so on.

Government regulations: HRM regulations, OSHA, EPA, and so on.

Technology: Changes in technology for manufacturing or service, electronic technologies, computers, and so on.

Social changes: Changes in consumer preference, age, attitudes; workforce considerations such as changes in educational or skill level, new attitudes; outside groups pressuring for changes, affirmative action, and so on.

Global marketplace: changes in customers, suppliers, competition, financial resources, industry, and so on.

*Adapted by Dorothy Marcic from Larry Miller, *A Workbook for Socio-Technical Design* (Miller Consulting Group, 1991), 82–83.

Relevant Factors for the Organizations

Organization	Economic conditions	Government regulations	Technology influences	Social changes	Global marketplace
1.	Past:				
	Future:				
2.	Past:				
	Future:				

4. As a group, discuss how these changes will impact on your organizations. Consider structure, roles, coordination, planning, interorganizational linkages, controlling the domain, and other things you think of.

5. Present your findings to the entire class and discuss implications for business in general.

Notes

1. John Keller, Leslie Cauley, and Douglas Lavin, "AT&T Job Cutbacks Are Just the First Shot in Global Telecom War," *Wall Street Journal Europe,* 5–6 January 1996, A1; Jaclyn Fierman, "When Genteel Rivals Become Mortal Enemies, *Fortune,* 15 May 1995, 90–100; John Greenwald, "MCI's New Extension," *Time*, 18 November 1996, 103; Richard S. Teitelbaum, "The New Race for Intelligence," *Fortune,* 2 November 1992, 104–107.

2. Kyle Pope, "Cable & Wireless, Hurt by Tougher Rivals, Is Losing Phone Wars," *Wall Street Journal*, 27 September 1995, A1.

3. Brent Schlender, "Paradise Lost: Apple's Quest for Life after Death," *Fortune*, 19 February 1996, 64–74.

4. Wendy Zellner, "Not Everyone Loves Wal-Mart's Low Price," *Business Week*, 12 October 1992, 36–38; Suzanne Alexander, "Feisty Yankees Resist Wal-Mart's Drive to Set Up Shops in New England Towns," *Wall Street Journal*, 16 September 1993, B1, B6.

5. Alan Deutschman, "What 25-Year-Olds Want," *Fortune,* 27 August 1990, 42–50; Dean Foust and Tim Smart, "The Merger Parade Runs into a Brick Wall," *Business Week* 14 May 1990; Michael Schroeder and Walecia Konrad, "Nucor: Rolling Right into Steel's Big Time," *Business Week,* 19 November 1990, 76–81.

6. Jonathan Berry, Zachary Schiller, Richard A. Melcher, and Mark Maremont, "Attack of the Fighting Brands," *Business Week,* 2 May 1994, 125.

7. Dana Milbank, "Aluminum Producers, Aggressive and Agile, Outfight Steelmakers," *Wall Street Journal*, 1 July 1992, A1.

8. Maria Mallory with Stephanie Anderson Forest, "Waking Up to a Major Market," *Business Week*, 23 March 1992, 70–73.

9. James Worsham, "Labor Comes Alive," *Nation's Business* (February 1996): 16–24.

10. Bela L. Musits, "When Big Changes Happen to Small Companies," *Inc.,* August 1994, 27–28.

11. Barbara Carton, "Gillette Faces Wrath of Children in Testing on Rats and Rabbits," *Wall Street Journal,* 5 September 1995, A1.

12. Lucinda Harper and Fred R. Bleakley, "An Era of Low Inflation Changes the Calculus for Buyers and Sellers," *Wall Street Journal,* 14 January 1994, A1, A3.

13. John Huey, "Waking Up to the New Economy," *Fortune,* 27 June 1994, 36–46.

14. Richard L. Daft, *Management,* 4th ed. (Ft. Worth, Texas: Dryden, 1997), 189.

15. Andrew Kupfer, "How American Industry Stacks Up," *Fortune,* 9 March 1992, 36–46.

16. Alan Farnham, "Global—or Just Globaloney?" *Fortune,* 27 June 1994, 97–100; William C. Symonds, Brian Bremner, Stewart Toy, and Karen Lowry Miller, "The Globetrotters Take Over," *Business Week,* 8 July 1996, 46–48; Carla Rapoport, "Nestlé's Brand Building Machine," *Fortune,* 19 September 1994, 147–156; "Execs with Global Vision," *USA Today,* International Edition, 9 February 1996, 12B.

17. Tom Peters, "Prometheus Barely Unbound," *Academy of Management Executive* 4 (1990): 70–84.

18. Clifford C. Hebard, "Managing Effectively in Asia," *Training & Development* (April 1996): 35–39.

19. Kupfer, "How American Industry Stacks Up."; Greenwald, "MCI's New Extension."

20. Symonds, et al., "The Globetrotters Take Over."

21. Tim Smart, "GE's Welch: 'Fighting Like Hell to Be No. 1'," *Business Week,* 8 July 1996, 48.

22. Allen C. Bluedorn, "Pilgrim's Progress: Trends and Convergence in Research on Organizational Size and Environment," *Journal of Management* 19 (1993): 163–91; Howard E. Aldrich, *Organizations and Environments* (Englewood, Cliffs, N.J.: Prentice-Hall, 1979); Fred E. Emery and Eric L. Trist, "The Casual Texture of Organizational Environments," *Human Relations* 18 (1965): 21–32.

23. Christine S. Koberg and Gerardo R. Ungson, "The Effects of Environmental Uncertainty and Dependence on Organizational Structure and Performance: A Comparative Study," *Journal of Management* 13 (1987): 725–37; Frances J. Milliken, "Three Types of Perceived Uncertainty About the Environment: State, Effect, and Response Uncertainty," *Academy of Management Review* 12 (1987): 133–43.

24. Robert B. Duncan, "Characteristics of Organizational Environment and Perceived Environmental Uncertainty," *Administrative Science Quarterly* 17 (1972): 313–27; Gregory G. Dess and Donald W. Beard, "Dimensions of Organizational Task Environments," *Administrative Science Quarterly* 29 (1984): 52–73; Ray Jurkovich, "A Core Typology of Organizational Environments," *Administrative Science Quarterly* 19 (1974): 380–94.

25. Jaclyn Fierman, "When Genteel Rivals Become Mortal Enemies."

26. Thomas M. Burton, "Anti-Depression Drug of Eli Lilly Loses Sales after Attack by Sect," *Wall Street Journal,* 19 April 1991, A1, A2.

27. J. A. Litterer, *The Analysis of Organizations*, 2d ed. (New York: Wiley, 1973), 335.

28. Joseph Pereira, "Toy Industry Finds It Harder and Harder to Pick the Winners," *Wall Street Journal,* 21 December 1993, A1, A5.

29. Rosalie L. Tung, "Dimensions of Organizational Environments: An Exploratory Study of Their Impact on Organizational Structure," *Academy of Management Journal* 22 (1979): 672–93.

30. Joseph E. McCann and John Selsky, "Hyperturbulence and the Emergence of Type 5 Environments," *Academy of Management Review* 9 (1984): 460–70.

31. Eric Schine with Gary McWilliams, "Mattel: Looking for a Few Good Boy Toys," *Business Week,* 17 February 1992, 116–18.

32. Judith Valente and Asra Q. Nomani, "Surge in Oil Price has Airlines Struggling, Some Just to Hang on," *Wall Street Journal,* 10 August 1990, A1, A4.

33. James D. Thompson, *Organizations in Action* (New York: McGraw-Hill, 1967), 20–21.

34. Sally Solo, "Whirlpool: How to Listen to Consumers," *Fortune,* 11 January 1993, 77–79.

35. David B. Jemison, "The Importance of Boundary Spanning Roles in Strategic Decision-Making," *Journal of Management Studies* 21 (1984): 131–52; Mohamed Ibrahim Ahmad At-Twaijri and John R. Montanari, "The Impact of Context and Choice on the Boundary-Spanning Process: An Empirical Extension," *Human Relations* 40 (1987): 783–98.

36. Robert C. Schwab, Gerardo R. Ungson, and Warren B. Brown, "Redefining the Boundary-Spanning Environment Relationship," *Journal of Management* 11 (1985): 75–86.

37. Ken Western, "Ethical Spying," *Business Ethics* (September/October 1995): 22–23; Stan Crock, Geoffrey Smith, Joseph Weber, Richard A. Melcher, and Linda Himelstein, "They Snoop to Conquer," *Business Week,* 28 October 1996,

172–176; Kenneth A. Sawka, "Demystifying Business Intelligence," *Management Review* (October 1996): 47–51.

38. Crock, et. al., "They Snoop to Conquer."

39. David Steitz, "Entrepreneur's Notebook: Let the Customer Be Your Guide," *Nation's Business* (March 1995): 6.

40. Jay W. Lorsch, "Introduction to the Structural Design of Organizations," in Gene W. Dalton, Paul R. Lawrence, and Jay W. Lorsch, eds., *Organizational Structure and Design* (Homewood, Ill.: Irwin and Dorsey, 1970), 5.

41. Paul R. Lawrence and Jay W. Lorsch, *Organization and Environment* (Homewood, Ill.: Irwin, 1969).

42. Lorsch, "Introduction to the Structural Design of Organizations," 7.

43. Jay W. Lorsch and Paul R. Lawrence, "Environmental Factors and Organizational Integration," in J. W. Lorsch and Paul R. Lawrence, eds., *Organizational Planning: Cases and Concepts* (Homewood, Ill.: Irwin and Dorsey, 1972), 45.

44. Tom Burns and G. M. Stalker, *The Management of Innovation* (London: Tavistock, 1961).

45. John A. Courtright, Gail T. Fairhurst, and L. Edna Rogers, "Interaction Patterns in Organic and Mechanistic Systems," *Academy of Management Journal* 32 (1989): 773–802.

46. Paul J. DiMaggio and Walter W. Powell, "The Iron Cage Revisited: Institutional Isomorphism and Collective Rationality in Organizational Fields," *American Sociological Review* 48 (1983): 147–60; Richard H. Hall, *Organizations: Structures, Processes, and Outcomes* (Englewood Cliffs, N.J.: Prentice-Hall, 1987); Christine Oliver, "Strategic Responses to Institutional Processes," *Academy of Management Review* 16 (1991): 145–79.

47. "Business Fads: What's In—and Out," *Business Week*, 20 January 1986, 52–61.

48. Thomas C. Powell, "Organizational Alignment as Competitive Advantage," *Strategic Management Journal* 13 (1992): 119–34. Mansour Javidan, "The Impact of Environmental Uncertainty on Long-Range Planning Practices of the U.S. Savings and Loan Industry," *Strategic Management Journal* 5 (1984): 381–92; Tung, "Dimensions of Organizational Environments," 672–93; Thompson, *Organizations in Action.*

49. David Ulrich and Jay B. Barney, "Perspectives in Organizations: Resource Dependence, Efficiency, and Population," *Academy of Management Review* 9 (1984): 471–81; Jeffrey Pfeffer and Gerald Salancik, *The External Control of Organizations: A Resource Dependent Perspective* (New York: Harper & Row, 1978).

50. Kathy Rebello with Richard Brandt, Peter Coy, and Mark Lewyn, "Your Digital Future," *Business Week,* 7 September 1992, 56–64.

51. Andrew H. Van de Ven and Gordon Walker, "The Dynamics of Interorganizational Coordination," *Administrative Science Quarterly* (1984): 598–621; Huseyin Leblebici and Gerald R. Salancik, "Stability in Interorganizational Exchanges: Rulemaking Processes of the Chicago Board of Trade," *Administrative Science Quarterly* 27 (1982): 227–42.

52. Kevin Kelly and Zachary Schiller with James B. Treece, "Cut Costs or Else: Companies Lay Down the Law to Suppliers," *Business Week,* 22 March 1993, 28–29.

53. G. Pascal Zachary, "Many Journalists See a Growing Reluctance to Criticize Advertisers," *Wall Street Journal,* 6 February 1992, A1, A9.

54. Richard Brandt, "Microsoft Is Like an Elephant Rolling around, Squashing Ants," *Business Week,* 30 October 1989, 148–52.

55. Judith A. Babcock, *Organizational Responses to Resource Scarcity and Munificence: Adaptation and Modification in Colleges within a University* (Ph.D. diss., Pennsylvania State University, 1981).

56. Peter Smith Ring and Andrew H. Van de Ven, "Developmental Processes of Corporative Interorganizational Relationships," *Academy of Management Review* 19 (1994): 90–118; Jeffrey Pfeffer, "Beyond Management and the Worker: The Institutional Function of Management," *Academy of Management Review* 1 (April 1976): 36–46; John P. Kotter, "Managing External Dependence," *Academy of Management Review* 4 (1979): 87–92.

57. Bryan Borys and David B. Jemison, "Hybrid Arrangements as Strategic Alliances: Theoretical Issues in Organizational Combinations," *Academy of Management Review* 14 (1989): 234–49.

58. Brian Bremmer with Kathy Rebello, Zachary Schiller, and Joseph Weber, "The Age of Consolidation," *Business Week*, 14 October 1991, 86–94.

59. Julie Cohen Mason, "Strategic Alliances: Partnering for Success," *Management Review* (May 1993): 10–15.

60. John F. Love, *McDonald's: Behind the Arches* (New York: Bantam Books, 1986).

61. Zachary Schiller and Wendy Zellner with Ron Stodghill II and Mark Maremont, "Clout! More

and More, Retail Giants Rule the Marketplace," *Business Week,* 21 December 1992, 66–73.

62. Borys and Jemison, "Hybrid Arrangements as Strategic Alliances."

63. Donald Palmer, "Broken Ties: Interlocking Directorates and Intercorporate Coordination," *Administrative Science Quarterly* 28 (1983): 40–55; F. David Shoorman, Max H. Bazerman, and Robert S. Atkin, "Interlocking Directorates: A Strategy for Reducing Environmental Uncertainty," *Academy of Management Review* 6 (1981): 243–51; Ronald S. Burt, *Toward a Structural Theory of Action* (New York: Academic Press, 1982).

64. James R. Lang and Daniel E. Lockhart, "Increased Environmental Uncertainty and Changes in Board Linkage Patterns," *Academy of Management Journal* 33 (1990): 106–28; Mark S. Mizruchi and Linda Brewster Stearns, "A Longitudinal Study of the Formation of Interlocking Directorates," *Administrative Science Quarterly* 33 (1988): 194–210.

65. "Dow Chemical: From Napalm to Nice Guy," *Fortune,* 12 May 1986, 75.

66. Linda Himelstein, Laura Zinn, Maria Mallory, John Carey, Richard S. Dunham, and Joan O'C. Hamilton, "Tobacco: Does It Have a Future?" *Business Week,* 4 July 1994, 24–29; Linda Himelstein and Nancy Walser, "Levi's Vs. the Dress Code," *Business Week,* 1 April 1996, 57–58.

67. Brenton R. Schlender, "How Toshiba Makes Alliances Work," *Fortune,* 4 October 1993, 116–20.

68. Kotter, "Managing External Dependence."

69. Daniel Pearl and Gabriella Stern, "How GM Managed to Wring Pickup Pact and Keep on Truckin'," *Wall Street Journal,* 5 December 1994, A1.

70. Rick Wartzman and John Harwood, "For the Baby Bells, Government Lobbying Is Hardly Child's Play," *Wall Street Journal,* 15 March 1994, A1.

71. Christi Harlan, "Accounting Proposal Stirs Unusual Uproar in Executive Suites," *Wall Street Journal,* 7 March 1994, A1.

72. David B. Yoffie, "How an Industry Builds Political Advantage," *Harvard Business Review* (May-June 1988): 82–89; Jeffrey H. Birnbaum, "Chief Executives Head to Washington to Ply the Lobbyist's Trade," *Wall Street Journal,* 19 March 1990, A1, A16.

73. David Whitford, "Built By Association," *Inc.* (July 1994): 71–75.

74. Anthony J. Daboub, Abdul M. A. Rasheed, Richard L. Priem, and David A. Gray, "Top Management Team Characteristics and Corporate Illegal Activity," *Academy of Management Review* 20, no. 1 (1995): 138–70.

75. Bryan Burrough, "Oil-Field Investigators Say Fraud Flourishes from Wells to Offices," *Wall Street Journal,* 15 January 1985, 1, 20; Irwin Ross, "How Lawless Are Big Companies?" *Fortune,* 1 December 1980, 57–64.

76. Stewart Toy, "The Defense Scandal," *Business Week,* 4 July 1988, 28–30.

77. Barry M. Staw and Eugene Szwajkowski, "The Scarcity-Munificence Component of Organizational Environments and the Commission of Illegal Acts," *Administrative Science Quarterly* 20 (1975): 345–54.

78. Kimberly D. Elsbach and Robert I. Sutton, "Acquiring Organizational Legitimacy through Illegitimate Actions: A Marriage of Institutional and Impression Management Theories," *Academy of Management Journal* 35 (1992): 699–738.

chapter four

Manufacturing, Service, and Advanced Information Technologies

A look inside

French Rags

In 1978, Brenda French started a scarf-making company in a spare bedroom of her home. Ten years later, leading department stores like Neiman Marcus, Bonwit Teller, and Bloomingdale's were showcasing her line of custom-made knitwear. French Rags seemed, to outsiders, like a booming success, but Brenda French knew better. Her business was beset by a multitude of problems and had difficulty competing against mass manufacturers with greater resources selling at lower prices. French Rags could offer customers the variety they wanted but production output was limited and costs were high.

Faced with closing the business, French began looking into new technology that offered a dazzling possibility: mass customization. She invested in a German-made Stoll knitting machine that combines new technology and timeless craft by using thousands of precisely angled needles to make clothes one stitch at a time. In addition, the company now uses computer-aided design and manufacturing technology, enabling French Rags to produce custom-made garments at virtually the same speed—and the same cost—as the cookie-cutter offerings of mass producers. Custom software produces knit-by-numbers templates that enable fast and easy switching from one garment to another. About one hundred employees at French Rags' Los Angeles factory augment the automated knitting line with the necessary human touch. The next step French took was to create a sales force of her most affluent customers, who sell French Rags out of their homes. After customers make their selections and pick out preferred color combinations, individual measurements are taken, the order is faxed or sent by modem to the French Rags factory, and the garment is custom made and shipped directly to the customer's home. Inventory costs and problems have been virtually eliminated.

Combining new technology with new ways of thinking turned Brenda French's small company into a $5 million full-line clothing manufacturer and put French Rags on the cutting edge of a revolution in manufacturing.[1]

Technology is the tools, techniques, and actions used to transform organizational inputs into outputs.[2] Technology is an organization's production process and includes machinery and work procedures. The technology at French Rags produces clothing.

Organization technology begins with raw materials of some type (for example, unfinished steel castings in a valve manufacturing plant). Employees take action on the raw material to make a change in it (they machine steel castings), which transforms the raw material into the output of the organization (control valves ready for shipment to oil refineries). For Federal Express, the production technology includes the equipment and procedures for delivering overnight mail.

Exhibit 4.1 features an example of production technology for a manufacturing plant. Note how the technology consists of raw material inputs, a transformation process that changes and adds value to these items, and the ultimate product or service output that is sold to consumers in the environment. In today's large,

Exhibit 4.1

Transformation Process for a Manufacturing Company

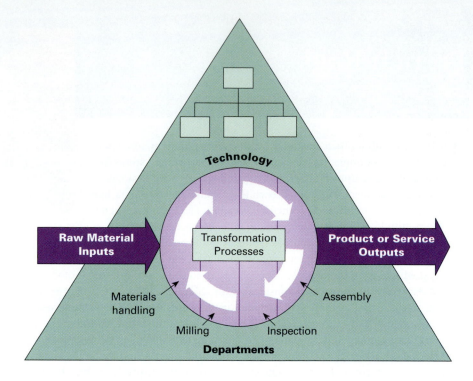

complex organizations, it can be hard to pinpoint technology. Technology can be partly assessed by examining the raw materials flowing into the organization,[3] the variability of work activities,[4] the degree to which the production process is mechanized,[5] the extent to which one task depends upon another in the work flow,[6] or the number of new product outputs.[7]

Recall from Chapter 3 that organizations have a technical core that reflects the organization's primary purpose. The technical core contains the transformation process that represents the organization's technology. As today's organizations try to become more flexible in a changing environment, new technology may influence organizational structure, but decisions about organizational structure may also shape or limit technology. Thus, the interaction between core technology and structure leads to a patterned relationship in many organizations.[8]

In today's large, complex organizations, many departments exist and each may employ a different technology for its own function. Thus, research and development transforms ideas into new product proposals, and marketing transforms inventory into sales, each using a different technology. Moreover, the administrative technology used by managers to run the organization represents yet another technology. Computers and advanced information technology have impact on the administrative arena.

Purpose of This Chapter

In this chapter, we will explore the nature of organizational technologies and the relationship between technology and organization structure. Chapter 3 described how the environment influences organization design. The question addressed in this chapter is, "How should the organization structure be designed to accommodate and facilitate the production process?" Form usually follows function, so the form of the organization's structure should be tailored to fit the needs of the production technology.

The remainder of the chapter will unfold as follows. First, we will examine how the technology for the organization as a whole influences organization structure and design. This discussion will include both manufacturing and service technologies and will introduce new concepts about computer-integrated manufacturing. Next, we will examine differences in departmental technologies and how the technologies influence the design and management of organizational subunits. Third, we will explore how interdependence—flow of materials and information—among departments affects structure. Finally, we will examine how new computer-based information technologies are influencing organization design by their impact on administration and management of the organization.

ORGANIZATION-LEVEL TECHNOLOGY

Organization-level technologies are of two types—manufacturing and service. Manufacturing technologies include traditional manufacturing processes and new computer-based manufacturing systems.

Manufacturing Firms

Woodward's Study.　　The first and most influential study of manufacturing technology was conducted by Joan Woodward, a British industrial sociologist. Her research began as a field study of management principles in south Essex. The prevailing management wisdom at the time (1950s) was contained in what was known as universal principles of management. These principles were "one best way" prescriptions that effective organizations were expected to adopt. Woodward surveyed one hundred manufacturing firms firsthand to learn how they were organized.[9] She and her research team visited each firm, interviewed managers, examined company records, and observed the manufacturing operations. Her data included a wide range of structural characteristics (span of control, levels of management) and dimensions of management style (written versus verbal communications, use of rewards) and the type of manufacturing process. Data were also obtained that reflected commercial success of the firms.

Woodward developed a scale and organized the firms according to technical complexity of the manufacturing process. **Technical complexity** represents the extent of mechanization of the manufacturing process. High technical complexity means most of the work is performed by machines. Low technical complexity means workers play a larger role in the production process. Woodward's scale of technical complexity originally had ten categories, as summarized in Exhibit 4.2. These categories were further consolidated into three basic technology groups:

- *Group I: Small-batch and unit production.* These firms tend to be job shop operations that manufacture and assemble small orders to meet specific needs of customers. Custom work is the norm. **Small-batch production** relies heavily on the human operator; it is thus not highly mechanized. Examples include many types of made-to-order manufactured products, such as specialized construction equipment, custom electronic equipment, and custom clothing.
- *Group II: Large-batch and mass production.* **Large-batch production** is a manufacturing process characterized by long production runs of standardized

Exhibit 4.2   *Woodward's Classification of One Hundred British Firms According to Their Systems of Production*

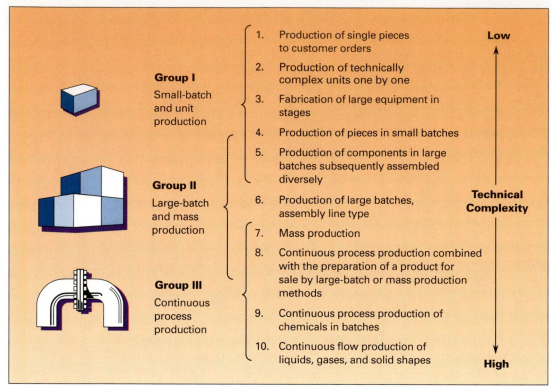

Source: Adapted from Woodward, *Management and Technology* (London: Her Majesty's Stationery Office, 1958). Used with permission of Her Britannic Majesty's Stationery Office.

parts. Output often goes into inventory from which orders are filled, because customers do not have special needs. Examples include most assembly lines, such as for automobiles or trailer homes.

• *Group III: Continuous process production.* In **continuous process production** the entire process is mechanized. There is no starting and stopping. This represents mechanization and standardization one step beyond those in an assembly line. Automated machines control the continuous process, and outcomes are highly predictable. Examples would include chemical plants, oil refineries, liquor producers, and nuclear power plants.

Using this classification of technology, Woodward's data made sense. A few of her key findings are given in Exhibit 4.3. The number of management levels and the manager/total personnel ratio, for example, show definite increases as technical complexity increases from unit production to continuous process. This indicates that greater management intensity is needed to manage complex technology. Direct/indirect labor ratio decreases with technical complexity because more indirect workers are required to support and maintain complex machinery. Other characteristics, such as span of control, formalized procedures, and centralization, are high for mass production technology but low for other technologies because the work is standardized. Unit production and continuous process technologies require highly skilled workers to run the machines and

Structural Characteristic	Technology		
	Unit Production	**Mass Production**	**Continuous Process**
Number of management levels	3	4	6
Supervisor span of control	23	48	15
Direct/indirect labor ratio	9:1	4:1	1:1
Manager/total personnel ratio	Low	Medium	High
Workers' skill level	High	Low	High
Formalized procedures	Low	High	Low
Centralization	Low	High	Low
Amount of verbal communication	High	Low	High
Amount of written communication	Low	High	Low
Overall structure	Organic	Mechanistic	Organic

Exhibit 4.3

Relationship Between Technical Complexity and Structural Characteristics

Source: Joan Woodward, *Industrial Organization: Theory and Practice* (London: Oxford University Press, 1965). Used with permission.

verbal communication to adapt to changing conditions. Mass production is standardized and routinized, so few exceptions occur, little verbal communication is needed, and employees are less skilled.

Overall, the management systems in both unit production and continuous process technology are characterized as organic. They are more free-flowing and adaptive, with fewer procedures and less standardization. Mass production, however, is mechanistic, with standardized jobs and formalized procedures. Woodward's discovery about technology thus provided substantial new insight into the causes of organization structure. In Joan Woodward's own words, "Different technologies impose different kinds of demands on individuals and organizations, and those demands had to be met through an appropriate structure."[10]

Strategy, Technology, and Performance. Another portion of Woodward's study examined the success of the firms along dimensions such as profitability, market share, stock price, and reputation. As indicated in Chapter 2, the measurement of effectiveness is not simple or precise, but Woodward was able to rank firms on a scale of commercial success according to whether they displayed above-average, average, or below-average performance on strategic objectives.

Woodward compared the structure-technology relationship against commercial success and discovered that successful firms tended to be those that had complementary structures and technologies. Many of the organizational characteristics of the successful firms were near the average of their technology category, as shown in Exhibit 4.3. Below-average firms tended to depart from the structural characteristics for their technology type. Another conclusion was that structural characteristics could be interpreted as clustering into organic and mechanistic management systems. Successful small-batch and continuous process organizations had organic structures, and successful mass production organizations had mechanistic structures. Subsequent research has replicated her findings.[11]

Exhibit 4.4
Co-alignment of Strategy, Technology, and Structure

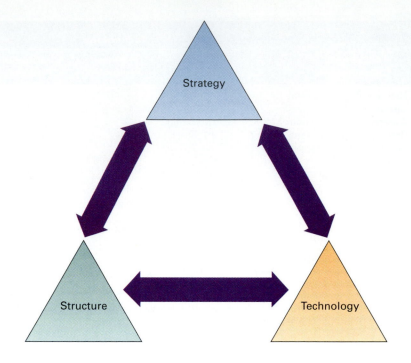

What this illustrates for today's companies is that strategy, structure, and technology need to be aligned, especially when competitive conditions change. Several researchers have argued that the strength of Japanese firms in many industries can be credited to a close alignment among strategy, structure, and technology,[12] as shown in Exhibit 4.4. Some insurance companies in the United States are currently realigning strategy, structure, and technology because of increased competition in the insurance business. Companies such as Geico and USAA are growing rapidly through the use of direct mail and phone solicitation, avoiding the costs associated with doing business through independent insurance agents. Agency-based companies like State Farm and Allstate have had to put new emphasis on a low-cost strategy and are adopting efficiency-oriented information technology to cut costs and more effectively serve customers.

Failing to adopt appropriate new technologies to support strategy, or adopting a new technology and failing to realign strategy to match it, can lead to poor performance. Today's increased global competition means more volatile markets, shorter product life cycles, and more sophisticated and knowledgeable consumers; and flexibility to meet these new demands has become a strategic imperative for many companies.[13] Manufacturing companies can adopt new technologies to support the strategy of flexibility. However, organization structures and management processes must also be realigned, as a highly mechanistic structure hampers flexibility and prevents the company from reaping the benefits of the new technology.[14] The need for new ways of thinking in today's manufacturing firms is discussed in Book Mark 4.0.

For utility companies, once the strategy and technology for providing electricity are chosen, the structure and management approach must also be aligned to achieve strategic objectives, as illustrated in the following example of nuclear power plants.

Book Mark 4.0

Have You Read About This?

Lean Thinking: Banish Waste and Create Wealth in Your Corporation

By James P. Womack and Daniel T. Jones

Even after North America has restructured and reengineered its companies, firms are still trying to pinpoint the best path to continuous growth and prosperity. The authors of *Lean Thinking* posit that, by relying on their current structures and old definitions for value, companies have created *muda*—a Japanese term meaning waste: a resource-using human activity that creates no value. Through an exploration of fifty mostly manufacturing firms, James Womack and Daniel Jones show that companies can banish this waste by employing lean thinking, which searches for ways to cut out the fat in the production process, extending from the design to the sale of a customer-desired product. Lean thinking can revitalize productivity, revenue, and employee satisfaction.

Five Principles of Lean Thinking

Womack and Jones offer five sequential principles to realize an organization characterized by lean thinking:

1. *Specify value.* Accurately define value based on a dialogue with customers.
2. *Identify value stream.* Map out all the activities entailed in bringing a specific product from design to the customer, eliminating wasteful steps.
3. *Flow.* Take the value-creating activities and make them move fluidly, continuously.
4. *Pull.* Allow the customer to demand a product as needed from the manufacturer. Don't push your products on customers.
5. *Perfection.* Strive for perfection with the first four principles working in a "virtuous circle"; this makes

value flow quicker and reveals hidden *muda* to be removed from the value stream.

Action Plan for Transformation

The authors provide a step-by-step action plan to achieve a lean thinking organization:

- *Get started.* Find a change agent, get lean knowledge, find a lever, map value streams, expand your scope.
- *Create a new organization.* Reorganize by product family, create a lean function, devise a policy for excess people, devise a growth strategy, remove anchor-draggers, instill a "perfection" mind-set.
- *Install business systems.* Introduce lean accounting, relate pay to firm performance, implement transparency, initiate policy deployment, introduce lean learning, find right-sized tools.
- *Complete the transformation.* Apply these steps to your suppliers/customers, develop global strategy, transition from top-down to bottom-up environment.

The Lean Enterprise

The authors close the book with a discussion of the *lean enterprise,* which is a combination of the best attributes of American, German, and Japanese industrial traditions. This collection of features can be used in every economic activity to produce lean-thinking companies—a new way of "thinking, being, and doing."

Lean Thinking: Banish Waste and Create Wealth in Your Corporation, by James P. Womack and Daniel T. Jones, is published by Simon and Schuster.

Northeast Utilities and Boston Edison Company

In Practice 4.1

Northeast Utilities' Millstone 1 nuclear plant, located in Waterford, Connecticut, is considered by the Nuclear Regulatory Commission (NRC) to be one of the best-managed plants in the industry. Northeast Utilities' management long ago realized that managing a nuclear power plant is different from managing a fossil fuel plant. Nuclear plants are bigger and more complex, and their complex technical systems and safety features require extensive maintenance. For these reasons, a large number of skilled workers are on the payroll, and each worker spends one week of every six in training classes. Northeast Utilities also assigns its best people to manage Millstone. The superintendent stays personally involved with employees by visiting the control room each day and chatting face-to-face with the staff.

Boston Edison Company's Pilgrim nuclear power plant, located just eight miles to the north of Millstone, is comparable in size, design, and vintage, but is considered by the NRC to be one of the worst-managed nuclear plants in the United States. Pilgrim hasn't had a major accident, but it was criticized by the NRC and has been shut down. Boston Edison didn't seem to realize that the complexity of nuclear technology required special management, that a nuclear plant is not just another boiler. At Pilgrim, operators rarely saw the superintendent face-to-face in the control room. A backlog of twelve thousand maintenance items indicated the need for more maintenance people. Moreover, Boston Edison traditionally did not assign its best managers to the nuclear plant. Edison is now trying to overcome its shortcomings by hiring a new plant manager, recruiting highly skilled operators, and doubling the maintenance staff.

The problem of managing nuclear plants was illustrated by the chairman of Georgia Power Company, who emphasized that "the world of a utility executive that has a nuclear power plant is different from one who doesn't, and if he doesn't understand that, he's in trouble."[15]

The nuclear power plant is a continuous process technology. Its automated equipment is highly complex and requires skilled employees along with a high number of maintenance personnel. Greater management skills and intensity are required to ensure close supervision and to provide backup expertise in a crisis. The failure of Boston Edison's management to diagnose the special management needs of nuclear technology cost the company and its ratepayers dearly. When the Pilgrim plant was closed for upgrading, Boston Edison spent $200,000 a day to buy electricity to replace what Pilgrim would have generated.[16]

Computer-Integrated Manufacturing

In the years since Woodward's research, new developments have occurred in manufacturing technology. New manufacturing technologies include robots, numerically controlled machine tools, and computerized software for product design, engineering analysis, and remote control of machinery. The ultimate technology is called **computer-integrated manufacturing** (CIM).[17] Also called *advanced manufacturing technology, agile manufacturing*, the *factory of the future*, *smart factories*, or *flexible manufacturing systems,* CIM links together manufacturing components that previously stood alone. Thus, robots, machines, product design, and engineering analysis are coordinated by a single computer.

The result has already revolutionized the shop floor, enabling large factories to deliver a wide range of custom-made products at low mass production costs.[18] As illustrated by the chapter opening case, computer-integrated manufacturing also enables small companies to go toe-to-toe with large factories and low-cost foreign competitors. Techknits, Inc., a small manufacturer located in New York City, competes successfully against low-cost sweater-makers in the Far East by using $8 million worth of computerized looms and other machinery. The work of designing sweaters, which once took two days, can now be accomplished in two hours. Looms operate round-the-clock and crank out 60,000 sweaters a week, enabling Techknits to fill customer orders faster than foreign competitors.[19]

Computer-integrated manufacturing is typically the result of three subcomponents.

- *Computer-aided design (CAD)*. Computers are used to assist in the drafting, design, and engineering of new parts. Designers guide their computer to draw specified configurations on the screen, including dimensions and component details. Hundreds of design alternatives can be explored, as can scaled-up or scaled-down versions of the original.[20]

- *Computer-aided manufacturing (CAM).* Computer-controlled machines in materials handling, fabrication, production, and assembly greatly increase the speed at which items can be manufactured. CAM also permits a production line to shift rapidly from producing one product to any variety of other products by changing the instruction tapes or software in the computer. CAM enables the production line to quickly honor customer requests for changes in product design and product mix.[21]
- *Administrative automation.* The computerized accounting, inventory control, billing, and shop-floor tracking systems allow managers to use computers to monitor and control the manufacturing process.

The combination of CAD, CAM, and administrative automation components represents the highest level of computer-integrated manufacturing. A new product can be designed on the computer, and a prototype can be produced untouched by human hands. The ideal factory can switch quickly from one product to another, working fast and with precision, without paperwork or recordkeeping to bog down the system.[22]

A company can adopt CAD in its engineering design department and/or CAM in its production area and make substantial improvements in efficiency and quality. However, when all three components are brought together in a truly advanced plant, the results are breathtaking. Companies such as Xerox, Westinghouse, Texas Instruments, Hewlett-Packard, and Boeing are leading the way. Boeing's new 777, the largest twin-engine plane ever built, has been called the first "paperless" jetliner. The company designed the plane with eight IBM mainframe computers supporting 2,200 workstations that eventually handled 3,500 billion bits of information. The digital design system reduced the possibility of human error and cut engineering changes and reworking of ill-fitting components by more than 50 percent over previous plane projects.[23]

This ultra-advanced system is not achieved piecemeal. CIM reaches its ultimate level to improve quality, customer service, and cost-cutting when all parts are used interdependently. The integration of CIM and flexible work processes is changing the face of manufacturing. The wave of the manufacturing future is mass customization, whereby factories are able to mass-produce products designed to exact customer specification. Levi Strauss recently began offering made-to-order jeans. A sales clerk enters a customer's measurements into a computer that creates a unique digital pattern. The pattern is then sent by modem to the factory, where robotic cutters and other advanced sewing and finishing equipment produce thousands of pairs of jeans, each tailored to a specific customer.[24] Ross Operating Valve, a seventy-year-old manufacturer of pneumatic valves in Troy, Michigan, invested millions in computerized design and automated production equipment to be able to tailor products to exact customer needs. Some U.S. business leaders envision a time in the near future when even cars can be custom-made in as little as three days.[25]

Performance. The awesome advantage of CIM is that products of different sizes, types, and customer requirements freely intermingle on the assembly line. Bar codes imprinted on a part enable machines to make instantaneous changes—such as putting a larger screw in a different location—without slowing

Exhibit 4.5 *Relationship of Computer-Integrated Manufacturing Technology to Traditional Technologies*

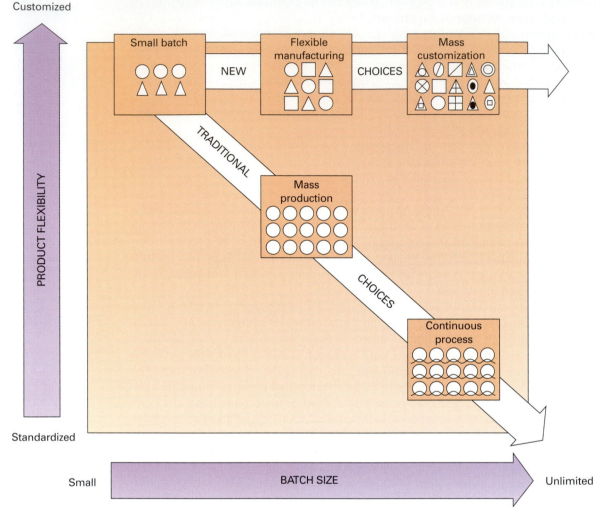

Source: Based on Jack Meredith, "The Strategic Advantages of New Manufacturing Technologies for Small Firms," *Strategic Management Journal* 8 (1987): 249–58; Paul Adler, "Managing Flexible Automation," *California Management Review* (Spring 1988): 34–56; and Otis Port, "Custom-made Direct from the Plant," *Business Week/21st Century Capitalism,* 18 November 1994, 158–59.

the production line. A manufacturer can turn out an infinite variety of products in unlimited batch sizes, as illustrated in Exhibit 4.5. In traditional manufacturing systems studied by Woodward, choices were limited to the diagonal. Small batch allowed for high product flexibility and custom orders, but because of the "craftsmanship" involved in custom-making products, batch size was necessarily small. Mass production could have large-batch size, but offered limited product flexibility. Continuous process could produce a single standard product in unlimited quantities. Computer-integrated manufacturing allows plants to break free of this diagonal and to increase both batch size and product flexibility at the same time. When taken to its ultimate level, CIM allows for mass customization, with each specific product tailored to customer specification. This high-level use of CIM has been referred to as *computer-aided craftsmanship* because computers tailor each product to meet a customer's exact needs.[26]

Studies suggest that with CIM, machine utilization is more efficient, labor productivity increases, scrap rates decrease, and product variety and customer satisfaction increase.[27] Many U.S. manufacturing companies are reinventing the factory using CIM and associated management systems to increase productivity.

Structural Implications.   Research into the relationship between CIM and organizational characteristics is beginning to emerge, and the patterns are summarized in Exhibit 4.6. Compared with traditional mass production technologies, CIM has a narrow span of control, few hierarchical levels, adaptive tasks, low specialization, decentralization, and the overall environment is characterized as organic and self-regulative. Employees need the skills to participate in teams, training is broad (so workers are not overly specialized) and frequent (so workers are up-to-date). Expertise tends to be cognitive so workers can process abstract ideas and solve problems. Interorganizational relationships in CIM firms are characterized by changing demand from customers—which is easily handled with the new technology—and close relationships with a few suppliers that provide top-quality raw materials.[28]

Technology alone cannot give organizations the benefits of flexibility, quality, increased production, and greater customer satisfaction. Recent research suggests that CIM can become a competitive burden rather than a competitive advantage unless organizational structures and management processes are redesigned to take advantage of the new technology.[29] Chrysler Corporation, for example, recognizes the crucial role of a highly trained, flexible, empowered workforce in computer-integrated manufacturing. According to Karl Branstner,

Characteristic	Mass Production	CIM
Structure		
Span of control	Wide	Narrow
Hierarchical levels	Many	Few
Tasks	Routine, repetitive	Adaptive, craftlike
Specialization	High	Low
Decision making	Centralized	Decentralized
Overall	Bureaucratic, mechanistic	Self-regulation, organic
Human Resources		
Interactions	Stand alone	Teamwork
Training	Narrow, one time	Broad, frequent
Expertise	Manual, technical	Cognitive, social Solve problems
Interorganizational		
Customer demand	Stable	Changing
Suppliers	Many, arm's length	Few, close relations

Exhibit 4.6

Comparison of Organizational Characteristics Associated with Mass Production and Computer Integrated Manufacturing

Source: Based on Patricia L. Nemetz and Louis W. Fry, "Flexible Manufacturing Organizations: Implications for Strategy Formulation and Organization Design," *Academy of Management Review* 13 (1988): 627–38; Paul S. Adler, "Managing Flexible Automation," *California Management Review* (Spring 1988): 34–56; Jeremy Main, "Manufacturing the Right Way," *Fortune,* 21 May 1990, 54–64.

human resources program coordinator at the UAW/Chrysler National Training Center, Chrysler had to "turn the power pyramid upside down," empowering workers on the factory floor to make decisions. To encourage hourly workers to learn new skills, Chrysler introduced *capability progression pay* at six plants, tying compensation to the ability to perform a variety of jobs.[30] Computer-integrated manufacturing can help companies be more competitive if top managers make a commitment to implement new structures and processes that empower workers and support a learning and knowledge-creating environment.[31]

The other major change occurring in the technology of organizations is a growing service sector. Service technologies are different from manufacturing technologies and, in turn, require a specific organization structure.

Service Firms

The United States and Canada are rapidly becoming service-oriented economies. In the United States, services now generate 74 percent of gross domestic product and account for 79 percent of all jobs. In addition, the Bureau of Labor Statistics expects services to account for all net job growth in the next decade.[32]

Definition.   Recent studies of service organizations focused on the unique dimensions of service technologies. **Service technologies** are defined based on the five elements in Exhibit 4.7. The first major difference is *simultaneous production and consumption,* which means a customer and an employee interact to provide the service. A client meets with a doctor or attorney, for example, and students and teachers come together in the classroom. This also means that customers tend to receive *customized output* and that *customers participate* in the production process. In manufacturing, by contrast, goods are produced at one time and inventoried for sale and consumption at another time; outputs tend to be standardized, and the production process tends to be removed and buffered from customers.

Exhibit 4.7   *Examples of Service Technology Versus Manufacturing Technology*

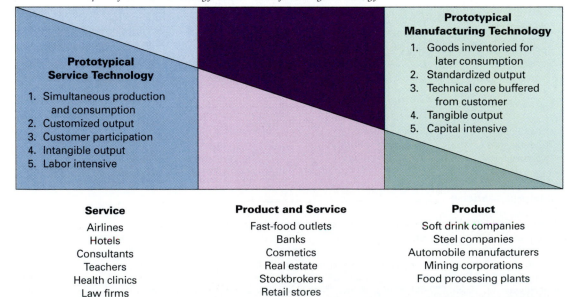

Service	Product and Service	Product
Airlines	Fast-food outlets	Soft drink companies
Hotels	Banks	Steel companies
Consultants	Cosmetics	Automobile manufacturers
Teachers	Real estate	Mining corporations
Health clinics	Stockbrokers	Food processing plants
Law firms	Retail stores	

Source: Based on David E. Bowen, Caren Siehl, and Benjamin Schneider, "A Framework for Analyzing Customer Service Orientations in Manufacturing," *Academy of Management Review* 14 (1989): 75–95.

Another major difference is *intangible output* in a service firm. A service is abstract and often consists of information or knowledge in contrast with the tangible physical products made by manufacturing firms. This typically means service firms are *labor intensive*, with many employees needed to meet the needs of customers, whereas manufacturing firms tend to be capital intensive, relying on mass production, continuous process, and CIM technologies.[33]

The characteristics in Exhibit 4.7 are prototypical, or the standard case, but exceptions arise. Some service firms try to take on characteristics of manufacturers, and vice versa. Some firms end up in the middle—such as fast-food outlets, banks, and stockbrokers, which provide both a product and service. These firms do not actually make a product, they provide it as a service, but a tangible product is part of the transaction. In addition, in today's competitive environment, manufacturers are placing a greater emphasis on service as well, which is one reason for the increased use of the CIM technology we have just discussed. Thus, manufacturers are shifting to organization structures and processes that have generally been characteristic of service firms.[34] The important point is that all organizations can be classified along a continuum that includes both manufacturing and service characteristics, as illustrated in Exhibit 4.7.

Structure. The feature of service technologies with a distinct influence on organizational structure and control systems is the need for technical core employees to be close to the customer.[35] The differences between service and product organizations necessitated by customer contact are summarized in Exhibit 4.8.

The impact of customer contact on organization structure is reflected in the use of boundary roles and structural disaggregation.[36] Boundary roles are used extensively in manufacturing firms to handle customers and to reduce disruptions for the technical core. They are used less in service firms because a service is intangible and cannot be passed along by boundary spanners, so service customers must interact directly with technical employees, such as doctors or brokers.

A service firm deals in information and intangible outputs and does not need to be large. Its greatest economies are achieved through disaggregation into small units that can be located close to customers. Stockbrokers, doctors' clinics, fast-food franchises, consulting firms, and banks disperse their facilities into regional and local offices. Some fast-food chains, such as Taco Bell, are taking this a step further, selling chicken tacos and bean burritos anywhere people gather—airports, supermarkets, college campuses, or street corners. Manufacturing firms, on the other hand, tend to aggregate operations in a single area that has raw materials and

Structure	Service	Product
1. Separate boundary roles	Few	Many
2. Geographical dispersion	Much	Little
3. Decision making	Decentralized	Centralized
4. Formalization	Lower	Higher
Human Resources		
1. Employee skill level	Higher	Lower
2. Skill emphasis	Interpersonal	Technical

Exhibit 4.8

Configuration and Structural Characteristics of Service Organizations Versus Product Organizations

The New Paradigm

Progressive Corp.

Within minutes after a car crash in Tampa, Florida, twenty-six-year-old Lance Edgy is on the scene, calming the victims and advising them on medical care, repair shops, police reports, and legal procedures. Before the tow trucks have even cleared the wreckage, Edgy, a senior claims representative for Progressive Corp., is offering his client a settlement for the market value of his totaled automobile. His "office" is an air-conditioned van equipped with a desk, cellular phones, and comfortable chairs.

Progressive Corp. illustrates internal organization characteristics that can keep service firms close to the customer. When Progressive, which specializes in high-risk drivers, ran into trouble in the late 1980s, CEO Peter Lewis saw both the need and the opportunity to create a new kind of company. "People get screwed seven ways from Sunday in auto insurance. They get dealt with adversarially, and they get dealt with slowly. I said, 'Why don't we just stop that? Why don't we start dealing with them nicely? It would be a revolution in the business.'" Today, through Progressive's Immediate Response Program, company representatives make contact with 80 percent of accident victims within nine hours; adjusters inspect 70 percent of damaged vehicles within one day; and most collision damage claims are wrapped up within one week.

Adjusters work in six-member teams and are given extensive training—not only in insurance regulations and legal intricacies but also in the art of negotiation and grief counseling, since part of the job involves dealing with relatives of dead crash victims. Teams have the authority to take care of any problem on the spot. Salaries are high, and a gain-sharing program gives workers the chance to increase their base salary by thousands of dollars. Progressive pays at the top of the market because it wants the best people at every level of the company.

Lewis has evidence that investing in people pays off. Progressive's net income, $267 million in one recent year, has increased at an average annual compound rate of 20 percent since 1989. For Progressive, training and keeping good employees is essential to keeping good customers.

Source: Ronald Henkoff, "Service Is Everybody's Business," *Fortune,* 27 June 1994, 48–60.

---

an available workforce. A large manufacturing firm can take advantage of economies derived from expensive machinery and long production runs.

Service technology also influences internal organization characteristics used to direct and control the organization. For one thing, the skills of technical core employees need to be higher. These employees need enough knowledge and awareness to handle customer problems rather than just enough to perform a single, mechanical task. Some service organizations give their employees the knowledge and freedom to make decisions and do whatever is needed to satisfy customers, whereas others, such as McDonald's, have set rules and procedures for customer service. Yet in all cases, service employees need social and interpersonal skills as well as technical skills.[37] Because of higher skills and structural dispersion, decision making often tends to be decentralized in service firms, and formalization tends to be low. Many Taco Bell outlets operate with no manager on the premises. Self-directed teams manage inventory, schedule work, order supplies, and train new employees.

Understanding the nature of service technology helps managers align strategy, structure, and management processes that may be quite different from those for a product-based or traditional manufacturing technology. Service companies are learning that what matters most is the brainpower and commitment of their employees and the loyalty of their customers. The New Paradigm box describes one organization that is a model of the modern service business.

Now let's turn to another perspective on technology, that of production activities within specific organizational departments. Departments often have characteristics similar to those of service technology, providing services to other departments within the organization.

DEPARTMENTAL TECHNOLOGY

This section shifts to the department level of analysis for departments not necessarily within the technical core. Each department in an organization has a production process that consists of a distinct technology. General Motors has departments for engineering, R&D, human resources, advertising, quality control, finance, and dozens of other functions. This section analyzes the nature of departmental technology and its relationship with departmental structure.

The framework that has had the greatest impact on the understanding of departmental technologies was developed by Charles Perrow.[38] Perrow's model has been useful for a broad range of technologies, which made it ideal for research into departmental activities.

Variety

Perrow specified two dimensions of departmental activities that were relevant to organization structure and process. The first is the number of exceptions in the work. This refers to task **variety**, which is the frequency of unexpected and novel events that occur in the conversion process. When individuals encounter a large number of unexpected situations, with frequent problems, variety is considered high. When there are few problems, and when day-to-day job requirements are repetitious, technology contains little variety. Variety in departments can range from repeating a single act, such as on an assembly line, to working on a series of unrelated problems or projects.

Analyzability

The second dimension of technology concerns the **analyzability** of work activities. When the conversion process is analyzable, the work can be reduced to mechanical steps and participants can follow an objective, computational procedure to solve problems. Problem solution may involve the use of standard procedures, such as instructions and manuals, or technical knowledge, such as that in a textbook or handbook. On the other hand, some work is not analyzable. When problems arise, it is difficult to identify the correct solution. There is no store of techniques or procedures to tell a person exactly what to do. The cause of or solution to a problem is not clear, so employees rely on accumulated experience, intuition, and judgment. The final solution to a problem is often the result of wisdom and experience and not the result of standard procedures. The brewmaster department at Heineken Brewery has an unanalyzable technology. Brewmasters taste each batch of product to identify the mix of ingredients and to see whether it fits within acceptable flavor limits. These quality control tasks require years of experience and practice. Standard procedures will not tell a person how to do such tasks.

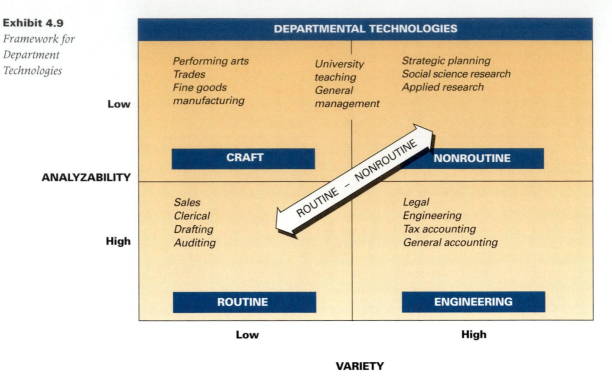

DEPARTMENTAL TECHNOLOGIES

Performing arts Trades Fine goods manufacturing	University teaching General management	Strategic planning Social science research Applied research
CRAFT		**NONROUTINE**
Sales Clerical Drafting Auditing		Legal Engineering Tax accounting General accounting
ROUTINE		**ENGINEERING**

ANALYZABILITY — Low / High

ROUTINE – NONROUTINE

VARIETY — Low / High

Source: Adapted with permission from Richard Daft and Norman Macintosh, "A New Approach to Design and Use of Management Information," *California Management Review* 21 (1978): 82–92. Copyright © 1978 by the Regents of the University of California. Reprinted by permission of the Regents.

Framework

The two dimensions of technology and examples of departmental activities on Perrow's framework are shown in Exhibit 4.9. The dimensions of variety and analyzability form the basis for four major categories of technology: routine, craft, engineering, and nonroutine.

Routine technologies are characterized by little task variety and the use of objective, computational procedures. The tasks are formalized and standardized. Examples include an automobile assembly line and a bank teller department.

Craft technologies are characterized by a fairly stable stream of activities, but the conversion process is not analyzable or well understood. Tasks require extensive training and experience because employees respond to intangible factors on the basis of wisdom, intuition, and experience. Although advances in machine technologies seem to have reduced the number of craft technologies in organizations, a few craft technologies remain. For example, steel furnace engineers continue to mix steel based on intuition and experience, pattern makers at apparel firms still convert rough designers' sketches into salable garments, and gas and oil explorationists use their internal divining rod to determine where millions will be spent on drilling operations.

Engineering technologies tend to be complex because there is substantial variety in the tasks performed. However, the various activities are usually handled on the basis of established formulas, procedures, and techniques. Employees normally refer to a well-developed body of knowledge to handle problems. Engineering and accounting tasks usually fall in this category.

Nonroutine technologies have high task variety, and the conversion process is not analyzable or well understood. In nonroutine technology, a great deal of effort is devoted to analyzing problems and activities. Several equally acceptable options typically can be found. Experience and technical knowledge are used to solve problems and perform the work. Basic research, strategic planning, and other work that involves new projects and unexpected problems are nonroutine.

Routine Versus Nonroutine. Exhibit 4.9 also illustrates that variety and analyzability can be combined into a single dimension of technology. This dimension is called routine versus nonroutine technology, and it is the diagonal line in Exhibit 4.9. The analyzability and variety dimensions are often correlated in departments, meaning that technologies high in variety tend to be low in analyzability, and technologies low in variety tend to be analyzable. Departments can be evaluated, along a single dimension of routine versus nonroutine that combines both analyzability and variety, which is a useful shorthand measure for analyzing departmental technology.

The following questions show how departmental technology can be analyzed for determining its placement on Perrow's technology framework in Exhibit 4.9.[39] Employees normally circle a number from one to seven in response to each question.

Variety
1. To what extent would you say your work is routine?
2. Does most everyone in this unit do about the same job in the same way most of the time?
3. Are unit members performing repetitive activities in doing their jobs?

Analyzability
1. To what extent is there a clearly known way to do the major types of work you normally encounter?
2. To what extent is there an understandable sequence of steps that can be followed in doing your work?
3. To do your work, to what extent can you actually rely on established procedures and practices?

If answers to the above questions indicate high scores for analyzability and low scores for variety, the department would have a routine technology. If the opposite occurs, the technology would be nonroutine. Low variety and low analyzability indicate a craft technology, and high variety and high analyzability indicate an engineering technology. As a practical matter, most departments fit somewhere along the diagonal and can be most easily characterized as routine or nonroutine.

DEPARTMENT DESIGN

Once the nature of a department's technology has been identified, then the appropriate structure can be determined. Department technology tends to be associated with a cluster of departmental characteristics, such as the skill level of employees, formalization, and pattern of communication. Definite patterns do exist in the relationship between work unit technology and structural characteristics, which are associated with departmental performance.[40] Key relationships

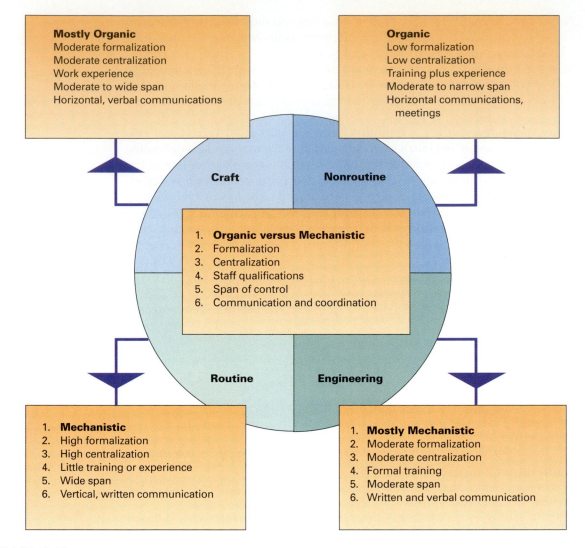

Mostly Organic
Moderate formalization
Moderate centralization
Work experience
Moderate to wide span
Horizontal, verbal communications

Organic
Low formalization
Low centralization
Training plus experience
Moderate to narrow span
Horizontal communications,
meetings

Craft   Nonroutine

1. **Organic versus Mechanistic**
2. Formalization
3. Centralization
4. Staff qualifications
5. Span of control
6. Communication and coordination

Routine   Engineering

1. **Mechanistic**
2. High formalization
3. High centralization
4. Little training or experience
5. Wide span
6. Vertical, written communication

1. **Mostly Mechanistic**
2. Moderate formalization
3. Moderate centralization
4. Formal training
5. Moderate span
6. Written and verbal communication

Exhibit 4.10

Relationship of De-partment Technology to Structural and Management Characteristics

between technology and other dimensions of departments are described in this section and are summarized in Exhibit 4.10.

1. Organic versus mechanistic. The single most persistent pattern is that routine technologies are associated with a mechanistic structure and processes and nonroutine technologies with an organic structure and processes. Formal rules and centralized management apply to routine units. When work is nonroutine, department administration is more organic and free-flowing. In the R&D lab at Datapoint Corporation, employees wear T-shirts and sandals, may wear beards, and ride to work on motorcycles. In the production department, employees wear more traditional dress, including shoes, shirts, and short haircuts, which reflects the more structured nature of the work.41

2. *Formalization.* Routine technology is characterized by standardization and division of labor into small tasks that are governed by formal rules and procedures. For nonroutine tasks, the structure is less formal and less standardized. When variety is high, as in a research department, fewer activities are covered by formal procedures.42

3. *Decentralization.* In routine technologies, most decision making about task activities is centralized to management.[43] In engineering technologies, employees with technical training tend to acquire moderate decision authority because technical knowledge is important to task accomplishment. Production employees who have long experience obtain decision authority in craft technologies because they know how to respond to problems. Decentralization to employees is greatest in nonroutine settings, where many decisions are made by employees.

4. *Worker skill level.* Work staff in routine technologies typically require little education or experience, which is congruent with repetitious work activities. In work units with greater variety, staff are more skilled and often have formal training in technical schools or universities. Training for craft activities, which are less analyzable, is more likely to be through job experience. Nonroutine activities require both formal education and job experience.[44]

5. *Span of control.* Span of control is the number of employees who report to a single manager or supervisor. This characteristic is normally influenced by departmental technology. The more complex and nonroutine the task, the more problems arise in which the supervisor becomes involved. Although the span of control may be influenced by other factors, such as skill level of employees, it typically should be smaller for complex tasks because on such tasks the supervisor and subordinate must interact frequently.[45]

6. *Communication and coordination.* Communication activity and frequency increase as task variety increases.[46] Frequent problems require more information sharing to solve problems and ensure proper completion of activities. The direction of communication is typically horizontal in nonroutine work units and vertical in routine work units.[47] The form of communication varies by task analyzability.[48] When tasks are highly analyzable, statistical and written forms of communication (memos, reports, rules, and procedures) are frequent. When tasks are less analyzable, information typically is conveyed face-to-face, over the telephone, or in group meetings.

Two important points are reflected in Exhibit 4.10. First, departments do differ from one another and can be categorized according to their workflow technology.[49] Second, structural and management processes differ based on departmental technology. Managers should design their departments so that requirements based on technology can be met. Design problems are most visible when the design is clearly inconsistent with technology. Studies have found that when structure and communication characteristics did not reflect technology, departments tended to be less effective.[50] Employees could not communicate with the frequency needed to solve problems. Sometimes employees have to deviate from misplaced rules to behave as needed to fit the technology, as in the following case.

*"M*A*S*H" Versus "E.R."*

In Practice 4.2

The *M*A*S*H* television series illustrated how well-intentioned army managers who imposed a tight, mechanistic structure on nonroutine hospital units worked against the requirements of the unit's technology. The humor in the *M*A*S*H* programs resulted from the efforts of Hawkeye, Potter, and O'Reilly to get their work done despite the army's bureaucracy, which was designed for routine infantry activities. Colonel Potter's ability to let the MASH unit run in free-flowing, organic fashion enabled the unit to be far more effective than would be the case if all rules and procedures were followed.[51]

The dramatic series *E.R.*, on the other hand, attempts to reveal the nature of the modern emergency room, where highly skilled employees have the authority to respond on their own initiative and discretion based on problems that arise. Following strict procedures would inhibit emergency room personnel from responding correctly to unexpected problems. Strict rules are appropriate, however, for routine hospital activities. Some of the tension in *E.R.* comes from the efforts of emergency room employees to maintain autonomy within a system that by necessity relies on rules and procedures.

WORKFLOW INTERDEPENDENCE AMONG DEPARTMENTS

So far, this chapter has explored how organization and department technologies influence structural design. The final characteristic of technology that influences structure is called interdependence. **Interdependence** means the extent to which departments depend on each other for resources or materials to accomplish their tasks. Low interdependence means that departments can do their work independently of each other and have little need for interaction, consultation, or exchange of materials. High interdependence means departments must constantly exchange resources.

Types

James Thompson defined three types of interdependence that influence organization structure.[52] These interdependencies are illustrated in Exhibit 4.11 and are discussed in the following sections.

Exhibit 4.11

Thompson's Classification of Interdependence and Management Implications

Form of Interdependence	Demands on Horizontal Communication, Decision Making	Type of Coordination Required	Priority for Locating Units Close Together
Pooled (bank) 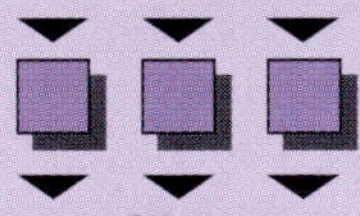 — Clients	Low communication	Standardization, rules, procedures	Low
Sequential (assembly line)  — Client	Medium communication	Plans, schedules, feedback	Medium
Reciprocal (hospital) 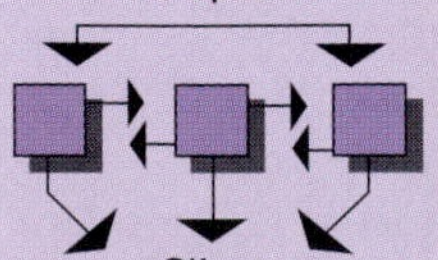 — Client	High communication	Mutual adjustment, cross-departmental meetings, teamwork	High

Pooled.   **Pooled interdependence** is the lowest form of interdependence among departments. In this form, work does not flow between units. Each department is part of the organization and contributes to the common good of the organization, but works independently. McDonald's restaurants or branch banks are examples of pooled interdependence. An outlet in Chicago need not interact with an outlet in Urbana. The connection between branches is that they share financial resources from a common pool, and the success of each branch contributes to the success of the organization.

Thompson proposed that pooled interdependence would exist in firms with what he called a mediating technology. A **mediating technology** provides products or services that mediate or link clients from the external environment and, in so doing, allows each department to work independently. Banks, brokerage firms, and real estate offices all mediate between buyers and sellers, but the offices work independently within the organization.

The management implications associated with pooled interdependence are quite simple. Thompson argued that managers should use rules and procedures to standardize activities across departments. Each department should use the same procedures and financial statements so the outcomes of all departments can be measured and pooled. Very little day-to-day coordination is required among units.

Sequential.   When interdependence is of serial form, with parts produced in one department becoming inputs to another department, then it is called **sequential interdependence**. The first department must perform correctly for the second department to perform correctly. This is a higher level of interdependence than pooled, because departments exchange resources and depend upon others to perform well.

Sequential interdependence occurs in what Thompson called **long-linked technology**, which "refers to the combination in one organization of successive stages of production; each stage of production uses as its inputs the production of the preceding stage and produces inputs for the following stage."[53] Large organizations that use assembly line production, such as in the automobile industry, use long-linked technologies and are characterized by sequential interdependence. For example, a labor strike by the UAW's Dayton, Ohio, local, where GM produces 90 percent of its brake assemblies, ultimately halted production at more than twenty General Motors assembly plants. Assembly plants were unable to continue work because they could not get the parts they needed.

The management requirements for sequential interdependence are more demanding than for pooled interdependence. Coordination among the linked plants or departments is required. Since the interdependence implies a one-way flow of materials, extensive planning and scheduling are generally needed. Plant B needs to know what to expect from Plant A so both can perform effectively. Some day-to-day communication among plants is also needed to handle unexpected problems and exceptions that arise.

Reciprocal.   The highest level of interdependence is **reciprocal interdependence**. This exists when the output of operation A is the input to operation B, and the output of operation B is the input back again to operation A. The outputs of departments influence those departments in reciprocal fashion.

Reciprocal interdependence tends to occur in organizations with what Thompson called **intensive technologies**, which provide a variety of products or services in combination to a client. Hospitals are an excellent example because they provide coordinated services to patients. A patient may move back and forth between X ray, surgery, and physical therapy as needed to be cured. A firm developing new products is another example. Intense coordination is needed between design, engineering, manufacturing, and marketing to combine all their resources to suit the customer's product need.

Management requirements are greatest in the case of reciprocal interdependence. The structure must allow for frequent horizontal communication and adjustment. Extensive planning is required in hospitals, for example, but plans will not anticipate or solve all problems. Daily interaction and mutual adjustment among departments are required. Managers from several departments are jointly involved in face-to-face coordination, teamwork, and decision making. Reciprocal interdependence is the most complex interdependence for organizations to handle.

Structural Priority

As indicated in Exhibit 4.11, since decision making, communication, and coordination problems are greatest for reciprocal interdependence, reciprocal interdependence should receive first priority in organization structure. New product development is one area of reciprocal interdependence that is of growing concern to managers as companies face increasing pressure to get new products to market fast. Many firms are revamping the design-manufacturing relationship by closely integrating computer-aided design (CAD) and computer-aided manufacturing (CAM) technologies discussed earlier in this chapter.[54] Activities that are reciprocally interdependent should be grouped close together in the organization so managers have easy access to one another for mutual adjustment. These units should report to the same person on the organization chart and should be physically close so the time and effort for coordination can be minimized. Poor coordination will result in poor performance for the organization. If the reciprocally interdependent units cannot be located close together, the organization should design mechanisms for coordination, such as daily meetings between departments or an electronic mail network to facilitate communication. The next priority is given to sequential interdependencies, and finally to pooled interdependencies.

This strategy of organizing keeps the communication channels short where coordination is most critical to organizational success. For example, Boise Cascade Corporation experienced poor service to customers because customer service reps located in New York City were not coordinating with production planners in Oregon plants. Customers couldn't get delivery as needed. Boise was reorganized, and the two groups were consolidated under one roof, reporting to the same supervisor at division headquarters. Now customer needs are met because customer service reps work with production planning to schedule customer orders.

Structural Implications

Most organizations experience various levels of interdependence, and structure can be designed to fit these needs, as illustrated in Exhibit 4.12.[55] In a manufacturing firm, new product development entails reciprocal interdependence among the design, engineering, purchasing, manufacturing, and sales departments. Perhaps a cross-departmental team could be formed to handle the back-

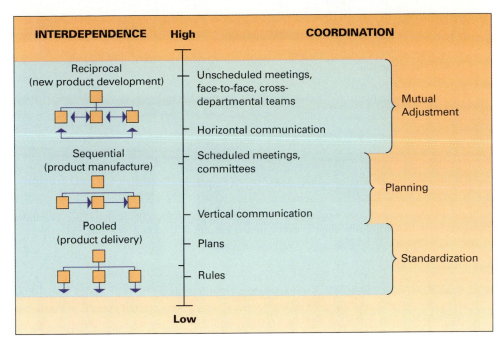

Source: Adapted from Andrew H. Van de Ven, Andre Delbecq, and Richard Koenig, "Determinants of Communication Modes within Organizations," *American Sociological Review* 41 (1976): 330.

Exhibit 4.12

Primary Means to Achieve Coordination for Different Levels of Task Interdependence in a Manufacturing Firm

and-forth flow of information and resources. Once a product is designed, its actual manufacture would be sequential interdependence, with a flow of goods from one department to another, such as among purchasing, inventory, production control, manufacturing, and assembly. The actual ordering and delivery of products is pooled interdependence, with warehouses working independently. Customers could place an order with the nearest facility, which would not require coordination among warehouses, except in unusual cases such as a stock outage.

When consultants analyzed NCR to learn why the development of new products was so slow, they followed the path from initial idea to implementation. The problem was that the development, production, and marketing of products took place in separate divisions, and communication across the three interdependent groups was difficult. NCR broke up its traditional organization structure and created several stand-alone units of about 500 people, each with its own development, production, and marketing people. This enabled new products to be introduced in record time.

A study of athletic teams reported that differences in team structure are closely related to interdependency among players. The following "In Practice" section illustrates how interdependence influences other aspects of baseball, football, and basketball teams.

Athletic Teams

In Practice 4.3

A major difference among baseball, football, and basketball is the interdependence among players. Baseball is low in interdependence, football is medium, and basketball represents the highest player interdependence. The relationships among interdependence and other characteristics of team play are illustrated in Exhibit 4.13.

	Baseball	**Football**	**Basketball**
Interdependence Physical dispersion of players	Pooled High	Sequential Medium	Reciprocal Low
Coordination	Rules that govern the sport	Game plan and position roles	Mutual adjustment and shared responsibility
Key management job	Select players and develop their skills	Prepare and execute game	Influence flow of game

Source: Based on William Passmore, Carol E. Francis, and Jeffrey Haldeman, "Sociotechnical Systems: A North American Reflection on the Empirical Studies of the 70s," *Human Relations* 35 (1982): 1179–1204.

Pete Rose said, "Baseball is a team game, but nine men who reach their individual goals make a nice team." In baseball, interdependence among team players is low and can be defined as pooled. Each member acts independently, taking a turn at bat and playing his or her own position. When interaction does occur, it is between only two or three players, as in a double play. Players are physically dispersed, and the rules of the game are the primary means of coordinating players. Players practice and develop their skills individually, such as by taking batting practice and undergoing physical conditioning. Management's job is to select good players. If each player is successful as an individual, the team should win.

In football, interdependence among players is higher and tends to be sequential. The line first blocks the opponents to enable the backs to run or pass. Plays are performed sequentially from first down to fourth down. Physical dispersion is medium, which allows players to operate as a coordinated unit. The primary mechanism for coordinating players is developing a game plan along with rules that govern the behavior of team members. Each player has an assignment that fits with other assignments, and management designs the game plan to achieve victory.

In basketball, interdependence tends to be reciprocal. The game is free-flowing, and the division of labor is less precise than in other sports. Each player is involved in both offense and defense, handles the ball, and attempts to score. The ball flows back and forth among players. Team members interact in a dynamic flow to achieve victory. Management skills involve the ability to influence this dynamic process, either by substituting players or by working the ball into certain areas. Players must learn to adapt to the flow of the game and to one another as events unfold.

Interdependence among players is a primary factor explaining the difference among the three sports. Baseball is organized around an autonomous individual, football around groups that are sequentially interdependent, and basketball around the free flow of reciprocal players.[56]

ADVANCED INFORMATION TECHNOLOGY

Organizations have rapidly moved from the computer age to the information age, brought about by the microprocessor revolution. A typical microprocessor contains semiconductor chips that can execute tens of thousands of calculations in the blink of an eye, all in a space no larger than a fingernail. This revolution enabled the emergence of computer-integrated manufacturing (CIM) systems described earlier in this chapter.

Microprocessors also enabled the disaggregation of large centralized computers into personal computers and workstations scattered around the organization, each having enormous computing power. Moreover, the solitary machines have become networks of interacting computers that greatly magnify their power and impact. Indeed, the impact of advanced information technologies on the administrative side of organizations is just as significant as that of CIM technologies on manufacturing. New corporate structures have combined with advanced information technology to increase productivity in many corporations.[57]

Those aspects of **advanced information technology** (AIT) most significant for administration are executive information systems, groupware, and workflow automation. An **executive information system** is the use of computer technology to support the information needs of senior managers. For example, the CEO of Duracell was able to use his personal computer to compare the performance of work forces in the United States and overseas. His computer produced a crisp table in color showing differences in productivity. Digging for more data, he discovered that overseas salespeople were spending too much time calling on small stores, prompting a decision to service small stores in less expensive ways.[58] Executive information systems have the capacity for supporting nonroutine decisions, such as company strategy and competitive responses.

Groupware enables employees on a network to interact with one another through their personal computers. The simplest form of groupware is *electronic mail,* which allows one-on-one communication from one PC to another. Other, more complex groupware programs allow numerous employees to communicate simultaneously. For example, a team of employees might sit around a conference table or even remain in their separate offices while each uses a computer terminal through which the comments of other members are registered. All participants may view the same display on their screens, thereby removing communication barriers in group meetings and facilitating the sharing of information.[59]

Workflow automation is a growing niche in advanced information technology. Workflow software enables computer networks to automatically send documents, such as invoices, check requests, or customer inquiries, to the correct location for processing. For example, an expense report can be filled out on a computer, which checks the details, alerts the appropriate manager for review, then prints the check and notifies the employee by electronic mail where to pick it up. Workflow automation allows the entire procedure to be completed via computer, without a single employee ever having to handle a paper document. The Federal National Mortgage Association (Fannie Mae) is linking three thousand lenders by computer and developing software that will cut processing time by putting the whole operation on computer networks. The paperless system not only cuts costs but improves customer service as well. Workflow automation also enables small companies to handle paperwork jobs that only firms with large numbers of employees could do in the past.[60]

For management, the rapid advancements in information technology call for new decisions on how it should be used in the organization. AIT makes the organization and the external environment more transparent to top managers. Should they use this power to centralize and tightly control the organization, or should they provide employees with the information needed to act autonomously? AIT can give employees all kinds of data about their customers, market, service, and efficiency. Some organizations use the new technology to simply reinforce rigid hierarchies, centralize decision making, and routinize work. For the most part, however, successful organizations are using this technology to decentralize, and its impact is being felt on management processes, organization design, and workplace culture.

Management Implications

Advanced information technology enables managers to be better connected with the organization, the environment, and each other. Specific improvements in management processes are:

1. *Broader participation in decision making.* Communication among managers takes time and effort, and AIT greatly reduces this effort, especially when managers are physically separated. For example, a product developer sent an electronic message asking for suggestions for a new product feature. He received more than 150 messages from every corner of the organization, almost all from people he did not know.[61] Moreover, research shows that AIT increases contact between the top of the organization and the bottom. Lower-level managers can communicate directly with the CEO, and a vice president can communicate directly with a project engineer. At Mrs. Fields, Inc., the world's largest retailer of cookies, branch employees use electronic mail to communicate directly to CEO Debbi Fields their opinions about products, competitors, and customer reactions. "On-line" at Wright-Patterson Air Force Base in Ohio, enlisted personnel can send messages directly to colonels, a level of communication that would have been unheard of five years ago.[62]

2. *Faster decision making.* AIT uses less of the organization's time for decision-related meetings.[63] The technology also reduces the time required to authorize organizational actions. Messages are handled fewer times, and interested parties can communicate directly. For example, Xerox dramatically reduced meeting time with its new computer system. Prior to a presentation, papers are no longer sent back and forth. Each unit submits a plan electronically five days in advance, which each top executive reads before the meeting. The meeting itself is short because time is spent on substantive issues.

3. *Better organizational intelligence, including more rapid identification of problems and opportunities.*[64] With AIT, organizational activities become visible to managers. For example, sales and market research data are now available from grocery store checkout scanners. Organizations can purchase access to hundreds of databases about industry, financial, and demographic patterns in their environments. AIT enables the accumulation and widespread communication of a larger volume as well as a larger range of information. For example, at MTV Networks, groupware became a new weapon for the affiliate sales force. When MTV was battling against rival Turner Broadcasting System's Cartoon Channel, trying to get operators to carry MTV's Comedy Central instead, salespeople encountered unexpectedly strong resistance. A saleswoman in Chicago discovered a cable system in her area had been offered a special two-year rock-bottom price by the Cartoon Channel. She shared this intelligence on the computer network so other salespeople could research pricing in their own areas. Ultimately MTV's top managers were able to counterattack by offering their own special pricing and terms, helping to close several deals that appeared lost.[65]

Organization Design

The impact of advanced information technology on the administrative structure of organizations is now being felt. Specific outcomes are:

1. *Flatter organization structure.* AIT has been enabling the lean structures many organizations are adopting. One organization in London that used information technology to empower employees rather than maintain a rigid hierarchy reduced the structure from thirteen to four layers. Hercules, a chemical company, adopted a combination of electronic messaging and groupware, after which the number of management levels between the president and plant foreman was reduced from a dozen to about seven, yet decision speed and effectiveness improved. New information technology has enabled Aetna Life and Casualty Company's sales force to replace its old hierarchy of supervisors and agents with small work teams.[66]

2. *Greater centralization or decentralization.* Depending on manager choices, AIT can either centralize or decentralize the organization. Managers who want to centralize can use the technology to acquire more information and make more decisions, often with greater responsiveness than previously. Likewise, managers can decentralize information to employees and increase participation and autonomy.[67] Management philosophy and corporate culture have substantial bearing on how AIT influences decision making, but enlightened companies seem to use it to empower employees whenever possible. For example, at the Chesebrough-Ponds, Inc. plant in Jefferson City, Missouri, line workers routinely tap the company's computer network to track shipments, schedule their own workloads, order production increases, and perform other functions that used to be the province of management.

3. *Improved coordination.* Perhaps one of the great outcomes of AIT is the ability to connect managers even when offices or stores are scattered worldwide. At Chase Manhattan Bank, groupware links 5,200 bankers throughout the world. The new technology enables managers to communicate with one another and be aware of organization activities and outcomes. It can help to break down barriers and create a sense of team and organizational identity that was not previously available, especially when people work at different locations.[68]

4. *Fewer narrow tasks.* Fewer administrative tasks under AIT will be subject to narrowly defined policies and job descriptions. Companies using AIT will closely resemble professional service firms. Remaining administrative and clerical tasks will provide intellectual engagement and more challenging work.[69]

5. *Larger professional staff ratio.* The implementation of sophisticated information systems means that employees have to be highly trained and professional to both operate and maintain such systems. For the most part, unskilled employees will be replaced by the new technology, such as when the North American Banking Group installed a customer service information system that shifted the staff mix from 30 percent professionals to 60 percent professionals. Many clerical personnel were replaced by AIT. Fewer employees were needed to type letters, file memos, and fill out forms. Middle- and upper-level managers can use the new technology to type their own memos and send them instantly through electronic mail.

The following example describes how information technology has changed the way Taco Bell operates.

In Practice 4.4	*Taco Bell*

When Susan Cramm was hired to develop a comprehensive technology strategy for PepsiCo's Taco Bell division, she focused on using advanced information technology to control costs and help employees do their jobs better by giving them the tools they needed to make smarter decisions. Her first challenge was revamping the way stores estimated labor needs for the coming week. Cramm knew local stores didn't really need help from headquarters to make their labor estimates, but she knew top management wouldn't give up control easily.

Cramm convinced a senior vice-president to endorse a test in fifty Taco Bells around the country. Local stores entered their sales data into computers and then zapped the data off to headquarters via modem, where a software program calculated labor needs on a restaurant-by-restaurant basis. The 1.5 percent reduction in labor costs per store persuaded top executives the new technology was worth further development. Eventually, each Taco Bell store was provided a copy of the labor scheduling software, so that local stores could make their own scheduling decisions without running their numbers through headquarters. Cramm then turned to implementing information technology in other operational areas—for example, a program that allows product usage to be monitored by computer, so ingredients can be shipped to stores just as they are needed.

Today, many Taco Bell stores are run by self-directed teams, with team members trained to handle all functions so they can rotate jobs. Information technology enables the sharing of information and coordination of tasks that make job rotation and employee participation possible. The new technology has contributed to a flatter organization and decentralization, with teams of front-line employees empowered to make decisions. Employees enjoy more challenging work because they have the information and training to perform a variety of jobs. In addition, the new technology has improved coordination among stores and between local stores and headquarters. The new systems increase efficiency and employee participation and enable workers to focus more time and energy on pleasing customers.[70]

Workplace Culture

All these changes in management processes and organization design also mean changes in office life. Corporate culture often changes with the introduction of advanced information technology. Depending on the approach of management, this can lead to a sense of empowerment when employees are given increased access to information previously available only to their bosses or to a loss of privacy for employees whose bosses now keep tabs on their every move. Relationships among workers are also affected when managers decide who within the organization should have access to what information and who should communicate with whom. It is important to remember that advanced information technology affects not just the structure of an organization but the people within it. In the following section, we will examine the impact of advanced information technology on people and jobs.

IMPACT OF TECHNOLOGY ON JOB DESIGN

So far, this chapter has described models for analyzing how manufacturing, service, department, and information technologies influence structure and management processes. The relation between a new technology and organization seems to follow a pattern, beginning with immediate effects on the content of jobs followed (after a longer period) by impact on design of the organization. The ultimate impact of technology on employees can be partially understood through the concepts of job design and sociotechnical systems.

Job Design

Research has studied whether new technologies tend to simplify or enrich jobs. New technologies change how jobs are done and the very nature of jobs.[71] Mass production technologies, for example, produce **job simplification**, meaning the number and difficulty of tasks performed by a single person are reduced. The consequence is boring, repetitive jobs that provide little satisfaction. More advanced technologies have caused **job enrichment**, meaning the jobs are designed to increase responsibility, recognition, and opportunities for growth and achievement.

Recent studies found that the introduction of computer-integrated manufacturing, for example, has had three noticeable results: greater opportunities for intellectual mastery and cognitive skills for workers; more worker responsibility for results; and greater interdependence among workers, enabling more social interaction and the development of teamwork and coordination skills.[72] One large bank that moved from a batch processing system to a fully on-line data entry transaction system found that teller skills became mental rather than manual, workers' increased feelings of responsibility for the whole task caused a sharp decrease in errors, and interdependence among workers resulted in workers helping one another find errors and improve their skills and accuracy.[73] A study of advanced information technology found that employees had to acquire higher-level skills to extract information from data and give it meaning rather than do activities based on physical labor.[74] Research also indicates that workers who are using advanced technologies generally earn 10 percent to 15 percent more than those who don't.[75] Thus, the findings about new technologies are encouraging, suggesting that jobs for workers are enriched rather than simplified, engaging higher mental capacities and providing greater satisfaction and income.

Sociotechnical Systems

The **sociotechnical systems approach** combines the needs of people with the needs of technical efficiency. The *socio* portion of the approach refers to the people and groups who work in organizations and how work roles are organized and coordinated. The *technical* portion of the approach refers to the materials, tools, machines, and processes used to transform organizational inputs into outputs.[76] The goal of the sociotechnical approach is **joint optimization**, which states that an organization will function best only if its social and technical systems are designed to fit the needs of one another.[77] Designing the structure to meet human needs while ignoring the technical system, or changing technology to improve efficiency while ignoring human needs, may inadvertently cause performance problems.

Sociotechnical principles evolved from work by the Tavistock Institute, a research organization in England, during the 1950s and 1960s.[78] Examples of organizational changes using sociotechnical principles have occurred in a railway maintenance depot, textile mills, a pet food plant, and new plants using computer-integrated manufacturing technologies.[79] In most of these applications, the joint optimization of changes in technology and structure to meet the needs of people as well as efficiency improves performance, safety, quality, absenteeism, and turnover. In some cases, work design was not the most efficient based on technical and scientific principles, but worker involvement and commitment more than made up for the difference. Thus, once again research shows that new technologies need not have a negative impact on workers, because the technology often requires higher-level mental and social skills and can be organized to encourage the involvement and commitment of employees, thereby benefiting both the employee and the organization.

The sociotechnical systems principle that people should be viewed as resources and provided with appropriate skills, meaningful work, and suitable rewards becomes even more important in today's world of growing technological complexity.[80] One recent study of paper manufacturers found that organizations that put too much faith in machines and technology and pay little attention to the appropriate management of people do not achieve advances in productivity and flexibility. Today's most successful companies strive to find the right mix of machines, computer systems, and people and the most effective way to coordinate them.[81] Systems based on maximum technical efficiency, tight top-down control, and assumptions that workers are irresponsible and mindless are increasingly ineffective.

Although many principles of sociotechnical systems theory are still valid, current scholars and researchers are also arguing for an expansion of the approach to capture the dynamic nature of today's organizations, the chaotic environment, and the shift from routine to nonroutine jobs brought about by advances in information technology.[82]

SUMMARY AND INTERPRETATION

This chapter reviewed several frameworks and key research findings on the topic of organizational technology. The potential importance of technology as a factor in organizational structure was discovered during the 1960s. During the 1970s and 1980s, a flurry of research activity was undertaken to understand more precisely the relationship of technology to other characteristics of organizations.

Five ideas in the technology literature stand out. The first is Woodward's research into manufacturing technology. Woodward went into organizations and collected practical data on technology characteristics, organization structure, and management systems. She found clear relationships between technology and structure in high-performing organizations. Her findings are so clear that managers can analyze their own organizations on the same dimensions of technology and structure. In addition, technology and structure can be co-aligned with organizational strategy to meet changing needs and provide new competitive advantages.

The second important idea is that service technologies differ in a systematic way from manufacturing technologies. Service technologies are characterized by intangible outcomes and direct client involvement in the production process. Service firms do not have the fixed, machine-based technologies that appear in manufacturing organizations; hence, organization design often differs also.

The third significant idea is Perrow's framework applied to department technologies. Understanding the variety and analyzability of a technology tells one about the management style, structure, and process that should characterize that department. Routine technologies are characterized by mechanistic structure and nonroutine technologies by organic structure. Applying the wrong management system to a department will result in dissatisfaction and reduced efficiency.

The fourth important idea is interdependence among departments. The extent to which departments depend on each other for materials, information, or other resources determines the amount of coordination required between them. As interdependence increases, demands on the organization for coordination increase. Organization design must allow for the correct amount of communication and coordination to handle interdependence across departments.

The fifth important idea is that new technologies—computer-integrated manufacturing and advanced information technologies—are being adopted by organizations and having impact on organization design. For the most part, the impact is positive, with shifts toward more organic structures both on the shop floor and in the management hierarchy. These technologies replace routine jobs, give employees more autonomy, produce more challenging jobs, encourage teamwork, and let the organization be more flexible and responsive. The new technologies are enriching jobs to the point where organizations are happier places to work.

Several principles of sociotechnical systems theory, which attempts to design the technical and human aspects of an organization to fit one another, are increasingly important as advances in technology alter the nature of jobs and social interaction in today's companies.

Key Concepts

advanced information technology
analyzability
computer-integrated manufacturing
continuous process production
craft technology
engineering technology
executive information system
groupware
intensive technology
interdependence
job enrichment
job simplification
joint optimization
large-batch production

long-linked technology
mediating technology
nonroutine technology
pooled interdependence
reciprocal interdependence
routine technology
sequential interdependence
service technology
small-batch production
sociotechnical systems approach
technical complexity
technology
variety
workflow automation

Discussion Questions

1. Where would your university or college department be located on Perrow's technology framework? Look for the underlying variety and analyzability characteristics when making your assessment. Would a department devoted exclusively to teaching be put in a different quadrant from a department devoted exclusively to research?

2. Explain Thompson's levels of interdependence. Identify an example of each level of interdependence in the university or college setting. What kinds of coordination mechanisms should an administration develop to handle each level of interdependence?

3. Describe Woodward's classification of organizational technologies. Explain why each of the three technology groups is related differently to organization structure and management processes.

4. What relationships did Woodward discover between supervisor span of control and technological complexity?

5. How does computer-integrated manufacturing differ from other manufacturing technologies? What is the primary advantage of CIM?

6. What is a service technology? Are different types of service technologies likely to be associated with different structures? Explain.

7. Edna Peterson is a colonel in the air force in charge of the finance section of an air base in New Mexico. Financial work in the military involves large amounts of routine matters and paperwork, and Peterson gradually developed a philosophy of management that was fairly mechanistic. She believed that all important decisions should be made by administrators, that elaborate rules and procedures should be developed and followed, and that subordinates should have little discretion and should be tightly controlled. The finance section is about to introduce advanced information technology that will take over most paperwork. Based on what you know about AIT, what advice would you give Edna Peterson?

8. A top executive claimed that top-level management is a craft technology because the work contains intangibles, such as handling personnel, interpreting the environment, and coping with unusual situations that have to be learned through experience. If this is true, is it appropriate to teach management in a business school? Does teaching management from a textbook assume that the manager's job is analyzable, and hence that formal training rather than experience is most important?

9. In which quadrant of Perrow's framework would a mass production technology be placed? Where would small-batch and continuous process technologies be placed? Why? Would Perrow's framework lead to the same recommendation about organic versus mechanistic structures that Woodward made?

10. To what extent does the development of new manufacturing and information technologies simplify and routinize the jobs of employees? Discuss.

Briefcase

As an organization manager, keep these guides in mind:

1. Relate organization structure to technology. Use the two dimensions of variety and analyzability to discover whether the work in a department is routine or nonroutine. If the work in a department is routine, use a mechanistic structure and process. If the work in a department is nonroutine, use an organic management process. Exhibit 4.10 illustrates this relationship between department technology and organization structure.

2. Use the categories developed by Woodward to diagnose whether the production technology in a manufacturing firm is small-batch, mass production, or continuous process. Use a more organic structure with small-batch or continuous process technologies, and with new computer-integrated manufacturing systems. Use a mechanistic structure with mass production technologies. When adopting a new technology, realign strategy, structure, and management processes to achieve top performance.

3. Use the concept of service technology to evaluate the production process in nonmanufacturing firms. Service technologies are intangible and must be located close to the customer. Hence, service organizations may have an organization structure with fewer boundary roles, greater geographical dispersion, decentralization, highly skilled employees in the technical core, and generally less control than in manufacturing organizations.

4. Evaluate the interdependencies among organizational departments. Use the general rule that, as interdependencies increase, mechanisms for coordination must also increase.

5. Analyze organizational and employee requirements when introducing advanced information technologies. Plan for greater participation in decision making, faster decisions, better organizational intelligence, a flatter organization, improved coordination, greater professional staff ratio, and more broadly defined tasks. AIT generally leads to job enrichment in much the same way as computer-integrated manufacturing. With both manufacturing and information technologies, the sociotechnical systems approach can be used to define the optimal fit between the social needs of employees and the technical needs of the organization.

Chapter Four Workbook *Bistro Technology**

You will be analyzing the technology used in three different restaurants—McDonald's, Burger King, and a typical family restaurant. Your instructor will tell you whether to do this assignment as individuals or in a group.

You must visit all three restaurants and infer how the work is done, according to the following criteria. You are not allowed to "interview" any employees, but instead you will be an observer. Take lots of notes when you are there.

*Adapted loosely by Dorothy Marcic from "Hamburger Technology," in Douglas T. Hall, et al., *Experiences in Management and Organizational Behavior,* 2nd ed. (New York: Wiley, 1982) 244–47, as well as "Behavior, Technology, and Work Design" in A.B. Shani and James B. Lau, *Behavior in Organizations* (Chicago: Irwin, 1996), M16–23–M16-26.

	McDonald's	Burger King	Family restaurant
Organization goals: Speed, service, atmosphere, etc.			
Authority structure			
Type of technology using Woodward's model			
Organization structure: Mechanistic or organic?			
Team versus individual: Do people work together or alone?			
Interdependence: How do employees depend on each other?			
Tasks: Routine versus nonroutine			
Specialization of tasks by employees			
Standardization: How varied are tasks and products?			
Expertise required: Technical versus social			
Decision making: Centralized versus decentralized			

Questions

1. Is the technology used the best one for each restaurant, considering its goals and environment?
2. From the preceding data, determine if the structure and other characteristics fit the technology.
3. If you were part of a consulting team assigned to improve the operations of each organization, what recommendations would you make?

Case for Analysis *Acetate Department**

The Acetate Department's product consisted of about twenty different kinds of viscous liquid acetate used by another department to manufacture transparent film to be left clear, or coated with photographic emulsion or iron oxide.

Before the change: The Department was located in an old four-story building as in Exhibit 4.14. The work flow was as follows:

1. Twenty kinds of powder arrived daily in 50 pound paper bags. In addition, storage tanks of liquid would be filled weekly from tank trucks.
2. Two or three Acetate Helpers would jointly unload pallets of bags into the storage area using a lift truck.
3. Several times a shift, the Helpers would bring the bagged material up the elevator to the third floor where it would be temporarily stored along the walls.
4. Mixing batches was under the direction of the Group Leader and was rather like baking a cake. Following a prescribed formula, the Group Leader, Mixers and Helpers operated valves to feed in the proper solvent and manually dump in the proper weight and mixture of solid material. The glob would be mixed by giant egg beaters and heated according to the recipe.

5. When the batch was completed, it was pumped to a finished product storage tank.
6. After completing each batch, the crew would thoroughly clean the work area of dust and empty bags because cleanliness was extremely important to the finished product.

To accomplish this work, the Department was structured as in Exhibit 4.15.

The Helpers were usually young men 18-25 years of age, the Mixers 25 to 40, and the Group Leaders and Foremen 40 to 60. Foremen were on salary, Group Leaders, Mixers and Helpers on hourly pay.

To produce 20,000,000 pounds of product per year, the Department operated 24 hours a day, 7 days a week. Four crews rotated shifts: for example, Shift Foreman A and his two Group Leaders and crews would work two weeks on the day shift 8:00 A.M. to 4:00 P.M., then two weeks on the evening shift 4:00 P.M. to midnight, then two weeks on the night shift midnight to 8:00 A.M. There were two days off between shift changes.

*From "Redesigning the Acetate Department," by David L. Hampton, Charles E. Summer, and Ross A. Webber, *Organizational Behavior and the Practice of Management* (Glenview, IL: Scott, Foresman and Company, 1982), 751–55. Used with permission.

Exhibit 4.14

Elevation View of Acetate Department Before Change

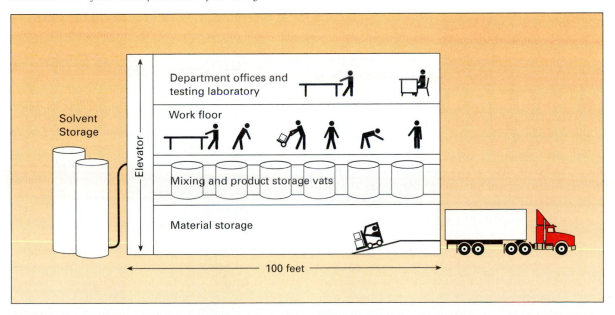

Exhibit 4.15

Organizational Chart of Acetate Department Before Change

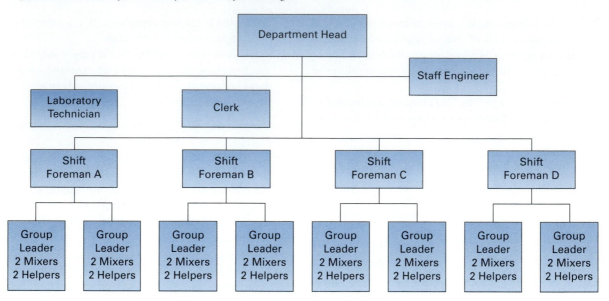

During a typical shift, a Group Leader and his crew would complete two or three batches. A batch would frequently be started on one shift and completed by the next shift crew. There was slightly less work on the evening and night shifts because no deliveries were made, but these crews engaged in a little more cleaning. The Shift Foreman would give instructions to the two Group Leaders at the beginning of each shift as to the status of batches in process, batches to be mixed, what deliveries were expected and what cleaning was to be done. Periodically throughout the shift, the Foreman would collect samples in small bottles, which he would leave at the laboratory technicians' desk for testing.

The management and office staff (Department Head, Staff Engineer, Lab Technician, and Department Clerk) only worked on the day shift, although if an emergency arose on the other shifts, the Foreman might call.

All in all, the Department was a pleasant place in which to work. The work floor was a little warm, but well-lighted, quiet and clean. Substantial banter and horseplay occurred when the crew wasn't actually loading batches, particularly on the nonday shifts. The men had a dartboard in the work area and competition was fierce and loud. Frequently a crew would go bowling right after work, even at 1:00 A.M., for the community's alleys were open 24 hours a day. Department turnover and absenteeism were low. Most employees spent their entire career with the Company, many in one department. The corporation was large, paternalistic, well-paying, and offered attractive fringe benefits including

large, virtually automatic bonuses for all. Then came the change. . . .

The new system: To improve productivity, the Acetate Department was completely redesigned; the technology changed from batches to continuous processing. The basic building was retained, but substantially modified as in Exhibit 4.16. The modified work flow is as follows:

1. Most solid raw materials are delivered via trucks in large aluminum bins holding 500 pounds.
2. One Handler (formerly Helper) is on duty at all times in the first floor to receive raw materials and to dump the bins into the semi-automatic screw feeder.
3. The Head Operator (former Group Leader) directs the mixing operations from his control panel on the fourth floor located along one wall across from the Department Offices. The mixing is virtually an automatic operation once the solid material has been sent up the screw feed; a tape program opens and closes the necessary valves to add solvent, heat, mixing, etc. Sitting at a table before his panel, the Head Operator monitors the process to see that everything is operating within specified temperatures and pressures.

This technical change allowed the Department to greatly reduce its manpower. The new structure is illustrated in Exhibit 4.17. One new position was created, that of a pump operator who is located in a small separate shack about 300 feet from the main building. He

Exhibit 4.16

Elevation View of Acetate Department After Change

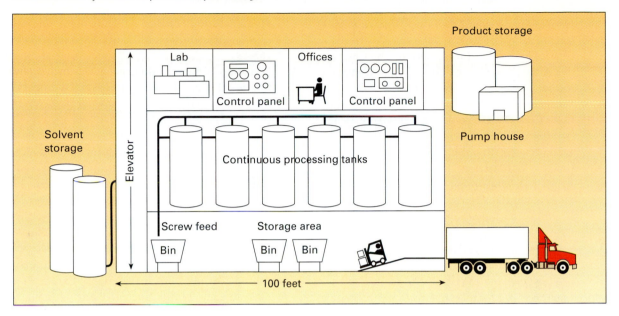

operates pumps and valves that move the finished product among various storage tanks.

Under the new system, production capacity was increased to 25,000,000 pounds per year. All remaining employees received a 15 percent increase in pay. Former personnel not retained in the Dope Department were transferred to other departments in the company. No one was dismissed.

Unfortunately, actual output has lagged well below capacity in the several months since the construction work and technical training was completed. Actual production is virtually identical with that under the old technology. Absenteeism has increased markedly, and several judgmental errors by operators have resulted in substantial losses.

Exhibit 4.17

Organizational Chart of Acetate Department After Change

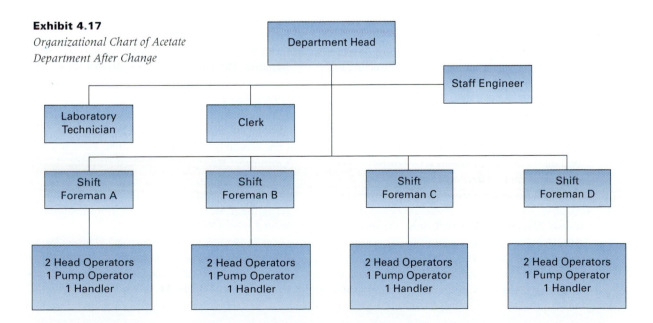

Notes

1. Hal Plotkin, "Riches From Rags," *Inc. Technology* (Summer 1995): 62–67.

2. Charles Perrow, "A Framework for the Comparative Analysis of Organizations," *American Sociological Review* 32 (1967): 194–208; Denise M. Rosseau, "Assessment of Technology in Organizations: Closed versus Open Systems Approaches," *Academy of Management Review* 4 (1979): 531–42.

3. Linda Argote, "Input Uncertainty and Organizational Coordination in Hospital Emergency Units," *Administrative Science Quarterly* 27 (1982): 420–34; Charles Perrow, *Organizational Analysis: A Sociological Approach* (Belmont, Calif.: Wadsworth, 1970); William Rushing, "Hardness of Material as Related to the Division of Labor in Manufacturing Industries," *Administrative Science Quarterly* 13 (1968): 229–45.

4. Lawrence B. Mohr, "Organizational Technology and Organization Structure," *Administrative Science Quarterly* 16 (1971): 444–59; David Hickson, Derek Pugh, and Diana Pheysey, "Operations Technology and Organization Structure: An Empirical Reappraisal," *Administrative Science Quarterly* 14 (1969): 378–97.

5. Joan Woodward, *Industrial Organization: Theory and Practice* (London: Oxford University Press, 1965); Joan Woodward, *Management and Technology* (London: Her Majesty's Stationery Office, 1958).

6. Hickson, Pugh, and Pheysey, "Operations Technology and Organization Structure"; James D. Thompson, *Organizations in Action* (New York: McGraw-Hill, 1967).

7. Edward Harvey, "Technology and the Structure of Organizations," *American Sociological Review* 33 (1968): 241–59.

8. Wanda J. Orlikowski, "The Duality of Technology: Rethinking the Concept of Technology in Organizations," *Organization Science* 3 (1992): 398–427.

9. Based on Woodward, *Industrial Organization* and *Management and Technology*.

10. Woodward, *Industrial Organization*, vi.

11. William L. Zwerman, *New Perspectives on Organizational Theory* (Westport, Conn.: Greenwood, 1970); Harvey, "Technology and the Structure of Organizations," 241–59.

12. Dean M. Schroeder, Steven W. Congden, and C. Gopinath, "Linking Competitive Strategy and Manufacturing Process Technology," *Journal of Management Studies* 32, no. 2 (March 1995): 163–89.

13. Fernando F. Suarez, Michael A. Cusumano, and Charles H. Fine, "An Empirical Study of Flexibility in Manufacturing," *Sloan Management Review* (Fall 1995): 25–32.

14. Raymond F. Zammuto and Edward J. O'Connor, "Gaining Advanced Manufacturing Technologies' Benefits: The Roles of Organization Design and Culture," *Academy of Management Review* 17, no. 4 (1992): 701–28; Dean Schroeder, Steven W. Congdon, and C. Gopinath, "Linking Competitive Strategy and Manufacturing Process Technology."

15. David Wessel, "Pilgrim and Millstone, Two Nuclear Plants, Have Disparate Fates," *Wall Street Journal*, 28 July 1987, 1, 18; Arlen J. Large, "Federal Agency Prods Nuclear-Plant Official to Raise Performance," *Wall Street Journal*, 10 May 1984, 1, 22.

16. Wessel, "Pilgrim and Millstone."

17. Jack R. Meredith, "The Strategic Advantages of the Factory of the Future," *California Management Review* 29 (Spring 1987): 27–41; Jack Meredith, "The Strategic Advantages of the New Manufacturing Technologies for Small Firms," *Strategic Management Journal* 8 (1987): 249–58; Althea Jones and Terry Webb, "Introducing Computer Integrated Manufacturing," *Journal of General Management* 12 (Summer 1987): 60–74.

18. Raymond F. Zammuto and Edward J. O'Connor, "Gaining Advanced Manufacturing Technologies' Benefits: The Roles of Organization Design and Culture," *Academy of Management Review* 17 (1992): 701–28.

19. John S. DeMott, "Small Factories' Big Lessons," *Nation's Business* (April 1995): 29–30.

20. Paul S. Adler, "Managing Flexible Automation," *California Management Review* (Spring 1988): 34–56.

21. Bela Gold, "Computerization in Domestic and International Manufacturing," *California Management Review* (Winter 1989): 129–43.

22. Graham Dudley and John Hassard, "Design Issues in the Development of Computer Integrated Manufacturing (CIM)," *Journal of General Management* 16 (1990): 43–53.

23. John Holusha, "Can Boeing's New Baby Fly Financially?" *New York Times*, 27 March 1994, Section 3, 1, 6.

24. Joel D. Goldhar and David Lei, "Variety is Free: Manufacturing In the Twenty-First Century," *Academy of Management Executive* 9, no. 4 (1995): 73–86.

25. Len Estrin, "The Dawn of Manufacturing," *Enterprise* (April 1994): 31–35; Otis Port, "The Responsive Factory," *Business Week/Enterprise* (1993): 48–52.

26. Joel D. Goldhar and David Lei, "Variety is Free: Manufacturing In the Twenty-First Century."

27. Meredith, "Strategic Advantages of the Factory of the Future."

28. Patricia L. Nemetz and Louis W. Fry, "Flexible Manufacturing Organizations: Implementations for Strategy Formulation and Organization Design," *Academy of Management Review* 13 (1988): 627–38; Paul S. Adler, "Managing Flexible Automation," *California Management Review* (Spring 1988): 34–56; Jeremy Main, "Manufacturing the Right Way," *Fortune*, 21 May 1990, 54–64; Frank M. Hull and Paul D. Collins, "High-Technology Batch Production Systems: Woodward's Missing Type," *Academy of Management Journal* 30 (1987): 786–97.

29. Joel D. Goldhar and David Lei, "Variety Is Free: Manufacturing In The Twenty-First Century"; P. Robert Duimering, Frank Safayeni, and Lyn Purdy, "Integrated Manufacturing: Redesign the Organization before Implementing Flexible Technology," *Sloan Management Review* (Summer 1993): 47–56; Zammuto and O'Connor, "Gaining Advanced Manufacturing Technologies' Benefits."

30. Len Estrin, "The Dawn of Manufacturing," *Enterprise*, (April 1994): 31–35.

31. Joel D. Goldhar and David Lei, "Variety is Free: Manufacturing In the Twenty-First Century," *Academy of Management Executive* 9, no. 4 (1995): 73–86.

32. Ronald Henkoff, "Service Is Everybody's Business," *Fortune*, 27 June 1994, 48–60; Ronald Henkoff, "Finding, Training, and Keeping the Best Service Workers," *Fortune*, 3 October 1994, 110–22.

33. David E. Bowen, Caren Siehl, and Benjamin Schneider, "A Framework for Analyzing Customer Service Orientations in Manufacturing," *Academy of Management Review* 14 (1989): 79–95; Peter K. Mills and Newton Margulies, "Toward a Core Typology of Service Organizations," *Academy of Management Review* 5 (1980): 255–65; Peter K. Mills and Dennis J. Moberg, "Perspectives on the Technology of Service Operations," *Academy of Management Review* 7 (1982): 467–78; G. Lynn Shostack, "Breaking Free from Product Marketing," *Journal of Marketing* (April 1977): 73–80.

34. Ronald Henkoff, "Service Is Everybody's Business," *Fortune*, 27 June 1994, 48–60.

35. Richard B. Chase and David A. Tansik, "The Customer Contact Model for Organization Design," *Management Science* 29 (1983): 1037–50.

36. *Ibid.*

37. David E. Bowen and Edward E. Lawler III, "The Empowerment of Service Workers: What, Why, How, and When," *Sloan Management Review* (Spring 1992): 31–39; Gregory B. Northcraft and Richard B. Chase, "Managing Service Demand at the Point of Delivery," *Academy of Management Review* 10 (1985): 66–75; Roger W. Schmenner, "How Can Service Businesses Survive and Prosper?" *Sloan Management Review* 27 (Spring 1986): 21–32.

38. Perrow, "Framework for Comparative Analysis" and *Organizational Analysis*.

39. Michael Withey, Richard L. Daft, and William C. Cooper, "Measures of Perrow's Work Unit Technology: An Empirical Assessment and a New Scale," *Academy of Management Journal* 25 (1983): 45–63.

40. Christopher Gresov, "Exploring Fit and Misfit with Multiple Contingencies," *Administrative Science Quarterly* 34 (1989): 431–53; Dale L. Goodhue and Ronald L. Thompson, "Task-Technology Fit and Individual Performance," *MIS Quarterly* (June 1995): 213–36.

41. Richard Cone, Bruce Snow, and Ricky Waclawcayk, *Datapoint Corporation* (Unpublished manuscript, Texas A&M University, 1981).

42. Gresov, "Exploring Fit and Misfit with Multiple Contingencies"; Charles A. Glisson, "Dependence of Technological Routinization on Structural Variables in Human Service Organizations," *Administrative Science Quarterly* 23 (1978): 383–95; Jerald Hage and Michael Aiken, "Routine Technology, Social Structure and Organizational Goals," *Administrative Science Quarterly* 14 (1969): 368–79.

43. Gresov, "Exploring Fit and Misfit with Multiple Contingencies"; A. J. Grimes and S. M. Kline, "The Technological Imperative: The Relative Impact of

Task Unit, Modal Technology, and Hierarchy on Structure," *Academy of Management Journal* 16 (1973): 583–97; Lawrence G. Hrebiniak, "Job Technologies, Supervision and Work Group Structure," *Administrative Science Quarterly* 19 (1974): 395–410; Jeffrey Pfeffer, Organizational Design (Arlington Heights, Ill.: AHM, 1978), ch. 1.

44. Patrick E. Connor, *Organizations: Theory and Design* (Chicago: Science Research Associates, 1980); Richard L. Daft and Norman B. Macintosh, "A Tentative Exploration into Amount and Equivocality of Information Processing in Organizational Work Units," *Administrative Science Quarterly* 26 (1981): 207–24.

45. Paul D. Collins and Frank Hull, "Technology and Span of Control: Woodward Revisited," *Journal of Management Studies* 23 (1986): 143–64; Gerald D. Bell, "The Influence of Technological Components of Work upon Management Control," *Academy of Management Journal* 8 (1965): 127–32; Peter M. Blau and Richard A. Schoenherr, *The Structure of Organizations* (New York: Basic Books, 1971).

46. W. Alan Randolph, "Matching Technology and the Design of Organization Units," *California Management Review* 22–23 (1980–81): 39–48; Daft and Macintosh, "Tentative Exploration into Amount and Equivocality of Information Processing"; Michael L. Tushman, "Work Characteristics and Subunit Communication Structure: A Contingency Analysis," *Administrative Science Quarterly* 24 (1979): 82–98.

47. Andrew H. Van de Ven and Diane L. Ferry, *Measuring and Assessing Organizations* (New York: Wiley, 1980); Randolph, "Matching Technology and the Design of Organization Units."

48. Richard L. Daft and Robert H. Lengel, "Information Richness: A New Approach to Managerial Behavior and Organization Design," in Barry Staw and Larry L. Cummings, eds., *Research in Organizational Behavior*, vol. 6 (Greenwich, Conn.: JAI Press, 1984), 191–233; Richard L. Daft and Norman B. Macintosh, "A New Approach into Design and Use of Management Information," *California Management Review* 21 (1978): 82–92; Daft and Macintosh, "Tentative Exploration in Amount and Equivocality of Information Processing"; W. Alan Randolph, "Organizational Technology and the Media and Purpose Dimensions of Organizational Communication," *Journal of Business Research* 6 (1978): 237–59; Linda Argote, "Input Uncertainty and Organizational Coordination in Hospital Emergency Units," *Administrative Science Quarterly* 27 (1982): 420–34; Andrew H. Van de Ven and Andre Delbecq, "A Task Contingent Model of Work Unit Structure," *Administrative Science Quarterly* 19 (1974): 183–97.

49. Peggy Leatt and Rodney Schneck, "Criteria for Grouping Nursing Subunits in Hospitals," *Academy of Management Journal* 27 (1984): 150–65; Robert T. Keller, "Technology-Information Processing *Academy of Management Journal* 37, no. 1 (1994): 167–79.

50. Gresov, "Exploring Fit and Misfit with Multiple Contingencies"; Michael L. Tushman, "Technological Communication in R&D Laboratories: The Impact of Project Work Characteristics," *Academy of Management Journal* 21 (1978): 624–45; Robert T. Keller, "Technology-Information Processing Fit and the Performance of R&D Project Groups: A Test of Contingency Theory," *Academy of Management Journal* 37, no. 1 (1994): 167–79.

51. Thanks to Gail Russ for suggesting this example of a technology-structure mismatch.

52. James Thompson, *Organizations in Action* (New York: McGraw-Hill, 1967).

53. *Ibid.*, 40.

54. Paul S. Adler, "Interdepartmental Interdependence and Coordination: The Case of the Design/Manufacturing Interface," *Organization Science* 6, no. 2 (March-April 1995): 147–67.

55. Christopher Gresov, "Effects of Dependence and Tasks on Unit Design and Efficiency," *Organization Studies* 11 (1990): 503–29; Andrew H. Van de Ven, Andre Delbecq, and Richard Koenig, "Determinants of Coordination Modes within Organizations," *American Sociological Review* 41 (1976): 322–38; Linda Argote, "Input Uncertainty and Organizational Coordination in Hospital Emergency Units"; Jack K. Ito and Richard B. Peterson, "Effects of Task Difficulty and Interdependence on Information Processing Systems," *Academy of Management Journal* 29 (1986): 139–49; Joseph L. C. Cheng, "Interdependence and Coordination in Organizations: A Role-System Analysis," *Academy of Management Journal* 26 (1983): 156–62.

56. Robert W. Keidel, "Team Sports Models as a Generic Organizational Framework," *Human Relations* 40 (1987): 591–612; Robert W. Keidel, "Baseball, Football, and Basketball: Models for Business," *Organizational Dynamics* (Winter 1984): 5–18; Richard L. Daft and Richard M.

Steers, *Organizations: A Micro-Macro Approach* (Glenview, Ill.: Scott, Foresman, 1986).

57. Howard Gleckman with John Carey, Russell Mitchell, Tim Smart, and Chris Roush, "The Technology Payoff," *Business Week*, 14 June 1993, 57–68; Michele Liu, Héléné Denis, Harvey Kolodny, and Benjt Stymne, "Organization and Design for Technological Change," *Human Relations* 43 (January 1990): 7–22; George P. Huber, "A Theory of the Effects of Advanced Information Technologies on Organizational Design, Intelligence, and Decision Making," *Academy of Management Review* 14 (1990): 47–71.

58. Jeremy Main, "At Last, Software CEOs Can Use," *Fortune*, 13 March 1989, 77–82.

59. Richard C. Huseman and Edward W. Miles, "Organizational Communication in the Information Age: Implementations of Computer-Based Systems," *Journal of Management* 14 (1988): 181–204.

60. John W. Verity, "Getting Work to Go with the Flow," *Business Week*, 21 June 1993, 156–61; Gleckman, et al., "The Technology Payoff"; Peter Coy, "Start with Some High-Tech Magic," *Business Week/Enterprise*, 1993, 24–32.

61. Huber, "A Theory of the Effects of Advanced Information Technologies"; Lee Sproull and Sara Keisler, "Reducing Social Context Cues: Electronic Mail in Organizational Communication," *Management Science* 32 (1986): 1492–512.

62. John R. Wilke, "Computer Links Erode Hierarchical Nature of Workplace Culture," *Wall Street Journal*, 9 December 1993, A1, A10; Huber, "A Theory of the Effects of Advanced Information Technologies"; Stephen D. Soloman, "Use Technology to Manage People," *Small Business Report* (September 1990): 46–51.

63. Huber, "A Theory of the Effects of Advanced Information Technologies."

64. *Ibid*.

65. John R. Wilke, "Computer Links Erode Hierarchical Nature of Workplace Culture."

66. Gleckman, et al., "The Technology Payoff"; Shoshanna Zuboff, *In the Age of the Smart Machine* (New York: Basic Books, 1984).

67. Lynda M. Applegate, James I. Cash, Jr., and D. Quinn Mills, "Information Technology and Tomorrow's Manager," *Harvard Business Review* (November–December 1988): 128–36.

68. Wilke, "Computer Links."

69. Applegate, Cash, and Mills, "Information Technology and Tomorrow's Manager."

70. Bronwyn Fryer, "Managing Technology When You're Not a Techie," *Working Woman* (October 1995): 24–25, 98.

71. Liu, Denis, Kolodny, and Stymne, "Organization Design for Technological Change."

72. Gerald I. Susman and Richard B. Chase, "A Sociotechnical Analysis of the Integrated Factory," *Journal of Applied Behavioral Science* 22 (1986): 257–70; Paul Adler, "New Technologies, New Skills," *California Management Review* 29 (Fall 1986): 9–28.

73. Adler, "New Technologies, New Skills."

74. Zuboff, *In the Age of the Smart Machine*.

75. Gleckman, et al., "The Technology Payoff."

76. William M. Fox, "Sociotechnical System Principles and Guidelines: Past and Present," *Journal Of Applied Behavioral Science* 31, no. 1 (March 1995): 91–105.

77. F. Emery, "Characteristics of Sociotechnical Systems," Tavistock Institute of Human Relations, document 527, 1959; Passmore, Francis, and Haldeman, "Sociotechnical Systems."

78. Eric Trist and K. Banforth, "Some Social and Psychological Consequences of the Long Wall Method of Coal-Getting," *Human Relations* (1951): 3–38; Eric Trist, C. Higgin, H. Murray, and A. Pollock, *Organizational Choice* (London: Tavistock Publications, 1963); Eric Trist and Hugh Murray, eds. *The Social Engagement of Social Science: A Tavistock Anthology* Vol. II (Philadelphia: University of Pennsylvania Press, 1993).

79. Lyman Katchum, "Sociotechnical Design in a Third World Country: The Railway Maintenance Depot at Scennar in the Sudan," *Human Relations* 37 (1984): 135–54; Passmore, Francis, and Haldeman, "Sociotechnical Systems."

80. William A. Pasmore, "Social Science Transformed: The Socio-Technical Perspective," *Human Relations* 48, no. 1 (1995) 1–21.

81. David M. Upton, "What Really Makes Factories Flexible?" *Harvard Business Review* (July-August 1995): 74–84.

82. Pasmore, "Social Science Transformed: The Socio-Technical Perspective"; and H. Scarbrough, "Review Article: *The Social Engagement of Social Science: A Tavistock Anthology*, Vol. II," *Human Relations* 48, no. 1 (1995): 23–33.

chapter five

Organization Size, Life Cycle, and Decline

A look inside

Matsushita Electric

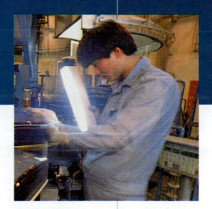

B y the early 1990s, Matsushita Electric, the world's largest consumer electronics company, was plagued by high costs, weak
sales, and falling profits. The company was slow to introduce new
products, depending heavily on televisions, VCRs, and stereos sold under brand names such as Panasonic, Technics, and Quasar. As rival companies began making the same products at lower cost, Matsushita's sales
slumped. Yet costs remained high, primarily due to runaway expansion of headquarters
staff during the rapid growth period of the 1980s.

When Yoichi Morishita took over as Matsushita's new president, he realized the plod-
ding bureaucracy that had developed over the years was threatening the company's future.
Morishita immediately propelled the company into the most aggressive management
overhaul in its history. Morishita wants to get this giant company acting with the speed
and simplicity of a small, entrepreneurial firm. Decentralizing management is the key to
Morishita's plan. He eliminated an entire line of management that traditionally oversaw
the company's 44 divisions and gave the division heads full responsibility for their own
businesses. One insider says presidents prior to Morishita often made decisions on everything from new light bulbs to import systems. The new decentralized structure enables division heads to save time and money by deciding independently whether to move operations
or switch suppliers based on their own division's competitive situation. Morishita is further
slashing headquarters staff by transferring thousands of corporate administrators to hands-
on marketing, sales, and production jobs. In addition, the CEO is challenging the sanctity
of lifetime employment by offering five-year contracts for scientists and engineers to work
on specific research and development projects to get new products to the marketplace.

Morishita hopes his strategy, which he calls "Four-S Management"—for simple, small,
speedy, and strategic—will put the company back on the fast track to increased sales and
profits.[1]

Matsushita Electric is an example of how companies around the world are combining the advantages of bigness with "the human scale, sharp focus, and fervent
entrepreneurship of smallness."[2] Today, many large companies are looking for
ways to be flexible and responsive in a rapidly changing marketplace. In the 1970s
and 1980s, growth and large size were considered natural and desirable; but in the
1990s, small—or at least the ability to behave as a small company—is beautiful.[3]

During the twentieth century, large organizations have become widespread,
and over the past thirty years, bureaucracy has been a major topic of study in organization theory.[4] Today, most large organizations have bureaucratic characteristics. They provide us with abundant goods and services, and they surprise us
with astonishing feats—astronauts to the moon, thousands of airline flights daily
without an accident—that are testimony to their effectiveness. On the other
hand, bureaucracy is also accused of many sins, including inefficiency, rigidity,
and demeaning, routinized work that alienates both employees and the customers an organization tries to serve.[5]

Purpose of This Chapter

In this chapter, we will explore the question of large versus small organization and how size is related to structural characteristics. Organization size is a contextual variable that influences organizational design and functioning just as do the contextual variables—technology, environment, goals—discussed in previous chapters. In the first section, we will look at the advantages of large versus small size. Then, we will examine the historical need for bureaucracy as a means to control large organizations and how managers today attack bureaucracy in some large organizations. Next, we will explore what is called an organization's life cycle and the structural characteristics at each stage. Finally, the causes of organizational decline and some methods for dealing with downsizing will be discussed. By the end of this chapter, you should understand the nature of bureaucracy, its strengths and weaknesses, and when to use bureaucratic characteristics to make an organization effective.

ORGANIZATION SIZE: IS BIGGER BETTER?

The question of big versus small begins with the notion of growth and the reasons so many organizations feel the need to grow large.

Pressures for Growth

Why do organizations grow? Why should they grow? The following are **reasons organizations grow**.

Organizational Goals.   In the early 1990s, America's management guru, Peter Drucker, declared that "the *Fortune* 500 is over"; yet the dream of practically every businessperson is still to have his or her company become a member of the *Fortune* 500 list—to grow fast and to grow large.[6] Sometimes this goal is more urgent than to make the best products or show the greatest profits. Some observers believe the United States is entering a new era of "bigness," as companies strive to acquire the size and resources to compete on a global scale, to invest in new technology and to control distribution channels and guarantee access to markets. In the first nine months of 1995 alone, more than $270 billion worth of mergers and acquisitions were announced.[7] For example, Kimberly Clark Corporation acquired Scott Paper Company because Scott had strength in European markets that Kimberly lacked. Pharmaceutical companies such as Upjohn and Sweden's Pharmacia are merging to gain stronger market presence and the clout to negotiate with large purchasers.

Executive Advancement.   Growth is often necessary to attract and keep quality managers. Growing organizations, both public and private, are exciting places to work. There are many challenges and opportunities for advancement when the number of employees is expanding.[8]

Economic Health.   Many executives have found that firms must grow to stay economically healthy. To stop growing is to suffocate. To be stable or to relax means customers may not have their demands fully met or that competitors will meet customer needs and increase market share at the expense of your company.

Hewlett-Packard, which continues to grow and succeed, has developed a philosophy of killing off its own products with new technology before its rivals have the chance to do so. Intel, an $11.5 billion company with a near monopoly on the lucrative microprocessor market, is able to lavish more than $1 billion a year on research and development, compared to around $275 million spent by Advanced Micro Devices, Intel's nearest competitor.[9] Scale is still crucial to economic health in some industries. For example, greater size gives marketing-intensive companies, such as beverage distributors Coca-Cola and Anheuser-Busch, power in the marketplace and thus increased revenues.[10]

Large Versus Small

Organizations feel compelled to grow, but how much and how large? What size organization is better poised to compete in a global environment? The arguments are summarized in Exhibit 5.1.

Large. Huge resources and economies of scale are needed for many organizations to compete globally. Only large organizations can build a massive pipeline in Alaska. Only a large corporation like Boeing can afford to build a 747, and only a large American Airlines can buy it. Only a large Merck can invest hundreds of millions in new drugs that must be sold worldwide to show a profit. Only a large McDonald's can open a new restaurant somewhere in the world every seventeen hours.

Large companies also are standardized, often mechanistically run, and complex. The complexity offers hundreds of functional specialties within the organization to perform complex tasks and to produce complex products. Moreover, large organizations, once established, can be a presence that stabilizes a

Exhibit 5.1

Differences Between Large and Small Organizations

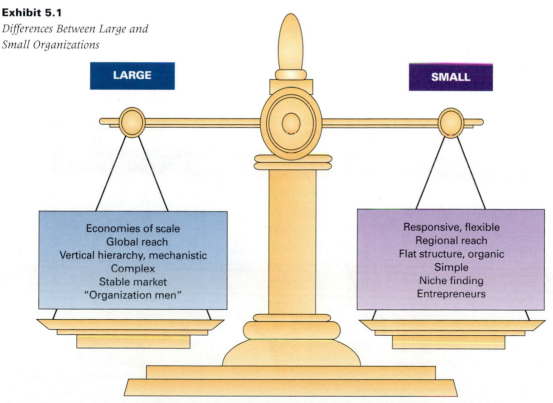

Source: Based on John A. Byrne, "Is Your Company Too Big?" *Business Week,* 27 March 1989, 84–94.

market for years. Managers can join the company and expect a career reminiscent of the "organization men" of the 1950s and 1960s. The organization can provide longevity, raises, and promotions.

Small.   The competing argument says small is beautiful because the crucial requirements for success in a global economy are responsiveness and flexibility in fast-changing markets. While the U.S. economy contains many large organizations, research shows that as global trade has accelerated, smaller organizations have become the norm. Huge investments are giving way to flexible manufacturing and niche marketing as the ways to succeed. The rapidly growing service sector, as discussed in the previous chapter, has also contributed to a decrease in average organization size, as most service companies remain small to be more responsive to customers.[11]

   Despite the fact that recent mergers are creating giant companies in some industries, the average size of organizations is decreasing, not only in the United States but in Britain and Germany as well. Exhibit 5.2 reflects the decrease in the average number of employees per firm for the three countries. Small organizations have a flat structure and an organic, free-flowing management style that encourages entrepreneurship and innovation. Today's leading biotechnological drugs, for example, were all discovered by small firms, such as Chiron, which de-

Exhibit 5.2

Average Size of Industrial Firms in Three Countries

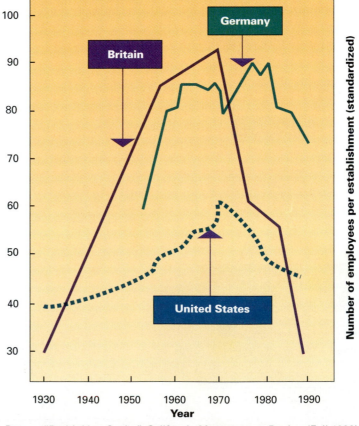

Source: Tom Peters, "Rethinking Scale," *California Management Review* (Fall 1992): 7–29. Used with permission.

veloped the hepatitis B vaccines, rather than by huge pharmaceutical companies, such as Merck.[12] Moreover, the personal involvement of employees in small firms encourages motivation and commitment because employees personally identify with the company's mission.

Big-Company/Small-Company Hybrid. The paradox is that the advantages of small companies enable them to succeed and, hence, grow large. *Fortune* magazine reported that the fastest growing companies in America are small firms characterized by an emphasis on putting the customer first and being fast and flexible in responding to the environment.[13] Small companies, however, can become victims of their own success as they grow large, shifting to a mechanistic structure emphasizing vertical hierarchies and spawning "organization men" rather than entrepreneurs.

The solution is what Jack Welch, chairman of General Electric, calls the "big-company/small-company hybrid" that combines a large corporation's resources and reach with a small company's simplicity and flexibility. This approach is being taken seriously by many large companies, including Johnson & Johnson, Hewlett-Packard, AT&T, and even General Motors. These companies have all undergone massive reorganizations into groups of small companies to capture the mind-set and advantages of smallness. The $14 billion giant Johnson & Johnson is actually a group of 168 separate companies. When a new product is created in one of J&J's fifty-six labs, a new company is created along with it.[14] Percy Barnevik, CEO of power equipment giant Asea Brown Boveri Ltd. (ABB), blasted a two hundred thousand-employee global enterprise into five thousand units, averaging just forty people each.[15] A good example of the shift to a hybrid form is Carrier Corporation, described in The New Paradigm box.

A full-service, global firm needs a strong resource base and sufficient complexity and hierarchy to serve clients around the world. Large or growing companies can retain the flexibility and customer focus of smallness by decentralizing authority and cutting layers of the hierarchy. At Nucor Corporation, a rapidly growing steelmaker with annual sales topping $2 billion, headquarters is staffed by only twenty-three people. Nucor's plant managers handle everything from marketing to personnel to production. Hewlett-Packard has decentralized almost every aspect of its business; for example, instead of relying on a central research and development staff, HP hands over most of its $2 billion research budget to its four operating groups to spend as they wish.[16]

ORGANIZATION SIZE AND BUREAUCRACY

The systematic study of bureaucracy was launched by Max Weber, a sociologist who studied government organizations in Europe and developed a framework of administrative characteristics that would make large organizations rational and efficient.[17] Weber wanted to understand how organizations could be designed to play a positive role in the larger society.

What Is Bureaucracy?

Although Weber perceived **bureaucracy** as a threat to basic personal liberties, he also recognized it as the most efficient possible system of organizing. He

The New Paradigm   Carrier Corporation

Imagine walking into a factory that's as clean and quiet as a research center. Imagine having to complete a tough, six-week training course before even being *considered* for a job there. And then, imagine you actually get a job on the shop floor and you end up interviewing applicants who could be your boss! What's going on here?

As strange as it may seem compared to the mass production factories of the past, the Carrier Corporation plant in Arkadelphia, Arkansas, may be the model for America's future factories. The plant was built because Carrier realized that to stay competitive, it had to make its own compressors for air conditioners. But the company already knew the huge factories it had built in the 1970s and 1980s, with their big costs, layers of management, and inflexible production lines, were money-losers. So it turned in a new direction, and the streamlined Arkadelphia model was born.

The highly automated plant employs only 150 workers, and each is trained in a variety of jobs so they can fill in for one another when necessary. Assembly-line workers have amazing autonomy. They don't punch a time clock, and they don't have to follow strict, inflexi-

ble rules regarding sick leave and other matters. One group recently rearranged a series of machines for increased efficiency after clearing it only with their immediate supervisor, rather than having to go through layers of management and then waiting for maintenance staff to do the job. Assembly-line workers can even order needed supplies without management approval.

Getting a job at Carrier's Arkadelphia plant isn't easy, but those who get one exercise a level of authority unheard of in traditional factories. Assembly-line workers even have a chance to influence future hiring decisions—they participate in interviewing all job applicants, even those who could end up being their boss.

Carrier's model plant is making compressors that cost less and are of higher quality than those produced by the old-style mass production factories. Carrier executives are confident that the plant will keep the company competitive in today's global environment.

Source: Erle Norton, "Small, Flexible Plants May Play Crucial Role in U.S. Manufacturing," *Wall Street Journal,* 13 January 1993, A1, A8.

predicted the triumph of bureaucracy because of its ability to ensure more efficient functioning of organizations in both business and government settings. Weber identified a set of organizational characteristics, listed in Exhibit 5.3, that could be found in successful bureaucratic organizations.

Rules and standard procedures enabled organizational activities to be performed in a predictable, routine manner. Specialized duties meant that each employee had a clear task to perform. Hierarchy of authority provided a sensible mechanism for supervision and control. Technical competence was the basis by which people were hired rather than friendship, family ties, and favoritism that dramatically reduced work performance. The separation of the position from the position holder meant that individuals did not own or have an inherent right to the job, thus promoting efficiency. Written records provided an organizational memory and continuity over time.

Although bureaucratic characteristics carried to an extreme are widely criticized today, the rational control introduced by Weber was a significant idea and a new form of organization. Bureaucracy provided many advantages over organization forms based upon favoritism, social status, family connections, or graft, which are often unfair. For example, in Mexico, a retired American lawyer had to pay a five-hundred-dollar bribe to purchase a telephone, then discovered that a government official had sold his telephone number to another family. In China, the tradition of giving government posts to relatives is widespread even under

Bureaucracy	Legitimate Bases of Authority
1. Rules and procedures 2. Specialization and division of labor 3. Hierarchy of authority 4. Technically qualified personnel 5. Separate position and incumbent 6. Written communications and records	1. Rational-legal 2. Traditional 3. Charismatic

Exhibit 5.3

Weber's Dimensions of Bureaucracy and Bases of Organizational Authority

communism. China's emerging class of educated people doesn't like seeing the best jobs going to children and relatives of officials.[18] By comparison, the logical and rational form of organization described by Weber allows work to be conducted efficiently and according to established rules.

Bases of Authority

The ability of an organization to function efficiently depends on its authority structure. Proper authority provides managers with the control needed to make the bureaucratic form of organization work. Weber argued that legitimate, rational authority was preferred over other types of control (for example, payoffs or favoritism) as the basis for internal decisions and activities. Within the larger society, however, Weber identified three types of authority that could explain the creation and control of a large organization.[19]

1. **Rational-legal authority** is based on employees' beliefs in the legality of rules and the right of those elevated to authority to issue commands. Rational-legal authority is the basis for both creation and control of most government organizations and is the most common base of control in organizations worldwide.
2. **Traditional authority** is the belief in traditions and in the legitimacy of the status of people exercising authority through those traditions. Traditional authority is the basis for control for monarchies and churches and for some organizations in Latin America and the Persian Gulf.
3. **Charismatic authority** is based upon devotion to the exemplary character or to the heroism of an individual person and the order defined by him or her. Revolutionary military organizations are often based on the leader's charisma, as are North American organizations led by charismatic individuals such as Lee Iacocca or Jack Welch.

More than one type of authority—such as long tradition and the leader's special charisma—may exist in today's organizations, but *rational-legal authority* is the most widely used form to govern internal work activities and decision making, especially in large organizations.

SIZE AND STRUCTURAL CHARACTERISTICS

In the field of organization theory, organization size has been described as an important variable that influences structural design. Should an organization become more bureaucratic as it grows larger? In what size organizations are bureaucratic characteristics most appropriate? More than one hundred studies have attempted to answer these questions.[20] Most of these studies indicate that large organizations are different from small organizations along several dimensions of bureaucratic structure, including formalization, centralization, complexity, and personnel ratios.

Formalization

Formalization, as described in Chapter 1, refers to rules, procedures, and written documentation, such as policy manuals and job descriptions, that prescribe the rights and duties of employees.[21] The evidence supports the conclusion that large organizations are more formalized. The reason is that large organizations rely on rules, procedures, and paperwork to achieve standardization and control across their large numbers of employees and departments, whereas top managers can use personal observation to control a small organization.[22] In large firms like IBM, Banc One, and AT&T, formal procedures allow top administrators to extend their reach, and rules are established to take the place of personal surveillance for such matters as sexual harassment, smoking bans, and flexible work hours. Formalization may also promote more formal and impersonal modes of behavior and interaction in large bureaucratic organizations, as opposed to the spontaneous, casual behavior and social interaction often observed in small, loosely-knit organizations.[23]

Decentralization

Centralization refers to the level of hierarchy with authority to make decisions. In centralized organizations, decisions tend to be made at the top. In decentralized organizations, similar decisions would be made at a lower level.

Decentralization represents a paradox because, in the perfect bureaucracy, all decisions would be made by the top administrator, who would have perfect control. However, as an organization grows larger and has more people and departments, decisions cannot be passed to the top, or senior managers would be overloaded. Thus, the research on organization size indicates that larger organizations (for example, Campbell Soup Company and American Airlines) permit greater decentralization.[24] CEO Mike Quinlan of McDonald's pushes decisions as far down the hierarchy as he can; otherwise, McDonald's decision making would be too slow. Moreover, McDonald's has many rules that define boundaries within which decisions can be made, thereby facilitating decentralization.

Complexity

As discussed in Chapter 1, **complexity** refers to both the number of levels in the hierarchy (vertical complexity) and the number of departments or jobs (horizontal complexity). Large organizations show a definite pattern of greater complexity.[25] The explanation for the relationship between size and complexity is straightforward. First, the need for additional specialties occurs more often in large organizations. For example, a study of new departments reported that new administrative departments were often created in response to problems of large size.[26] A planning department was established in a large organization because a greater need for planning arose after a certain size was reached. Second, as departments within the organization grow in size, pressure to subdivide arises. Departments eventually get so large that managers cannot control them effectively. At this point, subgroups will lobby to be subdivided into separate departments.[27]

Finally, vertical complexity traditionally has been needed to maintain control over a large number of people. As the number of employees increases, additional levels of hierarchy keep spans of control from becoming too large.

As we discussed earlier in this chapter, many large corporations are fighting against the effects of size by simplifying, reducing rules, and pushing decisions to even lower levels. However, bureaucratic characteristics can have positive impact on many firms. One of the most efficient large corporations in the United States and Canada is UPS, often called the Brown Giant for the color of packages it delivers and the trucks that deliver them.

United Parcel Service

In Practice 5.1

United Parcel Service took on the U.S. Postal Service at its own game—and won. The strongest force in the U.S. delivery business, UPS delivers ten million packages a day. With its 128,000 trucks and 458 aircraft, the company now controls more than three-fourths of the ground parcel market in the United States and is a growing force in air express.

How did the Brown Giant become so successful? Many efficiencies were realized through adoption of the bureaucratic model of organization. UPS is bound up in rules and regulations. It tells drivers how to step from their trucks (right foot first), how fast to walk (three feet per second), how to carry packages (under the left arm), even how to hold their keys (teeth up, third finger). There are safety rules for drivers, loaders, clerks, and managers. Strict dress codes are enforced—no beards, hair cannot touch the collar, no sideburns, mustaches must be trimmed evenly and cannot go below the corner of the mouth, and so on. Rules specify the cleanliness of buildings and property. All UPS delivery trucks must be washed inside and out at the end of every day. Each manager is given bound copies of policy books with the expectation that they will be used regularly. Jobs are broken down into a complex division of labor, including those of drivers, loaders, clerks, washers, sorters, and maintenance personnel. Each task is calibrated according to productivity standards. The hierarchy of authority is clearly defined and has eight levels, extending from a washer at the local UPS plant up to the president of the national organization. Drivers often are expected to make fifteen deliveries or pickups an hour, no matter what.

Technical qualification is the criterion for hiring and promotion. The UPS policy book says, "A leader does not have to remind others of authority by use of a title. Knowledge, performance, and capacity should be adequate evidence of position and leadership." Favoritism is forbidden. Moreover, UPS thrives on records. Daily worksheets specify performance goals and work outputs for every employee and department. New technology facilitates recordkeeping.

Another key to the Brown Giant's success is that, despite its huge size, it has never become impersonal to employees. Everyone is on a first-name basis. No one, not even the chairman, has a private secretary. Top executives started at the bottom, and they still do their own photocopying. The drivers are the real heroes of the company, and because UPS cares about its employees, employees care about the company and its customers.[28]

UPS illustrates how bureaucratic characteristics increase with large size. UPS is so productive and dependable that it dominates the small package delivery market. However, in recent years the company has suffered growing labor problems; new products and services put even more demands on workers, who are growing frustrated with UPS's excessive work rules and close monitoring.

Overseas, for example, the company's ban on beards has roiled workers in Spain and Germany. As UPS strives for a larger global presence, the company may face the need to adopt a more flexible approach.

Personnel Ratios

The next characteristic of bureaucracy is **personnel ratios** for administrative, clerical, and professional support staff. The most frequently studied ratio is the administrative ratio. In 1957, C. Northcote Parkinson published *Parkinson's Law,* which argued that work expands to fill the time available for its completion. Parkinson suggested that administrators were motivated to add more administrators for a variety of reasons, including the enhancement of their own status through empire building. Parkinson used his argument, called **Parkinson's law**, to make fun of the British Admiralty. During a fourteen-year period from 1914 to 1928, the officer corps increased by 78 percent, although the total navy personnel decreased by 32 percent and the number of warships in use decreased by approximately 68 percent.[29]

In the years since Parkinson's book, the administrative ratio has been studied in school systems, churches, hospitals, employment agencies, and other business and voluntary organizations.[30] Two patterns have emerged.

The first pattern is that the ratio of top administration to total employment is actually smaller in large organizations.[31] This is the opposite of Parkinson's argument and indicates that organizations experience administrative economies as they grow larger. Large organizations have large departments, more regulations, and a greater division of labor. These mechanisms require less supervision from the top. Increasing bureaucratization is a substitute for personal supervision from the administrators.

The second pattern concerns other staff support ratios. Recent studies have subdivided support personnel into subclassifications, such as clerical and professional staff.[32] These support groups tend to increase in proportion to organization size. The clerical ratio increases because of the greater communication (memos, letters) and paperwork requirements (policy manuals, job descriptions) in large organizations. The professional staff ratio increases because of the greater need for specialized skills in complex organizations. In a small organization, an individual may be a jack-of-all-trades. In a large organization, people are assigned full time to support activities to help make production employees more efficient.

Exhibit 5.4 illustrates administrative and support ratios for small and large organizations. As organizations increase in size, the administrative ratio declines and the ratios for other support groups increase.[33] The net effect for direct workers is that they decline as a percentage of total employees. Recent studies show that corporate America in general needs to reduce its overhead costs to remain competitive.

Large Japanese companies, such as Toyota Motor Corporation and Matsushita Electric, described at the beginning of this chapter, are also facing the need to reduce overhead costs. Japanese factories are highly productive, but companies are finding that profits are being dragged down by bloated administrative and clerical staffs. Shintaro Hori, a vice-president of Bain & Company Japan, estimates that Japanese companies in general have 15 to 20 percent more support workers than they need.[34]

An interesting pattern emerges from recent research on organizations during periods of growth and decline. In rapidly growing organizations, administrators

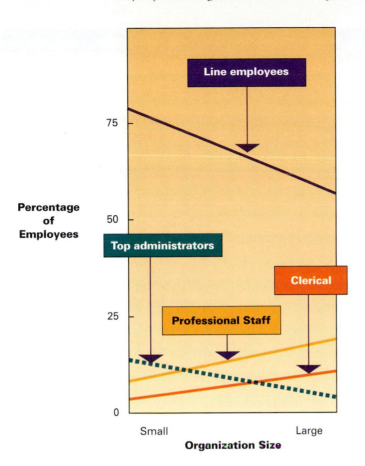

Exhibit 5.4
Percentage of Personnel Allocated to Administrative and Support Activities

grow faster than line employees; in declining organizations, they decline more slowly. This implies that administrative and staff personnel often are the first hired and last fired.[35] For example, when the University of Michigan was undergoing rapid growth, faculty increased by 7 percent, but professional nonfaculty employees increased by 26 percent, and executive, administrative, and managerial employees increased by 40 percent.[36] If the University of Michigan should suddenly decline rapidly, the administration may decline more slowly than professional and faculty employees.

In summary, top administrators typically do not comprise a disproportionate number of employees in large organizations; in fact, they are a smaller percentage of total employment. However, the idea that proportionately greater overhead is required in large organizations is supported. The number of people in clerical and professional departments increases at a faster rate than does the number of people who work in the technical core of a growing organization.

The differences between small and large organizations are summarized in Exhibit 5.5. Large organizations have many characteristics that distinguish them from small organizations: more rules and regulations; more paperwork, written communication, and documentation; greater specialization; more decentralization; a lower percentage of people devoted to top administration; and a larger percentage of people allocated to clerical, maintenance, and professional support staff.

However, size by itself does not cause these organizational characteristics. Recall from previous chapters that goals, environment, and technology also

Greater organization size is associated with:
1. Increased number of management levels (vertical complexity)
2. Greater number of jobs and departments (horizontal complexity)
3. Increased specialization of skills and functions
4. Greater formalization
5. Greater decentralization
6. Smaller percentage of top administrators
7. Greater percentage of technical and professional support staff
8. Greater percentage of clerical and maintenance support staff
9. Greater amount of written communications and documentation

influence structure. For example, an organization operating in a complex environment will need additional departments, and a changing environment creates the need for less formalization. Thus, while large organizations will appear different from small organizations, these relationships are not rigid. The impact of other contextual variables can modify bureaucratic structure.

BUREAUCRACY IN A CHANGING WORLD

Weber's prediction of the triumph of bureaucracy proved accurate. Bureaucratic characteristics have many advantages and have worked extremely well for many of the needs of the industrial age.[37] By establishing a hierarchy of authority and specific rules and procedures, bureaucracy provided an effective way to bring order to large groups of people and prevent abuses of power. Impersonal relationships based on roles rather than people reduced the favoritism and nepotism characteristic of many pre-industrial organizations. Bureaucracy also provided for systematic and rational ways to organize and manage tasks too complex to be understood and handled by a few individuals, thus greatly improving the efficiency and effectiveness of large organizations.

The world is rapidly changing, however, and the machinelike bureaucratic system of the industrial age no longer works so well as organizations face new challenges. With global competition and uncertain environments, many organizations are fighting against increasing complexity and professional staff ratios. The problems caused by large bureaucracies have perhaps nowhere been more evident than in the U.S. government. From the bureaucratic obstacles to providing emergency relief following Hurricane Andrew to the bungling by the U.S. Marshal's Service that put a convicted drug kingpin back on the streets, such actions by federal government agencies show how excessive bureaucracy can impede the effectiveness and productivity of organizations.[38]

Companies like Burlington Northern, Dana, and Hanson Industries have thirty-five to forty thousand employees and fewer than one hundred staff people working at headquarters. Aluminum Company of America (Alcoa) is cutting out two levels of top management, along with about two dozen headquarters staff jobs, giving business-unit managers unprecedented decision-making authority. The point is to not overload headquarters with accountants, lawyers, and financial analysts who will inhibit the autonomy and flexibility of divisions.[39] When Jack Welch laid off more than 100,000 employees during his tenure at General Electric, many of those affected were middle managers, senior managers, and staff professionals. Of course, many companies must be large to have sufficient resources and complexity to produce products for a global environment; but companies such as Johnson & Johnson, Wal-Mart, 3M, Coca-Cola, Emerson Electric, and Heinz are striving toward greater decentralization and leanness. They are giving front-line workers more authority and responsibility to define and direct their own jobs, often by creating self-directed teams that find ways to coordinate work, improve productivity, and better serve customers.

Another attack on bureaucracy is from the increasing professionalism of employees. Professionalism was defined in Chapter 1 as the length of formal training and experience of employees. More employees need college degrees, MBAs, and other professional degrees to work as attorneys, researchers, or doctors at General Motors, Kmart, and Bristol-Myers Squibb Company. Studies of professionals show that formalization is not needed because professional training regularizes a high standard of behavior for employees that acts as a substitute for bureaucracy.[40] Companies also enhance this trend when they provide ongoing training for *all* employees, from the front office to the shop floor, in a push for continuous individual and organizational learning. Increased training substitutes for bureaucratic rules and procedures that can constrain the creativity of employees to solve problems and increase organizational capability.

In addition, a form of organization called the *professional partnership* has emerged that is made up completely of professionals.[41] These organizations include medical practices, law firms, and consulting firms, such as McKinsey & Co. and Price Waterhouse. The general finding concerning professional partnerships is that branches have substantial autonomy and decentralized authority to make necessary decisions. They work with a consensus orientation rather than top-down direction typical of traditional business and government organizations. Thus, the trend of increasing professionalism combined with rapidly changing environments is leading to less bureaucracy in corporate North America.

ORGANIZATIONAL LIFE CYCLE

Stages of Life Cycle Development

A useful way to think about organizational growth and change is provided by the concept of a **life cycle**,[42] which suggests that organizations are born, grow older, and eventually die. As organizations mature, they may develop unadaptive patterns of thinking and behavior. Book Mark 5.0 discusses some of these patterns and how managers can help their companies avoid or correct them. Organization structure, leadership style, and administrative systems follow a fairly predictable pattern through stages in the life cycle. Stages are sequential in nature and follow a natural progression.

Recent work on organizational life cycle suggests that four major stages characterize organizational development.[43] These stages are illustrated in Exhibit 5.6 along with the problems associated with transition to each stage. Growth is not easy. Each time an organization enters a new stage in the life cycle, it enters a whole new ballgame with a new set of rules for how the organization functions internally and how it relates to the external environment.[44]

1. Entrepreneurial Stage. When an organization is born, the emphasis is on creating a product and surviving in the marketplace. The founders are

Have You Read About This?

The Self-Defeating Organization: How Smart Companies Can Stop Outsmarting Themselves

by Robert E. Hardy and Randy Schwartz

Organizations are similar to individuals in that as they mature they adopt patterns of behavior, both advantageous and unfavorable, that characterize how they act when presented with successes, challenges, and crises. Organizations may form inappropriate and habitual ways of confronting challenges that prevent future success. Robert Hardy and Randy Schwartz believe companies that consistently react poorly to challenges develop a systematic practice recognized as "self-defeating organizational behavior." *The Self-Defeating Organization* identifies detrimental organizational patterns and ways to correct deficiencies.

Five Types of Self-Defeating Organizations

1. *The Maintenance Crew*—values control and procedure above all; afraid of ritual-disrupting change; suffers from collective depression; performs chores via a grim, rigid schedule. This is a bad case of bureaucracy.
2. *The Funhouse Gang*—equates activity with productivity; undoes mistakes it has made; fears accountability; specializes in confusion and mix-ups. This is a teenager of sorts.
3. *The Pep Squad*—members display constant, strident, eerie optimism; pleasant to the world—unpleasant to each other; fears truth; frequently resorts to deceitful action to achieve its ends; has no sound core beliefs. Managers are in denial.
4. *The Alumni Club*—lives with constant regret; fears the future; resorts to reminiscing instead of thinking innovatively about today's problems. This is a case of old age.

5. *The Cargo Cult*—transforms virtue of eternal hope into an unhealthy vice; afraid of looking hard at present circumstances; engages in ritual self-denial; the focus on fantasized "dream work" leads to performance-inhibiting conflicts. This one is headed for decline.

Ways to Achieve High Performance

- *Define core beliefs.* Valid and positive beliefs help define a successful future for an organization.

- *Tell the truth.* Honesty and integrity provide accurate company assessment and group trust.

- *Be open-minded.* Open organizations view people, ideas, and methodologies as elements of their ongoing successes, pulling from internal "intellectual and spiritual capital."

- *Share costs and benefits equitably.* To evenly spread the costs and benefits among primary constituents promotes trust and accountability.

- *Maximize results.* Building upon successes helps to prove and support the value of this new thinking that provides benefits.

- *Own success.* Ownership promotes confidence and strengthens core beliefs to make success a habit.

Within the book, the authors present stories of managers who have led their organizations out of bureaucracy, denial, mistakes, and fear to success.

The Self-Defeating Organization: How Smart Companies Can Stop Outsmarting Themselves, by Robert E. Hardy and Randy Schwartz, is published by Addison-Wesley.

entrepreneurs, and they devote their full energies to the technical activities of production and marketing. The organization is informal and nonbureaucratic. The hours of work are long. Control is based on the owners' personal supervision. Growth is from a creative new product or service. Apple Computer was in the **entrepreneurial stage** when it was created by Steven Jobs and Stephen Wozniak in Wozniak's parents' garage. Software companies like Microsoft and Lotus Development were in the entrepreneurial stage when their original software programs were written and marketed.

Exhibit 5.6
Organizational Life Cycle

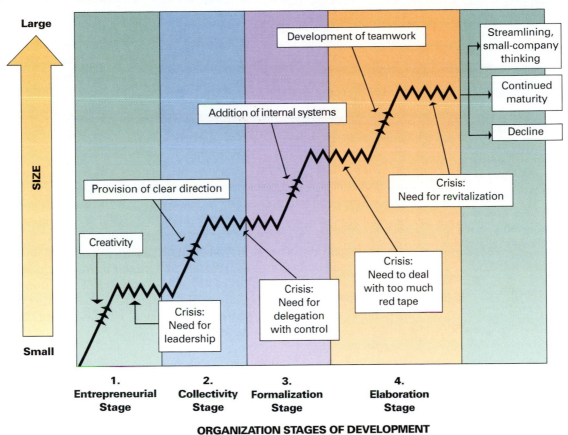

ORGANIZATION STAGES OF DEVELOPMENT

Source: Adapted from Robert E. Quinn and Kim Cameron, "Organizational Life Cycles and Shifting Criteria of Effectiveness: Some Preliminary Evidence," *Management Science* 29 (1983): 33–51; and Larry E. Greiner, "Evolution and Revolution as Organizations Grow," *Harvard Business Review* 50 (July–August 1972): 37–46.

Crisis: Need for Leadership. As the organization starts to grow, the larger number of employees causes problems. The creative and technically oriented owners are confronted with management issues, but they may prefer to focus their energies on making and selling the product or inventing new products and services. At this time of crisis, entrepreneurs must either adjust the structure of the organization to accommodate continued growth or else bring in strong managers who can do so. When Apple began a period of rapid growth, A. C. Markkula was brought in as a leader because neither Jobs nor Wozniak was qualified or cared to manage the expanding company.

2. Collectivity Stage. If the leadership crisis is resolved, strong leadership is obtained and the organization begins to develop clear goals and direction. Departments are established along with a hierarchy of authority, job assignments, and a beginning division of labor. Employees identify with the mission of the organization and spend long hours helping the organization succeed. Members feel part of a collective, and communication and control are mostly informal although a few formal systems begin to appear. Apple Computer was in the **collectivity stage** during the rapid growth years from 1978 to 1981. Employees threw themselves into the business as the major product line was established and more than two thousand dealers signed on.

Crisis: Need for Delegation. If the new management has been successful, lower-level employees gradually find themselves restricted by the strong top-down leadership. Lower-level managers begin to acquire confidence in their own functional areas and want more discretion. An autonomy crisis occurs when top managers, who were successful because of their strong leadership and vision, do not want to give up responsibility. Top managers want to make sure that all parts of the organization are coordinated and pulling together. The organization needs to find mechanisms to control and coordinate departments without direct supervision from the top.

3. *Formalization Stage.* The **formalization stage** involves the installation and use of rules, procedures, and control systems. Communication is less frequent and more formal. Engineers, human resource specialists, and other staff may be added. Top management becomes concerned with issues such as strategy and planning, and leaves the operations of the firm to middle management. Product groups or other decentralized units may be formed to improve coordination. Incentive systems based on profits may be implemented to ensure that managers work toward what is best for the overall company. When effective, the new coordination and control systems enable the organization to continue growing by establishing linkage mechanisms between top management and field units. Apple Computer was in the formalization stage in the mid-1980s.

Crisis: Too Much Red Tape. At this point in the organization's development, the proliferation of systems and programs may begin to strangle middle-level executives. The organization seems bureaucratized. Middle management may resent the intrusion of staff people. Innovation may be restricted. The organization seems too large and complex to be managed through formal programs. It was at this stage of Apple's growth that Jobs resigned from the company and CEO John Sculley took full control to face his own management challenges.

4. *Elaboration Stage.* The solution to the red tape crisis is a new sense of collaboration and teamwork. Throughout the organization, managers develop skills for confronting problems and working together. Bureaucracy may have reached its limit. Social control and self-discipline reduce the need for additional formal controls. Managers learn to work within the bureaucracy without adding to it. Formal systems may be simplified and replaced by manager teams and task forces. To achieve collaboration, teams are often formed across functions or divisions of the company. The organization may also be split into multiple divisions to maintain a small-company philosophy. Apple Computer is currently in the **elaboration stage** of the life cycle, as are such large companies as Caterpillar and Motorola.

Crisis: Need for Revitalization. After the organization reaches maturity, it may enter periods of temporary decline.[45] A need for renewal may occur every ten to twenty years. The organization shifts out of alignment with the environment or perhaps becomes slow moving and overbureaucratized and must go through a stage of streamlining and innovation. Top managers are often replaced during this period. At Apple, the top spot has changed hands twice in the company's struggle to revitalize. Both John Sculley and his successor, Michael Spindler, were forced to resign, and Gilbert Amelio took the reins to try to revive Apple's sales and profits.

Both Sculley and Spindler slashed thousands of jobs at Apple in an effort to control costs and improve profit margins. Amelio is facing some of the most daunting challenges of any Apple CEO to date.[46] The company faces the simultaneous needs for innovative new products and major cost cutting to remain competitive. Organizations need bold leadership to face the crisis at this stage of the life cycle and move forward into a new era. If mature organizations do not go through periodic revitalizations, they will decline, as shown in the last stage of Exhibit 5.6.

Summary.   Eighty-four percent of businesses that make it past the first year still fail within five years because they can't make the transition from the entrepreneurial stage.[47] The transitions become even more difficult as organizations progress through future stages of the life cycle. Organizations that do not successfully resolve the problems associated with these transitions are restricted in their growth and may even fail. From within an organization, the life cycle crises are very real, as illustrated by the nonprofit organization, Mothers Against Drunk Driving (MADD).

Mothers Against Drunk Driving

The drunk-driving problem has become a part of America's open political discourse, thanks largely to one angry, bereaved parent who gave a human face to the problem and eventually created a large, well-funded national organization called Mothers Against Drunk Driving (MADD). After her daughter was killed by a drunk driver, Candy Lightner and a few friends started MADD to push for stiffer penalties in her home state of California. People identified with Lightner's pain and anger, and within a year, MADD was a nationwide organization. After five years, MADD had over 350 local chapters and 600,000 members and donors.

As MADD began to grow in the collectivity stage, Lightner recognized the need for a board of directors and an executive director to help manage the expanding organization. As executive director, Philip Roos set up a departmentalized structure and recruited and developed specialists in public relations, law, social services, and non-profit advocacy. Roos' management helped take the organization to the formalization stage, but then he abruptly resigned, leaving Candy Lightner holding the titles of "President, Founder, Chairperson of the Board, and Chief Executive Officer." Lightner identified so strongly with the organization that she was unable to delegate authority to other managers; she rebelled against formalized coordination and control systems and was often accused of irrational or arbitrary decisions. Staff began referring to her as the MADD Queen, because of her autocratic leadership and refusal to follow consistent policies and operations. Conflicts with staff and board members continued to escalate until eventually Lightner was forced to resign and serve only as a consultant. A new president was brought in to get managers throughout the organization working together as a team to keep MADD growing and serving its mission.[48]

MADD reached a life cycle crisis at the end of the collectivity stage, when Candy Lightner was unable to delegate authority and responsibility. At this stage, top managers may need to be replaced when, like Lightner, they identify so strongly with the organization that they cannot share authority with lower-level managers.

Organizational Characteristics During the Life Cycle

As organizations evolve through the four stages of the life cycle, changes take place in structure, control systems, innovation, and goals. The organizational characteristics associated with each stage are summarized in Exhibit 5.7.

Entrepreneurial.   Initially, the organization is small, nonbureaucratic, and a one-person show. The top manager provides the structure and control system. Organizational energy is devoted to survival and the production of a single product or service.

Collectivity.   This is the organization's youth. Growth is rapid, and employees are excited and committed to the organization's mission. The structure is still mostly informal, although some procedures are emerging. Strong charismatic leaders like Bill Gates of Microsoft or Candy Lightner of MADD provide direction and goals for the organization. Continued growth is a major goal.

Formalization.   At this point, the organization is entering midlife. Bureaucratic characteristics emerge. The organization adds staff support groups, formalizes procedures, and establishes a clear hierarchy and division of labor. Innovation may be achieved by establishing a separate research and development department. Major goals are internal stability and market expansion. Top management has to delegate, but it also implements formal control systems.

At Dell Computer, for example, entrepreneurial whiz-kid Michael Dell has hired experienced managers, including some industry veterans from Apple, to help him develop and implement formal planning, management, and budgeting

Exhibit 5.7

Organization Characteristics During Four Stages of Life Cycle

Characteristic	1. Entrepreneurial Nonbureaucratic	2. Collectivity Prebureaucratic	3. Formalization Bureaucratic	4. Elaboration Very Bureaucratic
Structure	Informal, one-person show	Mostly informal, some procedures	Formal procedures, division of labor, new specialties added	Teamwork within bureaucracy, small-company thinking
Products or services	Single product or service	Major product or service, with variations	Line of products or services	Multiple product or service lines
Reward and control systems	Personal, paternalistic	Personal, contribution to success	Impersonal, formalized systems	Extensive, tailored to product and department
Innovation	By owner-manager	By employees and managers	By separate innovation group	By institutionalized R&D
Goal	Survival	Growth	Internal stability, market expansion	Reputation, complete organization
Top management style	Individualistic, entrepreneurial	Charismatic, direction-giving	Delegation with control	Team approach, attack bureaucracy

Source: Adapted from Larry E. Greiner, "Evolution and Revolution as Organizations Grow," *Harvard Business Review* 50 (July–August 1972): 37–46; G. L. Lippitt and W. H. Schmidt, "Crises in a Developing Organization," *Harvard Business Review* 45 (November–December 1967): 102–12; B. R. Scott, "The Industrial State: Old Myths and New Realities," *Harvard Business Review* 51 (March–April 1973): 133–48; Robert E. Quinn and Kim Cameron, "Organizational Life Cycles and Shifting Criteria of Effectiveness," *Management Science* 29 (1983): 33–51.

systems. Dell, who at the age of thirty-one is fourteen years younger than the youngest of his senior managers, says, "I'm very content to hire and delegate."[49] At the formalization stage, organizations may also develop complementary products to offer a complete product line.

Elaboration.   The mature organization is large and bureaucratic, with extensive control systems, rules, and procedures. Organization managers attempt to develop a team orientation within the bureaucracy to prevent further bureaucratization. Top managers are concerned with establishing a complete organization. Organizational stature and reputation are important. Innovation is institutionalized through an R&D department. Management may attack the bureaucracy and streamline it.

Summary.   Growing organizations move through stages of a life cycle, and each stage is associated with specific characteristics of structure, control systems, goals, and innovation. The life cycle phenomenon is a powerful concept used for understanding problems facing organizations and how managers can respond in a positive way to move an organization to the next stage.

ORGANIZATIONAL DECLINE AND DOWNSIZING

One reality facing leaders of today's organizations is that continual growth and expansion may not be possible. All around us we see evidence that some organizations have had to stop growing, and many are declining. Schools have decreasing enrollments, churches have closed their doors, municipal services have been curtailed, and industries have closed plants and laid off employees.[50]

Firms in decline often cut huge numbers of employees to reduce operating costs. For example, General Motors reduced its workforce by 99,000, and IBM slashed over 120,000 jobs, nearly 35 percent of its workforce.[51] Today, however, even profitable firms, such as GTE and Mobil Corp., are downsizing as part of an overall strategic plan to refocus on key business activities. AT&T has made massive job cutbacks at the same time it prepares for ambitious expansion into new global markets.[52]

In this section, we will examine the causes of organizational decline and then discuss how leaders in both declining and healthy firms can effectively manage the downsizing that is a reality of today's business world.

Definition and Causes

The term **organizational decline** is defined as a condition in which a substantial, absolute decrease in an organization's resource base occurs over a period of time.[53] Organizational decline is often associated with environmental decline in the sense that an organizational domain experiences either a reduction in size (such as shrinkage in customer demand or erosion of a city's tax base) or a reduction in shape (for example, shift in consumer demand). In general, three factors are considered to cause organization decline:

1. *Organizational atrophy.* Atrophy occurs when organizations grow older, become inefficient and overly bureaucratic, and lose muscle tone. The organization's ability to adapt to its environment deteriorates. Often atrophy follows a long period of success, because an organization takes success for

granted, becomes attached to practices and structures that worked in the past, and fails to adapt to changes in the environment.[54] Warning signals for organizational atrophy include excess staff personnel, cumbersome administrative procedures, lack of effective communication and coordination, and outdated organization structure.[55]

2. *Vulnerability.* Vulnerability reflects an organization's strategic inability to prosper in its environment. This often happens to small organizations that are not yet fully established. They are vulnerable to shifts in consumer tastes or in the economic health of the larger community. Some organizations are vulnerable because they are unable to define the correct strategy to fit the environment. Vulnerable organizations typically need to redefine their environmental domain to enter new industries and markets.

3. *Environmental decline or competition.* Environmental decline refers to reduced energy and resources available to support an organization. When the environment has less capacity to support organizations, the organization has to either scale down operations or shift to another domain.[56] For example, banks, real estate firms, oil service firms, and many other organizations found the total resource base in the Southwest declining after oil prices dropped. Companies had to divide up a shrinking pie, so several of them inevitably declined.

Increased global competition is also influencing many companies to scale down operations and cut back personnel as they strive for lean, nimble organizations. As discussed earlier, large companies have become bloated with too many administrative and support personnel and find that they need to slim down to remain competitive. Successful and profitable firms such as Procter & Gamble, American Home Products Corp., Sara Lee, and Banc One have all announced major layoffs, arguing that cutbacks are necessary in an era of cutthroat competition.[57]

A Model of Decline Stages

Based on an extensive review of organizational decline research, a model of decline stages has been proposed and is summarized in Exhibit 5.8. This model suggests that decline, if not managed properly, can move through five stages resulting in organizational dissolution.[58]

1. *Blinded stage.* The first stage of decline is the internal and external changes that threaten long-term survival and may require the organization to tighten up. The organization may have excess personnel, cumbersome procedures, or lack of harmony with customers. Leaders often miss the signals of decline at this point, and the solution is to develop effective scanning and control systems that indicate when something is wrong. With timely information, alert leaders can bring the organization back to top performance.

2. *Inaction stage.* The second stage of decline is called inaction, in which denial occurs despite signs of deteriorating performance. Leaders may try to persuade employees that all is well. Creative accounting may make things look well during this period. The solution is for leaders to recognize decline and take prompt action to realign the organization with the environment. Leadership actions can include new problem-solving approaches, increasing decision-making participation, and encouraging expression of dissatisfaction to learn what is wrong.

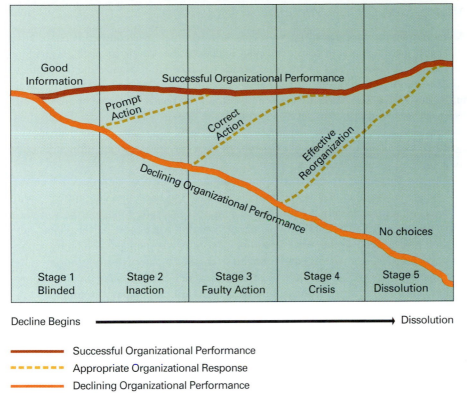

Exhibit 5.8
*Stages of Decline
and the Widening
Performance Gap*

Source: Reprinted from "Decline in Organizations: A Literature Integration and Extension," by William Weitzel and Ellen Jonsson, published in *Administrative Science Quarterly*, Vol. 34 (1), March 1989, by permission of *Administrative Science Quarterly*.

3. *Faulty action.* In the third stage, the organization is facing serious problems, and indicators of poor performance cannot be ignored. Failure to adjust to the declining spiral at this point can lead to organizational failure. Leaders are forced by severe circumstances to consider major changes. Actions may involve retrenchment, including downsizing personnel. Leaders should reduce employee uncertainty by clarifying values and providing information. A major mistake at this stage decreases the organization's chance for a turnaround.

4. *The crisis stage.* In stage four, the organization still has not been able to deal with decline effectively and is facing a panic. The organization may experience chaos, efforts to go back to basics, sharp changes, and anger. It is best for an organization to prevent a stage-four crisis, and the only solution is major reorganization. The social fabric of the organization is eroding, and dramatic action, such as replacing top administrators, and revolutionary changes in structure, strategy, and culture, are necessary. Workforce downsizing may be severe.

5. *Dissolution.* This stage of decline is irreversible. The organization is suffering loss of markets and reputation, the loss of its best personnel, and capital depletion. The only available strategy is to close down the organization in an orderly fashion and reduce the separation trauma of employees.

The following example of a once venerable law firm shows how failure to respond appropriately to signs of decline can lead to disaster.

In Practice 5.3   *Mudge, Rose, Guthrie, Alexander & Ferdon*

As the remaining partners in the New York law firm that once counted Richard Nixon among its members met to consider a plan of dissolution, the firm's problems had long been widely known in legal circles. Mudge's leaders failed to recognize the first signals of decline (blinded stage) as the firm gradually lost touch with customers and with changes in the law world. The company culture promoted the genteel, passive approach of the 1950s and 1960s and failed to develop partners who understood the need to hustle and retain business in the competitive legal world of the 1990s. Top leaders never even met with executives of Cigna Life Insurance Co., one of their top clients, which ultimately bolted for a more aggressive competitor.

As signs of trouble grew, executives responded with inaction. Unproductive partners were kept on, draining profits and morale, because the executive committee couldn't agree on what to do. Finally, the firm added a number of strong young partners in the areas of litigation, real estate, and white-collar defense, but when these partners later met to air their grievances over the firm's operations, executives responded with faulty action—supporting the weaker partners and trying to strengthen a paternalistic corporate culture that no longer worked. At the crisis stage, leaders were unable to make the revolutionary changes in structure, strategy, and culture that could turn the company around.

The departure of top-performing partners and significant clients sapped what strength remained in the 126-year-old firm. With little loyalty among partners or clients and with its reputation virtually destroyed, the only option for the organization was dissolution. As one partner put it: "You can't hold together something that no longer exists."[59]

As this example shows, properly managing organizational decline is necessary if an organization is to avoid dissolution. Leaders have a responsibility to detect the signs of decline, acknowledge them, implement necessary action, and reverse course. Some of the most difficult decisions pertain to **downsizing**—laying off employees to whom commitments have been made.

Downsizing Implementation

Downsizing has become a common practice in America's organizations and has affected hundreds of companies and millions of workers. For example, General Electric has cut its labor force by more than 150,000 since the early 1980s, and DuPont recently cut two layers of management and up to 25 percent of the employees in every department.[60] Downsizing has become such a part of the revitalization cycle of modern organizations that it is no longer considered only in connection with the decline and failure of organizations but as a routine part of management.[61]

When jobs are cut, managers must be prepared for conflict and decreased trust and morale. The following techniques can help smooth the downsizing process and ease the tensions for employees who leave as well as those who remain.[62]

1. *Consider voluntary programs.* The best way to cut jobs and still keep morale high among remaining employees is for some employees to leave voluntarily. For example, Hewlett-Packard, which has gone through major reorganization, has offered incentive packages for employees who choose to leave or retire. Dave Hill, human resources manager at Markem Corp., a privately owned manufacturer of in-plant printing systems, acknowledges

that his company's voluntary severance plan was much more expensive than involuntary layoffs would have been, but believes maintaining morale and support for the company made up for it.[63] Besides the expense, another possible downside to voluntary programs is that there is no way to predict which employees will accept the offer, and the company may lose employees with critical knowledge and skills.[64] Leaders at companies like Hewlett-Packard and Markem Corp. carefully manage voluntary programs to prevent the loss of key personnel.

2. *Communicate and overcommunicate.* Provide advance notice of layoffs with as much detailed information as possible. Even when managers are not certain about what's going to happen, they need to give employees periodic reports on the company's standing. Otherwise, employees assume the worst, and morale decreases as stress increases. At the Kansas City drug company Marion Merrell Dow, managers held frequent "town meetings" following the layoff of 13 percent of the workforce to explain the company's plan for fueling new growth.

3. *Allow employees to leave with dignity.* It is important that layoffs be handled appropriately and humanely; otherwise, employees sense that management does not value them as human beings. One communications company leaked the news of layoffs to the media before employees were told; thus, some people learned they were losing their jobs over the radio. This approach damaged the dignity of workers who left and the trust and morale of those who stayed. Employees should be allowed to say good-bye to coworkers and to express their sadness and anger. At Duracell, Inc. both laid-off workers and workers who remained met in groups with a senior management representative to express their feelings and grieve over the loss of colleagues.[65]

4. *Provide assistance to displaced workers.* Workers who lose their jobs can be given severance pay and extended benefits. Outplacement assistance and additional training eases the trauma of layoffs and helps workers find new jobs. Raychem, a California plastics and electronics company, offers career development programs not only to those who have been laid off but also to employees who stay, reasoning that if the company can't guarantee its workers employment, it should at least help them become more employable.

5. *Use ceremonies to reduce anger and confusion.* Important changes in people's lives are usually marked by rites and ceremonies to recognize the transition from one stage to another. Ceremonies connected with layoffs allow employees who are leaving as well as those remaining to acknowledge their feelings of grief, anxiety, guilt, or anger and thus better cope with this major transition. When layoffs at R. R. Donnelley, the world's largest printing company, broke the company's long tradition of lifetime employment, one manager likened the process to experiencing a death. Donnelley now offers off-site training courses and lectures that are designed partially to let employees vent their emotions.

Even the best managed companies may face the need to lay off workers in today's volatile environment. For organizations in decline, layoffs are often a first step toward turnaround and rejuvenation. Positive results can be obtained only if downsizing is handled in a way that enables remaining organization members to increase productivity and efficiency.

SUMMARY AND INTERPRETATION

The material covered in this chapter contains several important ideas about organizations. One is that bureaucratic characteristics, such as rules, division of labor, written records, hierarchy of authority, and impersonal procedures, become important as organizations grow large and complex. Bureaucracy is a logical form of organizing that lets firms use resources efficiently. However, in many large corporate and government organizations, bureaucracy has come under attack with attempts to decentralize authority, flatten organization structure, reduce rules and written records, and create a small-company mind-set. These companies are willing to trade economies of scale for responsive, adaptive organizations. Many companies are subdividing into small divisions to gain small-company advantages.

In large organizations, Parkinson's notion that top administrators build empires is not found. Greater support is required, however, from clerical and professional staff specialists in large organizations. This is a logical outcome of employee specialization and the division of labor. By dividing an organization's tasks and having specialists perform each part, the organization can become more efficient. Many organizations today need to reduce their overhead costs by cutting support personnel.

Organizations evolve through distinct life cycle stages as they grow and mature. Organization structure, internal systems, and management issues are different for each stage of development. Growth creates crises and revolutions along the way toward large size. A major task of managers is to guide the organization through the entrepreneurial, collectivity, formalization, and elaboration stages of development.

Organizations today are facing the reality that they cannot always continue to grow. Many organizations have stopped growing, and many are declining. One of the most difficult aspects is downsizing, or laying off employees. To smooth the downsizing process, managers can consider voluntary programs, keep employees informed, allow those who are laid off to leave with dignity, provide assistance to displaced workers, and use ceremonies to reduce feelings of anger and grief during the transition.

In the final analysis, large organization size and accompanying bureaucracy have many advantages, but they also have shortcomings. Large size and bureaucratic characteristics are important but can impede an organization that must act as if it is small, is a professional partnership, or needs to survive in a rapidly changing environment.

Key Concepts

bureaucracy	formalization stage
centralization	life cycle
charismatic authority	organizational decline
collectivity stage	Parkinson's law
complexity	personnel ratios
downsizing	rational-legal authority
elaboration stage	reasons organizations grow
entrepreneurial stage	traditional authority
formalization	

Discussion Questions

1. Describe the three bases of authority identified by Weber. Is it possible for each of these types of authority to function at the same time within an organization?
2. Discuss the key differences between large and small organizations. Which kinds of organizations would be better off acting as large organizations, and which are best trying to act as big-company/small-company hybrids?
3. How would you define organization size? What problems can you identify with using number of employees as a measure of size?
4. The manager of a medium-sized manufacturing plant once said, "We can't compete on price with the small organizations because they have lower overhead costs." Based upon the discussion in this chapter, would you agree or disagree with that manager? Why?
5. Why do large organizations tend to be more formalized?
6. If you were managing a department of college professors, how might you structure the department differently than if you were managing a department of bookkeepers? Why?
7. Do you think everyone would like to work in the new Carrier Corporation Arkadelphia factory (discussed in The New Paradigm box)? Would you? What type of employee would be best suited to a new factory like this versus a traditional mass production factory?
8. Apply the concept of life cycle to an organization with which you are familiar, such as a university or a local business. What stage is the organization in now? How did the organization handle or pass through its life cycle crises?
9. Discuss advantages and disadvantages of rules and regulations.
10. Should a "no-growth" philosophy of management be taught in business schools? Is a no-growth philosophy more realistic for today's economic conditions?

 Briefcase

As an organization manager, keep these guides in mind:

1. Decide whether your organization should act like a large or small company. To the extent that economies of scale, global reach, and complexity are important, introduce greater bureaucratization as the organization increases in size. As it becomes necessary, add rules and regulations, written documentation, job specialization, technical competence in hiring and promotion, and decentralization.
2. If responsiveness, flexibility, simplicity, and niche finding are important, subdivide the organization into simple, autonomous divisions that have freedom and a small-company approach.
3. Grow when possible. With growth, you can provide opportunities for employee advancement and greater profitability and effectiveness. Apply new management systems and structural configurations at each stage of an organization's development. Interpret the needs of the growing organization and respond with the management and internal systems that will carry the organization through to the next stage of development.
4. When layoffs are necessary, handle them with care. Treat departing employees humanely. Give them plenty of notice, allow them to leave with dignity, and offer assistance, such as severance pay and job leads.

Chapter Five Workbook *Life Cycle of Organizations* *

In this assignment, you will study one company in any of the high-tech industries, such as computers, telecommunications, and biotechnology. It should be a fairly successful organization that has been around for at least ten years. Your instructor will tell you whether you should work alone or with a partner.

You will need to either go to the library or use research resources on the Internet (probably one of the pay-as-you-use reference services). Find articles or annual reports on your organization from the current year and from eight to ten years ago. After you have done

your research, answer the following questions:

1. At what stage of the life cycle is the company? What evidence do you have for your inference?

2. Compare its size now to its size earlier. What stage was it in ten years ago? Again, on what evidence do you base your inference?

3. What issues are faced by management now versus ten years ago? Give examples. How are these issues being handled?

*Copyright 1996 by Dorothy Marcic. All rights reserved.

Case for Analysis *Mason & Lynch (A)* *

Two hundred fewer people, and change some attitudes toward performance and productivity . . . that's what it's going to take to turn this operation around.

John Piper looked at the sentence he had just written in his memo to the London managers work team (MWT). It sounded dramatic, but the loss of the detergent business three weeks ago had spelled it out quite clearly. An approach had to be found to downsize the plant and dramatically improve plant performance.

Company Background

Mason & Lynch was founded in London, England in 1837, and expanded to 28 countries with a product line that included confectionery, toiletries and detergents. M&L reached a 1986 net sales level of $15.4 billion, a 14 percent increase over the 1985 sales level.

International operations contributed approximately 20 percent to the 1986 net earnings level of $709 million. M&L international locations included Canada, Japan, the Middle East and Europe. Facilities in each of these countries and in the United States competed against one another for production rights to the various M&L products. Business was awarded to an M&L plant, or outsourced, based primarily on lowest manufacturing costs.

In 1986, M&L Canada employed approximately 3,500 people. The first Canadian plant opened in 1915 in London, Ontario, and additional plants were established in Montreal, Quebec, Kingston and Peterborough, Ontario. District sales offices were also located in Vancouver, Toronto, and Montreal with sales personnel in major centres across the country. Other Canadian

operations included a cellulose woodlands pulp mill facility and a sawmill producing quality bleached draft pulp and high-grade dimension lumber.

M&L London

The London plant was the oldest Canadian M&L facility. It produced the widest range of products and product sizes of any M&L plant and employed approximately 720 people. The average employee age was 42 and most people had well over eight years' seniority with the plant (Exhibit 5.9). No new non-managerial employees had been hired since 1979.

The plant's age showed in its relatively low flexibility and comparatively high manufacturing costs, and management was concerned that the plant's ability to

Exhibit 5.9
Projected Age and Service Demographics

Projected Age Demographics at December 31, 1986

Age Group	Number of Employees	Management (%)		Non-Management (%)		Percent of Total Population
25–29.9	54	26	(48%)	28	(52%)	7
30–34.9	119	16	(13%)	103	(87%)	16
35–39.9	108	12	(11%)	96	(89%)	14
40–44.9	118	3	(3%)	115	(97%)	16
45–49.9	107	9	(8%)	98	(92%)	14
50–54.9	102	7	(7%)	95	(93%)	14
55–59.9	104	16	(15%)	88	(85%)	14
60–64.9	42	8	(19%)	34 *	(81%)	5
	754	97	(13%)	657	(87%)	100

		Management	Non-Management
# Eligible for Early Retirement Incentive:	146	24	122
# Eligible for Voluntary Resignation Incentive:	608	73	535

Note: Excludes those who will retire prior to August 1, 1986.
*Includes 2 non-managers who will be age 65 at December 31, 1987.

Projected Age Demographics at December 31, 1986
Those Eligible for Early Retirement

Age	Number of Employees	Management	Non-Management
55	26	5	21
56	20	3	17
57	25	3	22
58	15	3	12
59	18	2	16
60	15	4	11
61	14	4	10
62	5	—	5
63	2	—	2
64	4	—	4
65	2	—	2
	146	24	122

Note: Excludes those who will retire prior to August 1, 1986.

(continued)

compete with other M&L facilities on bottom-line production costs was declining. Other M&L facilities were more modern, using new technology and technician task teams. The London plant, which was much older than these facilities, was more labour-intensive and trained and hired employees with single skills and traditional methods of supervision, as opposed to the newer facilities that used multiple-skilled employees

Exhibit 5.9
continued

Projected Service Demographics at December 31, 1986				
Years of Service	Number of Employees	Management (%)	Non-Management (%)	Percent of Total Population
0–4.9	24	23 (96%)	1 (4%)	3
5–9.9	73	22 (30%)	51 (70%)	10
10–14.9	242	10 (4%)	232 (96%)	32
15–19.9	125	4 (3%)	121 (97%)	17
20–24.9	90	3 (3%)	87 (97%)	12
25–29.9	98	11 (11%)	87 (89%)	13
30–34.9	71	16 (23%)	55 (77%)	9
35–39.9	17	6 (35%)	11 (65%)	2.2
40–44.9	13	2 (15%)	11 (85%)	1.7
45–49.9	1	0 —	1(100%)	0.1
	754	97	657	100

Note: Excludes those who will retire prior to August 1, 1986.

with better basic education, operating under self-management control systems.

In the spring of 1985, the London Management Work Team (MWT) held an offsite meeting to set some future direction for the plant. Through the course of their discussions, they developed a "vision" of the London plant for the year 1988. They documented this "vision" and presented it to employees in the fall of 1985.

The London Plant 1988 Vision

The 1988 vision was divided into five categories: tasks; structure; information and decision-making; people; and rewards.

Tasks

The vision called for broader, more flexible assignments than those performed in 1985. People with multiple skills and a broader knowledge of plant activities would be required to perform tasks within these assignments.

Business units, representing M&L product groups and support functions, would become self-sufficient once employees had expanded their skill base. Operating, technical and administrative responsibilities would be shared by all business unit members with each employee having core operating skills, such as operating, maintaining, and adjusting equipment, as well as at least one in-depth technical or administrative skill, and a co-

ordination role. In-depth skills would include production planning, pump overhaul, laboratory analyses and project management.

These new skills would enable employees to be responsible for achieving business results. They would set their own goals, monitor and track progress, and take corrective action when necessary. Managers would act as coaches, facilitators, and trainers, letting the business teams solve their own operating problems.

Structure

All plant employees would belong to a team consisting of approximately 12 people. Each team, formed within a business unit and organized to be self-sufficient, would focus on a specific area or subject. Focus areas would include specific brands, technology support and temporary tasks. (See Exhibit 5.10 for plant structure.)

Teams would perform most of the tasks associated with a business such as producing, packaging and shipping a product. This would increase the percentage of people directly tied to a business, and reduce general "support staff"—those not directly linked to a business—by about 50 percent over three years.

Additional employee reduction would be achieved through the business teams' examination of their functions. A function would be eliminated by questioning the need for it, by replacing it with improved technology, or through contracting it out. The required support functions

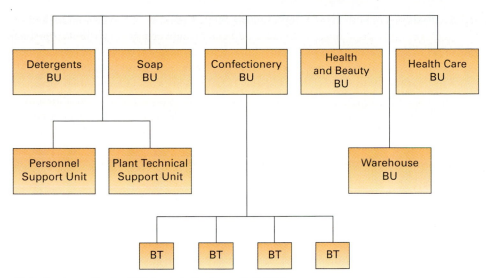

Exhibit 5.10
London Plant Structure

Note: Business Teams (BT) in each Business Unit (BU)

that remained would be tied to business units by rotating people from the units through the support functions.

New non-management employees would start their careers as members of production teams. They would acquire their operating skills first and then develop support skills through training and/or rotation to support functions.

Cross-sectional task teams would also be created to address most plant-wide issues and for some project work. Permanent task teams would have rotational membership to ensure the participation and development of all team members. Examples of possible task teams would include pay system task teams and teams commissioned to study opportunities.

Information and Decision-Making

All information relevant to the business and the teams would be broadly shared and well understood. Information would include profitability targets, market strategies, business plans and manufacturing's impact on the business. Regular and frequent team meetings would be held to share this information and to discuss goals and priorities, strategic planning and project management.

Decisions would be made by people throughout the company, including employees at the lowest possible organizational level. All tactical and some strategic decision-making, for example, would be made by team members. These decisions would be subject to plant-wide boundary conditions. Boundaries would be based on legal, moral and plant-imposed barriers, such as shift

differentials and the pay system. Local decision-making autonomy would be based on doing what's right for the business and the individuals affected. Examples of local team decisions would include vacation scheduling, hours of work and task assignments.

Tools to assist the decision-making and information collecting processes would include on-line/real-time data acquisition and computerized control systems. Approximately 50 percent of the teams would be using some real-time data to optimize their operations. Interactive information systems would also be available and include "what if" cost forecasting, and inventory control systems. The data that would be generated would be available to everyone.

An environment of open, two-way communication would have to exist within the plant to institute any changes. This would allow individuals to resolve problems and issues with those directly involved. If an individual or team couldn't reach a resolution, a formal problem-solving process would be available to assist.

People

London plant employees would need to be committed to the business and recognize and support the need for change. They would have to be flexible and committed to their own personal growth, while believing in the team approach.

A high quality search process would ensure that individuals with these characteristics were selected. Minority groups would also occupy "an appropriate percentage" of all skill and pay positions in both management and non-management areas. M&L wanted to hire more female department managers and process operators. They would also like to develop or hire more female employees with in-depth technical skills.

Once hired, employees would begin a training program to enhance their contribution to the business. Training would be accomplished through a training group and by training coordinators on each business team. Ten to twenty percent of an employee's time would be spent on training and development activities. This would include time spent on skill acquisition, coordinator activities, task force participation, business training and mentor systems for new team members.

Employee advancement would occur primarily within a business unit. Movement between business units would be infrequent. Interested people could apply and, if eligible, would be screened for ability and potential by the receiving team. The receiving team would accept the most appropriate candidate, based on performance and service. Individual needs would also be taken into account.

Movement would also occur at the company's request, based on business or site needs. For example, if the London plant was awarded a new brand's business, all employees possessing the necessary skills would be given the opportunity to move and form a new business team.

Regular feedback would also be provided to all employees. Performance appraisals, which would include peer input, would be used as well as improvement plans and team feedback sessions.

Rewards

All rewards would be based on an individual's measured contribution to business results. As the business results improved, employees would need to acquire more knowledge, skills and responsibilities in order to maintain their relative position in the plant.

The non-management pay system would be designed to reward the application of acquired skills. Applications would include training other employees, passing formal qualifications, and demonstrating the mastery and use of skills on an on-going basis. Examples of acquired skills would include leadership, project management, in-depth technical and administrative skills, and core operating skills.

A major portion of the reward system would be non-monetary in nature, rewarding the best performers first. Possible rewards would include more variety in assignments, travel, task-force participation, community work,

representing M&L to suppliers and customers, and individual movement between business units. Personal satisfaction would be the key reward. Promotion opportunities to management positions would also exist.

Existing management would be rewarded, based on their achievement of business results, and initiation of new concepts that would improve the business. Actual rewards would include pay, promotion, desirable assignments, high-profile opportunities, autonomy, professional development and an increased ability to influence the business.

Rewards, such as promotions, which would affect the pay system would be reviewed by a standing task team. This task team, which would also administer the pay system, would consist of a cross section of managers and non-managers, ensuring fairness and consistency across the plant.

Implementing the Vision

John Piper was promoted to London plant manager in September 1985, just after the MWT presented their "vision" to the employees. He had been with M&L for 12 years, most recently as the manager of employee relations in the London plant. His first job was to institute the changes outlined in the vision statement.

Piper approached the plant's Employees Association. This was an employee-elected body representing the London plant's non-management personnel. Normally, the MWT worked with the Employees Association to address the various issues that concerned plant employees. However, the Association resisted the idea of work system changes since the members of the Association believed that these would minimize the way in which seniority played a role in promotions and would threaten jobs of people who were unable or unwilling to learn new skills. Piper was convinced of the need for these changes and decided to bypass the Association and work directly with employees. He made several presentations at employee meetings and was successful in persuading most employees of the need for the changes. Piper felt that the key factor in getting employees to cooperate with these new changes was the general culture at M&L which stressed openness, trust, and individual employee security and dignity. When asked at the meeting whether these changes would mean layoffs, Piper said that M&L had always managed productivity improvements through attrition and he saw no reason why this could not be done in this case.

Plant employees were organized into 26 Business Teams. These teams studied and designed work systems within their business units. Designs had to be consistent with the vision statement and supportive of new technology before presentation to the MWT for approval. Two task teams were also commissioned to work with the business teams. They had to develop new movement and pay systems that complemented, rather than restricted, the business teams' designs. There were approximately 10 people on each team consisting of management personnel and business unit representatives.

Throughout the design process, Business Teams identified several employee surpluses. By January 1, 1988, 100 non-management positions would become redundant, as a result of the new work systems' productivity and technology improvements.

Loss of Market

In 1979, the London detergent division was at full capacity. Its principal product was a market leader in laundry detergents. M&L, with a 50-percent market share, expected continued market growth. In order to provide the additional production capacity, M&L decided to build a new plant in Peterborough, Ontario, devoted to detergent production.

The detergent market growth never materialized as forecast in 1979. Consumers were turning to denser, liquid products, and away from the type of powdered detergents that M&L manufactured. This left M&L with two producing plants and excess capacity.

In Febuary 1986, the company made an economic decision to consolidate detergent production at the Peterborough plant. They had facilities, work system and weight control advantages over the London plant, giving them lower manufacturing costs. This meant that M&L London would have 100 additional excess employees beyond the 100 identified as surplus if the vision was fully implemented.

Current Situation

By July 1, 1987, the transition of the detergent division to the Peterborough facility would be completed. This, coupled with productivity improvements from the implementation of the work system designs, meant that the London plant would have approximately 200 excess non-management personnel.

A M&L Excess Employee Reduction team was formed to develop an alternative downsizing plan. The team consisted of Steve Ronson, M&L London's personnel manager, John Piper, two plant employees and the corporate personnel manager. They also received input from senior management, the MWT and the U.K. parent company.

The team immediately made a 33-person reduction with the "term or task" employees; these employees worked on a temporary basis for specific terms and knew that in the event of an employee surplus, they would be the first to go. The lay-off of temporary employees meant that approximately 170 people were required to fill the 1988 reduction quota.

The reduction team had several downsizing alternatives for the remaining employee surplus. A severance pay package could be offered. A study of current severance pay practices indicated that the company should pay about one-month's base salary per year of service, up to a maximum of $75,000 (approximately two years' salary). Another option was an early retirement incentive plan (ERIP) in which an incentive, in addition to the normal early retirement supplement and the cost of benefits, could be offered. (See Exhibit 5.11 for regular retirement supplement data and suggested incentives.)

One senior M&L manager suggested that Piper and Ronson consider some form of educational program as a reduction method. M&L could offer an educational leave of absence (ELOA) to a limited number of employees. The company would pay for the employees'

Age	Regular Supplement	Incentive	Monthly Total
60–64	$700	$525	$1,225
55–59	$525	$525	$1,050
Note: Company continues to pay the cost of benefits.			

Exhibit 5.11

Early Retirement Incentive Plan

Exhibit 5.12

Suggested ELOA and LOA Formats

Suggested Format for an ELOA
• An ELOA is to be for a period of no less than one year.
• Company pays an $18,000/year salary, an education tuition refund, and a $1,000/year miscellaneous education expense.
• Company pays $2,000/year for basic benefits (i.e., OHIP, Supplemental, Dental and Group Life Insurance).
• Contributions to the Profit Sharing Pension Plan stop while an employee is on leave.
• An employee can return to work at any point during his/her ELOA and the company can recall employees after giving them six months' notice.
• If an employee decides to resign during his/her ELOA, the company will pay four months' severance.
• ELOA employees are given preference for summer work.
Suggested Format for a General LOA
Company pays $12,000/year and the cost of basic benefits. Other details are the same as in the ELOA program.

yearly tuition expense and provide a reduced salary. M&L management estimated that, on average, an employee cost the company $50,000/year. (See Exhibit 5.12 for a suggested ELOA format.)

Piper wasn't sure how an ELOA program should be structured, or if employees would even be interested. He wondered if a general leave of absence might be more appropriate. The reduction team had come up with a possible format for this type of leave of absence as well. (See Exhibit 5.12.)

Piper and Ronson would have to sell any idea(s) they came up with to senior management. They knew that management's approval would be based on a plan's perceived fairness to employees, and its rate of return.

Piper was also concerned about the employees' reactions. The MWT had to turn the plant around and downsizing was only one part of it. An approach had to be found that could dramatically improve plant performance and reduce employee enrollment by the desired numbers.

As Piper thought about the task before him, he picked up the phone to call another meeting of the Excess Employee Reduction team. They had to finalize a downsizing plan as soon as possible and put the vision into action before the London plant lost any more business.

Case for Analysis *Mason & Lynch (B)—Barb Jansen**

Barb Jansen had just finished talking to Bob Ryan, M&L's Education Leave of Absence Co-ordinator. Barb, who had wanted to be a veterinarian her entire life, had been assured by Bob that M&L would consider it an acceptable ELOA. Now with two weeks left on her maternity leave and the application due at the end of August, three days after her return, Barb had to decide whether she was ready to return to school after a 15 year absence and leave her job at M&L.

M&L London

In February 1986, M&L London had identified approximately 200 excess non-management employees. (See M&L London (A) for background information.) The company had already reduced this excess enrollment to 160 through a number of initiatives. They had replaced contractors, added new products and eliminated temporary employees.

Lay-offs were not an alternative for the remaining surplus of 160. M&L London had made a commitment to their employees that the plant's efforts to achieve productivity improvements would not result in a lay-off situation.

An M&L Excess Enrollment team was formed to develop a creative downsizing plan. They put together a reduction program consisting of three alternatives: an Early Retirement Incentive Plan (ERIP); an Educational Leave of Absence (ELOA); and a general Leave of Absence (LOA). All three options were voluntary and would be offered to employees in both phase one and two of the reduction program. (See Exhibit 5.13 for the details of each option.)

Phase one of the program was announced on July 28, 1986. Applications were due by the end of August. Employees would start leaving the business in September 1986, through to June 1987. Phase two of the program would be implemented on a similar time line commencing June, 1987.

In an effort to help employees make informed decisions, the London plant ran a three-hour session explaining the details of each option. They arranged contacts for employees at The University of Western Ontario and Fanshawe College in London. They also provided lifestyle counselling and a financial advisor to help employees understand the economics of each alternative in relation to their financial position.

Barb Jansen

Barb Jansen was away on maternity leave when the Excess Enrollment Reduction plan was announced. She didn't find out about the program until the beginning of August, when her father, a retired M&L London employee, phoned to tell her about the ELOA.

At first Barb wasn't interested in the program. She thought an ELOA had to be M&L related. To Barb, this meant taking engineering or machine maintenance courses, both of which she had no interest in.

It wasn't until the middle of August, that Barb found out that any registered degree program was considered acceptable. She had dropped by the plant with her two month old son, and had jokingly asked Bob Ryan if M&L would consider paying for her to become a veterinarian. She was shocked when he said 'yes'.

Barb had worked at M&L London for 13 years. She started when she was a student, working summers in the plant, and became a full time employee after completing high school. For the last nine years Barb had been the plant's Industrial Hygiene and Safety manager. Her salary had increased to $40,000 in 1986 and she thought that M&L was a fine employer with whom she could build a satisfying career.

Barb's husband, Eric, had recently started a new community newspaper in London. The couple had been married for three years. During that time, they had shared the dream of owning and operating a hobby farm. Barb would become a veterinarian, specializing in horses, and set up her practice on the farm while Eric would look after the business. With the M&L ELOA offer, Barb and Eric considered making their dream a reality.

Exhibit 5.13

The Excess Enrollment Reduction Plan

1. The Early Retirement Incentive Plan

Age	Regular Supplement	Incentive	Monthly Total
60–64	$700	$525	$1,225
55–59	$525	$525	$1,050

Company continues to pay the cost of benefits.

2. The Education Leave of Absence

- 30 positions offered to all non-management personnel, including those eligible for early retirement.
- An ELOA is to be for a period of no less than one year.
- Company pays an $18,000/year salary, an education tuition refund, and a $1,000/year miscellaneous education expense.
- Company pays $2,000/year for basic benefits (i.e. OHIP, Supplemental, Dental and Group Life Insurance).
- Contributions to the Profit Sharing Pension Plan stop while an employee is on leave.
- An employee can return to work at any point during their ELOA and the company can recall employees after giving them six months' notice.
- If an employee decides to resign during their ELOA, the company will pay them four months' severance.
- ELOA employees are given preference for summer work.

3. Other Leaves of Absence

- If 30 positions are not filled with the ELOA program, the company will offer other LOAs to fill the 30 positions.
- Approval of an LOA depends on the company's needs and employees' interests. Seniority is not a determining factor.
- Company pays $12,000/year and the cost of basic benefits. Other details are the same as in the ELOA program.

The Decision

The Jansens discussed the possibility of Barb taking an ELOA. She would have to upgrade her high school education before gaining admittance to a university program. Once accepted she would have to complete two years of a Bachelor of Science degree before applying to veterinarian school at the University of Guelph, Ontario.

It took four years to become a veterinarian and Barb wanted to specialize in surgery. This meant completing another three year course after obtaining her veterinarian license.

Over 600 students applied to Guelph's veterinarian program each year. The university accepted approximately 100 of these applications. Candidates needed an 80% average in their last two semesters in order to apply. Interviews were also required and practical experience was suggested.

Barb knew it would be a long and difficult process to become a veterinarian. At 32, with a two month old son, she wasn't sure she was prepared to take on the load.

She remembered her feelings when she left high school. The money M&L had offered her to become a full time employee was more attractive than continuing her education. Now, after a 15 year absence, Barb was considering returning to the academic life and giving up a job she enjoyed and had worked hard to obtain.

The application deadline was two weeks away. Bob Ryan had indicated to Barb that she stood a good chance of being accepted into the ELOA program. She would have to arrange for upgrading courses and get a guaranteed acceptance into a Bachelor of Science program at Guelph University before M&L could consider her application. With this in mind, Barb wondered whether or not the ELOA program was right for her.

Chapter Five Workshop *WINDSOCK, INC.**

1. *Introduction.* Class is divided into four groups: Central Office, Product Design, Marketing/Sales, and Production. Central Office is a slightly smaller group. If groups are large enough, assign observers to each one. Central Office is given 500 straws and 750 pins. Each person reads *only* the role description relevant to that group. (*Materials needed:* Plastic milk straws (500) and a box (750) of straight pins.)
2. *Perform task.* Depending on length of class, step 2 may take 30 to 60 minutes. Groups perform functions and prepare for a two-minute report for "stockholders."
3. *Group reports.* Each group gives a two-minute presentation to "stockholders."
4. *Observers' reports (optional).* Observers share insights with subgroups.
5. *Class discussion.*
   a. What helped or blocked intergroup cooperation and coordination?
   b. To what extent was there open versus closed communication? What impact did that have?
   c. What styles of leadership were exhibited?
   d. What types of team interdependencies emerged?

Roles

Central Office

Your team is the central management and administration of WINDSOCK, INC. You are the heart and pulse of the organization, because without your coordination and resource allocation, the organization would go under. Your task is to manage the operations of the organization, not an easy responsibility because you have to coordinate the activities of three distinct groups of personnel: the Marketing/Sales group, the Production group, and the Product Design group. In addition, you have to manage resources including materials (pins and straws), time deadlines, communications, and product requirements.

In this exercise, you are to do whatever is necessary in order to accomplish the mission and to keep the organization operating in a harmonious and efficient manner.

WINDSOCK, INC. has a total of thirty minutes (more if instructor assigns) to design an advertising campaign and ad copy, to design the windmill, and to produce the first windmill prototypes for delivery. Good luck to you all.

Product Design

Your team is the research and product design group of WINDSOCK, INC. You are the brain and creative aspect of the operation, because without an innovative and successfully designed product, the organization would go under. Your duties are to design products that will compete favorably in the marketplace, keeping in mind function, aesthetics, cost, ease of production, and available materials.

In this exercise, you are to come up with a workable plan for a product that will be built by your production team. Your windmill must be light, portable, easy to assemble, and aesthetically pleasing. Central Office controls the budget and allocates material for your division.

WINDSOCK, INC. as an organization has a total of thirty minutes (more if instructor assigns) to design an advertising campaign, to design the windmill (your group's task), and to produce the first windmill prototypes for delivery. Good luck to you all.

Marketing/Sales

Your team is the marketing/sales group of WINDSOCK, INC. You are the backbone of the operation, because without customers and sales the organization would go under. Your task is to determine the market, develop an advertising campaign to promote your company's unique product, produce ad copy, and develop a sales force and sales procedures for both potential customers and the public at large.

For the purpose of this exercise, you may assume that a market analysis has been completed. Your team is now in a position to produce an advertising campaign and ad copy for the product. To be effective, you have to become very familiar with the characteristics of the product and how it is different from those products already on the market. The Central Office controls your budget and allocates materials for use by your division.

WINDSOCK, INC. has a total of thirty minutes (more if instructor assigns) to design an advertising campaign and ad (your group's task), to design the windmill, and to produce the first windmill prototypes for delivery. Good luck to you all.

*Adapted by Dorothy Marcic from Christopher Taylor and Saundra Taylor in "Teaching Organizational Team-Building Through Simulations," *Organizational Behavior Teaching Review*, Vol. XI(3), pp. 86–87.

Production

Your team is the production group of WINDSOCK, INC. You are the heart of the operation, because without a group to produce the product, the organization would go under. You have the responsibility to coordinate and produce the product for delivery. The product involves an innovative "windmill" design that is cheaper, lighter, more portable, more flexible, and more aesthetically pleasing than other designs currently available in the marketplace. Your task is to build windmills within cost guidelines, according to specifications,

within a prescribed time period, using predetermined materials.

For the purpose of this exercise, you are to organize your team, set production schedules, and build the windmills. Central Office has control over your budget and materials, as well as the specifications.

WINDSOCK, INC. has a total of thirty minutes (more if instructor assigns) to design an advertising campaign, to design the windmill, and to produce the first windmill prototypes (your group's task) for delivery. Good luck to you all.

Notes

1. Robert Neff, "Tradition Be Damned," *Business Week*, 31 October 1994, 108–10.
2. Richard A. Melcher, "How Goliaths Can Act Like Davids," *Business Week/Enterprise*, 1993, 192–201.
3. Kim S. Cameron, "Organizational Downsizing," in George P. Huber and William H. Glick, eds., *Organizational Change and Redesign* (New York: Oxford University Press, 1992).
4. James Q. Wilson, *Bureaucracy* (Basic Books: 1989).
5. Charles Perrow, *Complex Organizations: A Critical Essay* (Glenview, Ill.: Scott, Foresman, 1979), 4.
6. Tom Peters, "Rethinking Scale," *California Management Review* (Fall 1992): 7–29.
7. Michael J. Mandel, Christopher Farrell, and Catherine Yang, "Land of the Giants," *Business Week*, 11 September 1995, 34–35; Michael J. Mandel, "A Dangerous Concentration?" *Business Week*, 29 April 1996, 96–97.
8. William H. Starbuck, "Organizational Growth and Development," in James March, ed., *Handbook of Organizations* (New York: Rand McNally, 1965), 451–522; John Child, *Organizations* (New York: Harper & Row, 1977), ch. 7.
9. Wendy Zellner, Robert D. Hof, Richard Brandt, Stephen Baker, and David Greising, "Go-Go Goliaths," *Business Week*, 13 February 1995, 64–70.
10. James B. Treece, "Sometimes, You've Still Gotta Have Size," *Business Week/Enterprise*, 1993, 200–201.
11. Glenn R. Carroll, "Organizations . . . The Smaller They Get," *California Management Review* 37, no. 1 (Fall 1994): 28–41.
12. Alan Deutschman, "America's Fastest Risers," *Fortune*, 7 October 1991, 46–57.
13. *Ibid.*
14. Melcher, "How Goliaths Can Act Like Davids."
15. Tom Peters, *The Pursuit of WOW: Every Person's Guide to Topsy-Turvy Times* (New York: Vintage, 1994), 31.
16. Wendy Zellner, Robert D. Hof, Richard Brandt, Stephen Baker, and David Greising, "Go-Go Goliaths."
17. Max Weber, *The Theory of Social and Economic Organizations*, translated by A. M. Henderson and T. Parsons (New York: Free Press, 1947).
18. John Crewdson, "Corruption Viewed as a Way of Life," *Bryan-College Station Eagle*, 28 November 1982, 13A; Barry Kramer, "Chinese Officials Still Give Preference to Kin, Despite Peking Policies," *Wall Street Journal,* 29 October 1985, 1, 21.
19. Weber, *Theory of Social and Economic Organizations,* 328–40.
20. Allen C. Bluedorn, "Pilgrim's Progress: Trends and Convergence in Research on Organizational Size and Environment," *Journal of Management Studies* 19 (Summer 1993): 163–91; John R. Kimberly, "Organizational Size and the Structuralist Perspective: A Review, Critique, and Proposal," *Administrative Science Quarterly* (1976): 571–97; Richard L. Daft and Selwyn W. Becker, "Managerial, Institutional, and Technical Influences on Administration: A Longitudinal Analysis," *Social Forces* 59 (1980): 392–413.
21. James P. Walsh and Robert D. Dewar, "Formalization and the Organizational Life Cycle," *Journal of Management Studies* 24 (May 1987): 215–31.
22. Nancy M. Carter and Thomas L. Keon, "Specialization as a Multidimensional Construct," *Journal of Management Studies* 26 (1989): 11–28; Cheng-Kuang Hsu, Robert M. March, and Hiroshi Mannari, "An Examination of the Determinants of

Organizational Structure," *American Journal of Sociology* 88 (1983): 975–96; Guy Geeraerts, "The Effect of Ownership on the Organization Structure in Small Firms," *Administrative Science Quarterly* 29 (1984): 232–37; Bernard Reimann, "On the Dimensions of Bureaucratic Structure: An Empirical Reappraisal," *Administrative Science Quarterly* 18 (1973): 462–76; Richard H. Hall, "The Concept of Bureaucracy: An Empirical Assessment," *American Journal of Sociology* 69 (1963): 32–40; William A. Rushing, "Organizational Rules and Surveillance: A Proposition in Comparative Organizational Analysis," *Administrative Science Quarterly* 10 (1966): 423–43.

23. David A. Morand, "The Role of Behavioral Formality and Informality in the Enactment of Bureaucratic Versus Organic Organizations," *Academy of Management Review* 20, no. 4 (1995): 831–72.

24. Jerald Hage and Michael Aiken, "Relationship of Centralization to Other Structural Properties," *Administrative Science Quarterly* 12 (1967): 72–91.

25. Guy Geeraerts, "The Effect of Ownership on the Organization Structure in Small Firms"; Hsu, Marsh, and Mannari, "An Examination of the Determinants of Organizational Structure"; Robert Dewar and Jerald Hage, "Size, Technology, Complexity, and Structural Differentiation: Toward a Theoretical Synthesis," *Administrative Science Quarterly* 23 (1978): 111–36.

26. Richard L. Daft and Patricia J. Bradshaw, "The Process of Horizontal Differentiation: Two Models," *Administrative Science Quarterly* 25 (1980): 441–56.

27. Peter M. Blau, *The Organization of Academic Work* (New York: Wiley Interscience, 1973).

28. Kathy Goode, Betty Hahn, and Cindy Seibert, *United Parcel Service: The Brown Giant* (Unpublished manuscript, Texas A&M University, 1981); Kenneth Labich, "Big Changes at Big Brown," *Fortune*, 18 January 1988, 56–64; Chuck Hawkins with Patrick Oster, "After a U-Turn, UPS Really Delivers," *Business Week*, 31 May 1993, 92–93; Robert Frank, "As UPS Tries to Deliver More To Its Customers, Labor Problems Grow," *Wall Street Journal*, 23 May 1994, A1.

29. Peter Brimelow, "How Do You Cure Injelitance?" *Forbes*, 7 August 1989, 42–44.

30. Jeffrey D. Ford and John W. Slocum, Jr., "Size, Technology, Environment and the Structure of Organizations," *Academy of Management Review* 2 (1977): 561–75; John D. Kasarda, "The Structural Implications of Social System Size: A Three-Level Analysis," *American Sociological Review* 39 (1974): 19–28.

31. Graham Astley, "Organizational Size and Bureaucratic Structure," *Organization Studies* 6 (1985): 201–28; Spyros K. Lioukas and Demitris A. Xerokostas, "Size and Administrative Intensity in Organizational Divisions," *Management Science* 28 (1982): 854–68; Peter M. Blau, "Interdependence and Hierarchy in Organizations," *Social Science Research* 1 (1972): 1–24; Peter M. Blau and R. A. Schoenherr, *The Structure of Organizations* (New York: Basic Books, 1971); A. Hawley, W. Boland, and M. Boland, "Population Size and Administration in Institutions of Higher Education," *American Sociological Review* 30 (1965): 252–55; Richard L. Daft, "System Influence on Organization Decision-Making: The Case of Resource Allocation," *Academy of Management Journal* 21 (1978): 6–22; B. P. Indik, "The Relationship between Organization Size and the Supervisory Ratio," *Administrative Science Quarterly* 9 (1964): 301–12.

32. T. F. James, "The Administrative Component in Complex Organizations," *Sociological Quarterly* 13 (1972): 533–39; Daft, "System Influence on Organization Decision-Making"; E. A. Holdaway and E. A. Blowers, "Administrative Ratios and Organization Size: A Longitudinal Examination," *American Sociological Review* 36 (1971): 278–86; John Child, "Parkinson's Progress: Accounting for the Number of Specialists in Organizations," *Administrative Science Quarterly* 18 (1973): 328–48.

33. Richard L. Daft and Selwyn Becker, "School District Size and the Development of Personnel Resources," *Alberta Journal of Educational Research* 24 (1978): 173–87.

34. Andrew Pollack, "Think Japan Inc. Is Lean and Mean? Step Into This Office," *The New York Times*, 20 March 1994, Section 3, p. 11.

35. Robert M. Marsh and Hiroshi Mannari, "The Size Imperative? Longitudinal Tests," *Organization Studies* 10 (1989): 83–95.

36. Karen Grassmuck, "U-M's Work Force: A Growth Industry," *Ann Arbor (Mich.) News,* 17 April 1989, A1, A4.

37. Based on Gifford and Elizabeth Pinchot, *The End of Bureaucracy and the Rise of the Intelligent Organization* (San Francisco: Berrett-Koehler Publishers, 1993), 21–29.

38. Bob Davis, "Federal Relief Agency Is Slowed by Infighting, Patronage, Regulations," *Wall Street Journal*, 31 August 1992, A1, A12; Paul M. Barrett, "Bureaucratic Bungling Helps Fugitives Evade Capture by Feds," *Wall Street Journal*, 7 August 1991, A1, A6.

39. Michael Schroder, "The Recasting of Alcoa," *Business Week,* 9 September 1991, 62–64; Thomas Moore, "Goodbye Corporate Staff," *Fortune*, 21 December 1987, 65–76.

40. Philip M. Padsakoff, Larry J. Williams, and William D. Todor, "Effects of Organizational Formalization on Alienation among Professionals and Nonprofessionals," *Academy of Management Journal* 29 (1986): 820–31.

41. Royston Greenwood, C. R. Hinings, and John Brown, "'P²-Form' Strategic Management: Corporate Practices in Professional Partnerships," *Academy of Management Journal* 33 (1990): 725–55; Royston Greenwood and C. R. Hinings, "Understanding Strategic Change: The Contribution of Archtypes," *Academy of Management Journal* 36 (1993): 1052–81.

42. John R. Kimberly, Robert H. Miles, and Associates, *The Organizational Life Cycle* (San Francisco: Jossey-Bass, 1980); Ichak Adices, "Organizational Passages—Diagnosing and Treating Lifecycle Problems of Organizations," *Organizational Dynamics* (Summer 1979): 3–25; Danny Miller and Peter H. Friesen, "A Longitudinal Study of the Corporate Life Cycle," *Management Science* 30 (October 1984): 1161–83; Neil C. Churchill and Virginia L. Lewis, "The Five Stages of Small Business Growth," *Harvard Business Review* 61 (May–June 1983): 30–50.

43. Larry E. Greiner, "Evolution and Revolution as Organizations Grow," *Harvard Business Review* 50 (July–August 1972): 37–46; Robert E. Quinn and Kim Cameron, "Organizational Life Cycles and Shifting Criteria of Effectiveness: Some Preliminary Evidence," *Management Science* 29 (1983): 33–51.

44. George Land and Beth Jarman, "Moving beyond Breakpoint," in Michael Ray and Alan Rinzler, eds., *The New Paradigm* (New York: Jeremy P. Tarcher/Perigee Books, 1993), 250–66; Michael L. Tushman, William H. Newman, and Elaine Romanelli, "Convergence and Upheaval: Managing the Unsteady Pace of Organizational Evolution," *California Management Review* 29 (1987): 1–16.

45. David A. Whetten, "Sources, Responses, and Effects of Organizational Decline," in John R. Kimberly, Robert H. Miles, and Associates, *The Organizational Life Cycle* (San Francisco: Jossey-Bass, 1980), 342–74.

46. Kathy Rebello, Robert D. Hof, and Peter Burrows, "Inside Apple's Boardroom Coup," *Business Week*, 19 February 1996, 28–30.

47. George Land and Beth Jarman, "Moving Beyond Breakpoint."

48. Frank J. Weed, "The MADD Queen: Charisma and the Founder of Mothers Against Drunk Driving," *Leadership Quarterly* 4, no. 3/4, (1993): 329–46.

49. Scott McCartney, "Michael Dell—and His Company—Grow Up," *Wall Street Journal*, 31 January 1995, B1.

50. Whetten, "Sources, Responses, and Effects of Organizational Decline"; David A. Whetten, "Organizational Decline: A Neglected Topic in Organizational Science," *Academy of Management Review* 5 (1980): 577–88.

51. Robert J. Grossman, "Damaged, Downsized Souls," *HR Magazine* (May 1996): 54–62.

52. Garry D. Bruton, J. Kay Keels, and Christopher L. Shook, Downsizing the Firm: Answering the Strategic Questions," *Academy of Management Executive* 10, no. 2 (1996): 38–45; Matt Murray, "Amid Record Profits, Companies Continue to Lay Off Employees," *Wall Street Journal*, 4 May 1995, A1, A6; John Keller, Leslie Cauley, and Douglas Lavin, "AT&T Job Cutbacks Are Just the First Shot in Global Telecom War," *Wall Street Journal*, 5-6 January 1996, A1.

53. Kim S. Cameron, Myung Kim, and David A. Whetten, "Organizational Effects of Decline and Turbulence," *Administrative Science Quarterly* 32 (1987): 222–40.

54. Danny Miller, "What Happens After Success: The Perils of Excellence," *Journal of Management Studies* 31, no. 3 (May 1994): 325–58.

55. Leonard Greenhalgh, "Organizational Decline," in Samuel B. Bacharach, ed., *Research in the Sociology of Organizations* 2 (Greenwich, Conn.: JAI Press, 1983), 231–76; Peter Lorange and Robert T. Nelson, "How to Recognize—and Avoid—Organizational Decline," *Sloan Management Review* (Spring 1987): 41–48.

56. Kim S. Cameron and Raymond Zammuto, "Matching Managerial Strategies to Conditions

of Decline," *Human Resources Management* 22 (1983): 359–75; Leonard Greenhalgh, Anne T. Lawrence, and Robert I. Sutton, "Determinants of Workforce Reduction Strategies in Declining Organizations," *Academy of Management Review* 13 (1988): 241–54.

57. Murray, "Amid Record Profits, Companies Continue to Lay Off Employees," *Wall Street Journal*.

58. William Weitzel and Ellen Jonsson, "Reversing the Downward Spiral: Lessons from W. T. Grant and Sears Roebuck," *Academy of Management Executive* 5 (1991): 7–21; William Weitzel and Ellen Jonsson, "Decline in Organizations: A Literature Integration and Extension," *Administrative Science Quarterly* 34 (1989): 91–109.

59. Amy Stevens and Edward Felsenthal, "Mudge Rose To Vote Today on Dissolution," *Wall Street Journal*, 2 October 1995, B1, B6.

60. Cascio, "Downsizing: What Do We Know? What Have We Learned?"; John A. Byrne, "Belt Tight-ening the Smart Way," *Business Week/Enterprise*, 1993, 34–38.

61. Sarah J. Freeman and Kim S. Cameron, "Organizational Downsizing: A Convergence and Reorientation Framework," *Organization Science* 4 (1993): 10–29.

62. Based on Joel Brockner, "Managing the Effects of Layoffs on Survivors," *California Management Review* (Winter 1992): 9–28; Ronald Henkoff, "Getting beyond Downsizing," *Fortune*, 10 January 1994, 58–64.

63. Alan Downs, "The Truth About Layoffs," *Management Review* (October 1995): 57–61; Robert J. Grossman, "Damaged, Downsized Souls," *HR Magazine* (May 1996): 54–62.

64. Kim S. Cameron, "Strategies for Successful Organizational Downsizing," *Human Resource Management* 33, no. 2 (Summer 1994): 189–211.

65. Marcela Kogan, "Rallying the Troops," *Government Executive* (January 1996): 22–27.

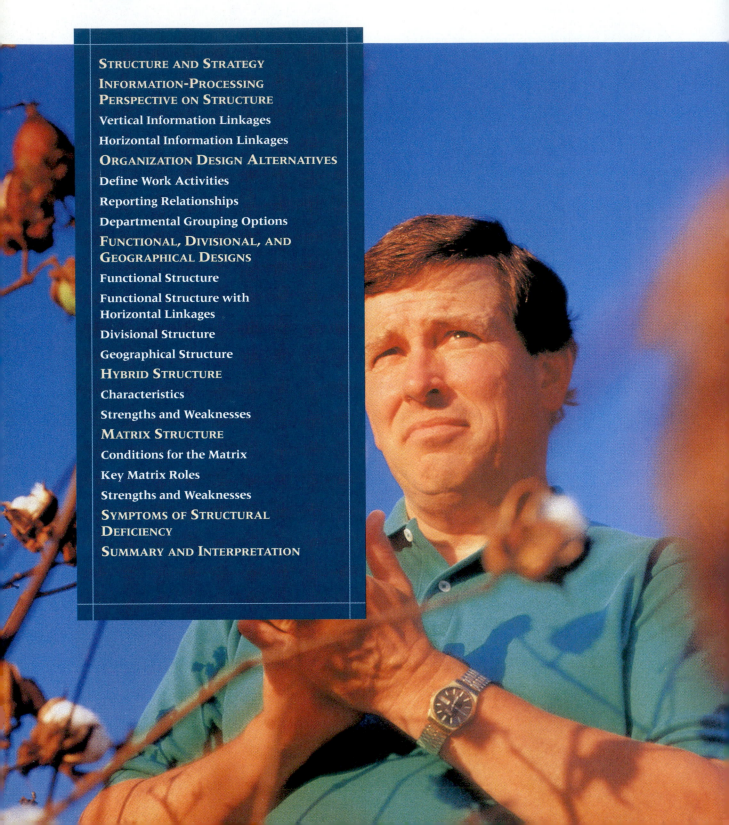

chapter six

Fundamentals of Organization Structure

A look inside

Zeneca
Agricultural Products

Top executives of the North American agrochemicals business of Britain's Imperial Chemical Industries met to consider the company's future. Profits were lousy and inventories were out of control. Matching a competitor's price cut had just cost $25 million. Things couldn't get any worse—but then, they did. Executives learned that the company would be part of a huge deconglomeration, when ICI spun off its pharmaceutical, agrochemical, and specialty chemical lines. They knew that, unless things turned around fast, their business might not survive the whirlwind.

Bob Woods presided over a traditional functional organization where managers were fiercely loyal to their own departments. Coordination between functional departments had to be improved, but Woods knew an immediate full-scale reorganization would arouse opposition and take time and money Zeneca didn't have. Everyone, however, agreed that the cash problem had to be solved, and that's where Woods found his opening. He first reached below the department heads, creating cross-functional teams of midlevel managers charged with getting working capital under control. Those teams later became the model for a larger transformation, as Zeneca Ag examined every business process—from product development to order fulfillment—and reorganized into teams designed to serve specific customers, for example, corn and soybean farmers. Again, Woods created teams from the middle, who soon became heroes in the organization as profits and customer satisfaction increased. Although some top managers squawked, most supported the improved departmental cooperation and eventually wanted to join the teams.

Horizontal teams have helped turn things around at Zeneca. The company entered 1995 with profits up 68 percent, head count down just 10 percent, and a leadership team poised for rapid response to further environmental changes.[1]

While Zeneca Ag retains elements of a functional structure, emphasis is on horizontal coordination to promote better and faster communication within the company and with customers.

Nearly every firm undergoes reorganization at some point, and today, many companies are almost continuously changing and reorganizing to meet new challenges. Structural changes are needed as the environment, technology, size or competitive strategy changes. The challenge for managers is to understand how to design organization structure to achieve their company's goals.

Purpose of This Chapter

The general concept of organization structure has been discussed in previous chapters. Structure includes such things as the number of departments in an organization, the span of control, and the extent to which the organization is formalized or centralized. The purpose of this chapter is to bring together these ideas to show how to design structure as it appears on the organization chart.

The material on structure is presented in the following sequence. First, structure is defined. Second, an information-processing perspective on structure explains how vertical and horizontal linkages are designed to provide needed information capacity. Third, basic organization design options are presented. Fourth, strategies for grouping organizational activities into functional, divisional, hybrid, or matrix structures are discussed. By the end of this chapter, you will understand how organization structure can help companies like Zeneca achieve their goals.

STRUCTURE AND STRATEGY

Organization **structure** is reflected in the organization chart. The organization chart is the visible representation for a whole set of underlying activities and processes in an organization. The three key components in the definition of organization structure are:

1. Organization structure designates formal reporting relationships, including the number of levels in the hierarchy and the span of control of managers and supervisors.
2. Organization structure identifies the grouping together of individuals into departments and of departments into the total organization.
3. Organization structure includes the design of systems to ensure effective communication, coordination, and integration of effort across departments.[2]

These three elements of structure pertain to both vertical and horizontal aspects of organizing. For example, the first two elements are the structural *framework*, which is the vertical hierarchy drawn on the organization chart.[3] The third element pertains to the pattern of *interactions* among organizational employees. An ideal structure encourages employees to provide horizontal information and coordination where and when it is needed.

Exhibit 6.1 illustrates that structural design is influenced by the environment, goals, technology, and size. Each of these key contextual variables was discussed at length in previous chapters. Recall that an environment can be stable or unstable; management's goals and strategies may stress internal efficiency or adaptation to external markets; production technologies can be routine or nonroutine; and an organization's size may be large or small. Each variable influences the correct structural design. Moreover, environment, technology, goals, and size may also influence one another, as illustrated by the connecting lines among these contextual variables in Exhibit 6.1. Human processes (such as leadership and culture) within the organization also influence structure as indicated in the center of Exhibit 6.1. These processes will be discussed in later chapters.

Of these contextual variables, the connection between competitive strategy and structure is of particular interest and has been widely studied. Structure typically reflects organizational strategy, and a change in product or market strategy frequently leads to a change in structure.[4] Once a company formulates a strategy by which it plans to achieve an advantage in the marketplace, leaders design or redesign the structure to coordinate organizational activities to best achieve that advantage. For example, an organization that adopts a strategy to produce a single or only a few products or services for a limited market generally operates

Exhibit 6.1
Organization Contextual Variables That Influence Structure

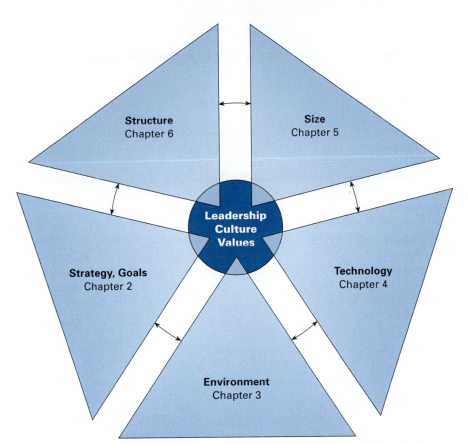

Source: Adapted from Jay R. Galbraith, *Competing with Flexible Lateral Organizations*, 2nd ed. (Reading, Mass.: Addison-Wesley, 1994), ch.1; Jay R. Galbraith, *Organization Design* (Reading, Mass.: Addison-Wesley, 1977), ch. 1.

well with a centralized, functional structure. Organizational goals stress internal efficiency and technical quality. Apple Computer in the 1980s provides an example: the company essentially produced a single product, the Macintosh, that was sold to a single type of customer, computer dealers.[5]

Often, a company's strategy will evolve to the greater complexity of producing multiple products or services and expanding to new markets. When organizations diversify, structure may evolve into a decentralized, divisional form to promote flexibility and speed decision making. Goals stress adaptation to the external environment. In the late 1980s, under John Sculley's leadership, Apple Computer shifted to a structure based on geographic divisions to facilitate manufacture and sales of a variety of computers to a larger customer base worldwide. Exhibit 6.2 illustrates the difference between the functional and the divisional structure as reflected in the organization chart.

Sometimes, an organization faces a simultaneous need for internal efficiency (a strength of the functional structure) and for external adaptation (a strength of the divisional structure). Strategy in this case may require that the organization evolve to the matrix structure, the most well-known dual-reporting structure used by organizations, also illustrated in Exhibit 6.2. The matrix and other basic organization designs will be discussed in detail later in this chapter.

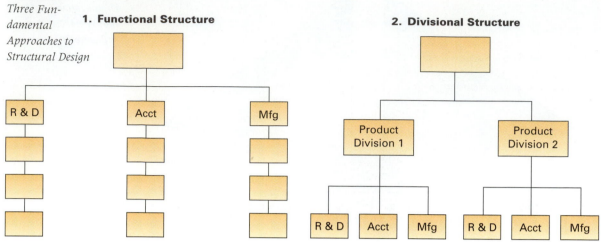

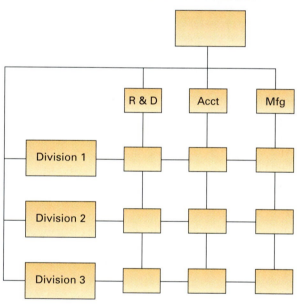

INFORMATION-PROCESSING PERSPECTIVE ON STRUCTURE

The concepts in previous chapters—technology, goals, environment, size—impose different information-processing requirements on organizations. A nonroutine technology or an uncertain environment, for example, requires employees to process more information to understand and respond to unexpected events. Reciprocal interdependence between departments requires substantially more communication and coordination than is needed for pooled interdependence. Thus, the organization must be designed to encourage information flow in both vertical and horizontal directions necessary to achieve the organization's

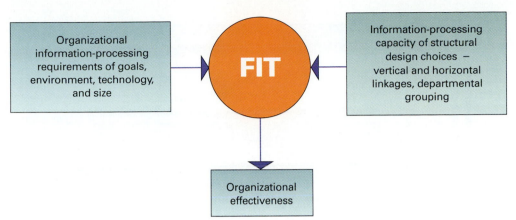

Exhibit 6.3
*Information-
Processing
Approach to
Structural
Design*

Source: Based on Richard L. Daft and Robert H. Lengel, "Organizational Information Requirements, Media Richness and Structural Design," *Management Science* 32 (1986): 554–71; and David Nadler and Michael Tushman, *Strategic Organization Design* (Glenview, Ill.: Scott Foresman, 1988).

overall task.[6] Exhibit 6.3 illustrates how structure should fit the information requirements of the organization. If it does not, people will either have too little information or will spend time processing information not vital to their tasks, thus reducing effectiveness.[7]

Vertical Information Linkages

Organization design should facilitate the communication among employees and departments that is necessary to accomplish the organization's overall task. *Linkage* is defined as the extent of communication and coordination among organizational elements. **Vertical linkages** are used to coordinate activities between the top and bottom of an organization. Employees at lower levels should carry out activities consistent with top-level goals, and top executives must be informed of activities and accomplishments at the lower levels. Organizations may use any of a variety of structural devices to achieve vertical linkage, including hierarchical referral, rules and procedures, plans and schedules, positions or levels added to the hierarchy, and formal management information systems.[8]

Hierarchical Referral.   The first vertical device is the hierarchy, or chain of command, which is illustrated by the vertical lines in Exhibit 6.2. If a problem arises that employees don't know how to solve, it can be referred up to the next level in the hierarchy. When the problem is solved, the answer is passed back down to lower levels. The lines of the organization chart act as communication channels.

Rules and Plans.   The next linkage device is the use of rules and plans. To the extent that problems and decisions are repetitious, a rule or procedure can be established so employees know how to respond without communicating directly with their manager. Rules provide a standard information source enabling employees to be coordinated without actually communicating about every job. A plan also provides standing information for employees. The most widely used plan is the budget. With carefully designed budget plans, employees at lower levels can be left on their own to perform activities within their resource allotment.

Exhibit 6.4

*Ladder of Mechanisms
for Vertical Linkage
and Control*

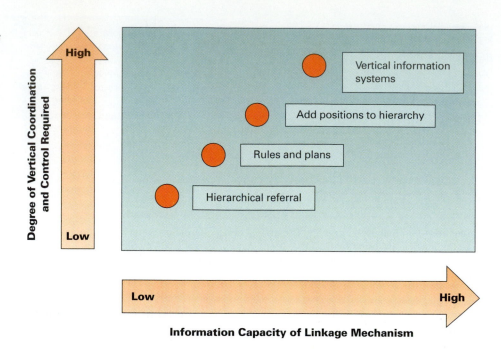

Information Capacity of Linkage Mechanism

Add Positions to Hierarchy. When many problems occur, planning and hierarchical referral may overload managers. In growing or changing organizations, additional vertical linkages may be required. One technique is to add positions to the vertical hierarchy. In some cases, an assistant will be assigned to help an overloaded manager. In other cases, positions in the direct line of authority may be added. Such positions reduce the span of control and allow closer communication and control.

Vertical Information Systems. Vertical information systems are another strategy for increasing vertical information capacity. **Vertical information systems** include the periodic reports, written information, and computer-based communications distributed to managers. Information systems make communication up and down the hierarchy more efficient. For example, Chairman Bill Gates of Microsoft communicates regularly with employees through his company's electronic mail system. He responds to a dozen individual messages each day. At Xerox, some forty thousand customers are polled each month, and this data is aggregated, summarized, and transferred up the hierarchy to managers.

Summary. Structural mechanisms that can be used to achieve vertical linkage and coordination are summarized in Exhibit 6.4. These structural mechanisms represent alternatives managers can use in designing an organization. Depending upon the amount of coordination needed in the organization, several of the linkage mechanisms in Exhibit 6.4 may be used.

Horizontal Information Linkages

Horizontal communication overcomes barriers between departments and provides opportunities for coordination among employees to achieve unity of effort and organizational objectives. **Horizontal linkage** refers to the amount of communication and coordination horizontally across organizational departments. Its importance was discovered by Lee Iacocca when he took over Chrysler Corporation.

> What I found at Chrysler were thirty-five vice presidents, each with his own turf. . . . I couldn't believe, for example, that the guy running engineering departments wasn't in constant touch with his counterpart in manufacturing. But that's how it was. Everybody worked independently. I took one look at that system and I almost threw up. That's when I knew I was in really deep trouble.
>
> . . . Nobody at Chrysler seemed to understand that interaction among the different functions in a company is absolutely critical. People in engineering and manufacturing almost have to be sleeping together. These guys weren't even flirting![9]

Today, horizontal communication has evolved to a high level at Chrysler and has had a significant positive impact. Chrysler puts everyone who's working on a specific vehicle project—designers, engineers, and manufacturers, along with representatives from marketing, finance, purchasing, and even outside suppliers—together on a single floor. The team concept has significantly improved horizontal coordination to help Chrysler become the world's most successful automaker.[10]

The need for horizontal coordination increases as the amount of uncertainty increases, such as when the environment is changing, the technology is nonroutine and interdependent, and goals stress innovation and flexibility. Horizontal linkage mechanisms often are not drawn on the organization chart, but nevertheless are part of organization structure. The following devices are structural alternatives that can improve horizontal coordination and information flow.[11] Each device enables people to exchange information.

Information Systems. A significant method of providing horizontal linkage in today's organizations is the use of cross-functional information systems. Computerized information systems can enable managers or front-line workers throughout the organization to routinely exchange information about problems, opportunities, activities, or decisions. Bow Valley Energy, a $264 million exploration and production company, redesigned its computer information system to improve cross-functional information flow among its geologists, geophysicists, production engineers, and contract managers worldwide.[12]

Direct Contact. A somewhat higher level of horizontal linkage is direct contact between managers or employees affected by a problem. To revive customer loyalty by improving service and quality, CEO Louis Morris began encouraging communication across department lines at Simplicity Pattern Company, so that creative design managers were talking with managers in sales and financing.[13] One way to promote direct contact is to create a special **liaison role**. A liaison person is located in one department but has the responsibility for communicating and achieving coordination with another department. Liaison roles often exist between engineering and manufacturing departments because engineering has to develop and test products to fit the limitations of manufacturing facilities.

Task Forces.   Direct contact and liaison roles usually link only two departments. When linkage involves several departments, a more complex device such as a task force is required. A **task force** is a temporary committee composed of representatives from each department affected by a problem.[14] Each member represents the interest of a department and can carry information from the meeting back to that department.

Task forces are an effective horizontal linkage device for temporary issues. They solve problems by direct horizontal coordination and reduce the information load on the vertical hierarchy. Typically, they are disbanded after their tasks are accomplished.

Xerox used a task force of twenty hand-picked members to develop its application for the Malcolm Baldrige National Quality Award. Book publishers coordinate the editing, production, advertising, and distribution of a special book with a temporary task force.

Full-time Integrator.   A stronger horizontal linkage device is to create a full-time position or department solely for the purpose of coordination. A full-time **integrator** frequently has a title, such as product manager, project manager, program manager, or brand manager. Unlike the liaison person described earlier, the integrator does not report to one of the functional departments being coordinated. He or she is located outside the departments and has the responsibility for coordinating several departments.

The brand manager for Planters Peanuts, for example, coordinates the sales, distribution, and advertising for that product. Gillette Company created product line managers for multinational coordination. A product line manager coordinates marketing and sales strategies for Trac II across fifteen countries, achieving savings by using similar advertising and marketing techniques in each country. As part of its recent restructuring, General Motors is setting up brand managers who will be responsible for marketing and sales strategies for each of GM's new models.[15]

The integrator can also be responsible for an innovation or change project, such as developing the design, financing, and marketing of a new product. An organization chart that illustrates the location of project managers for new product development is shown in Exhibit 6.5. The project managers are drawn to the side to indicate their separation from other departments. The arrows indicate project members assigned to the new product development. New Product A, for example, has a financial accountant assigned to keep track of costs and budgets. The engineering member provides design advice, and purchasing and manufacturing members represent their areas. The project manager is responsible for the entire project. He or she sees that the new product is completed on time, is introduced to the market, and achieves other project goals. The horizontal lines in Exhibit 6.5 indicate that project managers do not have formal authority over team members with respect to giving pay raises, hiring, or firing. Formal authority rests with the managers of the functional departments, who have formal authority over subordinates.

Integrators need excellent people skills. Integrators in most companies have a lot of responsibility but little authority. The integrator has to use expertise and persuasion to achieve coordination. He or she spans the boundary between departments and must be able to get people together, maintain their trust, confront problems, and resolve conflicts and disputes in the interest of the organization.[16] The integrator must be forceful in order to achieve co-

Exhibit 6.5

*Project Manager
Location in the
Structure*

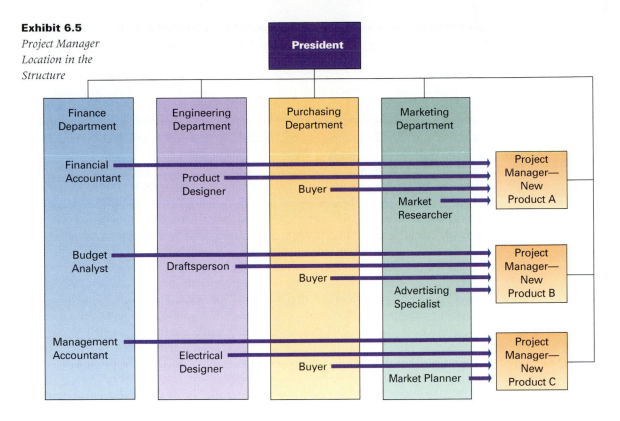

ordination, but must stop short of alienating people in the line departments. Some organizations, such as General Mills, have several integrators working simultaneously.

General Mills

In Practice 6.1

"When General Mills completed a ten-story tower at its suburban Minneapolis headquarters last summer, the company discovered that not all the telephones could be installed at once. 'Hook up the product managers' first,' the senior executive ordered. 'The business can't run without them.' "[17]

General Mills assigns a product manager to each of the more than twenty-five products in its line, including Cheerios, Wheaties, Bisquick, Softasilk Cake Mix, Stir-n-Frost Icing, Hamburger Helper, and Gold Medal Flour. Brand managers are also assigned to develop new products, name them, and test them in the marketplace.

Product managers at General Mills act as if they are running their own businesses. They set marketing goals and plot strategies to achieve those goals. They are responsible for product success, but they have no authority. Product management is management by persuasion. A good product manager is vibrant, challenging, and a little abrasive. He or she has to be to get things done without the aid of formal authority.

If the product manager for Cocoa Puffs needs special support from the sales force and additional output from the plant for a big advertising campaign, she has to sell the idea to people who report to managers in charge of sales and manufacturing. Product managers work laterally across the organization rather than within the vertical structure. When the product manager for Crispy Wheats 'n Raisins decides the product needs different packaging, a new recipe, a more focused commercial, or new ingredients, he must convince the departments to pay attention to his brand. The product manager can also expect to work with the procurement department, a controller, and the research lab at some point during the year.[18]

The product managers at General Mills are full-time integrators. They coordinate marketing, manufacturing, purchasing, research, and other functions relevant to their product lines. They provide horizontal linkages by persuading diverse departments to focus on the needs of their products. General Mills has been very profitable in a highly competitive industry, and one reason is the role played by product managers.

Teams.   Project teams tend to be the strongest horizontal linkage mechanism. **Teams** are permanent task forces and are often used in conjunction with a full-time integrator. When activities between departments require strong coordination over a long period of time, a cross-functional team is often the solution. Special project teams may be used when organizations have a large-scale project, a major innovation, or a new product line, such as Chrysler's Neon.

Boeing used around 250 teams to design and manufacture the new 777 aircraft. Some teams were created around sections of the plane, such as the wing, cockpit, or engines, while others were developed to serve specific customers, such as United Airlines or British Airways. Boeing's teams had to be tightly integrated and coordinated to accomplish this massive project. Even the U.S. Department of the Navy has discovered the power of cross-functional teams to improve horizontal coordination and increase productivity.[19]

The Rodney Hunt Company develops, manufactures, and markets heavy industrial equipment and uses teams to coordinate each product line across the manufacturing, engineering, and marketing departments. These teams are illustrated by the dashed lines and shaded areas in Exhibit 6.6. Members from each team meet the first thing each day as needed to resolve problems concerning customer needs, backlogs, engineering changes, scheduling conflicts, and any other problem with the product line.

A more intense use of teams was adopted by Hewlett-Packard's Terminals Division when the division found itself unable to compete in the fast-changing electronics industry. Permanent teams were combined with other linkage mechanisms to achieve remarkable coordination.

In Practice 6.2   *Hewlett-Packard Terminals Division*

The Terminals Division was created in 1983 to design and produce terminals for Hewlett-Packard systems, low-end personal computers, and video display systems. Although its terminals were ranked high in quality, they were quite expensive, and the division began rapidly losing market share to low-cost producers by 1985. Rather than sourcing terminals from the Far East, managers decided to radically alter the way the division did business to become a world-class, low-cost manufacturer and serve new customers on a global scale.

Close coordination and communication among all functions was needed to achieve the goal of becoming the highest quality, lowest cost producer, and even greater coordination was required to reduce the design and manufacturing time for development of a new global product. Cross-functional teams provided the solution. A cross-functional program team was created to serve as the integrating mechanism for a number of other teams, including a hardware design team, a software development team, and a team for the localization of hardware and software to meet various requirements in different countries. The hardware team was further subdivided into manufacturing teams around several assembly

Exhibit 6.6

Teams Used for Horizontal Coordination at Rodney Hunt Company

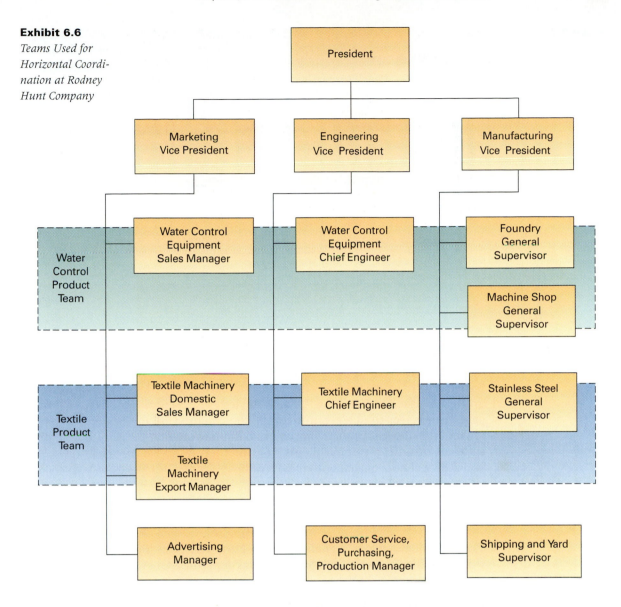

processes. In addition, there was a team for each major component that was to be purchased and a negotiating team to negotiate contracts for components to be shared across the division. Team members were carefully selected based on the goal of integrating products across functions, products across geographies, and components across products.

The program team responsible for coordinating all other teams was led by a program manager, who served as a full-time integrator and was chosen for his leadership abilities and his good relationships with all functional departments. Sharing leadership responsibilities with the program manager were two "architects," generalists who knew a great deal about hardware, software, and systems integration. Several engineers also served as liaisons between the hardware and software teams and between the localization teams and the design teams.

This complex, multidimensional team structure served its purpose. The division achieved the development of a new global product, dramatically reduced the cost of design and manufacture, and compressed development time to only eighteen months. The success of the effort led to refinements of the process to be used in developing future Hewlett-Packard products.[20]

Exhibit 6.7

Ladder of Mechanisms for Horizontal Linkage and Coordination

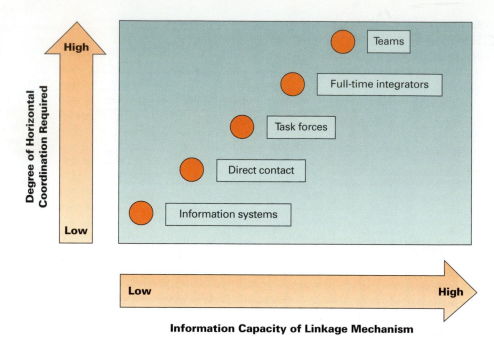

Summary.   The mechanisms for achieving horizontal linkages in organizations are summarized in Exhibit 6.7. These devices represent alternatives that managers can select to achieve horizontal coordination in any organization. The higher level devices provide more horizontal information capacity. If communication is insufficient, departments will find themselves out of synchronization, and they will not contribute to the overall goals of the organization.

ORGANIZATION DESIGN ALTERNATIVES

The overall design of organization structure indicates three things—needed work activities, reporting relationships, and departmental groupings.

Define Work Activities

Departments are created to perform tasks considered strategically important to the company. For example, when moving huge quantities of supplies in the Persian Gulf, the U.S. Army's logistics commander created a squad of fifteen soldiers called Ghostbusters who were charged with getting out among the troops, identifying logistics problems, and seeing that the problems got fixed. The fiberglass group at Manville set a priority on growth and, hence, created a department that was simply called Growth Department. Defining a specific department is a way to accomplish tasks deemed valuable by the organization to accomplish its goals.

Reporting Relationships

Reporting relationships, often called the chain of command, are represented by vertical lines on an organization chart. The chain of command should be an unbroken line of authority that links all persons in an organization and shows who reports to whom. In a large organization like Standard Oil Company, one hundred or more charts are required to identify reporting relationships among thousands of employees. The definition of departments and the drawing of reporting relationships defines how employees are to be grouped into departments.

Departmental Grouping Options

Options for departmental grouping, including functional grouping, divisional grouping, geographic grouping, and multifocused grouping, are illustrated in Exhibit 6.8. **Departmental grouping** has impact on employees because they share a common supervisor and common resources, are jointly responsible for performance, and tend to identify and collaborate with one another.[21] For example, at

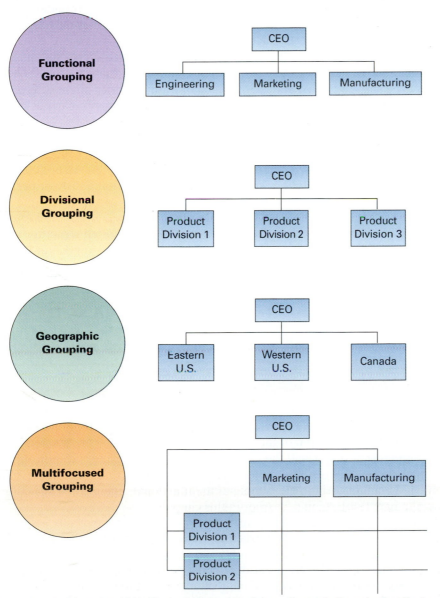

Exhibit 6.8

Structural Design Options for Grouping Employees into Departments

Source: Adapted from David Nadler and Michael Tushman, *Strategic Organization Design* (Glenview, Ill.: Scott Foresman, 1988), 68.

Albany Ladder Company, the credit manager was shifted from the finance department to the marketing department. By being grouped with marketing, the credit manager started working with sales people to increase sales, thus becoming more liberal with credit than when he was located in the finance department.

Functional grouping places employees together who perform similar functions or work processes or who bring similar knowledge and skills to bear. For example, all marketing people would work together under the same supervisor, as would manufacturing and engineering people. All people associated with the assembly process for generators would be grouped together in one department. All chemists may be grouped in a department different from biologists because they represent different disciplines.

Divisional Grouping means people are organized according to what the organization produces. All people required to produce toothpaste—including the marketing, manufacturing, and salespeople—are grouped together under one executive. In huge corporations such as PepsiCo, the product lines may represent independent businesses, such as Taco Bell, Frito Lay, and Pepsi Cola.

Geographic grouping means resources are organized to serve customers or clients in a particular geographical area. For example, all the activities required to serve the eastern United States or Canada or Latin America might be grouped together. This grouping focuses employees on meeting the specific needs of customers in a particular country or region.

Multifocused grouping means an organization embraces two structural grouping alternatives simultaneously. These structural forms are often called matrix or hybrid and will be discussed in more detail later in this chapter. An organization may need to group by function and product division simultaneously or perhaps by product division and geography.

The organizational forms described in Exhibit 6.8 provide the overall options within which the organization chart is drawn and the detailed structure is designed. Each structural design alternative has significant strengths and weaknesses, to which we now turn.

FUNCTIONAL, DIVISIONAL, AND GEOGRAPHICAL DESIGNS

Functional grouping and divisional grouping are the two most common approaches to structural design.

Functional Structure

In a **functional structure**, activities are grouped together by common function from the bottom to the top of the organization. All engineers are located in the engineering department, and the vice president of engineering is responsible for all engineering activities. The same is true in marketing, research and development, and manufacturing. An example of the functional organization structure is shown in part 1 of Exhibit 6.2 earlier in this chapter.

Exhibit 6.9 summarizes the organizational characteristics typically associated with the functional structure. This structure is most effective when the environment is stable and the technology is relatively routine with low interdependence across functional departments. Organizational goals pertain to internal efficiency and technical specialization. Size is small to medium. Each of these characteristics is associated with a low need for horizontal coordination. The stable environment, rou-

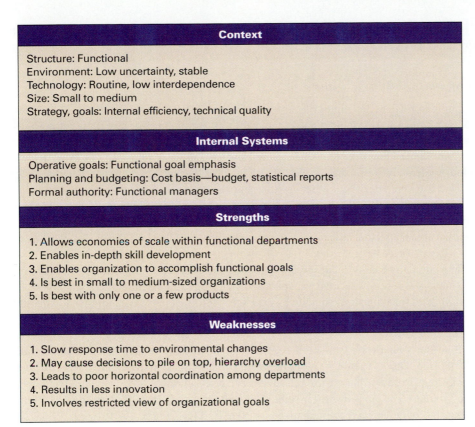

Exhibit 6.9

Summary of Functional Organization Characteristics

Context

Structure: Functional
Environment: Low uncertainty, stable
Technology: Routine, low interdependence
Size: Small to medium
Strategy, goals: Internal efficiency, technical quality

Internal Systems

Operative goals: Functional goal emphasis
Planning and budgeting: Cost basis—budget, statistical reports
Formal authority: Functional managers

Strengths

1. Allows economies of scale within functional departments
2. Enables in-depth skill development
3. Enables organization to accomplish functional goals
4. Is best in small to medium-sized organizations
5. Is best with only one or a few products

Weaknesses

1. Slow response time to environmental changes
2. May cause decisions to pile on top, hierarchy overload
3. Leads to poor horizontal coordination among departments
4. Results in less innovation
5. Involves restricted view of organizational goals

Source: Adapted from Robert Duncan, "What Is the Right Organization Structure? Decision Tree Analysis Provides the Answer," *Organizational Dynamics* (Winter 1979): 429.

tine technology, internal efficiency, and small size mean the organization can be controlled and coordinated primarily through the vertical hierarchy. Within the organization, employees are committed to achieving the operative goals of their respective functional departments. Planning and budgeting is by function and reflects the cost of resources used in each department. Formal authority and influence within the organization rests with upper managers in the functional departments.

One strength of the functional structure is that it promotes economy of scale within functions. Economy of scale means all employees are located in the same place and can share facilities. Producing all products in a single plant, for example, enables the plant to acquire the latest machinery. Constructing only one facility instead of separate facilities for each product line reduces duplication and waste. The functional structure also promotes in-depth skill development of employees. Employees are exposed to a range of functional activities within their own department. The functional form of structure is best for small to medium-sized organizations when only one or a few products are produced.[22]

The main weakness of the functional structure is a slow response to environmental changes that require coordination across departments. If the environment is changing or the technology is nonroutine and interdependent, the vertical hierarchy becomes overloaded. Decisions pile up, and top managers do not respond fast enough. Other disadvantages of the functional structure are that innovation is slow because of poor coordination, and each employee has a restricted view of overall goals.

Consider how the functional structure provides the coordination Blue Bell Creameries needs.

Blue Bell Creameries, Inc.

Within seconds, the old-timer on the radio had taken listeners out of their bumper-to-bumper Houston world and placed them gently in Brenham, Texas, with its rolling hills and country air, in the era when the town got its first traffic light.

"You know," he said, "that's how Blue Bell Ice Cream is. Old-fashioned, uncomplicated, homemade good." He paused. "It's all made in that little creamery in Brenham."

That little creamery isn't little anymore, but the desire for first-quality homemade ice cream is stronger than when Blue Bell started in 1907. Today, Blue Bell has more than eight hundred employees and will sell over $160 million in ice cream. The company has an unbelievable 60 percent share of the ice cream market in Houston, Dallas, and San Antonio—Texas's three largest cities.

The company cannot meet the demand for Blue Bell Ice Cream. It doesn't even try. Top managers recently decided to expand slowly into Louisiana and Oklahoma. Management refuses to compromise quality by expanding into regions that cannot be adequately serviced or by growing so fast that it can't adequately train employees in the art of making ice cream.

Blue Bell's major departments are sales, quality control, production, maintenance, and distribution. There is also an accounting department and a small research and development group. Product changes are infrequent because the orientation is toward tried-and-true products. The environment is stable. The customer base is well established. The only change has been the increase in demand for Blue Bell Ice Cream.

Blue Bell's quality control department tests all incoming ingredients and ensures that only the best products go into its ice cream. Quality control also tests outgoing ice cream products. After years of experience, quality inspectors can taste the slightest deviation from expected quality. It's no wonder Blue Bell has successfully maintained the image of a small-town creamery making homemade ice cream.[23]

The functional structure is just right for Blue Bell Creameries. The organization has chosen to stay medium-sized and focus on making a single product—quality ice cream. However, as Blue Bell expands, it may have problems coordinating across departments, requiring stronger horizontal linkage mechanisms.

Functional Structure with Horizontal Linkages

Today, there is a shift toward flatter, more horizontal structures because of the uncertain environment. Very few of today's successful companies can maintain a strictly functional structure. Organizations compensate for the vertical functional hierarchy by installing horizontal linkages, as described earlier in this chapter. Managers improve horizontal coordination by using information systems, direct contact between departments, full-time integrators or project managers (illustrated in Exhibit 6.5), task forces, or teams (illustrated in 6.6). Not-for-profit organizations are also recognizing the importance of horizontal linkages. An interesting example occurred at Karolinska Hospital in Stockholm, Sweden, where horizontal linkage mechanisms have dramatically improved productivity as well as patient care.

Karolinska Hospital

When Karolinska faced a 20 percent cut in state funding in the early 1990s, the hospital's then chief executive Jan Lindsten knew dramatic action was needed to maintain the quality of patient care. The hospital had only recently been through a major reorganization, which had created forty-seven separate functional departments, each marching to their own beat. Lindsten cut that number down to eleven, but coordination was still woefully inadequate. Patients had to scale the high walls between departments, often making multiple all-day visits to Karolinska for tests and procedures—in general, only 2 percent of the time a patient spent at the hospital involved actual treatment. So Lindsten and a consulting group set about to reorganize workflow at the hospital around patient care—instead of bouncing a patient from department to department, Karolinska now envisions the illness to recovery period as a process with pit stops in admissions, X ray, surgery, etc. For example, a patient now meets a surgeon and a doctor of internal medicine together rather than separately.

The most interesting aspect of Karolinska's approach was the creation of the new position of "nurse coordinator." Nurse coordinators serve as full-time integrators, looking for situations where the baton is dropped in the handoff between or within departments. This has created new career opportunities for nurses, but it's a difficult position and nurse coordinators need strong people skills to handle the inevitable conflicts. In effect, doctors at Karolinska are now reporting to nurses, a shift in thinking that has not always been easy for either side.

However, nurse coordinators free doctors from administrative and scheduling matters and allow them to concentrate on clinical work and research. Horizontal linkages have dramatically improved performance at Karolinska. Even though three out of fifteen operating theaters have been closed due to funding cuts, the high coordination has enabled the hospital to perform three thousand more operations annually, a 25 percent increase. On the patient side, things look better too. Waiting times for surgery have been reduced from eight months to only three weeks.[24]

Karolinska Hospital is using horizontal linkages to overcome some of the disadvantages of the functional structure. Full-time integrators span the boundaries between departments and coordinate activities to serve the needs of patients as well as the interests of the organization. We will talk more about this trend toward horizontal organizing in the next chapter.

Divisional Structure

The term **divisional structure** is used here as the generic term for what is sometimes called a *product structure* or *strategic business units*. With this structure, divisions can be organized according to individual products, services, product groups, major projects or programs, divisions, businesses, or profit centers. The distinctive feature of a divisional structure is that grouping is based on organizational outputs.

The difference between a divisional structure and a functional structure is illustrated in Exhibit 6.10. The functional structure can be redesigned into separate product groups, and each group contains the functional departments of R&D, manufacturing, accounting, and marketing. Coordination across functional departments within each product group is maximized. The divisional structure promotes flexibility and change because each unit is smaller and can adapt to the

Exhibit 6.10

Reorganization from Functional Structure to Divisional Structure at Info-Tech

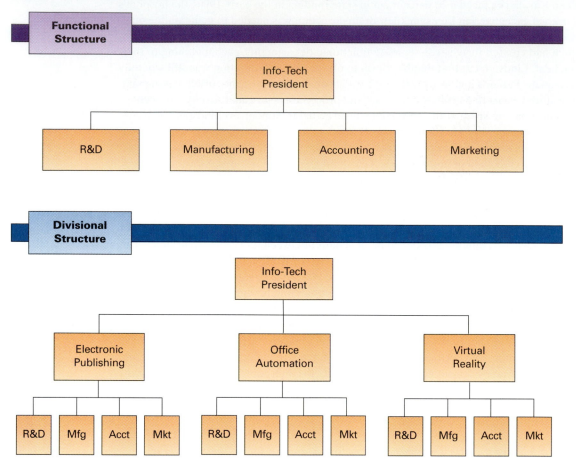

needs of its environment. Moreover, the divisional structure decentralizes decision making, because the lines of authority converge at a lower level in the hierarchy. The functional structure, by contrast, forces decisions all the way to the top before a problem affecting several functions can be resolved.

The divisional structure fits the context summarized in Exhibit 6.11.[25] This form of structure is excellent for achieving coordination across functional departments. When the environment is uncertain, the technology is nonroutine and interdependent across departments, and goals are external effectiveness and adaptation, then a divisional structure is appropriate.

Large size is also associated with divisional structure. Giant, complex organizations such as General Electric, PepsiCo, and Johnson & Johnson are subdivided into a series of smaller, self-contained organizations for better control and coordination. In these large companies, the units are sometimes called divisions, businesses, or strategic business units. The structure at Johnson & Johnson includes 168 separate operating units, including McNeil Consumer Products, makers of Tylenol; Ortho Pharmaceuticals, which makes Retin-A and birth control pills; and J & J Consumer Products, the company that brings us Johnson's

Context
Structure: Divisional Environment: Moderate to high uncertainty, changing Technology: Nonroutine, high interdependence among departments Size: Large Strategy, goals: External effectiveness, adaptation, client satisfaction

Internal Systems
Operative goals: Product line emphasis Planning and budgeting: Profit center basis—cost and income Formal authority: Product managers

Strengths
1. Suited to fast change in unstable environment 2. Leads to client satisfaction because product responsibility and contact points are clear 3. Involves high coordination across functions 4. Allows units to adapt to differences in products, regions, clients 5. Best in large organizations with several products 6. Decentralizes decision making

Weaknesses
1. Eliminates economies of scale in functional departments 2. Leads to poor coordination across product lines 3. Eliminates in-depth competence and technical specialization 4. Makes integration and standardization across product lines difficult

Exhibit 6.11

Summary of Divisional Organization Characteristics

Source: Adapted from Robert Duncan, "What Is the Right Organization Structure? Decision Tree Analysis Provides the Answer," *Organizational Dynamics* (Winter 1979): 431.

Baby Shampoo and Band-Aids. Each division is a separately chartered, autonomous company operating under the guidance of Johnson & Johnson's corporate headquarters.[26]

Another example of a divisional structure is Time Warner, Inc. Principal operating divisions include Warner Music, the world's largest record company, including the labels Warner Brothers, Elektra, and Atlantic; HBO, the leading pay cable television channel; Warner Brothers, maker of movies such as *Batman Forever* and television series such as *Friends*; and Time, Inc., which includes magazine publishers for *Time*, *Fortune*, and *People* as well as book publishers such as Little, Brown & Company.[27]

The divisional structure has several strengths. It is suited to fast change in an unstable environment and provides high product visibility. Since each product is a separate division, clients are able to contact the correct division and achieve satisfaction. Coordination across functions is excellent. Each product can adapt to requirements of individual customers or regions. The divisional structure typically works best in organizations that have multiple products or services and enough personnel to staff separate functional units. At corporations like Johnson & Johnson and PepsiCo, decision making is pushed down to the lowest levels. Each division is small enough to be quick on its feet, responding rapidly to changes in the market.

One disadvantage of using divisional structuring is that the organization loses economies of scale. Instead of fifty research engineers sharing a common facility in a functional structure, ten engineers may be assigned to each of five product divisions. The critical mass required for in-depth research is lost, and physical facilities have to be duplicated for each product line. Another problem is that product lines become separate from each other, and coordination across product lines can be difficult. As one Johnson & Johnson executive said, "We have to keep reminding ourselves that we work for the same corporation"[28]

Companies such as Hewlett-Packard, Xerox, and Digital Equipment have a large number of divisions and have had real problems with horizontal coordination. The software division may produce programs that are incompatible with business computers sold by another division. Customers are frustrated when a sales representative from one division is unaware of developments in other divisions. Task forces and other linkage devices are needed to coordinate across divisions. A lack of technical specialization is also a problem in a divisional structure. Employees identify with the product line rather than with a functional specialty. R&D personnel, for example, tend to do applied research to benefit the product line rather than basic research to benefit the entire organization.

Geographical Structure

Another basis for structural grouping is the organization's users or customers. The most common structure in this category is geography. Each region of the country may have distinct tastes and needs. Each geographic unit includes all functions required to produce and market products in that region. For multinational corporations, self-contained units are created for different countries and parts of the world.

As discussed earlier in the chapter, Apple Computer reorganized from a functional to a geographical structure to facilitate manufacture and delivery of Apple computers to customers around the world. Exhibit 6.12 contains a partial organization structure illustrating the geographical thrust. Apple used this structure to focus managers and employees on specific geographical customers and sales targets. In Canada, department stores frequently use a geographical structure with a separate entity for Quebec because customers there are physically smaller, use a different language, and have different tastes than those in Ontario or the Maritime Provinces. The regional structure allows Apple or a Canadian department store chain to focus on the needs of customers in a geographical area.

The strengths and weaknesses of a geographic divisional structure are similar to the divisional organization characteristics listed in Exhibit 6.11. The organization can adapt to specific needs of its own region, and employees identify with regional goals rather than with national goals. Horizontal coordination within a region is emphasized rather than linkages across regions or to the national office.

HYBRID STRUCTURE

As a practical matter, many structures in the real world do not exist in the pure form of functional, divisional, or geographic. An organization's structure may be multifocused in that both product and function, or product and geography, are

Exhibit 6.12
Geographical Structure for Apple Computer

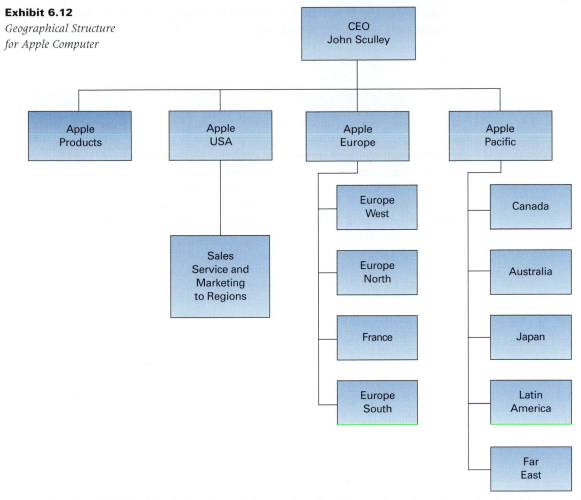

Source: Based on John Markoff, "John Sculley's Biggest Test," *New York Times,* 26 February 1989, sec. 3, pp. 1,26.

emphasized at the same time. One type of structure that combines characteristics of both is called the **hybrid structure**.

Characteristics

When a corporation grows large and has several products or markets, it typically is organized into self-contained units of some type. Functions that are important to each product or market are decentralized to the self-contained units. However, some functions are also centralized and located at headquarters. Headquarters functions are relatively stable and require economies of scale and in-depth specialization. By combining characteristics of the functional and divisional structures, corporations can take advantage of the strengths of each and avoid some of the weaknesses. Xerox Corporation recently reorganized into a hybrid structure, with nine nearly independent product divisions and three geographical sales divisions. CEO Paul Allaire thinks the hybrid structure can provide the coordination and flexibility needed to help Xerox get products to market faster and thrive in a competitive environment.[29]

Sun Petroleum Products restructured from a functional to a hybrid structure by combining three product divisions with several functional departments.

In Practice 6.5	*Sun Petroleum Products Company*

Sun Petroleum Products Company (SPPC) had sales of approximately $7 billion in the early 1980s and a workforce of 5,400 people. Its refineries produced about 500,000 barrels of products per day. The six refineries manufactured fuels, lubricants, and chemicals that were marketed by Sun's sales force.

SPPC was traditionally organized by function with each functional head reporting directly to the president or to the vice president of operations. Then a study revealed that Sun should be more responsive to changing markets. It recommended a reorganization into three major product lines of fuels, lubricants, and chemicals. Each product line served a different market and required a different strategy and management style.

The new hybrid organization structure adopted by SPPC is illustrated in Exhibit 6.13. Each product line vice president is now in charge of both marketing and manufacturing for that product, so coordination is easy to achieve. Each product line vice president also has planning, supply, and manufacturing departments reporting to him or her. The vice president in charge of refinery facilities is in charge of a functional department because there are major economies of scale by having all refineries work together. The output of these refineries becomes the input to the fuels, lubricants, and chemicals divisions. Other departments centralized as functional departments to achieve economies of scale are human resources, technology, financial services, and resources and strategy. Each of these departments provides services for the entire organization. The new structure is just right for SPPC because of the company's large size, moderate environmental change, interdependence, and goal of adapting to the environment.[30]

Strengths and Weaknesses

The hybrid structure typically appears in a context similar to that of the divisional structure. Hybrid structures tend to be used in an uncertain environment because product divisions are designed for innovation and external effectiveness. Technologies may be both routine and nonroutine, and interdependencies exist across the functions in product groupings. Size is typically large to provide sufficient resources for duplication of resources across product divisions. The organization has goals of client satisfaction and innovation, as well as goals of efficiency with respect to functional departments.

As summarized in Exhibit 6.14, a major strength of the hybrid structure is that it enables the organization to pursue adaptability and effectiveness within the product divisions simultaneously with efficiency in the functional departments. Thus, the organization can attain the best of both worlds. This structure also provides alignment between product division and corporate goals. The product groupings provide effective coordination within divisions, and the central functional departments provide coordination across divisions.

One weakness of the hybrid structure is administrative overhead. Some organizations experience a buildup of corporate staffs to oversee divisions. Some corporate functions duplicate activities undertaken within product divisions. If uncontrolled, administrative overhead can increase as the headquarters staff grows large. Decisions then become more centralized, and the product divisions

Exhibit 6.13
Sun Petroleum Products Company's Hybrid Organization

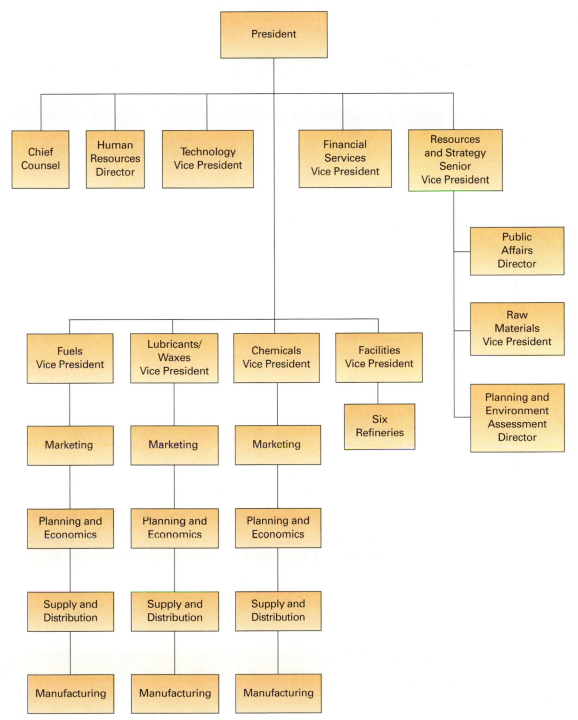

Exhibit 6.14
*Summary of Hybrid
Organization
Characteristics*

Context
Structure: Hybrid
Environment: Moderate to high uncertainty, changing customer demands
Technology: Routine or nonroutine, with some interdependencies between functions
Size: Large
Strategy, goals: External effectiveness and adaptation plus efficiency within some functions

Internal Systems
Operative goals: Product line emphasis, some functional emphasis
Planning and budgeting: Profit center basis for divisions; cost basis for central functions
Formal authority: Product managers; coordination responsibility resting with functional managers

Strengths
1. Allows organization to achieve adaptability and coordination in product divisions and efficiency in centralized functional departments
2. Results in better alignment between corporate and division-level goals
3. Achieves coordination both within and between product lines

Weaknesses
1. Has potential for excessive administrative overhead
2. Leads to conflict between division and corporate departments

lose the ability to respond quickly to market changes. As described in Chapter 5 on size, companies such as Nucor, Hanson Industries, and Burlington Northern have resisted administrative overhead by keeping headquarters staffs at fewer than one hundred people despite having as many as thirty-three thousand employees in product divisions. Managers in these companies minimize headquarters staffs to reduce bureaucracy and encourage division flexibility.[31]

An associated weakness is the conflict between corporate and divisional personnel. Headquarters functions typically do not have line authority over divisional activities. Division managers may resent headquarters intrusions, and headquarters managers may resent the desire of divisions to go their own way. Headquarters executives often do not understand the unique needs of the individual divisions that are trying to satisfy different markets.

The hybrid structure is often preferred to either the pure functional or pure divisional structure. It overcomes many of the weaknesses of these other structures and provides some advantages of both.

MATRIX STRUCTURE

Another way to achieve focus on multiple outcomes is with the **matrix structure**. The matrix can be used when one sector of the environment requires technological expertise, for example, and another sector requires rapid change within each product line. The matrix structure often is the answer when organizations find that neither the functional, divisional, geographical, nor hybrid structures combined with horizontal linkage mechanisms will work.

The matrix is a strong form of horizontal linkage. The unique characteristic of the matrix organization is that both product division and functional structures (horizontal and vertical) are implemented simultaneously, as shown in Exhibit 6.15. Rather than divide the organization into separate parts as in the hybrid structure, the product managers and functional managers have equal authority within the organization, and employees report to both of them. The matrix structure is similar to the use of full-time integrators or product managers described earlier in this chapter (Exhibit 6.5), except that in the matrix structure the product managers (horizontal) are given formal authority equal to that of the functional managers (vertical).

Conditions for the Matrix

A dual hierarchy may seem an unusual way to design an organization, but the matrix is the correct structure when the following conditions are met.[32]

- *Condition 1.* Pressure exists to share scarce resources across product lines. The organization is typically medium-sized and has a moderate number of product

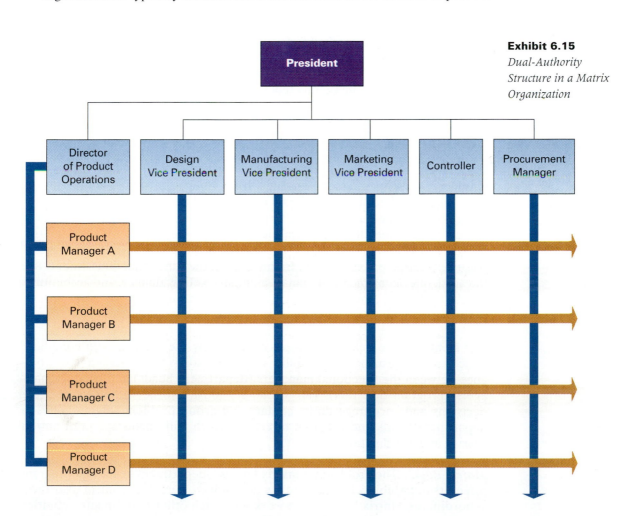

Exhibit 6.15
Dual-Authority Structure in a Matrix Organization

lines. It feels pressure for the shared and flexible use of people and equipment across those products. For example, the organization is not large enough to assign engineers full-time to each product line, so engineers are assigned part-time to several products or projects.

- *Condition 2.* Environmental pressure exists for two or more critical outputs, such as for technical quality (functional structure) and frequent new products (divisional structure). This dual pressure means a balance of power is needed between the functional and product sides of the organization, and a dual-authority structure is needed to maintain that balance.
- *Condition 3.* The environmental domain of the organization is both complex and uncertain. Frequent external changes and high interdependence between departments require a large amount of coordination and information processing in both vertical and horizontal directions.

Under these three conditions, the vertical and horizontal lines of authority must be given equal recognition. A dual-authority structure is thereby created so the balance of power between them is equal.

Referring again to Exhibit 6.15, assume the matrix structure is for a clothing manufacturer. Product A is footwear, product B is outerwear, product C is sleepwear, and so on. Each product line serves a different market and customers. As a medium-size organization, the company must effectively use people from manufacturing, design, and marketing to work on each product line. There are not enough designers to warrant a separate design department for each product line, so the designers are shared across product lines. Moreover, by keeping the manufacturing, design, and marketing functions intact, employees can develop the in-depth expertise to serve all product lines efficiently.

Key Matrix Roles

The unique aspect of matrix structure as reflected in Exhibit 6.15 is that some employees have two bosses. Working within a matrix structure is difficult for most managers because it requires a new set of skills compared with those required for a single-authority structure. For the matrix to succeed, managers in key roles have specific responsibilities. The key roles are top leaders, matrix bosses, and two-boss employees. These roles are illustrated in the College of Business matrix in Exhibit 6.16. In this matrix, the functional departments are the academic departments of management, marketing, finance, and accounting, which represent the vertical hierarchy. The horizontal reporting relationships are to the program directors for the undergraduate, MBA, and doctoral programs.

Top Leader.   The dean is the **top leader**, who is the head of both command structures. The primary responsibility for this person is to maintain a power balance between the functional managers (department heads) and product managers (program directors). The top leader must also be willing to delegate decisions and encourage direct contact and group problem solving between department heads and program directors, which will encourage information sharing and coordination.

Matrix Boss.   The problem for **matrix bosses**—department heads and program directors in Exhibit 6.16—is that they do not have complete control over their subordinates. Matrix bosses must work with each other to delineate activities

Exhibit 6.16
Key Positions in a College of Business Matrix Structure

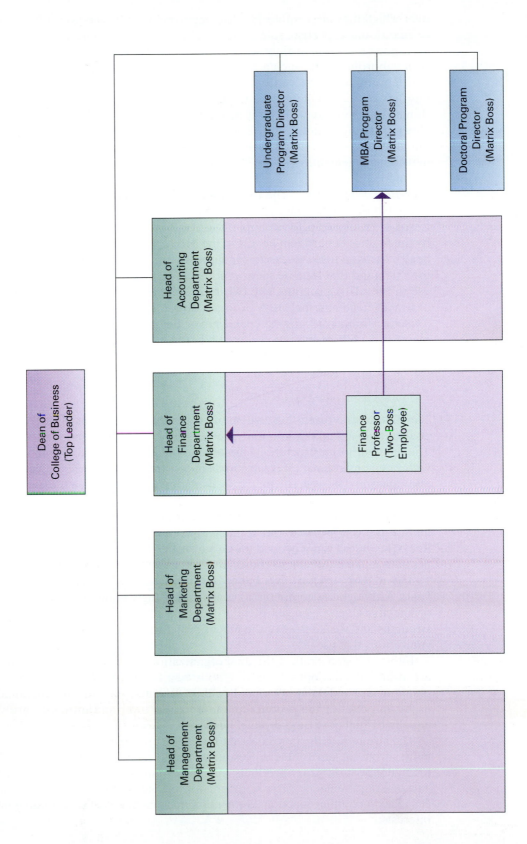

over which they are responsible. The department head's responsibilities pertain to functional expertise, rules, and teaching standards. The program director is responsible for coordinating the whole program. This person has authority over subordinates for such activities as class scheduling, exams, and preventing overlapping of course content. Matrix bosses must be willing to confront one another on disagreements and conflicts. They must also collaborate on such things as performance reviews, promotions, and salary increases, since professors report to both of them. These activities require a great deal of time, communication, patience, and skill at working with people, which are all part of matrix management.

Two-Boss Employees.   The **two-boss employee** often experiences anxiety and stress. Conflicting demands are imposed by the matrix bosses. The finance professor in Exhibit 6.16, for example, must cope with conflicting demands imposed by the finance department head and the MBA program director. The department head's demand to do research is in direct conflict with the MBA program director's demand that time be spent reading and developing teaching materials for use in the MBA program. The two-boss employee must confront both the department head and the MBA program director on these demands and reach a joint decision about how to spend his or her time. Two-boss employees must maintain an effective relationship with both managers, and they should display a dual loyalty toward both their departments and their programs.

Strengths and Weaknesses

The matrix structure is best when environmental uncertainty is high and when goals reflect a dual requirement, such as for both product and functional goals. The dual-authority structure facilitates communication and coordination to cope with rapid environmental change and enables an equal balance between product and functional bosses. The matrix is also good for nonroutine technologies that have interdependencies both within and across functions. The matrix is an organic structure that facilitates discussion and adaptation to unexpected problems. It tends to work best in organizations of moderate size with a few product lines. The matrix is not needed for only a single-product line, and too many product lines make it difficult to coordinate both directions at once.

The matrix structure has been used in organizations for more than thirty years. Although horizontal linkages are increasingly popular, empirical evidence of specific advantages is still relatively sparse. Exhibit 6.17 summarizes the strengths and weaknesses of the matrix structure based on what we know of organizations that use it.[33]

Internal systems reflect the dual organization structure. Two-boss employees are aware of and adopt subgoals for both their functions and their products. Dual planning and budgeting systems should be designed, one for the functional hierarchy and one for the product line hierarchy. Power and influence are shared equally by functional and product heads.

The strength of the matrix is that it enables an organization to meet dual demands from the environment. Resources (people, equipment) can be flexibly allocated across different products, and the organization can adapt to changing external requirements.[34] This structure also provides an opportunity for employees to acquire either functional or general management skills, depending on their interests.

Exhibit 6.17
*Summary of Matrix
Organization
Characteristics*

Context
Structure: Matrix Environment: High uncertainty Technology: Nonroutine, many interdependencies Size: Moderate, a few product lines Strategy, goals: Dual—product innovation and technical specialization
Internal Systems
Operative goals: Equal product and functional emphasis Planning and budgeting: Dual systems—by function and by product line Formal authority: Joint between functional and product heads
Strengths
1. Achieves coordination necessary to meet dual demands from environment 2. Flexible sharing of human resources across products 3. Suited to complex decisions and frequent changes in unstable environment 4. Provides opportunity for functional and product skill development 5. Best in medium-sized organizations with multiple products
Weaknesses
1. Causes participants to experience dual authority, which can be frustrating and confusing 2. Means participants need good interpersonal skills and extensive training 3. Is time-consuming; involves frequent meetings and conflict resolution sessions 4. Will not work unless participants understand it and adopt collegial rather than vertical-type relationships. 5. Requires dual pressure from environment to maintain power balance

Source: Adapted from Robert Duncan, "What Is the Right Organization Structure? Decision Tree Analysis Provides the Answer," *Organizational Dynamics* (Winter 1979): 429.

One disadvantage of the matrix is that some employees experience dual authority, which is frustrating and confusing. They need excellent interpersonal and conflict-resolution skills, which may require special training in human relations. The matrix also forces managers to spend a great deal of time in meetings.[35] If managers do not adapt to the information and power sharing required by the matrix, the system will not work. Managers must collaborate with one another rather than rely on vertical authority in decision making. The successful implementation of one matrix structure occurred at a steel company in Pittsburgh.

Pittsburgh Steel Company

In Practice 6.6

As far back as anyone can remember, the steel industry in the United States was stable and certain. If steel manufacturers could produce quality steel at a reasonable price, that steel would be sold. No more. Inflation, a national economic downturn, reduced consumption of autos, and competition from steelmakers in Germany and Japan forever changed the steel industry. Today, steelmakers have shifted to specialized steel products. They must market aggressively, make efficient use of internal resources, and adapt to rapid-fire changes.

Pittsburgh Steel employs 2,500 people, makes 300,000 tons of steel a year, and is 170 years old. For 160 of those years, functional structure worked fine. As the environment became more turbulent and competitive, however, Pittsburgh Steel managers realized they were not keeping up. Fifty percent of Pittsburgh's orders were behind schedule. Profits were eroded by labor, material, and energy cost increases. Market share declined.

In consultation with outside experts, the president of Pittsburgh Steel saw that the company had to walk a tightrope. Pittsburgh Steel had to specialize in a few high-value-added products tailored for separate markets, while maintaining economies of scale and sophisticated technology within functional departments. The dual pressure led to an unusual solution for a steel company: a matrix structure.

Pittsburgh Steel had four product lines: open-die forgings, ring-mill products, wheels and axles, and steelmaking. A business manager was given responsibility and authority of each line, which included preparing a business plan for each product line and developing targets for production costs, product inventory, shipping dates, and gross profit. They were given authority to meet those targets and to make their lines profitable. Functional vice presidents were responsible for technical decisions relating to their function. Functional managers were expected to stay abreast of the latest techniques in their areas and to keep personnel trained in new technologies that could apply to product lines. With twenty thousand recipes for specialty steels and several hundred new recipes ordered each month, functional personnel had to stay current. Two functional departments—field sales and industrial relations—were not included in the matrix because they worked independently. The final design was a hybrid matrix structure with both matrix and functional relationships, as illustrated in Exhibit 6.18.

Implementation of the matrix was slow. Middle managers were confused. Meetings to coordinate across functional departments seemed to be held every day. After about a year of training by external consultants, Pittsburgh Steel is on track. Ninety percent of the orders are now delivered on time. Market share has recovered. Both productivity and profitability are increasing steadily. The managers thrive on matrix involvement. Meetings to coordinate product and functional decisions have provided a growth experience. Middle managers now want to include younger managers in the matrix discussions as training for future management responsibility.[36]

Pittsburgh Steel Company illustrates the correct use of a matrix structure. The dual pressure to maintain economies of scale and to market four product lines gave equal emphasis to the functional and product hierarchies. Through continuous meetings for coordination, Pittsburgh Steel achieved both economies of scale and flexibility.

All kinds of organizations have experimented with the matrix, including consulting firms, hospitals, banks, insurance companies, government, and many types of industrial firms.[37] This structure has been used successfully by companies such as IBM, Unilever, and Ford Motor Company, which have fine-tuned the matrix to suit their particular goals and cultures. The matrix can be highly effective in a complex, rapidly changing environment where the organization needs to be flexible and adaptable.[38] However, the matrix is not a cure-all for structural problems. Many organizations have found the matrix described here, sometimes called a balanced matrix, difficult to install and maintain because one side of the authority structure often dominates. Recognizing this tendency, two variations of matrix structure have evolved—the **functional matrix** and the **project matrix**. In a functional matrix, the functional bosses have primary authority, and project or product managers simply coordinate product activities. In a project matrix, by contrast, the project or product manager has primary responsibility, and functional managers simply assign technical personnel to projects and provide advisory expertise as needed. For many organizations, one of these approaches works better than the balanced matrix and dual lines of authority.[39]

Exhibit 6.18

Matrix Structure for Pittsburgh Steel Company

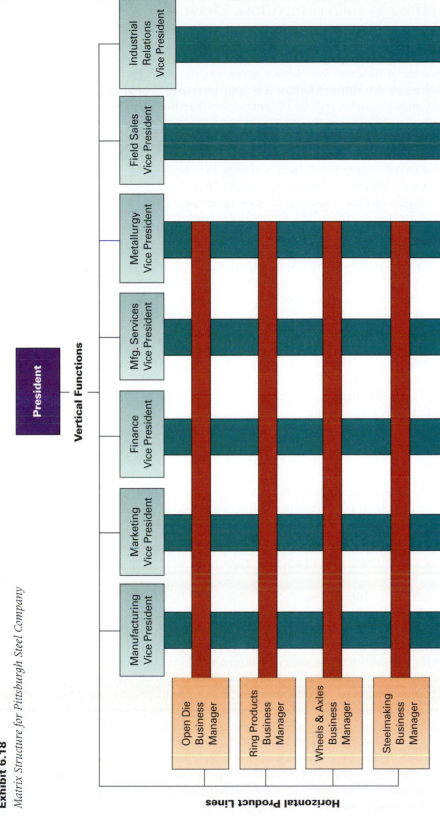

SYMPTOMS OF STRUCTURAL DEFICIENCY

Each form of structure—functional, divisional, hybrid, matrix—represents a tool that can help managers make an organization more effective depending on the demands of its situation. Senior managers periodically evaluate organization structure to determine whether it is appropriate to changing organization needs. Many organizations try one organization structure, then reorganize to another structure in an effort to find the right fit between internal reporting relationships and the needs of the external environment. Compaq Computer Corporation, for example, switched from a functional structure to a divisional structure for about a year to develop new products and then switched back to a functional structure to reduce competition among its product lines.[40]

As a general rule, when organization structure is out of alignment with organization needs, one or more of the following **symptoms of structural deficiency** appear.[41]

- *Decision making is delayed or lacking in quality.* Decision makers may be overloaded because the hierarchy funnels too many problems and decisions to them. Delegation to lower levels may be insufficient. Another cause of poor quality decisions is that information may not reach the correct people. Information linkages in either the vertical or horizontal direction may be inadequate to ensure decision quality.
- *The organization does not respond innovatively to a changing environment.* One reason for lack of innovation is that departments are not coordinated horizontally. The identification of customer needs by the marketing department and the identification of technological developments in the research department must be coordinated. Organization structure also has to specify departmental responsibilities that include environmental scanning and innovation.
- *Too much conflict is evident.* Organization structure should allow conflicting departmental goals to combine into a single set of goals for the entire organization. When departments act at cross purposes or are under pressure to achieve departmental goals at the expense of organizational goals, the structure is often at fault. Horizontal linkage mechanisms are not adequate.

SUMMARY AND INTERPRETATION

Organization structure must accomplish two things for the organization. It must provide a framework of responsibilities, reporting relationships, and groupings, and it must provide mechanisms for linking and coordinating organizational elements into a coherent whole. The structure is reflected on the organization chart. Linking the organization into a coherent whole requires the use of information systems and linkage devices in addition to the organization chart.

It is important to understand the information-processing perspective on structure. Organization structure can be designed to provide vertical and horizontal information linkages based upon the information processing required because of an uncertain environment, technology, size, or strategy and goals. Early organization theorists stressed vertical design and relied on vertical linkages, such as the hierarchy, planning, and new positions, to provide coordination. Vertical linkages are not sufficient for most organizations in today's complex and rapidly changing world.

The trend is toward flatter, more horizontal structures. Many organizations are breaking down the vertical hierarchy in favor of cross-functional teams. Other ways organizations provide horizontal linkages are through temporary task forces; regular, direct contact between managers across department lines; and through full-time integrators, such as product managers.

Alternatives for grouping employees and departments into overall structural design include functional grouping, divisional grouping, geographic grouping, and multifocused (hybrid, matrix) grouping. The best organization design achieves the correct balance between vertical and horizontal coordination. The choice among functional, divisional, and hybrid structures determines vertical priority and, hence, where coordination and integration will be greatest. Horizontal linkage mechanisms complement the vertical dimension to achieve the integration of departments and levels into an organizational whole. The matrix organization implements an equal balance between the vertical and horizontal dimensions of structure.

Finally, an organization chart is only so many lines and boxes on a piece of paper. A new organization structure will not necessarily solve an organization's problems. The organization chart simply reflects what people should do and what their responsibilities are. The purpose of the organization chart is to encourage and direct employees into activities and communications that enable the organization to achieve its goals. The organization chart provides the structure, but employees provide the behavior. The chart is a guideline to encourage people to work together, but management must implement the structure and carry it out.

Key Concepts

departmental grouping	matrix structure
divisional grouping	multifocused grouping
divisional structure	project matrix
functional grouping	structure
functional matrix	symptoms of structural deficiency
functional structure	task force
geographic grouping	teams
horizontal linkage	top leader
hybrid structure	two-boss employee
integrator	vertical information system
liaison role	vertical linkages
matrix bosses	

Briefcase

As an organization manager, keep these guides in mind:

1. Develop organization charts that describe task responsibilities, vertical reporting relationships, and the grouping of individuals into departments. Provide sufficient documentation so that all people within the organization know to whom they report and how they fit into the total organization picture.

2. Provide vertical and horizontal information linkages to integrate diverse departments into a coherent whole. Achieve vertical linkage through hierarchy referral, rules and plans, new positions, and vertical information systems. Achieve horizontal linkage through cross-functional information systems, direct contact, task forces, full-time integrators, and teams.

3. Choose between functional or divisional structures when designing overall organization structure. Use a functional structure in a small or medium-sized organization that has a stable environment. Use a divisional structure in a large organization that has multiple product lines and when you wish to give priority to product goals and to coordination across functions.

4. Implement hybrid structures, when needed, in large corporations by dividing the organization into self-contained product divisions and assigning to the product division each function needed for the product line. If a function serves the entire organization rather than a specific product line, structure that function as a central functional department. Use a hybrid structure to gain the advantages of both functional and divisional design while eliminating some of the disadvantages.

5. Consider a matrix structure in certain organization settings if neither the divisional nor the functional structure meets coordination needs. For best results with a matrix structure, use it in a medium-sized organization with a small number of products that has a changing environment and needs to give equal priority to both products and functions because of dual pressures from the environment. Do not use the matrix structure unless there is truly a need for a dual hierarchy and employees are well trained in its purpose and operation.

6. Consider a structural reorganization whenever the symptoms of structural deficiency are observed. Use organization structure to solve the problems of poor quality decision making, slow response to the external environment, and too much conflict between departments.

Discussion Questions

1. What is the definition of *organization structure*? Does organization structure appear on the organization chart? Explain.
2. How do rules and plans help an organization achieve vertical integration?
3. When is a functional structure preferable to a divisional structure?
4. Large corporations tend to use hybrid structures. Why?
5. How does organizational context influence the choice of structure? Are some contextual variables more important than others? Discuss.

6. What is the difference between a task force and a team? Between liaison role and integrating role? Which of these provides the greatest amount of horizontal coordination?
7. What conditions usually have to be present before an organization should adopt a matrix structure?
8. The manager of a consumer products firm said, "We use the brand manager position to train future executives." Do you think the brand manager position is a good training ground? Discuss.
9. In a matrix organization, how do the role requirements of the top leader differ from the role requirements of the matrix bosses?
10. In your opinion, what is the value of an information-processing perspective on structure?

Chapter Six Workbook *You and Organization Structure**

To better understand the importance of organization structure in your life, do the following assignment.

Select one of the following situations to organize:

1. The registration process at your university or college
2. A new fast-food franchise
3. A sports rental in an ocean resort area, such as jet skis
4. A bakery

Background

Organization is a way of gaining some power against an unreliable environment. The environment provides the organization with inputs, which include raw materials, human resources, and financial resources. There is a service or product to produce that involves technology. The output goes to clients, a group that must be nurtured. The complexities of the environment and the technology determine the complexity of the organization.

Planning Your Organization

1. Write down the mission or purpose of the organization in a few sentences.
2. What are the specific things to be done to accomplish the mission?
3. Based on the specifics in No. 2, develop an organizational chart. Each position in the chart will perform a specific task or is responsible for a certain outcome.
4. Add duties to each job position in the chart. These will be the job descriptions.
5. How can you make sure people in each position will work together?
6. What level of skill and abilities is required at each position and level in order to hire the right persons?
7. Make a list of the decisions that would have to be made as you developed your organization.
8. Who is responsible for customer satisfaction? How will you know if customers' needs are met?
9. How will information flow within the organization?

*Adapted by Dorothy Marcic from "Organizing," in Donald D. White and H. William Vroman, Action in Organizations, 2nd ed. (Boston: Allyn and Bacon, 1982) 154.

Case for Analysis *C & C Grocery Stores, Inc.**

The first C & C grocery store was started in 1947 by Doug Cummins and his brother Bob. Both were veterans who wanted to run their own business, so they used their savings to start the small grocery store in Charlotte, North Carolina. The store was immediately successful. The location was good, and Doug Cummins had a winning personality. Store employees adopted Doug's informal style and "serve the customer" attitude.

*Prepared by Richard L. Daft, from Richard L. Daft and Richard Steers, Organizations: a Micro/Macro Approach (Glenview, Ill.: Scott, Foresman, 1986). Reprinted with permission.

Exhibit 6.19

Organization Structure for C & C Grocery Stores, Inc.

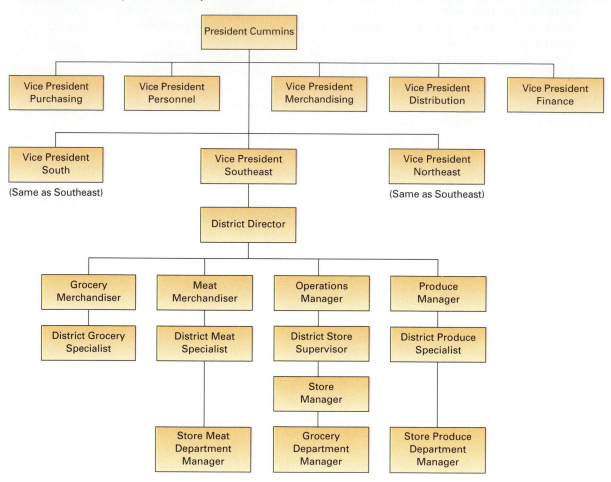

C & C's increasing circle of customers enjoyed an abundance of good meats and produce.

By 1984, C & C had over 200 stores. A standard physical layout was used for new stores. Company headquarters moved from Charlotte to Atlanta in 1975. The organization chart for C & C is shown in Exhibit 6.19. The central offices in Atlanta handled personnel, merchandising, financial, purchasing, real estate, and legal affairs for the entire chain. For management of individual stores, the organization was divided by regions. The southern, southeastern, and northeastern regions each had about seventy stores. Each region was divided into five districts of ten to fifteen stores each. A district director was responsible for supervision and coordination of activities for the ten to fifteen district stores.

Each district was divided into four lines of authority based upon functional specialty. Three of these lines reached into the stores. The produce department manager within each store reported directly to the produce specialist for the division, and the same was true for the meat department manager, who reported directly to the district meat specialist. The meat and produce managers were responsible for all activities associated with the acquisition and sale of perishable products. The store manager's responsibility included the grocery line, front-end departments, and store operations. The store manager was responsible for appearance of personnel, cleanliness, adequate check-out service, and price accuracy. A grocery manager reported to the store manger and maintained inventories and restocked shelves for grocery items. The district merchandising office was responsible for promotional campaigns, advertising circulars, district advertising, and for attracting customers into the stores. The grocery merchandisers were expected to coordinate their activities with each store in the district.

During the recession in 1980–81, business for the C & C chain dropped off in all regions and did not increase with the improved economic times in 1983–84. This caused concern among senior executives. They also were aware that other supermarket chains were adopting a trend toward one-stop shopping, which meant the emergence of super stores that included a pharmacy, dry goods, and groceries—almost like a department store. Executives wondered whether C & C should move in this direction and how such changes could be assimilated into the current store organization. However, the most pressing problem was how to improve business with the grocery stores they now had. A con-

sulting team from a major university was hired to investigate store structure and operations.

The consultants visited several stores in each region, talking to about fifty managers and employees. The consultants wrote a report that pinpointed four problem areas to be addressed by store executives.

1. The chain is slow to adapt to change. Store layout and structure were the same as had been designed fifteen years ago. Each store did things the same way, even though some stores were in low-income areas and other stores in suburban areas. A new grocery management system for ordering and stocking had been developed, but after two years was only partially implemented in the stores.

2. Roles of the district store supervisor and the store manager were causing dissatisfaction. The store managers wanted to learn general management

Exhibit 6.20

Proposed Reorganization of C & C Grocery Stores, Inc.

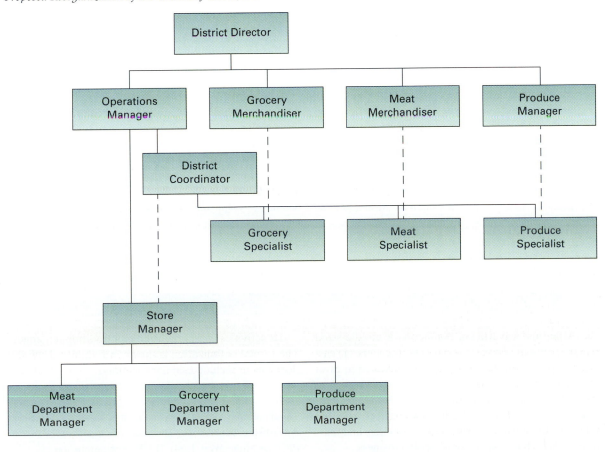

skills for potential promotion into district or regional management positions. However, their jobs restricted them to operational activities and they learned little about merchandising, meat, and produce. Moreover, district store supervisors used store visits to inspect for cleanliness and adherence to operating standards rather than to train the store manager and help coordinate operations with perishable departments. Close supervision on the operational details had become the focus of operations management rather than development, training, and coordination.

3. Cooperation within stores was low and morale was poor. The informal, friendly atmosphere originally created by Doug Cummins was gone. One example of this problem occurred when the grocery merchandiser and store manager in a Louisiana store decided to promote Coke and Diet Coke as a loss leader. Thousands of cartons of Coke were brought in for the sale, but the stockroom was not prepared and did not have room. The store manager wanted to use floor area in the meat and produce sections to display Coke cartons, but those managers refused. The produce department manager said that Diet Coke did not help his sales and it was okay with him if there was no promotion at all.

4. Long-term growth and development of the store chain would probably require reevaluation of long-term strategy. The percent of market share going to traditional grocery stores was declining nationwide due to competition from large super stores and convenience stores. In the future, C & C might need to introduce non-food items into the stores for one-stop shopping, and add specialty sections within stores. Some stores could be limited to grocery items, but store location and marketing techniques should take advantage of the grocery emphasis.

To solve the first three problems, the consultants recommended reorganizing the district and the store structure as illustrated in Exhibit 6.20. Under this reorganization, the meat, grocery, and produce department managers would all report to the store manager. The store manager would have complete store control and would be responsible for coordination of all store activities. The district supervisor's role would be changed from supervision to training and development. The district supervisor would head a team that included himself and several meat, produce, and merchandise specialists who would visit area stores as a team to provide advice and help for the store managers and other employees. The team would act in a liaison capacity between district specialists and the stores.

The consultants were enthusiastic about the proposed structure. By removing one level of district operational supervision, store managers would have more freedom and responsibility. The district liaison team would establish a cooperative team approach to management that could be adopted within stores. The focus of store responsibility on a single manager would encourage coordination within stores, adaptation to local conditions, and provide a focus of responsibility for store-wide administrative changes.

The consultants also believed that the proposed structure could be expanded to accommodate non-grocery lines if enlarged stores were to be developed in the future. Within each store, a new department manager could be added for pharmacy, dry goods, or other major departments. The district team could be expanded to include specialists in these departments who would act as liaison for stores in the district.

Case for Analysis *Aquarius Advertising Agency**

The Aquarius Advertising Agency is a middle-sized firm that offered two basic services to its clients: (1) customized plans for the content of an advertising campaign (for example, slogans, layouts) and (2) complete plans for media (such as radio, TV, newspapers, billboards, and magazines). Additional services included aid in marketing and distribution of products and marketing research to test advertising effectiveness.

Its activities were organized in a traditional manner. The formal organization is shown in Exhibit 6.21. Each department included similar functions.

*Adapted from John F. Veiga and John N. Yanouzas, "Aquarius Advertising Agency," *The Dynamics of Organization Theory* (St. Paul, Minn.: West, 1984), 212–17, with permission.

Exhibit 6.21
Aquarius Advertising Agency Organization Chart

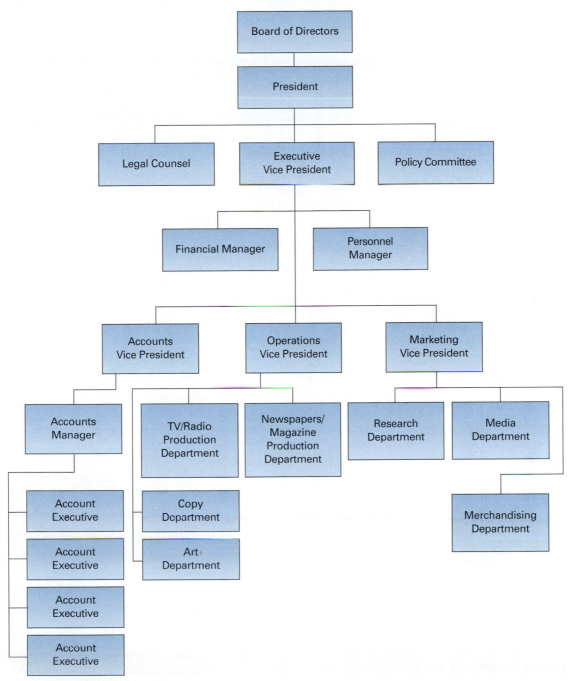

Each client account was coordinated by an account executive who acted as a liaison between the client and the various specialists on the professional staff of the operations and marketing divisions. The number of direct communications and contacts between clients and Aquarius specialists, clients and account executives, and Aquarius specialists and account executives is indicated in Exhibit 6.22. These sociometric data were gathered by a consultant who conducted a study of the patterns of formal and informal communication.

Exhibit 6.22

Sociometric Index of Contacts of Aquarius Personnel and Clients

	Clients	Account Manager	Account Executives	TV/Radio Specialists	Newspaper/Magazine Specialists	Copy Specialists	Art Specialists	Merchandising Specialists	Media Specialists	Research Specialists
Clients	X	F	F	N	N	O	O	O	O	O
Account Manager		X	F	N	N	N	N	N	N	N
Account Executives			X	F	F	F	F	F	F	F
TV/Radio Specialists				X	N	O	O	N	N	O
Newspaper/Magazine Specialists					X	O	O	N	O	O
Copy Specialists						X	N	O	O	O
Art Specialists							X	O	O	O
Merchandising Specialists								X	F	F
Media Specialists									X	F
Research Specialists										X

F = Frequent – daily
O = Occasional – once or twice per project
N = None

Each intersecting cell of Aquarius personnel and the clients contains an index of the direct contacts between them.

Although an account executive was designated to be the liaison between the client and specialists within the agency, communications frequently occurred directly between clients and specialists and bypassed the account executive. These direct contacts involved a wide range of interactions, such as meetings, telephone calls, letters, and so on. A large number of direct communications occurred between agency specialists and their counterparts in the client organization. For example, an art specialist working as one member of a team on a particular client account would often be contacted directly by the client's in-house art specialist, and agency research personnel had direct communication with research people of the client firm. Also, some of the unstructured contacts often led to more formal meetings with clients in which agency personnel made presentations, interpreted and defended agency policy, and committed the agency to certain courses of action.

Both hierarchical and professional systems operated within the departments of the operations and marketing divisions. Each department was organized hierarchically with a director, an assistant director, and several levels of authority. Professional communications were widespread and mainly concerned with sharing knowledge and techniques, technical evaluation of work, and development of professional interests. Control in each department was exercised mainly through control of promotions and supervision of work done by subordinates. Many account executives, however, felt the need for more influence, and one commented:

Creativity and art. That's all I hear around here. It is hard as hell to effectively manage six or seven hotshots who claim they have to do their own thing. Each of them tries to sell his or her idea to the client, and most of the time I don't know what has happened until a week later. If I were a despot, I would make all of them check with me first to get approval. Things would sure change around here.

The need for reorganization was made more acute by changes in the environment. Within a short period of time, there was a rapid turnover in the major accounts handled by the agency. It was typical for advertising agencies to gain or lose clients quickly, often with no advance warning as consumer behavior and life-style changes emerged and product innovations occurred.

An agency reorganization was one solution proposed by top management to increase flexibility in this unpredictable environment. The reorganization was aimed at reducing the agency's response time to environmental changes and at increasing cooperation and communication among specialists from different departments. The top managers are not sure what type of reorganization is appropriate. They would like your help analyzing their context and current structure and welcome your advice on proposing a new structure.

Notes

1. Thomas A. Stewart, "How To Lead a Revolution," *Fortune,* 28 November 1994, 48–61.

2. John Child, *Organization* (New York: Harper & Row, 1984).

3. Stuart Ranson, Bob Hinings, and Royston Greenwood, "The Structuring of Organizational Structures," *Administrative Science Quarterly* 25 (1980): 1–17; Hugh Willmott, "The Structuring of Organizational Structure: A Note," *Administrative Science Quarterly* 26 (1981): 470–74.

4. This discussion is based on Jay R. Galbraith, *Competing with Flexible Lateral Organizations*, 2nd ed. (Reading, Mass.: Addison-Wesley, 1994), ch. 2; Terry L. Amburgey and Tina Dacin, "As The Left Foot Follows The Right? The Dynamics of Strategic and Structural Change," *Academy of Management Journal* 37, no. 6 (1994): 427–52; Raymond E. Miles and W. E. Douglas Creed, "Organizational Forms and Managerial Philosophies: A Descriptive and Analytical Review," *Research in Organizational Behavior* 17 (1995): 333–72.

5. Galbraith, *Competing with Flexible Lateral Organizations.*

6. David Nadler and Michael Tushman, *Strategic Organization Design* (Glenview, Ill.: Scott Foresman, 1988).

7. *Ibid.*

8. Based on Jay R. Galbraith, *Designing Complex Organizations* (Reading, Mass.: Addison-Wesley, 1973) and *Organization Design* (Reading, Mass.: Addison-Wesley, 1977), 81–127.

9. Lee Iacocca with William Novak, *Iacocca: An Autobiography* (New York: Phantom Books, 1984), 152–53.

10. Alex Taylor III, "Will Success Spoil Chrysler?" *Fortune*, 10 January 1994, 88–92.

11. Based on Galbraith, *Designing Complex Organizations.*

12. Bob Lindgren, "Going Horizontal," *Enterprise,* April 1994, 20–25.

13. Barbara Ettorre, "Simplicity Cuts a New Pattern," *Management Review* (December 1993): 25–29.

14. Walter Kiechel III, "The Art of the Corporate Task Force," *Fortune,* 28 January 1991, 104–5; William J. Altier, "Task Forces: An Effective Management Tool," *Management Review* (February 1987): 52–57.

15. Keith Naughton and Kathleen Kerwin, "At GM, Two Heads May Be Worse Than One," *Business Week,* 14 August 1995, 46.

16. Paul R. Lawrence and Jay W. Lorsch, "New Managerial Job: The Integrator," *Harvard Business Review* (November-December 1967): 142–51.

17. Ann M. Morrison, "The General Mills Brand of Managers," *Fortune,* 12 January 1982, 99–107.

18. *Ibid.;* Daniel Rosenheim, "The Metamorphosis of General Mills," *Houston Chronicle,* 1 April 1982, sec. 3, p. 4.

19. Jay R. Galbraith, *Competing with Flexible Lateral Organizations,* 2nd ed. (Reading, Mass.: Addison-Wesley, 1994), 17–18; Laurie P. O'Leary, "Curing the Monday Blues: A U.S. Navy Guide for Structuring Cross-Functional Teams," *National Productivity Review* (Spring 1996): 43–51.

20. Galbraith, *Competing with Flexible Lateral Organizations,* 132–46.

21. Henry Mintzberg, *The Structuring of Organizations* (Englewood Cliffs, N.J.: Prentice-Hall, 1979).

22. Based on Robert Duncan, "What Is the Right Organization Structure?" *Organizational Dynamics* (Winter 1979): 59–80; W. Alan Randolph and Gregory G. Dess, "The Congruence Perspective of Organization Design: A Conceptual Model and Multivariate Research Approach," *Academy of Management Review* 9 (1984): 114–27.

23. Toni Mack, "The Ice Cream Man Cometh," *Forbes,* 22 January 1990, 52–56; David Abdalla, J. Doehring, and Ann Windhager, "Blue Bell Creameries, Inc.: Case and Analysis" (Unpublished manuscript, Texas A&M University, 1981); Jorjanna Price, "Creamery Churns Its Ice Cream into Cool Millions," *Parade,* 21 February 1982, 18–22.

24. Rahul Jacob, "The Struggle to Create an Organization for the 21st Century," *Fortune,* 3 April 1995, 90–99.

25. Based on Duncan, "What Is the Right Organization Structure?"

26. Joseph Weber, "A Big Company That Works," *Business Week,* 4 May 1992, 124–132; and Elyse Tanouye, "Johnson & Johnson Stays Fit by Shuffling Its Mix of Businesses," *Wall Street Journal,* 22 December 1992, A1, A4.

27. Mark Landler, "Shake-Up at Warner Music Group Results in Ouster of Its Chairman," *New York Times,* 4 May 1995, C1, C7.

28. Weber, "A Big Company That Works."

29. Lisa Driscoll, "The New, New Thinking at Xerox," *Business Week,* 22 June 1992, 120–21.

30. Adapted from Linda S. Ackerman, "Transition Management: An In-depth Look at Managing Complex Change," *Organizational Dynamics* (Summer 1982): 46–66.

31. Terrence P. Pare, "How to Cut the Cost of Headquarters," *Fortune,* 11 September 1989, 189–96; Thomas Moore, "Goodbye, Corporate Staff," *Fortune,* 21 December 1987, 65–76.

32. Stanley M. Davis and Paul R. Lawrence, *Matrix* (Reading, Mass.: Addison-Wesley, 1977), 11–24.

33. Robert C. Ford and W. Alan Randolph, "Cross-Functional Structures: A Review and Integration of Matrix Organizations and Project Management," *Journal of Management* 18 (June 1992): 267–94; Duncan, "What Is the Right Organization Structure?"

34. Lawton R. Burns, "Matrix Management in Hospitals: Testing Theories of Matrix Structure and Development," *Administrative Science Quarterly* 34 (1989): 349–68.

35. Christopher A. Bartlett and Sumantra Ghoshal, "Matrix Management: Not a Structure, a Frame of Mind," *Harvard Business Review* (July-August 1990): 138–45.

36. This case was inspired by John E. Fogerty, "Integrative Management at Standard Steel" (Unpublished manuscript, Latrobe, Pennsylvania, 1980); Bill Saporito, "Allegheny Ludlum has Steel Figured Out," *Fortune,* 25 June 1984, 40–44; "The Worldwide Steel Industry: Reshaping to Survive," *Business Week,* 20 August 1984, 150–54; Stephen Baker, "The Brutal Brawl Ahead in Steel," *Business Week,* 13 March 1995, 88–90, and "Why Steel Is Looking Sexy," *Business Week,* 4 April 1994, 106–8.

37. Davis and Lawrence, *Matrix,* 155–80.

38. Robert C. Ford and W. Alan Randolph, "Cross-Functional Structures: A Review and Integration of Matrix Organization and Project Manage-

ment," *Journal of Management* 18, no. 2 (1992): 267–94; Paula Dwyer with Pete Engardio, Zachary Schiller, and Stanley Reed, "Tearing Up Today's Organization Chart," *Business Week/21st Century Capitalism,* 18 November 1994, 80–90.

39. Erik W. Larson and David H. Gobeli, "Matrix Management: Contradictions and Insight," *Cali-* *fornia Management Review* 29 (Summer 1987): 126–38.

40. Jo Ellen Davis, "Who's Afraid of IBM?" *Business Week,* 29 June 1987, 68–74.

41. Based on Child, *Organization*, ch. 1.

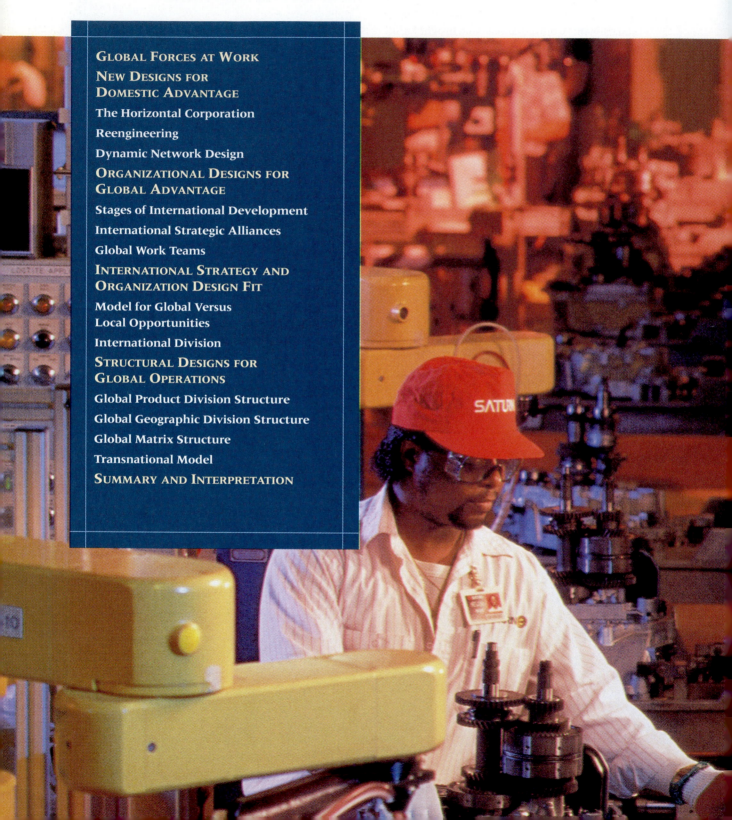

Contemporary Designs for Global Competition

A look inside

Ryder Systems, Inc.

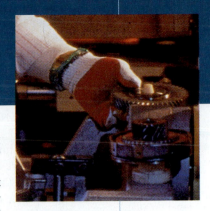

Every fifty-eight minutes, a tractor-trailer pulls into a loading dock at the Saturn plant in Spring Hill, Tennessee. A series of pallets containing car seats are automatically unloaded and moved along a conveyor belt to arrive at the right spot on the assembly line at the exact moment they are needed. The process has to work right every time, and it does, thanks to a just-in-time delivery system designed and operated by Ryder Systems, Inc.

As companies in all industries began feeling increased competition in the global marketplace, Ryder saw an untapped market for providing customized solutions to the growing complexity of coordinating transportation and distribution of materials. Yet Ryder's leaders knew they first had to take a long, hard look at how well their own processes worked. When the answer turned out to be "not very well," Ryder set out to reengineer its business processes to achieve significant performance improvements in the areas of customer service, quality, and cost. The company is striving for a boundaryless organization—one that is not based on vertical hierarchy but instead uses cross-functional teams organized around key business processes oriented toward customer needs. This is the only way Ryder can guarantee that car seats will arrive at Saturn at the exact moment they are needed, hour after hour, day after day. The company has invested heavily in leading-edge technology, employee training, and communication to support the team concept. New cultural values and management processes encourage continuous employee learning.

Ryder's reengineering efforts are ongoing, but the shift to a horizontal, learning-based organization is already showing results. Customer teams garner high customer satisfaction ratings. The productivity of salespeople assigned to contractual business has increased by 33 percent, and maintenance staff efficiency is up 11 percent. New customer start-up time for sophisticated integrated logistics contracts has been cut in half. Results are also showing up on Ryder's bottom line, as sales and revenues continue to grow. Ryder knows that staying in tune with customers worldwide is key to remaining competitive in a rapidly changing global marketplace.[1]

Ryder is not the only company looking for new ways to fight on the increasingly competitive global battleground. Dozens of America's top manufacturers, including Gillette, Xerox, Hewlett-Packard, Dow Chemical, 3M, and DuPont, sell more of their products outside of the United States than they do at home. In terms of profits, Coca-Cola made more money in both the Pacific and western Europe than it did in the United States, and nearly 70 percent of General Motors profit in recent years has been from non-U.S. operations.

Even more ominous for North American companies is the arrival on North American shores of foreign competitors in enormous numbers and strength. Companies such as Nestlé (Switzerland), Michelin (France), Sony and Honda (Japan), Bayer (Germany), Northern Telecom (Canada), and Unilever (United Kingdom) all receive more than 40 percent of annual sales from foreign countries.[2] They are in North America competing vigorously for markets.

Today, no company is isolated from global influence, and global competition continues to escalate with rapid advances in technology and communications. Consider Hong Kong's Johnson Electric Holdings Ltd., a $195 million producer of micromotors that power hair dryers, blenders, and automobile features such as power windows and door locks. With factories in South China and a research and development lab in Hong Kong, Johnson is thousands of miles away from a leading automaker. Yet the company has cornered the market for electric gizmos for Detroit's Big Three by using new information technology. Johnson design teams "meet" face-to-face for two hours each morning with their customers in the United States and Europe via videoconferencing. The company's processes and procedures are so streamlined that Johnson can take a concept and deliver a prototype to the United States in six weeks.[3] North American companies simply have no choice about global competition. No company is safe and no employee immune to its impact. For example, U.S. companies have held a virtual lock on unique products in software and multimedia, but foreign competition is heating up as companies throughout Asia quickly move into the industry. For example, Bilingual Education Computing, Inc., a company on the outskirts of Beijing, is rapidly selling its interactive CD-ROM programs for teaching English to institutes from Japan to Germany. Mainly because of lower wages, Bilingual can produce a CD-ROM product for anywhere from a quarter to one-tenth of the cost in the United States.[4]

Purpose of this Chapter

This chapter will introduce new approaches to organization design that enable organizations to compete effectively in a global environment. First, we will discuss the grim reality of worldwide competition. Then we will examine new designs for domestic advantage, including a shift from vertical to horizontal management, the radical redesign of business processes known as *reengineering,* and the use of network structures. Finally, we will discuss how companies can best organize for worldwide advantage, ranging from adding an export department to establishing a worldwide matrix structure or transnational model. By the end of the chapter, you will understand how to apply organization design innovations to a variety of domestic and international situations.

GLOBAL FORCES AT WORK

It is hard to deny the impact of globalization on each of us. We buy goods and services from around the world. Many U.S. workers are already working for foreign bosses. Even if you live and work in a small city, an international thrust for your company may be just around the corner, with rewards going to employees who can speak a foreign language or who have international abilities.

Globalization is so pervasive that it is hard to sort out, but the boxes in Exhibit 7.1 identify some of the key elements.[5] International forces at work today include the dominant economies of Japan and Germany, which sponsor powerhouse international companies and have huge positive trade balances with the United States. This means the end of U.S. company dominance and the onset of intense competition among high-wage nations. Newly industrialized countries such as Korea, Taiwan, and Spain are fast-growing and rapidly becoming industrialized. Their companies produce low-cost, high-quality commodities and are moving into high-value items, such as automobiles and high-technology electronic goods. The shift toward market economies in eastern Europe and the

Exhibit 7.1
Global Forces Influencing Domestic Organizations

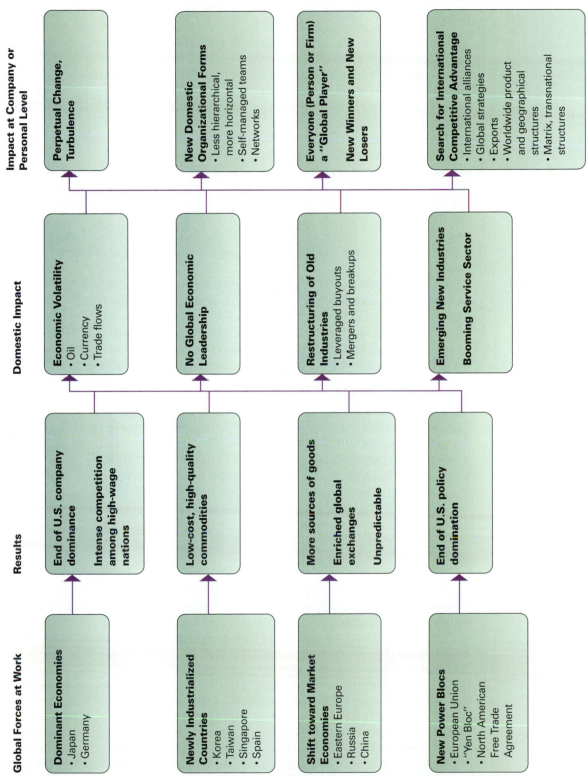

Source: Adapted from Tom Peters, "Prometheus Barely Unbound," *Academy of Management Executive* 4 (1990): 71.

former Soviet republics is rapidly producing more sources of goods, potential new markets, and, to some extent, an unpredictable future about how these countries will affect globalization.

More uncertainty will be caused by international blocs, including: the European Union agreement to drop internal trade barriers, spawning even larger, more competitive international companies and erecting barriers to outsiders; the "yen bloc" that includes Asian powerhouse nations; and the North American Free Trade Agreement. These power blocs will shape the world economy into the twenty-first century and will certainly mean the end of U.S. domination of international trade policy.

What are the outcomes for individuals and businesses within the United States and Canada—or any other country, for that matter? One outcome is economic volatility: No one knows whether oil will cost fifteen or twenty dollars a barrel next year. Likewise, currency values fluctuate based on inflation, trade balances, and capital investments over which no single country has control. Products we buy today, such as an IBM PC or a Black & Decker appliance, may include components from a dozen nations. No company or country can provide global economic leadership; every company and country is subordinate to larger economic forces.

No wonder we've seen the dramatic restructuring of traditional industries in the United States through leveraged buyouts, mergers, and breakups. These companies were striving for greater efficiency within an increasingly turbulent and competitive international environment. Indeed, the spinoffs and breakups of previous mergers may turn out to be a bigger story than the mergers, because the smaller players are efficient and well managed. Also, expect new and rapidly emerging industries—such as information technology that already contributes 20 percent directly to gross national product. Biotechnology is just underway and may foster its own industrial revolution. People who grew up feeling comfortable and secure working for a manufacturing firm appreciate just how elusive stability and security are in the new world order.

The impact at a personal level is illustrated in the righthand column of Exhibit 7.1. Companies operating nationally, such as Wal-Mart or Quad/Graphics, are adopting new organizational forms that include less hierarchy and more self-managed teams and dynamic network structures that provide autonomy to clusters of people and activities. These organizational forms utilize human resources better than ever before and enable companies to fend off international competition. One example of this shift is Ciba-Geigy Canada, described in The New Paradigm box.

Another outcome is perpetual change—enduring turbulence that organizations must learn to accept as the norm. Everyone—employees, organizations—needs to begin thinking of themselves as global players; they must try to use global alliances to advantage, sell to global markets, and be ready to meet global competition. This is especially true for Americans, who grew up believing in the superiority and invincibility of the U.S. economy.

All of this turbulence creates new winners and new losers. New winners are companies thriving under the new rules of the game—Nucor in steel, Dell in computers, MCI in telecommunications—companies not even in existence twenty-five years ago. Moreover, companies are learning to search for international competitive advantage through international alliances and joint ventures. Even small companies are learning to produce quality products that can compete overseas and, hence, are adding export departments. Larger companies have learned to organize themselves into worldwide product or geographical struc-

---

The New Paradigm   **Ciba-Geigy Canada, Ltd.**

By getting rid of the bosses, Ciba-Geigy's agricultural chemicals plant in Ontario has boosted productivity by up to 30 percent. Plant workers set schedules, manage jobs, create job descriptions, interview new job applicants, and handle numerous decisions and tasks once handled by their supervisors. For Director of Production Gerry Rich and his team of workers, the post-boss paradigm is a dream come true.

When Rich first came to Ciba-Geigy, he found twelve managers and supervisors watching over ninety employees who "seemed to be leaving their ability to think at the factory gate." Productivity was low, and standards of quality were slipping. Rich decided to throw out the management rulebook in a daring effort to turn the plant around. Production workers served on the design team along with representatives from management, the warehouse, the administrative office, and the chemical lab. Ultimately, the plant was redesigned

for participative management, with production, warehouse, and maintenance at the center of the new organization. The structure looks something like the rings on a dartboard, with administration and support services, such as the lab, forming layers surrounding the center. On the very outside are the managers—now called advisers—whose primary job is to facilitate teamwork and act as liaison between teams. Many of the old-style managers couldn't adapt; by the end of the reorganization, two of the plant's three foremen and half of the management staff had left the company. As Rich put it, "People who can't change, you have to ask to work in an authoritarian environment—somewhere else."

Clearly, the loss of the bosses hasn't hurt at Ciba-Geigy.

Source: John Southerst, "First, We Dump the Bosses," *Canadian Business,* April 1992, 46–51.

---

tures. A few global firms have attained a quality of being transnational—almost without a home country—and are held together through complex international matrix or transnational structures that allow them to be global and local in fifty or more countries at the same time.

These international forces and the impact on individuals and companies mean that things must be done faster, organizations must be flexible, and innovation and improvement are paramount. Companies must be designed for maximum domestic or worldwide advantage.

In the next section, we will discuss some new organizational designs for domestic advantage, and then we will look at worldwide organization designs.

NEW DESIGNS FOR DOMESTIC ADVANTAGE

The functional organization structure described in Chapter 6 was the first to be used by large firms and eventually became associated with bureaucracy. The product or divisional structure was the next innovation in structure and provided a way to subdivide huge firms like General Motors and Sears Roebuck into more manageable profit centers. Then came the notion of cross-functional teams that worked horizontally to coordinate across departments. Horizontal teams evolved into the matrix structure that has two hierarchies simultaneously.

The most recent organization design innovations are a significant shift toward horizontal rather than vertical management, the radical redesign of business processes referred to as reengineering, and the use of dynamic network structures. These approaches harness human resources in new ways to give companies a competitive advantage.

The Horizontal Corporation

Many of today's corporations are shifting away from the top-heavy functionally organized structures of the past to a form that virtually eliminates both the vertical hierarchy and old departmental boundaries. The newly emerging **horizontal corporation** is illustrated in Exhibit 7.2 and has the following characteristics:

1. Structure is created around workflows or processes rather than departmental functions. Boundaries between traditional departments are obliterated. At Chrysler, for example, the structure is designed around the core processes of new car development.
2. The vertical hierarchy is flattened, with perhaps only a few senior executives in traditional support functions, such as finance and human resources.
3. Management tasks are delegated to the lowest level. Most employees work in multidisciplinary, self-directed teams organized around a process, such as new product development. Kodak, for example, did away with its senior vice presidents in charge of such functions as administration, manufacturing, and R&D and replaced them with self-directed teams. The company has over one thousand such teams working on various processes and programs.
4. Customers drive the horizontal corporation. For the horizontal design to work, processes must be based on meeting customer needs. Employees are brought into direct, regular contact with customers as well as suppliers. Sometimes, representatives of these outside organizations serve as full-fledged team members.[6]

Self-Directed Teams.   Self-directed teams are the building blocks of the new horizontal organization. A **self-directed team** is an outgrowth of earlier team approaches.[7] For example, many companies have used cross-functional teams to achieve coordination across departments and task forces to accomplish temporary projects. Other companies have experimented with problem-solving teams of voluntary hourly employees who meet to discuss ways to improve quality, efficiency, and work environment.

Self-directed teams, also called self-managed teams, typically consist of five to thirty workers with different skills who rotate jobs and produce an entire product or service and who take over managerial duties, such as work and vacation scheduling, ordering materials, and hiring new members. To date, several hundred companies in Canada and the United States have experimented with a self-directed team design.[8] These companies include AT&T, Xerox, General Mills, Federal Express, Ryder Systems, and Motorola.

The self-directed team design consists of permanent teams that include the following three elements:

1. The team is given access to resources, such as materials, information, equipment, machinery, and supplies, needed to perform a complete task.
2. The team includes a range of employee skills, such as engineering, manufacturing, finance, and marketing. The team eliminates barriers between departments, functions, disciplines, or specialties. Team members are crosstrained to perform one another's jobs, and the combined skills are sufficient to perform a major organizational task.
3. The team is empowered with decision-making authority, which means members have the freedom to plan, solve problems, set priorities, spend money,

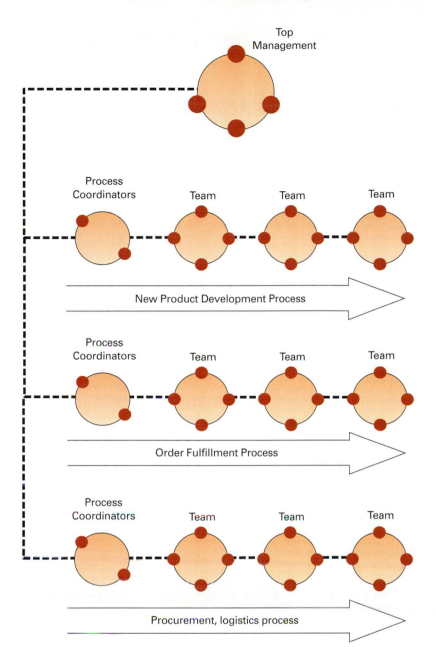

Exhibit 7.2
The Horizontal Corporation

Source: Based on John A. Byrne, "The Horizontal Corporation," *Business Week,* 20 December 1993, 76–81; and Thomas A. Stewart, "The Search for the Organization of Tomorrow," *Fortune,* 18 May 1992, 92–98.

monitor results, and coordinate activities with other departments or teams. The team must have autonomy to do what is necessary to accomplish the task.[9]

Volvo uses self-directed teams of seven to ten hourly workers, with each team assembling four cars per shift. Members are trained to handle all assembly jobs, creating greater employee motivation and decreased absenteeism.[10] In Canada,

Campbell Soup Company Ltd. designed self-directed teams to make its operations competitive with U.S. operations, achieving an "impossible" assignment of finding $700,000 of savings in three months.[11]

General Mills has increased the productivity of its plants by 40 percent by using self-directed teams. At its cereal plant in Lodi, California, workers are in charge of all activities, including designing the work process, purchasing equipment, and scheduling, operating, and maintaining machinery. The company has discovered that teams generally set higher goals for themselves than management would have set for them.[12]

From Vertical to Horizontal.   Experimentation with teams and horizontal structures often begins at the lower levels of organizations, but today, more companies are shifting their entire structure to a horizontal mode. Some start-up companies, such as Astra-Merck Group, a stand-alone company created to market anti-ulcer and blood-pressure medicine from Sweden's Astra, are structuring themselves as horizontal organizations from the beginning. Astra-Merck is organized around processes, such as drug development and product distribution, rather than divided into functional departments.

Eastman Chemical Company, a $3.5 billion stand-alone unit of Eastman-Kodak, replaced several of its senior vice presidents with self-directed teams. The company calls its new organization chart "the pizza chart," because it looks like a round pizza with several slices of pepperoni on top. Each slice of pepperoni (small circles) on the pizza represents a self-directed team that is responsible for a work flow, such as cellulose technology. The president of the company is in the center of the pizza. Surrounding him are the self-directed teams, with the white space in between reflecting where the interaction among teams should take place. As Ernest W. Deavenport, Jr., the "head pepperoni," says, "We did it in circular form to show that everyone is equal in the organization. No one dominates the other."[13]

Some companies, such as Canada's MacMillan Bloedel, have been evolving into team-based organizations over a period of many years.

In Practice 7.1

MacMillan Bloedel

MacMillan Bloedel has been weaving together the elements of a team-based organization since the late 1960s, when a labor disruption threatened the company's service to panelboard customers. In response to this problem, MacMillan Bloedel's training manager developed a plan to implement a team-based operation at the new plant in Thunder Bay, Ontario. In this highly unionized community, MacMillan Bloedel wanted to manage in such a way that employees would not feel the need to be represented by a third party. The company hired employees well before the scheduled start-up and provided them with lengthy training in technical, interpersonal, and group problem-solving skills. Teams of five to seven workers were organized around various parts of the production process and handled all day-to-day operating decisions, production adjustments, and hiring and firing. Although the flat organization structure was successful at Thunder Bay, it didn't spread to the rest of the organization and was considered by the company as something of a "special case."

In the early 1980s, however, MacMillan Bloedel decided to shut down its outdated and money-losing Chemainus sawmill in British Columbia after unsuccessful efforts to involve employees and their union in finding creative ways to keep the mill running. The Chemainus manager and several workers decided to visit the Thunder Bay operation in their search for a "better way." A new Chemainus plant using a team-oriented system became MacMillan Bloedel's most profitable mill. Since that time, two other MacMillan Bloedel operations have shifted to a team-based philosophy by actively involving workers and union leaders in discussions of what kind of environment they want to work in. One important way top management has supported the team-oriented philosophy has been by implementing a gainsharing program so that all employees share in the success of the company.

Although the evolutionary approach has some disadvantages, MacMillan Bloedel likes the fact that it doesn't dictate what is best for employees. Instead, it opens up possibilities for employees to experiment and develop the deep commitment that comes from working hard to create an organization that reflects their beliefs and values. After all, that's what true teamwork is all about.[14]

Advantages and Disadvantages. The horizontal structure with self-directed teams has yielded excellent results in many organizations. As with all structures, however, it has disadvantages as well as advantages. The most significant advantage is that it delivers dramatic improvements with speed and efficiency. Rapid response time and quicker decisions mean greater customer satisfaction. At Federal Express, organizing clerical workers into teams played a key role in achieving a major reduction in customer service problems such as incorrect bills and lost packages.[15]

Second, there are reduced, practically nonexistent barriers among departments, which means achieving cooperation with the total task in mind. Third, there is better morale because employees are enthused about their involvement and participation. Finally, administrative overhead is reduced because teams take on the administrative tasks.

But shifting to a horizontal structure can be a lengthy and difficult process, requiring major changes in job design, management philosophy, and information and reward systems.[16] Simply defining the processes around which teams are to be organized can be mind-boggling. AT&T's sixteen thousand employee Network Systems Division eventually counted up 130 processes, then began working to pare them down to thirteen core ones.[17]

In addition, managers need to be trained to understand the concept of participative management and develop new skills to become coaches and and facilitators rather than "supervisors." Employees need training to work effectively in a team environment. Information systems may need to be redesigned to give team members the information they need, not only from within the organization but from customers and suppliers as well. Employees have to spend more time in lengthy meetings to coordinate and reach consensual decisions. Finally, reward systems should support team performance and commitment.

In the shift to horizontal structures and self-directed teams, there is also a danger that the company will organize around processes without analyzing and linking processes to its key goals, in which case the new structure may bring about more negative than positive results. In the next section, we discuss reengineering, which can prevent this from happening.

Reengineering

The shift to a horizontal structure often goes hand-in-hand with reengineering, a popular management concept sweeping through corporate America. **Reengineering** is a cross-functional initiative involving the radical redesign of business processes to bring about simultaneous changes in organization structure, culture, and information technology and produce dramatic performance improvements in areas such as customer service, quality, cost, and speed.[18] Hoechst Celanese Corp., Union Carbide, DuPont Co., Pepsi-Cola North America, Pacific Bell, and BellSouth Telecommunications are among the dozens of companies involved in major reengineering efforts. After reengineering, Union Carbide cut $400 million out of fixed costs in just three years. Hoechst Celanese identified $70 million in cost savings and productivity improvements over a two year period, without making massive job cuts.[19] Many more organizations have reengineered one or a few specific processes; a 1994 Price Waterhouse poll, for example, revealed that an astounding 78 percent of *Fortune* 500 companies and 68 percent of British firms were reengineering one process or another.[20] Organizations are finding that the old ways of doing things no longer work in the emerging postmodern world. Reengineering is one method companies are using to reinvent themselves to meet new challenges. Book Mark 7.0 discusses other ways in which managers can meet the challenge of redefining and reinventing their companies for the twenty-first century.

Reengineering basically means taking a clean slate approach, pushing aside all the notions of how work is done now and looking at how work can best be designed for optimal performance. The idea is to squeeze out the dead space and time lags in workflows. Successful reengineering efforts are customer-driven. For example, looking at work processes "from the outside in" means BellSouth's cost cutting zeroes in on eliminating work content that is internally focused and does not add value for the customer—staff dealing with staff, hand-offs from one group to another, etc.[21] When reengineering forces companies to examine work and workflow in terms of customer value, the organization is more likely to organize processes around key goals and core competencies. Reengineering also brings about fundamental changes in organization structure, culture, and information systems.

Organization Structure.   Because reengineering examines work processes that cross functional boundaries, it is almost always associated with a shift to a more horizontal structure. Pepsi-Cola North America scrapped its functional, hierarchical organization for one designed around serving customers. Seven layers of management were cut to four. Similarly, after reengineering at Premier Bank of Louisiana, the organization structure is becoming increasingly flatter, with fewer management layers, the elimination of checking/reworking positions, and a reduction in centralized control both at headquarters and the regional levels. Exhibit 7.3 illustrates the evolution from the vertical to the horizontal organization as the design of work shifts from a focus on function to a focus on process. Most reengineering projects have landed companies somewhere in the middle of the evolutionary scale; few companies have shifted to an organization structure based entirely on horizontal processes.[22]

Culture.   As structure becomes flatter and more authority is pushed down to lower levels, corporate culture changes. Lower-level employees are empowered to make decisions and held accountable for performance improvements. Trust and tolerance of mistakes become key cultural values. Since reengineering at Bell-South, some employees have actually earned cash awards for their failures. According to Richard Harder, vice president for organization planning and development, "You need some worthy failures in your efforts to change behavior." At Premier

Book Mark 7.0

Have You Read About This?

Jumping the Curve: Innovation and Strategic Choice in an Age of Transition*

by Nicholas Imparato and Oren Harari

Nicholas Imparato and Oren Harari in their book, *Jumping the Curve,* explain that business success in the emerging world of the twenty-first century depends on "taking on the role of redefining, reinventing, repositioning, rethinking, and ultimately reforming organizations." Relying on extensive research and using case studies of companies such as All-Nippon Airways, Knight-Ridder, 3M, and Mrs. Fields Cookies, the authors help chart a path from the familiar world of the past to the unknown world of the future. They offer organizing principles that can help managers move from a mind-set of ineffective managerialism to postmodern leadership.

Organizing Principles

Jumping the Curve integrates thirteen critical success factors for managerial and organizational success: embracing change; attending to external realities; creating power; promoting a coaching style; expanding job responsibilities; developing expertise; driving out fear; exhibiting readiness for an entrepreneurial environment; keeping balance; maintaining a sense of continuity; demonstrating emotional maturity; providing the long-term view; and standing for an idea. Managers can embrace these success factors through four organizing principles:

- **Look a Customer Ahead:** Successful companies anticipate customers' needs before the customers do and anticipate and create new markets.
- **Build the Company Around the Software and the Software Around the Customer:** Organizations can develop processes that maximize the flow of knowledge and information. Information technology is used to link internal resources, external resources, and customers.
- **Ensure That Those Who Live the Values and Ideals of the Organization Are the Most Rewarded and the Most Satisfied:** Managers must truly embrace the philosophy that employees are the company's most valuable resource; and they must ensure that those who live the values and ideals of the organization are supported and rewarded.
- **Make the Customer the Final Arbiter of Quality:** Successful companies have a deep sense of commitment and responsibility to satisfy customers 100 percent.

Conclusion

Companies that organize around these four principles can build a framework for transition to the future. The principles can help managers "jump the curve" and build an organization that is based on trust, meaning, integrity, and commitment, oriented toward innovation, and guided by credible leadership. Imparato and Harari believe the elements of traditional management are inadequate in today's rapidly changing environment: ". . . Human imagination needs to fill the void, to invent new symbols for the world that has begun to stir."

*Thanks to Ken Friedman, Norwegian School of Management, Oslo, Norway, for providing this review.

Jumping the Curve: Innovation and Strategic Choice in an Age of Transition, by Nicholas Imparato and Oren Harari, is published by Jossey-Bass.

Bank, where teams have been empowered to make decisions to best serve customers, questioning and experimentation have become part of the culture.[23]

Information Systems. In traditionally organized companies, information systems have generally linked people within functional departments, but as workflow shifts to processes rather than functions, information systems need to cross boundaries as well.[24] The Gillette Company of Boston reengineered to cut its order cycle time from ten to fifteen days down to one or two days. Information

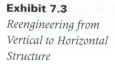

Exhibit 7.3

Reengineering from Vertical to Horizontal Structure

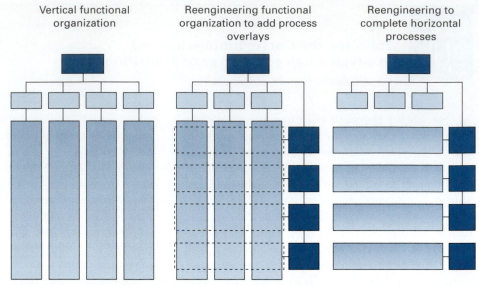

Source: George Stalk, Jr. and Jill E. Black, "The Myth of the Horizontal Organization," *Canadian Business Review* (Winter 1994): 26–31.

systems are being redesigned so that the customer service representative who takes the order can quickly access customer intelligence, up-to-date inventory information, pricing data, and worldwide delivery schedules from her PC or workstation.

Reengineering can lead to stunning results, but, as with all business ideas, it has its drawbacks. Reengineering is expensive, time-consuming, and usually painful. Leaders should be aware that it is a long-term process requiring major shifts in thinking and significant changes in organizational infrastructure.

Dynamic Network Design

Another major trend of the 1990s is the choice companies are making to limit themselves to only a few activities that they do extremely well and let outside specialists handle the rest. These network organizations, sometimes also called *modular corporations*, are flourishing particularly in fast-moving industries, such as apparel and electronics, but even companies in such industries as steel and chemicals are shifting toward this type of structure.[25]

The **dynamic network** structure incorporates a free market style to replace the traditional vertical hierarchy. A company keeps key activities in-house and then outsources other functions, such as sales, accounting, and manufacturing, to separate companies or individuals who are coordinated or brokered by a small headquarters. In most cases, these separate organizations are connected electronically to a central office.[26] Exhibit 7.4 illustrates how this organization might look.

For example, Lewis Galoob Toys, Inc., sold $58 million worth of toys with only 115 employees. Galoob contracts out manufacturing and packaging to contractors in Hong Kong, toy design to independent inventors, and sales to independent distribution representatives. Galoob never touches a product and does not even collect the money. The company is held together with phones, telexes, and other electronic technology.[27]

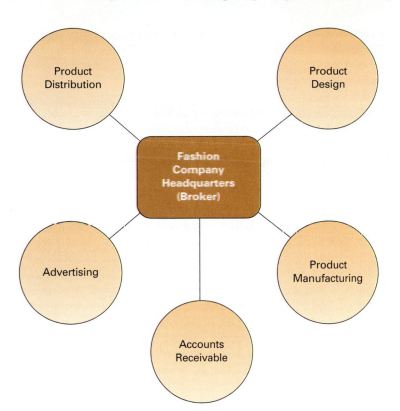

Exhibit 7.4
*Dynamic Network
Structure*

Companies like Nike and Reebok have succeeded by concentrating on their strengths in designing and marketing and contracting virtually all their footwear manufacturing to outside suppliers. Computer firms such as Dell, Gateway, and CompuAdd either purchase their products ready-made or buy all the parts and handle only the final assembly. Sun Microsystems relies so heavily on outside manufacturers and distributors that its own employees never touch one of its computers.[28]

The free market aspect means subcontractors flow in and out of the system as needed. Much like building blocks, parts of the network can be added or taken away to meet changing needs.[29] One company, TopsyTail, Inc., used the network approach to grow into an $80 million company with only two full-time employees.

TopsyTail, Inc.

In Practice 7.2

Thirty-seven-year-old entrepreneur Tomima Edmark was still working at IBM's Dallas office when she founded TopsyTail to make and sell the hair care gadget she had invented. At IBM, Edmark chafed at the amount of time she felt was wasted on office politics, countless meetings, and personnel issues. In her own business, she decided to keep full-time employees to a minimum and set up a network of outside vendors to do everything from manufacturing to public relations.

She started by farming out the tooling and injection molding of her plastic hair product, saving at least $5 million in start-up costs and giving her the freedom to explore the product's market potential. Today, TopsyTail's production partners include a tool maker, two injection molders, a package designer, a logo designer, freelance photographers, and a printer. The company also outsources packaging and shipping to three fulfillment houses;

television commercials to a video production company; customer mailings to a mailing list firm; and publicity to a public relations firm. Four distributing companies sell TopsyTail products in the United States, Canada, Mexico, the Pacific Rim, Europe, and South Africa. Headquarters maintains control of new product development and marketing strategy, the core competencies that form the heart of the company.

TopsyTail's current three full-time employees share an office in Dallas, where they focus on finding the right partners and coordinating network relationships. Edmark believes the network structure gives her a greater ability to respond quickly to changes in market demand. As her business continues to grow with new products, she will simply add the new partners needed to get the products to market.[30]

Advantages and Disadvantages.   The advantages of the dynamic network structure are several. The structure is unbelievably lean, with almost no administrative overhead because work activities are contracted and coordination is electronic.

As illustrated by the previous example, the approach can help new entrepreneurs get products to market quickly without having to incur huge start-up costs. In mature industries that are beginning to stagnate, the network structure can reinvigorate companies by enabling them to develop new products without huge investments. Another significant advantage of the network approach is its flexible, rapid response—the ability to arrange and rearrange resources to meet changing needs and best serve customers. Managerial and technical talent can be focused on key activities that provide competitive advantage, while other functions are outsourced.[31]

The disadvantages are related to the unusual nature of this organization design. For one thing, there is little hands-on control. Operations are not under one roof, and managers must adjust to relying on independent subcontractors to do the work. Companies can experience problems with quality control when many different subcontractors are involved. In addition, some companies have found that subcontractors tend to dramatically raise prices once the company becomes hooked on their products or services.[32] Moreover, it can be difficult with a network structure to define the organization, since it may change from week to week as the set of subcontractors changes. Likewise, the organization can occasionally lose a part if a subcontractor defects or goes out of business and can't be replaced. A final disadvantage is weakened employee loyalty. A cohesive corporate culture for the larger organization is difficult to establish. Turnover tends to be high because employees are committed only to their own task or subcontractor, and they may be dismissed at any time in favor of a new contractor.

ORGANIZATIONAL DESIGNS FOR GLOBAL ADVANTAGE

Companies in the 1990s must think globally to remain competitive. At least 70 to 85 percent of the U.S. economy is feeling the impact of foreign competition.[33] The global environment is a huge potential market. International expansion can lead to greater profits, efficiency, and responsiveness. Of course, no company can become a global giant overnight. The change from domestic to international usually occurs through stages of development, similar to the life cycle described in Chapter 5.

Stages of International Development

Exhibit 7.5 summarizes the four stages many companies go through as they evolve toward full-fledged global operations.[34] In stage one, the **domestic stage**, the company is domestically oriented, but managers are aware of the global envi-

	I. **Domestic**	II. **International**	III. **Multinational**	IV. **Global**
Strategic Orientation	Domestically oriented	Export-oriented, multidomestic	Multinational	Global
Stage of Development	Initial foreign involvement	Competitive positioning	Explosion	Global
Structure	Domestic structure, plus export department	Domestic structure, plus international division	Worldwide geographic, product	Matrix, transnational
Market Potential	Moderate, mostly domestic	Large, multidomestic	Very large, multinational	Whole world

Exhibit 7.5
Four Stages of International Evolution

Source: Based on Nancy J. Adler, *International Dimensions of Organizational Behavior* (Boston: PWS-KENT, 1991), 7–8; and Theodore T. Herbert, "Strategy and Multinational Organization Structure: An Interorganizational Relationships Perspective," *Academy of Management Review* 9 (1984): 259–71.

ronment and may want to consider initial foreign involvement to expand production volume. Market potential is limited and is primarily in the home country. The structure of the company is domestic, typically functional or divisional, and initial foreign sales are handled through an export department. The details of freight forwarding, customs problems, and foreign exchange are handled by outsiders.

In stage two, the **international stage**, the company takes exports seriously and begins to think multidomestically. **Multidomestic** means competitive issues in each country are independent of other countries; the company deals with each country individually. The concern is with international competitive positioning compared with other firms in the industry. At this point, an international division has replaced the export department, and specialists are hired to handle sales, service, and warehousing abroad. Multiple countries are identified as a potential market.

In stage three, the **multinational stage**, the company is becoming a truly multinational company, which means it has marketing and production facilities in many countries and has more than one-third of its sales outside the home country. Explosion occurs as international operations take off, and the company has business units scattered around the world along with suppliers, manufacturers, and distributors.

The fourth and ultimate stage is the **global stage**, which means the company transcends any single country. The business is not merely a collection of domestic industries; rather, subsidiaries are interlinked to the point where competitive position in one country significantly influences activities in other countries.[35] Truly **global companies** no longer think of themselves as having a single home country, and, indeed, have been called "stateless" corporations.[36] This represents a new and dramatic evolution from the multinational company of the 1960s and 1970s.

Global companies operate in truly global fashion, and the entire world is their marketplace. Organization structure at this stage can be extremely complex and often evolves into an international matrix or transnational model, which will be discussed later in this chapter.

Global companies such as Procter and Gamble, Unilever, and Matsushita Electric may operate in forty to seventy-five countries. The structural problem of holding together this huge complex of subsidiaries scattered thousands of miles apart is immense. Before turning to a discussion of specific structures, let's briefly consider two additional approaches to international activity, international alliances and global teams.

International Strategic Alliances

Strategic alliances are perhaps the hottest way to get involved in international operations. Typical alliances include licensing, joint ventures, and consortia.[37] Licensing agreements are frequently entered into by manufacturing firms to capitalize on the diffusion of new technology quickly and inexpensively while getting the advantage of lucrative worldwide sales. For example, Merck, Eli Lilly, and Bayer cross-license their newest drugs to one another to support industrywide innovation and advertising and offset the high fixed costs of research and distribution.[38] **Joint ventures** are separate entities created with two or more active firms as sponsors. This is another approach to sharing development and production costs and penetrating new markets. It is estimated that the rate of joint venture formation between U.S. and international companies has been growing by 27 percent annually since 1985. Joint ventures may be with either customers or competitors. Merck has put together major ventures with such competitors as Johnson & Johnson and AB Astra of Sweden.[39] A manufacturer may seek a joint venture to distribute its new technology and products through another country's distribution channels and markets.

The agreement between Toyota and General Motors to construct a Chevrolet Nova plant in California was Toyota's way of distributing its technology to the United States. Texas Instruments sought long-term alliances with its biggest customers in Japan, including Sony, to gain subsidiaries in Japan. Over time, TI bought out Sony's share and ended up with four major plants in Japan producing semiconductors for the rest of TI's worldwide operations.[40]

Given the expense of new technology, **consortia** of organizations are likely to be the wave of the future. Rather than one-on-one competition among individual firms, groups of independent companies—suppliers, customers, and even competitors—will join together to share skills, resources, costs, and access to one another's markets.

Managers must learn to cooperate as well as compete.[41] For example, Airbus Industrie is a European consortium of businesses backed by the governments of Germany, France, the United Kingdom, and Spain to produce commercial aircraft. Airbus is slowly gaining market share and is successfully selling aircraft worldwide. Consortia are often used in other parts of the world, such as the *keiretsu* families of corporations in Japan. In Korea, these interlocking company arrangements are called *choebol*.

A type of consortia, called the *virtual organization*, is increasingly being used in the United States and offers a promising avenue for worldwide competition in the future. The virtual organization is a continually evolving group of companies that unite to exploit specific opportunities or attain specific strategic advantages and then disband when objectives are met. A company may be involved in multiple alliances at any one time. Some U.S. executives believe shifting to a consortia or virtual approach is the best way for U.S. companies to remain competitive in the global marketplace.[42]

Global Work Teams

The reality of today's business world as a global work environment has led some companies to establish global work teams to expand their products and operations into international markets.[43] **Global teams**, also called *transnational teams*, are work groups made up of multinational members whose activities span multiple countries. For example, Heineken formed the European Production Task Force, a thirteen-member team representing five countries, to wrestle with the question of how the company's production facilities throughout Europe could best be configured to cope with the challenges of the twenty-first century.[44] Global teams have been used in various ways. Some, such as Heineken's, help organizations achieve global efficiencies by developing regional or worldwide cost advantages and standardizing designs and operations. Other global teams help their companies be more locally responsive by meeting the needs of different regional markets, consumer preferences, and political and legal systems. A third primary use of global teams is to contribute to continuous organizational learning and adaptation on a global level.[45] The most advanced use of global teams involves simultaneous contributions in all of these strategic areas.

Global work teams bring unique problems to the concept of teamwork. Team leaders and members must learn to accommodate one another's cultural values and backgrounds and work together smoothly, usually in conditions of rapid change. One model for global team effectiveness, called the GRIP model, suggests that teams focus on developing common understanding in four critical areas: goals, relationships, information, and work processes, thus enabling the team to "get a grip" on its collaborative work at a very high level.[46] The need for and use of global work teams is likely to grow. Teams that effectively blend their varied backgrounds and interests into a teamwork culture focused on serving the organization's international goals can significantly enhance a company's global competitiveness.

INTERNATIONAL STRATEGY AND ORGANIZATION DESIGN FIT

As we discussed in Chapter 6, an organization's structure must fit its situation by providing sufficient information processing for coordination and control while focusing employees on specific functions, products, or geographic regions. Organization design for international structure follows a similar logic, with special interest on global versus local strategic opportunities.

Model for Global Versus Local Opportunities

A major strategic issue for firms venturing into the international domain is whether (and when) to use a globalization rather than a multidomestic strategy. The **globalization strategy** means that product design and advertising strategy are standardized throughout the world.[47] For example, the Japanese took business away from Canadian and American companies by developing similar high-quality, low-cost products for all countries. The Canadian and American companies incurred higher costs by tailoring products to specific countries. Black & Decker became much more competitive internationally when it standardized its line of power hand tools. Other products, such as Coca-Cola and Levi blue jeans, are naturals for globalization, because only advertising and marketing need to be tailored for different regions.

A **multidomestic strategy** means that competition in each country is handled independently of competition in other countries. Thus, a multidomestic strategy would encourage product design, assembly, and marketing tailored to the specific needs of each country. Some companies have found that their products do not thrive in a single global market. The French do not drink orange juice for break-fast, and laundry detergent is used to wash dishes, not clothes, in parts of Mexico. Parker Pen experienced a disaster when it reduced from five hundred to one hundred pen styles because the different styles were valued in different countries.

The model in Exhibit 7.6 illustrates how organization design and international strategy fit.[48] Companies can be characterized by whether their product and service lines have potential for globalization, which means advantages through worldwide standardization. Companies that sell diverse products or services across many countries have a globalization strategy. On the other hand, some companies have products and services appropriate for a multidomestic strategy, which means local-country advantages through differentiation and customization.

As indicated in Exhibit 7.6, when a company is low with respect to developing either a globalization or multidomestic strategy, simply using an international division with the domestic structure is an appropriate way to handle international business. For some businesses, however, the basis for advantage may be a globalization strategy—selling the same products worldwide—in which case a global product structure is appropriate. This structure will provide product managers with authority to handle their product lines worldwide. When a company's strategy is multidomestic through locally based customization, then a worldwide geographical structure is appropriate, with each country or region having subsidiaries modifying products and services to fit that locale.

Exhibit 7.6

Model to Fit Organization Structure to International Advantages

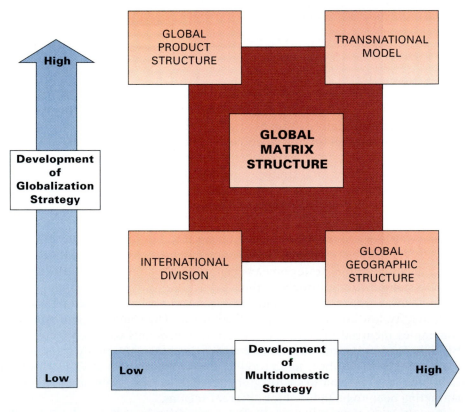

Source: Roderick E. White and Thomas A. Poynter, "Organizing for Worldwide Advantage," *Business Quarterly* (Summer 1989): 84-89. Adapted by permission of *Business Quarterly,* published by the Western Business School, the University of Western Ontario, London, Ontario, Canada.

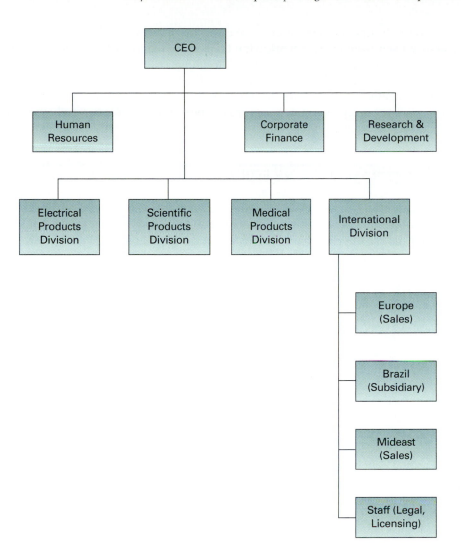

Exhibit 7.7
Domestic Hybrid Structure with International Division

In many instances, companies will have both global and local opportunities simultaneously, in which case the matrix structure or transnational model can be used. Part of the product line may need to be standardized globally, and other parts tailored to the needs of local countries, in which case the matrix structure may work. When the company achieves truly global size and scope beyond what can be handled by the matrix, the transnational model may be used. Next, we will discuss each of the structures in Exhibit 7.6 in more detail.

International Division

As companies begin to explore international opportunities, they typically start with an export department that grows into an **international division**. The international division has a status equal to the other major departments or divisions within the company and is illustrated in Exhibit 7.7. The international division has its own hierarchy to handle business (licensing, joint ventures) in various countries, selling the products and services created by the domestic divisions, opening subsidiary plants, and in general moving the organization into more sophisticated international operations.

Although functional structures are often used domestically, they are less frequently used to manage a worldwide business.[49] Lines of functional hierarchy running around the world would extend too long, so some form of product or geographical structure is used to subdivide the organization into smaller units. Firms typically start with an international department and, depending on their strategy, later use product or geographic divisional structures, to which we will now turn.

STRUCTURAL DESIGNS FOR GLOBAL OPERATIONS

The international arena produces complex structures because of defined national boundaries and great distances. The structures most typically used by international firms are the global product structure and global geographic structure.

Global Product Division Structure

In a **global product structure**, the product divisions take responsibility for global operations in their specific product area. Each product division can organize for international operations as it sees fit. Each division manager is responsible for planning, organizing, and controlling all functions for the production and distribution of its products for any market around the world. The product-based structure works best when a division handles products that are technologically similar and can be standardized for marketing worldwide. As we saw in Exhibit 7.6, the global product structure works best when the company has opportunities for worldwide production and sale of standard products for all markets, thus providing economies of scale and standardization of production, marketing, and advertising.

Eaton Corporation has used a form of worldwide product structure, as illustrated in Exhibit 7.8. In this structure, the automotive components group, industrial group, and so on are responsible for manufacture and sale of products worldwide. The vice president of international is responsible for coordinators in each region, including a coordinator for Japan, Australia, South America, and northern Europe. The coordinators find ways to share facilities and improve production and delivery across all product lines sold in their region. These coordinators provide the same function as integrators described in Chapter 6.

The product structure is great for standardizing production and sales around the globe, but it also has problems. Often the product divisions do not work well together, competing instead of cooperating in some countries; and some countries may be ignored by product managers. The solution adopted by Eaton Corporation of using country coordinators who have a clearly defined role is a superb way to overcome these problems.

Global Geographic Division Structure

A worldwide regional organization divides the world into regions, each of which reports to the CEO. Each region has full control of functional activities in its geographical area. Companies that use this **global geographic structure** tend to have mature product lines and stable technologies. They find low-cost manufacturing within countries as well as different needs across countries for marketing and sales. Strategically, this structure can exploit many opportunities for regional or locally based competitive advantages.[50]

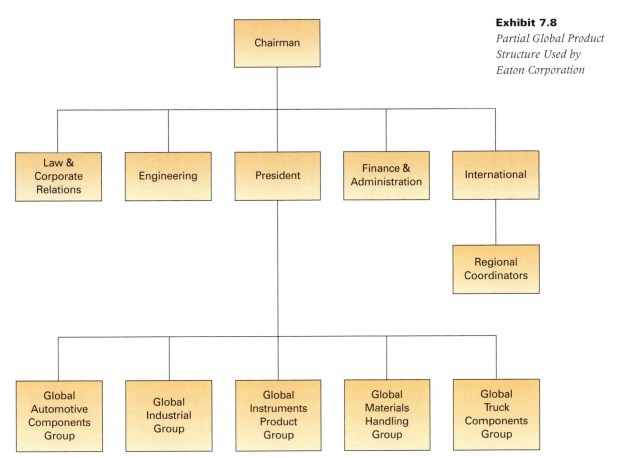

Source: Based on *New Directions in Multinational Corporate Organization* (New York: Business International Corp., 1981).

The problems encountered by senior management using a global geographic structure result from the autonomy of each regional division. For example, it is difficult to do planning on a global scale—such as new product R&D—because each division acts to meet only the needs of its region. New domestic technologies and products can be difficult to transfer to international markets because each division feels it will develop what it needs. Likewise, it is difficult to rapidly introduce products developed offshore into domestic markets; and there is often duplication of line and staff managers across regions. Companies such as Dow Chemical find ways to take advantage of the geographic structure while overcoming these problems.

Dow Chemical

In Practice 7.3

For several years, Dow Chemical used a geographic structure of the form illustrated in Exhibit 7.9. First, Dow Europe developed its own manufacturing, sales, and technical services that became an autonomous division. Subsequently the Pacific and Latin American areas developed as regional entities, also, as did Canadian operations. Dow handled the problems of coordination across regions by creating a corporate-level product department to provide long-term planning and worldwide product coordination and communication. It used six corporate product directors, each of whom had been a line manager with overseas experience. The product directors are essentially staff coordinators, but they

Exhibit 7.9
Global Geographic Division Structure

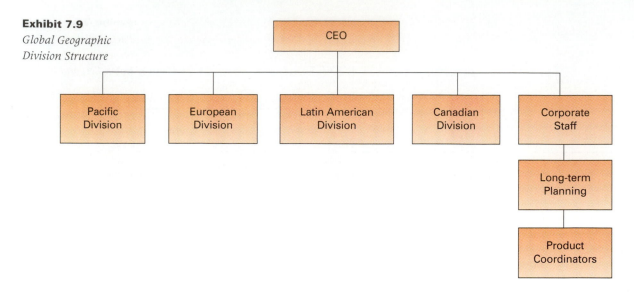

have authority to approve large capital investments and to move manufacturing of a product from one geographic location to another to best serve corporate needs. With this structure, Dow maintains its focus on each region and achieves coordination for overall planning, savings in administrative staff, and manufacturing and sales efficiency.[51]

Global Matrix Structure

We've discussed how Eaton used a global product division structure and found ways to coordinate across worldwide divisions. Dow Chemical used a global geographic division structure and found ways to coordinate across geographical regions. Each of these companies emphasized a single dimension. Recall from Chapter 6 that a matrix structure provides a way to achieve vertical and horizontal coordination simultaneously along two dimensions. Matrix structures used by multinational corporations are similar to those described in Chapter 6, except that geographical distances for communication are greater and coordination is more complex.

The matrix works best when pressure for decision making balances the interests of both product standardization and geographical localization and when coordination to share resources is important. An excellent example of a **global matrix structure** that works extremely well is ABB, an electrical equipment corporation headquartered in Zurich.

In Practice 7.4   *Asea Brown Boveri (ABB)*

ABB, which employs more than 200,000 people worldwide and has annual revenues of $29 billion, has given new meaning to the notion of "being local worldwide." ABB owns 1,300 subsidiary companies, divided into 5,000 profit centers located in 140 countries. ABB's average plant has fewer than 200 workers and most of the company's 5,000 profit centers contain only forty to fifty people, meaning almost everyone stays close to the customer. ABB uses a complex global matrix structure similar to Exhibit 7.10 to achieve worldwide economies of scale combined with local flexibility and responsiveness.

At the top are the chief executive officer and an international committee of eight top managers, who hold frequent meetings around the world. Along one side of the matrix are sixty-five or so business areas located worldwide, into which ABB's products and services

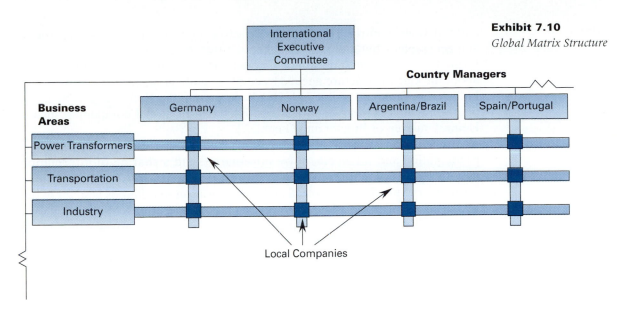

Exhibit 7.10
Global Matrix Structure

Local Companies

are grouped. Each business area leader is responsible for handling business on a global scale, allocating export markets, establishing cost and quality standards, and creating mixed-nationality teams to solve problems. For example, the leader for power transformers is responsible for twenty-five factories in sixteen countries.

Along the other side of the matrix is a country structure; ABB has more than one hundred country managers, most of them citizens of the country in which they work. They run national companies and are responsible for local balance sheets, income statements, and career ladders. The German president, for example, is responsible for thirty-six thousand people across several business areas that generate annual revenues in Germany of more than $4 billion.

The matrix structure converges at the level of the thirteen hundred local companies. The presidents of local companies report to two bosses—the business area leader, who is usually located outside the country, and the country president who runs the company of which the local organization is a subsidiary.

ABB's philosophy is to decentralize things to the lowest levels. Global managers are generous, patient, and multilingual. They must work with teams made up of different nationalities and be culturally sensitive. They craft strategy and evaluate performance for people and subsidiaries around the world. Country managers, by contrast, are regional line managers responsible for several country subsidiaries. They must cooperate with business area managers to achieve worldwide efficiencies and the introduction of new products. Finally, the presidents of local companies have both a global boss—the business area manager—and a country boss, and they learn to coordinate the needs of both.[52]

In the language of Chapter 6, the CEO is the "top leader," the business area and country managers are "matrix bosses," and the presidents of local company affiliates are "two-boss employees." ABB is a large, successful company that manages to achieve the benefits of both product and geographic organizations through this matrix structure.

Transnational Model

The **transnational model** of organization structure may occur for huge multinational firms with subsidiaries in many countries that try to exploit both global and local advantages, and perhaps technological superiority, rapid innovation, and functional control. The matrix is effective for handling two issues (product and geographic), but more than two competitive issues requires a more complex form of structure. The transnational model represents the most current thinking about the kind of structure needed by complex global organizations such as N. V. Philips, illustrated in Exhibit 7.11. Headquartered in the Netherlands, Philips has operating units in sixty countries and is typical of global companies, such as Heinz, Unilever, or Procter and Gamble.[53]

The units in Exhibit 7.11 are far-flung. Achieving coordination, a sense of participation and involvement by subsidiaries, and a sharing of information, new technologies, and customers requires a complex and multidimensional form of structure. For example, a global corporation like Philips is so large that size itself is a problem when coordinating global operations. In addition, some subsidiaries may become so large that they no longer fit a narrow strategic role assigned to them by headquarters. While being part of a large organization, they also need autonomy for themselves and need to have impact on other parts of the organization.

The transnational model is much more than just an organization chart. It is a state of mind, a set of values, a shared desire to make a worldwide system work, and an idealized organization structure for effectively managing such a system. The transnational model cannot be given a precise definition, but the following characteristics distinguish it from and move it beyond a matrix structure.[54]

1. *The transnational model differentiates into many centers of different kinds.* The matrix structure had a single headquarters, a single center of control for each country, and a single center for each product line. The transnational operates on a principle of "flexible centralization." A transnational may centralize some functions in one country, some in another, yet decentralize still other functions among its many geographically dispersed operations. An R&D center may be centralized in Holland and a purchasing center located in Sweden, while financial accounting responsibilities are decentralized to operations in many countries. A unit in Hong Kong may be responsible for coordinating activities across Asia, while activities for all other countries are coordinated by a large division headquarters in London.

2. *Subsidiary managers initiate strategy and innovations that become strategy for the corporation as a whole.* In traditional structures, managers have a strategic role only for their division. In a transnational, various centers and subsidiaries can shape the company from the bottom up because there is no notion of a single headquarters, no clear top-down corporate level responsibility. Managers at all levels in any country have authority to develop creative responses and initiate programs in response to emerging local trends, then disperse their innovations worldwide. Transnational companies recognize that different parts of the organization possess different capabilities. In addition, environmental demands and opportunities vary from country to country, and exposing the whole organization to this broader range of environmental stimuli can trigger greater learning and innovation. By ensuring that the entire organization has access to the combined knowledge, abilities, and intellectual capacities of all divisions and all employees, transnationals engage in continuous worldwide learning.

3. *Unification and coordination are achieved through corporate culture, shared vision and values, and management style rather than through the vertical hierarchy.* The transnational is essentially a horizontal structure. It is diverse, extended, and exists in a fluctuating environment so that standard rules,

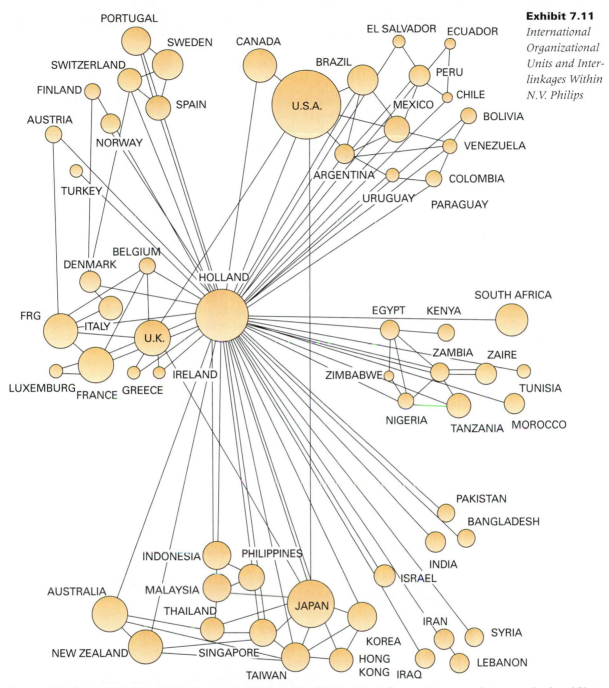

Exhibit 7.11
International Organizational Units and Inter-linkages Within N.V. Philips

Source: Sumantra Ghoshal and Christopher A. Bartlett, "The Multinational Corporation as an Interorganizational Network," *Academy of Management Review* 15 (1990): 605. Used by permission.

procedures, and close supervision are not appropriate. The very nature of the transnational organization dramatically expands the difficulty of unifying and coordinating operations. To achieve unity and coordination, organization leaders build a context of shared vision, values, and perspectives among managers, who in turn cascade these elements down through all parts of the organization. For example, people are often promoted by rotation through different jobs, divisions, and countries. Moreover, long experience with the company is highly valued because these people have been strongly socialized into the corporate culture. Experience plus rotation through different divisions and regions means that people share corporate culture and values sufficient for unity of purpose.

4. *Alliances are established with other company parts and with other companies.* Although resources and functions are widely dispersed, the transnational may integrate them through strong interdependencies. A world-scale production plant in Singapore may depend on world-scale component plants in Australia, Mexico, and Germany; major sales subsidiaries in turn depend on Singapore for finished products. In addition, each part of the organization can serve as an independent catalyst, bringing together unique elements with synergistic potential, perhaps other firms or subsidiaries from different countries, to improve its performance. These alliances may include joint ventures, cooperation with governments, and licensing arrangements.

The transnational model is truly a complex and "messy" way to conceptualize organization structure, but it is becoming increasingly relevant for large, global firms that treat the whole world as their playing field and do not have a single country base. The autonomy of organizational parts gives strength to smaller units and allows the firm to take advantage of rapid change and competitive opportunities. To achieve this end, a broad range of people throughout the global firm must develop capacity for strategic thinking and strategic action. Managers must follow their own instincts, using worldwide resources to achieve their local objectives. Strategy is the result of action in the sense that company parts seek to improve on their own rather than waiting for a strategy from the top. Indeed, each part of the company must be aware of the whole organization so its local actions will complement and enhance other company parts.

SUMMARY AND INTERPRETATION

The concepts about organization design in this chapter build upon the approaches to organizational structure and design described in Chapter 6. Significant global forces are causing American companies to find innovative designs and to extend operations overseas. The international forces include the dominant economies of Japan and Germany, newly industrialized countries, a shift toward market economies in Eastern Europe, and new power blocs. One response to these pressures is for domestic organizations to become more competitive. One significant innovation is the shift away from top-heavy, functionally organized structures toward horizontal structures. With a horizontal structure, the focus is on processes rather than function, the hierarchy is flattened, and self-directed teams are empowered to make the decisions necessary to satisfy the customer.

The shift to a horizontal structure often begins with *reengineering,* one of the hottest concepts in management today. Reengineering means looking at how work processes can be designed for optimal performance in today's rapidly changing environment. Reengineering brings about changes in organization structure, culture, and information systems, and can produce dramatic results.

Another innovation is the dynamic network structure, which uses a free market approach rather than a vertical hierarchy. Separate companies or individuals are coordinated through contracts with a small headquarters organization. New contractors can be added as needed to respond immediately to changes in the environment.

Many companies are developing overseas operations to take advantage of world markets. One way companies get involved internationally is through *international strategic alliances,* such as joint ventures or a consortia of independent organizations that share resources and access to one another's markets. *Global work teams,* made up of multinational members whose activities span multiple countries, are increasingly being used to help companies expand their operations into international markets.

Organizations typically evolve through four stages, beginning with a domestic orientation, shifting to an international orientation, then a multinational orientation, and finally to a global orientation that sees the whole world as a potential market. Organizations initially use an export department, then an international division, and finally develop into a worldwide geographic or product structure. Huge global companies may use a matrix or a transnational form of structure.

A global product structure is typically best when a company has many opportunities for globalization, which means products can be standardized and sold worldwide. A global geographic structure is typically used when a company's products and services have local country advantages, which means they do best when tailored to local needs and cultures. When an international company must succeed on two dimensions—global and local—simultaneously, the matrix structure is appropriate. When global companies must compete on multiple dimensions simultaneously, they may evolve toward a transnational model, which is a form of horizontal organization. The transnational differentiates into multiple centers; subsidiary managers initiate strategy and innovations for the company as a whole; and unity and coordination is achieved through corporate culture and shared values.

Key Concepts

consortia	horizontal corporation
domestic stage	international division
dynamic network	international stage
global company	joint venture
global geographic structure	multidomestic
global matrix structure	multidomestic strategy
global product structure	multinational stage
global stage	reengineering
global team	self-directed team
globalization strategy	transnational model

Discussion Questions

1. What do you see as the primary differences between horizontal corporations and traditional, functionally organized corporations?
2. What are the consequences to organizations of no single company or country being able to dominate global commerce?
3. How do self-directed teams differ from the cross-functional teams described in Chapter 6?

4. Would you like to work on a self-directed team where decisions are made by the team rather than by individuals and individual rewards are subordinated to team rewards? Discuss.
5. Because reengineering focuses on work processes that cut across functional boundaries, it leads to changes in organization structure. Why does this also cause significant changes in organizational culture and information systems?
6. How does the dynamic network structure enable an organization to respond rapidly in a changing, competitive environment?
7. Under what conditions should an organization consider a global product structure as opposed to a global geographic structure?
8. How does an international matrix structure differ from the domestic matrix structure described in Chapter 6?
9. Why do you think firms should join strategic alliances? Would they be better served to go it alone in international operations? Explain.
10. Describe the transnational model. Does this model seem workable in a huge global firm? Discuss.

Briefcase

As an organization manager, keep these guides in mind:

1. Analyze the global forces at work that influence your company, and respond by designing new domestic or international structures that enable international competitive advantage.
2. Move the organization through the four stages of international evolution, including domestic, international, multinational, and global. Maintain congruence between stage of development, strategic orientation, resource flow, structure, market potential, and facilities location.
3. Shift to a horizontal structure with self-directed teams or a dynamic network structure to maintain domestic competitiveness in the face of global competitive forces. Use self-directed teams to gain motivation and commitment of employees and a dynamic network structure to maintain a fluid responsiveness to the changing international environment.
4. Choose a global product structure when the organization can gain advantages with a globalization strategy. Choose a global geographic structure when the company has advantages with a multidomestic strategy. Choose an international division when the company is primarily domestic and has only a few international opportunities.
5. Develop international strategic alliances, such as licensing, joint ventures, and consortia, as fast and less expensive ways to become involved in international sales and operations.
6. Implement a matrix structure when the opportunities for globalization and multidomestic opportunities are about equal. Move to a transnational model when the organization is truly global and is responding to many global forces simultaneously.

Chapter Seven Workbook *Team Principles**

Think of a recent experience you had with a group project for a course or a team you were involved with at work. How did it operate? How effective was it? In order to answer these questions, fill out the following table:

Principles of an effective team are
- Sharing information
- Listening
- Active involvement of all
- Support and recognition
- Diversity of people and ideas
- Trust
- Reliability of members
- Fair distribution of work

Principle (from above list—those you consider important)	What it means to do this	How your team did (rate 1–10, with 1-low and 10-high)	Forces that worked against this principle	How could a team member help this principle to work?	What to do to ensure this principle when starting a new team
1.					
2.					
3.					
4.					
5.					

Questions

1. Consider you are on a horizontal team with each member from a different department. How might your answers in the last three columns change?

2. Consider you are on a global team with each member from a different country. How might your answers in the last three columns change?

3. *Optional:* In groups, share your experiences and discuss ways to develop more effective teams.

*Adapted by Dorothy Marcic from "Principles for Our Team by Which to Live," in Jennifer M. Howard and Lawrence M. Miller, *Team Management,* Miller Consulting Group, 1994, p. 38.

The Newsroom Reorganization Project

In January, 1991, the 33 managers and supervisors of the newsroom held an editorial management workshop to consider

- The priority of newsroom objectives, and
- Plans to overcome organizational barriers preventing their achievement.

The meeting represented phase two of the ongoing redesign project, phase one having been the cosmetic changes put in place earlier. The current phase was to deal with the production process by which editorial material was generated.

Overall goals for the workshop were

- To develop a list of issues facing the department and reach consensus on their relative importance;
- To identify organizational barriers to resolution of these issues; and,
- To determine how those barriers could be removed.

In terms of priorities, the workshop started with the premise that two sets of needs had to be met:

- The community's needs; a redesign content study had concluded that more diversity and relevance was required in the LFP news coverage and editorials.
- The company's needs; of importance to the editorial department, the latest strategic plan identified younger readers (ages 25 to 45) for special targeting in order to build a readership base for the future.

A final assumption directing the discussion at the workshop was that organizational barriers might be preventing the editorial staff from effectively meeting these needs. Issues tabled for discussion and resolution revolved around questions such as

- Does our management style inhibit cooperation?
- Are we too decentralized to be effective?
- Are we performing services unneeded (or unwanted) by today's readers?

The Home Base Cluster (HBC) Proposal

In his introductory memo to workshop participants, McLeod noted that the editorial department was, in 1991, still organized much as it had been in the 1920s when the daily newspaper was the only medium available for mass dissemination of information. Perhaps, he suggested, the time had come to change.

To establish a closer connection between the editorial staff and the community, and to avoid embarrassing oversights such as the failure to write about the WWF wrestling event, McLeod had determined that the traditional organization structure of the LFP should be changed. Based on research about teams at Spar Aerospace, Aetna Insurance, and Apple Computer, he proposed that workshop participants consider reorganizing the newsroom staff into small, self-contained work groups. Each group would "own" a story through the whole process up to its appearance in the paper: reporters, layout people, copy editors, and graphics staff would work together to create integrated, complete coverage of local news events. McLeod thought that by being intimately familiar with the entire process of producing a story, the work group might be less inclined than before to create material which was unreadable or uninteresting. He called the model "Home Based Clusters" (HBC).

Under the existing organization structure, reporters were assigned to a specific section and did all their work under the supervision and direction of that section's editor. But with the newsroom staff organized into work groups, section barriers would be broken down by allowing these clusters to "sell" their work to any section of the paper. If the paper were organized this way, a story that was newsworthy would become the responsibility of a group of people who had no formal ties to any part of the paper. They would feel a strong sense of ownership for the piece they were creating, without feeling as though it had to be portrayed from any particular "angle." Traditional classifications such as sports, business, entertainment, or local news would become almost irrelevant—a place would be found for any good, newsworthy story, even if it was difficult to classify by conventional newspaper standards. The overriding criterion for including a story in the paper would be whether it was interesting to the community, not its fit with the editorial policies of a narrowly defined section of the newspaper.

By being allowed to develop their own stories, as well as working on those assigned by senior editors, newsroom staff would become more sensitive to what kinds of issues the public wanted to see investigated and reported. They would no longer see themselves in the context of an abstract journalistic ideal, or worse, as slaves to an editorial prescription set down by the section editors they happened to be working for. They would, it was hoped, be working on stories that members of the community were interested in.

By May, 1991, the committees formed as a result of the workshop had decided that Home Based Clusters had the potential to be effective organizational building blocks for the LFP. The prototypical cluster would be self-contained, composed of a leader/coach, reporters, copy editors, designers, photographers, graphic artists, and support staff. But smaller clusters could also operate by sharing resources with others. In a clear break with tradition, clusters would perform both newsgathering and production functions. They would also not be formally associated with a particular section of the newspaper, thus erasing the old departmental boundaries.

Small-group work had the potential to enrich professional lives and relationships, and coordinating the efforts of a diverse group of people around a common end would result in better, more effective news coverage. Cluster members would tend to identify with their HBC, in terms of its goals, treatment of stories, and performance. While welcoming ideas from outside the group, they would be encouraged to generate their own story ideas, and to incorporate graphic and photo treatments into the concept right at the start, instead of as an afterthought. With copy editors, graphic designers, and photographers as equal members of the production team along with reporters, the final product would be more likely to represent the best possible treatment of a particular story.

Cluster members were expected to nurture relationships with established news sources, and to be more creative and proactive in finding fresh ones. An outreach mentality had to be fostered to develop better and more meaningful ties with the community; this, in turn, would enable the clusters to report stories with more relevance and meaning, leading to a higher level of interest on the part of readers. Being unbound from section or departmental constraints in terms of what is news would also help in the creation of new story angles, leading to new sources and fresh perspectives on issues of interest to readers.

This proposal seemed to fit the needs of an organization which was struggling to find a way to survive in the long term. A 1991 readership study conducted by the American Society of Newspaper Editors had identified two kinds of readers who "don't feel a strong commitment to the kinds of newspapers we are now producing." **At Risk Readers** were people who were currently buying newspapers, but were not very satisfied and thus were a shrinking group. **Potential Readers** were those which had all the demographic characteristics that, historically, had been associated with loyal readership, but who were not buying the paper. More than half of each group was in the 18 to 34 age category, and both together made up about 25 percent of the total reading audience in the United States.

The study went on to suggest that the way to attract these people was to listen to them and to respond to their wishes. At the LFP, the cluster model was thought to foster this kind of responsiveness, by focusing on the community and the news events occurring there, instead of on internal standards and norms about what constituted good journalism. Attention would shift from satisfying the requirements of section editors to reporting relevant events in ways that appealed to readers.

Pilot Cluster

In June, a second meeting of managers approved the cluster idea and agreed it should be tested. A Setup Group consisting of senior editorial staff was named to deal with the following issues:

1. Establish the parameters of the pilot—what it was expected to test, and what feedback and evaluation process would be applied to judge success or failure.
2. Deal with operational details such as
   - Cluster membership criteria;
   - News coverage guidelines, in accordance with a statement of shared values with respect to story treatment;
   - Job functions to be included in the cluster; and
   - Timeline for the test.

The pilot was run from October, 1991 to January, 1992, and was judged successful enough to push forward. Interesting stories were being written, and those individuals involved in the experiment were convinced it had possibilities. No major operational problems had surfaced that were thought to be insurmountable. The next step was to try it on a larger scale, which would result in the "clustering" of the city department, comprising about one-third of the newsroom staff and most of the reporters. A task force was struck to investigate how this might best be accomplished, in light of what had been learned from the pilot.

Some issues had emerged which needed to be addressed before the cluster concept could be applied to the rest of the newsroom. These included:

1. The need for a coordinator who would have an overview of the news topics covered, and who could mediate and adjudicate potential overlaps and conflicts. In the initial implementation phase, an overseer or observer would also be needed to help ensure an orderly transition from the old to the new system.

2. The need for cluster members to maintain contact with others in their functional areas. A process allowing professional alignments to be maintained outside individuals' clusters was necessary to ensure that the specialized skills represented in the groups could be nurtured and developed.

3. The section editors' relationships with the clusters had to be clarified. One internal document discussing this issue referred to section editors as "space barons," a reference to their ultimate authority in determining the content of their sections. At first glance, an unresolvable conflict existed between what clusters were being encouraged to produce and the residual authority of section editors to reject their work. However, the same document recognized that the real intent was to set up a "positive creative friction" between the two parties. A way of defining these roles had to be found.

4. A closely related issue was the role of the cluster leaders. Questions to be answered related to their autonomy in determining their news agenda, and to what extent this agenda should be influenced by section editors and others in positions of traditional authority. It was also not clear whether or to what extent cluster leaders should have an administrative role or formal authority.

Some critics interpreted McLeod's ideas as further evidence of a depersonalization of the relationship between management and the editorial staff. In Mr. Black-burn's day, these people felt, writers were treated with respect and dignity, did not have their jobs de-skilled to the point where they felt like technicians following a formula, and had pride in their collective output. Some also saw the benign paternalism which had characterized management in the past being abandoned in favour of a numbers-driven, results-oriented approach. The recent unionization of the LFP's newsroom was attributed by many to the anxieties, real or imagined, that resulted from the shift away from tradition.

The reorganization also appeared to conflict with the personal characteristics of reporters. Some of the qualities which newspapers prized highly when hiring reporters were the same ones which made them a challenging group to manage. Desirable attributes included skepticism, creativity, aggressiveness, individualism, idealism, and strong ego needs. But such traits as group-centeredness and team-playing had not been a priority in the past. Instead, reporters tended to be individualists who avoided becoming joiners or conformists. Any attempt by a management-minded editor to force a reporter into a new organizational structure had to be carefully orchestrated with full awareness of these potential problems.

Supporters of the change, on the other hand, viewed reorganization as an opportunity to experiment with the newspaper production process. They believed, first of all, that something had to change, because the status quo would lead to inexorable decline in readership, advertising revenue, and profit. Secondly, they were less convinced of the intrinsic rightness of the old way of doing things.

McLeod's Options

While McLeod thought that he was on the right track in challenging the traditional notions of journalistic process, he needed to deal with his employees' anxieties about the increased task ambiguity that the new work environment would produce, as well as their fears about job security and career development. His task was complicated by the fact that the LFP was, through 1991, still profitable, which might lead many of his colleagues and subordinates to wonder about the true motivation for change.

McLeod wondered whether the time had come to implement the cluster system across the whole newsroom. Some problems clearly still needed to be resolved, and resistance to the concept was still strongly felt in some circles. He could wait until his staff had become more accustomed to the idea, abandon it altogether in favour of a different alternative, or go ahead with wholesale change.

Case for Analysis *The London Free Press (B2)— Strategic Change**

The issues which surfaced as a result of the task force's discussions were still unresolved when the cluster model was being gradually put into place across the newsroom. However, it was felt by the group that the cluster model had many advantages over the old system, and that the unresolved issues and pockets of resistance would not go away with the passage of more time. They decided to go ahead with a full-scale implementation while actively searching for ways to overcome the obstacles.

The final reorganization plan was presented to all staff in October, 1992, through a series of individual and group meetings. Included was a "Statement of Intentions," a question-and-answer document intended to clarify the goals and the process, and a forecast outlining which of the jobs in the old system would become redundant under the reorganization.

During the last months of 1992, each section and each of the new clusters developed a set of goals and principles which would govern their operation. Finally, a schematic was produced to demonstrate graphically how the clusters would go together and who would work where.

Many thought that there was some truth to the notion that reporters had lost touch with the community, and that there was some room for decompartmentalizing the way stories were written. An example of a successful operation of the cluster system was the story of the London Tigers' baseball team. The Tigers were a minor-league affiliate of baseball's Detroit Tigers, and had come to London in 1986 amid great fanfare and with large financial concessions from the city. Some years later, they presented London's City Council with an ultimatum which demanded still more concessions. In the past, this news event might have been covered by a sports reporter who would have treated it as a story of interest mainly to baseball fans, and written it to fit the needs of the sports section. But the cluster given the assignment discovered the larger dimensions of this story which were of interest to all citizens of London. Treated in this way, the Tigers' departure was much more than just a sports story—it took on a political and community flavour which it would not have had under the old system.

A summation of the reorganization process made to date was contained in an internal memo authored by Mary Nesbitt, Associate Editor. She noted that the early cosmetic redesign of the LFP had been premature because it failed to recognize that the process of production was, perhaps, at the heart of the problem. Commenting on the cluster experiment, she wrote:

This series of redesigns are not skin-deep changes but radical—as in, from the root—shifts based on what we have learned, and must continue to learn, about ourselves and our readers. Education is life-long, and the real job for any organization is to learn how to learn.

[We thought that] if we could just produce better stuff, more relevant stuff, stuff people couldn't live without, we wouldn't have a problem. If we could just . . . but we just couldn't.

It wasn't for want of trying. We consulted ourselves, we consulted here, we consulted there, we consulted ourselves some more. (Our navels were the most thoroughly interviewed subjects in town.) But we rarely consulted our reader-customers.

The move to clusters, it was hoped, would bring about closer contact with the community while enabling news staff to exercise their creativity and professional skills without the constraints of a traditional newspaper organization. Nesbit provided an overview of how the system was expected to work, from a section editor's perspective:

Clusters are our radar in the community, attuned to a wide array of news and information, skilled in assessing its value, able to supply it. Section editors are the retailers, selecting news and information on the basis of marketplace needs and desires. It's their decision what gets into the newspaper and with what sort of prominence. Having so decided, they allot space to clusters.

*Detlev Nitsch prepared this case under the supervision of Professor Mary Crossan solely to provide material for class discussion. This case is not intended to illustrate either effective or ineffective handling of a managerial situation. Certain names and other identifying information may have been disguised to protect confidentiality. This material is not covered under authorization from CanCopy or any reproduction rights organization. Any form of reproduction, storage or transmittal of this material is prohibited without written permission from Western Business School. Copies or permission to reproduce may be obtained by contacting Case and Publication Services, Western Business School, The University of Western Ontario, London, Ontario, N6A 3K7 or by calling (519) 661-3208, or faxing (519) 661-3882. Copyright © 1995 The University of Western Ontario; 95/12/06.

In both theory and practice, it's in the interests of clusters (who have resources) and sections (who have the real estate, or space) to share information, learn how to negotiate, understand readers and work toward the same ends.

Such a focus on negotiation, sharing, overlapping roles, and teamwork promised to pose ongoing managerial challenges as the LFP tried to move profitably towards an uncertain future. There were still pockets of strong discontent among many editorial staff. They questioned, above all, the underlying motivation for the changes, feeling that profit goals were the true reason for the HBC implementation. Some admitted that the pilot cluster had seemed to work, but maintained that the conditions under which the experiment had been run were not replicated when the rest of the newsroom was "clustered." The pilot had been given all the material and human resources it needed, and made the theoretical case look quite favourable. In practice however, clusters were finding that they had to share key resources such as graphic artists and photographers, and that they were expected to do more with less. They concluded that management was simply using the HBC idea to cloak their true agenda, which they felt was reducing staff.

At the same time, real efforts to get closer to the community were being made in other areas. For example, the front page of each section now featured a box displaying a picture of its editor, and phone numbers where this person and other key people could be contacted. Readers were invited to call with their views on issues of the day, and to praise or criticise the paper. The opinion page was also more reader-centred, with an expanded "Letters" section and multiple gateways for the public to interact with the paper's staff. These initiatives were, for the most part, independent of the cluster organization, and were seen by some as having a greater and much more direct effect on reader loyalty than the reorganization.

McLeod's Decisions

McLeod faced more internal challenges in dealing with the problems that the changes had raised. Equally important, he had to assess whether these changes were having the desired effect externally, in terms of the ultimate objective of retaining and building readership for the paper. He had to reach a decision on whether to push ahead with a full-scale "clustering" of the entire newsroom, abandon the idea in favour of returning to a more traditional organization, or something in between.

Case for Analysis *Saint-Gobain-Pont-a-Mousson* *

Saint-Gobain-Pont-a-Mousson (SGPM) is a worldwide manufacturer of glass, paper, pipe, and related products. The corporate headquarters is in Paris. Over 50 percent of its Fr 50 billion in sales is from international business.

SGPM is organized into a three-tiered structure, as illustrated in Exhibit 7.12. The structure consists of five corporate functional vice presidents at headquarters, nine worldwide product group presidents, and seven "general delegates" or country managers.

Manufacturing operations exist in several countries and report to their respective product groups headquartered in France and to the country manager. Each product group has its own marketing staff and has more influence over country subsidiaries than do country managers, who are responsible for the finance, tax, and legal functions within their countries. The country manager is the political knowledge center for the country,

having an understanding of the environment, government regulations, pricing, labor negotiations, and the like. The worldwide product manager does the business planning, which reflects business and product goals rather than country-by-country requirements. Profit and loss responsibility is at the product manager level.

Most senior line and staff managers possess significant international experience—business, cultural, linguistic—although virtually all are French nationals, including the country managers. This broad scope arises from assignment rotation and from exposure to international situations.

*New Directions in Multinational Corporate Organization (New York: Business International Corporation, 1981), 44–45. Used by permission.

Exhibit 7.12

International Organization Structure for Saint-Gobain-Pont-a-Mousson

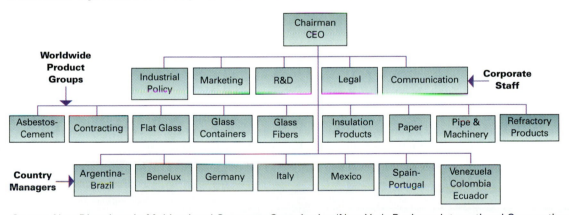

Source: New Directions in Multinational Corporate Organization (New York: Business International Corporation, 1981), 44–45. Used by permission.

Chapter Seven Workshop *The Poster Company**

You are a newly developed advertising agency specializing in poster development. The PR department of a local sports team has contacted you, along with some other companies, to develop a sample poster that will soon be placed in competition with the other companies' posters.

1. Form teams of ten to thirteen members (if a smaller class, you may go as low as eight).
2. Your team has been given various product "specs" that you must meet. The poster must have
   a. At least three colors
   b. Artwork/graphics/drawings
   c. A hard-hitting phrase or jingle to catch the audience's attention
3. Organize yourself. A consultant has recommended the following:
   a. Your company should have three subgroups specializing in
      i. Poster layout (size, colors, shape, and arrangement)
      ii. Artwork
      iii. Written materials (called copy)
   b. There should be some physical separation between the subgroups in order to reduce unnecessary interactions. Such distance will also help in reducing confusion about roles and responsibilities.
   c. A hierarchy of subgroup leaders (with a team leader) will handle coordination problems.

You will have fifteen to thirty minutes (depending on what your instructor tells you) to discuss your plan to organize in order to produce the poster. During this time, you should discuss the consultant's recommendations. At the end of the time, you must turn in a plan to the instructor on how you will organize yourselves. The plan should be either an organization chart or a specific statement.

4. The instructor will give you supplies, such as poster paper, scissors, markers, and so on.
5. You will have thirty to fifty minutes to produce the poster.
6. Halfway through the thirty to fifty minutes, you will be given ten minutes to decide whether you want to reorganize.
7. Posters are shown to the entire group.
8. Teams are given ten minutes to assess their design. Evaluate
   a. How the structure related to task uncertainty
   b. How uncertainty influenced coordination
   c. Whether there were trade-offs between specialization and coordination

Determine what would have been the "ideal" structure. What theories support that design?

9. General discussion on the exercise follows.

Total time: 75 to 100 minutes

*Adapted by Dorothy Marcic from J. Lawrence French's "Simulating Organizational Design Issues," *Journal of Management Education,* 17, no. 19 (February 1993): 110–13.

Notes

1. J. Ernie Riddle, "Reengineering Ryder to Meet Rising Customer Expectations," *National Productivity Review* (Winter 1995/96): 51–62.
2. William J. Holstein. "The Stateless Corporation," *Business Week*, 14 May 1990, 98–105.
3. Pete Engardio, with Robert D. Hof, Elisabeth Malkin, Neil Gross, and Karen Lowry Miller, "High-Tech Jobs All Over the Map," *Business Week/21st Century Capitalism,* 18 November 1994, 112–17.
4. *Ibid.*
5. Based on Tom Peters, "Prometheus Barely Unbound," *Academy of Management Executive* 4 (November 1990): 70–84.
6. John A. Byrne, "The Horizontal Corporation," *Business Week,* 20 December 1993, 76–81; Thomas A. Stewart, "The Search for the Organization of Tomorrow," *Fortune,* 18 May 1992, 92–98.
7. Jack D. Orsburn, Linda Moran, Ed Musselwhite, and John H. Zenger, *Self-Directed Work Teams: The New American Challenge* (Homewood, Ill.: Business One Irwin, 1990).

8. Charles C. Mainz, David E. Keating, and Anne Donnellon, "Preparing for an Organizational Change to Employee Self-Managed Teams: The Managerial Transition," *Organizational Dynamics* (Autumn 1990): 15–26.

9. Thomas Owens, "The Self-Managing Work Team," *Small Business Reports* (February 1991): 53–65; D. Brian Harrison and Henry P. Conn, "Mobilizing Abilities Through Teamwork," *Canadian Business Review* (Autumn 1994): 20–23.

10. Jonathan Kapstein, "Volvo's Radical New Plant: 'The Death of the Assembly Line'?" *Business Week,* 28 August 1989, 92–93.

11. Wendy Trueman, "Alternate Visions," *Canadian Business,* March 1991, 29–33.

12. Gregory G. Dess, Abdul M. A. Rasheed, Kevin J. McLaughlin, and Richard L. Priem, "The New Corporate Architecture," *Academy of Management Executive* 9, no. 3 (1995): 7–20.

13. Byrne, "The Horizontal Corporation."

14. Lorne Armstrong, "Evolution to a Team-Based Organization," *Canadian Business Review* (Autumn 1994): 14–17.

15. Gregory G. Dess, Abdul M. A. Rasheed, Kevin J. McLaughlin, and Richard L. Priem, "The New Corporate Architecture," *Academy of Management Executive* 9, no. 3 (1995): 7–20.

16. Susan G. Cohen, "New Approaches to Teams and Teamwork," in Jay R. Galbraith, Edward E. Lawler III & Associates, *Organizing for the Future: The New Logic for Managing Complex Organizations* (San Francisco, Calif.: Jossey-Bass, 1993), 194–226.

17. Byrne, "The Horizontal Corporation."

18. Donna B. Stoddard, Sirkka L. Jarvenpaa, and Michael Littlejohn, "The Reality of Business Reengineering: Pacific Bell's Centrex Provisioning Process," *California Management Review* 38, no. 3 (Spring 1996): 57–76.

19. Thomas A. Stewart, "Reengineering: The Hot New Managing Tool," *Fortune,* 23 August 1993, 41–48; Brian S. Moskal, "Reengineering Without Downsizing," *IW,* 19 February 1996, 23–28.

20. S. L. Mintz, "The Reengineers: A Guide for the Perplexed," *CFO,* October 1994, 42–54.

21. A. J. Vogl, "Plugging in Change," *Across the Board* (October 1995): 24–31.

22. George Stalk, Jr. and Jill E. Black, "The Myth of the Horizontal Organization," *Canadian Business Review* (Winter 1994): 26–31.

23. A. J. Vogl, "Plugging in Change"; T. Wood Parker, "Real-World Reengineering: Supporting Organizational Change at Premier Bank," *National Productivity Review* (Spring 1996): 67–80.

24. Bob Lindgren, "Going Horizontal," *Enterprise* (April 1994): 20–25.

25. Charles C. Snow, Raymond E. Miles, and Henry J. Coleman, Jr., "Managing 21st Century Network Organizations," *Organizational Dynamics* 20 (Winter 1992): 5–19; Shawn Tully, "The Modular Corporation," *Fortune,* 8 February 1993, 106–14.

26. Raymond E. Miles and Charles C. Snow, "Fit, Failure and the Hall of Fame," *California Management Review* 26 (Spring 1984): 10–28.

27. Richard L. Daft, *Management* 2d ed. (Chicago: Dryden Press, 1991).

28. Gianni Lorenzoni and Charles Baden-Fuller, "Creating a Strategic Center to Manage a Web of Partners," *California Management Review* 37 no. 3 (Spring 1995): 146–63; Shawn Tully, "You'll Never Guess Who Really Makes . . .," *Fortune,* 3 October 1994, 124–28; G. Pascal Zachary, "High-Tech Firms Find It's Good to Line Up Outside Contractors," *Wall Street Journal,* 29 July 1992, A1, A5.

29. Gregory G. Dess, Abdul M. A. Rasheed, Kevin J. McLaughlin, and Richard L. Priem, "The New Corporate Architecture," *Academy of Management Executive* 9, no. 3 (1995): 7–20.

30. Echo Montgomery Garrett, "Innovation + Outsourcing = Big Success," *Management Review* (September 1994): 17–20.

31. Raymond E. Miles and Charles C. Snow, "The New Network Firm: A Spherical Structure Built on a Human Investment Philosophy," *Organizational Dynamics* (Spring 1995): 5–18; and Gregory G. Dess, Abdul M. A. Rasheed, Kevin J. McLaughlin, and Richard L. Priem, "The New Corporate Architecture."

32. Donna Brown, "Outsourcing: How Corporations Take Their Business Elsewhere," *Management Review* (February 1992): 16–19.

33. Snow, Miles, and Coleman, "Managing 21st Century Network Organizations."

34. Based heavily on Nancy J. Adler, *International Dimensions of Organizational Behavior,* 2d ed. (Boston: PWS-Kent, 1991); Theodore T. Herbert, "Strategy and Multinational Organizational Structure: An Interorganizational Relationships Perspective," *Academy of Management Review* 9 (1984): 259–71; Laura K. Rickey, "International

Expansion—U.S. Corporations: Strategy, Stages of Development and Structure," (Unpublished manuscript, Vanderbilt University, 1991.)

35. Michael E. Porter, "Changing Patterns of International Competition," *California Management Review* 28 (Winter 1986): 9–40.

36. Holstein, "The Stateless Corporation."

37. David Lei and John W. Slocum, Jr., "Global Strategic Alliances: Payoffs and Pitfalls," *Organizational Dynamics* (Winter 1991): 17–29.

38. *Ibid.*

39. Stratford Sherman, "Are Strategic Alliances Working?" *Fortune,* 21 September 1992, 77–78; David Lei, "Strategies for Global Competition," *Long-Range Planning* 22 (1989): 102–09.

40. Lei, "Strategies For Global Competition."

41. Kathryn Rudie Harrigan, "Managing Joint Ventures: Part I," *Management Review* (February 1987): 24–41.

42. Kevin Kelly and Otis Port, with James Treece, Gail DeGeorge, and Zachary Schiller, "Learning from Japan," *Business Week,* 27 January 1992, 52–60; Dess, Rasheed, McLaughlin, and Priem, "The New Corporate Architecture."

43. Mary O'Hara-Devereaux and Robert Johansen, *Globalwork: Bridging Distance, Culture & Time* (San Francisco: Jossey-Bass, 1994).

44. Charles C. Snow, Scott A. Snell, Sue Canney Davison, and Donald C. Hambrick, "Use Transnational Teams to Globalize Your Company," *Organizational Dynamics* 24, no. 4 (Spring 1996): 50–67.

45. *Ibid.*

46. Mary O'Hara-Devereaux and Robert Johansen, *Globalwork: Bridging Distance, Culture & Time,* pp. 227–28.

47. Kenichi Ohmae, "Managing in a Borderless World," *Harvard Business Review* (May-June 1989): 152–61.

48. Sumantra Ghoshal and Nitin Nohria, "Horses for Courses: Organizational Forms for Multinational Corporations," *Sloan Management Review* (Winter 1993): 23–35; Roderick E. White and Thomas A. Poynter, "Organizing for Worldwide Advantage," *Business Quarterly* (Summer 1989): 84–89.

49. John D. Daniels, Robert A. Pitts, and Marietta J. Tretter, "Strategy and Structure of U.S. Multinationals: An Exploratory Study," *Academy of Management Journal* 27 (1984): 292–307.

50. *New Directions in Multinational Corporate Organization* (New York: Business International Corporation, 1981).

51. *Ibid.*

52. William Taylor, "The Logic of Global Business: An Interview with ABB's Percy Barnevik," *Harvard Business Review* (March-April 1991): 91–105; Carla Rappaport, "A Tough Swede Invades the U.S.," *Fortune,* 29 January 1992, 76–79; Raymond E. Miles and Charles C. Snow, "The New Network Firm: A Spherical Structure Built on a Human Investment Philosophy," *Organizational Dynamics* (Spring 1995): 5–18; Manfred F. R. Kets de Vries, "Making a Giant Dance," *Across the Board* (October 1994): 27–32.

53. Sumantra Ghoshal and Christopher A. Bartlett, "The Multinational Corporation as an Interorganizational Network," *Academy of Management Review* 15 (1990): 603–25.

54. Gunnar Hedlund and Dag Rolander, "Action in Heterarchies: New Approaches to Managing the MNC," in Christopher A. Bartlett, Yves Doz, and Gunnar Hedlund, eds., *Managing the Global Firm* (New York: Routledge, 1990), 15–46; Gunnar Hedlund, "The Hypermodern MNC—A Heterarchy?" *Human Resource Management* 25 (Spring 1986): 9–35; Christopher A. Bartlett and Sumantra Ghoshal, *Managing Across Borders: The Transnational Solution* (Boston, Mass.: Harvard Business School Press, 1989).

Organization Design Process

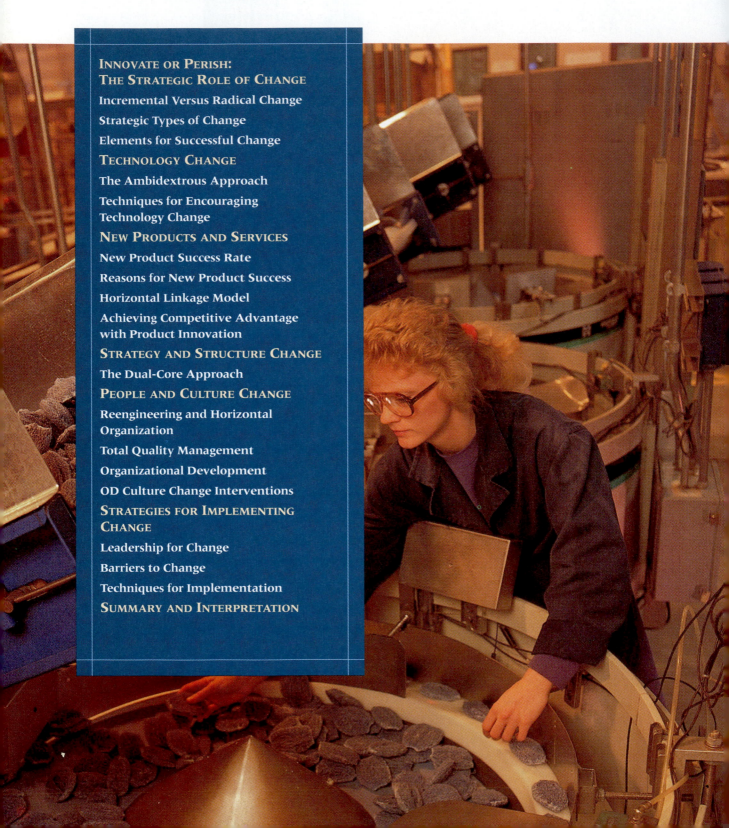

chapter eight

Innovation and Change

A look inside

3M

When asked about 3M's strategy, CEO L. D. "Desi" DiSimone says, "We're going to do two principal things: be very innovative, and satisfy our customers in all aspects." 3M, a company whose name is synonymous with innovation, has three approaches to new product development: "skunkworks" projects, which are spearheaded by employees and are not overseen by management; traditional development, in which business managers and researchers work together to create new products or improve existing ones; and pacing programs, which consist of a small number of products and technologies the company thinks will produce substantial profits fast and are thus given extra attention and resources. The process works. 3M has achieved its goal of getting 30 percent of sales from products less than four years old so consistently that it is considering raising the bar.

3M also maintains a close connection with customers—company lore tells salespeople to head for the smokestacks, where the end users of products are, rather than the offices where the purchasing department sits. "Major-customer teams" that include representatives from various functions, from R&D to sales, not only look for ways to push existing products but also try to understand customers' unarticulated needs so 3M can develop products to meet them. For example, a new fabric that allows water vapor to pass through but blocks liquids is being used for surgical gowns that protect doctors from patients' blood but don't leave them soaked in their own sweat.

One reason 3M is bubbling over with new ideas and new products is that the culture supports innovation and risk-taking. Any employee with a new product or technology idea can always find someone to give advice and moral support. Ideas and knowledge are shared throughout the organization—a new technology that isn't useful in one division may lead to a series of new products in another. All new employees attend a class on risk-taking where they're actually encouraged to defy their supervisors. They hear stories of success won despite opposition from the boss—such as how DiSimone himself five times tried to kill the project that became the highly successful Thinsulate. They also hear stories of "failures" that became hot new products—such as the not-very-sticky glue that led to development of the popular Post-it Notes. 3M has remained a highly successful company for ninety-three years by supporting a risk-taking, entrepreneurial spirit and by following where its researchers and customers lead.[1]

At 3M, innovation is a primary goal preached by top management and supported throughout the organization. Managers also recognize the importance of staying in touch with customers. Strong cross-functional coordination and communication helps identify customer needs, turn new ideas into new products, and get them to the marketplace fast.

Innovation is not limited to 3M. Today, every organization must change to survive. New discoveries and inventions quickly replace standard ways of doing things. The pace of change is revealed in the fact that the parents of today's college-age students grew up without cable television, VCRs, crease-resistant clothing, personal computers, compact disc players, video games, and talking checkout machines in supermarkets.

Purpose of This Chapter

This chapter will explore how organizations change and how managers direct the innovation and change process. The next section describes the difference between incremental and radical change, the four types of change—technology, product, structure, people—occurring in organizations, and how to manage change successfully. The organization structure and management approach for facilitating each type of change is then discussed. Management techniques for influencing both the creation and implementation of change are also covered.

INNOVATE OR PERISH: THE STRATEGIC ROLE OF CHANGE

If there is one theme or lesson that emerges from previous chapters, it is that organizations must run fast to keep up with changes taking place all around them. Organizations must modify themselves not just from time to time, but all of the time. Large organizations must find ways to act like small, flexible organizations. Manufacturing firms need to reach out for new computer-integrated manufacturing technology and service firms for new information technology. Today's organizations must poise themselves to innovate and change, not only to prosper but merely to survive in a world of increased competition.[2] As illustrated in Exhibit 8.1, there are a number of environmental forces driving this need for major organizational change. Powerful forces associated with advancing technology, international economic integration, the maturing of domestic markets, and the shift to capitalism in formerly communist regions have brought about a globalized economy that impacts every business, from the largest to the smallest, creating more threats as well as more opportunities. To recognize and manage the threats and take advantage of the opportunities, today's companies are undergoing dramatic changes in all areas of their operations.

As we saw in Chapter 7, many organizations are responding to global forces by reengineering business processes and shifting to a horizontal organization structure with self-directed teams. Some are adopting structural innovations such as the network, to focus on their core competencies while outside specialists handle other activities. Others become involved in joint ventures, consortia, or "virtual organizations" to extend operations and markets internationally. In addition to these structural changes, today's organizations face the need for dramatic strategic and cultural change, and for rapid innovations in technology and products.

In the past, stability was the norm and change occurred incrementally and infrequently. Today, organizational change is often dramatic and constant. For example, a key element in the success of PepsiCo in recent years has been its passion for change. Former CEO Wayne Calloway insisted that the worst rule of management is "if it ain't broke, don't fix it." Calloway preached that in today's economy, "if it ain't broke, you might as well break it yourself, because it soon will be."[3]

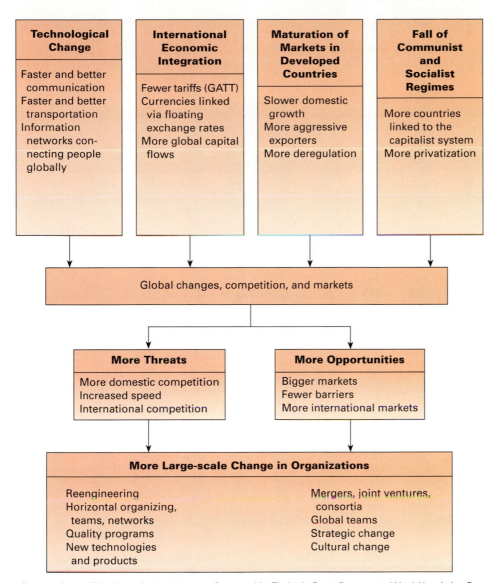

Source: From *The New Rules: How to Succeed in Today's Post-Corporate World* by John P. Kotter. Copyright © 1995 by John P. Kotter. Adapted with permission of The Free Press, a Division of Simon & Schuster.

Incremental Versus Radical Change

The changes used to adapt to the environment can be evaluated according to scope—that is, the extent to which changes are incremental or radical for the organization.[4] As summarized in Exhibit 8.2, **incremental change** represents a series of continual progressions that maintain the organization's general equilibrium and often affect only one organizational part. **Radical change**, by contrast, breaks the frame of reference for the organization, often creating new equilibrium because the entire organization is transformed. For example, an incremental change is the implementation of sales teams in the marketing department, whereas a radical change is reengineering the organization to develop new

Exhibit 8.2

Incremental Versus
Radical Change

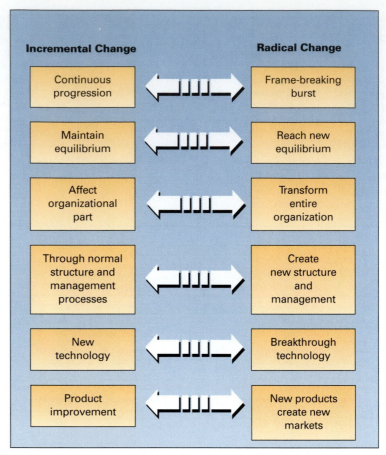

Source: Based on Alan D. Meyer, James B. Goes, and Geoffrey R. Brooks, "Organizations in Disequilibrium: Environmental Jolts and Industry Revolutions," in George Huber and William H. Glick, eds., *Organizational Change and Redesign* (New York: Oxford University Press, 1992), 66–111; and Harry S. Dent, Jr., "Growth through New Product Development," *Small Business Reports* (November 1990): 30–40.

products in only one year instead of four and maintaining one year as the new equilibrium.

For the most part, incremental change occurs through the established structure and management processes, and it may include new technologies—such as computer-integrated manufacturing technologies—and product improvements. Radical change involves the creation of a new structure and management processes. The technology is likely to be breakthrough, and new products thereby created will establish new markets.

As we have just discussed, there is a growing emphasis on the need for radical change because of today's turbulent, unpredictable environment.[5] Indeed, some experts argue that firms must be constantly changing their structures and management processes in response to changing demands. The health-care industry, for example, is facing tremendous upheaval, and companies likely will have to implement radical change to survive. One example of radical change was the revolution at Motorola that achieved an astounding six sigma quality (only 3.4 mistakes per million parts produced). This level of quality, previously considered impossible, became the new norm. Motorola is now aiming for the same level of quality in its administrative functions, such as financial recordkeeping and reporting.[6]

Corporate transformations and turnarounds are also considered radical change. A good example of a radical corporate transformation is Globe Metallurgical, Inc., which was a typical Rust Belt company in the early 1980s: old-fashioned, bureaucratic, slow-moving, and unresponsive to customers. Costs were high and quality was low. When Arden Sims took over as chief executive in 1984, the company was in a death spiral, sure to be run out of business by foreign competition. Over a period of eight years, Sims transformed Globe into today's top source for specialty metals for the chemical and foundry industries worldwide. The transformation involved fundamental changes in management systems, work structures, products, technology, and worker attitudes. Globe became the first small company to win a Malcolm Baldrige National Quality Award.[7]

Strategic Types of Change

Managers can focus on four types of change within organizations to achieve strategic advantage. These four types of changes are summarized in Exhibit 8.3 as products and services, strategy and structure, people and culture, and technology. We touched on overall leadership and organizational strategy in Chapter 2, and we will touch these topics again along with corporate culture in Chapter 10. These factors provide an overall context within which the four types of change serve as a competitive wedge to achieve an advantage in the international environment. Each company has a unique configuration of products and services, strategy and structure, people and culture, and technologies that can be focused for maximum impact upon the company's chosen markets.[8]

Technology changes are changes in an organization's production process, including its knowledge and skill base, that enable distinctive competence. These changes are designed to make production more efficient or to produce greater volume. Changes in technology involve the techniques for making products or services. They include work methods, equipment, and work flow. For example, in

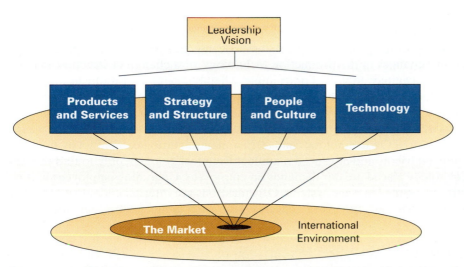

Exhibit 8.3
The Four Types of Change Provide a Strategic Competitive Wedge

Source: Joseph E. McCann, "Design Principles for an Innovating Company," *Academy of Management Executive* 5 (May 1991): 76–93. Used by permission.

a university, technology changes are changes in techniques for teaching courses. As another example, Globe Metallurgical changed its production process using breakthrough furnace technology.

Product and service changes pertain to the product or service outputs of an organization. New products include small adaptations of existing products or entirely new product lines. New products are normally designed to increase the market share or to develop new markets, customers, or clients. Globe Metallurgical shifted its product line to high-margin specialty metals, which helped take the company global and into highly profitable niche markets. The Saturn automobile developed by General Motors is a product change.

Strategy and structure changes pertain to the administrative domain in an organization. The administrative domain involves the supervision and management of the organization. These changes include changes in organization structure, strategic management, policies, reward systems, labor relations, coordination devices, management information and control systems, and accounting and budgeting systems. Structure and system changes are usually top-down, that is, mandated by top management, whereas product and technology changes may often come from the bottom up. The structure at Globe Metallurgical was changed after managers discovered the power of flexible work teams when they were forced to run the furnaces during a year-long strike. When workers came back on the job, management instituted a new team structure. A system change instituted by management in a university might be a new merit pay plan. Corporate downsizing is another example of top-down structure change.

People and culture changes refer to changes in the values, attitudes, expectations, beliefs, abilities, and behavior of employees. An organization may wish to hire only the best people or to upgrade the leadership ability of key managers. Changes in communication networks and improved problem-solving and planning skills of employees are people changes. In transformations and turnarounds, the entire culture of the organization is changed. In the old days at Globe Metallurgical, employees were suspicious of management, who dictated new policies without consulting workers. One of the results of Globe's transformation is a new culture that values employee empowerment and involvement, a new respect for management, and a new commitment to quality.

Change Interdependence.   The four types of changes in Exhibit 8.3 are interdependent—a change in one often means a change in another. A new product may require changes in the production technology, or a change in structure may require new employee skills. For example, when Shenandoah Life Insurance Company acquired new computer technology to process claims, the technology was not fully utilized until clerks were restructured into teams of five to seven members that were compatible with the technology. The structural change was an outgrowth of the technology change. In a manufacturing company, engineers introduced robots and advanced manufacturing technologies, only to find that the technology placed greater demands on employees. Upgrading employee skills required a change in wage systems. Organizations are interdependent systems, and changing one part often has implications for other organization elements.

Elements for Successful Change

Regardless of the type or scope of change, there are identifiable stages of innovation, which generally occur as a sequence of events, though innovation stages may overlap.[9] In the research literature on innovation, **organizational change** is considered the adoption of a new idea or behavior by an organization.[10] **Organizational innovation**, in contrast, is the adoption of an idea or behavior that is new to the organization's industry, market, or general environment.[11] The first organization to introduce a new product is considered the innovator, and organizations that copy are considered to adopt changes. For purposes of managing change, however, the terms *innovation* and *change* will be used interchangeably because the **change process** within organizations tends to be identical whether a change is early or late with respect to other organizations in the environment.

Innovations typically are assimilated into an organization through a series of steps or elements. Organization members first become aware of a possible innovation, evaluate its appropriateness, and then evaluate and choose the idea.[12] The required elements of successful change are summarized in Exhibit 8.4. For a change to be successfully implemented, managers must make sure each element occurs in the organization. If one of the elements is missing, the change process will fail.

1. *Ideas.* Although creativity is a dramatic element of organizational change, creativity within organizations has not been widely and systematically studied. No company can remain competitive without new ideas; change is the outward expression of those ideas.[13] An idea is a new way of doing things. It may be a new product or service, a new management concept, or a new procedure for working together in the organization. Ideas can come from within or from outside the organization.

Exhibit 8.4

Sequence of Elements for Successful Change

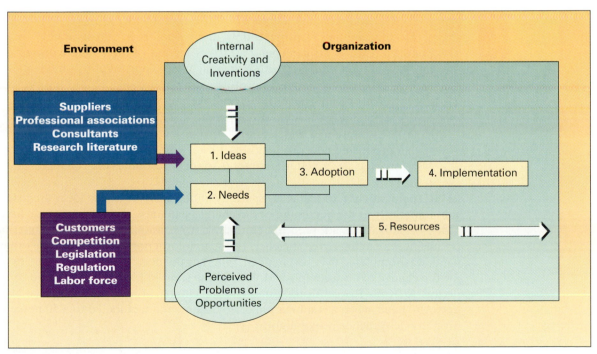

2. *Need.* Ideas are generally not seriously considered unless there is a perceived need for change. A perceived need for change occurs when managers see a gap between actual performance and desired performance in the organization. For example, IBM executives perceived a strong need for structural change after the company posted operating losses for two consecutive years. Sometimes, ideas are generated to meet a perceived need; other times, a new idea occurs first and will stimulate consideration of problems it will solve or opportunities it provides. For example, at 3M, discussed in the chapter opening, employees are encouraged to constantly come up with new ideas, even when there is no perceived need or purpose. The ideas then encourage consideration of new products.

3. *Adoption.* Adoption occurs when decision makers choose to go ahead with a proposed idea. Key managers and employees need to be in agreement to support the change. For a major organizational change, the decision might require the signing of a legal document by the board of directors. For a small change, adoption might occur with informal approval by a middle manager. When Ray Kroc was CEO of McDonald's, he made the adoption decision about innovations such as the Big Mac and Egg McMuffin.

4. *Implementation.* Implementation occurs when organization members actually use a new idea, technique, or behavior. Materials and equipment may have to be acquired, and workers may have to be trained to use the new idea. Implementation is a very important step because without it, previous steps are to no avail. Implementation of change is often the most difficult part of the change process. Until people use the new idea, no change has actually taken place.

5. *Resources.* Human energy and activity are required to bring about change. Change does not happen on its own; it requires time and resources, for both creating and implementing a new idea. Employees have to provide energy to see both the need and the idea to meet that need. Someone must develop a proposal and provide the time and effort to implement it.

   3M has an unwritten but widely understood rule that its eighty-three hundred researchers can spend up to 15 percent of their time working on any idea of their choosing, without management approval. Most innovations go beyond ordinary budget allocations and require special funding. At 3M, exceptionally promising ideas become "pacing programs" and receive high levels of funding for further development.

   At S. C. Johnson & Son, a $250,000 seed fund has been set up for anyone with a promising new product idea. Other companies use committees and task forces, as described in Chapter 6, to focus resources on a change.

One point about Exhibit 8.4 is especially important. Needs and ideas are listed simultaneously at the beginning of the change sequence. Either may occur first. Many organizations adopted the computer, for example, because it seemed a promising way to improve efficiency. The search for a polio vaccine, on the other hand, was stimulated by a severe need. Whether the need or the idea occurs first, for the change to be accomplished, each of the steps in Exhibit 8.4 must be completed. At Rolls-Royce Motor Company, the change process was triggered by a powerful need, when a combination of environmental factors led to a 50 percent drop in sales practically overnight.

Rolls-Royce Motor Company

1990 was the most successful year in the history of Rolls-Royce, but within a year sales dropped by half and the company was forced to reduce its workforce by 50 percent. The combination of the Gulf War, a new luxury tax in the United States, and the scale of the recession in the United Kingdom and the United States, followed by Japan and Europe, meant Rolls-Royce had to change to survive. Managers needed to increase flexibility to speed production and lower costs.

One idea was a new approach to labor practices for both shop-floor workers and managers. The company had hundreds of precise job descriptions and different trade union spheres of influence. For example, because a car battery has an electrical connection, only an electrician was allowed to connect or install one. The new contract developed by labor and management specifies that all employees will do anything within their capabilities and will undertake any training necessary, regardless of their trade or union membership. With the survival of the company at stake, both management and trade union officials agreed to adopt the new contract within only twelve weeks of negotiations. Implementation occurred as Rolls-Royce cut three levels of management and set up ten-member cross-functional teams led by a team leader, who is a shop-floor worker rather than a manager. Each manager is responsible for ten teams, meaning he or she has to effectively manage through the team leaders rather than like an old-style foreman. Resources were invested in training to help workers and managers work effectively in the new cross-functional team environment.

The next revolution was the implementation of the "change team" concept, designed to get managers and shop workers from all functions continuously communicating and developing new ideas, enabling Rolls-Royce to continue to change. Over the past three years, the company has had more than twenty-five hundred continuous improvement initiatives, many based on the ideas of shop workers. As a result of the initiatives, the time it takes to make a car has been cut from seventy to less than thirty days, without any appreciable capital investment. Cross-functional teams have also cut new product development time in half, as well as halved project costs and reduced errors and rework. On-time delivery to dealers is up from 50 percent to almost 100 percent.

This successful change process enabled Rolls-Royce to weather the turbulence of the early 1990s and once again become a successful manufacturer that exemplifies top-quality British craftsmanship and engineering.[14]

Rolls-Royce changed because it had to in order to survive. Beyond survival, the most important outcome may be that the change team philosophy supports continuous change in response to new threats or opportunities. The cross-functional communication and the empowerment of shop-floor workers creates a steady flow of new ideas. As Rolls-Royce's managing director of operations put it, successful change is "about energy and determination and getting lots of people committed and trying lots of things."[15]

TECHNOLOGY CHANGE

In today's rapidly changing world, any company that isn't constantly developing, acquiring, or adapting new technology will likely be out of business in a few years. However, organizations face a contradiction when it comes to technology change, for the conditions that promote new ideas are not generally the best for implementing those ideas for routine production. An innovative organization is characterized by flexibility, empowered employees, and the absence of rigid work rules.[16] As discussed earlier in this book, an organic, free-flowing organization is typically associated with change and is considered the best organization form for adapting to a chaotic environment.

The flexibility of an organic organization is attributed to people's freedom to create and introduce new ideas. Organic organizations encourage a bottom-up innovation process. Ideas bubble up from middle- and lower-level employees because they have the freedom to propose ideas and to experiment. A mechanistic structure, on the other hand, stifles innovation with its emphasis on rules and regulations, but it is often the best structure for efficiently producing routine products. The challenge for organizations is to create both organic and mechanistic conditions within organizations to achieve both innovation and efficiency. To achieve both aspects of technological change, many organizations use the ambidextrous approach.

The Ambidextrous Approach

Recent thinking has refined the idea of organic versus mechanistic structures with respect to innovation creation versus innovation utilization. For example, sometimes an organic structure generates innovative ideas but is not the best structure for using those ideas.[17] In other words, the initiation and the utilization of change are two distinct processes. Organic characteristics such as decentralization and employee freedom are excellent for initiating ideas; but these same conditions often make it hard to use a change because employees are less likely to comply. Employees can ignore the innovation because of decentralization and a generally loose structure.

How does an organization solve this dilemma? One approach is for the organization to be **ambidextrous**—to incorporate structures and management processes that are appropriate to both the creation and use of innovation.[18] The organization can behave in an organic way when the situation calls for the initiation of new ideas and in a mechanistic way to implement and use the ideas.

An example of the ambidextrous approach is the Freudenberg-NOK auto-parts factory in Ligonier, Indiana. Shifting teams of twelve, including plant workers, managers, and outsiders, each spend three days creating ideas to cut costs and boost productivity in various sections of the plant. At the end of the three days, team members go back to their regular jobs, and a new team comes in to look for even more improvements. Over a year's time, there are approximately forty of these GROWTTH (Get Rid of Waste Through Team Harmony) teams roaming through the sprawling factory. Management has promised that no one will be laid off as a result of suggestions from GROWTTH teams, which further encourages employees to both create and use innovations.[19]

Techniques for Encouraging Technology Change

Freudenberg-NOK has created both organic and mechanistic conditions in the factory. Some of the techniques used by many companies to maintain an ambidextrous approach are switching structures, separate creative departments, venture teams, and corporate entrepreneurship.

Switching Structures. **Switching structures** means an organization creates an organic structure when such a structure is needed for the initiation of new ideas.[20] Some of the ways organizations have switched structures to achieve the ambidextrous approach are as follows.

- Philips Corporation, a building materials producer in Ohio, each year creates groups of five employees from various departments—up to 150 teams—to work together for five days to improve Philips products. After the five days of organic brainstorming and problem solving, the company switches back to running things on a more mechanistic basis as the improvements are implemented into the system.[21]

- Lockheed's famous Skunk Works, a secret research and development subsidiary, was purposely isolated from the corporation's sprawling bureaucracy. Staffed with creative mavericks not afraid to break conventions, Skunk Works has been responsible for some of Lockheed's greatest innovations. Chief Executive Daniel M. Tellup counts on the innovators at Skunk Works to help Lockheed maintain its technological edge as the defense industry shrinks and becomes more competitive.[22]

- Apple Computer designates highly paid Apple Fellows who are free to brainstorm for new ideas as they please. One fellow is studying how children learn to create artificial intelligence, and another is looking for ways to combine video devices and computers.[23] As these ideas take shape, they are gradually taken over for implementation by Apple's traditional structure.

- The NUMMI plant, a Toyota subsidiary located in Fremont, California, creates a separate, organically organized cross-functional subunit, called the Pilot Team, to design production processes for new car and truck models. When the model they are preparing moves into production, workers return to their regular jobs on the shop floor.[24]

Each of these organizations found creative ways to be ambidextrous, establishing organic conditions for developing new ideas in the midst of more mechanistic conditions for implementing and using those ideas.

Creative Departments. In many large organizations the initiation of innovation is assigned to separate **creative departments**.[25] Staff departments, such as research and development, engineering, design, and systems analysis, create changes for adoption in other departments. Departments that initiate change are organically structured to facilitate the generation of new ideas and techniques. Departments that use those innovations tend to have a mechanistic structure more suitable for efficient production. Exhibit 8.5 indicates how one department is responsible for creation and another department implements the innovation.

Raytheon's New Products Center, in operation for twenty-five years, illustrates how creativity and entrepreneurial spirit can coexist with discipline and controls. The center has been responsible for many technical innovations, including industry-leading combination ovens, which added microwave capabilities to conventional stoves. The New Products Center provides autonomy and freedom for staff to explore new ideas, yet staff must also establish a working relationship with other departments so that innovations meet a genuine need for Raytheon departments.[26]

Exhibit 8.5

Division of Labor Between Departments to Achieve Changes in Technology

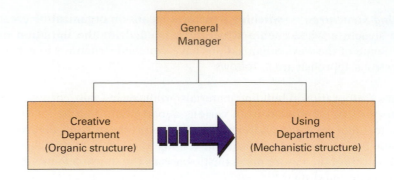

Venture Teams.   **Venture teams** are a recent technique used to give free reign to creativity within organizations. Venture teams are often given a separate location and facilities so they are not constrained by organizational procedures. Dow Chemical created an innovation department that has virtually total license to establish new venture projects for any department in the company. Convergent Technologies uses the name "strike force" for a separate team that will develop a new computer. The team is cut loose to set up its own company and pursue members' ideas. The venture groups are kept small so they have autonomy and no bureaucracy emerges.

A new venture team is a small company within a large company. To giant companies like Eastman Kodak and AT&T, new venture teams are essential to free creative people from the bureaucracy. Eastman Kodak has launched fourteen new ventures since 1984. Each is like a company-within-a-company that explores such ideas as computerized photo imaging, lithium batteries, or technology to project computer images on a large screen. AT&T has created eleven venture companies, one of which developed Pixel Machines, which offer striking capability to produce sharp pictures on a computer terminal. These venture companies are carefully nurtured and are given freedom from the AT&T bureaucracy.[27]

Corporate Entrepreneurship.   Corporate entrepreneurship attempts to develop an internal entrepreneurial spirit, philosophy, and structure that will produce a higher than average number of innovations.[28] Corporate entrepreneurship may involve the use of creative departments and new venture teams as described above, but it also attempts to release the creative energy of all employees in the organization. The most important outcome is to facilitate **idea champions** which go by a variety of names, including advocate, intrapreneur, or change agent. Idea champions provide the time and energy to make things happen. They fight to overcome natural resistance to change and to convince others of the merit of a new idea.[29] For example, when Texas Instruments reviewed fifty successful and unsuccessful technical projects, one fascinating finding emerged. Every failure was characterized by the absence of a volunteer champion. There was no one who passionately believed in the idea, who pushed the idea through all the necessary obstacles to make it work. Texas Instruments took this finding so seriously that now its number one criterion for approving new technical projects is the presence of a zealous champion.[30]

Companies encourage idea champions by providing freedom and slack time to creative people. IBM and General Electric allow employees to develop new technologies without company approval. Known as "bootlegging," the unauthorized research often pays big dividends. As one IBM executive said, "We wink at it. It pays off. It's just amazing what a handful of dedicated people can do when they are really turned on."[31]

Idea champions usually come in two types. The **technical or product champion** is the person who generates or adopts and develops an idea for a technological innovation and is devoted to it, even to the extent of risking position or prestige. The **management champion** acts as a supporter and sponsor to shield and promote an idea within the organization.[32] The management champion sees the potential application and has the prestige and authority to get it a fair hearing and to allocate resources to it. Technical and management champions often work together because a technical idea will have a greater chance of success if a manager can be found to sponsor it. At Black & Decker, Peter Chaconas is a technical champion. He invented the Piranha circular saw blade, which is a best-selling tool accessory. Next, he invented the Bullet, which is a bit for home power drills and is the first major innovation in this product in almost one hundred years. Chaconas works full-time designing products and promoting their acceptance. Randy Blevins, his boss, acts as management champion for Chaconas's ideas.[33]

The following example illustrates the integral roles of technical and management champions and the obstacles they often face, even in companies that are supportive of innovation.

Hewlett-Packard

In Practice 8.2

As a young engineer at Hewlett-Packard, Chuck House helped develop oscilloscope technology for use in an improved airport control tower monitor for the Federal Aviation Administration. Although the HP monitor ultimately lost out to competitors, House saw some features of the prototype that deserved further investigation. For example, the Hewlett-Packard monitor was smaller and lighter in weight than its competitors; it was twenty times as fast; and it provided a brighter, energy-efficient picture. In his efforts to demonstrate the value of the prototype, House broke a number of organization rules and boundaries. In conducting his own market research on potential applications, he violated functional boundaries by bypassing HP's marketing department, and he breached company security, which forbade the showing of prototypes to customers. House's enthusiasm was not shared by company founder David Packard, who said: "When I come back next year, I don't want to see that project in the lab!"

With the clandestine support of his boss, Das Howard, House managed to get the time and resources to complete the project within a year, and when Packard returned for the next annual review, the monitor was in the marketplace. Packard, rather than firing House and Howard for insubordination, revealed his own maverick tendencies by supporting the project and giving the team permission to develop further applications. Eventually, the Hewlett-Packard monitor was used for the National Aeronautics and Space Administration's moon mission and was the medical monitor used during the first artificial heart transplant. Without the dedication of technical champion Chuck House and the support and sponsorship of management champion Das Howard, these landmark innovations would probably never have come about.[34]

The development of the NASA moon mission monitor illustrates how technical and management champions work together and how they sometimes break the rules to support and develop technological innovations. Champions who are willing to risk their jobs and their prestige are crucial for technology change.

NEW PRODUCTS AND SERVICES

Many of the concepts described for technology change are also relevant to the creation of new products and services. However, in many ways, new products and services are a special case of innovation because they are used by customers outside the organization. Since new products are designed for sale in the environment, uncertainty about the suitability and success of an innovation is very high.

New Product Success Rate

Research has explored the enormous uncertainty associated with the development and sale of new products.[35] To understand what this uncertainty can mean to organizations, just consider such flops as RCA's VideoDisc player, which lost an estimated $500 million, or Time Incorporated's *TV-Cable Week,* which lost $47 million. Producing new products that fail is a part of business in all industries. One survey examined two hundred projects in nineteen chemical, drug, electronics, and petroleum laboratories to learn about success rates. To be successful, the new product had to pass three stages of development: technical completion, commercialization, and market success. The findings about success rates are given in Exhibit 8.6.

On the average, only 57 percent of all projects undertaken in the R&D laboratories achieved technical objectives, which means all technical problems were solved and the projects moved on to production. Of all projects that were started, however, less than one-third (31 percent) were fully marketed and commercialized. Several projects failed at this stage because production estimates or test market results were unfavorable.

Finally, only 12 percent of all projects originally undertaken achieved economic success. Most of the commercialized products did not earn sufficient returns to cover the cost of development and production. This means that only about one project in eight returns a profit to the company. New product development is thus very risky.

Reasons for New Product Success

The next question to be answered by research was, "Why are some products more successful than others?" Further studies indicated that innovation success was related to collaboration between technical and marketing departments. Successful new products and services seemed to be technologically sound and also carefully tailored to customer needs.[36] A study called Project SAPPHO exam-

Exhibit 8.6

Probability of New Product Success

	Probability
Technical completion (technical objectives achieved)	.57
Commercialization (full-scale marketing)	.31
Market success (earns economic returns)	.12

Source: Based on Edwin Mansfield, J. Rapaport, J. Schnee, S. Wagner, and M. Hamburger, *Research and Innovation in Modern Corporations* (New York: Norton, 1971), 57.

ined seventeen pairs of new product innovations, with one success and one failure in each pair, and concluded the following.

1. Successful innovating companies had a much better understanding of customer needs and paid much more attention to marketing.
2. Successful innovating companies made more effective use of outside technology and outside advice, even though they did more work in-house.
3. Top management support in the successful innovating companies was from people who were more senior and had greater authority.

Thus, there is a distinct pattern of tailoring innovations to customer needs, making effective use of technology, and having influential top managers support the project. These ideas taken together indicate that the effective design for new product innovation is associated with horizontal linkage across departments.

Horizontal Linkage Model

The organization design for achieving new product innovation involves three components—departmental specialization, boundary spanning, and horizontal linkages. These components are similar to the differentiation and integration ideas in Chapter 3 and the information linkage mechanisms in Chapter 6. Exhibit 8.7 illustrates these components in the **horizontal linkage model**.

Specialization. The key departments in new product development are R&D, marketing, and production. The specialization component means that the personnel in all three of these departments are highly competent at their own tasks. The three departments are differentiated from each other and have skills, goals, and attitudes appropriate for their specialized functions.

Exhibit 8.7
Horizontal Linkage Model for New Product Innovations

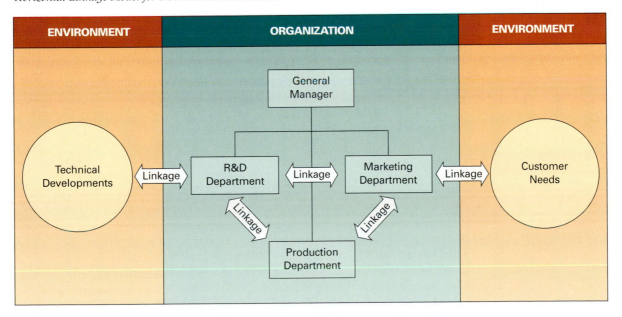

Boundary Spanning.   This component means each department involved with new products has excellent linkage with relevant sectors in the external environment. R&D personnel are linked to professional associations and to colleagues in other R&D departments. They are aware of recent scientific developments. Marketing personnel are closely linked to customer needs. They listen to what customers have to say, and they analyze competitor products and suggestions by distributors. For example, Worlds of Wonder had astonishing success with its Teddy Ruxpin and Laser Tag toys because of market research, which meant working with some one thousand families chosen at random to learn their needs.[37]

Horizontal Linkages.   This component means that technical, marketing, and production people share ideas and information. Research people inform marketing of new technical developments to learn whether the developments are applicable to customers. Marketing people provide customer complaints and information to R&D to use in the design of new products. People from both R&D and marketing coordinate with production because new products have to fit within production capabilities so costs are not exorbitant. The decision to launch a new product is ultimately a joint decision among all three departments.

   At General Electric, members of the R&D department have a great deal of freedom to imagine and invent, and then they have to shop their ideas around other departments and divisions, sometimes finding applications for new technologies that are far from their original intentions. As a result, one study shows that of 250 technology products GE undertook to develop over a four-year period, 150 of them produced major applications, far above the U.S. average of about one success out of ten. Boeing's engineers and manufacturers worked side-by-side on the new 777 project, sometimes bringing in representatives from outside suppliers, airline customers, maintenance, and finance.[38] Famous innovation failures—such as Weyerhaeuser's UltraSoft diapers, General Mills's Benefit cereal, Anheuser-Busch's LA Beer, and RJR Nabisco's Premier smokeless cigarettes—usually violate the horizontal linkage model. Employees fail to connect with customer needs, or internal departments fail to adequately share needs and coordinate with one another.

   Companies are increasingly using cross-functional teams for product development to ensure a high level of communication and coordination from the beginning. The functional diversity increases both the amount and the variety of information for new product development, enabling the design of products that meet customer needs and circumventing manufacturing and marketing problems.[39] IBM has recognized the need for stronger horizontal coordination to revive the company's struggling personal computer business.

In Practice 8.3   *IBM PC Company*

Once the overwhelming revenue leader in the personal computer market, IBM's PC division slid to No. 4 in the United States and to No. 2, behind Compaq, around the world. Products trickled out of development, and market forecasting was inept. While the industry was racking up double-digit revenue growth, IBM was writing off $700 million in obsolete inventory, with no potentially hot-selling new products to make up for it.

   However, Richard Thoman, head of the division, is working overtime to change that. A new approach to product development is central to Thoman's plans to bring new products out quickly, build them in sufficient volume at lower prices, and replace them before they become unsalable. New products are now created by teams from research, design, procurement, logistics, and manufacturing, all working side by side in Raleigh, North Carolina, rather than being spread out across the country in nine different locations. Now, when an engineer selects a part, there's someone right there who knows how much it will cost, how long it will take to get the parts to the plant, and whether using that component will cause manufacturing problems.

The cross-functional process has already produced some head-turning new products, the most promising of which is the Think-Pad 701 laptop, code-named Butterfly because of an innovative full-size keyboard that folds like the wings of a butterfly to tuck neatly into the compact four and one-half pound subnotebook. Researcher John Karides, who came up with the idea for the Butterfly, and two colleagues joined a cross-functional design team in Raleigh and the product metamorphosed from idea sketch to finished product in a smooth eighteen months. Although this isn't particularly impressive in an industry with nine-month product cycles, the Butterfly is IBM's first on-time product in years and is a badly needed smash hit. The division is now revamping the entire ThinkPad portable line to share the new keyboard as well as launching a new line of Aptiva home computers. IBM is counting on successful new product development to help the division regain its position as market leader.[40]

Companies such as IBM, Rubbermaid, General Electric, and Honda are using the horizontal linkage model to achieve competitive advantage in today's global marketplace.

Achieving Competitive Advantage with Product Innovation

For many companies, creating new products is a critical way to adapt and survive in a rapidly changing environment.[41] Getting new products to market fast and developing products that can compete in a competitive international market are key issues for companies like Xerox, Hewlett-Packard, and Chrysler. One authority on time-based competition has said that the old paradigm for success— "provide the most value for the least cost"—has been updated to "provide the most value for the least cost in the least elapsed time."[42]

To gain business, companies are learning to develop new products and services incredibly fast. Whether the approach is called the horizontal linkage model, concurrent engineering, companies without walls, the parallel approach, or simultaneous coupling of departments, the point is the same—get people working together simultaneously on a project rather than in sequence. Many companies are learning to sprint to market with new products.

By breaking down the walls between functions, Chrysler delivered its new Neon in a speedy forty-two months and has now cut the time it takes to go from concept to production to less than three years.[43] Hewlett-Packard has made speed a top priority, getting products out the door twice as fast and urging employees to rethink every process in terms of speed. A printer that once took fifty-four months to develop is now on the market in twenty-two. Speed is becoming a major competitive issue and requires the use of cross-functional teams and other horizontal linkages.[44]

Another critical issue is designing products that can compete on a global scale and successfully marketing those products internationally. Chrysler is already making and selling fifty thousand Jeep Cherokees a year in China and is opening a small factory in Vietnam. Ford is enhancing its global competitiveness by using global teleconferencing to link car design teams into a single unified group.

Black & Decker has also been redesigning its product development process to become a stronger international player. To make global product development faster and more effective, new products are developed by cross-functional project delivery teams, which are answerable to a global business unit team.[45]

Failing to pay attention to global horizontal linkages can hurt companies trying to compete internationally. The Dutch giant Philips Electronics NV was certain its compact disk interactive player called The Imagination Machine would be a hit in the crucial U.S. market, and ultimately, the rest of the world. Five years later, the product, which was promoted as an interactive teaching aid and was so complex it required a thirty-minute sales demonstration, had all but disappeared from the shelves. Marketing employees, salespeople, and major customers had crucial information that would have helped Philips understand the U.S. market, but by the time the executives gathered the information and tried to change course, it was too late. "We should have done things differently," said one Philips executive. "The world isn't as easy as it seems."[46] When companies enter the arena of intense international competition, horizontal coordination across countries is essential to new product development.

STRATEGY AND STRUCTURE CHANGE

The preceding discussion focused on new production processes and products, which are based in the technology of an organization. The expertise for such innovation lies within the technical core and professional staff groups, such as research and engineering. This section turns to an examination of structural and strategy changes.

All organizations need to make changes in their strategies and structures from time to time. In the past, when the environment was relatively stable, most organizations focused on small, incremental changes to solve immediate problems or take advantage of new opportunities. However, over the past decade, companies throughout the world have faced the need to make radical changes in strategy, structure, and management processes to adapt to new competitive demands.[47] Many organizations are reducing the workforce, cutting out layers of management, and decentralizing decision making. There is a strong shift toward more horizontal structures, with teams of front-line workers empowered to make decisions and solve problems on their own. Some companies are breaking totally away from traditional organization forms and moving toward network strategies and structures. Global competition and rapid technological change will likely lead to even greater strategy-structure realignments over the next decade.

These types of changes are the responsibility of the organization's top managers, and the overall process of change is typically different from the process for innovation in technology or new products.

The Dual-Core Approach

The dual-core approach compares administrative and technical changes. Administrative changes pertain to the design and structure of the organization itself, including restructuring, downsizing, teams, control systems, information systems, and departmental grouping. Research into administrative change suggests two things. First, administrative changes occur less frequently than do technical changes. Second, administrative changes occur in response to different environmental sectors and follow a different internal process than do technology-based changes.[48] The **dual-core approach** to organizational change identifies the unique processes associated with administrative change.[49]

Organizations—schools, hospitals, city governments, welfare agencies, government bureaucracies, and many business firms—can be conceptualized as having two cores: a technical core and an administrative core. Each core has its own employees, tasks, and environmental domain. Innovation can originate in either core.

The administrative core is above the technical core in the hierarchy. The responsibility of the administrative core includes the structure, control, and coordination of the organization itself and concerns the environmental sectors of government, financial resources, economic conditions, human resources, and competitors. The technical core is concerned with the transformation of raw materials into organizational products and services and involves the environmental sectors of customers and technology.[50]

The findings from research comparing administrative and technical change suggest that a mechanistic organization structure is appropriate for frequent administrative changes, including changes in goals, strategy, structure, control systems, and personnel.[51] For example, administrative changes in policy, regulations, or control systems are more critical than technical changes in many government organizations that are bureaucratically structured. Organizations that successfully adopt many administrative changes often have a larger administrative ratio, are larger in size, and are centralized and formalized compared with organizations that adopt many technical changes.[52] The reason is the top-down implementation of changes in response to changes in the government, financial, or legal sectors of the environment. In contrast, if an organization has an organic structure, lower-level employees have more freedom and autonomy and, hence, may resist top-down initiatives. An organic structure is more often used when changes in organizational technology or products are important to the organization.

The innovation approaches associated with administrative versus technical change are summarized in Exhibit 8.8. Technical change, such as changes in production techniques and innovation technology for new products, is facilitated by an organic structure, which allows ideas to bubble upward from lower- and

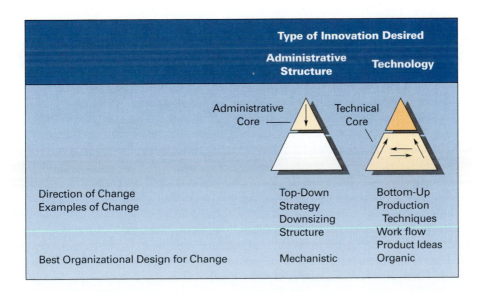

Exhibit 8.8

Dual-Core Approach to Organization Change

middle-level employees. Organizations that must adopt frequent administrative changes tend to use a top-down process and a mechanistic structure. For example, policy changes, such as the adoption of tough no-smoking policies by companies like Park Nicollet Medical Center in Minnesota, are facilitated by a top-down approach. Downsizing and restructuring are nearly always managed top-down, such as when Ronald E. Compton, CEO of Aetna Life and Casualty Company, announced plans to slash over four thousand jobs and drop two of the company's product lines.[53]

The point of the dual-core approach is that many organizations—especially not-for-profit and government organizations—must adopt frequent administrative changes, so a mechanistic structure may be appropriate. For example, research into civil service reform found that the implementation of administrative innovation was extremely difficult in organizations that had an organic technical core. The professional employees in a decentralized agency could resist civil service changes. By contrast, organizations that were considered more bureaucratic in the sense of high formalization and centralization adopted administrative changes readily.[54]

What about business organizations that are normally technologically innovative in bottom-up fashion but suddenly face a crisis and need to reorganize? Or consider a technically innovative, high-tech firm that must reorganize frequently or must suddenly cut back to accommodate changes in production technology or the environment. Technically innovative firms may suddenly have to restructure, reduce the number of employees, alter pay systems, disband teams, or form a new division.[55] The answer is to use a top-down change process. The authority for strategy and structure change lies with top management, who should initiate and implement the new strategy and structure to meet environmental circumstances. Employee input may be sought, but top managers have the responsibility to direct the change. *Downsizing*, *restructuring*, and *reorganizing* are common terms for what happens in times of rapid change and global competition. Often, strong top-down changes follow the installation of new top management. At Autodesk, Inc., a new top leader faced the need to make strong top-down changes in a technologically innovative, organically organized company.

In Practice 8.4   *Autodesk, Inc.*

When Carol Bartz left Sun Microsystems, Inc. to run Autodesk, the world's sixth largest PC software company and a leader in sales of computer-aided design software, she introduced a first for the company: a management hierarchy. For the freethinkers at Autodesk, who brought their dogs to work and sent endless memos through e-mail trying to reach consensus on strategy decisions, it was a shock that has sent them reeling.

But when Bartz was hired, profits were falling, Autodesk's growth was continuing to slow, and stock prices were declining sharply. Something had to be done. Bartz came in with a mandate for change and is taking a strong top-down approach to try to build a billion-dollar company in a highly competitive industry. While the company's programmers are not happy with the new hierarchy, sales and marketing are pleased to have someone setting priorities to get the company back on track as far as sales are concerned.

Bartz knows any change, particularly one this momentous, is stressful, so she's instituted a series of "brown-bag chats" with employees to hear their side of things and try to build faith in the new structure as one that will have a positive outcome. As Bartz put it, "It's safe to say there are good ways to manage change and bad ways to manage change, and we have to get on the right side of that paradigm."[56]

Carol Bartz knows that while it is important to communicate with employees, top management is responsible for firmly directing restructuring changes. Restructuring and especially downsizing can be painful and difficult, so top managers should move quickly and authoritatively to make both as humane as possible.[57]

PEOPLE AND CULTURE CHANGE

Organizations are made up of people and their relationships with one another. Changes in strategy, structure, technologies, and products do not happen on their own, and changes in any of these areas involve people changes as well. People change targets the values, skills, and attitudes of individual employees. Employees must learn how to use new technologies, or market new products, or work effectively in a team-based structure.

In a world where any organization can purchase new technology, the motivation, skill, and commitment of employees can provide the competitive edge. Human resource systems can be designed to attract, develop, and maintain an efficient force of employees.

Sometimes achieving a new way of thinking requires a focused change on the underlying corporate culture values and norms. In the last decade, numerous large corporations, including DuPont, Rockwell, and Amoco, have undertaken some type of culture change initiative. Changing corporate culture fundamentally shifts how work is done in an organization and generally leads to renewed commitment and empowerment of employees and a stronger bond between the company and its customers.[58]

Some recent trends that generally lead to significant changes in corporate culture are reengineering, the shift to horizontal forms of organizing, and the implementation of total-quality management programs, all of which require employees to think in new ways about how work is done.

Organizational development programs also focus on changing old culture values to new ways of thinking, including greater employee participation and empowerment and developing a shared companywide vision.

Reengineering and Horizontal Organization

As described in the previous chapter, reengineering is a cross-functional initiative involving the radical redesign of business processes to produce dramatic performance improvements. Because the focus is on process rather than function, reengineering generally leads to a shift in organization structure from vertical to horizontal, requiring major changes in corporate culture and management philosophy. In his book, *The Reengineering Revolution*, Michael Hammer refers to people change as "the most perplexing, annoying, distressing, and confusing part" of reengineering.[59] Managers may confront powerful emotions as employees react to rapid, massive change with fear or anger. Top leaders at Jaguar of North America coped with resistance to reengineering by putting their loudest dissenters in charge of solutions and then getting out of the way. They implemented employee suggestions that corrected so many of Jaguar's shortcomings that even the most skeptical dealers accepted that the company truly cared about its employees and its customers.[60]

In the horizontal organization, managers and front-line workers need to understand and embrace the concepts of teamwork, empowerment, and cooperation.

Everyone throughout the organization needs to share a common vision and goals so they have a framework within which to make decisions and solve problems. Managers shift their thinking to view workers as colleagues rather than cogs in a wheel; and workers learn to accept not only greater freedom and power, but also the higher level of responsibility—and stress—that comes with it. Mutual trust, risk-taking, and tolerance for mistakes become key cultural values in the horizontal organization. Most top managers have little experience dealing with the complexities of human behavior; yet, they should remember that significant people and culture changes are crucial to the success of reengineering and the shift to horizontal forms of organization.

Total Quality Management

The approach known as **total quality management** infuses quality values throughout every activity within a company. The concept is simple: workers, not managers, are handed the responsibility for achieving standards of quality. No longer are quality control departments and other formal control systems in charge of checking parts and improving quality. Companies are training their workers and then trusting them to infuse quality into everything they do. The results of TQM programs can be staggering. After noticing that Ford Motor Company cut $40 billion out of its operating budget by adopting quality principles and changing corporate culture, the Henry Ford Health System recently instituted a quality program. CEO Gail Warden says of quality programs at Henry Ford and other U.S. health-care institutions, "We have to change the way we practice medicine" to get health-care costs down and remain competitive in the rapidly changing health-care industry.[61]

By requiring organizationwide participation in quality control, TQM requires a major shift in mind-set for both managers and workers. In TQM, workers must be trained, involved, and empowered in a way that many managers at first find frightening. One way in which workers are involved is through **quality circles**, groups of six to twelve volunteer workers who meet to analyze and solve problems.

Another technique of total quality management is known as **benchmarking**, a process whereby companies find out how others do something better than they do and then try to imitate or improve on it. Through research and field trips by small teams of workers, companies compare their products, services, and business practices with those of their competitors and other companies. AT&T, Xerox, DuPont, Eastman Kodak, and Motorola are constantly benchmarking. Ford Motor Company shamelessly benchmarked more than two hundred features of the Ford Taurus against seven competitors, including the Honda Accord, Chevy Lumina, and Nissan Maxima, helping to make the Taurus one of the top-selling cars.[62]

While the focus of total quality programs is generally on improving quality and productivity, it always involves a significant people and culture change. Managers should be prepared for this aspect before undertaking quality programs.

Organizational Development

One method of bringing about culture change is known as organizational development, which focuses on the development and fulfillment of people to bring about improved performance. In the 1970s, **organizational development** evolved as a separate field in the behavioral sciences focused on examining how work is done and how people who do the work feel about their efficiency and effectiveness. Rather than using a step-by-step procedure to solve a specific problem, organizational development is a process of fundamental change in an organization's culture.[63]

OD uses knowledge and techniques from the behavioral sciences to improve performance through trust, open confrontation of problems, employee empowerment and participation, the design of meaningful work, cooperation between groups, and the full use of human potential. OD practitioners believe the best performance occurs by breaking down hierarchical and authoritarian approaches to management. In terms of the competing values effectiveness model described in Chapter 2, OD places high value on internal processes and human relationships. However, consistent with the arguments in the environment and technology chapters, research has shown that the OD approach may not enhance performance or satisfaction in stable business environments and for routine tasks.[64]

The spirit of the people change OD tries to accomplish is illustrated by efforts of the U.S. Agriculture Department's Animal and Plant Health Inspection Service (APHIS) to overcome the problems of bureaucracy and develop a culture that supports learning and change. The OD program at APHIS is described in The New Paradigm box.

Changing organizational culture is not easy, but organizational development techniques can smooth the process. For example, OD can help managers and employees think in new ways about human relationships, making the transition to more participative management less stressful. At Hewlett-Packard's direct marketing organization, self-confessed "authoritarian" manager Sharon Jacobs used concepts based in organizational development to create a better quality of life and participation for employees as well as improve the organization's performance. Spurred by pleas from new staffers who felt constricted by the excessive top-down control, Jacobs is doing her best to let go, to ask her telemarketers for solutions, to listen to the ideas of even lowest level staff members. Despite the difficulties in the beginning, the new style has resulted in a 40 percent increase in productivity, a rise in employee morale significant enough to warrant a note from HP's president, and a 44 percent decline in the unit's annual attrition rate.[65]

OD Culture Change Interventions

OD interventions involve training of specific groups or of everyone in the organization. For OD intervention to be successful, senior management in the organization must see the need for OD and provide enthusiastic support for the change. Techniques used by many organizations for improving people skills through OD include the following.

Survey Feedback. Organizational personnel are surveyed about their job satisfaction, attitudes, performance, leader behavior, climate, and quality of work relationships. A consultant feeds back the data to stimulate a discussion of organizational problems. Plans are then made for organizational change.[66]

Off-site Meetings. The process of change may begin with an off-site meeting to formulate a vision for the desired outcome of the process, create a microcosm of the new culture, and devise ways to instill new cultural values throughout the organization. Off-site meetings limit interference and distractions, enabling

The New Paradigm

U.S. Agriculture Department's Animal and Plant Health Inspection Service

A federal agency might seem an unlikely hotbed of management reform, but that's exactly what the Agriculture Department's Animal and Plant Health Inspection Service (APHIS) has become. A self-designated group of change agents is constantly stirring things up at APHIS, yet far from being seen as troublemakers, these employees are viewed by leaders as crucial to keeping people in the organization active, energized, and empowered. The agency has won a series of Hammer Awards from Vice President Al Gore for its aggressive approach to reinventing government.

According to APHIS Director Lonnie King, in today's difficult world, "the status quo is not acceptable. . . . You can be the driver, the passenger, or the road kill. We want to be the driver." He and other leaders at APHIS attribute the agency's aptitude for change in part to its organization development (OD) unit. APHIS created the unit to help deal with the problems that were overwhelming federal agencies. For example, Plant Protection and Quarantine workers at Miami International Airport, one of the least desirable work sites within APHIS, wanted to organize into self-directed teams. Yet when the experiment was tried, workers became frustrated and demoralized because neither they nor their supervisors had the necessary skills. Rather than counting the teamwork experiment a failure, APHIS pumped additional resources into the effort, hiring OD specialists to make it successful.

Since then, the agency's OD unit has continued to grow. OD specialists are now helping the agency coordinate a planning process known as *future search*, to develop a vision and strategy for the future and break down boundaries between functions, divisions, and field offices. APHIS is using OD to create a culture in which change and continuous learning are primary values and where employees have the attitude that "we're all in this together." Rather than cutting OD when resources go down, the agency protects the unit as the best way to help APHIS remain flexible. When managers rated the agency's support services on the degree to which they added value to their operations, OD got one of the highest ratings. According to Dan Stone, head of the unit, "People experienced OD as helping them to solve real problems. When this kind of support is available, people are willing to bite off more. There is a more profound level of change."

Source: James Thompson, "Rogue Workers, Change Agents," *Government Executive,* April 1996, 46–49.

participants to focus on a new way of doing things. At MasterBrand Industries, for example, the culture change process began with an off-site meeting of seventy-five key managers who would be the catalysts for remaking MasterBrand into a cross-functional team-based organization. The managers formed into *advocate teams* that examined all the company's activities from a cross-functional perspective and began to develop a cooperative team spirit. The goal of the three-day conference was to break down vertical walls that had isolated departments and sow the seeds of a self-sustaining team culture from top management down to the shop floor.[67]

Team Building.   **Team building** activities promote the idea that people who work together can work as a team. A work team can be brought together to discuss conflicts, goals, the decision-making process, communication, creativity, and leadership. The team can then plan to overcome problems and improve results.[68] Team building activities are also used in many companies to train task forces, committees, and new product development groups.

Intergroup Activities.   Representatives from different groups are brought together in a mutual location to surface conflict, diagnose its causes, and plan improvement in communication and coordination. This type of intervention has been applied to union-management conflict, headquarters-field office conflict, interdepartmental conflict, and mergers.[69]

In today's world, the workforce is becoming more and more diverse, and organizations are constantly changing in response to environmental uncertainty and increasing international competition. OD interventions can respond to these new realities as organizations head toward the twenty-first century.[70]

STRATEGIES FOR IMPLEMENTING CHANGE

This chapter began by looking at incremental versus radical change, the four types of changes managers can use to gain a competitive edge, and the five elements that must be present for any change to succeed—idea, need, adoption, implementation, and resources. In this final section, we are going to briefly discuss the need for strong leadership to support change, resistance to change at the organizational level, and some techniques managers can use to implement change.

Leadership for Change

As the world becomes increasingly complex, the need for change within organizations and the need for managers who can successfully deal with change continues to grow. As we discussed in Chapter 1, coping with rapid change is one of the greatest challenges facing today's organizations. Organizations need to continuously change and adapt in response to a turbulent environment. They need leaders who can clearly recognize the need for change and make it happen, who can develop and communicate a vision for what the organization can be and provide the motivation and guidance to take it there. Leaders who can effect the kind of continuous adaptation needed in today's world recognize that change is painful for employees, and they learn to put themselves in their employees' shoes and develop partnerships that make successful change possible.[71]

Successful change can happen only when employees are willing to devote the time and energy needed to reach new goals as well as endure possible stress and hardship. Having a clearly communicated vision that embodies flexibility and openness to new ideas, methods, and styles sets the stage for a change-oriented organization and helps employees cope with the chaos and tension associated with change.[72] Leaders also build organizationwide commitment by taking employees through three stages of the change commitment process, illustrated in Exhibit 8.9.[73] In the first stage, preparation, employees hear about the change through memos, meetings, speeches, or personal contact and become aware that the change will directly affect their work. In the second stage, leaders should help employees develop an understanding of the full impact of the change and the positive outcomes of making the change. When employees perceive the change as positive, the decision to implement is made. In the third stage the true commitment process begins. The installation step, a trial process for the change, gives leaders an opportunity to discuss problems and employee concerns and build commitment to action. In the final stage, institutionalization, employees view the

Exhibit 8.9

Stages of Commitment to Change

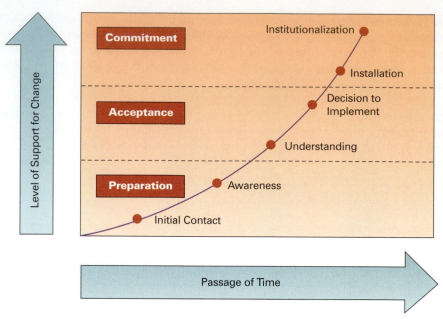

Source: Adapted from Daryl R. Conner, *Managing at the Speed of Change* (New York: Villard Books, 1992), 148. Used with permission.

change not as something new but as a normal and integral part of organizational operations.

The pressures on organizations to change will likely increase over the next few decades and leaders must develop the personal qualities, skills, and methods needed to help their companies remain competitive. Book Mark 8.0 further discusses this growing need for change leadership.

Barriers to Change

Visionary leadership is crucial for change; however, leaders should expect to encounter resistance as they attempt to take the organization through the three stages of the change commitment process. It is natural for people to resist change, and many barriers to change exist at the organizational level.[74]

1. *Excessive focus on costs.* Management may possess the mind-set that costs are all-important and may fail to appreciate the importance of a change that is not focused on costs—for example, a change to increase employee motivation or customer satisfaction.
2. *Failure to perceive benefits.* Any significant change will produce both positive and negative reactions. Education may be needed to help managers and employees perceive more positive than negative aspects of the change. In addition, if the organization's reward system discourages risk-taking, a change process may falter because employees feel that the risk of making the change is too high.
3. *Lack of coordination and cooperation.* Organizational fragmentation and conflict often result from the lack of coordination for change implementation. Moreover, in the case of new technology, the old and new systems must be compatible.

Book Mark 8.0

Have You Read About This?

Real Change Leaders: How You Can Create Growth and High Performance at Your Company

By Jon R. Katzenbach and the RCL Team

In today's chaotic business world, successful organizational change is becoming everyone's problem and everyone's responsibility. Jon Katzenbach argues that middle managers, far from becoming dispensable baggage as organizations trim hierarchies and cut costs, can emerge as leaders who make a real difference by changing the behaviors of workers and generating better results for customers faster than the competition. *Real Change Leaders* examines successful midlevel change agents at real organizations, ranging from Compaq Computer to State Farm Insurance to the New York City Transit Authority. Katzenbach studied more than 150 *real change leaders* (RCLs)—front-line managers who emerged during a time of flux or crisis with the skills needed to motivate and inspire workers to go beyond the norm.

What Is a Real Change Leader?

Katzenbach found that while these change agents run the gamut of personalities and backgrounds, they share certain core characteristics, including commitment, courage, initiative, motivation, caring, modesty, and humor. RCLs act as the linchpin connecting three critical forces for organizational change: the aspirations of top leadership (What are we trying to become?), the energy and productivity of the workforce (How can we get there?), and the reality of the marketplace (What do our customers really want?).

Real change leaders exhibit several characteristics and behaviors:

- They understand the bottom line but also realize that developing and nurturing people is critical.

- They challenge workers by setting "stretch" goals, believing that people will meet them most of the time and will learn from those they don't meet.
- They recognize the importance of developing and communicating a strong, meaningful vision for the future.
- They set clear objectives, put the right people in the right positions, create a structured-but-flexible employee participation process, and design effective methods of communication.
- They have the courage to take risks in order to build credibility, instill courage in others, and influence top leaders when it counts.

How to Be a Real Change Leader

The final section of the book, "Extended Leadership Capacity," shows how ordinary managers can develop the skills needed to become RCLs. Katzenbach highlights the major difference between good managers and RCLs: "Most managers still see the organization structure as the primary alignment mechanism for channeling behaviors and skills . . . RCLs use whatever works, but they seldom start with structure." Katzenbach's chapters on building and sustaining momentum, developing RCL skills and approaches, and adopting a no-excuses mind-set enable front-line managers as well as top leaders to meet the challenge of leading their organizations through successful change.

Real Change Leaders by Jon Katzenbach and the RCL Team is published by Times Books, a division of Random House.

4. *Uncertainty avoidance.* At the individual level, many employees fear the uncertainty associated with change. Constant communication is needed so that employees know what is going on and understand how it impacts their jobs.
5. *Fear of loss.* Managers and employees may fear the loss of power and status or even their jobs. In these cases, implementation should be careful and incremental, and all employees should be involved as closely as possible in the change process.

Implementation can typically be designed to overcome many of the organizational and individual barriers to change.

Techniques for Implementation

Top leaders articulate the vision and set the tone, but managers and employees throughout the organization are involved in the process of change. There are a number of techniques that can be used to successfully implement change.

1. *Identify a true need for change.* A careful diagnosis of the existing situation is necessary to determine the extent of the problem or opportunity. If the people affected by the change do not agree with a problem, the change process should not proceed without further analysis and communication among all employees. A perceived problem or opportunity is necessary to unfreeze participants and make them willing to invest the time and energy to adopt new techniques or procedures.[75] For example, at Land's End, Inc. of Dodgeville, Wisconsin, new management wanted to try some of today's hottest management trends, such as teams, peer reviews, and the elimination of time clocks and strict rules. But employees were happy with the familiar family-like atmosphere and uncomplicated work environment, which had, they pointed out, made the company number one in specialty catalog sales in the United States. They did not see any need for changing things and balked at the new initiatives, which were ultimately shelved.[76]

2. *Find an idea that fits the need.* Finding the right idea often involves search procedures—talking with other managers, assigning a task force to investigate the problem, sending out a request to suppliers, or asking creative people within the organization to develop a solution. The creation of a new idea requires organic conditions. This is a good opportunity to encourage employee participation, because they need the freedom to think about and explore new options.[77]

3. *Get top management support.* Successful change requires the support of top management. Top managers should articulate clear innovation goals. For a single large change, such as a structural reorganization, the president and vice presidents must give their blessing and support. For smaller changes, the support of influential managers in relevant departments is required. The lack of top management support is one of the most frequent causes of implementation failure.[78]

4. *Design the change for incremental implementation.* When a large bank in South Carolina installed a complete new $6 million system to computerize processing, it was stunned that the system didn't work very well. The prospect for success of such a large change is improved if the change can be broken into subparts and each part adopted sequentially. Then designers can make adjustments to improve the innovation, and hesitant users who see success can throw support behind the rest of the change program. An incremental approach also reduces the cost of failure because only a few resources are lost on a bad idea.

5. *Develop plans to overcome resistance to change.* Many good ideas are never used because managers failed to anticipate or prepare for resistance to change by consumers, employees, or other managers. No matter how impressive the performance characteristics of an innovation, its implementation will conflict with some interests and jeopardize some alliances in the organization. To increase the chance of successful implementation, management must acknowledge the conflict, threats, and potential losses perceived by employees. Several strategies can be used by managers to overcome the resistance problem:

- *Alignment with needs and goals of users.* The best strategy for overcoming resistance is to make sure change meets a real need. Employees in R&D often come up with great ideas that solve nonexistent problems. This happens because initiators fail to consult with the people who use a change. Resistance can be frustrating for managers, but moderate resistance to change is good for an organization. Resistance provides a barrier to frivolous changes or to change for the sake of change. The process of overcoming resistance to change normally requires that the change be good for its users.

- *Communication and training.* Communication informs users about the need for change and about the consequences of a proposed change, preventing false rumors, misunderstanding, and resentment. In one study of change efforts, the most commonly cited reason for failure was that employees learned of the change from outsiders. Top managers concentrated on communicating with the public and with shareholders, but failed to communicate with the people who would be most intimately involved and most affected by the changes—their own employees.[79] Open communication often gives management an opportunity to explain what steps will be taken to ensure that the change will have no adverse consequences for employees. Training is also needed to help employees understand and cope with their role in the change process.

- *Participation and involvement.* Early and extensive participation in a change should be part of implementation. Participation gives those involved a sense of control over the change activity. They understand it better, and they become committed to successful implementation. One recent study of the implementation and adoption of computer technology at two companies showed a much smoother implementation process at the company that introduced the new technology using a participatory approach.[80]

- *Forcing and coercion.* As a last resort, managers may overcome resistance by threatening employees with loss of jobs or promotions or by firing or transferring them. In other words, management power is used to overwhelm resistance. In most cases, this approach is not advisable because it leaves people angry at change managers, and the change may be sabotaged. However, this technique may be needed when speed is essential, such as when the organization faces a crisis. It may also be required for needed administrative changes that flow from the top down, such as downsizing the workforce.[81]

6. *Create change teams.* Throughout, this chapter has discussed the need for resources and energy to make change happen. Separate creative departments, new venture groups, or an ad hoc team or task force are ways to focus energy on both creation and implementation. A separate department has the freedom to create a new technology that fits a genuine need. A task force can be created to see that implementation is completed. The task force can be responsible for communication, involvement of users, training, and other activities needed for change.

7. *Foster idea champions.* One of the most effective weapons in the battle for change is the idea champion. The most effective champion is a volunteer champion who is deeply committed to a new idea. The idea champion sees that all technical activities are correct and complete. An additional champion, such as a manager sponsor, may also be needed to persuade people about implementation, even using coercion if necessary. For example, John

Cunningham was the idea champion at Chesebrough-Ponds who developed the polishing pen through which nail polish is applied. Management supporters at Chesebrough-Ponds then solved the implementation problems of manufacturing, packaging, and marketing.[82] Both technical and management champions may break the rules and push ahead even when others are nonbelieving, but the enthusiasm pays off.[83]

SUMMARY AND INTERPRETATION

Organizations face a dilemma. Managers prefer to organize day-to-day activities in a predictable, routine manner. However, change—not stability—is the natural order of things in today's global environment. Thus, organizations need to build in change as well as stability, to facilitate innovation as well as efficiency.

Most change in organizations is incremental, but there is a growing emphasis on the need for radical change. Four types of change—products and services, strategy and structure, people and culture, and technology—may give an organization a competitive edge, and managers can make certain each of the necessary ingredients for change is present.

For technical innovation, which is of concern to most organizations, an organic structure that encourages employee autonomy works best because it encourages a bottom-up flow of ideas. Other approaches are to establish a separate department charged with creating new technical ideas, establish venture teams, and encourage idea champions. New products and services generally require cooperation among several departments, so horizontal linkage is an essential part of the innovation process.

For changes in strategy and structure, a top-down approach is typically best. These innovations are in the domain of top administrators who take responsibility for restructuring, for downsizing, and for changes in policies, goals, and control systems.

People changes are also generally the responsibility of top management. Sometimes, the entire corporate culture must change. Some recent trends that lead to significant changes in corporate culture are reengineering, the shift to horizontal forms of organizing, and the implementation of total-quality management programs, all of which require employees to think in new ways. Organizational development is another process for bringing about culture change by focusing on the development and fulfillment of people to bring about improved performance. All of these approaches typically favor organic conditions that lead to employee participation in decisions, interesting work, and the freedom to initiate ideas to improve their jobs.

Finally, the implementation of change can be difficult. Strong leadership is needed to guide employees through the turbulence and uncertainty and build organizationwide commitment to change. A number of barriers to change exist, including excessive focus on cost, failure to perceive benefits, lack of organizational coordination, and individual uncertainty avoidance and fear of loss. Managers can thoughtfully plan how to deal with resistance to increase the likelihood of success. Techniques that will facilitate implementation are to obtain top management support, implement the change incrementally, align change with the needs and goals of users, include users in the change process through communication and participation, and, in some cases, to force the innovation, if necessary. Change teams and idea champions are also effective.

Key Concepts

ambidextrous approach	people and culture changes
benchmarking	product and service changes
change process	quality circles
creative departments	radical change
dual-core approach	strategy and structure changes
horizontal linkage model	switching structures
idea champion	team building
incremental change	technical or product champion
management champion	technology changes
organizational change	total quality management
organizational development	venture teams
organizational innovation	

Discussion Questions

1. How is the management of radical change likely to differ from the management of incremental change?
2. How are organic characteristics related to changes in technology? To administrative changes?
3. Describe the dual-core approach. How does administrative change normally differ from technology change? Discuss.
4. How might organizations manage the dilemma of needing both stability and change? Discuss.
5. Why do organizations experience resistance to change? What steps can managers take to overcome this resistance?
6. "Bureaucracies are not innovative." Discuss.
7. A noted organization theorist said, "Pressure for change originates in the environment; pressure for stability originates within the organization." Do you agree? Discuss.
8. Of the five elements required for successful change, which element do you think managers are most likely to overlook? Discuss.
9. Why do total quality management programs lead to significant culture changes when these programs are aimed at improving quality and productivity? Discuss.
10. The manager of R&D for a drug company said only 5 percent of the company's new products ever achieve market success. He also said the industry average is 10 percent and wondered how his organization might increase its success rate. If you were acting as a consultant, what advice would you give him concerning organization structure?
11. Review the stages of commitment to change illustrated in Exhibit 8.9 and the seven techniques for implementing change discussed at the end of the chapter. At which stage of change commitment would each of the seven techniques most likely be used?

Briefcase

As an organization manager, keep these guides in mind:

1. Facilitate frequent changes in internal technology by adopting an organic organizational structure. Give technical personnel freedom to analyze problems and develop solutions or create a separate organically structured department or venture group to conceive and propose new ideas.
2. Facilitate changes in strategy and structure by adopting a top-down approach. Use a mechanistic structure when the organization needs to adopt frequent administrative changes in a top-down fashion.
3. Work with organization development consultants for large-scale changes in the attitudes, values, or skills of employees. Adopt total quality management programs to facilitate change in company culture toward greater quality and productivity.
4. Encourage marketing and research departments to develop linkages to each other and to their environments when new products or services are needed.
5. Make sure every change undertaken has a definite need, idea, adoption, decision, implementation strategy, and resources. Avoid failure by not proceeding until each element is accounted for.
6. Lead employees through the three stages of commitment to change—preparation, acceptance, and commitment—and use techniques to achieve successful implementation. These include obtaining top-management support, implementing the change in a series of steps, assigning change teams or idea champions, and overcoming resistance by actively communicating with workers and encouraging their participation in the change process.

Chapter Eight Workbook *Innovation Climate**

In order to examine differences in the level of innovation encouragement in organizations, you will be asked to rate two organizations. You may choose one in which you have worked or the university. The other should be someone else's workplace, either that of a family member, a friend, or an acquaintance. You will have to interview that person to answer the questions on the next page. You should put your own answers in column A, your interviewee's answers in column B, and what you think would be the ideal in column C. Use a scale of 1 to 5: 1 = don't agree at all to 5 = agree completely.

*Adapted by Dorothy Marcic from Susanne G. Scott and Reginald A. Bruce, "Determinants of Innovative Behavior: A Path Model of Individual Innovation in the Workplace," *Academy of Management Journal* 37, no. 3 (1994): 580–607.

Innovation Measures

Item of Measure	Column A Your Organization	Column B Other Organization	Column C Your Ideal
1. Creativity is encouraged here.*			
2. People are allowed to solve the same problems in different ways.*			
3. I get free time to pursue creative ideas.#			
4. The organization publicly recognizes and also rewards those who are innovative.#			
5. Our organization is flexible and always open to change.*			
Below score items on the opposite scale: 1 = agree completely to 5 = don't agree at all			
6. The primary job of people here is to follow orders that come from the top.*			
7. The best way to get along here is to think and act like the others.*			
8. This place seems to be more concerned with the status quo than with change.*			
9. People are rewarded more if they don't rock the boat.#			
10. New ideas are great, but we don't have enough people or money to carry them out.#			

Note: *Starred items indicate the organization's innovation climate.

   # Pound sign items show resource support.

Questions

1. What comparisons about innovative climates can you make from these two organizations?
2. How might productivity differ between a climate that supports innovation versus a climate that does not?
3. For which type of place would you rather work? Why?

Case for Analysis *The Bay Kitchener**

On Monday, May 8, 1995, Emree Siaroff, the new Human Resources/Operations Manager at the Bay store in Kitchener, Ontario, Canada, was thinking about the mission statement he had just finished typing:

The Bay Kitchener will offer the best in customer satisfaction that can be offered by any retailer in the Kitchener-Waterloo area or by any Bay store in the Ontario Region.

After two weeks in his new position, Emree had decided this statement would constitute his personal objective for the upcoming year. During the next week, Emree wanted to ascertain what this goal would mean to the Bay Kitchener and how this goal could be met.

The Retail Industry

Retailers in Canada faced increasing competition as American retailers continued to enter the Canadian market. This competition ultimately resulted in consumers who expected lower retail prices and higher levels of customer service. Consequently, many Canadian retailers were forced to restructure their organizations in order to remain competitive. Some retailers declared bankruptcy because they could not adapt quickly enough to the changes in their competitive environment. Other retailers thrived in this environment.

Overall, the retail industry in Canada achieved relatively strong sales growth in 1994. A key measure of this performance, Department Store Sales (DSS), rebounded from a 1.7 percent decrease in 1993 to a 3.8 percent increase in 1994. This increase was attributed to strong sales in junior department stores while, on average, major department stores continued to experience decreased sales. Junior department stores, such as Zellers, Kmart and Bi-Way, sold a more limited selection of merchandise than major department stores; for example, junior department stores did not sell appliances or furniture.

The Hudson's Bay Company

The Hudson's Bay Company (HBC) was Canada's oldest corporation and largest retail department store. It had two major operating divisions: Zellers and the Bay. Since 1994, Zellers' strategies included combatting the impact of new competitors, such as Wal-Mart, from the United States. Simultaneously, the Bay continued its strategic plan to be Canada's best fashion department store.

Through these two divisions, HBC covered the Canadian retail market from British Columbia to Nova Scotia and targeted consumers at all price levels. In 1994, HBC's sales and revenues increased by 7.1 percent to $5.8 billion and operating profits increased by 1.5 percent to $369 million over 1993. As well, HBC increased its market share of DSS from 39.5 percent in 1993 to 40.6 percent in 1994. HBC planned to continue this substantial growth in the future.

On January 1, 1995, there were 103 Bay stores all across Canada. In support of the Bay's objective to be Canada's leading fashion department store, renovations were completed in 17 locations in 1994, with plans to renovate additional stores in 1995. Contrary to the general trend of decreased sales in major department stores that was observed in DSS calculations, the Bay's sales and revenues increased by 7.8 percent to $2.2 billion in 1994 and operating profits increased by 32.5 percent to $161 million over 1993. The large increase in operating profits was attributed to several factors including increased sales, a higher gross profit and the controlling of expenses.

The Bay Kitchener

The Tri-City area of Kitchener, Waterloo and Cambridge was located in southwestern Ontario and had a population of 379,900 people as of June 1, 1994. The area had been growing at an average rate of 2.5 percent since 1986. The average income per capita in Kitchener was $18,800, 5 percent above the national average income in Canada. While 79 percent of the citizens spoke English as their first language, historically there were many German people that settled in Kitchener as well.

*Krista Wylie prepared this case under the supervision of Elizabeth M. A. Grasby, Pre-Business Program Director, solely to provide material for class discussion. The case is not intended to illustrate either effective or ineffective handling of a managerial situation. Certain names and other identifying information may have been disguised to protect confidentiality. This material is not covered under authorization from CanCopy or any reproduction rights organization. Any form of reproduction, storage or transmittal of this material is prohibited without written permission from Western Business School. Copies or permission to reproduce may be obtained by contacting Case and Publication Services, Western Business School, The University of Western Ontario, London, Ontario, N6A 3K7, or by calling (519) 661-3208, or faxing (519) 661-3882. Copyright © 1996 The University of Western Ontario; Revision Date 96/05/16.

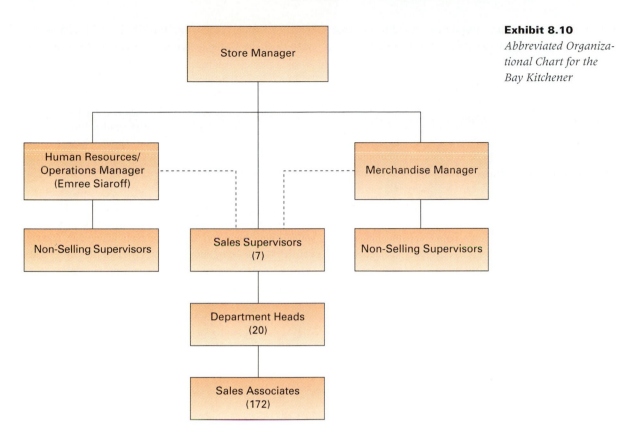

Exhibit 8.10
Abbreviated Organizational Chart for the Bay Kitchener

Four percent of Kitchener's population spoke German as their first language.

Located in Fairview Park Mall, off Ontario Highway 8, the Bay Kitchener was a larger than average-sized suburban store, covering 185,000 square feet over three floors. It served customers in and around Kitchener, Waterloo, Cambridge, Guelph and Woodstock. This market was likely going to be affected by a new Bay store opening in Waterloo, 15 kilometres away from the Bay Kitchener. Located in Conestoga Mall, the new store was 110,000 square feet covering a single floor and was scheduled to open in August 1995.

The Bay Kitchener operated with a total staff of 232 people, including a team of four executives. The majority of staff were in sales. Of those, there were 172 sales associates, 20 department heads and 7 sales supervisors (see Exhibit 8.10). The remaining employees provided retail support such as loss prevention, receiving, in-store marketing, visual presentation, and various clerical duties including sales audit, cash office, switchboard, and inventory management.

Sales Associates

According to the job description, a Sales Associate's role was to be courteous, to maintain customer service standards and to continually improve his or her selling skills. The Bay had developed specific customer service standards (Exhibit 8.11) that sales associates were

1. Acknowledge every customer within 20 seconds.
2. Make the customer feel welcome or encourage them to wait.
3. Ask "Is that on your Bay card?".
4. Offer an "add-on item" or service.
5. Ensure the sales transaction is efficient.
6. Thank the customer by name.
7. Invite them to return.
8. Be friendly and courteous.

Exhibit 8.11
Customer Service Standards

expected to follow. These standards served to increase sales and profitability in a variety of ways. For instance, prompt customer acknowledgment not only increased sales by turning browsers into buyers but also increased profitability by discouraging thefts since customers in the presence of an attentive sales associate were unlikely to steal merchandise. As well, since customers generally spent three times more money if they made a purchase using a credit card instead of cash, a sales associate who regularly asked customers if they would like to make their purchase on their Bay card helped to increase sales.

Sales associates were evaluated after being employed at the Bay for 30, 60, and 90 days, and then annually, by their supervisors. These evaluations were based on each sales associate's customer service skills, sales support behaviour, attendance, appearance and professionalism (see Exhibit 8.12). Although evaluations were not used to determine wage increases, they were used when considering people for promotions. To help supervisors evaluate the customer skills behaviour of each sales associate, two tools were used: Mystery Shops and Mini-Shops.

Mystery Shops involved people employed by a company that was contracted by the Bay. These people made purchases, like actual customers, observing and, therefore, evaluating, whether the sales associate had complied with customer service standards. Mystery Shopping could occur any time and provided a snapshot of both appropriate and inappropriate employee behaviours. During Mini-Shops, supervisors observed a sales associate throughout a customer transaction and evaluated the associate's performance against the same customer service standards that a mystery shopper used (see Exhibit 8.13).

Between the formal Mystery Shops and informal Mini-Shops, an employee's customer skills behaviour was thoroughly evaluated. As well, these tools provided an opportunity for interim feedback to employees. In addition to the supervisors' immediate feedback regarding how the employee handled the transaction during a Mini-Shop, the Human Resources/Operations Manager or Store Manager tried to speak to each employee within 48 hours of their having been "Mystery Shopped." Since they received frequent feedback, employees knew continually how they were performing. If necessary, they could make improvements to their customer skills behavior.

Mystery Shop results provided the only quantifiable data for comparison of the Bay Kitchener's performance to other Bay stores. These results were calculated by adding up the number of "yes" responses on the evaluation form and dividing by the total number of criteria for which "yes" could have been achieved. As of May 1995, the Bay Kitchener had been scoring Mystery Shop results averaging 79 percent. One of the 28 stores in the Ontario region had been averaging 97 percent. In order for the Bay Kitchener to be able to offer the best in customer satisfaction, sales associates would need to improve their Mystery Shop results significantly.

The company also believed that these front-line employees should be empowered to handle more of the customers' needs. For example, if a customer would not buy a shirt that had a small stain on it unless they received a 10 percent discount, the sales associates should be able to meet the customer's request immediately rather than having to approach their supervisor for approval. It was believed this empowerment would help sales associates gain a better understanding of the rationale behind the Bay's customer service standards and that if they truly understood these standards they would be better equipped to follow through on them. It would, however, be difficult to quantify how this empowerment would improve customer satisfaction.

Department Heads

Department Heads were expected to perform the same tasks as sales associates and, additionally, to be involved in the display of merchandise, to have superior knowledge of stock levels and products, to be aware of upcoming sales plans, to help sales associates meet customer needs and to act as coaches to sales associates. Department heads were evaluated in the same way as sales associates, using the same criteria outlined in Exhibit 8.12. Their additional duties were also evaluated. Due to their additional responsibilities, department heads earned a higher wage than sales associates.

The department heads at the Bay Kitchener needed to be supported more in their role as coaches to the sales associates. The department heads were in an ideal position to act as coaches since they spent more time on the sales floor working with sales associates than sales supervisors. Management wanted to ensure that department heads took full advantage of the opportunities they had to assist sales associates in becoming better salespeople. Specifically, they wanted to see department heads guide sales associates through the process of meeting the customer service standards. For instance, if a department head heard a sales associate close a sale without suggesting additional appropriate merchandise, they wanted the department head to discuss the transaction with the sales associate, providing assistance on how a sales associate might have gone about suggesting additional merchandise.

Exhibit 8.12

Sales Associate Performance Review

Part A:

Name:	Unit/Location:
Position:	Date:
Department:	Review Period: From To

Part B: Customer Skills Behavior:
{enter the appropriate level of performance from the expert system: Distinguished, Commendable, Competent, Adequate, Provisional}.

	Selling Skill:	Rating:	Comment:
1.	Acknowledgment		
2.	Friendliness		
3.	Offer Help/ Determine Needs		
4.	Product Knowledge		
5.	Add-on Selling		
6.	Multiple Customers		
7.	Listening Skills		
8.	Clientele/Full Service Selling		

Overall Summary of Customer Skills Behavior:

Sales Support Behavior Rating:

Housekeeping, stock, paperwork, systems, policy, cooperation, dependability.

SUMMARY RATING: Total Performance:

(Continued)

Exhibit 8.12 (continued)

Part C: Standards Review:
Attendance:

Commendable	Meets Standard	Area of Concern	Improve/Alternative

Dress Code (business dress attire):

Commendable	Meets Standard	Area of Concern	Improve/Alternative

Professionalism (suitable conduct for customer satisfaction):

Commendable	Meets Standard	Area of Concern	Improve/Alternative

Part D: Overall Summary of Previous Performance:

After discussion with the Associate, complete this area:

Part E: Major Challenges/Objectives on the Job:

Description	Target Date

Part F: Personal Skills/Knowledge Development Objectives:

Description	Target Date

Part G:

	Signature:	Date:
Sales Associate:		
Supervisor:		
Human Resources Manager:		

Exhibit 8.13

Customer Satisfaction Shopping Report

Shopper's Letter	Store		Department		Month	Week
Sales Associate Name				Clerk Number		

1. Acknowledgment/Greeting		Yes	No
a)	When you came into view of an associate were you acknowledged within 20 seconds?		
b)	Did the acknowledgment make you feel welcome, and/or encourage you to wait? (eg. "Hi, how are you today", "thanks for waiting")		
Comment:			

2. 1 On 1 Service		N/A	Yes	No
a)	Were you approached and offered help promptly?			
b)	Did the associate display curiosity and genuine interest in determining your needs?			
c)	Did the associate offer/demonstrate product knowledge?			
d)	Did the associate add-on related merchandise to build a multiple sale?			
e)	Were you invited to fill out a clientele card (if applicable)?			
f)	Did the associate display enthusiasm and desire to make the sale?			
Comment:				

3. The Sales Transaction		N/A	Yes	No
a)	Were you asked to use your Bay card or if not, were you offered an application?			
b)	Did the associate offer an extra ITEM (add-on) or SERVICE?			
c)	Was the transaction efficient?			
d)	Were you THANKED by NAME?			
e)	Were you INVITED to RETURN?			
Comment:				

4. Overall Impression		Yes	No
a)	Did the associate favorably impact your shopping experience? (Extra care given and/or extra polite)		
Comment:			

5. General Comments

6. Regional Focus Question	Yes	No

Reviewed With Sales Associate By	Date M D Y

06032   (0594)   Part 1-Employee's File   Part 2-Store Manager   Part 3-Training Dept.

Furthermore, it was felt that department heads could be more involved in sharing information with sales associates than they were currently. Department heads were generally full-time employees and were, therefore, present for most meetings where information was passed on to employees. Many sales associates, however, worked on a part-time basis and were often unable to attend these meetings. Given this, department heads were in the best position to consistently and accurately relay information from these meetings. With this information exchange in place, the Bay Kitchener would be in a better position to meet its objective of offering the best in customer service.

Sales Supervisors

Based on their job description, Sales Supervisors were responsible for all customer service activities and presentation of merchandise. As well, they were responsible for supervising sales associates and department heads in order to ensure that the Bay provided superior customer service while achieving maximum profitability. Specifically, sales supervisors were responsible for their area's discipline, training and development, scheduling, payroll and sales. Supervisors were also responsible for their own hiring.

In order for sales supervisors to be effective in their positions, they needed to spend the majority of their time managing and coaching the people working in their area. Because supervisors chose the people who worked in their area, they were more likely to do a better job of coaching and managing their team. However, supervisors were currently not completely involved in the hiring process. In the future, the Bay Kitchener wanted to provide both the opportunity and the training necessary to allow supervisors to do all of their own hiring.

Meeting the Goal

After analyzing their roles in the store, it was apparent that each of the aforementioned groups would play a unique role in meeting the goal that he had set. In order for the Bay Kitchener sales team to be ready to meet the challenge, some specific training and development had to be provided to each group of employees. As well, each group had to be motivated to work towards achieving the goal.

Training and Development

Computer Based Training (CBT) modules were one resource available to provide interactive training in spe-cific areas to any Bay employee. There were numerous courses (see Exhibit 8.14); however, not all courses were appropriate for all employees. Therefore, before anyone took a CBT course, it was important to ensure that the course would be beneficial to the employee in the role that he or she would play in achieving the goal.

Another common training practice used by the Bay was Sales Clinics. These clinics were 15–20 minute training sessions which focused on meeting a specific customer service standard. They included an introduction, a brief lecture, a role play or some other activity, and a conclusion. Generally, sales clinics were run by sales supervisors but could, theoretically, be run just as effectively by department heads.

Motivation

Management often walked around the store talking to employees on a regular basis. This practice was valuable in building good working relationships with the staff so that they felt comfortable relaying ideas, feedback or concerns. These interactions could be used to motivate employees to work towards the main objective of improved customer satisfaction.

Regarding other motivational tools, management was willing to explore any possibility if they felt that it would increase the employees' desire to offer superior customer service. They knew that empowering employees was often an effective motivator. As well, a staff room that was frequented by almost all employees and morning meetings which were attended by everyone in the store at the time seemed like opportune times to somehow motivate the employees.

The Next Step

Based on his two and a half years of experience in the same position at a different Bay store, Emree was aware that setting a goal was the first, and perhaps the easiest, step in effecting change. Some points that required consideration included:

1. Communicating the objective so that everyone supported and felt committed to the goal.
2. Determining a way to measure the employees' efforts to achieve the goal and to provide feedback to employees.
3. Devising a training and development plan that would be effective for each of the sales associates, department heads, and supervisors in meeting the goal.

Exhibit 8.14
CBT Courses

ORIENTATION COURSES	SELF-DEVELOPMENT COURSES	PRODUCT KNOWLEDGE COURSES
Corporate Perspectives (corper)	Time Management (gstimx)	Service Insurance (insur)
Designing Your Career (career)	Decision Making Skills (gsdecx)	Jewelry (jewel)
Keyboard Skills (keycbt)	Effective English for Business Writing (gsengx)	China (china)
Workplace Hazardous Material Information System (whmis)	Letter, Memo and Report Writing (gslmrx)	Communication Technology (comtec)
	Strategies for Business Writing (gsbusx)	Toys (toys)
MERCHANDISE EDUCATION	Management Performance (gsmgtx)	Sporting Goods (sports)
	Financial Skills (gsfinx)	Nursery Accessories (baby)
Retail Marketing in the Future (rtlmrk)	Dealing With Stress (stress)	Shoes (shoes)
Retail Method of Inventory (retail)	Controlling Your Time (time)	Linens (linens)
Sales Leadership (leader)		Small Appliances (small)
Merchandise Information Management (cmim)	**SUPERVISORY COURSES**	Cameras/Small Electronics (camera)
Support Departments (supdep)		Women's Fashions (wfash)
Human Resources (human)	Corporate Ethics (ethics)	Men's Fashions (shirt)
Professional Selling (sell)	Supervisory Practices Program (sppl)	Women's Fashion Accessories (wfacc)
Advanced Professional Selling (sell2)	Interviewing Skills (inview)	Electronics (elect)
Employee Development (empdev)	Presentation Skills (pres)	
Merchandise Strategy (merch)	Negotiation Skills (snegot)	**SYSTEMS COURSES**
Merchandise Perspectives (merper)	How to Answer Employee Questions (bquest)	
Customer Satisfaction (custom)	How to Coach (coach)	Electronic Mail (email)
Customer Satisfaction for Auxilliary Staff (auxcus)	How to Delegate (deleg)	Big Ticket Inventory Sales Floor Procedure (btis)
Bay Card Dollars (baydol)	How to do Perf. Appraisals (parcbt)	Basic Automated Stock Inventory Control System (basics)
Customer Refunds (refund)	Managing Employee Safeguards (bguard)	Purchase Order Inquiry (poms)
Buyer Negotiations (negot)	How to Motivate (motiv)	Purchase Order Entry System (poes)
Stock Shortage (short)		National Vendor System (msonvs)
Purchase Journal Checker (pjchec)	**OPERATIONAL COURSES**	National Stock Assortment List (nsal)
Sales Promotion (promo)		Line Budget (line)
Cheque Authorization (cheque)	Health, Safety and the Law (hslaw)	Gift Registry (regis)
Sales Associate Commission System (sacs)	Health and Safety Representative (hsrep)	Price Management (price)
	Accident Investigation (hsacc)	Managing Unit Food Cost (food)

4. Motivating each of these groups within the sales team to attain the goal.

The next step required a concrete action plan that would enable the Bay Kitchener to offer the best in customer satisfaction. Although Emree recognized that his plan would take months to implement, he wanted to complete an outline before the end of the week.

Notes

1. L. D. DiSimone, comments about 3M in "How Can Big Companies Keep the Entrepreneurial Spirit Alive?" *Harvard Business Review* (November-December 1995): 184–85, and Thomas A. Stewart, "3M Fights Back," *Fortune,* 5 February 1996, 94–99.

2. Based on John P. Kotter, *Leading Change* (Boston, Mass.: Harvard Business School Press, 1996), 18–20.

3. Laura Zinn, "Pepsi's Future Becomes Clearer," *Business Week,* 1 February 1993, 74–75; Patricia Sellers, "Pepsi Keeps on Going after No. 1," *Fortune,* 11 March 1991, 61–70.

4. David A. Nadler and Michael L. Tushman, "Organizational Frame Bending: Principles for Managing Reorientation," *Academy of Management Executive* 3 (1989): 194–204.

5. William A. Davidow and Michael S. Malone, *The Virtual Corporation* (New York: HarperBusiness, 1992); Gregory G. Dess, Abdul M. A. Rasheed, Kevin J. McLaughlin, and Richard L. Priem, "The New Corporate Architecture," *Academy of Management Executive* 9, no. 3 (1995): 7–20.

6. Barbara Ettorre, "How Motorola Closes Its Books In Two Days," *Management Review,* March 1995, 40–44.

7. Bruce Rayner, "Trial-by-Fire Transformation: An Interview with Globe Metallurgical's Arden C. Sims," *Harvard Business Review* (May–June 1992): 117–29.

8. Joseph E. McCann, "Design Principles for an Innovating Company," *Academy of Management Executive* 5 (May 1991): 76–93.

9. Richard A. Wolfe, "Organizational Innovation: Review, Critique and Suggested Research Directions," *Journal of Management Studies* 31, no. 3 (May 1994): 405–31.

10. John L. Pierce and Andre L. Delbecq, "Organization Structure, Individual Attitudes and Innovation," *Academy of Management Review* 2 (1977): 27–37; Michael Aiken and Jerald Hage, "The Organic Organization and Innovation," *Sociology* 5 (1971): 63–82.

11. Richard L. Daft, "Bureaucratic versus Nonbureaucratic Structure in the Process of Innovation and Change," in Samuel B. Bacharach, ed., *Perspectives in Organizational Sociology: Theory and Research* (Greenwich, Conn.: JAI Press, 1982), 129–66.

12. Alan D. Meyer and James B. Goes, "Organizational Assimilation of Innovations: A Multilevel Contextual Analysis," *Academy of Management Journal* 31 (1988): 897–923.

13. Richard W. Woodman, John E. Sawyer, and Ricky W. Griffin, "Toward a Theory of Organizational Creativity," *Academy of Management Review* 18 (1993): 293–321; Alan Farnham, "How to Nurture Creative Sparks," *Fortune,* 10 January 1994, 94–100.

14. Charles Matthews, "How We Changed Gear to Ride the Winds of Change," *Professional Manager* (January 1995): 6–8.

15. *Ibid.*

16. D. Bruce Merrifield, "Intrapreneurial Corporate Renewal," *Journal of Business Venturing* 8 (September 1993): 383–89; Linsu Kim, "Organizational Innovation and Structure," *Journal of Business Research* 8 (1980): 225–45; Tom Burns and G. M. Stalker, *The Management of Innovation* (London: Tavistock Publications, 1961).

17. James Q. Wilson, "Innovation in Organization: Notes toward a Theory," in James D. Thompson, ed., *Approaches to Organizational Design* (Pittsburgh: University of Pittsburgh Press, 1966), 193–218.

18. J. C. Spender and Eric H. Kessler, "Managing the Uncertainties of Innovation: Extending Thompson (1967)," *Human Relations* 48, no. 1 (1995): 35–56; Robert B. Duncan, "The Ambidextrous Organization: Designing Dual Structures for Innovation," in Ralph H. Killman, Louis R. Pondy, and Dennis Slevin, eds., *The Management of Organization,* vol. 1 (New York: North-Holland, 1976), 167–88.

19. James B. Treece, "Improving the Soul of an Old Machine," *Business Week,* 25 October 1993, 134–36.

20. Edward F. McDonough III and Richard Leifer, "Using Simultaneous Structures to Cope with Uncertainty," *Academy of Management Journal* 26 (1983): 727–35.

21. John McCormick and Bill Powell, "Management for the 1990s," *Newsweek,* 25 April 1988, 47–48.

22. Eric Schine, "Out at the Skunk Works, the Sweet Smell of Success," *Business Week,* 26 April 1993, 101.

23. Brenton R. Schlender, "Apple Computer Tries to Achieve Stability by Remaining Creative," *Wall Street Journal,* 16 July 1987, 1, 21.

24. Paul S. Adler, Barbara Goldoftas, and David I. Levine, "Flexibility Versus Efficiency? A Case Study of Model Changeovers in the Toyota Production System" (Working Paper, School of Business Administration, University of Southern California, Los Angeles, 1996).

25. Judith R. Blau and William McKinley, "Ideas, Complexity, and Innovation," *Administrative Science Quarterly* 24 (1979): 200–19.

26. Rosabeth Moss Kanter, Jeffrey North, Lisa Richardson, Cynthia Ingols, and Joseph Zolner, "Engines of Progress: Designing and Running Entrepreneurial Vehicles in Established Companies: Raytheon's New Product Center, 1969–1989," *Journal of Business Venturing* 6 (March 1991): 145–63.

27. Rosabeth Moss Kanter, Lisa Richardson, Jeffrey North, and Erika Morgan, "Engines of Progress: Designing and Running Entrepreneurial Vehicles in Established Companies: The New Venture Process at Eastman Kodak, 1983–1989," *Journal of Business Venturing* 6 (January 1991): 63–82; Gene Bylinsky, "The New Look at America's Top Lab," *Fortune,* 1 February 1988, 60–64.

28. Daniel F. Jennings and James R. Lumpkin, "Functioning Modeling Corporate Entrepreneurship: An Empirical Integrative Analysis," *Journal of Management* 15 (1989): 485–502.

29. Jane M. Howell and Christopher A. Higgins, "Champions of Technology Innovation," *Administrative Science Quarterly* 35 (1990): 317–41; Jane M. Howell and Christopher A. Higgins, "Champions of Change: Identifying, Understanding, and Supporting Champions of Technology Innovations," *Organizational Dynamics* (Summer 1990): 40–55.

30. Thomas J. Peters and Robert H. Waterman, Jr., *In Search of Excellence* (New York: Harper & Row, 1982).

31. *Ibid.,* p. 205.

32. Peter J. Frost and Carolyn P. Egri, "The Political Process of Innovation," in L. L. Cummings and Barry M. Staw, eds., *Research in Organizational Behavior,* vol. 13 (New York: JAI Press, 1991), 229–95; Jay R. Galbraith, "Designing the Innovating Organization," *Organizational Dynamics* (Winter 1982): 5–25; Marsha Sinatar, "Entrepreneurs, Chaos, and Creativity—Can Creative People Really Survive Large Company Structure?" *Sloan Management Review* (Winter 1985): 57–62.

33. "Black & Decker Inventory Makes Money for Firm by Just Not 'Doing the Neat Stuff,'" *Houston Chronicle,* 25 December 1987, sec. 3, p. 2.

34. Frost and Egri, "The Political Process of Innovation."

35. Christopher Power with Kathleen Kerwyn, Ronald Grover, Keith Alexander, and Robert D. Hof, "Flops," *Business Week,* 16 August 1993, 76–82; Modesto A. Maidique and Billie Jo Zirger, "A Study of Success and Failure in Product Innovation: The Case of the U.S. Electronics Industry," *IEEE Transactions in Engineering Management* 31 (November 1984): 192–203; Edwin Mansfield, J. Rapaport, J. Schnee, S. Wagner, and M. Hamburger, Research and Innovation in Modern Corporations (New York: Norton, 1971); Antonio J. Bailetti and Paul F. Litva, "Integrating Customer Requirements into Product Designs," *Journal of Product Innovation Management* (1995): 12: 3–15.

36. Shona L. Brown and Kathleen M. Eisenhardt, "Product Development: Past Research, Present Findings, and Future Directions," *Academy of Management Review* 20, no. 2 (1995): 343–78; F. Axel Johne and Patricia A. Snelson, "Success Factors in Product Innovation: A Selective Review of the Literature," *Journal of Product Innovation Management* 5 (1988): 114–28; Science Policy Research Unit, University of Sussex, *Success and Failure in Industrial Innovation* (London: Centre for the Study of Industrial Innovation, 1972).

37. Jerry Jakubobics, "Rising Stars in Toys and Togs," *Management Review* (May 1987): 19–21.

38. Amal Kumar Naj, "GE's Latest Invention: A Way to Move Ideas from Lab to Market," *Wall Street Journal,* 14 June 1990, A1, A9; Dora Jones Yang, "Boeing Knocks Down the Walls between the Dreamers and the Doers," *Business Week,* 28 October 1991, 120–21.

39. Shona L. Brown and Kathleen M. Eisenhardt, "Product Development: Past Research, Present Findings, and Future Directions," *Academy of Management Review* 20, no. 2 (1995): 343–78; Dan Dimancescu and Kemp Dwenger, "Smoothing the Product Development Path," *Management Review* (January 1996): 36–41.

40. Ira Sager, "The Man Who's Rebooting IBM's PC Business," *Business Week,* 24 July 1995, 68–72.

41. Kathleen M. Eisenhardt and Behnam N. Tabrizi, "Accelerating Adaptive Processes: Product Innovation in the Global Computer Industry," *Administrative Science Quarterly* 40 (1995): 84–110.

42. George Stalk, Jr., "Time and Innovation," *Canadian Business Review,* Autumn 1993, 15–18.

43. Marshall Loeb, "Empowerment That Pays Off," *Fortune,* 20 March 1995, 145–46.

44. Robert D. Hof, "From Dinosaur to Gazelle: HP's Evolution Was Painful but Necessary," *Business Week/Reinventing America,* 1992, 65; Karne Bronikowski, "Speeding New Products to Market," *Journal of Business Strategy* (September–October 1990): 34–37; Brian Dumaine, "How Managers Can Succeed through Speed," *Fortune,* 13 February 1989, 54–59; Otis Port, Zachary Schiller, and Resa W. King, "A Smarter Way to Manufacture," *Business Week,* 30 April 1990, 110–17; Tom Peters, "Time-Obsessed Competition," *Management Review* (September 1990): 16–20.

45. Dan Dimancescu and Kemp Dwenger, "Smoothing the Product Development Path," *Management Review,* January 1996, 36–41.

46. Jeffrey A. Trachtenberg, "How Philips Flubbed Its U.S. Introduction of Electronic Product," *Wall Street Journal,* 28 June 1996, A1.

47. Raymond E. Miles, Henry J. Coleman, Jr., and W. E. Douglas Creed, "Keys to Success in Corporate Redesign," *California Management Review* 37, no. 3 (Spring 1995): 128–45.

48. Fariborz Damanpour and William M. Evan, "Organizational Innovation and Performance: The Problem of 'Organizational Lag,'" *Administrative Science Quarterly,* 29 (1984): 392–409; David J. Teece, "The Diffusion of an Administrative Innovation," *Management Science* 26 (1980): 464–70; John R. Kimberly and Michael J. Evaniski, "Organizational Innovation: The Influence of Individual, Organizational and Contextual Factors on Hospital Adoption of Technological and Administrative Innovation," *Academy of Management Journal* 24 (1981): 689–713; Michael K. Moch and Edward V. Morse, "Size, Centralization, and Organizational Adoption of Innovations," *American Sociological Review* 42 (1977): 716–25; Mary L. Fennell, "Synergy, Influence, and Information in the Adoption of Administrative Innovation," *Academy of Management Journal* 27 (1984): 113–29.

49. Richard L. Daft, "A Dual-Core Model of Organizational Innovation," *Academy of Management Journal* 21 (1978): 193–210.

50. Daft, "Bureaucratic versus Nonbureaucratic Structure"; Robert W. Zmud, "Diffusion of Modern Software Practices: Influence of Centralization and Formalization," *Management Science* 28 (1982): 1421–31.

51. Daft, "A Dual-Core Model of Organizational Innovation"; Zmud, "Diffusion of Modern Software Practices."

52. Fariborz Damanpour, "The Adoption of Technological, Administrative, and Ancillary Innovations: Impact of Organizational Factors," *Journal of Management* 13 (1987): 675–88.

53. Mark Landler with Ronald Grover, "Aetna's Heavy Ax," *Business Week,* 14 February 1994, 32.

54. Gregory H. Gaertner, Karen N. Gaertner, and David M. Akinnusi, "Environment, Strategy, and the Implementation of Administrative Change: The Case of Civil Service Reform," *Academy of Management Journal* 27 (1984): 525–43.

55. Claudia Bird Schoonhoven and Mariann Jelinek, "Dynamic Tension in Innovative, High Technology Firms: Managing Rapid Technology Change through Organization Structure," in Mary Ann Von Glinow and Susan Albers Mohrman, eds., *Managing Complexity in High Technology Organizations* (New York: Oxford University Press, 1990), 90–118.

56. Lawrence M. Fisher, "Imposing a Hierarchy on a Gaggle of Techies," *New York Times,* 29 November 1992, F4.

57. David Ulm and James K. Hickel, "What Happens after Restructuring?" *Journal of Business Strategy* (July–August 1990): 37–41; John L. Sprague, "Restructuring and Corporate Renewal: A Manager's Guide," *Management Review* (March 1989): 34–36.

58. Benson L. Porter and Warrington S. Parker, Jr., "Culture Change," *Human Resource Management* 31 (Spring–Summer 1992): 45–67.

59. Anne B. Fisher, "Making Change Stick," *Fortune,* 17 April 1995, 122.

60. *Ibid.*

61. Ron Winslow, "Healthcare Providers Try Industrial Tactics to Reduce Their Costs," *Wall Street Journal,* 3 November 1993, A1, A16.

62. Jeremy Main, "How to Steal the Best Ideas Around," *Fortune,* 19 October 1992, 102–06.

63. W. Warner Burke, *Organization Development: A Process of Learning and Changing*, 2nd ed. (Reading, Mass.: Addison-Wesley, 1994).

64. Michael Beer and Elisa Walton, "Developing the Competitive Organization: Interventions and

Strategies," *American Psychologist* 45 (February 1990): 154–61.

65. Joseph Weber, "Letting Go Is Hard to Do," *Business Week/Enterprise,* 1993, 218–19.

66. David A. Nadler, *Feedback and Organizational Development: Using Data-based Methods* (Reading, Mass.: Addison-Wesley, 1977), 5–8.

67. Patrick Flanagan, "The ABCs of Changing Corporate Culture," *Management Review* (July 1995): 57–61.

68. Wendell L. French and Cecil H. Bell, Jr., *Organization Development* (Englewood Cliffs, N.J.: Prentice-Hall, 1978), 117–29.

69. Paul F. Buller, "For Successful Strategic Change: Blend OD Practices with Strategic Management," *Organizational Dynamics* (Winter 1988): 42–55.

70. Jyotsna Sanzgiri and Jonathan Z. Gottlieb, "Philosophic and Pragmatic Influences on the Practice of Organization Development, 1950–2000," *Organizational Dynamics* (Autumn 1992): 57–69.

71. John P. Kotter, *Leading Change* (Boston, Mass.: Harvard Business School Press, 1996); Paul Strebel, "Why Do Employees Resist Change?" *Harvard Business Review* (May-June 1996): 86–92; Michael Beer and Russell A. Eisenstat, "Developing an Organization Capable of Implementing Strategy and Learning," *Human Relations* 49, no. 5 (1996): 597–619.

72. Ronald Recardo, Kathleen Molloy, and James Pellegrino, "How the Learning Organization Manages Change," *National Productivity Review* (Winter 1995/96): 7–13.

73. Based on Daryl R. Conner, *Managing at the Speed of Change* (New York: Villard Books, 1992), 146–160.

74. Based on Carol A. Beatty and John R. M. Gordon, "Barriers to the Implementation of CAD/CAM Systems," *Sloan Management Review* (Summer 1988): 25–33.

75. Michael Aiken, Samuel B. Bacharach, and Lawrence J. French, "Organizational Structure, Work Process and Proposal-Making in Administrative Bureaucracies," *Academy of Management Journal* 23 (1980): 631–52; Gerald Zaltman, Robert Duncan, and Jonny Holbek, *Innovations and Organizations* (New York: Wiley, 1973), 55–58.

76. Gregory A. Patterson, "Land's End Kicks Out Modern New Managers, Rejecting a Makeover," *Wall Street Journal*, 3 April 1995, A1, A6.

77. Richard L. Daft and Selwyn W. Becker, *Innovation in Organizations* (New York: Elsevier, 1978); John P. Kotter and Leonard A. Schlesinger, "Choosing Strategies for Change," *Harvard Business Review* 57 (1979): 106–14.

78. Everett M. Rogers and Floyd Shoemaker, *Communication of Innovations: A Cross Cultural Approach,* 2d ed. (New York: Free Press, 1971); Stratford P. Sherman, "Eight Big Masters of Innovation," *Fortune,* 15 October 1984, 66–84.

79. Peter Richardson and D. Keith Denton, "Communicating Change," *Human Resource Management* 35, no. 2 (Summer 1996): 203–16.

80. Philip H. Mirvis, Amy L. Sales, and Edward J. Hackett, "The Implementation and Adoption of New Technology in Organizations: The Impact on Work, People, and Culture," *Human Resource Management* 30 (Spring 1991): 113–39; Arthur E. Wallach, "System Changes Begin in the Training Department," *Personnel Journal* 58 (1979): 846–48, 872; Paul R. Lawrence, "How to Deal with Resistance to Change," *Harvard Business Review* 47 (January–February 1969): 4–12, 166–76.

81. Dexter C. Dunphy and Doug A. Stace, "Transformational and Coercive Strategies for Planned Organizational Change: Beyond the O. D. Model," *Organizational Studies* 9 (1988): 317–34; Kotter and Schlesinger, "Choosing Strategies for Change."

82. "How Chesebrough-Ponds Put Nail Polish in a Pen," *Business Week,* 8 October 1984: 196–200.

83. Richard L. Daft and Patricia J. Bradshaw, "The Process of Horizontal Differentiation: Two Models," *Administrative Science Quarterly* 25 (1980): 441–56; Alok K. Chakrabrati, "The Role of Champion in Product Innovation," *California Management Review* 17 (1974): 58–62.

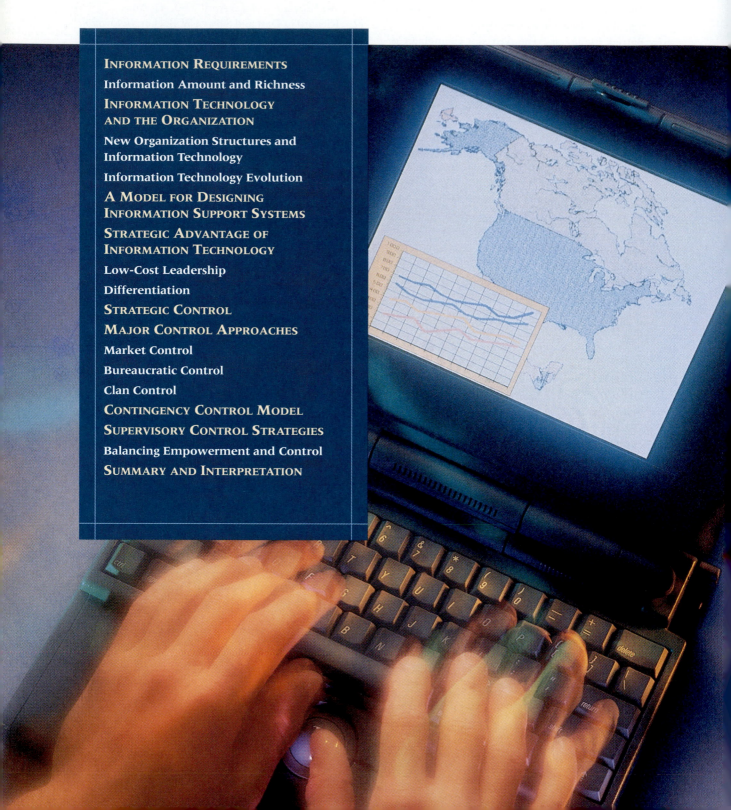

chapter nine

Information Technology and Organizational Control

KPMG Peat Marwick

When KPMG Peat Marwick consultants go to a client's office, they take the knowledge and experience of seventy-five thousand KPMG professionals with them. The company's computer system, called Knowledge Manager, gives employees access to detailed information about client experiences, proposals, résumés, methodologies, best practices, vendors, and more. In addition, a feature called Help Wanted allows a consultant to post a request for help on a particular project and receive immediate feedback from consultants around the world.

In a business where knowledge is everything, the ability to rapidly share information on a global scale gives Peat Marwick a competitive advantage by bringing the best ideas from all over the world to serve each individual client. The Knowledge Manager system was key to helping one consultant close a major deal with a national real estate organization. Firms that wanted to bid on the job had only two weeks to respond with a proposal. John Klaffky, a partner in Peat Marwick's Washington office, used Knowledge Manager to tap expertise worldwide, and within four days the team had put together a winning, customized proposal without ever meeting face-to-face.

At Peat Marwick, technology provides much more than a way to house data; sharing knowledge through groupware enables employees to respond to client needs better and faster. As partner Allan Frank explains it: "We're the quintessential knowledge organization. We don't sell widgets. We're the product. . . . [Knowledge Manager] is multiple pieces of information linked together with golden threads."[1]

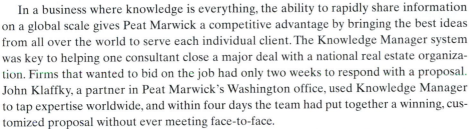

Information technology has become a crucial weapon in many companies' efforts to maintain a competitive edge in the face of increasing global competition and rising customer demands for speed, quality, and value. In knowledge-based firms like Peat Marwick, effectively using information technology is fundamental to the business. Companies in all industries are taking advantage of new information technology to improve responsiveness, decision making, and organizational control. Information technology can empower employees by giving them the complete information they need to do their jobs well and opportunities to propose new ways of doing things. It can also increase the brainpower of the organization and enable the company to move to a higher level of quality and customer service.

Purpose of This Chapter

Information and control are essential components of organizations. Managers spend 80 percent of their time actively exchanging information.[2] They need this information to hold the organization together. For example, the vertical and horizontal information linkages described in Chapter 6 are designed to provide managers with relevant data for decision making and evaluation. Moreover, control systems depend on information. The first part of this chapter examines information processing requirements in organizations and then evaluates how technology helps meet the requirements and provides a strategic advantage. Then we will examine mechanisms of organizational control and how information technology assists in management control.

INFORMATION REQUIREMENTS

Information is the lifeblood of organizations because information feeds decision making about such things as structure, technology, and innovation and because information is the lifeline to suppliers and customers. Organizations should be designed to provide both the correct amount and richness of information to managers. Before moving into information technology and design, however, one must understand what is information.

Information is that which alters or reinforces understanding, while **data** is the input of a communication channel.[3] Data is tangible and includes the number of words, telephone calls, or pages of computer printout sent or received. Data does not become information unless people use it to improve their understanding. Managers want information, not data. Organizational information systems should provide information rather than data to managers.

Information Amount and Richness

The factors that shape organizational information processing are summarized in Exhibit 9.1. Changes in the environment, large size, and nonroutine or interdependent technologies may create both higher uncertainty and higher ambiguity for managers in organizations.[4] **Uncertainty** is the absence of information; when

Exhibit 9.1

Uncertainty and Ambiguity Influence Information-Processing Amount and Channels

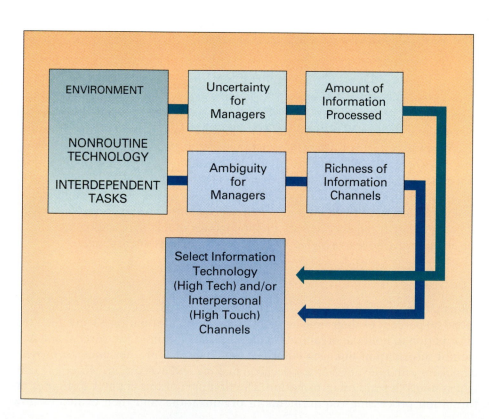

uncertainty is high, a greater amount of information has to be acquired and processed.[5] **Information amount** is the volume of data about organizational activities that is gathered and interpreted by organization participants. Under conditions of high uncertainty, data can be gathered that will answer questions and reduce uncertainty. Often this data can be provided by technology-based information systems, called **high tech** for short.

Information ambiguity means issues cannot be objectively analyzed and understood, and additional data cannot be gathered that will resolve an issue. Encountering an ambiguous situation means managers process richer information and discuss the situation with each other to create a solution, since external data does not provide an answer. Face-to-face discussion is **high touch** and enables managers to understand ill-defined issues and reach agreement to the best of their ability about how to respond.

The formal definition of **information richness** is the information carrying capacity of data.[6] Some data is highly informative and provides deeper, richer understanding to managers, especially for ambiguous issues. The communication channels used in organizations can be roughly organized into a continuum of four categories ranging from highest to lowest in richness. Channels low in richness are considered lean because they are effective for conveying a large amount of data and facts.

1. Face-to-face is the richest medium. It provides many cues, such as body language and facial expression. Immediate feedback allows understanding to be checked and corrected. This channel is best for mitigating ambiguity, enabling managers to create a shared understanding.
2. Telephone and other personal electronic media such as voice mail are next in richness, representing a relatively rich channel because feedback is fast and messages are personally focused, although visual cues are missing.
3. Written, addressed documents—such as letters, memos, notes, and faxes—are lower still in richness. Feedback is slow compared with richer media, and visual cues are minimal.
4. Written, impersonally addressed documents—including bulletins, standard computer reports, computer databases, and printouts—are the leanest channels. These documents are not amenable to feedback and are often quantitative in nature. This channel is best for conveying a large amount of precise data to numerous people.

At Connor Formed Metal Products, a job-shop manufacturer of springs and other components, computer technology is used to automatically figure price, production, and delivery answers when a customer calls with a new order. A lean channel such as impersonal computer technology is effective for this application because uncertainty is high and a substantial amount of data must be processed to calculate answers.

When a managerial problem is ambiguous, however, computer technology is not as effective as face-to-face communication. For example, a company wanted to develop a new concept for a restaurant and there was no database that would tell it which concept would succeed. The response was to pick a date or a place as a restaurant theme and to form a team of experts to *create* a solution. The team included chefs, architects, designers, and artists. The group stayed focused on this issue and brainstormed for several days until they created all of the details for the restaurant. The result, Ed Debevic's, has been a smashing success in Beverly Hills and Chicago.[7]

In today's global business world, face-to-face communication may not always be possible. New forms of communication such as videoconferencing and groupware, which enable colleagues around the world to share information and ideas, are increasingly and effectively being used for ambiguous problems.

INFORMATION TECHNOLOGY AND THE ORGANIZATION

Recall from Chapter 4 that advanced information technology—including executive information systems, groupware, and workflow automation—has impact on organization structure. We will first examine this impact on structure and then discuss how information systems have gradually evolved toward a variety of applications at all levels in organizations.

New Organization Structures and Information Technology

An important aspect of organizational structure is the way in which the parts of an organization communicate and coordinate with one another and with other organizations.[8] As we discussed in previous chapters, vertical linkages coordinate activities between the top and bottom of the organization, while horizontal linkages are used to coordinate activities across departments. Advances in information technology can reduce the need for middle managers and administrative support staff, resulting in leaner organizations with fewer hierarchical levels. In some organizations, such as Microsoft and Andersen Consulting, front-line employees communicate directly with top managers through e-mail. Information technology can also provide stronger linkages across departments and plays a significant role in the shift to horizontal forms of organizing. Coordination no longer depends on physical proximity; teams of workers from various functions can communicate and collaborate electronically.

New technology enables the electronic communication of richer, more complex information and removes the barriers of time and distance that have traditionally defined organization structure. A special kind of team, the virtual team, uses computer technology to tie together geographically distant members working toward a common goal. Virtual teams can be formed within an organization whose plants and offices are scattered across the country or around the world. Whirlpool Corp.'s North American Appliance Group in Evansville, Indiana, used a virtual team made up of members from the United States, Brazil, and Italy to develop its chlorofluorocarbon-free refrigerator. A company may also use virtual teams in partnership with suppliers or even competitors to pull together the best minds to complete a project or speed a new product to market.[9]

An organizational structure that takes the virtual approach a step further is the network, described in Chapter 7. Key activities are performed by a headquarters organization, with other functions outsourced to separate companies or individuals connected electronically to the central office. The speed and ease of electronic communication makes networking a viable option for companies looking for ways to keep costs low but expand activities or market visibility. Nu Skin International's visionary use of information technology helped the company grow from zero to $500 million in sales in a decade.

Nu Skin International

In the mid-1980s, Nu Skin began with a line of skin and hair care products made by an Arizona company and hand-spooned by the three founders into used jars and containers. Today, the company has $500 million in sales, has added a division with vitamin supplements, nutrition bars, and a sports drink, and has expanded into Canada, Hong Kong, Taiwan, Australia, New Zealand, Japan, and Mexico.

Advanced information technology supports the far-flung marketing and distribution network that made that growth possible. Each day, detailed distributor and sales order information pours into Nu Skin's Provo, Utah, headquarters from every corner of the globe via satellite and fiber optics. The company's computer calculates commissions for each of the 250,000 distributors and transmits results back to each market, where checks are cut in the local currency. So that distributors can easily access needed information, Nu Skin invested in a software application that translates screen prompts into each country's native language.

The technological infrastructure enables Nu Skin to open a new market in just ninety days, and insiders predict the company will be in at least six new countries within the next three years.[10]

Nu Skin's rapid international growth depended heavily on advanced information technology, which enables creative forms of organizing and communicating not previously possible. Almost every organization today uses some level of information technology to support its activities and enhance vertical and horizontal coordination. The following section examines the specific evolution of information technology applications within organizations.

Information Technology Evolution

The evolution of information technology is illustrated in Exhibit 9.2. First-line management is typically characterized with well-defined, programmed problems about operational issues and past events. Top management, by contrast, is concerned with uncertain, ambiguous issues, such as strategy, planning, and other nonprogrammed events, about which decisions must be made. As the complexity of computer-based information technology has increased, applications have grown to include nonprogrammed issues at top management levels.[11]

The initial applications were based on the notion of machine room efficiency—that is, current tasks could be performed more efficiently with the use of computer technology. The goal was to reduce labor cost by having computers take over some tasks. These systems became known as **transaction processing systems** (TPS), which automate the organization's routine, day-to-day business transactions. Routine transactions include sending bills to customers, depositing checks in the bank, or placing orders. For example, American Airlines introduced Sabre in the 1960s to keep track of customer reservations, by far its biggest set of daily transactions.

In the next stage, technology became a business resource. Through the application of management information systems and decision support systems, managers had tools to improve performance of departments and the organization as a whole. As databases accumulated from transaction processing systems, managers began envisioning ways the computer could help them make important decisions by using data in summary form.

A **management information system** (MIS) is a system that generally contains comprehensive data about all transactions within an organization. MISs can

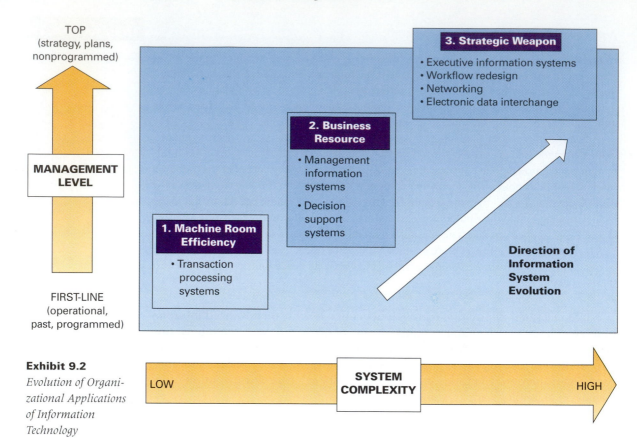

TOP
(strategy, plans,
nonprogrammed)

MANAGEMENT
LEVEL

FIRST-LINE
(operational,
past, programmed)

3. Strategic Weapon
• Executive information systems
• Workflow redesign
• Networking
• Electronic data interchange

2. Business Resource
• Management information systems
• Decision support systems

1. Machine Room Efficiency
• Transaction processing systems

Direction of Information System Evolution

LOW   **SYSTEM COMPLEXITY**   HIGH

Exhibit 9.2
Evolution of Organizational Applications of Information Technology

provide data to help managers make decisions and perform their management functions. However, while these vast, comprehensive databases are vital to businesses, they do not present information in the fast and flexible ways most managers regularly need. An **executive information system** (EIS) is a higher-level application because it focuses on information as opposed to data: this interactive system helps top managers monitor and control organizational operations by processing and presenting data in usable form. A **decision support system** (DSS) provides specific benefits to managers at all levels of the organization because it enables them to retrieve, manipulate, and display information from integrated databases for making specific decisions.[12] For example, Frito-Lay, Inc. uses information technology so well that the DSS has become a strategic weapon, enabling the company to gain market share. Frito-Lay has developed a huge database that draws on information fed into it by ten thousand salespeople reporting each day with handheld computers on about one hundred product lines selling in four hundred thousand stores. This database builds a powerful decision support system for managers. In one case, sales were observed to be slumping in San Antonio and Houston, and an analysis of data for the south Texas area showed that something was clearly wrong. Executives learned that a competitor had introduced a white-corn tortilla chip that was winning shelf space and market share. Having identified the problem, Frito-Lay introduced within three months a white-corn version of Tostitos and soon won back its market share.[13]

Using information technology, such as executive information systems, as a strategic weapon is the highest level of application (Exhibit 9.2). Workflow redesign, networks, and electronic data interchange systems are other ways organizations use information technology in their strategy. **Networking,** which links computers within or between organizations and enables coworkers within a business or even in separate companies to share information and cooperate on projects, is rapidly becoming a primary strategic weapon for many companies.

Networks take many forms. Companies can establish their own local area network (LAN) or wide area network (WAN) or communicate directly via the Internet, an amorphous, rapidly growing web of corporate, educational, and research computer networks around the world. For Sterling Software, Inc., a Dallas software maker, the Internet enables thirty-six hundred employees across seventy-five worldwide offices to keep in touch with each other, with headquarters, and with customers.[14] The fastest growing form of corporate networking is called the **intranet**, a private internal network that uses the infrastructure and standards of the Internet and the World Wide Web but is cordoned off from the public with the use of software programs known as *firewalls*.[15] The New Paradigm box describes intranets in more detail.

Before turning to a further discussion of the strategic use of information technology, let's explore a model for tailoring information support systems to organizational needs.

A MODEL FOR DESIGNING INFORMATION SUPPORT SYSTEMS

Organizations can be designed to provide the right kind of information to managers. So can information support systems. Frito-Lay enjoys success with its decision support system because it applied technology to measurable, analyzable problems. Some problems, especially at the top management level, are handled by face-to-face discussions. The application of MIS, EIS, and DSS to the right task is essential for its successful application.

A framework for applying information concepts to organizational departments is given in Exhibit 9.3. This framework is based upon Perrow's concept of department technology, which was discussed in Chapter 4. Technology represents the pattern of issues and tasks performed in different parts of the organization. Exhibit 9.3 identifies the two relationships that determine information requirements based on the type of task performed by a department.

1. When task variety is high, problems are frequent, wide ranging, and unpredictable. Uncertainty is greater, so the amount of information needed also will be greater. Employees spend more time processing information, and they need access to high tech sources and large databases. When variety is low, the amount of information processed is less.[16]
2. When tasks are unanalyzable and hence lead to ambiguous problems, employees need rich, high touch information.[17] Face-to-face discussions and telephone conversations transmit multiple information cues in a short time. When tasks are simple, managers will use lean media. Then the underlying problem is clear, so only simple, written or computer-based information is needed.

The implication of these relationships is reflected in the framework in Exhibit 9.3. Organization structure and information support systems should be designed

The New Paradigm

Information on Demand—The Intranet

Squirrels are wreaking havoc on phone lines in Golden, Colorado. As soon as US West repairmen arrive on the scene, they begin sharing information and a map of the damage with headquarters in Denver via the company's internal Web site. Meanwhile, at the Denver office, a project manager is clicking onto US West's lab page to "test drive" software being designed for a new service she wants to offer, while a sales consultant checks the on-line newsletter for the day's updates. These US West employees, as well as fifteen thousand others, rely on the company's network, known as Global Village, all day long to share information, collaborate on projects, and give their customers the best possible service.

Businesses of every kind have used the World Wide Web to get information to customers, partners, or investors. Now, companies as diverse as General Electric, Chevron, Levi Strauss, Pfizer, and Turner Broadcasting are finding that the World Wide Web also offers an inexpensive yet extremely powerful way to improve internal communications and unlock hidden information. By setting up internal webs that use the infrastructure of the Internet, with software to prevent unauthorized access by the general public, companies are transforming the way they view and use information. These *intranets* present information in the same way to every computer, pulling all the varied computers, software, and databases of the company into a single system, enabling employees to find information wherever it resides. Scientists working in fields such as genetics and biotechnology credit intranets with allowing them to

share information with colleagues and rapidly sift through volumes of data that might have taken days to find in the past. In addition, intranets allow workers to venture out onto the Internet for even more information.

So far, most intranet Web sites are used for basic information sharing, such as job listings, training manuals, phone directories, and benefits information. However, more companies are discovering how intranets can provide a strategic advantage by enabling unprecedented levels of collaboration. The most advanced intranets are even being linked to the proprietary systems that govern a company's business functions. For example, the web at US West will soon make it easy for a sales rep to immediately provide a customer with a service such as call waiting.

Intranets are likely to replace traditional networking and groupware in most large corporations that operate on a global scale. In addition, small companies are drawn to intranets because they are less expensive and time-consuming than setting up and training for traditional networks. According to John Swartzendruber, an information consultant who linked three thousand of pharmaceutical giant Eli Lilly's employees in two dozen countries, "Intranets aren't the Holy Grail of computing. But for now, they're hard to beat."

Source: Amy Cortese, "Here Comes the Intranet," *Business Week,* 26 February 1996, 76–84; Alison L. Sprout, "The Internet Inside Your Company," *Fortune,* 27 November 1995, 161–168.

---

to provide department managers and employees with the appropriate amount and richness of information. *Routine* activities have only a few problems, which are well understood. For such activities, the amount of information can be small and directed toward clear applications. Written procedures and economic order quantity (EOQ) reorder systems for inventory control are examples of information support used for a routine task.

Engineering tasks have high variety, which increases the demand for information. With these tasks, managers and employees typically need access to large databases and high tech decision support systems. A large information base is appropriate. The huge number of engineering blueprints that support an engineering project is an example of a large database that can be stored on a computer. So is the large database made available to airline reservation agents.

Exhibit 9.3   *Task Characteristics and Information Processing Requirements*

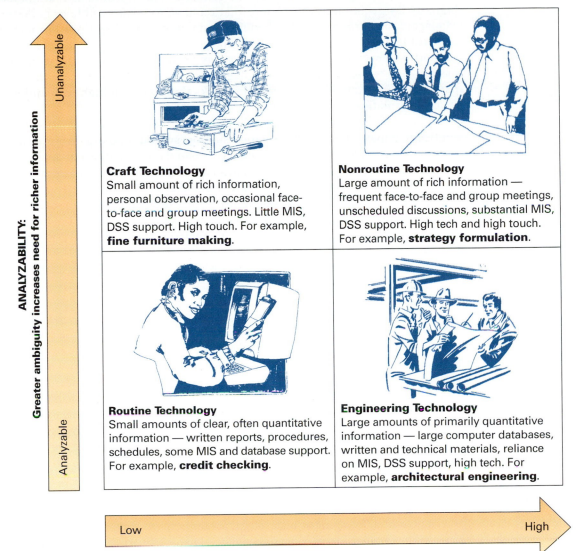

ANALYZABILITY:
Greater ambiguity increases need for richer information

Unanalyzable

Craft Technology
Small amount of rich information, personal observation, occasional face-to-face and group meetings. Little MIS, DSS support. High touch. For example, **fine furniture making**.

Nonroutine Technology
Large amount of rich information — frequent face-to-face and group meetings, unscheduled discussions, substantial MIS, DSS support. High tech and high touch. For example, **strategy formulation**.

Routine Technology
Small amounts of clear, often quantitative information — written reports, procedures, schedules, some MIS and database support. For example, **credit checking**.

Engineering Technology
Large amounts of primarily quantitative information — large computer databases, written and technical materials, reliance on MIS, DSS support, high tech. For example, **architectural engineering**.

Analyzable

Low   High

TASK VARIETY:
Greater uncertainty increases need for more information

Source: Adapted from Richard L. Daft and Norman B. Macintosh, "A New Approach to Design and Use of Management Information," *California Management Review* 21 (1978): 82–92. Copyright © 1978 by the Regents of the University of California. Reprinted by permission of the Regents.

Craft departments require a different form of information. Here, task variety is not high, but problems are ambiguous and hard to analyze. Problems are handled on the basis of high touch experience and judgment. There are many intangibles, so managers need rich information. An example of a craft organization is a psychiatric care unit. The process of therapeutic change is not well understood. MIS information about costs and benefits cannot be directly related to the healing process. When psychiatrists are unclear about an issue, they discuss it face-to-face among themselves to reach a solution.

Nonroutine departments are characterized by many problems that are ambiguous. Large amounts of rich information have to be accessible or gathered. Managers spend time in both scheduled and unscheduled meetings. For technical problems in these departments, management information and decision support systems are valuable. Managers may need to interact directly with databases to ask "what if" questions. Strategic planning units and basic research departments are examples of nonroutine tasks that use both high tech and high touch information.

The underlying tasks determine the pattern of issues and information needs confronting managers. The information support systems and organization structure should provide information to managers based on the pattern of decisions to be made. More information should be available when tasks have many problems, and richer information should be provided when tasks are poorly defined and unanalyzable. When information systems are poorly designed, problem solving and decision processes will be ineffective, and managers may not understand why.

The following case illustrates how an organization can be designed to provide the correct information for engineering tasks.

In Practice 9.2

Ingersoll Milling Machine Co.

Ingersoll Milling is an extraordinarily successful machine tool builder. It makes large-scale custom machines and machining systems for special applications, such as a $50 million system for computer-controlled auto assembly recently ordered by General Motors. Ingersoll is the only company in the industry that eschews government protection. The boss believes companies that can't handle foreign competition should be allowed to go under.

The company's success is due to supersophisticated planning and information systems that are nearly paperless. Ingersoll was first in the industry to use computers. Designers draw blueprints on computer screens rather than on drafting tables. Programmers write instructions to accompany a blueprint, and the computer generates a tape with those instructions. The tape is used to control machinery that shapes the metal to build the machine. Ingersoll builds some of the most sophisticated production lines in the world, including highly computerized systems for GE and Ford.

Ingersoll's smart move was to get rid of drafting tables and everything else that could be computerized. Everyone at Ingersoll speaks the same computer language. All three U.S. divisions are linked to a common computer database. Every department—accounting, engineering, shipping, purchasing—in each division exchanges design, product, and financial information. When an engineer designs a cutting tool, the computer generates a list of materials needed, which goes to purchasing. The next step is to computerize Ingersoll's tool sales force. Salespeople will use briefcase terminals to call in specifications from the field. The central computer will then instruct the machinery to turn out an order.

Ingersoll's computer technology is so sophisticated that other machine tool builders are barely able to compete. Boeing and other aerospace companies prefer Ingersoll because the company is efficient and accurate. The specialty orders that carry big profits come Ingersoll's way. Ingersoll's huge but highly quantified information system is perfectly tailored to the very complicated yet analyzable task of designing sophisticated machine tool systems.[18]

Large databases are appropriate when a task is well understood but is complex and has to answer many questions. For Ingersoll, a huge amount of computer-based data was just right. Competitors in the machine tool industry that used seat-of-the-pants guesswork never achieved the same efficiency. Quantitative computer-based information is not suitable for many ambiguous tasks, however, such as those associated with top management. However, information technology in recent years has been adapted to a strategic role at the top of organizations as illustrated in Exhibit 9.2.

Studies have shown that the appropriate use of information technology, such as executive information systems and decision support systems, can improve the efficiency and effectiveness of the strategic decision-making process. Information technology enhances the ability of top managers to identify problems as well as the speed at which they generate solutions.[19]

STRATEGIC ADVANTAGE OF INFORMATION TECHNOLOGY

Managers are increasingly considering the role of information management in their constant search for the right combination of strategy, motivation, technology, and business design to maintain a competitive edge.[20]

Recall from Chapter 2 that two of the competitive strategies firms can adopt are *low-cost leadership* and *differentiation*. The low-cost leader incurs low production costs and can price its product or service offerings low enough so it makes a profit while rival firms are sustaining losses. Differentiation means a firm offers a unique product or service based on product features, superb service, or rapid delivery. An important question for top managers is whether information technology can be used to achieve cost leadership or differentiation. Information technology might be used to create barriers to entry for new firms, high product switching costs for competitors, or efficient relationships with suppliers that can alter competitive balance with respect to cost leadership or differentiation.[21]

The American Airlines Sabre system, originally installed to keep track of reservations, evolved into a strategic weapon. More than 85,000 Sabre terminals have been installed at travel agencies in 47 countries, keeping track of fares and schedules for 665 airlines, 20,000 hotels, and 52 rental car companies. This information service differentiates American and is an enormous profit maker. It has also increased American's efficiency by enabling it to load as many as 1.5 million new fares daily to meet competition and to make precise calculations for flight plans, aircraft weight, fuel requirements, and takeoff power settings for 2,300 American flights each day.[22]

Other organizations find other ways of using information technology for strategic advantage. Wal-Mart's pioneering use of computer networks to conduct business electronically squeezed time and costs out of unwieldy supply chains and made the company the largest retailer in the world. Wal-Mart uses technology to convert information into action almost immediately, keeping it a step ahead of the competition.[23]

Exhibit 9.4 lists a few ways information technology can be used to give companies a strategic edge over competitors.

Low-Cost Leadership	Differentiation
Operational efficiency	Lock in customers
Interdepartmental coordination	Customer service
Rapid resupply	Product development, market niches

Exhibit 9.4

Strategic Advantages from Information Technology

Low-Cost Leadership

Perhaps the most obvious way information technology can lower cost is through *operational efficiency;* but this means more than simply doing the same work faster. One element of operational efficiency has been the development of executive information systems, as discussed earlier in this chapter. Executive information systems use computer technology to facilitate the highest levels of strategic decision making, helping senior managers diagnose problems and develop solutions. Executive information systems can shape masses of numbers into simple, colorful charts and can be operated without in-depth computer skills. For example, the CEO of Duracell used EIS to compare the performance of hourly and salaried workforces in the United States and overseas. Within seconds, he had a crisp color table showing that U.S. workers produced more sales. Asking for more data, he discovered that salespeople overseas spent too much time calling on small stores. The EIS provided sufficient information to diagnose and solve this problem.[24]

Another way to improve efficiency is **work flow redesign**, which means reengineering (described in Chapter 7) work processes to fit new information technology rather than simply layering new computerized workflow systems on top of the old work processes.

For example, at Texas Commerce Bank, workflow redesign is part of a $42 million reengineering effort. Consumers seeking a loan used to wait at least two weeks before their applications were approved. Thanks to workflow redesign, nine out of ten customers now have their applications processed in just three hours, and rush applications are handled in as little as thirty minutes. A sophisticated computer system and workflow software routes applications for processing to whichever loan officer is available.[25] Workflow redesign of the expense report system for Xerox's fleet of service vehicles eliminated the need for eighty-five clerical workers and improved management of maintenance schedules and fuel costs, saving the company around $3 million a year. The company has gone from a completely manual system to an almost totally electronic one. According to Bob Brown, manager of vehicle fleet operations, the company is "still looking for ways to prevent sending any paper anywhere."[26]

Advances in information technology are also leading to greater *interdepartmental coordination* as well as growing linkages between organizations. Thanks to networks and intranets, boundaries between departments within organizations as well as between organizations seem to dissolve, making a division or company across the world seem as close as one down the hall. Networks allow computers to talk to one another about all aspects of business, such as customer orders, parts requirements, invoices, manufacturing dates, and market share slippage.[27]

One specific type of interorganizational linkage, **electronic data interchange** (EDI), ties businesses with suppliers. EDI, which links a computer at one company to a computer at another for the transmission of business data, such as sales statistics, without human interference, can enable businesses to achieve low-cost leadership through *rapid resupply*. One study found that the use of EDI to coordinate material movements by Chrysler assembly plants and its suppliers resulted in annual savings of about $220 million.[28] Campbell Soup Company invested $30 million to redesign its order-processing system around EDI, a move the company predicts will save $18 million a year and speed deliveries. The EDI system can detect when a customer like Flemings Co. runs low on Campbell's tomato soup, for instance, and ensure that the warehouse is restocked automatically.[29] Some large retailers with a low-cost strategy, such as Wal-Mart and JCPenney, are requiring that suppliers become EDI-capable.

Differentiation

A way to differentiate a company is to *lock in customers* with information technology. The innovator of this strategy was American Hospital Supply Corporation. Senior executives decided to give computer terminals free to hospitals around the country, linking hospital purchasers directly with AHS, enabling customers to directly place orders for any of more than 100,000 products. AHS immediately gained sales and market share at competitors' expense.[30]

Fruit of the Loom is connecting its wholesalers to the Internet at virtually no cost to them to compete with Hanes and other brands in the market for blank T-shirts sold through novelty stores and at special events. Fruit of the Loom's Activewear Online displays colorful catalogs, processes electronic orders twenty-four hours a day, and manages inventories. If a silk screener needs one thousand black T-shirts in a hurry for a Megadeth concert and the wholesaler is low, Fruit of the Loom's central warehouse can rapidly ship the shirts directly to the customer.[31]

This approach can be upgraded to electronic data interchange so supplies are reordered automatically. EDI is gradually replacing traditional paper document flows. It is estimated that by the end of the decade, at least 75 percent of all interorganization transactions will be handled via EDI, over either private networks or the Internet.[32]

Exhibit 9.5 shows how EDI can be used to connect several organizations to facilitate trade on both domestic and international levels. Companies that are not plugged into this technology will be at a competitive disadvantage.

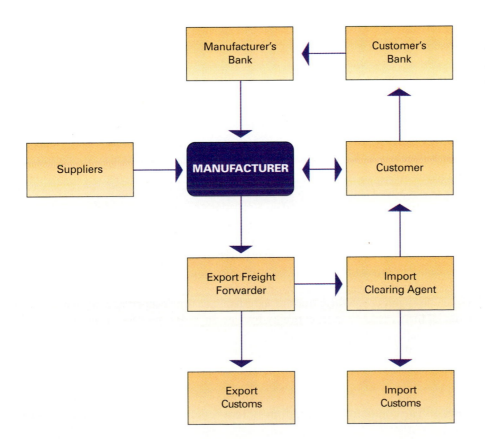

Exhibit 9.5

Electronic Data Interchange for International Transactions

Improving customer service can differentiate a company from competitors. For example, automating the sales force can dramatically reduce the time it takes to close an order as well as increase the rate of successful closes. Deere Power Systems, a division of John Deere that makes diesel engines and other heavy equipment, found that its salespeople might spend a full day logging into various computer systems and calling different departments for information before going on a call. In the meantime, competitors would step in and beat Deere to the deal. With new information technology, departments that once kept information to themselves are sharing it on a network, and a salesperson is generally able to get all the information needed for a call in half a day or less.[33]

A third dimension of differentiation is *new product development for specialized market niches*. Coleco, for example, used computers to design millions of its wildly successful Cabbage Patch dolls, each of which was unique. Moreover, many companies, like J. P. Morgan, General Electric, and Xerox, are using the resources of the Internet to spot unutilized niches, detect needs for new projects or services, learn about their competitors, and stay up-to-date on the latest technological advances.[34]

Companies constantly look for new ways to use information technology to gain a step on competitors. Trucking company Schneider National harnessed new technology to drive costs down and service quality up.

| In Practice 9.3 | *Schneider National* |

Staying on the road in the trucking industry isn't easy these days. Because of deregulation, the number of licensed interstate trucking companies has grown from seventeen thousand in 1980 to more than sixty thousand today. Increased competition has triggered expensive price wars at the same time customers are demanding better service. Schneider National pioneered the industry's use of wireless communication systems in an effort to remain competitive. The company initially invested $20 million to launch the system, including laptop computing devices and satellite dishes for each of its ten thousand trucks.

Today, more than 450 employees at Schneider's Green Bay, Wisconsin, headquarters monitor the location and status of each truck. Key pickup and delivery information, last-minute changes in orders, or warnings of dangerous driving conditions or potential traffic tie-ups can be relayed to truckers immediately by satellite. The operation runs twenty-four hours a day, every day of the year. At 8 A.M. each day, top executives meet to analyze information and reduce deadhead mileage—unproductive trips in which trucks travel without a load—and redirect traffic to pick up additional business. For example, if a portion of the western United States is shaded red on Schneider's computer map (indicating that there are too many orders and too few trucks in the area) and a portion of the southeast is shaded purple (indicating a surplus of available rigs), executives can rapidly move trucks from east to west. "Before, we didn't know where trucks were," explains Dick Ritchie, network center manager. "Now we can tell where they are within one hundred feet."

Schneider believes the effective use of information technology is the best way to survive in the highly competitive trucking industry. Each driver supervisor can manage an average of forty truckers, up from twenty-five several years ago. The advanced technology has cut internal costs as well as improved Schneider's on-time reliability from below 90 percent to about 99 percent. The company's revenues doubled, to around $1.4 billion, in the seven years since going wireless.[35]

Schneider's use of information technology also plays a role in organizational control. The company's information systems enable top managers to make effective decisions and direct activities to meet Schneider's strategic goals. A large part of organizational information processing pertains to control, a major responsibility of management to which we now turn.

STRATEGIC CONTROL

Strategic control is the overall evaluation of the strategic plan, organizational activities, and results that provides information for future action.[36] Exhibit 9.6 illustrates a simplified model of strategic control. The cycle of control includes the strategic plan, measuring production activities to determine whether they are on target, and assuring control by correcting or changing activities as needed. Note in Exhibit 9.6 that strategic control also includes the measurement of inputs to the production activity, as well as outputs, and continuous information about the external environment to determine whether the strategic plan is responding to emerging developments.

Strategic control differs from **operational control**, which is a short-term cycle that includes the four stages of target-setting, measurement of performance, comparison of performance against standards, and feedback.[37] Operational control tends to focus on a specific department or activity and to be short-term.

Strategic control typically uses both feedback and *feedforward* information. Feedback control measures outputs, and control information is fed back and compared to targets to make required changes. Feedforward control measures inputs on the front end of the process, both with respect to production activities

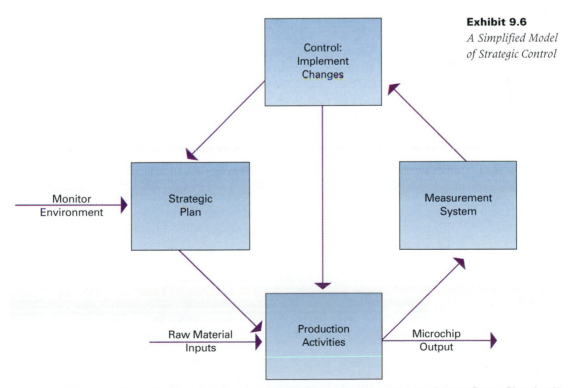

Exhibit 9.6

A Simplified Model of Strategic Control

Source: Adapted from David Asch, "Strategic Control: A Problem Looking for a Solution," *Long Range Planning* 25 (1992): 105–10.

and environmental changes that may affect strategic plans. Feedforward control enables the organization to be proactive and change plans earlier than would be possible with output data alone and before the organization gets out of alignment with external needs. Strategic control is an ongoing process that requires monitoring not only conditions within the organization but also in the external environment.

Strategic control directs the activities of the firm toward strategic objectives. For example, Frito-Lay uses the information system described earlier for strategic control. Frito-Lay establishes targets in each region of the country for snack food sales. The hand-held computers used by ten thousand salespeople provide daily information on actual sales levels. This data is compared, and feedback is used to change strategies, products, or marketing approaches to improve sales as needed. The control system reflects the strategic direction of the firm.[38]

MAJOR CONTROL APPROACHES

Managers at the top and middle levels of an organization can choose among three overall approaches for control. These approaches come from a framework for organizational control proposed by William Ouchi of the University of California at Los Angeles. Ouchi suggested three control strategies that organizations could adopt—market, bureaucratic, and clan.[39] Each form of control uses different types of information. However, all three types may appear simultaneously in an organization. The requirements for each control strategy are given in Exhibit 9.7.

Market Control

Market control occurs when price competition is used to evaluate the output and productivity of an organization. The idea of market control originated in economics.[40] A dollar price is an efficient form of control because managers can compare prices and profits to evaluate the efficiency of their corporation. Top managers nearly always use the price mechanism to evaluate performance in corporations. Corporate sales and costs are summarized in a profit-and-loss statement that can be compared against performance in previous years or with that of other corporations.

The use of market control requires that outputs be sufficiently explicit for a price to be assigned and that competition exist. Without competition, the price will not be an accurate reflection of internal efficiency. A few traditionally not-for-profit organizations are turning to market control. For example, the city of Indianapolis requires its departments to bid against private companies. When the

Exhibit 9.7

Three Organizational Control Strategies

Type	Requirements
Market	Prices, competition, exchange relationship
Bureaucracy	Rules, standards, hierarchy, legitimate authority
Clan	Tradition, shared values and beliefs, trust

Source: Based upon William G. Ouchi, "A Conceptual Framework for the Design of Organizational Control Mechanisms," *Management Science* 25 (1979): 833–48.

city's transportation department was underbid by a private company on a contract to fill potholes, the city's union workers made a counterproposal that involved eliminating most of the department's middle managers and reengineering union jobs to save money. Eighteen supervisors were laid off, costs were cut by 25 percent, and the department won the bid.[41]

Market control is used primarily at the level of the entire organization, but it also can be used in product divisions. Profit centers are self-contained product divisions, such as those described in Chapter 6. Each division contains resource inputs needed to produce a product. Each division can be evaluated on the basis of profit or loss compared with other divisions. Asea Brown Boveri (ABB), a multinational electrical contractor and manufacturer of electrical equipment, includes three different types of profit centers, all operating according to their own bottom line and all interacting through buying and selling with one another and with outside customers.[42]

Some firms even require that individual departments interact with one another at market prices—buying and selling products or services among themselves at prices equivalent to those quoted outside the firm. To make the market control system work, internal units also have the option to buy and sell with outside companies. Imperial Oil Limited of Canada (formerly Esso), transformed its R & D department into a semiautonomous profit center several years ago.

Imperial Oil Limited

In Practice 9.4

In the early 1990s, Imperial Oil's R & D was a monopoly service provider allocated an annual budget of about $45 million. Imperial felt that this method of operating gave the two hundred scientists and staff little incentive to control costs or advance quality. Today, R & D receives a much smaller budget and essentially supports itself through applied research and lab-services contracts negotiated with internal and external customers. Contracts spell out the costs of each program, analysis, or other service, and cost-conscious Imperial managers can shop for lower prices among external labs.

R & D has even introduced competition within its own small unit. For example, research teams are free to buy some lab services outside the company if they feel their own laboratories are overpriced or inefficient. However, quality and efficiency have dramatically improved at Imperial R & D, and the unit's high-quality, low-cost services are attracting a great deal of business from outside the company. Canadian companies routinely send samples of used motor oil to the R & D labs for analysis. Manufacturers use R & D to autopsy equipment failures. Vehicle makers like GM and Ford test new engines at Imperial R & D's chassis dynamometer lab. According to John Charlton, Imperial's corporate strategic planning manager, applying market control to R & D has led to an increase in the amount of work the unit does, as well as a 12 percent reduction in internal costs.[43]

Market control can only be used when the output of a company, division, or department can be assigned a dollar price and when there is competition. Companies are finding that they can apply the market control concept to internal departments such as accounting, data processing, legal departments, and information services.

The trend toward creating internal markets, such as the R & D unit at Imperial, is closely related to current trends toward outsourcing and network structures, described in Chapter 7. With outsourcing, companies farm out certain tasks to other firms that can provide high-quality services at low costs. Electronic Data Systems Corp. has taken over running the computers and communication systems for numerous companies that prefer to focus their energies on their core business and outsource the data processing. Many banks outsource the processing of credit cards to companies that can do it more cheaply. Ford Motor Company has cut costs by developing good outsourcing relationships with independent suppliers of auto parts. One survey found that about 86 percent of major corporations, including American Airlines, DuPont, Exxon, Honda, IBM, and Johnson & Johnson, now outsource some of their services.[44]

Bureaucratic Control

Bureaucratic control is the use of rules, policies, hierarchy of authority, written documentation, standardization, and other bureaucratic mechanisms to standardize behavior and assess performance. Bureaucratic control uses the bureaucratic characteristics defined by Weber and discussed in Chapter 5 on bureaucracy. The primary purpose of bureaucratic rules and procedures is to standardize and control employee behavior.

Within a large organization, thousands of work behaviors and information exchanges take place both vertically and horizontally. Rules and policies evolve through a process of trial and error to regulate these behaviors. Bureaucratic control mechanisms are used when behavior and methods of processing information are too complex or ill-defined to be controlled with a price mechanism.

Some degree of bureaucratic control is used in virtually every organization. Rules, regulations, and directives contain information about a range of behaviors. Bureaucratic mechanisms are especially valuable in not-for-profit organizations for which prices and competitive markets often do not exist.

Management Control Systems.   **Management control systems** are broadly defined as the formalized routines, reports, and procedures that use information to maintain or alter patterns in organizational activity.[45] The management information and strategic control systems discussed earlier in this chapter are critical tools to help managers control organizational operations. Control systems include the formalized information-based activities for planning, budgeting, performance evaluation, resource allocation, and employee rewards. These systems operate as feedback systems, with the targets set in advance, outcomes compared with targets, and variance reported to managers for remedial actions.[46] Advances in technology have dramatically improved the efficiency and effectiveness of these systems.

In the past, most organizations relied largely on financial accounting measures as the basis for measuring organization performance, but today's companies realize that a balanced view of both financial and operational measures is needed for successful organization control in a competitive and rapidly changing environment.[47] The four control system elements listed in Exhibit 9.8 are often considered the core of management control systems. These four elements include the budget, periodic nonfinancial statistical reports, reward systems, and standard operating procedures.[48] The management control system elements enable middle and upper management to both monitor and influence major departments.

The operating budget is used to set financial targets for the year and then report costs on a monthly or quarterly basis. Periodic statistical reports are used to evaluate and monitor nonfinancial performance. These reports typically are computer-based and may be available daily, weekly, or monthly.

Exhibit 9.8
Management Control Systems Used as Part of Bureaucratic Control

Subsystem	Content and Frequency
Budget	Financial, resource expenditures, monthly
Statistical reports	Nonfinancial outputs, weekly or monthly, often computer-based
Reward systems	Annual evaluation of managers based on department goals and performance
Operating procedures	Rules and regulations, policies that prescribe correct behavior, continuous

Source: Based on Richard L. Daft and Norman B. Macintosh, "The Nature and Use of Formal Control Systems for Management Control and Strategy Implementation," *Journal of Management* 10 (1984): 43–66.

Reward systems offer incentives for managers and employees to improve performance and meet departmental goals. Managers and superiors may sit down and evaluate how well previous goals were met, set new goals for the year, and establish rewards for meeting the new targets. Operating procedures are traditional rules and regulations. Managers use all of these systems to correct variances and bring activities back into line.

One finding from research into management control systems is that each of the four control systems focuses on a different aspect of the production process. These four systems thus form an overall management control system that provides middle managers with control information about resource inputs, process efficiency, and output.[49] Moreover, the use of and reliance on control systems depend on the strategic targets set by top management. The relationship of strategy, management control systems, and departmental activities is illustrated in Exhibit 9.9.

The budget is used primarily to allocate resource inputs. Managers use the budget for planning the future and reducing uncertainty about the availability of human and material resources needed to perform department tasks. Organizations coping with continuous change, such as those pursuing a differentiation strategy through ongoing new product development, often find that the standard annual budget is not an effective control tool because revenue and spending targets evolve so quickly. The HON Company, the largest maker of mid-priced office furniture in the United States and Canada, overcomes this problem through the use of a continuous three-month budget cycle. Quarterly budgets have become the integral planning and control device for achieving HON's strategic goals of ongoing new product and service development and rapid continuous improvement.[50]

Whereas the budget deals with resource inputs, computer-based statistical reports are used to control outputs. These reports contain data about output volume and quality and other indicators that provide feedback to middle management about departmental results. The reward system and the policies and procedures are directed at the production process. Operating procedures give explicit guidelines about appropriate behaviors. Reward systems provide incentives to meet goals and can help guide and correct employee activities. Managers also use direct supervision to keep departmental work activities within desired limits.

Exhibit 9.9

*Four Management
Control Subsystems
and Focus of Control*

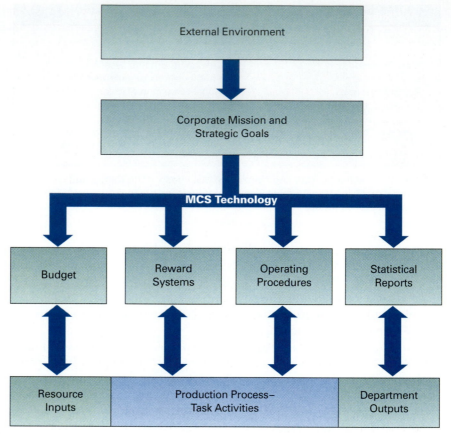

Source: Adapted from Richard L. Daft and Norman B. Macintosh, "The Nature and Use of Formal Control Systems for Management Control and Strategy Implementation," *Journal of Management* 10 (1984): 43–66.

Technology Overcontrol.   Taken together, the management control subsystems described in Exhibit 9.9 provide important information within the overall bureaucratic control framework used to monitor and influence departmental performance. However, the information technology described earlier in this chapter can be used to increase the speed and intensity of control over employees. As businesses continue to try to squeeze out more productivity in today's competitive environment, they sometimes turn to electronic technology to track workers' every move.

At Schneider National, described earlier, each truck's speed is constantly monitored by computer; if drivers stay within the speed limit, the company offers financial rewards. In addition to lowering accident rates, Schneider has cut fuel costs by preventing truckers from speeding. Some organizations have taken the use of computer control to the point of overkill, believing that carefully monitored workers will perform more efficiently. Organizations count the number of elapsed seconds per phone call, the number of keystrokes per minute, and every other measurable behavior related to the job, creating stress for employees.

Unions and employee associations are fighting back, and several organizations have reduced control and discovered that performance actually improved.[51] Canada Bell started monitoring employees in groups rather than individually, responding only if the group average fell below target levels. This has not been needed, however, because overall performance increased. Northwestern Bell and Federal Express decreased monitoring and found that productivity remained high and employee satisfaction increased. In one study, monitored service workers reported that production quantity was high but work quality was poor. Unmonitored employees reported that work quality, service, accuracy, and teamwork were more important than work quantity. On average, the unmonitored workers provided better customer service, taking more time to do the job right rather than trying to save seconds at the expense of customers or fellow employees.[52]

Cypress Semiconductor uses technology-based management control systems that are extremely powerful, but it uses them in concert with employee needs, not against them.

Cypress Semiconductor Corporation

T.J. Rogers, president and CEO of Cypress, says Cypress's management control systems track corporate, departmental, and individual performance so regularly and in such detail that no manager can possibly claim to be in the dark about critical problems. Things are monitored so closely that "no surprises" is a way of life. Strategic managers cannot see five years, or even one year, into the future, but revenue and profit budgets and sales production targets for each quarter must be met. Product shipments and revenues are tracked on a daily basis and compared with targets, enabling managers to identify adjustments to make.

The system is anything but an "electronic treadmill," because it is designed to encourage collective thinking and problem solving. For example, one system is designed to encourage everyone in the organization to set challenging goals and then measure and meet them. Each of the fourteen hundred employees sets his or her own goals every week and commits to achieving them by a specific date. These goals and ways of measuring them are all entered into a database. Employees help each other achieve goals.

The budget system allocates key resources—people, capital, operating expenses—for maximum productivity. Departments can obtain additional resources as the company grows, but top management expects ever-increasing revenue per employee, higher productivity ratios, and ever-lower expense ratios.

The employee performance appraisal system rank-orders employees according to performance. A committee is formed to rank all shipping clerks, circuit designers, or vice presidents. Using a committee takes the pressure off the immediate manager and provides a broader perspective. Then salary increases are allocated according to rank-order performance.

All of these control systems are computerized. The president can review the raises of every employee in two hours. Top managers can review recent trends—such as quality level—in each product line. The trends enable strategic adjustments in databases or work procedures in the next quarter.

The control systems have enabled Cypress to become large without waste or bureaucracy. The control system is rigorous, but it works.[53]

Clan Control

Clan control is the use of social characteristics, such as corporate culture, shared values, commitment, traditions, and beliefs, to control behavior. Organizations that use clan control require shared values and trust among employees.[54] Clan control is important when ambiguity and uncertainty are high. High uncertainty means the organization cannot put a price on its services, and things change so fast that rules and regulations are not able to specify every correct behavior.

Under clan control, people may be hired because they are committed to the organization's purpose, such as in a religious organization. New employees may be subjected to a long period of socialization to gain acceptance by colleagues. Clan control is most often used in small, informal organizations or in organizations with a strong culture, because of personal involvement in and commitment to the organization's purpose. In addition, the increasing use of computer networks, which can lead to a democratic spread of information throughout the organization, may force many companies to depend less on bureaucratic control and more on shared values that guide individual actions for the corporate good.[55]

Traditional control mechanisms based on strict rules and close supervision are ineffective for controlling behavior in conditions of high uncertainty and rapid change.[56] Companies that shift to the new management paradigm of decentralization, horizontal teams, network structures, and employee participation generally use clan control or *self-control*.

Whereas clan control is a function of being socialized into a group, self-control stems from individual values, goals, and standards. The organization attempts to induce a change such that individual employees' own internal values and work preferences are brought in line with the organization's values and goals.[57] With self-control, employees generally set their own goals and monitor their own performance, yet companies relying on self-control need strong leaders who can clarify boundaries within which employees can exercise their own knowledge and discretion.

Clan or self-control may also be used in certain departments, such as strategic planning, where uncertainty is high and performance is difficult to measure. Managers of departments that rely on these informal control mechanisms must not assume that the absence of written, bureaucratic control means no control is present. Clan control is invisible yet very powerful. One recent study found that the actions of employees were controlled even more powerfully and completely with clan control than with a bureaucratic hierarchy.[58] When clan control works, bureaucratic control is not needed, as in the following case.

In Practice 9.6   *Metallic, Inc.*

Stuart Tubbs came up through the manufacturing ranks at Metallic, Inc., a huge producer of chrome finishes and specialty metals with several product divisions. He was accustomed to the use of lengthy budgets and statistical reports, in which almost every manufacturing activity was counted and evaluated weekly. When Tubbs was promoted to executive vice president, one of the first things he wanted to do was get the strategic planning department "under control." The department was responsible for strategic planning for the organization as a whole, as well as for the numerous divisions. Because planners were involved in investigating strategic initiatives and opportunities for all divisions, they had multiple projects underway simultaneously. Tubbs had noticed that the department was run very loosely and people had the freedom to do as they pleased, even working at night instead of during regular business hours if they preferred.

Tubbs's first step was to install a detailed budget system. A budget was established for each project. Even minor expenditures had to be budgeted. The strategic planning director was expected to keep each expense category on target. Statistical reports were implemented to keep track of all nonfinancial items, such as how employees spent their time and the productivity level for each project. The amount of computer time used, travel, and use of equipment were all measured and monitored.

As the detail and intensity of the bureaucratic control system increased, satisfaction and productivity within the department decreased. At least once a week the executive vice president and the strategic planning director battled over differences between actual expenditures and budget or over the interpretation of activity reports. After about a year, the director resigned. This was followed by the resignations of several key planners.

The board of directors asked that a management consultant examine the problems in the department. She found that the control procedures were not appropriate in a strategic planning department characterized by a long time horizon, frequent change, and uncertainty. Precise, detailed reports may work for a stable manufacturing department, but they do not capture the uncertain nature of strategic planning activities. Minor deviations from budget are the rule rather than the exception. A less precise control system used just to plan future projects and keep output consistent with company needs would be more effective. The consultant recommended that the bureaucratic control be reduced so that the shared values and commitment of professional employees regulate behavior.

Stuart Tubbs had failed to recognize and understand the strong system of clan control that was operating in the strategic planning department at Metallic. Employees were socialized into professional norms and practices and shared a strong departmental culture. Most planners worked extra hours at night to finish projects because they were deeply committed and liked the chance to talk informally among themselves about strategic initiatives they were exploring. The lack of bureaucratic control mechanisms did not mean lack of control.

CONTINGENCY CONTROL MODEL

A question for organization designers is when to emphasize each control strategy. A **contingency control model** that describes contingencies associated with market, bureaucratic, and clan control is shown in Exhibit 9.10. Each type of control often appears in the same organization, but one form of control will usually dominate.[59]

Bureaucratic control mechanisms are by far the most widely used control strategy. Some form of bureaucratic control combined with internal management control systems is found in almost every organization. Bureaucratic control is used more exclusively when organizations are large and when the environment and technology are certain, stable, and routine. It is also associated with the functional structure described in Chapter 6. Bureaucratic control emphasizes a vertical information and control process.

Clan control is almost the opposite of bureaucratic control. When organizations are small and when the environment and technology are uncertain, unstable, and nonroutine, then trust, tradition, and shared culture and values are important sources of control. Clan control is best when horizontal information sharing and coordination are needed, as they are with a matrix, team-based, or horizontal organization structure. Rules and budgets will be used, of course, but trust, values, and commitment will be the primary reasons for employee compliance.

Research on self-control is just emerging, but this type of control seems most appropriate in organizations that are shifting to what has been called the learning organization, an organization in which everyone is engaged in identifying and solving problems, enabling the organization to continuously experiment, improve, and increase its capability. The learning organization involves

Exhibit 9.10
*Contingency Model for
Organizational Control
Strategies*

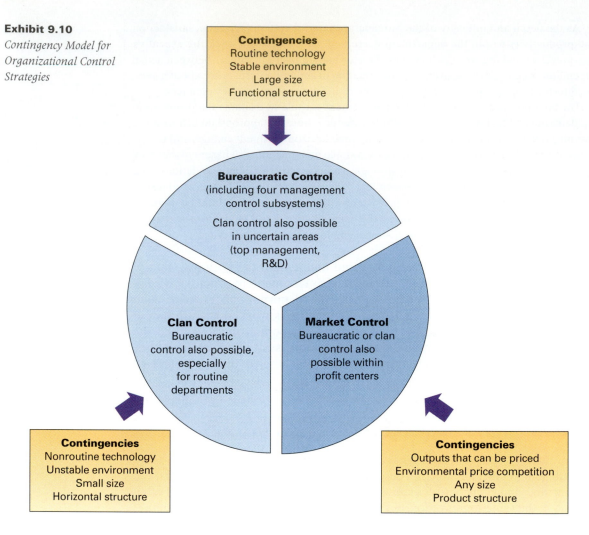

changing employee behaviors and attitudes and will be discussed in detail in Chapter 15.

Market control has limited applications, but its use is growing. It is used when costs and outputs can be priced and a market is available for price competition. The technology must produce outputs that can be defined and priced, and competition must exist in the environment. Market control can be used in organizations of any size so long as costs can be identified and outputs are competitively priced. It is frequently used in the self-contained product divisions of a business corporation, as described in Chapter 6. Each such division is a profit center. When applicable, market control is efficient because performance information is summarized in a profit-and-loss statement.

The balance among control strategies may differ from organization to organization. The use of each strategy reflects the structure, technology, and environment, as well as the ability to price output. When managers emphasize the correct type of control, the outcome can be very positive. For example, using the right approach to control helped Allegheny Ludlum Steel ride a crest of profitability during the toughest years of the steel industry. Bureaucratic control is the primary control mechanism at Allegheny. A computer-based information system measures every aspect of operations, and strict rules, budgets, and statistical reports monitor all activities. This is appropriate for Allegheny because the technology is well defined and is measurable. The company also uses market control. Outputs can be priced, and the industry is very competitive, so cost efficiency and bottom-line profits are the most important criteria of company success.[60]

SUPERVISORY CONTROL STRATEGIES

The control strategies described so far apply to the top and middle levels of an organization where the concern is for the entire organization or major departments. Control is also an issue at the lower, operational level in organizations where supervisors must directly control employee subordinates, which is called supervisory control. **Supervisory control** focuses on the performance of individual employees. Three types of supervisory control available to managers are output control, behavior control, and input control.[61]

Output control is based upon written records that measure employee outputs and productivity. It is used when the outputs of individual workers can be easily measured, such as for piece-rate jobs where the number of units per hour can be easily calculated. At Lincoln Electric Co., a manufacturer in Euclid, Ohio, for example, factory workers don't belong to a union and are paid by the piece rather than by union wage rates. Each job is rated according to skill, required effort, and responsibility. A base wage comparable to those for similar jobs in the Cleveland area is assigned to the job and then Lincoln's time-study department sets piece prices so that an average worker producing at an average pace can earn the base wage. Supervisors can easily calculate the output of each individual worker. One reason this control system works so well at Lincoln is that there is virtually no limit to what an ambitious worker can earn on the piece-rate system.[62]

Behavior control is based on personal observation of employee behavior to see whether an employee follows correct procedures. Behavior control usually takes more time than output control because it requires personal surveillance. Managers must observe employees at work. Behavior control is used when outputs are not easily measured. High school and college teaching is often monitored and influenced through behavior control. The outputs of teaching are the amount of student learning, which is very difficult to measure. Consequently, teachers are usually evaluated on the procedures or behavior they use in teaching. A high school principal may personally observe teachers to learn whether they follow accepted practices. Student evaluations are often used at universities to provide information to managers about the classroom behavior of teachers.

Input control uses employee selection and training to regulate the knowledge, skills, abilities, values, and motives of employees. This type of control attempts to align the goals of individual employees with those of the company. Input control is used when neither procedures nor outcomes are easily measurable. Some not-for-profit service organizations, such as welfare departments, use input control as a primary means of control because the helping professions cannot be perfectly programmed and their outcomes are not measurable. Managers therefore socialize employees into correct knowledge and values. Input control involves rigorous staff selection and ongoing training and development programs.[63]

The choice of supervisory control depends on the nature of employee tasks. A simple model of when each control approach can be used is shown in Exhibit 9.11. The two dimensions are the extent to which task outcomes are measurable and the extent to which task procedures are programmable.[64] When tasks are

Exhibit 9.11
*Relationship of
Supervisory Control
to Employee Task
Characteristics*

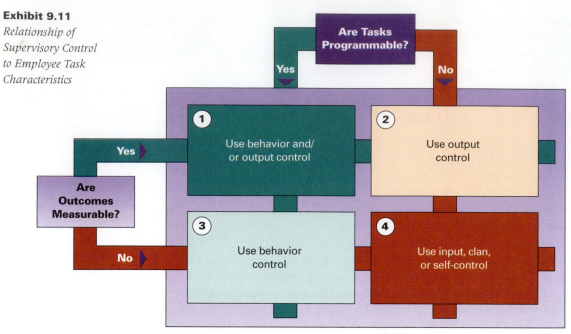

Source: Based on William Ouchi, "A Conceptual Framework for Design of Organization Control Mechanisms," *Management Science* 25 (1979): 833–48; and Kathleen M. Eisenhardt, "Control: Organizational and Economic Approaches," *Management Science* 31 (1985): 134–49.

programmable and outcomes are measurable, as in quadrant 1, then managers can use behavior control, output control, or both. Piece-rate work in a manufacturing plant is often of this variety, and managers typically choose output control because output is easier to measure than is behavior. In quadrant 2, when outcomes are measurable and the tasks are not programmable—such as in research—then output control has to be used. The outcomes of a research project are measured, not the techniques used to develop it.

In quadrant 3, outcomes are difficult to measure, but the task is programmable. This occurs in university teaching, for example, and behavior control has to be used. Customer satisfaction from service in a department store is another hard-to-measure output. Many stores use behavior control by prescribing explicit procedures for how employees are to deal with customers, stock shelves, and keep things clean and tidy.

In quadrant 4 of Exhibit 9.11, neither procedures nor outcomes are measurable. This situation is fairly rare at the operational level, but when it occurs, managers usually rely on input control to regulate employee performance. In addition, organizations may emphasize clan control or self-control by building a strong culture with shared performance values. Some not-for-profit service organizations must rely totally on input, clan, or self-control to guide employees to high performance.

Balancing Empowerment and Control

Many managers are giving up some of their control and empowering workers at low organization levels to make decisions and act independently. Tight management control can constrain creativity and limit flexibility and innovation, organizational characteristics that are becoming increasingly important in an era of

Book Mark 9.0

Have You Read About This?

Levers of Control: How Managers Use Innovative Control Systems to Drive Strategic Renewal

by Robert Simons

Balancing the need to encourage creativity and innovation with the need to minimize surprises and correct deviations is a challenge for today's managers. In *Levers of Control,* Robert Simons examines the tensions that exist in today's empowered organizations operating in highly competitive markets: tensions between freedom and constraint, empowerment and accountability, top-down direction and bottom-up creativity, and experimentation and efficiency. Based on decade-long research of numerous companies in ten industries, Simons proposes a theory of how managers can balance these tensions using four levers of control.

Levers of Control

Simons's four levers of control provide a way to balance three facets of an organization—the dynamics of creating value, the dynamics of making strategy, and the dynamics of human behavior—to drive strategic renewal. The levers are

- *Belief systems.* Belief systems often manifest themselves in a firm's mission or credo. Belief systems communicate core values and motivate employees to search for new opportunities to create value.
- *Boundary systems.* These limit risk by delineating the acceptable domains of organizational activity. Boundary systems consist of both business conduct boundaries (such as codes of conduct or industry standards) and strategic boundaries (such as strategic planning and capital budgeting).
- *Diagnostic control systems.* Diagnostic controls focus on results by monitoring performance according to intended plans of action and correcting problems or deviations.
- *Interactive control systems.* These systems focus attention on strategic uncertainties and consist of the information systems that managers use to make decisions and regularly participate in the bottom-up emergence of strategy. Interactive systems promote open dialogue and organizationwide learning.

Pulling the Levers to Push Strategy

Using case studies, graphs, and charts based on his research, Simons makes the case that managers can no longer rely solely on traditional control techniques such as budgeting and performance appraisals. *Levers of Control* shows managers how to create an environment that balances the need for creativity, innovation, and flexibility with the requirement for goal-oriented achievement. In times of rapid change, effective managers can use the four levers of control to help their companies forge ahead strategically while minimizing risk.

Levers of Control: How Managers Use Innovative Control Systems to Drive Strategic Renewal, by Robert Simons, is published by Harvard Business School Press.

rapid change. Yet managers must still maintain adequate control to ensure that departments and organizations meet their goals.

Most managers are accustomed to relying on control systems that measure the progress of individuals and departments toward strategically important goals. Although such systems are still an important part of control in empowered companies, they should be balanced with other mechanisms, including shared belief systems, boundary systems that set the limits for employee behavior (including ethical statements and codes of conduct), and interactive information systems that enable managers to stay abreast of what is happening in the organization and involve themselves regularly and personally in the activities and decisions of employees. This balanced approach to control, which can help managers unleash the creativity of employees while still ensuring that activities are directed toward meeting strategic goals, is discussed in more detail in Book Mark 9.0.

SUMMARY AND INTERPRETATION

An organization's situation creates uncertainty and ambiguity for managers, which translates into requirements for information amount and richness. Determining how manager and department information needs differ along these two dimensions and how to design information support systems are key problems for organizations to solve. Generally, as ambiguity of managerial tasks increases, more rich, personal information is required. Well-defined tasks that are complex and of high variety require a large amount of precise, quantitative data.

Information technology impacts organization structure by removing barriers of time and distance. Advanced technology has played a significant role in the shift to horizontal forms of organizing, with fewer hierarchical levels and more self-directed teams, and in the trend toward network structures. Within organizations, information systems have evolved to a variety of applications to meet information needs.

Initial transaction processing systems were applied to well-defined tasks at lower levels, and they increased efficiency. Then management information systems and decision support systems were developed as business resources at the middle- and upper-management levels. Finally, executive information systems are being used at top levels of management as a strategic weapon. Advances in networking technology are leading to greater cooperation between departments as well as between organizations. Interorganization linkages, such as electronic data interchange and communication via the Internet, also provide strategic advantages.

Information technology plays an important role in helping organizations achieve a competitive advantage through low-cost leadership or differentiation. Information technology can increase operational efficiency, coordination, and the speed of resupply, and can lock in customers, improve customer service, and enhance product development.

A large part of information processing pertains to control. The concepts of market, bureaucratic, clan, output, behavior, and input control help explain how control is exercised in organizations. Market control is used where product or service outputs can be priced and competition exists. Clan control, and more recently self-control, are associated with uncertain and rapidly changing organizational processes and rely on commitment, tradition, and shared values for control. Bureaucratic control relies on the bureaucratic characteristics of organizations described in Chapter 5, as well as on the four internal management control systems of budgets, statistical reports, operating procedures, and reward systems. At the supervisory level, managers use output, behavior, clan, self-, or input control or some combination to control the performance of individual employees. In organizations where employees are empowered to make decisions and act independently, managers are taking a balanced approach to control, helping to unleash employee creativity while also ensuring that activities are directed toward meeting organizational goals.

Key Concepts

behavior control	input control
bureaucratic control	intranet
clan control	management control systems
contingency control model	management information system
data	market control
decision support system	networking
electronic data interchange	operational control
executive information system	output control
high tech	strategic control
high touch	supervisory control
information	transaction processing systems
information ambiguity	uncertainty
information amount	work flow redesign
information richness	

Discussion Questions

1. How do uncertainty and ambiguity affect information processing requirements and the design of information support systems?

2. To what extent can information technology meet the needs of top managers for rich information? Do you think technology will ever enable top managers to do their job without face-to-face communication? Discuss.

3. How might the Internet provide a competitive advantage to a company?

4. The manager of a computer processing department told his employees: "Top managers need the same control data everyone else needs, except that we'll aggregate it for the company as a whole." Agree or disagree with the manager's philosophy, and explain why.

5. An organization consultant argued that managers need information that is independent of computers. Explain why you agree or disagree with her point of view.

6. In writing about types of control, William Ouchi said, "The Market is like the trout and the Clan like the salmon, each a beautiful highly specialized species which requires uncommon conditions for its survival. In comparison, the bureaucratic method of control is the catfish—clumsy, ugly, but able to live in the widest range of environments and ultimately, the dominant species." Discuss what Ouchi meant with that analogy.

7. What type of controls do most professors use to control students—output, input, behavior, clan, or all of these?

8. Government organizations often seem more bureaucratic than for-profit organizations. Could this partly be the result of the type of control used in government organizations? Explain.

9. Discuss the following statements: "Things under tight control are better than things under loose control." "The more data managers have, the better decisions they make."

10. Discuss how the use of intranets may affect the control processes used in organizations.

BRIEFCASE

As an organization manager, keep these guides in mind:

1. Provide managers and employees with information support that reflects the frequency and the type of problems with which they deal. Design both the amount and the richness of information to meet the problem-solving needs of managers.
2. Use information technology as a strategic weapon. Use technology to achieve differentiation or low-cost leadership by becoming more efficient, locking in customers and suppliers, and developing new products.
3. Implement one of the three basic choices—bureaucratic, clan, market—as the primary means of organizational control. Use bureaucratic control when organizations are large, have a stable environment, and use routine technology. Use clan control in small, uncertain departments. Use market control when outputs can be priced and when competitive bidding is available.
4. Use management control systems to monitor and influence department-level activities. The budget controls resources into the department, and statistical reports control the product and service outcomes of the department. Reward systems and operating procedures can be used to control work activities within departments.
5. Take a balanced approach to control in organizations where lower-level workers are empowered to make decisions and act independently. Combine traditional performance measurement with mechanisms such as belief systems, boundary systems, and interactive information systems to encourage creativity and flexibility while keeping activities directed toward strategic goals.

Chapter Nine Workbook *Control Mechanisms**

Think of two situations in your life: your work and your school experiences. How is control exerted? Fill out the tables on the next page.

On the Job

Your job responsibilities	How your boss controls	Positives of this control	Negatives of this control	How you would improve control
1.				
2.				
3.				
4.				

At the University

Item	How professor A (small class) controls	How professor B (large class) controls	How these controls influence you	What you think is a better control
1. Exams				
2. Assignments /papers				
3. Class participation				
4. Attendance				
5. Other				

Questions

1. What are advantages and disadvantages of the various controls?
2. What happens when there is too much control? Too little?
3. Does the type of control depend on the situation and the people involved?
4. *Optional:* How do the control mechanisms in your tables compare to those of other students?

Case for Analysis *Sunflower Incorporated**

Sunflower Incorporated is a large distribution company with more than five thousand employees and gross sales of more than $550 million (1992). The company purchases salty snack foods and liquor and distributes them to independent retail stores throughout the United States and Canada. Salty snack foods include corn chips, potato chips, cheese curls, tortilla chips, and peanuts. The United States and Canada are divided into twenty-two regions, each with its own central warehouse, sales people, finance department, and purchasing department. The company distributes national as well as local brands, and packages some items under private labels. Competition in this industry is intense. The demand for liquor has been declining, and competitors like Procter & Gamble and Frito-Lay develop new snack foods to gain market share from smaller companies like Sunflower. The head office encourages each region to be autonomous because of local tastes and practices. In the northeast United States, for example, people consume a greater percentage of Canadian whisky and American bourbon, while in the West, they consume more light liquors, such as vodka, gin, and rum. Snack foods in the Southwest are often seasoned to reflect Mexican tastes.

Early in 1988, Sunflower began using a financial reporting system that compared sales, costs, and profits across company regions. Each region was a profit center, and top management was surprised to learn that profits varied widely. By 1990, the differences were so great that management decided some standardization was necessary. Managers believed highly profitable regions were sometimes using lower-quality items, even seconds, to boost profit margins. This practice could hurt Sunflower's image. Most regions were facing cutthroat price competition to hold market share. Triggered by price cuts by Anheuser-Busch Company's Eagle Snacks division, national distributors, such as Frito-Lay, Borden, Nabisco, Procter & Gamble (Pringles), and Standard Brands (Planters Peanuts), were pushing to hold or increase market share by cutting prices and launching new products.

As these problems accumulated, Joe Steelman, president of Sunflower, decided to create a new position to monitor pricing and purchasing practices. Loretta Williams was hired from the finance department of a competing organization. Her new title was director of pricing and purchasing, and she reported to the vice president of finance, Peter Langly. Langly gave Williams great latitude in organizing her job and encouraged her

to establish whatever rules and procedures were necessary. She was also encouraged to gather information from each region. Each region was notified of her appointment by an official memo sent to the twenty-two regional directors. A copy of the memo was posted on each warehouse bulletin board. The announcement was also made in the company newspaper.

After three weeks on the job, Williams decided two problems needed her attention. Over the long term, Sunflower should make better use of information technology. Williams believed information technology could provide more information to headquarters for decision making. Top managers in the divisions were connected to headquarters by an electronic messaging system, but lower employees and sales people were not connected. Only a few senior managers in about half the divisions used the system regularly.

In the short term, Williams decided fragmented pricing and purchasing decisions were a problem and these decisions should be standardized across regions. This should be undertaken immediately. As a first step, she wanted the financial executive in each region to notify her of any change in local prices of more than 3 percent. She also decided that all new contracts for local purchases of more than five thousand dollars should be cleared through her office. (Approximately 60 percent of items distributed in the regions were purchased in large quantities and supplied from the home office. The other 40 percent were purchased and distributed within the region.) Williams believed the only way to standardize operations was for each region to notify the home office in advance of any change in prices or purchases. She discussed the proposed policy with Langly. He agreed, so they submitted a formal proposal to the president and board of directors, who approved the plan. The changes represented a complicated shift in policy procedures, and Sunflower was moving into peak holiday season, so Williams wanted to implement the

---

*This case was inspired by "Frito-Lay May Find Itself in a Competition Crunch," *Business Week,* 19 July 1982, 186; "Dashman Company," in Paul R. Lawrence and John A. Seiler, *Organizational Behavior and Administration: Cases, Concepts, and Research Findings* (Homewood, Ill: Irwin and Dorsey, 1965), 16–17; and Laurie M. Grossman, "Price Wars Bring Flavor to Once-Quiet Snack Market," *Wall Street Journal,* 23 May 1991, B1, B3.

new procedures right away. She decided to send an electronic mail message followed by a fax to the financial and purchasing executives in each region notifying them of the new procedures. The change would be inserted in all policy and procedure manuals throughout Sunflower within four months.

Williams showed a draft of the message to Langly and invited his comments. Langly said the message was a good idea but wondered if it was sufficient. The regions handled hundreds of items and were used to decentralized decision making. Langly suggested that Williams ought to visit the regions and discuss purchasing and pricing policies with the executives. Williams refused, saying that such trips would be expensive and time-consuming. She had so many things to do at headquarters that trips were impossible. Langly also suggested waiting to implement the procedures until after the annual company meeting in three months, when Williams could meet the regional directors personally. Williams said this would take too long, because the procedures would then not take effect until after the

peak sales season. She believed the procedures were needed now. The messages went out the next day.

During the next few days, electronic mail replies came in from seven regions. The managers said they were in agreement and said they would be happy to cooperate.

Eight weeks later, Williams had not received notices from any regions about local price or purchase changes. Other executives who had visited regional warehouses indicated to her that the regions were busy as usual. Regional executives seemed to be following usual procedures for that time of year. She telephoned one of the regional managers and discovered that he did not know who she was and had never heard of the position called director of pricing and purchasing. Besides, he said, "we have enough to worry about reaching profit goals without additional procedures from headquarters." Williams was chagrined that her position and her suggested changes in procedure had no impact. She wondered whether field managers were disobedient or whether she should have used another communication strategy.

Notes

1. Stephanie Stahl, "Hire on One, Get 'Em All," *Information Week*, 20 March 1995, 120–24.

2. Henry Mintzberg, *The Nature of Managerial Work* (New York: Harper & Row, 1972), 39.

3. Richard L. Daft and Norman B. Macintosh, "A Tentative Exploration into the Amount and Equivocality of Information Processing in Organizational Work Units," *Administrative Science Quarterly* 26 (1981): 207–24.

4. Michael L. Tushman and David A. Nadler, "Information Processing as an Integrating Concept in Organization Design," *Academy of Management Review* 3 (1978): 613–24; Samuel B. Bacharach and Michael Aiken, "Communication in Administrative Bureaucracies," *Academy of Management Journal* 20 (1977): 365–77.

5. Jay R. Galbraith, *Organization Design* (Reading, Mass.: Addison-Wesley, 1977), 35–36; William E. Souder and Ruby K. Moenaert, "Integrating Marketing and R&D Project Personnel within Innovation Projects: An Information Uncertainty Model," *Journal of Management Studies* 29 (July 1992): 485–512.

6. Richard L. Daft, Robert H. Lengel, and Linda Klebe Trevino, "Message Equivocality, Media Se-

lection, and Manager Performance: Implications for Information Systems," *MIS Quarterly* 11 (1987): 355–66; Richard L. Daft and Robert H. Lengel, "Information Richness: A New Approach to Managerial Behavior and Organization Design," in Barry Staw and Larry L. Cummings, eds., *Research in Organizational Behavior,* vol. 6 (Greenwich, Conn.: JAI Press, 1984), 191–233; Robert H. Lengel, "Managerial Information Processing and Communication-Media Source Selection Behavior" (Unpublished Ph.D. dissertation, Texas A&M University, 1982).

7. Erik Larson, "The Man with the Golden Touch," *Inc.,* October 1988, 67–77.

8. Based on Janet Fulk and Gerardine DeSanctis, "Electronic Communication and Changing Organizational Forms," *Organization Science* 6, no. 4 (July-August 1995): 337–49.

9. Beverly Geber, "Virtual Teams," *Training* (April 1995): 36–40.

10. Niklas von Daehne, "Techno-Boom," *Success* (December 1994): 43–46.

11. David W. L. Wightman, "Competitive Advantage through Information Technology," *Journal of General Management* 12 (Summer 1987): 36–45; M. J.

Bissett, "Competitive Advantage—through Controlling the Middle Ground," (Paper presented at Southcourt Conference: Improving Business-Based IT Strategy, October 1986).

12. Robin Matthews and Anthony Shoebridge, "EIS: A Guide for Executives," *Long Range Planning* 25, no. 6 (1992): 94–101; Jeffrey P. Stamen, "Decision Support Systems Help Planners Hit Their Targets," *Journal of Business Strategy* (March/April 1990): 30–33.

13. Jeffrey Rothfeder, Jim Bartimo and Lois Therrien, "How Software Is Making Food Sales a Piece of Cake," *Business Week,* 2 July 1990, 54–55.

14. Rick Tetzeli, "The Internet and Your Business," *Fortune,* 7 March 1994, 86–96.

15. Amy Cortese, "Here Comes the Intranet," *Business Week,* 26 February 1996, 76–84; Alison L. Sprout, "The Internet Inside Your Company," *Fortune*, 27 November 1995, 161–68.

16. Richard L. Daft and Robert H. Lengel, "Organizational Information Requirements, Media Richness and Structural Design," *Management Science* 32 (1986): 554–71; Daft and Macintosh, "A Tentative Exploration"; W. Alan Randolph, "Matching Technology and the Design of Organization Units," *California Management Review* 22–23 (1980–81): 39–48; Michael L. Tushman "Technical Communications in R&D Laboratories: The Impact of Project Work Characteristics," *Academy of Management Journal* 21 (1978): 624–45.

17. Robert H. Lengel and Richard L. Daft, "The Selection of Communication Media as an Executive Skill," *Academy of Management Executive* 2 (August 1988): 225–32.

18. Michael McFadden, "The Master Builder of Mammoth Tools," *Fortune,* 3 September 1984, 58–64.

19. Steve Molloy and Charles R. Schwenk, "The Effects of Information Technology on Strategic Decision Making," *Journal of Management Studies* 32:3 (May 1995): 283–311; Dorothy E. Leidner and Joyce J. Elam, "The Impact of Executive Information Systems on Organizational Design, Intelligence, and Decision Making," *Organization Science* 6, no. 6 (November-December 1995): 645–64.

20. Renae Broderick and John W. Boudreau, "Human Resource Management, Information Technology and the Competitive Edge," *Academy of Management Executive* 6, no. 2 (1992): 7–17.

21. Mark C. S. Lee and Dennis A. Adams, "A Manager's Guide to the Strategic Potential of Information Systems," *Information and Management* (1990): 169–82; Wightman, "Competitive Advantage through Information Technology."

22. Kenneth Labich, "America Takes on the World," *Fortune,* 24 September 1990, 40–48.

23. John W. Verity, "Invoice? What's An Invoice?" *Business Week,* 10 June 1995, 110–12; Bill Saporito, "What Sam Walton Taught America," *Fortune,* 4 May 1992, 104–05.

24. Fess Crockett, "Revitalizing Executive Information Systems," *Sloan Management Review* (Summer 1992): 39–47; Jeremy Main, "At Last, Software CEOs Can Use," *Fortune,* 13 March 1989, 77–81.

25. Doug Bartholomew, "A Better Way to Work," *Information Week,* 11 September 1995, 32–40.

26. Peter Bradley, "The Road to Wealth," *Success* (April 1995): 47–52.

27. Myron Magnet, "Who's Winning the Information Revolution," *Fortune,* 30 November 1992, 110–17; Jeremy Main, "Computers of the World, Unite!" *Fortune,* 24 Steptember 1990, 114–22.

28. Tridas Mukhopadhyay, Sunder Kekre, and Suresh Kalathur, "Business Value of Information Technology: A Study of Electronic Data Interchange," *MIS Quarterly* (June 1995): 137–56.

29. Verity, "Invoice? What's An Invoice?"

30. Robert I. Benjamin, John F. Rockart, Michael S. Scott Morton, and John Wyman, "Information Technology: A Strategic Opportunity," *Sloan Management Review* 25 (Spring 1984): 3–10.

31. Verity, "Invoice? What's An Invoice?"

32. N. Venketraman, "IT-Enabled Business Transformation: From Automation to Business Scope Redefinition," *Sloan Management Review* (Winter 1994): 73–87.

33. John W. Verity, "Taking a Laptop on a Call," *Business Week,* 25 October 1993, 124–25.

34. Rick Tetzeli, "The Internet and Your Business," *Fortune,* 7 March 1994, 86–96.

35. Warren Cohen, "Taking It to the Highway," *U.S. News and World Report,* 18 September 1995, 84–87.

36. John F. Preble, "Towards a Comprehensive System of Strategic Control," *Journal of Management Studies* 29 (July 1992): 391–409; David Asch, "Strategic Control: A Problem Looking for a Solution," *Long Range Planning* 25, no. 2 (1992): 105–10.

37. T. K. Das, "Organizational Control: An Evolutionary Perspective," *Journal of Management Studies* 26 (1989): 459–75; Kenneth A. Merchant, *Control in Business Organizations* (Marshfield, Mass: Pit-

man, 1985); William G. Ouchi, "The Relationship between Organizational Structure and Organizational Control," *Administrative Science Quarterly* 22 (1977): 95–113.

38. Michael Goold, "Strategic Control in the Decentralized Firm," *Sloan Management Review* (Winter 1991): 69–81: Robert Simons, "Strategic Orientation and Top Management Attention to Control Systems," *Strategic Management Journal* 12 (1991): 49–62.

39. William G. Ouchi, "Markets, Bureaucracies, and Clans," *Administrative Science Quarterly* 25 (1980): 129–41;—idem, "A Conceptual Framework for the Design of Organizational Control Mechanisms," *Management Science* 25 (1979): 833–48.

40. Oliver A. Williamson, *Markets and Hierarchies: Analyses and Antitrust Implications* (New York: Free Press, 1975).

41. Anita Micossi, "Creating Internal Markets," *Enterprise* (April 1994): 43–44.

42. Raymond E. Miles, Henry J. Coleman, Jr., and W. E. Douglas Creed, "Keys to Success in Corporate Redesign," *California Management Review* 37, no. 3 (Spring 1995): 128–45.

43. Anita Micossi, "Creating Internal Markets," *Enterprise* (April 1994): 43–44.

44. John A. Byrne, "Has Outsourcing Gone Too Far?" *Business Week,* 1 April 1996, 26–28.

45. Simons, "Strategic Organizations and Top Management Attention to Control Systems."

46. Stephen G. Green and M. Ann Welsh, "Cybernetics and Dependents: Reframing the Control Concept," *Academy of Management Review* 13 (1988): 287–301.

47. Robert S. Kaplan and David P. Norton, "The Balanced Scorecard—Measures That Drive Performance," *Harvard Business Review* (January-February 1992): 71–79; Robert G. Eccles, "The Performance Measurement Manifesto," *Harvard Business Review,* (January-February 1991): 131–37.

48. Richard L. Daft and Norman B. Macintosh, "The Nature and Use of Formal Control Systems for Management Control and Strategy Implementation," *Journal of Management* 10 (1984): 43–66.

49. Ibid.; Scott S. Cowen and J. Kendall Middaugh II, "Matching an Organization's Planning and Control System to Its Environment," *Journal of General Management* 16 (1990): 69–84.

50. Ralph Drtina, Steve Hoeger, and Jon Schaub, "Continuous Budgeting at the HON Company," *Management Accounting* (January 1996): 20–24.

51. Marlene C. Piturro, "Employee Performance Monitoring . . . or Meddling?" *Management Review* (May 1989): 31–33.

52. Rebecca A. Grant, Christopher A. Higgins, and Richard H. Irving, "Computerized Performance Monitors: Are They Costing You Customers?" *Sloan Management Review* (Spring 1988): 39–45.

53. T. J. Rodgers, "No Excuses Management," *Harvard Business Review* (July-August 1990): 84–98.

54. Ouchi, "Markets, Bureaucracies, and Clans."

55. Stratford Sherman, "The New Computer Revolution," *Fortune,* 14 June 1993, 56–80.

56. Richard Leifer and Peter K. Mills, "An Information Processing Approach for Deciding Upon Control Strategies and Reducing Control Loss in Emerging Organizations," *Journal of Management* 22, no. 1 (1996): 113–37.

57. Leifer and Mills, "An Information Processing Approach for Deciding Upon Control Strategies"; Laurie J. Kirsch, "The Management of Complex Tasks in Organizations: Controlling the Systems Development Process," *Organization Science* 7, no. 1 (January-February 1996): 1–21.

58. James R. Barker, "Tightening the Iron Cage: Concertive Control in Self-Managing Teams," *Administrative Science Quarterly* 38 (1993): 408–37.

59. Carol R. Snodgrass and Edward J. Szewczak, "The Substitutability of Strategic Control Choices: An Empirical Study," *Journal of Management Studies* 27 (1990): 535–53.

60. Bill Saporito, "Allegheny Ludlum Has Steel Figured Out," *Fortune,* 25 June 1984, 40–44.

61. Scott A. Snell, "Control Theory in Strategic Human Resource Management: The Mediating Effect of Administrative Information," *Academy of Management Journal* 35 (1992): 292–327; Ouchi, "Relationship between Organizational Structure and Organizational Control," William G. Ouchi and Mary Ann McGuire, "Organizational Control: Two Functions," *Administrative Science Quarterly* 20 (1975): 559–69.

62. Anita Lienert, "A Dinosaur of a Different Color," *Management Review* (February 1995): 24–29.

63. Snell, "Control Theory in Strategic Human Resource Management."

64. Kathleen M. Eisenhardt, "Control: Organizational and Economic Approaches," *Management Science* 31 (1985): 134–49; Ouchi and McGuire, "Organizational Control."

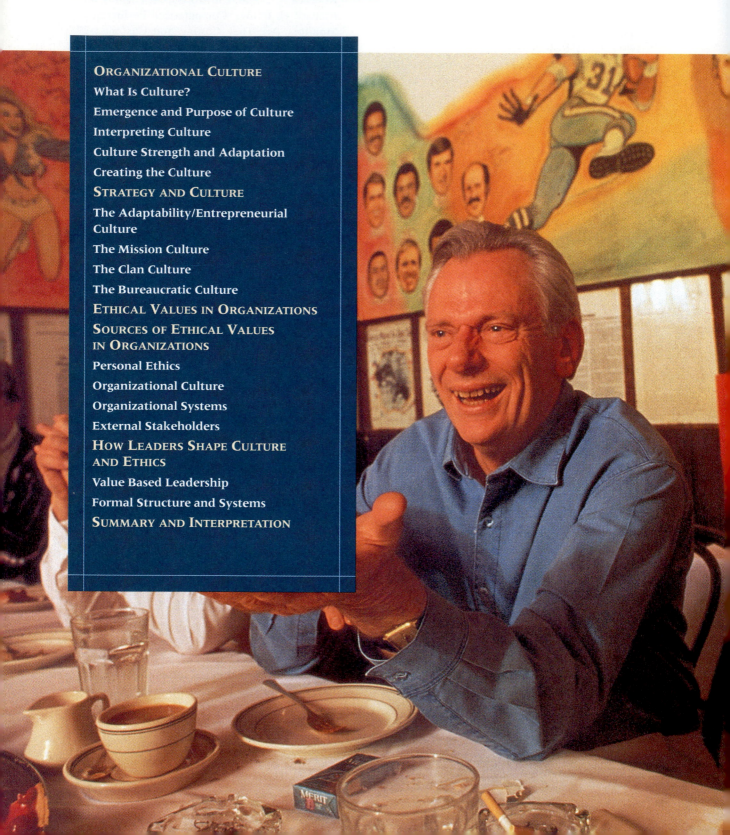

chapter ten

Organizational Culture and Ethical Values

Southwest Airlines

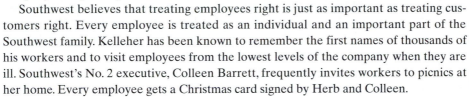

Herb Kelleher, CEO and president of Southwest Airlines, believes the key to good business is to do what your customer wants and to be happy in your work. It's a philosophy that has made Southwest the most consistently profitable airline in the industry and earned the company a string of awards from the U.S. Department of Transportation. Although other airlines may imitate some of Southwest's low-cost operating practices, the characteristic that truly makes Southwest successful can never be cloned. That characteristic, known as the "Southwest Spirit," is the company's unique corporate culture.

Southwest believes that treating employees right is just as important as treating customers right. Every employee is treated as an individual and an important part of the Southwest family. Kelleher has been known to remember the first names of thousands of his workers and to visit employees from the lowest levels of the company when they are ill. Southwest's No. 2 executive, Colleen Barrett, frequently invites workers to picnics at her home. Every employee gets a Christmas card signed by Herb and Colleen.

When recruiting employees, what Southwest's "People Department" looks for first and foremost is a positive attitude and a sense of humor. One ad featuring Kelleher dressed as the King of Rock reads, "Work in a Place Where Elvis Has Been Spotted." Orientation for new hires begins with a scavenger hunt and a video entitled "The Southwest Airlines Shuffle," which incorporates rap music performed by various employees describing their jobs and an appearance by Kelleher as Big Daddy-O.

Southwest believes a fun atmosphere builds a strong sense of community, counterbalances the stress of hard work, and enhances customer service. Employees are given the flexibility to let their own individual personalities come out in serving customers. Passengers on a recent Southwest flight, for example, had a bunny-eared flight attendant pop out of an overhead bin to greet them. Celebrations are an important part of work at Southwest Airlines, from impromptu "fun sessions" to a lavish annual awards banquet where the company officially celebrates employees who go above and beyond the call of duty. Red "LUV" hearts emblazon the company's training manuals and other materials, symbolizing the Southwest spirit of employees caring about themselves, each other, and the customer.[1]

Southwest Airlines has definite values that make it unique. Southwest has created a culture that engages employees' hearts and minds as well as their bodies. A Culture Committee, made up of employees representing a cross-section of departments, meets four times a year to make sure the Southwest Spirit stays alive.

Organizational success or failure is often attributed to culture. The new CEO at Black & Decker was credited with transforming an entire corporate culture, replacing the complacent manufacturing mentality with an almost manic market-driven way of doing things. Firms such as 3M and Johnson & Johnson have been praised for their innovative cultures. Corporate culture also has been implicated in problems faced by IBM, Sears, Bank of America, and General Motors, where changing their cultures is considered essential for ultimate success.[2]

Purpose of This Chapter

This chapter explores ideas about corporate culture and associated ethical values and how these are influenced by organizations. The first section will describe the nature of corporate culture, its origins and purpose, and how to identify and interpret culture through ceremonies, stories, and symbols. Then we turn to ethical values in organizations and how managers can implement ethical structures that will shape employee behavior. In the last section, we will discuss how leaders shape cultural and ethical values in a direction suitable for strategy and performance outcomes.

ORGANIZATIONAL CULTURE

The popularity of the organizational culture topic raises a number of questions. Can we identify cultures? Can culture be aligned with strategy? How can cultures be managed or changed? The best place to start is by defining culture and explaining how it can be identified in organizations.

What Is Culture?

Culture is the set of values, guiding beliefs, understandings, and ways of thinking that is shared by members of an organization and is taught to new members as correct.[3] It represents the unwritten, feeling part of the organization. Everyone participates in culture, but culture generally goes unnoticed. It is only when organizations try to implement new strategies or programs that go against basic culture norms and values that they come face to face with the power of culture.

Organizational culture exists at two levels, as illustrated in Exhibit 10.1. On the surface are visible artifacts and observable behaviors—the ways people dress and act and the symbols, stories, and ceremonies organization members share. The visible elements of culture, however, reflect deeper values in the minds of organization members. These underlying values, assumptions, beliefs, and thought processes are the true culture.[4] For example, at Southwest Airlines, red "LUV" hearts are a visible symbol; the underlying value is that "we are one family of people who truly care about each other." The attributes of culture display themselves in many ways but typically evolve into a patterned set of activities carried out through social interactions.[5] Those patterns can be used to interpret culture.

Emergence and Purpose of Culture

Culture provides members with a sense of organizational identity and generates a commitment to beliefs and values that are larger than themselves. Though ideas that become part of culture can come from anywhere within the organization, an organization's culture generally begins with a founder or early leader who articulates and implements particular ideas and values as a vision, philosophy, or business strategy. When these ideas and values lead to success, they become institutionalized, and an organizational culture emerges that re-

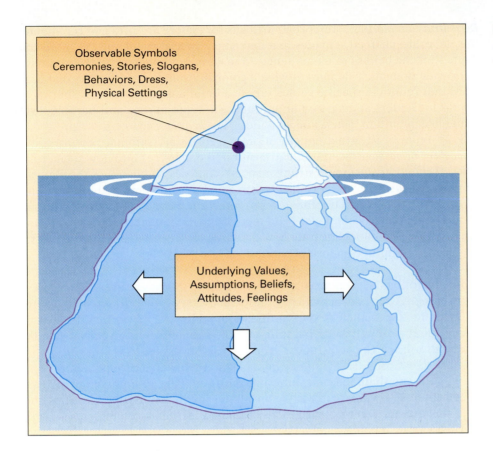

Exhibit 10.1

Levels of Corporate Culture

flects the vision and strategy of the founder or leader, as it did at Southwest Airlines.[6]

Cultures serve two critical functions in organizations: (1) to integrate members so that they know how to relate to one another, and (2) to help the organization adapt to the external environment. **Internal integration** means that members develop a collective identity and know how to work together effectively. It is culture that guides day-to-day working relationships and determines how people communicate within the organization, what behavior is acceptable or not acceptable, and how power and status is allocated. **External adaptation** refers to how the organization meets goals and deals with outsiders. Culture helps guide the daily activities of workers to meet certain goals. It can help the organization respond rapidly to customer needs or the moves of a competitor. We will discuss culture and adaptation in more detail later in the chapter.

Interpreting Culture

To identify and interpret the content of culture requires that people make inferences based on observable artifacts. Artifacts can be studied but are hard to decipher accurately. An award ceremony in one company may have a different meaning than in another company. To decipher what is really going on in an organization requires detective work and probably some experience as an insider. Some of the typical and important observable aspects of culture are rites and ceremonies, stories, symbols, and language.

Rites and Ceremonies.   Important artifacts for culture are **rites and ceremonies**, the elaborate, planned activities that make up a special event and are often conducted for the benefit of an audience. Managers can hold rites and ceremonies to provide dramatic examples of what a company values. These are special occasions that reinforce specific values, create a bond among people for sharing an important understanding, and anoint and celebrate heroes and heroines who symbolize important beliefs and activities.[7]

Four types of rites that appear in organizations are summarized in Exhibit 10.2. *Rites of passage* facilitate the transition of employees into new social roles. *Rites of enhancement* create stronger social identities and increase the status of employees. *Rites of renewal* reflect training and development activities that improve organization functioning. *Rites of integration* create common bonds and good feelings among employees and increase commitment to the organization. The following examples illustrate how these rites and ceremonies are used by top managers to reinforce important cultural values.

- In a major bank, election as an officer was seen as the key event in a successful career. A series of activities accompanied every promotion to bank officer, including a special method of notification, taking the new officer to the officers' dining room for the first time, and the new officer buying drinks on Friday after his or her notification.[8] This is a rite of passage.
- Mary Kay Cosmetics Company holds elaborate awards ceremonies, presenting gold and diamond pins, furs, and pink Cadillacs to high-achieving sales consultants. The most successful consultants are introduced by film clips, such as the kind used to introduce award nominees in the entertainment industry.[9] This is a rite of enhancement.
- An important annual event at McDonald's is the nationwide contest to determine the best hamburger cooking team in the country. The contest encourages all stores to reexamine the details of how they cook hamburgers. The ceremony is highly visible and communicates to all employees the McDonald's value of hamburger quality.[10] This is a rite of renewal.

Exhibit 10.2

A Typology of Organizational Rites and Their Social Consequences

Type of Rite	Example	Social Consequences
Passage	Induction and basic training, U.S. Army	Facilitate transition of persons into social roles and statuses that are new for them
Enhancement	Annual awards night	Enhance social identities and increase status of employees
Renewal	Organizational development activities	Refurbish social structures and improve organization functioning
Integration	Office Christmas party	Encourage and revive common feelings that bind members together and commit them to the organization

Source: Adapted from Harrison M. Trice and Janice M. Beyer, "Studying Organizational Cultures through Rites and Ceremonials," *Academy of Management Review* 9 (1984): 653–59. Used with permission.

- Whenever a Wal-Mart executive visits one of the stores, he or she leads employees in the Wal-Mart cheer: "Give me a W! Give me an A! Give me an L! Give me a squiggly! (all do a version of the twist) Give me an M! Give me an A! Give me an R! Give me a T! What's that spell? Wal-Mart! What's that spell? Wal-Mart! Who's No. 1? THE CUSTOMER!" The cheer strengthens bonds among employees and reinforces their commitment to common goals.[11] This is a rite of integration.

Stories.   **Stories** are narratives based on true events that are frequently shared among organizational employees and told to new employees to inform them about an organization. Many stories are about company **heroes** who serve as models or ideals for serving cultural norms and values. Some stories are considered **legends** because the events are historic and may have been embellished with fictional details. Other stories are **myths**, which are consistent with the values and beliefs of the organization but are not supported by facts.[12] Stories keep alive the primary values of the organization and provide a shared understanding among all employees. Examples of how stories shape culture are as follows:

- Two stories that symbolize the "HP way" at Hewlett-Packard involve the hero founders, David Packard and Bill Hewlett. After work hours one evening, Packard was wandering around the Palo Alto lab. He discovered a prototype constructed of inferior materials. Packard destroyed the model and left a note saying, "That's not the HP way. Dave." Similarly, Bill Hewlett is said to have gone to a plant on Saturday and found the lab stockroom door locked. He cut the padlock and left a note saying, "Don't ever lock this door again. Thanks, Bill." Hewlett wanted the engineers to have free access to components, and even to take them home, to stimulate the creativity that is part of the HP way.[13]
- For years, workers at U.S. Paper Mills Corporation have been hearing this story about the company's founder and principal stockholder: One morning, when Walter Cloud saw a worker trying to unclog the drain of a blending vat using an extension pole, he quickly jumped over the edge of the vat and reached through the three-feet-deep muck to unclog the drain with his hand. Brushing himself off, Cloud then asked the worker, "Now, what are you going to do the next time you need to unclog a drain?" By telling and retelling this story, workers at the mill communicate the importance of jumping in to do whatever needs to be done.[14]

Symbols.   Another tool for interpreting culture is the symbol. A **symbol** is something that represents another thing. In one sense, ceremonies, stories, slogans, and rites are all symbols. They symbolize deeper values of an organization. Another symbol is a physical artifact of the organization. Physical symbols are powerful because they focus attention on a specific item. Examples of physical symbols are as follows:

- Nordstrom department store symbolizes the importance of supporting lower-level employees with the organization chart in Exhibit 10.3. Nordstrom's is known for its extraordinary customer service, and the organization chart symbolizes that managers are to support the employees who *give* the service rather than be managers who control them.[15]
- President Bill Arnold of Nashville's Centennial Medical Center symbolized his commitment to an open door policy by ripping his office door from its hinges and suspending it from the ceiling where all employees could see it. At

Exhibit 10.3
Organization Chart for Nordstrom, Inc.

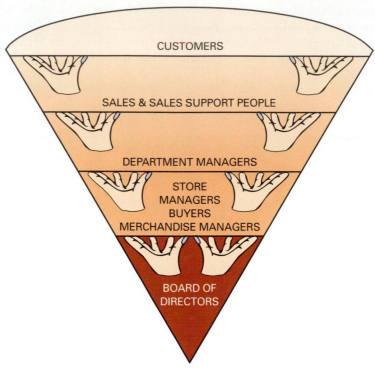

CUSTOMERS

SALES & SALES SUPPORT PEOPLE

DEPARTMENT MANAGERS

STORE MANAGERS BUYERS MERCHANDISE MANAGERS

BOARD OF DIRECTORS

Source: Used with permission of Nordstrom, Inc.

Sequint Computer Systems, all employees are expected to pitch in and help anyone wearing a red button. The red button symbolizes that a critical project is behind schedule.[16]

Language. The final technique for influencing culture is **language**. Many companies use a specific saying, slogan, metaphor, or other form of language to convey special meaning to employees. Slogans can be readily picked up and repeated by employees as well as customers of the company. At Speedy Muffler in Canada, the saying "At Speedy you're somebody" applies to employees and customers alike. Other significant uses of language to shape culture are as follows:

- T. J. Watson, Jr., son of the founder of International Business Machines, used the metaphor "wild ducks" to describe the type of employees needed by IBM. His point was, "You can make wild ducks tame, but you can never make tame ducks wild again."[17] Wild ducks symbolized the freedom and opportunity that must be available to keep from taming creative employees at IBM.
- At Sequins International, where 80 percent of the employees are Hispanic, words from W. Edwards Deming, "You don't have to please the boss; you have to please the customer," are embroidered in Spanish on the pockets of workers' jackets. Employees work in teams and are empowered to make quality and customer satisfaction improvements.[18]

Recall that culture exists at two levels—the underlying values and assumptions and the visible artifacts and observable behaviors. The slogans, symbols, and ceremonies described above are artifacts that reflect underlying company values.

These visible artifacts and behaviors can be used by managers to shape company values and to strengthen organizational culture. Now we will discuss how a strong corporate culture can have either positive or negative outcomes.

Culture Strength and Adaptation

When an organizational culture is strong, it can have a powerful impact, though not necessarily always a positive one. **Culture strength** refers to the degree of agreement among members of an organization about the importance of specific values. If widespread consensus exists about the importance of those values, the culture is cohesive and strong; if little agreement exists, the culture is weak.[19]

A strong culture is typically associated with the frequent use of ceremonies, symbols, stories, heroes, and slogans. These elements increase employee commitment to the values and strategy of a company.

However, research into some two hundred corporate cultures found that a strong culture does not ensure success unless the culture is one that encourages a healthy adaptation to the external environment.[20] A strong culture that does not encourage adaptation can be more damaging to an organization's success than having a weak culture. Consider the case of IBM in Chapter 1, where a strong corporate culture actually precluded adaptation.

As illustrated in Exhibit 10.4, adaptive corporate cultures have different values and behavior patterns than unadaptive cultures. In adaptive cultures, managers are concerned about customers and employees, and they strongly value processes that contribute to useful change. Behavior is flexible; managers initiate change when needed, even if it involves risk. In an unadaptive corporate culture, on the other hand, managers are more concerned about themselves or some pet project. Their values discourage risk-taking and change. Thus, strong, healthy cultures help

	Adaptive Corporate Cultures	**Unadaptive Corporate Cultures**
Core Values	Managers care deeply about customers, stockholders, and employees. They also strongly value people and processes that can create useful change (for example, leadership initiatives up and down the management hierarchy).	Managers care mainly about themselves, their immediate work group, or some product (or technology) associated with that work group. They value the orderly and risk-reducing management process much more highly than leadership initiatives.
Common Behavior	Managers pay close attention to all their constituencies, especially customers, and initiate change when needed to serve their legitimate interests, even if it entails taking some risks.	Managers tend to be somewhat isolated, political, and bureaucratic. As a result, they do not change their strategies quickly to adjust to or take advantage of changes in their business environments.

Exhibit 10.4
Adaptive Versus Nonadaptive Corporate Cultures

Source: Adapted and reprinted with the permission of The Free Press, an imprint of Simon & Schuster, from *Corporate Culture and Performance* by John P. Kotter and James L. Heskett. Copyright © 1992 by Kotter Associates, Inc. and James L. Heskett.

Book Mark 10.0

Have You Read About This?

Built to Last: Successful Habits of Visionary Companies

by James C. Collins and Jerry I. Porras

In a six-year study comparing eighteen companies that have experienced long-term success with eighteen similar companies that have not performed as well, James Collins and Jerry Porras found a key determining factor in the successful companies to be a culture in which employees share such a strong vision that they know in their hearts what is right for the company. *Built to Last* describes how companies such as 3M, Boeing, Wal-Mart, Merck, Nordstrom, Hewlett-Packard, and others have successfully adapted to a changing world without losing sight of the core values that guide the organization. Collins and Porras found that the successful companies were guided by a "core ideology"—values and a sense of purpose that go beyond just making money and that provide a guide for employee behavior.

Timeless Fundamentals

The book offers four key concepts that show how managers can contribute to building successful companies.

- *Be a clock builder, not a time teller.* Products and market opportunities are vehicles for building a great organization, not the other way around. Visionary leaders concentrate on building adaptive cultures and systems that remain strong despite changes in products, services, or markets.

- *Embrace the "Genius of the AND."* Successful organizations simultaneously embrace two extremes, such as continuity and change, stability and revolution, predictability and chaos.
- *Preserve the core/Stimulate progress.* The core ideology is balanced with a relentless drive for progress. Successful companies set ambitious goals and create an atmosphere that encourages experimentation and learning.
- *Seek consistent alignment.* Strive to make all aspects of the company work in unison with the core ideology. At Disneyland, employees are "cast members" and customers are "guests." Hewlett-Packard's policies reinforce its commitment to respect for each individual.

Conclusion

Built to Last offers important lessons on how managers can build organizations that stand the test of time. By concentrating on the timeless fundamentals, organizations can adapt and thrive in a changing world.

Built to Last: Successful Habits of Visionary Companies, by James C. Collins and Jerry I. Porras, is published by HarperCollins.

organizations adapt to the external environment, whereas strong, unhealthy cultures can encourage an organization to march resolutely in the wrong direction.

As discussed in Book Mark 10.0, a strong adaptive culture is a key determining factor in the success of companies such as Wal-Mart, Johnson & Johnson, and Hewlett-Packard. The Hewlett-Packard stories described earlier reinforced an adaptive internal culture consistent with the "HP Way." Insistence on product quality, recognition of employee achievement, and respect for individual employees are the values responsible for HP's success. Rhone-Poulenc, Inc., the U.S. subsidiary of France's leading chemical and pharmaceutical manufacturer, provides another example of a strong, adaptive culture.

In Practice 10.1   *Rhone-Poulenc, Inc.*

When asked what can help Rhone-Poulenc remain competitive in an ever-changing global world, CEO Peter Neff speaks almost entirely in terms of corporate culture: "You need an atmosphere of openness and respect, you need to let people make mistakes, and you need to reward risk-taking." Under Neff's leadership, Rhone-Poulenc has broken down the walls between functional departments and set up teams of employees empowered to solve problems and make decisions. Employees are guided in their decision making by the company's core values—integrity, safety, innovation, partnership, and quality/customer focus. According to Neff, these values act as a social glue that provides stability in a world of rapid change and gives employees the confidence to take risks. Neff has created a culture in which change is embraced rather than feared.

A basic cultural assumption at Rhone-Poulenc is that all employees want to do a good job and want to make a contribution to the organization. Ideas, big or small, are valued. The company has a spot-bonus program for employees who display creativity in their jobs and each year officially recognizes and celebrates one or more of its teams for innovativeness. Managers at the company view their role as enabling each employee to do and be their best and to continue to learn and grow. "Our success depends on people," says Neff. ". . . on our ability to tap the collective wisdom—that is, the accumulated judgments, perceptions, experiences, intuition, and intelligence—of all our employees."

Rhone-Poulenc's culture involves and empowers each employee, leading not only to some breakthrough products but also to continuous learning throughout the organization, ensuring that the company can adapt to rapid changes in the global environment.[21]

Creating the Culture

How do managers infuse and maintain strong, adaptive corporate cultures at companies like Southwest Airlines, Rhone-Poulenc, or JCPenney?[22] The techniques described earlier of using symbols, stories, language, and ceremonies are important. In addition, emphasis can be given to the selection and socialization of new employees. For example, at Southwest, prospective employees are subjected to rigorous interviewing, sometimes even by Southwest's regular customers, so that only those who fit the culture are hired. In a company such as Procter & Gamble, new employees are assigned minor tasks while they learn to question their prior behaviors, beliefs, and values. Then they have room to assimilate the beliefs and values of P&G. Through extensive training, new recruits constantly hear about the company's transcendent values and overarching purposes, about watershed events in the company's history, and about exemplary individuals—the heroes. These procedures enable organizations to develop strong cultures and use them as a strategic weapon.

STRATEGY AND CULTURE

Strategy and the external environment are big influences on corporate culture. Corporate culture should embody what the organization needs to be effective within its environment. For example, if the external environment requires flexibility and responsiveness, the culture should encourage adaptability. The correct relationship among cultural values and beliefs, organizational strategy, and the business environment can enhance organizational performance.

Studies of culture and effectiveness have proposed that the fit among strategy, environment, and culture is associated with four categories of culture, which are illustrated in Exhibit 10.5.[23] These categories are based on two factors: (1) the extent to which the competitive environment requires flexibility or stability and (2) the extent to which the strategic focus and strength is internal or external. The

Exhibit 10.5

Relationship of Environment and Strategy to Corporate Culture

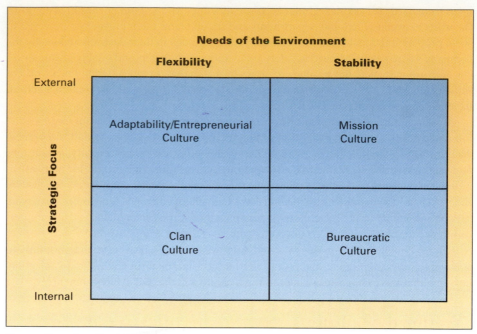

Source: Based on Daniel R. Denison and Aneil K. Mishra, "Toward a Theory of Organizational Culture and Effectiveness," *Organization Science* 6, no. 2 (March-April 1995): 204–23; R. Hooijberg and F. Petrock, "On Cultural Change: Using the Competing Values Framework to Help Leaders Execute a Transformational Strategy," *Human Resource Management* 32 (1993): 29–50; and R. E. Quinn, *Beyond Rational Management: Mastering the Paradoxes and Competing Demands of High Performance* (San Francisco: Jossey-Bass, 1988).

four categories associated with these differences are adaptability/entrepreneurial, mission, clan, and bureaucratic.

The Adaptability/Entrepreneurial Culture

The **adaptability/entrepreneurial culture** is characterized by strategic focus on the external environment through flexibility and change to meet customer needs. The culture encourages norms and beliefs that support the capacity of the organization to detect, interpret, and translate signals from the environment into new behavior responses. This type of company, however, doesn't just react quickly to environmental changes—it actively creates change. Innovation, creativity, and risk-taking are valued and rewarded

An example of the adaptability/entrepreneurial culture is 3M, a company whose values promote individual initiative and entrepreneurship. All new employees attend a class on risk-taking, where they are told to pursue their ideas even if it means defying their supervisors. Another example is Rhone-Poulenc, described earlier in the chapter. After years of steady growth and a number of acquisitions, Rhone-Poulenc found that its culture, which emphasized internal efficiency and consistency in following established policies and procedures, was no longer suitable to meet the demands of the rapidly changing global environment in which it operated. Rhone-Poulenc shifted to an external focus emphasizing the importance of employee flexibility and initiative to meet customer needs. Marketing, electronics, and cosmetic companies may also use this type of culture because they must move quickly to satisfy customers.

The Mission Culture

An organization concerned with serving specific customers in the external environment, but without the need for rapid change, is suited to the mission culture. The **mission culture** is characterized by emphasis on a clear vision of the organization's purpose and on the achievement of goals, such as sales growth, profitability, or market share, to help achieve the purpose. Individual employees may be responsible for a specified level of performance, and the organization promises specified rewards in return. Managers shape behavior by envisioning and communicating a desired future state for the organization. Because the environment is stable, they can translate the vision into measurable goals and evaluate employee performance for meeting them. In some cases, mission cultures reflect a high level of competitiveness and a profit-making orientation.

One example is PepsiCo, where former CEO Wayne Calloway set a vision to be the best consumer products company in the world. Managers who met the high performance standards were generously rewarded—first class air travel, fully loaded company cars, stock options, bonuses, and rapid promotion. Annual performance reviews focus specifically on meeting performance goals, such as sales targets or marketing goals.[24]

The Clan Culture

The **clan culture** has a primary focus on the involvement and participation of the organization's members and on rapidly changing expectations from the external environment. This culture is similar to the clan form of control described in Chapter 9. More than any other, this culture focuses on the needs of employees as the route to high performance. Involvement and participation create a sense of responsibility and ownership and, hence, greater commitment to the organization.

Southwest Airlines, described at the beginning of this chapter, is an example of a clan culture. The most important value is taking care of employees. In so doing, the organization is able to adapt to competition and changing markets. Companies in the fashion and retail industries also use this culture because it releases the creativity of employees to respond to rapidly changing tastes.

The Bureaucratic Culture

The **bureaucratic culture** has an internal focus and a consistency orientation for a stable environment. This organization has a culture that supports a methodical approach to doing business. Symbols, heroes, and ceremonies support cooperation, tradition, and following established policies and practices as a way to achieve goals. Personal involvement is somewhat lower here, but that is outweighed by a high level of consistency, conformity, and collaboration among members. This organization succeeds by being highly integrated and efficient.

One example of a bureaucratic culture is Safeco Insurance Company, considered by some to be stuffy and regimented. Employees take their coffee breaks at an assigned time, and the dress codes specify white shirts and suits for men and no beards. However, employees like this culture. Reliability counts. Extra work is not required. The culture is appropriate for the insurance company, which succeeds because it can be trusted to deliver on insurance policies as agreed.[25]

Ethical Values in Organizations

Of the values that make up an organization's culture, ethical values are now considered among the most important. Ethical standards are becoming part of the formal policies and informal cultures of many organizations, and courses in ethics are taught in many business schools. **Ethics** is the code of moral principles and values that governs the behaviors of a person or group with respect to what is right or wrong. Ethical values set standards as to what is good or bad in conduct and decision making.[26]

Ethics is distinct from behaviors governed by law. The **rule of law** arises from a set of codified principles and regulations that describe how people are required to act, are generally accepted in society, and are enforceable in the courts.[27]

The relationship between ethical standards and legal requirements is illustrated in Exhibit 10.6. Ethical standards for the most part apply to behavior not covered by the law, and the rule of law covers behaviors not necessarily covered by ethical standards. Current laws often reflect combined moral judgments, but not all moral judgments are codified into law. The morality of aiding a drowning person, for example, is not specified by law, and driving on the righthand side of the road has no moral basis; but in areas such as robbery or murder, rules and moral standards overlap.

Many people believe that if you are not breaking the law, then you are behaving in an ethical manner, but ethics often go far beyond the law.[28] Many behaviors have not been codified, and managers must be sensitive to emerging norms and values about those issues. **Managerial ethics** are principles that guide the decisions and behaviors of managers with regard to whether they are right or wrong in a moral sense. The notion of **social responsibility** is an extension of this idea and refers to management's obligation to make choices and take action so that the organization contributes to the welfare and interest of society as well as to itself.[29]

Examples of the need for managerial ethics are as follows:[30]

• The supervisor of a travel agency was aware that her agents and she could receive large bonuses for booking one hundred or more clients each month with an auto rental firm, although clients typically wanted the rental agency selected on the basis of lowest cost.

Exhibit 10.6

Relationship Between the Rule of Law and Ethical Standards

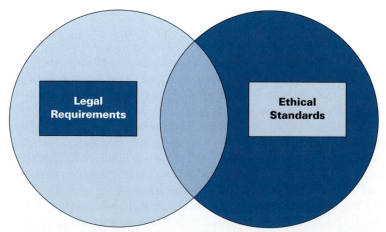

Source: LaRue Tone Hosmer, *The Ethics of Management,* 2d ed. (Homewood, Ill.: Irwin, 1991).

- The executive in charge of a parts distribution facility told employees to tell phone customers that inventory was in stock even if it was not. Replenishing the item only took one to two days, no one was hurt by the delay, and the business was kept from competitors.
- The project manager for a consulting project wondered whether some facts should be left out of a report because the marketing executives paying for the report would look bad if the facts were reported.
- A North American manufacturer operating abroad was asked to make cash payments (a bribe) to government officials and was told it was consistent with local customs, despite being illegal in North America.

These issues are exceedingly difficult to resolve and often represent dilemmas. An **ethical dilemma** arises when each alternative choice or behavior seems undesirable because of a potentially negative ethical consequence. Right or wrong cannot be clearly identified. These choices can be aided by establishing ethical values within the organization as part of corporate culture. Corporate culture can embrace the ethical values needed for business success.

SOURCES OF ETHICAL VALUES IN ORGANIZATIONS

The standards for ethical or socially responsible conduct are embodied within each employee as well as within the organization itself. In addition, external stakeholders can influence standards of what is ethical and socially responsible. The immediate forces that impinge on ethical decisions are summarized in Exhibit 10.7. Individual beliefs and values, a person's ethical decision framework, and moral development influence personal ethics. Organization culture, as we

Exhibit 10.7
Forces That Shape Managerial Ethics

Personal Ethics

Beliefs and Values
Moral Development
Ethical Framework

Organizational Culture

Rituals, Ceremonies
Stories, Heroes
Language, Slogans
Symbols
Founder, History

Is Decision or Behavior Ethical and Socially Responsible?

Organizational Systems

Structure
Policies, Rules
Code of Ethics
Reward System
Selection, Training

External Stakeholders

Government Regulations
Customers
Special Interest Groups
Global Market Forces

have already discussed, shapes the overall framework of values within the organization. Moreover, formal organization systems influence values and behaviors according to the organization's policy framework and reward systems.

Companies also respond to numerous stakeholders in determining what is right. They consider how their actions may be viewed by customers, government agencies, shareholders, and the general community, as well as the impact each alternative course of action may have on various stakeholders. All of these factors can be explored to understand ethical decisions in organizations.[31]

Personal Ethics

Every individual brings a set of personal beliefs and values into the workplace. Personal values and the moral reasoning that translates these values into behavior are an important aspect of ethical decision making in organizations.[32]

The family backgrounds and spiritual values of managers provide principles by which they carry out business. In addition, people go through stages of moral development that affect their ability to translate values into behavior. For example, children have a low level of moral development, making decisions and behaving to obtain rewards and avoid physical punishment. At an intermediate level of development, people learn to conform to expectations of good behavior as defined by colleagues and society. Most managers are at this level, willingly upholding the law and responding to societal expectations. At the highest level of moral development are people who develop an internal set of standards. These are self-chosen ethical principles that are more important to decisions than external expectations. Only a few people reach this high level, which can mean breaking laws if necessary to sustain higher moral principles.[33]

The other personal factor is whether managers have developed an *ethical framework* that guides their decisions. *Utilitarian theory,* for example, argues that ethical decisions should be made to generate the greatest benefits for the largest number of people. This framework is often consistent with business decisions because costs and benefits can be calculated in dollars. The *personal liberty* framework argues that decisions should be made to ensure the greatest possible freedom of choice and liberty for individuals. Liberties include freedom to act on one's conscience, free speech, due process, and the right to privacy. The *distributive justice* framework holds that moral decisions are those that promote equity, fairness, and impartiality with respect to the distribution of rewards and the administration of rules, which are essential for social cooperation.[34]

Organizational Culture

Rarely can ethical or unethical business practices be attributed entirely to the personal ethics of a single individual. Because business practices reflect the values, attitudes, and behavior patterns of an organization's culture, ethics is as much an organizational issue as a personal one. Though Johnson & Johnson's handling of the Tylenol-poisoning crisis has sometimes been attributed to the ethical standards of then-CEO James Burke, Burke himself has pointed out that the decisions in connection with that crisis reflected a set of values and principles that has been deeply ingrained throughout the company since its early days. Several years ago, Johnson & Johnson won a Business Ethics Award for sustaining ethical decision making over four decades.[35]

General Mills is another company whose ethical standards have been maintained from its beginning through seven CEOs, multiple acquisitions, and geographical expansion. The legal department always advises managers not to enter into a proposed move if there is any question about legality. Investments in equipment to ensure environmental safety are considered less expensive than risking contamination. A toy called Riviton was pulled from the market because of two children's deaths in one year, although obvious misuse by the customers was the cause and there was no request for a recall. These decisions are part of the General Mills ethical culture.[36]

Organizational Systems

The third category of influences that shape managerial ethics is formal organizational systems. This includes the basic architecture of the organization, such as whether ethical values are incorporated in policies and rules; whether an explicit code of ethics is available and issued to members; whether organizational rewards, including praise, attention, and promotions, are linked to ethical behavior; and whether ethics is a consideration in the selection and training of employees. These formal efforts can reinforce ethical values that exist in the informal culture.

Today, more and more companies are establishing formal ethics programs. NYNEX Corporation, embarrassed by scandal when a group of managers was discovered to have attended supplier-sponsored parties that included paid sexual services, has worked overtime to prevent future ethical problems. The company has provided extensive training in ethical standards to ninety-five thousand employees, created a sixty-page "Code of Business Conduct," started a monthly ethics newsletter, and set up a toll-free, confidential ethics hot line. The Boeing Company provides all employees with written materials that familiarize them with the company's high ethical standards and help them recognize and handle ethical dilemmas in their day-to-day work.[37]

External Stakeholders

Managerial ethics and social responsibility are also influenced by a variety of external stakeholders, groups outside the organization that have a stake in the organization's performance. Ethical and socially responsible decision making recognizes that the organization is part of a larger community and considers the impact of a decision or action on all stakeholders.[38] Important external stakeholders are government agencies, customers, special interest groups such as those concerned with the natural environment, and global market forces.

Companies must operate within the limits of certain government regulations, such as safety laws, environmental protection requirements, and many other laws and regulations. Customers are concerned about the quality, safety, and availability of goods and services. For example, even though Dow Corning has an ambitious ethics program, the company's reputation as an ethical company was seriously damaged by the failure to keep customers satisfied with the safety of its silicone breast implants.[39]

Special interest groups continue to be one of the largest stakeholder concerns that companies face. Today, those concerned with corporate responsibility to the natural environment are particularly vocal. Thus, environmentalism is becoming an integral part of organizational planning and decision making for leading companies such as Johnson & Johnson, Hewlett-Packard, Pitney Bowes, and Colgate

The New Paradigm   Starbucks Coffee

Starbucks Coffee has always projected itself as a progressive and socially responsible business, touting its "Bean Stock" employee ownership plan, full medical benefits for even part-time workers, and an idealistic mission of contributing to society while also running a successful business. Starbucks makes an annual six-figure donation to the non-profit international aid organization, CARE, in support of educational and social programs in coffee-growing regions. Yet the company was targeted by the Chicago-based U.S./Guatemala Labor Education Project, claiming that Guatemalan workers toil in inhumane conditions, earning two cents a pound for beans that Starbucks sells for up to $8 a pound. Activists began passing out leaflets to customers entering Starbucks coffee bars, and hundreds of letters demanding action poured in from customers, investors, and the general public.

Soon, management was being asked to adopt a code of conduct that would encourage Third World employers to ban child labor and to provide workers with higher wages, better working conditions, and at least minimal health care. Starbucks responded with the first-ever agricultural code of conduct. In addition to upholding general ethical guidelines, such as aspiring to purchase coffee from suppliers who share a commitment to treating workers with dignity and respect, the company developed a list of concrete, measurable goals. These include a strategic plan for implementing a "coffee mission" for each country in which Starbucks does business. Guatemala became the initial focus, where Starbucks is working to develop a set of industry standards in collaboration with Anacafe, the Guatemala coffee producers organization. Starbucks is also seeking collaboration with other specialty coffee companies to identify specific actions to improve the lives of coffee workers.

Although it is likely that Starbucks will continue to face challenges on ethical issues, the company has shown a commitment to develop organizational systems and policies that respond to the interests of external as well as internal stakeholders.

Source: Mary Scott, "Interview: Howard Schultz," *Business Ethics,* November/December 1995, 26–29; and Susan Gaines, "Growing Pains," *Business Ethics,* January/February 1996, 20–23.

Palmolive. Over a four-year period, Hewlett-Packard eliminated all ozone-depleting agents from its manufacturing process. Patagonia, a California-based outdoor apparel company, developed a list of nine environmental goals for the company, three of which were eliminating all solid waste sent to landfills, reducing the use of nonrenewable energy, and including environmental costs in company accounting and production systems.[40]

Another growing pressure on organizations is related to the rapidly changing global market. Companies operating globally face difficult ethical issues. Thousands of U.S. workers have lost jobs or earning power because companies can get the same work done overseas for lower costs. For example, Yakima Products, located in Arcata, California, transferred all production of its cartop carrying systems for bikes, skis and other sporting gear to Mexico. Although the decision was financially sound and clearly served the interests of shareholders, employees and the local community felt angry and betrayed.[41] Levi Strauss contracted for low-cost labor in Burma and China but later felt ethically compelled to pull out of those contracts because of human rights violations in those countries. As the business world becomes increasingly global, issues of ethics and social responsibility will likely become even more difficult.[42] The New Paradigm box describes how Starbucks Coffee Company is facing these issues head-on.

HOW LEADERS SHAPE CULTURE AND ETHICS

A report issued by the Business Roundtable—an association of chief executives from 250 large corporations—discussed ethics, policy, and practice in one hundred member companies, including GTE, Xerox, Johnson & Johnson, Boeing, and Hewlett-Packard.[43] In the experience of the surveyed companies, the single most important factor in ethical decision making was the role of top management in providing commitment, leadership, and example for ethical values. The CEO and other top managers must be committed to specific values and must give constant leadership in tending and renewing those values. Values can be communicated in a number of ways—speeches, company publications, policy statements, and, especially, personal actions. Top leaders are responsible for creating and sustaining a culture that emphasizes the importance of ethical behavior for all employees every day. When the CEO engages in unethical practices or fails to take firm and decisive action in response to the unethical practices of others, this attitude filters down through the organization. Formal ethics codes and training programs are worthless if leaders do not set and live up to high standards of ethical conduct.[44]

The following sections examine how managers signal and implement values through leadership as well as through the formal systems of the organization.

Value Based Leadership

The underlying value system of an organization cannot be managed in the traditional way. Issuing an authoritative directive, for example, has little or no impact on an organization's value system. Organizational values are developed and strengthened primarily through **value based leadership**, a relationship between a leader and followers that is based on shared, strongly internalized values that are advocated and acted upon by the leader.[45] Leaders influence cultural and ethical values by clearly articulating a vision for organizational values that employees can believe in, communicating the vision throughout the organization, and institutionalizing the vision through everyday behavior, rituals, ceremonies, and symbols, as well as through organizational systems and policies.

Leaders must remember that every statement and action has impact on culture and values, perhaps without their realizing it. Employees learn about values, beliefs, and goals from watching managers, just as students learn which topics are important for an exam, what professors like, and how to get a good grade from watching professors. To be effective value based leaders, executives often use symbols, ceremonies, speeches, and slogans that match the values. Most important, actions speak louder than words, so value based leaders "walk their talk."[46] At Eastman Kodak, for example, CEO George Fischer has emphasized the organization's commitment to social responsibility by linking a portion of his own pay to social factors.[47]

Value based leaders engender a high level of trust and respect from employees, based not only on their stated values but also on the courage, determination, and self-sacrifice they demonstrate in upholding those values. Leaders can use this respect and trust to motivate employees toward high performance and a sense of purpose in achieving the organizational vision. When leaders are willing to make personal sacrifices for the sake of values, employees also become more willing to do so. This element of self-sacrifice puts a somewhat spiritual connotation on the process of leadership. Indeed, one writer in organization theory, Karl Weick, has said that, "Managerial work can be viewed as managing myth, symbols, and labels . . . ; because managers traffic so often in images, the appropriate role for the manager may be evangelist rather than accountant."[48]

An excellent example of a value based leader is Max De Pree, retired CEO of Herman Miller, whose books, *Leadership Is an Art* and *Leadership Jazz,* offer insights into his success as a leader.

In Practice 10.2	*Herman Miller*

Herman Miller, a manufacturer of office furniture, was founded on the strong values of D. J. De Pree, who believed in employee participation and the importance of treating each individual with respect. The company adopted a plan as early as 1950 to provide workers extra pay when their unit's goals were met. Another noteworthy characteristic was limiting the CEO's salary to twenty times the amount made by the average factory worker, far less than the 117 times that a typical *Fortune* 500 CEO earns.

D. J. De Pree's son, Max, served in a number of capacities at the company, eventually becoming CEO. Max De Pree built upon the values of worker participation espoused by his father in his "covenant" model of leadership. He defines a *covenant* as an emotional bond creating mutual trust built on shared goals and values. De Pree believes effective leadership can occur only when there is a "sacred" relationship between leaders and followers. For De Pree, leadership and ethics intersect at these primary points:

1. Ethical leadership withers without justice. There should be a fair distribution of profits, and leaders should recognize their indebtedness to those who follow.
2. Leaders assume stewardship of limited resources and exercise personal restraint so that meaningful relationships in the lives of followers are honored.
3. Leaders subsume their needs to those of their followers and learn how to make a commitment to the common good.
4. Leaders know how to bear, not inflict, pain.

Max De Pree was a hero to his workers. He symbolized hard work, integrity, and a constant awareness of how his decisions affected those who followed his leadership. He believed that leadership should "[liberate] people to do what is required of them in the most effective and humane way possible." De Pree worked to create and sustain an environment in which each employee wanted to do his or her best, helping the company gain recognition by *Fortune* magazine as one of the ten best-managed, most innovative companies in America.[49]

Formal Structure and Systems

Another set of tools leaders can use to shape cultural and ethical values is the formal structure and systems of the organization. These systems have been especially effective in recent years for influencing managerial ethics.

Structure. Managers can assign responsibility for ethical values to a specific position. This not only allocates organization time and energy to the problem but symbolizes to everyone the importance of ethics. One example is an **ethics committee**, which is a group of executives appointed to oversee company ethics. The committee provides rulings on questionable ethical issues and assumes responsibility for disciplining wrongdoers.

Many companies are setting up ethics offices that go beyond a "police" mentality to act more as counseling centers. Northrup Grumman, a Los Angeles defense contractor, set up an ethics office in the mid-1980s primarily to ferret out wrongdoers. Today, however, the department spends most of its time dealing with day-to-day ethical dilemmas, questions, and appeals for advice. The department is also responsible for training employees based on a statement of values intended to guide behavior.[50]

Another example is an **ethics ombudsperson**, who is a single manager, perhaps with a staff, who serves as the corporate conscience. As workforces become more diverse and organizations continue to emphasize greater employee involvement, it is likely that more and more companies will assign ombudspersons to listen to grievances, investigate ethical complaints, and point out employee concerns and possible ethical abuses to top management. For the system to work, it is necessary for the person in this position to have direct access to the chairman or CEO, as does the corporate ombudsperson for Pitney Bowes.[51]

Disclosure Mechanisms.   The ethics office, committee, or ombudsperson provides mechanisms for employees to voice concerns about ethical practices. One important function is to establish supportive policies and procedures about whistle-blowing. **Whistle-blowing** is employee disclosure of illegal, immoral, or illegitimate practices on the part of the organization.[52] One value of corporate policy is to protect whistle-blowers so they will not be transferred to lower-level positions or fired because of their ethical concerns. A policy can also encourage whistle-blowers to stay within the organization—for instance, to quietly blow the whistle to responsible managers.[53] Whistle-blowers have the option to stop organizational activities by going to newspaper or television reporters, but as a last resort.

Although whistle-blowing has become widespread in recent years, it is still risky for employees, who can lose their jobs or be ostracized by co-workers. Sometimes managers believe a whistle-blower is out of line and think they are acting correctly to fire or sabotage that employee. As ethical problems in the corporate world increase, many companies are looking for ways to protect whistle-blowers. In addition, calls are increasing for legal protection for those who report illegal or unethical business activities.[54]

When there are no protective measures, whistle-blowers suffer, and the company may continue its unethical or illegal practices. After exposing fraud in the real estate funds he managed for Prudential Insurance Company of America, Mark Jorgensen suffered ostracism by his supervisor and colleagues, was accused by company lawyers of breaking the law, and was eventually dismissed. Although the company later offered Jorgensen an apology and his job back (which he declined), this could not make up for the months of despair he and his family suffered.[55]

Although many whistle-blowers are prepared to suffer financial loss to maintain ethical standards, many companies have created a climate in which employees feel free to point out problems. A growing number of corporations, including Texas Instruments, NYNEX, Raytheon, Pacific Bell, and Northern Telecom, are setting up ethics hot lines that give employees a confidential way to report misconduct. These hot lines also serve as help lines. According to Gary Edwards, president of the Ethics Resource Center, about 65 to 85 percent of calls to hot lines in the organizations he advises are calls for counsel on ethical issues rather than calls to blow the whistle on wrongdoers. Northrup Grumman's "Openline" fields about 1,400 calls a year, of which only one-fourth are reports of misdeeds.[56]

Code of Ethics.   A recent study by the Center for Business Ethics found that 90 percent of *Fortune* 500 companies and almost half of all other companies have developed a corporate code of ethics.[57] The code clarifies company expectations of employee conduct and makes clear that the company expects its personnel to recognize the ethical dimensions of corporate behavior.

Some companies use broader mission statements within which ethics is a part. These statements define ethical values as well as corporate culture and contain language about company responsibility, quality of product, and treatment of employees. GTE, Norton, and Chemical Bank all have established statements of cultural and ethical values.[58] Northern Telecom's *Code of Business Conduct*, which is provided to all employees in booklet form and is also available on the Internet, is a set of standards and guidelines that illustrates how the company's core values and mission translate into ethical business practices.

A code of ethics states the values or behaviors that are expected as well as those that will not be tolerated or backed up by management's action. A code of ethics or larger mission statement is an important tool in the management of organizational values.

Training Programs.   To ensure that ethical issues are considered in daily decision making, companies can supplement a written code of ethics with employee training programs.[59] A recent survey showed that 45 percent of responding companies were including ethics training in employee seminars. McDonnell Douglas has a corporatewide ethics training program that all management and nonmanagement employees attend.[60] These training programs include case examples to give employees a chance to wrestle with ethical dilemmas. Training also provides rules or guidelines for decision making, and it discusses codes of ethics and mission statements. Citicorp has developed an ethics board game, which teams of employees use to solve hypothetical ethical problems.[61]

In an important step, ethics programs also include frameworks for ethical decision making, such as the utilitarian approach described earlier in this chapter. Learning these frameworks helps managers act autonomously and still think their way through a difficult decision. In a few companies, managers are also taught about the stages of moral development, which helps to bring them to a high stage of ethical decision making. This training has been an important catalyst for establishing ethical behavior and integrity as critical components of strategic competitiveness.[62]

One company that has made a strong commitment to incorporating ethics into its formal systems for more than thirty years is Texas Instruments, which today spends more than $750,000 annually to support a six-member ethics department.

In Practice 10.3	*Texas Instruments*

Employees at this high-tech electronics firm work in a rapidly changing environment where difficult decisions with no clear right or wrong answer often have to be made on a daily basis. Texas Instruments (TI) developed a formal code of ethics in 1961 but has now gone far beyond that initial step to hold the company and its employees to high standards of integrity. TI's ethics department spends much of its time and budget on ethics awareness. In addition to regular newsletters and supplemental publications, weekly news articles on ethics topics are sent to sixty thousand employees worldwide on the company's electronic mail system. The company has also produced a series of more than fifty short videotapes on ethical dilemmas, which managers can use as a way to encourage discussion of ethical issues.

TI's ethics office has been extraordinarily successful in maintaining direct dialog with the company's global workforce. Employees may contact the office through a toll-free confidential hot line, send messages or questions to an ethics post office box (separate from the corporate mail system), or communicate through a secure e-mail address. Unlike some companies that operate ethics hot lines only during business hours, Texas Instruments keeps its hot line open twenty-four hours a day and makes it available to suppliers and customers as well as employees. Anyone wishing to express a concern about the company is encouraged to call.

Texas Instruments also makes effective use of training. In addition to an eight-hour ethics training course, TI is incorporating an ethical component into every course it offers. For example, a new course on how to use Windows 95 included information on when it is permissible to copy and distribute software.

Investing in ethics has paid off for Texas Instruments. Employees say they are proud to work for a company that holds them to the highest standards. TI hasn't experienced the same legal troubles many other large defense contractors have, and the company has earned a string of awards for its ethics programs. According to Carl Skooglung, ethics director, there are solid, strategic reasons for investing in ethics: "We believe our reputation for integrity is every bit as important as the technology base we've developed."[63]

Texas Instruments believes weaving ethics into all the systems of the organization is essential to building and sustaining a highly ethical company. By integrating ethics throughout the organization, companies like TI make personal and organizational integrity a part of day-to-day business.

SUMMARY AND INTERPRETATION

This chapter covered a range of material on corporate culture, the importance of cultural and ethical values, and techniques managers can use to influence these values. Culture is the set of key values, beliefs, and understandings shared by members of an organization. Organizational cultures serve two critically important functions—to integrate members so that they know how to relate to one another and to help the organization adapt to the external environment. Culture can be observed and interpreted through rites and ceremonies, stories and heroes, symbols, and language. Strong corporate cultures can be either adaptive or unadaptive. Adaptive cultures have different values and different behavior patterns than unadaptive cultures. Strong but unhealthy cultures can be detrimental to a company's chances for success. Four types of cultures that may exist in organizations are adaptability/entrepreneurial culture, mission culture, clan culture, and bureaucratic culture.

An important aspect of organizational values is management ethics, which is the set of values governing behavior with respect to what is right or wrong. Ethical decision making in organizations is shaped by many factors: personal characteristics, which include personal beliefs, moral development, and the adoption of ethical frameworks for decision making; organizational culture, which is the extent to which values, heroes, traditions, and symbols reinforce ethical decision making; organizational systems, which pertain to the formal structure, policies, codes of ethics, and reward systems that reinforce ethical or unethical choices; and the interests and concerns of external stakeholders, which include government agencies, customers, special interest groups, and global market forces.

Finally, the chapter discussed how leaders can shape culture and ethics. One important idea is value based leadership, which means leaders define a vision of proper values, communicate it throughout the organization, and institutionalize it through everyday behavior, rituals, ceremonies, and symbols. We also discussed formal systems that are important for shaping ethical values. Formal systems include an ethics committee, an ethics ombudsperson, disclosure mechanisms for whistle-blowing, ethics training programs, and a code of ethics or mission statement that specifies ethical values.

Key Concepts

adaptability/entrepreneurial culture	language
bureaucratic culture	legends
clan culture	managerial ethics
culture	mission culture
culture strength	myths
ethical dilemma	rites and ceremonies
ethics	rule of law
ethics committee	social responsibility
ethics ombudsperson	stories
external adaptation	symbol
heroes	value based leadership
internal integration	whistle-blowing

Discussion Questions

1. Describe observable symbols, ceremonies, dress, or other aspects of culture and the underlying values they represent for an organization where you have worked.
2. Discuss how a strong corporate culture could be negative as well as positive for an organization.
3. Do you think a bureaucratic culture would be less employee-oriented than a clan culture? Discuss.
4. Discuss the differences among rites of enhancement, renewal, and integration.
5. Why is value based leadership so important to the influence of culture? Does a symbolic act communicate more about company values than an explicit statement? Discuss.
6. Are you aware of a situation where either you or someone you know was confronted by an ethical dilemma, such as being encouraged to inflate an expense account? Do you think the person's decision was affected by individual moral development or by the accepted values within the company? Explain.
7. From where do managers derive ethical values? From where have you derived your ethical values? Do you think managers use ethical decision frameworks as a part of their decision making? Why?
8. What importance would you attribute to leadership statements and actions for influencing ethical values and decision making in an organization?
9. How do external stakeholders influence ethical decision making in an organization? Discuss why globalization has contributed to more complex ethical issues for today's organizations.
10. Codes of ethics have been criticized for transferring responsibility for ethical behavior from the organization to the individual employee. Do you agree? Do you think a code of ethics is valuable for an organization?

Briefcase

As an organization manager, keep these guides in mind:

1. Pay attention to corporate culture. Understand the underlying values, assumptions, and beliefs on which culture is based as well as its observable manifestations. Evaluate corporate culture based on rites and ceremonies, stories and heroes, symbols, and language.

2. Make sure corporate culture is consistent with strategy and environment. Culture can be shaped to fit the needs of both. Four types of culture are adaptability/entrepreneurial culture, mission culture, clan culture, and bureaucratic culture.

3. Take control of ethical values in the organization. Ethics is not the same as following the law. Ethical decisions are influenced by management's personal background, by organizational culture, and by organizational systems.

4. Act as a leader for the internal culture and ethical values that are important to the organization. Influence the value system through value based leadership, including the use of ceremonies, slogans, symbols, and stories. Communicate important values to employees to enhance organizational effectiveness, and remember that actions speak louder than words.

5. Use the formal systems of the organization to implement desired cultural and ethical values. These systems include an ethics committee, ethics ombudsperson, disclosure mechanisms, a code of ethics, a mission statement, and training in ethical decision-making frameworks.

Chapter Ten Workbook *Shop 'til You Drop: Corporate Culture in the Retail World**

To understand more about corporate culture, visit two retail stores and compare them according to various factors. Go to one discount/low-end store, such as Kmart or Wal-Mart, and to one high-end store, such as Saks Fifth Avenue, Dayton/Hudson's, Goldwater's, or Dillard's. Do not interview any employees, but instead be an observer or a shopper. After your visits, fill out the table on p. 390 for each store. Spend at least two hours in each store on a busy day and be very observant.

*Copyright 1996 by Dorothy Marcic. All rights reserved.

Culture Item	Discount Store	High-End Department Store
1. Mission of store: What is it, and is it clear to employees?		
2. Individual initiative: Is it encouraged?		
3. Reward system: What are employees rewarded for?		
4. Teamwork: Do people within one department or across departments work together or talk with each other?		
5. Company loyalty: Is there evidence of loyalty or of enthusiasm to be working there?		
6. Dress: Are there uniforms? Is there a dress code? How strong is it? How do you rate employees' personal appearance in general?		
7. Diversity or commonality of employees: Is there diversity or commonality in age, education, race, personality, and so on?		
8. Service orientation: Is the customer valued or tolerated?		
9. Human resource development: Is there opportunity for growth and advancement?		

Questions

1. How does the culture seem to influence employee behavior in each store?
2. What effect does employees' behavior have on customers?
3. Which store was more pleasant to be in? How does that relate to the mission of the store?

Case for Analysis *Dinner for Four (A)* *

Professor Erskine heard the beep and saw the *Ctrl-Enter* message signal flashing. He displayed the message and began to read.

To: jerskine@novell.business.uwo.ca
Subject: Re: Ethics for discussion
From: s4anutrs@sms.business (Siriporn Anutrsothi)
Date: Thu, 07 Apr 94 15:33:14 EST
In-Reply-To: <CnuLFK.138@exnet.com>
Organization: University of Western Ontario
Newsgroups: soc.culture.thai
From: s01g@exnet.com (L Godfrey)
Subject: Re: Ethics for discussion
Organization: ExNet Public-Access News, London, UK +44 81 244 0077
References: <ygOckc1w165w@sms.business.uwo.ca>
Date: Wed, 6 Apr 1994 17:18:51 GMT

s4anutrs@sms.business.uwo.ca (Siriporn Anutrsothi) writes:

> This is not to say that any action is right or wrong.
> I just want to get some opinion on the following
> incidence. Recently I heard that a sub-committee
> of the MBA Association in my university did the
> following. One group in the MBA Association was
> to take care of organizing the MBA orientation
> last fall. At the end, four of the organisers saw that
> there were some money left, so they let them-
> selves have a dinner and drinks which cost $450-.
> This was charged to the organization but the As-
> sociation did not agree with the expense. The four
> people were asked to pay the money back. Only
> one paid back because he was elected to the Asso-
> ciation. The other three did not even feel anything
> for their action.
>
> I said it is unfair. The worst is when I asked
> around for some of my friends' opinions on this
> point, they don't care less. (These are all Canadi-
> ans. There are no Thais here in the MBA pro-
> gram.) I think the problem here is the empathy.
> People around here are indifferent about this
> incident.
>
> There is a saying "Those who know but didn't do
> anything to stop it are as sinful as those who did
> it." I didn't say that this does not happen in Thai-
> land. At least we accept that these things happen.

> What I am concerned about is that North Ameri-
> cans preach that they have a higher ethical stan-
> dard than the Asians', but they cannot live up to it
> and don't even accept it.
>
> Now I would like to ask the Thais who are study-
> ing here: what would you feel if this happened in
> your university here? (I forgot to tell you that the
> money in the MBA Association is donated by the
> MBA students only. The University has no claim
> on it. The Faculty say they can't control these peo-
> ple. I think the school's reputation is at stake
> here!!!)
>
> How about if this happened in Thailand? What
> will your reaction be? Will you do anything or
> even think about it?
>
> Thanks and I will read all the feedback.
> Siriporn

Professor Erskine knew Siriporn since she had taken his fall elective course. The course was focused essentially on "becoming a manager," and on several occasions the class had discussed ethical issues for newly appointed managers.

Siriporn, who had just finished her MBA program at Western, was a quiet spoken but regular contributor to the class and her classmates had listened attentively when she softly offered her opinions and views in class discussions.

Professor Erskine paused before reading further a reply from L. Godfrey.

*Siriporn Anutrsothi allowed Professor James A. Erskine to present her information in case form solely to provide material for class discussion. The case is not intended to illustrate either effective or ineffective handling of a managerial situation. Certain names and other identifying information may have been disguised to protect confidentiality. Any form of reproduction, storage or transmittal of this material is prohibited without the written permission of the Western Business School. To order, call (519) 661-3208 or write Case and Publication Services, Western Business School, London, Ontario, Canada, N6A 3K7. Copyright © 1994 The University of Western Ontario; 94/10/20.

Case for Analysis *Dinner for Four (B)**

Professor Erskine continued to read the E-mail message sent by Siriporn Anutrsothi.

> s4anutrs@sms.business.uwo.ca (Siriporn Anutrsothi)
> Western Business School—London, Ontario

As I'm sure you know, I'm not a Thai, but nonetheless I have an opinion on what you should do. Write a letter to the president (chair or whatever) of the MBA association saying the same as you have said above, and insist that the money be collected from those who have not paid back, and redistributed amongst those who donated it. Send a copy of this letter to the Dean of the faculty, and a copy to the office of the University president. You might point out that in Canada, obtaining money by deception is illegal, as is embezzlement (what you describe falls into one or the other of these categories, depending on whether or not there was an intention to misspend the money at the time it was collected).

If you do as I say, it is almost certain that the authorities will be forced to investigate the matter, and the culprits will be asked to repay. While the university may have no direct control over the association, they do have a duty of care to their students, and they have the authority to recognize or bar any particular organisation on their campus. If you don't have any success, you might consider reporting the matter to the police (who will almost certainly not want to act, but will if you press the point).

I suggest this matter is not so much an example of corruption, as one of ignorance of the students about what is permissible. Canadians are, as you know, not so very bright, and they have to be shown what is the right way to do things.

A gentle hint—the word you want in your text above is apathy, not empathy.

laurence

Now what, thought Erskine!

*Siriporn Anutrsothi allowed Professor James A. Erskine to present her information in case form solely to provide material for class discussion. The case is not intended to illustrate either effective or ineffective handling of a managerial situation. Certain names and other identifying information may have been disguised to protect confidentiality. Any form of reproduction, storage or transmittal of this material is prohibited without the written permission of the Western Business School. To order, call (519) 661-3208 or write Case and Publication Services, Western Business School, London, Ontario, Canada, N6A 3K7. Copyright © 1994 The University of Western Ontario; 94/10/20.

Case for Analysis *Implementing Strategic Change**

On October 15, 1987, James Fulmer, chief executive officer of Allied Industries, reviewed three notes he had exchanged with Frank Curtis, president of a company owned by Allied. The two men were going to meet in a few minutes to discuss problems that had recently surfaced. During the past decade, Allied had aggressively pursued a growth objective based on a conglomerate strategy of acquiring companies in distress. Chairman Fulmer's policy was to appoint a new chief operating officer for each acquisition with instructions to facilitate a turnaround. Mr. Fulmer reviewed two of the notes he wrote to Curtis.

*John M. Champion and John H. James, Critical Incidents in Management: Decision and Policy Issues, 6th ed. (Homewood, Ill.: Irwin, 1989), 138–40.

DATE: *January 15, 1986: Memorandum*

TO: *Frank Curtis, Director of Fiscal Affairs, Allied Industries*

FROM: *James Fulmer, Chairman, Allied Industries*

SUBJECT: *Your Appointment as President, Lee Medical Supplies*

You are aware that Allied Industries recently acquired Lee Medical Supplies. Mr. John Lee, founder and president of the company, has agreed to retire, and in line with our earlier discussions, I am appointing you to replace him. Our acquisitions group will brief you on the company, but I want to warn you that Lee Medical Supplies has a history of mismanagement. As a distributor of medical items, the company's sales last year totaled approximately $300 million, with net earnings of only $12 million. Your job is to make company sales and profits compatible with Allied standards. You are reminded that it is my policy to call for an independent evaluation of company progress and your performance as president after 18 months.

DATE: *September 10, 1987: Memorandum*

TO: *Frank Curtis, President, Lee Medical Supplies*

FROM: *James Fulmer, Chairman, Allied Industries*

SUBJECT: *Serious Problems at Lee Medical Supplies*

In accord with corporate policy, consultants recently conducted an evaluation of Lee Medical Supplies. In a relatively short period of time, you have increased sales and profits to meet Allied's standards, but I am alarmed at other aspects of your performance, as revealed by the consultant's report. I am told that during the past 18 months, three of your nine vice presidents have resigned and that you have terminated four others. An opinion survey conducted by the consultants indicates that a low state of morale exists and that your managerial appointees are regarded by their subordinates as hard-nosed perfectionists obsessed with quotas and profits. Employees report that ruthless competition now exists between divisions, regions, and districts. They also note that the collegial, family-oriented atmosphere fostered by Mr. Lee has been replaced by a dog-eat-dog situation characterized by negative management attitudes toward employee feelings and needs. After you have studied the enclosed report from the consultants, we will meet to

discuss their findings. I am particularly concerned with their final conclusion that "a form of corporate cancer seems to be spreading throughout Lee Medical Supplies."

As Chairman Fulmer prepared to read the third note, written by Frank Curtis, he reflected on his exit interview with the consultants. While Fulmer considered Curtis to be a financial expert and a turnaround specialist, his subordinates characterized Curtis as an autocrat, a hatchetman, and better suited to be a marine boot camp commander.

DATE: *September 28, 1987: Memorandum*

TO: *Mr. James Fulmer*

FROM: *Mr. Frank Curtis*

SUBJECT: *The so-called "Serious Problems" at Lee Medical Supplies*

I have received your memorandum dated September 10, 1987, and reviewed the consultant's report. When you appointed me to my present position, I was instructed to take over an unprofitable company and make it profitable. I have done so in 18 months, although I inherited a family-owned business that by your own admission had been mismanaged for years. I found a group of managers and salespeople with an average company tenure of 22 years. They believed their jobs were guaranteed for life. Mr. Lee had centralized all personnel decisions so that only he could terminate an employee. He tolerated mediocre performance. All employees were paid on a straight salary basis with seniority the sole criterion for advancement. Some emphasis was given to increasing sales each year, but none was given to reducing costs and increasing profits. Employees did indeed find the company a fun place to work, did express undying loyalty and love for Lee, and a feeling of being a part of a family did permeate the company. Such attitudes were, however, accompanied by mediocrity, incompetency, and poor performance.

I found it necessary to implement immediate strategic changes in five areas: the organization's structure, employee rewards and incentives, management information systems, allocation of resources, and managerial leadership style. As a result, sales areas were reorganized into divisions, regions, and districts. Managers that I felt were incompetent and/or lacking in commitment to my objectives and methods were replaced. Unproductive and mediocre employees were encouraged to find jobs elsewhere. Authority for staffing and compensation decisions was decentralized to units at the division, region, and district levels. Managers of those units were informed that along with their authority went responsibility for reducing costs, and increasing sales and profits. Each unit was established as a profit center. A new department was established and charged with reviewing performance of those units. Improved accounting and control systems were implemented. A management-by-objectives program was developed to establish standards and monitor performance. Performance appraisals are now required for all employees. To encourage more aggressive action, bonuses and incentives are offered to managers of units showing increased profits. A commission plan based on measurable sales and profit performances has replaced straight salaries. Resources are allocated to units based on their performance.

My own leadership style has probably represented the most traumatic change for employees. Internal competition is a formally mandated policy throughout the company. It has been responsible for much of the progress achieved to date. Progress, however, is never made without costs, and I recognize that employees are not having as much fun as in the past. I was employed to achieve results and not to ensure that employees remain secure and happy in their work. Don't let a few crybabies unable to adjust to changes lead you to believe that problems take precedence over profits. Does it mean that I am not people oriented if I believe it is unlikely that a spirit of aggressiveness and competitiveness can coexist with an atmosphere of cooperativeness and family orientation? Do you feel that we are obligated to employees because of past practices? Frankly, I thought I had your support to do whatever was necessary to get this company turned around. In our meeting, tell me if you think my approaches have been wrong, and if so, tell me what I should have done differently.

Just as Chairman Fulmer finished reviewing the third memorandum, his secretary informed him that Curtis had arrived for their scheduled meeting. He realized that he was undecided how to communicate to Curtis his ideas and beliefs regarding how changes in an organization can best be implemented. One thing he did know was that he didn't appreciate how Curtis expressed his views in his memorandum, but he recognized that he probably should set aside emotions and respond to the questions Curtis posed.

Chapter Ten Workshop *The Power of Ethics**

This exercise will help you to better understand the concept of ethics and what it means to you.

1. Spend about five minutes individually answering the questions below.
2. Divide into groups of four to six members.
3. Have each group try to achieve consensus with answers to each of the four questions. For question 3, choose one scenario to highlight. You will have twenty to forty minutes for this exercise, depending on the instructor.
4. Have groups share their answers with the whole class, after which the instructor will lead a discussion on ethics and its power in business.

Questions

1. In your own words, define the concept of ethics in one or two sentences.

2. If you were a manager, how would you motivate your employees to follow ethical behavior? Use no more than two sentences.
3. Describe a situation in which you were faced with an ethical dilemma. What was your decision and behavior? How did you decide to do that? Can you relate your decision to any concept in the chapter?
4. What do you think is a powerful ethical message for others? Where did you get it from? How will it influence your behavior in the future?

*Adapted by Dorothy Marcic from Allayne Barrilleaux Pizzolatto's "Ethical Management: An Exercise in Understanding Its Power," *Journal of Management Education* 17 no. 1 (February 1993): 107–9.

Notes

1. Brenda Paik Sunoo, "How Fun Flies At Southwest Airlines," *Personnel Journal* (June 1995): 62–73; Kristin Dunlap Godsey, "Slow Climb to New Heights: Combine Strict Discipline with Goofy Antics and Make Billions," *Success* (October 1996): 20–26; "Southwest Airlines' Herb Kelleher: Unorthodoxy at Work," an interview with William G. Lee, *Management Review* (January 1995): 9–12; Scott McCartney, "Airline Industry's Top-Ranked Woman Keeps Southwest's Small-Fry Spirit Alive," *Wall Street Journal*, 30 November 1995, B1.

2. Charles O'Reilly, "Corporations, Culture, and Commitment: Motivation and Social Control in Organizations," *California Management Review* 31 (Summer 1989): 9–25.

3. W. Jack Duncan, "Organizational Culture: 'Getting a Fix' on an Elusive Concept," *Academy of Management Executive* 3 (1989): 229–36; Linda Smircich, "Concepts of Culture and Organizational Analysis," *Administrative Science Quarterly* 28 (1983): 339–58; Andrew D. Brown and Ken Starkey, "The Effect of Organizational Culture on Communication and Information," *Journal of Management Studies* 31 no. 6 (November 1994): 807–28.

4. Edgar H. Schein, "Organizational Culture," *American Psychologist* 45 (February 1990): 109–19.

5. Harrison M. Trice and Janice M. Beyer, "Studying Organizational Cultures through Rites and Ceremonials," *Academy of Management Review* 9 (1984): 653–69; Janice M. Beyer and Harrison M. Trice, "How an Organization's Rites Reveal Its Culture," *Organizational Dynamics* 15 (Spring 1987): 5–24; Steven P. Feldman, "Management in Context: An Essay on the Relevance of Culture to the Understanding of Organizational Change," *Journal of Management Studies* 23 (1986): 589–607; Mary Jo Hatch, "The Dynamics of Organizational Culture," *Academy of Management Review* 18 (1993): 657–93.

6. This discussion is based on Edgar H. Schein, *Organizational Culture and Leadership,* 2d ed. (Homewood, Ill.: Richard D. Irwin, 1992); John P. Kotter and James L. Heskett, *Corporate Culture and Performance* (New York: Free Press, 1992).

7. Charlotte B. Sutton, "Richness Hierarchy of the Cultural Network: The Communication of Corporate Values" (Unpublished manuscript, Texas A & M University, 1985); Terrence E. Deal and Allan A. Kennedy, "Culture: A New Look through Old Lenses," *Journal of Applied Behavioral Science* 19 (1983): 498–505.

8. Thomas C. Dandridge, "Symbols at Work" (Working paper, School of Business, State University of New York at Albany, 1978), 1.

9. Alan Farnham, "Mary Kay's Lessons in Leadership," *Fortune,* 20 September 1993, 68–77.

10. Thomas J. Peters and Robert H. Waterman, Jr., *In Search of Excellence* (New York: Harper & Row, 1982).

11. Don Hellriegle and John W. Slocum, Jr., *Management,* 7th ed. (Cincinnati, Ohio: South-Western, 1996), 537.

12. Trice and Beyer, "Studying Organizational Cultures through Rites and Ceremonials."

13. Sutton, "Richness Hierarchy of the Cultural Network"; Deal and Kennedy, *Corporate Cultures.*

14. Gregory M. Bounds, Gregory H. Dobbins, and Oscar S. Fowler, *Management: A Total Quality Perspective* (Cincinnati, Ohio: South-Western 1995), 353–54.

15. "FYI," *Inc.,* April 1991, 14.

16. Nancy K. Austin, "Wacky Management Ideas That Work," *Working Woman,* November 1991, 42–44; Susan Benner, "Culture Shock," *Inc.,* August 1985, 73–82.

17. Richard Ott, "Are Wild Ducks Really Wild: Symbolism and Behavior in the Corporate Environment" (Paper presented at the Northeastern Anthropological Association, March 1979).

18. Barbara Ettorre, "Retooling People and Processes," *Management Review* (June 1995): 19–23.

19. Bernard Arogyaswamy and Charles M. Byles, "Organizational Culture: Internal and External Fits," *Journal of Management* 13 (1987): 647–59.

20. Kotter and Heskett, *Corporate Culture and Performance.*

21. Michael A. Verespej, "Lead, Don't Manage," *IW,* 4 March 1996, 55–60.

22. Based on Richard Pascale, "Fitting New Employees into the Company Culture," *Fortune,* 28 May 1984, 28–39; and Richard Pascale, "The Paradox of 'Corporate Culture': Reconciling Ourselves to Socialization," *California Management Review* 27 (Winter 1985): 26–41.

23. Based on Daniel R. Denison, *Corporate Culture and Organizational Effectiveness* (New York: Wiley, 1990), 11–15; Daniel R. Denison and Aneil K. Mishra, "Toward a Theory of Organizational Culture and Effectiveness," *Organization Science* 6,

no. 2 (March-April 1995): 204–23; R. Hooijberg and F. Petrock, "On Cultural Change: Using the Competing Values Framework to Help Leaders Execute a Transformational Strategy," *Human Resource Management* 32 (1993), 29–50; R. E. Quinn, *Beyond Rational Management: Mastering the Paradoxes and Competing Demands of High Performance* (San Francisco: Jossey-Bass, 1988).

24. Brian Dumaine, "Those High Flying PepsiCo Managers," *Fortune,* 10 April 1989; L. Zinn, J. Berry, and G. Burns, "Will the Pepsi Brass Be Drinking Hemlock?" *Business Week,* 25 July 1994, 31; S. Lubove, "We Have a Big Pond to Play In," *Forbes,* 12 September 1993, 216–24; J. Wolfe, "PepsiCo and the Fast Food Industry," in M. A. Hitt, R. D. Ireland, and R. E. Hoskisson, eds., *Strategic Management: Competitiveness and Globalization* (St. Paul, Minn.: West Publishing, 1995), 856–79.

25. Carey Quan Jelernter, "Safeco: Success Depends Partly on Fitting the Mold," *Seattle Times,* 5 June 1986, D8.

26. Gordon F. Shea, *Practical Ethics* (New York: American Management Association, 1988); Linda K. Trevino, "Ethical Decision Making in Organizations: A Person–Situation Interactionist Model," *Academy of Management Review* 11 (1986): 601–17.

27. LaRue Tone Hosmer, *The Ethics of Management,* 2d ed., (Homewood, Ill.: Irwin, 1991).

28. Dawn-Marie Driscoll, "Don't Confuse Legal and Ethical Standards," *Business Ethics,* July/August 1996, 44.

29. Eugene W. Szwajkowski, "The Myths and Realities of Research on Organizational Misconduct," in James E. Post, ed., *Research and Corporate Social Performance and Policy,* vol. 9 (Greenwich, Conn.: JAI Press, 1986), 103–22.

30. These incidents are from Hosmer, *The Ethics of Management.*

31. Linda Klebe Trevino, "A Cultural Perspective on Changing and Developing Organizational Ethics," in Richard Woodman and William Pasmore, eds., *Research and Organizational Change and Development,* vol. 4 (Greenwich, Conn.: JAI Press, 1990); Lynn Sharp Paine, "Managing for Organizational Integrity," *Harvard Business Review* (March/April 1994), 106–17.

32. James Weber, "Exploring the Relationship between Personal Values and Moral Reasoning," *Human Relations* 46 (1993): 435–63.

33. L. Kohlberg, "Moral Stages and Moralization: The Cognitive-Developmental Approach," in T.

Likona, ed., *Moral Development and Behavior: Theory, Research, and Social Issues* (New York: Holt, Rinehart & Winston, 1976).

34. Hosmer, *The Ethics of Management.*

35. "James Burke: The Fine Art of Leadership," an interview with Barbara Ettorre, *Management Review* (October 1996): 13–16; Margaret Kaeter, The 5th Annual Business Ethics Awards for Excellence in Ethics," *Business Ethics,* November-December 1993, 26–29.

36. *Corporate Ethics: A Prime Business Asset* (New York: The Business Roundtable, February 1988).

37. Mark Henricks, "Ethics in Action," *Management Review* (January 1995): 53–55.

38. David M. Messick and Max H. Bazerman, "Ethical Leadership and the Psychology of Decision Making," *Sloan Management Review* (Winter 1996): 9–22; Dawn-Marie Driscoll, "Don't Confuse Legal and Ethical Standards," *Business Ethics,* July/August 1996, 44.

39. Max B. E. Clarkson, "A Stakeholder Framework for Analyzing and Evaluating Corporate Social Performance," *Academy of Management Review* 20, no. 1 (1995): 92–117.

40. Kathleen Dechant and Barbara Altman, "Environmental Leadership: From Compliance to Competitive Advantage," *Academy of Management Executive* 8, no. 3 (1994): 7–20; "The Sixth Annual Business Ethics Awards," *Business Ethics,* November/December 1994, 29; Mary Scott, "Interview: Yvon Chouinard," *Business Ethics,* May/June 1995, 31–34.

41. Howard Rothman, "A Growing Dilemma," *Business Ethics,* July/August 1996, 18–21.

42. Susan Gaines, "Growing Pains," *Business Ethics,* January/February 1996, 20–23.

43. *Corporate Ethics: A Prime Business Asset.*

44. Andrew W. Singer, "The Ultimate Ethics Test," *Across the Board,* March 1992, 19–22; Ronald B. Morgan, "Self and Co-Worker Perceptions of Ethics and Their Relationships to Leadership and Salary," *Academy of Management Journal,* 36, no.1 (February 1993): 200–14; Joseph L. Badaracco, Jr. and Allen P. Webb, "Business Ethics: A View From the Trenches," *California Management Review* 37, no. 2 (Winter 1995): 8–28.

45. This discussion is based on Robert J. House, Andre Delbecq, and Toon W. Taris, "Value Based Leadership: An Integrated Theory and an Empirical Test" (Working paper).

46. Peters and Waterman, *In Search of Excellence.*

47. "Best Moves of 1995," *Business Ethics,* January/February 1996, 23.

48. Karl E. Weick, "Cognitive Processes in Organizations," in B. M. Staw, ed., *Research in Organizations,* vol. 1 (Greenwich, Conn.: JAI Press, 1979), 42.

49. Patrick E. Murphy and George Enderle, "Managerial Ethical Leadership: Examples Do Matter," *Business Ethics Quarterly* 5, no. 1 (January 1995): 117–28.

50. Beverly Geber, "The Right and Wrong of Ethics Offices," *Training,* October 1995, 102–18.

51. Justin Martin, "New Tricks for an Old Trade," *Across the Board,* June 1992, 40–44.

52. Janet P. Near and Marcia P. Miceli, "Effective Whistle-Blowing," *Academy of Management Review* 20, no. 3 (1995): 679–708.

53. Richard P. Nielsen, "Changing Unethical Organizational Behavior," *Academy of Management Executive* 3 (1989): 123–30.

54. Jene G. James, "Whistle-Blowing: Its Moral Justification," in Peter Madsen and Jay M. Shafritz, eds., *Essentials of Business Ethics* (New York: Meridian Books, 1990), 160–90; Janet P. Near, Terry Morehead Dworkin, and Marcia P. Miceli, "Explaining the Whistle-Blowing Process: Suggestions from Power Theory and Justice Theory," *Organization Science* 4 (1993): 393–411.

55. Kurt Eichenwald, "He Told, He Suffered, Now He's a Hero," *New York Times,* 29 May 1994, Section 3, 1.

56. Beverly Geber, "The Right and Wrong of Ethics Offices," *Training,* October 1995, 102–18.

57. Carolyn Wiley, "The ABC's of Business Ethics: Definitions, Philosophies, and Implementation," *IM,* January/February 1995, 22–27.

58. Saul W. Gellerman, "Managing Ethics from the Top Down," *Sloan Management Review* (Winter 1989): 73–79; Donald Robin, Michael Giallourakis, Fred R. David, and Thomas E. Moritz, "A Different Look at Codes of Ethics," *Business Horizons* (January–February 1989): 66–71.

59. James Weber, "Institutionalizing Ethics into Business Organizations: A Model and Research Agenda," *Business Ethics Quarterly* 3 (1993): 419–36.

60. Susan J. Harrington, "What Corporate America Is Teaching about Ethics," *Academy of Management Executive* 5 (1991): 21–30.

61. Labich, "The New Crisis in Business Ethics."

62. Harrington, "What Corporate America Is Teaching about Ethics."

63. Mark Henricks, "Ethics in Action," *Management Review* (January 1995): 53–55; Dorothy Marcic, *Management and the Wisdom of Love* (San Francisco: Jossey-Bass, 1997); Beverly Geber, "The Right and Wrong of Ethics Offices," *Training,* October 1995, 102–18.

Managing Dynamic Processes

Decision-Making Processes

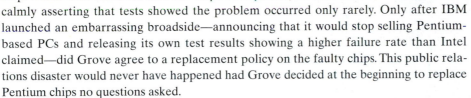

A look inside

Intel Corporation

With more than 70 percent of the microprocessor market and $11.5 billion in sales, Intel Corporation is a leader in the computer industry and its top executive, Andrew Grove, is one of the most admired CEOs in America. Grove, however, made a serious blunder when news surfaced about minor flaws in Intel's Pentium chip. Faced with demands that the chips be replaced, Grove refused, calmly asserting that tests showed the problem occurred only rarely. Only after IBM launched an embarrassing broadside—announcing that it would stop selling Pentium-based PCs and releasing its own test results showing a higher failure rate than Intel claimed—did Grove agree to a replacement policy on the faulty chips. This public relations disaster would never have happened had Grove decided at the beginning to replace Pentium chips no questions asked.

Although Intel's business was not seriously damaged, this incident cast a black mark against the company's customer service reputation. Some observers believe Andrew Grove's doggedly analytical style hampered his ability to consider all sides of the situation to determine the true nature of the problem and carefully consider his decision choices. Grove also failed to listen to employees who had a better feel for the situation, as many of the company's two thousand employees expressed disagreement with the harsh initial policy. Intuition is not highly valued at Intel—as Grove puts it, "Intuition is not going to get you a three-million transistor microprocessor."

Eventually, Grove implemented the replacement policy and conceded that Intel needs to get in closer touch with consumers. The company opened a hot line staffed by engineers to cut through the layers between chip designers and customers and give the company better information for making decisions. Grove recognizes that the decisions he and other executives make today affect Intel's ability to remain competitive in the rapidly changing computer industry.[1]

Every organization grows, prospers, or fails as a result of decisions by its managers, and decisions can be risky and uncertain, without any guarantee of success. Decision making must be done amid constantly changing factors, unclear information, and conflicting points of view. Andy Grove's failure to listen to other employees led to a faulty decision in the Pentium case. However, a decision Grove made in the 1980s over the strong objections of other executives propelled the company to its current dominance. At that time, Grove decided to take Intel out of the DRAM memory chip business—a technology Intel had invented—and focus relentlessly on microprocessors. The decision ultimately served the corporation well, but the outcome was certainly not clear in 1985.

Many organizational decisions are complete failures. For example, Coca-Cola thought it had a sure-fire winner in its BreakMate, a miniature soda fountain designed for office use and targeted to small offices without enough workers to support a standard vending machine. Maintaining the machines, however, proved to be a major headache. After pumping some $30 million into the biggest development project in its history, Coke never saw a profit and BreakMate fountains now sit gathering dust in storage sheds. Apple Computer is facing serious trouble because of a series of poor decisions, perhaps the most damaging being the failure to license its technology to other computer makers and permit Mac clones. If the decision had gone the other direction, many observers believe that Apple, not Microsoft, would now be ruling the computer business.[2]

Managers also make many successful decisions every day. For example, Pepsi-Cola's quick and open response to reports of syringes found in cans of Pepsi enhanced the company's reputation. Lee Iacocca's decision to forgo an alliance with foreign automakers and instead have Chrysler build the new Dodge Neon revived not only the company but perhaps the entire U.S. auto industry.[3]

Purpose of This Chapter

At any time, an organization may be identifying problems and implementing alternatives for hundreds of decisions. Managers and organizations somehow muddle through these processes.[4] The purpose here is to analyze these processes to learn what decision making is actually like in organizational settings. Decision-making processes can be thought of as the brain and nervous system of an organization. Decision making is the end use of the information and control systems described in Chapter 9. Decisions are made about organization strategy, structure, innovation, and acquisitions. This chapter explores how organizations can and should make decisions about these issues.

The first section of the chapter defines decision making. The next section examines how individual managers make decisions. Then several models of organizational decision making are explored. Each model is used in a different organizational situation. The final section in this chapter combines the models into a single framework that describes when and how they should be used and discusses special issues, such as decision mistakes.

DEFINITIONS

Organizational decision making is formally defined as the process of identifying and solving problems. The process contains two major stages. In the **problem identification** stage, information about environmental and organizational conditions is monitored to determine if performance is satisfactory and to diagnose the cause of shortcomings. The **problem solution** stage is when alternative courses of action are considered and one alternative is selected and implemented.

At Intel, mistakes were made at both the problem identification and problem solution stages. Although Andrew Grove considered flaws in the Pentium chip to be minor, the real problem concerned customer perception as much as technical quality. Thus, at the problem solution stage, Grove failed to consider alternatives that addressed the customer relations side of the problem.

Organizational decisions vary in complexity and can be categorized as programmed or nonprogrammed.[5] **Programmed decisions** are repetitive and well defined, and procedures exist for resolving the problem. They are well structured because criteria of performance are normally clear, good information is available about current performance, alternatives are easily specified, and there is relative certainty that the chosen alternative will be successful. Examples of programmed decisions include decision rules, such as when to replace an office copy machine, when to reimburse managers for travel expenses, or whether an applicant has sufficient qualifications for an assembly-line job. Many companies adopt rules based on experience with programmed decisions. For example, general pricing rules in the restaurant industry are that food is marked up three times direct cost, beer four times, and liquor six times. A rule for large hotels staffing banquets is to allow one server per thirty guests for a sit-down function and one server per forty guests for a buffet.[6]

Nonprogrammed decisions are novel and poorly defined, and no procedure exists for solving the problem. They are used when an organization has not seen a problem before and may not know how to respond. Clear-cut decision criteria do not exist. Alternatives are fuzzy. There is uncertainty about whether a proposed solution will solve the problem. Typically, few alternatives can be developed for a nonprogrammed decision, so a single solution is custom-tailored to the problem.

The decision about how to deal with charges of faulty Pentium chips was a nonprogrammed decision. Intel had never faced this kind of problem and had no rules for dealing with it. Many nonprogrammed decisions involve strategic planning, because uncertainty is great and decisions are complex. For example, at Continental Airlines, new CEO Gordon M. Bethune decided to ground forty-one planes, cut more than forty-two hundred jobs, and abolish cut-rate fares as part of his strategy to make the ailing airline profitable again. Bethune and other top managers had to analyze complex problems, evaluate alternatives, and make a choice about how to pull Continental out of its slump.[7]

Particularly complex nonprogrammed decisions have been referred to as "wicked" decisions, because simply defining the problem can turn into a major task. Wicked problems are associated with manager conflicts over objectives and alternatives, rapidly changing circumstances, and unclear linkages among decision elements. Managers dealing with a wicked decision may hit on a solution that merely proves they failed to correctly define the problem to begin with.[8]

Today's managers and organizations are dealing with a higher percentage of nonprogrammed decisions because of the rapidly changing business environment. As outlined in Exhibit 11.1, today's environment has increased both the number and complexity of decisions that have to be made and created a need for new decision-making processes. One example of how the environment affects organizations is the recent increase in the minimum wage. Managers at Popeyes Chicken & Biscuits have estimated that paying the higher wage will decrease operating profits by 25 percent or more and are considering decision alternatives such as cutting jobs or raising prices to meet the new conditions. Another example is globalization. The trend toward moving production to low-wage countries has managers all over corporate America struggling with ethical decisions concerning working conditions in the Third World and the loss of manufacturing jobs in small American communities. In one Tennessee community where the unemployment rate is 18 percent, six hundred workers recently lost their jobs because most garment manufacturing is now sent overseas.[9]

Exhibit 11.1

*Decision Making in
Today's Environment*

Today's Business Environment
• Demands more large-scale change via new strategies, reengineering, restructuring, mergers, acquisitions, downsizing, new product or market development, and so on

Decisions Made Inside the Organization
• Are based on bigger, more complex, more emotionally charged issues • Are made more quickly • Are made in a less certain environment, with less clarity about means and outcomes • Require more cooperation from more people involved in making and implementing decisions

A New Decision-Making Process
• Is required because no one individual has the information needed to make all major decisions • Is required because no one individual has the time and credibility needed to convince many people to implement the decision • Relies less on hard data as a base for good decisions • Is guided by a powerful coalition that can act as a team • Permits decisions to evolve through trial and error and incremental steps as needed

Source: Adapted from John P. Kotter, *Leading Change* (Boston, Mass.: Harvard Business School Press, 1996), 56. Used with permission.

INDIVIDUAL DECISION MAKING

Individual decision making by managers can be described in two ways. First is the **rational approach**, which suggests how managers should try to make decisions. Second is the **bounded rationality perspective**, which describes how decisions actually have to be made under severe time and resource constraints. The rational approach is an ideal managers may work toward but never reach.

Rational Approach

The rational approach to individual decision making stresses the need for systematic analysis of a problem followed by choice and implementation in a logical step-by-step sequence. The rational approach was developed to guide individual decision making because many managers were observed to be unsystematic and arbitrary in their approach to organizational decisions. According to the rational approach, the decision process can be broken down into the following eight steps.[10]

1. *Monitor the decision environment.* In the first step, a manager monitors internal and external information that will indicate deviations from planned or acceptable behavior. He or she talks to colleagues and reviews financial

statements, performance evaluations, industry indices, competitors' activities, and so forth. For example, during the pressure-packed five-week Christmas season, Linda Koslow, general manager of Marshall Fields's Oakbrook, Illinois, store, checks out competitors around the mall, eyeing whether they are marking down merchandise. She also scans printouts of her store's previous day's sales to learn what is or is not moving.[11]

2. *Define the decision problem.* The manager responds to deviations by identifying essential details of the problem: where, when, who was involved, who was affected, and how current activities are influenced. For Koslow, this means defining whether store profits are low because overall sales are less than expected or because certain lines of merchandise are not moving as expected.

3. *Specify decision objectives.* The manager determines what performance outcomes should be achieved by a decision.

4. *Diagnose the problem.* In this step, the manager digs below the surface to analyze the cause of the problem. Additional data may be gathered to facilitate this diagnosis. Understanding the cause enables appropriate treatment. For Koslow at Marshall Fields, the cause of slow sales may be competitors' marking down of merchandise or Marshall Fields's failure to display hot-selling items in a visible location.

5. *Develop alternative solutions.* Before a manager can move ahead with a decisive action plan, he or she must have a clear understanding of the various options available to achieve desired objectives. The manager may seek ideas and suggestions from other people. Koslow's alternatives for increasing profits could include buying fresh merchandise, running a sale, or reducing the number of employees.

6. *Evaluate alternatives.* This step may involve the use of statistical techniques or personal experience to assess the probability of success. The merits of each alternative are assessed as well as the probability that it will reach the desired objectives.

7. *Choose the best alternative.* This step is the core of the decision process. The manager uses his or her analysis of the problem, objectives, and alternatives to select a single alternative that has the best chance for success. At Marshall Fields, Koslow may choose to reduce the number of staff as a way to meet the profit goals rather than increase advertising or markdowns.

8. *Implement the chosen alternative.* Finally, the manager uses managerial, administrative, and persuasive abilities and gives directions to ensure that the decision is carried out. The monitoring activity (step 1) begins again as soon as the solution is implemented. For Linda Koslow, the decision cycle is a continuous process, with new decisions made daily based on monitoring her environment for problems and opportunities.

The first four steps in this sequence are the problem identification stage, and the next four steps are the problem solution stage of decision making, as indicated in Exhibit 11.2. All eight steps normally appear in a manager's decision, although each step may not be a distinct element. Managers may know from experience exactly what to do in a situation, so one or more steps will be minimized. The following case illustrates how the rational approach is used to make a decision about a personnel problem.

Exhibit 11.2

Steps in Rational Approach to Decision Making

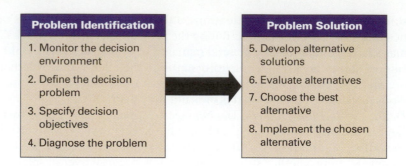

Problem Identification	**Problem Solution**
1. Monitor the decision environment	5. Develop alternative solutions
2. Define the decision problem	6. Evaluate alternatives
3. Specify decision objectives	7. Choose the best alternative
4. Diagnose the problem	8. Implement the chosen alternative

In Practice 11.1   *Alberta Manufacturing*

1. *Monitor the decision environment.* It is Monday morning, and Joe DeFoe, one of Alberta's most skilled cutters, is absent again.

2. *Define the decision problem.* This is the sixth consecutive Monday DeFoe has been absent. Company policy forbids unexcused absenteeism, and DeFoe has been warned about his excessive absenteeism on the last three occasions. A final warning is in order but can be delayed, if warranted.

3. *Specify decision objectives.* DeFoe should attend work regularly and establish the production and quality levels of which he is capable. The time period for solving the problem is two weeks.

4. *Diagnose the problem.* Discreet discussions with DeFoe's co-workers and information gleaned from DeFoe indicate that DeFoe has a drinking problem. He apparently uses Mondays to dry out from weekend benders. Discussion with other company sources confirms that DeFoe is a problem drinker.

5. *Develop alternative solutions.* (1) Fire DeFoe. (2) Issue a final warning without comment. (3) Issue a warning and accuse DeFoe of being alcoholic to let him know you are aware of his problem. (4) Talk with DeFoe to see if he will discuss his drinking. If he admits he has a drinking problem, delay the final warning and suggest that he enroll in Alberta's new employee assistance program for help with personal problems, including alcoholism. (5) Talk with DeFoe to see if he will discuss his drinking. If he does not admit he has a drinking problem, let him know that the next absence will cost him his job.

6. *Evaluate alternatives.* The cost of training a replacement is the same for each alternative. Alternative 1 ignores cost and other criteria. Alternatives 2 and 3 do not adhere to company policy, which advocates counseling where appropriate. Alternative 4 is designed for the benefit of both DeFoe and the company. It might save a good employee if DeFoe is willing to seek assistance. Alternative 5 is primarily for the benefit of the company. A final warning might provide some initiative for DeFoe to admit he has a drinking problem. If so, dismissal might be avoided, but further absences will no longer be tolerated.

7. *Choose the best alternative.* DeFoe does not admit that he has a drinking problem. Choose alternative 5.

8. *Implement the chosen alternative.* Write up the case and issue the final warning.[12]

In the preceding case, issuing the final warning to Joe DeFoe was a programmable decision. The standard of expected behavior was clearly defined, information on the frequency and cause of DeFoe's absence was readily available, and acceptable alternatives and procedures were described. The rational procedure works best in such cases, when the decision maker has sufficient time for an orderly, thoughtful process. Moreover, Alberta Manufacturing had mechanisms in place to implement the decision, once made.

When decisions are nonprogrammed, ill defined, and piling on top of one another, the individual manager should still try to use the steps in the rational approach, but he or she often will have to take shortcuts by relying on intuition and experience. Deviations from the rational approach are explained by the bounded rationality perspective.

Bounded Rationality Perspective

The point of the rational approach is that managers should try to use systematic procedures to arrive at good decisions. When organizations are facing little competition and are dealing with well-understood issues, managers generally use rational procedures to make decisions.[13] Yet research into managerial decision making shows managers often are unable to follow an ideal procedure. In today's competitive environment, decisions often must be made very quickly. Time pressure, a large number of internal and external factors affecting a decision, and the ill-defined nature of many problems make systematic analysis virtually impossible. Managers have only so much time and mental capacity and, hence, cannot evaluate every goal, problem, and alternative. The attempt to be rational is bounded (limited) by the enormous complexity of many problems. There is a limit to how rational managers can be. For example, an executive in a hurry may have a choice of fifty ties on a rack but will take the first or second one that matches his suit. The executive doesn't carefully weigh all fifty alternatives because the short amount of time and the large number of plausible alternatives would be overwhelming. The manager simply selects the first tie that solves the problem and moves on to the next task.

Large organizational decisions are not only too complex to fully comprehend, but many other constraints impinge on the decision maker, as illustrated in Exhibit 11.3. The circumstances are ambiguous, requiring social support, a shared perspective on what happens, and acceptance and agreement. For example, in a study of the decision making surrounding the Cuban missile crisis, the executive committee in the White House knew a problem existed but was unable to specify exact goals and objectives. The act of discussing the decision led to personal objections and finally to the discovery of desired objectives that helped clarify the desired course of action and possible consequences.[14] In addition, personal constraints—such as decision style, work pressure, desire for prestige, or simple feelings of insecurity—may constrain either the search for alternatives or the acceptability of an alternative. All of these factors constrain a perfectly rational approach that should lead to an obviously ideal choice.[15] Recent research on the importance of personal decision style is discussed in Book Mark 11.0. Even seemingly simple decisions, such as selecting a job on graduation from college, can quickly become so complex that a bounded rationality approach is used. Graduating students have been known to search for a job until they have two or three acceptable job offers, at which point their search activity rapidly diminishes. Hundreds of firms may be available for interviews, and two or three job offers are far short of the maximum number that would be possible if students made the decision based on perfect rationality.

The bounded rationality perspective is often associated with intuitive decision processes. In **intuitive decision making**, experience and judgment rather than

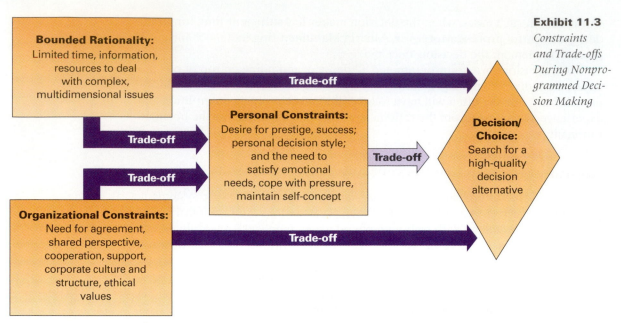

Exhibit 11.3
Constraints and Trade-offs During Nonprogrammed Decision Making

Source: Adapted from Irving L. Janis, *Crucial Decisions* (New York: Free Press, 1989); and A. L. George, *Presidential Decision Making in Foreign Policy: The Effective Use of Information and Advice* (Boulder, Colo.: Westview Press, 1980).

sequential logic or explicit reasoning are used to make decisions.[16] Intuition is not arbitrary or irrational because it is based on years of practice and hands-on experience, often stored in the subconscious. When managers use their intuition based on long experience with organizational issues, they more rapidly perceive and understand problems, and they develop a gut feeling or hunch about which alternative will solve a problem, speeding the decision-making process.[17] Indeed, many universities are offering courses in creativity and intuition so business students can learn to understand and rely on these processes.

In a situation of great complexity or ambiguity, previous experience and judgment are needed to incorporate intangible elements at both the problem identification and problem solution stages.[18] A study of manager problem finding showed that thirty of thirty-three problems were ambiguous and ill defined.[19] Bits and scraps of unrelated information from informal sources resulted in a pattern in the manager's mind. The manager could not "prove" a problem existed but knew intuitively that a certain area needed attention. A too simple view of a complex problem is often associated with decision failure,[20] and research shows managers are more likely to respond intuitively to a perceived threat to the organization than to an opportunity.[21]

For example, although IDS Financial Services was very profitable and grew rapidly in the early 1990s, a manager perceived a high turnover rate among the company's financial planners. She interpreted this as a weakness that could seriously threaten IDS's position in the increasingly competitive financial services industry. Other examples of problems that might be discovered through informal, intuitive processes are the possibility of impending legislation against the company, the need for a new product, customer dissatisfaction, and a need for reorganization by creating new departments.[22]

Book Mark 11.0

Have You Read About This?

The Dynamic Decisionmaker

by Michael J. Driver, Kenneth R. Brousseau, and Philip L. Hunsaker

The Dynamic Decisionmaker discusses the thought processes and decision styles managers use when making decisions. The authors develop a model based on two decision factors that combine into five decision styles.

Two Key Factors

The basic decision style model presented by the authors is based on two decision elements—the amount of information used in making a decision (called information use) and the number of alternatives considered (called focus). With respect to information use, managers may be maximizers or satisficers. The maximizer wants as much relevant information as possible before making a decision; the satisficer, in contrast, is a fast-action person who wants just enough information to get on with the decision.

Moreover, some decision makers are unifocused, which means they look at the problem with the idea of coming up with a single solution. Others are multifocused, wanting to develop a variety of options and related pros and cons before deciding.

Five Decision Styles

The underlying elements can appear in various combinations to form five decision making styles.

The **decisive style** is satisficing and unifocused. This style uses minimum information and perhaps a single alternative to solve a problem quickly. Attention quickly shifts to the next problem.

The **flexible style** is satisficing and multifocused. This style moves fast also but often changes focus, interpreting information to see multiple alternatives.

The **hierarchic style** is maximizing and unifocused. This style uses lots of information and analysis to create a detailed, specific solution to a problem. This style exerts control with emphasis on quality and perfection to reach the "best" solution.

The **integrative style** is maximizing and multifocused. Lots of information is collected but is used to develop many possible solutions. Emphasis is on creativity and exploration and on openness to new options.

The **systemic style** is the most complex of all. This style is both multifocused and unifocused and prefers maximum information while looking at different perspectives and alternative solutions. This style sees the big picture and handles complex decisions well.

Conclusion

Learning one's personal style and the style of co-workers will increase a manager's effectiveness as a leader and in interpersonal relationships. For example, a supervisor and employee may have a "style clash." A multifocused manager is seen by a unifocused subordinate as wishy-washy, and the unifocused subordinate is seen by the manager as having tunnel vision.

While the authors suggest there is no best style, people should adapt their style to the decision. Managers fail not because they make wrong decisions but because they use the wrong style for the situation—deciding too quickly and impulsively, gathering too much information, or postponing action too long.

The Dynamic Decisionmaker by Michael J. Driver, Kenneth R. Brousseau, and Phillip L. Hunsaker is published by Ballinger.

Intuitive processes are also used in the problem solution stage. A survey found that executives frequently made decisions without explicit reference to the impact on profits or to other measurable outcomes.[23] As we saw in Exhibit 11.3, many intangible factors—such as a person's concern about the support of other executives, fear of failure, and social attitudes—influence selection of the best alternative. These factors cannot be quantified in a systematic way, so intuition guided the choice of a solution. Managers may make a decision based on what they sense to be right rather than on what they can document with hard data.

A number of important decisions, some quite famous, have been based on hunch and intuition. For example, the movie *M*A*S*H* and the television programs *All in the Family, Hill Street Blues,* and *Cheers* would never have been made if producers Robert Altman, Norman Lear, and Stephen Bochco hadn't gone with their gut feelings and pushed the projects. Referring to the movie and television spinoff that made more than $1 billion for 20th Century Fox, Altman put it this way, "I always say *M*A*S*H* wasn't released; it escaped." Some years later, researchers who analyzed hard data warned film director George Lucas that his choice of *Star Wars* as the title of his film would turn away crowds at the box office, but Lucas stuck with his intuitive feeling that the title would work.[24]

Managers may walk a fine line between two extremes: on the one hand, making arbitrary decisions without careful study and on the other, relying obsessively on numbers and rational analysis.[25] Remember that the bounded rationality perspective and the use of intuition applies mostly to nonprogrammed decisions. The novel, unclear, complex aspects of nonprogrammed decisions mean hard data and logical procedures are not available. A study of executive decision making found that managers simply could not use the rational approach for nonprogrammed decisions, such as when to buy a CT scanner for an osteopathic hospital or whether a city had a need for and could reasonably adopt a data processing system.[26] In those cases, managers had limited time and resources, and some factors simply couldn't be measured and analyzed. Trying to quantify such information could cause mistakes because it may oversimplify decision criteria. When Michael Eisner was president of Paramount Pictures, he learned to rely on intuition for making nonprogrammed decisions. His decision approach was astonishingly successful at Paramount and, more recently, at Disney.

In Practice 11.2	*Paramount Pictures Corporation*

When Barry Diller and Michael Eisner went to the movies, it wasn't for entertainment. They were checking audience reaction on one of their new movies. Barry Diller was chairman and Michael Eisner was president of Paramount Pictures Corporation.

Some of Paramount's successes under their leadership were *Indiana Jones and the Temple of Doom, Raiders of the Lost Ark, An Officer and a Gentleman, Trading Places, 48 Hours, Flashdance,* and *Terms of Endearment.* A major reason for the string of hits was the excellent choice of films. Paramount decision makers were attuned to the tastes of eighteen- to twenty-four-year olds, who count most. Paramount had also gotten into other ventures, such as selling its films to Showtime. And *Entertainment Tonight,* Paramount's entertainment-news TV show, was also hugely successful.

Why was Paramount so successful at selecting films? Diller and Eisner claim they relied on gut reaction when picking films or other projects. Their tastes were shaped while they were executives at ABC, where they were responsible for the "Movie of the Week." Their experience paid off. Columbia Pictures, then a division of Coca-Cola, used market research to identify what people want to see. "We don't use Coca-Cola type research. We think it's junk," said Eisner. He thinks about what he likes, not what the public likes. "If I ask Miss Middle America if she wants to see a movie about religion, she'll say yes. If I say, 'Do you want to see a movie about sex,' she'll say no. But she'll be lying."

Experience is so important, Eisner said, because "you tend not to make the same mistakes twice." Eisner and Diller made their share of mistakes, and they frequently disagreed about the right path. They hammered out the best decision and combined their intuition through intense arguments. One bomb was *The Keep,* which ran for only three weeks. *Flashdance* went the other way because no one realized it would be a smash. The experience of both successes and failures helped Diller and Eisner develop an intuition for projects the public wanted.

Eisner's remarkable success led to his selection as president of Disney. After he took over, Disney's studio, Touchstone, moved from last place to being a top studio in the industry. Eisner's intuitive decision skills have made two studios successful, an incredible record in an unpredictable business.[27]

ORGANIZATIONAL DECISION MAKING

Organizations are composed of managers who make decisions using both rational and intuitive processes; but organization-level decisions are not usually made by a single manager. Many organizational decisions involve several managers. Problem identification and problem solution involve many departments, multiple viewpoints, and even other organizations, which are beyond the scope of an individual manager.

The processes by which decisions are made in organizations are influenced by a number of factors, particularly the organization's own internal structures as well as the degree of stability or instability of the external environment.[28] Research into organization-level decision making has identified four types of organizational decision-making processes: the management science approach, the Carnegie model, the incremental decision process model, and the garbage can model.

Management Science Approach

The **management science approach** to organizational decision making is the analog to the rational approach by individual managers. Management science came into being during World War II.[29] At that time, mathematical and statistical techniques were applied to urgent, large-scale military problems that were beyond the ability of individual decision makers. Mathematicians, physicists, and operations researchers used systems analysis to develop artillery trajectories, antisubmarine strategies, and bombing strategies such as salvoing (discharging multiple shells simultaneously). Consider the problem of a battleship trying to sink an enemy ship several miles away. The calculation for aiming the battleship's guns should consider distance, wind speed, shell size, speed and direction of both ships, pitch and roll of the firing ship, and curvature of the earth. Methods for performing such calculations using trial and error and intuition are not accurate, take far too long, and may never achieve success.

This is where management science came in. Analysts were able to identify the relevant variables involved in aiming a ship's guns and could model them with the use of mathematical equations. Distance, speed, pitch, roll, shell size, and so on could be calculated and entered into the equations. The answer was immediate, and the guns could begin firing. Factors such as pitch and roll were soon measured mechanically and fed directly into the targeting mechanism. Today, the human element is completely removed from the targeting process. Radar picks up the target, and the entire sequence is computed automatically.

Management science yielded astonishing success for many military problems. This approach to decision making diffused into corporations and business schools, where techniques were studied and elaborated. Today, many corporations have assigned departments to use these techniques. The computer department develops quantitative data for analysis. Operations research departments use mathematical models to quantify relevant variables and develop a quantitative representation of alternative solutions and the probability of each one solving the problem. These departments also use such devices as linear programming, Bayesian statistics, PERT charts, and computer simulations.

Management science is an excellent device for organizational decision making when problems are analyzable and when the variables can be identified and measured. Mathematical models can contain a thousand or more variables, each one relevant in some way to the ultimate outcome. Management science techniques have been used to correctly solve problems as diverse as finding the right spot for a church camp, test marketing the first of a new family of products, drilling for oil, and radically altering the distribution of telecommunications services.[30] Other problems amenable to management science techniques are the scheduling of airline employees, telephone operators, and turnpike toll collectors.[31] As illustrated in the following case, management science techniques can also be applied to a situation as complicated as scheduling ambulance technicians.

In Practice 11.3	*Urgences Santé*

Urgences Santé, the public agency responsible for coordinating ambulance service in the Montréal area, schedules vehicle time and working hours for approximately eighty ambulances and seven hundred technicians. The agency does not own any of the vehicles or directly employ any technicians, but rents these services from fifteen private companies. Urgences Santé wanted to optimize the schedule to keep costs as low as possible, realizing that, with ambulance rental fees at $55 an hour, a daily excess of ten hours represents more than $200,000 a year.

Two types of calls require ambulance service—emergency calls from the public, which occur randomly throughout the day and require immediate attention, and calls from hospitals, which are concentrated in specific time periods and are generally not urgent. In addition, demand for ambulance service is generally higher in the winter, but with more emergency calls on weekends during the summer months. Besides meeting shifting demand, a number of other constraints governed the design of a new schedule, for example, the fair distribution of work hours among the fifteen service companies; the provisions of the union contract; the number of ambulances available; and the quality and consistency of work schedules for technicians.

Urgences Santé applied mathematical formulations and techniques to first build workday schedules for each type of day (weekday or weekend) for each season, then equitably assign workdays to the fifteen service companies, and finally to build individual schedules for the seven hundred service technicians. The agency is able to create at least 85 percent of the individual schedules automatically. Implementing the new system has had two positive effects. First, Urgences Santé was able to meet ambulance demand while cutting rental hours per week by up to 110 hours, thus saving approximately $250,000 a year. Second, the quality of the ambulance technicians' schedules has been vastly improved. This has led to an increase in the number of full-time rather than part-time technicians and a decrease in turnover for the service companies. Impressed with these results, Urgences Santé continues to use management science techniques to adapt to new demands and shifts in operational methods.[32]

Management science can accurately and quickly solve problems that have too many explicit variables for human processing. This system is at its best when applied to problems that are analyzable, are measurable, and can be structured in a logical way.

Management science has also produced many failures.[33] In recent years, many banks have begun using computerized scoring systems to rate those applying for credit, but some argue that human judgment is needed to account for extenuating circumstances. In one case, a member of the Federal Reserve Board, the agency that sets interest rates and regulates banks, was denied a Toys 'R' Us credit card based on his computerized score.[34] One problem with the management science approach, as discussed in Chapter 9, is that quantitative data are not rich. Informal cues that indicate the existence of problems have to be sensed on a more personal basis by managers.[35] The most sophisticated mathematical analyses are of no value if the important factors cannot be quantified and included in the model. Such things as competitor reactions, consumer "tastes," and product "warmth" are qualitative dimensions. In these situations, the role of management science is to supplement manager decision making. Quantitative results can be given to managers for discussion and interpretation along with their informal opinions, judgment, and intuition. The final decision can include qualitative factors as well as quantitative calculations.

Carnegie Model

The **Carnegie model** of organizational decision making is based on the work of Richard Cyert, James March, and Herbert Simon, who were all associated with Carnegie-Mellon University.[36] Their research helped formulate the bounded rationality approach to individual decision making as well as provide new insights about organization decisions. Until their work, research in economics assumed that business firms made decisions as a single entity, as if all relevant information were funneled to the top decision maker for a choice. Research by the Carnegie group indicated that organization-level decisions involved many managers and that a final choice was based on a coalition among those managers. A **coalition** is an alliance among several managers who agree about organizational goals and problem priorities.[37] It could include managers from line departments, staff specialists, and even external groups, such as powerful customers, bankers, or union representatives.

Management coalitions are needed during decision making for two reasons. First, organizational goals are often ambiguous, and operative goals of departments are often inconsistent. When goals are ambiguous and inconsistent, managers disagree about problem priorities. They must bargain about problems and build a coalition around the question of which problems to solve. For example, months of discussion, bargaining, and planning took place before Chrysler decided not to abandon small-car production and began working on the new Neon.[38]

The second reason for coalitions is that individual managers intend to be rational but function with human cognitive limitations and other constraints, as described earlier. Managers do not have the time, resources, or mental capacity to identify all dimensions and to process all information relevant to a decision. These limitations lead to coalition-building behavior. Managers talk to each other and exchange points of view to gather information and reduce ambiguity. People who have relevant information or a stake in a decision outcome are consulted. Building a coalition will lead to a decision that is supported by interested parties.

The process of coalition formation has several implications for organizational decision behavior. First, decisions are made to satisfice rather than to optimize problem solutions. **Satisficing** means organizations accept a "satisfactory" rather than a maximum level of performance, enabling them to achieve several goals simultaneously. In decision making, the coalition will accept a solution that is perceived as satisfactory to all coalition members. Second, managers are concerned with immediate problems and short-run solutions. They engage in what Cyert and March called problemistic search.[39] **Problemistic search** means managers look around in the immediate environment for a solution to quickly resolve a problem. Managers don't expect a perfect solution when the situation is ill defined and conflict-laden. This contrasts with the management science approach, which assumes that analysis can uncover every reasonable alternative. The Carnegie model says search behavior is just sufficient to produce a satisfactory solution and that managers typically adopt the first satisfactory solution that emerges. Third, discussion and bargaining are especially important in the problem identification stage of decision making. Unless coalition members perceive a problem, action will not be taken. The decision process described in the Carnegie model is summarized in Exhibit 11.4.

The Carnegie model points out that building agreement through a managerial coalition is a major part of organizational decision making. This is especially true at upper management levels. Discussion and bargaining are time-consuming, so search procedures are usually simple and the selected alternative satisfices rather than optimizes problem solution. When problems are programmed—are clear and have been seen before—the organization will rely on previous procedures and routines. Rules and procedures prevent the need for renewed coalition formation and political bargaining. Nonprogrammed decisions, however, require bargaining and conflict resolution.

One of the best and most visible coalition builders of recent years was former President George Bush, who would seek a broad-based coalition at the start of an important decision process. During the decision process regarding the Persian Gulf War, President Bush kept up a barrage of personal calls and visits to world leaders to gain agreement for his vision of forcing Saddam Hussein from Kuwait and for shaping a "new world order."[40]

When senior managers are unable to build a coalition around goals and problem priorities, the results can be a disaster, as illustrated by the case of Greyhound Bus Lines.

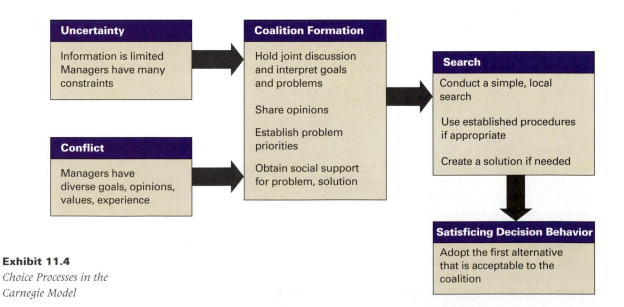

Exhibit 11.4

Choice Processes in the Carnegie Model

Greyhound Lines, Inc.

Everyone agreed that Greyhound Lines had problems. The company was operating on paper-thin margins and could not afford to dispatch nearly empty vehicles or have buses and drivers on call to meet surges in demand. In the terminals, employees could be observed making fun of passengers, ignoring them, and handling their baggage haphazardly. To reduce operating costs and improve customer service, Greyhound's top executives put together a reorganization plan that called for massive cuts in personnel, routes, and services, along with the computerization of everything from passenger reservations to fleet scheduling.

However, middle managers disagreed with the plan. Many felt that huge workforce reductions would only exacerbate the company's real problem regarding customer satisfaction. Managers in computer programming urged a delay in introducing the computerized reservations system, called Trips, to work out bugs in the highly complex software. The human resources department pointed out that terminal workers generally had less than a high school education and would need extensive training before they could use the system effectively. Terminal managers warned that many of Greyhound's low-income passengers didn't have credit cards or even telephones to use Trips. Despite the disagreements, executives went ahead with the rollout, promising that it would improve customer service, make ticket buying more convenient, and allow customers to reserve space on specific trips.

A nightmare resulted. The time Greyhound operators spent responding to phone calls dramatically increased. Many callers couldn't even get through because of problems in the new switching mechanism. Most passengers arrived to buy their tickets and get on the bus just as they always had, but the computers were so swamped that it sometimes took forty-five seconds to respond to a single keystroke and five minutes to print a ticket. The system crashed so often that agents frequently had to handwrite tickets. Customers stood in long lines, were separated from their luggage, missed connections, and were left to sleep in terminals overnight. Discourtesy to customers increased as a downsized workforce struggled to cope with a system they were ill-trained to operate. Ridership plunged sharply. As regional rivals continue to pick off Greyhound's dissatisfied customers, the future of the huge bus company remains uncertain.[41]

The Carnegie model is particularly useful at the problem identification stage. At Greyhound, a few top executives jumped in with a solution before reaching agreement with other managers regarding the nature of the problem and alternatives for solving it. A coalition of key department managers is needed for smooth implementation of a major reorganization. When top managers perceive a problem or want to make a major decision, they need to reach agreement with other managers to support the decision.[42]

Incremental Decision Process Model

Henry Mintzberg and his associates at McGill University in Montreal approached organizational decision making from a different perspective. They identified twenty-five decisions made in organizations and traced the events associated with these decisions from beginning to end.[43] Their research identified each step in the decision sequence. This approach to decision making, called the **incremental decision process model**, places less emphasis on the political and social factors described in the Carnegie model, but tells more about the structured sequence of activities undertaken from the discovery of a problem to its solution.[44]

Sample decisions in Mintzberg's research included choosing which jet aircraft to acquire for a regional airline, developing a new supper club, developing a new container terminal in a harbor, identifying a new market for a deodorant, installing a controversial new medical treatment in a hospital, and firing a star announcer.[45] The scope and importance of these decisions are revealed in the length of time taken to complete them. Most of these decisions took more than a year, and one-third of them took more than two years. Most of these decisions were nonprogrammed and required custom-designed solutions.

One discovery from this research is that major organization choices are usually a series of small choices that combine to produce the major decision. Thus, many organizational decisions are a series of nibbles rather than a big bite. Organizations move through several decision points and may hit barriers along the way. Mintzberg called these barriers *decision interrupts*. An interrupt may mean an organization has to cycle back through a previous decision and try something new. Decision loops or cycles are one way the organization learns which alternatives will work. The ultimate solution may be very different from what was initially anticipated.

The pattern of decision stages discovered by Mintzberg and his associates is shown in Exhibit 11.5. Each box indicates a possible step in the decision sequence. The steps take place in three major decision phases: identification, development, and selection.

Identification Phase.   The identification phase begins with *recognition*. Recognition means one or more managers become aware of a problem and the need to make a decision. Recognition is usually stimulated by a problem or an opportunity. A problem exists when elements in the external environment change or when internal performance is perceived to be below standard. In the case of firing a radio announcer, comments about the announcer came from listeners, other announcers, and advertisers. Managers interpreted these cues until a pattern emerged that indicated a problem had to be dealt with.

The second step is *diagnosis*, which is where more information is gathered if needed to define the problem situation. Diagnosis may be systematic or informal, depending upon the severity of the problem. Severe problems do not have time for extensive diagnosis; the response must be immediate. Mild problems are usually diagnosed in a more systematic manner.

Development Phase.   The development phase is when a solution is shaped to solve the problem defined in the identification phase. The development of a solution takes one of two directions. First, *search* procedures may be used to seek out alternatives within the organization's repertoire of solutions. For example, in the case of firing a star announcer, managers asked what the radio station had done the last time an announcer had to be let go. To conduct the search, organization participants may look into their own memories, talk to other managers, or examine the formal procedures of the organization.

The second direction of development is to *design* a custom solution. This happens when the problem is novel so that previous experience has no value. Mintzberg found that in these cases, key decision makers have only a vague idea of the ideal solution. Gradually, through a trial-and-error process, a custom-designed alternative will emerge. Development of the solution is a groping, incremental procedure, building a solution brick by brick.

Exhibit 11.5 *The Incremental Decision Process Model*

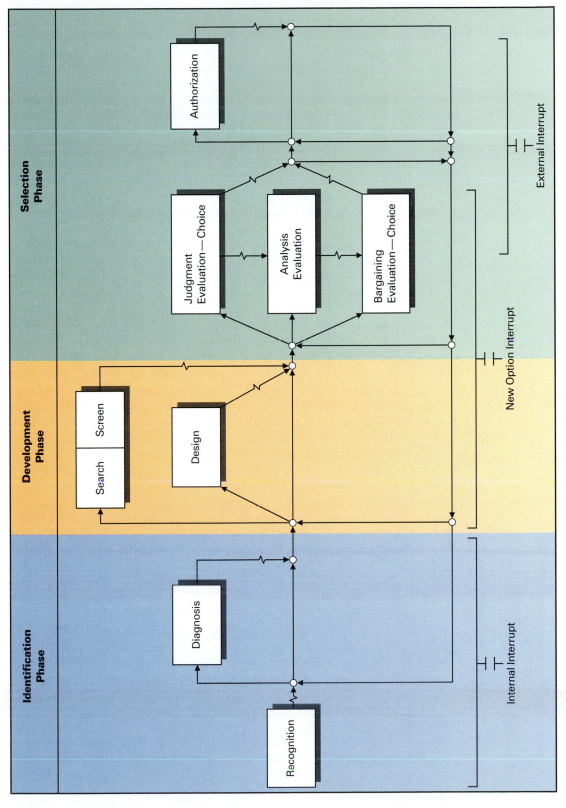

Source: Adapted and reprinted from "The Structure of Unstructured Decision Processes" by Henry Mintzberg, Duru Raisinghani, and André Théorêt, published in *Administrative Science Quarterly* 21, no. 2 (1976), 266, by permission of *The Administrative Science Quarterly.* Copyright © 1976 Cornell University.

Selection Phase.   The selection phase is when the solution is chosen. This phase is not always a matter of making a clear choice among alternatives. In the case of custom-made solutions, selection is more an evaluation of the single alternative that seems feasible.

Evaluation and choice may be accomplished in three ways. The *judgment* form of selection is used when a final choice falls upon a single decision maker, and the choice involves judgment based upon experience. In analysis, alternatives are evaluated on a more systematic basis, such as with management science techniques. Mintzberg found that most decisions did not involve systematic analysis and evaluation of alternatives. *Bargaining* occurs when selection involves a group of decision makers. Each decision maker may have a different stake in the outcome, so conflict emerges. Discussion and bargaining occur until a coalition is formed, as in the Carnegie model described earlier.

When a decision is formally accepted by the organization, *authorization* takes place. The decision may be passed up the hierarchy to the responsible hierarchical level. Authorization is often routine because the expertise and knowledge rest with the lower decision makers who identified the problem and developed the solution. A few decisions are rejected because of implications not anticipated by lower-level managers.

Dynamic Factors.   The lower part of the chart in Exhibit 11.5 shows lines running back toward the beginning of the decision process. These lines represent loops or cycles that take place in the decision process. Organizational decisions do not follow an orderly progression from recognition through authorization. Minor problems arise that force a loop back to an earlier stage. These are decision interrupts. If a custom-designed solution is perceived as unsatisfactory, the organization may have to go back to the very beginning and reconsider whether the problem is truly worth solving. Feedback loops can be caused by problems of timing, politics, disagreement among managers, inability to identify a feasible solution, turnover of managers, or the sudden appearance of a new alternative. For example, when a small Canadian airline made the decision to acquire jet aircraft, the board authorized the decision, but shortly after, a new chief executive was brought in and he canceled the contract, recycling the decision back to the identification phase. He accepted the diagnosis of the problem but insisted upon a new search for alternatives. Then a foreign airline went out of business and two used aircraft became available at a bargain price. This presented an unexpected option, and the chief executive used his own judgment to authorize the purchase of the aircraft.[46]

Because most decisions take place over an extended period of time, circumstances change. Decision making is a dynamic process that may require a number of cycles before a problem is solved. An example of the incremental process and cycling that can take place is illustrated in Gillette's decision to create a new razor.

In Practice 11.5   *Gillette Company*

A bright idea developed at Gillette Company's British research facility finally became the Sensor razor thirteen years later, after more twists and turns than shaving a craggy face. The bright idea was to create a thinner razor blade that would make Gillette's cartridges easier to clean (recognition). The technical development cost for the idea ran $200 million.

The technical demands of building a razor with thin blades and floating parts to follow a man's face had several blind alleys. Engineers first tried to find established techniques (search, screen), but none fit the bill. One idea called for the blades to sit on tiny rubber tubes, perhaps filled with fluid, but that was too costly and complicated to manufacture (new option interrupt). Eventually, a prototype was built (design), and five hundred men liked it. The next problem was manufacturing (diagnosis), which again required an entirely new process to laser weld each blade to a support (design).

Top management gave the go-ahead to develop manufacturing equipment (judgment, authorization). Then a conflict broke out between two groups of Gillette executives. One group wanted to orient the product toward inexpensive disposables, whereas the other group fought for a heavier, more permanent razor (internal interrupt). Then Gillette was threatened with an outside takeover, reducing resources allocated to the project (external interrupt). A new executive vice president made the choice to deemphasize disposables (judgment). A nine-member task force was then authorized to live with the razor for fifteen months to get it to market (authorization). Another $100 million was authorized for advertising and marketing promotions.

The razor has been a smashing success, smoothly sliding off shelves, and Gillette expects to recover its huge investment in record time. Now Gillette is starting the process over again, experimenting with a curved blade and perhaps a new ceramic blade, moving ahead in increments until the new razors are ready, probably not before the turn of the century.[47]

At Gillette, the identification phase occurred because executives were aware of the need for a new razor and became aware of the idea for floating, thin blades. The development phase was characterized by the trial-and-error custom design leading to the Sensor. During the selection phase, certain approaches were found unacceptable, causing Gillette to recycle back, redesign the razor, and reappraise whether it should be a permanent or disposable razor. Advancing once again to the selection phase, the Sensor passed the judgment of executives, and manufacturing and marketing budgets were quickly authorized. This decision took thirteen years, reaching completion in January 1990.

Integrating the Incremental Process and Carnegie Models

At the beginning of this chapter, decision making was defined as occurring in two stages: problem identification and problem solution. The Carnegie description of coalition building is especially relevant for the problem identification stage. When issues are ambiguous, or if managers disagree about problem severity, discussion, negotiation, and coalition building are needed. Once agreement is reached about the problem to be tackled, the organization can move toward a solution.

The incremental process model tends to emphasize the steps used to reach a solution. After managers agree on a problem, the step-by-step process is a way of trying various solutions to see what will work. When problem solution is unclear, a trial-and-error solution may be designed.

The two models do not disagree with one another. They describe how organizations make decisions when either problem identification or solution is uncertain. The application of these two models to the stages in the decision process is illustrated in Exhibit 11.6. When both parts of the decision process are highly

Exhibit 11.6

Organizational Decision Process When Either Problem Identification or Problem Solution Is Uncertain

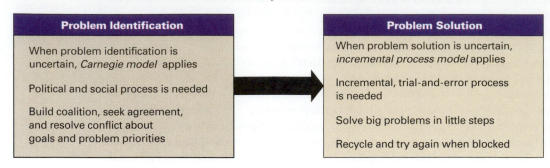

uncertain simultaneously, the organization is in an extremely difficult position. Decision processes in that situation may be a combination of Carnegie and incremental process models, and this combination may evolve into a situation described in the garbage can model.

Garbage Can Model

The **garbage can model** is one of the most recent and interesting descriptions of organizational decision processes. It is not directly comparable to the earlier models, because the garbage can model deals with the pattern or flow of multiple decisions within organizations, whereas the incremental and Carnegie models focus on how a single decision is made. The garbage can model helps you think of the whole organization and the frequent decisions being made by managers throughout.

Organized Anarchy.   The garbage can model was developed to explain the pattern of decision making in organizations that experience extremely high uncertainty. Michael Cohen, James March, and Johan Olsen, the originators of the model, called the highly uncertain conditions an **organized anarchy**, which is an extremely organic organization.[48] Organized anarchies do not rely on the normal vertical hierarchy of authority and bureaucratic decision rules. They are caused by three characteristics:

1. *Problematic preferences.* Goals, problems, alternatives, and solutions are ill defined. Ambiguity characterizes each step of a decision process.
2. *Unclear, poorly understood technology.* Cause-and-effect relationships within the organization are difficult to identify. An explicit database that applies to decisions is not available.
3. *Turnover.* Organizational positions experience turnover of participants. In addition, employees are busy and have only limited time to allocate to any one problem or decision. Participation in any given decision will be fluid and limited.

The organized anarchy describes organizations characterized by rapid change and a collegial, nonbureaucratic environment. No organization fits this extremely organic circumstance all the time. Many organizations will occasionally find themselves in positions of making decisions under unclear, problematic circumstances. The garbage can model is useful for understanding the pattern of these decisions.

Streams of Events. The unique characteristic of the garbage can model is that the decision process is not seen as a sequence of steps that begins with a problem and ends with a solution. Indeed, problem identification and problem solution may not be connected to each other. An idea may be proposed as a solution when no problem is specified. A problem may exist and never generate a solution. Decisions are the outcome of independent streams of events within the organization. The four streams relevant to organizational decision making are as follows:

1. *Problems.* Problems are points of dissatisfaction with current activities and performance. They represent a gap between desired performance and current activities. Problems are perceived to require attention. However, they are distinct from solutions and choices. A problem may lead to a proposed solution or it may not. Problems may not be solved when solutions are adopted.
2. *Potential solutions.* A solution is an idea somebody proposes for adoption. Such ideas form a flow of alternative solutions through the organization. Ideas may be brought into the organization by new personnel or may be invented by existing personnel. Participants may simply be attracted to certain ideas and push them as logical choices regardless of problems. Attraction to an idea may cause an employee to look for a problem to which the idea can be attached and, hence, justified. The point is that solutions exist independent of problems.
3. *Participants.* Organization participants are employees who come and go throughout the organization. People are hired, reassigned, and fired. Participants vary widely in their ideas, perception of problems, experience, values, and training. The problems and solutions recognized by one manager will differ from those recognized by another manager.
4. *Choice opportunities.* Choice opportunities are occasions when an organization usually makes a decision. They occur when contracts are signed, people are hired, or a new product is authorized. They also occur when the right mix of participants, solutions, and problems exists. Thus, a manager who happened to learn of a good idea may suddenly become aware of a problem to which it applies and, hence, can provide the organization with a choice opportunity. Match-ups of problems and solutions often result in decisions.

With the concept of four streams, the overall pattern of organizational decision making takes on a random quality. Problems, solutions, participants, and choices all flow through the organization. In one sense, the organization is a large garbage can in which these streams are being stirred, as illustrated in Exhibit 11.7. When a problem, solution, and participant happen to connect at one point, a decision may be made and the problem may be solved; but if the solution does not fit the problem, the problem may not be solved. Thus, when viewing the organization as a whole and considering its high level of uncertainty, one sees problems arise that are not solved and solutions tried that do not work. Organization decisions are disorderly and not the result of a logical, step-by-step sequence. Events may be so ill defined and complex that decisions, problems, and solutions act as independent events. When they connect, some problems are solved, but many are not.[49]

Exhibit 11.7

Illustration of Independent Streams of Events in the Garbage Can Model of Decision Making

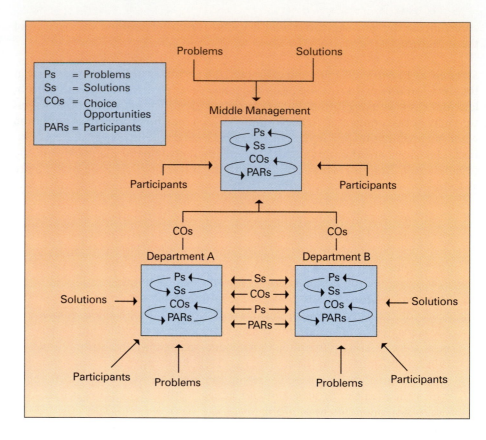

Consequences.   Four consequences of the garbage can decision process for organizational decision making are as follows:

1. *Solutions may be proposed even when problems do not exist.* An employee may be sold on an idea and may try to sell it to the rest of the organization. An example was the adoption of computers by many organizations during the 1970s. The computer was an exciting solution and was pushed by both computer manufacturers and systems analysts within organizations. The computer did not solve any problems in those initial applications. Indeed, some computers caused more problems than they solved.

2. *Choices are made without solving problems.* A choice such as creating a new department may be made with the intention of solving a problem; but, under conditions of high uncertainty, the choice may be incorrect. Moreover, many choices just seem to happen. People decide to quit, the organization's budget is cut, or a new policy bulletin is issued. These choices may be oriented toward problems but do not necessarily solve them.

3. *Problems may persist without being solved.* Organization participants get used to certain problems and give up trying to solve them; or participants may not know how to solve certain problems because the technology is unclear. A university in Canada was placed on probation by the American Association of University Professors because a professor had been denied tenure without due process. The probation was a nagging annoyance that the administrators wanted to remove. Fifteen years later, the nontenured professor died. The probation continues because the university did not ac-

quiesce to the demands of the heirs of the association to reevaluate the case. The university would like to solve the problem, but administrators are not sure how, and they do not have the resources to allocate to it. The probation problem persists without a solution.

4. *A few problems are solved.* The decision process does work in the aggregate. In computer simulation models of the garbage can model, important problems were often resolved. Solutions do connect with appropriate problems and participants so that a good choice is made. Of course, not all problems are resolved when choices are made, but the organization does move in the direction of problem reduction.

The effects of independent streams and the rather chaotic decision processes of the garbage can model can be seen in the production of the classic film *Casablanca*.

Casablanca

The public flocked to see *Casablanca* when it opened in 1942. The film won Academy Awards for best picture, best screenplay, and best director, and is recognized today by film historians and the public alike as a classic. But up until the filming of the final scene, no one involved in the production of the now-famous story even knew how it was going to end.

In Practice 11.6

Everybody Comes to Rick's wasn't a very good play, but when it landed on Hal Wallis's desk at Warner Brothers, Wallis spotted some hot-from-the-headlines potential, purchased the rights, and changed the name to *Casablanca* to capitalize on the geographical mystique the story offered. A series of negotiations led to casting Humphrey Bogart as Rick, even though studio chief Jack Warner questioned his romantic appeal. The casting of Ingrid Bergman as Ilsa was largely by accident. A fluke had left an opening in her usually booked schedule. The screenplay still wasn't written.

Filming was chaotic. Writers made script changes and plot revisions daily. Actors were unsure of how to develop their characterizations, so they just did whatever seemed right at the time. For example, when Ingrid Bergman wanted to know which man should get most of her on-screen attention, she was told, "We don't know yet—just play it, well . . . in between." Scenes were often filmed blindly with no idea of how they were supposed to fit in the overall story. Amazingly, even when it came time to shoot the climactic final scene, no one involved in the production seemed to know who would "get the girl"; a legend still persists that two versions were written. During filming, Bogart disagreed with director Michael Curtiz's view that Rick should kiss Ilsa good-bye, and Hal Wallis was summoned to mediate. Because the cast received their scripts only hours before filming began, they couldn't remember their lines, causing continual delays.

Some industry analysts predicted disaster, but the haphazard process worked. Ingrid Bergman plays it "in between" just right. Bogart's characterization of Rick is perfect. The tale of love and glory and heartbreaking romance couldn't have been told better than it was in *Casablanca*. In addition, fortuitous circumstances outside the studio contributed to the film's commercial success. Just eighteen days before the premiere on Thanksgiving Day, 1942, the Allies invaded North Africa and fought the Battle of Casablanca. Then, when the film opened nationwide, President Franklin D. Roosevelt and Prime Minister Winston Churchill presided over the Casablanca Conference, a historical coincidence that was clearly a boon to the film, helping to push its initial gross to $3.7 million.[50]

The production of *Casablanca* was not a rational process that started with a clear problem and ended with a logical solution. Many events occurred by chance and were intertwined, which characterizes the garbage can model. Everyone from the director to the actors continuously added to the stream of new ideas to the story. Some solutions were connected to emerging problems: the original script arrived just when Hal Wallis was looking for topical stories; and Bergman was surprisingly available to be cast in the role of Ilsa. The actors (participants) daily made personal choices regarding characterization that proved to be perfect for the story line. Other events that contributed to *Casablanca's* success were not even connected to the film—for example, the invasion of North Africa only eighteen days before the premiere. Overall, the production of *Casablanca* had a random, chancy flavor that is characteristic of the garbage can model. As evidenced by the film's huge success and continuing popularity after more than fifty years, the random, garbage can decision process did not hurt the film or the studio.

The garbage can model, however, doesn't always work—in the movies or in organizations. A similar haphazard process during the filming of *Waterworld* led to the most expensive film in Hollywood history and a decided box-office flop for Universal Pictures.[51]

CONTINGENCY DECISION-MAKING FRAMEWORK

This chapter has covered several approaches to organizational decision making, including management science, the Carnegie model, the incremental decision process model, and the garbage can model. It has also discussed rational and intuitive decision processes used by individual managers. Each decision approach is a relatively accurate description of the actual decision process, yet all differ from each other. Management science, for example, reflects a different set of decision assumptions and procedures than does the garbage can model.

One reason for having different approaches is that they appear in different organizational situations. The use of an approach is contingent on the organization setting. Two characteristics of organizations that determine the use of decision approaches are (1) goal consensus and (2) technical knowledge about the means to achieve those goals.[52] Analyzing organizations along these two dimensions suggests which approach will be used to make decisions.

Goal Consensus

Goal consensus refers to the agreement among managers about which organizational goals and outcomes to pursue. This variable ranges from complete agreement to complete disagreement. When managers agree, the goals of the organization are clear and so are standards of performance. When managers disagree, organization direction and performance expectations are in dispute. One example of goal uncertainty occurred among cabinet members and presidential advisors during the Cuban missile crisis. Participants fought intensely over what goals should be pursued.[53] Another example of goal uncertainty occurred within the Penn Central Railroad after it went bankrupt. Some managers wanted to adopt the goal of becoming more efficient and profitable as a railroad. Other managers wanted to diversify into other businesses. Eventually, a strong coalition formed in favor of diversification, and that goal was adopted.

Goal consensus tends to be low when organizations are differentiated, as described in Chapter 3. Recall that uncertain environments cause organizational departments to differentiate from one another in goals and attitudes to special-ize in specific environmental sectors. This differentiation leads to disagreement and conflict about organizational goals. When differentiation among depart-ments or divisions is high, managers must make a special effort to build coali-tions during decision making.

Goal consensus is especially important for the problem identification stage of decision making. When goals are clear and agreed on, they provide clear stan-dards and expectations for performance. When goals are not agreed on, problem identification is uncertain and management attention must be focused on gain-ing agreement about goals and problem priorities.

Technical Knowledge

Technical knowledge refers to understanding and agreement about how to reach organizational goals. This variable can range from complete agreement and cer-tainty to complete disagreement and uncertainty about cause-effect relationships leading to goal attainment. An example of low technical knowledge was reflected in market strategies at 7-Up. The goal was clear and agreed on—increase market share from 6 percent to 7 percent, but the means for achieving this increase in market share were not known or agreed on. A few managers wanted to use dis-count pricing in supermarkets. Other managers believed they should increase the number of soda fountain outlets in restaurants and fast-food chains. A few other managers insisted that the best approach was to increase advertising through radio and television. Managers did not know what would cause an increase in market share. Eventually, the advertising judgment prevailed at 7-Up, but it did not work very well. The failure of its decision reflected 7-Up's low technical knowledge about how to achieve its goal.

Technical knowledge is especially important to the problem-solution stage of decision making. When means are well understood, the appropriate alternatives can be identified and calculated with some degree of certainty. When means are poorly understood, potential solutions are ill defined and uncertain. Intuition, judgment, and trial and error become the basis for decisions.

Contingency Framework

The **contingency decision-making framework** brings together the two organiza-tional dimensions of goal consensus and technical knowledge. Exhibit 11.8 shows how these two variables influence the decision situation. Goals and technical knowledge determine the extent to which problem identification and solution stages are uncertain. Depending on the situation, an organization may have to focus on gaining goal consensus, increasing technical knowledge, or both. Low uncertainty means that rational, analytical procedures can be used. High uncer-tainty leads to greater use of judgment, bargaining, and other less systematic pro-cedures.

Exhibit 11.9 describes the contingency decision framework. Each cell repre-sents an organizational situation that is appropriate for the decision-making approaches described in this chapter.

Cell 1.   In cell 1 of Exhibit 11.9, rational decision procedures are used because goals are agreed on, and cause-effect relationships are well understood. Deci-sions can be made in a computational manner. Alternatives can be identified and

Exhibit 11.8
*Contingency Decision
Situations*

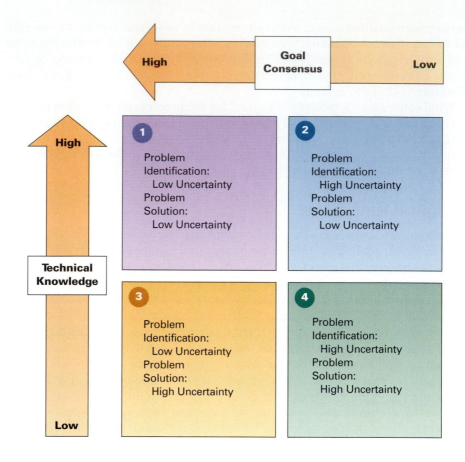

the best solution adopted through analysis and calculations. The rational models described earlier in this chapter, both for individuals and for the organization, are appropriate when goals and technical means are well defined. When problems occur, a logical process can be used to decide on the solutions.

Cell 2.   In cell 2, bargaining and compromise are used to reach consensus about goals and priorities. Diverse opinions are present in this situation. Achieving one goal would mean the exclusion of another goal. The priorities given to respective goals are decided through discussion, debate, and coalition building.

Managers in this situation should use broad participation to achieve goal consensus in the decision process. Opinions should be surfaced and discussed until compromise is reached. The organization will not otherwise move forward as an integrated unit. In the case of Penn Central Railroad, the diversification strategy was eventually adopted but only after much bargaining. During the Cuban missile crisis, debate finally led to the goal of establishing a blockade to prevent Soviet ships from reaching Cuba. At Gillette, much debate surrounded the struggle between executives favoring disposable versus permanent Sensor razors, eventually consolidating toward the permanent.

The Carnegie model applies when there is dissension about organizational goals. When groups within the organization disagree, or when the organization is in conflict with constituencies (government regulators, suppliers, unions), bargaining and negotiation are required. The bargaining strategy is especially

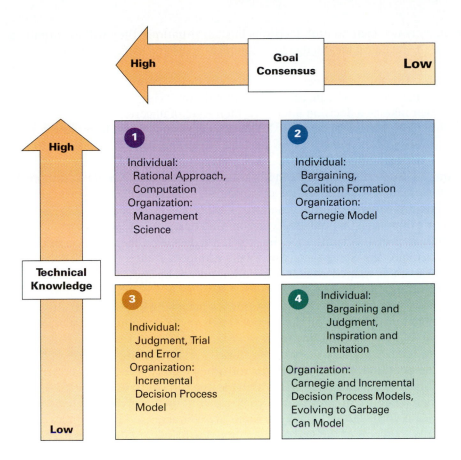

Exhibit 11.9
Contingency Frame-work for Using Deci-sion Models

relevant to the problem identification stage of the decision process. Once bargaining and negotiation are completed, the organization will have support for one direction.

Cell 3.   In a cell 3 situation, goals and standards of performance are certain, but alternative technical solutions are vague and uncertain. Techniques to solve a problem are ill defined and poorly understood. When an individual manager faces this situation, intuition will be the decision guideline. The manager will rely on past experience and judgment to make a decision. Rational, analytical approaches are not effective because the alternatives cannot be identified and calculated. Hard facts and accurate information are not available.

The incremental decision process model reflects trial and error on the part of the organization. Once a problem is identified, a sequence of small steps enables the organization to learn a solution. As new problems arise, the organization may recycle back to an earlier point and start over. Eventually, over a period of months or years, the organization will acquire sufficient experience to solve the problem in a satisfactory way. Solving the engineering and manufacturing problems for the Sensor razor, described earlier, is an example of a cell 3 situation. Gillette engineers had to use trial and error to develop an efficient manufacturing process.

The situation in cell 3, of senior managers agreeing about goals but not knowing how to achieve them, occurs frequently in business organizations. If managers use incremental decisions in such situations, they will eventually acquire the technical knowledge to accomplish goals and solve problems.

Cell 4.   The situation in cell 4, characterized by low consensus and low technical knowledge, occurs infrequently but is difficult for decision making. An individual manager making a decision under this high level of uncertainty can employ techniques from both cell 2 and cell 3. The manager can attempt to build a coalition to establish goals and priorities and use judgment or trial and error to solve problems. Additional techniques, such as inspiration and imitation, also may be required. **Inspiration** refers to an innovative, creative solution that is not reached by logical means. **Imitation** means adopting a decision tried elsewhere in the hope that it will work in this situation.

For example, in one university, accounting department faculty were unhappy with their current circumstances but could not decide on the direction the department should take. Some faculty members wanted a greater research orientation, whereas others wanted greater orientation toward business firms and accounting applications. The disagreement about goals was compounded because neither group was sure about the best technique for achieving its goals. The ultimate solution was inspirational on the part of the dean. An accounting research center was established with funding from Big Eight accounting firms. The funding was used to finance research activities for faculty interested in basic research and to provide contact with business firms for other faculty. The solution provided a common goal and unified people within the department to work toward that goal.

When an entire organization is characterized by low goal consensus and low technical knowledge and many decisions are characterized by a high level of uncertainty, elements of the garbage can model will appear. Managers may first try techniques from both cells 2 and 3, but logical decision sequences starting with problem identification and ending with problem solution will not occur. Potential solutions will precede problems as often as problems precede solutions. In this situation, managers should encourage widespread discussion of problems and idea proposals to facilitate the opportunity to make choices. Eventually, through trial and error, the organization will solve some problems.

SPECIAL DECISION CIRCUMSTANCES

In a highly competitive world beset by global competition and rapid change, decision making seldom fits the traditional rational, analytical model. To cope in today's world, managers must learn to make decisions fast, especially in high-velocity environments, to learn from decision mistakes, and to avoid escalating commitment to an unsatisfactory course of action.

High-Velocity Environments

In some industries today, the rate of competitive and technological change is so extreme that market data is either unavailable or obsolete, strategic windows open and shut quickly, perhaps within a few months, and the cost of a decision error is company failure. Recent research has examined how successful companies make decisions in these **high-velocity environments**, especially to understand whether organizations abandon rational approaches or have time for incremental implementation.[54]

Comparing successful with unsuccessful decisions in high-velocity environments suggests the following guidelines.

- Successful decision makers track information in real time to develop a deep and intuitive grasp of the business. Two to three intense meetings per week with all key players are usual. Decision makers track operating statistics about cash, scrap, backlog, work in process, and shipments to constantly feel the pulse of what is happening. Unsuccessful firms were more concerned with future planning and forward-looking information, with only a loose grip on immediate happenings.
- During a major decision, successful companies began immediately to build multiple alternatives. Implementation may run in parallel before finally settling on a final choice. Slow-decision companies developed only a single alternative, moving to another only after the first one failed.
- Fast, successful decision makers sought advice from everyone and depended heavily on one or two savvy, trusted colleagues as counselors. Slow companies were unable to build trust and agreement among the best people.
- Fast companies involved everyone in the decision and tried for consensus; but if consensus did not emerge, the top manager made the choice and moved ahead. Waiting for everyone to be on board created more delays than warranted. Slow companies delayed decisions to achieve a uniform consensus.
- Fast, successful choices were well integrated with other decisions and the overall strategic direction of the company. Less successful choices considered the decision in isolation from other decisions; the decision was made in the abstract.[55]

When speed matters, a slow decision is as ineffective as the wrong decision. As we discussed in Chapter 8, speed is a crucial competitive weapon in a growing number of industries, and companies can learn to make decisions fast. Managers must be plugged into the pulse of the company, must seek consensus and advice, and then be ready to take the risk and move ahead.

Decision Mistakes and Learning

Organizational decisions produce many errors, especially when made under high uncertainty. Managers simply cannot determine or predict which alternative will solve a problem. In these cases, the organization must make the decision—and take the risk—often in the spirit of trial and error. If an alternative fails, the organization can learn from it and try another alternative that better fits the situation. Each failure provides new information and learning. The point for managers is to move ahead with the decision process despite the potential for mistakes. "Chaotic action is preferable to orderly inaction."[56]

In many cases, managers have been encouraged to instill a climate of experimentation, even foolishness, to facilitate creative decision making. If one idea fails, another idea should be tried. Failure often lays the groundwork for success, as when technicians at 3M developed Post-it Notes based on a failed product—a not-very-sticky glue. Companies such as Pepsi-Cola believe that if all their new products succeed, they're doing something wrong, not taking the necessary risks to develop new markets.[57]

Only by making mistakes can managers and organizations go through the process of **decision learning** and acquire sufficient experience and knowledge to perform more effectively in the future. Robert Townsend, who was president at Avis Corporation, gives the following advice:

> Admit your mistakes openly, maybe even joyfully. Encourage your associates to do likewise by commiserating with them. Never castigate. Babies learn to walk by falling down. If you beat a baby every time he falls down, he'll never care much for walking.
>
> My batting average on decisions at Avis was no better than a .333. Two out of every three decisions I made were wrong. But my mistakes were discussed openly and most of them corrected with a little help from my friends.[58]

Escalating Commitment

A much more dangerous mistake is to persist in a course of action when it is failing. Research suggests that organizations often continue to invest time and money in a solution despite strong evidence that it is not working. Two explanations are given for why managers **escalate commitment** to a failing decision. The first is that managers block or distort negative information when they are personally responsible for a negative decision. They simply don't know when to pull the plug. In some cases, they continue to throw good money after bad even when a strategy seems incorrect and goals are not being met.[59] An example of this distortion is the reaction at Borden when the company began losing customers following its refusal to lower prices on dairy products. When the cost of raw milk dropped, Borden hoped to boost the profit margins of its dairy products, convinced that customers would pay a premium for the brand name. Borden's sales plummeted as low-priced competitors mopped up, but top executives stuck with their premium pricing policy for almost a year. By then, the company's dairy division was operating at a severe loss. Other companies have done the same, such as when Emery Air Freight Corporation acquired Consolidated Freightways, Inc. In the year since acquiring Consolidated, Emery lost $100 million on it, but executives were reluctant to admit it was a bad choice, believing things were about to get better.[60] Negative information often doesn't sink in.

As another example, consider the increasing investment of the Canadian Imperial Bank of Commerce in the ill-fated Canary Wharf project, an $8 billion development in London's remote Docklands area. CIBC had already lent over $1 billion for Canary Wharf to the now-failed Olympia & York Developments Ltd. and its subsidiaries. Despite loads of negative information that led CEO Al Flood to pronounce Canary Wharf a project that "would not meet our lending criteria today," CIBC turned around and invested an additional $36 million in the project. Flood said the move was designed to "protect our investment . . . and try to make the project work."[61] These additional millions now seem like a terrible choice.

A second explanation for escalating commitment to a failing decision is that consistency and persistence are valued in contemporary society. Consistent managers are considered better leaders than those who switch around from one course of action to another. Even though organizations learn through trial and error, organizational norms value consistency. These norms may result in a course of action being maintained, resources being squandered, and learning being inhibited. Emphasis on consistent leadership was partly responsible for the Long Island Lighting Company's refusal to change course in the construction of the Shoreham Nuclear Power Plant, which was eventually abandoned—after an investment of more than $5 billion—without ever having begun operation. Shoreham's cost was estimated at $75 million when the project was announced in 1966, but by the time a construction permit was granted, LILCO had already spent $77 million. Opposition to nuclear power was growing. Critics continued to decry the huge sums of money being pumped into Shoreham. Customers complained that LILCO was cutting back on customer service and maintenance of current operations. Shoreham officials, however, seemed convinced that they would triumph in the end; their response to criticism was, "If people will just wait until the end, they are going to realize that this is a hell of an investment."

The end came in 1989, when a negotiated agreement with New York led LILCO to abandon the $5.5 billion plant in return for rate increases and a $2.5 billion tax write-off. By the time Governor Mario Cuomo signed an agreement with the company, LILCO had remained firmly committed to a losing course of action for more than twenty-three years.[62]

Failure to admit a mistake and adopt a new course of action is far worse than an attitude that encourages mistakes and learning. Based on what has been said about decision making in this chapter, one can expect companies to be ultimately successful in their decision making by adopting a learning approach toward solutions. They will make mistakes along the way, but they will resolve uncertainty through the trial-and-error process.

SUMMARY AND INTERPRETATION

The single most important idea in this chapter is that most organizational decisions are not made in a logical, rational manner. Most decisions do not begin with the careful analysis of a problem, followed by systematic analysis of alternatives, and finally implementation of a solution. On the contrary, decision processes are characterized by conflict, coalition building, trial and error, speed, and mistakes. Managers operate under many constraints that limit rationality; hence, intuition and hunch often are the criteria for choice.

Another important idea is that individuals make decisions, but organizational decisions are not made by a single individual. Organizational decision making is a social process. Only in rare circumstances do managers analyze problems and find solutions by themselves. Many problems are not clear, so widespread discussion and coalition building take place. Once goals and priorities are set, alternatives to achieve those goals can be tried. When a manager does make an individual decision, it is often a small part of a larger decision process. Organizations solve big problems through a series of small steps. A single manager may initiate one step but should be aware of the larger decision process in which it is embedded.

The greatest amount of conflict and coalition building occurs when goals are not agreed on. Priorities must be established to indicate which goals are important and what problems should be solved first. If a manager attacks a problem other people do not agree with, the manager will lose support for the solution to be implemented. Thus, time and activity should be spent building a coalition in the problem identification stage of decision making. Then the organization can move toward solutions. Under conditions of low technical knowledge, the solution unfolds as a series of incremental trials that will gradually lead to an overall solution.

The most novel description of decision making is the garbage can model. This model describes how decision processes can seem almost random in highly organic organizations. Decisions, problems, ideas, and people flow through organizations and mix together in various combinations. Through this process, the organization gradually learns. Some problems may never be solved, but many are, and the organization will move toward maintaining and improving its level of performance.

Finally, many organizations must make decisions with speed, which means staying in immediate touch with operations and the environment. Moreover, in an uncertain world, organizations will make mistakes, and mistakes made through trial and error should be encouraged. Encouraging trial-and-error increments facilitates organizational learning. On the other hand, an unwillingness to change from a failing course of action can have serious negative consequences for an organization. Norms for consistency and the desire to prove one's decision correct can lead to continued investment in a useless course of action.

Key Concepts

bounded rationality perspective	intuitive decision making
Carnegie model	management science approach
coalition	nonprogrammed decisions
contingency decision-making framework	organizational decision making
decision learning	organized anarchy
escalating commitment	problem identification
garbage can model	problem solution
goal consensus	problemistic search
high velocity environment	programmed decisions
imitation	rational approach
incremental decision process model	satisficing
inspiration	technical knowledge

Discussion Questions

1. A professional economist once told his class, "An individual decision maker should process all relevant information and select the economically rational alternative." Do you agree? Why or why not?
2. Why is intuition used in decision making?
3. The Carnegie model emphasizes the need for a political coalition in the decision-making process. When and why are coalitions necessary?
4. What are the three major phases in Mintzberg's incremental decision process model? Why might an organization recycle through one or more phases of the model?

5. An organization theorist once told her class, "Organizations never make big decisions. They make small decisions that eventually add up to a big decision." Explain the logic behind this statement.

6. Why would managers in high-velocity environments worry more about the present than the future? Discuss.

7. How does goal consensus influence problem identification in an organization?

8. Describe the four streams of events in the garbage can model of decision making. Why are they considered to be independent?

9. Are there decision-making situations in which managers should be expected to make the "correct" decision? Are there situations in which decision makers should be expected to make mistakes? Discuss.

10. Why are decision mistakes usually accepted in organizations but penalized in college courses and exams that are designed to train managers?

Briefcase

As an organization manager, keep these guides in mind:

1. Adopt decision processes to fit the organizational situation.

2. Use a rational decision approach—computation, management science—when a problem situation is well understood.

3. Use a coalition-building approach when organizational goals and problem priorities are in conflict. When managers disagree about priorities or the true nature of the problem, they should discuss and seek agreement about priorities. The Carnegie model emphasizes the need for building a coalition and maintaining agreement about goals and problems.

4. Take risks and move the company ahead by increments when a problem is defined but solutions are uncertain. Try solutions step-by-step to learn whether they work.

5. Apply both the Carnegie model and the incremental process model in a situation with low goal consensus and low technical knowledge. Decision making may also employ garbage can procedures. Move the organization toward better performance by proposing new ideas, spending time working in important areas, and persisting with potential solutions.

6. Track real-time information, build multiple alternatives simultaneously, and try to involve everyone—but move ahead anyway when making decisions in a high-velocity environment.

7. Do not persist in a course of action that is failing. Some actions will not work out if uncertainty is high, so encourage organizational learning by readily trying new alternatives. Seek information and evidence that indicates when a course of action is failing, and allocate resources to new choices rather than to unsuccessful ventures.

Chapter Eleven Workbook *Decision Styles*

Think of some recent decisions that have influenced your life. Choose two significant decisions that you made and two decisions that other people made. Fill out the following table, using Exhibit 11.9 to determine decision styles.

*Adapted by Dorothy Marcic from "Action Assignment" in Jennifer M. Howard and Lawrence M. Miller, *Team Management,* Miller Consulting Group, 1994, p. 205.

Your decisions	Approach used	Advantages and disadvantages	Your recommended decision style
1.			
2.			
Decisions by others			
1.			
2.			

Questions

1. How can decision approach influence the outcome of the decision? What happens when the approach fits the decision? When it doesn't fit?

2. How can you know what approach is best?

Case for Analysis *Equal Employment Reaction**

Pleasantville, a southeastern city of 100,000 residents, earned the coveted designation of "All-American City" last year as a progressive municipality. Among other notable accomplishments, the city has established human rights councils and has supported affirmative action and equal employment opportunity programs. In fact, the first female firefighter ever to complete training in the city recently has been assigned to duty at Fire Station No. 5. Rookie firefighter Nancy Williams was welcomed for duty as a fully qualified combat firefighter by Fire Chief Dunmore.

The firefighters' work schedule of 24 hours on duty followed by 48 hours off duty required them to eat and sleep at the fire station. Station living facilities, designed for males only, included an open bay with closely spaced single beds, one toilet, a large unpartitioned shower room, and a common kitchen for cooking and eating. The only private bedroom was assigned to and occupied by the shift lieutenant. To accommodate Williams' presence, a shower schedule was arranged to afford her solitary showering privileges, and most of the men voluntarily began wearing bathrobes over their underwear, which they usually slept in.

This system worked well and seemed satisfactory until the firefighters' wives began to complain bitterly that they didn't want another woman living with their husbands under the conditions at Fire Station No. 5. It's only a matter of time until some romance blossoms, they argued. Besides that, the wives insisted, under intimate living conditions, the presence of Williams infringed upon their husbands' right to privacy. These complaints and others became front page news in the local press. Neither the husbands nor Williams commented publicly on the issue. In rapid succession, the wives banded together and hired a prominent lawyer, who implied that legal action was being considered; the city manager (see organization chart, Exhibit 11.10) stated publicly that the fire chief ran the fire department and was solely responsible for resolving the issue; and the city commissioners declared the problem beyond their jurisdiction under the city manager form of government.

Realizing that he had been tossed the ball but not knowing what to do with it, the chief pondered his options, which included, but were not limited to: reassigning Williams to the fire department's Administration and Fire Prevention unit, where she would have day-shift duty only; moving the shift lieutenant out of his private bedroom and assigning it to the female rookie; meeting personally with the wives and assuring them their complaints were unfounded; suspending Williams from duty, with pay, until the furor blew over; seeking a solution through the local firefighter's union; doing nothing; or doing whatever would best protect his position as fire chief.

As several wives began picketing Fire Station No. 5, Chief Dunmore felt increased pressure for an immediate decision and action.

Exhibit 11.10

Fire Department Organization

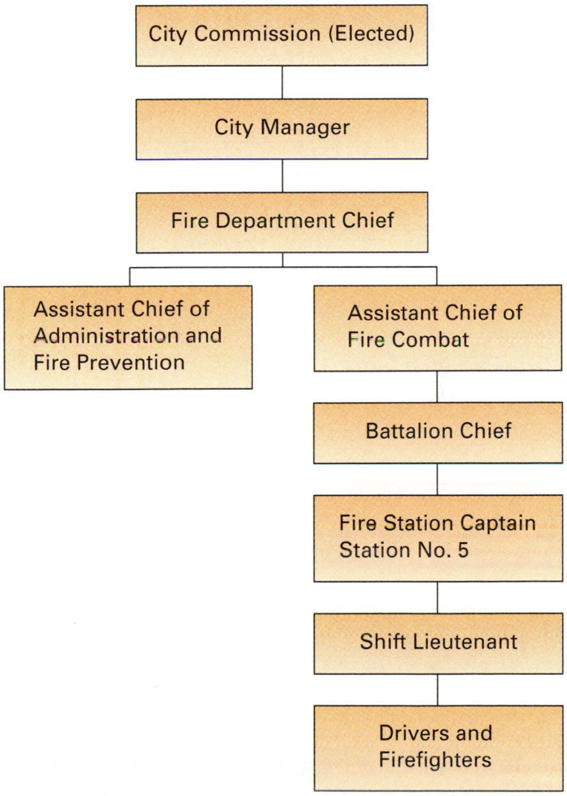

*John M. Champion and John H. James, *Critical Incidents in Management: Decision and Policy Issues,* 6th ed. (Homewood, Ill.: Irwin, 1989), 99-101.

Case for Analysis *The Dilemma of Aliesha State College: Competence Versus Need**

Until the 1980s, Aliesha was a well-reputed, somewhat sleepy State Teachers College located on the outer fringes of a major metropolitan area. Then with the rapid expansion of college enrollments, the state converted Aliesha to a four-year state college (and the plans called for its becoming a state university with graduate work and perhaps even with a medical school in the 1990s). Within ten years, Aliesha grew from 1,500 to 9,000 students. Its budget expanded even faster than the enrollment, increasing twenty-fold during that period.

The only part of Aliesha that did not grow was the original part, the teachers college; there enrollment actually went down. Everything else seemed to flourish. In addition to building new four-year schools of liberal arts, business, veterinary medicine, and dentistry, Aliesha developed many community service programs. Among them were a rapidly growing evening program, a mental-health clinic, and a speech therapy center for children with speech defects—the only one in the area. Even within education one area grew—the demonstration high school attached to the old teachers college. Even though it enrolled only 300 students, this high school was taught by the leading experts in teacher education and was considered the best high school in the whole area.

Then in 1986, the budget was suddenly cut quite sharply by the state legislature. At the same time the faculty demanded and got a fairly hefty raise in salary. It was clear that something had to give—the budget deficit was much too great to be covered by ordinary cost reductions. When the faculty committee sat down with the President and the Board of Trustees, two candidates for abandonment emerged after long and heated wrangling: the speech therapy program and the demonstration high school. Both cost about the same—and both were extremely expensive.

The speech-therapy clinic, everyone agreed, addressed itself to a real need and one of high priority. But—and everyone had to agree as the evidence was overwhelming—it did not do the job. Indeed it did such a poor, sloppy, disorganized job that pediatricians, psychiatrists, and psychologists hesitated to refer their patients to the clinic. The reason was that the clinic was a college program run to teach psychology students rather than to help children with serious speech impediments.

The opposite criticism applied to the high school. No one questioned its excellence and the impact it made on the education students who listened in on its classes and on many young teachers in the area who came in as auditors. But what need did it fill? There were plenty of perfectly adequate high schools in the area.

"How can we justify," asked one of the psychologists connected with the speech clinic, "running an unnecessary high school in which each child costs as much as a graduate student at Harvard?"

"But how can we justify," asked the Dean of the School of Education, himself one of the outstanding teachers in the demonstration high school, "a speech clinic that has no results even though each of its patients costs the state as much as one of our demonstration high school students, or more?"

*Peter F. Drucker, *Management Cases* (New York: Harper's College Press, 1977), 23–24.

Notes

1. Robert D. Hof, "The Education of Andrew Grove," *Business Week,* 16 January 1995, 60–62.
2. John M. Emshwiller and Michael J. McCarthy, "Coke's Soda Fountain For Offices Fizzles, Dashing High Hopes," *Wall Street Journal,* 14 June 1993, A1, A6; Walter S. Mossberg, "Apple of America's Eye Falls Victim to Pride," *Wall Street Journal,* 24 January 1996, B1; Kathy Rebello, Peter Burrows, and Ira Sager, "The Fall of an American Icon," *Business Week,* 5 February 1996, 34–42.
3. David Woodruff with Karen Lowry Miller, "Chrysler's Neon," *Business Week,* 3 May 1993, 116–26.
4. Charles Lindblom, "The Science of 'Muddling Through,'" *Public Administration Review* 29 (1954): 79–88.

5. Herbert A. Simon, *The New Science of Management Decision* (Englewood Cliffs, N.J.: Prentice-Hall, 1960), 1–8.

6. Paul J. H. Schoemaker and J. Edward Russo, "A Pyramid of Decision Approaches," *California Management Review* (Fall 1993): 9–31.

7. Wendy Zellner, "Back to Coffee, Tea, or Milk?" *Business Week,* 3 July 1995, 52–56.

8. Michael Pacanowsky, "Team Tools for Wicked Problems," *Organizational Dynamics* 23, no. 3 (Winter 1995): 36–51.

9. Bernard Wysocki, Jr., "A Popeyes Chain Frets Over How to Handle A Minimum-Pay Rise," *Wall Street Journal,* 24 April 1996, A1; Doug Wallace, "What Would You Do? Southern Discomfort," *Business Ethics,* March/April 1996, 52–53; Renee Elder, "Apparel Plant Closings Rip Fabric of Community's Employment," *The Tennessean,* 3 November 1996, 1E.

10. Earnest R. Archer, "How to Make a Business Decision: An Analysis of Theory and Practice," *Management Review* 69 (February 1980): 54–61; Boris Blai, "Eight Steps to Successful Problem Solving," *Supervisory Management* (January 1986): 7–9.

11. Francine Schwadel, "Christmas Sales' Lack of Momentum Test Store Managers' Mettle," *Wall Street Journal,* 16 December 1987, 1.

12. Adapted from Archer, "How to Make a Business Decision," 59–61.

13. James W. Dean, Jr., and Mark P. Sharfman, "Procedural Rationality in the Strategic Decision-Making Process," *Journal of Management Studies* 30 (1993): 587–610.

14. Paul A. Anderson, "Decision Making by Objection and the Cuban Missile Crisis," *Administrative Science Quarterly* 28 (1983): 201–22.

15. Irving L. Janis, *Crucial Decisions: Leadership in Policymaking and Crisis Management* (New York: The Free Press, 1989); Paul C. Nutt, "Flexible Decision Styles and the Choices of Top Executives," *Journal of Management Studies* 30 (1993): 695–721.

16. Herbert A. Simon, "Making Management Decisions: The Role of Intuition and Emotion," *Academy of Management Executive* 1 (February 1987): 57–64; Daniel J. Eisenberg, "How Senior Managers Think," *Harvard Business Review* 62 (November-December 1984): 80–90.

17. Sefan Wally and J. Robert Baum, "Personal and Structural Determinants of the Pace of Strategic Decision Making," *Academy of Management Journal* 37, no. 4 (1994): 932–56; Orlando Behling and Norman L. Eckel, "Making Sense Out of Intuition," *Academy of Management Executive* 5, no. 1 (1991): 46–54.

18. Thomas F. Issack, "Intuition: An Ignored Dimension of Management," *Academy of Management Review* 3 (1978): 917–22.

19. Marjorie A. Lyles, "Defining Strategic Problems: Subjective Criteria of Executives," *Organizational Studies* 8 (1987): 263–80; Marjorie A. Lyles and Ian I. Mitroff, "Organizational Problem Formulation: An Empirical Study," *Administrative Science Quarterly* 25 (1980): 102–19.

20. Marjorie A. Lyles and Howard Thomas, "Strategic Problem Formulation: Biases and Assumptions Embedded in Alternative Decision-Making Models," *Journal of Management Studies* 25 (1988): 131–45.

21. Susan E. Jackson and Jane E. Dutton, "Discerning Threats and Opportunities," *Administrative Science Quarterly* 33 (1988): 370–87.

22. David A. Cowan, "Developing a Classification Structure of Organizational Problems: An Empirical Investigation," *Academy of Management Journal* 33 (1990): 366–90; David Greising, "Rethinking IDS from the Bottom Up, *Business Week,* 8 February 1993, 110–12.

23. Ross Stagner, "Corporate Decision-Making: An Empirical Study," *Journal of Applied Psychology* 53 (1969): 1–13.

24. Annetta Miller and Dody Tsintar, "A Test for Market Research," *Newsweek,* 28 December 1987, 32–33; Oren Harari, "The Tarpit of Market Research," *Management Review* (March 1994): 42–44.

25. Ann Langley, "Between 'Paralysis By Analysis' and 'Extinction By Instinct,'" *Sloan Management Review* (Spring 1995): 63–76.

26. Paul C. Nutt, "Types of Organizational Decision Processes," *Administrative Science Quarterly* 29 (1984): 414–50.

27. "How Paramount Keeps Turning Out Winners," *Business Week,* 11 June 1984, 148–151; Ron Grover, "Michael Eisner's Hit Parade," *Business Week,* 1 February 1988, 27.

28. Nandini Rajagopalan, Abdul M. A. Rasheed, and Deepak K. Datta, "Strategic Decision Processes: Critical Review and Future Decisions," *Journal of Management* 19 (1993): 349–84; Paul J.

H. Schoemaker, "Strategic Decisions in Organizations: Rational and Behavioral Views," *Journal of Management Studies* 30 (1993): 107–29; Charles J. McMillan, "Qualitative Models of Organizational Decision Making," *Journal of Management Studies* 5 (1980): 22–39; Paul C. Nutt, "Models for Decision Making in Organizations and Some Contextual Variables Which Stimulate Optimal Use," *Academy of Management Review* 1 (1976): 84–98.

29. Hugh J. Miser, "Operations Analysis in the Army Air Forces in World War II: Some Reminiscences," *Interfaces* 23 (September-October 1993): 47–49; Harold J. Leavitt, William R. Dill, and Henry B. Eyring, *The Organizational World* (New York: Harcourt Brace Jovanovich, 1973), chap. 6.

30. Stephen J. Huxley, "Finding the Right Spot for a Church Camp in Spain," *Interfaces* 12 (October 1982): 108–14; James E. Hodder and Henry E. Riggs, "Pitfalls in Evaluating Risky Projects," *Harvard Business Review* (January-February 1985): 128–35.

31. Edward Baker and Michael Fisher, "Computational Results for Very Large Air Crew Scheduling Problems," *Omega* 9 (1981): 613–18; Jean Aubin, "Scheduling Ambulances," *Interfaces* 22 (March-April, 1992): 1–10.

32. Jean Aubin, "Scheduling Ambulances."

33. Harold J. Leavitt, "Beyond the Analytic Manager," *California Management Review* 17 (1975): 5–12; C. Jackson Grayson, Jr., "Management Science and Business Practice," *Harvard Business Review* 51 (July-August 1973): 41–48.

34. David Wessel, "A Man Who Governs Credit Is Denied a Toys 'R' Us Card," *Wall Street Journal,* 14 December 1995, B1.

35. Richard L. Daft and John C. Wiginton, "Language and Organization," *Academy of Management Review* (1979): 179–91.

36. Based on Richard M. Cyert and James G. March, *A Behavioral Theory of the Firm* (Englewood Cliffs, N.J.: Prentice-Hall, 1963); and James G. March and Herbert A. Simon, *Organizations* (New York: Wiley, 1958).

37. William B. Stevenson, Joan L. Pearce, and Lyman W. Porter, "The Concept of 'Coalition' in Organization Theory and Research," *Academy of Management Review* 10 (1985): 256–68.

38. David Woodruff with Karen Lowry Miller, "Chrysler's Neon," *Business Week,* 3 May 1993, 116–26.

39. Cyert and March, *Behavioral Theory of the Firm,* 120–22.

40. Ann Reilly Dowd, "How Bush Decided," *Fortune,* 11 February 1991, 45–46.

41. Robert Tomsho, "How Greyhound Lines Re-Engineered Itself Right Into a Deep Hole," *Wall Street Journal,* 30 October 1994, A1.

42. Lawrence G. Hrebiniak, "Top-Management Agreement and Organizational Performance," *Human Relations* 35 (1982): 1139–58; Richard P. Nielsen, "Toward a Method for Building Consensus during Strategic Planning," *Sloan Management Review* (Summer 1981): 29–40.

43. Based on Henry Mintzberg, Duru Raisinghani, and André Théorêt, "The Structure of 'Unstructured' Decision Processes," *Administrative Science Quarterly* 21 (1976): 246–75.

44. Lawrence T. Pinfield, "A Field Evaluation of Perspectives on Organizational Decision Making," *Administrative Science Quarterly* 31 (1986): 365–88.

45. Mintzberg, et al, "The Structure of 'Unstructured' Decision Processes."

46. Ibid., 270.

47. Keith H. Hammonds, "How a $4 Razor Ends up Costing $300 Million," *Business Week,* 29 January 1990, 62–63.

48. Michael D. Cohen, James G. March, and Johan P. Olsen, "A Garbage Can Model of Organizational Choice," *Administrative Science Quarterly* 17 (March 1972): 1–25; Michael D. Cohen and James G. March, *Leadership and Ambiguity: The American College President* (New York: McGraw-Hill, 1974).

49. Michael Masuch and Perry LaPotin, "Beyond Garbage Cans: An AI Model of Organizational Choice," *Administrative Science Quarterly* 34 (1989): 38–67.

50. David Krouss, "Casablanca," *Sky,* November 1992, 82–91

51. Thomas R. King, "Why 'Waterworld,' with Costner in Fins, Is Costliest Film Ever," *Wall Street Journal,* 31 January 1995, A1.

52. Adapted from James D. Thompson, *Organizations in Action* (New York: McGraw-Hill, 1967), chap. 10; and McMillan, "Qualitative Models of Organizational Decision Making," 25.

53. Anderson, "Decision Making by Objection and the Cuban Missile Crisis."

54. L. J. Bourgeois III and Kathleen M. Eisenhardt, "Strategic Decision Processes in High Velocity Environments: Four Cases in the Microcomputer Industry," *Management Science* 34 (1988): 816–35.

55. Kathleen M. Eisenhardt, "Speed and Strategic Course: How Managers Accelerate Decision Making," *California Management Review* (Spring 1990): 39–54.

56. Karl Weick, *The Social Psychology of Organizing,* 2d ed. (Reading, Mass.: Addison-Wesley, 1979), 243.

57. Power, et al., "Flops."

58. Robert Townsend, *Up the Organization* (New York: Knopf, 1974), 115.

59. Helga Drummond, "Too Little Too Late: A Case Study of Escalation in Decision Making," *Organization Studies* 15, no. 4 (1994): 591–607; Joel Brockner, "The Escalation of Commitment to a Failing Course of Action: Toward Theoretical Progress," *Academy of Management Review* 17 (1992): 39–61; Barry M. Staw and Jerry Ross, "Knowing When to Pull the Plug," *Harvard Business Review* 65 (March-April 1987): 68–74; Barry M. Staw, "The Escalation of Commitment to a Course of Action," *Academy of Management Review* 6 (1981): 577–87.

60. Elizabeth Lesly, "Why Things Are So Sour at Borden," *Business Week,* 22 November 1993, 78–85; Joan O'C. Hamilton, "Emery Is One Heavy Load for Consolidated Freightways," *Business Week,* 26 March 1990, 62–64.

61. Shona McKay, "When Good People Make Bad Choices," *Canadian Business,* February 1994, 52–55.

62. Jerry Ross and Barry M. Staw, "Organizational Escalation and Exit: Lessons from the Shoreham Nuclear Power Plant," *Academy of Management Journal* 36 (1993): 701–32.

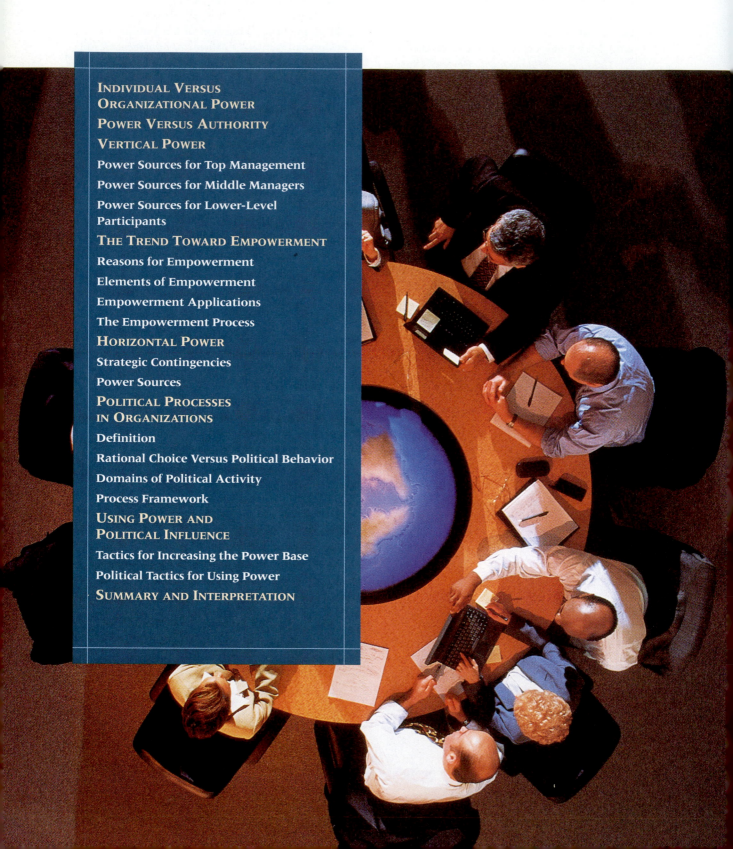

chapter twelve

Power and Politics

United States Information Agency

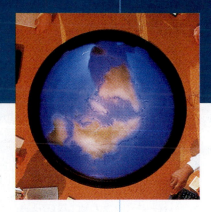

The creation of yet another bureau is nothing new in the U.S. government. When the U.S. Information Agency (USIA) set up its Information Bureau to replace the Bureau of Policy and Programs, however, it signalled a new era in government work. In place of the traditional bureaucratic hierarchy that piles layers of authority on top of one another, USIA formed twenty-one self-directed work teams, wiped out branches and divisions, downgraded managers, cut supervisory levels, and abolished the positions of deputies and special assistants.

In the past, managers passed information up and down the hierarchy, issued orders based on decisions made at the top, and "spent time breathing down people's necks" to make sure decisions were implemented. Today, teams iron out problems and make decisions together. Authority is no longer derived from title, and leadership is based on the ability to create an environment that brings out the best in workers. Throughout the Information Bureau, power is cascaded downward from the highest levels. In discussing his role of team leader compared to the old-style manager, Bill Peters said, "It came to me [the other day] that the team is the leader, not me. That is what we are striving for."

The team-based approach has given the Information Bureau greater flexibility to respond to current challenges and enhanced the motivation and commitment of workers. Team members constantly come up with new ideas and new ways to perform their work. Although the transition to team-based management has not been easy, especially for managers who had to give up power and authority, few employees feel any desire to return to the old hierarchy. As one team leader put it, "For the first time in my professional career, I don't have to ask permission. This is a new way of doing business."[1]

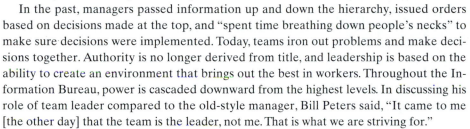

The United States Information Agency represents a trend that is sweeping North America, as well as other parts of the world—turning power over to workers. Rather than top managers taking responsibility for making the company work, using power and authority to the fullest, many managers are giving power away as fast as they can, with astonishing results. Sometimes it's done by creating a high-involvement corporate culture, or perhaps through self-directed teams, or by using clan control, all of which have been discussed in previous chapters. The implications are enormous because if this trend continues, managers will have to learn power sharing rather than power grabbing, a new way to manage effectively in today's world.

Purpose of This Chapter

Most organizations still operate under the old rules of power and politics. This chapter will explore power in organizations as a way to get things done. The following sections examine sources of power in organizations and the way power is used to attain organizational goals. Vertical and horizontal power are quite different, so these are discussed separately. We will also explore the new trend of worker empowerment to understand how it works. The latter part of the chapter looks at politics, which is the application of power and authority to achieve desired outcomes.

The study of power and politics is a natural extension of the previous chapter on decision making. Like decision making, politics involves the development of coalitions among executives. The dynamic processes associated with power and politics are thus similar in some respects to the processes associated with decision making.

INDIVIDUAL VERSUS ORGANIZATIONAL POWER

In popular literature, power is often described as a personal characteristic, and a frequent topic is how one person can influence or dominate another person.[2] You probably recall from an earlier management or organizational behavior course that managers have five sources of personal power.[3] *Legitimate power* is the authority granted by the organization to the formal management position a manager holds. *Reward power* stems from the ability to bestow rewards—promotion, raise, pat on the back—to other people. The authority to punish or recommend punishment is called *coercive power*. *Expert power* derives from a person's higher skill or knowledge about the tasks being performed. The last one, *referent power,* derives from personal characteristics such that people admire the manager and want to be like or identify with the manager out of respect and admiration. Each of these sources may be used by individuals within organizations.

Power in organizations, however, is often the result of structural characteristics.[4] Organizations are large, complex systems that contain hundreds, even thousands, of people. These systems have a formal hierarchy in which some tasks are more important regardless of who performs them. In addition, some positions have access to greater resources, or their contribution to the organization is more critical. Thus, the important power processes in organizations reflect larger organizational relationships, both horizontal and vertical, and organizational power usually is vested in the position, not in the person.

POWER VERSUS AUTHORITY

Power is an intangible force in organizations. It cannot be seen, but its effect can be felt. Power is often defined as the potential ability of one person (or department) to influence other persons (or departments) to carry out orders[5] or to do something they would not otherwise have done.[6] Other definitions stress that power is the ability to achieve goals or outcomes that power holders desire.[7] The achievement of desired outcomes is the basis of the definition used here: **Power** is the ability of one person or department in an organization to influence other people to bring about desired outcomes. It is the potential to influence others within the organization but with the goal of attaining desired outcomes for power holders.

Power exists only in a relationship between two or more people, and it can be exercised in either vertical or horizontal directions. The source of power often derives from an exchange relationship in which one position or department provides scarce or valued resources to other departments. When one person is dependent on another person, a power relationship emerges in which the person with the resources has greater power.[8] When power exists in a relationship, the power holders can achieve compliance with their requests. For example, the following outcomes are indicators of power in an organization:

- Obtain a larger increase in budget than other departments
- Obtain above-average salary increases for subordinates
- Obtain production schedules that are favorable to your department
- Get items on the agenda at policy meetings[9]

The inability to achieve a desired outcome came as a shock to Steve Jobs when he tried to oust John Sculley from Apple Computer. Sculley wrested control from Jobs after Jobs tried to fire him. The board of directors and senior managers supported Sculley, so Sculley, not Jobs, effectively had power.[10] Shortly after, Jobs, who had created Apple Computer, was forced from the company.

The concept of formal authority is related to power but is narrower in scope. **Authority** is also a force for achieving desired outcomes, but only as prescribed by the formal hierarchy and reporting relationships. Three properties identify authority:

1. *Authority is vested in organizational positions.* People have authority because of the positions they hold, not because of personal characteristics or resources.
2. *Authority is accepted by subordinates.* Subordinates comply because they believe position holders have a legitimate right to exercise authority.[11] Richard Ferris resigned as chairman of Allegis Corporation (now UAL, Inc.) because few people accepted his strategy of making Allegis a travel empire. Other senior managers, airline pilots, and board members preferred to see the company concentrate on its major business, United Airlines, and didn't accept Ferris's authority to implement his strategy.
3. *Authority flows down the vertical hierarchy.*[12] Authority exists along the formal chain of command, and positions at the top of the hierarchy are vested with more formal authority than are positions at the bottom.

Organizational power can be exercised upward, downward, and horizontally in organizations. Formal authority is exercised downward along the hierarchy and is the same as vertical power and legitimate power. The next section examines the use of vertical power as well as sources of power for lower participants. A later section examines the use of horizontal power in organizations, which is not defined by the vertical hierarchy and is determined by power relationships across departments.

VERTICAL POWER

All employees along the vertical hierarchy have access to some sources of power. Although any person may have access to almost any source of power, each level in the hierarchy tends to be concerned with different power issues and to rely on somewhat different power sources.

Power Sources for Top Management

The formal pyramid of authority provides power and authority to top management. Top management is responsible for a great number of people and many resources, and its authority is equal to those responsibilities. The chain of command converges at the top of the organization, so authority is great for top offices. The authority to govern granted to top management is reflected in both the formal organization structure and the decision authority defined by that structure.

> The design of an organization, its structure, is first and foremost the system of control and authority by which the organization is governed. In the organizational structure, decision discretion is allocated to various positions and the distribution of formal authority is established. Furthermore, by establishing the pattern of prescribed communication and reporting requirements, the structure provides some participants with more and better information and more central locations in the communication network. . . . Thus, organizational structures create formal power and authority by designating certain persons to do certain tasks and make certain decisions, and create informal power through the effect on information and communication structures within the organization. Organizational structure is a picture of the governance of the organization and a determinant of who controls and decides organizational activities.[13]

A large amount of power is allocated to senior management positions by the traditional organizational structure. The power of top management comes from four major sources: formal position, resources, control of decision premises and information, and network centrality.[14]

Formal Position.   Certain rights, responsibilities, and prerogatives accrue to top positions. People throughout the organization accept the legitimate right of top managers to set goals, make decisions, and direct activities. Thus, the power from formal position is sometimes called legitimate power.

Senior managers often use symbols and language to perpetuate their legitimate power. Reserving the top floor for senior executives and giving them wood-paneled offices are ways to communicate legitimate authority to others in the organization. When James Dutt was chairman of Beatrice, he had his picture hung in every facility worldwide. Such symbols reinforce the legitimacy of top management's authority.

Most Americans accept the legitimate right of top managers to direct an organization. They believe that "those in authority have the right to expect compliance; those subject to authority have the duty to obey."[15]

Resources.   Organizations allocate huge amounts of resources. Buildings are constructed, salaries are paid, and equipment and supplies are purchased. Each year, new resources are allocated in the form of budgets. These resources are allocated downward from top managers. In many companies, top managers own stock, which gives them property rights over resource allocation. A senior vice president with large shareholdings may sometimes be more powerful than the CEO.[16]

Top managers control the resources and, hence, can determine their distribution. Resources can be used as rewards and punishments, which are also sources of power. Resource allocation also creates a dependency relationship. Lower-level participants depend on top managers for the financial and physical resources needed to perform their tasks. Top management can exchange resources in the form of salaries, personnel, promotion, and physical facilities for compliance with the outcomes they desire.

Control of Decision Premises and Information. Control of **decision premises** means that top managers place constraints on decisions made at lower levels by specifying a decision frame of reference and guidelines. For example, when he was president of McDonnell Douglas, Sandy McDonnell prescribed a value of participative management, which was a frame of reference for the decisions of other managers. In one sense, top managers make big decisions, whereas lower-level participants make small decisions. Top management decides which goal an organization will try to achieve, such as increased market share. Lower-level participants then decide how the goal is to be reached. In one company, top management appointed a committee to select a new marketing vice president. The CEO provided the committee with detailed qualifications that the new vice president should have. He also selected people to serve on the committee. In this way, the CEO shaped the decision premises within which the marketing vice president would be chosen. Top manager actions and decisions such as these place limits on the decisions of lower-level managers and thereby influence the outcome of their decisions.[17]

The control of information can also be a source of power. Managers in today's organizations recognize that information is a primary business resource and that by controlling what information is collected, how it is interpreted, and how it is shared, they can influence how decisions are made.[18] Top managers often have access to more information than do other managers. This information can be released as needed to shape the decision outcomes of other people. For example, during the bidding war between Viacom Inc. and QVC Network Inc. to acquire Paramount Communications Inc., Paramount chairman Martin S. Davis was determined to accept the friendly Viacom offer and reject QVC's offer. Speaking to the board of directors, Davis attacked the QVC bid and had investment advisors provide a positive written opinion about Viacom's offer. Directors felt they weren't given the full story because Davis wanted Viacom to win.[19]

In another organization, Clark, Ltd., the senior manager controlled information given to the board of directors and thereby influenced the board's decision to purchase a large computer system.[20] The board of directors had formal authority to decide from which company the computer would be purchased. The management services group was asked to recommend which of six computer manufacturers should receive the order. Jim Kenny was in charge of the management services group, and Kenny disagreed with other managers about which computer to purchase. As shown in Exhibit 12.1, other managers had to go through Kenny to have their viewpoints heard by the board. Kenny shaped the board's thinking to select the computer he preferred by controlling information given to them.

Network Centrality. Top managers can locate themselves centrally in an organization. They can surround themselves with a network of loyal subordinates and use their networks to learn about events throughout the organization.[21] By placing managers they know in critical positions, top managers increase their power. They gain power by being well informed, having access to other people in the network, and having multiple people dependent on them. They can use their central positions to build alliances and loyalty and, hence, be in a position to wield substantial power in the organization.

When Harvey Golub was named chief executive officer of American Express, the board of directors put him on a short leash, naming a board member as

Exhibit 12.1

Information Flow for Computer Decision at Clark Ltd.

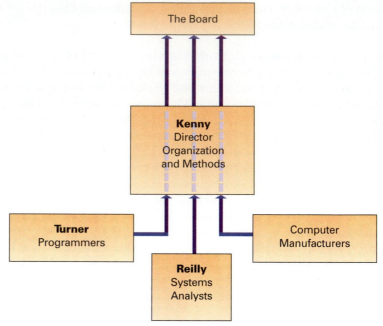

Source: Andrew M. Pettigrew, *The Politics of Organizational Decision-Making* (London: Tavistock, 1973), 235, with permission.

chairman and assigning a committee to keep tabs on the new CEO. But Golub moved quickly to put his imprint on the company and establish friendships and support among board members. He was named chairman within five months and then moved to surround himself with hand-picked top managers he trusted to be loyal and supportive.[22]

The following example illustrates a successful power play at Time Warner, where president and co-CEO Nicholas J. Nicholas, Jr., was ousted and replaced by a long-time rival.

In Practice 12.1 *Time Warner*

The board meeting that changed the line of succession at the world's largest media and entertainment company lasted less than an hour. However, the internal conflicts and struggles for power that led to that meeting had been building up since the merger of Time, Inc. and Warner Communications in 1990. At that time, Steven J. Ross, the Warner chairman, and Nicholas J. Nicholas, Jr., who had been designated heir by Time's chairman, were put in the rather awkward position of being co-CEOs. As a part of the merger negotiation, Nicholas was to become sole CEO in August 1994, on the eve of Ross's sixty-seventh birthday. However, while Nicholas was enjoying a family skiing trip in early 1992, the directors at a specially called meeting moved to oust him as president and co-CEO and replace him with vice chairman and chief operating officer Gerald M. Levin, a supporter of Ross.

Nicholas had complained that Ross controlled most of the directors, but the extent of Ross's power was never more clear than when Nicholas was given the sad and shocking news that his twenty-eight-year career at Time and Time Warner had come to an end. Ross and Levin had moved quickly, building support among executives and board members, so that by the time Levin approached retired Time chairman J. Richard Munro, the move to oust Munro's named successor had already gained so much momentum that a pragmatic Munro agreed to support Levin in the move.

Levin and Ross first contacted the directors they knew they could rely on, then gradually expanded the network so that those who were reluctant felt they had little choice but to go along. By the time of the fateful meeting, only one director voted against the ouster.[23]

Though at least one board member felt that the evidence produced to remove Nicholas didn't constitute cause, Ross and Levin had developed sufficient **network centrality** to push the co-CEO out. Moreover, once things were set in motion, they moved quickly, not allowing Nicholas time to mount a defense and gain his own support among directors.

Power Sources for Middle Managers

The distribution of power down the hierarchy is influenced by organization design factors. Top managers will almost always have more power than middle managers, but the amount of power provided to any given position or organizational group can be built into the organization's structural design.

The allocation of power to middle managers and staff is important because power enables employees to be productive. Managers need sufficient power and latitude to perform their jobs well. When positions are powerless, middle managers may seem ineffective and may become petty, dictatorial, and rules-minded.[24] Several factors that influence the amount of power along the hierarchy are shown in Exhibit 12.2. Power is the result of both task activities and network interactions. When a position is nonroutine, it encourages discretion, flexibility, and creativity. When a job pertains to pressing organizational problems, power is

Exhibit 12.2

Ways in Which Vertical Design Contributes to Power at Middle-Manager Levels

Design Factor	Generates Power When Factor Is	Generates Powerlessness When Factor Is
Task Activities		
Rules, precedents, and established routines in the job	Few	Many
Task variety and flexibility	High	Low
Rewards for unusual performance and innovation	Many	Few
Approvals needed for nonroutine decisions	Few	Many
Relation of tasks to current problem areas	Central	Peripheral
Network Interactions		
Physical location	Central	Distant
Publicity about job activities and contact with senior officials	High	Low
Participation in programs, conferences, meetings	High	Low
Participation in problem-solving task forces	High	Low

Source: Based on Rosabeth Moss Kanter, "Power Failure in Management Circuits," *Harvard Business Review* 57 (July–August 1979): 65–75.

more easily accumulated. Power is also increased when a position encourages contact with high-level people, brings visibility and recognition to employees, and facilitates peer networks both inside and outside the organization.

The variables in Exhibit 12.2 can be designed into specific roles or departments. For example, funds can be allocated to a department so members can attend professional meetings, thereby increasing their visibility and stature. Allowing people to approve their own decisions gives more discretion, reduces dependence on others, and increases power.

The logic of designing positions for more power assumes an organization does not have a limited amount of power to be allocated among high-level and low-level employees. The total amount of power in an organization can be increased by designing tasks and network interactions along the hierarchy so everyone has more influence. If the distribution of power is too heavily skewed toward the top so middle managers are powerless, research suggests the organization will be less effective. A study by Rosabeth Moss Kanter showed that design factors prevented some middle managers and staff personnel from having enough power to accomplish their jobs.

> Decision factors can leave an entire level of the hierarchy, such as first line supervisors, in a position of powerlessness. Their jobs may be overwhelmed with rules and precedents, and they may have little opportunity to develop an interaction network in the organization. Minority group members often have little power because management is overprotective, and thereby precludes opportunities for initiative and exposure needed for power accumulation. The same fate can befall staff specialists.

> As advisors behind the scenes, staff people must sell their programs and bargain for resources, but unless they get themselves entrenched in organizational power networks, they have little in the way of favors to exchange. They are not seen as useful to the primary tasks of the organization. . . . Lacking growth prospects themselves and working alone or in very small teams, they are not in a position to develop others or pass on power to them. They miss out on an important way in which power can be accumulated.[25]

Without sufficient power, middle-level people cannot be productive. Power can be built into positions and departments through the design of task activities and interaction opportunities.

Power Sources for Lower-Level Participants

Positions at the bottom of an organization have less power than positions at higher levels. Often, however, people at the bottom levels obtain power disproportionate to their positions and are able to exert influence in an upward direction. Secretaries, maintenance people, word processors, computer programmers, and others find themselves being consulted in decisions or having great latitude and discretion in the performance of their jobs. The power of lower-level employees often surprises managers. The vice president of a university may be more reluctant to fire a secretary than to fire an academic department head. Why does this happen?

People at lower levels obtain power from several sources. Some of these sources are individual because they reflect the personality and skill of employees.[26] Other power sources are position based, as indicated in Exhibit 12.3. One study found that unexpectedly high levels of power came from expertise, physi-

Personal Sources	Position Sources
Expertise	Physical Location
Effort	Information Flow
Persuasion	Access
Manipulation	

Exhibit 12.3

Power Sources for Lower-Level Participants

cal location, information, and personal effort.[27] When lower-level participants become knowledgeable and expert about certain activities, they are in a position to influence decisions. Sometimes individuals take on difficult tasks and acquire specialized knowledge, and then become indispensable to managers above them. Power accumulation is also associated with the amount of effort and interest displayed. People who show initiative, work beyond what is expected, take on undesirable but important projects, and show an interest in learning about the company and the industry often find themselves with influence.[28] Physical location also helps because some locations are in the center of things. Central location lets a person be visible to key people and become part of interaction networks. Likewise, certain positions are in the flow of organizational information. One example is the secretary to a senior executive. He or she can control information that other people want and will be able to influence those people.

Additional personal sources of upward influence are persuasion and manipulation.[29] Persuasion is a direct appeal to upper management and is the most frequent type of successful upward influence.[30] Manipulation means arranging information to achieve the outcome desired by the employee. It differs from persuasion because, with manipulation, the true objective for using influence is concealed. The final source of power is a position that provides access to other important people.[31] Access to powerful people and the development of a relationship with them provide a strong base of influence. However, access, persuasion, and manipulation only work as sources of power if employees are willing to make influence attempts that will provide desired outcomes.

THE TREND TOWARD EMPOWERMENT

A vertical hierarchy with greater power centralized at the top has been a distinctive feature of organizations almost since the appearance of the first large organization. Now we see a major shift away from this approach. Whether we are talking about organic structures, self-directed teams, or high-involvement cultures, the attempts to diffuse and share power are widespread. The notion of encouraging employees to participate fully in the organization is called empowerment. **Empowerment** is power sharing, the delegation of power or authority to subordinates in the organization.[32] It means giving power to others in the organization so they can act more freely to accomplish their jobs.

In an environment characterized by intense global competition and new technology, many top managers believe giving up centralized control will promote speed, flexibility, and decisiveness. Indeed, fully 74 percent of CEOs reported in a recent survey that they are more participatory, more consensus-oriented, and now rely more on communication than on command. They are finding less value in being dictatorial, autocratic, or imperial.[33] The trend is clearly toward moving power out of the executive suite and into the hands of employees. This trend can be seen in a variety of manufacturing and service industries, including some of the best known companies in the world, such as Hewlett-Packard, Southwest Airlines, Boeing, General Electric, and Caterpillar.[34]

Reasons for Empowerment

Why are so many organizations empowering workers and what advantages do these organizations achieve? One study suggests three primary reasons firms adopt empowerment: (1) as a strategic imperative to improve products or services; (2) because other firms in their industry are doing so (recall from Chapter 3 how firms tend to imitate similar organizations in the same environment); and (3) to create a unique organization with superior performance capabilities. Of the three reasons, the most compelling in terms of durability and success is the third—to create a unique organization that becomes the basis of sustainable competitive advantage.[35] The best known example is Southwest Airlines, discussed in the opening case in Chapter 10. The strength of Southwest comes not from products or services but from a unique culture and management philosophy that emphasizes employee involvement and empowerment.[36]

Empowerment provides a basis of sustainable competitive advantage in several ways. For one thing, empowerment *increases* the total amount of power in the organization. Many managers mistakenly believe power is a zero-sum game, which means they must give up power in order for someone else to have more. Not true. Both research and the experience of managers indicate that delegating power from the top creates a bigger power pie, so that everyone has more power.[37] Ralph Stayer, CEO of Johnsonville Foods, believes a manager's strongest power comes from committed workers: "Real power comes from giving it up to others who are in a better position to do things than you are."[38] The manager who gives away power gets commitment and creativity in return. Employees find ways to use their knowledge and abilities to make good things happen. Front-line workers often have a better understanding than do managers of how to improve a work process, satisfy a customer, or solve a production problem. In addition, employees are more likely to be committed to a decision or course of action when they are closely involved in the decision-making process.[39] Management's fear of power loss is the biggest barrier to empowerment of employees; however, by understanding they will actually gain power, delegation should be easy.

Empowerment also increases employee motivation. Research indicates that individuals have a need for *self-efficacy,* which is the capacity to produce results or outcomes, to feel they are effective. Increasing employee power heightens motivation for task accomplishment because people improve their own effectiveness, choosing how to do the task and using their creativity.[40] Most people come into the organization with the desire to do a good job, and empowerment enables them to release the motivation already there. Their reward is a sense of personal mastery and competence. One company that recognizes the benefits of empowerment is Chrysler Corporation.

In Practice 12.2   *Chrysler Corporation*

In recent years, Chrysler has turned out a string of hot-selling new cars and sales and earnings have risen rapidly. Ask CEO Robert Eaton how he does it and he answers with one word: empowerment.

Eaton has continued the empowerment efforts begun by Lee Iacocca in the late 1980s, and the efforts are clearly paying off. Eaton says that since he came to Chrysler he has basically never been involved in a product decision. When Chrysler decides to build a new model or revamp an old one, it forms a self-directed team to do it. Management essentially works out a contract with the team—sketching a vision for the vehicle and setting aggressive goals—and then turns workers loose to do the job as they see fit. When problems arise and disputes erupt, they're worked out within the team rather than by management. As Eaton says, "Because we stay out of it, it becomes their vehicle, and they work much, much harder, with much more pride, and the success or failure is theirs." One result is that every vehicle has come in below its total investment target and cost-per-car target. Another payoff has been speed to market. Chrysler's five-year concept-to-production time has been cut to three years and is still declining.

Robert Eaton believes that the success of any company comes down to people. "There's no magic," he says. "What will make all the difference in business will be how well you train your workforce, how well you motivate—and how well you empower."[41]

Elements of Empowerment

Empowering employees means giving them four elements that enable them to act more freely to accomplish their jobs: information, knowledge, power, and rewards.[42]

1. *Employees receive information about company performance.* In companies where employees are fully empowered, such as Semco S/A, Brazil's largest manufacturer of marine and food processing equipment, no information is secret. At Semco, every employee has access to the books and any other information, including executive salaries. To show they're serious about sharing information, Semco management works with the labor union that represents its workers to train employees—even messengers and cleaning people—to read balance sheets and cash flow statements.

2. *Employees have knowledge and skills to contribute to company goals.* Companies use training programs to give employees the knowledge and skills they need to personally contribute to company performance. For example, regular quality awareness workshops are held at Chrysler Canada's assembly plant in Bramalea, Ontario, so that employees can initiate quality improvements on their own. Xerox gives its workers what the company calls "line of sight" training, in which employees familiarize themselves with how their job fits into upstream and downstream activities. The training helps empowered employees make better decisions that support other workers and contribute to the organization's goals.[43]

3. *Employees have the power to make substantive decisions.* Many of today's most competitive companies are giving workers the power to influence work procedures and organizational direction through quality circles and self-directed work teams. At Prudential Insurance Company's Northeastern Group Operations, teams made up of clerical, processing, technical, and quality control specialists are empowered to approve claims of a certain type or for a certain customer up to a dollar amount representing 95 percent of all claim submissions. Another team decided employees could save the company money by processing claims from home. Workers, free to set their own hours, are setting new records for productivity.[44]

The New Paradigm   **Reflexite Corporation**

Once or twice a month, Cecil Ursprung gets a call from someone who wants to buy Reflexite Corporation. Ursprung tells them the company's already been sold—to its employees. Reflexite employees own 59 percent of the company's stock. Reflexite pushes employee ownership to the limit, unlike big-company ESOPs, in which employees hold only 5 to 10 percent of company stock.

And at Reflexite, stock ownership allows workers to behave like owners instead of wage earners. Reflexite manufactures retroreflective material (which coats highway signs and barricades). The technology is extremely complex—the tooling, machinery, and chemicals have to work together just right. As one manager said, "There are so many little things to pay attention to. We've got to have the hearts of the employees to make this thing run." The company has created a "culture of ownership," where employees truly feel a sense of proprietorship and long-term stake in the company. Reflexite employees aren't likely to forget the stake they own—it's reflected in a supplementary paycheck, which may be several hundred dollars a month for an experienced employee. In addition, every letterhead reads, "An ESOP company . . . where employees are owners." Regular meetings provide information about the company's performance and priorities. At the annual meeting, employees vote for the board of directors.

The structure and culture of ownership helps the company retain experienced employees, a critical asset for a company dependent on complex technology. When the company was facing a financial crisis and potential layoffs because of an economic downturn, the employee-owners devised a voluntary leave-of-absence plan, combined with a pay cut for top and middle management and a cut in manufacturing costs that saved the company more than $200,000. The year ended with profitability intact. When the company comes back strong, everyone will share in the rewards.

Back in the mid-1980s, Cecil Ursprung believed giving employees "some power" made good business sense. Time is proving him right. Though Reflexite competes with the giant 3M Company, which once tried to buy it out, the smaller company has more than doubled its sales, tripled its workforce, and increased its profits sixfold.

Source: John Case, "Collective Effort," *Inc.,* January 1992, 32–43.

4. *Employees are rewarded based on company performance.* Two of the ways in which organizations can reward employees financially based on company performance are through profit sharing and employee stock ownership plans (ESOPs). At W. L. Gore & Associates, makers of Gore-Tex, compensation takes three forms—salary, profit sharing, and an associates stock ownership program.[45] Reflexite Corporation, a growing and profitable technology-based business described in The New Paradigm box, is taking the concept of employee empowerment to new levels with its ESOP.

Empowerment Applications

Many of today's organizations are implementing empowerment programs, but they are empowering workers to varying degrees. At some companies, empowerment means encouraging employee input while managers maintain final authority for decisions; at others it means giving front-line workers almost complete power to make decisions and exercise initiative and imagination.[46] At Nordstrom (a department store chain), for example, employees are given the following guidelines: "Rule No. 1: Use your good judgment in all situations. There will be no additional rules."[47]

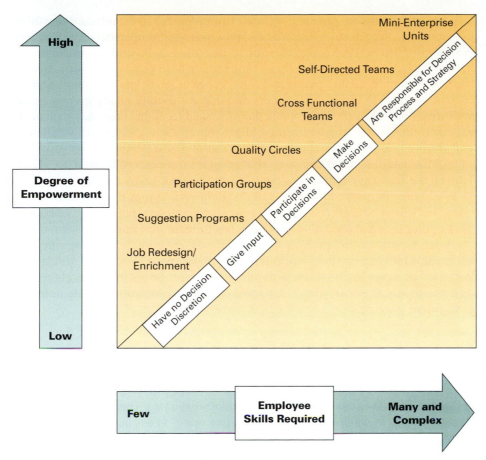

Exhibit 12.4
*The Empowerment
Continuum*

Source: Based on Robert C. Ford and Myron D. Fottler, "Empowerment: A Matter of Degree," *Academy of Management Executive* 9, no. 3 (1995): 21–31; Lawrence Holpp, "Applied Empowerment," *Training* (February 1994): 39–44; and David P. McCaffroy, Sue R. Faerman, and David W. Hart, "The Appeal and Difficulties of Participative Systems," *Organization Science* 6, no. 6 (November-December 1995): 603–27.

Exhibit 12.4 shows a continuum of empowerment, from a situation where front-line workers have no discretion (for example, a traditional assembly line) to full empowerment, where workers actively participate in determining organizational strategy. Current methods of empowering workers fall along this continuum. When employees are fully empowered, they are given decision-making authority and control over how they do their own jobs, as well as the power to influence and change such areas as organizational goals, structures, and reward systems. An example is when self-directed teams are given the power to hire, discipline, and dismiss team members and to set compensation rates. Few organizations have moved to this level of empowerment. One that has is W. L. Gore and Associates. The company, which operates with no titles, hierarchy, or any of the conventional structures associated with a company of its size, has remained highly successful and profitable under this empowered system for more than thirty years. The culture emphasizes teamwork, mutual support, freedom, motivation, independent effort, and commitment to the total organization rather than to narrow jobs or departments.[48]

Empowerment programs are difficult to implement in established organizations because they destroy hierarchies and upset the familiar balance of power. A study of *Fortune* 1000 companies found that the empowerment practices that have diffused most widely are those that redistribute power and authority the least, for example, quality circles and other types of participation groups and job enrichment and redesign.[49] Managers may have difficulty giving up power and authority; and although workers like the increased freedom, they may balk at the added responsibility freedom brings. Most organizations begin with small steps and gradually increase employee empowerment. For example, at Recyclights, a small Minneapolis-based company that recycles fluorescent lights, CEO Keith Thorndyke first gave employees control of their own tasks. As employee skills grew and they developed a greater interest in how their jobs fit into the total picture, Thorndyke recognized that workers also wanted to help shape corporate goals rather than having a plan handed down to them as a finished package.[50]

The trend toward empowering lower-level workers is likely to grow, with more companies moving up the continuum of empowerment shown in Exhibit 12.4. Whether an organization starts with job redesign or moves immediately to self-directed teams, there are steps managers can take to smoothly implement empowerment programs.

The Empowerment Process

When managers decide that delegation of power is important, the process can be accomplished in three stages. The first stage is to diagnose conditions within the organization that cause powerlessness for subordinates. The second stage is to engage in empowerment practices that will increase power at lower levels. Stage three involves feedback to employees that reinforces their success and feelings of effectiveness.

The first stage of diagnosis means looking carefully at organizational and job design elements at the middle and lower levels that reduce power. Recall from Exhibit 12.2 that such factors as too many rules, little task variety, being stuck in a remote location, rewards for routine output rather than innovation, and no opportunity for participating in task forces all reduce power. By analyzing these factors within organizations, the necessary changes for empowerment can be identified.

In stage two of empowerment, the old factors that generate powerlessness are changed, and employees are given access to the elements described in the previous section: information, knowledge and skills, power to make decisions, and rewards based on company performance. This stage usually starts with a clear goal or vision, from the top, publicly stated. Top managers make clear their desire for empowerment, and they articulate clear organizational goals. Employees no longer need to walk in step, but they should all head in the same direction. Next is widespread communication and information sharing. Employees must understand what's going on, otherwise they will not use power.

Employees must also be educated in the knowledge and skills they need to contribute to meeting organizational performance goals. In addition, a systematic change in structure is needed to increase employee power. This means jobs will be given more variety, rules will be withdrawn, high-level approvals will no longer be needed, physical locations can be consolidated, levels of the hierarchy can be eliminated, and employees can participate in teams and task forces as they see fit. These structural changes provide the basis for enlarged jobs and enlarged decision making. With clarity on overall company direction and goals, complete information, and a structure that provides latitude, employees can make decisions that use their power to enact task accomplishment.

At Hampton Inns, for example, employees are empowered to do whatever is necessary to honor the company's "100% Satisfaction Guarantee." They are given comprehensive ongoing training so that they understand the mission and rationale behind the guarantee and have the knowledge to make effective decisions that meet organizational goals. Training programs emphasize the importance of each job and each employee to the overall success of the company and instill a fix-it mentality that encourages employees to solve any guest problem on the spot, even if the problem isn't the hotel's fault. In one instance, a business traveler had forgotten to bring a tie and the stores weren't yet open. A front desk employee drove home and got one of his own ties for the guest to wear to an important meeting.[51]

In the third stage, feedback, employees learn how they are doing. Many companies place new emphasis on pay for performance, so employees' success is immediately rewarded. Career advancement is also encouraged as another way to reward excellence. At each Hampton Inn, managers set aside discretionary bonuses to be given to employees who go above and beyond the call of duty. The company also has a nationwide awards program to recognize workers who raise the standards of customer service to a higher level. Positive feedback reinforces employee feelings of self-efficacy, so they become comfortable and prosper under empowerment. The organization that has empowered employees will look and act differently from before, with major changes in structure, information sharing, and decision-making responsibility.

More organizations can be expected to push power down the vertical hierarchy in the future. As discussed in Book Mark 12.0, some scholars believe expanding employee power and participation is the only way companies can achieve long-term success.

HORIZONTAL POWER

Horizontal power pertains to relationships across departments. All vice presidents are usually at the same level on the organization chart. Does this mean each department has the same amount of power? No. Horizontal power is not defined by the formal hierarchy or the organization chart. Each department makes a unique contribution to organizational success. Some departments will have greater say and will achieve their desired outcomes, whereas others will not. For example, Charles Perrow surveyed managers in several industrial firms.[52] He bluntly asked, "Which department has the most power?" among four major departments: production, sales and marketing, research and development, and finance and accounting. Partial survey results are given in Exhibit 12.5. In most firms, sales had the greatest power. In a few firms, production was also quite powerful. On average, the sales and production departments were more powerful than R&D and finance, although substantial variation existed. Differences in the amount of horizontal power clearly occurred in those firms.

Horizontal power is difficult to measure because power differences are not defined on the organization chart. However, some initial explanations for departmental power differences, such as those shown in Exhibit 12.5, have been found. The theoretical concept that explains relative power is called strategic contingencies.[53]

Exhibit 12.5
*Ratings of Power
Among Departments
in Industrial Firms*

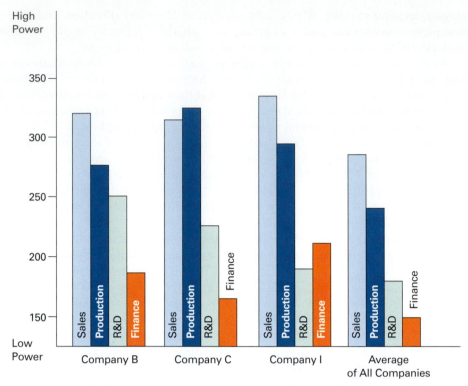

Source: Charles Perrow, "Departmental Power and Perspective in Industrial Firms," in Mayer N. Zald, ed., *Power in Organizations* (Nashville, Tenn.: Vanderbilt University Press, 1970), 64.

Strategic Contingencies

Strategic contingencies are events and activities both inside and outside an organization that are essential for attaining organizational goals. Departments involved with strategic contingencies for the organization tend to have greater power. Departmental activities are important when they provide strategic value by solving problems or crises for the organization. For example, if an organization faces an intense threat from lawsuits and regulations, the legal department will gain power and influence over organizational decisions because it copes with such a threat. If product innovation is the key strategic issue, the power of R&D can be expected to be high.

The strategic contingency approach to power is similar to the resource dependence model described in Chapter 3. Recall that organizations try to reduce dependency on the external environment. The strategic contingency approach to power suggests that the departments most responsible for dealing with key resource issues and dependencies in the environment will become most powerful.

Power Sources

Jeffrey Pfeffer and Gerald Salancik, among others, have been instrumental in conducting research on the strategic contingency theory.[54] Their findings indicate that a department rated as powerful may possess one or more of the characteristics illustrated in Exhibit 12.6.[55] In some organizations these five **power sources** overlap, but each provides a useful way to evaluate sources of horizontal power.

Book Mark 12.0

Have You Read About This?

The Age of Participation: New Governance for the Workplace and the World

by Patricia McLagan and Christo Nel

The authors of *The Age of Participation* argue that, as information technology, global economic and ecological interdependence, stakeholder demands, and other powerful forces in today's world converge, participation is the only viable option for the long-term success of human institutions. Their primary emphasis is on the workplace: "The shift to participative governance in the workplace . . . is necessary because the issues that we face . . . are too complex and interdependent to be solved by a few people in authority."

Moving Toward Participation

The authors review the history of participative governance and present a persuasive argument, along with mounting evidence, that participative systems outperform authoritarian ones. Numerous examples from companies in the United States, Europe, and Africa give life to their discussion of the theory and principles of empowerment and participation that are emerging in today's organizations. The book emphasizes the importance of a systems approach, pointing out that isolated and disconnected participative practices have little impact on a company's bottom line.

Written from the viewpoint of a practicing manager, *The Age of Participation* offers several practical guidelines on how to make the shift toward a participative workplace:

- Don't expect to find a perfect time or place to start the change process.
- Work on several key areas at a time, emphasizing a systems approach.
- Move to action as quickly as possible.
- Don't try to control everything.
- Get everyone throughout the organization involved as soon as possible.
- Balance planning with action learning.
- Take a deep breath and acknowledge that transforming the workplace requires a long-term commitment.

Guidelines for the Journey

The appendixes include a guide for assessing an organization's current level of participation and a worksheet examining authoritarian and participative practices in nine crucial areas: values, structures, leadership, management processes, information, employee relationships, core competencies, control, and compensation systems. Managers can use these worksheets to begin their journey toward participative governance. Although the authors acknowledge that the climb toward true participation in the workplace can seem daunting, they present compelling arguments that making the trip is both inevitable and necessary.

The Age of Participation, by Patricia McLagan and Christo Nel, is published by Berrett Koehler Publishers.

Dependency.   Interdepartmental dependency is a key element underlying relative power. Power is derived from having something someone else wants. The power of department A over department B is greater when department B depends on A.[56]

Many dependencies exist in organizations. Materials, information, and resources may flow between departments in one direction, such as in the case of sequential task interdependence (Chapter 4). In such cases, the department receiving resources is in a lower power position than the department providing them. The number and strength of dependencies are also important. When seven or eight departments must come for help to the engineering department, for example, engineering is in a strong power position. In contrast, a department that depends on many other departments is in a low power position.

Exhibit 12.6
Strategic Contingencies That Influence Horizontal Power Among Departments

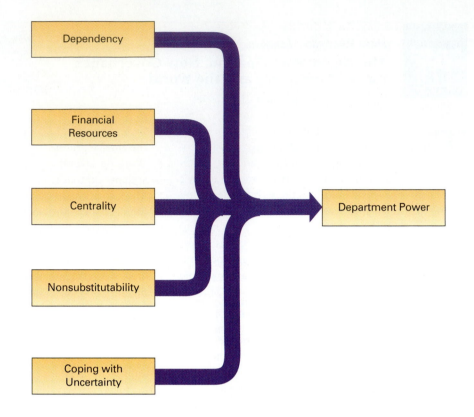

In a cigarette factory, one might expect that the production department would be more powerful than the maintenance department, but this was not the case in a cigarette plant near Paris.[57] The production of cigarettes was a routine process. The machinery was automated and production jobs were small in scope. Production workers were not highly skilled and were paid on a piece-rate basis to encourage high production. On the other hand, the maintenance department required skilled workers. These workers were responsible for repair of the automated machinery, which was a complex task. They had many years of experience. Maintenance was a craft because vital knowledge to fix machines was stored in the minds of maintenance personnel.

Dependency between the two groups was caused by unpredictable assembly line breakdowns. Managers could not remove the breakdown problem; consequently, maintenance was the vital cog in the production process. Maintenance workers had the knowledge and ability to fix the machines, so production managers became dependent on them. The reason for this dependence was that maintenance managers had control over a strategic contingency—they had the knowledge and ability to prevent or resolve work stoppages.

Financial Resources. There's a new golden rule in the business world: "The person with the gold makes the rules."[58] Control over various kinds of resources, and particularly financial resources, is an important source of power in organizations. Money can be converted into other kinds of resources that are needed by other departments. Money generates dependency; departments that provide financial resources have something other departments want. Departments that generate income for an organization have greater power. The survey of industrial firms reported in Exhibit 12.5 showed sales as the most powerful unit in most of those firms. Sales had power because salespeople find customers and sell the product, thereby removing an important problem for the organization. The sales department ensures the inflow of money. An ability to provide financial resources also explains why certain departments are powerful in other organizations, such as universities.

<table>
<tr><td>

University of Illinois

</td><td>

In Practice 12.3

</td></tr>
</table>

You might expect budget allocation in a state university to be a straightforward process. The need for financial resources can be determined by such things as the number of undergraduate students, the number of graduate students, and the number of faculty in each department.

In fact, resource allocation at the University of Illinois is not clear-cut. The University of Illinois has a relatively fixed resource inflow from state government. Beyond that, important resources come from research grants and the quality of students and faculty. University departments that provide the most resources to the university are rated as having the most power. Some departments have more power because of their resource contribution to the university. Departments that generate large research grants are more powerful because research grants contain a sizable overhead payment to university administration. This overhead money pays for a large share of the university's personnel and facilities. The size of a department's graduate student body and the national prestige of the department also add to power. Graduate students and national prestige are nonfinancial resources that add to the reputation and effectiveness of the university.

How do university departments use their power? Generally, they use it to obtain even more resources from the rest of the university. Very powerful departments receive university resources, such as graduate student fellowships, internal research support, and summer faculty salaries, far in excess of their needs based on the number of students and faculty.[59]

As shown in the example of the University of Illinois, power accrues to departments that bring in or provide resources that are highly valued by an organization. Power enables those departments to obtain more of the scarce resources allocated within the organization. "Power derived from acquiring resources is used to obtain more resources, which in turn can be employed to produce more power—the rich get richer."[60]

Centrality. **Centrality** reflects a department's role in the primary activity of an organization.[61] One measure of centrality is the extent to which the work of the department affects the final output of the organization. For example, the production department is more central and usually has more power than staff groups (assuming no other critical contingencies). Centrality is associated with power because it reflects the contribution made to the organization. The corporate finance department of an investment bank generally has more power than the stock research department. At Morgan Stanley Group, research analysts say they've been pressured to alter negative research reports on the stocks of the firm's corporate clients. "We were held accountable to corporate finance," a former Morgan Stanley analyst said, "playing the game the way corporate finance dictated."[62] By contrast, in the manufacturing firms described in Exhibit 12.5, finance tends to be low in power. When the finance department has the limited task of recording money and expenditures, it is not responsible for obtaining critical resources or for producing the products of the organization.

Nonsubstitutability.   Power is also determined by **nonsubstitutability**, which means that a department's function cannot be performed by other readily available resources. Nonsubstitutability increases power. If an employee cannot be easily replaced, his or her power is greater. If an organization has no alternative sources of skill and information, a department's power will be greater. This can be the case when management uses outside consultants. Consultants might be used as substitutes for staff people to reduce the power of staff groups.

The impact of substitutability on power was studied for programmers in computer departments.[63] When computers were first introduced, programming was a rare and specialized occupation. People had to be highly qualified to enter the profession. Programmers controlled the use of organizational computers because they alone possessed the knowledge to program them. Over a period of about ten years, computer programming became a more common activity. People could be substituted easily, and the power of programming departments dropped.

Today, however, the power of computer programming departments has increased again, as organizations battle the "millenium problem." Most large corporations use computer systems that were programmed thirty years ago to deal only in two-digit dates, which will convert the year 2000 into 00, throwing the entire system out of whack. The complex conversion process has to be done manually, and programmers with the skills to handle the conversion are highly prized.[64]

Coping with Uncertainty.   The chapters on environment and decision making described how elements in the environment can change swiftly and can be unpredictable and complex. In the face of uncertainty, little information is available to managers on appropriate courses of action. Departments that cope with this uncertainty will increase their power.[65] Just the presence of uncertainty does not provide power, but reducing the uncertainty on behalf of other departments will. When market research personnel accurately predict changes in demand for new products, they gain power and prestige because they have reduced a critical uncertainty. Forecasting is only one technique for **coping with uncertainty**. Sometimes uncertainty can be reduced by taking quick and appropriate action after an unpredictable event occurs.

Three techniques departments can use to cope with critical uncertainties are (1) obtaining prior information, (2) prevention, and (3) absorption.[66] *Obtaining prior information* means a department can reduce an organization's uncertainty by forecasting an event. Departments increase their power through *prevention* by predicting and forestalling negative events. *Absorption* occurs when a department takes action after an event to reduce its negative consequences. In the following case, the industrial relations department increased its power by absorbing a critical uncertainty. It took action after the event to reduce uncertainty for the organization.

| In Practice 12.4 | *Crystal Manufacturing* |

Although union influence has been declining in recent years, unions are still actively seeking to extend their membership to new organizations. A new union is a crucial source of uncertainty for many manufacturing firms. It can be a countervailing power to management in decisions concerning wages and working conditions.

In 1990, the workers in Crystal Manufacturing Company voted to become part of the Glassmakers Craft Union. Management had been aware of union organizing activities, but it had not taken the threat seriously. No one had acted to forecast or prevent the formation of a union.

The presence of the union had potentially serious consequences for Crystal. Glassmaking is a delicate and expensive manufacturing process. The float-glass process cannot be shut down even temporarily except at great expense. A strike or walkout would mean financial disaster. Therefore, top management decided that establishing a good working relationship with the union was critically important.

The industrial relations department was assigned to deal with the union. This department was responsible for coping with the uncertainties created by the new union. The industrial relations group quickly developed expertise in union relationships. It became the contact point on industrial relations matters for managers throughout the organization. Industrial relations members developed a network throughout the organization and could bypass the normal chain of command on issues they considered important. Industrial relations had nearly absolute knowledge and control over union relations.

In Crystal Manufacturing Company, the industrial relations unit coped with the critical uncertainty by absorption. It took action to reduce the uncertainty after it appeared. This action gave the unit increased power.

Horizontal power relationships in organizations change as strategic contingencies change. For example, in recent years, a few unions have increased their power by involving themselves in companies' strategic contingencies. In addition to the normal activities of work stoppages and strikes, these unions have become involved in pressuring companies' banks and creditors, challenging applications for financing and industrial revenue bonds, and using boycotts of products, banks, and health insurance companies. Unions have gone so far as to embarrass directors and executives by picketing their homes, opposing management in proxy battles, and communicating directly with stockholders.[67] These activities create new uncertainties and strategic issues for an organization, which can be reduced with the union's cooperation—thereby increasing union influence.

POLITICAL PROCESSES IN ORGANIZATIONS

Politics, like power, is intangible and difficult to measure. It is hidden from view and is hard to observe in a systematic way. Two recent surveys uncovered the following reactions of managers toward political behavior.[68]

1. Most managers have a negative view toward politics and believe that politics will more often hurt than help an organization in achieving its goals.
2. Managers believe political behavior is common to practically all organizations.
3. Most managers think political behavior occurs more often at upper rather than lower levels in organizations.
4. Political behavior arises in certain decision domains, such as structural change, but is absent from other decisions, such as handling employee grievances.

Based on these surveys, politics seems more likely to occur at the top levels of an organization and around certain issues and decisions. Moreover, managers do not approve of political behavior. The remainder of this chapter explores more fully what is political behavior, when it should be used, the type of issues and decisions most likely to be associated with politics, and some political tactics that may be effective.

Definition

Power has been described as the available force or potential for achieving desired outcomes. *Politics* is the use of power to influence decisions in order to achieve those outcomes. The exercise of power and influence has led to two ways to define politics—as self-serving behavior or as a natural organizational decision process. The first definition emphasizes that politics is self-serving and involves activities that are not sanctioned by the organization.[69]

In this view, politics involves deception and dishonesty for purposes of individual self-interest and leads to conflict and disharmony within the work environment. This dark view of politics is widely held by laypeople. Recent studies have shown that workers who perceive this kind of political activity at work within their companies often have related feelings of anxiety and job dissatisfaction. Studies also support the belief that inappropriate use of politics is related to low employee morale, inferior organizational performance, and poor decision making.[70] This view of politics explains why managers in the surveys described above did not approve of political behavior.

Although politics can be used in a negative, self-serving way, the appropriate use of political behavior can serve organizational goals.[71] The second view sees politics as a natural organizational process for resolving differences among organizational interest groups.[72] Politics is the process of bargaining and negotiation that is used to overcome conflicts and differences of opinion. In this view, politics is very similar to the coalition-building decision processes defined in Chapter 11 on decision making.

The organization theory perspective views politics as described in the second definition—as a normal decision-making process. Politics is simply the activity through which power is exercised in the resolution of conflicts and uncertainty. Politics is neutral and is not necessarily harmful to the organization. The formal definition of organizational politics is as follows: **organizational politics** involves activities to acquire, develop, and use power and other resources to obtain the preferred outcome when there is uncertainty or disagreement about choices.[73]

Political behavior can be either a positive or a negative force. Politics is the use of power to get things accomplished—good things as well as bad. Uncertainty and conflict are natural and inevitable, and politics is the mechanism for reaching agreement. Politics includes informal discussions that enable participants to arrive at consensus and make decisions that otherwise might be stalemated or unsolvable.

One reason for a negative view of politics is that political behavior is compared with more rational procedures in organizations. Rational procedures are considered by many managers to be more objective and reliable and to lead to better decisions than political behavior. Rational approaches are effective but only in certain situations. Both rational and political processes are normally used in organizations.

Rational Choice Versus Political Behavior

Rational Model.   The **rational model** of organization is an outgrowth of the rational approach to decision making described in Chapter 11. It describes a number of activities beyond decision making, as summarized in Exhibit 12.7. Behavior in the rational organization is not random or accidental. Goals are clear and choices are made in a logical way. When a decision is needed, the goal is defined, alternatives are identified, and the choice with the highest probability of achieving the desired outcome is selected. The rational model of organization is also characterized by

Exhibit 12.7

Rational Versus Political Models of Organization

Organizational Characteristic	Rational Model	Political Model
Goals, preference	Consistent across participants	Inconsistent, pluralistic within the organization
Power and control	Centralized	Decentralized, shifting coalitions and interest groups
Decision process	Orderly, logical, rational	Disorderly, characterized by push and pull of interests
Rules and norms	Norm of optimization	Free play of market forces; conflict is legitimate and expected
Information	Extensive, systematic, accurate	Ambiguous; information used and withheld strategically
Beliefs about cause-effect relationships	Known, at least to a probability estimate	Disagreements about causes and effects
Decisions	Based on outcome-maximizing choice	Result of bargaining and interplay among interests
Ideology	Efficiency and effectiveness	Struggle, conflict, winners and losers

Source: Based on Jeffrey Pfeffer, *Power in Organizations* (Marshfield, Mass.: Pitman, 1981), 31.

extensive, reliable information systems, central power, a norm of optimization, uniform values across groups, little conflict, and an efficiency orientation.[74]

Political Model. The opposite view of organizational processes within organizations is the **political model**, outlined in Exhibit 12.7. This model assumes organizations are made up of coalitions that disagree about goals and have poor information about alternatives. The political model defines the organization as made up of groups that have separate interests, goals, and values. Disagreement and conflict are normal, so power and influence are needed to reach decisions. Groups will engage in the push and pull of debate to decide goals and to reach decisions. Decisions are disorderly. Information is ambiguous and incomplete. Bargaining and conflict are the norm. The political model applies to organizations that strive for democracy and participation in decision making by empowering workers. Purely rational procedures do not work in democratic organizations.

Mixed Model. In many organizations neither the rational model nor the political model characterizes things fully, but each will be observed some of the time. This might be called a **mixed model**. One model may dominate, depending on organizational environment and context. The important thing is that both models apply to organizational processes. Managers may strive to adopt rational processes, but it is wishful thinking to assume an organization can be run without politics. Bargaining and negotiation should not be avoided for fear they are improper. The political model is an effective mechanism for reaching decisions under conditions of uncertainty and disagreement.

The rational model applies best to organizations in stable environments with well-understood technologies. It is inadequate when there is uncertainty and conflict, as illustrated in the following case.

| In Practice 12.5 | *Britt Technologies, Inc.* |

Britt Technologies was a new manufacturer of computer peripheral equipment, including tape and disk drives. The company's target was to sell equipment to manufacturers of complete computer systems. The strategy was working and the company was initially quite successful, but a problem emerged.

The problem pertained to the extent to which products should be custom-designed for customers. A manufacturer might be interested in a tape or disk product, but only if it could be reengineered to change some operating characteristics. This reengineering was expensive and time-consuming, and some managers felt it would be better to sell only what had already been designed. Indeed, almost every customer would ask for some modifications rather than accept the standard models that were available.

The design problem led to disagreement among executives. The marketing vice president believed engineering and production should produce whatever the market demanded. The vice president of production disagreed, saying that efficiencies would never be achieved unless the company developed a standard product line. The controller agreed with the production vice president, because profit margins would be reduced if redesigned units were continually produced. The engineering vice president was willing to redesign products so long as doing so didn't result in engineering overload.

Rather than hammer out this problem among themselves, Britt's executives decided to retain an outside consultant. They believed an outside consultant with experience in these matters would know how to rationally arrive at the correct answer, which each manager would accept. The consultant did some market research, competitive analysis, and strategic planning. Another consultant was hired to examine manufacturing operations.

Unfortunately, the company was left in a state of drift while the consultants did their research. Without a clear strategy, Britt Technologies was not excelling at either standard products or custom-designed peripherals. Marketing would sometimes accept custom orders, but manufacturing would refuse to produce them. The consultants' reports arrived in due course and were very logical, but Britt executives still disagreed among themselves. A clear strategy was delayed. In this highly competitive industry, once the company fell behind the competition, bankruptcy was inevitable.[75]

Britt Technologies was searching for a logical, correct answer through an orderly decision process that used precise data. Executives tried to apply the rational model to a situation that required a political model. The managers had to bargain and negotiate, use whatever information was available, and build a coalition among themselves. They couldn't do it. The search for rational answers was a time-consuming process that caused the company's failure.

Domains of Political Activity

Politics is a mechanism for arriving at consensus when uncertainty is high and there is disagreement over goals or problem priorities. Thus, political activity tends to emerge when managers confront nonprogrammed decisions, as discussed in Chapter 11, and is related to the Carnegie model of decision making. Because managers at the top of an organization generally deal with more nonprogrammed decisions than do managers at lower levels, more political activity will appear. Moreover, some issues are associated with inherent disagreement. Resources, for example, are critical for the survival and effectiveness of departments, so resource allocation often becomes a political issue. "Rational" methods of allocation do not satisfy participants. Four **domains of political activity** (areas in which politics plays a role) in most organizations are structural change, interdepartmental coordination, management succession, and resource allocation.

Structural reorganizations strike at the heart of power and authority relationships. Reorganizations such as those discussed in Chapter 6 change responsibilities and tasks, which also affects the underlying power base from strategic contingencies. For these reasons, a major reorganization can lead to an explosion of political activity.[76] Managers may actively bargain and negotiate to maintain the responsibilities and power bases they have.

Another area of political activity is interdepartmental coordination. Relationships among major organizational departments typically are not well defined. When joint issues arise, managers have to meet and work out solutions on an ad hoc basis. Uncertainty and conflict are common, especially when the issues are departmental territory and responsibility. Political processes help define respective authority and task boundaries.[77]

Organizational changes such as hiring new executives, promotions, and transfers have great political significance, particularly at top organizational levels where uncertainty is high and networks of trust, cooperation, and communication among executives are important.[78] Hiring decisions can generate uncertainty, discussion, and disagreement. Managers can use hiring and promotion to strengthen network alliances and coalitions by putting their own people in prominent positions.

The fourth area of political activity is resource allocation. Resource allocation decisions encompass all resources required for organizational performance, including salaries, operating budgets, employees, office facilities, equipment, use of the company airplane, and so forth. Resources are so vital that disagreement about priorities exists, and political processes help resolve the dilemmas.

Process Framework

The framework in Exhibit 12.8 summarizes the political processes described so far. Uncertainty and disagreement are the antecedent conditions that influence whether the political model is used. The political approach typically will be used

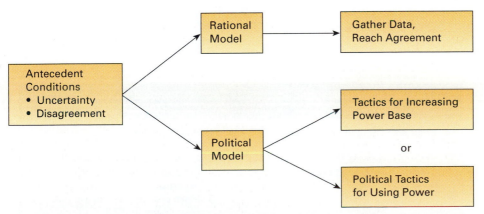

Exhibit 12.8

A Process Framework of Organizational Politics

Source: Adapted from Donald J. Vredenburgh and John G. Maurer, "A Process Framework of Organizational Politics," *Human Relations* 37 (1984): 47–66.

in specific areas, such as structural change, interdepartmental coordination, management succession, and resource allocation. Political behavior is often used for reaching decisions in these areas because the areas are uncertain and are associated with conflict. Managers who ignore political processes in these situations will have little influence over final outcomes.

Exhibit 12.8 also illustrates that when the political model is used, managers may wish to adopt specific tactics for increasing power or for using their power politically. The next section examines specific factors that managers can adopt to increase or use power.

USING POWER AND POLITICAL INFLUENCE

One theme in this chapter has been that power in organizations is not primarily a phenomenon of the individual. It is related to the resources departments command, the role departments play in an organization, and the environmental contingencies with which departments cope. Position and responsibility more than personality and style determine a manager's influence on outcomes in the organization.

Power is used through individual political behavior, however. Individual managers seek agreement about a strategy to achieve their departments' desired outcomes. Individual managers negotiate decisions and adopt tactics that enable them to acquire and use power.

Thus, to fully understand the use of power within organizations, it is important to look at both structural components and individual behavior.[79] Although the power base comes from larger organizational forms and processes, the political use of power involves individual-level activities. This section briefly summarizes tactics managers can use to increase the power base of their departments and political tactics they can use to achieve desired outcomes. These tactics are summarized in Exhibit 12.9.

Tactics for Increasing the Power Base

Four **tactics for increasing the power base** are as follows:

1. *Enter areas of high uncertainty.* One source of departmental power is to cope with critical uncertainties.[80] If department managers can identify key uncertainties and take steps to remove those uncertainties, the department's power base will be enhanced. Uncertainties could arise from stoppages on

Exhibit 12.9

Power and Political Tactics in Organizations

Tactics for Increasing the Power Base	Political Tactics for Using Power
1. Enter areas of high uncertainty	1. Build coalitions
2. Create dependencies	2. Expand networks
3. Provide resources	3. Control decision premises
4. Satisfy strategic contingencies	4. Enhance legitimacy and expertise
	5. Make preferences explicit, but keep power implicit

an assembly line, from the needed quality of a new product, or from the inability to predict a demand for new services. Once an uncertainty is identified, the department can take action to cope with it. By their very nature, uncertain tasks will not be solved immediately. Trial and error will be needed, which is to the advantage of the department. The trial-and-error process provides experience and expertise that cannot easily be duplicated by other departments.

2. *Create dependencies.* Dependencies are another source of power.[81] When the organization depends on a department for information, materials, knowledge, or skills, that department will hold power over the others. This power can be increased by incurring obligations. Doing additional work that helps out other departments will obligate the other departments to respond at a future date. The power accumulated by creating a dependency can be used to resolve future disagreements in the department's favor. An equally effective and related strategy is to reduce dependency on other departments by acquiring necessary information or skills. For example, data processing departments have created dependencies in many health-care organizations because of the enormous amount of paperwork. Doing paperwork fast and efficiently has created a dependency, giving data processing more power.

3. *Provide resources.* Resources are always important to organizational survival. Departments that accumulate resources and provide them to an organization in the form of money, information, or facilities will be powerful. For example, In Practice 12.3 described how university departments with the greatest power are those that obtain external research funds for contributions to university overhead. Likewise, marketing departments are powerful in industrial firms because they bring in financial resources.

4. *Satisfy strategic contingencies.* The theory of strategic contingencies says that some elements in the external environment and within the organization are especially important for organizational success. A contingency could be a critical event, a task for which there are no substitutes, or a central task that is interdependent with many others in the organization. An analysis of the organization and its changing environment will reveal strategic contingencies. To the extent that contingencies are new or are not being satisfied, there is room for a department to move into those critical areas and increase its importance and power.

In summary, the allocation of power in an organization is not random. Power is the result of organizational processes that can be understood and predicted. The abilities to reduce uncertainty, increase dependency on one's own department, obtain resources, and cope with strategic contingencies will all enhance a department's power. Once power is available, the next challenge is to use it to attain helpful outcomes.

Political Tactics for Using Power

The use of power in organizations requires both skill and willingness. Many decisions are made through political processes because rational decision processes do not fit. Uncertainty or disagreement is too high. **Political tactics for using power** to influence decision outcomes include the following:

1. *Build coalitions.* Coalition building means taking the time to talk with other managers to persuade them to your point of view.[82] Most important decisions are made outside formal meetings. Managers discuss issues with each other and reach agreements on a one-to-one basis. Effective managers are those who huddle, meeting in groups of twos and threes to resolve key issues.[83] An important aspect of coalition building is to build good relationships. Good interpersonal relationships are built on liking, trust, and respect. Reliability and the motivation to work with others rather than exploit others are part of coalition building.[84]

2. *Expand networks.* Networks can be expanded (1) by reaching out to establish contact with additional managers and (2) by co-opting dissenters. The first approach is to build new alliances through the hiring, transfer, and promotion process. Placing in key positions people who are sympathetic to the outcomes of the department can help achieve departmental goals.[85] On the other hand, the second approach, co-optation, is the act of bringing a dissenter into one's network. One example of co-optation involved a university committee whose membership was based on promotion and tenure. Several female professors who were critical of the tenure and promotion process were appointed to the committee. Once a part of the administrative process, they could see the administrative point of view and learned that administrators were not as evil as suspected. Co-optation effectively brought them into the administrative network.[86]

3. *Control decision premises.* To control decision premises means to constrain the boundaries of a decision. One technique is to choose or limit information provided to other managers. A common method is simply to put your department's best foot forward, such as selectively presenting favorable criteria. A variety of statistics can be assembled to support the departmental point of view. A university department that is growing rapidly and has a large number of students can make claims for additional resources by emphasizing its growth and large size. Such objective criteria do not always work, but they are a valuable step.

   Decision premises can be further influenced by limiting the decision process. Decisions can be influenced by the items put on an agenda for an important meeting or even by the sequence in which items are discussed.[87] Items discussed last, when time is short and people want to leave, will receive less attention than those discussed early. Calling attention to specific problems and suggesting alternatives also will affect outcomes. Stressing a specific problem to get it—rather than problems not relevant to your department—on the agenda is an example of agenda setting.

4. *Enhance legitimacy and expertise.* Managers can exert the greatest influence in areas in which they have recognized legitimacy and expertise. If a request is within the task domain of a department and is consistent with the department's vested interest, other departments will tend to comply. Members can also identify external consultants or other experts within the organization to support their cause.[88] For example, a financial vice president in a large retail firm wanted to fire the director of human resource management. She hired a consultant to evaluate the human resource management projects undertaken to date. A negative report from the consultant provided sufficient legitimacy to fire the director, who was replaced with a director loyal to the financial vice president.

5. *Make preferences explicit, but keep power implicit.* If managers do not ask, they seldom receive. Political activity is effective only when goals and needs are made explicit so the organization can respond. Managers should bargain aggressively and be persuasive. An assertive proposal may be accepted because other managers have no better alternatives. Moreover, an explicit proposal will often receive favorable treatment because other alternatives are ambiguous and less well defined. Effective political behavior requires sufficient forcefulness and risk taking to at least try to achieve desired outcomes.

The use of power, however, should not be obvious.[89] If one formally draws upon his or her power base in a meeting by saying, "My department has more power, so the rest of you have to do it my way," the power will be diminished. Power works best when it is used quietly. To call attention to power is to lose it. Explicit claims for power are made by the powerless, not by the powerful. People know who has power. There is substantial agreement on which departments are more powerful. Explicit claims to power are not necessary and can even harm the department's cause.

When using any of the preceding tactics, recall that most people feel self-serving behavior hurts rather than helps an organization. If managers are perceived to be throwing their weight around or are perceived to be after things that are self-serving rather than beneficial to the organization, they will lose respect. On the other hand, managers must recognize the relational and political aspect of their work. It is not sufficient to be rational and technically competent. Politics is a way to reach agreement. When managers ignore political tactics, they may find themselves failing without understanding why. This happened to Jeff Glover, a new manager with a firm in California's Silicon Valley.

Halifax Business Machines

In Practice 12.6

Jeff Glover was promoted to group leader at Halifax Business Machines because of his reputation as a well-respected technical specialist. Glover was interested in medical applications of the electronic business machines manufactured by his company. After visiting a hospital several times during his wife's illness, he developed specifications for a new piece of medical equipment. It was a clever modification of one of Monarch's existing products, and Glover's bosses were enthusiastic. They gave him permission to work half time on the new product and asked for cooperation from appropriate people in engineering, marketing, and manufacturing to develop a prototype.

A month after the project began, Glover was told that the engineer assigned to the project had to reduce his time to only five hours a week. Then Glover discovered that the manufacturing engineer who was supposed to do cost estimates was temporarily reassigned to a small crisis in a New York plant. Three days later, Glover was hit with the most damaging blow. His boss said that marketing had redone the market potential analysis and found the projected market was only one-fifth the size originally forecast. The project would have to be stopped immediately. Glover was furious. He resigned at the end of the day.

A few weeks later, Glover learned from a friend that the sales manager had immediately disliked Glover's idea when it was proposed. He didn't want his people to develop new knowledge about hospitals and medical purchasing practices. He had gotten one of his people to develop pessimistic numbers about market potential and had suggested to top management that time not be wasted on Glover's project.[90]

Glover's problem was that he naively assumed the logic and technical merits of his proposed machine would carry the day. He ignored political relationships, especially with the sales manager. He did not take the time to build a network of support for the project among key managers. He should have devoted more time to building a coalition and enhancing the legitimacy of his proposal, perhaps with his own market research.

SUMMARY AND INTERPRETATION

This chapter presented two views of organization. One view, covered only briefly, is the rational model of organization. This view assumes that organizations have specific goals and that problems can be logically solved. The other view, discussed throughout most of the chapter, is based upon a power and political model of organization. This view assumes the goals of an organization are not specific or agreed upon. Organizational departments have different values and interests, so managers come into conflict. Decisions are made on the basis of power and political influence. Bargaining, negotiation, persuasion, and coalition building decide outcomes.

The most important idea from this chapter is the reality of power and political processes in organizations. Differences in departmental tasks and responsibilities inevitably lead to differences in power and influence. Power differences determine decision outcomes. Uncertainty and disagreement lead to political behavior. Understanding sources of power and how to use politics to achieve outcomes for the organization are requirements for effective management.

Many managers prefer the rational model of decision making. This model is clean and objective. Rational thinking is effective when decision factors are sharply specified because of manager agreement and good information. Political processes, however, should not be ignored. Political decision processes are used in situations of uncertainty, disagreement, and poor information. Decisions are reached through the clash of values and preferences and by the influence of dominant departments.

Other important ideas in this chapter pertain to power in organizations. The traditional view of vertical power, with power centralized at the top, still applies to most organizations. However, as today's organizations face increasing global competition and environmental uncertainty, top managers are finding that empowering lower-level employees helps their organizations run leaner and more profitably, fight off competition, and move rapidly into new markets.

Research into horizontal power processes has uncovered characteristics that make some departments more powerful than others. Such factors as dependency, resources, and the removal of strategic contingencies determine the influence of departments. Political strategies, such as coalition building, expanded networks, and control of decision premises, help departments achieve desired outcomes. Organizations can be more effective when managers appreciate the realities of power and politics.

Finally, despite its widespread use in organizations, many people distrust political behavior. They fear political behavior may be used for selfish ends that benefit the individual but not the organization. If politics is used for personal gain, other managers will become suspicious and will withdraw their support. Politics will be accepted when it is used to achieve the legitimate goal of a department or an organization.

Key Concepts

authority
centrality
coping with uncertainty
decision premises
domains of political activity
empowerment
mixed model
nonsubstitutability
network centrality

organizational politics
political model
political tactics for using power
power
power sources
rational model
strategic contingencies
tactics for increasing the power base

Discussion Questions

1. If an organization decides to empower lower-level workers, are future decisions more likely to be made using the rational or political model of organization? Discuss.
2. Explain how control over decision premises gives power to a person.
3. In Exhibit 12.5, research and development has greater power in company B than in the other firms. Discuss possible strategic contingencies that give R&D greater power in this firm.
4. If you are a lower-level employee in an organization, how might you increase your power base?
5. Some positions are practically powerless in an organization. Why would this be? How could those positions be redesigned to have greater power?
6. State University X receives 90 percent of its financial resources from the state and is overcrowded with students. It is trying to pass regulations to limit student enrollment. Private University Y receives 90 percent of its income from student tuition and has barely enough students to make ends meet. It is actively recruiting students for next year. In which university will students have greater power? What implications will this have for professors and administrators? Discuss.
7. Do you believe it is possible to increase the total amount of power in an organization by delegating power to employees? Explain.
8. Why do you think most managers have a negative view of politics?
9. The engineering college at a major university brings in three times as many government research dollars as does the rest of the university combined. Engineering appears wealthy and has many professors on full-time research status. Yet, when internal research funds are allocated, engineering gets a larger share of the money, even though it already has substantial external research funds. Why would this happen?
10. Would the rational model, political model, or mixed model be used in each of the following decision situations: quality-control testing in a production department, resource allocation in an executive suite, and deciding which division will be in charge of a recently built plant.

Briefcase

As an organization manager, keep these guides in mind:

1. Do not leave lower organization levels powerless. If vertical power is too heavy in favor of top management, empower lower levels by giving them the tools they need to perform better: information about the company's performance; knowledge and skills that help them contribute to company goals; the power to make decisions; and rewards based on company performance.
2. Be aware of the less visible, but equally important, horizontal power relationships that come from the ability of a department to deal with strategic contingencies that confront the organization. Increase the horizontal power of a department by increasing involvement in strategic contingencies.
3. Expect and allow for political behavior in organizations. Politics provides the discussion and clash of interests needed to crystallize points of view and to reach a decision. Build coalitions, expand networks, control decision premises, enhance legitimacy, and make preferences explicit to attain desired outcomes.
4. Use the rational model of organization when alternatives are clear, when goals are defined, and when managers can estimate the outcomes accurately. In these circumstances, coalition building, cooptation, or other political tactics are not needed and will not lead to effective decisions.

Chapter Twelve Workbook *Power of Lower-Level Participants**

This assignment is designed to help you understand the effects of powerlessness. Choose a group of relatively powerless people, such as

> The homeless
>
> Elderly people
>
> Teenage mothers
>
> Retarded citizens
>
> Some minority group

Interview at least three people. Two of these should be members of the target group; also interview at least one person who works on behalf of that group, such as a nurse, social worker, or community organizer. If you are assigned to do this as a group, expand the number of people interviewed accordingly. For example, a group of four would interview twelve people, including eight members of the target group and four people who work on their behalf.

Answer the following questions:

1. What problems does this group face? What factors cause these problems?
2. What are the main sources for powerlessness for this group? What do you think needs to be done to help members of this group acquire more power?
3. Who are the people involved in trying to help this group? What strategies or tactics do they use to achieve their goals? What are the sources of resistance to their changes?
4. Can you think of ways members of your target group might increase their power?

*Adapted by Dorothy Marcic from "Down and Out in Evanston: Teaching About Power and Powerlessness to MBA Students" by Robert J. Bies, in *Organizational Behavior Teaching Review* 12 (3) (1987-88): 68–74; and R. Richard Ritti and G. Ray Funkhouser, *The Ropes to Skip and the Ropes to Know* (Columbus, Ohio: Grid Publishing, 1977), 172–75.

Case for Analysis *Dual Lines of Authority**

James A. Grover, retired land developer and financier, is president of the Chiefland Memorial Hospital Board of Trustees. Chiefland Memorial is a 200-bed voluntary, short-term general hospital serving an area of approximately 50,000 persons. Grover has just begun a meeting with the hospital administrator, Edward M. Hoffman. The purpose of the meeting is to seek an acceptable solution to an apparent conflict-of-authority problem within the hospital between Hoffman and the chief of surgery, Dr. Lacy Young.

The problem was brought to Grover's attention by Young during a golf match between the two men. Young had challenged Grover to the golf match at the Chiefland Golf and Country Club, but it was only an excuse for Young to discuss a hospital problem with Grover.

The problem that concerned Young involved the operating room supervisor, Ms. Geraldine Werther. Werther, a registered nurse, schedules the hospital's operating suite according to policies that she "believes" were established by the hospital's administration. One source of irritation to the surgeons is her attitude of maximum utilization for the hospital's operating rooms to reduce hospital costs. She therefore schedules operations so that idle time is minimized. Surgeons complain that the operative schedule often does not permit them sufficient time to complete a surgical procedure in the manner they think desirable. All too often, there is insufficient time between operations for effective preparation of the operating room for the next procedure. Such scheduling, the surgical staff maintains, contributes to low-quality patient care. Furthermore, some surgeons have complained that Werther shows favoritism in her scheduling, allowing some doctors more use of the operating suite than others.

The situation reached a crisis when Young, following an explosive confrontation with Werther, told her he was firing her. Werther than made an appeal to the hospital administrator, who in turn informed Young that discharge of nurses was an administrative prerogative. In effect, Young was told he did not have the authority to fire Werther. But Young asserted that he did have authority over any issue affecting medical practice and good patient care in Chiefland Hospital. He considered this a medical problem and threatened to take the matter to the hospital's board of trustees.

When Grover and Hoffman met, Hoffman explained his position on the problem. He stressed the point that a hospital administrator is legally responsible for patient care in the hospital. He also contended that quality patient care cannot be achieved unless the board of trustees authorizes the administrator to make decisions, develop programs, formulate policies, and implement procedures. While listening to Hoffman, Grover recalled the belligerent position taken by Young, who contended that surgical and medical doctors holding staff privileges at Chiefland would never allow a "layman" to make decisions impinging on medical practice. Young also had said that Hoffman should be told to restrict his activities to fund-raising, financing, maintenance, and housekeeping—administrative problems rather than medical problems. Young had then requested that Grover clarify in a definitive manner the lines of authority at Chiefland Memorial.

As Grover ended his meeting with Hoffman, the severity of the problem was unmistakably clear to him, but the solution remained quite unclear. Grover knew a decision was required—and soon. He also recognized that the policies Werther professed to follow were only implied policies that had never been fully articulated, formally adopted by board action, or communicated to employees. He also intended to correct that situation.

*John M. Champion and John H. James, *Critical Incidents in Management: Decision and Policy Issues,* 6th ed. (Homewood, Ill.: Irwin, 1989), 70–71.

Pierre Dux sat quietly in his office considering the news. A third appointment to regional management had been announced and, once again, the promotion he had expected had been given to someone else. The explanations seemed insufficient this time. Clearly, this signaled the end to his career at INCO. Only one year ago, the company president had arrived at Dux's facility with national press coverage to publicize the success of the innovation he had designed and implemented in the management of manufacturing operations. The intervening year had brought improved operating results and further positive publicity for the corporation but a string of personal disappointments for Pierre Dux.

Four years earlier, the INCO manufacturing plant had been one of the least productive of the 13 facilities operating in Europe. Absenteeism and high employee turnover were symptoms of the low morale among the work group. These factors were reflected in mediocre production levels and the worst quality record in INCO. Pierre Dux had been in his current position one year and had derived his only satisfaction from the fact that these poor results might have been worse had he not instituted minor reforms in organizational communication. These allowed workers and supervisors to vent their concerns and frustrations. Although nothing substantial had changed during that first year, operating results had stabilized, ending a period of rapid decline. But this "honeymoon" was ending. The expectation of significant change was growing, particularly among workers who had been vocal in expressing their dissatisfaction and suggesting concrete proposals for change.

The change process, which had begun three years before, had centered on a redesign of production operations from a single machine-paced assembly line to a number of semi-autonomous assembly teams. Although the change had been referred to as the INCO "Volvo project" or "INCO's effort at Japanese-style management," it had really been neither of these. Rather, it had been the brainchild of a group of managers, led by Dux, who believed that both productivity and working conditions in the plant could be improved through a single effort. Of course, members of the group had visited other so-called "innovative production facilities," but the new work groups and job classifications had been designed with the particular products and technology at INCO in mind.

After lengthy discussions among the management group, largely dedicated to reaching agreement on the general direction that the new project would take, the actual design began to emerge. Equally lengthy discussions (often referred to as negotiations) with members of the workforce, supervisors, and representatives of the local unions were part of the design process. The first restructuring into smaller work groups was tried in an experimental project that received tentative approval from top management in INCO headquarters and a "wait and see" response from the union. The strongest initial resistance had come from the plant engineers. They were sold neither on the new structure nor on the process of involving the workforce in the design of operating equipment and production methods. Previously, the engineering group had itself fulfilled these functions, and it felt the problems now present were a result of a lack of skill among employees or managerial unwillingness to make the system work.

The experiment was staffed by volunteers supported by a few of the better trained workers in the plant. The latter were necessary to ensure a start-up of the new equipment, which had been modified from the existing technology on the assembly line.

The initial experiment met with limited success. Although the group was able to meet the productivity levels of the existing line within a few weeks, critics of the new plan attributed the minor success to the unrepresentative nature of the experimental group or the newness of the equipment on which they were working. However, even this limited success attracted the attention of numerous people at INCO headquarters and in other plants. All were interested in visiting the new "experiment." Visits soon became a major distraction, and Dux declared a temporary halt to permit the project to proceed, although this produced some muttering at headquarters about his "secretive" and "uncooperative" behavior.

Because of the experiment's success, Dux and his staff prepared to convert the entire production opera-

*This case was prepared by Michael Brimm, Associate Professor at INSEAD. It is intended to be used as a basis for class discussion rather than to illustrate either effective or ineffective handling of an administrative situation. Copyright © 1983 INSEAD Fountainbleau, France. Revised 1987.

tion to the new system. The enthusiasm of workers in the plant grew as training for the changeover proceeded. In fact, a group of production workers asked to help with the installation of the new equipment as a means of learning more about its operation.

Dux and his staff were surprised at the difficulties encountered at this phase. Headquarters seemed to drag their feet in approving the necessary funding for the changeover. Even after the funding was approved, there was a stream of challenges to minor parts of the plan. "Can't you lay the workers off during the changeover?" "Why use workers on overtime to do the changeover when you could hire temporary workers more cheaply?" These criticisms reflected a lack of understanding of the basic operating principles of the new system, and Dux rejected them.

The conversion of the entire assembly line to work groups was finally achieved, with the local management group making few concessions from their stated plans. The initial change and the first days of operation were filled with crisis. The design process had not anticipated many of the problems that arose with full scale operations. However, Dux was pleased to see managers, staff, and workers clustered together at the trouble areas, fine-tuning the design when problems arose. Just as the start-up finally appeared to be moving forward, a change in product specifications from a headquarters group dictated additional changes in the design of the assembly process. The new change was handled quickly and with enthusiasm by the workforce. While the period was exhausting and seemingly endless to those who felt responsible for the change, the new design took only six months to reach normal operating levels (one year had been forecast as the time needed to reach that level—without the added requirement for a change in product specification).

Within a year, Dux was secure that he had a major success on his hands. Productivity and product quality measures for the plant had greatly improved. In this relatively short period his plant had moved from the worst, according to these indicators, to the third most productive in the INCO system. Absenteeism had dropped only slightly, but turnover had been reduced substantially. Morale was not measured formally but was considered by all members of the management team to be greatly improved. Now, after three years of full operations, the plant was considered the most productive in the entire INCO system.

Dux was a bit surprised when no other facility in INCO initiated a similar effort or called upon him for help. Increases of the early years had leveled off, with the peak being achieved in the early part of year three. Now the facility seemed to have found a new equilibrium. The calm of smoother operations had been a welcome relief to many who had worked so hard to launch the new design. For Dux it provided the time to reflect on his accomplishment and think about his future career.

It was in this context that he considered the news that he had once again been bypassed for promotion to the next level in the INCO hierarchy.

Notes

1. Mark A. Abramson, "First Teams," *Government Executive* (May 1996): 53–58.

2. Examples are Michael Korda, *Power: How to Get It, How To Use It* (New York: Random House, 1975), and Robert J. Ringer, *Winning through Intimidation* (Los Angeles: Los Angeles Book Publishing, 1973).

3. John R. P. French, Jr., and Bertram Raven, "The Bases of Social Power," in *Group Dynamics,* D. Cartwright and A. F. Zander, eds. (Evanston, Ill.: Row Peterson, 1960), 607–23.

4. Ran Lachman, "Power from What? A Reexamination of Its Relationships with Structural Conditions," *Administrative Science Quarterly* 34 (1989): 231–51; Daniel J. Brass, "Being in the Right Place: A Structural Analysis of Individual Influence in an Organization," *Administrative Science Quarterly* 29 (1984): 518–39.

5. Robert A. Dahl, "The Concept of Power," *Behavioral Science* 2 (1957): 201–15.

6. W. Graham Astley and Paramjit S. Sachdeva, "Structural Sources of Intraorganizational Power: A Theoretical Synthesis," *Academy of Management Review* 9 (1984): 104–13; Abraham Kaplan, "Power in Perspective," in Robert L. Kahn and Elise Boulding, eds., *Power and Conflict in Organizations* (London: Tavistock, 1964), 11–32.

7. Gerald R. Salancik and Jeffrey Pfeffer, "The Bases and Use of Power in Organizational Decision-Making: The Case of the University," *Administrative Science Quarterly* 19 (1974): 453–73.

8. Richard M. Emerson, "Power-Dependence Relations," *American Sociological Review* 27 (1962): 31–41.

9. Rosabeth Moss Kanter, "Power Failure in Management Circuits," *Harvard Business Review* (July-August 1979): 65–75.

10. Bro Uttal, "Behind the Fall of Steve Jobs," *Fortune,* 5 August 1985, 20–24; Deborah C. Weise, "Steve Jobs versus Apple: What Caused the Final Split," *Business Week,* 30 September 1985, 48.

11. A. J. Grimes, "Authority, Power, Influence, and Social Control: A Theoretical Synthesis," *Academy of Management Review* 3 (1978): 724–35.

12. Astley and Sachdeva, "Structural Sources of Intraorganizational Power."

13. Jeffrey Pfeffer, "The Micropolitics of Organizations," in Marshall W. Meyer, et al., *Environments and Organizations* (San Francisco: Jossey-Bass, 1978): 29–50.

14. Jeffrey Pfeffer, *Managing with Power: Politics and Influence in Organizations* (Boston: Harvard Business School Press, 1992).

15. Robert L. Peabody, "Perceptions of Organizational Authority," *Administrative Science Quarterly* 6 (1962): 479.

16. Sydney Finkelstein, "Power in Top Management Teams: Dimensions, Measurement, and Validation," *Academy of Management Journal* 35 (1992): 505–38.

17. Jeffrey Pfeffer, *Power in Organizations* (Marshfield, Mass.: Pitman, 1981).

18. Erik W. Larson and Jonathan B. King, "The Systemic Distortion of Information: An Ongoing Challenge to Management," *Organizational Dynamics* 24, no. 3 (Winter 1996): 49–61; Thomas H. Davenport, Robert G. Eccles, and Lawrence Prusak, "Information Politics," *Sloan Management Review* (Fall 1992): 53–65.

19. Johnnie L. Roberts and Randall Smith, "Who Gets the Blame for Paramount Gaffes: Big Cast of Characters," *Wall Street Journal*, 13 December 1993, A1.

20. Andrew M. Pettigrew, *The Politics of Organizational Decision-Making* (London: Tavistock, 1973).

21. Astley and Sachdeva, "Structural Sources of Intraorganizational Power"; Noel M. Tichy and Charles Fombrun, "Network Analysis in Organizational Settings," *Human Relations* 32 (1979): 923–65.

22. Steven Lipin, "Golub Solidifies Hold at American Express, Begins to Change Firm," *Wall Street Journal*, 30 June 1993, A1.

23. Ann M. Morrison, "After the Coup at Time Warner," *Fortune,* 23 March 1992, 82–89.

24. Kanter, "Power Failure in Management Circuits."

25. Ibid., p. 70.

26. David C. Wilson and Graham K. Kenny, "Managerially Perceived Influence over Intradepartmental Decisions," *Journal of Management Studies* 22 (1985): 155–73; Warren Keith Schilit, "An Examination of Individual Differences as Moderators of Upward Influence Activity in

Strategic Decisions," *Human Relations* 39 (1986): 933–53.

27. David Mechanic, "Source of Power in Lower Participants in Complex Organizations," *Administrative Science Quarterly* 7 (1962): 349–64.

28. Peter Moroz and Brian H. Kleiner, "Playing Hardball in Business Organizations," *IM* (January/February 1994): 9–11.

29. Richard T. Mowday, "The Exercise of Upward Influence in Organizations," *Administrative Science Quarterly* 23 (1978): 137–56.

30. Warren K. Schilit and Edwin A. Locke, "A Study of Upward Influence in Organizations," *Administrative Science Quarterly* 27 (1982): 304–16.

31. Richard S. Blackburn, "Lower Participant Power: Toward a Conceptual Integration," *Academy of Management Review* 6 (1981): 127–31.

32. Edwin P. Hollander and Lynn R. Offermann, "Power and Leadership in Organizations," *American Psychologist* 45 (February 1990): 179–89.

33. Thomas A. Stewart, "New Ways to Exercise Power," *Fortune,* 6 November 1989, 52–64; Thomas A. Stewart, "CEOs See Clout Shifting," *Fortune,* 6 November 1989, 66.

34. Frank Shipper and Charles C. Manz, "Employee Self-Management without Formally Designated Teams: An Alternative Road to Empowerment," *Organizational Dynamics* (Winter 1992): 48–61; Bob Filipczak, "Ericsson General Electric: The Evolution of Empowerment," *Training,* September 1993, 21–27.

35. David E. Bowen and Edward E. Lawler III, "Empowering Service Employees," *Sloan Management Review* (Summer 1995): 73–84.

36. Ibid., and "Southwest Airlines' Herb Kelleher: Unorthodoxy at Work," an interview with William G. Lee, *Management Review* (January 1995): 9–12.

37. Arnold S. Tannenbaum and Robert S. Cooke, "Organizational Control: A Review of Studies Employing the Control Graph Method," in Cornelius J. Lamners and David J. Hickson, eds., *Organizations Alike and Unlike* (Boston: Rutledge and Keegan Paul, 1980), 183–210.

38. Stewart, "New Ways to Exercise Power."

39. David P. McCaffrey, Sue R. Faerman, and David W. Hart, "The Appeal and Difficulties of Participative Systems," *Organization Science* 6, no. 6 (November-December 1995): 603–27.

40. Jay A. Conger and Rabindra N. Kanungo, "The Empowerment Process: Integrating Theory and Practice," *Academy of Management Review* 13 (1988): 471–82.

41. Marshall Loeb, "Empowerment That Pays Off," *Fortune,* 20 March 1995, 145–46.

42. David E. Bowen and Edward E. Lawler III, "Empowering Service Employees," *Sloan Management Review* (Summer 1995): 73–84.

43. Gordon Brockhouse, "Can This Marriage Succeed?" *Canadian Business,* October 1992, 128–35; Bowen and Lawler, "Empowering Service Employees."

44. Peter C. Fleming, "Empowerment Strengthens the Rock," *Management Review* (December 1991): 34–37.

45. Shipper and Manz, "An Alternative Road to Empowerment."

46. Robert C. Ford and Myron D. Fottler, "Empowerment: A Matter of Degree," *Academy of Management Executive* 9, no. 3 (1995): 21–31.

47. Jeffrey Pfeffer, "Producing Sustainable Competitive Advantage Through the Effective Management of People," *Academy of Management Executive* 9, no. 1 (1995): 55–69.

48. Robert C. Ford and Myron D. Fottler, "Empowerment: A Matter of Degree."

49. David P. McCaffrey, Sue R. Faerman, and David W. Hart, "The Appeal and Difficulties of Participative Systems," *Organization Science* 6, no. 6 (November-December 1995): 603–27.

50. Michael Barrier, "The Changing Face of Leadership," *Nation's Business* (January 1995): 41–42.

51. Jules Sowder, "The 100% Satisfaction Guarantee: Ensuring Quality at Hampton Inn," *National Productivity Review* (Spring 1996): 53–66.

52. Charles Perrow, "Departmental Power and Perspective in Industrial Firms," in Mayer N. Zald, ed., *Power in Organizations* (Nashville, Tenn.: Vanderbilt University Press, 1970), 59–89.

53. D. J. Hickson, C. R. Hinings, C. A. Lee, R. E. Schneck, and J. M. Pennings, "A Strategic Contingencies Theory of Intraorganizational Power," *Administrative Science Quarterly* 16 (1971): 216–29; Gerald R. Salancik and Jeffrey Pfeffer, "Who Gets Power—and How They Hold onto It: A Strategic-Contingency Model of Power," *Organizational Dynamics* (Winter 1977): 3–21.

54. Pfeffer, *Managing with Power*; Salancik and Pfeffer, "Who Gets Power"; C. R. Hinings, D. J. Hickson, J. M. Pennings, and R. E. Schneck, "Structural Conditions of Intraorganizational Power," *Administrative Science Quarterly* 19 (1974): 22–44.

55. Carol Stoak Saunders, "The Strategic Contingencies Theory of Power: Multiple Perspectives," *Journal of Management Studies* 27 (1990): 1–18; Warren Boeker, "The Development and Institutionalization of Sub-Unit Power in Organizations," *Administrative Science Quarterly* 34 (1989): 388–510; Irit Cohen and Ran Lachman, "The Generality of the Strategic Contingencies Approach to Sub-Unit Power," *Organizational Studies* 9 (1988): 371–91.

56. Emerson, "Power-Dependence Relations."

57. Michel Crozier, *The Bureaucratic Phenomenon* (Chicago: University of Chicago Press, 1964).

58. Pfeffer, *Managing with Power*.

59. Jeffrey Pfeffer and Gerald Salancik, "Organizational Decision-Making as a Political Process: The Case of a University Budget," *Administrative Science Quarterly* (1974): 135–51.

60. Salancik and Pfeffer, "Basis and Use of Power in Organizational Decision-Making," 470.

61. Hickson, et al., "Strategic Contingencies Theory."

62. Michael Siconolfi, "At Morgan Stanley, Analysts Were Urged to Soften Harsh Views," *Wall Street Journal*, 14 July 1992, A1.

63. Pettigrew, *Politics of Organizational Decision-Making*.

64. Thanks to Frank W. Edwards for suggesting this example.

65. Hickson, et al., "Strategic Contingencies Theory."

66. Ibid.

67. Aaron Bernstein, "The Unions Are Learning to Hit Where It Hurts," *Business Week,* 17 March 1986, 112–14; and James Worsham, "Labor Comes Alive," *Nation's Business,* February 1996, 16–24.

68. Jeffrey Gantz and Victor V. Murray, "Experience of Workplace Politics," *Academy of Management Journal* 23 (1980): 237–51; Dan L. Madison, Robert W. Allen, Lyman W. Porter, Patricia A. Renwick, and Bronston T. Mayes, "Organizational Politics: An Exploration of Managers' Perception," *Human Relations* 33 (1980): 79–100.

69. Gerald R. Ferris and K. Michele Kacmar, "Perceptions of Organizational Politics," *Journal of Management* 18 (1992): 93–116; Parmod Kumar and Rehana Ghadially, "Organizational Politics and its Effects on Members of Organizations," *Human Relations* 42 (1989): 305–14; Donald J. Vredenburgh and John G. Maurer, "A Process Framework of Organizational Politics," *Human Relations* 37 (1984): 47–66; Gerald R. Ferris, Dwight D. Frink, Maria Carmen Galang, Jing Zhou, Michele Kacmar, and Jack L. Howard, "Perceptions of Organizational Politics: Prediction, Stress-Related Implications, and Outcomes," *Human Relations* 49, no. 2 (1996): 233–66.

70. Ferris, et. al., "Perceptions of Organizational Politics: Prediction, Stress-Related Implications, and Outcomes"; John J. Voyer, "Coercive Organizational Politics and Organizational Outcomes: An Interpretive Study," *Organization Science* 5, no. 1 (February 1994): 72–85; James W. Dean, Jr., and Mark P. Sharfman, "Does Decision Process Matter? A Study of Strategic Decision-Making Effectiveness," *Academy of Management Journal* 39, no. 2 (1996): 368–96.

71. Jeffrey Pfeffer, *Managing With Power: Politics and Influence in Organizations* (Boston, Mass.: Harvard Business School Press, 1992); Moroz and Kleiner, "Playing Hardball in Business Organizations."

72. Amos Drory and Tsilia Romm, "The Definition of Organizational Politics: A Review," *Human Relations* 43 (1990): 1133–54; Vredenburgh and Maurer, "A Process Framework of Organizational Politics."

73. Pfeffer, Power in Organizations, p. 70.

74. Ibid.

75. Adapted from Don Hellriegel, John W. Slocum, Jr., and Richard W. Woodman, *Organizational Behavior* (St. Paul: West, 1986); and Pfeffer, *Power in Organizations*, 339–41.

76. Madison, et al., "Organizational Politics;" Jay R. Galbraith, *Organizational Design* (Reading, Mass.: Addison-Wesley, 1977).

77. Gantz and Murray, "Experience of Workplace Politics," 248.

78. Gantz and Murray, "Experience of Workplace Politics"; Pfeffer, *Power in Organizations*.

79. Daniel J. Brass and Marlene E. Burkhardt, "Potential Power and Power Use: An Investigation of Structure and Behavior," *Academy of Management Journal* 38 (1993): 441–70.

80. Hickson, et al., "A Strategic Contingencies Theory."

81. Pfeffer, *Power in Organizations*.
82. Ibid.
83. V. Dallas Merrell, *Huddling: The Informal Way to Management Success* (New York: AMACON, 1979).
84. Vredenburgh and Maurer, "A Process Framework of Organizational Politics."
85. Ibid.
86. Pfeffer, *Power in Organizations*.
87. Ibid.
88. Ibid.
89. Kanter, "Power Failure in Management Circuits"; Pfeffer, *Power in Organizations*.
90. Based on John P. Kotter, "How to Win Friends and Influence Comanagers," *Canadian Business,* October 1985, 29–30, 100–107.

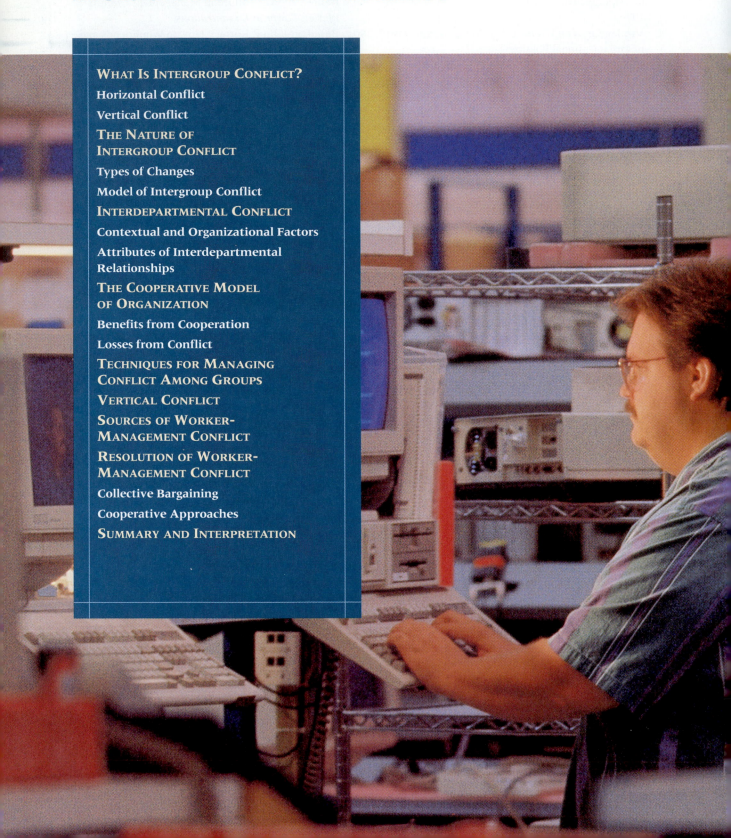

chapter thirteen

Interdepartmental Relations and Conflict

Techno Project

Top executives at a *Fortune* 500 communications company launched the Techno Project to develop a new core technology that would shape a diverse array of products and services and perhaps help the firm diversify into new businesses such as database storage or a multimedia network. They assigned a senior R&D executive the job of assembling a team of technical specialists, then located the team at a research facility several hundred miles from headquarters. The team was given its own budget and freedom from usual administrative controls so it could focus on the task. Top executives had high hopes, believing the new technology would improve productivity, cut costs, and give the company a stronger competitive position.

Other managers in the organization, however, saw the project as a threat to their departmental budgets, existing strategies and goals, and even their job security. Although representatives from the functional areas were linked to Techno as advisors, they were not considered members of the team and felt left out of important decisions. Clashes between the Techno R&D team and other functional departments, particularly marketing, emerged early in the process. Early efforts, which centered on increasing computer automation to enable customers to order products and services without the intervention of a salesperson, posed an ominous threat to the sales and marketing budget. The team also envisioned numerous other applications of the new technology, which, if implemented, could mean massive job cuts, reorganizing the firm's traditional structure, and upsetting the balance of power among departments.

Techno team members were so committed to the project that they wanted to maintain complete control over the technology and its applications, whereas marketing managers were furious that R&D should be calling the shots on matters that impacted customers. Although the physical separation of the Techno project increased the team's solidarity, it seriously hampered efforts to communicate and cooperate with the rest of the company. As unfounded rumors spread about what the Techno group was up to, the battle lines grew more entrenched. Top executives realized the turf war had to be stopped if the Techno Project was to meet the goals they had envisioned for it.[1]

Conflict can thwart the mission of any organization, as executives at this organization realized. In discussing their original decision to physically isolate the R&D team, one top executive remarked: "How could something as simple as location have been the one Achilles' heel? I'm afraid that is what it has become." The isolation created strong team cohesion and enabled the team to rapidly overcome technological hurdles, but this progress was offset because top managers had failed to put in place mechanisms that recognized departmental interdependencies throughout the firm. They moved quickly to resolve the conflicts by clarifying the goals of the Techno project, creating a compelling vision that both R&D and marketing could identify with, and involving other departments more closely with the decision-making process.

Managers regularly deal with decisions about how to get the most out of employees, enhance job satisfaction and team identification, and realize high organizational performance. One question is whether conflict or collaboration should be encouraged across departments. Will people be more highly motivated when they are urged to cooperate with one another or when they compete?

Purpose of This Chapter

This chapter will discuss the nature of conflict among groups and whether conflict is healthy or unhealthy for organizations. The notion of conflict has appeared in previous chapters. In Chapter 6, we talked about horizontal linkages, such as teams and task forces, that encourage coordination among functional departments. Chapter 7 examined the trend in today's globally competitive companies toward flatter, more horizontal structures that emphasize cooperation rather than competition among employees in self-directed teams. In Chapter 11 on decision making, coalition building was proposed as one way to resolve disagreements among departments. Chapter 12 examined power and political processes for managing competing claims on scarce resources. The very nature of organizations invites conflict, because organizations are composed of departmental groupings that have diverse and conflicting interests.

This chapter examines the nature and resolution of conflict more closely. Organizational conflict comes in many forms. Departments differ in goals, work activities, and prestige, and their members differ in age, education, and experience. The seeds of conflict are sown in these differences. As in the Techno project, conflict has to be effectively managed or an organization may fail completely to achieve its goals.

In the first sections of this chapter, intergroup conflict is defined, and the consequences of conflict are identified. Then the causes of interdepartmental conflict in organizations are analyzed, followed by a detailed discussion of techniques for preventing and reducing conflict between departments. The final sections turn to vertical conflict, such as between management and unions, and consider techniques for controlling and resolving this conflict.

WHAT IS INTERGROUP CONFLICT?

Intergroup conflict requires three ingredients: group identification, observable group differences, and frustration. First, employees have to perceive themselves as part of an identifiable group or department.[2] Second, there has to be an observable group difference of some form. Groups may be located on different floors of the building, members may have gone to different schools, or members may work in different departments. The ability to identify oneself as a part of one group and to observe differences in comparison with other groups is necessary for conflict.[3]

The third ingredient is frustration. Frustration means that if one group achieves its goal, the other will not; it will be blocked. Frustration need not be severe and only needs to be anticipated to set off intergroup conflict. Intergroup conflict will appear when one group tries to advance its position in relation to other groups. **Intergroup conflict** can be defined as the behavior that occurs among organizational groups when participants identify with one group and perceive that other groups may block their group's goal achievement or expectations.[4] Conflict means that groups clash directly, that they are in fundamental opposition. Conflict is similar to competition but more severe. **Competition**

Exhibit 13.1
Types of Intergroup Conflict

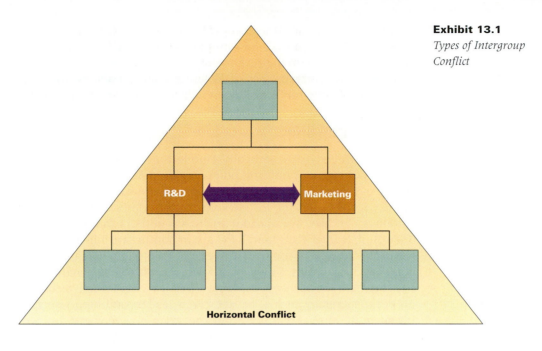

Horizontal Conflict

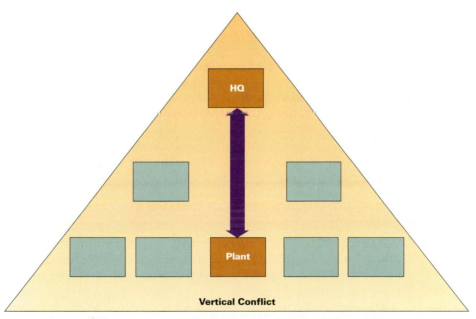

Vertical Conflict

means rivalry among groups in the pursuit of a common prize, while *conflict* presumes direct interference with goal achievement. Intergroup conflict within organizations can occur in both horizontal and vertical directions.

Horizontal Conflict

As shown in Exhibit 13.1, **horizontal conflict** occurs among groups or departments at the same level in the hierarchy, such as between line and staff.[5] Production may have a dispute with quality control because new quality procedures reduce production efficiency. The sales department may disagree with finance about credit policies that make it difficult to win new customers. R&D and marketing may fight over the design for a new product. Horizontal conflict between R&D and marketing occurred in the Techno project described at the beginning of this chapter, and this is a common area of dispute in high-technology firms.[6] Horizontal coordination of some sort is needed to reduce conflict and achieve collaboration.

Vertical Conflict

Conflict also arises vertically among hierarchical levels.[7] **Vertical conflict** arises over issues of control, power, goals, and wages and benefits. A typical source of vertical conflict is between headquarters executives and regional plants or franchises. For example, one study found conflict between a local television station and its New York headquarters. As another example, franchise owners for Taco Bell, Burger King, and KFC are in conflict with headquarters because of the rapid increase of company-owned stores, often in neighborhoods where they compete directly with franchisees. Some franchisees have gone so far as to take headquarters to court over this issue.[8] Vertical conflict can occur among any levels of the hierarchy, such as between crew leaders and supervisors. The most visible form of vertical conflict occurs between management and workers and is often formalized by union-management relations.

THE NATURE OF INTERGROUP CONFLICT

Intergroup conflict in both vertical and horizontal directions has been studied in a variety of settings. Experimenters and consultants have been able to observe conflict and to test methods for reducing or resolving conflict. This research has provided several insights into the behavioral dynamics that occur within and between groups.

At one time, the U.S. air-traffic controllers union became embroiled in a conflict with the Federal Aviation Administration (FAA). The mismanagement of that intergroup conflict was a disaster for the air-traffic controllers.

In Practice 13.1 *PATCO*

In the early 1980s, twelve thousand of the United States' air-traffic controllers joined together in a strike against the federal government. They were striking for higher pay and better working conditions. The controllers were supremely confident, dedicated to their cause, and certain they would win.

One month later, the controllers' strike seemed to symbolize a suicide march rather than a courageous mission. The controllers' self-confidence was badly eroded. The reaction of the FAA had been seriously miscalculated. The Professional Air Traffic Controllers Organization (PATCO) was frantically seeking a salvage operation that would save the jobs of the controllers and the dignity of the union.

One year later, the union was dead. Most of its members were fired from their government jobs. The union was found by the courts to have broken the law by striking against the government. It was decertified.

What happened to bring about such a dramatic shift in the prospects of PATCO union members? Why did PATCO leaders miscalculate so badly?

Union members badly overestimated their importance to air travel and their worth to the government. Members genuinely believed the government could not operate the nation's air transport system without the controllers. They also believed their enormous demands were justified. Even though controllers probably do endure more stress than ordinary government workers, they were more highly paid than other workers and also had job security. An average salary of thirty-three thousand dollars didn't seem that low to outsiders.

Several other reasons for PATCO's failure also surfaced. One was extreme internal cohesiveness. When the government issued an ultimatum with the backing of the full power of the presidency and the federal government, PATCO didn't flinch. Instead of compromising, PATCO members pulled together to stick it out. The emotional commitment to union solidarity became more important than the logical rationale for the strike.

Moreover, PATCO members didn't listen. They refused to believe President Ronald Reagan, who insisted that federal strikes were illegal and would be broken regardless of cost. Drew Lewis, secretary of transportation, said that, if a strike were called, the strikers would be dismissed and there would be no amnesty. PATCO didn't gain the support of other unions, such as the Airline Pilots Association or the International Machinists' Union. They were overconfident to the point of believing they could shut down the airline system by themselves.

The Professional Air Traffic Controllers Organization made several blunders and miscalculations, with tragic human and financial costs. The union members lost their jobs as air-traffic controllers, and the union itself was dead at the tender age of thirteen.[9]

Types of Changes

The **behavioral changes** that took place among PATCO officials and union members during the strike are similar to changes that take place in most conflict situations. The types of changes frequently observed during intergroup conflict are as follows:[10]

1. People strongly identify with a group when members share a common mission or value. Members think of their group as separate and distinct from other groups. They develop pride and show signs of the "we feelings" that characterize an in-group. This in-group identification was very visible among members of PATCO.
2. The presence of another group invites comparison between "we" and "they." Members prefer the in-group to the out-group. The "they" for PATCO members was the Federal Aviation Administration.
3. If a group perceives itself in intense conflict with another group, its members become more closely knit and cohesive. Members pull together to present a solid front to defeat the other group. A group in conflict tends to become more formal and accepting of autocratic leader behavior. This strong internal cohesiveness was clearly visible among members of PATCO.
4. Group members tend to see some other groups as the enemy rather than as a neutral object. PATCO perceived the FAA and the Department of Transportation as adversaries, and members displayed negative sentiments toward them.
5. Group members tend to experience a "superiority complex." They overestimate their own strengths and achievements and underestimate the strength and achievements of other groups. This certainly took place in PATCO. Overconfidence in their ability and strengths was the biggest mistake PATCO members made.
6. Communication between competing groups will decrease. If such communication does take place, it tends to be characterized by negative statements

and hostility. Members of one group do not listen or give credibility to statements by the other group. PATCO, for example, did not fully assimilate the statements made by President Reagan and Transportation Secretary Lewis.

7. When one group loses in a conflict, members lose cohesion. Group members experience increased tension and conflict among themselves and look for a scapegoat to blame for the group's failure. After the failed strike, PATCO members blamed one another and their leaders for the strike's failure and their loss of jobs.

8. Intergroup conflict and associated changes in perception and hostility are not the result of neurotic tendencies on the part of group members. These processes are natural and occur when group members are normal, healthy, and well-adjusted.

These behavioral outcomes of intergroup conflict research were vividly displayed in PATCO. They also can be observed in other organizations. Members of one high school or college often believe their school is superior to a rival school. Employees in one plant perceive themselves as making a greater contribution to the organization than do employees in other plants. Once these perceptions are understood, they can be managed as a natural part of intergroup dynamics.

Model of Intergroup Conflict

Exhibit 13.2 illustrates a **model of intergroup conflict**. The circles toward the left of the model are the organizational and intergroup factors that set the stage for intergroup conflict. An intergroup situation typically leads to conflict when a

Exhibit 13.2

Model of Intergroup Conflict in Organizations

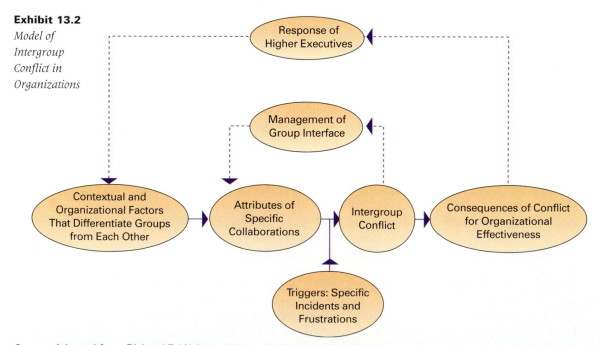

Source: Adapted from Richard E. Walton and John E. Dutton, "The Management of Interdepartmental Conflict," *Administrative Science Quarterly* 14 (1969): 73–84; and Louis R. Pondy, "Organizational Conflict: Concepts and Models," *Administrative Science Quarterly* 12 (1967): 296–320.

specific incident or frustration triggers a dispute. The circles at the top indicate the responses managers can make to control emergent conflict.

As discussed in Chapter 3, there are a number of factors that contribute to differentiation among departments within an organization. Departments pursue different goals and cope with different elements of the external environment, and employees develop behaviors and attitudes that will lead to success in their specific department. For example, a research and development department is characterized by a long-time horizon, whereas a sales department is focused on short-term results. Physical separation also contributes to differentiation, as occurred in the Techno project described at the beginning of this chapter. A conflict at Apple Computer between the Apple II and Macintosh groups reflects the model in Exhibit 13.2. Organizational factors that led to the conflict were physical separation of the two groups and different goals. The trigger for conflict was an annual meeting in which senior executives devoted most of the program to Macintosh products and ignored Apple II's innovations, which were the backbone of the company at that time. The consequence for Apple was poor morale and decreased performance in the Apple II division. Management responded by paying more attention to Apple II and by changing conditions so the Apple II group would not be physically removed from the rest of the organization.

Differentiation also occurs between lower-level workers and management. Workers often feel uninvolved in the organization, powerless and alienated, and perceive that management doesn't care about their needs. For example, triggered by pilot frustration over on-the-job fatigue, a conflict is brewing between pilots and airline executives concerning pilots' rest time. Some pilots fly as many as sixteen hours straight, with as little as eight hours of free time between flights. The pilots' union has enlisted the help of the National Transportation Safety Board and the Federal Aviation Administration to impose stronger rest rules. Airline executives, already facing constant cost pressure, stringently oppose the new rules, which would translate directly into economic and lifestyle benefits for the pilots.[11]

The remainder of this chapter discusses the organizational factors that lead to conflict, and the responses managers can use to manage or prevent conflict.

INTERDEPARTMENTAL CONFLICT

Contextual and Organizational Factors

The potential for horizontal conflict exists in any situation in which separate departments are created, members have an opportunity to compare themselves with other groups, and the goals and values of respective groups appear mutually exclusive. Several of the topics covered in previous chapters explain why organizational groups are in conflict with one another. Five of these topics are reviewed here.

Environment.   Recall from Chapter 3 that departments are established to interact with major domains in the external environment. As the uncertainty and complexity of the environment increase, greater differences in skills, attitudes, power, and operative goals develop among departments. Each department is tailored to fit its environmental domain and, thus, is differentiated from other organizational groups. Moreover, increased competition, both domestically and internationally, has led to demands for lower prices, improved quality, and better service. These demands translate into more intense goal pressures within an organization and, hence, greater conflict among departments.

Size. As organizations increase in size, subdivision into a larger number of departments takes place. Members of departments begin to think of themselves as separate, and they erect walls between themselves and other departments. Employees feel isolated from other people in the organization. The lengthening hierarchy also heightens power and resource differences among departments.

Technology. Technology determines task allocation among departments as well as interdependence among departments. Groups that have interdependent tasks interact more often and must share resources. Interdependence creates frequent situations that lead to conflict.

Goals. The overall goals of an organization are broken down into operative goals that guide each department. Operative goals pursued by marketing, accounting, legal, and human resources departments often seem mutually exclusive. The accomplishment of operative goals by one department may block goal accomplishment by other departments and, hence, cause conflict. Goals of innovation also often lead to conflict because change requires coordination across departments. Innovation goals cause more conflict than do goals of internal efficiency.

Structure. Organization structure reflects the division of labor as well as the systems to facilitate coordination and control. It defines departmental groupings and, hence, employee loyalty to the defined groups. The choice of a divisional structure, for example, means divisions may be placed in competition for resources from headquarters, and headquarters may devise pay incentives based on competition among divisions.

At Lantech, a small manufacturer of packaging machinery in Louisville, Kentucky, pay incentives led to gang warfare among manufacturing divisions.

| In Practice 13.2 | *Lantech* |

When Pat Lancaster founded Lantech in the early 1970s, it was the first manufacturer of machines used to wrap huge bundles of products (such as Kellogg's Corn Flakes or Pampers) in plastic film for shipment to retailers. The company was also a pioneer in the use of incentive pay. Lancaster believed basing bonuses on individual performance would increase motivation and enthusiasm, but the program only led to anxiety among workers.

Determined to make incentive pay work, Lancaster decided to give each of the company's five manufacturing divisions a bonus, to be divided among employees, based on how much profit the division made. However, the divisions were so interdependent that it proved almost impossible to determine which was entitled to what profits. For example, the division that built standard machines and the one that added custom design features depended on each other for parts, engineering, expertise, and so forth. The two groups spent most of their time trying to assign costs to the other division and claim credit for the revenues. They argued so long over who would get charged for overhead cranes for hauling heavy equipment around the factory floor that installation of the machines was delayed by several years.

An argument over who would pay for the toilet paper was the final straw—one aspiring accountant suggested that costs be divided based on the sexual makeup of the division, on the shaky theory that one gender uses more tissue than the other. According to Lancaster, "I was spending 95 percent of my time on conflict resolution instead of on how to serve our customers." Furious passions subsided only when the company abandoned individual and division performance pay in favor of a profit-sharing system that doesn't pit groups against one another for bonuses.[12]

Attributes of Interdepartmental Relationships

Environment, size, technology, goals, and structure are elements of the organizational context that lead to more or less horizontal conflict among departments. These contextual dimensions determine the specific organizational characteristics that generate conflict, as illustrated in Exhibit 13.3. The organizational context translates into eight attributes of interdepartmental relationships that influence the frequency, extent, and intensity of conflict among departments. These eight **sources of interdepartmental conflict** are operative goal incompatibility, differentiation, task interdependence, resource scarcity, power distribution, uncertainty, international context, and reward system.

Operative Goal Incompatibility.   Goal incompatibility is probably the greatest cause of intergroup conflict in organizations.[13] The operative goals of each department reflect the specific objectives members are trying to achieve. The achievement of one department's goals often interferes with another department's goals. University police, for example, have a goal of providing a safe and secure campus. They can achieve their goal by locking all buildings on evenings and weekends and not distributing keys. Without easy access to buildings, however, progress toward the science department's research goals will proceed slowly. On the other hand, if scientists come and go at all hours and security is ignored, police goals for security will not be met. Goal incompatibility throws the departments into conflict with each other.

The potential for conflict is perhaps greater between marketing and manufacturing than between other departments because the goals of these two

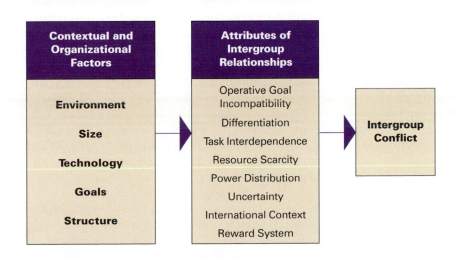

Exhibit 13.3

Sources of Horizontal Conflict Between Departments

Exhibit 13.4

Marketing-Manufacturing Areas of Potential Goal Conflict

Goal Conflict	MARKETING versus Operative goal is customer satisfaction.	MANUFACTURING Operative goal is production efficiency.
Conflict Area	*Typical Comment*	*Typical Comment*
1. Breadth of product line	"Our customers demand variety."	"The product line is too broad—all we get are short, uneconomical runs."
2. New product introduction	"New products are our lifeblood."	"Unnecessary design changes are prohibitively expensive."
3. Production scheduling	"We need faster response. Our lead times are too long."	"We need realistic customer commitments that don't change like wind direction."
4. Physical distribution	"Why don't we ever have the right merchandise in inventory?"	"We can't afford to keep huge inventories."
5. Quality	"Why can't we have reasonable quality at low cost?"	"Why must we always offer options that are too expensive and offer little customer utility?"

Source: Based on Benson S. Shapiro, "Can Marketing and Manufacturing Coexist?" *Harvard Business Review* 55 (September–October 1977): 104–14; and Victoria L. Crittenden, Lorraine R. Gardiner, and Antonie Stam, "Reducing Conflict Between Marketing and Manufacturing," *Industrial Marketing Management* 22 (1993): 299–309.

departments are frequently at odds. Exhibit 13.4 shows examples of goal conflict between typical marketing and manufacturing departments. Marketing strives to increase the breadth of the product line to meet customer tastes for variety. A broad product line means short production runs, so manufacturing has to bear higher costs.[14] Other areas of goal conflict are quality, cost control, and new products. Goal incompatibility exists among departments in most organizations.

Differentiation.   Differentiation was defined in Chapter 3 as "the differences in cognitive and emotional orientations among managers in different functional departments." Functional specialization requires people with specific education, skills, attitudes, and time horizons. For example, people may join a sales department because they have ability and aptitude consistent with sales work. After becoming members of the sales department, they are influenced by departmental norms and values.

Departments or divisions within an organization often differ in values, attitudes, and standards of behavior, and these cultural differences lead to horizontal conflicts.[15] Consider an encounter between a sales manager and an R&D scientist about a new product:

The sales manager may be outgoing and concerned with maintaining a warm, friendly relationship with the scientist. He may be put off because the scientist seems withdrawn and disinclined to talk about anything other than the problems in which he is interested. He may also be annoyed that the scientist seems to have such freedom in choosing what he will work on. Furthermore, the scientist is probably often late for appointments, which, from the salesman's point of view, is no way to run a business. Our scientist, for his part, may feel uncomfortable because the salesman seems to be pressing for immediate answers to technical questions that will take a long time to investigate. All the discomforts are concrete manifestations of the relatively wide differences between these two men in respect to their working and thinking styles. . . .[16]

Cultural differences can be particularly acute in the case of mergers or acquisitions. Employees in the acquired company may have completely different work styles and attitudes, and a "we against them" attitude can develop. One reason for the failure of many mergers is that although managers can integrate financial and production technologies, they have difficulty integrating the unwritten norms and values that have an even greater impact on company success.[17] The New Paradigm box describes how GE Plastics overcame cultural differences after acquiring rival Borg-Warner Chemicals.

Task Interdependence.   Task interdependence refers to the dependence of one unit on another for materials, resources, or information. As described in Chapter 4 on technology, pooled interdependence means little interaction; sequential interdependence means the output of one department goes to the next department; and reciprocal interdependence means departments mutually exchange materials and information.[18]

Generally, as interdependence increases, the potential for conflict increases.[19] In the case of pooled interdependence, units have little need to interact. Conflict is at a minimum. Sequential and reciprocal interdependence require employees to spend time coordinating and sharing information. Employees must communicate frequently, and differences in goals or attitudes will surface. Conflict is especially likely to occur when agreement is not reached about the coordination of services to each other. Greater interdependence means departments often exert pressure for a fast response because departmental work has to wait on other departments.[20]

Resource Scarcity.   Another major source of conflict involves competition between groups for what members perceive as limited resources.[21] Organizations have limited money, physical facilities, staff resources, and human resources to share among departments. In their desire to achieve goals, groups want to increase their resources. This throws them into conflict. Managers may develop strategies, such as inflating budget requirements or working behind the scenes, to obtain a desired level of resources. Resources also symbolize power and influence within an organization. The ability to obtain resources enhances prestige. Departments typically believe they have a legitimate claim on additional resources. However, exercising that claim results in conflict. For example, in almost every organization, conflict occurs during the annual budget exercise, often creating the political activities described in Chapter 12.

Power Distribution.   As explained in the previous chapter, power differences evolve even when departments are at the same level on the organization chart. Some departments provide a more valuable service or reduce critical uncertainties for the organization. For example, sometimes a conflict builds up between sales and marketing departments because of power differences. Over the past decade, the role of marketing has expanded into the realm of strategic planning,

The New Paradigm

GE Plastics/Borg-Warner

GE Plastics, with headquarters in Pittsfield, Massachusetts, recognized the importance of team building, but it took on new urgency after the company purchased a long-time rival, Borg-Warner Chemicals, based in Parkersville, West Virginia. The acquisition gave GE Plastics a real boost in technical and manufacturing strength, new products, and domestic and international marketing facilities. However, the two former competitors had very different corporate cultures. Borg-Warner had a paternalistic atmosphere and a group of loyal, older employees who wanted to stay put in Parkersville. In contrast to this familylike atmosphere, GE Plastics was described as youthful, aggressive, a little tougher, and a little colder than Borg-Warner.

Many Borg-Warner employees still considered GE "the competition" and didn't feel like a part of the company—and what's more, they weren't sure they wanted to. Executives considered team-building activities they had used in the past—rowing events, donkey races, wilderness experiences—and realized what they really needed was an event that would make a lasting impression on employees while serving a larger purpose and creating something of enduring value. The decision was made that employees would renovate five nonprofit facilities, using many of GE's materials, borrowing equipment when possible, and purchasing other supplies and tools in the local community. Teams were carefully formed to give employees a chance to meet and work with new people, to combine executives with lower-level workers, and, above all, to mix former Borg-Warner employees with GE workers. In one twelve-hour day, thirty teams completely renovated the run-down Copley Family YMCA, located in a low-income San Diego neighborhood riddled with gangs and drugs. Together they scraped and painted walls, cleaned graffiti, laid tile, replaced windows, landscaped the grounds, and even restored a twenty-year-old mural covering a two-story outer wall.

The teams had arrived at the site ready to compete with one another, but as the day wore on they noticed something different about this team-building exercise—they wanted *all* the teams to win, and any team that finished its project first gladly pitched in to help others. The final effect on the community was impressive, but what was most phenomenal was the impact on employees. The event proved to be the turning point in the integration of GE Plastics and Borg-Warner employees. After a day of pounding nails and painting walls, they shed their rivalries to become teammates working toward a common cause they all felt proud of. As one former Borg-Warner worker said, ". . . any questions I had about whether or not this was the kind of company I wanted to work for were gone, absolutely. For us to be able to pull this off and to want to do this really made all the difference."

Source: David Bollier, "Building Corporate Loyalty While Rebuilding the Community," *Management Review* (October 1996): 17–22.

which means more involvement in analyzing the competition with senior management. Sales, meanwhile, focuses on customer needs. Marketing's growing influence has elevated the conflict with sales departments in some companies to a battle for dominance.

Power differences often provide a basis for conflict, especially when actual working relationships do not reflect perceived power.[22] For example, in one company, an engineering department was perceived by the more powerful production department as telling production what to do and when to do it. The production department focused much of its energies on the impropriety of a less powerful department calling the tune for a supposedly more powerful department, devoting a great deal of time to rebalancing power relationships. The engineering department was made up of people with skills no greater than those possessed by production workers, and production workers felt capable of performing engineering's tasks better than they did. Production managers spent an inordinate amount of time checking for consistency among the various materials produced by engineering, and whenever an error was discovered a messenger would quickly be dispatched to carry the material back to engineering with a message about the stupidity that had produced such a mistake.[23] Production felt that its power could be maintained only by calling more tunes than it danced.

Uncertainty. Another factor for predicting intergroup conflict is the uncertainty and change experienced by organizational departments. When activities are predictable, departments know where they stand. They can rely on rules or previous decisions to resolve disputes that arise. When factors in the environment are rapidly changing or when problems arise that are poorly understood, departments may have to renegotiate their respective tasks.[24] Managers have to sort out how new problems should be handled. The boundaries of a department's territory or jurisdiction become indistinct. Members may reach out to take on more responsibility, only to find other groups feel invaded. In a study of hospital purchasing decisions, managers reported significantly higher levels of conflict when purchases were nonroutine than when purchases were routine.[25] Generally, as uncertainty about departmental relationships increases, conflict can be expected to increase.

International Context. The increasing importance of the international sector of the business environment has created another source of conflict within organizations. In companies operating globally, cultural differences provide a breeding ground for conflict among organizational units. For example, although an alliance between Northwest Airlines and KLM Royal Dutch Airlines is highly successful from a financial perspective, it has been referred to as a "marriage from hell" because of conflicts based largely on a clash of cultures. "It's the European way versus the American way," says KLM President Pieter Bouw. The Dutch collect modest salaries, disdain glitz, and believe in minimizing debt and investing for the long haul, whereas the American owners of Northwest draw huge salaries, live in Beverly Hills mansions, and believe risky, on-the-edge dealmaking is the right way to run a business.[26]

Some companies are finding that cultural differences provide more potential for conflict than any other single factor. Research done by Geert Hofstede on IBM employees in forty countries discovered that mind-set and cultural values on issues such as individualism versus collectivism strongly influence organizational and employee relationships and vary widely among cultures.[27] IBM discovered this when it attempted an ambitious team project, known as Triad, with Siemens AG of Germany and Toshiba Corporation of Japan.

The Triad Project

The Triad Project was a great idea: IBM, Toshiba, and Siemens brought together scientists with diverse backgrounds to develop a revolutionary memory chip. The cross-cultural team approach was expected to generate creative leaps and lead to dazzling discoveries. However, culture got in the way.

Siemens scientists were shocked to find Toshiba colleagues closing their eyes and appearing to sleep during meetings, a common practice in Japan. The Japanese, accustomed to working in large, informal groups, found it almost painful to be forced to schedule meetings in small, individual offices. The Germans were appalled by the offices, saying no one in their country would be expected to work in a room without a window. IBMers complained that the Germans planned too much and that the Japanese, who like to constantly review ideas, wouldn't make a decision. Because German and Japanese workers sometimes found it difficult to communicate their ideas clearly in English, they began talking among themselves in their native languages. Suspicions began to circulate that some researchers were withholding information, and conflicts among the three groups grew. Although Triad continues to work through cultural differences, results of the project have been disappointing.[28]

Reward System.   The reward system governs the degree to which subgroups cooperate or conflict with one another.[29] An experiment with student groups illustrates how incentives influence conflict.[30] In one-half of the groups, called cooperative groups, each student's grade was the grade given for the group's project. All students in those groups, regardless of individual contribution, received the same grade. In the remaining groups, called competitive groups, students were rewarded on the basis of their personal contribution to the group project. Each student was graded individually and could receive a high or low grade regardless of the overall group score.

The outcome of these incentives on conflict was significant. When the incentive system rewarded members for accomplishing the group goal (cooperative groups), coordination among members was better, communication among members was better, productivity was greater, and the quality of the group product was better. When individuals were graded according to their personal contributions to the group (competitive groups), they communicated less with each other and were more frequently in conflict. Members tried to protect themselves and to succeed at the expense of others in the group. Quality of the group project and productivity were lower.

As illustrated by the Lantech case (In Practice 13.2), incentives and rewards have similar impact on conflict among organizational departments. When departmental managers are rewarded for achieving overall organization goals rather than departmental goals, cooperation among departments is greater.[31] Bechtel, for example, provides a bonus system to division managers based on the achievement of Bechtel's profit goals. Regardless of how well a manager's division does, the manager isn't rewarded unless the corporation performs well. This incentive system motivates division managers to cooperate with each other. If departments are rewarded only for departmental performance, managers are motivated to excel at the expense of the rest of the organization.

THE COOPERATIVE MODEL OF ORGANIZATION

The preceding section looked at several causes and examples of horizontal conflict. The very nature of an organization, with goal incompatibility, task interdependence, scarce resources, and power differences, invites conflict. Conflict is natural and inevitable. Indeed, research suggests that when conflict is focused on substantive organizational rather than personal issues, it can be beneficial because it helps organization members clarify objectives, expectations, and behaviors and make better decisions about how to achieve organizational goals.[32] Top managers dealing with complex, nonprogrammed decisions, for example, make better choices when they discuss rather than ignore conflicting points of view. When conflict in teams is suppressed rather than acknowledged, *groupthink* may emerge, in which team members are reluctant to disagree with one another and poor decisions are made for the sake of consensus and group harmony.[33]

Have You Read About This?

The We-Force in Management: How to Build and Sustain Cooperation

by Lawrence G. Hrebiniak

The U.S. culture has traditionally valued individualism, and Lawrence Hrebiniak contends that this emphasis on individual achievement contributes to the mediocre performance of U.S. firms in today's global market. Whereas aggressive individualism has special merit in the early stages of a company's life cycle, greater cooperation and coordination are required as the organization expands and grows more complex. To endure in a global economy, companies can create a "We-Force" to replace the "I-Force" emphasis on individual efforts and rewards.

Traditional organizational systems, including performance evaluations, employee compensation, and communication systems, are based on the individual's desire to gain recognition, promotions, and power, and encourage differences across functional areas. Hrebiniak defines a We-Force as "a cooperative, teamwork-driven mind-set that influences managerial motivation, company culture, decision processes, and important strategic and operating results."

Embracing the We-Force Mind-set

Hrebiniak illustrates how the emphasis on individual achievement damages firms and then provides a framework for creating a more cooperative organization:

- *Understand the barriers to cooperation.* Recognize the current organizational obstacles, such as compensation systems, that stand in the way of cooperation.

- *Plan through visionary leadership.* Create a vision that unites managers from all functional areas.
- *Promote interdependence and communication.* Get everyone throughout the organization involved; develop systems that support cross-functional communication and collaboration.
- *Monitor the process using measurable outcomes.* Evaluate the results of enhanced cooperation through outcomes such as customer satisfaction, market share changes, or company profits.
- *Reward employees for cooperation.* Ensure that performance evaluations and compensation systems reflect a cooperative mind-set. Reward collaboration, not competition.

Call to Action

Hrebiniak offers sobering words of caution to companies that do not shift to a collective view of organization. If managers continue to rely on past practices that encourage and reward individual accomplishment, he says, "the next decade will be brutal and costly." To compete in today's global market, managers must eliminate the barriers to effective communication, coordination, and cooperation.

The We-Force in Management: How to Build and Sustain Cooperation, by Lawrence G. Hrebiniak, is published by Lexington Books.

However, whereas in the past managers often encouraged conflict and competition, the emerging view is that cooperation is the best way to achieve high performance. To compete in today's global market, organizations can shift from structures and systems that promote individual competition to those that encourage collaboration and teamwork, as discussed further in Book Mark 13.0. The new trends in management discussed in previous chapters—including clan control, high-involvement corporate cultures, time-based competition, and self-directed teams—all assume employee cooperation is a good thing. This means successful organizations must find healthy ways to confront and resolve conflict. Managers champion a **cooperative model** of organization, meaning they foster cooperation and don't stimulate competition or conflict, which work against the achievement of overall company goals.

Consider the company studied by Rosabeth Moss Kanter, a Harvard professor and consultant. This was a high-flying financial services company that she called Fastbuck. Conflict was initiated to increase performance—and led to disastrous failure.

In Practice 13.4   *Fastbuck, Incorporated*

Top management at Fastbuck took advantage of deregulation to acquire a company that would serve as a hedge against a downturn in the core business. The new and old businesses were set up to compete for resources and the attention of the CEO, and the two business heads were asked to fight for the big prize, taking over the CEO's job. In this organization, cooperation was seen as something soft, for sissies. Survival of the fittest was the style in this company.

Each business was treated as a totally separate organization. Nothing was done to create ties among the people in each group. The two business chiefs developed a strong personal rivalry. Gradually, George, head of the new business, got more attention than Fred, head of the traditional core business. The CEO was enthralled with the risky direction of the new business. George became more outspoken and aggressive; Fred started withdrawing and avoiding the CEO. George got the confidence of his own people and the board of directors. Fred and his business lost stature.

The major problem for Fastbuck was that most revenues and profits were from the traditional business, but those employees perceived themselves as losers and lost energy. Executives became passive, assuming George would soon take over as CEO and things would get even worse. Revenues declined, and a negative cycle began. At this point, George and his division managers were sure he was winning the competition.

Within a few months, Fastbuck hit a major financial crisis because overall business plummeted 20 percent. Something dramatic was needed, so the CEO fired both Fred and George, and the company was reorganized to integrate the two lines of business into one group. A few months later, parts of the new business were sold off because the traditional business was a more important mainstay. Only now the company was weaker and less valuable than before, thanks to the exercise in competition.[34]

The case of Fastbuck illustrates the consequences of conflict described earlier in the chapter. Groups in conflict develop mistrust of one another and pay more attention to beating their rivals than to performing their task. When that happens, the stronger party begins to feel invincible. Competition can sometimes have a healthy effect, but carried to an extreme, it can lead to long-term losses and a detrimental impact on the entire organization.

If an organization achieves an ideal of no conflict, it is probably in trouble. Conflict is a sign of an active, ongoing, forceful organization. However, conflict becomes a problem when there is too much and when it is used for motivational purposes. Exhibit 13.5 summarizes several benefits from cooperation and losses from conflict.

Benefits from Cooperation

The new viewpoint about cooperation proposes that internal competition is bad for organizations. The Vince Lombardi philosophy, "Winning isn't everything. It's

Exhibit 13.5

Organizational Benefits from Cooperation and Losses from Conflict

Benefits from Cooperation	Losses from Conflict
1. Productive Task Focus	1. Diversion of Energy
2. Cohesion and Satisfaction	2. Altered Judgment
3. Goal Attainment	3. Loser Effects
4. Innovation and Adaptation	4. Poor Coordination

the only thing," may do more harm than good within companies. One expert argues the ideal amount of competition among departments is zero—none at all.[35] Managers should discourage even informal competition, designing work to encourage cooperation. The reason is that competition prevents the free exchange of ideas, resources, and skills. Competition and conflict should be with other companies. Employees should identify with the entire organization as one team.

To achieve the cooperative state, for example, managers can design bonuses and incentive systems to enhance cooperation. Incentives should never be designed as prizes that only one department can win, because no department will help any other department. The result will be ill will and declining productivity. Incentives should be designed so that any department that reaches a certain goal is eligible for the bonus.[36]

The **benefits from cooperation** are as follows:

1. *Productive task focus.* Departmental employees do not become preoccupied with achieving their own goals. Instead, they are able to focus on the overall goals of the organization. For example, research in employment agencies found that when interviewers worked cooperatively to fill positions, they filled significantly more jobs than did interviewers in an agency that competed fiercely to fill job openings. The sharing of information about candidates and job openings far outweighed the intense effort generated by competition. A study of managers in an engineering firm and a utility company found that a goal of cooperation was associated with more cooperative assistance, exchange of resources and information, and more progress on tasks.[37]

2. *Employee cohesion and satisfaction.* Under conditions of cooperation, "we-feelings" and in-group identification occur for employees throughout the organization. Members are attracted to the organization as a whole, not just the group, and receive satisfaction from both memberships. Members across departments cooperate with each other and link the achievement of departmental tasks to organizational goals. One study of twenty organizational units found strong social ties among groups in low-conflict organizations and an image of order and meaning about the organization. High-conflict organizations were seen as chaotic by employees, who had only weak ties to other groups.[38] Other research suggests conflict creates stress that often produces negative results. Although some employees may seem to work hard under competition, they are less satisfied and are less likely to worry about company goals. A study of supervisors found that supervisors who engendered competitiveness were seen as less effective and as managing less effective departments. Supervisors rated high were able to engender a cooperative orientation. Employees simply enjoyed the cooperative arrangement more. Their jobs were more satisfying, partly because they achieved more.

3. *Organizational goal attainment.* Under the cooperative model, the organization is able to achieve overall goals because energy is not wasted on interdepartmental rivalries. Competition and conflict are created toward other organizations, not toward other departments within the organization. Moderate competition and conflict against other organizations stimulate participants to work hard.[39] Cohesion results in an enjoyable work atmosphere. The intensity of an athletic team achieving its goal is an example of benefits of competition against other organizations. Cooperation does not mean

complacency, which can be as big a problem as internal conflict. An organization can prosper and achieve its overall goals when subgroups are doing their tasks well and cooperating with one another.

4. *Innovation and adaptation.* Cooperation encourages creativity and innovation, helping organizations develop new technologies, products, and services quickly. As discussed in Chapter 8, when technical, marketing, and production people are sharing information and ideas and working simultaneously on projects, companies are able to speed new products to market for time-based competition. In addition, cooperation among departments is essential for companies to keep pace in today's rapidly changing, competitive environment. When employees are obsessed with their own department's task and with defeating other departments, innovation is stifled, and organizations are not poised to change and grow with the environment. Today's most successful companies are pushing cooperation to the limit. General Electric is on the cutting edge, striving to totally eliminate boundaries both within the organization and between GE and its suppliers and customers.

| In Practice 13.5 | *General Electric* |

Jack Welch, chairman and CEO of General Electric, believes that to win in today's competitive global environment, his company must involve, energize, and reward everyone throughout the company's twelve businesses. One of the principles guiding GE in its efforts to involve everyone is the concept of "boundaryless behavior," which Welch explained to employees and stockholders in GE's 1993 annual report:

"**Boundaryless behavior** is the soul of today's GE. . . . Simply put, people seem compelled to build layers and walls between themselves and others, and that human tendency tends to be magnified in large, old institutions like ours. These walls cramp people, inhibit creativity, waste time, restrict vision, smother dreams, and, above all, slow things down.

"The challenge is to chip away and eventually break down these walls and barriers, both among ourselves and between ourselves and the outside world. . . .

"Internally, boundaryless behavior means piercing the walls of 100-year-old fiefdoms and empires called finance, engineering, manufacturing, marketing, and gathering teams from all those functions in one room, with one shared coffee pot, one shared vision and one consuming passion—to design the world's best jet engine, or ultrasound machine, or refrigerator.

"Boundaryless behavior shows up in the actions of a woman from our appliances business in Hong Kong helping NBC with contacts needed to develop a satellite television service in Asia. On a larger scale, it means labor and management joining hands in the unprofitable Appliance Park complex in Louisville in a joint effort to 'Save the Park,' with a combination of labor practice changes and GE investment—not two people making a 'deal,' but 10,721 making a commitment.

"And finally, boundaryless behavior means exploiting one of the unmatchable advantages a multibusiness GE has over almost every other company in the world. Boundaryless behavior combines twelve huge global businesses—each number one or number two in its markets—into a vast laboratory whose principal product is new ideas, coupled with a commitment to spread them throughout the Company."[40]

Losses from Conflict

When conflict is too strong or is not managed appropriately, several negative consequences for organizations may arise. These **losses from conflict** are as follows:

1. *Diversion of energy.* One serious consequence is the diversion of a department's time and effort toward winning a conflict rather than toward achieving organizational goals.[41] When the most important outcome becomes defeating other departments, no holds barred, resources are wasted. This certainly occurred at Fastbuck. In extreme cases, sabotage, secrecy, and even illegal activities occur. At the Centers for Disease Control AIDS laboratory, for example, the important battle against this disease was slowed when a noted virologist actually ordered another scientist's experiments thrown away because of conflicts among departments about the type of research the lab should be conducting.[42]

2. *Altered judgment.* One finding from intergroup research is that judgment and perceptions become less accurate when conflict becomes more intense. The overconfidence and unrealistic expectations of PATCO members in In Practice 13.1 is an example. Moreover, when a group makes a mistake, it may blame perceived opponents within the organization rather than acknowledge its own shortcomings. People involved in conflict also have a poor understanding of ideas offered by competitors.[43]

3. *Loser effects.* Another unfortunate aspect of intense interdepartmental conflict is that someone normally loses. The losing department undergoes substantial change. Losers may deny or distort the reality of losing. They may withdraw. They often seek scapegoats, perhaps even members or leaders in their own department. Dissension replaces cohesion. Losers generally tend toward low cooperation and low concern for the needs and interests of other department members.[44]

4. *Poor coordination.* The final problem with conflict is the emphasis given to achieving departmental goals. Departmental goals serve to energize employees, but these goals should not become an all-consuming priority. Departmental goals must be integrated with the goals of the organization. Under intense conflict, coordination does not happen. Collaboration across groups decreases. Groups have less contact, and they are not sympathetic to other points of view. Under intense conflict, achieving departmental goals and defeating the enemy take priority. There is no room for compromise.[45] This lack of cooperation produced the disastrous result at Fastbuck.

TECHNIQUES FOR MANAGING CONFLICT AMONG GROUPS

The ideal situation for most organizations is to have only moderate interunit competition and conflict. Managers should not let conflict get so great that losses from conflict occur. To the extent possible, they should strive to stimulate cooperation to encourage productive task focus and organizational goal attainment.

Reducing extant conflict is often a challenge. When conflict has been too great, participants may actively dislike each other and may not want to change. The target of conflict management techniques can be either the *behavior* or the *attitude* of group members.[46] By changing behavior, open conflict is reduced or eliminated, but departmental members may still dislike people in other departments. A change in behavior makes the conflict less visible or keeps the groups separated. A change in attitude is deeper and takes longer. A new attitude is difficult to achieve and requires a positive change in perceptions and feelings about other departments. A change in attitude is the basis for a *true* cooperative organization.

Exhibit 13.6
*Strategies for
Managing Conflict
Among Groups*

Source: Adapted from Eric H. Neilsen, "Understanding and Managing Conflict," in Jay W. Lorsch and Paul R. Lawrence, eds., *Managing Group and Intergroup Relations* (Homewood, Ill.: Irwin and Dorsey, 1972), 329–43.

The techniques available for managing conflict are arranged along a scale in Exhibit 13.6. Techniques near the top of the scale, such as formal authority, will change behavior but not attitudes. Techniques near the bottom of the scale, such as rotating group members or providing intergroup training, are designed to bring about positive change in cooperative attitudes between groups.

Formal Authority.   Formal authority means senior management invokes rules, regulations, and legitimate authority to resolve or suppress a conflict. For example, the advertising and sales departments may disagree about advertising strategy. The sales force may want a strategy based on direct mail, whereas advertising prefers to use radio and television. This type of conflict can be resolved by passing it to the marketing vice president, who uses legitimate authority to resolve the conflict.

At Continental Airlines, top managers used formal authority to force cooperation between marketing and operations when the departments disagreed over flight scheduling. Cooperation between the two units dramatically improved Continental's on-time performance, moving the airline from near the bottom of the U.S. Department of Transportation ranking to the top.[47] The disadvantage of this technique is that it does not change attitudes toward cooperation and may treat only the immediate problem. The formal authority method is effective in the short run when members cannot agree on a solution to a specific conflict.[48]

Limited Communication.   Encouraging some communication among conflicting departments prevents the development of misperceptions about the abilities, skills, and traits of other departments. When departments are in severe conflict, controlled interaction can be used to resolve the conflict. Often the interaction can be focused on issues about which the departments have a common goal. A common goal means the departments must talk and cooperate, at least for the achievement of that goal. For example, Datapoint Corporation experiences frequent conflict between the research and development and manufacturing divisions. Because senior managers in these divisions are located in the same city, a forum was devised for them to resolve differences. "Summit meetings" were created where managers could bring their disagreements for discussion and resolution. A dispute about R&D security in a new building was resolved in this fashion. This technique may make a small impact on attitude change.[49]

Integration Devices.   As described in Chapter 6, teams, task forces, and project managers who span the boundaries between departments can be used as integration devices. Bringing together representatives from conflicting departments in joint problem-solving teams is an effective way to reduce conflict because the representatives learn to understand each other's point of view.[50] Sometimes a full-time integrator is assigned to achieve cooperation and collaboration by meeting with members of the respective departments and exchanging information. The integrator has to understand each group's problems and must be able to move both groups toward a solution that is mutually acceptable.[51]

As an outgrowth of teams and task forces, many organizations today are restructuring into permanent multidisciplinary, self-directed work teams focused on horizontal process rather than function. Chapter 7 describes these self-directed teams, which eliminate old boundaries between departments by bringing together employees from several functions, such as design, engineering, production, sales, supply, and finance. At Saturn Corporation, teams of about fifteen employees handle everything from production schedules and new car quality to budgeting and hiring new workers.[52]

Teams and task forces reduce conflict and enhance cooperation because they integrate people from different departments. An old-line insurance company, Aid Association for Lutherans, reorganized into cross-functional teams to try to reduce misunderstanding among departments that led to delays in processing claims or inquiries. Each team now has specialists who can handle any of the 167 tasks required for policyholder sales and service. Misunderstandings that once led to interdepartmental conflict are now worked out quickly within the teams, and procedures that once took almost a month are now completed in just five days.[53]

Confrontation and Negotiation.   **Confrontation** occurs when parties in conflict directly engage one another and try to work out their differences. **Negotiation** is the bargaining process that often occurs during confrontation and that enables the parties to systematically reach a solution. These techniques bring appointed representatives from the departments together to work out a serious dispute.

Confrontation and negotiation involve some risk. There is no guarantee that discussions will focus on a conflict or that emotions will not get out of hand. However, if members are able to resolve the conflict on the basis of face-to-face discussions, they will find new respect for each other, and future collaboration becomes easier. The beginnings of relatively permanent attitude change are possible through direct negotiation.

For example, one technique used by companies is to have each department head meet face-to-face once a month with each of the other department heads and list what he or she expects from that department. After discussion and negotiation, department heads sign off on their commitment to perform the services

Exhibit 13.7
Negotiating Strategies

Win-Win Strategy	Win-Lose Strategy
1. Define the conflict as a mutual problem	1. Define the conflict as a win-lose situation
2. Pursue joint outcomes	2. Pursue own group's outcomes
3. Find creative agreements that satisfy both groups	3. Force the other group into submission
4. Use open, honest, and accurate communication of group's needs, goals, and proposals	4. Use deceitful, inaccurate, and misleading communication of group's needs, goals, and proposals
5. Avoid threats (to reduce the other's defensiveness)	5. Use threats (to force submission)
6. Communicate flexibility of position	6. Communicate high commitment (rigidity) regarding one's position

Source: Adapted from David W. Johnson and Frank P. Johnson, *Joining Together: Group Theory and Group Skills* (Englewood Cliffs, N.J.: Prentice-Hall, 1975), 182–83.

on the list. The regular contact develops managers' skills as well as their desire to work out conflicts and solve problems among themselves.[54]

Confrontation is successful when managers engage in a "win-win" strategy. Win-win means both departments adopt a positive attitude and strive to resolve the conflict in a way that will benefit each other.[55] If the negotiations deteriorate into a strictly win-lose strategy (each group wants to defeat the other), the confrontation will be ineffective. Top management can urge group members to work toward mutually acceptable outcomes. The differences between win-win and win-lose strategies of negotiation are shown in Exhibit 13.7. With a win-win strategy—which includes defining the problem as mutual, communicating openly, and avoiding threats—understanding can be changed while the dispute is resolved.

Third-Party Consultants.   When conflict is intense and enduring, and department members are suspicious and uncooperative, a third-party consultant can be brought in from outside the organization to meet with representatives from both departments. Such consultants should be experts on human behavior, and their advice and actions must be valued by both groups. Third-party consultants can make great progress toward building cooperative attitudes and reducing conflict.[56] Sometimes called *workplace mediation*, the use of third-party consultants is growing as companies recognize the costs of intense workplace conflict. The Saskatchewan Research Council makes regular use of outside counselors. According to Jonathan France of the human resources department, "When we've got a squeaky wheel, we prefer to oil it than to replace it."[57]

Typical activities of third-party consultants are as follows:

- Reestablish broken communication lines between groups.
- Act as interpreter so that messages between groups are correctly understood and are not distorted by preconceived biases.
- Challenge and bring into the open the stereotyping done by one group or the other. Exposing stereotypes often leads to their dissolution.
- Bring into awareness the positive acts and intentions of the other group. This forces a cognitive reassessment of one group's stance toward the other group.
- Define, focus, and resolve the specific source of conflict.

With negative emotions removed, a cooperative attitude can be established and nurtured to replace the previous conflict.[58]

Member Rotation. Rotation means individuals from one department can be asked to work in another department on a temporary or permanent basis. The advantage is that individuals become submerged in the values, attitudes, problems, and goals of the other department. In addition, individuals can explain the problems and goals of their original departments to their new colleagues. This enables a frank, accurate exchange of views and information.

Rotation works slowly to reduce conflict but is very effective for changing the underlying attitudes and perceptions that promote conflict.[59] The following case illustrates the successful use of member rotation in one company.

Canadian-Atlantic

In Practice 13.6

Canadian-Atlantic, a transportation conglomerate headquartered in Vancouver, British Columbia, experienced intense conflict between research managers and operating managers at the home office. Research managers were responsible for developing operational innovations, such as for loading railroad cars, to increase efficiency. Operations managers were responsible for scheduling and running trains.

Operations managers disliked research personnel. They claimed research personnel took far too long to do projects. One manager said, "A 50 percent solution when we need it is much better than a 100 percent solution ten years from now when the crisis is over." Operating managers were also offended by the complicated terminology and jargon used by research personnel. Researchers had developed several useful innovations, such as automated loading platforms and training simulators, but resistance to their innovations was great. Research personnel wanted to cooperate with operations managers but could not go along with certain requests. They refused to release half-completed innovations or to water down their ideas for less well-educated employees in operations. One manager commented that the extent of communication between research and operations "was just about zero, and both groups like it that way."

The vice president of research and development was worried. He believed intergroup hostility was sharply reducing the effectiveness of R&D. Morale in R&D was low, and operations managers had little interest in new developments. The vice president persuaded the president to try rotating managers between operations and research. Initially, one manager from each department was exchanged. Later, two and three were exchanged simultaneously. Each rotation lasted about six months. After two and one-half years, the relationship between the departments was vastly improved. Key individuals now understood both points of view and could work to integrate the differences that existed. One operations manager enjoyed the work in research so much that he asked to stay on, and the operations vice president tried to hire two R&D managers to work permanently in his division.

Shared Mission and Superordinate Goals. Another strategy is for top management to create a shared mission and establish superordinate goals that require cooperation among departments.[60] As discussed in Chapter 10, organizations with strong, adaptive cultures, where employees share a larger vision for their company, are more likely to have a united, cooperative workforce. Recent studies have shown that when employees from different departments see that their goals are linked together, they will openly share resources and information.[61] To be effective, superordinate goals must be substantial, and employees must be granted the time to work cooperatively toward those goals. The reward system can also be redesigned to encourage the pursuit of the superordinate goals rather than departmental subgoals.

Perhaps the most powerful superordinate goal is company survival. If an organization is about to fail and jobs will be lost, groups forget their differences and try to save the organization. The goal of survival has improved relationships among groups in meat packing plants and auto supply firms that have been about to go out of business.

Intergroup Training.   A strong intervention to reduce conflict is intergroup training. This technique has been developed by such psychologists as Robert Blake, Jane Mouton, and Richard Walton.[62] When other techniques fail to reduce conflict to an appropriate level or do not fit the organization in question, special training of group members may be required. This training requires that department members attend an outside workshop away from day-to-day work problems. The training workshop may last several days, and various activities take place. This technique is expensive, but it has the potential for developing a companywide cooperative attitude.

Intergroup training is similar to the OD approach described in Chapter 8 on innovation and change. The steps typically associated with an intergroup training session are as follows:

1. The conflicting groups are brought into a training setting with the stated goal of exploring mutual perceptions and relationships.
2. The conflicting groups are then separated, and each group is invited to discuss and make a list of its perceptions of itself and the other group.
3. In the presence of both groups, group representatives publicly share the perceptions of self and other that the groups have generated, and the groups are obligated to remain silent. The objective is simply to report to the other group as accurately as possible the images that each group has developed in private.
4. Before any exchange takes place, the groups return to private sessions to digest and analyze what they have heard; there is great likelihood that the representatives' reports have revealed to each group discrepancies between its self-image and the image the other group holds of it.
5. In public session, again working through representatives, each group shares with the other what discrepancies it has uncovered and the possible reasons for them, focusing on actual, observable behavior.
6. Following this mutual exposure, a more open exploration is permitted between the two groups on the now-shared goal of identifying further reasons for perceptual distortions.
7. A joint exploration is then conducted of how to manage future relations in such a way as to encourage cooperation among groups.[63]

Intergroup training sessions can be quite demanding for everyone involved. It is fairly easy to have conflicting groups list perceptions and identify discrepancies. However, exploring their differences face-to-face and agreeing to change is more difficult. If handled correctly, these sessions can help department employees understand each other much better and lead to improved attitudes and better working relationships for years to come.

VERTICAL CONFLICT

The discussion so far in this chapter has dealt with horizontal conflict among departments. Vertical conflict occurs among groups at different levels along the vertical hierarchy. Several of the same concepts apply to vertical conflict, but the groups and issues may be different.

Vertical conflict can take various forms. Student groups may find themselves in conflict with faculty or administration about the teaching versus research goals of a university. Individual employees may have conflicts with their bosses. Managers of international divisions often experience conflict with senior executives located at domestic headquarters. Dealers for large computer companies have found themselves in conflict with corporate headquarters in recent years. As computer companies attempt to increase sales by shifting distribution to mail-order sales and volume retailers, their traditional dealers are often left unable to obtain adequate inventory rapidly enough to serve even their long-term customers.[64]

One visible and sometimes troublesome area of conflict within organizations is between management and workers, who are often represented by a union. All too often we see union or management representatives on television explaining why the other side is wrong and why a strike or lockout is necessary. These conflicts often occur in major industries, such as transportation and steel, and in specialized groups, such as football players or television writers. As an example, the United Auto Workers' struggle to save jobs for its members is in serious conflict with General Motors Corporation's strategy to improve domestic productivity and profitability in ways that could eliminate up to ninety thousand blue-collar jobs by the late 1990s.[65]

Status and power differences among groups are often greater for vertical conflict than for horizontal conflict. Part of the reason vertical conflict occurs is to equalize power differences; for example, unions try to give workers more power over wages or working conditions. Moreover, the ground rules for conflict between workers and management are formalized by laws and regulations. Formal negotiation procedures are available in which appointed representatives work to resolve differences. The conflict between union and management is thus different from conflict that occurs horizontally across departments.

The following sections explore some of the reasons for worker-management conflicts and techniques for the reduction of those conflicts.

SOURCES OF WORKER-MANAGEMENT CONFLICT

Vertical conflict can exist with or without a union, but conflict is more visible when workers join a union. The union formalizes vertical differences and provides a mechanism for resolving those differences. Workers form into unions for a variety of reasons, which reflect the **sources of vertical conflict**:

1. *Psychological distance.* Workers often do not feel involved in the organization. They perceive that their needs are not being met. A union is a way of giving voice to those needs. It provides workers with a clear group identity. Once the union is formed, members identify with the union, not the

company, and try to achieve gains through the union. This often throws union and management into a win-lose conflict situation.

2. *Power and status.* Workers are at the bottom of the hierarchy and often feel powerless and alienated. They have little say in decisions about issues that directly affect their lives, such as wages and benefits. Standing together in a union gives them strength that equalizes their power with management's. This power is restricted to areas directly affecting workers, but it is still more power than workers have alone.[66]

   For example, by standing together in their demands and going on strike, machinists at Boeing plants gained power and got most of what they wanted from management, including pay raises, bonuses, and changes in health insurance benefits. Because Boeing had a number of orders from major airlines, they felt the need to settle quickly and get the machinists back to work.[67]

3. *Ideology.* One basic difference between management and workers pertains to values and ideology. This difference represents basic beliefs about the purpose and goals of organizations and unions.[68] Major ideological differences identified in a survey of managers and union members are listed in Exhibit 13.8. Union members strongly believe in seniority, the right to engage in a strike, and union security. Managers believe more strongly in the free enterprise system, the right to work during a strike, management rights, and the use of quotas to measure performance.

   Though recent conflicts between union and management at Caterpillar focused on a host of issues ranging from wages to health care benefits, the real clash was ideological. Although the UAW insisted on *pattern bargaining*, a process whereby all companies within an industry accept similar union contracts, Caterpillar management refused, firmly reasserting the company's "right to manage." Basic value differences between union and management represent a major conflict that must be overcome before the groups can cooperate successfully.[69]

4. *Scarce resources.* Another important issue between unions and management is financial resources. Salary, fringe benefits, and working conditions are dominant bargaining issues. Workers look to the union to obtain financial benefits. Unions may strike if necessary to get the pay and benefits they

Exhibit 13.8

Differences in Union and Management Beliefs

Ideological Belief	Strength of Belief	
	Union Members	**Management**
1. Seniority	High	Low
2. Right to engage in a legal strike or boycott	High	Low
3. Union security	High	Low
4. Free enterprise system	Low	High
5. Right to continue work during a legal strike or boycott	Low	High
6. Management rights	Low	High
7. Use of work quotas to measure performance	Low	High

Source: Based on Roger S. Wolters, "Union-Management Ideological Frames of Reference," *Journal of Management* 8 (1982): 21–33.

want. Management, by contrast, feels pressure to reduce costs by holding the line on wages in order to maintain low prices. For example, the United Food and Commercial Workers has squared off with Food Lion, claiming that the chain's steadily growing earnings are due to Food Lion willfully avoiding paying overtime to thousands of hourly workers, in violation of federal labor laws. Food Lion itself is not unionized; the UFCW's primary motive is to slow the chain's rapid expansion, which takes market share—and UFCW members' jobs—away from unionized supermarkets.[70]

RESOLUTION OF WORKER-MANAGEMENT CONFLICT

One study that explored the underlying dynamics in union-management relationships was conducted by Blake and Mouton.[71] It involved managers who were placed in groups of nine to twelve persons. Each group produced a solution to a problem. To simulate the negotiation strategies of unions and management, each group was then asked to elect a representative who would negotiate with a representative from a competing group. The two representatives were asked to select one solution as the winner. An interesting thing happened: representatives stayed loyal to their own group's solution. In thirty-three incidents of having group representatives meet, thirty-one representatives remained loyal to their own group's solution, regardless of solution quality. The representatives never did agree on a winning solution.

These findings are striking because they emphasize just how difficult it can be for elected representatives to reach a solution when conflict is severe. The first priority for representatives is loyalty to their group. In a nonunion example, J. Hugh Liedtke, CEO of Pennzoil, and James W. Kinnear, CEO of Texaco, tried to settle the $10 billion debt Texaco owed Pennzoil. The two representatives were unwilling to reach a compromise; each was afraid to give in to the opposition. Ultimately, after almost two years of negotiation, the two sides settled for $3 billion, and Texaco was driven into bankruptcy. Some commentators believed both companies lost because of the long struggle.[72]

Collective Bargaining

The primary approach to resolving union-management conflict is collective bargaining. **Collective bargaining** is the negotiation of an agreement between management and workers. The bargaining process is usually accomplished through a union, and it follows a prescribed format. Collective bargaining involves at least two parties that have a defined interest. The collective bargaining activity usually begins with the presentation by one party of demands or proposals that are evaluated by the other parties. This is followed by counterproposals and concessions. A rigid agreement is ultimately reached that defines each party's responsibilities for the next two or three years.

Cooperative Approaches

Today's economic environment has led to a more cooperative rather than confrontational approach to labor-management relations. These changes have grown from the unions' need to prevent loss of employment and the companies' need to curb labor and production costs. Some of the new approaches to resolving union-management conflict are as follows:

- *Gain sharing.* Union members receive bonuses and profit sharing rather than guaranteed, flat-rate increases. **Gain sharing** is designed to provide a connection between organization performance and worker compensation. At Volkswagen, for example, workers are paid an annual bonus that reflects a combination of individual performance and company performance.[73]

- *Labor-management teams.* **Labor-management teams** are designed to increase worker participation and provide a "cooperative model" for union-management problems. The main function of teams is to tap workers' knowledge of their jobs to improve productivity. These teams exist at three levels: (1) On the shop floor, teams of perhaps ten workers identify problems and implement solutions, similar to a quality circle approach. At Saturn Corporation, for example, teams of factory workers actively make decisions on tools, supplies and suppliers, factory layout, and other plant matters; (2) Middle managers and local union leaders serve as an advisory team to coordinate programs and implement team suggestions; and (3) At the top, senior corporate executives and top union leaders set long-term policy and plan alternatives to layoffs. This coordinated approach engages union members' participation in the company and increases their identification with the company.[74]

- *Employment security.* The new trend is away from job security and toward employment security, which means unions allow workers to be reassigned to different positions. Employment security also means there can be no jobs unless the firm is successful. Managers and workers create a "common fate" culture that means they succeed or fail together. This superordinate goal increases employee concern about company productivity and profits. Moreover, employees are given meaningful information on the company's performance.

These new approaches have helped shift management and union leaders away from win-lose negotiating positions toward a win-win attitude to benefit both company and employees.[75] The win-win approach was described in Exhibit 13.7. For example, teams that include both workers and managers are now being tried in hundreds of companies, including AT&T, Goodyear, Ford Motor Company, and Xerox. Union Camp's giant paper plant in Savannah, Georgia, created labor-management teams to find cost-cutting measures that would keep the declining plant from closing. Management agreed to new work rules that give workers more power, and the union agreed to cuts in vacation and lower pay for overtime; working together, management and labor saved thousands of jobs in Savannah. In the steel industry, both LTV and Inland Steel have signed pacts that give labor representatives seats on the board, profit sharing, and strong job security guarantees in return for simpler work rules and job reductions through attrition.[76]

These innovative approaches do not eliminate collective bargaining, but they broaden the bargaining philosophy. SSI Services, Inc. used a combination of labor-management teams and a new approach to collective bargaining to bury old tensions and reach win-win agreements with unions.

| In Practice 13.7 | *SSI Services, Inc.* |

When SSI Services, Inc. took over the mission support contract for the U.S. Air Force Material Command's Arnold Engineering Development Center (AEDC), the company hired workers represented by thirteen different unions (headed by the Air Engineering Metal

Trades Council) to provide facilities maintenance, fire protection, security, logistics, and other services. Hostile negotiations and a disruptive fifty-seven-day strike in 1990 left a fallout of bitterness, mistrust, and animosity.

Both SSI and the AEMTC recognized that the negative feelings in the workplace had to be changed, so SSI's general manager and six union leaders began seeking ways to improve relationships. These individuals and others, including union representatives, managers, and human resources staff, met monthly (and sometimes even weekly), forming into teams to tackle such issues as options to reduce health insurance costs, changing sick leave policies, or ways to implement a four-day work week. Communication between labor and management gradually improved as each side learned to see problems from the other perspective. During one of the sessions, team members decided to "bury the hatchet," holding a symbolic funeral during which managers and union representatives buried a tiny coffin containing a real hatchet.

Soon after the "funeral," representatives heard of a new team-based approach to collective bargaining, called *target-specific bargaining*, a process whereby labor and management narrow down problems to a few key issues and jointly work for their resolution *before* the actual contract talks begin. One of the first issues faced with target-specific bargaining was insufficient voice from labor about how the business was run, so SSI implemented cross-functional employee-involvement teams. For the first time, craft employees had a voice in long-range planning, solutions to technical problems, and the best process for doing their jobs. The internal environment of the organization evolved from adversarial to cooperative. With all this preliminary cooperation, formal negotiations between SSI and AEMTC were completed in record time—three months prior to contract expiration—and with a five-year agreement, the longest in the AEDC's history.[77]

As traditional barriers between union and management are broken down through collaboration and teamwork, companies get increased productivity and workers receive a better quality of work life. The win-win approach is being applied to union-management relationships more than managers would have believed possible just a few years ago.

SUMMARY AND INTERPRETATION

This chapter contains several ideas that complement the topics of power and decision making in the two previous chapters. The most important idea is that interdepartmental conflict is a natural outcome of organizing. Differences in goals, backgrounds, and tasks are necessary for departmental excellence. These differences throw groups into conflict. Some conflict is healthy and should be directed toward successful outcomes for everyone. Understanding the role of organizational conflict and the importance of achieving appropriate levels of conflict are important lessons from this chapter.

The most recent thinking suggests managers should encourage cooperation within the organization. Conflict and competition should be directed toward other organizations. This approach increases cohesion, satisfaction, and performance for the organization as a whole. Too severe conflict among departments can lead to disregard and dislike for other groups, seeing other departments as inferior, as the enemy; hence, cooperation will decrease. Organizations can manage conflict with techniques such as member rotation or intergroup training. Some organizations are pushing cooperation even further by establishing permanent cross-functional work teams that virtually eliminate boundaries between departments.

Much of the work in organization theory has been concerned with horizontal rather than vertical conflict. Horizontal conflict is the day-to-day preoccupation of most managers. Vertical conflict is reflected most clearly in union-management relationships and is also important. Indeed, some of the most exciting developments taking place in the organizational world are techniques for improving union-management relationships. Problem-solving teams, employee gain sharing, and even union membership on the board of directors are steps to achieving collaboration between management and workers.

Key Concepts

behavioral changes
benefits from cooperation
collective bargaining
competition
confrontation
cooperative model
gain sharing
horizontal conflict

intergroup conflict
labor-management teams
losses from conflict
model of intergroup conflict
negotiation
sources of interdepartmental conflict
sources of vertical conflict
vertical conflict

Discussion Questions

1. Define *intergroup conflict*. How does this definition compare with that of *competition*? What is vertical as opposed to horizontal conflict?
2. Briefly describe how differences in tasks, personal background, and training lead to conflict among groups. How does task interdependence lead to conflict among groups?
3. What impact does conflict have on people within conflicting groups?
4. Discuss the organizational losses from interdepartmental conflict.
5. Intergroup training is located at a higher level on the scale of conflict-resolution techniques than is member rotation. What does this mean in terms of the impact the two techniques have on behavior versus attitudes? Can you think of situations in which rotation might have greater impact on attitudes than would intergroup training? Discuss.
6. What techniques can be used to overcome conflict between workers and management? Are there similarities to the techniques used to deal with horizontal conflict? Discuss.
7. Do you believe cooperation will stimulate higher performance than competition among departments? Discuss.
8. Discuss why some conflict is considered beneficial to organizations.

Briefcase

As an organization manager, keep these guides in mind:

1. Recognize that some interdepartmental conflict is natural but that cooperation among departments is associated with higher performance. Cooperation enhances productive task focus, employee satisfaction, and the attainment of organizational goals more than does competition or conflict.

2. Associate the organizational design characteristics of goal incompatibility, differentiation, task interdependence, resource scarcity, power distribution, international context, uncertainty, and reward systems with greater conflict among groups. Expect to devote more time and energy to resolving conflict in these situations.

3. Do not allow intense conflict to persist. Intense conflict is harmful to an organization because departments direct their resources toward sabotaging or defeating other groups rather than toward working with other departments to achieve company goals. Intervene forcefully with conflict resolution techniques.

4. Manage conflict among departments. Conflict can be reduced with formal authority, limited interaction, integration devices, confrontation, third-party consultants, member rotation, superordinate goals, and intergroup training. Select the techniques that fit the organization and the conflict.

5. Avoid placing groups in direct win-lose situations when managing either horizontal or vertical conflict. Direct the conflict toward enabling both groups to be partial winners. When negotiating, do not place representatives in the dilemma of choosing between loyalty to their group or loyalty to the best interest of the company as a whole. Representatives usually will be loyal to their group, even if their proposals are not the best solutions for the entire company.

Chapter Thirteen Workbook *How Do You Handle Conflict?**

Think of some disagreements you have had with a friend, relative, manager, or co-worker. Then indicate how frequently you engage in each of the following described behaviors. For each item, select the number that represents the behavior you are *most likely* to exhibit. There are no right or wrong answers. Respond to all items using the scale. The responses from 1 to 7 are

Scale

Always	Very often	Often	Sometimes	Seldom	Very seldom	Never
1	2	3	4	5	6	7

____ 1. I blend my ideas to create new alternatives for resolving a disagreement.

____ 2. I shy away from topics that are sources of disputes.

____ 3. I make my opinion known in a disagreement.

____ 4. I suggest solutions that combine a variety of viewpoints.

____ 5. I steer clear of disagreeable situations.

____ 6. I give in a little on my ideas when the other person also gives in.

____ 7. I avoid the other person when I suspect that he or she wants to discuss a disagreement.

*From "How Do You Handle Conflict?" in Robert E. Quinn, et al., *Becoming a Master Manager* (New York: Wiley, 1990), 221–23. Used with permission.

_____ 8. I integrate arguments into a new solution from the issues raised in a dispute.
_____ 9. I will go 50-50 to reach a settlement.
_____ 10. I raise my voice when I'm trying to get the other person to accept my position.
_____ 11. I offer creative solutions in discussions of disagreements.
_____ 12. I keep quiet about my views in order to avoid disagreements.
_____ 13. I give in if the other person will meet me halfway.
_____ 14. I downplay the importance of a disagreement.
_____ 15. I reduce disagreements by making them seem insignificant.
_____ 16. I meet the other person at a midpoint in our differences.
_____ 17. I assert my opinion forcefully.
_____ 18. I dominate arguments until the other person understands my position.
_____ 19. I suggest we work together to create solutions to disagreements.
_____ 20. I try to use the other person's ideas to generate solutions to problems.
_____ 21. I offer trade-offs to reach solutions in disagreements.
_____ 22. I argue insistently for my stance.
_____ 23. I withdraw when the other person confronts me about a controversial issue.
_____ 24. I sidestep disagreements when they arise.
_____ 25. I try to smooth over disagreements by making them appear unimportant.
_____ 26. I insist my position be accepted during a disagreement with the other person.
_____ 27. I make our differences seem less serious.
_____ 28. I hold my tongue rather than argue with the other person.
_____ 29. I ease conflict by claiming our differences are trivial.
_____ 30. I stand firm in expressing my viewpoints during a disagreement.

Scoring and Interpretation: Three categories of conflict-handling strategies are measured in this instrument: solution-oriented, nonconfrontational, and control. By comparing your scores on the following three scales, you can see which of the three is your preferred conflict-handling strategy.

To calculate your three scores, add the individual scores for the items and divide by the number of items measuring the strategy. Then subtract each of the three mean scores from seven.

Solution-oriented: Items 1, 4, 6, 8, 9, 11, 13, 16, 19, 20, 21 (Total = 11)

Nonconfrontational: Items 2, 5, 7, 12, 14, 15, 23, 24, 25, 27, 28, 29 (Total = 12)

Control: Items 3, 10, 17, 18, 22, 26, 30 (Total = 7)

Solution-oriented strategies tend to focus on the problem rather than on the individuals involved. Solutions reached are often mutually beneficial, with neither party defining himself or herself as the winner and the other party as the loser.

Nonconfrontational strategies tend to focus on avoiding the conflict by either avoiding the other party or by simply allowing the other party to have his or her way. These strategies are used when there is more concern with avoiding a confrontation than with the actual outcome of the problem situation.

Control strategies tend to focus on winning or achieving one's goals without regard for the other party's needs or desires. Individuals using these strategies often rely on rules and regulations in order to win the battle.

Questions

1. Which strategy do you find easiest to use? Most difficult? Which do you use more often?
2. How would your answers have differed if the other person was a friend, family member, or co-worker?
3. What is it about the conflict situation or strategy that tells you which strategy to use in dealing with a conflict situation?

Case for Analysis *Cherie Cosmetics Limited Elegante Division**

Heather King, general manager of the Elegante Division of Cherie Cosmetics Limited, had been waiting more than three weeks for a reply to the memo she had written on August 11, 1993 to Bob Shaw, vice-president of Operations. Her objective was to elicit some response from Operations that would lead to better communications between Marketing and Operations. Bob Shaw had always been responsive and Heather was unable to explain the three weeks of silence. It was now only three days until the next meeting with Operations, and Heather felt she had not made any progress towards improving the communications process.

Cherie Canada Ltd.

Cherie Canada Ltd., a wholly-owned subsidiary of the International Cherie Company of New York, was directed by Ralph Nolk, executive vice-president and managing director. From its Toronto head office, the company marketed both men's and women's fragrance and cosmetic products in four distinctive product lines. Each division was headed by a general manager who reported to Ralph Nolk, as did Bob Shaw (see Exhibit 13.9).

*Professor Kathleen E. Slaughter prepared this case solely to provide material for class discussion. The case is not intended to illustrate either effective or ineffective handling of a managerial situation. Certain names and other identifying information may have been disguised to protect confidentiality. This material is not covered under authorization from CanCopy or any Reproduction Rights Organization. Any form of reproduction, storage or transmittal of this material is prohibited without written permission from Western Business School. Permission to reproduce or copies may be obtained by contacting Case and Publication Services, Western Business School, The University of Western Ontario, London, Ontario, N6A, 3K7, or calling 519-661-3208, or faxing 519-661-3882. Copyright © 1985 The University of Western Ontario; 94/05/12.

Exhibit 13.9

Organization Chart

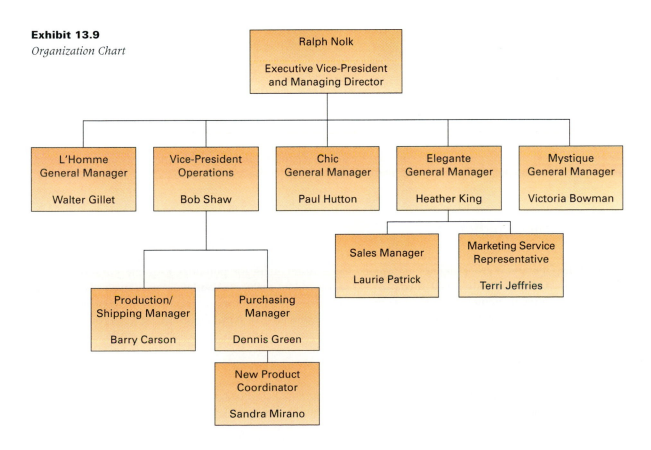

Heather King had joined Cherie Canada Ltd. nine years ago when she made a career change from teaching school. She was proud of the progress that she had made from her early start as an inexperienced, young sales representative for the Mystique division to general manager of the new Elegante Division.

Elegante Division

The international Cherie Company already had a worldwide image for high quality when it launched the Elegante line in February of 1989 in New York. The Elegante product line was the most exclusive cosmetic line of the prestigious company. Distribution was expanded from the United States market to include the United Kingdom in 1990 and Italy, Austria and Canada in 1991. Canada, with only ten retail outlets in 1993 permitted to carry the product, represented 35 percent of Elegante's international business but only 1.5 percent of Cherie Canada Ltd.'s total sales in all product lines.

Elegante was the first new product line that Cherie Company had announced in twelve years; therefore, Heather wanted to insure a smooth introduction of the new line. Heather knew that there would be difficulties in introducing a new product with new formulae, new packaging and new containers. In preparation for the product launch, Heather had prepared and presented a demonstration and slide presentation of the product to the operations group in November of 1990, before the Canadian Elegante launch in February of 1991. She included operation managers, support staff and the assembly line workers involved in preparing the product. The presentation was enthusiastically received by all participants, and Heather felt confident about the product launch.

New Product Challenges

From the first days of production, however, Heather felt that the Operations group did not understand the product line. Although Heather had attempted to prepare them with the demonstration and slide presentation, Operations personnel did not appear to be fully aware of the complexities of the product and seemed unable to deal with resulting difficulties.

Heather's main contact with Operations was Dennis Green, the purchasing manager. Although Dennis had been a purchasing agent with Cherie for twelve years, Heather was concerned that he might lack the flexibil-ity and sense of urgency necessary to understand the marketing of a fledgling product in the 1990s.

While production for all of Cherie's products was driven by sales forecasting, in the volatile cosmetic industry forecasting was, at the best of times, a shot in the dark. A lack of sales history and the dynamics of a new product line made forecasting for the Elegante line even more difficult.

Operations needed to be responsive to marketing changes in advertising and distribution as well as general marketing strategy. Production runs for Elegante products were only 200 units, compared to 5,000 units per run for other Cherie products. Elegante was, therefore, most vulnerable to errors in shipping, warehousing, purchasing, production or planning. Any errors would be highly visible and costly in the restricted Elegante market.

From the beginning, errors in shipping and warehousing had resulted in short shipments to stores; errors in production had resulted in Elegante's exclusive distributors receiving products with loose caps or missing components; and errors in purchasing had at times delayed product availability. These costly errors had not only affected sales, but had also dampened employee morale within the division. Members of the Elegante division felt that it was necessary to double and triple check everything that they requested from Operations.

In January of 1992, Bob Shaw hired Sandra Mirano to fill a new position reporting to Dennis Green within the Operations group: that of new product coordinator. Bob hoped that the new position would improve communication between Marketing and Operations not only for the Elegante line but also for all Cherie product lines.

After Sandra's appointment, however, the communication process continued to deteriorate. The tester unit difficulties finally broke the already strained relationship between Sandra and Heather.

The Tester Units Situation

Tester units for potential Elegante consumers were used by each retail outlet across Canada. These tester units were vital to the success of the high-priced Elegante line, for they allowed trial of the product by consumers prior to purchase. The tester units had, however, been delayed for several months and Heather was unable to determine the cause of the delay.

The basic makeup tester units had arrived from Italy in January, 1993. In April, they were still not ready for distribution because the screening and filling necessary for their use had not been completed by Elegante's supplier. Five phone calls and three memos over the next month to Sandra Mirano requesting the reasons for the delay were ignored.

On May 25, 1993, Heather bypassed Sandra and wrote to Dennis Green requesting the status of the tester units. Heather did not receive any reply from Dennis and her many subsequent phone calls to him were ignored. Finally, on August 1, Heather bypassed Dennis and called the supplier, Ryan Casey, directly, to request a status report on the tester units. Ryan Casey said that he had not received a direction from Dennis to finish the tester units. He said Dennis sometimes "dragged his heels" but reminded Heather that her direct request would annoy Dennis. Heather said that she would accept full responsibility for any problems. Ryan Casey was instantly responsive and said that he would begin the screening immediately.

Communication Breakdown

At the Marketing and Operations (MOPS) meeting of August 10, 1993, Dennis verbally attacked Heather for her breach of procedure in calling Ryan Casey directly. Dennis stated that he was "not going to be run by Marketing" and that "Casey is my supplier and I alone will deal with him." He finished by noting "I don't only work for Elegante. I have other brands and other priorities to worry about."

Dennis's outburst took place just as the meeting was breaking up and Heather was stunned by his verbal abuse. Heather's feelings were highly charged; she felt it was time to lay her case before Bob Shaw, Dennis's boss. If she didn't find a solution to the current difficulties, she faced another quarter of missed sales opportunities.

Heather expected that her memo to Bob Shaw (Exhibit 13.10 on pages 516–517) would produce some immediate response. Bob was proactive; he was accessible to Heather and never made her feel that Marketing was an interruption. Bob had been only two years with the Canadian operation, but he had worked for Cherie's Australian operation for several years and had developed a reputation for being a top operations manager with an appreciation for marketing dynamics. He showed his understanding of marketing as soon as he assumed his Canadian position in 1991 by making marketing a working part of the operations meetings. He changed the monthly operations (OPS) meeting to the MOPS meeting. Bob attended all MOPS meetings and he was aware of how upset Heather was after the August 10 meeting.

Although Heather had talked to Bob on several occasions during the three weeks since she had written the memo, he had never mentioned the memo to her. She was unable to explain his lack of responsiveness. Heather wondered if she should raise the issue with Bob Shaw before the September 8 MOPS meeting or discuss the situation and a solution at the meeting.

Exhibit 13.10

Interoffice correspondence

Toronto, Canada

INTEROFFICE CORRESPONDENCE

TO: Bob Shaw

FROM: Heather King

DATE: August 11, 1993

RE: OPERATIONS AND SALES/MARKETING RELATIONS—ELEGANTE CANADA

Dear Bob:

Success in business depends upon various functions of an organization working harmoniously toward the same goal. I feel that success, therefore, will continue to elude Elegante in Canada unless both the Operations and Sales/Marketing groups get back on track leading to the same end…to make Elegante a profitable business!

In recent months, Bob, I've felt that relations between our two groups have been strained. Serious problems have covered the gamut of shipping, warehousing, purchasing, production, planning—and you know that we could both produce files of correspondence to show that the brand has suffered the impact of these problems.

For example:

a) Shipping
- Gift with purchase items for Holt Renfrew shipped to The Bay, Vancouver
- Short-shipments of items in stock, both saleable and collateral
- Errors in picking (French collaterals sent when English is requested by code)

b) Warehousing
- Misplacement of Cosmetic Zipper Bags, Lip and Eye Pencils, Makeup Brush collection, all resulting in lost sales
- Confusion of old formula with new formula, lotions and creams

c) Production
- Loose caps
- Poor gluing
- Empty lipstick in Elegante carton
- Missing items in gift items and saleable items (puffs, components, etc.)

d) Planning
- Lack of response for several months to requests for balance-out sheets on phase-outs and discontinuations

e) Purchasing
- Three months to reservice vital tester units, collaterals, etc.
- Misplacement of original carton artboards
- Inaccessibility of key staff

All of the above have had a negative impact on Elegante SALES, not to mention our credibility and morale.

Exhibit 13.10 (continued)

Relations continue to deteriorate . . . yesterday's incident with Dennis Green—indignant that I had "breached procedures" by calling Ryan Casey directly—serves to underscore the fact that we do not "have our eyes on the same target." Dennis was concerned more about procedures than results, even after his department had failed to respond to a memo dating back to May 25 and several later phone calls pertaining to the tester units in question. I was more concerned with meeting commitments to open a new door on schedule with all the necessary selling tools.

Procedures notwithstanding, we need and want results on the Elegante brand. The tester units are a vital element in a successful launch; without them, our corporate investment of newspaper advertising, direct mail, training, demonstration, construction, etc. is jeopardized. If Dennis Green is prepared to accept responsibility for this huge investment, then I suggest he take up the matter with Mr. Nolk.

Lest the intention of this memo be misunderstood, let me clearly state that some progress has been made on the Elegante brand in the Operations area in the past year. That success is due, in large part, to your personal involvement and you know that I appreciate that very much. I would like to believe that everyone in the Operations area shares your commitment to our success. I would like to believe that everyone in Operations is as concerned with results as they are with procedures.

Bob, I fully appreciate the workload of your people. However, I can't understand, nor can I accept, the lack of attention to the recent "Tester" situation and others of its ilk. Elegante may not be the top priority brand in the eyes of many departments but if people continue to ignore it and continue to look upon it as a "step-sister brand," then we shall never make it the success it has the potential to be. This "second class" attitude will only lead to further erosion of profits, which will ultimately have to be absorbed by the corporation in one way or another. The ramifications of that on future growth and progress of our company are, needless to say, very many indeed!

In the interest of promoting a better understanding of each other's day-to-day pressures and responsibilities, I would like to propose an exchange: an invitation for Sandra Mirano (and anyone else you wish) to spend one or two days with us at the Bloor Street office and, in return, the opportunity for Terri and Laurie to take time at the plant with various departments. In this way, perhaps we will be able to recognize our objectives as mutual ones . . .

I am looking forward to discussing the above or any other positive action to get Elegante back into a profitable, success-oriented position.

Regards

Heather
HK/sd
encl.

P.S. Hope I do not have to wait until our next MOPS meeting for an apology from Dennis.

Notes

1. Michael D. Hunt, Beth A. Walker, and Gary L. Frankwick, "Hurdle the Cross-Functional Barriers to Strategic Change," *Sloan Management Review* (Spring 1995): 22–30.

2. Clayton T. Alderfer and Ken K. Smith, "Studying Intergroup Relations Imbedded in Organizations," *Administrative Science Quarterly* 27 (1982): 35–65.

3. Muzafer Sherif, "Experiments in Group Conflict," *Scientific American* 195 (1956): 54–58; Edgar H. Schein, *Organizational Psychology,* 3d ed. (Englewood Cliffs, N.J.: Prentice-Hall, 1980).

4. M. Ascalur Rahin, "A Strategy for Managing Conflict in Complex Organizations," *Human Relations* 38 (1985): 81–89; Kenneth Thomas, "Conflict and Conflict Management," in M. D. Dunnette, ed.,

Handbook of Industrial and Organizational Psychology (Chicago: Rand McNally, 1976); Stuart M. Schmidt and Thomas A. Kochan, "Conflict: Toward Conceptual Clarity," *Administrative Science Quarterly* 13 (1972): 359–70.

5. L. David Brown, "Managing Conflict among Groups," in David A. Kolb, Irwin M. Rubin, and James M. McIntyre, eds., *Organizational Psychology: A Book of Readings* (Englewood Cliffs, N.J.: Prentice-Hall, 1979), 377–89.

6. Hunt, et al., "Hurdle the Cross-Functional Barriers to Strategic Change"; Nathaniel Gilbert, "The Missing Link in Sales and Marketing: Credit Management," *Management Review* (June 1989): 24–30; Robert W. Ruekert and Orville C. Walker, Jr., "Interactions between Marketing and R&D Departments in Implementing Different Business Strategies," *Strategic Management Journal* 8 (1987): 233–48.

7. Brown, "Managing Conflict among Groups."

8. Amy Barrett, "Indigestion at Taco Bell," *Business Week,* 14 December 1994, 66–67; Susan V. Lourenco and John C. Glidewell, "A Dialectical Analysis of Organizational Conflict," *Administrative Science Quarterly* 20 (1975): 489–508.

9. Harry Bernstein, "Union Misjudged Government," *Houston Chronicle,* 4 September 1981, copyright © Los Angeles Times—Washington Post News Service; Paul Galloway, "Negotiating Consultant Says Air Controllers Can't Win Strike," *Houston Chronicle,* 25 August 1981, copyright © Chicago Sun-Times; Susan B. Garland, "Air-Traffic Controllers: Getting Organized Again," *Business Week,* 18 May 1987, 52.

10. These conclusions are summarized from Sherif, "Experiments in Group Conflict"; M. Sherif, O. J. Harvey, B. J. White, W. R. Hood, and C. W. Sherif, *Intergroup Conflict and Cooperation* (Norman, Okla.: University of Oklahoma Books Exchange, 1961); M. Sherif and C. W. Sherif, *Social Psychology* (New York: Harper & Row, 1969); and Schein, *Organizational Psychology.*

11. Andy Pasztor, "An Air-Safety Battle Brews over the Issues of Pilots' Rest Time," *Wall Street Journal,* 1 July 1996, A1.

12. Peter Nulty, "Incentive Pay Can Be Crippling," *Fortune,* 13 November 1995, 235.

13. Thomas A. Kochan, George P. Huber, and L. L. Cummings, "Determinants of Intraorganizational Conflict in Collective Bargaining in the Public Sector," *Administrative Science Quarterly* 20 (1975): 10–23.

14. Victoria L. Crittenden, Lorraine R. Gardiner, and Antonie Stam, "Reducing Conflict between Marketing and Manufacturing," *Industrial Marketing Management* 22 (1993): 299–309; Benson S. Shapiro, "Can Marketing and Manufacturing Coexist?" *Harvard Business Review* 55 (September-October 1977): 104–14.

15. Eric H. Neilsen, "Understanding and Managing Intergroup Conflict," in Jay W. Lorsch and Paul R. Lawrence, eds., *Managing Group and Intergroup Relations* (Homewood, Ill.: Irwin and Dorsey, 1972), 329–43; Richard E. Walton and John M. Dutton, "The Management of Interdepartmental Conflict: A Model and Review," *Administrative Science Quarterly* 14 (1969): 73–84.

16. Jay W. Lorsch, "Introduction to the Structural Design of Organizations," in Gene W. Dalton, Paul R. Lawrence, and Jay W. Lorsch, eds., *Organization Structure and Design* (Homewood, Ill.: Irwin and Dorsey, 1970), 5.

17. Morty Lefkoe, "Why So Many Mergers Fail," *Fortune,* 20 June 1987, 113–14. Afsaneh Nahavandi and Ali R. Malekzadeh, "Acculturation in Mergers and Acquisitions," *Academy of Management Review* (1988): 79–90.

18. James D. Thompson, *Organizations in Action* (New York: McGraw-Hill, 1967), 54–56.

19. Walton and Dutton, "Management of Interdepartmental Conflict."

20. Joseph McCann and Jay R. Galbraith, "Interdepartmental Relationships," in Paul C. Nystrom and William H. Starbuck, eds., *Handbook of Organizational Design,* vol. 2 (New York: Oxford University Press, 1981), 60–84.

21. Roderick M. Cramer, "Intergroup Relations and Organizational Dilemmas: The Role of Categorization Processes," in L. L. Cummings and Barry M. Staw, eds., *Research in Organizational Behavior,* vol. 13 (New York: JAI Press, 1991), 191–228; Neilsen, "Understanding and Managing Intergroup Conflict"; Louis R. Pondy, "Organizational Conflict: Concepts and Models," *Administrative Science Quarterly* 12 (1968): 296–320.

22. Richard Devine, "Overcoming Sibling Rivalry between Sales and Marketing," *Management Review,* (June 1989): 36–40; John A. Seiler, "Diagnosing Interdepartmental Conflict," *Harvard Business Review* 41 (September-October 1963): 121–32.

23. Seiler, "Diagnosing Interdepartmental Conflict," 126–27.

24. Walton and Dutton, "Management of Interdepartmental Conflict"; Pondy, "Organizational Conflict"; Kenneth W. Thomas and Louis R. Pondy, "Toward an 'Intent' Model of Conflict Management among Principal Parties," *Human Relations* 30 (1977): 1089–102.

25. Daniel S. Cochran and Donald D. White, "Intraorganizational Conflict in the Hospital Purchasing Decision Making Process," *Academy of Management Journal* 24 (1981): 324–32.

26. Shawn Tully, "Northwest and KLM—The Alliance from Hell," *Fortune,* 24 June 1996, 64–72.

27. Geert Hofstede, "The Interaction between National and Organizational Value Systems," *Journal of Management Studies* 22 (1985): 347–57; Geert Hofstede, "The Cultural Relativity of the Quality of Life Concept," *Academy of Management Review* 9 (1984): 389–98.

28. E. S. Browning, "Computer Chip Project Brings Rivals Together, But the Cultures Clash," *Wall Street Journal,* 3 May 1994, A1.

29. Walton and Dutton, "Management of Interdepartmental Conflict."

30. Morton Deutsch, "The Effects of Cooperation and Competition upon Group Process," in Dorwin Cartwright and Alvin Zander, eds., *Group Dynamics* (New York: Harper & Row, 1968), 461–82.

31. Gordon Cliff, "Managing Organizational Conflict," *Management Review* (May 1987): 51–53.

32. Allen C. Amason, "Distinguishing the Effects of Functional and Dysfunctional Conflict on Strategic Decision Making: Resolving a Paradox for Top Management Teams," *Academy of Management Journal* 39, no. 1 (1996): 123–48; Karen A. Jehn, "A Multimethod Examination of the Benefits and Detriments of Intragroup Conflict," *Administrative Science Quarterly* 40 (June 1995): 256–82; and Allen C. Amason, Kenneth R. Thompson, Wayne A. Hochwarter, and Allison W. Harrison, "Conflict: An Important Dimension in Successful Management Teams," *Organizational Dynamics* 24, no. 2 (Autumn 1995): 20–55.

33. Amason, et al., "Conflict: An Important Dimension in Successful Management Teams."

34. Rosabeth Moss Kanter, *When Giants Learn to Dance* (New York: Simon & Schuster, 1989).

35. Alfie Kohn, "No Contest," *Inc.*, November 1987, 145–48.

36. Alfie Kohn, *No Contest: The Case against Competition* (Boston: Houghton Mifflin, 1986).

37. Dean Tjosvold, "Cooperative and Competitive Interdependence: Collaboration between Departments to Serve Customers," *Group and Organizational Studies* 13 (1988): 274–89.

38. Reed E. Nelson, "The Strength of Strong Ties: Social Networks and Intergroup Conflict in Organizations," *Academy of Management Journal* 32 (1989): 377–401.

39. Joe Kelly, "Make Conflict Work for You," *Harvard Business Review* 48 (July-August 1970): 103–13; Stephen P. Robbins, *Managing Organizational Conflict: A Nontraditional Approach* (Englewood Cliffs, N.J.: Prentice-Hall, 1974).

40. Jack Welch, "Letter to Shareholders," *General Electric 1993 Annual Report,* p. 2. Used with permission of General Electric.

41. Seiler, "Diagnosing Interdepartment Conflict."

42. Jonathan Kwitny, "At CDC's AIDS Lab: Egos, Power, Politics, and Lost Experiments," *Wall Street Journal,* 12 December 1986, A1.

43. Blake and Mouton, "Reactions to Intergroup Competition."

44. Schein, *Organizational Psychology*; Blake and Mouton, "Reactions to Intergroup Competition," 174–75.

45. Pondy, "Organizational Conflict."

46. Neilsen, "Understanding and Managing Intergroup Conflict."

47. Scott McCartney, "How to Make an Airline Run on Schedule," *Wall Street Journal,* 22 December 1995, B1.

48. Pondy, "Organizational Conflict."

49. Neilsen, "Understanding and Managing Intergroup Conflict."

50. Robert R. Blake and Jane S. Mouton, "Overcoming Group Warfare," *Harvard Business Review* (November–December 1984): 98–108.

51. Blake and Mouton, "Overcoming Group Warfare"; Paul R. Lawrence and Jay W. Lorsch, "New Management Job: The Integrator," *Harvard Business Review* 45 (November–December 1967): 142–51.

52. David Woodruff, "Saturn: Labor's Love Lost?" *Business Week,* 8 February 1993, 122–24; David Woodruff, James Treece, Sunita Wadekar Bhargava, and Karen Lowry, "Saturn," *Business Week,* 17 August 1992, 87–91.

53. John Hoerr, "Work Teams Can Rev Up Paper Pushers, Too," *Business Week,* 28 November 1988, 64–72.

54. Wilson Harrell, "Inspire Action—What Really Motivates Your People to Excel?" *Success,* September 1995, 100.

55. Robert R. Blake, Herbert A. Shepard, and Jane S. Mouton, *Managing Intergroup Conflict in Industry* (Houston: Gulf Publishing, 1964).

56. Leonard Greenhalgh, "Managing Conflict," *Sloan Management Review* 27 (Summer 1986): 45–51.

57. Tamsen Tillson, "War in the Work Zone," *Canadian Business,* September 1995, 40–42.

58. Thomas, "Conflict and Conflict Management."

59. Neilsen, "Understanding and Managing Intergroup Conflict"; Joseph McCann and Jay R. Galbraith, "Interdepartmental Relations."

60. Neilsen, "Understanding and Managing Intergroup Conflict"; McCann and Galbraith, "Interdepartmental Relations"; Sherif et al., *Intergroup Conflict and Cooperation.*

61. Dean Tjosvold, Valerie Dann, and Choy Wong, "Managing Conflict between Departments to Serve Customers," *Human Relations* 45 (1992): 1035–54.

62. Robert R. Blake and Jane S. Mouton, "Overcoming Group Warfare"; Schein, *Organizational Psychology*; Blake, Shepard, and Mouton, *Managing Intergroup Conflict in Industry*; Richard E. Walton, *Interpersonal Peacemaking: Confrontation and Third-Party Consultations* (Reading, Mass.: Addison-Wesley, 1969).

63. Mark S. Plovnick, Ronald E. Fry, and W. Warner Burke, *Organizational Development* (Boston: Little, Brown, 1982), 89–93; Schein, *Organizational Psychology,* 177–78, reprinted by permission of Prentice-Hall, Inc.

64. Kyle Pope, "Dealers Accuse Compac of Jilting Them," *Wall Street Journal,* 7 April 1993, B1.

65. Neal Templin and Joseph B. White, "GM Drive to Step Up Efficiency is Colliding with UAW Job Fears," Wall Street Journal, 23 June 1993, A1.

66. Leon C. Megginson, *Personal and Human Resources Administration* (Homewood, Ill.: Irwin, 1977), 519–20.

67. James Worsham, "Labor Comes Alive," *Nation's Business,* February 1996, 16–24.

68. Roger S. Wolters, "Union-Management Ideological Frames of Reference," *Journal of Management* 8 (1982): 21–33.

69. Kevin Kelly, Aaron Bernstein, and Robert Neff, "Caterpillar's Don Fites: Why He Didn't Blink," *Business Week,* 10 August 1992, 56–57; Kevin Kelly, "Cat May Be Trying to Bulldoze the Immovable," *Business Week,* 2 December 1991, 116.

70. Walecia Konrad, "Much More Than a Day's Work—for Just a Day's Pay?" *Business Week,* 23 September 1991, 40.

71. Blake and Mouton, "Reactions to Intergroup Competition."

72. Stratford P. Sherman, "The Gambler Who Refused $2 Billion," *Fortune,* 11 May 1987, 50–58.

73. Alexander B. Trowbridge, "Avoiding Labor-Management Conflict," *Management Review* (February 1988): 46–49.

74. Barbara Ettorre, "Will Unions Survive?" *Management Review* (August 1993): 9–15; Richard B. Peterson, "Lessons from Labor-Management Cooperation," *California Management Review* (Fall 1988): 40–53.

75. Blake and Mouton, "Reactions to Intergroup Competition."

76. Peter Nulty, "Look What the Unions Want Now," *Fortune,* 8 February 1993, 128–35; Kevin Kelly and Aaron Bernstein, "Labor Deals That Offer a Break from 'Us versus Them'," *Business Week,* 2 August 1993, 30.

77. Donald D. Tippett and Joseph Costa, "Labor Adversaries Bury the Hatchet," *Personnel Journal* (May 1996): 100–107.

part six

Strategy and Structure for the Future

chapter fourteen

Interorganizational Relationships

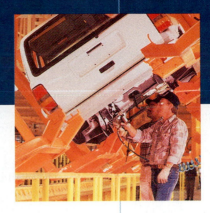

A look inside

Chrysler Corporation

Chrysler Corporation and its supplier companies long treated each other with distrust and suspicion. Chrysler selected parts suppliers strictly on their ability to build components at the lowest possible cost and exploited suppliers by pitting one against the other. Relationships with suppliers were competitive and contractual and were designed to squeeze price concession. Then Chrysler hit bottom with its fourth quarter loss in 1989 of $664 million. New car development was running $1 billion over budget, and the company was in dire financial straits.

From this crisis, Chrysler's senior executives asked whether a new kind of relationship with suppliers could be created. They wanted a more personal, collaborative relationship in which both parties shared in risk and rewards to create value jointly. Chrysler managed to transform the contentious supplier relationships by virtually eliminating supplier bidding. Trusted, capable suppliers were brought onto Chrysler's car design development teams early. Suppliers used their own engineers to design components for new cars and made substantial investments to meet Chrysler's needs more efficiently. In return, Chrysler gave suppliers long-term contracts and recognized the need for suppliers to make a fair profit. Both sides welcomed the other's help with improvements. One supplier learned to produce eight hundred oil pans a day using two workers compared to five hundred pans a day using four workers previously. The savings accrued to both companies.

The transformation of supplier relationships from an adversarial game to one of cooperation and trust has boosted Chrysler to the lead in the U.S. auto industry. Its return on investment outstrips rivals, and it is now considered one of the most innovative and well-managed companies in the world.[1]

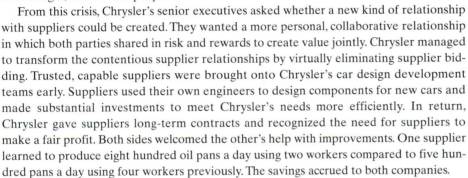

The shift in Chrysler's relationship with suppliers is a major reason for its resurgence as a leading manufacturer. Organizations are rethinking how to cope with a chaotic and turbulent environment. Chapter 13 described how to reduce boundaries and increase cooperation within companies. A more recent trend is to reduce boundaries and increase collaboration *among* organizations to survive in a wildly changing environment. In this new economy, webs of organizations are emerging. A large company like Wal-Mart develops a special relationship with a supplier such as Procter & Gamble that eliminates middlemen by sharing complete information and reducing the costs of salespersons and distributors. You can see the results of interorganizational collaboration when a movie such as *The Hunchback of Notre Dame* is launched. Prior to seeing the movie, you may read a cover story in *People* magazine, see a preview clip on a television program such as *ET*, find action toys being given away at a fast food franchise, and notice retail stores loaded with movie-related merchandise. For a movie like *The Lion King*, coordinated action among companies yielded $200 million in addition to box-office and video profits. In the new economy, organizations think of themselves as teams that create value jointly rather than as autonomous companies that are in competition with all others.

Purpose of This Chapter

This chapter explores the most recent trend in organizing, which is the increasingly dense web of relationships among organizations. Companies have always been dependent on other organizations for supplies, materials, and information. The question is how these relationships are managed. At one time it was a matter of a large, powerful company like General Motors tightening the screws on small suppliers. Today a company can choose, like Chrysler, to develop positive, trusting relationships. Or a large company like General Motors may find it difficult to adapt to the environment and create a new organizational form, such as Saturn, to operate with a different structure and culture. The notion of horizontal relationships described in Chapter 7, and the understanding of environmental uncertainty in Chapter 3, are leading to the next stage of organizational evolution, which is horizontal relationships *across* organizations. Organizations can choose to build relationships in many ways, such as appointing preferred suppliers, establishing agreements, business partnering, joint ventures, or even mergers and acquisitions.

Interorganizational research has yielded perspectives such as resource dependence, networks, population ecology, and institutionalism. The sum total of these ideas can be daunting, because it means managers no longer can rest in the safety of managing a single organization. They have to figure out how to manage a whole set of interorganizational relationships, which is a great deal more challenging and complex.

ORGANIZATIONAL ECOSYSTEMS

Interorganizational relationships are the relatively enduring resource transactions, flows, and linkages that occur among two or more organizations.[2] Traditionally, these transactions and relationships have been seen as a necessary evil to obtain what an organization needs. The presumption has been that the world is composed of distinct businesses that thrive on autonomy and compete for supremacy. A company may be forced into interorganizational relationships depending on its needs and the stability of the environment.

A new view described by James Moore argues that organizations are now evolving into business ecosystems. An **organizational ecosystem** is a system formed by the interaction of a community of organizations and their environment. An ecosystem cuts across traditional industry lines. A company can create its own ecosystem. Microsoft travels in four major industries: consumer electronics, information, communications, and personal computers. Its ecosystem also includes hundreds of suppliers, including Hewlett-Packard and Intel, and millions of customers across many markets.[3] Traditional boundaries are dissolving. Circuit City uses its expertise gained from selling televisions and stereos to sell used cars. Shell Oil is the largest seller of packaged sausages in the Scandinavian countries. Wal-Mart created an ecosystem based on well-known brands and low prices in rural and small-town markets. Today, Wal-Mart cannot be categorized simply as a retailer. It is also a wholesaler, a logistics company, and an information services company. Wal-Mart, like other business ecosystems, develops relationships with hundreds of organizations cutting across traditional business boundaries.

Is Competition Dead?

No company can go it alone under a constant onslaught of international competitors, changing technology, and new regulations. Thus competition, which assumes a distinct company competing for survival and supremacy with other stand-alone businesses, no longer exists. In that sense competition is dead. However, a new form of competition is in fact intensifying.[4]

For one thing, companies now need to coevolve with others in the ecosystem so that everyone gets stronger. Consider the wolf and the caribou. Wolves cull weaker caribou, which strengthens the herd. A strong herd means that wolves must become stronger themselves. With coevolution, the whole system becomes stronger. In the same way, companies coevolve through discussion with each other, shared visions, alliances, and managing complex relationships, as we saw between Chrysler and its suppliers in the opening case. As another example, AT&T, America Online, Microsoft, and Netscape developed a set of overlapping alliances to provide Internet services.

In today's world, conflict and cooperation exist at the same time. In New York City, Time Warner refused to carry Fox's twenty-four-hour news channel on its New York City cable systems. The two companies engaged in all-out war that included court lawsuits and front page headlines. This all-out conflict, however, masked a simple fact: the two companies can't live without each other. Fox and Time Warner are wedded to one another in separate business deals around the world. They will never let the local competition in New York upset their larger interdependence on a global scale. Mutual dependencies and partnerships have become a fact of life in business ecosystems. Companies no longer operate autonomously or with a single voice. A senior executive at DreamWorks sued Disney, but that hasn't stopped Disney's ABC network from acquiring television shows from DreamWorks. Companies today may use their strength to win conflicts and negotiations, but ultimately cooperation carries the day.[5]

The Changing Role of Management

Within business ecosystems managers learn to move beyond traditional responsibilities of corporate strategy and designing hierarchical structures and control systems. If a top manager looks down to enforce order and uniformity, the company is missing opportunities for new and evolving external relationships.[6] In this new world, managers think about horizontal processes rather than vertical structures. Important initiatives are not just top down, they cut across the boundaries separating organizational units. Moreover, horizontal relationships now include linkages with suppliers and customers, who become part of the team. Book Mark 14.0 further discusses the need for today's managers to break down traditional organizational boundaries. Business leaders can learn to lead economic coevolution. Managers learn to see and appreciate the rich environment of opportunities that grow from cooperative relationships with other contributors to the ecosystem. Rather than trying to force suppliers into low prices or customers into high prices, managers strive to strengthen the larger system evolving around them, finding ways to understand this big picture and how to contribute.

This is a broader leadership role than ever before. For example, the CEO of Advanced Circuit Technologies in Nashua, New Hampshire, formed a coalition of ten electronic firms to jointly package and market noncompeting products.

Book Mark 14.0

Have You Read About This?

The Boundaryless Organization: Breaking the Chains of Organizational Structure

by Ron Ashkenas, Dave Ulrich, Todd Jick, and Steve Kerr

The authors of this book argue that fluid boundaries both within and between organizations are necessary to achieve the speed, flexibility, integration, and innovation critical to company success. Managers must become "boundary-aware" and learn new leadership skills to find the right balance of permeability for their organizations. Two chapters on creating permeable boundaries between organizations are particularly useful because these boundaries are the least understood by most managers. *The Boundaryless Organization* uses case studies of well-known companies such as General Electric and SmithKline Beecham to illustrate the importance of creating boundaryless behavior in four essential areas.

Four Boundaries That Block Success

The authors describe four types of boundaries, examine the impact of each, and offer questionnaires, checklists, and mini-models that can help managers create cross-boundary linkages.

- *Vertical boundaries.* Four critical dimensions required to span vertical boundaries are information sharing, building competence, delegating authority, and distributing rewards.
- *Horizontal boundaries.* The best way to permeate horizontal boundaries is by focusing on the customer; teams should be formed and re-formed as needed to serve customers.
- *External boundaries.* To create essential relationships with customers, suppliers, regulators, and other organizations, companies can determine where opportunities exist for collaboration and align and integrate systems, structure, and processes.
- *Geographic boundaries.* To attain globalization, companies must be committed to spanning geographic boundaries, identifying challenges and opportunities in the international marketplace, and recalibrating human resource practices and other organizational systems and processes.

Conclusion

The authors acknowledge that boundaries are necessary and will always exist, but they argue that traditional boundaries within and between organizations are dysfunctional in today's complex world. As the authors put it: "Boundaryless behavior is not about eliminating all administrative procedures and rules. . . . it is about substituting permeable structures for concrete walls."

The Boundaryless Organization, by Ron Ashkenas, Dave Ulrich, Todd Jick, and Steve Kerr, is published by Jossey-Bass.

This coalition even adopted a single name: Electronic Packaging Team. Members can still conduct their own business, but they now bid on projects larger than they could deliver individually and call on the other partners for elements they can't do themselves. The coalition landed a job with Compaq Computer Corp. to design and build a specialized computer board that none of the companies could have handled alone.[7]

Interorganizational Framework

Understanding this larger organizational ecosystem is one of the most exciting areas of organization theory. The models and perspectives for understanding interorganizational relationships ultimately help managers change their role from top-down management to horizontal management across organizations. A framework for analyzing the different views of interorganizational relationships is in Exhibit 14.1. Relationships among organizations can be characterized by

Organization Type

Exhibit 14.1
*A Framework of
Interorganizational
Relationships**

	Dissimilar	**Similar**
Competitive	Resource Dependence	Population Ecology
Cooperative	Collaborative Network	Institutionalism

(Organization Relationship)

*Thanks to Anand Narasimhan for suggesting this framework.

whether the organizations are dissimilar or similar, and whether relationships are competitive or cooperative. By understanding these perspectives, managers can assess their environment and adopt strategies to suit their needs. The first perspective is called resource dependence theory, which was briefly described in Chapter 3. It describes rational ways organizations deal with each other to reduce dependence on the environment. The second perspective is about collaborative networks, wherein organizations allow themselves to become dependent on other organizations to increase value and productivity for both. The third perspective is population ecology, which examines how new organizations fill niches left open by established organizations, and how a rich variety of new organizational forms benefit society. The final approach is called institutionalism and explains why and how organizations legitimate themselves in the larger environment and design structures by borrowing ideas from each other. These four approaches to the study of interorganizational relationships will be described in the remainder of this chapter.

RESOURCE DEPENDENCE

Resource dependence represents the traditional view of relationships among organizations. As described in Chapter 3, **resource dependence** theory argues that organizations try to minimize their dependence on other organizations for the supply of important resources and try to influence the environment to make resources available.[8] When threatened by greater dependence, organizations will assert control over external resources to minimize that dependence. Resource dependence theory argues that organizations do not want to become vulnerable to other organizations because of negative effects on performance.

The amount of dependence on a resource is based on two factors. First is the importance of the resource to the firm, and second is how much discretion or monopoly power those who control a resource have over its allocation and use.[9] For example, a Wisconsin manufacturer made scientific instruments with internal electronics. It acquired parts from a supplier that provided adequate quality at the lowest price. The supplier was not involved in the manufacturer's product design but was able to provide industry-standard capacitors at fifty cents each. As industry standards changed, other suppliers of the capacitor switched to other products, and in one year the cost of the capacitor increased to $2 each. The Wisconsin firm had no choice but to pay the higher price. Within eighteen months, the price of the capacitor increased to $10 each, and then the supplier discontinued production altogether. Without capacitors, production came to a halt for six months. The scientific instruments manufacturer allowed itself to become dependent on a single supplier and made no plans for redesign to use substitute capacitors or to develop new suppliers. A single supplier had sufficient power to increase prices beyond reason and to almost put the Wisconsin firm out of business.[10]

Organizations aware of resource dependence tend to develop strategies to reduce their dependence on the environment and learn how to use their power differences.

Resource Strategies

When organizations feel resource or supply constraints, the resource dependence perspective says they maneuver to maintain their autonomy through a variety of strategies, several of which were described in Chapter 3. One strategy is to adapt to or alter the interdependent relationships. This could mean purchasing ownership in suppliers, developing long-term contracts or joint ventures to lock in necessary resources, or building relationships in other ways. For example, interlocking directorships occur when boards of directors include members of the boards of supplier companies. Organizations may join trade associations to coordinate their needs, sign trade agreements, or merge with another firm to guarantee resource and material supplies. Some organizations may take political action, such as lobbying for new regulations or deregulation, favorable taxation, tariffs, or subsidies, or push for new standards that make resource acquisition easier. Organizations operating under the resource dependence philosophy will do whatever is needed to avoid excessive dependence on the environment to maintain control of resources and hence reduce uncertainty.

Power Strategies

In resource dependence theory, large, independent companies have power over small suppliers. For example, power in consumer products has shifted from vendors such as Rubbermaid and Procter & Gamble to the big discount retail chains such as Wal-Mart and Kmart. In manufacturing, behemoths like General Electric and Ford can account for 10 to 50 percent of many suppliers' revenue, giving the large company enormous power. When one company has power over another, it can ask suppliers to absorb more costs, ship more efficiently, and provide more services than ever before, often without a price increase. For example, Rubbermaid, Inc. derives about 15 percent of its revenues from Wal-Mart. When Rubbermaid's raw material costs increased, Wal-Mart would not accept a higher price. Wal-Mart also offered more shelf space to Rubbermaid's competitors. As a result, Rubbermaid earnings dropped 30 percent and it shut nine facilities. In manufacturing, a company like General Motors can use its power to tighten the screws on suppliers. It can force suppliers into competition with one another for low prices and then drop vendors, virtually putting them out of business. General Electric called in three hundred suppliers to its appliance division and told them they must slash costs by 10 percent. Often the suppliers have no alternative but to go along, and those who fail to do so may go out of business.[11]

The resource power of large companies means that small companies must be lean and nimble and not count on price competition alone. A small supplier should not depend on a large company as a sole customer, because it can be put out of business if its product goes out of style or if the customer changes its mind. When Totes, Inc. created a new product called slipper socks, they sold $14 million a year largely through Kmart and Wal-Mart. Within two years, however, both discount retailers found suppliers that made knockoff slipper socks for 25 percent less, and they turned to these new suppliers. Totes had to be ready for this eventuality, developing new products and finding alternative ways to distribute products to consumers. Being on the receiving end of a power imbalance means building relationships with other customers, innovating constantly, and perhaps joining forces with other small suppliers.[12]

COLLABORATIVE NETWORKS

North American companies typically have worked alone, competing with each other and believing in the tradition of individualism and self-reliance. Today, however, thanks to an uncertain international environment, a realignment in corporate relationships is taking place. The **collaborative network** perspective is an emerging alternative to resource dependence theory. Companies join together to become more competitive and to share scarce resources. As a new wave of technology based on digital communications builds, for example, computer manufacturers, local phone companies, cable television operators, cellular phone companies, and even water and gas utilities have been teaming up.[13] As companies move into their own uncharted territory, they are also racing into alliances as a way to share risks and cash in on rewards. In many cases companies are learning to work closely together. Consider the following examples:

- AT&T, the world's largest telecommunications company, is reaching out everywhere these days, dropping its traditional do-it-from-scratch approach to team up with such major, established companies as Viacom, Inc. as well as small pioneering companies, ensconcing itself in almost every corner of the rapidly changing communications industry.[14]
- Many big companies, such as Motorola, Sony, Time Warner, IBM, and Kodak, are joining forces with smaller firms to obtain innovative new technologies and markets. Small, pioneering companies get the benefit of the larger firm's financing and marketing capabilities.[15]
- Canada's garment manufacturers and retailers have formed high-level strategic partnerships. Electronic reordering as products are sold helps retailers display the right products at the right times, and gives Canadian manufacturers a competitive speed and flexibility advantage over low-cost factories in other parts of the world.[16]
- With corporate research budgets under pressure, the hottest R&D trend is collaboration. Companies are figuring out how to fruitfully connect with outside experts in other companies, consortiums, universities, and government labs. With technology more complex, no single company can do it all. IBM, Siemens, and Toshiba are teaming up to develop a new memory chip. General Motors, Ford, and Chrysler have formed twelve research consortiums on such topics as electric vehicle batteries and better crash dummies.[17]

International Origins

Why all this interest in interorganizational collaboration? Major reasons are sharing risks when entering new markets, mounting expensive new programs and reducing costs, and enhancing organizational profile in selected industries or technologies. Cooperation is a prerequisite for greater innovation, problem solving, and performance.[18] In addition, partnerships are a major avenue for entering global markets, with both large and small firms developing partnerships overseas and in North America.

North Americans have learned from their international experience just how effective interorganizational relationships can be. Both Japan and Korea have long traditions of corporate clans or industrial groups that collaborate and assist each other. In Japan this grouping is called *keiretsu*. A *keiretsu* is a collection of companies that share holdings in one another, have interlocking boards of directors, and undertake joint ventures in long-term business relationships. A *keiretsu* has long-term historical linkages through educational backgrounds of executives that literally create a family of companies.[19] North Americans typically have considered interdependence a bad thing, believing it would reduce competition. In a *keiretsu*, no single company dominates, and competition is fierce. It's as if the brothers and sisters of a single family went into separate businesses and want to outdo one another, but they still love one another and will help each other when needed. Companies in a *keiretsu* enjoy a safety net that encourages long-term investment and risk-taking for entering new markets and trying new technologies. The interorganizational linkage is so powerful that it is believed to be one of the major reasons for Japan's success in world markets. Perhaps the most famous *keiretsu* is Mitsubishi.

| In Practice 14.1 | *Mitsubishi* |

The Mitsubishi group is well-known in North America. This *keiretsu* extends all the way back to prewar industrial Japan. The group comprises literally hundreds of companies, but at its heart are twenty-eight core members whose company presidents regularly meet. The three major companies are Mitsubishi Corporation, Mitsubishi Bank, and Mitsubishi Heavy Industry. Other companies—heavily connected by cross-ownership, other financial ties, interlocking directors, and long-term business relationships—are Mitsubishi Plastic Industries, Mitsubishi Petro Chemical, Kirin Brewery, Mitsubishi Oil, Mitsubishi Construction, Asahi Glass, Tokio Marine and Fire Insurance, Mitsubishi Motors, and Mitsubishi Rayon. From 17 percent to 50 percent of each of the twenty-eight core companies is owned by other companies in the family.

The coalition of companies, partially illustrated in Exhibit 14.2, gives Mitsubishi enormous clout. Mitsubishi Estate Company recently paid almost $1 billion for 58 percent of Rockefeller Center. Mitsubishi Corporation bought control of Aristech Chemical Corporation for about $875 million, and other Mitsubishi companies bought most of Verbatim from Kodak for $200 million, closed a $400 million power plant deal in Virginia, bought a San Francisco oil company for $75 million, and invested hundreds of million dollars in other ventures. Mitsubishi Trust and Banking was the main lender in the almost $1 billion deal to purchase the famed Pebble Beach Gold Course in California. This kind of clout is unattainable by a single company operating alone in North America. To reach the ultimate in interorganizational coordination, Mitsubishi has linked up with Germany's Daimler-Benz, one of the largest and most powerful industry groups in Europe.[20]

Exhibit 14.2
A Portion of the
Mitsubishi Keiretsu

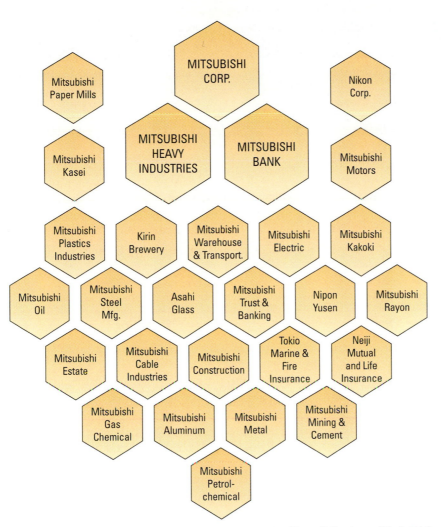

Source: Based on Robert Neff, "Mighty Mitsubishi Is on the Move," *Business Week*, 24 September 1990, 98–101.

Although North American companies may never collaborate to the extent that Mitsubishi does, interorganizational linkages can help firms achieve higher levels of innovation and performance, especially as they learn to shift from an adversarial to a partnership mind-set.[21]

From Adversaries to Partners

Fresh flowers are blooming on the battle-scarred landscape where once-bitter rivalries among suppliers, customers, and competitors took place. In North America, collaboration among organizations initially occurred in not-for-profit social service and mental health organizations where public interest was involved. Community organizations collaborated to achieve greater effectiveness for each party and better utilize scarce resources.[22] With the push from international competitors and international examples, hard-nosed American managers are shifting to a new partnership paradigm on which to base their relationships.

Exhibit 14.3
Changing Characteristics of Interorganizational Relationships

Traditional Orientation: Adversarial	New Orientation: Partnership
Suspicion, competition, arm's length	Trust, addition of value to both sides, high commitment
Price, efficiency, own profits	Equity, fair dealing, all profit
Limited information and feedback	Electronic linkages to share key information, problem feedback, and discussion
Legal resolution of conflict	Mechanisms for close coordination, people on site
Minimal involvement and up-front investment	Involvement in partner's product design and production
Short-term contracts	Long-term contracts
Contract limiting the relationship	Business assistance beyond the contract

Source: Based on Jeffrey H. Dyer, "How Chrysler Created an American *Keiretsu*," *Harvard Business Review* (July–August 1996): 42–56; Myron Magnet, "The New Golden Rule of Business," *Fortune*, 21 February 1994, 60–64; and Peter Grittner, "Four Elements of Successful Sourcing Strategies," *Management Review* (October 1996): 41–45.

Consider the example of Digital Equipment Corporation. When chief executive Robert Palmer took over, Digital was in horrible shape, and one of his strategies was to build alliances with previous enemies, such as Microsoft. Palmer expected to announce an alliance with MCI Communications Corporation and Microsoft to provide products and services to companies needing internal networking systems. As Palmer said, "The model that existed in the 1970s and that we carried on too long in the 1980s was that you do everything yourself. Don't share technology, don't cooperate with other companies. Get all the benefit by being the do-all be-all end-all yourself. That model doesn't work in the 1990s."[23]

A summary of this change in mind-set is in Exhibit 14.3. More companies are changing from a traditional adversarial mind-set to a partnership orientation. More and more evidence from studies of General Electric, Corning, Amoco, and Whirlpool indicate that partnering allows reduced cost and increased value for both parties in a predatory world economy.[24] The new model is based on trust and the ability of partners to develop equitable solutions to conflicts that inevitably arise. In the new orientation, people try to add value to both sides and believe in high commitment rather than suspicion and competition. Companies work toward equitable profits for both sides rather than just for their own benefit. The new model is characterized by lots of shared information, including electronic linkages for automatic ordering and face-to-face discussions to provide corrective feedback and solve problems. Sometimes people from other companies are on site to enable very close coordination. Partners are involved in each other's product design and production and invest for the long term. It's not unusual for business partners to help each other outside whatever is specified in the contract.[25]

For example, AMP, a manufacturer of electronic and electrical connectors, was contacted by a customer about a broken connector that posed serious problems. It wasn't even AMP's connector, but the vice president and his sales manager went to a warehouse on a weekend and found replacement parts to get the customer back on line. They provided the service with no charge as a way to enhance the relationship. Indeed, this kind of teamwork treats partner companies almost like departments of one's own company.[26]

Companies like Whirlpool Corporation use suppliers to design new products. The design work for the gas burner system for a new Whirlpool gas range was done by supplier Eaton Corporation. In this new view of partnerships, dependence on another company is seen to reduce rather than increase risks. Greater value can be achieved by both parties. By being imbedded in a system of interorganizational relationships, similar to a Japanese *keiretsu*, everyone does better by helping each other. This is a far cry from the belief that organizations do best by being autonomous and independent. Sales representatives may have a desk on the customer's factory floor, and they have access to information systems and the research lab.[27] Coordination is so intimate that it's hard to tell one organization from another. An example of how partnership can boost both parties is Empire Equipment.

Empire Equipment Company

In Practice 14.2

"[Empire Equipment], a New York equipment manufacturer, decided to introduce a more analytical approach to its supply-chain management, with the goal of reducing procurement costs of filters, an important but expensive component. The New York firm was happy with the quality of its supplier's product, but felt it was paying too much for the part.

A team of experts and managers was put together, visited the supplier and explained the study goal: to better understand the functions, activities and demands that added cost to the filter they built, and to explore potential avenues for reducing those costs. Based on a commitment from the manufacturer that the supplier would be a partner in the strategy and would share in any cost-saving measures that emerged, the supplier agreed to cooperate.

The team toured the supplier's operation, tracking each step of the production process: raw materials cost, direct labor, equipment usage, set-up time, order processing, production planning and overhead costs. It became obvious that the direct-manufacturing costs were a fraction of the total product costs—about 30 percent. The other 70 percent was buried in the contribution margin supporting the indirect functions of marketing, developing, engineering, testing, packaging and shipping [Empire's] filter. But which indirect functions added the most cost, and why?

To answer that question, the team met with engineering staff, production managers, quality inspectors and other personnel—including top management—involved in servicing the New York company. They learned that much of the indirect costs were attributable to two factors: erratic and inefficient ordering patterns, and excessive and redundant post-production specifications for quality measurement and testing.

By making long-term volume commitments, improving forecasting, coordinating order size and altering quality specifications that were inefficient or overlapping, the team was able to reduce total product costs from $7,300 to $4,000, a 46 percent savings."[28]

By becoming intimately involved in the supplier's production with the attitude of fair dealing and adding value to both sides, Empire Equipment achieved savings for itself and additional value for its supplier. In the next generation of collaborative networks, suppliers may build products from components that arrive at one point to be assembled into a final product. Germany's Volkswagen is attempting to achieve this new form of organization in the automobile industry, as described in The New Paradigm box.

The New Paradigm

Volkswagen

Volkswagen executives dream of a new industrial revolution (initiated by José López, formerly of General Motors) that will start in a Volkswagen plant in the Brazilian hinterland. Automakers such as Chrysler have created closer partnerships with key suppliers. Volkswagen, however, is moving to another level: the company plans on seven international suppliers to make their own components and then to fasten them together into finished trucks and buses. This approach, if successful, will be a model for new automotive factories around the world.

The problems in achieving this vision are immense. In this system, hundreds of suppliers are reduced to seven final assemblers that will work in the Brazilian factory. Each of the seven will have second- and third-tier suppliers, which must be coordinated for on-time delivery and provide top-notch quality. The seven final assemblers bring parts and expertise from around the world:

Engine and transmission	Motoren-Werke Mannheim (Germany), Cummins (United States)
Chassis	Iochpe-Maxion (Brazil)
Cab	Tamet (Brazil)
Steering and instruments	VDO Kienzle (Germany)
Axles, brakes, suspension	Rockwell (United States)
Wheels and tires	Iochpe-Maxion (Brazil), Bridgestone (Japan), Borlen (Brazil)
Painting	Eisenmann (Germany)

Each assembler will have a marked off area on the plant floor. For example, VDO Kienzle will have two hundred workers install everything from seats to instrument panels in the steel shell of a truck cab. The cab will move down the assembly line to other suppliers' spaces. When the factory is up to speed with fourteen hundred workers, only two hundred will be VW employees; the rest will be provided by the suppliers. It seems to many observers that an international collection of suppliers could never assemble a defect-free vehicle. The solution is to shift from the traditional plant hierarchy to partnership and teamwork. The plant manager holds a daily roundtable discussion with suppliers; and he sees himself as just a partner at the table, not the owner. Working as partners requires the breakdown of competitive mind-sets but may enable the new concept to succeed.

Called *coproduction* and a *modular consortium,* the new approach is appealing because VW's capital investment drops because suppliers provide needed equipment and inventory. The number of hours it takes to build each vehicle will also decrease.

Is this factory of the future going to produce a dream or a nightmare? If the assemblers can become true partners, the dream is possible, and López will have started a revolution as well as created a model for new car factories around the world.

Source: Based on David Woodruff with Ian Katz and Keith Naughton, "VW's Factory of the Future," *Business Week*, 7 October 1996, 52–56; and Diana Jean Schemo, "Is VW's New Plant Lean, or Just Mean?" *New York Times*, 19 November 1996, D1.

POPULATION ECOLOGY

This section introduces a different perspective on relationships among organizations. The **population ecology** perspective differs from the other perspectives because it focuses on organizational diversity and adaptation within a population of organizations.[29] A **population** is a set of organizations engaged in similar activities with similar patterns of resource utilization and outcomes. Organizations within a population compete for similar resources or similar customers, such as financial institutions in the Seattle area.

Within a population, the question asked by ecology researchers is about the large number and variation of organizations in society. Why are new organizational forms constantly appearing that create such diversity? Their answer is that individual organizational adaptation is severely limited compared to the changes demanded by the environment. Innovation and change in a population of organizations take place through the birth of new forms and kinds of organizations more so than by the reform and change of existing organizations. Indeed, organizational forms are considered relatively stable, and the good of a whole society is served by the development of new forms of organization through entrepreneurial initiatives. New organizations meet the new needs of society more so than established organizations that are slow to change.[30]

What does this theory mean in practical terms? It means that large established organizations often become dinosaurs. GM, Sears, and IBM are so large that adaptation to a rapidly changing environment becomes nearly impossible. Hence new organizational forms that fit the current environment will emerge, such as Toyota, Wal-Mart, and Microsoft, that fill a new niche and over time take away business from established companies.

Why do established organizations have such a hard time adapting to a rapidly changing environment? Michael Hannan and John Freeman, originators of the population ecology model of organization, argue that there are many limitations on the ability of organizations to change. The limitations come from heavy investment in plant, equipment, and specialized personnel, limited information, established viewpoints of decision makers, the organization's own successful history that justifies current procedures, and the difficulty of changing corporate culture. True transformation is a rare and unlikely event in the face of all these barriers.[31]

At this very moment new organizations are appearing in the used car industry. One example is CarMax, which provides huge lots with fixed price cars that take the pain out of shopping. CarMax and similar companies make traditional used car dealers look like dinosaurs. Another recent change is the development of corporate universities within large companies like Motorola and Fedex. There are more than one thousand corporate universities, compared to just two hundred a few years ago. One reason they've developed so fast is that companies can't get desired services from established universities, which are too stuck in traditional ways of thinking and teaching. Another example is the steel industry, which two decades ago was dominated by a few huge firms. Then a new organizational form, called the minimill, emerged, led by companies such as Nucor, that created highly efficient steel production that is taking business away from the giants.[32]

According to the population ecology view, when looking at an organizational population as a whole, the changing environment determines which organizations survive or fail. The assumption is that individual organizations suffer from structural inertia and find it difficult to adapt to environmental changes. Thus, when rapid change occurs, old organizations are likely to decline or fail, and new organizations emerge that are better suited to the needs of the environment.

Currently, huge AT&T is working hard to renew itself in the rapidly changing telecommunications world. A part of this strategy is the appointment of a new chief executive who will replace long-time CEO Robert Allen. AT&T analysts say this change is long overdue, because the many restructurings and downsizings initiated by Allen have not produced effective results. Based on the history of telephone companies, population ecology researchers would say that successful change is unlikely.[33] For example, in the early 1900s when the telephone industry was new, over four hundred telephone companies existed in Pennsylvania alone. Most used magneto technology, which means each telephone carried its own battery. A major innovation was a common battery—a power source located within the central office used for voice transmission among all telephones connected there. This was a powerful innovation, but most phone companies failed to adapt. Thus as the common battery became more popular, the magneto-based companies went out of business.[34] Over the years consolidation occurred until only a few phone companies are left, and now AT&T, the dominant long-distance carrier, may be in the twilight of its dominance.

The population ecology model is developed from theories of natural selection in biology, and the terms *evolution* and *selection* are used to refer to the underlying behavioral processes. Theories of biological evolution try to explain why certain life forms appear and survive whereas others perish. Some theories suggest the forms that survive are typically best fitted to the immediate environment.

Forbes magazine recently reported a study of American businesses over seventy years, from 1917 to 1987. Do you recall Baldwin Locomotive, Studebaker, and Lehigh Coal & Navigation? These companies were among 78 percent of the top one hundred in 1917 that did not see 1987. Of the twenty-two that remained in the top one hundred, only eleven did so under their original names. The environment of the 1940s and 1950s was suitable to Woolworth, but new organizational forms like Wal-Mart and Kmart became dominant in the 1980s. In 1917, most of the top one hundred companies were huge steel and mining industrial organizations, which were replaced by high-technology companies such as IBM and Merck.[35] Two companies that seemed to prosper over a long period were Ford and General Motors, but they are now being threatened by world changes in the automobile industry. No company is immune to the processes of social change. From just 1979 to 1989, 187 of the companies on the *Fortune* 500 list ceased to exist as independent companies. Some were acquired, some merged, and some were liquidated.[36]

Organizational Form and Niche

The population ecology model is concerned with organizational forms. **Organizational form** is an organization's specific technology, structure, products, goals, and personnel, which can be selected or rejected by the environment. Each new organization tries to find a **niche** (a domain of unique environmental resources and needs) sufficient to support it. The niche is usually small in the early stages of an organization but may increase in size over time if the organization is successful. If a niche is not available, the organization will decline and may perish.

From the viewpoint of a single firm, luck, chance, and randomness play important parts in survival. New products and ideas are continually being proposed by both entrepreneurs and large organizations. Whether these ideas and organizational forms survive or fail is often a matter of chance—whether external circumstances happen to support them. A woman who started a small electrical contracting business in a rapidly growing Florida community would have an excellent chance of success. If the same woman were to start the same business in a declining community elsewhere in the United States, the chance of success would be far less. Success or failure of a single firm thus is predicted by the characteristics of the environment as much as by the skills or strategies used by the organization.

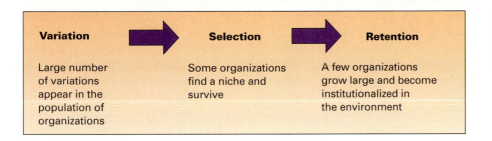

Exhibit 14.4
Elements in the Population Ecology Model of Organizations

Process of Change

The population ecology model assumes that new organizations are always appearing in the population. Thus, organization populations are continually undergoing change. The process of change in the population is defined by three principles that occur in stages: **variation**, **selection**, and **retention**. These stages are summarized in Exhibit 14.4

- *Variation.* New organizational forms continually appear in a population of organizations. They are initiated by entrepreneurs, established with venture capital by large corporations, or set up by a government seeking to provide new services. Some forms may be conceived to cope with a perceived need in the external environment. In your own neighborhood, for example, a new restaurant may be started to meet a perceived need. In recent years, a large number of new firms have been initiated to develop computer software, to provide consulting and other services to large corporations, and to develop new kinds of toys. Other new organizations produce a traditional product such as steel, but do it using minimal technology and new management techniques that make the new steel companies far more able to survive. Organizational variations are analogous to mutations in biology, and they add to the scope and complexity of organizational forms in the environment.
- *Selection.* Some variations will suit the external environment better than others. Some prove beneficial and thus are able to find a niche and acquire the resources from the environment necessary to survive. Other variations fail to meet the needs of the environment and perish. When there is insufficient demand for a firm's product and when insufficient resources are available to the organization, that organization will be "selected out." Only a few variations are "selected in" by the environment and survive over the long term.
- *Retention.* Retention is the preservation and institutionalization of selected organizational forms. Certain technologies, products, and services are highly valued by the environment. The retained organizational form may become a dominant part of the environment. Many forms of organizations have been institutionalized, such as government, schools, churches, and automobile manufacturers. McDonald's, which owns a huge share of the fast-food market and provides the first job for many teenagers, has become institutionalized in American life.

Institutionalized organizations like McDonald's seem to be relatively permanent features in the population of organizations, but they are not permanent in the long run. The environment is always changing, and, if the dominant organizational forms do not adapt to external change, they will gradually diminish and be replaced by other organizations. Already, Taco Bell, owned by PepsiCo, has been drawing in McDonald's customers because the Mexican fast-food chain kept lowering prices while McDonald's consistently raised them. Unless it adapts, McDonald's might no longer be price-competitive in the fast-food market.[37]

From the population ecology perspective, the environment is the important determinant of organizational success or failure. The organization must meet an environmental need, or it will be selected out. The process of variation, selection, and retention leads to the establishment of new organizational forms in a population of organizations.

Strategies for Survival

Another principle that underlies the population ecology model is the **struggle for existence**, or competition. Organizations and populations of organizations are engaged in a competitive struggle over resources, and each organizational form is fighting to survive. The struggle is most intense among new organizations, and both the birth and survival frequencies of new organizations are related to factors in the larger environment. Factors such as size of urban area, percentage of immigrants, political turbulence, industry growth rate, and environmental variability have influenced the launching and survival of newspapers, telecommunication firms, railroads, government agencies, labor unions, and even voluntary organizations.[38]

In the population ecology perspective, **generalist** and **specialist** strategies distinguish organizational forms in the struggle for survival. Organizations with a wide niche or domain, that is, those that offer a broad range of products or services or that serve a broad market, are generalists. Organizations that provide a narrower range of goods or services or that serve a narrower market are specialists.

In the natural environment, a specialist form of flora and fauna would evolve in protective isolation in a place like Hawaii, where the nearest body of land is two thousand miles away. The flora and fauna are heavily protected. In contrast, a place like Costa Rica, which experienced wave after wave of external influences, developed a generalist set of flora and fauna that has better resilience and flexibility for adapting to a broad range of circumstances. A corporate example of a specialist is Olmec Corporation, a New York-based toy manufacturer that markets more than sixty African-American and Hispanic dolls. Mattel, on the other hand, is a generalist, marketing a broad range of toys, including a Disney line, Barbie, and a new African-American doll that is more than a Barbie with darker skin.[39]

Specialists are generally more competitive than generalists in the narrow area in which their domains overlap. However, the breadth of the generalist's domain serves to protect it somewhat from environmental changes. Though demand may decrease for some of the generalist's products or services, it usually increases for others at the same time. In addition, because of the diversity of products, services, and customers, generalists are able to reallocate resources internally to adapt to a changing environment, whereas specialists are not. However, because specialists are often smaller companies, they can sometimes move faster and be more flexible in adapting to a changing environment.[40]

Managerial impact on company success often comes from selecting a strategy that steers a company into an open niche in the environment. In Practice 14.3 illustrates how a company in the computer industry found a new niche that may replace current powerhouses like Microsoft and Intel.

Sun Microsystems, Inc.

In a scene reminiscent of the old west, with large ranchers battling small farmers among shifting alliances and coalitions, Sun Microsystems is leading a great new wave in computing. CEO Scott McNealy has been preaching his vision of network computing for years. The true value of computers is only realized when they work together in networks, and Sun became tops in networked workstations for engineers. Stand-alone PCs are nothing compared to networked computers because the power multiplies geometrically. People can tap the power of other machines, making an entire network their computer.

Corporations now are scrambling to get on the Internet and are using Java, Sun's red-hot Internet softwave. The Java programming language can run without modification on any kind of computer. Moreover, people can download whatever applications they need off the Internet, saving space in their own computer. In addition, Java is available to users for free.

Why is Sun upsetting the established order in the industry? Many consumers are tired of the lock placed on the industry by Microsoft with its Windows software and Intel with its microprocessors. Companies spend more than $6,000 a year to upkeep a PC that runs the Microsoft operating system. Java enables hardware to last longer, and software can be taken from the Internet. Java simplifies applications because companies can keep their old computers. What works for Apple also works for IBM, because they can talk to each other. The Java system also lets a company's customers and suppliers communicate directly with a company's own information system, thereby shortening the supply chain, reducing costs, and adding to the bottom line.

Sun is in the right place at the right time as the world rushes toward it. The dominance of Microsoft and Intel has meant huge profits for them, whereas profits have shrunk at IBM, Apple, and other companies. IBM dominated in the 1960s and 1970s and Microsoft took over in the 1980s and 90s. Now another new era is emerging. Federal Express, Gap and Charles Schwab now use Sun networks. Companies are devoting thousands of programmers and millions of dollars to write new programming applications for Java, taking away dominance from Microsoft and Intel. If Sun dominates, companies once again will be able to operate with few restrictions, equalizing opportunity for both the traditional large cattle ranchers and the influx of small farmers.[41]

Microsoft and Intel are holding onto the status quo by resisting Sun's changes where they can. Sun has found an important new niche and may lead the next wave in computing by harnessing the Internet for everyone.

INSTITUTIONALISM

The institutional perspective provides yet another view of interorganizational relationships.[42] Organizations are highly interconnected. Just as companies need efficient production to survive, the institutional view argues that organizations need legitimacy from their stakeholders. Companies perform well when they are perceived by the larger environment to have a legitimate right to exist. Thus the **institutional perspective** describes how organizations survive and succeed through congruence between an organization and the expectations from its environment. The **institutional environment** is composed of norms and values from stakeholders (customers, investors, associations, boards, government, collaborating organizations). Thus the institutional view believes that organizations adopt structures and processes to please outsiders, and these activities come to take on rulelike status in organizations. The institutional environment reflects what the greater society views as correct ways of organizing and behaving.[43]

Legitimacy is defined as the general perspective that an organization's actions are desirable, proper, and appropriate within the environment's system of norms, values, and beliefs.[44] Institutional theory thus is concerned with the set of intangible norms and values that shape behavior as opposed to the tangible elements of technology and structure focused on in early chapters of this book. Organizations must fit within the cognitive and emotional expectations of their audience. For example, people will not deposit money in a bank unless it sends signals of safety and compliance with norms of wise financial management.

Another example is the widespread interest among business firms in the annual *Fortune* magazine survey that ranks corporations based on their reputation. Consider also your local government and whether it could raise property taxes for increased school funding if community residents did not approve of the school district's policies and activities. The Soviet Union collapsed and communism quickly disappeared because communism held little legitimacy in the minds of citizens in Russia and Eastern Europe. Just as important, when Westerners tried to construct a market-based economy in the Soviet Union, those efforts failed because citizens did not have a mental framework that saw competitive organizations as legitimate. Gradually institutions will grow and flourish in the Soviet Union consistent with the values held in the larger culture.

The notion of legitimacy answers an important question for institutional theorists. Why is there so much homogeneity in the forms and practices of established organizations? For example, visit banks, high schools, hospitals, government departments, business firms in a similar industry, in any part of the country, and they will look strikingly similar. When an organizational field is just getting started, such as in the computer industry of which Sun Microsystems is a part, then diversity is the norm. New organizations fill emerging niches. However, once an industry becomes established, there is an invisible push toward similarity. Isomorphism is the term used to describe this move toward similarity.

The institutional view also sees organizations as having two essential dimensions—technical and institutional. The technical dimension is the day-to-day work technology and operating requirements. The institutional structure is that part of the organization most visible to the outside public. Moreover, the technical dimension is governed by norms of rationality and efficiency, but the institutional dimension is governed by expectations from the external environment. As a result of pressure to do things in a proper and correct way, the formal structures of many organizations reflect the expectations and values of the environment rather than the demand of work activities. This means that an organization may incorporate positions or activities (equal employment officer, strategic planning group) perceived as important by the larger society and thus increase its legitimacy and survival prospects, even though these elements may decrease efficiency. Thus the formal structure and design of an organization is not rational with respect to workflow and products or services, but it will assure survival in the larger environment.

Organizations adapt to the environment by signaling their congruence with the demands and expectations stemming from cultural norms, standards set by professional bodies, funding agencies, and customers. Structure is something of a facade disconnected from technical work through which the organization obtains approval, legitimacy, and continuing support. The adoption of structures thus may not be linked to actual production needs, and may occur regardless of whether specific internal problems are solved. Formal structure is separated from technical action in this view.[45]

Institutional Isomorphism

Organizations have a strong need to appear legitimate. In so doing, many aspects of structure and behavior may be targeted toward environmental acceptance rather than toward internal technical efficiency. Interorganizational relationships thus are characterized by forces that cause organizations in a similar population to look like one another. **Institutional isomorphism** is the emergence of a common structure and approach among organizations in the same field. Isomorphism is the process that causes one unit in a population to resemble other units that face the same set of environmental conditions.[46]

Exactly how does increasing similarity occur? How are these forces realized? A summary of three mechanisms for institutional adaptation are summarized in Exhibit 14.5. There are three core mechanisms: mimetic isomorphism, which results from responses to uncertainty, normative isomorphism, which results from common training and professionalism, and coercive isomorphism, which stems from political influence.[47]

Mimetic Isomorphism. Most organizations, especially business organizations, face great uncertainty. It is not clear to senior executives exactly what products, services, or technologies will achieve desired goals, and sometimes the goals themselves are not clear. In the face of this uncertainty, **mimetic isomorphism** occurs, which is the copying or modeling of other organizations.

Executives see an innovation in a firm generally regarded as successful, so the management practice is quickly copied. This modeling is done without any clear proof that performance will be improved. Mimetic processes explain why fads and fashions occur in the business world. Once a new idea starts, many organizations grab onto it, only to learn that the application is difficult and may cause more problems than it solves. This was the case with the recent frenzy around reengineering and the merger wave that swept many industries. Of course there were successes reported in both instances but also a large number of failures.

Exhibit 14.5
Three Mechanisms for Institutional Adaptation

	Mimetic	Coercive	Normative
Reason to adapt	Uncertainty	Dependence	Duty, obligation
Carrier	Innovation visibility	Political law, rules, sanctions	Professionalism—certification, accreditation
Social basis	Culturally supported	Legal	Moral
Example	Reengineering, benchmarking	Pollution controls, school regulations	Accounting standards, consultant training

Source: Adapted from W. Richard Scott, *Institutions and Organizations* (Thousand Oaks, Calif.: Sage, 1995).

Techniques such as job enrichment, zero-based budgeting, and total quality management have all been adopted without clear evidence for efficiency or effectiveness. The one certain benefit is that management's feelings of uncertainty will be reduced, and the company's image will be enhanced because the firm is seen as using the latest management techniques.

Perhaps the clearest example of official copying is the technique of benchmarking that occurs as part of the total quality movement. *Benchmarking* means identifying who's best at something in an industry and then duplicating the technique for creating excellence, perhaps even improving it in the process. Rank Xerox, the subsidiary of Xerox that sells copiers in Europe, uses benchmarking to find out what competitors are doing and then copies the best techniques.[48]

The mimetic process works because organizations face continuous high uncertainty, they are aware of innovations occurring in the environment, and the innovations are culturally supported, thereby giving legitimacy to adopters. This is a strong mechanism by which a group of banks, or high schools, or manufacturing firms begin to look and act like one another.

Coercive Isomorphism.   All organizations are subject to pressure, both formal and informal, from government, regulatory agencies, and other important organizations in the environment, especially those on which a company is dependent. **Coercive isomorphism** is external pressure exerted on organizations to adopt structures, techniques, or behaviors similar to other organizations. Some pressures may have the force of law, such as government mandates to adopt new pollution control equipment. Health and safety regulations may demand that a safety officer be appointed. As with other changes, coercive isomorphism does not mean that the organization becomes more effective, but it will "look" more effective and will be accepted as legitimate in the environment.

Coercive pressures occur between organizations where there is a power difference, as described in the resource dependence section earlier in this chapter. It is not unusual for a large retailer like Wal-Mart or a manufacturer like General Motors to insist on certain policies, procedures, and techniques used by its suppliers. When Honda picked Donnelly Corporation to make all the mirrors for its U.S.-manufactured cars, Honda insisted that Donnelly empower its workers. Because Donnelly had already taken major steps in this direction, they won the contract. Unless an organization knows how to foster collaborative relationships internally, Honda believes the company won't be good at making a partnership work between the two companies.

Coercive isomorphism occurs when an organization is dependent on another, when there are political factors such as rules, laws, and sanctions involved, or when some other contractual or legal basis defines the relationship. Organizations operating under those constraints will adopt changes and relate to one another in a way that increases homogeneity and limits diversity.

Normative Isomorphism.   The third reason organizations change according to the institutional view is normative. **Normative isomorphism** means that organizations change to achieve standards of professionalism, to adopt techniques that are considered by the professional community to be up-to-date and effective. Changes may be in any area, such as information technology, accounting requirements, or marketing techniques. Professionals share a body of formal education based on university degrees and professional networks through which ideas are exchanged by consultants and professional leaders. Universities, consulting firms, and professional training institutions develop norms among professional managers. People are exposed to similar training and standards, and adopt shared values, which are implemented in organizations with which they work. Business schools teach finance, marketing, and human resource majors that certain techniques are better than others, so using those techniques becomes a standard in the field. In one study, for example, a radio station changed from a functional to a multidivisional structure because a consultant recommended it as a "higher standard" of doing business. There was no proof that this structure was better, but the radio station wanted legitimacy and to be perceived as fully professional and up-to-date in its management techniques. As another example, studies show great homogeneity among superintendents in the U.S. public school system and among board members of *Fortune* 500 companies. Through education and experience, people are subjected to considerable pressure to gain legitimacy by acting exactly the same way as people already in those positions.

Companies accept normative pressure to become like one another through a sense of obligation or duty to high standards of performance based on professional norms shared by managers and specialists in their respective organizations. These norms are conveyed through professional education and certification and have almost a moral or ethical requirement based on the highest standards accepted by the profession at that time.

A company may use any or all of the mechanisms of mimetic, coercive, or normative isomorphism to change itself for greater legitimacy in the institutional environment. Firms tend to use these mechanisms when they feel dependence, uncertainty, ambiguous goals, and reliance on professional credentials. The outcome of these processes is that organizations become far more homogeneous than would be expected from the natural diversity among managers and environments.

SUMMARY AND INTERPRETATION

This chapter has been about the important evolution in interorganizational relationships. At one time organizations considered themselves autonomous and separate, trying to outdo other companies. Today more organizations see themselves as part of an ecosystem. The organization may span several industries and will be anchored in a dense web of relationships with other companies. In this ecosystem, collaboration is as important as competition. Indeed, organizations may compete and collaborate at the same time depending on the location and issue. In this business ecosystem, the role of management is changing to include the development of horizontal relationships with other organizations.

Four perspectives have been developed to explain relationships among organizations. The resource dependence perspective is the most traditional, arguing that organizations try to avoid excessive dependence on other organizations. In this view, organizations devote considerable effort to controlling the environment to assure ample resources while maintaining independence. Moreover, powerful organizations will exploit the dependence of small companies. The collaborative network perspective is an emerging alternative. Organizations welcome collaboration and interdependence with other organizations to enhance value for both. The success of collaboration has been revealed in not-for-profit organizations and in international industrial groups such as the Japanese *keiretsu*. Many executives are changing mind-sets away from autonomy toward collaboration, often with previous corporate enemies. The new mind-set emphasizes trust, fair dealing, and achieving profits for all parties in a relationship.

The population ecology perspective explains why organizational diversity continuously increases with the appearance of new organizations filling niches left open by established companies. This perspective says that large companies cannot adapt to meet a changing environment, hence new companies emerge with the appropriate form and skills to serve new needs. Through the process of variation, selection, and retention, some organizations will survive and grow while others perish. Companies may adopt a generalist or specialist strategy to survive in the population of organizations.

The institutional perspective argues that interorganizational relationships are shaped as much by a company's need for legitimacy as by the need for providing products and services. The need for legitimacy means that the organization will adopt structures and activities that are perceived as valid, proper, and up-to-date by external stakeholders. In this way, established organizations copy techniques from one another and begin to look very similar. The emerging common structures and approaches in the same field is called institutional isomorphism. There are three core mechanisms that explain increasing organizational homogeneity: mimetic isomorphism, which results from responses to uncertainty; normative isomorphism, which results from common training and professionalism; and coercive isomorphism, which stems from power differences and political influences.

Each of these four perspectives is valid. They represent different lenses through which the world of interorganizational relationships can be viewed: organizations experience a competitive struggle for autonomy; they can thrive through collaborative relationships with others; the slowness to adapt provides openings for new organizations to flourish; and organizations seek legitimacy as well as profits from the external environment. The important thing is for managers to be aware of interorganizational relationships and to consciously manage them.

Key Concepts

coercive isomorphism	organizational ecosystem
collaborative network	organizational form
generalist	population
institutional environment	population ecology
institutional isomorphism	resource dependence
institutional perspective	retention
interorganization relationships	selection
legitimacy	specialist
mimetic isomorphism	struggle for existence
niche	variation
normative isomorphism	

Discussion Questions

1. The concept of business ecosystems implies that organizations are more interdependent than ever before. From personal experience do you agree? Explain.
2. How do you feel about the prospect of becoming a manager and having to manage a set of relationships with other companies rather than just managing your own company? Discuss.

3. Assume you are the manager of a small firm that is dependent on a large manufacturing customer that uses the resource dependence perspective. Put yourself in the position of the small firm, and describe what actions you would take to survive and succeed. What actions would you take from the perspective of the large firm?

4. Many managers today were trained under assumptions of adversarial relationships with other companies. Do you think operating as adversaries is easier or more difficult than operating as partners with other companies? Discuss.

5. Discuss how the adversarial versus partnership orientations work among students in class. Is there a sense of competition for grades? Is it possible to develop true partnerships in which your work depends on others? Discuss.

6. The population ecology perspective argues that it is healthy for society to have new organizations emerging and old organizations dying as the environment changes. Do you agree? Why would European countries pass laws to sustain traditional organizations and inhibit the emergence of new ones?

7. How might the process of variation, selection, and retention explain innovations that take place within an organization? Explain.

8. Do you believe that legitimacy really motivates organizations? Is acceptance by other people a motivation for individuals? Explain.

9. How does the desire for legitimacy result in organizations becoming more similar over time?

10. How does mimetic isomorphism differ from normative isomorphism? Give an example of each.

Briefcase

As an organization manager, keep these guides in mind:

1. Look for and develop relationships with other organizations. Don't limit your thinking to a single industry or business type. Build an ecosystem of which your organization is a part.

2. Reach out and control external sectors that threaten needed resources. Adopt strategies to control resources especially when your organization is dependent and has little power. Assert your company's influence when you have power and control over resources.

3. Seek collaborative partnerships that enable mutual dependence and enhance value and gain for both sides. Get deeply involved in your partner's business, and vice versa, to benefit both.

4. Adapt your organization to new variations being selected and retained in the external environment. If you are starting a new organization, find a niche that contains a strong environmental need for your product or service, and be prepared for a competitive struggle over scarce resources.

5. Pursue legitimacy with your organization's major stakeholders in the external environment. Adopt strategies, structures, and new management techniques that meet the expectations of significant parties, thereby assuring their cooperation and resources. Enhance legitimacy by borrowing good ideas from other firms, complying with laws and regulations, and following procedures considered best for your company.

Chapter Fourteen Workbook *Management Fads**

Look up one or two articles on current trends or fads in management. Then, find one or two articles on a management fad from several years ago. Finally, surf the Internet for information on both the current and previous fads.

1. How were these fads used in organizations? Use real examples from your readings.
2. Why do you think the fads were adopted? To what extent were the fads adopted to truly improve

productivity and morale versus the company's desire to appear current in its management techniques compared to the competition?

3. Give an example in which a fad did not work as expected. Explain the reason it did not work.

Case for Analysis *Hugh Russel Inc.**

The following story is a personal recollection by David Hurst of the experience of a group of managers in a mature organization undergoing profound change. . . . The precipitating event in this change was a serious business crisis. . . .

When I joined Hugh Russel Inc. in 1979, it was a medium-sized Canadian distributor of steel and industrial products. With sales of CDN$535 million and three thousand employees, the business was controlled by the chairman, Archie Russel, who owned 16 percent of the common shares. The business consisted of four groups—the core steel distribution activities (called "Russelsteel"), industrial bearings and valves distribution, a chain of wholesalers of hardware and sporting goods, and a small manufacturing business. . . .

The company was structured for performance. . . . The management was professional, with each of the divisional hierarchies headed by a group president reporting to Peter Foster in his capacity as president of the corporation. Jobs were described in job descriptions, and their mode of execution was specified in detailed standard operating procedures. Three volumes of the corporate manual spelled out policy on everything from accounting to vacation pay. Extensive accounting and data-processing systems allowed managers to track the progress of individual operations against budgets and plans. Compensation was performance-based, with return on net assets (RONA) as the primary measure and large bonuses (up to 100 percent of base) for managers who made their targets.

At the senior management level, the culture was polite but formal. The board of directors consisted of Archie's friends and associates together with management insiders. Archie and Peter ran the organization as if they were majority owners. Their interaction with management outside of the head office was restricted to the occasional field trip. . . .

Crisis

Nine months after I joined the company as a financial planner, we were put "in play" by a raider and, after a fierce bidding war, were acquired in a hostile takeover. Our acquirer was a private company controlled by the eldest son of an entrepreneur of legendary wealth and ability, so we had no inkling at the time of the roller-coaster ride that lay ahead of us. We were unaware that not only did the son not have the support of his father in this venture but he had also neglected to consult his two brothers, who were joint owners of the acquiring company! As he had taken on $300 million of debt to do the deal, this left each of the brothers on the hook for a personal guarantee of $100 million. They were not amused, and it showed!

Within days of the deal, we were inundated by waves of consultants, lawyers, and accountants: each shareholder seemed to have his or her own panel of advisers. After six weeks of intensive analysis, it was clear that far too much had been paid for us and that the transaction was vastly overleveraged. At the start of the deal, the acquirer had approached our bankers and asked

*Source: David K. Hurst, *Crisis and Renewal: Meeting the Challenge of Organizational Change* (Boston: Harvard Business School Press, 1995).

them if they wanted a piece of the "action." Concerned at the possible loss of our banking business and eager to be associated with such a prominent family, our bankers had agreed to provide the initial financing on a handshake. Now, as they saw the detailed numbers for the first time and became aware of the dissent among the shareholders, they withdrew their support and demanded their money back. We needed to refinance $300 million of debt—fast. . . .

Change

The takeover and the subsequent merger of our new owner's moribund steel-fabricating operations into Hugh Russel changed our agenda completely. We had new shareholders (who fought with each other constantly), new bankers, and new businesses in an environment of soaring interest rates and plummeting demand for our products and services. Almost overnight, the corporation went from a growth-oriented, acquisitive, earnings-driven operation to a cash-starved cripple, desperate to survive. Closures, layoffs, downsizing, delayering, asset sales, and "rationalization" became our new priorities. . . . At the head office, the clarity of jobs vanished. For example, I had been hired to do financial forecasting and raise capital in the equity markets, but with the company a financial basket case, this clearly could not be done. For all of us, the future looked dangerous and frightening as bankruptcy, both personal and corporate, loomed ahead.

And so it was in an atmosphere of crisis that Wayne Mang, the new president (Archie Russel and Peter Foster left the organization soon after the deal), gathered the first group of managers together to discuss the situation. Wayne Mang had been in the steel business for many years and was trusted and respected by the Hugh Russel people. An accountant by training, he used to call himself the "personnel manager" to underscore his belief in both the ability of people to make the difference in the organization and the responsibility of line management to make this happen. The hastily called first meeting consisted of people whom Wayne respected and trusted from all over the organization. They had been selected without regard for their position in the old hierarchy.

The content and style of that first meeting were a revelation to many! Few of them had ever been summoned to the head office for anything but a haranguing over their budgets—"To have the shit kicked out of us," as they put it. Now they were being told the complete gory details of the company's situation and, for the first time, being treated as if they had something to contribute. Wayne asked for their help.

During that first meeting, we counted nineteen major issues confronting the corporation. None of them fell under a single functional area. We arranged ourselves into task forces to deal with them. I say "arranged ourselves" because that was the way it seemed to happen. Individuals volunteered without coercion to work on issues in which they were interested or for which their skills were relevant. They also "volunteered" others who were not at the meeting but, it was thought, could help. There was some guidance—each task force had one person from the head office whose function it was to report what was happening back to the "center"—and some members found themselves on too many task forces, which required that substitutes be found. But that was the extent of the conscious management of the process.

The meeting broke up at 2:00 A.M., when we all went home to tell our incredulous spouses what had happened. . . .

The cross-functional project team rapidly became our preferred method of organizing new initiatives, and at the head office, the old formal structure virtually disappeared. The teams could be formed at a moment's notice to handle a fast-breaking issue and dissolved just as quickly. We found, for example, that even when we weren't having formal meetings, we seemed to spend most of our time talking to each other informally. Two people would start a conversation in someone's office, and almost before you knew it, others had wandered in and a small group session was going. Later on, we called these events "bubbles"; they became our equivalent of the Bushmen's campfire meetings. . . .

Later, when I became executive vice president, Wayne and I deliberately shared an office so we could each hear what the other was doing in real time and create an environment in which "bubbles" might form spontaneously. As people wandered past our open door, we would wave them in to talk; others would wander in after them. The content of these sessions always had to do with our predicament, both corporate and personal. It was serious stuff, but the atmosphere was light and open. Our fate was potentially a bad one, but at least it would be shared. All of us who were involved then cannot remember ever having laughed so much. We laughed at ourselves and at the desperate situation. We laughed at the foolishness of the bankers in having financed such a mess, and we laughed at the antics of the feuding shareholders, whose outrageous manners and language we learned to mimic to perfection.

I think it was the atmosphere from these informal sessions that gradually permeated all our interactions—with employees, bankers, suppliers, everyone with whom we came into contact. Certainly, we often had tough meetings, filled with tension and threat, but we were always able to "bootstrap" ourselves back up emotionally at the informal debriefings afterward. . . .

Perhaps the best example of both the change in structure and the blurring of the boundaries of the organization was our changing relationships with our bankers. In the beginning, at least for the brief time that the loan was in good standing, the association was polite and at arm's length. Communication was formal. As the bank realized the full horror of what it had financed (a process that took about eighteen months), the relationship steadily grew more hostile. Senior executives of the bank became threatening, spelling out what actions they might take if we did not solve our problem. This hostility culminated in an investigation by the bank for possible fraud (a standard procedure in many banks when faced with a significant loss).

Throughout this period, we had seen a succession of different bankers, each of whom had been assigned to our account for a few months. As a result of our efforts to brief every new face that appeared, we had built a significant network of contacts within the bank with whom we had openly shared a good deal of information and opinion. When no fraud was found, the bank polled its own people on what to do. Our views presented so coherently by our people (because everyone knew what was going on), and shared so widely with so many bankers, had an enormous influence on the outcome of this process. The result was the formation of a joint company-bank team to address a shared problem that together we could solve. The boundary between the corporation and the bank was now blurred: to an outside observer, it would have been unclear where the corporation ended and the bank began. . . .

Our corporation had extensive formal reporting systems to allow the monitoring of operations on a regular basis. After the takeover, these systems required substantial modifications. For example, . . . we had to report our results to the public every quarter at a time when we were losing nearly two million dollars a week! We knew that unless we got to our suppliers ahead of time, they could easily panic and refuse us credit. Hasty moves on their part could have had fatal consequences for the business.

In addition, our closure plans for plants all over Canada and the United States brought us into contact with unions and governments in an entirely different way. We realized that we had no option but to deal with these audiences in advance of events.

I have already described how our relationship with the bankers changed as a result of our open communication. We found exactly the same effect with these new audiences. Initially, our major suppliers could not understand why we had told them we were in trouble before we had to. We succeeded, however, in framing the situation in a way that enlisted their cooperation in our survival, and by the time the "war story" was news, we had their full support. Similarly, most government and union organizations were so pleased to be involved in the process before announcements were made that they bent over backward to be of assistance. Just as had been the case with the bank, we set up joint task forces with these "outside" agencies to resolve what had become shared problems. A significant contributor to our ability to pull this off was the high quality of our internal communication. Everyone on the teams knew the complete, up-to-date picture of what was happening. An outside agency could talk to anyone on a team and get the same story. In this way, we constructed a formidable network of contacts, many of whom had special skills and experience in areas that would turn out to be of great help to us in the future.

The addition of multiple networks to our information systems enhanced our ability both to gather and to disseminate information. The informality and openness of the networks, together with the high volume of face-to-face dialogues, gave us an early warning system with which to detect hurt feelings and possible hostile moves on the part of shareholders, suppliers, nervous bankers, and even customers. This information helped us head off trouble before it happened. The networks also acted as a broadcast system through which we could test plans and actions before announcing them formally. In this way, we not only got excellent suggestions for improvement, but everyone felt that he or she had been consulted before action was taken. . . .

We had a similar experience with a group of people outside the company during the hectic last six months of 1983, when we were trying to finalize a deal for the shareholders and bankers to sell the steel distribution business to new owners. The group of people in question comprised the secretaries of the numerous lawyers and accountants involved in the deal. . . .

We made these secretaries part of the network, briefing them in advance on the situation, explaining why things were needed, and keeping them updated on the progress of the deal. We were astounded at the cooperation we received: our calls were put through, our messages received prompt responses, drafts and opinions were produced on time. In the final event, a complex deal that should have taken nine months to complete was done in three. All of this was accomplished by ordinary people going far beyond what might have been expected of them. . . .

We had been thrust into crisis without warning, and our initial activities were almost entirely reactions to issues that imposed themselves upon us. But as we muddled along in the task forces, we began to find that we had unexpected sources of influence over what was happening. The changing relationship with the bank illustrates this neatly. Although we had no formal power in that situation, we found that by framing a confusing predicament in a coherent way, we could, via our network, influence the outcomes of the bank's decisions. The same applied to suppliers: by briefing them ahead of time and presenting a reasonable scenario for the recovery of their advances, we could influence the decisions they would make.

Slowly we began to realize that, although we were powerless in a formal sense, our networks, together with our own internal coherence, gave us an ability to get things done invisibly. As we discussed the situation with all the parties involved, a strategy began to emerge. A complicated financial/tax structure would allow the bank to "manage" its loss and give it an incentive not to call on the shareholders' personal guarantees. The core steel distribution business could be refinanced in the process and sold to new owners. The wrangle between the shareholders could be resolved, and each could go his or her own way. All that had to be done was to bring all the parties together, including a buyer for the steel business, and have them agree that this was the best course to follow. Using our newfound skills, we managed to pull it off.

It was not without excitement: at the last minute, the shareholders raised further objections to the deal. Only the bank could make them sell, and they were reluctant to do so, fearful that they might attract a lawsuit. Discreet calls to the major suppliers, several of whose executives were on the board of the bank, did the trick. "This business needs to be sold and recapitalized," the suppliers were told. "If the deal does not go through, you should probably reduce your credit exposure." The deal went through. By the end of 1983, we had new owners, just in time to benefit from the general business recovery. The ordeal was over . . .

Chapter Fourteen Workshop *Ugli Orange Case**

1. Form groups of three members. One person will be Dr. Roland, one person will be Dr. Jones, and the third person will be an observer.
2. Roland and Jones will read only their own roles, but the observer will read both.
3. Role play: Instructor announces: "I am Mr./Ms. Cardoza, the owner of the remaining Ugli oranges. My fruit export firm is based in South America. My country does not have diplomatic relations with your country, although we do have strong trade relations."

   The groups will spend about ten minutes meeting with the other firm's representative and will decide on a course of action. Be prepared to answer the following questions:
   a. What do you plan to do?
   b. If you want to buy the oranges, what price will you offer?
   c. To whom and how will the oranges be delivered?
4. The observers will report the solutions reached. The groups will describe the decision-making process used.
5. The instructor will lead a discussion on the exercise addressing the following questions:
   a. Which groups had the most trust? How did that influence behavior?
   b. Which groups shared more information? Why?
   c. How are trust and disclosure important in negotiations?

Role of "Dr. Jones"

You are Dr. John W. Jones, a biological research scientist employed by a pharmaceutical firm. You have

*By Dr. Robert House, University of Toronto. Used with permission.

recently developed a synthetic chemical useful for curing and preventing Rudosen. Rudosen is a disease contracted by pregnant women. If not caught in the first four weeks of pregnancy, the disease causes serious brain, eye, and ear damage to the unborn child. Recently there has been an outbreak of Rudosen in your state, and several thousand women have contracted the disease. You have found, with volunteer patients, that your recently developed synthetic serum cures Rudosen in its early stages. Unfortunately, the serum is made from the juice of the Ugli orange, which is a very rare fruit. Only a small quantity (approximately four thousand) of these oranges were produced last season. No additional Ugli oranges will be available until next season, which will be too late to cure the present Rudosen victims.

You've demonstrated that your synthetic serum is in no way harmful to pregnant women. Consequently, there are no side effects. The Food and Drug Administration has approved production and distribution of the serum as a cure for Rudosen. Unfortunately, the present outbreak was unexpected, and your firm had not planned on having the compound serum available for six months. Your firm holds the patent on the synthetic serum, and it is expected to be a highly profitable product when it is generally available to the public.

You have recently been informed on good evidence that Mr. R. H. Cardoza, a South American fruit exporter, is in possession of three thousand Ugli oranges in good condition. If you could obtain the juice of all three thousand you would be able to both cure present victims and provide sufficient inoculation for the remaining pregnant women in the state. No other state currently has a Rudosen threat.

You have recently been informed that Dr. P. W. Roland is also urgently seeking Ugli oranges and is also aware of Mr. Cardoza's possession of the three thousand available. Dr. Roland is employed by a competing pharmaceutical firm. He has been working on biological warfare research for the past several years. There is a great deal of industrial espionage in the pharmaceutical industry. Over the past several years, Dr. Roland's firm and yours have sued each other for infringement of patent rights and espionage law violations several times.

You've been authorized by your firm to approach Mr. Cardoza to purchase the three thousand Ugli oranges. You have been told he will sell them to the highest bidder. Your firm has authorized you to bid as high as $250,000 to obtain the juice of the three thousand available oranges.

Role of "Dr. Roland"

You are Dr. P. W. Roland. You work as a research biologist for a pharmaceutical firm. The firm is under contract with the government to do research on methods to combat enemy uses of biological warfare.

Recently several World War II experimental nerve gas bombs were moved from the United States to a small island just off the U.S. coast in the Pacific. In the process of transporting them, two of the bombs developed a leak. The leak is presently controlled by government scientists, who believe that the gas will permeate the bomb chambers within two weeks. They know of no method of preventing the gas from getting into the atmosphere and spreading to other islands and very likely to the West Coast as well. If this occurs, it is likely that several thousand people will incur serious brain damage or die.

You've developed a synthetic vapor that will neutralize the nerve gas if it is injected into the bomb chamber before the gas leaks out. The vapor is made with a chemical taken from the rind of the Ugli orange, a very rare fruit. Unfortunately, only four thousand of these oranges were produced this season.

You've been informed on good evidence, that a Mr. R. H. Cardoza, a fruit exporter in South America, is in possession of three thousand Ugli oranges. The chemicals from the rinds of all three thousand oranges would be sufficient to neutralize the gas if the serum is developed and injected efficiently. You have also been informed that the rinds of these oranges are in good condition.

You have also been informed that Dr. J. W. Jones is also urgently seeking purchase of Ugli oranges, and he is aware of Mr. Cardoza's possession of the three thousand available. Dr. Jones works for a firm with which your firm is highly competitive. There is a great deal of industrial espionage in the pharmaceutical industry. Over the years, your firm and Dr. Jones' have sued each other for violations of industrial espionage laws and infringement of patent rights several times. Litigation on two suits is still in process.

The federal government has asked your firm for assistance. You've been authorized by your firm to approach Mr. Cardoza to purchase three thousand Ugli oranges. You have been told he will sell them to the highest bidder. Your firm has authorized you to bid as high as $250,000 to obtain the rind of the oranges.

Before approaching Mr. Cardoza, you have decided to talk to Dr. Jones to influence him so that he will not prevent you from purchasing the oranges.

Notes

1. Jeffrey H. Dyer, "How Chrysler Created an American Keiretsu," *Harvard Business Review* (July-August 1996): 42–56; James Bennett, "Detroit Struggles to Learn Another Lesson From Japan," *New York Times*, 19 June 1994, F5

2. Christine Oliver, "Determinants of Interorganizational Relationships: Integration and Future Directions," *Academy of Management Review* 15 (1990) 241–65.

3. James Moore, *The Death of Competition: Leadership and Strategy in the Age of Business Ecosystems* (New York: HarperCollins, 1996).

4. James Moore, "The Death of Competition," *Fortune*, 15 April 1996, 142–44.

5. Elizabeth Jensen and Eben Shapiro, "Time Warner's Fight with News Corp. Belies Mutual Dependence," *Wall Street Journal*, 28 October 1996, A1, A6.

6. Sumantra Ghoshal and Christopher A. Bartlett, "Changing the Role of Top Management: Beyond Structure and Process," *Harvard Business Review* (January-February 1995): 86–96.

7. Jessica Lipnack and Jeffrey Stamps, "One Plus One Equals Three," *Small Business Reports* (August 1993): 49–58.

8. J. Pfeffer and G. R. Salancik, *The External Control of Organizations: A Resource Dependence Perspective* (New York: Harper & Row, 1978).

9. Derek S. Pugh and David J. Hickson, *Writers on Organizations*, 5th ed. (Thousand Oaks, Calif.: Sage, 1996).

10. Peter Grittner, "Four Elements of Successful Sourcing Strategies," *Management Review* (October 1996): 41–45.

11. This discussion is based on Matthew Schifrin, "The Big Squeeze," *Forbes*, 11 March 1996, 45–46; Wendy Zellner with Marti Benedetti, "CLOUT!" *Business Week*, 21 December 1992, 62–73; Kevin Kelly and Zachary Schiller with James B. Treece, "Cut Costs or Else," *Business Week*, 22 March 1993, 28–29; Lee Berton, "Push From Above," *Wall Street Journal*, 23 May 1996, R24.

12. Ibid.

13. Kathy Rebello with Richard Brandt, Peter Coy, and Mark Lewyn, "Your Digital Future," *Business Week*, 7 September 1992, 56–64.

14. Edmund L. Andrews, "AT&T Reaches Out (and Grabs Everyone)," *New York Times*, 8 August 1993, Section 3, 1, 6.

15. Rebello, et al., "Your Digital Future"; Mark Lander with Bart Ziegler and Ronald Grover, "Time Warner's Techie at the Top," *Business Week*, 10 May 1993, 60–63.

16. Mark Stevenson, "Virtual Mergers," *Canadian Business*, September 1993, 20–26.

17. Peter Coy with Neil Gross, Silvia Sansoni and Kevin Kelly, "What's the Word in the Lab? Collaborate," *Business Week*, 27 June 1994, 78–80.

18. Christine Oliver, "Determinants of Interorganizational Relationships: Integration and Future Directions," *Academy of Management Review*, 15 (1990): 241–65; Ken G. Smith, Stephen J. Carroll, and Susan Ashford, "Intra- and Interorganizational Cooperation: Toward a Research Agenda," *Academy of Management Journal*, 38 (1995): 7–23; Timothy M. Stearns, Alan N. Hoffman, and Jan B. Heide, "Performance of Commercial Television Stations as an Outcome of Interorganizational Linkages and Environmental Conditions," *Academy of Management Journal* 30 (1987): 71–90; Keith G. Provan, "Technology and Interorganizational Activity as Predictors of Client Referrals," *Academy of Management Journal* 27 (1984): 811–29; David A. Whetten and Thomas K. Kueng, "The Instrumental Value of Interorganizational Relations: Antecedents and Consequences of Linkage Formation," *Academy of Management Journal* 22 (1979): 325–44.

19. Michael L. Gerlach, "The Japanese Corporate Network: A Blockmodel Analysis," *Administrative Science Quarterly* 37 (1992): 105–39.

20. Robert Neff, "Mighty Mitsubishi is on the Move," *Business Week*, 24 September 1990, 98–101.

21. Smith et al., "Intra- and Interorganizational Cooperation: Toward a Research Agenda."

22. Keith G. Provan and H. Brinton Milward, "A Preliminary Theory of Interorganizational Network Effectiveness: A Comparative of Four Community Mental Health Systems," *Administrative Science Quarterly* 40 (1995): 1–33.

23. Audrey Choi, "Digital's New Attitude Toward Old Enemies Puts It Back in the Game," *Wall Street Journal*, 9 April 1996, A1, A10.

24. Myron Magnet, "The New Golden Rule of Business," *Fortune*, 21 February 1994, 60–64; Grittner, "Four Elements of Successful Sourcing Strategies."

25. Peter Smith Ring and Andrew H. Van de Ven, "Developmental Processes of Corporate Interorganizational Relationships," *Academy of Management Review* 19 (1994): 90–118; Dyer, "How Chrysler Created an American Keiretsu"; Magnet, "The New Golden Rule of Business"; Grittner, "Four Elements of Successful Sourcing Strategies."

26. Magnet, "The New Golden Rule of Business"; Grittner, "Four Elements of Successful Sourcing Strategies."

27. Fred R. Blekley, "Some Companies Let Suppliers Work on Site and Even Place Orders," *Wall Street Journal*, 13 January 1995, A1, A6.

28. Peter Grittner, "Four Elements of Successful Sourcing Strategies," *Management Review* (October 1996): 42. Used with permission.

29. This section draws from Joel A. C. Baum, "Organizational Ecology," in Steward R. Clegg, Cynthia Hardy, and Walter R. Nord, eds., *Handbook of Organization Studies* (Thousand Oaks, Calif.: Sage, 1996); Jitendra V. Singh, *Organizational Evolution: New Directions* (Newbury Park, Calif.: Sage, 1990); Howard Aldrich, Bill McKelvey, and Dave Ulrich, "Design Strategy from the Population Perspective," *Journal of Management* 10 (1984): 67–86; Aldrich, *Organizations and Environments*; Michael Hannan and John Freeman, "The Population Ecology of Organizations," *American Journal of Sociology* 82 (1977): 929–64; Dave Ulrich, "The Population Perspective: Review, Critique, and Relevance," *Human Relations* 40 (1987): 137–52; Jitendra V. Singh and Charles J. Lumsden, "Theory and Research in Organizational Ecology," *Annual Review of Sociology* 16 (1990): 161–95; Howard E. Aldrich, "Understanding, Not Integration: Vital Signs from Three Perspectives on Organizations," in Michael Reed and Michael D. Hughes, eds., *Rethinking Organizations: New Directories in Organizational Theory and Analysis* (London: Sage: forthcoming); Jitendra V. Singh, David J. Tucker, and Robert J. House, "Organizational Legitimacy and the Liability of Newness," *Administrative Science Quarterly* 31 (1986): 171–93; Douglas R. Wholey and Jack W. Brittain, "Organizational Ecology: Findings and Implications," *Academy of Management Review* 11 (1986): 513–33.

30. Derek S. Pugh and David J. Hickson, *Writers on Organizations*; Lex Donaldson, *American Anti-Management Theories of Organization* (New York: Cambridge University Press, 1995).

31. Michael T. Hannan and John Freeman, "The Population Ecology of Organizations."

32. Stephen Baker, "The Minimill that Acts Like a Biggie," *Business Week*, 30 September 1996, 100–4; Thomas Moore, "The Corporate University: Transforming Management Education" (Presentation in August, 1996. Thomas Moore is the Dean of the Arthur D. Little University).

33. John J. Keller, "A Telecom Novice Is Handed Challenge of Remaking AT&T," *Wall Street Journal*, 24 October 1996, A1, A6.

34. William P. Barnett, "The Organizational Ecology of a Technology System," *Administrative Science Quarterly*, 35 (1990): 31–60.

35. Peter Newcomb, "No One is Safe," *Forbes*, 13 July 1987, 121; "It's Tough Up There," *Forbes*, 13 July 1987, 145–60.

36. Stewart Feldman, "Here One Decade, Gone the Next," *Management Review* (November 1990): 5–6.

37. Patricia Sellers, "Pepsi Keeps on Going after No. 1." *Fortune*, 11 March 1991, 61–70.

38. David J. Tucker, Jitendra V. Singh, and Agnes G. Meinhard, "Organizational Form, Population Dynamics, and Institutional Change: The Founding Patterns of Voluntary Organizations," *Academy of Management Journal* 33 (1990): 151–78; Glenn R. Carroll and Michael T. Hannan, "Density Delay in the Evolution of Organizational Populations: A Model and Five Empirical Tests," *Administrative Science Quarterly* 34 (1989): 411–30; Jacques Delacroix and Glenn R. Carroll, "Organizational Foundings: An Ecological Study of the Newspaper Industries of Argentina and Ireland," *Administrative Science Quarterly* 28 (1983): 274–91; Johannes M. Pennings, "Organizational Birth Frequencies: An Empirical Investigation," *Administrative Science Quarterly* 27 (1982): 120–44; David Marple, "Technological Innovation and Organizational Survival: A Population Ecology Study of Nineteenth-Century American Railroads," *Sociological Quarterly* 23 (1982): 107–16; Thomas G. Rundall and John O. McClain, "Environmental Selection and Physician Supply," *American Journal of Sociology* 87 (1982): 1090–1112.

39. Maria Mallory with Stephanie Anderson Forest, "Waking Up to a Major Market," *Business Week*, 23 March 1992, 70–73.

40. Arthur G. Bedeian and Raymond F. Zammuto, *Organizations: Theory and Design* (Orlando, Fla.:

Dryden Press, 1991); Richard L. Hall, *Organizations: Structure, Process and Outcomes* (Englewood Cliffs, N.J.: Prentice-Hall, 1991).

41. Robert D. Hof and John Verity, "Scott McNealy's Rising Sun," *Business Week*, 22 January 1996, 66–73; Brent Schlender, "Sun's Java: The Threat to Microsoft is Real," *Fortune*, 11 November 1996, 165–70.

42. Thanks to Tina Dacin for her material and suggestions for this section of the chapter.

43. J. Meyer and B. Rowan, "Institutionalized Organizations: Formal Structure as Myth and Ceremony," *American Journal of Sociology* 83 (1990): 340–63.

44. Mark C. Suchman, "Managing Legitimacy: Strategic and Institutional Approaches," *Academy of Management Review* 20 (1995): 571–610.

45. Pamela S. Tolbert and Lynne G. Zucker, "The Institutionalization of Institutional Theory," in Stewart R. Clegg, Cynthia Hardy, and Walter R. Nord, eds., *Handbook of Organization Studies* (Thousand Oaks, Calif.: Sage, 1996).

46. Pugh and Hickson, *Writers on Organizations*; Paul J. DiMaggio and Walter W. Powell, "The Iron Cage Revisited: Institutional Isomorphism and Collective Rationality in Organizational Fields," *American Sociological Review* 48 (1983): 147–60.

47. This section is based largely on DiMaggio and Powell, "The Iron Cage Revisited"; Pugh and Hickson, *Writers on Organizations*; and W. Richard Scott, *Institutions and Organizations* (Thousand Oaks, Calif.: Sage, 1995).

48. Thomas A. Stewart, "Beat the Budget and Astound Your CFO," *Fortune*, 28 October 1996, 187–89.

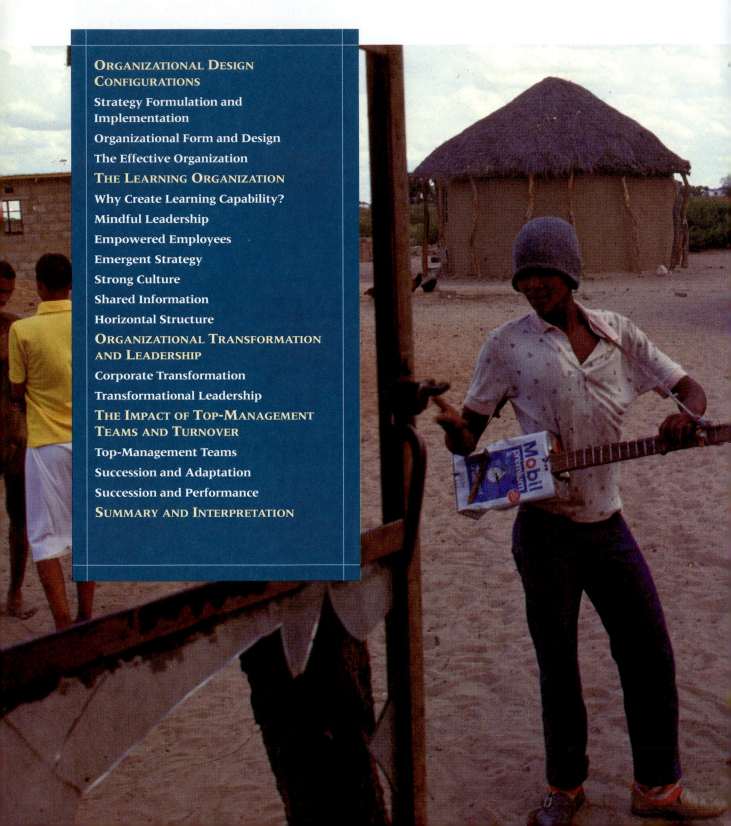

chapter fifteen

Toward the
Learning Organization

A look inside

Kalahari Bushmen

For hundreds of years, the Kalahari Bushmen were nomadic hunters and foragers in the harsh, unpredictable Southern African desert. The Bushmen developed the skills to find water during a drought, to live on reptiles and plants in the absence of game, and to fashion bows and arrows from limited sources. They traveled in bands bound together by ties of kinship and friendship. Their mobility and few possessions enabled Bushmen to switch easily to more successful bands, in this way capitalizing on success wherever it was found over a wide geographical area. The flexible band system was enhanced by values of equality, sharing, and gift giving. A hunter's kill would be used to feed neighbors, who would later reciprocate. Gift giving meant that useful artifacts and utensils were widely shared. Hunting camps had grass huts facing the center of a circle where the cooking hearths were hubs of continuous discussion and social exchanges. The Bushmen also bonded through a deep culture in their camps of shared mythology, stories, and dances.

Enter civilization. In recent years, exposure to material wealth has fostered a transformation. Bushmen now accumulate possessions, which hamper mobility, forcing a life-style shift from foraging to farming. A new community structure has evolved, with families living in separate, permanent huts. Entrances are located for privacy, and hearths have been moved inside. Survival skills have deteriorated, with bows and arrows produced only for curio shops. Without sharing and communication, a hierarchy of authority—the chief—is used to resolve disputes. Tension and conflicts have increased, and the tribe's ability to handle drought and disaster today is nonexistent. No longer are there shared stories and mythology that bind the tribespeople into a community.[1]

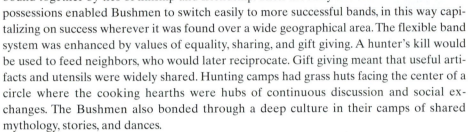

The emerging herder-farmer society resembles a bureaucracy that excels in a stable, safe environment, leaving the Bushmen vulnerable to sudden environmental changes. The hunter-forager society resembles today's entrepreneurial and learning organization, based on little hierarchy, equality of rewards, shared culture, and a flowing, adaptable structure designed to seize opportunities and handle crises.

Many organizations in industrialized societies have evolved toward bureaucratic forms, as discussed in Chapter 5. However, in the face of complex, shifting environments, these organizations no longer work. The hunter-forager society of the Kalahari Bushmen is a metaphor for the learning organization that many companies want to become. Can a bureaucratic herder-farmer society be transformed backward to a skilled, flowing, adaptable hunter-forager society? How can traditional organization structures be transformed into fluid, learning systems?

Purpose of This Chapter

The previous chapter described how today's companies respond to increasing uncertainty and instability through interorganizational collaboration. The purpose of this chapter is to examine another way companies cope with and adapt to rapid changes—by increasing their own ability to learn and change. The chapter integrates materials from previous chapters about organizational design to describe the coming generation of learning organizations. The first section describes how structure, technology, strategy, and other characteristics fit together for organizational effectiveness and identifies the key issues each organization must resolve. Then the learning organization, which resembles the original bands of Kalahari Bushmen, is described. The final sections briefly examine corporate transformation, the role of organizational leadership in revitalizing stagnant companies, and the extent to which top management teams and turnover affect organizational performance.

ORGANIZATIONAL DESIGN CONFIGURATIONS

In this section, we will integrate concepts from earlier chapters. A key task for top leaders is to decide on goals and strategy and then to design the organizational form appropriate for the strategy. By fitting the pieces together into the right configuration, an organization can maintain a high level of effectiveness.

Strategy Formulation and Implementation

The starting point for defining organizational configuration is **strategy**, which is the current set of plans, decisions, and objectives that has been adopted to achieve the organization's goals. **Strategy formulation** includes the activities that lead to establishment of a firm's overall goals and mission and the development of a specific strategic plan as described in Chapter 2.[2] For example, a firm might formulate a strategy of differentiation, low-cost leadership, or focus. **Strategy implementation** is the use of managerial and organizational tools to direct and allocate resources to accomplish strategic objectives.[3] It is the administration and execution of the strategic plan. The concepts of organizational design are especially relevant for implementation. The direction and allocation of resources are accomplished with the tools of organizational structure, control systems, culture, technology, and human resources.

Organizational Form and Design

Organizational form and design are the ultimate expression of strategy implementation. Each chapter of this book has dealt with some aspect of design. Top leaders must design the organization so all parts fit together into a coherent whole to achieve the organization's strategy and purpose.

A framework proposed by Henry Mintzberg[4] suggests that every organization has five parts, as illustrated in Exhibit 15.1. Top management is located at the top of the organization. Middle management is at the intermediate levels, and the technical core includes the people who do the basic work of the organization. The technical support staff are the engineers, researchers, and analysts who are responsible for the formal planning and control of the technical core. The administrative support staff provides indirect services and includes clerical, maintenance, and mail room employees. The five parts of the organization may vary in size and importance depending on the overall environment, strategy, and technology.

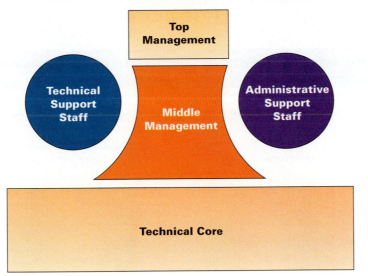

Exhibit 15.1
*The Five Basic Parts
of an Organization*

Source: Based on Henry Mintzberg, *The Structuring of Organizations* (Englewood Cliffs, N.J.: Prentice-Hall, 1979), 215–97; and Henry Mintzberg, "Organization Design: Fashion or Fit?" *Harvard Business Review* 59 (January–February 1981): 103–16.

Mintzberg proposed that these five organizational parts could fit together in five basic configurations, in which environment, goals, power, structure, formalization, technology, and size hang together in identifiable clusters. This framework defines key organizational variables and tells managers the appropriate configuration for specific environments and strategies.

The **five organizational configurations** proposed by Mintzberg are entrepreneurial structure, machine bureaucracy, professional bureaucracy, divisional form, and "adhocracy."[5] A brief description of each configuration follows. Specific organizational characteristics associated with the appropriate configuration for strategy implementation are summarized in Exhibit 15.2.

1. *Entrepreneurial structure.* The organization with an **entrepreneurial structure** is typically a new, small company in the first stage of the organizational life cycle, described in Chapter 5. The organization consists of a top manager and workers in the technical core. Only a few support staffs are required. There is little specialization or formalization. Coordination and control come from the top. The founder has the power and creates the culture. Employees have little discretion, although work procedures are typically informal. This organization is suited to a dynamic environment. It can maneuver quickly and compete successfully with larger, less adaptable organizations. Adaptability is required to establish its market. The organization is not powerful and is vulnerable to sudden changes. Unless adaptable, it will fail.

2. *Machine bureaucracy.* **Machine bureaucracy** describes the bureaucratic organization, also discussed in Chapter 5. This organization is very large, and the technology is routine, often oriented to mass production. Extensive specialization and formalization are present, and key decisions are made at the top. The environment is simple and stable because this organization is not adaptable. The machine bureaucracy is distinguished by large technical and

Exhibit 15.2

Dimensions of Five Organizational Types

Dimension	Entrepreneurial Structure	Machine Bureaucracy	Professional Bureaucracy	Divisional Form	Adhocracy
Strategy and goals:	Growth, survival	Defender; efficiency	Analyzer; effectiveness, quality	Portfolio; profit	Prospector; innovation
Age and size:	Typically young and small	Typically old and large	Varies	Typically old and very large	Typically young
Technology:	Simple	Machines but not automated	Service	Divisible, like machine bureaucracy	Very sophisticated, often automated
Environment:	Simple and dynamic; sometimes hostile	Simple and stable	Complex and stable	Relatively simple and stable; diversified markets	Complex and dynamic
Formalization:	Little	Much	Little	Within divisions	Little
Structure:	Functional	Functional	Functional or product	Product, hybrid	Functional and product (matrix)
Coordination:	Direct supervision	Vertical linkage	Horizontal linkage	Headquarters (HQ) staff	Mutual adjustment
Control:	Clan	Bureaucratic	Clan and bureaucratic	Market and bureaucratic	Clan
Culture:	Developing	Weak	Strong	Subcultures	Strong
Technical support staff:	None	Many	Few	Many at HQ for performance control	Small and within project work
Administrative support staff:	Small	Many	Many to support professionals	Split between HQ and divisions	Many but within project work
Key part of organization:	Top management	Technical staff	Production core	Middle management	Support staff and technical core

Source: Adapted and modified from Henry Mintzberg, *The Structuring of Organizations: A Synthesis of the Research* (Englewood Cliffs, N.J.: Prentice-Hall, 1979), 466–71.

administrative support staffs. Technical support staffs, including engineers, market researchers, financial analysts, and systems analysts are used to scrutinize, routinize, and formalize work in other parts of the organization. The technical support staff is the dominant group in the organization. Machine bureaucracies are often criticized for lack of control by lower employees, lack of innovation, a weak culture, and an alienated workforce, but they are suited to large size, a stable environment, and the goal of efficiency.

3. *Professional bureaucracy.* The distinguishing feature of a **professional bureaucracy** is that the production core is composed of professionals, as in hospitals, universities, and consulting firms. Although the organization is bureaucratized, people within the production core have autonomy. Long training and experience encourage clan control and a strong culture, thereby reducing the need for bureaucratic control structures. These organizations often provide services rather than tangible products, and they exist in complex environments. Most of the power rests with the professionals in the production core. Technical support groups are small or nonexistent, but a large administrative support staff is needed to handle the organization's routine administrative affairs.

4. *Divisional form.* Organizations with a **divisional form** are typically large and are subdivided into product or market groups, as discussed in Chapter 6 on designing organizational structures. There are few liaison devices for coordination among divisions, and the divisional emphasis is on market control using profit and loss statements. The divisional form can be quite formalized within divisions because technologies are often routine. The environment for any division will tend to be simple and stable, although the total organization may serve diverse markets. Many large corporations, such as General Motors, Procter & Gamble, Ford, and Westinghouse, are divisional organizations. Each division is somewhat autonomous, with its own subculture. Centralization exists within divisions, and a headquarters staff may retain some functions, such as planning and research.

5. *Adhocracy.* An **adhocracy** develops to survive in a complex, dynamic environment. The adhocracy resembles the global matrix or transnational structure described in Chapter 7. The technology is sophisticated, as in the aerospace and electronic industries. Adhocracies are typically young or middle-aged and quite large but need to be adaptable. A team-based structure typically emerges with many horizontal linkages and empowered employees. Both technical support staff and the production core have authority over key production elements. The organization has an elaborate division of labor but is not formalized. Employee professionalism is high, cultural values are strong, and clan control is stressed. With decentralization, people at any level may be involved in decision making. The adhocracy is almost the opposite of the machine bureaucracy in terms of structure, power relationships, and environment.

The point of the five configurations is that top management can design an organization to achieve harmony and fit among key elements. For example, a machine bureaucracy is appropriate for a strategy of efficiency in a stable environment; but to impose a machine bureaucracy in a hostile and dynamic environment is a mistake. Managers can implement strategy by designing the correct structural configuration to fit the situation.

The Effective Organization

An additional idea proposed by Mintzberg is that for an organization to be effective, it must manage the interplay of seven basic forces.[6] The organization's form can be designed to help manage this interplay as illustrated in Exhibit 15.3.

Exhibit 15.3
*A System of Forces
and Forms in
Organizations*

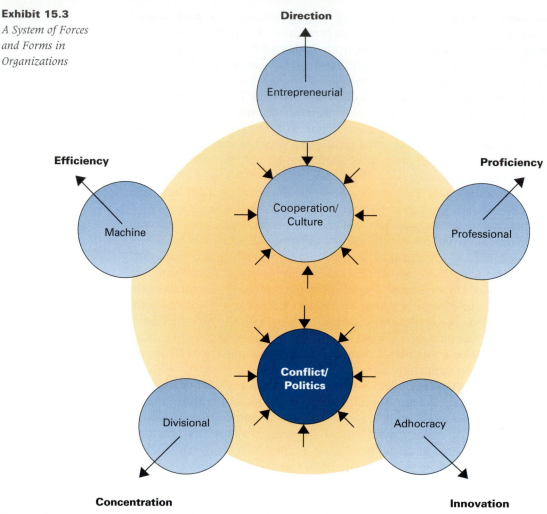

The first force is direction, which is the sense of vision, goals, and mission for the organization. Chapter 2 described how managers set a strategic direction for the organization by establishing a mission and goals. The entrepreneurial form best typifies a single organizational direction and common purpose.

The next force is efficiency, which is the need to minimize costs and increase benefits. The best known structure for efficiency is the machine bureaucracy because it focuses on rationalization and standardization.

The third force, proficiency, means carrying out tasks with a high level of knowledge and skill. Proficiency is the advantage of the professional bureaucracy, which uses highly trained professionals to achieve excellence. Recall from Chapter 2 that managers can also develop internal organization characteristics of strategic orientation, top management, organization design, and corporate culture that contribute to excellence.

The fourth force, innovation, discussed in detail in Chapter 8, refers to the organization's need to develop new products and services to adapt to a changing external environment. The adhocracy form of organization is best for meeting the need for innovation and change.

The fifth force in Exhibit 15.3 is concentration, which means focusing organizational efforts on particular markets. As we learned in Chapter 6, divisional organizations achieve the advantage of concentration by focusing activities on specific products or markets.

Two additional forces within the pentagon of Exhibit 15.3 are cooperation/culture and conflict/politics. Cooperation is the result of common culture values and reflects the need for harmony and cooperation among a diverse set of people. Chapter 10 described how leaders can build strong, adaptive corporate cultures, and Chapter 13 examined the emerging view that cooperation, not competition or conflict, is the best way to achieve high performance. Conflict can cause negative politics (discussed in Chapter 12) and a splitting apart of individuals and departments because of the need for individual success and recognition.

An important purpose of organizational form is to enable an organization to achieve the right balance among the seven forces. An effective organization such as 3M stresses innovation, whereas an organization such as Wal-Mart stresses efficiency and proficiency in its design. A conglomeration such as Hanson Industries stresses concentration; Southwest Airlines succeeds by creating a strong culture based on participation and cooperation.

Each organization has to find out what works. It cannot maximize all needs simultaneously. By understanding these forces and designing the right structure to achieve strategic outcomes, leaders can create effective organizations. This is a continual leadership process, because a configuration may work for a period of time and then need to be reorganized to achieve a new period of harmony and effectiveness.[7] Ultimately, organizational form will fit the needs of formulated strategy and the environment.

THE LEARNING ORGANIZATION

The field of management is undergoing a worldwide, fundamental shift. This shift was described in Chapter 1 as a transition from a modern to a postmodern organization paradigm and is reflected in The New Paradigm boxes throughout this book that describe how companies are transforming away from traditional, hierarchical management toward full participation by every employee. The shift is also reflected in new organizational forms, such as the network organization, virtual corporation, and horizontal organization described in Chapter 7. The remainder of this chapter focuses on the newest way of thinking about organizations brought about by this paradigm shift.

The management shift has been prompted by two accelerating trends. The first is the increasing rate of change brought by global competition. Organizations must adapt faster and be able to do more things well. The second trend is a fundamental change in organizational technologies. Traditional organizations were designed to manage machine-based technologies, with a primary need for stable and efficient use of physical resources, such as in mass production. However, new organizations are knowledge-based, which means they are designed to handle ideas and information, with each employee becoming an expert in one or several conceptual tasks. Rather than striving for efficiency, each employee in knowledge-based companies must continuously learn and be able to identify and solve problems in his or her domain of activity.[8]

In this new world order, the responsibility of management is to create organizational learning capability. In many industries, the ability to learn and change faster than competitors may be the only sustainable competitive advantage. Hence, many companies are redesigning themselves toward something called the learning organization.

Managers began thinking about the concept of the learning organization after the publication of Peter Senge's book, *The Fifth Discipline: The Art and Practice of Learning Organizations*, in which Senge describes the kinds of changes managers need to undergo to help their organizations adapt to an increasingly chaotic world.[9] His original concepts about how managers build learning capability have evolved to include characteristics of the organization itself. There is no single model of the learning organization. The learning organization is an attitude or philosophy about what an organization is and the role of employees. The notion of the learning organization may replace any of the designs described in Exhibit 15.2. The learning organization is a paradigm shift to a new way of thinking about organizations.

In the **learning organization**, everyone is engaged in identifying and solving problems, enabling the organization to continuously experiment, improve, and increase its capability. The essential value of the learning organization is problem solving, in contrast to the traditional organization that was designed for efficiency. In the learning organization, employees engage in problem identification, which means understanding customer needs. Employees also solve problems, which means putting things together in unique ways to meet customer needs. The organization in this way adds value by defining new needs and solving them, which is accomplished more often with ideas and information than with physical products. When physical products are produced, ideas and information still provide the competitive advantage because products are changing to meet new and challenging needs in the environment.[10]

Why Create Learning Capability?

Consider three traditional ways of gaining competitive advantage through financial, marketing, and technological capabilities, as illustrated in Exhibit 15.4.[11] These traditional sources of competitive advantage are taught in most business schools. Financial capability pertains to financial efficiencies as reflected in wise investment decisions and a profitable return to investors. Marketing capability pertains to building the right products, establishing a close relationship with customers, and effectively marketing products and services. Technology capability refers to technical innovation, research and development, new products, and up-to-date production technologies.

In a world that is shifting from machines to ideas, however, these traditional capabilities now require organizational learning capability, also illustrated in Exhibit 15.4. The learning component of competitive advantage refers to the ability to advance financial, marketing, and technological capabilities to a higher level by disengaging employees from traditional notions of efficiency and engaging them in active problem solving that helps the organization change. The more learning capability is increased, the more adaptable and successful the organization.

Learning capability is not about learning the principles of accounting or marketing. It means enhancing the organization's and each person's capacity to do things they were not able to do previously. This is knowledge acquired not from textbooks and past experience but from actually engaging in independent action, experimenting, and using trial and error. Experimentation extends from an accounting clerk trying a new software program to the organization's strategy to

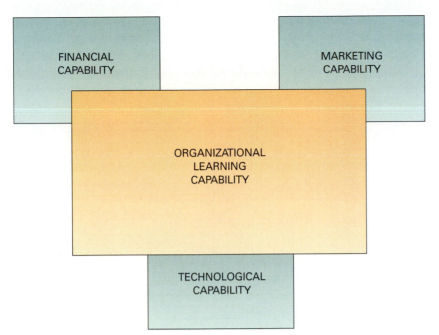

Exhibit 15.4
Organizational Learning Capability—A Critical Source of Competitive Advantage

Source: Adapted from Dave Ulrich and Dale Lake, "Organizational Capability: Creating Competitive Advantage," *Academy of Management Executive* 5, no. 1 (1991): 77. Used by permission.

always modify and update products to meet changing customer needs. Increasing knowledge is not something stored intellectually or in computers; it reflects expanding know-how, similar to the increase in capability gained from learning to ride a bike or paint a portrait.[12]

Although the learning organization cannot be precisely defined, it is an extension of the concepts described in this book and is typically associated with certain characteristics. Exhibit 15.5 indicates how the learning organization goes beyond both the traditional hierarchy and the horizontal organization described in Chapters 6 and 7. In the traditional hierarchy, top management was responsible for directing organizational strategy and took responsibility for thinking and acting. Employees were simply factors of efficient production to be assigned to routine tasks that did not change. The breakthrough of the horizontal organization is that employees are empowered to think and act to design work methods on behalf of the organization. Although top managers still provide a primary strategic direction, employees have great latitude in executing this direction and can sometimes identify and anticipate customer needs.

The further breakthrough of the learning organization is that employees contribute to strategic direction to an extent not before achieved. Employees identify needs so that strategy emerges from the accumulated activities of employee teams serving customers.[13] The strategy emerges within the overall vision of the organization's future that all employees share, so innovations and improvements by respective teams add to the organizational whole. The learning organization resembles a web in which different parts of the organization are adapting and changing independently while at the same time contributing to the company mission.

In addition to increased employee responsibility over both organizational means and ends, the shift to a learning organization philosophy is associated with

Exhibit 15.5

Evolution of the Learning Organization

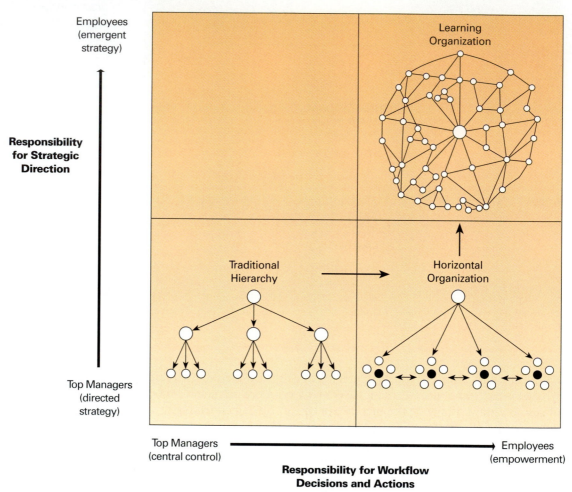

mindful leadership, a strong culture, widespread information sharing, and a systematic shift in formal structures and systems. These characteristics of the learning organization are illustrated in Exhibit 15.6, and each is described in the following sections.

Mindful Leadership

The learning organization starts in the minds of the organization's leaders. The learning organization requires mindful leadership—people who understand it and can help other people succeed. Leaders in a learning organization have three distinct roles.

1. *Design the social architecture.* The social architecture pertains to behind-the-scenes behavior and attitudes. The first task of organization design is to develop the governing ideas of purpose, mission, and core values by which employees will be guided. The mindful leader defines the foundation of pur-

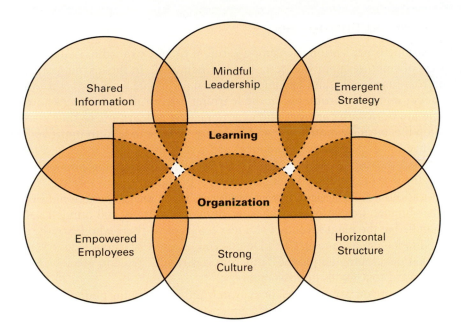

Exhibit 15.6
Interacting Elements in a Learning Organization

pose and core values. Second, new policies, strategies, and structures that support the learning organization are designed and put into place. These structures reinforce new behavior. Third, leaders design effective learning processes. Creating learning processes and ensuring they are improved and understood require leader initiative. With these design actions, the learning organization idea can take hold.[14]

2. *Create a shared vision.* The shared vision is a picture of an ideal future for the organization. This may be created by the leader or by employee discussion, but the company vision must be widely understood and imprinted throughout the organization. This vision represents desired long-term outcomes, hence employees are free to identify and solve immediate problems on their own that help achieve the vision. However, without a shared vision that provides harmony and unity of mind, employee actions will not add to the whole. Without a strong vision, employees may fragment and move in different directions.

3. *Servant leadership.* Learning organizations are built by servant leaders who devote themselves to others and to the organization's vision. The image of a leader as a single actor who builds an organization by herself is not appropriate for the learning organization. Leaders give away power, ideas, and information. The learning organization requires leaders who devote themselves to the organization. Indeed, many people become leaders who serve others and the organization.[15] One example of a servant leader is George Sztykiel, chairman of Spartan Motors. Spartan builds chassis for fire trucks and motor homes. Sztykiel's attitude is reflected in his statements to new employees: "Welcome. We think this is a good corporation. It is run on the same principles that a family is, because we think that's the most effective way human beings have managed to get along." Sztykiel also said, "I am not the boss. I am the number one servant of this corporation." At Spartan, everyone has equal opportunity, and all share in the gains of continuous learning.[16]

Empowered Employees

The learning organization uses empowerment to an extraordinary degree. The process of empowerment was described in Chapter 12. In the learning organization, cross-functional teams become the basic unit. People work together to identify needs and solve problems. In the learning organization, leaders know that people are born with curiosity and experience joy in learning, so they strive to develop this intrinsic motivation and curiosity, which can lead to improved performance. When Monsanto's chemical and nylon plant in Pensacola, Florida, gave teams the responsibility and authority for hiring, purchasing, and job assignments, the plant experienced increases in both profitability and safety.[17] At AES Corporation, a Connecticut power producer, there are no functional departments—finance, operations, purchasing, human resources, and public relations are handled at the plant level by volunteer teams of workers who learn the skills needed to handle each task. CEO Dennis Bakke and Chairman Roger Sant believe that developing employees' inherent desire to learn and grow is the best route toward continuous improvement.[18]

Learning organizations invest heavily in training, providing abundant learning opportunities for everyone.[19] For example, at Foldcraft, a manufacturer of institutional seating in Kenyon, Minnesota, president Chuck Mayhew teaches a six-hour class in the basics of business. Working with groups of thirty to thirty-five employees at a time, Mayhew first focuses on employees' personal finances and gradually leads workers into discussion of Foldcraft's financial statements. The class ends with Mayhew talking individually with workers about their specific job and how it impacts the company's profitability.[20]

Training workers to understand the business and giving them the power to make decisions based on what they know helps to create a sense of ownership and pride among employees. At Springfield Remanufacturing Corporation, 30 percent of everyone's job is learning. People are expected to think and act as owners of their part of the business, because real owners need not be told what to do. They can figure it out for themselves. Employees are given the knowledge and information needed to make a decision and are trusted to act in the best interest of the company.[21]

AES Corporation pushes empowerment to a remarkable level to create a sense of ownership and a climate of trust among workers. Not only do teams of workers make virtually all operational decisions, but an ad hoc team of coal handlers and maintenance workers actually manages a $33 million investment fund for AES. The team has consistently matched, and once bettered, the returns of its corporate counterparts.[22] The learning organization increases individual responsibility for achieving the company's vision, allowing workers to be intellectually excited and engaged in the struggles and successes that come from difficult challenges.

Emergent Strategy

Business strategy emerges bottom up as well as top down. Since many employees are in touch with customers, suppliers, and new technologies, they identify needs and solutions. Customer needs may result in new products that define the company's strategy. Employees at the top and the bottom develop sensitive antennae for technological and market change. They look at what customers ask for, and they look at what the customer may need tomorrow. Hundreds, perhaps thousands of people are in touch with the environment, providing much data about external needs. This information accumulates into the strategy. For example, Nucor Steel developed a strategy of low-cost production that reflects the vision of CEO Ken Iverson, who heard about and took a $270 million chance on new technology for a thin-slab minimill. Employees, however, helped acquire the new technology and found new products and processes that used it. The result was astonishing, with Nucor producing a ton of sheet steel in forty-five man-minutes versus three man-hours for big steelmakers.[23]

Strategy also emerges from a network of partnerships with suppliers, customers, and even competitors. As discussed in Chapter 14, organizations develop partnerships—sometimes with legal contracts, sometimes with informal agreements—that share information and create emerging strategies. The learning organization does not act autonomously. Information from partners provides data to the organization about new strategic needs and directions.[24] More companies are evolving into alliances, joint ventures, and electronic linkages, which were discussed in Chapters 7 and 9. Organizations become collaborators rather than competitors, experimenting to find the best way to learn and adapt.

Some companies, such as Chevron, Andersen Windows, and Springfield Remanufacturing, encourage a free exchange of information with other organizations, allowing teams to regularly visit and observe their "best practices." These leading edge companies believe that a mutual sharing of good ideas is the best way to keep their organizations competitive.[25] Strategy in the learning organization can emerge from anywhere.

Strong Culture

What does the culture of a learning organization look like? Corporate cultures were described in Chapter 10, and the learning organization reflects those values and more. To really become a learning organization, a company must have the following values:

1. *The whole is more valuable than the part, and boundaries are minimized.*[26] The learning organization stresses the company as a whole system. Only by understanding the overall vision and learning to improve the whole will the learning organization succeed. The culture also reduces boundaries, as Jack Welch is trying to do at General Electric. Welch clearly recognized the importance of culture when he told a group of employees: "A company can boost productivity by restructuring, removing bureaucracy, and downsizing, but it cannot sustain high productivity without cultural change."[27] Welch wants to create a culture of "boundarylessness," and is striving to break down barriers among departments, divisions, and with external organizations. Removing boundaries enables the free flow of people, ideas, and information that allows coordinated action to innovate and adapt to an uncertain and changing environment. Reducing boundaries also means more partnerships with suppliers, customers, and competitors.

2. *The culture also values a sense of community and compassion and caring for one another.*[28] People like to belong to something, and the learning organization becomes a place for creating a web of relationships that nurtures and develops each person within the community. People learn and experiment as part of a team and as part of a larger community.

Activities that create differences among people are discarded. At Intel Corporation, everyone has a small, open cubicle, including CEO Andrew Grove. This open environment, which is increasingly being used at companies including Aluminum Company of America, Procter & Gamble, and Hewlett-Packard, reflects the dissolution of old hierarchies and the emphasis on interaction and cooperation.[29] The learning organization also discards status symbols such as executive dining rooms and reserved parking spots. Caring, egalitarian cultures provide the safety for experimentation, frequent mistakes, and failures that enable learning.

Shared Information

The learning organization is flooded with information. To identify needs and solve problems, people have to be aware of what's going on. Formal data about budgets, profits, and departmental expenses are available to everyone. Each person is free to exchange information with anyone in the company. In the move toward information- and idea-based organizations, information sharing reaches extraordinary levels. Like the oil in a car's engine, information is not allowed to get low. Managers believe too much information sharing is better than too little. Employees can pick what they need for their tasks.

The president of Quad/Graphics is hooked via e-mail to sixty-five hundred employees. He receives and answers approximately sixty messages a day.[30] Emery Olcott, president and CEO of Canberra Industries, Inc., prefers to communicate in person with employees, particularly when the company is facing difficult issues such as downsizing or relocation.[31]

The learning organization also encourages widespread communication among all employees; ideas are shared throughout the organization and may be implemented anywhere. At the Danish company Oticon, all incoming mail is scanned into a computer and, with few exceptions, anyone can access anyone else's mail. The same applies to financial documents.[32]

At Granite Rock Company, employees are flooded with information that includes survey feedback from customers, the charting of one hundred operational variables within the company, and outside speakers talking about changes in the industry. Each employee is informed of events in the company and its environment.[33] Employees at Springfield Remanufacturing meet in group sessions where department heads go over all production and financial figures, encouraging questions. Employees also have access to daily printouts from cost accounting that detail every job in the plant.[34] The days of managers hoarding data to make decisions are long gone in learning organizations. This trend toward complete information sharing is discussed further in Book Mark 15.0.

Horizontal Structure

In the learning organization, the formal vertical structure that created distance between managers and workers is disbanded. So too are pay and budget systems that pit individual against individual and department against department. As described in Chapter 7, teams are the fundamental structure in a horizontal organization. People work together along a production process to create an output for a customer. Teams of employees produce the product or service, and they deal with the customer, making changes and improvements as they go along. In learning companies, bosses are practically eliminated, with team members taking responsibility for training, safety, scheduling vacations, purchases, and decisions

Book Mark 15.0

Have You Read About This?

Open-Book Management: The Coming Business Revolution

by John Case

Information—particularly financial information—is power, and the traditional approach to business has treated financial data as the exclusive property of management. Yet throughout the business world, today's managers are sharing information and power with employees at all levels of the company. By sharing financial information with employees, teaching them what the numbers mean, and then giving them a financial stake in the business, open-book management helps to create empowered workers who act more like owners than hired hands.

The Open Book Philosophy

John Case presents open-book management as a philosophy, not a magic formula, and emphasizes that it requires a fundamental shift in the culture of most organizations. His book, *Open-Book Management: The Coming Business Revolution*, is a straightforward guide to help companies make the transition. Case focuses on five basic principles needed to successfully implement open-book management:

- *Get the information out there.* Companies must identify the financial data crucial to success and share it with all employees.
- *Teach employees business literacy.* Employees need to be taught what the numbers mean and what effect their own performance has on the bottom line.
- *Create an atmosphere of trust.* Managers should expect employees to be skeptical and work to develop the trust necessary to make open-book management succeed.
- *Develop a system of accountability and responsibility.* Case calls this "empowerment with brains" because it tells employees "what the destination is and how to gauge their progress toward it."
- *Give everyone a stake in the company's success.* The only way employees can think like owners is when they participate in the success of the company. Employees should reap the rewards of improved performance.

Making the Transition

The book offers a number of case studies that show how open-book management has led to increased productivity, improved motivation, and higher profits. Case emphasizes, however, that this "new way of thinking about business" is not easy to execute in the complex social structure of organizations. He offers two suggestions: (1) have a champion who is responsible for keeping open-book management a top priority; and (2) start slowly—you don't need to scrap your current system all at once. Finally, Case offers this word of advice: "Be patient." It takes time for employees to understand the financial data, to take responsibility for results, and to start thinking like owners, but the success stories presented here suggest it's well worth the effort.

Open-Book Management, by John Case, is published by HarperBusiness.

---

about work and pay. Boundaries between departments are reduced or eliminated. In addition, boundaries between organizations become more diffuse. As discussed in the previous chapter, companies are collaborating in unprecedented ways. The network organization and the emerging virtual organization, also described in Chapter 7, consist of groups of companies that join together to attain certain goals or exploit specific opportunities. These new structures provide the flexibility needed to adapt to rapidly changing competitive conditions.

Incentive systems are also changed in the learning organization. Studies have shown a connection between pay systems and worker commitment and performance.[35] In addition, as we learned in Chapter 13, incentive systems can dramatically affect whether employees cooperate or compete with one another. The learning organization encourages a cooperative model to keep employees learning and growing. Solar Press, Inc. went through a series of pay system transformations to find an incentive system that encourages growth and learning of employees. The initial system gave a bonus to each employee without regard to company performance or employee learning. A new system awarded production bonuses by team. This increased productivity but also pitted teams against one another and became an administrative nightmare. The final system gives profit-sharing bonuses to everyone in the company based on company performance. This system emphasizes teamwork and interdepartmental coordination.[36]

Employees at Spartan Motors also share in company profits. Perhaps even more important, the chief executive earns only four times as much as the lowest paid worker.[37] This narrow pay range signals the egalitarian nature of the company. At Springfield Remanufacturing, workers get 10 percent bonuses when the company goals are met. Learning is further enhanced by paying $500 for each new idea adopted; one employee made a quick $7,500 and appreciated being rewarded for thinking and acting.[38] Some companies are moving to a system called pay for knowledge, which gives workers a raise for each new task learned.

Although no organization represents a perfect example of a learning organization, one excellent example is Chaparral Steel, which has been called a learning laboratory.

In Practice 15.1   *Chaparral Steel*

Chaparral Steel is the tenth largest U.S. steel producer, and it has won significant international recognition for quality and productivity. Chaparral produces eleven hundred tons of steel per worker each year compared to the U.S. average of 350 tons. Started nearly twenty years ago, it has become an experimental laboratory for the latest techniques of learning organizations.

What makes Chaparral so effective? Managers articulate a clear vision—to lead the world in the low-cost, safe production of high-quality steel—along with the values of egalitarianism and respect for the individual. Everyone participates. Everyone takes responsibility for solving problems. When a cooling hose burst, a group of operators, a welder, a foreman, and a buyer all responded because they saw the problem. There is no assumption that other people are expected to do a job. Because employees know the vision and values, supervisors do not micromanage. The organization has few supervisors, and only two levels of hierarchy separate the CEO from operators in the rolling mill.

Employees are rewarded for learning new skills and for performance. Ideas are contributed by just about everybody. Everyone is paid a salary rather than an hourly wage—hence, everyone acts like owners and managers. People are also rewarded with bonuses from company profits, which are shared with the entire community, including janitors and secretaries.

Everyone contributes to developing and sharing knowledge. A steel plant is deliberately held to fewer than one thousand employees so that people can share information easily. An employee experimenting with new equipment will tell other people how it works. Employees who visit a competitor explain to others what they learned. There are no staff positions and no boundaries between departments because there are few departments. Everyone is considered a salesperson and is free to interact with potential customers. Security guards do data entry while on night duty. There is no research and development department because employees on the line are responsible for experimenting with new techniques and products. To reinforce continuous learning, most employees attend some school, and many are teachers of other employees in formal classes. Moreover, using new ideas to benefit the company takes precedence over individual ownership of ideas, so knowledge is shared liberally.

Experimentation is rampant. The cultural value is if you have an idea, try it. First-level managers can authorize thousands of dollars for employee experiments. Everyone is encouraged to push beyond current knowledge. This involves risk, which is another cultural value. Employees learn to tolerate, even welcome, risk on a production line that is very expensive to shut down.

Chaparral also networks outside the organization. Employees travel constantly, scanning for new ideas at trade shows and other companies. Teams of employees that include vice presidents and shop people travel together to investigate a new technology.

Chaparral is so good at what it does that it welcomes competitors to visit. A competitor can be shown everything it does and yet take away nothing. The reason is that the learning organization must be created by leadership, culture, and empowered people. Most other steelmakers have been unable to achieve this, because they don't have the commitment or the vision.[39]

Chaparral Steel illustrates the extension of an organization beyond horizontal organizing toward a true learning organization. The leadership provides organization design, a shared vision, and an attitude of serving employees. The culture emphasizes community values, providing the caring and compassion that supports risk taking. In addition, there are no boundaries separating departments. People are empowered to the point where no one has to take orders if he or she feels the order is wrong. Everyone operates autonomously yet is part of a team and a community doing what is best for the whole. Chaparral is flooded with information from internal experiments and external companies. The formal structure and systems reinforce horizontal teams and companywide performance.

ORGANIZATIONAL TRANSFORMATION AND LEADERSHIP

Almost every organization today is struggling to adapt to rapid social and economic changes, and many are incorporating elements of the learning organization, moving toward greater information sharing, empowering employees, and changing corporate cultures and structures to be more flexible and adaptive. Yet, many organizations are not ready to implement the learning organization philosophy. They don't know how; or they are just struggling to survive and managers are busy cutting costs and revising procedures to improve efficiency. Companies may be in a period of decline because of poor economic conditions, global competition, or bad management. Some top executives do not understand the skills needed to implement the learning organization philosophy. For companies like these, the dominant issue is transformation, which can set their companies on the road toward becoming learning organizations. Transformation is typically completed in three stages under the guidance of a transformational leader.

Corporate Transformation

As the head of one large U.S. corporation said: "The tragedy of top management . . . is that it is so much more reassuring to stay as you are, even though you know the result will be certain failure, than to try to make a fundamental change when you cannot be certain that the effort will succeed."[40] The process of organizational change is complex and messy, and many top managers stick with the known because of fear of the unknown. For organizations to transform, there often has to be intense pressure to improve or even a threat to the company's very survival. More organizations than ever before are facing such a threat today because of complex and rapid changes, as we have discussed throughout this book. Today's organizations must confront the "chaos of constant change," to survive the whirlwind.[41]

The transformation of a company suffering from decline or needing major change typically involves three phases.[42] The first is **crisis**, in which managers realize that the company is now or will soon be uncompetitive unless changes are made. In this stage, managers often downsize the workforce, cut out several layers of management, and lower production costs. The old mold is broken. Moving through the crisis involves simplification by reducing functions and product lines. Costs are reduced by instituting controls and lowering expenses. Assets may be sold and some units may be relocated or shut down. Also during this period the problems are analyzed by leaders to plan the subsequent turnaround. Leaders also create a new vision about what the organization can become in the future.

The second phase is to **reinvest** organizational capability. Now that the firm's competitive scope has been simplified, expenses are under control, and size has been reduced, the organization stabilizes. Top leaders will mobilize commitment to the new vision, using symbolic management techniques described in Chapter 10. Organization structure and corporate culture will be changed to reflect the new mission and goals. Leaders will invest in new equipment to enhance technological capability and in new marketing and financial programs to improve sales and show a profit. The most important focus of this phase, however, is investing in human factors and organizational capability by implementing a shared mindset, empowering workers, and creating capacity for change and future growth.

The final phase is **rebuilding**, wherein the organization begins to grow. The focus shifts away from efficiency toward innovation and branching out for growth. New cultural values and behavior patterns have become institutionalized so that the organization can continue to adapt and change.[43] Leaders may reposition products or decrease prices to penetrate new markets or may add new product lines. Organizational expansion becomes the priority, with new people hired and support functions such as research and development and human resource management increased.

Each company undergoes transformation in its own way, but some aspects of these three stages are typically present. A major corporate transformation took place for Navistar International Corporation, previously known as International Harvester, during the 1980s.

| In Practice 15.2 | *Navistar International Corporation* |

In the early 1980s, Navistar was forced to the brink of bankruptcy by mismanagement, a strike, soaring interest rates, and increased competition. To stave off bankruptcy, the company was restructured and downsized. Several businesses were divested, plants were closed, and staff was reduced. In one decision, fully half of the company was divested by the sale of its tractor division to Tenneco.

The reduction in workforce was handled well. Outplacement centers were established to help all employees, severance pay was provided, and health and life insurance benefits were extended.

After the initial crisis and trauma, Navistar moved into a stable position and began reinvesting in organizational capability. Team-building workshops and staff effectiveness sessions were held. These activities mobilized commitment against the traditional hierarchical, nonparticipative management philosophy that had been deeply ingrained. Even some board members went to off-site retreats to identify new values for the future. A new statement of values was written, as was a new mission statement, which helped institutionalize the new concern for employees. More power was given to the human resource department, and corporate decision making was decentralized.

By 1987, Navistar was growing again. It introduced three new truck products. A new performance evaluation and compensation system was installed that gave leaders flexibility to reward high performance. Continuous improvement teams were formed to make Navistar competitive. Moreover, Navistar focused exclusively on truck and engine manufacturing, devoting all of its energies to grow in those businesses rather than branch out to other fields.

The outcome was an astonishing success. Against all odds, Navistar went from precipitous decline to revitalization and is now a growing, healthy, self-renewing organization.[44]

Navistar had reached a crisis and yet was able to rebound through decisive contraction, the intelligent reconstruction of organizational capability, and rebuilding with a new focus on trucks and engines. It is an exceptional story of what leaders can do to save a major company.

Transformational Leadership

Leadership is perhaps the most widely studied topic in the organization sciences. What kind of people can lead an organization through major changes? One type of leadership that has a substantial impact on organizations is transformational leadership.

Transformational leaders are characterized by the ability to bring about change, innovation, and entrepreneurship. Transformational leaders motivate followers to not just follow them personally but to believe in the vision of corporate transformation, to recognize the need for revitalization, to sign on for the new vision, and to help institutionalize a new organizational process.[45]

Throughout previous chapters, we have discussed the need for large-scale changes in organizations—whether to implement a new corporate culture or self-managed team structure, grow to a new stage in the life cycle, or expand internationally. A massive administrative change involves a fundamental transformation of mission, structure, and the political and cultural systems of an organization to provide a new level of organizational capability.[46] In a situation of crisis or rapid change, a transformational leader should emerge who can impose major changes on the organization. To do so, the transformational leader must successfully achieve the following three activities.[47]

1. *Creation of a new vision.* The vision of a desired future state will articulate that the organization must break free of previous patterns and that old structures, processes, and activities are no longer useful. The leader must be able to spread the vision throughout the organization. At AT&T, a new strategic vision was articulated under the leadership of CEO Robert Allen. Following the breakup of AT&T in 1984, the company quickly lost market share and was a dinosaur on the brink of extinction when Allen was hired. He spent time and energy spreading his new vision throughout the organization, seeing his primary goal as "helping our people learn how to win again."[48] Although leaders must involve managers and employees throughout the organization through task forces or other mechanisms, they alone are ultimately responsible for initiating a new vision.

2. *Mobilization of commitment.* Widespread acceptance of the new mission and vision is critical. At General Motors, Roger Smith took nine hundred top executives on a five-day retreat to discuss his vision and gain their commitment. At Siemens Rolm, a U.S. telecommunications business owned by Siemens AG of Germany, six hundred managers attended a three-day institute and then went back and mobilized commitment to the new vision in their own units.[49] Large scale, discontinuous change requires special commitment, or it will be resisted as inconsistent with traditional organizational goals and activities.

3. *Institutionalization of change.* The new practices, actions, and values must be permanently adopted. This means major resources must be devoted to training programs, retreats, and employee gatherings to implement the new organizational style. Changes may involve the technical, financial, and marketing systems as well as administrative structures and control systems. A long time period, perhaps several years, may be required for the leader to bring about full implementation. The transformational leader must be persistent to move the organization toward a new way of doing and thinking. The new system may alter power and status and revise interaction patterns. New executives may be hired who display values and behaviors appropriate for the new order of things. The new system is then institutionalized and made permanent.

One example of a leader with transformational qualities is the CEO of Corsair Communications.

In Practice 15.3	*Corsair Communications Inc.*

Like big defense contractors everywhere, California-based TRW was forced to find commercial applications for many of its products. One good prospect, developed by the top-secret ESL division, was a technology for identifying the source of electronic transmissions, which had significant commercial potential for inhibiting fraudulent cellular telephone use. Corsair Communications was created as a spinoff company, to be owned 20 percent by TRW, 60 percent by venture capitalists, and 20 percent by its employees. When Mary Ann Byrnes was hired as CEO, Corsair already had a product (although it was far from perfected), a multimillion dollar contract with a cellular carrier, and a group of first-rate engineers. Everything was in place to build the new business except the glue that would hold it together.

Byrnes knew she had to teach a group of government contract engineers, who were accustomed to working what one called a "10%-of-the-day kind of job," to compete as entrepreneurs. Today, Corsair is thriving and growing rapidly, and most agree it is due to Byrnes's leadership. Byrnes's vision was to create a culture that communicated a sense of shared responsibility and destiny—of everyone pulling together to serve the customer and sharing in the success or failure. She started by allowing workers to make the decisions they would have to live with—for example, out of a group of sixty engineers, Byrnes had to pick thirty, so she allowed the engineers themselves to decide who would stay and who would go. Later, she let those who stayed help select the new vice president of engineering. She set up cross-functional teams that work face-to-face with customers and began sharing all information with employees. Companywide pizza lunches enhance information sharing as well as team spirit. And, when a big check comes in, employees don't just hear about it—the check gets passed around so everyone can see it, touch it, and realize they had a part in making it happen. The sense of ownership and shared destiny is strengthened because employees themselves own part of the company.

Corsair's culture has become its major competitive weapon. By trusting her workers, Byrnes has created an environment that motivates employees and allows them to get the job done. For example, when engineers told Byrnes they would need six months to solve one particular technological problem, she took them at their word and told them to get to work. At ESL, managers had insisted they do it in six weeks, and the problem *never* got solved. At Corsair, the engineers made their six-month deadline, and subsequent goals have been met even earlier than projected.[50]

THE IMPACT OF TOP-MANAGEMENT TEAMS AND TURNOVER

So far, this chapter has described how top managers are responsible for defining organizational design configurations, creating organizational learning capability, and leading an organization. Two additional issues related to leadership are whether top management can truly have an impact on organizational performance and how executive turnover impacts organizations.

Top-Management Teams

Recent research on organizational leadership has explored the notion of top-management teams—as opposed to an individual executive being responsible for the entire company. The makeup of the top-management group is believed to affect the development of organizational capability and the ability to exploit strategic opportunities. A team provides a range of aptitudes and skills to deal with complex organizational situations. The configuration of the top-management team is believed by many researchers to be more important for organizational success than the personality characteristics of the CEO. For example, the size, diversity, attitudes, and skills of the team affect patterns of communication and collaboration, which in turn affect company performance.[51]

The emerging focus on top-management teams is more realistic in some ways than focusing on individual leadership. In a complex environment, a single leader cannot do all things. An effective team has a better chance of identifying and implementing a successful strategy, of providing an accurate interpretation of the environment, and of developing internal capability based on empowered employees and a shared mind-set. Without a capable and effectively interacting top-management team, a company cannot adapt readily in a shifting environment.

There are a number of issues that can prevent top-management teams from providing effective leadership. Four common problems are fragmentation, intense conflict, the emergence of groupthink, and inadequate capabilities of one or more top executives.[52] The most damaging problem may be *fragmentation*, which means the top-management team is not a team at all, but rather a group of executives each pursuing his or her own agenda. This can lead to the negative use of political activity, as discussed in Chapter 12. In addition, as we saw in Chapter 13, *conflict* that is too strong or becomes focused on personal rather than organizational issues can seriously limit team effectiveness. However, the complete suppression of conflict is also detrimental to performance because it can lead to *groupthink*, in which members agree, for the sake of harmony and cohesion, to decisions that prove to be unsound. Top-management teams need to engage in serious debate to reach sound decisions. Finally, when one or more team members do not perform effectively or engage in shortsighted thinking and be-havior, the team and the company can suffer.

An effective top-management team is a balancing act, as is an effective organ-ization. The top executive still plays a critical role as leader of the team and can help to ensure effectiveness by striving for gradual staggered turnover of team members, setting up incentive systems and other mechanisms that encourage col-laboration rather than conflict, and providing frequent opportunities for interac-tion and communication.[53] The top-management team at Johnson & Johnson, for example, meets almost daily for lunch. Although the agenda is flexible, the team is always focused on significant organizational issues. At General Electric, Jack Welch's commitment to candor and open information promotes a healthy de-bate of ideas among top executives. Considering that no one manager can do it alone in today's complex business world, bringing unity of purpose to the top-management team may be the most important challenge a top executive faces. In the following sections, we turn to a discussion of how changes in top manage-ment affect organizations.

Succession and Adaptation

One finding from succession research is that, for an organization as a whole, pe-riodic management turnover is a form of organizational adaptation. In organiza-tions characterized by turbulent environments, the turnover of organizational leaders is greater.[54] Such organizations are more difficult to manage, so new en-ergy and vitality are needed on a frequent basis. Today, for example, firms in high-tech industries, such as Apple Computer, America Online, and Novell, are turning over CEOs at a rapid rate. Apple has replaced its top executive twice within three years.

Top manager turnover also allows an organization to cope with new contin-gencies. The selection of a new chief executive may reflect the need for a specific skill or specialization.[55] For example, if the dominant issue confronting an organ-ization is financing mergers, choosing a finance person as chief executive gives priority to financial activities. Historically, CEO backgrounds have changed with business conditions. Early in this century, large firms were controlled by people who came up through manufacturing. In the middle decades, sales and market-ing people were more frequently selected as chief executive officers. In the past twenty years, finance personnel have become increasingly dominant.[56] The ma-jor issues confronting business organizations were first manufacturing technol-ogy, then sales, and now finance.

Turnover every few years can have a positive effect. If a chief executive and top management team serve too long, say over ten years, organizational stagna-tion may begin. New executives are not coming in to provide fresh energy, new strategies, or expertise for new environmental situations.

One example of how management succession is used for adaptation is Coca-Cola Company. Until a few years ago, Coca-Cola was a tradition-bound, stag-nating corporation. The firm was not adapting to its turbulent international environment and was losing ground to PepsiCo in the U.S. market. That all changed with the appointment of new top executives who provided new blood and an international perspective. The new chief executive of Coca-Cola was born in Havana, Cuba. The chief financial officer is Egyptian. The president of Coke USA is an Argentine. The marketing vice president is a Mexican. These changes in top management revitalized Coca-Cola in both the U.S. and foreign markets.[57]

Succession and Performance

In recent years, companies such as Continental Airlines, Kodak, DEC, Celanese, Tiger International, Baldwin-United, and Northwest Energy had turnover at the top.[58] Turnover at the top is of particular interest to organization studies because the CEO has a pervasive impact on an organization. In addition, there are often symbolic aspects connected with CEO succession, and turnover at the top may be associated with firm decline and eventual transformation.[59]

Athletic Team Performance. One type of organization that can help answer the question of whether manager turnover influences performance is an athletic team. The coach is the top manager of the team, and coaches are regularly replaced in both college and professional sports. Several studies have analyzed coaching changes to see whether they lead to an improvement in performance. The general finding is that manager (coach) turnover does not lead to improved performance unless the new coach is exceptionally competent.[60] If the coach has prior experience and has brought about improvements in other teams, then the coach can make a difference. However, most manager replacements do not lead to improved performance.

Another finding from those studies is that performance leads to turnover.[61] Teams with poor records experience greater succession because a poor record often leads to the firing of the old coach. Firing the previous coach serves as a symbol that the team is trying to improve. The term **ritual scapegoating** describes how turnover signals to fans and others that efforts are being made to improve the team's performance record.[62] Corporations also use ritual scapegoating, in the sense that poor performance causes turnover.[63] For example, the board fired the CEO at Allegheny to signal to stockholders and the press that it was attempting to make changes that would correct ethical problems and improve performance.

Corporations and Performance. A corporation is much larger and more diverse than an athletic team. Can the chief executive make a difference to performance in a corporate setting? Several studies of chief executive turnover have been conducted, including a sample of 167 corporations studied over a twenty-year period, 193 manufacturing companies, a large sample of Methodist churches, and retail firms in the United Kingdom.[64] These studies found that leader succession was associated with improved profits and stock prices and, in the case of churches, by improved attendance, membership, and donations. It was also found that performance was improved by good economic conditions and industry circumstances, but the chief executive officer had impact beyond these environmental factors. Overall, when research has been carefully done, there has been a finding that leadership succession explains 20 percent to 45 percent of the variance in an organization's outcomes.[65]

An interesting corollary is that the importance of chief executives means turnover in some cases may lead to poorer performance. In a study of managerial succession in local newspapers, when the founder who created and developed the organization left, performance dropped. In the early stages of the organizational life cycle, an organization depends heavily on the special skills of its founder. A new top manager is unable to achieve the same level of performance.[66]

A realistic interpretation of these findings is the conclusion that corporate performance is the result of many factors. General economic and industry conditions outside the control of the chief executive do affect sales and net earnings.

However, outcomes under the control of executive strategy—such as net profit—are influenced by the chief executive. The impact of chief executives on performance is also greater in smaller organizations where chief executives can directly formulate and implement strategy and can use symbolic action to affect the direction and performance of the company.

SUMMARY AND INTERPRETATION

This chapter covered several topics concerning organizational forms relevant to the future, the trend toward learning organizations, and organizational transformation and leadership. Top leaders are responsible for the organization's design configuration. They decide on strategy formulation and then implement strategy by selecting organizational structure and form. Five forms described in the chapter are entrepreneurial, professional bureaucracy, adhocracy, divisional form, and machine bureaucracy. The selection of the configurations among these forms helps managers deal with basic forces, such as efficiency, direction, and innovation.

The paradigm shift occurring in the field of management has resulted in the learning organization. Enhanced learning capability is associated with mindful leadership, empowered people, emergent strategy, strong culture, shared information, and horizontal structure.

Some organizations are engaged in transformation, which includes the three stages of crisis, reinvestment, and rebuilding. The process of revitalization or transformation is often led by a transformational leader.

Finally, recent research has explored the impact of top-management teams and turnover on organizations. Rather than a single executive being responsible for the entire company, the makeup of the top-management group is believed to affect organizational capability. Four problems that can limit top-management team effectiveness are fragmentation, intense conflict, groupthink, and inadequate capabilities of one or more top executives. Top leaders can implement systems that help to overcome these problems. Turnover at the top provides new energy and perspectives for organizational leadership. Succession also provides new skills to cope with changing environmental conditions and may symbolize a new organizational direction.

Key Concepts

adhocracy	rebuilding
crisis	reinvest
divisional form	ritual scapegoating
entrepreneurial structure	strategy
five organizational configurations	strategy formulation
learning organization	strategy implementation
machine bureaucracy	transformational leadership
professional bureaucracy	

Discussion Questions

1. Do you agree that creating organizational learning capability is more important for competitive advantage than is creating financial, marketing, or technological capability? Explain.
2. How do the five organizational forms proposed by Mintzberg help an organization deal with the system of seven primary forces?
3. What do you think of the concept of the learning organization? Which aspects seem least realistic? Would you like to work in one?
4. What might managers do during the rebuilding stage of transformation to prevent the problems of the past? Discuss.
5. Why are cultural values of minimal boundaries and compassion and caring important to a learning organization? Discuss.
6. How might top management succession be used for adaptation and ritual scapegoating? Explain.
7. A consultant said, "The individual who occupies the chief executive position can have more impact on profits than on total sales." Explain why you agree or disagree with this statement.
8. Do you see any conflict between the concept of an individual transformational leader and the current emphasis on the importance of top-management teams? Discuss.

Briefcase

As an organization manager, keep these guides in mind:

1. Take responsibility for designing organizational form to fit strategy and environment. Five organizational types to choose from are entrepreneurial, machine bureaucracy, professional bureaucracy, divisional form, and adhocracy.
2. Make sure the organization is effective by managing the interplay among and needs for the seven basic forces of direction, proficiency, innovation, concentration, efficiency, cooperation/culture, and conflict/politics.
3. Create organizational learning capability beyond that provided by technology, financial, and marketing capabilities by developing mindful leadership, empowered employees, emergent strategy, strong culture, information sharing, and horizontal structures.
4. When an organization needs transformation, begin implementing the three stages of crisis, reinvestment, and rebuilding. Act as a transformational leader to motivate followers to believe in the vision of corporate transformation, recognize the need for revitalization, sign on for the new vision, and help institutionalize a new organizational process.
5. Recognize the importance of the top-management team, and implement mechanisms to bring unity of purpose, promote cooperation, and encourage a healthy debate of ideas.
6. Encourage periodic top management succession to ensure a flow of fresh energy and ideas into the upper ranks. Adapt to specific problems by bringing needed skills and experience into the chief executive position. Remember that chief executive succession is typically associated with improved organizational performance.

Chapter Fifteen Workbook *Creating a Learning Organization**

Imagine you are working in the ideal learning organization. What would it be like and how is that different from a recent work experience you have had (or your experience in the "job" of student)? What keeps your workplace from becoming more learning oriented? Complete the following table:

What are aspects of the ideal learning organization?	What are behaviors for this aspect?	What would be the result of these behaviors?	What are blocks to achieving these?	How would I know if progress has been made?
1. (Example): Employees feel what they do has some meaning.	They display energy and enthusiasm when they work.	The team is more motivated and new ideas are generated.	There is a lack of clarity on how tasks help fulfill the overall mission.	Employees talk about how they are fulfilling an important mission.
2.				
3.				
4.				
5.				
6.				

Further Work

1. Choose the three aspects that are the most compelling to you and the organization.
2. How can the organization achieve these? What are the major blocks?
3. *Optional:* Form groups and compare your table and the three aspects you chose with those of other students. Are there some common themes? What is most important in creating a learning organization? What are reasons for not having a learning organization—what are the blocks?

*Adapted by Dorothy Marcic from "Defining Your Learning Organization," in Peter Senge, et al., *The Fifth Discipline Fieldbook* (New York: Doubleday, 1994), 50–52.

Case for Analysis *W. L. Gore & Associates, Inc.**

On July 26, 1976, Jack Dougherty, a newly minted MBA from the College of William and Mary, bursting with resolve and dressed in a dark blue suit, reported to his first day at W. L. Gore & Associates. He presented himself to Bill Gore, shook hands firmly, looked him in the eye, and said he was ready for anything.

What happened next was one thing for which Dougherty was not ready. Gore replied, "That's fine, Jack, fine. Why don't you look around and find something you'd like to do." Three frustrating weeks later he found that something, dressed in jeans, loading fabric into the mouth of a machine that laminates the company's patented GORE-TEX[1] membrane to fabric. By 1982, Dougherty had become responsible for all advertising and marketing in the fabrics group.

This story is part of the folklore that is heard over and over about W. L. Gore. Today the process is slightly more structured. New Associates[2] take a journey through the business before settling into their own positions, regardless of the specific position for which they are hired. A new sales Associate in the Fabric Division may spend six weeks rotating through different areas before beginning to concentrate on sales and marketing. Among other things he or she may learn is how GORE-TEX fabric is made; what it can and cannot do; how Gore handles customer complaints; and how it makes its investment decisions.

Anita McBride related her early experience at W. L. Gore & Associates this way:

Before I came to Gore, I had worked for a structured organization and I came here, and for the first month it was fairly structured because I was going through training, and this is what we do and this is how Gore is and all of that, and I went to Flagstaff for that training. After a month, I came down to Phoenix and my sponsor said, "Well, here's your office"—it's a wonderful office—and "Here's your desk" and walked away. And I thought, Now what do I do, you know? I was waiting for a memo or something, or a job description. Finally after another month I was so frustrated, I felt what have I gotten myself into, and so I went to my sponsor and I said, "What the heck do you want from me? I need something from you," and he said, "If you don't know what you're supposed to do, examine your commitment and opportunities."

Background

W. L. Gore & Associates is a company that evolved from the late Wilbert L. Gore's experiences personally, organizationally, and technically. Gore was born in Meridian, Idaho, near Boise, in 1912. By age six, he claimed that he had become an avid hiker in the Wasatch Mountain Range in Utah. In those mountains, at a church camp, he met Genevieve, his future wife. She is called Vieve by everyone. In 1935 they got married—in their eyes, a partnership. He would make breakfast, and she would make lunch. The partnership lasted a lifetime.

Gore received both a bachelor of science degree in chemical engineering in 1933 and a masters of science in chemistry in 1935 from the University of Utah. He began his professional career at American Smelting and Refining in 1936. He moved to Remington Arms Company in 1941. He moved once again, to E. I. Du Pont de Nemours in 1945, where he was research supervisor and head of operations research. While at Du Pont he worked on a team to develop applications for polytetrafluoroethylene, frequently referred to as PTFE in the scientific community and known as "Teflon" by Du Pont's consumers (it is known by consumers under other

---

*Frank Shipper, Salisbury State University, and Charles Manz, Arizona State University. A number of sources were especially helpful in providing background material for this case. The most important sources of all were the W. L. Gore Associates who generously shared their time and viewpoints about the company. We especially appreciate the input received from Anita McBride, who spent hours with us sharing her personal experiences as well as providing many resources including internal documents and videotapes. In addition, Trish Hearn and Dave McCarter also added much to this case through sharing their personal experiences as well as ensuring that the case accurately reflected the Gore company and culture.

[1]GORE-TEX is a registered trademark of W. L. Gore & Associates.

[2]In this case the word *Associate* is used and capitalized because in W. L. Gore & Associates' literature the word is always used instead of *employees* and is capitalized. In fact, the case writers were told that Gore "never had 'employees'—always 'Associates.'"

names from other companies). On this team Gore felt a sense of excited commitment, personal fulfillment, and self-direction. He followed the development of computers and transistors and felt that PTFE had the ideal insulating characteristics for use with such equipment.

He tried a number of ways to make a PTFE-coated ribbon cable, but without success. A breakthrough came in his home basement laboratory. He was explaining the problem to his son, Bob. Bob saw some PTFE sealant tape made by 3M and asked his father, "Why don't you try this tape?" His father then explained to his son that everyone knows you cannot bond PTFE to itself. Bob went on to bed.

Gore remained in his basement lab and proceeded to try what everyone knew would not work. At about 4:00 A.M., he woke up his son waving a small piece of cable around, saying excitedly, "It works, it works!" The following night father and son returned to the basement lab to make ribbon cable coated with PTFE.

By this time in his career, Gore knew some of the decision makers at Du Pont. For the next four months, he tried to persuade Du Pont to make a new product— PTFE-coated ribbon cable. It became clear after talking to several people that Du Pont wanted to remain a supplier of raw materials and not a fabricator.

Gore began to discuss with Vieve the possibility of starting their own insulated wire and cable business. On January 1, 1958, their wedding anniversary, they founded W. L. Gore & Associates. The basement of their home served as their first facility. After finishing dinner on their anniversary, Vieve said, "Well, let's clear up the dishes, go downstairs, and get to work." They viewed this as another partnership.

Gore was 45 years old with five children to support when he left Du Pont. He left behind a career of 17 years and a good, secure salary. To finance the first two years of the business, the Gores mortgaged their house and took $4,000 from savings. All of their friends told them not to do it.

The first few years were rough. In lieu of salary, some of their Associates accepted room and board in the Gore home. At one point 11 Associates were living and working under one roof. The order that was almost lost and that put the company on a profitable footing came from Denver's water department. One afternoon, Vieve answered a phone call while sifting PTFE powder. The caller indicated that he was interested in the ribbon cable but wanted to ask some technical questions. Gore was out running some errands. The caller asked for the product manager. Vieve explained that he was out at the moment. Next he asked for the sales manager and finally, the president. Vieve said that they were also out. The caller became outraged and hollered, "What kind of company is this anyway?" With a little diplomacy, the Gores were able eventually to secure an order for $100,000. This order put the company over the hump, and it began to take off.

W. L. Gore & Associates has continued to grow and develop new products primarily derived from PTFE, including its best known product, GORE-TEX fabric. In 1986 Gore died while backpacking in the Wind River Mountains of Wyoming. Before he died he had become chairman and his son Bob, president, a position he continues to occupy. Vieve remains as the only other officer, secretary-treasurer.

The Operating Company

W. L. Gore & Associates is a company without titles, hierarchy, or any of the conventional structures associated with enterprises of its size. The titles of president and secretary-treasurer are used only because they are required by the laws of incorporation. In addition, Gore does not have a corporatewide mission or code of ethics statement, although Gore does not require or prohibit business units from developing such statements for themselves. Thus, the Associates of some business units who have felt a need for such statements have developed them for themselves. The majority of business units within Gore do not have such statements. When questioned about this issue, one Associate stated, "The company belief is that (1) its four basic operating principles cover ethical practices required of people in business; and (2) it will not tolerate illegal practices." Gore's management style has been referred to as un-management. The organization has been guided by Gore's experiences on teams at Du Pont and has evolved as needed.

For example, in 1965 W. L. Gore & Associates was a thriving and growing company with a facility on Paper Mill Road in Newark, Delaware, with about 200 Associates. One warm Monday morning in the summer, Gore was taking his usual walk through the plant when he realized that he did not know everyone in the plant. The team had become too big. As a result, the company has a policy that no facility will have over 200 Associates. Thus was born the expansion policy of "Get big by staying small." The purpose of maintaining small plants is to accentuate a close-knit and interpersonal atmosphere.

Today, W. L. Gore & Associates consists of 44 plants worldwide with over 5,300 Associates. In some cities the plants are clustered together on the same site, as in

Flagstaff, Arizona, with four plants on the same site. Twenty-seven of those plants are in the United States, and 17 are overseas. The company's overseas plants are located in Scotland, Germany, France, and Japan, manufacturing electronics, medical, industrial, and fabric products.

Gore electronic products are found in unconventional places where conventional products will not do—in space shuttles, for example, where Gore wire and cable assemblies withstood the heat of ignition and the cold of space. In addition, they are found in fast computers, transmitting signals at up to 90 percent of the speed of light. Gore cables are even underground, in oil-drilling operations, and undersea, on submarines that require superior microwave signal equipment and no-fail cables that can survive high pressure. The Gore Electronic Products Division has a history of anticipating future customer needs with innovative products. Gore electronic products are well known in the industry for their ability to last under adverse conditions.

In the medical arena, GORE-TEX-expanded PTFE is considered an ideal replacement for human tissue in many situations. In patients suffering from cardiovascular disease, the diseased portion of arteries are often replaced by tubes of expanded PTFE that are strong, biocompatible, and able to carry blood at arterial pressures. Gore has a dominant share in this market. Other Gore medical products include patches that can literally mend broken hearts by patching holes and repairing aneurysms, a synthetic knee ligament that provides stability by replacing the natural anterior cruciate ligament, and sutures that allow for tissue attachment and offer the surgeon silklike handling coupled with extreme strength. In 1985 Gore won Britain's Prince Philip Award for Polymers in the Service of Mankind. The award recognized especially the life-saving achievements of the Gore medical products team.

The Industrial Products Division produces a number of products including sealants, filter bags, cartridges, clothes, and coatings. These products tend to have specialized and critical applications. Gore's reputation for quality appears to influence the industrial purchasers of these products.

The Gore Fabrics Division, which is the largest division, supplies laminates to manufacturers of foul-weather gear, ski wear, running suits, footwear, gloves, and hunting and fishing garments. Firefighters and U.S. Navy pilots wear GORE-TEX fabric gear, as do some Olympic athletes. And the U.S. Army has adopted a total garment system built around a GORE-TEX fabric component.

GORE-TEX membrane has 9 billion pores randomly dotting each square inch and is feather light. Each pore is 700 times larger than a water vapor molecule yet thousands of times smaller than a water droplet. Wind and water cannot penetrate the pores, but perspiration can escape. As a result, fabrics bonded with GORE-TEX membrane are waterproof, windproof, and breathable. The laminated fabrics bring protection from the elements to a variety of products—from survival gear to high-fashion rain wear. Recently, other manufacturers including 3M have brought out products to compete with GORE-TEX fabrics. Gore, however, continues to have a commanding share of this market.

Gore wanted to avoid smothering the company in thick layers of formal "management." He felt that they stifled individual creativity. As the company grew, he knew that a way had to be devised to assist new people to get started and to follow their progress. This was seen as particularly important when it came to compensation. Gore has developed what they call their "sponsor" program to meet these needs. When people apply to Gore, they are initially screened by personnel specialists as in most companies. For those who meet the basic criteria, there are interviews with other Associates. Before anyone is hired, an Associate must agree to be their sponsor. The sponsor is both a coach and an advocate who takes a personal interest in the new Associate's contributions, problems, and goals. He or she tracks the new Associate's progress, helping and encouraging, dealing with weaknesses and concentrating on strengths. Sponsoring is not a short-term commitment. All Associates have sponsors, and many have more than one. When individuals are hired initially, they will have a sponsor in their immediate work area. If they move to another area, they will have a sponsor in that work area. As Associates' responsibilities grow, they may require additional sponsors.

Because the sponsoring program looks beyond conventional views of what makes a good Associate, some anomalies occur in the hiring practices. Gore has proudly told the story of "a very young man" of 84 who walked in, applied, and spent five very good years with the company. The individual had 30 years of experience in the industry before joining Gore. His other Associates had no problems accepting him, but the personnel computer did. It insisted that his age was 48. The individual success stories at Gore come from diverse backgrounds.

An internal memo by Gore described three kinds of sponsorship expected and how they might work as follows:

1. The sponsor who helps a new Associate *get started* on his job. Also, the sponsor who helps a present Associate get started on a new job (starting sponsor).
2. The sponsor who sees to it the Associate being sponsored *gets credit* and recognition for contributions and accomplishments (advocate sponsor).
3. The sponsor who sees to it that the Associate being sponsored is *fairly paid* for contributions to the success of the enterprise (compensation sponsor).

A single sponsor can perform any one or all three kinds of sponsorship. A sponsor is a friend and an Associate. All the supportive aspects of the friendship are also present. Often (perhaps usually) two Associates sponsor each other as advocates.

In addition to the sponsor program, Gore Associates are asked to follow four guiding principles:

1. Try to be fair.
2. Use your freedom to grow.
3. Make your own commitments, and keep them.
4. Consult with other Associates prior to any action that may adversely effect the reputation or financial stability of the company.

The four principles are often referred to as fairness, freedom, commitment, and waterline. The waterline terminology is drawn from an analogy to ships. If someone pokes a hole in a boat above the waterline, the boat will be in relatively little real danger. If someone pokes a hole below the waterline, however, the boat is in immediate danger of sinking.

The company's operating principles were put to a test in 1978. By this time, the word about the qualities of GORE-TEX fabric [was] being spread throughout the recreational and outdoor markets. Production and shipment had begun in volume. At first a few complaints were heard, then some of the clothing started coming back. Finally, much of the clothing was being returned. The trouble was that the GORE-TEX fabric was leaking. Waterproofness was one of the two major properties responsible for GORE-TEX fabric's success. The company's reputation and credibility were on the line. Peter W. Gilson, who led Gore's Fabrics Division said, "It was an incredible crisis for us at that point. We were really starting to attract attention; we were taking off—and then this." Gilson and a number of his Associates in the next few months made many of those below-the-waterline decisions.

First, the researchers determined that oils in human sweat were responsible for clogging the pores in the GORE-TEX fabric and altering the surface tension of the membrane. Thus, water could pass through. They also discovered that a good washing could restore the waterproof property. At first this solution, known as the "Ivory Snow Solution," was accepted.

A single letter from "Butch," a mountain guide in the Sierras, changed the company's position. Butch wrote that he had been leading a group and, "My parka leaked and my life was in danger." As Gilson said, "That scared the hell out of us. Clearly our solution was no solution at all to someone on a mountaintop." All of the products were recalled. "We bought back, at our own expense, a fortune in pipeline material—anything that was in the stores, at the manufacturers, or anywhere else in the pipeline," Gilson said.

In the meantime, Gore and other Associates set out to develop a permanent fix. One month later, a second-generation GORE-TEX fabric had been developed. Gilson, furthermore, told dealers that if at any time a customer returned a leaky parka, they should replace it and bill the company. The replacement program alone cost Gore roughly $4 million.

Organizational Structure

W. L. Gore & Associates has not only been described as un-managed but also as un-structured. Gore referred to the structure as a lattice organization. A lattice structure is portrayed in Exhibit 15.7 and has the following characteristics:

1. Direct lines of communication are direct, person to person, with no intermediary.
2. No fixed or assigned authority.
3. Sponsors, not bosses.
4. Natural leadership defined by followership.
5. Objectives set by those who must "make them happen."
6. Tasks and functions organized through commitments.

The structure within the lattice is described by the people at Gore as complex and evolves from interpersonal interactions, self-commitment to group-known responsibilities, natural leadership, and group-imposed discipline. Gore once explained this structure by saying, "Every successful organization has an underground lattice. It's where the news spreads like lightning, where people can go around the organization to get things done." Another description of what is occurring within the lattice structure is constant cross-area teams—the equivalent of quality circles going on all the time. When

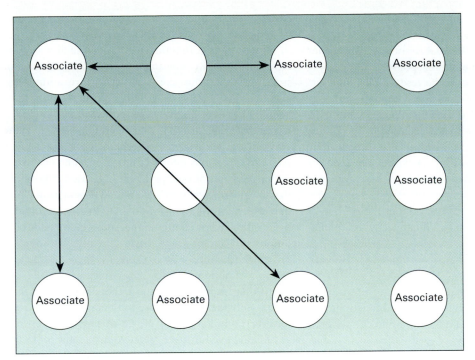

Exhibit 15.7
W. L. Gore's Lattice Structure

Source: W. L. Gore & Associates, Inc.

a puzzled interviewer told Gore that he was having trouble understanding how planning and accountability worked, Gore replied with a grin, "So am I. You ask me how it works—every which way."

The lattice structure does have some similarities to traditional management structures. For instance, a group of 30 to 40 Associates who make up an advisory group meets every six months to review marketing, sales, and production plans. As Gore conceded, "The abdication of titles and rankings can never be 100 percent."

One thing that might strike an outsider in the meetings and the other places in Gore's organization is the informality and amount of humor. Meetings tend to be only as long as necessary. As Trish Hearn, an Associate in Newark, Delaware, said, "No one feels a need to pontificate." Words such as *responsibilities* and *commitments* are, however, commonly heard. This is an organization that seems to take what it does very seriously, but its members do not take themselves too seriously.

Gore, for a company of its size, may have the shortest organizational pyramid. The pyramid consists of Bob Gore, the late Bill Gore's son, as president, and Vieve, Gore's widow, as secretary-treasurer. All the other members of the Gore organization are referred to as Associates. Words such as *employees*, *subordinates*, and *managers* are taboo in the Gore culture.

Gore does not have any managers, but it does have many leaders. Gore described in an internal memo the kinds of leadership and the role of leadership as follows:

1. The Associate is recognized by a team as having a special knowledge, or experience (for example, this could be a chemist, computer expert, machine operator, salesman, engineer, lawyer). This kind of leader gives the team *guidance in a special area.*

2. The team looks to the Associate for coordination of individual activities in order to achieve the agreed upon objectives of the team. The role of this leader is to persuade team members to *make the commitments* necessary for success (commitment seeker).

3. The Associate proposes necessary objectives and activities and seeks agreement and team *consensus on objectives.* This leader is perceived by the team members as having a good grasp of how the objectives of the team fit in with the broad objective of the enterprise. This kind of leader is often also the "commitment seeking" leader in 2. above.

4. The leader evaluates relative contribution of team members (in consultation with other sponsors), and reports these contribution evaluations to a compensation committee. This leader may also

participate in the compensation committee on relative contribution and pay and *reports changes in compensation* to individual Associates. This leader is then also a compensation sponsor.

5. The leader coordinates the research, manufacturing, and marketing of one product type within a business, interactive with team leaders and individual Associates who have commitments regarding the product type. These leaders are usually called *product specialists*. They are respected for their knowledge and dedication to their products.

6. *Plant leaders* help coordinate activities of people within a plant.

7. *Business leaders* help coordinate activities of people in a business.

8. *Functional leaders* help coordinate activities of people in a "functional" area.

9. *Corporate leaders* help coordinate activities of people in different businesses and functions and try to promote communication and cooperation among all Associates.

10. *Intrapreneuring Associates organize new teams* for new businesses, new products, new processes, new devices, new marketing efforts, new or better methods of all kinds. These leaders invite other Associates to "sign up" for their project.

Leaders are not authoritarians, managers of people, or supervisors who tell us what to do or forbid us doing things, nor are they "parents" to whom we transfer our own self-responsibility. However, they do often advise us of the consequences of actions we have done or propose to do. Our actions result in contributions, or lack of contribution, to the success of our enterprise. Our pay depends on the magnitude of our contributions. This is the basic discipline of our lattice organization.

Many other aspects of Gore's operations are arranged along egalitarian lines. The parking lot does not have any reserved parking spaces except for customers and the handicapped. There is only one area in each plant in which to eat. The lunchroom in each new plant is designed to be a focal point for Associate interaction. Davd McCarter of Phoenix explained, "The design is no accident. The lunchroom in Flagstaff has a fireplace in the middle. We want people to like to be here." The location of the plant is also no accident. Sites are selected based on transportation access, a nearby university, beautiful surroundings, and climate appeal. Land cost is never a primary consideration. McCarter justified the selection by stating, "Expanding is not

costly in the long run. The loss of money is what you make happen by stymieing people into a box."

Not all people function well under such a system, especially initially. For those accustomed to a more structured work environment, there are adjustment problems. As Gore said, "All our lives, most of us have been told what to do, and some people don't know how to respond when asked to do something—and have the very real option of saying no—on their job. It's the new Associate's responsibility to find out what he or she can do for the good of the operation." The vast majority of the new Associates, after some initial floundering, adapt quickly.

For those who require more structured working conditions and cannot adapt, Gore's flexible workplace is not for them. According to Gore, for those few "it's an unhappy situation, both for the Associate and the sponsor. If there is no contribution, there is no paycheck." Anita McBride, an Associate in Phoenix, said, "It's not for everybody. People ask me do we have turnover, and yes we do have turnover. What you're seeing looks like utopia, but it also looks extreme. If you finally figure the system, it can be real exciting. If you can't handle it, you gotta go. Probably by your own choice, because you're going to be so frustrated."

In rare cases an Associate "is trying to be unfair," in Gore's own words. In one case the problem was chronic absenteeism, and in another the individual was caught stealing. "When that happens, all hell breaks loose," said Gore. "We can get damned authoritarian when we have to."

Over the years, Gore has faced a number of unionization drives. The company neither tries to dissuade an Associate from attending an organizational meeting nor retaliates when flyers are passed out. Each attempt has been unsuccessful. None of the plants have been organized to date. Gore believed that no need exists for third-party representation under the lattice structure: "Why would Associates join a union when they own the company? It seems rather absurd."

Overall, the Associates appear to have responded positively to the Gore system of un-management and un-structure. Gore estimated the year before he died that "the profit per Associate is double" that of Du Pont. However, the lattice structure is not without its critics. As Gore stated, "I'm told from time to time that a lattice organization can't meet a crisis well because it takes too long to reach a consensus when there are no bosses. But this isn't true. Actually, a lattice, by its very nature, works particularly well in a crisis. A lot of useless effort is avoided because there is no rigid management hierarchy to conquer before you an attack a problem."

The lattice has been put to the test on a number of occasions. For example, in 1975 Dr. Charles Campbell, the University of Pittsburgh's senior resident, reported that a GORE-TEX arterial graft had developed an aneurysm. An aneurysm is a bubblelike protrusion that is life-threatening. If it continues to expand, it will explode. Obviously, this kind of problem has to be solved quickly and permanently.

Within only a few days of Dr. Campbell's first report, he flew to Newark to present his findings to Bill and Bob Gore and a few other Associates. The meeting lasted two hours. Dan Hubis, a former policeman who had joined Gore to develop new production methods, had an idea before the meeting was over. He returned to his work area to try some different production techniques. After only three hours and 12 tries, he had developed a permanent solution; in other words, a potentially damaging problem to both patients and the company was resolved. Furthermore, Hubis's redesigned graft has gone on to win widespread acceptance in the medical community.

Other critics have been outsiders who had problems with the idea of no titles. Sarah Clifton, an Associate at the Flagstaff facility, was being pressed by some outsiders as to what her title was. She made one up and had it printed on some business cards: SUPREME COMMANDER. When Gore learned what she did, he loved it and recounted the story to others.

Another critic, Eric Reynolds, founder of Marmot Mountain Works Ltd. of Grand Junction, Colorado, and major Gore customer, said "I think the lattice has its problems with the day-to-day nitty-gritty of getting things done on time and out the door. I don't think Bill realizes how the lattice system affects customers. I mean, after you've established a relationship with someone about product quality, you can call up one day and suddenly find that someone new to you is handling your problem. It's frustrating to find a lack of continuity." He went on to say, "But I have to admit that I've personally seen at Gore remarkable examples of people coming out of nowhere and excelling."

Gore was asked a number of times if the lattice structure could be used by other companies. His answer was "No. For example, established companies would find it very difficult to use the lattice. Too many hierarchies would be destroyed. When you remove titles and positions and allow people to follow who they want, it may very well be someone other than the person who has been in charge. The lattice works for us, but it's always evolving. You have to expect problems." He maintained that the lattice system works best when put in place in start-up companies by dynamic entrepreneurs.

Research and Development

Research and development like everything else at Gore are unstructured. There is no formal research and development department. Yet the company holds many patents, although most inventions are held as proprietary or trade secrets. Any Associate can ask for a piece of raw PTFE, known as a silly worm, with which to experiment. Gore believed that all people had it within themselves to be creative.

The best way to understand how research and development works is to see how inventiveness has previously occurred at Gore. By 1969, the wire and cable division was facing increased competition. Gore began to look for a way to straighten out the PTFE molecules. As he said, "I figured out that if we ever unfold those molecules, get them to stretch out straight, we'd have a tremendous new kind of material." He thought that if PTFE could be stretched, air could be introduced into its molecular structure. The result would be greater volume per pound of raw material without affecting performance. Thus, fabricating costs would be reduced and the profit margins would be increased. Going about this search scientifically with his son, Bob, Gore heated rods of PTFE to various temperatures and then slowly stretched them. Regardless of the temperature or how carefully they stretched them, the rods broke.

Working alone late one night after countless failures, Bob in frustration yanked at one of the rods violently. To his surprise, it did not break. He tried it again and again with the same results. The next morning Bob demonstrated his breakthrough to his father, but not without some drama. As Gore recalled, "Bob wanted to surprise me so he took a rod and stretched it slowly. Naturally, it broke. Then he pretended to get mad. He grabbed another rod and said, 'Oh the hell with this' and gave it a pull. It didn't break—he'd done it." The new arrangement of molecules changed not only the wire and cable division but led to the development of GORE-TEX fabric and what is now the largest division at Gore plus a host of other products.

Initial field-testing of GORE-TEX fabric was conducted by Gore and Vieve in the summer of 1970. Vieve made a hand-sewn tent out of patches of GORE-TEX fabric. They took it on their annual camping trip to the Wind River Mountains in Wyoming. The very first night in the wilderness, they encountered a hailstorm. The hail tore holes in the top of the tent, but the bottom filled up like a bathtub from the rain. As Gore stated, "At least we knew from all the water that the tent was waterproof. We just need to make it stronger, so it could withstand hail."

The second largest division began on the ski slopes of Colorado. Gore was skiing with his friend Dr. Ben Eiseman of the Denver General Hospital. As Gore told the story, "We were just to start a run when I absentmindedly pulled a small tubular section of GORE-TEX out of my pocket and looked at it. 'What is that stuff?' Ben asked. So I told him about its properties. 'Feels great,' he said. 'What do you use it for?' 'Got no idea,' I said. 'Well give it to me,' he said, 'and I'll try it in a vascular graft on a pig.' Two weeks later, he called me up. Ben was pretty excited. 'Bill,' he said, 'I put it in a pig and it works. What do I do now?' I told him to get together with Pete Cooper in our Flagstaff plant and let them figure it out." Now hundreds of thousands of people throughout the world walk about with GORE-TEX vascular grafts.

Every Associate is encouraged to think, experiment, and follow a potentially profitable idea to its conclusion. For example, at a plant in Newark, Delaware, a machine that wraps thousands of feet of wire a day was designed by Fred L. Eldreth, an Associate with a third-grade education. The design was done over a weekend. Many other Associates have contributed their ideas through both product and process breakthroughs. Without a research and development department, innovations and creativity work very well at Gore. The year before he died, Gore claimed, "The creativity, the number of patent applications and innovative products is triple" that of Du Pont.

Associate Development

Ron Hill, an Associate in Newark, said, Gore "will work with Associates who want to advance themselves." Associates are offered many in-house training opportunities. They do tend to be technical and engineering focused because of the type of organization Gore is, but it also offers in-house programs in leadership development. In addition, the company has cooperative programs with their Associates to obtain training through universities and other outside providers. Gore will pick up most of the costs for the Associates. The emphasis in Associate development as in many parts of Gore is that the Associate must take the initiative.

Products

The products that Gore makes are arranged into four divisions—electronics, medical, industrial, and fabrics. The Electronic Products Division produces wire and cable for various demanding applications in aerospace, defense, computers, and telecommunications. The wire and cable products have earned a reputation for unequaled reliability. Most of the wire and cable is used where conventional cables cannot operate. For example, Gore wire and cable assemblies were used in the space shuttle *Columbia* because they would stand the heat of ignition and the cold of space. Gore wire was used in the moon vehicle shuttle that scooped up samples of moon rocks, and Gore's microwave coaxial assemblies have opened new horizons in microwave technology. Back on earth, the electrical wire products help make the world's fastest computers possible because electrical signals can travel through them at up to 90 percent of the speed of light. Because of the physical properties of the GORE-TEX material used in their construction, the electronic products are used extensively in defense systems, electronic switching for telephone systems, scientific and industrial instrumentation, microwave communications, and industrial robotics. Reliability is a watchword for all Gore products.

In medical products, reliability is literally a matter of life and death. GORE-TEX-expanded PTFE is an ideal material used to combat cardiovascular disease. When human arteries are seriously damaged or plugged with deposits that interrupt the flow of blood, the diseased portions can often be replaced with GORE-TEX artificial arteries. GORE-TEX arteries and patches are not rejected by the body because the patient's own tissues grow into the graft's open porous spaces. GORE-TEX vascular grafts come in many sizes to restore circulation to all areas of the body. They have saved limbs from amputation and saved lives. Some of the tiniest grafts relieve pulmonary problems in newborns. GORE-TEX-expanded PTFE is also used to help people with kidney disease. Associates are developing a variety of surgical reinforcing membranes, known as GORE-TEX cardiovascular patches, which can literally mend broken hearts, by patching holes and repairing aneurysms.

Through the Fabrics Division, Gore technology has traveled to the roof of the world on the backs of renowned mountaineers. GORE-TEX fabric is waterproof and windproof yet breathable. Those features have qualified GORE-TEX fabric as essential gear for mountaineers and adventurers facing extremely harsh environments. The PTFE membrane blocks wind and water but allows sweat to escape, which makes GORE-TEX fabric ideal for anyone who works or plays hard in foul weather. Backpackers have discovered that a single lightweight GORE-TEX fabric shell will replace a poplin jacket and a rain suit and dramatically outperform both. Skiers, sailors, runners, bicyclists, hunters, fishermen, and other outdoor enthusiasts have also become big customers of garments made of GORE-TEX fabric. General sportswear, as well as women's fashion footwear and handwear of GORE-TEX fabric, are as functional as they are beautiful. Boots and gloves, both for work and recreation, are waterproof thanks to GORE-TEX liners. GORE-TEX garments are even becoming standard items issued to many military personnel. Wetsuits, parkas, pants, headgear, gloves, and boots keep the troops warm and dry in foul-weather missions. Other demanding jobs also require the protection of GORE-TEX fabric because of its unique combination of chemical and physical properties.

The GORE-TEX fibers products, like the fabrics, end up in some pretty tough places. The outer protective layer of NASA's spacesuit is woven from GORE-TEX fibers. GORE-TEX fibers are in many ways the ultimate in synthetic fibers. They are impervious to sunlight, chemicals, heat, and cold. They are strong and uniquely resistant to abrasion.

The Industrial Products Division produces joint sealant, a flexible cord of porous PTFE that can be applied as a gasket to the most complex shapes, sealing them to prevent leakage of corrosive chemicals even at extreme temperature and pressure. Steam valves packed with GORE-TEX valve-stem packing are guaranteed for the life of the valve when used properly. Industrial filtration products, such as GORE-TEX filter bags, reduce air pollution and recover valuable solids from gases and liquids more completely than alternatives; they also do it more economically. They could make coal-burning plants completely smoke free, contributing to a cleaner environment.

The coatings division applies layers of PTFE to steel castings and other metal articles by a patented process. Called Fluroshield[3] protective coatings, this fluorocarbon polymer protects processing vessels in the production of corrosive chemicals.

GORE-TEX microfiltration products are used in medical devices, pharmaceutical manufacturing, and chemical processing. These membranes remove bacteria and other microorganisms from air or liquids making them sterile and bacteria free.

Compensation

Compensation at Gore takes three forms: salary, profit sharing, and an Associates' Stock Ownership Program (ASOP).[4] Entry-level salary is in the middle for comparable jobs. According to Sally Gore, daughter-in-law of the founder, "We do not feel we need to be the highest paid. We never try to steal people away from other companies with salary. We want them to come here because of the opportunities for growth and the unique work environment." Associates' salaries are reviewed at least once a year and more commonly twice a year. The reviews are conducted by a compensation team for most workers in the facility in which they work. The sponsors for all Associates act as their advocate during this review process. Prior to meeting with the compensation committee, the sponsor checks with customers or whoever uses the results of the person's work to find out what contribution has been made. In addition, the evaluation team will consider the Associate's leadership ability, his or her willingness to help others to develop to their fullest.

Besides salaries, Gore has profit-sharing and ASOP plans for all Associates. Profit-sharing typically occurs twice a year but is dependent on profitability. The amount also depends on time in service and annual rate of pay. In addition, the firm buys company stock equivalent to 15 percent of the Associates' annual income and places it in an ASOP retirement fund. Thus, an Associate becomes a stockholder after being at Gore for one year. Gore wanted every Associate to feel that they themselves are the owners.

The principle of commitment is seen as a two-way street. Gore tries to avoid layoffs. Instead of cutting pay, which is seen at Gore as disastrous to morale, the company has used a system of temporary transfers within a plant or cluster of plants and voluntary layoffs.

Marketing Strategy

Gore's marketing strategy is based on making the determination that it can offer the best-valued products to a marketplace, that people in that marketplace appreciate what it manufactures, and that Gore can become a

[3]Fluroshield is a registered trademark of W. L. Gore & Associates.
[4]Gore's ASOP is similar legally to an ESOP (Employee Stock Ownership Plan). Gore simply does not use the word *employee* in any of its documentation.

leader in that area of expertise. The operating procedures used to implement the strategy follow the same principles as other functions at Gore.

First, the marketing of a product revolves around a leader who is referred to as a "product champion." According to Dave McCarter, "You've got to marry your technology with the interests of your champions, as you've got to have champions for all these things no matter what. And that's the key element within our company. Without a product champion you can't do much anyway, so it is individually driven. If you get a person interested in a particular market or a particular product for the marketplace, then there is no stopping them."

Second, a product champion is responsible for marketing the product through the commitments with sales representatives. "We have no quota system," said McCarter. "Our marketing and our salespeople make their own commitments as to what their forecasts are. There is no person sitting around telling them that that is not high enough, you have to increase it by 10 percent, or whatever somebody feels is necessary. You are expected to meet your commitment, which is your forecast, but nobody is going to tell you to change it. . . . There is no order of command, no chain involved. These are groups of independent people who come together to make unified commitments to do something and sometimes when they can't make those agreements. . . . You may pass up a market place. . . . but that's OK because there's much more advantage when the team decides to do something."

Third, the sales representatives are on salary. They are not on commission. They participate in the profit-sharing and ASOP plans in which all other Associates participate.

As in other areas of Gore, individual success stories come from diverse backgrounds. McCarter related one of these success stories as follows:

I interviewed Sam one day. I didn't even know why I was interviewing him actually. Sam was retired from AT&T. After twenty-five years, he took the golden parachute and went down to Sun Lakes to play golf. He played golf a few months and got tired of that. He was selling life insurance.

I sat reading the application; his technical background interested me. . . . He had managed an engineering department with 600 people. He'd managed manufacturing plants for AT&T and had a great wealth of experience at AT&T. He said, "I'm retired. I like to play golf but I just can't do it every day, so I want to do something else. Do you have something around here I can do?" I was thinking to myself, This is one of these guys I would sure like to hire, but I don't know what I would do with him. The thing that triggered me was the fact that he said he sold insurance, and here is a guy with a high degree of technical background selling insurance. He had marketing experience, international marketing experience. So, the bell went off in my head that we were trying to introduce a new product into the marketplace that was a hydrocarbon leak protection cable. You can bury it in the ground, and in a matter of seconds it could detect a hydrocarbon (gasoline, etc.). I had a couple of other guys working on it who hadn't been very successful with marketing it. We were having a hard time finding a customer. Well, I thought that kind of a product would be like selling insurance. If you think about it, why should you protect your tanks? It's an insurance policy that things are not leaking into the environment. That has implications, big-time monetary. So, actually, I said, "Why don't you come back Monday? I have just the thing for you." So he did. We hired him; he went to work, a very energetic guy. Certainly a champion of the product, he picked right up on it, ran with it single-handed. . . . Now it's a growing business. It certainly is a valuable one, too, for the environment.

In the implementation of its marketing strategy, Gore relies on cooperative and word-of-mouth advertising. Cooperative advertising is especially used to promote GORE-TEX fabric products. Those products are sold through a number of clothing manufacturers and distributors, including Apparel Technologies, Lands' End, Austin Reed, Timberland, Woolrich, The North Face, Grandoe, and Michelle Jaffe. Gore engages in cooperative advertising because the Associates believe positive experiences with any one product will carry over to purchases of other and more GORE-TEX fabric products.

The power of informal marketing techniques extends beyond consumer products. According to McCarter, "In the technical end of the business, company reputation probably is most important. You have to have a good reputation with your company." He went on to say that without a good reputation, a company's products would not be considered seriously by many industrial customers. In other words, the sale is often made before the representative calls. Using its marketing strategies, Gore has been very successful in securing a market leadership position in a number of areas ranging from waterproof outdoor clothing to vascular grafts.

Financial Information

Gore is a closely held private corporation. Financial information is as closely guarded as proprietary information on products and processes. About 90 percent of the stock is owned by Associates who work at Gore. According to Shanti Mehta, an Associate, Gore's return on assets and sales rank it among the top 10 percent of the Fortune 500 companies. According to another source, Gore is working just fine by any financial measure. It has had 31 straight years of profitability and positive return on equity. The compounded growth rate for revenues at Gore from 1969 to 1989 was over 18 percent discounted for inflation. In comparison, only 11 of the 200 largest companies in the Fortune 500 have had positive return on equity each year from 1970 to 1988, and only two other companies missed only one year. The revenue growth rate for these 13 companies was 5.4 percent compared to 2.5 percent for the entire Fortune 500. Moreover, in 1969 Gore's total sales were about $6 million and in 1990, $660 million. This growth has been financed without debt.

Conclusion

Some analysts are beginning to question whether a large, multinational organization such as Gore can prosper in the 1990s without formal strategic planning and with such an unstructured, unusual management style. Do you feel the analysts' concerns are legitimate, or would you conclude from the case that Gore's strategic management process, or lack thereof, is effective?

References

Aburdene, Patricia, and John Nasbitt. *Re-inventing the Corporation.* New York: Warner Books, 1985.

Agrist, S. W. "Classless Capitalists." *Forbes*, May 9, 1983, pp. 123–24.

Franlesca, L. "Dry and Cool." *Forbes*, August 27, 1984, p. 126.

"The Future Workplace." *Management Review*, July 1986, pp. 22–23.

Hoerr, J. "A Company Where Everybody Is the Boss." *Business Week*, April 15, 1985, p. 98.

McKendrick, Joseph. "The Employees as Entrepreneur." *Management World*, January 1985, pp. 12–13.

Milne, M. J. "The Gorey Details." *Management Review*, March 1985, pp. 16–17.

Posner, B. G. "The First Day on the Job." *Inc.*, June 1986, pp. 73–75.

Price, Kathy. "Firm Thrives without Boss." *AZ Republic*, February 2, 1986.

Rhodes, Lucien. "The Un-manager." *Inc.*, August 1982, p. 34.

Simmons, J. "People Managing Themselves: Unmanagement at W. L. Gore Inc." *Journal for Quality and Participation*, December 1987, pp. 14–19.

Trachtenberg, J. A. "Give Them Stormy Weather." *Forbes*, March 24, 1986, pp. 172–74.

Ward, Alex. "An All-Weather Idea." *The New York Times Magazine*, November 10, 1985, sec. 6.

Weber, Joseph. "No Bosses. And Even 'Leaders' Can't Give Orders." *Business Week*, December 10, 1990, pp. 196–97.

"Wilbert L. Gore." *Industry Week*, October 17, 1983, pp. 48–49.

Notes

1. David K. Hurst, "Cautionary Tales from the Kalahari: How Hunters Become Herders (and May Have Trouble Changing Back Again)," *Academy of Management Executive* 3, no. 5 (1991): 74–86.

2. Milton Leontiades, "The Confusing Words of Business Policy," *Academy of Management Review* 7 (1982): 45–48.

3. Lawrence G. Hrebiniak and William F. Joyce, *Implementing Strategy* (New York: Macmillan, 1984).

4. Henry Mintzberg, *The Structure of Organizations* (Englewood Cliffs, N.J.: Prentice-Hall, 1979), 215–97; idem, "Organization Design: Fashion or Fit?" *Harvard Business Review* 59 (January-February 1981): 103–16.

5. Mintzberg, *The Structure of Organizations*; idem, "Organization Design."

6. Based on Henry Mintzberg, "The Effective Organization: Forces and Forms," *Sloan Management Review* (Winter 1991): 54–67.

7. Danny Miller, "Organizational Configurations: Cohesion, Change, and Prediction," *Human Relations* 43 (1990): 771–89.

8. Peter M. Senge, "Transforming the Practice of Management," *Human Resource Development Quarterly* 4 (Spring 1993): 5–32.

9. Peter Senge, *The Fifth Discipline: The Art and Practice of Learning Organizations* (New York: Doubleday/Currency, 1990).

10. Robert B. Reich, "The Real Economy," *Atlantic Monthly*, February 1991, 35–52.

11. Dave Ulrich and Dale Lake, "Organizational Capability: Creating Competitive Advantage," *Academy of Management Executive* 5, no. 1 (1991): 77–92.

12. Senge, "Transforming the Practice of Management."

13. Ken Peattie, "Strategic Planning: Its Role in Organizational Politics," *Long Range Planning* 26, no. 3 (1993): 10–17.

14. Peter M. Senge, "The Leader's New Work: Building Learning Organizations," *Sloan Management Review* (Fall 1990): 7–23.

15. Ibid.

16. Edward O. Welles, "The Shape of Things to Come," *Inc.*, February 1992, 66–74.

17. Jeffrey Pfeffer, "Producing Sustainable Competitive Advantage through the Effective Management of People," *Academy of Management Executive* 9, no. 1 (1995): 55–72.

18. Alex Markels, "A Power Producer Is Intent on Giving Power to Its People," *Wall Street Journal*, 3 July 1995, A1.

19. Lucien Rhodes with Patricia Amend, "The Turnaround," *Inc.*, August 1986, 42–48.

20. John Case, "The Open Book Revolution," *Inc.*, June 1995, 26–43.

21. Jack Stack, "The Great Game of Business," *Inc.*, June 1992, 53–66.

22. Markels, "A Power Producer Is Intent on Giving Power to Its People."

23. Myron Magnet, "Meet the New Revolutionaries," *Fortune*, 24 February 1992, 94–101.

24. Marc S. Gerstein and Robert B. Shaw, "Organizational Architectures for the Twenty-First Century," in David A. Nadler, Marc S. Gerstein, Robert B. Shaw, and associates, eds., *Organizational Architecture: Designs for Changing Organizations* (San Francisco: Jossey-Bass, 1992), 263–74.

25. Justin Martin, "Are You as Good as You Think You Are?," *Fortune*, 30 September 1996, 142–52; John A. Byrne, "Management Meccas," *Business Week*, 18 September 1995, 122–34.

26. Mary Anne Devanna and Noel Tichy, "Creating the Competitive Organization of the 21st Century: The Boundaryless Corporation," *Human Resource Management* 29 (Winter 1990): 455–71; Fred Kofman and Peter M. Senge, "Communities of Commitment: The Heart of Learning Organizations," *Organizational Dynamics* (Autumn 1993): 4–23.

27. Sumantra Ghoshal and Christopher A. Bartlett, "Rebuilding Behavioral Context: A Blueprint for Corporate Renewal," *Sloan Management Review* (Winter 1996): 23–36.

28. Kofman and Senge, "Communities of Commitment."

29. Joan O'C. Hamilton, Stephen Baker, and Bill Vlasic, "The New Workplace," *Business Week*, 29 April 1996, 106–17.

30. "Interview with Harry V. Quadracci," *Business Ethics* (May-June 1993): 19–21.

31. Ronald Recardo, Kathleen Molloy, and James Pellegrino, "How the Learning Organization Manages Change," *National Productivity Review* (Winter 1995/96): 7–13.

32. Oren Harari, "Open the Doors, Tell the Truth," *Management Review* (January 1995): 33–35.

33. Case, "The Change Masters."

34. Rhodes with Amend, "The Turnaround."

35. Stephen Wood, "High Commitment Management and Payment Systems," *Journal of Management Studies* 33, no. 1 (January 1996): 53–77.

36. Bruce G. Posner, "If at First You Don't Succeed," *Inc.*, May 1989, 132–34.

37. Welles, "The Shape of Things of Come."

38. Rhodes with Amend, "The Turnaround."

39. Dorothy Leonard-Barton, "The Factory as a Learning Laboratory," *Sloan Management Review* (Fall 1992): 23–38.

40. Sumantra Ghoshal and Christopher A. Bartlett, "Rebuilding Behavioral Context: A Blueprint for Corporate Renewal," *Sloan Management Review* (Winter 1996): 23–36.

41. Tom Broersma, "In Search of the Future," *Training and Development* (January 1995): 38–43.

42. Brian Dumaine, "The New Turnaround Champs," *Fortune*, 16 July 1990, 36–44; John M. Stopford and

Charles Baden-Fuller, "Corporate Rejuvenation," *Journal of Management Studies* 27 (1990): 399–415; Richard C. Hoffman, "Strategies for Corporate Turnarounds: What Do We Know about Them?" *Journal of General Management* 14 (Spring 1989): 46–66.

43. Barbara Blumenthal and Philippe Haspeslagh, "Toward a Definition of Corporate Transformation," *Sloan Management Review* (Spring 1994): 101–6.

44. Chet Borucki and Carole K. Barnett, "Restructuring for Self-Renewal: Navistar International Corporation," *Academy of Management Executive* 4 (February 1990): 36–49.

45. Robert J. House and Jitendra V. Singh, "Organizational Behavioral: Some New Directions for I/O Psychology," *Annual Review of Psychology* 38 (1987): 669–718; Bernard M. Bass, *Bass & Stogdill's Handbook of Leadership: Theory, Research, and Managerial Applications*, 3d ed. (New York: Free Press, 1990); Joseph Seltzer and Bernard M. Bass, "Transformational Leadership: Beyond Initiation and Consideration," *Journal of Management* 16 (1990): 693–703.

46. Noel M. Tichy and Mary Ann Devanna, *The Transformational Leader* (New York: John Wiley, 1986).

47. Noel M. Tichy and David O. Ulrich, "The Leadership Challenge—A Call for the Transformational Leader," *Sloan Management Review* 26 (Fall 1984): 59–64.

48. Ghoshal and Bartlett, "Rebuilding Behavioral Context."

49. Gillian Flynn, "On Track to a Comeback," *Personnel Journal* (February 1996): 58–69.

50. Alessandra Bianchi, "Mission Improbable," *Inc.* September 1996, 69–75.

51. Ken G. Smith, Ken A. Smith, Judy D. Olian, Henry P. Sims, Jr., Douglas P. O'Bannon, and Judith A. Scully, "Top Management Team Demography and Process: The Role of Social Integration and Communication," *Administrative Science Quarterly* 39 (1994): 412–38.

52. This discussion is based on Donald C. Hambrick, "Fragmentation and the Other Problems CEOs Have with Their Top Management Teams," *California Management Review* 37, no. 3 (Spring 1995): 110–27.

53. Ibid.

54. Gerald R. Salancik, Barry M. Staw, and Louis R. Pondy, "Administrative Turnover as a Response to Unmanaged Organizational Interdependence," *Academy of Management Journal* 23 (1980): 422–37; Jeffrey Pfeffer and William L. Moore, "Average Tenure of Academic Department Heads: The Effects of Paradigm, Size, and Departmental Philosophy," *Administrative Science Quarterly* 25 (1980): 387–406.

55. Jeffrey Pfeffer and Gerald R. Salancik, "Organizational Context and the Characteristics and Tenure of Hospital Administrators," *Academy of Management Journal* 20 (1977): 74–88.

56. Neil Fligstein, "The Intraorganizational Power Struggle: Rise of Finance Personnel to Top Leadership in Large Corporations, 1919–1979," *American Sociological Review* 52 (1987): 44–58.

57. Ann B. Fischer, "Coke's Brand-Loyalty Lesson," *Fortune*, 5 August 1985, 44–46; John Huey, "New Top Executives Shake up Old Order at Soft-Drink Giant," *Wall Street Journal,* 6 November 1981, 1.

58. "Turnover at the Top," *Business Week*, 19 December 1983, 104–10.

59. Idalene F. Kesner and Terrence C. Sebora, "Executive Succession: Past, Present & Future," *Journal of Management* 20, no. 2 (1994): 327–72.

60. Jeffrey Pfeffer and Alison Davis-Blake, "Administrative Succession and Organizational Performance: How Administrator Experience Mediates the Succession Effect," *Academy of Management Journal* 29 (1986): 72–83; Michael Patrick Allen, Sharon K. Panian, and Roy E. Lotz, "Managerial Succession and Organizational Performance: A Recalcitrant Problem Revisited," *Administrative Science Quarterly* 24 (1979): 167–80; M. Craig Brown, "Administrative Succession and Organizational Performance: The Succession Effect," *Administrative Science Quarterly* 27 (1982): 1–16.

61. David R. James and Michael Soref, "Profit Constraints on Managerial Autonomy: Managerial Theory and the Unmaking of the Corporation President," *American Sociological Review* 46 (1981): 1–18; Oscar Grusky, "Managerial Succession and Organizational Effectiveness," *American Journal of Sociology* 69 (1963): 21–31.

62. Brown, "Administrative Succession and Organizational Performance"; William Gamson and Norman Scotch, "Scapegoating in Baseball," *American Journal of Sociology* 70 (1964): 69–72.

63. J. Richard Harrison, David L. Torres, and Sal Kukalis, "The Changing of the Guard: Turnover and Structural Change in the Top-Management

Positions," *Administrative Science Quarterly* 33 (1988): 211–32.

64. Stanley Lieberson and James F. O'Connor, "Leadership and Organizational Performance: A Study of Large Corporations," *American Sociological Review* 37 (1972): 119; Nan Weiner and Thomas A. Mahoney, "A Model of Corporate Performance as a Function of Environmental, Organizational, and Leadership Influences," *Academy of Management Journal* 24 (1981): 453–70; Jonathan E. Smith, Kenneth P. Carson, and Ralph A. Alexander, "Leadership: It Can Make a Difference," *Academy of Management Journal* 27 (1984): 765–76; Alan Berkeley Thomas, "Does Leadership Make a Difference to Organizational Performance?" *Administrative Science Quarterly* 33 (1988): 388–400.

65. David V. Day and Robert G. Lord, "Executive Leadership and Organizational Performance: Suggestions for a New Theory and Methodology," *Journal of Management* 14 (1988): 453–64.

66. Glenn E. Carroll, "Dynamics of Publishers Succession in Newspaper Organizations," *Administrative Science Quarterly* 29 (1984): 93–113.

Integrative Cases

Integrative Case 1.0 *Victoria Heavy Equipment Limited (Revised)**

Brian Walters sat back in the seat of his Lear jet as it broke through the clouds en route from Squamish, a small town near Vancouver, British Columbia, to Sacramento, California. As chairman of the board, majority shareholder, and chief executive officer, the 51-year-old Walters had run Victoria Heavy Equipment Limited as a closely held company for years. During this time Victoria had become the second-largest producer of mobile cranes in the world, with 1985 sales of $100 million and exports to more than 70 countries. But in early 1986 the problem of succession was in his thoughts. His son and daughter were not yet ready to run the organization, and he personally wanted to devote more time to other interests. He wondered about the kind of person he should hire to become president. There was also a nagging thought that there might be other problems with Victoria that would have to be worked out before he eased out of his present role.

Company History

Victoria Heavy Equipment was established in 1902 in Victoria, British Columbia, to produce horse-drawn log skidders for the forest industry. The young firm showed a flair for product innovation, pioneering the development of motorized skidders and later, after diversifying into the crane business, producing the country's first commercially successful hydraulic crane controls. In spite of these innovations, the company was experiencing severe financial difficulties in 1948 when it was purchased by Brian Walters Sr., the father of the current chairman. By installing tight financial controls and paying close attention to productivity, Walters was able to turn the company around, and in the mid-1950s he decided that Victoria would focus its attention exclusively on cranes, and go after the international market.

By the time of Brian Walters Sr.'s retirement in 1968, it was clear that the decision to concentrate on the crane business had been a good one. The company's sales and profits were growing, and Victoria cranes were beginning to do well in export markets. Walters Sr. was succeeded as president by his brother James, who began to exercise very close personal control over the company's operations. However, as Victoria continued to grow in size and complexity, the load on James became so great that his health began to fail. The solution was to appoint an assistant general manager, John

Rivers, through whom tight supervision could be maintained while James Walters' workload was eased. This move was to no avail, however. James Walters suffered a heart attack in 1970 and Rivers became general manager. At the same time, the young Brian Walters, the current chairman and chief executive officer, became head of the U.S. operation.

When Brian Walters took responsibility for Victoria's U.S. business the firm's American distributor was selling 30–40 cranes per year. Walters thought the company should be selling at least 150. Even worse, the orders that the American firm did get tended to come in large quantities—as many as 50 cranes in a single order—which played havoc with Victoria's production scheduling. Walters commented, "We would rather have ten orders of ten cranes each than a single order for 100." In 1975, when the U.S. distributor's agreement expired, Walters offered the company a five-year renewal if it would guarantee sales of 150 units per year. When the firm refused, Walters bought it, and in the first month fired 13 of the 15 employees and canceled most existing dealerships. He then set to work to rebuild—only accepting orders for 10 cranes or less. His hope was to gain a foothold and a solid reputation in the U.S. market before the big U.S. firms even noticed him.

This strategy quickly showed results, and in 1976 Walters came back to Canada. As Rivers was still general manager, there was not enough to occupy him fully, and he began traveling three or four months a year. While he was still very much a part of the company, it was not a full-time involvement.

Exhibit 1

Victoria Balance Sheet for the Years 1981–85 ($000s)

	1981	1982	1983	1984	1985
Assets					
Current Assets					
Accounts receivable	$ 8,328	$ 7,960	$ 9,776	$10,512	$10,951
Allowance for doubtful accounts	(293)	(310)	(282)	(297)	(316)
Inventories	21,153	24,425	24,698	25,626	27,045
Prepaid expenses	119	104	156	106	129
Total current assets	29,307	32,179	34,343	35,947	37,809
Advances to shareholders	1,300	1,300	1,300	1,300	1,300
Fixed assets: property plant and equipment	6,840	6,980	6,875	7,353	7,389
Total assets	$37,447	$40,459	$42,518	$44,600	$46,598
Liabilities and Shareholders' Equity					
Current Liabilities					
Notes payable to bank	$ 7,733	$ 8,219	$ 9,258	$10,161	$11,332
Accounts payable	9,712	11,353	10,543	10,465	10,986
Accrued expenses	1,074	1,119	1,742	1,501	1,155
Deferred income tax	419	400	396	408	345
Income tax payable	545	692	612	520	516
Current portion of long-term debt	912	891	867	888	903
Total current liabilities	$20,395	$22,674	$23,418	$23,943	$25,237
Long-term debt	6,284	6,110	6,020	6,005	6,114
Total liabilities	26,679	28,784	29,438	29,948	31,351
Shareholders' Equity					
Common shares	200	290	295	390	435
Retained earnings	10,568	11,385	12,790	14,262	14,812
Total shareholders' equity	10,768	11,675	13,080	14,652	15,247
Total liabilities and shareholders' equity	$37,447	$40,459	$42,518	$44,600	$46,598

Victoria in the 1980s

Victoria entered the 1980s with sales of approximately $50 million and by 1985, partly as a result of opening the new plant in California, had succeeded in doubling this figure. Profits reached their highest level ever in 1983, but declined somewhat over the next two years as costs rose and the rate of sales growth slowed. Financial statements are presented in Exhibits 1 and 2. The following sections describe the company and its environment in the 1980s.

Product Line

The bulk of Victoria's crane sales in the 1980s came from a single product line, the LTM 1000, which was produced both in the company's Squamish facility (the firm had moved from Victoria to Squamish in the early 1900s) and its smaller plant in California, built in 1979. The LTM 1000 line consisted of mobile cranes of five basic sizes, averaging approximately $500,000 in price. Numerous options were available for these cranes, which could provide uncompromised on-site performance, precision lifting capabilities, fast highway travel, and effortless city driving. Because of the numerous choices available, Victoria preferred not to build them to stock. The company guaranteed 60-day delivery and "tailor-made" cranes to customer specifications. This required a large inventory of both parts and raw material.

Exhibit 2

*Victoria Income State-
ment for the Years
1981–85 ($000s)*

	1981	1982	1983	1984	1985
Revenue					
Net sales	$63,386	$77,711	$86,346	$94,886	$100,943
Costs and Expenses					
Cost of sales	49,238	59,837	63,996	71,818	75,808
Selling expense	7,470	9,234	10,935	11,437	13,104
Administrative expense	2,684	3,867	5,490	5,795	7,038
Engineering expense	1,342	1,689	1,832	1,949	2,109
Gross income	2,652	3,084	4,093	3,887	2,884
Income taxes	1,081	1,281	1,630	1,505	1,254
Net income	$ 1,571	$ 1,803	$ 2,463	$ 2,382	$ 1,630

Walters had used a great deal of ingenuity to keep Victoria in a competitive position. For example, in 1982, he learned that a company trying to move unusually long and heavy logs from a new tract of redwood trees in British Columbia was having serious problems with its existing cranes. A crane with a larger than average height and lifting capacity was required. Up to this point, for technical reasons, it had not been possible to produce a crane with the required specifications. However, Walters vowed that Victoria would develop such a crane, and six months later it had succeeded.

Although the LTM 1000 series provided almost all of Victoria's crane sales, a new crane had been introduced in 1984 after considerable expenditure on design, development and manufacture. The $650,000 A-100 had a 70-tonne capacity and could lift loads to heights of 61 meters, a combination previously unheard of in the industry. Through the use of smooth hydraulics even the heaviest loads could be picked up without jolts. In spite of these features, and an optional ram-operated tilt-back cab designed to alleviate the stiff necks which operators commonly developed from watching high loads, sales of the A-100 were disappointing. As a result, several of the six machines built were leased to customers at unattractive rates. The A-100 had, however, proven to be a very effective crowd attraction device at equipment shows.

Markets

There were two important segments in the crane market—custom-built cranes and standard cranes—and although the world mobile crane market was judged to be $630 million in 1985, no estimates were available as to the size of each segment. Victoria competed primarily in the custom segment, in the medium- and heavy-capacity end of the market. In the medium-capacity custom crane class Victoria's prices were approximately 75% of those of its two main competitors. The gap closed as the cranes became heavier, with Victoria holding a 15% advantage over Washington Cranes in the heavy custom crane business. In heavy standard cranes Victoria did not have a price advantage.

Victoria's two most important markets were Canada and the United States. The U.S. market was approximately $240 million in 1985, and Victoria's share was about 15%. Victoria's Sacramento plant, serving both the U.S. market and export sales involving U.S. aid and financing, produced 60 to 70 cranes per year. The Canadian market was much smaller, about $44 million in 1985, but Victoria was the dominant firm in the country, with a 60% share. The Squamish plant, producing 130 to 150 cranes per year, supplied both the Canadian market and all export sales not covered by the U.S. plant. There had been very little real growth in the world market since 1980.

The primary consumers in the mobile crane industry were contractors. Because the amount of equipment downtime could make the difference between showing a profit or loss on a contract, contractors were very sensitive to machine dependability as well as parts and service availability. Price was important, but it was not everything. Independent surveys suggested that Washington Crane, Victoria's most significant competitor, offered somewhat superior service and reliability, and if Victoria attempted to sell similar equipment at prices comparable to Washington's, it would fail. As a result, Victoria tried to reduce its costs through extensive backward integration, manufacturing 85% of its crane components in-house, the highest percentage in the industry. This drive to reduce costs was somewhat offset, however, by the fact that much of the equipment in the Squamish plant was very old. In recent years, some of the slower and less versatile machinery had been replaced, but by 1985 only 15% of the machinery in the plant was new, efficient, numerically controlled equipment.

Victoria divided the world into eight marketing regions. The firm carried out little conventional advertising, but did participate frequently at equipment trade shows. One of the company's most effective selling tools was its ability to fly in prospective customers from all over the world in Walters' executive jet. Victoria believed that the combination of its integrated plant, worker loyalty, and the single-product concentration evident in their Canadian plant produced a convinced customer. There were over 14 such visits to the British Columbia plant in 1985, including delegations from The People's Republic of China, Korea, France and Turkey.

Competition

Victoria, as the world's second largest producer of cranes, faced competition from five major firms, all of whom were much larger and more diversified. The industry leader was the Washington Crane Company with 1985 sales of $400 million and a world market share of 50%. Washington had become a name synonymous around the world with heavy-duty equipment and had been able to maintain a sales growth-rate of over 15% per annum for the past five years. It manufactured in the U.S., Mexico and Australia. Key to its operations were 100 strong dealers worldwide with over 200 outlets. Washington had almost 30% of Canada's crane market.

Next in size after Victoria was Texas Star, another large manufacturer whose cranes were generally smaller than Victoria's and sold through the company's extensive worldwide equipment dealerships. The next two largest competitors were both very large U.S. multinational producers whose crane lines formed a small part of their overall business. With the exception of Washington, industry observers suggested that crane sales for these latter firms had been stable (at best) for quite some time. The exception was the Japanese crane producer Toshio which had been aggressively pursuing sales worldwide and had entered the North American market recently. Sato, another Japanese firm, had started in the North American market as well. Walters commented:

> *My father laid the groundwork for the success that this company has enjoyed, but it is clear that we now have some major challenges ahead of us. Washington Cranes is four times our size and I know that we are at the top of their hit list. Our Japanese competitors,*

> *Toshio and Sato, are also going to be tough. The key to our success is to remain flexible—we must not develop the same kind of organization as the big U.S. firms.*

Organization

In 1979, a number of accumulating problems had ended Brian Walters' semi-retirement and brought him back into the firm full time. Although sales were growing, Walters saw that work was piling up and things were not getting done. He believed that new cranes needed to be developed, and he wanted a profit-sharing plan put in place. One of his most serious concerns was the development of middle managers. Walters commented, "we had to develop middle-level line managers—we had no depth." The root cause of these problems, Walters believed, was that the firm was overly centralized. Most of the functional managers reported to Rivers, and Rivers made most of the decisions. Walters concluded that action was necessary—"We have to change," he said. "If we want to grow further we have to do things."

Between 1979 and 1982 Walters reorganized the firm by setting up separate operating companies and a corporate staff group. In several cases, senior operating executives were placed in staff/advisory positions, while in others executives held positions in both operating and staff groups. Exhibit 3 illustrates Victoria's organizational chart as of 1983.

By early 1984 Walters was beginning to wonder "if I had made a very bad decision." The staff groups weren't working. Rivers had been unable to accept the redistribution of power and had resigned. There was "civil war in the company." Politics and factional disputes were the rule rather than the exception. Line managers were upset by the intervention of the staff VPs of employee relations, manufacturing, and marketing. Staff personnel, on the other hand, were upset by "poor" line decisions.

As a result, the marketing and manufacturing staff functions were eradicated with the late-1985 organizational restructuring illustrated in Exhibit 4. The services previously supplied by the staff groups were duplicated to varying extent inside each division.

In place of most of the staff groups, an executive committee was established in 1984. Membership in this group included the president and head of all staff groups and presidents (general managers) of the four divisions. Meeting monthly, the executive committee was intended to evaluate the performance of the firm's profit and cost problems, handle mutual problems such as transfer prices, and allocate capital expenditures among the four operating divisions. Subcommittees handled subjects such as R&D and new products.

Exhibit 3

Victoria Organizational Structure, 1979–83

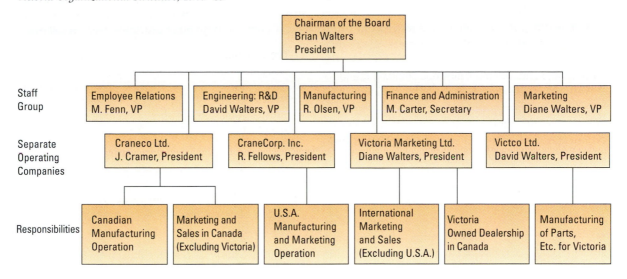

The new organization contained seven major centers for performance measurement purposes. The cost centers were

1. Engineering; R&D (reporting to Victco Ltd.).
2. International Marketing (Victoria Marketing Ltd.).
3. Corporate staff.

The major profit centers were

4. CraneCorp. Inc. (U.S. production and sales).
5. Victco Ltd. (supplying Victoria with components).
6. Craneco (Canadian production and marketing).
7. Victoria-owned Canadian sales outlets (reporting to Victoria Marketing Ltd.).

Exhibit 4

Victoria Organizational Structure, Late 1985

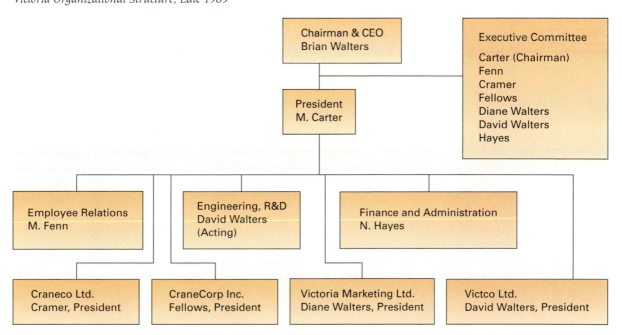

The major profit centers had considerable autonomy in their day-to-day operations and were motivated to behave as if their division was a separate, independent firm.

By mid-1985, Brian Walters had moved out of his position as president, and Michael Carter—a long-time employee close to retirement—was asked to take the position of president until a new one could be found.

Walters saw his role changing. "If I was anything, I was a bit of an entrepreneur. My job was to supply that thrust but to let people develop on their own accord. I was not concerned about things not working, but I was concerned when nothing was being done about it."

In the new organization Walters did not sit on the executive committee. However, as chairman of the board and chief executive officer, the committee's recommendations came to him and ". . . they tried me on six ways from Sunday." His intention was to monitor the firm's major activities rather than to set them. He did have to sit on the product development subcommittee, however, when "things were not working . . . there was conflict . . . the engineering group (engineering, R&D) had designed a whole new crane and nobody including me knew about it." Mr. McCarthy, the V.P. of engineering and R&D, called only five to six committee meetings. The crane his group developed was not to Walters' liking. (There had been a high turnover rate in this group, with four V.P.s since 1983.) Recognizing these problems, Walters brought in consultants to tackle the problems of the management information system and the definition of staff/line responsibilities.

In spite of these moves, dissatisfaction still existed within the company in 1986. The new organization had resulted in considerable dissension. Some conflict centered around the establishment of appropriately challenging budgets for each operating firm and even more conflict had erupted over transfer pricing and allocation of capital budgets. In 1985-86, even though requested budgets were cut equally, lack of central control over spending resulted in overexpenditures by several of the profit and cost centers.

The views of staff and the operating companies' presidents varied considerably when they discussed Victoria's organizational evolution and the operation of the present structure.

Diane Walters, the president of Victoria International Marketing, liked the autonomous system because it helped to identify the true performance of sections of the company. "We had separate little buckets and could easily identify results." Furthermore, she felt that there was no loss of efficiency (due to the duplication of certain staff functions within the divisions) since there was little duplication of systems between groups, and each group acted as a check and balance on the other groups so that "manufacturing won't make what marketing won't sell." Comments from other executives were as follows:

> The divisionalized system allowed me to get closer to my staff because we were a separate group.

> We ended up with sales and marketing expertise that was much better than if we had stayed under manufacturing.

> If you (run the firm) with a manufacturing-oriented organization, you could forget what people want.

> In a divisionalized system there was bound to be conflict between divisions, but that was not necessarily unhealthy.

Some executives saw the decentralized, semiautonomous operating company structure as a means of giving each person the opportunity to grow and develop without the hindrance of other functional executives. Most, if not all, of the operating company presidents and staff V.P.s were aware that decentralization brought benefits, especially in terms of the autonomy it gave them to modify existing practices. One senior executive even saw the present structure as an indicator of their basic competitive stance: "Either we centralize the structure and retract, or we stay as we are and fight with the big guys." With minimal direction supplied from Brian Walters, presidents were able to build up their staff, establish priorities and programs, and, essentially, were only held responsible for the bottom line.

Other executives believed that Victoria's structure was inappropriate. As one executive put it, "The semi-independence of the operating companies and the lack of a real leader for the firm have resulted in poor coordination of problem solving and difficulty in allocating responsibility." As an example, he noted how engineering's response to manufacturing was often slow and poorly communicated. Even worse, the executive noted, was how the priorities of different units were not synchronized. "When you manufacture just one product line all your activities are interrelated. So when one group puts new products first on a priority list while another is still working out bugs in the existing product, conflict and inefficiencies have to develop."

The opposing group argued that the present organization was more appropriate to a larger, faster growing and more complex company. As one senior executive put it, "We're too small to be as decentralized as we are now. All of this was done to accommodate the Walters kids anyway, and it's now going to detract from profitability and growth." Another of these executives stated that rather than being a president of an operating company he would prefer to be a general manager at the head of a functional group, reporting to a group head. "If we had the right Victoria Heavy Equipment president," he said, "we wouldn't need all these divisional presidents." Another continued,

> *Right now the players (divisional presidents and staff V.P.s) run the company. Brian Walters gives us a shot of adrenaline four or six times a year but doesn't provide any active leadership. When Brian leaves, things stop. Instead, Brian now wants to monitor the game plan rather than set it up for others to run. As we still only have an interim president (Carter), it is the marketplace that leads us, not any strategic plan or goal.*

The New President

Individual views about the appropriate characteristics of a new president were determined by what each executive thought was wrong with Victoria. Everyone realized that the new president would have to accommodate Brian Walters' presence and role in the firm and the existence of his two children in the organization. They all generally saw Brian as wanting to supply ideas and major strategies but little else.

All but one of Victoria's executives agreed that the new president should not get involved in day-to-day activities or in major decision making. Instead, he should "arbitrate" among the line general managers (subsidiary presidents) and staff VPs and become more of a "bureaucrat-cum-diplomat" than an aggressive leader. As another put it, "The company will drive itself; only once in a while he'll steer a little."

The 1986 Situation

Industry analysts predicted a decline of 10% in world crane sales—which totaled 1200 units in 1985—and as much as a 30% decrease in the North American market in 1986. Victoria's sales and production levels were down. Seventy-five shop-floor employees had been laid off at Squamish, bringing total employment there to 850, and similar cuts were expected in Sacramento. Worker morale was suffering as a result, and the profit sharing plan, which had been introduced in early 1985 at Walters' initiative, was not helping matters. In spite of the optimism conveyed to workers when the plan was

initiated, management had announced in October that no bonus would be paid for the year. Aggravating the problem was the workforce's observation that while certain groups met their budget, others did not, and hence all were penalized. This problem arose because each bonus was based on overall as well as divisional profits.

Many of the shop-floor workers and the supervisory staff were also disgruntled with the additions to the central and divisional staff groups, which had continued even while the workforce was being reduced. They felt that the paperwork these staff functions created was time-consuming and of little benefit. They noted, for example, that there were four or five times as many people in production control in 1986 as there were in 1980 for the same volume of production. In addition, they pointed out that despite all sorts of efforts on the part of a computer-assisted production control group, inventory levels were still too high.

Brian Walters commented on the 1986 situation and his view of the company's future:

> *What we are seeing in 1986 is a temporary decline in the market. This does not pose a serious problem for us, and certainly does not impact on my longer term goals for this company, which are to achieve a 25% share of the world market by 1990, and reach sales of $250 million by 1999. We can reach these goals as long as we don't turn into one of these bureaucratic, grey-suited companies that are so common in North America. There are three keys for success in this business—a quality product, professional people and the motivation for Victoria to be the standard of excellence in our business. This means that almost everything depends on the competence and motivation of our people. We will grow by being more entrepreneurial, more dedicated, and more flexible than our competitors. With our single product line we are also more focused than our competitors. They manage only by the numbers—there is no room in those companies for an emotional plea, they won't look at sustaining losses to get into a new area, they'll turn the key on a loser . . . we look at the longer term picture.*

"The hazard for Victoria," Walters said as he looked out of his window toward the Sacramento airstrip, "is that we could develop the same kind of bureaucratic, quantitatively oriented, grey-suited managers that slow down the large U.S. competitors. But that," he said, turning to his audience, "is something I'm going to watch like a hawk. We need the right people."

Integrative Case 2.1 *Littleton Manufacturing (A)**

Rule #1 for business organizations: People, not structure, make a business work or fail. Blindly following organizational concepts that have worked elsewhere is a sure way to waste talent and get poor results. Organizational change alone achieves nothing, while dedicated people can make any structure work. This doesn't mean that organizational changes shouldn't happen. But design any changes to get the most out of people in the company's unique circumstances. Top management should never dictate change as a cure-all to avoid facing fundamental problems.

> Quotation from the *Harvard Business Review* (title and author uncited) posted on the wall of Bill Larson, Plant Manager of Littleton Manufacturing

On June 21, 1990, Paul Winslow, the Director of Human Resources at Littleton Manufacturing, was told by his boss, Bill Larson, to put together a team of employees to address a number of issues that Larson thought were hurting Littleton's bottom line. Winslow's assignment had come about as a result of his making a presentation on those problems to Larson. Larson had then met with his executive staff, and he and Winslow had subsequently gone to the plant's Quality Steering Committee to discuss what to do. It was decided to form a Human Resources Process Improvement Team (PIT) to prioritize the issues and propose a corrective course of action. Winslow, who had been at the plant for seventeen years, had been asked by Larson to chair the PIT.

The Quality Steering Committee decided that the PIT should include two representatives each from Sales and Marketing, Fabrication, and Components. Two managers from each of these areas were chosen, including Dan Gordon, the Fabrication Manufacturing Manager, and Phil Hanson, the Components Manufacturing Manager. There were no supervisors or hourly employees on the team.

At the first meeting, the PIT discussed the six widely recognized problem areas that Winslow had identified to Larson. Each member's assignment for the next meeting, on June 28, was to prioritize the issues and propose an action plan.

The Problems

A course in management and organizational studies carried out by students at a nearby college had started the chain of events that led to the formation of the Human Resources PIT. In late 1989, Winslow was approached by a faculty member at a local college who was interested in using Littleton as a site for a field-project course. Because of ongoing concerns about communication at the plant by all levels, Winslow asked that the students assess organizational communication at Littleton. Larson gave his approval, and in the spring of 1990 the students carried out the project, conducting individual and group interviews with employees at all levels of the plant.

Winslow and his staff combined the results of the students' assessment with the results of an in-house survey done several years earlier. The result was the identification of six problem areas that they thought were critical for the plant to address:

- Lack of organizational unity
- Lack of consistency in enforcing rules and procedures
- Supervisor's role poorly perceived
- Insufficient focus on Littleton's priorities
- Change is poorly managed
- Lack of a systematic approach to training

The Company

Littleton Manufacturing, located in rural Minnesota, was founded in 1925. In 1942, Littleton was bought by Brooks Industries, a major manufacturer of domestic appliances and their components. At that time, Littleton manufactured custom-made and precision-machined components from special metals for a variety of industries.

In 1983, through the purchase of a larger competitor, Frühling, Inc., Brooks was able to increase its domestic market share from 8 percent to about 25 percent.

---

*By David E. Whiteside, organizational development consultant. This case was written at Lewiston-Auburn College of the University of Southern Maine with the cooperation of management, solely for the purpose of stimulating student discussion. Data are based on field research; all events are real, although the names of organizations, locations, and individuals have been disguised. Faculty members in nonprofit institutions are encouraged to reproduce this case for distribution to their students without charge or written permission. All other rights reserved jointly to the author and the North American Case Research Association (NACRA). Copyright © 1994 by the *Case Research Journal* and David E. Whiteside.

Brooks then decided to have only one facility produce the components that were used in most of the products it made in the United States. The site chosen was Littleton Manufacturing. To do this, Brooks added a whole new business (Components) to Littleton's traditional activity. To accommodate the new line, a building of 80,000 square feet was added to the old Littleton plant, bringing the total to 220,000 square feet of plant space. Because of the addition of this new business, Littleton went from 150 employees in 1984 to 600 in 1986. In mid-1990, there were about 500 employees.

The older part of the plant (the Fabrication side) manufactured its traditional custom-made products and sold them to a variety of industrial customers. It also supplied the newer side of the plant (the Components side) with a variety of parts that were further processed and used to make electrical components. These components were used by all other Brooks plants in the assembly of domestic appliances that were sold worldwide. About 95 percent of the products made on the Components side of the plant originated on the Fabrication side.

The plant was also headquarters for Brooks Industries' sales and marketing department, known as the "commercial group," which had worldwide sales responsibilities for products made by the Fabrication side. These included international and domestic sales of products to several industries, including the semiconductor, consumer electronics, and nuclear furnace industry. This group marketed products made not only by Littleton Manufacturing but also those made by Brooks's other fourteen plants, all located in the United States.

Bill Larson, the plant manager, reported to the executive vice president of manufacturing of Brooks, whose corporate office was in Chicago, Illinois. Larson met once a month with his boss and the other plant managers. Reporting directly to Larson were six functional line managers and the manager of the Quality Improvement System (QIS). This group of seven managers, known as the "staff," met weekly to plan and discuss how things were going. (See Exhibit 1 for an organizational chart.)

In December 1989, there were 343 hourly and 125 salaried employees at the plant. About 80 percent of the work force was under 45. Seventy-seven percent were male, and 23 percent were female. Seventy-six percent had been at the plant 10 years or less. All of the hourly workers were represented by the Teamsters union.

The Financial Picture

Brooks Industries

Brooks was the second largest producer of its kind of domestic appliances in the United States. Its three core business units were commercial/industrial, consumer, and original equipment manufacturing. The major U.S. competitors for its domestic appliances were Eagleton, Inc., and Universal Appliances, Inc. In the United States, Eagleton's market share was 47 percent; Brooks had about 23 percent; and Universal Appliances and a

Exhibit 1

Littleton Manufacturing Organizational Chart (Littleton Manufacturing)

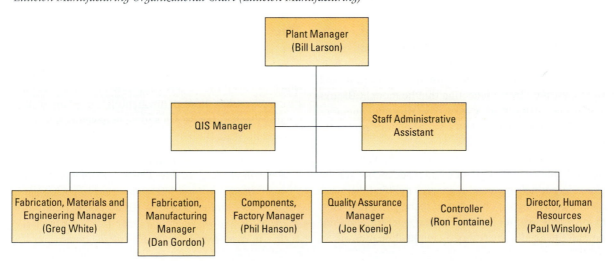

number of small companies had the remaining 30 percent. However, U.S. manufacturers were facing increasing competition, primarily based on lower prices, from companies in Asia and eastern Europe.

In 1989, Brooks's sales declined 4 percent, and in 1990, they declined another 5 percent, to $647 million. Their 1989 annual report contained the following statement about the company's financial condition: "There was fierce competition . . . which led to a decline in our share of a stable market and a fall in prices, resulting in a lower level of sales. . . . With sales volume showing slower growth, we failed to reduce our costs proportionately and there was underutilization of capacity." In May 1990, after announcing unexpected first-quarter losses, Brooks started a corporationwide efficiency drive, including planned layoffs of 16 percent of its work force, a corporate restructuring, and renewed emphasis on managerial accountability for bottom-line results.

Because of its worsening financial condition, for the past few years Brooks had been reducing the resources available to Littleton. For example, Larson's budget for salaries had been increased by only 4 percent each year for the past several years. As a result, supervisors and middle managers complained strongly that recent salary increases had been too little and that plant salaries were too low. They also felt that the forced-ranking performance appraisal system used by the plant, which was based on a bell curve, did not reward good performance adequately. One middle manager commented: "All we get now for good performance is a card and a turkey." In April 1990, the company cut Littleton's capital budget by half and stipulated that any new project involving nonessential items had to have a one-year payback.

In addition, in both 1988 and 1989 Brooks had charged the Littleton plant around $300,000 for various services provided, such as technical support, but in 1990 this charge was increased by $1 million. Many of the Littleton plant managers felt that this was done to help offset Brooks's deteriorating financial condition and were frustrated by it. Indicating that he thought Brooks was using Littleton as a cash cow, one staff member said, "The more profitable we get, the more corporate will charge us."

Many managers, especially those on the Fabrication side, felt that even though they had made money for the plant, corporate's increase in charges nullified their success and hard work. A number of managers on the Fabrication side also feared that if their operation did not do well financially, the company might close it down.

In discussing the increasing lack of resources available from corporate and the plant's own decline in profits, Larson said: "There needs to be a change in the way people here think about resources. They have to think more in terms of efficiency." He was proud of the fact that the company had achieved its goal of reducing standard costs by 1 percent for each of the past three years and that in 1990 cost reductions would equal 5 percent of production value. He thought that if the company reduced the number of reworks, costs could be lowered by another 20 to 30 percent.

Littleton Manufacturing

The Fabrication and the Components operations at Littleton Manufacturing were managed as cost centers by Brooks while the commercial group was a profit center. (A *profit center* is part of an organization that is responsible for accumulating revenues as well as costs. A *cost center* is an organizational division or unit of activity in which accounts are maintained containing direct costs for which the center's head is responsible.) In 1989 and 1990, the Fabrication side of Littleton had done well in terms of budgeted costs, while the Components side had incurred significant losses for both years.

Littleton's net worth increased from $319,000 in 1989 to $3,094,000 in 1990 due to the addition of a new Fabrication-side product that was sold on the external market and had required no additional assets or resources. In 1990, sales for the plant as a whole were $41,196,000, with an operating profit of 3.7 percent, down from 7.3 percent in 1989. Larson estimated that the current recession, which was hurting the company, would lower sales in 1991 by 10 percent. Exhibit 2 presents an operating statement for Littleton Manufacturing from 1988 to 1990.

The Quality Improvement System

In 1985, corporate mandated a total quality management effort, the Quality Improvement System (QIS), which replaced the quality circles that the plant had instituted in 1980. Posted throughout the plant was a Quality Declaration, which had been developed by Larson and his staff. It read:

We at Littleton Manufacturing are dedicated to achieving lasting quality. This means that each of us must understand and meet the requirements of our customers and co-workers. We all must continually strive for improvement and error-free work in all we do—in every job . . . on time . . . all the time.

Exhibit 2

Littleton Manufacturing Operating Profit Statement

	1988	1989	1990
Fabrication			
Sales	$16,929	$18,321	$19,640
Direct costs	11,551	11,642	11,701
Contribution margin	5,378	6,679	7,939
% to sales	31.8%	36.5%	40.4%
All other operating costs	4,501	4,377	4,443
Operating profit	877	2,301	3,496
% to sales	5.2%	-12.6%	17.8%
Components			
Sales	$20,468	$15,590	$21,556
Direct costs	16,049	10,612	18,916
Contribution margin	4,419	4,978	2,640
% to sales	21.6%	31.9%	12.2%
All other operating costs	4,824	4,797	4,628
Operating profit	(405)	180	(1,988)
% to sales	-2.0%	1.2%	-9.2%
Total Littleton Manufacturing			
Sales	$37,397	$33,911	$41,196
Direct costs	27,599	22,254	30,617
Contribution margin	9,798	11,656	10,579
% to sales	26.2%	34.4%	25.7%
All other operating costs	9,326	9,175	9,071
Operating profit	472	2,482	1,508
% to sales	1.3%	7.3%	3.7%

Note: Changes in Operating Profit from year to year are posted to retained earnings (net worth) account on the corporate balance sheet. It must be noted, however, that the balance sheet figures include the impact of headquarters, national organization charges, and extraordinary income from other operations, which are not reflected on the operating profit statement shown above.

Source: Controller, Littleton Manufacturing.

Bill Larson was enthusiastic about QIS. He saw QIS as a total quality approach affecting not just products but all of the plant's processes, one that would require a long-term effort at changing the culture at the plant. He felt that QIS was already reaping benefits in terms of significant improvements in quality, and that the system had also greatly helped communication at the plant.

In the QIS all employees were required to participate in Departmental Quality Teams (DQTs) that met in groups of 6 to 12 every 2 weeks for at least an hour to identify ways to improve quality. Most hourly employees were on only one DQT; middle managers were, on average, on three DQTs. Some managers were on as many as six. The results of each team's efforts were ex-hibited in graphs and charts by their work area and updated monthly. There were about sixty teams in the plant.

The leader from each Departmental Quality Team, a volunteer, served also as a member of a Quality Improvement Team (QIT), whose goals were to support the DQTs and help them link their goals to the company's goals. QITs consisted of six to eight people; each was chaired by a member of the executive staff. These staff members, along with Bill Larson, composed the Quality Steering Committee (QSC) for the plant. The QSC's job was to oversee the direction and implementation of the Quality Improvement System for the plant and to coordinate with corporate's quality improvement programs. The QSC also sometimes formed corrective action teams to work on special projects. Unlike DQTs, which were composed of employees from a single department or work area, corrective action teams had members from different functions or departments. By 1986, there were nine corrective action teams, but by 1989, none were functioning. When asked about them, Winslow said, "I'm not sure what happened to them. They just sort of died out."

Larson and most managers believed that the QIS had improved quality. On most of its Fabrication products, the company competed on the basis of quality and customer service, and the vice president of sales and marketing thought that their quality was the best in the industry. In 1988 and 1989, the plant won several Brooks awards for quality and was publicly cited by a number of customers for quality products.

Hourly employees in general also thought that QIS had improved quality, although they were less enthusiastic about the system than management. A number of hourly employees complained that since participation was mandatory, many groups were held back by unmotivated members. They thought participation should be voluntary. Another complaint was that there was inadequate training for group leaders, with the result that some groups were not productive.

In the spring of 1990, the company decided that the QIS effort was "stagnating" and that DQTs should be changed to include members from different departments. It was thought this would improve communication and coordination between departments and lead to further improvements in quality, productivity, and on-time delivery. DQTs became known is IDQTs (Interdepartmental Quality Teams). IDQTs were scheduled to begin in November 1990. In addition, the company decided to begin Process Improvement Teams (PITs), which would focus on various ongoing processes at the plant, such as budgeting and inventory management. A PIT, composed of managers from different functions, would not be ongoing but only last as long as it took to achieve its particular goals.

How Different Levels Perceived the Problems

In order to choose the issues to tackle first and to devise a tentative plan for addressing them, Winslow reflected on the background information he had on the six problem areas that he and his staff had identified on the basis of their own analysis and the students' assessment of organizational communication.

A Lack of Organizational Unity

People often talked about "this side of the wall and that side of the wall" in describing the plant. They were referring to the wall separating the newer, Components side and the older, Fabrication side of the plant. (Some parts of the Fabrication side had been built in the twenties.) The Components side was brighter, cleaner, and more open, and, in summer, it was cooler. In comparing the two sides one manager said, "At the end of the shift in Fabrication, you come out looking like you've been through the wringer." On the whole, the equipment in the Components side was also newer, with most of it dating from the 1970s and 1980s and some of it state-of-the-art machinery that was developed at the plant. Much of the equipment on the Fabrication side went back to the 1950s and 1960s. These differences in age meant that, in general, the machinery on the Fabrication side required more maintenance.

It was generally agreed that Components jobs were cleaner and easier, and allowed more social interaction. On the Fabrication side many of the machines could run only 2 to 3 hours before needing attention, whereas on the Components side the machines might run for days without worker intervention. On the Fabrication side, because of the placement of the machines and the need for frequent maintenance, people tended to work more by themselves and to "be on the go all the time." It was not uncommon for senior hourly employees in Fabrication to request a transfer to Components.

Hourly workers described Components as "a country club" compared to the Fabrication side. Many attributed this to how the different sides were managed. Enforcement of rules was more lax on the Components side. For example, rules requiring safety shoes and goggles were not as strictly enforced, and some operators were allowed to eat on the job.

One Human Resources staff member described Components supervisors as "laid-back about sticking to the rules" and those in Fabrication as "sergeants." He saw the manufacturing manager of Fabrication, Dan Gordon, as having a clear vision of what he wanted for the Fabrication side and a definite plan on how to get there. He also saw Gordon as keeping a tight rein on his supervisors and holding them accountable. The same Human Resources employee described the factory manager of Components, Phil Hanson, as dealing with things as they came up—as more reactive. Hanson allowed his supervisors more freedom and did not get involved on the floor unless there was a problem. When there was a problem, however, he reacted strongly and swiftly. For example, to combat a recent tendency for employees to take extended breaks, he had begun posting supervisors outside of the bathrooms right before and after scheduled breaks.

Bill Larson attributed the differences in the two sides "to the different performance and accountability needs dictated by their business activities and by the corporate office." Components met the internal production needs of Brooks by supplying all of the other Brooks plants with a product that they, in turn, used to manufacture a household product that sold in the millions each year. Fabrication, however, had to satisfy the needs of a variety of industrial customers while competing on the open market. Larson felt that Fabrication had to have a more entrepreneurial ethic than Components because "Fabrication lives or dies by how they treat their customers—they have to woo them and interact well with them," whereas Components had a ready-made market.

Larson also thought that some of the differences were due to the fact that the plant was "held prisoner by what goes on in corporate." Although the corporate office set financial targets for both sides of the plant, it exercised more control over the financial and productivity goals of the Components side because no other Brooks plant was in the Fabrication business and Brooks understood the Components business much better. In addition, corporate was dependent on the Components side for the standardized parts—primarily wire coils—used in many of its finished products. The Components side produced as many as 2 million of some of these small parts a day.

Larson also indicated that the requirements for the number of workers on the two sides of the plant were different. For example, depending upon what business was like for each side, the overtime requirements could vary. Hourly employees on the side of the plant that had more overtime felt the side that was working less was getting "easier" treatment. Larson knew that the overtime disparity was due to need, not preferential treatment of one side over the other, but as he put it: "You can talk your head off, but you're not going to be able to explain it to them to their satisfaction. So that causes a lot of frustration among the ranks down there."

The Manager of QIS traced the differences between the Fabrication side and the Components side to the consolidation at Littleton of all of Brooks's production of wire coils needed for its domestic appliances after Brooks bought Frühling, Inc., in 1984. Most of the upper managers hired to start the Components business were brought in from Frühling, and, as he put it, "They had a different way of doing things. It wasn't a tightly

run ship." He said that some of the old managers at the plant wondered about the wisdom of bringing in managers from a company that had not been successful. People asked, "Why use them here? They must have been part of what was wrong." One Fabrication manager added that the manager brought in to start the Components business, Bob Halperin, had the view: "We're going to start a new business here and do whatever is necessary to make it run and to hell with Littleton Manufacturing policies." Also, when the new Components business was started, its manager reported directly to the Brooks corporate office and not to the plant manager. In 1986 the structure was changed so that the factory manager of Components reported to the Littleton Manufacturing plant manager.

A union steward at the plant attributed some of the differences between the two sides to the fact that the work force on the Components side tended to be younger and had more women with young children (67 percent of the hourly women in the plant worked in Components). The demands of raising children, he thought, resulted in the women needing to take more time off from work. One of the Fabrication supervisors thought that since the supervisors on the Components side were younger, they expected more from management and were more outspoken, especially about how much an hour they should be paid. A number of these supervisors had also been brought in from Frühling, and were not originally from Littleton.

Lack of Consistency in Enforcing Rules and Procedures

A major complaint of both hourly and salaried workers was the inconsistent application of policies and procedures. Although most people mentioned the differences from one side of the plant to the other, there were also differences from one department to another. As the chief union steward put it, "This is the number one problem here—nobody is the same!" Some Components supervisors were letting people take longer breaks and going for breaks earlier than they were supposed to. Some supervisors allowed hourly employees to stand around and talk for a while before getting them to start their machines. In some departments on the Components side, employees were allowed to gather in the bathrooms and "hang out" anywhere from 5 to 20 minutes before quitting time. The chief steward cited an example where, contrary to previous policy, some workers on the Components side were allowed to have radios. "When people on the Fabrication side found out," he said, "they went wild."

Some other examples of inconsistencies cited by employees were as follows:

1. Fighting in the plant was supposed to result in automatic dismissal, but the Human Resources administrator recalled two incidents of fighting where the people involved were not disciplined.
2. Another incident that had been much discussed throughout the plant involved an employee who was "caught in a cloud of marijuana smoke" by his supervisor. Since the supervisor did not observe the man smoking but just smelled the marijuana, the person was only given a written warning. One manager said, "We need to take a stand on these things. We need to make a statement. That way we would gain some respect." Describing the same incident, another manager said, "It makes us close to thinking we're giving them (hourly employees) the key to the door."
3. Several people also mentioned the case of a mother who claimed she missed work several times because of doctor's appointments for her children and was suspended for 3 days, which they compared with the case of an operator who also missed work several times, and was suspected of drug or alcohol abuse, but was not disciplined.

In discussing differences in the enforcement of safety regulations throughout the plant, the administrator of plant safety and security said that when he confronted people who were wearing sneakers, often they would just say they forgot to wear their safety shoes. He said, "If I had to punish everyone, I'd be punishing 50 to 100 people a day."

There were also differences in absenteeism for the two sides of the plant. Absenteeism on the Components side was around 2.2 percent, whereas it was slightly less than 1 percent on the Fabrication side. Some attributed this to a looser enforcement of the rules governing absenteeism by supervisors on the Components side.

Winslow had tried to estimate the annual cost of failure to enforce the rules governing starting and stopping work. His estimate was that the plant was losing $2,247.50 per day, for a total of $539,400 a year. Winslow's memo detailing how he arrived at his overall estimate had been part of his presentation to Larson; it is included as Exhibit 3. Although Winslow had not said so in the memo, he later estimated that 70 percent of the total loss occurred on the Components side of the plant.

Supervisors complained that when they tried to discipline subordinates, they often did not feel confident of backing by management. They referred to incidents where they had disciplined hourly employees only to have their decision changed by management or the Human Resources department. One supervisor told of an incident in which he tried to fire someone in accordance with what he thought was company policy, but the termination was changed to a suspension. He was told he had been too harsh. In a subsequent incident he had another decision overruled and was told he had been too lenient. He said, "We feel our hands are tied; we're not sure what we can do." Supervisors' decisions that were changed were usually communicated directly to the union by the Human Resources department. In these instances, the supervisors felt they wound up with "egg on their face."

Winslow attributed some of these problems to a lack of communication regarding the company's policies and procedures. He thought that if the supervisors understood company policy better, their decisions would not need to be changed so frequently. There was no Human Resources policy manual, for example, although the work rules were contained in the union contract.

Dan Gordon disagreed with the view that these problems were a result of the supervisors' lack of understanding of the plant's policies and procedures. He claimed: "Ninety-nine percent of the supervisors know the policies but they lack the skills and willingness to enforce them. Just like a police officer needs to be trained to read a prisoner his rights, the supervisors need to be taught to do their jobs." He thought that in some of the cases where a supervisor's decision was changed, the supervisor had made a mistake in following the proper disciplinary procedure. Then, when the supervisor's decision was overturned, no explanation was provided, so the supervisor would be left with his or her own erroneous view of what happened.

The Human Resources administrator thought that some of the supervisors were reluctant to discipline or confront people because "They're afraid to hurt people's feelings and want to stay on their good side."

Supervisor's Role Is Poorly Perceived

On the first shift in Fabrication there were about 70 hourly workers and 7 supervisors, and in Components there were about 140 hourly workers and 11 supervisors. Supervisors were assisted by group leaders, hourly employees who were appointed by the company and who received up to an extra 10 cents an hour.

All levels of the plant were concerned about the role of supervisors. "Supervisors feel like a nobody," said one senior manager. In the assessment of organizational communication done by the students, hourly employees,

Exhibit 3

Memo from Paul Winslow to Bill Larson

MEMORANDUM

From: Paul Winslow, Director of Human Resources

To: Bill Larson

Subject: Estimated Cost of Loss of Manufacturing Time

Date: 6/18/90

Loss of Manufacturing Time*

(Based on 348 Hourly Employees)

Delay at start of shift	10 Minutes x 25% (87) =	14.50 hours
Wash-up before AM break	5 Minutes x 75% (261) =	21.75 hours
Delayed return from break	10 Minutes x 50% (174) =	29.00 hours
Early wash-up—Lunch	avg. 10 Minutes x 50% (174) =	29.00 hours
Delayed return from Lunch	10 Minutes x 25% (87) =	14.50 hours
Early wash-up before PM break	5 Minutes x 75% (261) =	21.75 hours
Delayed return from break	10 Minutes x 50% (174) =	29.00 hours
Early wash-up—end of shift	5 Minutes x 75% (261) =	65.25 hours
	Total =	224.75 hours/day

Cost: 224.75 x Avg. $10/hr. = $2,247.50/day

240 days x $2,247.50 = $539,400.00/year

---

* 1. Does not include benefits.
   2. Does not include overtime abuses.
   3. Does not include instances of employees exiting building while punched in.

Source: Littleton Manufacturing

---

middle managers, and supervisors all reported that supervisors had too much to do and that this limited their effectiveness. A typical observation by one hourly employee was: "The supervisors can't be out on the floor because of meetings and paperwork. They have a tremendous amount of things on their mind. . . . The supervisor has become a paperboy, which prevents him from being able to do his job." In speaking about how busy the supervisors were and how they responded to suggestions by hourly employees, another hourly person said, "The supervisor's favorite word is 'I forgot.'"

Supervisors also wanted more involvement in decision making. "You will! You will! You will!" is the way one supervisor characterized the dominant decision-making style of managers at the plant. He thought that most managers expected supervisors to just do what they were told to do. "We have a lot of responsibility but little authority," was how another supervisor put it. Many supervisors felt that they were ordered to do things by their managers, but when something went wrong, they were blamed.

Another factor contributing to the low morale of supervisors was a perceived lack of the resources that they felt were necessary to do a good job. Many complained that they were often told there was no money to make changes to improve things. They also complained of too few engineering, housekeeping, and maintenance personnel. Some supervisors thought there were too few supervisors on the second and third shifts. They thought this resulted in inadequate supervision and allowed some hourly workers to "goof off," since the employees knew when these few supervisors would and would not be around.

The combination of these factors—job overload, too much paperwork, lack of authority, not enough involvement in decision making, lack of resources to make changes, inadequate training, and few rewards—made it difficult to find hourly people at the plant who would accept an offer to become a supervisor.

In discussing the role of supervisors, Larson said, "We don't do a good job of training our supervisors. We tell them what we want and hold them accountable, but we don't give them the personal tools for them to do what we want them to do. They need to have the confidence and ability to deal with people and to hold them accountable without feeling badly." He continued by praising one supervisor who he thought was doing a good job. In particular, Larson felt, this supervisor's subordinates knew what to expect from him. This person had been a chief petty officer in the Navy for many years, and Larson thought this had helped him feel comfortable enforcing rules. Reflecting on this, he said, "Maybe we should just look for people with military backgrounds to be supervisors."

Insufficient Focus on Littleton's Priorities

The phrase "insufficient focus on Littleton's priorities" reflected two concerns expressed by employees. First, there was a lack of understanding of Littleton's goals. Secondly, there was a questioning of the plant's commitment to these goals. However, various levels saw these matters differently.

Although the plant had no mission statement, senior managers said that they thought that they understood Littleton's priorities. A typical senior management description of the plant's goals was, "To supply customers with quality products on time at the lowest possible cost in order to make a profit."

Each year, Larson and the executive staff developed a 4-year strategic plan for Littleton. Sales and marketing would first project the amounts and types of products that they thought they could sell. Then manufacturing would look at the machine and labor capabilities of the plant. The sales projections and capabilities were then adjusted as necessary. Throughout the process, goals were set for improving quality and lowering costs. Larson then took the plan to Brooks for revision and/or approval. Next, Larson turned the goals in the strategic plan into specific objectives for each department. These departmental objectives were used to set measurable objectives for each executive staff member. These then formed the basis for annual performance appraisals. Because of this process, all of the executive staff felt that they knew what was expected of them and how their jobs contributed to achieving the company's goals.

At the same time, both senior and middle managers thought there was insufficient communication and support from corporate headquarters. They mentioned not knowing enough about corporate's long-term plans for the company. A number of the managers on the Fabrication side wondered about corporate's commitment to the Fabrication business. They thought that if their operation did not do well financially, the company might end it. In discussing the status of the Fabrication side of the plant, Gordon said that Brooks considered it a "noncore business." The Quality Assurance manager felt that corporate was not providing enough support and long-term direction for the QIS. Winslow was concerned about the lack of consistency in corporate's Human Resources policies and felt that he did not have enough say in corporate Human Resources planning efforts.

All levels below the executive staff complained that they did not have a good understanding of Littleton's own long-range goals. Some middle managers thought there was a written, long-range plan for the company but others disagreed. One member of the executive staff reported that as far as he knew, the entire strategic plan was seen only by the executive staff, although some managers would see the portions of it that concerned their department. He also reported that the strategic plan was never discussed at operations review meetings. Most hourly employees said that they relied on the grapevine for information about "the big picture." In discussing the flow of information at the plant, one union steward said, "Things get lost in the chain of command." He said he got more than 80 percent of his information from gossip on the floor.

The primary mechanism used to communicate Littleton's goals and the plant's status with regard to achieving them was the operations review meeting held once a month by the plant manager, to which all salaried employees were ostensibly invited. At these meetings, usually attended by about eighty people, the plant manager provided figures on how closely the plant had hit selected business indicators. At one recent and typical meeting, for example, the Manager of QIS described various in-place efforts to improve quality. Bill Larson then reviewed "the numbers." He presented data on budgeted versus actual production, variances between budgeted and actual manufacturing costs, profits, the top ten products in sales, standard margins on various products, shipments of products, information on backlogs, and the top ten customers.* When he asked for questions at the end of his presentation, there were none.

The students' organizational assessment reported that all levels appreciated the intent of the operations review meetings, but there were a number of concerns. Everyone interviewed wanted more two-way communication but thought the size and format of the meetings inhibited discussion. Middle managers thought the meetings focused too much on what had happened and not enough on the future. As one manager said: "It's like seeing Lubbock in the rearview mirror. We want to know where we're going—not where we've been. We want to know what's coming up, how it's going to affect our department, and what we can do to help." Others, including some of the executive staff, complained about the difficulty of understanding the financial jargon. Some hourly employees interviewed did not know there were operations review meetings, and others did not know what was discussed at them.

A number of middle managers in manufacturing thought that having regular departmental meetings would improve communication within their departments. They also said that they would like to see minutes of the executive staff meetings.

When interviewed by the students for their assessment of organizational communication, a number of middle managers, supervisors, and hourly workers thought the company was not practicing what it preached with regard to its stated goals. A primary goal was supposed to be a quality product; however, they reported that there was too much emphasis on "hitting the numbers," or getting the required number of products shipped, even if there were defects. They said this especially occurred toward the end of the month when production reports were submitted. One worker's comment reflected opinions held by many hourly employees: "Some foremen are telling people to push through products that are not of good quality. This passes the problem from one department to another and the end result is a lousy product. They seem too interested in reaching the quota and getting the order out on time rather than quality. It's a big problem because when the hourly workers believe that quality isn't important, they start not to care about their work. They pass it on to the next guy, and the next guy gets mad."

The perception by a number of hourly workers that their suggestions to improve quality were not responded to because of a lack of money also resulted in their questioning the company's commitment to quality.

Change Is Poorly Managed

Most of the employees interviewed by the students thought there were too many changes at the plant and that the numerous changes resulted in confusion. Among the changes cited were:

1. QIS was initiated in 1985.
2. In 1986, 100 hourly employees were laid off.
3. In 1984, there were 154 managers; in 1990, there were 87 managers.
4. In 1989, corporate initiated a restructuring which changed the reporting relationships of several senior managers.
5. In 1989, as part of QIS, the plant began using statistical process control techniques and began efforts to attain ISO certification. (ISO is an internationally recognized certification of excellence.)
6. In 1989, a new production and inventory control system was introduced, with the help of a team of outside consultants who were at the plant for almost a year studying its operations.
7. In 1990, the Components side reorganized its production flow.

A number of complaints were voiced about the effect of all the changes. People felt that some roles and responsibilities were not clear. There was a widespread belief that the reasons for changes were not communicated well enough and that people found out about changes affecting them too late. In addition, many were uncertain how long a new program, once started, would be continued. Larson thought that many hourly employees were resistant to the changes being made because they thought the changes would require more work for them and they were already "running all the time." One union steward observed, "There's never a gradual easing in of things here." A middle manager said: "We're mandated for speed. We pride ourselves on going fast. We rush through today to get to tomorrow."

Larson thought the culture of the plant was gradually changing due to the implementation of QIS, but he noted that a lot of time had to be spent giving the employees reasons for changes.

---

* At Littleton, the manufacturing, engineering, and accounting departments estimated the standard labor costs for making each of the plant's products and a budget was prepared based on those estimates. The budgeted costs were plant goals. A variance is the difference between actual and standard costs. A variance could be positive (less than) or negative (greater than) with respect to the budgeted costs.

Dan Gordon thought the plant needed to "communicate change in a single voice." He said that Larson's style was to leave it to the staff to tell others about upcoming changes. He commented, "By the time it gets to the last person, it's lost something." He felt that Larson needed to communicate changes to those on lower levels in person.

The QIS manager thought that Brooks did not provide enough resources and support for changes at the plant. In explaining his view of corporate's approach to change, he said, "Step one is to not give much. Step two is to not give anything. Step three is they take what's left away." Another middle manager commented, "We're always being asked to do more with less, but the requirements by corporate don't get cut back."

A frequently mentioned example of change that was frustrating to many people was the introduction of the Manufacturing Assisted Production and Inventory Control System (MAPICS) in 1989. MAPICS was a computerized system that was supposed to keep track of materials, productivity, and labor efficiency. Theoretically, it tracked orders from time of entry to payment of the bill, and one could find out where an order was at any point in the system by calling it up on a computer. However, the system was time-consuming (data had to be entered manually by the supervisors), and was not as well suited to the Fabrication side of the plant as it was to the Components side, where production was more standardized. One senior manager commented, "MAPICS was sold as the savior for the supervisors, and the company was supposed to get all of the data it needed. But it's never happened. It's only half-installed, and there are systems problems and input problems." Recently, there had been some question as to whether MAPICS was giving an accurate inventory count.

Hourly workers felt put upon by the way in which changes were made. One person said, "We were all of a sudden told to start monitoring waste and then all of a sudden we were told to stop." Another said, "One day the MAPICS room is over here, and then the next day it's over there. They also put a new system in the stock room, and we didn't know about it." Many resented the outside consultants that had been brought in by corporate, reporting that they did not know why the consultants were brought in or what they were doing. They feared that the consultants' recommendations might result in layoffs.

Hourly people felt that a lot of their information about upcoming changes came through the grapevine. "Rumors fly like crazy" is the way one hourly person described communication on the floor. Another said,

"The managers don't walk through the plant much. We only see them when things are going bad."

In discussing communication about changes, one middle manager said: "It's a standing joke. The hourly know what's going to happen before we do." One steward said, "Lots of times, you'll tell the supervisor something that's going to happen and they will be surprised. It raises hell with morale and creates unstable working conditions. But nine out of ten times it's true."

Hourly workers also felt that they were not involved enough in management decisions about changes to be made. One hourly worker said, "They don't ask our input. We could tell them if something is not going to work. They should keep us informed. We're not idiots."

Lack of a Systematic Approach to Training

The company had carried out a well-regarded training effort when employees were hired to begin the Components side of the plant and when the QIS program was started. In addition, every 2 years each employee went through refresher training for the QIS. There was no other formal company training or career development at the plant.

Hourly employees and supervisors in particular complained about the lack of training. One hourly employee expressed the predominant view: "When you start work here, it's sink or swim." In discussing the promotion of supervisors, the chief union steward said he did not know how people got to be a supervisor and that as far as he knew there was no training that one had to have to become a supervisor.

When they were hired, new hourly and salaried employees attended an orientation session in which they were informed about benefits, attendance policies, their work schedule, parking regulations, and safety issues. After the orientation session, further training for new salaried employees was left up to individual departments. Standard practice was for the department supervisor to assign the hourly person to an experienced hourly operator for one-on-one job training for 2 weeks. Winslow expressed some of his reservations about this approach by commenting, "You don't know if the department is assigning the best person to train the new employee or if they always use the same person for training."

The Human Resources department had no separate training budget. Individual departments, however, did sometimes use their money for training and counted the money used as a variance from their budgeted goals. The training that did occur with some regularity tended to be technical training for maintenance personnel.

When asked to explain why there was not more training, Winslow replied, "We would like to do more but we haven't been able to because of the cost and manpower issues." For example, in 1986 Winslow's title was manager of training and development, and he had been responsible for the training program for all of the new employees hired to begin the Components unit. After the initial training was completed, he requested that the plant provide ongoing training for Components operators. However, his request was turned down by Larson, who did not want to spend the money. Winslow also recalled the over 160 hours he had spent the previous year developing a video training package for hourly workers in one part of the Components side of the plant. He said that the program had been piloted, but when it came time to send people through the training course, production management was unwilling to let people take time off the floor.

Winslow also cited a lack of support from corporate as a factor in the plant's sporadic training efforts. At one time Brooks had employed a director of training for its plants, but in 1987, the person left and the company never hired anyone to replace him. Now, Brooks had no training department; each plant was expected to provide its own training. The training Brooks did provide, according to Winslow, was for the "promising manager" and was purchased from an outside vendor.

Top Management

As he sat in his office thinking about what to do, Winslow knew that any plan would have to be acceptable to Larson, Gordon, and Hanson—the plant manager and the two factory managers—and he spent some time thinking about their management styles.

Bill Larson was in his late forties, had a B.S. in mechanical engineering, and had started at Littleton in 1970. He had been plant manager since 1983. His direct reports considered him bright, analytical, and down-to-earth. When asked once how he would describe himself to someone who didn't know him, he said, "I keep my emotions out of things. I can remember when I was in the Army, standing at attention in my dress blues at the Tomb of the Unknown Soldier. People would come up a foot from my face and look me in the eye and try to get me to blink. But I was able to remove myself from that. I wouldn't even see it." He added that he had built most of his own home and repaired his own equipment, including the diesels on a cabin cruiser he used to own. Being raised on a farm in the rural Midwest, he said he learned at an early age how to repair equipment with baling wire to keep it going.

Although Larson was considered accessible by the executive staff, he rarely got out on the floor to talk to people. Many managers saw him as a "numbers" man who readily sprinkled his conversations about the plant with quantitative data about business indicators, variances, budgeted costs, etc. In referring to his discomfort discussing personal things, he somewhat jokingly said about himself, "I can talk on the phone for about thirty-five seconds and then I can't talk any longer."

In describing his own management style, Larson said, "I like to support people and get them involved. I like to let them know what I am thinking and what they need to accomplish. I like to let ideas come from them. I want them to give me recommendations, and if I feel they're O.K., I won't change them. They need to be accountable, but I don't want them to feel I'm looking over their shoulder. I don't want to hamper their motivation." He estimated that 40 percent of his job responsibility consisted of managing change.

Dan Gordon, who was 38, had been at Littleton for 15 years and had been manufacturing manager of Fabrication for 7 years. In describing himself, he said, "I'm a stickler for details, and I hate to not perform well. My superiors tell me I'm a Theory X manager and that I have a 'strong' personality—that I can intimidate people."

In speaking about how much he communicated with hourly employees, Gordon said that he didn't do enough of it, adding that "Our platters are all so loaded, we don't spend as much time talking to people as we should." He said he seldom walked through the plant and never talked to hourly workers one-on-one. Once a year, though, he met formally with all the hourly employees on the Fabrication side to have an operations review meeting like the salaried people had in order to discuss what the plant was doing, profits, new products, etc. "The hourly people love it," he reported.

Reflecting on why he didn't communicate more with hourly workers, Gordon said, "Since the accounting department's data depends, in part, on our data collection, a lot of my time is eaten up with this. Maybe I'm too busy with clerical activities to be more visible." He based his management decisions on documented data and regularly studied the financial and productivity reports issued by the accounting department. He said he would like to see the supervisors go around in the morning to just talk to people but acknowledged that they had too many reports to fill out and too many meetings to attend.

When asked to explain what one needed to do to succeed as a manager at Littleton, Gordon answered, "You have to get things done. Bill Larson wants certain things done within a certain time span. If you do this, you'll succeed."

Phil Hanson, in his early fifties, had been at Littleton for 7 years. He was hired as materials manager for Components and was promoted to Components factory manager in mid-1989. Phil estimated that he spent 50 percent of his time on the factory floor talking to people. He felt it gave him a better insight as to what was going on at the plant and created trust. He thought that too many of the managers at the plant were "office haunts"—they felt it was beneath them to talk with hourly workers. It appeared to other managers that Hanson often made decisions based on what he learned in informal conversations with hourly employees. He tried to delegate as much as he could to his managers. When asked what a manager had to do to succeed there, he said, "You have to be a self-starter and make things happen."

Winslow remembered how a few years ago, when he was manager of training and development, the executive staff had gone to one of those management development workshops where you find out about your management style. All of the staff had scored high on the authoritarian end of the scale.

This triggered a memory of a recent debate in which he had passed along a suggestion by his staff to the executive staff to "do something nice for the workers on the floor." To celebrate the arrival of summer, his staff wanted the company to pay for buying hamburgers, hot dogs, and soft drinks so the workers could have a cookout during their lunch break. Those on the executive staff who resisted the idea cited the "jelly bean theory of management." As one manager explained it, "If you give a hungry bear jelly beans, you can keep it happy and get it to do what you want. But watch out when you run out of jelly beans! You're going to have a helluva angry bear to deal with!" The jelly bean argument carried the day, and the cookout was not held.

Recommendation Time

As Winslow turned on the computer to write down his recommendations concerning the six problem areas, he recalled how Larson had reacted when the students made their presentation on organizational communication at Littleton. After praising the students' efforts, Larson had said, in an offhanded way, "This mainly confirms what we already knew. Most of this is not a surprise." Winslow was hopeful that now some of these issues would be addressed.

One potential sticking point, he knew, was the need for the meetings that would be necessary to discuss the problems and plan a strategy. People were already strapped for time and complaining about the number of meetings. Yet unless they took time to step back and look at what they were doing, nothing would change.

On a more hopeful note, he recalled that Larson had been impressed when the Human Resources staff emphasized in their presentation to him that these issues were impacting Littleton's bottom line. Winslow felt that the decline in sales and profits at Brooks, the increasing domestic and foreign competition, the current recession, and declining employee morale made it even more important that the issues be dealt with. People at all levels of the plant were starting to worry about the possibility of more layoffs.

Integrative Case 2.2 *Littleton Manufacturing (B)* *

Winslow met with his staff to develop a list of proposed corrective actions. Exhibit 1 is the memo that Winslow sent, in June 1990, to the Human Resources PIT, outlining suggested corrective actions. (The action steps were not prioritized.)

The PIT did not meet to discuss what to do about the six issues identified by the Human Resources department until the middle of September. The first issue the PIT decided to address was the inconsistent application of disciplinary policies and procedures. They chose this issue first because they thought that if this could be improved, many of the other issues would be resolved as well.

The PIT decided to first find out how well supervisors understood the work rules and the extent to which they had different interpretations of them. To do this they developed a quiz covering Littleton's twenty-eight work rules and gave the quiz to all supervisors. One question, for example, was "If you came in and found an employee who had just dozed off at his/her workstation, what would you do?" The supervisor then had to choose from several alternatives. This question was followed by "If you came in and found an employee away from the job and asleep on top of some packing materials, what would you do?" Again, there was a choice of several responses. After taking the exam, the answers were discussed and the correct answer explained by Winslow and the Human Resources staff. The results revealed to the PIT that there was much less knowledge of these rules and how to apply them than management had expected.

The PIT then theorized that a number of supervisors were not comfortable with confronting employees about their failure to follow the company's policies and procedures, especially the wearing of safety shoes and goggles. They decided to seek the assistance of an outside consultant to help them develop a training program for the supervisors. However, on September 1, 1991, as a continuation of its "efficiency drive," Brooks had imposed a freeze on salaries and a reduction in travel, and prohibited the use of outside consultants at all of its plants. When Winslow asked Bill Larson for approval to hire the consultant, he was reminded that because of the freeze they would have to do the training in-house.

As a consequence, Winslow began a series of meetings with union stewards and supervisors—called "Sup and Stew" meetings—to discuss what the work rules were, different interpretations of them, and how violations of work rules should be handled. For scheduling reasons, it was planned so that half of the supervisors and the stewards would attend each meeting. These meetings were held biweekly for over a year. Winslow believed that the meetings were helping to clarify and support the role of the supervisors and were beginning to have a positive effect on the enforcement of policies and procedures.

In 1991, because the plants that bought the wire coils made by Components had excess finished goods inventory, Brooks shut them down for a month during the Christmas holidays, leading Littleton to eliminate 125 positions from the Components side for the same month, to reduce production. "If we hadn't," Winslow said, "we would have had a horrendous amount of inventory." The employees filling those positions had, in general, less seniority than their counterparts from Fabrication, and no one from the Fabrication side was laid off. A few of the more senior employees from the Components side were hired to work on the Fabrication side. At the time of the layoffs, business on the Fabrication side was "booming." In January, the plant started rehiring the laid-off workers, and by the end of June, all of them had been rehired.

In November 1991, Bill Larson learned that he had cancer, and in June, 1992, he died. Because of Larson's illness, the lack of resources, and time pressures, there was no formal attempt to address any of the issues identified by Winslow other than inconsistent enforcement of policies and procedures.

The new plant manager, Bob Halperin, took over in the fall of 1992; Halperin had been managing another Brooks plant in the south for 3 years. One of the

*By David E. Whiteside, organizational development consultant. This case was written at Lewiston-Auburn College of the University of Southern Maine with the cooperation of management, solely for the purpose of stimulating student discussion. Data are based on field research; all events are real, although the names of organizations, locations, and individuals have been disguised. Faculty members in nonprofit institutions are encouraged to reproduce this case for distribution to their students without charge or written permission. All other rights reserved jointly to the author and the North American Case Research Association (NACRA). Copyright © 1994 by the *Case Research Journal* and David E. Whiteside.

Exhibit 1

Memorandum from Paul Winslow to Human Resources

Memorandum

From: Paul Winslow

To: Human Resources Process Improvement Team

Subject: Proposed Corrective Actions

Date: 6/24/90

Lack of Organizational Unity

1. Use job shadowing or rotation to help people understand each other's jobs, e.g., do this across functions.

2. Reformat the Operations Review meetings, e.g., have a program committee.

3. Have a smaller group forum, e.g., have supervisors from the two sides meet.

4. Provide teamwork training for salaried employees.

Lack of Consistency in Enforcing Rules and Procedures

1. Hold meetings with department managers and supervisors to discuss how to enforce policies and procedures. Have these led by BIll Larson.

2. Develop a policy and procedures review and monitoring system.

Supervisor's Role Poorly Perceived

1. Have department managers meet with supervisors to determine priorities or conflicts between priorities.

2. Have supervisory training for all manufacturing supervisors.

3. Time assessment. (How is their time being spent?)

Insufficient Focus on Littleton's Priorities

1. Use the in-house newsletter to communicate priorities.

2. Develop an internal news sheet.

3. Have a question box for questions to be answered at Operations Review meetings.

4. Have a restatement of Littleton's purpose (do at Operations Review).

5. Have an Operations Review for hourly workers.

6. Use payroll stuffers to communicate information about goals.

7. Hold department meetings; have the manager of the department facilitate the meeting.

Lack of a Systematic Approach to Training

1. Establish annual departmental training goals.

2. Link training goals to organizational priorities.

3. Have a systematic approach to training the hourly work force.

4. Have a training plan for each salaried employee.

5. Have an annual training budget.

Change is Poorly Managed

1. Provide training in managing change.

2. Communicate changes.

HR Dept.

6/90

reasons he was chosen was his familiarity with Littleton. He had been at Littleton as an industrial engineer from 1973 to 1980, when he left to manage another facility. In 1984 he was sent back to Littleton to start and manage Components. He held this position for 4 years before leaving to manage the plant in the southern United States.

Shortly after Halperin arrived, Winslow acquainted him with the problem areas defined the previous year, gave him a copy of the (A) case, and met with him to discuss the issues. At that time, although Winslow felt that progress had been made on having more consistent enforcement of policies and procedures from one side of the plant to the other, he did not feel much had changed with regard to the other issues. With the exception of the Sup and Stew meetings, none of the specific action steps recommended by him and his staff had been implemented.

Integrative Case 3.0 *Shoe Corporation of Illinois**

Shoe Corporation of Illinois produces a line of women's shoes that sell in the lower-price market for $11.95 to $13.95 per pair. Profits averaged twenty-five cents to thirty cents per pair ten years ago, but according to the president and the controller, labor and materials costs have risen so much in the intervening period that profits today average only fifteen cents to twenty cents per pair.

Production at both the company's plants totals 12,500 pairs per day. The two factories are located within a radius of sixty miles of Chicago: one at Centerville, which produces 4,500 pairs per day, and the other at Meadowvale, which produces 8,000 pairs per day. Company headquarters is located in a building adjacent to the Centerville plant.

It is difficult to give an accurate picture of the number of items in the company's product line. Shoes change in style perhaps more rapidly than any other style product, including garments. This is so chiefly because it is possible to change production processes quickly and because, historically, each company, in attempting to get ahead of competitors, gradually made style changes ever more frequently. At present, including both major and minor style changes, S.C.I. offers 100 [to] 120 different products to customers each year.

A partial organizational chart, showing the departments involved in this case, appears in Exhibit 1.

Competitive Structure of the Industry

Very large general shoe houses, such as International and Brown, carry a line of ladies' shoes and are able to undercut prices charged by Shoe Corporation of Illinois, principally because of the policy in the big companies of producing large numbers of "stable" shoes, such as the plain pump and the loafer. They do not attempt to change styles as rapidly as their smaller competitors. Thus, without constant changes in production processes and sales presentations, they are able to keep costs substantially lower.

Charles F. Allison, the president of Shoe Corporation of Illinois, feels that the only way for a small independent company to be competitive is to change styles frequently, taking advantage of the flexibility of a small organization to create designs that appeal to customers. Thus, demand can be created, and a price set high enough, to make a profit. Allison, incidentally, appears to have an artistic talent in styling and a record of successful judgments in approving high-volume styles over the years.

Regarding [SCI's] differences from its large competitors, Allison says:

> You see, Brown and International Shoe Company both produce hundreds of thousands of the same pair of shoes. They store them in inventory at their factories. Their customers, the large wholesalers and retailers, simply know their line and send in orders. They do not have to change styles nearly as often as we do. Sometimes I wish we could do that, too. It makes for a much more stable and orderly system. There is also less friction between people inside the company. The [sales people] always know what they're selling, the production people know what is expected of them. The plant personnel are not shook up so often by someone coming in one morning and tampering with their machine lines or their schedules. The styling people are not shook up so often by the plant saying, "We can't do your new style the way you want it."

Major Style Changes

The decision about whether to put a certain style into production requires information from a number of different people. Here is what typically happens in the company. It may be helpful to follow the organization chart in tracing the procedure.

M. T. Lawson, the style manager, and his designer, John Flynn, originate most of the ideas about shape, size of heel, use of flat sole or heels, and findings (the term used for ornaments attached to, but not part of, the shoes—bows, straps, and so forth). They get their ideas principally from reading style and trade magazines or by copying a top-flight designer. Lawson corresponds with publications and friends in large stores in New York, Rome, and Paris in order to obtain by air mail pictures and samples of up-to-the-minute style innovations.

When Lawson decides on a design, he takes a sketch to Allison, who either approves or disapproves it. If Allison approves, he (Allison) then passes the sketch on to Shipton, the sales manager, to find out what lasts

*Written by Charles E. Summer. Copyright 1978. Used with permission.

Exhibit 1
Partial Organization Chart of Shoe Corporation of Illinois

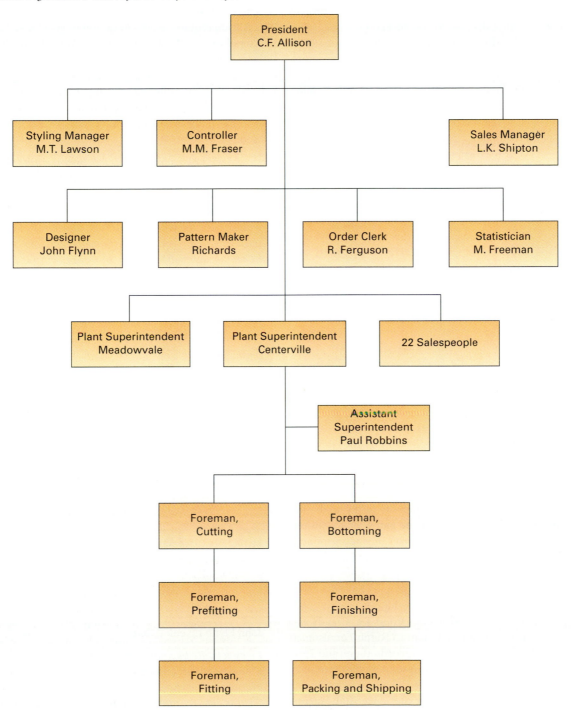

(widths) should be chosen. Shipton, in turn, simply forwards the design to Martin Freeman, a statistician in the sales department, who maintains summary information on customer demand for colors and lasts.

To compile this information, Freeman visits [sales people] twice a year to get their opinions on the colors and lasts that are selling best, and he keeps records of shipments by color and by last. For these needs, he simply totals data that is sent to him by the shipping foreman in each of the two plants.

When Freeman has decided on the lasts and colors, he sends Allison a form that lists the colors and lasts in which the shoe should be produced. Allison, if he approves this list, forwards the information to Lawson, who passes it on to Richards, an expert pattern maker. Richards makes a paper pattern and constructs a prototype in leather and paper, sends this to Lawson, who in turn approves or disapproves it. He forwards any approved prototype to Allison. Allison, if he too approves, notifies Lawson, who takes the prototype to Paul Robbins, assistant to the superintendent of the Centerville plant. Only this plant produces small quantities of new or experimental shoe styles. Such production is referred to as a "pilot run" by executives at the plant.

Robbins then literally carries the prototype through the six production departments of the plant—from cutting to finish—discussing it with each foreman, who in turn works with men on the machines in having a sample lot of several thousand pairs made.

When the finished lot is delivered by the finishing foreman to the shipping foreman (because of the importance of styling, Allison has directed that each foreman personally deliver styling goods in process to the foreman of the next department), the latter holds the inventory in storage and sends one pair each to Allison and Lawson. If they approve of the finished product, Allison instructs the shipping foreman to mail samples to each of the company's twenty-two [sales people] throughout the country. [Sales people] have instructions to take the samples immediately (within one week) to at least ten customers. Orders for already established shoes are normally sent to Ralph Ferguson, a clerk in Shipton's office, who records them and forwards them to the plant superintendents for production. In the case of first orders on new styles, however, [sales people] have found by experience that Martin Freeman has a greater interest in the success of new "trials," so they rush orders to him, air mail, and he in turn places the first orders for a new style in the interoffice mail to the plant superintendents. He then sends a duplicate of the order, mailed in by the [sales people], to Ferguson for entering in his statistical record of all orders received by the company.

Three weeks after the [sales people] receive samples, Allison requires Ralph Ferguson to give him a tabulation of orders. At that time, he decides whether the [sales people] should push the item and the superintendents should produce large quantities, or whether he will tell them that although existing orders will be produced, the item will be discontinued in a short time.

The procedures outlined here have, according to Allison:

. . . worked reasonably well. The average time from when Lawson decides on a design until we notify the Centerville plant to produce the pilot run is two weeks to a month. Of course, if we could speed that up, it would make the company just that much more secure in staying in the game against the big companies, and in taking sales away from our competitors. There seems to be endless bickering among people around here involved in the styling phase of the business. That's to be expected when you have to move fast— there isn't much time to stop and observe all of the social amenities. I have never thought that a formal organization chart would be good in this company— we've worked out a customary system here that functions well.

M. T. Lawson, manager of styling, says that within his department all work seems to get out in minimum time; he also states that both Flynn and Richards are good employees and skilled in their work. He mentioned that Flynn had been in to see him twice in the last year:

. . . to inquire about his (Flynn's) future in the company. He is thirty-three years old and has three children. I know that he is eager to make money, and I assured him that over the years we can raise him right along from the $35,000 we are now paying. Actually, he has learned a lot about shoe styles since we hired him from the design department of a fabric company six years ago.

John Flynn revealed that:

I was actually becoming dissatisfied with this job. All shoe companies copy styles—it's generally accepted practice within the industry. But I've picked up a real feel for designs, and several times I've suggested that the company make all its own original styles. We could make [SCI] a style leader and also increase our volume. When I ask Lawson about this, he says it takes too much time for the designer to create originals—that we have all we can handle to do research in trade magazines and maintain contracts feeding us the results of experts. Beside, he says our styles are standing the test of the marketplace.

"Projects X and Y"

Flynn also said that he and Martin Freeman had frequently talked about the styling problem. They felt that:

Allison is really a great president, and the company surely would be lost without him. However, we've seen times when he lost a lot of money on bad judgments in styles. Not many times—perhaps six or seven times in the last 18 months. Also, he is, of course, extremely busy as president of the corporation. He must look after everything from financing from the banks to bargaining with the union. The result is that he is sometimes unavailable to do his styling approvals for several days, or even two weeks. In a business like this, that kind of delay can cost money. It also makes him slightly edgy. It tends, at times when he has many other things to do, to make him look quickly at the styles we submit, or the prototypes Richards makes, or even the finished shoes that are sent for approval by the shipping foreman. Sometimes I worry that he makes two kinds of errors. He simply rubber stamps what we've done, in which sending them to him is simply a waste of time. At other times he makes snap judgments of his own, overruling those of us who have spent so much time and expertise on the shoe. We do think he has good judgment, but he himself has said at times that he wishes he had more time to concentrate on styling and approval of prototypes and final products.

Flynn further explained (and this was corroborated by Freeman) that the two had worked out two plans, which they referred to as "project X" and "project Y." In the first, Flynn created an original design that was not copied from existing styles. Freeman then gave special attention to color and last research for the shoe and recommended a color line that didn't exactly fit past records on consumer purchases—but one he and Flynn thought would provide "great consumer appeal." This design and color recommendation were accepted by Lawson and Allison; the shoe went into production and was one of the three top sellers during the calendar year. The latter two men did not know that the shoe was styled in a different way from the usual procedure.

The result of a second, similar project (Y) was put into production the next year, but this time sales were discontinued after three weeks.

Problem Between Lawson and Robbins

Frequently, perhaps ten to twelve times a year, disagreement arises between Mel Lawson, manager of styling, and Paul Robbins, assistant to the superintendent of the Centerville plant. Robbins says that:

The styling people don't understand what it means to produce a shoe in the quantities that we do, and to make the changes in production that we have to. They dream up a style quickly, out of thin air. They do not realize that we have a lot of machines that have to be adjusted, and that some things they dream up take much longer on certain machines than others, thus creating a bottleneck in the production line. If they put a bow or strap in one position rather than others, it may mean we have to keep people idle on later machines while there is a pile-up on the sewing machines on which this complicated little operation is performed. This costs the plant money. Furthermore, there are times when they get the prototype here late, and the foremen and I either have to work overtime or the trial run won't get through in time to have new production runs on new styles, to take the plant capacity liberated by our stopping production on old styles. Lawson doesn't know much about production and sales and the whole company. I think all he does is to bring shoes down here to the plant sort of like a messenger boy. Why should he be so hard to get along with? He isn't getting paid any more than I am, and my position in the plant is just as important as his.

Lawson, in turn says that he has a difficult time getting along with Robbins:

There are many times when Robbins is just unreasonable. I take prototypes to him five or six times a month, and other minor style changes to him six or eight times. I tell him every time that we have problems in getting these ready, but he knows only about the plant, and telling him doesn't seem to do any good. When we first joined the company, we got along all right, but he has gotten harder and harder to get along with.

Certain Other Problems That Have Arisen

Ralph Ferguson, the clerk in the sales department who receives orders from [sales people] and forwards totals for production schedules to the two plant superintendents, has complained that the [sales people] and

Freeman are bypassing him in their practice of sending experimental shoe orders to Freeman. He insists that his job description (one of only two written descriptions in the company) gives him responsibility for receiving all orders throughout the company and for maintaining historical statistics on shipments.

Both the [sales people] and Freeman, on the other hand, say that before they started the new practice (that is, when Ferguson still received the experimental shoe orders), there were at least eight or ten instances a year when these were delayed from one to three days on Ferguson's desk. They report that Ferguson just wasn't interested in new styles, so the [sales people] "just started sending them to Freeman." Ferguson acknowledged that there were times of short delay, but there were good reasons for them:

They ([sales people] and Freeman) are so interested in new designs, colors, and lasts, that they can't understand the importance of a systematic handling of the whole order procedure, including both old and new shoe styles. There must be accuracy. Sure, I give some priority to experimental orders, but sometimes when rush orders for existing company products are piling up, and when there's a lot of planning I have to do to allocate production between Centerville and Meadowvale, I decide which comes first—processing of these, or processing the experimental shoe orders. Shipton is my boss, not the [sales people] or Freeman. I'm going to insist that these orders come to me.

Integrative Case 4.0 *Bhiwar Enterprises**

Pratap Bhiwar[1] had been working as a consultant to the family business between the two years of his M.B.A. program. Near the end of his summer's efforts, he had prepared a report for his cousin who was Managing Director of the Rori Company, one of several businesses owned and operated by the Bhiwar family. His recommendations were intended to rationalize company operations to increase effectiveness and efficiency. Instead, they seemed to have stimulated a rash of arguments among his cousins and uncles that threatened to destroy forty years of solidarity and business success. As the time drew near to return to North America, Pratap wondered what he could do to resolve the problems his report had generated.

History of the Bhiwar Family in Africa

Mohan Bhiwar emigrated from India with his wife and family to avoid starvation and to start a new life in the British colony of Kenya. However, in Kenya Mohan could not farm as his family had done in India. Agriculture, especially the cultivation of cash crops, was a white man's monopoly. Africans and Asians[2] were prohibited from farming by the colonial government. Mohan, therefore, became a retail peddler in the area around the village in which he had settled.

For twenty years Mohan rose daily at 4:00 A.M. and rode his bicycle into the countryside, where he purchased surplus fruit and vegetables from Africans. Mohan brought the produce back to his village and sold it. Then he purchased hardware and cloth, which he sold in the more rural villages.

After a few years Mohan was able to afford to bring over from India his three younger brothers—Anil, Vijay, and Sanjay—and their families. Together the brothers expanded the retail operation and assured themselves of economic survival in their adopted country. The family relationships are shown in Exhibit 1.

[1]Names of people, places, and companies have been disguised.
[2]In this country blacks are referred to as Africans. Asian is a term that refers to people of East Indian origin, and European is the term used for Caucasians. See Appendix A for a brief discussion of the Asian experience in this multiracial milieu.
[3]Appendix B contains a description of some elements of the extended family system.

All four brothers and their families lived together under one roof. In addition to the economic benefits, this arrangement was also a form of social security. For example, in the case of accident or sickness, other members of the family were available to help. This role of the extended family was particularly important in Kenya where no state welfare structure existed. Living together was also culturally acceptable in the Asian community.[3]

For years the brothers continued their retail peddling and saved a little money from the business every year. Eventually the family bought its first car, and three years later they purchased their first truck. When Mohan died of a heart attack, the family leadership passed to Anil, the oldest surviving brother.

The year Mohan died was also the year the fortunes of the family business picked up. In October, a group of African freedom fighters (or terrorists according to the colonists) began a campaign to end colonial rule and white domination in Kenya. The colonial government, which represented white interests in the colony, responded to the terrorism by declaring a state of martial law. As part of its response, the government constructed large prison camps in which to confine captured rebels. These camps had to be supplied with food, clothing, and other provisions. Competitive bids were invited from various firms for the monopoly of supplying the camps. Through an elaborate system of bribery, a common practice in the colony, the Bhiwar brothers successfully obtained the contract.

Their business dealings, however, were not confined to the government. The rebels needed materials for the

Exhibit 1

Bhiwar Family Structure

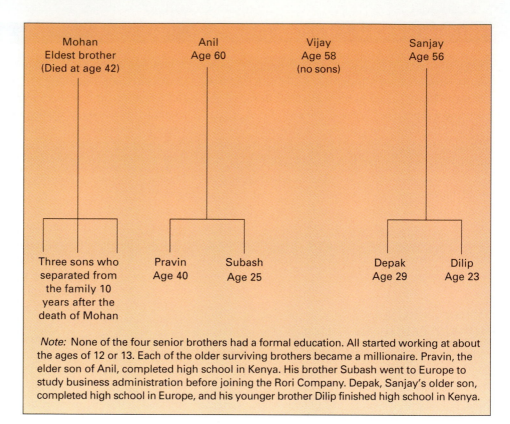

Note: None of the four senior brothers had a formal education. All started working at about the ages of 12 or 13. Each of the older surviving brothers became a millionaire. Pravin, the elder son of Anil, completed high school in Kenya. His brother Subash went to Europe to study business administration before joining the Rori Company. Depak, Sanjay's older son, completed high school in Europe, and his younger brother Dilip finished high school in Kenya.

manufacture of weapons that the brothers were able to supply. The Bhiwars did not consider these activities treasonable. As Asians, they identified with neither the Europeans nor the Africans. They saw the relationship as merely buyer-seller. In their dealings with both the rebels and the government, the brothers were able to name their own prices since their services were in such high demand.

Because of their success during the rebellion and the fact that the brothers had established valuable contacts, they were in a favorable position to buy up surplus agricultural produce to sell to European wholesalers in Kenya. The surpluses resulted from improved agricultural techniques introduced after the rebellion had ended. The techniques were part of an economic revitalization program to reduce inequalities which had been central in originally bringing about the conflict. However, although many farmers were able to produce a surplus, few had the transportation facilities necessary to move their goods to market. The Bhiwar brothers, on the other hand, had both equipment and capital. They were, therefore, able to take advantage of this unusual opportunity.

Family Breakup and a New Company

Five years after the rebellion had ended, the older generation of brothers—Anil, Vijay, and Sanjay—decided to retire from active participation in the business. According to tradition, the leadership of the family should have passed to Mohan's oldest son. However, since Anil had been the head of the family unit, his influence and guidance were powerful forces in the transition of leadership. Furthermore, only two of the three sons of Mohan were involved in the business, and both of these were located some distance from the head office where Anil's sons operated.

As the health of the older generation declined, Pravin showed increasing initiative. In addition, he received recognition and credit for the steady success of the business by virtue of his physical location, position in the firm, and family status as Anil's older son. As the gradual transition in leadership occurred, it became clear that Pravin would succeed his father. Mohan's sons, resentful of being deprived of a right they saw as belonging to their oldest brother, refused to work in the family business any longer. Their feelings of bitterness were heightened by their judgment that the surviving uncles had not done a conscientious job of looking after them (one was expected to protect the sons of a deceased brother). The result was the breaking away of Mohan's widow and sons from the main body of the Bhiwar family. To some extent, this was encouraged by the mother who, according to the Bhiwars, never had liked her brothers-in-law.

The breakup of the family was psychologically traumatic for all parties concerned. Such an event was unusual and discouraged in the Asian community. Socially, it was considered a sign of deterioration in the stability of the family. Personally, it diminished the reputations of all the individuals involved. Within the family, it left a great deal of bad feeling between the parties.

After the breakup, Pravin, on the advice of his father and uncles, bought a food processing business (Rori Company) from another Asian family. There were two reasons for this acquisition. First, the Bhiwar brothers felt that they could process food cheaply and add to their revenues. Secondly, the purchase of Rori would provide the sons of Anil and Sanjay with an opportunity to develop a business of their own.

Two years after the acquisition, Depak, Sanjay's older son, was made Managing Director of the Rori Company when he returned from finishing his education in Europe. Over the next decade, he expanded the business primarily through his successful marketing efforts in the United States and Canada. But, in spite of this success, Depak was not entirely satisfied, because his cousin Pravin would not permit him to have full control over operations. All changes proposed by Depak had to be reviewed and ratified by Pravin before being implemented. An organization chart for the company is shown in Exhibit 2.

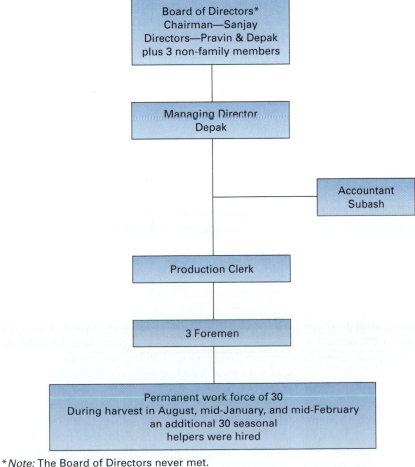

Exhibit 2
Organization of Rori Company

Board of Directors*
Chairman—Sanjay
Directors—Pravin & Depak
plus 3 non-family members

Managing Director
Depak

Accountant
Subash

Production Clerk

3 Foremen

Permanent work force of 30
During harvest in August, mid-January, and mid-February
an additional 30 seasonal
helpers were hired

*Note: The Board of Directors never met.

The situation worsened when Pravin's younger brother, Subash, returned to Kenya following completion of his education and was made accountant of the Rori Company. Subash used his position to spy on Depak for his brother Pravin, whose interference in the business and ultimate control of all financial allocations in the family business kept Depak from operating autonomously and efficiently in his own sphere of responsibility. The situation was exacerbated by the fact that personal relations between Depak and the two brothers were strained. Further, it appeared that Pravin was to some extent envious of Depak's ability to work hard and make a success of his operation.

A Nephew as Consultant

Pratap Bhiwar, a nephew through marriage to the older generation (Anil, Vijay, and Sanjay), was home in Kenya for a vacation. He was currently an M.B.A. student in a North American university. While he was visiting with his uncle Sanjay, his cousin Depak arrived and asked him how his studies were going. As the two men began to talk about business in general and the operations of the Rori Company in particular, it occurred to Pratap that he might be able to help Depak with some of the problems he was having in the business. He suggested to Depak that he be hired to do consulting work while he was home for the vacation. Depak was delighted and consulted with his father, Sanjay. The older man also thought the idea had merit, but said that it would be necessary to check with Pravin, who after all was the head of the family interests now that the older generation of men had retired. Pravin made some remarks about outside interference in the affairs of the family, but did not attempt to stop Pratap from helping.

As Pratap started the consulting job, he approached his work using the tough-minded framework of analysis that he was being taught in North America. He viewed the consulting assignment as an opportunity to implement rigorous North American management practices. He decided that any inefficiencies in the operation would be uprooted. He would recommend the firing of poor performers.

After making some preliminary investigations of the operations, Pratap concluded that although the marketing system that Depak had set up was good, the company's costing system was sloppy. In addition, the production setup of the plant was not well-integrated with the rest of the operation because of poor planning and haphazard expansion. However, Pratap told Depak, in order to proceed further, it would now be necessary to analyze in some detail the past financial statements of the company. Depak told him that would be difficult since he did not have the data. In fact, he continued, he had never seen any of the financial statements of the Rori Company. He told Pratap that Pravin kept all the statements to himself. Pratap then asked Depak how, as Managing Director of Rori Company, he made his financial decisions. Depak replied that it was simple. Whenever it was necessary to make an expenditure, he relayed his request for money through Subash who then made the representation to his older brother on Depak's behalf. Pravin would then make a decision and tell Subash what it was; Subash would, in turn, inform Depak.

A little amazed by this system, but quite prepared to work within its constraints for the time being, Pratap approached Subash and asked him to obtain the financial statements. Subash, however, misrepresented Pratap to Pravin, who refused to issue the statements. Pratap then approached his uncle Sanjay to help him. Sanjay went to Pravin and persuaded him to hand over the statements. Pravin, however, was not happy about the whole affair. While reluctantly parting with the financial data, he insinuated that Pratap was simply out to make trouble.

After Pratap had analyzed the financial statements, he discovered that a substantial amount of money had disappeared. When asked, Depak said he didn't know anything about it, since he had no control over expenditures. Pratap told Depak that, as Managing Director of Rori, it was his responsibility to know how and where money was spent. Depak agreed and went to see Pravin. But when he asked Pravin about the money, Pravin exploded in anger and told Depak that he was inefficient as a Managing Director, knew nothing of the business, and had wasted his last six years with the firm. Depak retorted that Pravin had never helped him with the business, so how could he expect him to learn? He added heatedly that whenever he asked Pravin a few questions, he never received any answers. As usual, the meeting ended without Pravin answering any of Depak's questions, and bad feelings continued to exist between the two men.

In these circumstances, Pratap felt that the quarrel over the missing money was not worth further straining the family relationships. He told Depak that he would be able to complete his report with the information he had available.

Pratap's Report

Several days later, Pratap finished the report. He had come to two major conclusions. First, the capital acquisition policy of the Rori Company was poor and bore no relation to the overall profit objectives of the firm. He felt that the reason was Pravin's absolute financial control. Depak was unable to make necessary capital acquisitions because he could not obtain the money or approval from Pravin. Secondly, Pratap found that Subash was incompetent as an accountant. In failing to gather and to analyze properly the cost data essential to the business, Subash had proven useless to Depak. In short, Pratap concluded that the Rori Company could function neither efficiently nor effectively. The power to make critical financial decisions was in the hands of a man who for all practical purposes was an absentee landlord who refused to listen to his manager.

It was clear to Pratap that he should make two recommendations:

1. Pravin should give Depak control of the financial statements and decisions related to Rori.
2. The incompetent Subash should be removed.

When Pratap showed his report to Depak, Depak said it should be hidden. He felt that the recommendations to rationalize the operations were unacceptable and would result in family conflict. Pratap admitted that he knew it to be true, but was interested in approaching the business problems rigorously and pushing through to logical conclusions. Agreeing that there were some parts of the report that could be implemented without disturbing the family, both men were willing to let the full report "die" in Depak's office.

However, the matter was not resolved so easily. Sanjay kept inquiring about the progress of the report and told Pratap that he would like to see it when it was completed. Eventually, under continual pressure from Sanjay, Pratap brought the report to his uncle. But since Sanjay could not read English, Pratap read the report aloud to him. When Pratap finished, Sanjay agreed with his nephew's conclusions and asked for his recommendations.

Pratap answered that, in his opinion, the Rori Company should be separated from the Bhiwar Enterprises and placed under the complete control of Depak. He said Depak should be totally responsible for profits and free from outside interference. He also stated that Subash should be fired, since he was incapable of doing his job.

Sanjay listened to the recommendations quietly, but told Pratap that they were unacceptable. If Subash were fired, Sanjay continued, Anil would ask why his son had been discharged. If told that his son was incompetent, he would most certainly become angry, and conflict among the elder brothers would inevitably result. Besides, in the eyes of the Asian community in Kenya, Subash was a big executive. What would they think of the solidarity of the Bhiwar family if he were fired from the family business? Sanjay asked if it would be worth breaking up a close partnership between the brothers that had lasted for forty years just for the sake of more efficiency. Was it really worth all this trouble, Sanjay concluded, for a few thousand dollars of inefficiency?

Although Pratap said that he understood his uncle's point of view, he asked the older man if it was worth sacrificing Depak's future in a business where he was going to be constantly constrained. Pratap argued that Depak would eventually become fed up with the whole situation. In fact, he was fed up now. But as the elder son with the burden of responsibility for the Sanjay household in the Bhiwar family he was unlikely to rebel against a situation that helped preserve the stability of the extended family as a strongly integrated social unit. Pratap concluded that Depak would likely leave Rori in frustration. Sanjay replied that he understood all this, but could not really accept the solution proposed by Pratap.

Another factor in the situation was Dilip, the younger brother of Depak. Unlike Depak, he had gone into business on his own, although he worked out of the premises of the Rori Company. Dilip was disgusted with watching his older brother being dominated by Pravin and Subash. He felt so strongly, he stated, that if his father did not resolve the problem soon, he was going to tell Sanjay that he would not speak to him again until he broke away from Anil.

Pratap felt partially responsible for the state of near-crisis in the Bhiwar family and business, since his report had brought to the surface these problems that had previously remained suppressed. Furthermore, he knew that any additional action by him would have to be taken soon, since he had to return to North America shortly. As the time to make flight reservations drew near, Pratap wondered what he should do.

Appendix A: A Note on Asians Among Africans and Europeans in Kenya

When the English colonists originally came to Kenya, they came to farm fertile land. Although the native Africans were displaced from their land by the whites in the early days before World War I, the small numbers involved had minimal effects, especially since there was plenty of land. As time passed, however, the whites took more and more land—mainly through the legislative mechanism of the colonial government, which favored the powerful, agricultural white minority. The African majority in the colony helplessly watched this encroachment and stealing of the land for which they received no remuneration. The Africans were generally regarded as savages by the whites, and, in the colony, had no significant political or economic rights. For the most part, Africans were forced either to farm noncash crops on poor land (cash crops were a white monopoly) or to find work in the towns that sprang up in Kenya as the century progressed.

In this social system of inequality, the Asian community formed a third group. Many Asians had first come to the colony as contracted labor before World War I, primarily to build the railway. After their contracts had expired, many chose to remain in the colony rather than return to India and be faced with poor land and widespread starvation. In the colony, however, Asians, like Africans, were prohibited from farming cash crops. Consequently, many Asians met the growing demand for civil servants, merchants, and professionals. The Asians proved to be brilliant commercial entrepreneurs and, by the 1930s, virtually monopolized the commercial life of Kenya—principally as retail merchants in the towns.

However, although they were a successful commercial community, they were politically less powerful than the whites. During the first half of the twentieth century, they constantly fought for equal rights in Kenya. At the same time, as a community, they remained socially aloof from both the whites and the Africans, identifying strongly with their traditional Indian background. Many hoped one day to return to India after they had become financially successful. Because of this orientation to their homeland, their involvement and identity with the colony were limited to those areas they regarded as being in their interest for political and economic survival.

Their aloofness, economic success, and constant battle for political recognition endeared them neither to the Europeans nor to the Africans. The whites saw them as a threat to their political and economic dominance, while the Africans coveted the Asian commercial success and advancement in the professions and civil service, which many Africans regarded as rightfully belonging to them.

During the colonial period, therefore, the Asians were discriminated against by white legislation which denied them equal access to the political arena. After independence, which followed the rebellion, the new black majority government sought to weaken Asian privileges in the colony by taking over Asian enterprises and giving them to African entrepreneurs. Although there currently are many Africans involved in business, the Asian community has remained an important part of commerce and industry in Kenya. Out of economic necessity, the government of Kenya tolerates Asian businesses and merchants. The number of Africans capable of running commercial operations has been growing constantly so that the position of the Asians remains insecure. Intense nationalism among some African governments also has weakened the status of Asians, as the unilateral expulsion of Asians from Uganda in 1972 illustrated. Taking all these factors together, Asians in Kenya today face a dramatically different situation from the colonial period when, at least in the retail sector, their economic survival was certain.

Appendix B: The Extended Family System

Traditionally, the Asian communities in Kenya were organized according to the extended family system. This consisted of all the brothers of a generation and their sons living together either under one roof or in close proximity. By staying together in this way, the males of one family were able to maintain a powerful social unit. In the case of marriage, the wives lived with their husbands' family.

This tightly knit kinship structure was closely bound up with the commercial enterprises of the families. For example, the structure of the business organization was based less on the ability of the various personnel in the firm than on the family relationships of the personnel to each other. Given this type of organization, it was possible for a family containing a great deal of business talent to be a very unified and powerful force in commercial affairs.

Within the extended family, the leadership traditionally lay with the eldest brother of the oldest generation still in power. In the case of the Bhiwar brothers, this power originally was in Mohan's hands. When he died, the power stayed in his generation and was passed to Anil. When the older brothers retired, tradition dictated that the family leadership be passed to the oldest son of the oldest brother. Note that this does not read "oldest son of the oldest *surviving* brother," which was the rule of succession used by the Bhiwars and resulted in the first family breakup. As head of the household, the oldest man of any generation holding power was the ultimate authority on all matters relating to the family. This power was exercised in many areas, including marriage decisions.

Recently, the extended family structure has been challenged. Although not yet widespread, there is a growing tendency for some Asians to break from the traditional extended family and adopt the North American nuclear form consisting of a father and mother and their children. Sometimes this breaking away can be done in a way that leaves the parties on amicable terms. More often, however, it is accompanied by considerable trauma, since it is not a practice widely accepted by the Asian community at present.

Integrative Case 5.0 *National Bank of San Francisco**

The National Bank of San Francisco operates seven branches that receive deposits and make loans to both businesses and individual depositors. Deposits have grown from $14 million to $423 million within the past twenty years, and the directors have opened more branches as population and business activity in the Bay area have increased.

The Bank has generally been characterized by aggressive marketing including give-away promotions for new deposits and extremely competitive interest rates on loans. President E. F. Wellington has prided himself on his ability to appoint entrepreneurial branch managers and loan officers who have pushed new business development.

In response to a question at a board meeting two years ago concerning a noticeable rate of increase in operating and overhead expenses, Wellington announced that he would undertake a study of ways the bank might lower, or at least hold the line on, these costs.

Shortly thereafter, he called in James Nicholson, one of his two assistants, described the general problem of reducing costs, and told him that the bank had reached the size where it needed someone to devote full time to operating methods and facilities. He said that he had talked this matter over with Ms. Simmons, manager of personnel, and that both of them had agreed "that you would be ideal for this position." He also explained that Ms. Simmons would be simultaneously promoted to vice president and put in charge of all equipment purchases, the maintenance of all bank buildings, and personnel relations. "Simmons and I feel that you might have a permanent advisory committee made up of one person from each branch, and that such a group can be really effective in deciding on ways to utilize our banking buildings and equipment, and our people, more effectively. Unless you have some objection, each of the branch managers will appoint a representative to meet with you regularly."

Within three months of the original reference to the subject at the directors' meeting, Simmons had been promoted to vice president, Nicholson received the title of manager of personnel and equipment planning, and all branch managers had appointed, at Wellington's request, an employee to what became known as the "systems committee." At the present time, two years later, the committee appears to have taken its work seriously, as evidenced by

1. a record of regular meetings held over a period of eighteen months;
2. the transcripts of those meetings and exhibits, which show that all seven committee members entered the discussions;
3. seventeen recommendations in writing, supported by a total of 1,800 pages of research data and reasoning;
4. the fact that meetings often lasted four to five hours, extending after working hours; and
5. the statements of all seven members of the committee to the effect that they enjoyed the work, felt that they were accomplishing something for the bank, and had personally enjoyed being on the committee with the other members.

All members have also expressed their high regard for Jim Nicholson and feel that he has done a good job.

The seventeen recommendations cover such matters as salary scales, a policy on days off for personal business, a policy on central purchasing of janitorial supplies, and a recommendation that certain models of personal computers and software be adopted uniformly in all branches.

Office Space and Furnishings

About a year ago, both Simmons and Nicholson had made inspection trips to the branches and had come to the conclusion that there was much wasted space in branch offices and that this situation had been brought about principally because office personnel and clerical personnel had been, over a period of years, buying equipment—such as desks, telephone stands, and extra tables—that pleased them personally but that, in many instances, was also "too large and expensive" for what the bank needed to keep up its public appearance. In addition, loan officers in some branches had succeeded in having the managers construct walls for unnecessary private offices. Nicholson had obtained the services of the bank's architect and also of systems engineers from two large equipment manufacturers; together they made a "general estimate, to be confirmed by further fact-finding" that the bank could save $80,000 a year

*Written by Charles E. Summer. Copyright 1978. Used with permission.

over a thirty-year period if (1) furniture were to be standardized with functional equipment that was modest in design but met the essential requirements of dignity for the branches and if (2) henceforth, only branch managers could have private offices.

Before the meeting of the systems committee last week, Simmons expressed concern to Nicholson that his committee had not taken up these two problems.

Your committee could have done some real research on these questions. I hope that you will put them on the agenda right away and agree, let's say in six months, on standard layouts and equipment. You and I both know, for instance, that the loan officers at San Mateo and Menlo Park have entirely too much space, should not be in those large offices, and perhaps should have three standard pieces of equipment—a desk, chair, and small bookcase. There should be no telephone stands like those that were purchased there last year for $90 each.

Relations with Branch Managers

Branch managers have been kept informed of the committee's general work over the eighteen-month period. Most managers selected a loan officer (assistant manager) to represent them, and these officers made a real effort to let their managers know what was going on. Dick May, representative of the Burlingame branch, reports that he has been spending at least an hour a week with his boss telling him what the committee is doing and asking for his ideas. Janice Strickland of the Market Street branch says that she has been able to confer briefly with her boss about once a week on the subjects the committee is working on. Other members report that they, too, have been able to keep their managers informed and that the latter exhibit a good deal of interest in the committee's work. In all cases except Burlingame, however, representatives say that their managers quite naturally do not have the time to go into the details of committee recommendations and that they, the managers, have not been particularly aggressive or enthusiastic about putting any of these recommendations into effect.

The committee has talked about the best way to get its recommendations adopted. Dick May claims that his manager is ready to put many of them into effect immediately and that it is up to each representative to convince his or her own manager. All others say they believe that the president should issue the recommen-

dations as instructions over his signature. The reason given by Strickland is typical:

We're convinced that the recommendations are best for the bank, but the managers just won't buy them. The only way to get the managers to carry them out is to have Mr. Wellington lay them out as official and let it be known that they are going to be put into effect. Of course, they would have to be acknowledged as being drawn up by the Department of Personnel and Equipment, with some advice from our committee.

James Nicholson reported in his own weekly meeting with the president that it looked as if it is going to be "rather touchy" to get managers to accept the recommendations. Mr. Wellington thereupon stated that his own knowledge of the committee recommendations was rather sketchy, even though he had discussed them in part with Nicholson each week for a year. He therefore decided to call a meeting of all branch managers and committee members at the same time so that he and everyone concerned could be acquainted in detail with them. This meeting took place one week ago.

Informal Comments of Branch Managers

Most of the branch managers dropped in to the officers' dining room for lunch before the meeting. After the usual banter, the conversation naturally drifted onto the proposals of the systems committee.

Sure hope my secretary likes those new computers. I can't spell, and if Sally left I'd be sunk.

So what, Karen, you always talk better than you write. Say, I sure hated to come in here this afternoon. Ever since Smedley Scott became president of Menlo Laboratories I've been trying to convince him to do all his banking with us. Had to break a date with him, and in my office, too. If we start spending all our time buying mops, our development program goes out the window. How are you making out with your two (officer) trainees, Carl? I have a smart one coming right along, but she won't be happy under the proposed salary schedule.

The best employee we have came from the credit department a year ago. He sure gets around. Tennis matches, hospital drives, U.N. meetings; always on the go. I thought of him when I read that proposal for days off. How do you decide when a guy like that is working? Granted his work gets behind sometimes.

That's better than drawing pay for just sitting at his desk. I get a kick out of bringing a young employee like that along. And he is building a lot of good will for the bank in my area.

Well, I kind of like that days-off rule. It would save a lot of complaints and conversation about grandfather's weak heart.

It might be just fine for you, Tyson, but not so good for Ann. Why not let each manager decide? After all, each of us is paid to run our branch in the best interests of the bank, and we wouldn't be in our present positions if we weren't doing it. What do you think, Oscar?

Guess I have longer service than any of the rest of you. It will be thirty-nine years in September. But I'd say there isn't a manager who doesn't run his branch just as though it was his own business.

And the record is not bad either. Deposits are going up and the bank is making money.

It's making money that counts. (This from a manager of one of the slower-growing branches.)

I heard from somebody about a year ago that the committee was going to study office space and equipment and that someone figured they could save $1 million over a period of years. But apparently they didn't get around to that.

Don't worry. We're building a real base for the future. By the way, did you see the latest report on Zenith Radio?

Just before the meeting with the systems committee, Simmons called Jim Nicholson into her office to have a brief discussion of the recommendations. The two read over the list of seventeen final recommendations; then Nicholson explained briefly the reasons why each recommendation was made and how it would help the bank to reduce costs.

The Meeting of the Committee and Branch Managers

The meeting started at 2:00 PM and was scheduled to last until 5:00 PM, but actually ran over until six o'clock. The committee, branch managers, Wellington, and Simmons were present. Wellington opened the meeting by stating that its purpose was to study the committee recommendations and, it was hoped, to arrive at a decision on whether they should be accepted and put into effect.

In fact, however, after a reading of the seventeen recommendations, the entire meeting was taken up by a discussion of the first two recommendations.

1. It is recommended that the following pay scales be adopted for clerical and nonofficer personnel in all branches. (This was followed by a list of positions and grades—the bank had had some uniformity before, but the recommendations specified absolute uniformity and also changed some of the classifications, thus meaning, for instance, that head tellers would in the future receive more than head bookkeepers, whereas both had received the same in the past.)

2. Employees should be allowed two days per year off with pay for miscellaneous personal business, such days to be granted at the discretion of managers. Because of the possibility of abuse of this privilege, days in excess of two must be taken without pay. This limitation does not apply to sickness or death in the immediate family.

In the discussion, the branch managers found a great many points on which (a) they disagreed among themselves, and (b) they agreed among themselves but disagreed with the committee. For instance, they all agreed that uniformity was in the interest of the bank but disagreed on many of the salary scales and classifications. On this point, they cited many instances in which one competent employee would feel hurt if the scales were arranged in the way the committee recommended.

The committee members had talked confidentially among themselves before the meeting and agreed that Jim Nicholson must be the one to present the findings and, by and large, the one to defend them. This plan was carried out, and after the meeting, the president remarked to Jim that

the combined thinking of the managers, with all of their experience, made quite an impression on Simmons and me. We have confidence in you, and you know that, but I can't help but wonder if your committee really worked out the "best" recommendation for all on this salary matter. If you had, why couldn't you convince the managers instead of raising all of the criticism?

Yesterday, Wellington and Simmons met to consider the recommendations privately. Simmons again expressed the same idea that Wellington passed on to Nicholson, wondered out loud whether the committee should be sent back to do more research on the recommendations. Both were concerned that two years had elapsed since the committee was established without any recommendations having been accepted and put into effect.

Integrative Case 6.0 *The Audubon Zoo, 1993**

The Audubon Zoo was the focus of national concern in the early 1970s, with well documented stories of animals kept in conditions which were variously termed an "animal ghetto,"[1] "the New Orleans antiquarium," and even "an animal concentration camp."[2] In 1971, the Bureau of Governmental Research recommended a $5.6 million zoo improvement plan to the Audubon Park Commission and the City Council of New Orleans. The local Times Picayune commented on the new zoo: "It's not going to be quite like the Planet of the Apes situation in which the apes caged and studied human beings but something along those broad general lines."[3] The new zoo confined people to bridges and walkways while the animals roamed amidst grass, shrubs, trees, pools, and fake rocks. The gracefully curving pathways, generously lined with luxuriant plantings, gave the visitor a sense of being alone in a wilderness, although crowds of visitors might be only a few yards away.

The Decision

The Audubon Park Commission launched a $5.6 million development program, based on the Bureau of Governmental Research plan for the zoo, in March 1972. A bond issue and a property tax dedicated to the zoo were put before the voters on November 7, 1972. When it passed by an overwhelming majority, serious discussions began about what should be done. The New Orleans City Planning Commission finally approved the master plan for the Audubon Park Zoo in September 1973. But the institution of the master plan was far from smooth.

The Zoo Question Goes Public

Over two dozen special interests were ultimately involved in choosing whether to renovate/expand the existing facilities or move to another site. Expansion became a major community controversy. Some residents opposed the zoo expansion, fearing "loss of green space" would affect the secluded character of the neighborhood. Others opposed the loss of what they saw as an attractive and educational facility.

Most of the opposition came from the zoo's affluent neighbors. Zoo Director John Moore ascribed the criticism to "a select few people who have the money and power to make a lot of noise." He went on to say "[T]he real basis behind the problem is that the neighbors who

live around the edge of the park have a selfish concern because they want the park as their private back yard." Legal battles over the expansion plans continued until early 1976. At that time, the 4th Circuit Court of Appeals ruled that the expansion was legal.[3] An out-of-court agreement with the zoo's neighbors (the Upper Audubon Association) followed shortly.

Physical Facilities

The expansion of the Audubon Park Zoo took it from fourteen to fifty-eight acres. The zoo was laid out in geographic sections: the Asian Domain, World of Primates, World's Grasslands, Savannah, North American Prairie, South American Pampas, and Louisiana Swamp, according to the zoo master plan developed by the Bureau of Governmental Research. Additional exhibits included the Wisner Discovery Zoo, Sea Lion exhibit, and Flight Cage. Exhibit 1 is a map of the new zoo.

Purpose of the Zoo

The main outward purpose of the Audubon Park Zoo was entertainment. Many of the promotional efforts of the zoo were aimed at creating an image of the zoo as an entertaining place to go. Obviously, such a campaign was necessary to attract visitors to the zoo. Behind the scenes, the zoo also preserved and bred many animal species, conducted research, and educated the public. The mission statement of the Audubon Institute is given in Exhibit 2.

New Directions

A chronology of major events in the life of the Audubon Zoo is given in Exhibit 3. One of the first significant changes made was the institution of an admission charge in 1972. Admission to the zoo had been free to anyone prior to the adoption of the renovation plan. Ostensibly, the initial purpose behind instituting the admission charge was to prevent vandalism,[4] but the need

---

*By Claire J. Anderson, Old Dominion University, and Caroline Fisher, Loyola University, New Orleans. © 1993, 1991, 1989, 1987, Claire J. Anderson and Caroline Fisher. This case was designed for classroom discussion only, not to depict effective or ineffective handling of administrative situations.

Exhibit 1

The Audubon Park Zoo

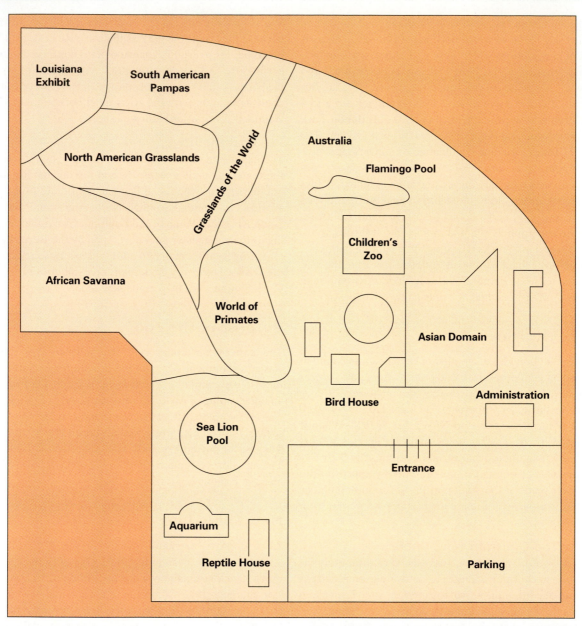

for additional income was also apparent. Despite the institution of and increases in admission charges, attendance increased dramatically (see Exhibit 4).

Operations

Friends of the Zoo

The Friends of the Zoo was formed in 1974 and incorporated in 1975 with four hundred members. The stated purpose of the group was to increase support and awareness of the Audubon Park Zoo. Initially, the Friends of the Zoo tried to increase interest in and commitment to the zoo, but its activities increased dramatically over the following years to where it was involved in funding, operating, and governing the zoo.

The Friends of the Zoo had a 24-member governing board. Yearly elections were held for six members of

Exhibit 2
Audubon Institute Mission Statement

The mission of the Audubon Institute is to cultivate awareness and appreciation of life and the earth's resources and to help conserve and enrich our natural world. The Institute's primary objectives toward this are:

Conservation: To participate in the global effort to conserve natural resources by developing and maintaining captive stocks of endangered plants, animals and marine life, and by cooperating with related projects in the wild.

Education: To impart knowledge and understanding of the interaction of nature and man through programs, exhibits and publications and to encourage public participation in global conservation efforts.

Research: To foster the collection and dissemination of scientific information that will enhance the conservation and educational objectives of the facilities of the Audubon Institute.

Economics: To insure long-range financial security by sound fiscal management and continued development, funding through creative means that encourage corporate, foundation and individual support.

Leadership: To serve as a model in the civic and professional communities. To foster a spirit of cooperation, participation and pride.

Source: The Audubon Institute

Exhibit 3
Chronology of Major Events for the Zoo

1972	Voters approved a referendum to provide tax dollars to renovate and expand the Zoo. The first Zoo-To-Do was held. An admission charge was instituted.
1973	The City Planning Commission approved the initial master plan for the Audubon Park Zoo calling for $3.4 million for upgrading. Later phases called for an additional $2.1 million.
1974	Friends of the Zoo formed with 400 members to increase support and awareness of Zoo.
1975	Renovations began with $25 million public and private funds; 14 acres to be expanded to 58 acres.
1976	The Friends of the Zoo assumed responsibility for concessions.
1977	John Moore went to Albuquerque, Ron Forman took over as Park and Zoo director.
1980	First full-time education staff assumed duties at the Zoo.
1980	Last animal removed from antiquated cage, a turning point in Zoo history.
1981	Contract signed allowing New Orleans Steamboat Company to bring passengers from downtown to the Park.
1981	Delegates from the American Association of Zoological Parks and Aquariums ranked the Audubon Zoo as one of the top three zoos in America of its size.
1981	Zoo accredited.
1982	The Audubon Park Commission reorganized under Act 352 which required the Commission to contract with a non-profit organization for the daily management of the Park.
1985	The Zoo was designated as a Rescue Center for Endangered and Threatened Plants.
1986	Voters approved a $25 million bond issue for the Aquarium.
1988	The Friends of the Zoo became The Audubon Institute.
1990	The Aquarium of the Americas opened in September.

Source: The Audubon Institute

Exhibit 4

Admission Charges

Year	ADMISSION CHARGES Adult	Child
1972	$0.75	$0.25
1978	1.00	0.50
1979	1.50	0.75
1980	2.00	1.00
1981	2.50	1.25
1982	3.00	1.50
1983	3.50	1.75
1984	4.00	2.00
1985	4.50	2.00
1986	5.00	2.50
1987	5.50	2.50
1988	5.50	2.50
1989	6.00	3.00
1990	6.50	3.00
1991	7.00	3.25

Year	ADMISSIONS Number of Paid Admissions	Number of Member Admissions
1972	163,000	
1973	310,000	
1974	345,000	
1975	324,000	
1976	381,000	
1977	502,000	
1978	456,000	
1979	561,000	
1980	707,000	
1981	741,000	
1982	740,339	78,950
1983	835,044	118,665
1984	813,025	128,538
1985	856,064	145,020
1986	916,865	187,119
1987	902,744	193,926
1988	899,181	173,313
1989	711,709	239,718
1990	725,469	219,668

Source: The Audubon Institute

the board, who served four-year terms. The board oversaw the policies of the zoo and set guidelines for memberships, concessions, fund-raising, and marketing. Actual policy making and operations were controlled by the Audubon Park Commission, however, which set zoo hours, admission prices, and so forth.

Through its volunteer programs, the Friends of the Zoo staffed many of the zoo's programs. Members of the Friends of the Zoo served as "edZOOcators," education volunteers who were specially trained to conduct interpretive educational programs, and "Zoo Area Pa-

trollers," who provided general information at the zoo and helped with crowd control. Other volunteers assisted in the commissary, the Animal Health Care Center and Wild Bird Rehabilitation Center or helped with membership, public relations, graphics, clerical work, research, or horticulture.

In 1988, the name of the Friends of the Zoo was changed to the Audubon Institute to reflect its growing interest in activities beyond the zoo alone. It planned to promote the development of other facilities and manage these facilities once they were a reality.

Exhibit 5

Membership Fees and Membership

Year	Family Membership Fees	Individual Membership Fees	Number of Memberships
1979	$ 20	$ 10	1,000
1980	20	10	7,000
1981	20	10	11,000
1982	25	15	18,000
1983	30	15	22,000
1984	35	20	26,000
1985	40	20	27,000
1986	45	25	28,616
1987	45	25	29,318
1988	45	25	33,314
1989	49	29	35,935
1990	49	29	38,154

Source: The Audubon Institute

Fund-Raising. The Audubon Park Zoo and the Friends of the Zoo raised funds through five major types of activities: Friends of the Zoo membership, concessions, "Adopt an Animal," "Zoo-to-Do," and capital fund drives. Zoo managers from around the country came to the Audubon Park Zoo for tips on fund-raising.

Membership. Membership in the Friends of the Zoo was open to anyone. The membership fees increased over the years as summarized in Exhibit 5, yet the number of members increased steadily from the original four hundred members in 1974 to thirty-eight thousand members in 1990, but declined to 28,000 in 1992. Membership allowed free entry to the Audubon Park Zoo and many other zoos around the United States. Participation in Zoobilations (annual members-only evenings at the zoo) and the many volunteer programs described earlier were other benefits of membership.

Expanding membership required a special approach to marketing the zoo. Chip Weigand, director of marketing for the zoo, stated,

. . . [I]n marketing memberships we try to encourage repeat visitations, the feeling that one can visit as often as one wants, the idea that the zoo changes from visit to visit and that there are good reasons to make one large payment or donation for a membership card, rather than paying for each visit. . . . . [T]he overwhelming factor is a good zoo that people want to visit often, so that a membership makes good economical sense.

Results of research on visitors to the zoo are contained in Exhibits 6 and 7.

In 1985, the zoo announced a new membership designed for business, the Audubon Zoo Curator Club, with four categories of membership: bronze, $250; silver, $500; gold, $1,000; and platinum, $2,500 and more.

Concessions. The Friends of the Zoo took over the Audubon Park Zoo concessions for refreshments and gifts in 1976 through a public bidding process. The concessions were run by volunteer members of the Friends of the Zoo and all profits went directly to the zoo. Before 1976, concession rentals brought in fifteen hundred dollars in a good year. Profits from operation of the concessions by the Friends of the Zoo brought in $400,000 a year by 1980 and almost $700,000 in profits in 1988. In 1993, FOTZ was considering leasing the concessions to a third party vendor.

Adopt an Animal. Zoo Parents paid a fee to "adopt" an animal, the fee varying with the animal chosen. Zoo Parents' names were listed on a large sign inside the zoo. They also had their own annual celebration, Zoo Parents Day.

Zoo-to-Do. Zoo-to-Do was an annual black-tie fund-raiser held with live music, food and drink, and original, high-class souvenirs, such as posters or ceramic necklaces. Admission tickets, limited to three thousand annually, were priced starting at one hundred dollars per person. A raffle was conducted in conjunction with the Zoo-to-Do, with raffle items varying from an opportunity to be zoo curator for a day to the use of a Mercedes-Benz for a year. Despite the rather stiff price, the Zoo-to-Do was a popular sellout every year. Local restaurants and other businesses donated most of the necessary supplies, decreasing the cost of the affair. In 1985, the Zoo-to-Do raised almost $500,000 in one night, more money than any other nonmedical fund-raiser in the county.[5]

Exhibit 6

Respondent Characteristics of Zoo Visitors According to Visitation Frequency (in %)

Number of Zoo visits over past two years Respondent Characteristic	Four or More	Two or Three	One or None	Never Visited Zoo
Age				
Under 27	26	35	31	9
27 to 35	55	27	15	3
36 to 45	48	32	11	9
46 to 55	18	20	37	25
Over 55	27	29	30	14
Marital Status				
Married	41	28	20	11
Not Married	30	34	24	13
Children at Home				
Yes	46	30	15	9
No	34	28	27	12
Interest in Visiting New Orleans Aquarium				
Very, with Emphasis	47	26	18	9
Very, without Emphasis	45	24	23	12
Somewhat	28	37	14	11
Not Too	19	32	27	22
Member of Friends of the Zoo				
Yes	67	24	5	4
No, but Heard of It	35	30	24	12
Never Heard of It	25	28	35	13
Would You Be Interested in Joining FOTZ (Non-Members Only)				
Very/Somewhat	50	28	14	8
No/Don't Know	33	29	26	12

Source: The Audubon Institute

Advertising

The Audubon Zoo launched impressive marketing campaigns in the 1980s. The zoo received ADDY awards from the New Orleans Advertising Club year after year.[6] In 1986, the film Urban Eden, produced by Alford Advertising and Buckholtz Productions Inc. in New Orleans, finished first among fifty entries in the "documentary films, public relations" category of the Eighth Annual Houston International Film Festival. The first-place Gold Award recognized the film for vividly portraying Audubon Zoo as a conservation, rather than a confining, environment.

During the same year, local television affiliates of ABC, CBS and NBC produced independent TV spots using the theme: "One of the World's Greatest Zoos Is in Your Own Back Yard . . . Audubon Zoo!" Along with some innovative views of the Audubon Zoo being in someone's "backyard," local news anchor personalities enjoyed "monkeying around" with the animals, and the zoo enjoyed some welcome free exposure.[7]

In 1993 the marketing budget was over $800,000, including group sales, public relations, advertising, and special events. Not included in this budget was developmental fund-raising or membership. Percentage breakdowns of the marketing budget can be found in Exhibit 8.

The American Association of Zoological Parks and Aquariums reported that most zoos find the majority of

Exhibit 7

Relative Importance of Seven Reasons as to Why Respondent Does Not Visit the Zoo More Often (in %)

Reason (Closed Ended)	Very Imp. w/ Emphasis	Very Imp. w/o Emphasis	Somewhat Important	Un-Important
The distance of the Zoo's location from where you live	7	11	21	60
The cost of a Zoo visit	4	8	22	66
Not being all that interested in Zoo animals	2	12	18	67
The parking problem on weekends	7	11	19	62
The idea that you get tired of seeing the same exhibits over and over	5	18	28	49
It's too hot during the summer months	25	23	22	30
Just not having the idea occur to you	8	19	26	48

Source: The Audubon Institute

their visitors live within a single population center in close proximity to the park.[8] Thus, to sustain attendance over the years, zoos must attract the same visitors repeatedly. A large number of the zoo's promotional programs and special events were aimed at just that.

Progress was slow among non-natives. For example, Simon & Schuster, a reputable publishing firm, in its 218-page [Frommer's] 1983–84 Guide to New Orleans, managed only a three-word allusion to a "very nice zoo." A 1984 study found that only 36 percent of the visitors were tourists, and even this number was probably influenced to some extent by an overflow from the World's Fair.

Promotional Programs

The Audubon Park Zoo and the Friends of the Zoo conducted a multitude of very successful promotional programs. The effect was to have continual parties and celebrations going on, attracting a variety of people to the zoo (and raising additional revenue). Exhibit 9 lists the major annual promotional programs conducted by the zoo.

In addition to these annual promotions, the zoo scheduled concerts of well-known musicians, such as Irma Thomas, Pete Fountain, The Monkeys, and Manhattan Transfer, and other special events throughout the year. As a result, a variety of events occurred each month.

Many educational activities were conducted all year long. These included (1) a junior zoo keeper program for seventh and eighth graders, (2) a student intern program for high school and college students, and (3) a ZOOmobile that took live animals to such locations as special education classes, hospitals, and nursing homes.

Admission Policy

The commission recommended the institution of an admission charge. Arguments generally advanced against such a charge held that it results in an overall decline in attendance and a reduction of nongate revenues. Proponents held that gate charges control vandalism, produce greater revenues, and result in increased public awareness and appreciation of the facility. In the early 1970s, no major international zoo failed to charge admission, and 73 percent of the 125 zoos in the United States charged admission.

The commission argued that there is no such thing as a free zoo; someone must pay. If the zoo is tax-

Exhibit 8

1991 Marketing Budget

Marketing

General and Administrative	$ 30,900
Sales	96,300
Public Relations	109,250
Advertising	304,800
Special Events	157,900
TOTAL	$ 699,150

Public Relations

Education, Travel and Subscriptions	$ 5,200
Printing and Duplicating	64,000
Professional Services	15,000
Delivery and Postage	3,000
Telephone	1,250
Entertainment	2,000
Supplies	16,600
Miscellaneous	2,200
TOTAL	$ 109,250

Advertising

Media	$ 244,000
Production	50,000
Account Service	10,800
TOTAL	$ 304,800

Special Events

General and Administrative	$ 27,900
LA Swamp Fest	35,000
Earthfest	25,000
Ninja Turtle Breakfast	20,000
Jazz Search	15,000
Fiesta Latina	10,000
Crescent City Cats	10,000
Other Events	15,000
TOTAL	$ 157,900

Source: The Audubon Institute

supported, then locals carry a disproportionate share of the cost. At the time, neighboring Jefferson Parish was growing by leaps and bounds and surely would bring a large, non-paying [constituency] to the new zoo. Further, since most zoos are tourist attractions, tourists should pay since they contribute little to the local tax revenues.

The average yearly attendance for a zoo may be estimated using projected population figures multiplied by a "visitor generating factor." The average visitor generating factor of fourteen zoos similar in size and climate to the Audubon Zoo was 1.34, with a rather wide range from a low of 0.58 in the cities of Phoenix and Miami to a high of 2.80 in Jackson, Mississippi.

Attracting More Tourists and Other Visitors

A riverboat ride on the romantic paddle wheeler Cotton Blossom took visitors from downtown New Orleans to the zoo. Originally, the trip began at a dock in the French Quarter, but it was later moved to a dock immediately adjacent to New Orleans's newest attraction, the Riverwalk, a Rouse development, on the site of the 1984 Louisiana World Exposition. Not only was the riverboat ride great fun, it also lured tourists and conventioneers from the downtown attractions of the French Quarter and the new Riverwalk to the zoo, some six miles upstream. A further allure of the riverboat ride was a return trip to downtown on the New Orleans Streetcar, one of the few remaining trolley cars

Exhibit 9

Selected Audubon Park Zoo Promotional Programs

Month	Activity
March	Louisiana Black Heritage Festival. A two day celebration of Louisiana's Black history and its native contributions through food, music, and arts and crafts.
March	Earth Fest. The environment and our planet are the focus of this fun-filled and educational event. Recycling, conservation displays, and puppet shows.
April	Jazz Search. This entertainment series is aimed at finding the best new talent in the area with the winners featured at the New Orleans Jazz & Heritage Festival.
April	Zoo-To-Do for Kids. At this "pint-sized" version of the Zoo-To-Do, fun and games abound for kids.
May	Zoo-To-Do. Annual black tie fundraiser featuring over 100 of New Orleans' finest restaurants and three music stages.
May	Irma Thomas Mother's Day Concert. The annual celebration of Mother's Day with a buffet.
August	Lego Invitational. Architectural firms turn thousands of Lego pieces into original creations.
September	Fiesta Latina. Experience the best the Hispanic community has to offer through music, cuisine, and arts and crafts.
October	Louisiana Swamp Festival. Cajun food, music, and crafts highlight this four-day salute to Louisiana's bayou country; features hands-on contact with live swamp animals.
October	Boo at the Zoo. This annual Halloween extravaganza features games, special entertainment, trick or treat, a haunted house, and the Zoo's Spook Train.

Source: The Audubon Institute

in the United States. The Zoo Cruise not only drew more visitors but also generated additional revenue through landing fees paid by the New Orleans Steamboat Company and [helped keep] traffic out of uptown New Orleans.[9]

Financial

The zoo's ability to generate operating funds has been ascribed to the dedication of the Friends of the Zoo, continuing increases in attendance, and creative special events and programs. A history of adequate operating funds allowed the zoo to guarantee capital donors that their gifts would be used to build and maintain top-notch exhibits. A comparison of the 1989 and 1990 Statements of Operating Income and Expense for the Audubon Institute is in Exhibit 10.

Capital Fund Drives

The Audubon Zoo Development Fund was established in 1973. Corporate/Industrial support of the zoo has been very strong—many corporations have underwritten construction of zoo displays and facilities. A partial list of major corporate sponsors is in Exhibit 11. A sponsorship was considered to be for the life of the exhibit. The development department operated on a 12 percent overhead rate, which meant 88 cents of every dollar raised went toward the projects. By 1989,

the master plan for development was 75 percent complete. The fund-raising goal for the zoo in 1989 was $1,500,000.

Management

The Zoo Director

Ron Forman, Audubon Zoo director, was called a "zoomaster extraordinaire" and was described by the press as a "cross between Doctor Doolittle and the Wizard of Oz," as a "practical visionary," and as "serious, but with a sense of humor."[10] A native New Orleanian, . . . Forman quit an MBA program to join the city government as an administrative assistant and found himself doing a business analysis project on the Audubon Park. Once the city was committed to a new zoo, Forman was placed on board as an assistant to the zoo director, John Moore. In early 1977, Moore gave up the battle between the "animal people" and the "people people,"[11] and Forman took over as park and zoo director.

Forman was said to bring an MBA-meets-menagerie style to the zoo, which was responsible for transforming it from a public burden into an almost completely self-sustaining operation. The result not only benefited the citizens of the city but also added a major tourist attraction to the economically troubled city of the 1980s.

Exhibit 10

The Audubon Institute, Inc. The Audubon Park and Zoological Garden Statement of Operating Income and Expenses

	1989	1990 (ZOO)	1990 (AQU.)
Operating Income			
Admissions	$2,952,000	$3,587,000	$3,664,000
Food & Gift Operations	$2,706,000	$3,495,500	$711,000
Membership	$1,476,000	$1,932,000	$2,318,000
Recreational Programs	$410,000	$396,000	$0
Visitor Services	$246,000	$218,000	$0
Other	$410,000	$32,000	$650,000
TOTAL INCOME	$8,200,000	$9,660,500	$7,343,000
Operating Expenses			
Maintenance	$1,394,000	$1,444,000	$1,316,000
Educational/Curatorial	$2,296,000	$2,527,500	$2,783,000
Food & Gift Operations	$1,804,000	$2,375,000	$483,000
Membership	$574,000	$840,000	$631,000
Recreational	$328,000	$358,000	$362,000
Marketing	$410,000	$633,000	$593,000
Visitor Services	$574,000	$373,000	$125,000
Administration	$820,000	$1,110,000	$1,050,000
TOTAL EXPENSES	$8,200,000	$9,660,500	$7,343,000

Staffing

The zoo used two classes of employees, civil service, through the Audubon Park Commission, and noncivil service. The civil service employees included the curators and zoo keepers. They fell under the jurisdiction of the city civil service system but were paid out of the budget of the Friends of the Zoo. Employees who worked in public relations, advertising, concessions, fund-raising, and so on were hired through the Friends of the Zoo and were not part of the civil service system. See Exhibit 12 for further data on staffing patterns.

The Zoo in the Late '80s

A visitor to the new Audubon Park Zoo could quickly see why New Orleanians were so proud of their zoo. In a city that was termed among the dirtiest in the nation, the zoo was virtually spotless. This was a result of adequate staffing and the clear pride of both those who worked at and those who visited the zoo. One of the first points made by volunteers guiding school groups was that anyone seeing a piece of trash on the ground must pick it up.[12] A 1986 city poll showed that 93 percent of the citizens surveyed gave the zoo a high approval rating—an extremely high rating for any public facility.

Kudos came from groups outside the local area as well. Delegates from the American Association of Zoological Parks and Aquariums ranked the Audubon Park Zoo as one of the three top zoos of its size in America. In 1982, the American Association of Nurserymen gave the zoo a Special Judges Award for its use of plant materials. In 1985, the Audubon Park Zoo received the Phoenix Award from the Society of American Travel Writers for its achievements in conservation, preservation, and beautification.

By 1987, the zoo was virtually self-sufficient. The small amount of money received from government grants amounted to less than 10 percent of the budget. The master plan for the development of the zoo was 75 percent complete, and the reptile exhibit was scheduled for completion in the fall. The organization had expanded with a full complement of professionals and managers. (See Exhibit 13 for the organizational structure of the zoo.)

While the zoo made great progress in fifteen years, all was not quiet on the political front. In a court battle, the city won over the state on the issue of who wielded ultimate authority over Audubon Park and Zoo.

Amoco Foundation
American Express
Anheuser-Busch, Inc.
Arthur Anderson and Company
J. Aron Charitable Foundation, Inc.
Bell South Corporation
BP America
Chevron USA, Inc.
Conoco, Inc.
Consolidated Natural Gas Corporation
Entergy Corporation
Exxon Company, USA
Freeport-McMoRan, Inc.
Host International, Inc.
Kentwood Spring Water
Louisiana Coca-Cola Bottling Company, Ltd.
Louisiana Land and Exploration Company
Martin Marietta Manned Space Systems
McDonald's Operators of New Orleans
Mobil Foundation, Inc.
National Endowment for the Arts
National Science Foundation
Ozone Spring Water
Pan American Life Insurance Company
Philip Morris Companies Inc.
Shell Companies Foundation, Inc.
Tenneco, Inc.
Texaco USA
USF&G Corporation
Wendy's of New Orleans, Inc.

Exhibit 11
Major Corporate Sponsors

Source: The Audubon Institute

Year	# of Paid Employees	Number of Volunteers
1972	36	
1973	49	
1974	69	
1975	90	
1976	143	
1977	193	
1978	184	
1979	189	
1980	198	
1981	245	
1982	305	
1983	302	56
1984	419	120
1985	454	126
1986	426	250
1987	431	300
1988	462	310
1989	300	270
1990	450	350

Exhibit 12
Employee Structure

Source: The Audubon Institute

Indeed, the zoo benefited from three friendly mayors in a row, starting with Moon Landrieu, who championed the new zoo, to Ernest "Dutch" Morial, to Sidney Barthelemy who threw his support to both the zoo and the aquarium proposal championed by Ron Forman.

The Future

New Directions for the Zoo

Zoo Director Ron Forman demonstrated that zoos have almost unlimited potential. A 1980 New Orleans magazine article cited some of Forman's ideas, ranging from a safari train to a breeding center for rare animals. The latter has an added attraction as a potential money-maker since an Asiatic lion cub, for example, sells for around ten thousand dollars. This wealth of ideas was important because expanded facilities and programs are required to maintain attendance at any public attraction. The most ambitious of Forman's ideas was for an aquarium and riverfront park to be located at the foot of Canal Street.

Although the zoo enjoyed political support in 1992, New Orleans was still suffering from a high unemployment rate and a generally depressed economy resulting from the slump in the oil industry. Some economists predicted the beginning of a gradual turnaround in 1988, but any significant improvement in the economy was still forecasted to be years away in 1993. (A few facts about New Orleans are given in Exhibit 14.) In addition, the zoo operated in a city where many attractions competed for the leisure dollar of citizens and visitors. The Audubon Zoological Garden had to vie with the French Quarter, Dixieland jazz, the Superdome, and even the greatest of all attractions in the city—Mardi Gras.

The New Orleans Aquarium

In 1986, Forman and a group of supporters proposed the development of an aquarium and riverfront park to the New Orleans City Council. In November 1986, the electorate voted to fund an aquarium and a riverfront park by a 70 percent margin—one of the largest margins the city has ever given to any tax proposal. Forman[13] hailed this vote of confidence from the citizens as a mandate to build a world-class aquarium that would produce new jobs, stimulate the local economy, and create an educational resource for the children of the city.

The Aquarium of the Americas opened in September 1990. The $40 million aquarium project was located providing a logical pedestrian link for visitors between [major] attractions of the Riverwalk and the Jax Brewery, a shopping center in the French Quarter. Management of the aquarium was placed under the Audubon Institute, the same organization that ran the Audubon Zoo. A feasibility study prepared by Harrison Price Company[14] projected a probable 863,000 visitors by the year 1990, with 75 percent of the visitors coming from outside the metropolitan area. That attendance figure was reached in only four months and six days from the grand opening. Attendance remained strong through 1992, after a slight drop from the initial grand opening figures.

Meanwhile, the zoo had its own future to plan. The new physical facilities and professional care paid off handsomely in increased attendance and new animal births. But the zoo could not expand at its existing location because of lack of land within the city. Forman and the zoo considered several alternatives. One was little "neighborhood" zoos to be located all over the city. A second was a special survival center, a separate breeding area to be located outside the city boundaries where land was available.

Forman presented . . . plans for a project called Riverfront 2000, which included expansion of the aquarium, the Woldenberg Riverfront Park, a species survival center, an arboretum, an insectarium, a natural history museum, and a further expansion of the zoo. With the zoo running smoothly, the staff seemed to need new challenges to tackle, and the zoo needed new facilities or programs to continue to increase attendance.

Notes

1. Millie Ball, "The New Zoo of '82," Dixie Magazine, Sunday Times-Picayune, 24 June 1979.
2. Merikaye Presley, "Neighbors Objecting to Audubon Zoo Expansion Project in Midst of Work," Times-Picayune, 30 March 1975, p. A3.
3. "Zoo Expansion Is Ruled Illegal," Times-Picayune, 20 January 1976.
4. "Society Seeks Change at Zoo," Times-Picayune, 29 April 1972, p. D25.
5. "Zoo Thrives Despite Tough Times in New Orleans," Jefferson Business, August 1985, p. A1.
6. Ibid.
7. Sharon Donovan, "New Orleans Affiliates Monkey Around for Zoo," Advertising Age, 17 March 1986.
8. Karen Sausmann, ed., Zoological Park and Aquarium Fundamentals (Wheeling, W. Va.: American Association of Zoological Parks and Aquariums, 1982), p. 111.

Exhibit 13
Audubon Park Commission

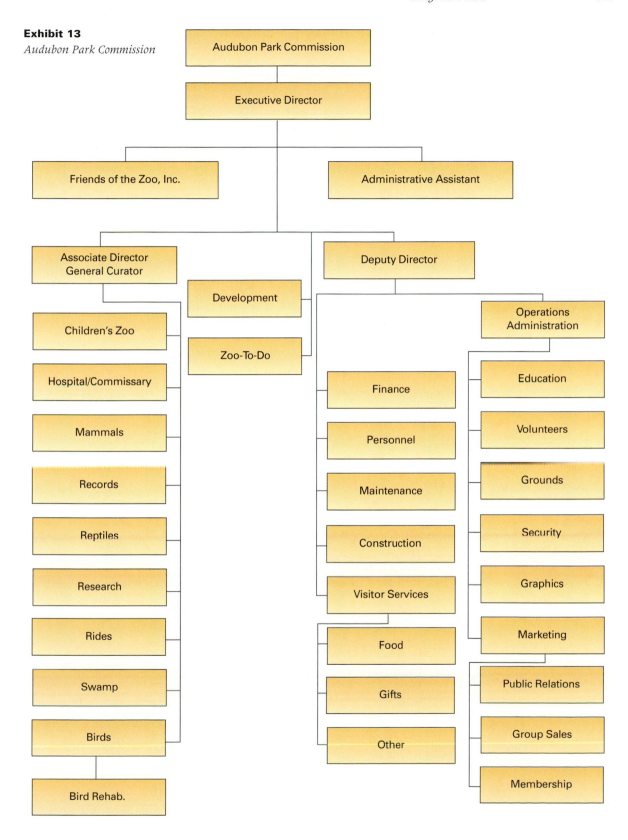

Exhibit 14

A Few Facts About the New Orleans MSA

Population	1,324,400
Households	489,900
Median Age	30.8 years
Median Household EBI	$29,130
Average Temperature	70 degrees
Average Annual Rainfall	63 inches
Average Elevation	5 feet below sea level
Area	363.5 square miles
	199.4 square miles of land

Major Economic Activities

Tourism (5 million visitors per year)
Oil and Gas Industry
The Port of New Orleans (170 million tons of cargo/year)

Taxes

State Sales Tax	4.0%
Parish (County) Sales Tax	5.0% (Orleans)
	4.0% (Jefferson)
State Income Tax	2.1–2.6% on first $20,000
	3.0–3.5% on next $30,000
	6.0% on $51,000 & over

Parish Property Tax of 126.15 mills (Orleans) is based on 10% of appraised value over $75,000 homestead exemption.

Source: Sales and Marketing Management. South Central Bell Yellow Pages, 1991.

9. Diane Luope, "Riverboat Rides to Zoo Are Planned," Times-Picayne, 30 November 1981, p. A17.
10. Steve Brooks, "Don't Say 'No Can Do' to Audubon Zoo Chief," Jefferson Business, 5 May 1986, p. 1
11. Ross Yuchey, "No Longer Is Heard a Discouraging Word at the Audubon Zoo," New Orleans, August 1980, p. 53.
12. Ibid., p. 49.
13. At the Zoo, Winter 1987.
14. Feasibility Analysis and Conceptual Planning for a Major Aquarium Attraction, prepared for the City of New Orleans, March 1985.

References

Beaulieu, Lovell. "It's All Happening at the Zoo," The Times Picayune, Sunday, January 28, 1978.

Ball, Millie. "The New Zoo of '82," Dixie Magazine, Sunday Times Picayune, June 24, 1978.

Brooks, Steve. "Don't Say 'No Can Do' to Audubon Zoo Chief," Jefferson Business, May 5, 1986.

Bureau of Governmental Research, City of New Orleans. Audubon Park Zoo Study, Part I, Zoo Improvement Plan. August 1971. New Orleans: Bureau of Governmental Research.

Bureau of Governmental Research, City of New Orleans. Audubon Park Zoo Study, Part II, An Operational Analysis. August 1971 New Orleans: Bureau of Governmental Research.

Donovan, S. "The Audubon Zoo: A Dream Come True," New Orleans, May 1986, pp. 52–66.

Feasibility Analysis and Conceptual Planning for a Major Aquarium Attraction, prepared for the City of New Orleans, March 1985.

Forman, R., J. Logsdon and J. Wilds. Audubon Park: An Urban Eden, 1985, New Orleans: The Friends of the Zoo.

Poole, Susan. Frommer's 1983–84 Guide to New Orleans, 1983, New York: Simon & Schuster.

Sausmann, K., ed., Zoological Park and Aquarium Fundamentals, 1982, Wheeling, West Virginia: American Association of Zoological Parks and Aquariums.

Yuckey, R. "No Longer Is Heard a Discouraging Word at the Audubon Zoo," New Orleans, August, 1980, pp. 49–60.

Zuckerman, S., ed., Great Zoos of the World, 1980, Colorado: Westview Press.

Integrative Case 7.1 *The Food Terminal (A)**

In July 1991, three months after graduating from the Western Business School, 23-year-old Mike Bellafacia knew that he was in for a rough ride.

> When I arrived at the store, the staff morale was terrible. The previous manager had made a mess of things, the recession was hitting home, sales were spiraling downward quickly, and my store was losing $10,000 per week. To make matters worse, most of the key people in the company felt that I didn't deserve the Store Manager's position.

As the recently appointed Store Manager of the newest Foodco location in St. Catharines, Ontario, Mike knew that he had to turn the store around by improving its financial performance and the employee morale. He also knew that something had to be done immediately because the losses at this store were seriously affecting the entire company.

Foodco Ltd.

Foodco Ltd. (FC), with its head office located in St. Catharines, Ontario, was a large player in the Niagara Peninsula grocery retailing industry. FC, a retailer in this market since 1962, was currently made up of seven stores: three St. Catharines locations, one Welland location, one Port Colborne location, and two Lincoln locations. Most of the ownership and key management positions were held by Frank Bellafacia, Tony Bellafacia, and Rocco Bellafacia as shown in Exhibit 1. Selected financial ratios for FC are shown in Exhibit 2.

FC had created a powerful presence in this industry by developing and refining a strategy that worked. Their product offering was that of any typical supermarket: groceries, meats, bakery and dairy items, packaged foods and non-food items. Each store carried eight to ten thousand different items. FC planned to widen the selection available by adding more lines, and to follow a general trend in consumer preferences towards an increased percentage of non-food items in the product mix. Central to FC's strategy was a well-managed marketing effort. Weekly flyers were distributed that highlighted five or six items. FC priced these items below cost to draw customers. The rest of the flyer's products were representative of all the product groups (see Exhibit 3). FC's ability to differentiate itself from the other competitors centered around its corporate vision: low food prices and fast, friendly service. Central to the

FC competitive strategy was the mandate to be the low-price leader among conventional supermarkets, during good and bad economic times. Mike Bellafacia stated: "This is a no frills and low price store for a no frills and low price clientele. Most markets are shifting in this direction." FC had developed aggressive expansion plans with six stores being considered for development.

The Retail Grocery Industry

The job of managing the store and the staff became crucial to the overall success of FC given the demanding challenges in the industry. The industry was shifting from a simple mass market to a spectrum of distinct, serviceable segments. A recent statistic stated that 30% of consumers switch stores every year. Moreover, a new Food Marketing Institute study found that consumers buy on the basis of the following criteria (ranked in decreasing priority): service, quality products, variety, and low prices. Thus, there was now more opportunity for competitive differentiation based on service and on quality than on price alone.

There were tremendous opportunities for niche players to enter the market, and such entrants had been observed. Health and organic food stores, fruit markets, and independent single-commodity stores (i.e., pet food stores) emerged and were servicing their target segments more effectively than the supermarkets were willing or able to do. Consumer demands varied from region to region, and many small independent retail grocers emerged to meet these demands both in the Niagara

---

*Leo J. Klus prepared this case under the supervision of John F. Graham, Pre-Business Program Director, solely to provide material for class discussion. The case is not intended to illustrate either effective or ineffective handling of a managerial situation. Certain names and other identifying information may have been disguised to protect confidentiality. This material is not covered under authorization from CanCopy or any reproduction rights organization. Any form of reproduction, storage or transmittal of this material is prohibited without written permission from Western Business School. Copies or permission to reproduce may be obtained by contacting Case and Publication Services, Western Business School, The University of Western Ontario, London, Ontario, N6A 3K7, or by calling (519) 661-3208, or faxing (519) 661-3882. Copyright 1992 © The University of Western Ontario; Revision Date 95/06/12.

Exhibit 1
Personnel Organization Chart

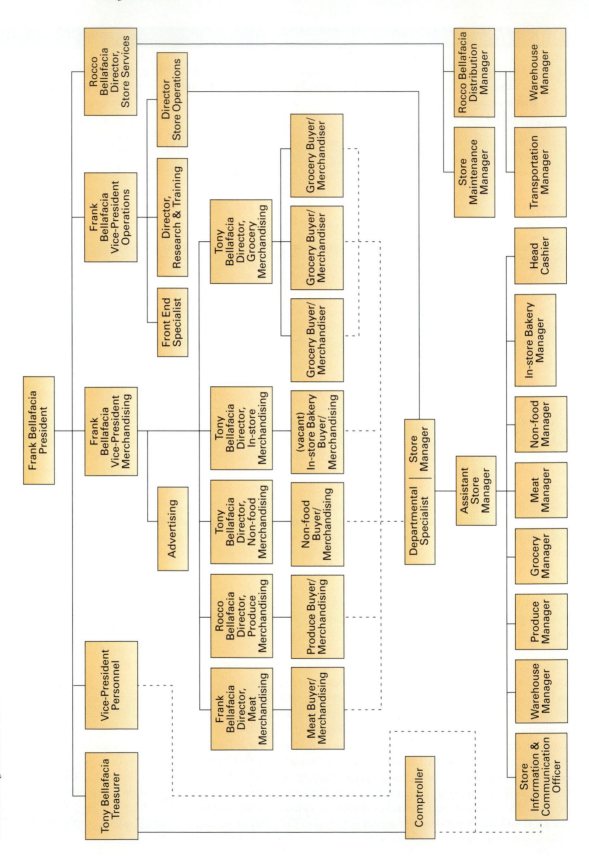

	1986	1987	1988	1989	1990
Profitability					
Cost of Goods Sold	81.2%	80.2%	79.7%	78.7%	78.3%
Operating Expenses	19.4%	18.7%	19.1%	19.6%	19.8%
Net Income Before Tax	-1.1%	0.5%	0.3%	0.7%	0.7%
Return					
After-Tax Return on Equity	0.0%	715.0%	n/a	725.0%	94.2%
Stability					
Interest Coverage*	1.28×	1.36×	1.05×	1.19×	2.37×
Liquidity					
Net Working Capital ($000)*	-1,447	-2,051	-13	-316	-243
Growth					
Sales		26.0%	10.7%	14.1%	15.5%
Assets*		16.7%	3.8%	11.2%	9.6%
Equity*		-0.3%	1.2%	4.9%	19.5%

*Denotes a ratio calculated from the statements of Bellafacia's Consolidated Holdings Inc.

Exhibit 2
Selected Financial Ratios

Peninsula and across all of Ontario. These independents managed not only to survive, but to take sizable portions of market share from the major chains. This shift towards niche marketing and catering to the local market outlined the need to employ Store Managers who understood how to please and retain the local customer.

The Role of the Store Manager

The success of FC depended upon each of the seven Store Managers operating his/her store consistently with the corporate strategy. Traditionally, the road to Store Manager (SM) began within one of the stores at a lower management position. The family culture within each Food Terminal location was very important to FC management. Thus, Store Managers were selected from within the company to ensure a leader who understood the FC vision and values. Five managers reported directly to the SM as shown in Exhibit 4, and their development was an important job for the SM. The SM position became increasingly more important at FC. Many of the current SM functions that used to be handled by the head office were delegated downward to the store level to allow the head office to focus on overall company strategy. The stores were now more attuned to the local market they serve. An SM was responsible for the following:

1. Ensuring that merchandising skills were strong among all department managers

2. Monitoring local market information
3. Focusing staff on organizational goals (such as sales, gross margin, and profit goals)
4. Organizing weekly staff meetings
5. Developing all employees and encouraging staff training
6. Generating and producing sales, gross margin and profit objectives
7. Meeting cost objectives (motivating the staff to be cost conscious)
8. Analyzing the performance of each inter-store department
9. Attending FC "Top Management Meetings" (TMMs)

Mike Bellafacia's Background

Mike Bellafacia graduated from the University of Western Ontario with an Honors Business Administration degree (HBA). During his summers at University, he was assigned special projects from his father that focused on a variety of company problems. Mike would combine the analytical skills developed in the business school with his knowledge of the family business to address these issues. In his last year in the HBA program, Mike and a team of student consultants spent the year focusing on the long-term strategy and competitive advantage of FC. They examined every aspect of the company and developed many strategic recommendations for the top management at FC.

Exhibit 3

Front Page of a Weekly Flyer

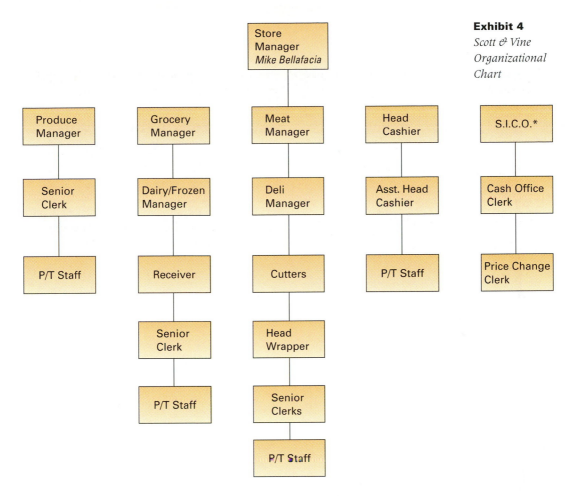

Exhibit 4
Scott & Vine Organizational Chart

* *Store Information and Communications Officer.* Responsible for maintaining the lines of communication between the store and head office.

Upon graduation, Mike decided to work for FC. He planned to start off working in some of the various departments (i.e., the Produce department) at different stores within FC, and work his way up in order to get the experience he needed to manage a store. This would have allowed him the opportunity to work under some of the most knowledgeable managers in the company. He didn't expect to be Store Manager so soon.

The Scott & Vine Location: The First Month

Mike's career at FC was supposed to begin in one of the departments in the company. Both Mike and FC management felt strongly about that. However, while Mike was on vacation in May, FC management made a chancy decision. As of June 1, 1991, Mike Bellafacia would take over the SM position at the Scott and Vine

location from the existing SM. The store's performance was deteriorating, and Mike was expected to change things. Mike reflected on the first week at the three-month old location:

When I first started I was extremely nervous. The District Supervisor brought me to the store to have a meeting with the department managers, and I could see the look of disappointment in their eyes. Most of these managers had been forced to move to this new store from other locations. The staff morale was definitely low to begin with. Combined with the fact that I am the boss's son, they probably assumed that I was sent to check on them.

After getting settled in, Mike began to realize that something was terribly wrong at the Scott & Vine Food Terminal. The store was not producing a bottom line, and many of the 95 employees were not performing well. Mike commented: "This building used to be a Food City that was on the verge of closing down. We acquired it, and picked up where they left off. The task I had was to get above average performance from an average staff. They were just not driven to succeed, were poorly trained, and many of them, especially the managers, didn't want to be there." The previous manager had performed poorly by FC standards. Although he had been a SM at other grocery stores, he was unable to create a productive atmosphere at this one. When this location opened, the sales level was $160,000 per week, but by Mike's first month it had dropped by 17%. FC management expected this location to be operating at over $200,000 per week. The other St. Catharines stores were operating at over $350,000 per week. They had a long way to go.

What took place at the Scott & Vine location was a symptom of a more serious problem: the performance of FC as a whole. Mike explained the situation:

Some of what was happening here can be attributed to FC. They became fat cats and, in the process, they lost touch with the customers. Pricing had gone way out of line, cross-border shopping was cutting into our bottom line, and our marketing efforts were poor. The weekly ads which are developed by head office for all the stores were not drawing in customers like they used to. As a result, we had no word-of-mouth advertising which is so essential to a retail outlet. When our sales across the board went down, we had only ourselves to blame.

Sorting Through the Disorder

The job of managing the Food Terminal was overwhelming, and the problems were endless. Some of the more prevalent problems are listed below:

1. Product rotation (a job monitored by department managers and very important for customer satisfaction) was handled improperly.
2. It was not uncommon to find empty counters and shelves.
3. The staff paid very little attention to cleanliness. (Customers complained about this.)
4. Customers were not treated with respect by those employees who had frequent contact with them.
5. Department Managers were doing a poor job of managing and motivating the employees in their departments.
6. Department sales and gross profit results were poor. (See Exhibit 5 for a breakdown of departmental sales and gross profit figures.)

Exhibit 5

Selected Financial Indicators—Scott & Vine Location for the Week Ending June 9, 1991

DEPARTMENTAL PERFORMANCE			
Department	Sales ($)	Gross profit ($)	% of Sales
Produce	22,677	4,602	20.3
Grocery	77,363	12,467	16.1
Meat	32,963	7,629	23.1
Non-Food	4,784	1,228	25.7
IS-Bakery	2,337	934	40.0
TOTAL	140,124	28,860	19.2

OVERALL STORE PERFORMANCE (ONE WEEK)		
Weekly Indicators	Budget ($)	Actual ($)
Sales	155,000	140,124
Gross Profit	33,683	26,860
Expenses:		
Wages	16,483	19,600
Supplies	1,895	1,410
Other Expenses	17,091	16,257
Total Expenses	35,469	37,267
Net Income	(1,786)	(10,407)
# Of Customers	7,723/WEEK	

Difficulties arose within the staff that made the SM job even more strenuous. Mike described the situation:

> *There was a lot of people problems that I had to face. The weekly staff meetings we had together were a joke. Instead of a time to interact and solve problems together, it was just a waste of time. As well, the entire staff was demoralized due to the continual failure to meet monthly performance goals since the store opened. We had the worst performance in the FC organization. The controller of the company told me that the Scott & Vine location was hurting the entire company. I felt as though head office was blaming me for the store's poor performance and I knew that I had to set some goals that we could all rally behind.*
>
> *For the first month I was very autocratic. I had to be! I replaced all the cashiers that month, because of the numerous customer complaints about their attitude, but that was just the beginning of my problems. The part-time staff were continually standing around doing nothing. The receiver was not handling the deliveries very well. I found it tough to get along with the department managers. My worst employee problems came from the produce and meat managers (see Exhibit 4). They just were not doing their jobs well. I tried going over the product orders with them, developing schedules, and assisting with their product display plans. I even brought in some of FC's department experts to go over things with them. They would not listen to any of my suggestions. Even though I had some problems with my Grocery manager, I began to see that he had real potential for managing. There was some resentment towards me for being a family member and getting the SM position so young, and as a result, people would not open up to me. I also knew that some of the other SMs at other locations didn't want me to succeed, and I found myself conveniently left out of important SM meetings. To make matters worse, after two months here, the General Manager of FC made it known that I should be pulled out of this job.*

Facing the Future

It was a tough season to compete in the retail grocery business. Mike Bellafacia found this out after only two months at the Food Terminal and the situation was now grave. The Scott & Vine location was losing over $10,000 per week, and the sales level was stagnant. The staff morale had changed very little. Customers were not responding to advertisement efforts, and things looked as if they were going to worsen. Mike reflected on what had happened during these last two months and where things were going. He wondered if he was responsible for the mess the store was in—had he mismanaged his managers, thereby making the situation worse? Had FC made a big mistake putting him in the position of SM? Thinking back on his education, Mike commented: "The business school helped me understand the decision-making process. I'm not afraid to make decisions, do analysis and pin-point problem areas. But, it didn't teach me how to get the job done, the execution of a decision. More importantly, I was not prepared to deal with people who didn't have the training I did, or the desire to succeed as I did."

Although he was unsure about these issues, he focused on what he should do to get the Scott & Vine Food Terminal operating profitably, with good management and with a growing customer base. As he looked over the financial data, he wondered if he should lay off some employees to bring the wages expense down. Mike reflected on this: "We didn't have the sales to support the exorbitant number of employees we had at the store." He was concerned about how he would handle these lay-offs. He also thought about the serious morale problem. Many of the employees were lazy and demotivated and customers complained regularly about cleanliness and service. He wondered if there was a way to use the weekly meetings to his advantage. Things seemed just as complicated as they did in June.

Integrative Case 7.2 *The Food Terminal (B)**

"I'm really just starting to have fun here, and the staff is working more like a team every day." In June 1992, Mike Bellafacia was able to look out over the store floor with a smile on his face. Things had really changed at the youngest Food Terminal. The staff was working well together, the customer base had increased by 45%, and the marketing strategy had been improved. More obvious was the drastic improvement in sales to $193,000 per week and net profit to $1,300 per week.

> *The major problems that we had a year ago had much to do with the fact that we weren't established in our market as a store to deal with the environmental changes. The entire FC lost much of its customer-driven focus, and the results were immediate. I had a staff that was incompetent, and managers who weren't managing. We had to increase the customer base, and this meant improving the word of mouth advertising that was desperately needed.*

Evaluating the Staff

Mike's first priority was to stop the bleeding in the store and establish a bottom line. In a business that focuses on selling at the lowest price, poor cost control could be detrimental to the bottom line. This meant taking a hard look at all expenses, especially wages. Mike explained this process: "Although the fixed costs weren't too bad, the wages were by far our largest expense. With the help of the FC General Manager, I analyzed our past performance and developed a way of determining the staffing needs based on sales volume. Unfortunately, this meant reducing the staff. I set up meetings with each department head to discuss the need for lower staff levels, and to get their input. I pushed them to evaluate their own staff and determine who should leave. We then proceeded to transfer, lay off and terminate various employees. By the time the managers and I were through we were down to 50 employees from 95. This process forced the managers to manage their departments. It was not long before the managers were coming to me with staffing suggestions, especially when the sales started rising. At this point a certain level of trust began to develop between me and the managers, and I began to challenge them to do more managing and less working."

Developing the Staff

Mike's first year at the Food Terminal gave him a profound insight into the art of managing people. "People need to be treated with respect. If you don't help them to make decisions on their own, the changes and improvements you have introduced will fall apart as soon as you leave. All of the wonderful things we learn at business school are useless unless we put these ideas into the language of the people we are managing. To assume that they understand what we are doing and why we are doing it is very dangerous."

After addressing the financial issues, Mike concentrated on improving the service at the Scott Street location. In order to beat the competition, he decided that the Food Terminal would need higher standards than the competition. This meant adherence to three simple, yet powerful, principles:

1. Having a cleaner store.
2. Serving people with a friendlier staff.
3. Doing the job faster than the competition.

Mike reflected on this mandate: "The major chain stores don't do these things as well because they are not customer-driven. I know that I will beat my competition when I adhere to these principles." His challenge was to make these principles a priority to the staff.

Mike began by revamping the weekly meetings. Instead of simply meeting together to deal with small problems, Mike turned this into a motivational and

*This case was prepared by Leo J. Klus, Instructor, under the supervision of Professor John F. Graham for the sole purpose of providing material for class discussion at the Western Business School. Certain names and other identifying information may have been disguised to protect confidentiality. It is not intended to illustrate either effective or ineffective handling of a managerial situation. This material is not covered under authorization from CanCopy or any Reproduction Rights Organization. Any form of reproduction, storage or transmittal of this material is prohibited without written permission from Western Business School. Permission to reproduce or copies may be obtained by contacting Case and Publication Services, Western Business School, The University of Western Ontario, London, Ontario, N6A 3K7, or calling 519-661-3208, or faxing 519-661-3882. Copyright 1992 © The University of Western Ontario.

team-building session. They are still so important to him that he spends six or seven hours preparing for them. Each week a different issue of strategic importance to the store was introduced and discussed with the staff, simply and effectively. Mike's goal was to get the managers and staff talking among themselves to solve problems together. Merchandising plans, scheduling, store problems were all discussed with everyone. After a few weeks, this became very successful, and the three principles were understood by all. "As managers, we are not there to serve ourselves, or do the workers' job for them, as many leaders mistakenly think. We are there to serve them by giving them the skills to do their jobs."

Other Development Initiatives

Mike began posting a series of motivational statements that could always be seen by the staff. These sayings encouraged the staff to focus on the vision Mike was trying to instill: *Making the Customer Everybody's Top Priority*. The entire staff memorized Mike's most customer-driven vision: The 10 Commandments. (See Exhibit 1 A & B for other examples of these motivators.)

Developing employees to reach levels of excellence was Mike's toughest and most rewarding task. In order to understand the goals and objectives of his staff, he conceived the Food Terminal "Career Path Form" to be filled out by all the full-time employees. Mike talked about this process: "I picked out six people from the pile who I felt were the most committed to advancement and excellence at FC. We are now taking a course in Customer Relations together and meet weekly to discuss class issues. I can recognize potential in people, and I want to help them realize their goals."

Interpersonal Conflict

The problems with the managers did not disappear. The produce and meat managers were replaced by September 1991. The second manager in the grocery department was dismissed due to a problem with alcoholism, and much of Mike's time was devoted to helping the inexperienced grocery manager manage his department better. "The key thing when managing people is to catch them doing things right!" The Scott & Vine Food Terminal had handled the turnaround well. The staff was now ready to handle increases in sales and customers, service was a store vision, the morale was

strong, and the financial indicators were positive and improving. (See Exhibit 2.)

When asked about the way he managed the store that year, Mike responded:

I thought I could be successful from day one. I didn't expect it to be as hard as it was. In retrospect, I should have listened more to my staff at the beginning, rather than handle it like a maverick. I would have liked to have seen other great departments in the FC organization and gathered knowledge, rather than trying to reinvent the wheel. There were times that I concentrated too hard on the after-the-fact numbers, instead of reinforcing values and running a business. I now know that I have to spend my time perfecting the art of merchandising. However, I am glad that I focused on the customer the entire time. When you walk into this store, you can feel the sense of customer commitment that we all have. It was a difficult job laying off people, but the wage expense was too high for the sales level we were at. It really hurt our gross profit figure. We now add employees as we grow in sales and profits. I am glad that I learned to handle this with a hands off approach, as this allowed me to focus on developing people.

The Weekly Flyers

Making changes to this process was lengthy. Mike kept making suggestions to the head office about the problems with the ads, but no one seemed to listen to his suggestions. Eventually, FC decided to implement some of these suggestions and the flyers began advertising products at incredibly low prices. The entire FC organization started an advertising blitz on February 25, 1992. The goal was to get back to being a customer-driven organization. Eventually, people started asking for those locally famous FC flyers. The Scott & Vine location saw a 45% increase in the number of customers over the next 5 months, and overall FC sales increased 32% that quarter. Mike commented on this growth: "The staff was prepared to handle this growth. We were all so aware of the little details at the store that when the people started coming in, we were ready for them."

As Mike considered the future of the Scott & Vine location, he wondered if there was anything else he could do to improve the performance of his staff, become more customer-driven, and continue to improve sales and profits.

THE 10 COMMANDMENTS
FROM THE BOOK OF SCOTT...

1. THE CUSTOMER IS THY LORD, OUR ONLY PURPOSE IN LIFE IS TO SERVE HIM.
2. THOU SHALT NEVER SELL A PRODUCT THAT YOU YOURSELF WOULD NOT BUY.
3. THOU SHALT NOT BE OUT OF STOCK ON ANY ITEM AT ANY TIME.
4. THOU SHALT RESPECT YOUR CO-WORKERS AS THYSELF.
5. CLEANLINESS IS SACRED. YOUR DEPARTMENTS MUST BE CLEAN AND SAFE AT ALL TIMES.
6. SCANNING IS SACRED. WE WILL NOT SELL ANYTHING AT AN INCORRECT PRICE.
7. MERCHANDISING IS SACRED. THE JOB OF SELLING IS NEVER COMPLETE.
8. THOU SHALT NOT STEAL—MERCHANDISE OR TIME.
9. THOU SHALT ALWAYS ACT AS PROFESSIONAL MANAGERS. COMMUNICATE, MOTIVATE, MEDIATE, DISCIPLINE, TRAIN, INVOLVE, EVALUATE AND COACH EACH EMPLOYEE CONSTANTLY.
10. THOU SHALT NEVER QUIT, FOR THE RISK OF FAILURE IS THE MOTHER OF SUCCESS.

WAR ON SHORTS

10 + 10 + 10

**TOGETHER AS A MANAGEMENT TEAM
WE MUST WAGE A CONCENTRATED WAR ON
OUT OF STOCK ITEMS. THE FIRST
STAGE OF THE WAR IS TO ASK...**

WHY ARE THE SHORTS OCCURRING?

MIKE'S LAW
KEEP IT SIMPLE...

**BUY IT RIGHT,
PRICE IT RIGHT,
SELL IT RIGHT
IN A
FULL STORE,
CLEAN STORE,
NEAT STORE**

...THAT'S WHAT WE DO

10 + 10 + 10 PLAN

- Steal 10 ideas from our competitors each period and implement them immediately.

- Interview 10 customers each period and implement their suggestions immediately.

- Commit to a $10,000 average weekly sales improvement each period.

COMMIT TO THIS...

PERIOD	SALES ($k)
5	$ 110
6	$ 120
7	$ 130
8	$ 140
9	$ 150
10	$ 160
11	$ 170
12	$ 180
13	$ 190

Exhibit 2

The Food Terminal: Selected Financial Comparisons for the Week Ending June 9

	1991 Actual	1992 Actual	1992 Budget
Sales	141,124	193,467	168,369
Gross Profit	26,860	38,241	30,949
Expenses:			
Wages	19,600	20,203	15,318
Supplies	1,410	2,305	1,851
Other	16,257	14,337	13,644
TOTAL	37,267	36,845	30,813
Net Profit	(10,407)	1,396	136
Customers/Week	7,723	11,243	N/A

Glossary

adaptability/entrepreneurial culture   a culture characterized by strategic focus on the external environment through flexibility and change to meet customer needs.

adhocracy   a sophisticated organization that typically uses teams and is designed to survive in a complex, dynamic environment.

administrative principles   a closed systems management perspective that focuses on the total organization and grows from the insights of practitioners.

advanced information technology   microprocessors and other computer-related information-transmitting devices and systems that have enabled organizations to revolutionize their operations and increase productivity.

ambidextrous approach   a characteristic of an organization that can behave both in an organic and a mechanistic way.

analyzability   a dimension of technology in which work activities can be reduced to mechanical steps and participants can follow an objective, computational procedure to solve problems.

authority   a force for achieving desired outcomes that is prescribed by the formal hierarchy and reporting relationships.

behavior control   control that is based on personal observation of employee behavior to see whether an employee follows correct procedures.

behavioral changes   alterations in behavior that occur during intergroup conflict.

benchmarking   a process whereby companies find out how others do something better than they do and then try to imitate or improve on it.

benefits from cooperation   positive consequences of cooperation, including productive task focus, employee cohesion and satisfaction, organizational goal attainment, and innovation and adaptation.

boundary-spanning roles   activities that link and coordinate an organization with key elements in the external environment.

bounded rationality perspective   how decisions are made when time is limited, a large number of internal and external factors affect a decision, and the problem is ill-defined.

buffering roles   activities that absorb uncertainty from the environment.

bureaucracy   an organizational framework marked by rules and procedures, specialization and division of labor, hierarchy of authority, technically qualified personnel, separate position and incumbent, and written communications and records.

bureaucratic control   the use of rules, policies, hierarchy of authority, written documentation, standardization, and other bureaucratic mechanisms to standardize behavior and assess performance.

bureaucratic culture   a culture that has an internal focus and a consistency orientation for a stable environment.

Carnegie model   organizational decision making involving many managers and a final choice based on a coalition among those managers.

centrality   a trait of a department whose role is in the primary activity of an organization.

centralization   refers to the level of hierarchy with authority to make decisions.

change process   the way in which changes occur in an organization.

chaos theory   a new science that recognizes that randomness and disorder occur within larger patterns of order.

charismatic authority   based in devotion to the exemplary character or heroism of an individual and the order defined by him or her.

clan control   the use of social characteristics, such as corporate culture, shared values, commitment, traditions, and beliefs, to control behavior.

clan culture   a culture that focuses primarily on the involvement and participation of the organization's members and on rapidly changing expectations from the external environment.

closed system   a system that is autonomous, enclosed, and not dependent on its environment.

coalition   an alliance among several managers who agree through bargaining about organizational goals and problem priorities.

coercive isomorphism adopting structures, techniques, or behaviors similar to other organizations because of external pressures, such as legal requirements.

collaborative network an emerging perspective whereby organizations allow themselves to become dependent on other organizations to increase value and productivity for all.

collective bargaining the negotiation of an agreement between management and workers.

collectivity stage the life cycle phase in which an organization has strong leadership and begins to develop clear goals and direction.

competing values approach a perspective on organizational effectiveness that combines diverse indicators of performance that represent competing management values.

competition rivalry between groups in the pursuit of a common prize.

complexity refers to the number of levels in a hierarchy and the number of departments or jobs.

computer-integrated manufacturing computer systems that link together manufacturing components, such as robots, machines, product design, and engineering analysis.

confrontation a situation in which parties in conflict directly engage one another and try to work out their differences.

consortia groups of firms that venture into new products and technologies together.

contextual dimensions traits that characterize the whole organization, including its size, technology, environment, and goals.

contingency a theory meaning one thing depends on other things; the organization's situation dictates the correct management approach.

contingency control model a model that describes contingencies associated with market, bureaucratic, and clan control.

contingency decision-making framework a perspective that brings together the two organizational dimensions of goal consensus and technical knowledge.

continuous process production a completely mechanized manufacturing process in which there is no starting or stopping.

cooperative model a model of organization in which managers foster cooperation rather than competition and find healthy ways to confront and resolve conflict.

cooptation occurs when leaders from important sectors in the environment are made part of an organization.

coping with uncertainty a source of power for a department that reduces uncertainty for other departments by obtaining prior information, prevention, and absorption.

craft technology technology characterized by a fairly stable stream of activities but in which the conversion process is not analyzable or well understood.

creative departments organizational departments that initiate change, such as research and development, engineering, design, and systems analysis.

crisis the first of three phases in the revitalization and turnaround of an organization suffering from decline in which managers downsize the work force and lower production costs.

culture the set of values, guiding beliefs, understandings, and ways of thinking that is shared by members of an organization and is taught to new members as correct.

culture strength the degree of agreement among members of an organization about the importance of specific values.

data the input of a communication channel.

decision learning a process of recognizing and admitting mistakes that allows managers and organizations to acquire the experience and knowledge to perform more effectively in the future.

decision premises constraining frames of reference and guidelines placed by top managers on decisions made at lower levels.

decision support system a system that enables managers at all levels of the organization to retrieve, manipulate, and display information from integrated data bases for making specific decisions.

departmental grouping a structure in which employees share a common supervisor and resources, are jointly responsible for performance, and tend to identify and collaborate with each other.

differentiation the cognitive and emotional differences among managers in various functional departments of an organization and formal structure differences among these departments.

differentiation strategy a strategy in which organizations attempt to distinguish their products or services from others in the industry.

direct interlock a situation that occurs when a member of the board of directors of one company sits on the board of another.

divisional form   large organizations that are subdivided into product or market groups.

divisional grouping   a grouping in which people are organized according to what the organization produces.

divisional structure   the structuring of the organization according to individual products, services, product groups, major projects, or profit centers; also called product structure or strategic business units.

domain   an organization's chosen environmental field of action.

domains of political activity   areas in which politics plays a role. The four domains in organizations are: structural change, interdepartmental coordination, management succession, and resource allocation.

domestic stage   the first stage of international development in which a company is domestically oriented while managers are aware of the global environment.

downsizing   the laying off of employees to whom commitments have been made.

dual-core approach   an organizational change perspective that identifies the unique processes associated with administrative change compared to those associated with technical change.

dynamic network   a structure in which a free market style replaces the traditional vertical hierarchy.

effectiveness   the degree to which an organization realizes its goals.

efficiency   the amount of resources used to produce a unit of output.

elaboration stage   the organizational life cycle phase in which the red tape crisis is resolved through the development of a new sense of teamwork and collaboration.

electronic data interchange   the linking of organizations through computers for the transmission of data without human interference.

empowerment   power sharing; the delegation of power or authority to subordinates.

engineering technology   technology in which there is substantial variety in the tasks performed, but the activities are usually handled on the basis of established formulas, procedures, and techniques.

entrepreneurial stage   the life cycle phase in which an organization is born and its emphasis is on creating a product and surviving in the marketplace.

entrepreneurial structure   typically, a new, small entrepreneurial company consisting of a top manager and workers in the technical core.

escalating commitment   persisting in a course of action when it is failing; occurs because managers block or distort negative information and because consistency and persistence are valued in contemporary society.

ethical dilemma   one in which each alternative choice or behavior seems undesirable because of a potentially negative ethical consequence.

ethics   the code of moral principles and values that governs the behavior of a person or group with respect to what is right or wrong.

ethics committee   a group of executives appointed to oversee company ethics.

ethics ombudsperson   a single manager who serves as the corporate conscience.

executive information systems   interactive systems that help top managers monitor and control organizational operations by processing and presenting data in usable form.

external adaptation   the manner in which an organization meets goals and deals with outsiders.

five organizational configurations   these are entrepreneurial structure, machine bureaucracy, professional bureaucracy, divisional form, and adhocracy.

focus   an organization's dominant perspective value, which may be internal or external.

focus strategy   a strategy in which an organization concentrates on a specific regional market or buyer group.

formalization   the degree to which an organization has rules, procedures, and written documentation.

formalization stage   the phase in an organization's life cycle involving the installation and use of rules, procedures, and control systems.

functional grouping   the placing together of employees who perform similar functions or work processes or who bring similar knowledge and skills to bear.

functional matrix   a structure in which functional bosses have primary authority and product or project managers simply coordinate product activities.

functional structure   the grouping of activities by common function.

gain sharing   an approach to resolving union-management conflict in which union members receive bonuses and profit sharing rather than guaranteed, flat-rate increases.

garbage can model   a model that describes the pattern or flow of multiple decisions within an organization.

general environment   includes those sectors that may not directly affect the daily operations of a firm but will indirectly influence it.

generalist   an organization with a wide niche or domain.

geographic grouping   the organizing of resources to serve customers or clients in a particular geographic area.

global company   a company that no longer thinks of itself as having a home country.

global geographic structure   a form in which an organization divides its operations into world regions, each of which reports to the CEO.

global matrix structure   a form of horizontal linkage in an international organization in which both product and functional structures (horizontal and vertical) are implemented simultaneously.

global product structure   a form in which product divisions take responsibility for global operations in their specific product areas.

global stage   the stage of international development in which the company transcends any one country.

global teams   work groups made up of multinational members whose activities span multiple countries; also called transnational teams.

globalization strategy   the standardization of product design and advertising strategy throughout the world.

goal approach   an approach to organizational effectiveness that is concerned with output and whether the organization achieves its output goals.

goal consensus   the agreement among managers about which organizational goals and outcomes to pursue.

groupware   programs that enable employees on a computer network to interact with one another through their PCs.

heroes   organizational members who serve as models or ideals for serving cultural norms and values.

high tech   technology-based information systems.

high touch   face-to-face discussion.

high-velocity environments   industries in which competitive and technological change is so extreme that market data is either unavailable or obsolete, strategic windows open and shut quickly, and the cost of a decision error is company failure.

horizontal conflict   behavior that occurs between groups or departments at the same level in the hierarchy.

horizontal corporation   a structure in which vertical hierarchy and departmental boundaries are virtually eliminated.

horizontal linkage   the amount of communication and coordination that occurs horizontally across organizational departments.

horizontal linkage model   a model of the three components of organizational design needed to achieve new product innovation: departmental specialization, boundary spanning, and horizontal linkages.

human relations model   an organizational model that incorporates the values of an internal focus and a flexible structure.

hybrid structure   a structure that combines characteristics of both product and function or geography.

idea champions   organizational members who provide the time and energy to make things happen; sometimes called "advocates," "intrapreneurs," and "change agents."

imitation   the adoption of a decision tried elsewhere in the hope that it will work in the present situation.

incremental change   a series of continual progressions that maintain an organization's general equilibrium and often affect only one organizational part.

incremental decision process model   a model that describes the structured sequence of activities undertaken from the discovery of a problem to its solution.

indirect interlock   a situation that occurs when a director of one company and a director of another are both directors of a third company.

information   that which alters or reinforces understanding.

information ambiguity   a situation in which issues cannot be objectively analyzed and understood and additional data cannot be gathered that will resolve the issues.

information amount   the volume of data about organizational activities that is gathered and interpreted by organization participants.

information richness   the information carrying capacity of data.

input control   control that uses employee selection and training to regulate the knowledge, skills, abilities, values, and motives of employees.

inspiration   an innovative, creative solution that is not reached by logical means.

institutional environment   norms and values from stakeholders (customers, investors, boards, government, etc.) that organizations try to follow in order to please stakeholders.

institutional isomorphism   the emergence of common structures, management approaches, and behaviors among organizations in the same field.

institutional perspective   an emerging view that holds that under high uncertainty, organizations imitate others in the same institutional environment.

integration   the quality of collaboration between departments of an organization.

integrator   a position or department created solely to coordinate several departments.

intensive technology   a variety of products or services provided in combination to a client.

interdependence   the extent to which departments depend on each other for resources or materials to accomplish their tasks.

intergroup conflict   behavior that occurs between organizational groups when participants identify with one group and perceive that other groups may block their group's goal achievement or expectations.

interlocking directorate   a formal linkage that occurs when a member of the board of directors of one company sits on the board of another company.

internal integration   a state in which organization members develop a collective identity and know how to work together effectively.

internal process approach   an approach that looks at internal activities and assesses effectiveness by indicators of internal health and efficiency.

internal process model   an organizational model that reflects the values of internal focus and structural control.

international division   a division that is equal in status to other major departments within a company and has its own hierarchy to handle business in various countries.

international stage   the second stage of international development, in which the company takes exports seriously and begins to think multidomestically.

interorganization relationships   the relatively enduring resource transactions, flows, and linkages that occur among two or more organizations.

intranet   a private, internal network that uses the infrastructure and standards of the Internet but is cordoned off from the public with the use of software programs known as *firewalls*.

intuitive decision making   the use of experience and judgment rather than sequential logic or explicit reasoning to solve a problem.

job enrichment   the designing of jobs to increase responsibility, recognition, and opportunities for growth and achievement.

job simplification   the reduction of the number and difficulty of tasks performed by a single person.

joint optimization   the goal of the sociotechnical systems approach, which states that an organization will function best only if its social and technical systems are designed to fit the needs of one another.

joint venture   a separate entity for sharing development and production costs and penetrating new markets that is created with two or more active firms as sponsors.

labor-management teams   a cooperative approach designed to increase worker participation and provide a cooperative model for union-management problems.

language   slogans, sayings, metaphors, or other expressions that convey a special meaning to employees.

large-batch production   a manufacturing process characterized by long production runs of standardized parts.

learning organization   an organization in which everyone is engaged in identifying and solving problems, enabling the organization to continuously experiment, improve, and increase its capability.

legends   stories of events based in history that may have been embellished with fictional details.

legitimacy   the general perspective that an organization's actions are desirable, proper, and appropriate within the environment's system of norms, values, and beliefs.

level of analysis   in systems theory, the subsystem on which the primary focus is placed; four levels of analysis normally characterize organizations.

liaison role   the function of a person located in one department who is responsible for communicating and achieving coordination with another department.

life cycle   a perspective on organizational growth and change that suggests organizations are born, grow older, and eventually die.

long-linked technology   the combination within one organization of successive stages of production, with each stage using as its inputs the production of the preceding stage.

losses from conflict   negative consequences of conflict for organizations, including diversion of energy, altered judgment, loser effects, and poor coordination.

low-cost leadership   a strategy that tries to increase market share by emphasizing low cost compared to competitors.

machine bureaucracy   a very large organization in which the technology is routine and often oriented to mass production.

management champion   a manager who acts as a supporter and sponsor of a technical champion to shield and promote an idea within the organization.

management control systems   the formalized routines, reports, and procedures that use information to maintain or alter patterns in organizational activity.

management information system   a system that generally contains comprehensive data about all transactions within an organization.

management science approach   organizational decision making that is the analog to the rational approach by individual managers.

managerial ethics   principles that guide the decisions and behaviors of managers with regard to whether they are morally right or wrong.

market control   a situation that occurs when price competition is used to evaluate the output and productivity of an organization.

matrix bosses   department heads and program directors who have complete control over their subordinates.

matrix structure   a strong form of horizontal linkage in which both product and functional structures (horizontal and vertical) are implemented simultaneously.

mechanistic   an organization system marked by rules, procedures, a clear hierarchy of authority, and centralized decision making.

mediating technology   the provision of products or services that mediate or link clients from the external environment and allow each department to work independently.

meso theory   a new approach to organization studies that integrates both micro and macro levels of analysis.

mimetic isomorphism   under conditions of uncertainty, the copying of techniques or processes from other organizations in the environment that appear successful.

mission   the organization's reasons for its existence.

mission culture   a culture that places emphasis on a clear vision of the organization's purpose and on the achievement of specific goals.

mixed model   a description of an organization that displays both rational and political model characteristics.

model of intergroup conflict   a graphic representation of the organizational and intergroup factors that set the stage for intergroup conflict, the triggers that set off a dispute, and the responses managers can make to control emergent conflict.

multidomestic company   a company that deals with competitive issues in each country independent of other countries.

multidomestic strategy   one in which competition in each country is handled independently of competition in other countries.

multifocused grouping   a structure in which an organization embraces structural grouping alternatives simultaneously.

multinational stage   the stage of international development in which a company has marketing and production facilities in many countries and more than one-third of its sales outside its home country.

myths   stories that are consistent with the values and beliefs of the organization but are not supported by facts.

negotiation   the bargaining process that often occurs during confrontation and enables the parties to systematically reach a solution.

network centrality   top managers increase their power by locating themselves centrally in an organization and surrounding themselves with loyal subordinates.

networking   linking computers within or between organizations.

niche   a domain of unique environmental resources and needs.

nonprogrammed decisions novel and poorly defined, these are used when no procedure exists for solving the problem.

nonroutine technology technology in which there is high task variety and the conversion process is not analyzable or well understood.

nonsubstitutability a trait of a department whose function cannot be performed by other readily available resources.

normative isomorphism adopting structures, techniques, or management processes considered by the professional community to be up-to-date and effective.

official goals the formally stated definition of business scope and outcomes the organization is trying to achieve; another term for **mission**.

open system a system that must interact with the environment to survive.

open systems model an organizational model that reflects a combination of external focus and flexible structure.

operational control a short-term control cycle that includes the four stages of setting targets, measuring performance, comparing performance against standards, and feedback.

operative goals descriptions of the ends sought through the actual operating procedures of the organization; these explain what the organization is trying to accomplish.

organic an organization system marked by free-flowing, adaptive processes, an unclear hierarchy of authority, and decentralized decision making.

organization theory a macro approach to organizations that analyzes the whole organization as a unit.

organizational behavior a micro approach to organizations that focuses on the individuals within organizations as the relevant units of analysis.

organizational change the adoption of a new idea or behavior by an organization.

organizational decision making the organizational process of identifying and solving problems.

organizational decline a condition in which a substantial, absolute decrease in an organization's resource base occurs over a period of time.

organizational development a behavioral science field devoted to improving performance through trust, open confrontation of problems, employee empower-ment and participation, the design of meaningful work, cooperation between groups, and the full use of human potential.

organizational ecosystem a system formed by the interaction of a community of organizations and their environment, usually cutting across traditional industry lines.

organizational environment all elements that exist outside the boundary of the organization and have the potential to affect all or part of the organization.

organizational form an organization's specific technology, structure, products, goals, and personnel.

organizational goal a desired state of affairs that the organization attempts to reach.

organizational innovation the adoption of an idea or behavior that is new to an organization's industry, market, or general environment.

organizational politics activities to acquire, develop, and use power and other resources to obtain one's preferred outcome when there is uncertainty or disagreement about choices.

organizations social entities that are goal-directed, deliberately structured activity systems linked to the external environment.

organized anarchy extremely organic organization characterized by highly uncertain conditions.

output control control that is based on written records that measure employee outputs and productivity.

paradigm a shared mind-set that represents a fundamental way of thinking, perceiving, and understanding the world.

Parkinson's law a view that holds that work expands to fill the time available for its completion.

people and culture changes changes in the values, attitudes, expectations, beliefs, abilities, and behavior of employees.

personnel ratios the proportions of administrative, clerical, and professional support staff.

political model a definition of an organization as being made up of groups that have separate interests, goals, and values in which power and influence are needed to reach decisions.

political tactics for using power these include: build coalitions, expand networks, control decision premises, enhance legitimacy and expertise, and make preferences explicit while keeping power implicit.

pooled interdependence   the lowest form of interdependence among departments in which work does not flow between units.

population   a set of organizations engaged in similar activities with similar patterns of resource utilization and outcomes.

population ecology model   a perspective in which the focus is on organizational diversity and adaptation within a community or population of organizations.

power   the ability of one person or department in an organization to influence others to bring about desired outcomes.

power sources   there are five sources of horizontal power in organizations: dependency, financial resources, centrality, nonsubstitutability, and the ability to cope with uncertainty.

problem identification   the decision-making stage in which information about environmental and organizational conditions is monitored to determine if performance is satisfactory and to diagnose the cause of shortcomings.

problem solution   a decision-making stage in which alternative courses of action are considered and one alternative is selected and implemented.

problemistic search   occurs when managers look around in the immediate environment for a solution to resolve a problem quickly.

product and service changes   changes in an organization's product or service outputs.

professional bureaucracy   an organization in which the production core is composed of professionals.

programmed decisions   repetitive and well-defined procedures that exist for resolving problems.

project matrix   a structure in which the project or product manager has primary responsibility, and functional managers simply assign technical personnel to projects and provide advisory expertise.

quality circles   groups of six to twelve volunteer workers who meet to analyze and solve problems.

radical change   a breaking of the frame of reference for an organization, often creating a new equilibrium because the entire organization is transformed.

radical-Marxism   a perspective on organizations that holds that managers make decisions to maintain themselves in the capitalist class, keeping power and resources for themselves.

rational approach   a process of decision making that stresses the need for systematic analysis of a problem followed by choice and implementation in a logical sequence.

rational-contingency perspective   an approach to organizations that assumes that managers try to do what is logically best for the organization.

rational goal model   an organizational model that reflects values of structural control and external focus.

rational-legal authority   one based on employees' beliefs in the legality of rules and the right of those in authority to issue commands.

rational model   a description of an organization characterized by a rational approach to decision making, extensive and reliable information systems, central power, a norm of optimization, uniform values across groups, little conflict, and an efficiency orientation.

reasons organizations grow   growth occurs because it is an organizational goal; it is necessary to attract and keep quality managers; or it is necessary to maintain economic health.

rebuilding   the final phase in turnaround and recovery in which the organization begins to grow, moving away from efficiency toward innovation.

reciprocal interdependence   the highest level of interdependence in which the output of one operation is the input of a second, and the output of the second operation is the input of the first (for example, a hospital).

reengineering   a cross-functional initiative involving the radical redesign of business processes to bring about simultaneous changes in organization structure, culture, and information technology and produce dramatic performance improvements.

reinvest   the turnaround and recovery phase in which the organization stabilizes, and its structure and culture are changed to reflect its new mission and goals.

resource dependence   a situation in which organizations depend on the environment but strive to acquire control over resources to minimize their dependence.

retention   the preservation and institutionalization of selected organizational forms.

rites and ceremonies   the elaborate, planned activities that make up a special event and often are conducted for the benefit of an audience.

ritual scapegoating   the functioning of manager turnover as a sign that the organization is trying to improve.

routine technology technology characterized by little task variety and the use of objective, computational procedures.

rule of law that which arises from a set of codified principles and regulations that describe how people are required to act, are generally accepted in society, and are enforceable in the courts.

satisficing the acceptance by organizations of a satisfactory rather than a maximum level of performance.

scientific management a classical approach that claims decisions about organization and job design should be based on precise, scientific procedures.

sectors subdivisions of the external environment that contain similar elements.

selection the process by which organizational variations are determined to fit the external environment; variations that fail to fit the needs of the environment are "selected out" and fail.

self-directed team a group of workers with different skills who rotate jobs and assume managerial responsibilities as they produce an entire product or service.

sequential interdependence a serial form of interdependence in which the output of one operation becomes the input to another operation.

service technology technology characterized by simultaneous production and consumption, customized output, customer participation, intangible output, and being labor intensive.

simple-complex dimension the number and dissimilarity of external elements relevant to an organization's operations.

small-batch production a manufacturing process, often custom work, that is not highly mechanized and relies heavily on the human operator.

social responsibility management's obligation to make choices and take action so that the organization contributes to the welfare and interest of society as well as itself.

sociotechnical systems approach an approach that combines the needs of people with the needs of technical efficiency.

sources of interdepartmental conflict eight factors that generate conflict, including operative goal incompatibility, differentiation, task interdependence, resource scarcity, power distribution, uncertainty, international context, and reward system.

sources of vertical conflict factors within an organization, usually involving workers and management, that cause conflict, including psychological distance, power and status, ideology, and scarce resources.

specialist an organization that has a narrow range of goods or services or serves a narrow market.

stable-unstable dimension the state of an organization's environmental elements.

stakeholder any group within or outside an organization that has a stake in the organization's performance.

stakeholder approach also called the constituency approach, this perspective assesses the satisfaction of stakeholders as an indicator of the organization's performance.

stories narratives based on true events that are frequently shared among organizational employees and told to new employees to inform them about an organization.

strategic contingencies events and activities inside and outside an organization that are essential for attaining organizational goals.

strategic control the overall evaluation of the strategic plan, organizational activities, and results that provides information for future action.

strategy the current set of plans, decisions, and objectives that have been adopted to achieve the organization's goals.

strategy and structure changes changes in the administrative domain of an organization, including structure, policies, reward systems, labor relations, coordination devices, management information control systems, and accounting and budgeting.

strategy formation the activities that lead to the establishment of an organization's overall goals and mission and the development of a specific strategic plan.

strategy implementation the use of managerial and organizational tools to direct and allocate resources to accomplish strategic objectives.

structural dimensions descriptions of the internal characteristics of an organization indicating whether stability or flexibility is the dominant organizational value.

structure the formal reporting relationships, groupings, and systems of an organization.

struggle for existence a principle of the population ecology model that holds that organizations are engaged in a competitive struggle for resources and fighting to survive.

subsystems divisions of an organization that perform specific functions for the organization's survival; organizational subsystems perform the essential functions of boundary spanning, production, maintenance, adaptation, and management.

supervisory control control that focuses on the performance of individual employees.

switching structures an organization creates an organic structure when such a structure is needed for the initiation of new ideas.

symbol something that represents another thing.

symptoms of structural deficiency signs of the organizational structure being out of alignment, including delayed or poor-quality decision making, failure to respond innovatively to environmental changes, and too much conflict.

system a set of interacting elements that acquires inputs from the environment, transforms them, and discharges outputs to the external environment.

system resource approach an organizational perspective that assesses effectiveness by observing the beginning of the process and evaluating whether the organization effectively obtains resources necessary for high performance.

tactics for increasing the power base these include: enter areas of high uncertainty, create dependencies, provide resources, and satisfy strategic contingencies.

task environment sectors with which the organization interacts directly and that have a direct effect on the organization's ability to achieve its goals.

task force a temporary committee composed of representatives from each department affected by a problem.

team building activities that promote the idea that people who work together can work together as a team.

teams permanent task forces often used in conjunction with a full-time integrator.

technical complexity the extent of mechanization in the manufacturing process.

technical knowledge understanding and agreement about how to reach organizational goals.

technical or product champion a person who generates or adopts and develops an idea for a technological innovation and is devoted to it, even to the extent of risking position or prestige.

technology the tools, techniques, and actions used to transform organizational inputs into outputs.

technology changes changes in an organization's production process, including its knowledge and skills base, that enable distinctive competence.

top leader the head of both functional and product command structures in a matrix.

total quality management an organizational approach in which workers, not managers, are handed the responsibility for achieving standards of quality.

traditional authority based in the belief in traditions and the legitimacy of the status of people exercising authority through those traditions.

transaction-cost economics a perspective that assumes that individuals act in their self-interest and that exchanges of goods and services theoretically could occur in the free marketplace.

transaction processing systems automation of the organization's routine, day-to-day business transactions.

transformational leadership the ability of leaders to motivate followers to not just follow them personally but to believe in the vision of organizational transformation, to recognize the need for revitalization, to commit to the new vision, and to help institutionalize a new organizational process.

transnational model a form of horizontal organization that has multiple centers, subsidiary managers who initiate strategy and innovations for the company as a whole, and unity and coordination achieved through corporate culture and shared vision and values.

two-boss employees employees who must maintain effective relationships with both department heads and program directors in a matrix structure.

uncertainty occurs when decision makers do not have sufficient information about environmental factors and have a difficult time predicting external changes.

value-based leadership a relationship between a leader and followers that is based on strongly shared values that are advocated and acted upon by the leader.

variation appearance of new organizational forms in response to the needs of the external environment; analogous to mutations in biology.

variety in terms of tasks, the frequency of unexpected and novel events that occur in the conversion process.

venture teams a technique to foster creativity within organizations in which a small team is set up as its own company to pursue innovations.

vertical conflict   behavior between groups that arises over issues of control, power, goals, and wages and benefits.

vertical information system   the periodic reports, written information, and computer-based communications distributed to managers.

vertical linkages   communication and coordination activities connecting the top and bottom of an organization.

whistle-blowing   employee disclosure of illegal, immoral, or illegitimate practices on the part of the organization.

work flow automation   a form of advanced information technology in which documents are automatically sent to the correct location for processing.

work flow redesign   reengineering work processes to fit new information technology.

Name Index

Corporate Name Index

Subject Index

Photo Credits